The Palgrave Handbook of Popular Culture as Philosophy

David Kyle Johnson
Editor-in-Chief

Dean A. Kowalski · Chris Lay ·
Kimberly S. Engels
Editors

The Palgrave Handbook of Popular Culture as Philosophy

Volume 2

With 1 Figure and 2 Tables

Editor-in-Chief
David Kyle Johnson
King's College
Wilkes Barre, PA
USA

Editors
Dean A. Kowalski
University School of Milwaukee
Waukesha, WI, USA

Chris Lay
Young Harris College
Young Harris, GA, USA

Kimberly S. Engels
Molloy University
Rockville Centre, NewYork, NY, USA

ISBN 978-3-031-24684-5   ISBN 978-3-031-24685-2 (eBook)
https://doi.org/10.1007/978-3-031-24685-2

© Springer Nature Switzerland AG 2024

This work is subject to copyright. All rights are reserved by the Publisher, whether the whole or part of the material is concerned, specifically the rights of translation, reprinting, reuse of illustrations, recitation, broadcasting, reproduction on microfilms or in any other physical way, and transmission or information storage and retrieval, electronic adaptation, computer software, or by similar or dissimilar methodology now known or hereafter developed.

The use of general descriptive names, registered names, trademarks, service marks, etc. in this publication does not imply, even in the absence of a specific statement, that such names are exempt from the relevant protective laws and regulations and therefore free for general use.

The publisher, the authors, and the editors are safe to assume that the advice and information in this book are believed to be true and accurate at the date of publication. Neither the publisher nor the authors or the editors give a warranty, expressed or implied, with respect to the material contained herein or for any errors or omissions that may have been made. The publisher remains neutral with regard to jurisdictional claims in published maps and institutional affiliations.

This Palgrave Macmillan imprint is published by the registered company Springer Nature Switzerland AG. The registered company address is: Gewerbestrasse 11, 6330 Cham, Switzerland

If disposing of this product, please recycle the paper.

For my wife and son, who demonstrated exceptional patience with me during the five years this project took to complete.

Preface: A Brief Defense of Pop Culture as Philosophy

If you want to tell people the truth, make them laugh, otherwise they'll kill you.
—George Bernard Shaw[1]

Abstract

This introductory chapter articulates the overarching objectives and methodology of the Palgrave Handbook of Popular Culture as Philosophy. Its primary aim is to treat works of popular culture as philosophical works, essentially considering them to be works of art that aspire to articulate philosophical arguments or provoke profound philosophical inquiries. The chapter also defends the concept that creative works, including but not limited to films, possess the capacity to do philosophy – an idea characterized by Paisley Livingston as the "Bold Thesis." A persuasive case in favor of the Bold Thesis is articulated and objections to it are considered and answered.

Introduction

William Irwin started the "Pop Culture and Philosophy" craze with *Seinfeld and Philosophy* in 1999; the second volume of the series, *The Simpsons and Philosophy (2001)*, ended up selling over 200,000 copies. (Because it was published in 2001, at the time it might have been the best-selling philosophy book of the twenty-first century.) Later volumes, like *The Matrix and Philosophy* (2002) and *The Lord of the Rings and Philosophy* (2003), were also highly successful (and impeccably timed with popular movie sequels). And it was around that time, at a point when Irwin started to bring in other editors to help with the workload (Eric Bronson and Greg Bassham were volume editors of the *Lord of the Rings* book), that the series really took off. Regardless of how you count, to date, there are at least 200 "pop and phil" books.

Although I had taught a "Simpsons, South Park, and Philosophy" class at the University of Oklahoma as a graduate student ca. 2004, my first published chapter was in Robert Arp's *South Park and Philosophy* in 2006; the first words I ever published were "Cartman is an ass." I went on to write almost 30 pop culture chapters, attend multiple pop-culture conferences, and edit three books in Irwin's

Blackwell *Philosophy and Pop Culture* series: *Heroes and Philosophy* (2009), *Inception and Philosophy* (2011), and *Black Mirror and Philosophy* (2019). Irwin also graciously asked me to co-edit his textbook *Introducing Philosophy Through Pop Culture* (2010), which is a collection of select chapters from his Blackwell series, organized by subject so that it can be used in the classroom. We published an updated edition in 2022, and I have used chapters from it, and other chapters from the series, in my classroom for many years.

I mention all this not to demonstrate my "bona fides" (others have certainly edited and published on pop culture more) but to emphasize that this current project – *The Palgrave Handbook of Popular Culture as Philosophy* – is NOT a continuation of that series. As should be obvious, I am a big fan of the "pop and phil" approach; but it is decidedly not the approach that this handbook takes. The astute reader might have noticed the difference in its title – it's "*as*" philosophy, not "and." It's subtle, but that "as" makes a lot of difference.

The Difference Between "As" and "And"

The goal of the "pop *and* phil" approach is to use popular culture as a kind of springboard to introduce and discuss philosophical concepts and arguments. If the show has an android – like *Data* from *Star Trek* – we can introduce the reader to the philosophical debate about artificial intelligence by discussing whether Data has a mind. If the show has characters waging war and vying for political power – like *Game of Thrones* – we can examine their actions to introduce the reader to just war theory and political philosophy. *The Matrix* can be used to explain Descartes' dream problem, *Inception* can be used to discuss the acceptability of faith, and *The Good Place* can be used to explore ethical theories and the possibility of an afterlife. I'm oversimplifying, of course, and the number of philosophical issues explored in any one "pop and phil" book is broad and diverse. But the "and philosophy" approach treats the pop culture it engages as a kind of thought experiment – one that is already known and loved and so makes the task of introducing the reader to philosophy easier. As Irwin has often said about his series, "A spoonful of sugar helps the medicine go down" (Written Voices n.d.).

The "as philosophy" approach is different. The basic idea is that the creators of popular culture – the directors, the writers – can actually *do* philosophy while playing at their craft. They can not only be inspired by philosophy, or use ideas they learned in philosophy class, but they can convey philosophical points, raise philosophical questions, and even make philosophical arguments.[2] Consequently, the works they produce can *be* philosophy, and as a result are worth philosophical examination. Ruppert Read and Jerry Goodenough's *Film as Philosophy: Essays on Cinema after Wittgenstein and Cavell* (2005), Murry Smith and Thomas Wartenberg's *Thinking through Cinema: Film as Philosophy* (2006), Thomas Wartenberg's *Thinking on Screen: Film as Philosophy* (2007), and Bernd Herzogenrath's *Film as Philosophy* (2017), all embrace the "as philosophy" approach.

Of course, not all pop culture is philosophy; but quite a bit is, with some examples greatly standing out in this respect – like *The Matrix* and *Inception*. In fact, these two movies are perfect examples. While both movies could be used to explain Descartes' dream problem, they seem to argue for completely different conclusions. *The Matrix*, by making a villain out of the one character (Cypher) who willfully embraces ignorance, seems to be arguing that one should care for and strive to embrace reality – to obtain objectively true beliefs. *Inception* on the other hand, by having Cobb turn away from his spinning top (his test of reality) in the final scene and instead choose to believe that his children are real, seems to suggest that, in the end, it is only "your truth" that matters. Other examples of obviously philosophical films include *2001: A Space Odyssey, Lord of the Rings, Star Wars, Blade Runner, Groundhog Day, The Shawshank Redemption, Tenet, Ex Machina, Don't Look Up, AI: Artificial Intelligence, Fight Club,* and *Gattaca,* all of which (and much more) are covered in this handbook.

Going Beyond Films

It's not only films, of course. Most people recognize that series (what used to be relegated to television but now also exist on streaming services) like *Star Trek, South Park, Black Mirror, House of Cards, Doctor Who, The Handmaid's Tale,* and *The Good Place* can do something similar. (All of these and more are also covered in this handbook.) But one thing that generally goes unappreciated, even by philosophers, is that other kinds of popular culture can be philosophy as well – like graphic novels and video games. Both have long since ceased being "for kids only," and the creators of both enjoy certain kinds of creative freedom that make them an especially welcome medium for philosophical reflection. The graphic novel *V for Vendetta*, for example, does a much better job of articulating exactly when violent political rebellion is warranted than the movie it inspired. And modern video games, with their interactive features and story-telling, can make points about, say, political choice and free will that their strictly scripted movie counterparts cannot. (The game *Papers Please*, where you choose whether to cooperate with a fascist regime or resist it – and can "win" the game either way – is most notable in this regard.) What's more, while common wisdom will tell you that graphic novels and video games aren't as "popular" as TV series and films, graphic novels serve as the groundwork for some of the most popular movies and TV of all time (*The Avengers, X-Men, Justice League, Watchmen, 300, The Walking Dead,* etc.) and the video game industry dwarfs all other entertainment industries in terms of profit (grossing $160 billion in 2020).

Because of its reliance on spoken word, another medium that is prime for the doing of philosophy is stand-up comedy. On the *Comedy Gold Minds* podcast (2021), Hasan Minhaj elaborated on how his experience with competitive debate – the same thing that helped prepare me for a career in philosophy – helped prepare him for his career as a comedian. "Comedians," he says, are "just normal philosophers," tasked with turning "coffee into espresso" (i.e., taking what's difficult to understand and compressing it into something comprehensible). In an interview with Khan Academy (2020), he elaborated a bit more: "Stand-up comedy is just funny speech and debate ... The most important thing for comedy is the argument. You are making a funny joke, but at the core, what is your argument? So great jokes at their essence are great philosophical positions said in a funny way."

Some comedians, like Jerry Seinfeld, shy away from this responsibility. "Ok, fine, fine." he said on the HBO special *George Carlin's American Dream*, "you want the comedian to be your lens on society. Go…enjoy it. But, for me, I never heard a comic bit that changed my opinion on anything" (Apatow & Bonfiglo 2022). But the promotional featurette for the very special in which Seinfeld speaks these words begins with multiple comedians not only saying that George Carlin was the smartest man they ever met, but that he was also a "genius at making you laugh and *changing your mind*" (HBO 2022). In the special itself, Chris Rock was more specific.

> I remember one time Carlin said to me, "I'm not in show business, I'm a comedian." ... I took it to mean that comedians were thinkers. But, when you think about the history of [hu]man[ity], [hu]man[ity] used to love philosophers. We don't really have philosophers anymore. But we have comedians. So, Carlin encompassed all those things; that's what he meant. Like, this is what we do, this is the life we've chosen, we're, you know, a kind a secret society in a sense. (Apatow & Bonfiglo 2022)

In his last comedy special, "Nothing Special," Norm McDonald (2022) was a bit more kind to living philosophers.

> Like nowadays, I've heard ... "The comedian is the modern-day philosopher," you know? Which, first of all, it always makes me feel sad for the actual modern-day philosophers, who exist, you know.

Thanks for the shout-out Norm; indeed, we do exist. But what Rock was getting at still stands: the public doesn't listen to philosophers anymore – at least not like they used to. Don't get me wrong, philosophers still influence society; but the public doesn't crowd event halls to go listen to philosophers speak, as they used to do with academics in the past. But they *do* watch comedians; and many comedians – from George Carlin and Dave Chappell to Amy Schumer and Hannah Gadsby – are presenting philosophical arguments that change people's minds. (Sometimes they are explicit, like Carlin's arguments against religion; other times they are implicit, like Schumer's arguments about feminism. But the arguments are there.) They may not always mean to. Carlin himself said that "try[ing] to make people think ... would be the kiss of death" for a comedian; he only aims "to let them know I'm thinking." But they are doing it, nonetheless – comedians are making people think. And so, it should be worth the real-world (existing) modern philosopher's time to examine what comedians are saying, and the arguments they are making, to see whether they are onto something – or whether they are full of (sh)it.

The same holds for philosophy that is being done in movies, television/streaming series, graphic novels, and video games. While the people who make these things are doing philosophy, they usually are not professional philosophers; they don't always have a philosophy degree; they might not have even had a philosophy class. So, they

Preface: A Brief Defense of Pop Culture as Philosophy   xi

may be getting things wrong.³ They might also be getting them right; but how can we know unless those who know the subject best take a closer look, identify what argument being made, and evaluate whether it is any good – or identify the question being raised and explore the answers it might have? That is what I tried to do in my course for *The Great Courses* (now known as *Wondrium*) *Sci-Phi: Science Fiction as Philosophy*, and that's what I tried to have my authors do in *Exploring The Orville* (which I edited with Michael Berry) and in *Black Mirror and Philosophy* (even though it was in an "and philosophy" series). And that is what this handbook aims to do: identify and evaluate the philosophy that is being done in and by popular culture.

This is important to do not only because pop culture can be very influential, but because it can be easily misinterpreted and misused. Think of how the term "snowflake" has become ubiquitous in right–wing political circles, to describe those who they think are easily offended. They stole the term from the mouth of Tyler Durden in *Fight Club*; but those who use it today don't seem to recognize that (a) Durden is the villain of the film, not the hero and (b) he uses the term to solidify obedience in his communistic commune – and communism is something that the right decries. (For more on *Fight Club*, see Alberto Oya's magnificent chapter in this volume. For more on how snowflakey (easily offended) many in right-wing political circles are, see the second half of my chapter on *South Park*.)

Speaking of *South Park,* almost every episode of *South Park* is some kind of argument on some social or political issue – and a lot of young impressionable viewers think Matt Stone and Trey Parker make good points. And sometimes they do. *South Park: Bigger, Longer, and Uncut* effectively argues that parents skirt responsibility for their children's behavior by blaming cartoons, and their film *Team America: World Police* effectively criticizes America's militaristic role as "world police" (while also arguing, through a very vulgar (but seemingly accurate) analogy, that it is sometimes necessary). When I was younger, Matt and Trey definitely changed my view about a few things. But Matt and Trey also get things very wrong. In season 10's *ManBearPig* (2006) they made fun of Al Gore (and his 2006 film *An Inconvenient Truth*) and equated his concerns about climate change with concerns about a mythical creature called ManBearPig that didn't actually exist. Their argument was that Gore just wanted attention. But in Season 22, Stone and Parker admitted they were wrong with two episodes, "Time to Get Cereal" and "Nobody Got Cereal?," that revealed that ManBearPig was indeed real, is now murdering and destroying the town, and thus that Al Gore was right (about climate change) all along (see Miller 2018).

Perhaps one might argue that this is more of a scientific, rather than a philosophic, issue. But a scene in "Time to Get Cereal" makes clear that they have a philosophical point in mind. A patron at Red Lobster tries to mansplain to his wife why ManBearPig is not real – "What you need to understand, Susan, is that everyone has an agenda, mmmkay?" – as ManBearPig actively kills the other patrons in the restaurant and his wife yells "he's real!" The patron eventually turns around – yet when he sees ManBearPig with his own eyes, he only begrudgingly admits he was wrong and immediately shifts to "What are we going to do about it now, huh? What are we going to do that's going to make any difference now, Susan? What can we do that everyone else will also do?," only to then be eaten alive by ManBearPig.[4] Matt and Trey go on to show townhall meetings where, as ManBearPig destroys the town, the people calmly agree that, perhaps, they should, maybe, begin to consider thinking about possibly being worried. And when it's revealed that ManBearPig is attacking because Stan's grandpa and his generation made a deal with ManBearPig (for cars and premium boutique ice cream because they "didn't think they would have to live with the consequences"), and Stan tries to renegotiate the contract, Stan goes to the townspeople with the new terms of the deal:

Stan (to the townspeople)	Um, [ManBearPig] says he'll never come back again, but, we have to give up soy sauce and *Red Dead Redemption 2*.
Townspeople (in unison, disappointed)	Ohhh.... A long silence
A single townsperson	Just plain rice?
Stan (pauses, but is unsurprised)	Yeah, that's what I thought.

The scene is hilarious and so on the nose that it's depressing. Stan has to strike another deal.

Lawyer	Sign here that ManBearPig has rights to the lives of all children in third world countries.
Stan	Ok, got it.
Lawyer	And you agree to ignore ManBearPig until he returns in five years, in which time the carnage will be a thousand-fold.
Stan	Ok, where do I sign that?

Parker and Stone are not known for being subtle, and clearly they are making a philosophical point; yet one might still struggle to put it into words so that it can be examined – hence the need for professional philosophers to step in. A chapter on these episodes would show that the Red Lobster scene is making a philosophical point about how climate change denial is epistemically bankrupt; no matter how obvious the evidence is, or how imminent the threat, their denial and excuses will continue. Such a chapter would point out that the townhall meeting scene is making the point that, because of people's epistemic tendency toward self-denial when it comes to things so overwhelmingly unpleasant, even those who recognize the severity of the threat are afraid to say that people should be even worried for fear of being labeled "alarmist." And it would point out that the negotiation scene shows how human selfishness makes us collectively incapable of giving up even the most basic comforts for the good of others (like children in third world countries), future generations, or even ourselves five years from now. (My chapter on *South Park* in this volume covers a different topic, but check out this handbook's chapter on *Don't Look Up* to see that Parker and Stone are essentially right on these topics.)

The Handbook's Approach

I've divided the handbook into five sections – cinema, series, comedians, video games, and graphic novels – but the basic approach of each chapter will be similar.

1. A short introduction to the pop culture work and the philosophical issue it raises
2. A quick summary of the work itself
3. An attempt to identify exactly what argument the work is making or what question it is raising
4. An evaluation of that argument or an attempt to answer the relevant philosophical question

Now, there is a lot of variation; I tried to give the author of each chapter the freedom to evaluate the philosophy being done by their selected piece of pop culture in the most appropriate way. But each has the goal of treating the pop culture in question as philosophy – or, in the case of a comedian, as a philosopher.

Another thing I tried to make consistent throughout is the writing style. Each author, of course, has their own flair and approach – but while this handbook is more academic in nature, and some of its chapters are quite long, I intended the handbook for classroom use. So, each chapter is written with the goal of being understandable to the average college student. (If the chapter is long, its sections make it divisible into readable parts.) What's more, the reason that I made sure that each chapter contains a summary of the pop culture in question is so the instructor does not have to assign it or spend valuable class time screening it. That's not to say that doing so wouldn't enhance the student's experience; but a familiarity with the pop culture in question is not required to understand, learn from, or enjoy any chapter.

Defending a Bold Thesis

Despite the popularity of viewing films as philosophy, the notion that films can do philosophy, which of course would entail that popular culture (e.g., TV, graphic novels, etc.) can do philosophy, has its detractors. I, however, have never found the arguments against the notion very convincing. After all, my guess is that most readers would agree that the novels *To Kill a Mockingbird* and *1984* are arguments against racism and fascism – so why can't the movies based on them be the same? And why couldn't something that is even more overtly philosophical, like *The Matrix*, be presenting an argument?

Bruce Russell (2000) would argue that *The Matrix* (and *To Kill a Mockingbird* and *1984* for that matter) doesn't do philosophy but merely inspires viewers (or readers) to do their own philosophy – to construct their own arguments and raise their own questions. I have three responses to this charge. First, even if Russell's claim is true and pop culture can't do philosophy (but instead merely inspires people to do philosophy), this handbook is still warranted, as it essentially contains the philosophy that pop culture inspired professional philosophers to do. Second, inspiring others to do philosophy can be (and often is) philosophy itself. Philosophy is often aimed at simply changing our perspective, making us think about the world or a situation in a way that we have not before. As any philosophy instructor will tell you, that is the goal of nearly every philosophy class. So, even if inspiring others to do philosophy is all a piece of popular culture does, that work of popular culture is still doing philosophy.

The third response is that this claim is simply false. Films can do more than inspire philosophy; they can do philosophy. To take a rather obvious example (anticipated by Smuts 2009), suppose someone took one of Plato's dialogues and turned it into a movie – which, of course, could be done because they are dialogues complete with characters and settings. Wouldn't it undeniably be philosophy? And couldn't the story of Plato's cave be made into a movie; and if it was, wouldn't it have just as much of a philosophical point as the story does in Plato's *Republic*? Or take the article, "A Debate Between a Theist and a Santa Clausist," that Ruth Tallman and I divided into two "acts" and published in the journal *Think* in 2015. It was written (and originally delivered at a conference) as a sketch, and could easily be turned into a short film that has the express purpose of convincing the audience that many of the arguments given in favor of theism could be given in defense in Santa Claus – and thus that theistic belief is on shaky ground. The quality of such a film might be questionable, but such a film would undoubtedly be philosophy.

In reply, skeptics might insist that a film can't be philosophy by simply putting philosophical arguments in the mouths of characters. But, again, I would object. First, why not? I mean, it would be one thing for a painter to say that he had a painting that "did philosophy," only to find out that he had just written a philosophical treatise on a canvas with a paint brush. That's not a painting. In the same way, just recording a video of someone giving a philosophy lecture wouldn't count as an example of "film as philosophy." That's not really a film; it's not cinema. (A recorded lecture lacks certain defining features of cinema at both an aesthetic and technical level.) But to have a character give a philosophical argument at a crucial moment that delivers the film's philosophical message doesn't disqualify a piece of media from being cinema. Take the film *God's Not Dead* for example. It not only contains a student – on three separate occasions – presenting formal arguments for God's existence, but it has the conclusion the movie is arguing for in the damn title! It may have lazy writing and be a really bad movie – and as one chapter in this handbook will show, the arguments it presents are pretty bad – but that doesn't mean it's not philosophy. (Bad philosophy is still philosophy.)

At this point in the debate, skeptics might argue that *good* film can't be philosophy. "Without just putting arguments in characters' mouths, films can't do philosophy. A *real* film would be able to show the argument without having a character 'spell it out' for the audience." There are two problems with claims like this. First, such a line of argument would be fallacious, something akin to the no-true-Scotsman fallacy. If I say that no Scotsmen lie, and then you produce a clear, obvious example of a lying Scotsman, I can't refute your counter example by simply claiming "he's not a *true* Scotsman." That's a fallacy. That's just me claiming, arbitrarily, that your example doesn't count so I don't have to admit I'm wrong. In the same way, those skeptical of the idea that films can be philosophy can't just say that movies like *My Dinner with Andre,* which involves two people having a philosophical dinner conversation, don't count "as philosophical films" because they contain people bluntly making philosophical arguments and thus aren't *true* films. In fact, *My Dinner with Andre* is frequently regarded as a masterpiece of a film – in part *because* of its philosophical content.

What's more, there seem to be clear examples of films, even very good films, doing philosophy without simply putting the argument for the film's thesis in the mouths of its characters. My favorite example might be *Contact*, the movie based on Carl Sagan's novel of the same name, in which aliens (seem to) make contact with Earth and give us instructions for building a device to visit them. Carl Sagan was a famous skeptic and science communicator who was labeled as an atheist by religious conservatives but who was, in reality, merely agnostic. In 2021, in chapter six of William Anderson's *Film, Philosophy and Religion*, I showed how *Contact* is an argument for a thesis that Sagan often defended in public: science and religion are compatible. The film has Dr. Arroway dismiss Rev. Palmer's belief in God because it is based solely on his personal experience, only to have Dr. Arroway turn around and believe that she visited aliens based solely on her personal experience. The argument Dr. Arroway uses against Rev. Palmer (based in Occam's razor) is turned back on her, and she answers it in almost the same way he answered her: "Everything I am tells me it was real. It changed me forever." The movie is an argument from analogy that it never formally states: if Arroway's beliefs based in her personal experience about aliens are justified, and they are, then Palmer's beliefs (and the beliefs of those like him in the real world) in God, based in personal experience, are justified as well. And such beliefs are as compatible with science as Dr. Arroway's are. As I try to explain in my aforementioned chapter, it's not a good argument – Dr. Arraoways' belief is not scientific and science and religion are not compatible in the way that Sagan or the movie suggests – but it is an argument, the kind that are made by philosophers every day. To deny that *Contact* is doing philosophy seems ludicrous.

Or take an even better example: *No Exit*, the play by Jean Paul Sartre that everyone agrees conveys very clearly his intended message: "Hell is other people." Although those words are spoken by the character Garcin, no formal argument for that thesis is put forth; yet the message is clearly there and the play (and thus the movie based on it) is very clearly doing philosophy. A film must do more than just illustrate a position or worldview to be philosophy; after all, mysticism and religion can merely state positions. But when films actually argue for a position, whether it be directly or indirectly, they seem to be doing philosophy.

Now, to be fair, pop culture may not be able to explore every nuance philosophers can in print; but (a) that is what projects like this handbook are for and (b) they might be able to explore other nuances in a way that philosophers can't in print. Think of how *Contact* is able to make the viewer experience Dr. Arroway's contact with her deceased "father" (or the alien she believes is taking his form) and thereby make them feel the same emotions she does – all to make the analogy stick in a way that the mere printed word can't. Or think of how a videogame – because of its immersive qualities and choice-making – can provide the player with a phenomenological experience that reading an argument simply cannot.

When Paisley Livingston (2006) entered the debate on this issue, he argued that doing philosophy in film required some very specific conditions. For film to really be considered philosophy, it must make an innovative, independent contribution to philosophy using only means "exclusive to the cinematic medium" – sounds, images, camera angles, visual setting, and the like – no spoken words (at least, not to convey the philosophical message). He called the idea that films could do this the "Bold Thesis." Since it seems that arguments and questions can only be made and raised with words, it seems that the Bold Thesis is false; film doing philosophy, in the way that Livingston says is must, would seem to be an impossible task. But, again, I have objections.

First, even if pop culture isn't making independent, innovative contributions to philosophy and instead is just putting already existing philosophical arguments into another form, so what? Pop culture has brought those arguments to the public's attention, so the arguments are still worth identifying and evaluating. Even if that's all this handbook does, it's still something that needs to be done.

Second, why use the restrictive definition that Livingston demands? Why must film be making *innovative, independent* contributions to philosophy to be doing philosophy? My introduction to philosophy course doesn't do that, yet I and my students are still doing philosophy. If a film makes an argument, then it is doing philosophy, even if someone else made that argument first. Further, why must a film only use elements unique to film to do philosophy? Yes, one might argue that there is no good way to disentangle the language from the cinema-exclusive elements, so there's no way to determine if the philosophy we find in a film gets its philosophical worth from the language the film uses or from its specifically cinematic elements. So, one might argue, the film isn't doing the philosophical work – it's just a delivery vehicle for language to do philosophy. But language is still an essential part of film; so why must language be excluded as a means by which filmmakers can do philosophy? Wouldn't that be like demanding that, if a song is going to rhyme (like poetry rhymes), it has to do with only with musical notes? "It can't use lyrics to rhyme, since notes are unique to songs but words are not!" That's ridiculous. Sure, musical notes can't rhyme, but musical notes are not all that is essential to a song. In the same way, maybe camera angles can't do philosophy – but that is just one element of a film.

Or think of it this way: Are comedians not doing philosophy when they use words to tell a joke with a philosophical point because words are not unique to comedy? Wouldn't this be like saying that philosophers can't make jokes while doing philosophy because jokes are not something unique to philosophy? Comedians aren't the only ones who get to use jokes to make people laugh, so why are philosophers the only ones who get to use language to do philosophy?

What's more, it seems that Livingston's burden can be met. In his defense of the bold thesis in his book *Joss Whedon as Philosopher*, Dean Kowalski (2017) persuasively argues that the *Buffy the Vampire* episode "Hush" coveys a message about the limitations inherent in propositional knowledge while containing not only no formal argument but almost no dialogue at all (p. 144-8). Now Livingston might object because the philosophical message of the episode can be put into words (e.g., "there are inherent limitations to propositional knowledge"), and (Livingston would argue) it is only once an argument is put into words that it has any value, or is even an argument to begin with. But notice that I have only been able to put the conclusion of the argument into words, not its premises. If the episode can make a conclusion arise within my mind without using language or any articulable premises, this seems to not only be a prime example of a film doing philosophy well, but doing it in exactly the way that Livingston says it must (to be philosophy). If Livingston would still insist that it "doesn't count" simply because I can understand the episode's non-linguistic argument well enough to put its conclusion into words, he has arbitrarily selected standards that would make film doing philosophy impossible. (This is something Livingston seemed to later acknowledge, in that he eventually admitted that Ingmar Bergman's films do philosophy; see Livingston 2009.)

Other criticisms of the "film as philosophy" thesis are answerable as well. Does the fact that works of popular culture are open to interpretation mean that they can't be doing philosophy? Why would it? The works of continental philosophers (such as Hegel, Schopenhauer, Nietzsche, Sartre, Foucault, and Deleuze) are definitely open to interpretation – as are the works of, say, Kant and Spinoza. But even as frustrating as some (like myself) find their works to be, no one will say that they aren't philosophy. Even if film always does its philosophy implicitly, rather than explicitly, well, so do a lot of philosophers. Does the fact that films are fictional while philosophy is supposed to reveal truth about the world mean that films can't do philosophy? Again, why would it? Philosophical thought experiments are fictional, but philosophers use them all the time – not only to reveal our intuitions but also philosophical truths about the world. Nozick's experience machine thought experiment, for example, is thought to be an effective refutation of hedonism. And wouldn't that mean that famous written philosophical works like *No Exit*, *The Stranger,* or *The Metamorphosis* are not philosophy just because they are works of fiction?

What's more, while the arguments against pop culture being philosophy seem to be aimed at preserving the integrity of philosophy, in reality they seem to undercut it. Consider *Saving Private Ryan*, Steven Spielberg's World War II movie that preceded his creation of the landmark HBO series *Band of Brothers*. After depicting the horrors of the war, including D-Day, and how a band of soldiers sacrificed themselves to save another – Private Ryan (Matt Damon), whose three brothers have all died in the war – Spielberg has Capt. Miller (Tom Hanks) simply give Ryan two dying words: "Earn this." An elderly Ryan then stands above Miller's grave in the present day and asks his wife to assure him that he led a good life. It's an obvious ethical call for Americans to (better) appreciate "the greatest generation," because of the sacrifices it made in its fight against fascism, and to better appreciate the life free of the influences of fascism that they earned us – to appreciate it both intellectually and emotionally and also in how they live. Given the rise of fascism in America and around the world more than 20 years later, the film takes on a new significance. But in 1998, it fundamentally changed my perspective on, and my appreciation of (and my relationship with), my (now) late grandfather, who earned a bronze star serving in the war's European theater. To insist that the ethical argument the movie makes is not actually a case of Spielberg doing philosophy seems to suggest that film can do better what philosophy is supposed to do best: affect people's beliefs and change the way they live.

Let me put it another way; this is an important point. Since the time of the ancients, the stated goal of philosophy has been to lead those who do it to "the good life" and an appreciation of what really matters. And philosophy is supposed to do this like nothing else; it is unique in that respect. But as Julian Baggini (2003) points out, fictional stories can and do accomplish this as well (p. 18). If film can do this without doing or being philosophy, then philosophy not only fails to be unique, it is superfluous: it's not really needed. If, instead, we recognize that when films do this, they are doing philosophy, then the uniqueness and indispensability of philosophy are preserved. Films can only change people's lives in this way because they can do philosophy. Yes, they can change my life in a raw, phenomenological way, by appealing to my emotions. But what makes media like film, games, and graphic novels so beautiful is that they can combine that kind of affective response with an intellectual (philosophical) one, so as to have a more genuine and long-lasting effect.

In the end, those who deny works of popular culture can be philosophy may simply have too rigid and inflexible a view of what philosophy is. Just like there are many ways for something to be a religion, and no one definition of religion captures them all, there are many different ways to do philosophy, many of which popular culture can and does engage in. How a piece of pop culture is philosophy may not always be obvious, but we can discern whether and how it is by taking a closer look at what is being conveyed – which is exactly what this handbook intends to do with nearly 100 pieces of pop culture that, I think, most readers will come to agree, are obviously doing philosophy.

"Let's Go to Work"

My goal here is not to give a detailed review of the debate surrounding the bold thesis or even a full defense of it. Christopher Falzon (n.d.) already has a well-informed overview of the debate on *The Internet Encyclopedia of Philosophy*, and much more knowledgeable philosophers than myself – like Stephen Mulhall (2008) and Dean Kowalski (2017), the latter of whom helped edit numerous chapters in this handbook – have elsewhere done a much better job of defending it. Instead, my goal here is to merely defend the idea that pop culture can be philosophy enough to justify the existence of this handbook. If you remain unconvinced, I highly recommend Mulhall (2008) and chapters six and seven of Kowalski's 2017 book. If you still remain unconvinced, I guess this handbook is not for you. But if you are – or if you didn't need convincing in the first place – you will find this handbook worthwhile. At least I hope so. While it was a labor of love, it took over five years to complete!

But before we begin, many thanks are in order. I'd like to thank Ruth Lefevre and Rekha Sukumar at Palgrave, the former of which set up this little project, and the latter of which helped with the logistics of pulling it off. I'd like to thank the other editors of the project – Chris Lay, Kimberly S. Engels, and Dean Kowalski – who helped out with the enormous workload, especially in the latter years of the project (after I finally realized that, without help, I couldn't complete it). You are all wonderful philosophers, careful editors, and great persons; the handbook is ten times better thanks to your involvement. I can't express enough my gratitude for your time, wisdom, and efforts. I'd also like to thank numerous colleagues that I roped into giving feedback on certain chapters, as well as many student aides and others who helped with formatting and proofing over the years. I'd also like to thank King's College for granting me a sabbatical to finally complete the project. I couldn't be more thankful to work at such a wonderful institution.

Finally, but most importantly, I'd like to thank every last one of the authors who contributed to this handbook, for their tireless efforts and for their patience in putting up with me as their editor. Much of the work on this handbook was done during the COVID pandemic; COVID even cost it a few chapters, as the pressures the pandemic brought made it impossible for some potential authors to complete their work. Indeed, even though the handbook has nearly 100 chapters, there are countless pieces of pop culture and comedians that I wanted covered but couldn't find an author for. But to those who did contribute, you all have my heartfelt thanks. Your work was fantastic! Although I know it took a long time to finally see the handbook in print, I hope that it was worth the wait.

Notes

1. The original source of this quote is debatable, but it is credibly attributed to Shaw. See https://quoteinvestigator.com/2016/03/17/truth-laugh/.
2. They can even take you on confusing but potentially enlightening philosophical journeys, like the continental philosophers Deleuze or Derrida do in their works. Admittedly, this volume does not deal with continental philosophy to a large degree. Perhaps that topic deserves its own volume.
3. I don't mean to imply that professional philosophers always get things right; only that non-professional philosophers doing philosophy are more likely to make philosophical mistakes, and thus the philosophical works of non-philosophers deserve an expert eye.
4. You can watch the clip here – and you should: https://southpark.cc.com/video-clips/mqwfxt/south-park-it-s-right-there

April 2024　　　　　　　　　　　　　　　　　　　　　　　　David Kyle Johnson

References

Apatow, Judd, and Michael Bonfiglo. 2022. *George Carlin's American Dream*. HBO.

Arp, Robert. 2006. South Park and philosophy. Wiley-Blackwell.

Baggini, Julian. 2003. Alien ways of thinking: Muhall's on film. *Film-Philosophy* 7 (24).

Basham, Greg, and Eric Bronson. 2003. *The Lord of the rings and philosophy*. Open Court.

Comedy Gold Minds (podcast, hosted by Kevin Hart). 2021. Hasan Minhaj. 18 Feb. https://comedy-gold-minds-with-kevin-hart.simplecast.com/episodes/hasan-minhaj-Lb_YEYiw

Falzon, Christopher. n.d. Philosophy through film. *Internet Encyclopedia of Philosophy*. https://iep.utm.edu/phi-film/

HBO (YouTube). 2022. *George Carlin's American dream: What George meant to me, featurette*. 20 May. https://www.youtube.com/watch?v=T_L3mDG9r4I

Herzogenrath, Bernd. 2017. *Film as philosophy*. Minneapolis/London: University of Minnesota Press.

Irwin, William, ed. 1999. *Seinfeld and philosophy*. Open Court.

———, ed. 2001. *The Simpsons and philosophy*. Open Court.

——— (ed.) 2002. The matrix and philosophy.

Irwin, William, and David Kyle Johnson, eds. 2022. *Introducing philosophy through pop culture: From socrates to star wars and beyond*. 2nd ed Wiley-Blackwell.

Johnson, David Kyle. 2009. *Heroes and philosophy*. Wiley-Blackwell.

———. 2011. *Inception and philosophy*. Wiley-Blackwell.

———. 2019. Black mirror and philosophy.. Wiley-Blackwell.

———. 2021. Contact and the incompatibility of science and religion. In *Film, philosophy and religion*, ed. William Anderson's. Vernon Press.

Khan Academy. 30 July 2020. Hasan Minhaj on finding your gifts, being authentic, & understanding yourself, Homeroom with Sal. YouTube video, 32:26. https://youtu.be/mm0Y3ym-JUg.

Kowalski, Dean. 2017. *Joss Whedon as philosopher*. Lexington Books.

Livingston, Paisley. 2006. Thesis on cinema as philosophy. In *Thinking through Cinema: Film as philosophy*, ed. Murry Smith and Thomas E. Wartenberg, 11–18. Hoboken: Wiley-Blackwell.

———. 2009. *Cinema, philosophy, Bergman: On film as philosophy*. 1st ed. Oxford University Press.

MacDonald, Norm. 2022. Nothing special. *Netflix*.

Miller, M. 2018. In a rare move, South Park admits it was wrong about climate change. *Esquire*, 15 Nov. https://www.esquire.com/entertainment/tv/a25127458/south-park-climate-change-manbearpig-apology-season-22-episode-7/

Mulhall, Stephen. 2008. *On Film*. New York: Routledge.

Read, Ruppert, and Jerry Goodenough. 2005. *Film as Philosophy: Essays on Cinema after Wittgenstien and Cavell*. Palgrave Macmillan.

Russell, Bruce. 2000. The philosophical limits of film. *Film and philosophy* (special edition): pp. 163–167.

Smith, Murry, and Thomas E. Wartenberg, eds. 2006. *Thinking through cinema: Film as philosophy.* Hoboken: Wiley-Blackwell.

Smuts, Aaron. 2009. Film as philosophy: In defense of a bold thesis. *The Journal of Aesthetics and Art Criticism* 67 (4): 409–420.

Tallman, Ruth, and David Kyle Johnson. 2015a. A debate between a theist and a Santa Clausist: Act I (co-authored with Ruth Tallman). *Think* 14 (40): 9–25. https://doi.org/10.1017/s147717561500010x.

Tallman, R., and D.K. Johnson. 2015b. A debate between a theist and a Santa Clausist: Act II (co-authored with Ruth Tallman). *Think* 14 (40): 27–41. https://doi.org/10.1017/s1477175615000111.

Wartenberg, Thomas. 2007. *Thinking on screen: Film as philosophy.* Routledge.

Written Voices. (n.d.) *About William Irwin with George A. Dunn and Rebecca Housel.* http://mail.writtenvoices.com/author_display.php?auth_id=Dunn

Contents

Volume 1

Part I Television and Streaming 1

1. *The Good Place* as Philosophy: Moral Adventures in the Afterlife 3
   Kimberly S. Engels

2. Twilight Zone as Philosophy 101 23
   Mimi Marinucci

3. *Star Trek* as Philosophy: Spock as Stoic Sage 41
   Massimo Pigliucci

4. *Star Trek: The Next Generation* as Philosophy: Gene Roddenberry's Argument for Humanism 65
   Kevin S. Decker

5. *Battlestar Galactica* as Philosophy: Breaking the Biopolitical Cycle 93
   Jason T. Eberl and Jeffrey P. Bishop

6. *Black Sails* as Philosophy: Pirates and Political Discourse 113
   Clint Jones

7. *Doctor Who* as Philosophy: Four-Dimensionalism and Time Travel 135
   Kevin S. Decker

8. *Breaking Bad* as Philosophy: The Moral Aesthetics of the Anti-hero's Journey 163
   David Koepsell

9. *The Handmaid's Tale* as Philosophy: Autonomy and Reproductive Freedom 185
   Rachel Robison-Greene

10 *Mister Rogers' Neighborhood* as Philosophy: Children as
    Philosophers 211
    David Baggett

11 *Futurama* as Philosophy: Wisdom from the Ignorance of a
    Delivery Boy 233
    Courtland D. Lewis

12 *Firefly* as Philosophy: Social Contracts, Political Dissent, and
    Virtuous Communities 259
    Dean A. Kowalski

13 *Arrested Development* as Philosophy:
    Family First? What We Owe Our Parents 283
    Kristopher G. Phillips

14 The Doctor as Philosopher: The Collectivist-Realist Pacifism of the
    Doctor and the Quest for Social Justice 311
    Paula Smithka

15 *Grey's Anatomy* as Philosophy: Ethical Ambiguity in Shades
    of Grey 341
    Kimberly S. Engels and Katie Becker

16 *House of Cards* as Philosophy: Democracy on Trial 361
    Brendan Shea

17 *Last Week Tonight* as Philosophy: The Importance of Jokalism ... 383
    Christelle Paré

18 *Russian Doll* as Philosophy: Life Is Like a Box of Timelines 407
    Richard Greene

19 *The Orville* as Philosophy: The Dangers of Religion ... 425
    Darren M. Slade and David Kyle Johnson

20 *Westworld* as Philosophy: A Commentary on Colonialism 453
    Matthew P. Meyer

21 *Black Mirror* as Philosophy: A Dark Reflection of Human
    Nature 479
    Chris Lay

22 *Rick & Morty* as Philosophy: Nihilism in the Multiverse 503
    Sergio Genovesi

23 *The X-Files* as Philosophy: Navigating the "Truth Out There" ... 519
    Dean A. Kowalski

24 *Game of Thrones* as Philosophy: Cynical Realpolitiks 541
    Eric J. Silverman and William Riordan

25	*The Mandalorian* as Philosophy: "This Is the Way" Lance Belluomini	555
26	*Midnight Mass* as Philosophy: The Problems with Religion David Kyle Johnson	581
27	*Squid Game* as Philosophy: The Myths of Democracy Leander Penaso Marquez and Rola Palalon Ombao	609
28	*South Park* as Philosophy: Blasphemy, Mockery, and (Absolute?) Freedom of Speech David Kyle Johnson	633
29	*Frank Herbert's Dune* as Philosophy: The Need to Think for Yourself Greg Littmann	673
30	*The Boys* as Philosophy: Superheroes, Fascism, and the American Right David Kyle Johnson	703

Volume 2

Part II Films **751**

31	*Inception* as Philosophy: Choose Your Dreams or Seek Reality David Kyle Johnson	753
32	*Okja* as Philosophy: Why Animals Matter Randall M. Jensen	773
33	*2001* as Philosophy: A Technological Odyssey Jerold J. Abrams	795
34	*The Lord of the Rings* as Philosophy: Environmental Enchantment and Resistance in Peter Jackson and J.R.R. Tolkien John F. Whitmire Jr and David G. Henderson	827
35	*Star Wars* as Philosophy: A Genealogy of the Force Jason T. Eberl	855
36	*The Godfather* as Philosophy: Honor, Power, Family, and Evil Raymond Angelo Belliotti	873
37	*Groundhog Day* as Philosophy: Phil Connors Says "No" to Eternal Return Kimberly Blessing	897

38	*The Big Lebowski*: Nihilism, Masculinity, and Abiding Virtue .... Peter S. Fosl	917
39	*Harry Potter* as Philosophy: Five Types of Friendship .... James M. Okapal	951
40	*Deadpool* as Philosophy: Using Humor to Rebel Against the System .... Matthew Brake	967
41	*Blade Runner* as Philosophy: What Does It Mean to Be Human? .... Timothy Shanahan	983
42	*Up in the Air* as Philosophy: Buddhism and the Middle Path .... Leigh Duffy	1005
43	*Ex Machina* as Philosophy: Mendacia *Ex Machina* (Lies from a Machine) .... Jason David Grinnell	1025
44	*Gattaca* as Philosophy: Genoism and Justice .... Jason David Grinnell	1043
45	*A.I.: Artificial Intelligence* as Philosophy: Machine Consciousness and Intelligence .... David Gamez	1061
46	*The Shawshank Redemption* as Philosophy: Freedom and Panopticism .... Alexander E. Hooke	1091
47	*Snowpiercer* as Philosophy: The Danger to Humanity .... Leander Penaso Marquez	1109
48	*The Matrix* as Philosophy: Understanding Knowledge, Belief, Choice, and Reality .... Edwardo Pérez	1131
49	*A Serious Man* as Philosophy: The Elusiveness of Moral Knowledge .... Shai Biderman	1151
50	*The Cabin in the Woods* as Philosophy: Cinematic Reflections on Ethical Complexity, Human Nature, and Worthwhile Horror .... Dean A. Kowalski	1169
51	*Magnolia* As Philosophy: Meaning and Coincidence .... Bart Engelen	1193

52	*Fight Club* as Philosophy: I Am Jack's Existential Struggle Alberto Oya	1217
53	Tarantino as Philosopher: Vengeance – Unfettered, Uncensored, but Not Unjustified David Kyle Johnson	1235
54	*The Man from Earth* as Philosophy: The Desirability of Immortality Kiki Berk	1271
55	*Avatar* as Philosophy: The Metaphysics of Switching Bodies Joshua L. Tepley	1289
56	*Pulp Fiction* as Philosophy: Bad Faith, Authenticity, and the Path of the Righteous Man Bradley Richards	1311
57	*Tenet* as Philosophy: Fatalism Isn't an Excuse to Do Nothing Lance Belluomini	1327
58	Tom Sawyer as Philosopher: Lying and Deception on the Mississippi Don Fallis	1349
59	*Don't Look Up* as Philosophy: Comets, Climate Change, and Why the Snacks Are Not Free Chris Lay and David Kyle Johnson	1373
60	*Little Women* as Philosophy: Death or Marriage and the Meaning of Life Kimberly Blessing	1411
61	*God's Not Dead* as Philosophy: Trying to Prove God Exists David Kyle Johnson	1435

Volume 3

Part III	Comedians	1467
62	Hannah Gadsby as Philosopher: Is Comedy Really Such a Good Thing? Mark Ralkowski	1469
63	Amy Schumer as Philosopher: Fuck the Feminine Mystique Charlene Elsby	1491
64	George Carlin as Philosopher: It's All Bullshit. Is It Bad for Ya? Kimberly S. Engels	1511

65	**Louis CK as Philosopher: The King and His Fall** .... 1533 Jennifer Marra Henrigillis	
66	**Marc Maron as Philosopher: Comedy, Therapy, and Identification** .... 1563 Steven S. Kapica	
67	**Hari Kondabolu as Philosopher: Enacting a Philosophy of Liberation** .... 1583 Brandyn Heppard	
68	**Richard Pryor as Philosopher: Stand-Up Comedy and Gramsci's Organic Intellectual** .... 1603 Cori Hall Healy	
69	**Larry David as Philosopher: Interrogating Convention** .... 1619 Noël Carroll	
70	**Jerry Seinfeld as Philosopher: The Assimilated Sage of New Chelm** .... 1631 Stephen Stern and Steven Gimbel	
71	**Dave Chappelle as Philosopher: Standing Up to Racism** .... 1643 Steven A. Benko and Reagan Scout Burch	
72	**Ricky Gervais as Philosopher: The Comedy of Alienation** ...... 1669 Catherine Villanueva Gardner	
73	**Hasan Minhaj as Philosopher: Navigating the Struggles of Identity** .... 1685 Pankaj Singh	
74	**Stephen Fry as Philosopher: The Manic Socrates** .... 1701 Christopher M. Innes	
75	**Phoebe Waller-Bridge as Philosopher: Conscious Women Making Choices** .... 1719 Neha Pande and Kimberly S. Engels	

Part IV   Video Games **1739**

76	*The Last of Us* **as Moral Philosophy: Teleological Particularism and Why Joel Is Not a Villain** .... 1741 Charles Joshua Horn	
77	*Journey* **as Philosophy: Meaning, Connection, and the Sublime** .... 1757 Russ Hamer	
78	*The Witness* **as Philosophy: How Knowledge Is Constructed** ..... 1771 Luke Cuddy	

79	*Cyberpunk 2077* as Philosophy: Balancing the (Mystical) Ghost in the (Transhuman) Machine Chris Lay	1789
80	*Detroit Become Human* as Philosophy: Moral Reasoning Through Gameplay Kimberly S. Engels and Sarah Evans	1811
81	*Papers, Please* as Philosophy: Playing with the Relations between Politics and Morality Juliele Maria Sievers	1833
82	*Planescape: Torment* as Philosophy: Regret Can Change the Nature of a Man Steven Gubka	1847
83	*Disco Elysium* as Philosophy: Solipsism, Existentialism, and Simulacra Diana Khamis	1865
84	*The Legend of Zelda: Breath of the Wild* as Philosophy: Teaching the Player to Be Comfortable Being Alone Chris Lay	1883
85	*Persona 5 Royal* as Philosophy: Unmasking (Persona)l Identity and Reality Alexander Atrio L. Lopez and Leander Penaso Marquez	1907
86	*God of War* as Philosophy: Prophecy, Fate, and Freedom Charles Joshua Horn	1929
Part V	**Graphic Novels**	**1947**
87	Frank Miller's Batman as Philosophy: "The World Only Makes Sense When You Force It To" Steve Bein	1949
88	*Watchmen* as Philosophy: Illustrating Time and Free Will Nathaniel Goldberg and Chris Gavaler	1969
89	The Joker as Philosopher: Killing Jokes Matthew Brake	1987
90	*From Hell* as Philosophy: Ripping Through Structural Violence James Rocha and Mona Rocha	2003
91	*Deadpool's* Killogy as Philosophy: The Metaphysics of a Homicidal Journey Through Possible Worlds Tuomas W. Manninen	2025

92	*V for Vendetta* as Philosophy: Victory Through the Virtues of Anarchy Clara Nisley	2043
93	Asterios Polyp as Philosophy: Master of Two Worlds Bradley Richards	2065
94	*Yes, Roya* and Philosophy: The Art of Submission Nathaniel Goldberg, Chris Gavaler, and Maria Chavez	2085
95	*The Walking Dead* as Philosophy: Rick Grimes and Community Building in an Apocalypse Clint Jones	2103
Index		2119

About the Editor-in-Chief

David Kyle Johnson is Professor of Philosophy at King's College (PA) who earned his Ph.D. at the University of Oklahoma and specializes in metaphysics, philosophy of religion, and scientific/critical reasoning. He also produces lecture series for Wondrium's *The Great Courses* (such as *Sci-Phi: Science Fiction as Philosophy*, *The Big Questions of Philosophy*, and *Exploring Metaphysics*) and has published in journals such as *Sophia*, *Religious Studies*, *Think*, *Philo*, *Religions, SHERM (Socio-Historical Examination of Religion and Ministry)*, and *Science, Religion, and Culture*. In addition to other duties, he regularly contributes chapters to and edits volumes for Blackwell's Philosophy and Pop Culture series (such as *Black Mirror and Philosophy: Dark Reflections*), and also co-edited *Introducing Philosophy Through Popular Culture* with the series editor William Irwin. He maintains two blogs for *Psychology Today: Plato on Pop* and *A Logical Take*.

About the Editors

Dean A. Kowalski is Professor of Philosophy and Chair of the Arts and Humanities Department in the College of General Studies at the University of Wisconsin-Milwaukee. He earned his Ph.D. in Philosophy from the University of Wisconsin-Madison. He specializes in the Philosophy of Religion and Metaphysics and has published articles in such academic journals as *Religious Studies* and *Philosophy and Theology*. He regularly teaches philosophy of religion, Asian philosophy, and ethics.

Prof. Dean has written extensively on philosophy and popular culture – both philosophy in popular culture and popular culture as philosophy – specializing in film and television. He has published articles in *The Journal of Whedon Studies* and *Film and Philosophy*, and more than 30 book chapters in volumes dedicated to popular culture. He is the author of *Joss Whedon as Philosopher* (2017), *Classic Questions and Contemporary Film*, 2nd edition (2016), and *Moral Theory at the Movies* (2012). He is the editor of *Indiana Jones and Philosophy* (2023), *The Big Bang Theory and Philosophy* (2012), *The Philosophy of The X-Files*, revised edition (2009), and *Steven Spielberg and Philosophy* (2008), and he is the co-editor of *The Philosophy of Joss Whedon* (2011).

Chris Lay earned his Ph.D. from the University of Georgia in 2018 and has held teaching positions at UGA, the University of Texas at El Paso, and Young Harris College in northeast Georgia. Currently, he runs the YHC philosophy program as Assistant Professor of Philosophy, offering courses like Science Fiction and Philosophy, Video Games as Philosophy, and Feminism in Horror Films. Professor Lay specializes in metaphysics – especially issues of personal identity and mereology – and the philosophy of popular culture generally, and he has published numerous "pop culture" volumes that bring the two subjects together.

Kimberly S. Engels is Associate Professor of Philosophy at Molloy University. She received her Ph.D. in Philosophy from Marquette University in 2017. Her research interests include existentialism, Native American philosophy, philosophy and pop culture, and UAP studies. She is the editor of *The Good Place and Philosophy: Everything Is Forking Fine!* and co-editor of *Westworld and Philosophy: If You Go Looking for the Truth, Get the Whole Thing*.

Contributors

Jerold J. Abrams Creighton University, Omaha, NE, USA

David Baggett School of Christian Thought, Houston Baptist University, Houston, TX, USA

Katie Becker Greensboro, NC, USA

Steve Bein Philosophy Department, University of Dayton, Dayton, OH, USA

Raymond Angelo Belliotti The State University of New York, Emeritus, Fredonia, NY, USA

Lance Belluomini San Francisco Bay Area, CA, USA

Steven A. Benko Meredith College, Raleigh, NC, USA

Kiki Berk Southern New Hampshire University, Manchester, NH, USA

Shai Biderman Beit-Berl College, Kfar Saba, Israel
Tel Aviv University, Tel Aviv, Israel

Jeffrey P. Bishop Center for Health Care Ethics and Department of Philosophy, Saint Louis University, St Louis, MO, USA

Kimberly Blessing Philosophy, SUNY Buffalo State, Buffalo, NY, USA

Matthew Brake Northern Virginia Community College, Manassas, VA, USA

Reagan Scout Burch Meredith College, Raleigh, NC, USA

Noël Carroll Philosophy Program, The Graduate Center, City University of New York, New York, NY, USA

Maria Chavez Charlottesville, VA, USA

Luke Cuddy Southwestern College, Chula Vista, CA, USA

Kevin S. Decker Eastern Washington University, Cheney, WA, USA

Leigh Duffy SUNY Buffalo State College, Buffalo, NY, USA

Jason T. Eberl Center for Health Care Ethics, Saint Louis University, St Louis, MO, USA

Charlene Elsby University of Ottawa, Ottawa, ON, Canada

Bart Engelen Tilburg Center for Moral Philosophy, Epistemology and Philosophy of Science (TiLPS), Tilburg University, Tilburg, The Netherlands

Kimberly S. Engels Molloy University, Rockville Centre, NY, USA

Sarah Evans Molloy University, Rockville, NY, USA

Don Fallis Philosophy, Northeastern University, Boston, MA, USA

Peter S. Fosl Transylvania University, Lexington, KY, USA

David Gamez Department of Computer Science, Middlesex University, London, UK

Catherine Villanueva Gardner University of Massachusetts Dartmouth, North Dartmouth, MA, USA

Chris Gavaler W&L University, Lexington, VA, USA

Sergio Genovesi University of Bonn, Bonn, Germany

Steven Gimbel Gettysburg College, Gettysburg, PA, USA

Nathaniel Goldberg W&L University, Lexington, VA, USA

Richard Greene Weber State University, Ogden, UT, USA

Jason David Grinnell Philosophy Department, SUNY Buffalo State, Buffalo, NY, USA

Steven Gubka Florida Atlantic University, Boca Raton, Florida, United States

Cori Hall Healy Bowling Green State University, Bowling Green, OH, USA

Russ Hamer Mount St. Mary's University, Emmitsburg, MD, USA

David G. Henderson Western Carolina University, Cullowhee, NC, USA

Brandyn Heppard Raritan Valley Community College, Somerville, NJ, USA

Alexander E. Hooke Stevenson University, Stevenson, MD, USA

Charles Joshua Horn University of Wisconsin-Stevens Point, Stevens Point, WI, USA

Christopher M. Innes Philosophy Department, Boise State University, ID, Boise, USA

Randall M. Jensen Northwestern College, Orange City, IA, USA

David Kyle Johnson Department of Philosophy, King's College, Wilkes-Barre, PA, USA

Clint Jones Plover, WI, USA
Capital University, Columbus, OH, USA

Steven S. Kapica Keuka College, Keuka Park, NY, USA

Diana Khamis Nijmegen, Netherlands

David Koepsell Department of Philosophy, Texas A&M, College Station, TX, USA

Dean A. Kowalski Arts and Humanities Department, University of Wisconsin-Milwaukee, College of General Studies, Waukesha, WI, USA

Chris Lay Young Harris College, Young Harris, GA, USA

Courtland D. Lewis Philosophy, Pellissippi State Community College, Knoxville, TN, USA

Greg Littmann Southern Illinois University Edwardsville, Edwardsville, IL, USA

Alexander Atrio L. Lopez University of the Philippines Diliman, Quezon City, Philippines

Tuomas W. Manninen Arizona State University, Glendale, AZ, USA

Mimi Marinucci Eastern Washington University, Cheney, WA, USA

Leander Penaso Marquez College of Social Sciences and Philosophy, University of the Philippines Diliman, Quezon City, Philippines

Jennifer Marra Henrigillis St. Norbert College, De Pere, WI, USA

Matthew P. Meyer University of Wisconsin–Eau Claire, Eau Claire, WI, USA

Clara Nisley Atlanta, GA, USA

James M. Okapal Missouri Western State University, Saint Joseph, MO, USA

Rola Palalon Ombao College of Social Sciences and Philosophy, University of the Philippines Diliman, Quezon City, Philippines

Alberto Oya IFILNOVA – Instituto de Filosofia da Nova (Universidade Nova de Lisboa), Lisboa, Portugal

Neha Pande Royal Roads University, Victoria, BC, Canada

Christelle Paré Department of Communication, University of Ottawa, Ottawa, ON, Canada
École nationale de l'humour, Montréal, Québec, Canada

Edwardo Pérez Tarrant County College, Fort Worth, TX, USA
The University of Texas at Arlington, Arlington, TX, USA

Kristopher G. Phillips Southern Utah University, Cedar City, UT, USA
Eastern Michigan University, Ypsilanti, MI, USA

Massimo Pigliucci Department of Philosophy, The City College of New York, New York, NY, USA

Mark Ralkowski George Washington University, Washington, DC, USA

Bradley Richards Department of Philosophy, York University, Toronto, ON, Canada

William Riordan Christopher Newport University, Newport News, VA, USA

Rachel Robison-Greene Utah State University, Logan, UT, USA

James Rocha California State University, Fresno, CA, USA

Mona Rocha Clovis Community College, Clovis, CA, USA

Timothy Shanahan Department of Philosophy, Loyola Marymount University, Los Angeles, CA, USA

Brendan Shea Rochester Community and Technical College, Rochester, MN, USA

Juliele Maria Sievers Federal University of Alagoas, Maceió, Brazil

Eric J. Silverman Christopher Newport University, Newport News, VA, USA

Pankaj Singh School for Life (SFL), University of Petroleum and Energy Studies, Dehradun, India

Darren M. Slade Global Center for Religious Research (GCRR), Denver, CO, USA

Paula Smithka University of Southern Mississippi, Hattiesburg, MS, USA

Stephen Stern Gettysburg College, Gettysburg, PA, USA

Joshua L. Tepley Saint Anselm College, Manchester, NH, USA

John F. Whitmire Jr Western Carolina University, Cullowhee, NC, USA

Part II

Films

Inception as Philosophy: Choose Your Dreams or Seek Reality

31

David Kyle Johnson

Contents

Introduction	754
Summarizing *Inception*	754
Figuring Out the Ending	757
Interpreting the Entire Movie	758
The Moral of *Inception*	761
Evaluating *Inception*'s Moral	764
Defense 1: Knowledge Is Completely Impossible	765
Defense 2: Reality Does Not Exist	766
Defense 3: While Some Knowledge Is Possible, the True Nature of Reality Is Beyond Us	767
Defense 4: Taking a Leap of Faith	768
Defense 5: It's Acceptable to Place the Best Wager	769
Defense 6: Soften the Moral	770
Conclusion: Applying the Moral	771
References	771

Abstract

Christopher Nolan' *Inception* is more than its folding cityscapes and mind-bending ambiguous ending. It's a film that makes its viewer question the very nature of reality. Not only is it possible that the entire movie is a dream, but multiple viewings of *Inception* leaves one wondering whether the same might be true of one's experience. Indeed, according to the author of "The Fiction of Christopher Nolan" Todd McGowan, *Inception* calls its viewers to abandon any concern they have for knowledge of reality and instead choose to believe what they want. But does this moral hold up? Is it philosophically defensible? In this

---

D. K. Johnson (✉)
Department of Philosophy, King's College, Wilkes-Barre, PA, USA
e-mail: davidjohnson@kings.edu

© Springer Nature Switzerland AG 2024
D. K. Johnson et al. (eds.), *The Palgrave Handbook of Popular Culture as Philosophy*,
https://doi.org/10.1007/978-3-031-24685-2_5

chapter, after a close inspection of the movie itself, this moral will be identified and evaluated. An examination of a number of related arguments by important philosophers will reveal that, although knowledge of reality is sometimes difficult to attain, it should always be sought.

Keywords

Inception · Quest for reality · Knowledge of reality · True belief · Christopher Nolan · Dom Cobb · Hans Zimmer · Edith Piaf's "Non, Je Ne Regette Rien" · Film ambiguity · Rene Descartes · The dream problem · The skeptical problem · Descartes' evil demon · Kierkegaard's leap of faith · Jacques Lacan · Plato's cave allegory · Nozick's experience machine · Abduction · Kantian categories · Pascal's wager · William Clifford · David Hume · Problem of induction · Fictionalism

Introduction

> The dream has become their reality. Who are you to say otherwise, sir?
> —Elderly Bald Man

Christopher Nolan's 2010 film *Inception* became a classic almost as soon as it was projected on silver screens. Although it only won Academy Awards for its cinematography, visual effects, sound mixing, and sound editing, it was much more than its famous folding cityscapes and zero gravity fights. Its story was truly mind-bending. It's ambiguous ending not only left one unsure of whether the protagonist Dom Cobb was really reunited with his children – but the multiple viewings *Inception* demanded left one wondering whether the entirely of the movie was a dream. Interestingly, Nolan was completely aware of this question, and actually had a particular answer to it in mind as he made the film–but he also intends to never reveal it.

The philosophical meaning of *Inception* – the moral of the story – is equally illusive. Is it some kind of psychological allegory? An exploration of whether one should be more dedicated to their kids than their spouse? A commentary on how movies incept ideas into us? A suggestion that life might be a dream? A call to embrace dreams and abandon reality? Finding and evaluating *Inception*'s moral shall be the goal of this chapter, but any attempt to understand *Inception* must begin with a quick summary for even those who have seen it could still be confused by its plot.

Summarizing *Inception*

Inception is set in a world in which teams of people known as "extractors" steal secrets from people's minds using a dream sharing technology known as a PASIV (Portable Automated Somnacin IntraVenous) device. Extraction usually takes a team of two or three – an architect to design the dream that the target will be pulled into, another to dream it, and yet another to explore the dream and find "the safe" where the target has hidden their secrets. Any other persons in the dream are projections of the target's subconscious – or in some cases, the team member's. To wake, a person has to either die in the dream, experience a "kick" outside the dream (e.g., a falling sensation), or the PASIV device's timer has to run out. Time also passes more quickly in a dream such that being hooked up to a PASIV device for only 5 min might produce a dream that seems like it lasts an hour.

The film follows Dom Cobb, the world's most skilled extractor, who was forced to abandon his children and flee the country after being charged with murdering his wife (who committed suicide by jumping out a window and tried to force Cobb to follow her by making it look like murder). He makes his living doing extractions but desperately hopes to be cleared of the charges and reunited with his children.

The film opens with Cobb awakening on a beach and then being dragged away by guards to a large house on a cliff. There he meets Saito, an elderly man who seems to recognize Cobb. Then, all of a sudden, although they are still in the same house, Saito is young and Cobb (alongside his partner Arthur) is explaining to Saito the resilient nature of ideas and offering to teach him how to protect himself from extraction.

We soon learn, however, that the scene is a dream and Cobb and Arthur are there to extract an idea from Saito's mind. Indeed, to do so, they have subjected Saito to a dream within a dream – a fact that impresses Saito to no end. Although the extraction fails, partly because the first dream was sabotaged by a subconscious projection of Cobb's dead wife Mal, Saito tracks them down and reveals that he wants to hire Cobb to perform an "*inception.*" Instead of extracting an idea, he wants Cobb to implant one – in the mind of Robert Fisher, the son of his main business competitor. If Cobb can get Fisher to break up the energy company that he is about to inherit, Saito says he can get the charges against Cobb dropped with a single phone call. Cobb doubts that he can deliver, but Saito convinces him my pointing out that Cobb can either "take a leap of faith" and believe that he can, or "become an old man, filled with regret, waiting to die alone" (Nolan 2010a).

In addition to Arthur, the team Cobb assembles includes Ariadne, a star architecture student (of Cobb's father-in-law, Miles); Eames, a dream forger (who can take on the persona of other people in a dream), and Yusuf, a chemist (who can mix a sedative strong enough for the inception, which will require a three-layered dream). As part of her training, Arthur teaches Ariadne about paradoxical dream architecture (e.g., Penrose steps) and totems – small objects team members keep in their pocket to determine whether they are in someone else's dream. Cobb's totem is a top, which perpetually spins in other's dreams. Arthur's is a loaded die, of which only he knows the weight and feel. Ariadne fashions one out of a chess bishop.

While recruiting Eames in Mombasa, Cobb is almost apprehended by Cobol, the company which hired him to perform the extraction on Saito – who is also inexplicably in Mombasa and rescues Cobb from Cobol's clutches. Saito, Cobb, and Eames then visit Yusuf, who shows them how well his sedative works on a cove of dreamers in his basement who use it every day to share dreams. Indeed, it is so strong that it compounds the time slippage in dreams by a factor of 20; 10 hours in the real world will mean a week on the first level of the inception dream, 6 months on the second, and 10 years on the third. They won't be able to wake up until the sedative wears off, but once the inception is successful the team will "synchronize kicks" in each of the dream levels to get them back up to the first.

They attempt to incept Fisher on a flight from Sydney to Los Angeles, as Fisher accompanies his father's body back home. Everyone goes in: Cobb, Arthur, Ariadne, Saito, Yusuf, and Eames. In the first layer, which happens in a city, the team intends to kidnap Robert and put him alongside his godfather Peter Browning – or, more accurately, Eames disguised as Fisher's godfather Peter Browning. Eames will lead Fischer to believe that his father left him an alternate will that would break up the company; this will bring to mind the idea that Fischer "shouldn't follow in his father's footsteps." The hope is that, in the second layer of the dream (which happens in a hotel), Fisher's own subconscious projection of Browning will feed a version of that idea back to him. That way it will "seem self-generated." And, indeed, it works; in the second layer, Fischer's projection of Browning tells him that his father wanted him "to create something for himself."

In the process of kidnapping Fisher in the first layer, however, Saito gets shot and wounded. Cobb then revels that if anyone dies under Yusuf's heavy sedative, they won't wake up but instead descend into limbo – an unconstructed subconscious dream space below the third dream layer, where time has almost no meaning and one could go insane. In an aside, Cobb tells Ariadne how he once spent (what seemed like) 50 years in limbo with Mal. Indeed, that is what led to her death. When they awoke, she still thought they were dreaming, and that she had to die to wake up.

The team decides that the only way to save Saito is to press on. In the third dream layer, they hope Fischer will place a projection of his dying father into the safe of a mountain fortress. But just as Fisher is about to enter the safe, Cobb's projection of Mal appears and shoots Fisher, causing him to descend into limbo. Cobb and Ariadne follow, and find Fischer held captive by Cobb's projection of Mal. Mal pleads with Cobb to stay with her in limbo, but Cobb counters by revealing that he was responsible for the idea that killed her. When they were in limbo, she intentionally forgot she was dreaming. To get her to leave, Cobb incepted into her the idea that her world wasn't real – that to awaken, she had to kill herself. But the incepted idea stuck even after they awoke. That's how Cobb knew inception was possible and why Mal committed suicide. Ariadne shoots Mal and Cobb decides to stay behind to rescue Saito, who has by now died and thus and decended into limbo.

To return them to the mountain fortress dream, Ariadne kills Fisher and then herself. Once there, Fisher does indeed find his dying father in the safe, who clarifies his last word to Fischer. His father wasn't "disappointed" that Fisher wasn't more like him, but that he had tried to be. This cements Fisher's decision to break up his father's company. With the inception complete, Fisher, Ariadne, Eames, and the rest of the team (minus Cobb and Saito who are still stuck in limbo) "ride the kicks" back up to the first dream layer.

The film then ends where it began: Cobb with Saito as an old man, filled with regret, waiting to die alone in his house on a cliff – having been stuck in limbo for

31 Inception as Philosophy: Choose Your Dreams or Seek Reality

decades. Cobb asks Saito to take a leap of faith. Saito reaches for Cobb's gun...and then we cut to Cobb dreamingly awakening on the plane. He looks across to Saito, who places a phone call. Cobb safely makes his way through immigration and then to his home. He spins his top to see whether he is dreaming...but when he sees his children, he leaves it behind. While they greet him, the camera pans down to the still spinning top – and cuts to black before we see whether it falls.

Figuring Out the Ending

That ending of course left audiences wondering. Did the top fall? Knowing the answer would seem to reveal whether Cobb really returned to his kids. A closer examination of the film, however, reveals that this is not the case – and understanding why is the key to a deeper understanding of the film.

First, as Arthur makes clear in his first scene with Ariadne, a person's totems can only tell them whether they are in *someone else's dream* – not their own. It only works if neither the dreamer nor the architect knows how it functions. This is why Arthur won't let Ariadne hold his die, and why Cobb praises her for not letting him hold her bishop. Since Cobb knows how it functions, even if Cobb's top falls, he could still be in his own dream.

Second, Cobb is not the only one who knows how his totem works. Right after he praised Ariadne for not letting him know how her totem works, he revealed to her the function of his: "This one was Mal's. She would spin it in a dream, and it would just spin and spin." His top is therefore useless as a means of telling whether he escaped the inception; Ariadne designed every one of the inception's dreams.

Third, Cobb's top cannot be effective as a reality detector because it's backwards. In order for the dreamer to not know how it works, it must have unique property in reality – one that the dreamer would not know it has. Arthur's weighted die, for example, falls on a particular number in the real world, but falls like normal in a dream (because that's how a dreamer would assume it works). So too with Eames' totem, a Mombasa poker chip with an extra "s" in Mombasa. (It is not seen in the film, but official prop replicas were seen at comic-cons.) If he looked down and didn't see "Mombassa," he would know that he was in someone else's dream, because they would spell it correctly. The behavior of Cobb's totem, on the other hand, is ordinary in the real world but unique in a dream. If he spun it in say, Saito's dream, it would fall – because that is what Saito believes tops do.

This is important because, at film's end, Cobb could very well be in Saito's dream. Why? Consider what Ariadne and Fischer dying in limbo, during the inception, reveals about where one goes when one dies in limbo. They do not wake back up into the real world. They go "one layer up" (to Eames' snow fortress dream) and then "ride the kicks" back up to Yusuf's kidnap dream. When Cobb finds Saito in limbo as an old man, Saito presumably shoots himself and Cobb follows suit. But, if this movie is consistent, this would only send them "one layer up," to where Eames' Snow fortress dream was. Believing that he had awoken, Saito could easily fill this layer with a dream of returning to the plane, and Cobb could just as easily find himself in it.

Now it's possible that, by the time Cobb and Saito exited limbo, the timer on the PASIV device had expired and thus killing themselves in limbo would awaken Cobb and Saito into the real world. And the way the end of the film is cut, that certainly is one interpretation. But this is by no means guaranteed. Recall the temporal relationship between the inceptions' dreams and the real world. The plane ride is 10 hours and they can't awake until that time is up. Yusuf's Kidnap dream is a week; Arthur's hotel dream is 6 months, and Eames snow fortress dream is 10 years. But by the time the *Inception* on Fischer is complete, and everyone but Cobb and Saito are back up to Yusuf's kidnap dream, only an hour (at most) has passed in that dream. So they still have nearly a week to spend there! Therefore, if Saito did go one layer up (to Eames' abandoned snow fortress dream level) and make it his own, even after exiting limbo, Cobb could still have 10 years to spend in that dream. His "kids" could be teenagers before he awakes on the plane.

That it was exactly this that happened is suggested by the last line of the film. Not only is the entire end sequence "dreamy," with little dialogue, and abrupt cuts – and not only are Cobb's children initially in the exact position he always dreams seeing them in – but when Cobb turns his back on his totem to greet his kids, and asks them what they are doing, his son says "we're building a house on a cliff." This is significant because of what the film establishes regarding how subconscious elements work their way through dreams. The train that killed Mal and Cobb in limbo also appears in Yusuf's kidnap dream; the number of its front (3502) is even the same number as their hotel suit. The number Fischer gives Cobb in the first layer (528,491) is the room numbers in the second (528 and 491) and ends up being the combination of the safe in the third. It would seem quite coincidental, then, for Saito to have spent years in limbo living in a house on a cliff, and then for Cobb's children to just so happen to be building a house on a cliff in the real world.

Taken together, this all reveals that even if the camera stayed on a few seconds longer and revealed that the top fell, Cobb could still be dreaming. This is what makes the ending of *Inception* so brilliant. It's a magic trick; it's misdirection. Everyone was watching what the top is doing in the lower left to find out whether Cobb is still dreaming, but they should have been listening to what was going on in the upper right.

Interpreting the Entire Movie

The realization that dying in limbo only sends a person one "layer" up – to the dream via which that person entered limbo – raises another question: Did Cobb and Mal actually make it back to the real world? When Cobb explains how they entered limbo, he specifically says that they were "exploring the concept of a dream within a dream." They lay their heads down onto the train track in limbo, and then wake up on an apartment floor; but if one only goes one layer up upon awaking from limbo, wouldn't that be the deepest layer of the multilevel dream they used to enter limbo in the first place? If so, Mal was right; they were dreaming and she awoke after jumping from the hotel-room ledge.

Awareness of the possibility that the entire movie is dream reveals a host of other interesting things about it. For example, given that extractors and inceptors create dreams that are like mazes, it seems a little on the nose that the overhead shots of the Mombasa chase scene make Mombasa look exactly like a maze. Indeed, many of elements of the chase scene are very dreamlike – like when the walls seem to close in around Cobb, when Cobb can't get the shopkeeper to be quiet, when the people chasing Cobb literally come out of nowhere, and when Saito shows up inexplicably to rescue him.

That this was supposed to make one question the reality of the supposed real world was articulated by Nolan himself. "The idea of showing Mombasa as mazelike was, for me, a very specific narrative point in the film. When Cobb finally confronts Mal at the end and she brings up the idea that Cobb no longer believes in one reality, you need to have shown the audience the potential for the real world to have the same rule set as the dreams. The mazelike nature of Mombasa was very important for this" (Nolan 2010).

And Nolan didn't stop there. Eames seems to not only be able to forge objects in dreams but also in the supposed real world. In the Mombasa casino, Eames loses what the script calls "his last two chips" in a bet (Nolan 2010b). But he then immediately has two giant stacks of chips to cash in. Cobb even recognizes them as forgeries. "I see your spelling hasn't improved." Apparently, they have the extra "s." What's more, Eames seems to be able to lift Fisher's passport in the real world (on the plane) in exactly the same way that he lifts Fisher's wallet in Arthur's hotel dream: without even touching him.

Or consider what Cobb says about how dreams are often strange in obvious ways that we don't recognize in the moment. "Dreams, they feel real while we're in them, right? It's only when we wake up that we realize something was actually strange." With this in mind, think of where Mal is before she leaps to her supposed death in front of Cobb. We are led to believe that she trashed their hotel room to make it look like they struggled and then crawled out onto the ledge of their hotel room window. But she is actually sitting in the window of *another hotel room* opposite theirs – one just like theirs but that is not trashed. I suppose it's possible she rented a second hotel room and went to it after she trashed theirs; but Cobb keeps motioning to her to come back inside their hotel room, as if she can just float across. He doesn't recognize the oddity.

In the movie, during what is known to be dreams, there are jump cuts – where the characters, mid conversation, just appear in new rooms or places without explanation. For example, when Cobb is talking to Mal for the first time in the film, they go from the outside ledge, to inside a room, mid-conversation. This is a function of how dreams work. As Cobb points out to Ariadne in their first shared dream, "You never really remember the beginning of a dream, do you? You always wind up right in the middle of what's going on." And yet, in the supposed real world, there are a barrage of exactly these kinds of cuts. For example, when Cobb visits Miles' classroom in

Paris, he is standing outside the classroom looking in – and then without opening the door, or even moving at all, he is suddenly, inexplicably, there in the classroom.

Lines and facts in the film also seem to suggest that the "real world" is a dream. During his classroom visit, Miles' implores Cobb to "come back to reality" and Cobb's projection of Mal repeatedly telling him that he knows what he has to do to get back to her seems to indicate that, to find her, he must die to wake up. And the fact that Cobb cannot sleep or dream anymore unless he is hooked up to a PASIV device makes one wonder: can he not sleep or dream anymore because he already is? And Fisher's subconscious is trained even though such training did not appear in Arthur's research. Was Arthur inept – or does Fisher know how to defend against extraction because he's really just a projection of Cobb's subconscious?

Speaking of which, could all the characters just be projections of Cobb's subconscious? After all, Arthur, Ariadne, Eames, Saito, Yusuf – these one-dimensional characters, that only seem to be there to do Cobb's bidding – don't even have last names. But their names do have symbolic significance. In Greek mythology, Ariadne guided her brother through a circular labyrinth (a maze) to defeat the Minotaur. Arthur, who tries to keep Cobb grounded in reality, means "rock" in English. Saito, who cleanses Cobb's record, means "purifying flower" in Japanese. "Yusuf" is Arabic for Joseph, the biblical character known for dreaming and dream interpretation. And isn't "Eames" a little too close to "dreams?"

Then there is the music. The song Cobb's team uses to signal the end of a dream is Edith Piaf's "Non, Je Ne Regette Rien" (which translates as "No, I regret nothing"). Hans Zimmer, who wrote the musical score for the film, based his composition on how different parts of that song sounds at different speeds (just like a dreamer would hear it in a time-altered dream). "[A]ll the music in the score is subdivisions and multiplications of the tempo of the Edith Piaf track," he said in the New York Times (Itzkoff 2010). The iconic deep pulsating score that opens the film is based on how the beginning of Piaf's song sounds when it is slowed down by about a factor of 10 (just like a dreamer would hear it) – a fact he hinted at during end of the credit sequence, when Piaf's song is played one last time, and then seemingly slowed down and faded out as the pulsating score kicks back in. What's more, the original famous live recording of Piaf's song the movie uses is 2 min and 28 seconds long (0:2.28). And the movie *Inception* is, to the second, 2 hours and 28 minutes long (2:28.00) – almost as if the movie is longer than the song by a *factor of 10*. The math is not exact, but those who notice these details are clearly meant to suspect that the entire movie takes place during one playing of Piaf's song – and when the song is done, the dream is over.

Realizing that Nolan payed attention to details like this make oddities that one first attributed to editing errors start to look like subtle clues. When Cobb's top is spinning for the final time in the film, the number of paintbrushes in the glass inexplicably multiply. As the team plans the inception, the newspaper articles about Fischer in Cobb's folder change without him turning the page. Are these even more subtle hints that Cobb is dreaming?

Of course, none of this proves that the entire movie is a dream. But it certainly does raise the possibility. At the least, it is a legitimate question. Nolan himself certainly had this possibility in mind as he made the film. To him it was "very important that the dream worlds reflect the same rules as what's presented as reality." Indeed, Nolan likely had an answer to this question in mind as he made the film. When Wired Magazine's Robert Capps asked Nolan about the end of the film, he replied.

> Oh no, I've got an answer... I've always believed that if you make a film with ambiguity, it needs to be based on a sincere interpretation. If it's not, then it will contradict itself, or it will be somehow insubstantial and end up making the audience feel cheated. I think the only way to make ambiguity satisfying is to base it on a very solid point of view of what you think is going on, and then allow the ambiguity to come from the inability of the character to know, and the alignment of the audience with that character. (Nolan 2010)

That which has been considered up to this point certainly seems to suggest that he was doing this with the entire film.

The Moral of *Inception*

There are multiple messages and morals that one can find in *Inception*. One centers on the possibility of inception itself. Is it possible to implant an idea in a person's mind in such a way that the person thinks they came up with it themselves? Cobb initially says it is impossible, but of course he does pull it off. And to pull it off, Cobb and his team do something so similar to producing a movie that one wonders if Nolan is suggesting that movies can and do incept us. Cobb, who assembles and directs the team, is like a director. Ariadne, who creates the worlds her audience will inhabit, is the screenwriter. Arthur, who organizes and sets everything up, is the producer and Saito, who bankrolls the entire endeavor, is the production company. Eames, who pretends to be Peter Browning and the sexy blonde, is the actor. Yusuf, whose technical savvy allows them to pull the whole thing off, is special effects. And Fisher, of course, is the audience. As Nolan himself says, "I think that there's a fairly strong relationship in a lot of ways between what the team is trying to provide for their subject, Fischer, and what we're trying to do as filmmakers" (Nolan 2010).

Recall what *Inception* is: implanting an idea in someone in such a way that they think they came up with it themselves. This way the idea "sticks." It could even "define him; it may come to change...well it may come to change everything about him." And movies change people's lives all the time. Indeed, media of all kinds is used to incept us. Advertisements implant the idea to buy or use their products; one often doesn't even remember why they are craving certain foods. Politicians incept ideas into people about their opponents by using ominous music and pictures. Indeed, instead of calling it "hacking," one could accurately describe the outcome of the misinformation campaign that Russia launched (on Facebook and Twitter) to help elect Donald Trump in 2016 as a successful inception of the American people.

One idea that *Inception* incepts into its audience is the idea that Cobb incepted into Mal: the idea that one might actually be dreaming – that one can't know what is real. This is especially true if one watches the movie multiple times and realizes that, contrary to first appearances, the entire movie might be a dream. This idea, and its consequences, can feel like something one realized or came up with all on one's own – when, in reality, Nolan intentionally made the movie ambiguous on this very point to make the viewer question the nature of their reality.

Of course Nolan was not the first to recognize this worry. It was most famously articulated by Rene Descartes, in his "Meditations on First Philosophy," where he searched for an undoubtable belief on which he could ground scientific inquiry. The idea that the world was real was an early candidate for such a belief, but he then realized that he could be dreaming. What he was experiencing felt real of course; but he'd also had dreams in which he had felt the same assuredness – dreams in which he was just as convinced that he was awake (when, of course, he was not).

Now this didn't drive him to the conclusion that the external world didn't exist; after all, the ideas in his dreams had to come from somewhere. But he then went on to consider the possibility that all that existed was him and an evil demon – an evil demon who, like Cobb had in Mal, entered his mind to incept into Descartes a false idea. But while Cobb incepted into Mal the idea that the world wasn't real, Descartes was worried that a demon had incepted into him the idea that the world was real when it was not. "[What if] some malicious deomon of the utmost power and cunning has employed all his energies in order to deceive me, [what if] the sky, the air, the earth, colors, shapes, sounds, and all external things are merely the delusions of dreams which he has devised to ensare my judgment?" (Cottingham 2013, p. 15). Indeed, Descartes argued, the demon could even make it seem to Descartes that $2 + 3 = 5$ when in fact it did not. Descartes thought that the fact that he could not prove any of this false threatened his ability to have any knowledge at all.

This is called the skeptical problem. And the moral message of *Inception* seems to revolve around this issue. How should one respond to the threat of ignorance...to one's inability to have knowledge, not only about the existence of the world but about the myriad of things in it? Should one press on in an attempt to discover the truth, or should one abandon the quest and simply choose what to believe for the sake of one's own sanity or convenience?

At first, *Inception* seems to defend the former approach. Cobb's projection of Mal, the antagonist of the film, pleads with Cobb to embrace ignorance and simply choose to believe what he wants. As she says to him in limbo, at the end of the film: "admit it, Dom. You don't believe in one reality anymore. So choose. Choose your reality like I did. Choose to be here. Choose me." But our protagonist Cobb, it seems, is endlessly concerned with making sure his world is real and getting back to his children in the real world. "Our children. I have to get back to them. Because you left them. You left us...our real children are waiting for me up above." Since the viewer should identify with the protagonist, it seems this is the viewpoint the movie means for the viewer to embrace.

But that same scene undermines this interpretation. When Mal points out that what Cobb thinks of as the real world could actually be a dream – because he is being "chased around the globe by anonymous corporations and police forces, the way the projections persecute the dreamer" – he dismisses the possibility out of hand. He doesn't even consider it; indeed, in the shooting script, after he initially says "I know what's real," he immediately admits that he has merely "chosen" to believe that his real children are waiting for him up above.

The ending of the movie, where Cobb supposedly rejoins his children, signifies this choice. Cobb briefly worries that he is still dreaming and spins his top to determine whether he is; but as soon as he hears his children approaching, he loses interest and looks away. As Nolan himself said about this ending, "sometimes I think people lose the importance of the way the thing is staged with the spinning top at the end. Because the most important emotional thing is that Cobb's not looking at it. He doesn't care." Cobb has abandoned his search for reality.

But the moral of *Inception* is not just about how one should react to the skeptical problem; it's about how one should react any time one realizes that one lacks knowledge. Again, as Nolan says, "without getting too wild and woolly about it, the idea is that by the end of the film people will start to realize that the situation is very much like real life. We don't know what comes next; we don't know what happens to us after we die. And so the idea of the leap of faith is the leap into the unknowability of where the characters find themselves" (Nolan 2010).

The leap of faith indeed does play a prominent role in the film. And just like Cobb takes a leap of faith at the beginning of the film to believe "Saito can deliver on his promise to reunite me with my children," Cobb takes a leap at the end to believe "I have returned to the real world and been reunited with my children." In both cases, it seems that without such a leap, Cobb will become an "old man, filled with regret, waiting to die alone." And this, it seems, is the moral of the film: when faced with uncertainty about anything, instead of searching for reality, one should simply choose to believe what is most advantageous to believe – even to just believe what one wants. As Todd McGowan, author of "The Fiction of Christopher Nolan," puts it.

> *Inception* ... suggests ... a marginalization of the question of reality for the sake of one's object [of desire] ... an object that comes to the fore[front] in the dream or in the fiction. Instead of seeking new answers in the real world, we must change the question in a way that obviates our obsession with reality. The point is not whether one inhabits the real world but whether one has betrayed or remained faithful to one's object [of desire]. (McGowan 2012, p. 170)

According to McGowan, the point of *Inception* is not the question of whether Cobb is still dreaming. Instead, it illustrates Jacques Lacan's idea that dreams are what contain the truth, and that one wakes from them and enters the real world to hide oneself from the truths they contain. For example, dreams can reveal one's true desires that one doesn't want to admit; awakening from the dream shields one from facing them and thus from the truth. But one *should* face them; one should thus abandon their quest to determine what is real and embrace the dream. For McGowan, Mal "is the de facto hero of the film" (McGowan 2012, p. 167) because (while in limbo) she abandoned her concern for reality in exchange for her object of desire: to be with Cobb. The villain is Cobb, who caused her to abandon this desire, by implanting in her an obsession for reality. "Reality is the real retreat," McGowan says, and he's very serious about it.

> One must instead follow the dream or deception wherever it leads, even when it leads to self-destruction. When spectators invest themselves in the fate of the top in the film's final shot, they share in Cobb's betrayal. Fidelity demands sustaining the dream even when it leads to certain destruction. (McGowan 2012, p. 170)

When read this way, Cobb doesn't embrace the moral of the film until the end, when he stops caring about whether he has returned to reality and instead focuses on the object of his desire, his children (even though he might be destroyed one day by learning that they aren't real). (According to McGowan, Cobb's object of desire is Mal, not his children. "Desire isn't aroused by the object that it seeks but by the obstacle that renders this object inaccessible. In this sense, Cobb's true object is not the successful heist or the reunion with his children but Mal herself, who obstructs both of these possibilities." To defend this idea, he suggests that "desire finds its satisfaction not through the success of attaining its aim but through the repetition of failing to do so" (p. 148). I find this interpretation so contrary to the film itself, I have omitted it from my analysis.)

Interestingly, the catharsis Cobb achieves by doing this resembles the catharsis Fisher accomplishes by believing that his father was not disappointed because Fisher was not like him, but disappointed because he had tried to be like him – even though this belief will destroy his father's legacy and Fisher's inheritance. Fisher has deceived himself in order to reconcile his relationship with his father to his own detriment.

In any event, according to McGowan, the moral of *Inception* is clear: since one can't be sure what is real, one should just choose the reality one wants. As the old man who guards the dreamers in Yusuf's basement puts it, "they come to be woken up. The dream has become their reality. Who are you to say otherwise, sir?"

Evaluating *Inception*'s Moral

But is this moral philosophically defensible? Should one abandon the quest for reality to embrace the truths that fictions like dreams can reveal and believe what one wants?

Initially, it seems not. For example, the idea that reality can be an escape from the truth that dreams can reveal is interesting, but certainly is not universally true. Indeed, sometimes it's the reverse: dreams provide a respite from the harsh truths of reality. This is likely true, in fact, for the dreamers in Yusuf's basement. And even when dreams do reveals truth, one need not abandon the quest for realty to face them. There's a false dichotomy here; one need not choose between the truths revealed about oneself in dreams and truths about reality. One can quest for and face both. Besides, even truths about oneself are truths about reality – for every person is a part of reality.

But the argument that one should abandon the quest for reality and believe what one wants could go much deeper. And to see whether it is defensible, it will be necessary to evaluate every feasible way of defending it. In doing so, it should become clear that – although more sophisticated defenses are available – the seeming moral of *Inception* does not hold true.

Defense 1: Knowledge Is Completely Impossible

Descrates' skeptical problem suggests that knowledge of reality is impossible because knowledge itself is impossible, because we can never be sure that we aren't being fooled by a demon or a dream. From this it might seem to follow that one should abandon the quest for reality, but it decidedly does not. Even if knowledge is impossible, it's only because one can't be sure that one's beliefs are true; but one's quest for reality could still lead one to have true beliefs, and having true beliefs is still valuable in and of itself.

The value of true belief was made clear by Plato more than 2000 years ago in *The Republic* (Plato 2008). With his allegory of the cave, Plato imagined prisoners, trapped in a cave, watching shadows on a wall cast by a fire. Because it's all they've ever known, they think they are real and are perfectly happy. But when one prisoner breaks loose, learns the truth, and makes his way to the outside world, he looks back on his former situation as pitiful. The moral? It's better to be the person who has escaped the cave than the person still trapped, watching the shadows, erroneously thinking they are real. And this is true even if life is a little rougher on the outside. Since those inside don't know they are trapped, subjectively they might be happier. But objectively, their life is not meaningful; they can never flourish. If they knew the truth, they would want to be freed.

A similar point was made more recently by Harvard philosopher Robert Nozick in *Anarchy, State, and Utopia* (Nozick 1974). Nozick imagines a choice between living life in the physical world and living a life plugged into an experience machine – a machine capable of giving a person any set of experiences they would like all the while fooling them into thinking it is real. Nozick argues that, while it might be fun to plug in for a while, no one would choose to plug in for life. Why? Because there is something intrinsically valuable about "living in contact with reality" (p. 45). We don't want to be fooled. We want to have true beliefs.

Another problem with using Descartes' skeptical problem as a defense of *Inception*'s moral is that Descartes' skeptical problem is not as insoluble as it is often made out to be. It suggests that knowledge is impossible because one can't be certain that one isn't being fooled, but philosophers have never considered certainty to be required for knowledge. Since Plato, knowledge has been defined as justified true belief: to know something one must believe it, it must be true, and one must have good reason to think it's true (e.g., it can't be a guess). (Edmond Gettier (1963) pointed out that a fourth component might is required for knowledge, but because he did not show that knowledge requires certainty, his argument is irrelevant to the one made here.) But one can have good reason to think something is true even if it's not certain. Indeed, one can be justified in believing something if it is merely beyond a reasonable doubt; and the veracity of one's waking experiences are beyond a reasonable doubt.

As Ted Schick and Lewis Vaughn point out in chapter four of their book *How To Think About Weird Things*, a hypothesis is beyond a reasonable doubt when it provides the best explanation of something; and that one is awake and not dreaming – that one's experience is caused by an outside world which others too can experience – is the best explanation for one's experience (Schick and Vaughn 2014). Why?

To determine what is the best explanation, one must compare multiple explanations to the criteria of adequacy: testability, fruitfulness, scope, parsimony, and conservatism. By definition, a good explanation will make novel observable predictions (i.e., be testable), get those predictions right (i.e., be fruitful), unify one's knowledge and not raise unanswerable questions (i.e., have wide scope), not require extra assumptions or invoke extra entities (i.e., be parsimonious), and align with what one already have good reason to believe (i.e., be conservative). When one explanation does these things more than another, it is preferable.

Now, when it comes to comparing the waking and dreaming hypotheses, testability and fruitfulness are not useful; the problem is created by the fact that there is no test one can perform to delineate between the two. And assuming that the waking hypothesis aligns with what we already believe would seem to beg the question. But the dream hypothesis is inferior because it lacks both scope and simplicity. Rather than unifying one's knowledge, it fractures it, raising a host of questions that cannot be answered (e.g., what is the purpose of the deception?) and requiring a host of assumptions and extra entities to pull off the deception. On the other hand, if the world is real, how the world is known is understood and no extra entities are required; the real world hypothesis unifies knowledge in a grandiose way and is parsimonious. It is thus preferable and one is justified in believing it.

This method of reasoning is called abduction – inference to the best explanation – and this abductive solution to Descartes' dream problem has been expertly defended by the dissertations of Bryan C. Appley (2016) and Kevin McCain (2011). Since knowledge is indeed possible, the impossibility of knowledge cannot be used to defend the notion that one should abandon the quest for reality.

Defense 2: Reality Does Not Exist

Those who argue against the notion that we should be concerned with reality are usually those that think there is no such thing – like Jean Baudrillard (1995), who famously argued in *Simulacra and Simulation* that knowledge was impossible because there was no such thing as reality or truth. Since WWII and the invention of things like film and television, Baudrillard argued, humanity no longer interacts with things but with what he calls "simulacra" – images and representations of things: signs, copies, and models. Politicians and the media inundate the populace with propaganda and deception. From this, he concludes, there is no real world or truth to seek. As David Detmer translated Baudrillard's words from *La Pensee*

Radicale, "Truth is what should be laughed at...simulacra have become reality... The simulacrum now hides, not the truth, but the fact that there is none" (Detmer 2005, p. 96).

Now Baudrillard certainly has a point about how far removed people often are, in the modern world, from the objects they perceive. And electronic technology has certainly altered people's perception of reality, and made it easier for politicians and the media to mislead them. But from these things it does not follow that there is no reality and no truths about it. Reality may be harder to ascertain, sure. But even if it was impossible, it would still be there. Notice how even Baudrillard's own conclusion reveals this: it can't be "a fact that there is no truth" because that fact itself would be true. In order for reality to be in the state that Baudrillard describes, reality must exist to be in that state. All postmodern denials of reality and truth – such as the arguments of Jean-François Lyotard and Jacques Derrida, who ground their arguments in an understanding of the way language works – are haunted by these same basic problems. It's impossible to successfully argue for the fact that there are no facts. So as a defense for the idea that the quest for reality should be abandoned, the argument that there is no reality falls short.

Defense 3: While Some Knowledge Is Possible, the True Nature of Reality Is Beyond Us

A better defense of *Inception*'s moral might be found in the idea it's impossible to know the way the world is. Contrary to what Descartes suggested, perhaps we can know that the world exists and that things like "$2 + 3 = 5$" are true. But perhaps the true nature of the world, the way it is rather than the way it seems, is impossible to grasp.

To understand this notion, consider the distinction John Locke drew between primary and secondary qualities in *An Essay Concerning Human Understanding* (Locke 1997). Primary qualities are qualities that objects have which resemble the ideas we have of those objects. Solidity and shape, for example, are primary qualities. The solidity and cylindricalness of an iron rod and the idea that quality causes in one's mind are similar; they are both solid and cylindrical. Secondary qualities, on the other hand, are properties that objects have which do not resemble those that they cause in one's mind. Heat, for example, is a secondary quality. What causes the rod to feel hot when touched is the excited motion of its molecules. But molecular motion is not hot; motion is not what heat feels like. Motion transfers energy to nerves, and that sends a signal the brain, but the only thing that is actually hot is one's experience – the experience touching the rod causes. The same is true for things like color, and taste, and sound. The qualities objects have that cause such experiences do not, at all, resemble the experiences themselves. To the extent that these experiences cause one to believe that objects themselves are hot, have color, or are salty or sweet, they cause one to have an inaccurate conception of the way the world is.

Since Locke, the problem has become worse because many of the qualities Locke thought were primary are now known to be secondary. Take solidity for example.

Objects like tables and chairs are perceived as solid when in reality, they are mostly empty space; they are made of atoms, and the majority of every atom consists of the void between its nucleus and its surrounding electrons. And yet one cannot help but perceive things like tables and chairs as solid.

But this expansion of the problem actually reveals its solution. In the same way that the true nature of objects can be revealed, despite appearances, as empty space, the true nature of reality can be revealed, despite appearances: through science. Indeed, As Ernan McMullin points out in his short book *The Inference that Makes Science*, the process science uses to discover such things is the same one we used to solve Descartes skeptical problem: abduction (inference to the best explanation) (McMullin 1992). Science progresses by comparing multiple hypotheses to the criteria of adequacy. Indeed, to get at the way the world really is, abduction actively guards against the many ways human senses can mislead us. And by doing so, it gets beyond the illusions created by secondary qualities and reveals the way the world is.

A similar response could be proposed to Immanuel Kant's arguments in a *Critique of Pure Reason* (Kant 1998). Kant argued that everything humans experience is filtered through categories – such as quantity, quality, relation, and modality – and thus humans will always be separated in their knowledge from what he called "the noumenal world" (the way the world actually is). According to Kant, all one can know is the phenomenal world – the world as it is appears (as it is interpreted through the categories). But, again, it seems that science can move beyond these categories and reveal the world as it is. Indeed, quantum mechanics, which tells us that things like electrons primarily exist as wave-functions and cannot have both location and momentum at the same time, completely defies the Kantian categories – and yet, thanks to science, we know the world is that way.

So as a defense of *Inception*'s seeming moral, that the quest for reality should be abandoned, the argument that the true nature reality cannot be known also falls short.

Defense 4: Taking a Leap of Faith

In order to find the best defense of *Inception*'s moral, one would think that Søren Kierkegaard holds the answer. He is, after all, the philosopher best known for the film's key philosophical concept: the leap of faith. Unfortunately, however, Kierkegaard's arguments seem to only be applicable in the realm of religion, and even then only when religion is understood in a particular way.

Although Kierkegaard is difficult to interpret, he is usually understood to have admitted that belief in God is irrational but called Christians to take a leap of faith and believe anyway – not despite the fact, but because it is absurd. For Kierkegaard, religion is an arena in which reason is not applicable, and thus asking someone to justify their religious beliefs is completely inappropriate. Thus, in the realm of religion, one can take a leap of faith and believe whatever one wants.

But this is true only on a certain understanding of the nature of religious language. If it is completely nonliteral, akin to that used in a fictional story, then yes reason does not apply. In the same way that it would not make sense to ask a fan of *Lord of the Rings* to provide evidence for their belief that Frodo lives, it would not make sense to ask a Christian to justify their belief that Jesus lives. If the importance of religious dogma and scriptures lies solely in their moral message, and not their literal truth or happening, then "proof" of their literal truth would not be necessary.

If, however, the literal truth of religious claims matters – for example, if the claims of Christianity are void unless Jesus actually, physically, rose from the dead – then asking for proof is completely appropriate. In the same way and for the same reason that one would be right to ask a person for evidence if they said that Elvis was still alive, it would be perfectly appropriate to ask a Christian to justify their belief that Jesus was resurrected.

But there are two problems here. First, except for a handful and religious scholars – like Peter Lipton (2007) and Robin Le Poidevin (2016) who embrace a view of religious language called fictionalism – very few Christians accept anything like the former view. When the average Christian says they believe that Jesus rose, they mean it literally – just like they mean it when they say that that miracles occur or (in some cases) that the Earth is only 6000 years old. In each case reason is applicable, and it would be irrational to believe such things without justification (i.e., by faith), just like it would be irrational to believe most anything else without justification.

Second, even if religious language is nonliteral, Kierkegaard's argument would only defend religious leaps of faith – or, at the most, leaps to nonliteral beliefs. It would not defend a broad scoping dismissal of reality or the right to believe whatever one wants in the face of uncertainty. Cobb's belief that Saito could deliver on his promise, or Cobb's belief that he returned to his children, certainly are not nonliteral beliefs. Thus Kierkegaard's philosophy cannot be used defend them.

Defense 5: It's Acceptable to Place the Best Wager

Perhaps the best defense of *Inception*'s moral can be found in the works of Blasé Pascal (Pascal 2004). In what is now known as "Pascal's Wager," he suggested that, when reason cannot settle a matter, you can choose to believe what you want based on personal risk and reward. He then applied this to belief in God. For Pascal, belief in God was risk free – if you're right you go to heaven, and being wrong costs you nothing. Atheism, on the other hand, is all risk and no reward – if you're right you get nothing, and if you're wrong you burn in hell. For this reason, even though he admitted that reason could not settle the matter of God's existence, Pascal concluded that belief in God was rational.

The success of Pascal's argument as a defense of the rationality of theism is highly contested. He did not, for example, seem to properly recognize the benefits of atheistic belief (e.g., a better appreciation for the only life you have), or the risks of theistic belief (even if you believe in God, you still might end up in hell because you belonged to the wrong religion). Still, he seems to have a point about having the right to choose to believe what you want based on personal benefit, if reason cannot point you in the right direction.

His point is complicated, however, by the arguments of William Clifford who famously argued that "it is wrong, always, everywhere, and for anyone, to believe anything on insufficient evidence" (Clifford 1877). Now Pascal actually proves this is wrong; since there are situations where believing without evidence is inevitable, it can't *always* be wrong. But Clifford reaches his conclusion by appreciating how the consequences of beliefs, and how they affect others, are relevant to the ethics of what we choose to believe. Choosing to believe, for example, without evidence that a ship is seaworthy could end up costing the passengers their lives.

So we cannot say, as *Inception* seems to, that a person should simply choose to believe by faith whatever is most beneficial to them. Beliefs are not merely a private affair; they affect how one behaves, and how such behavior would affect others must also be taken into account. For example, even though Cobb's choice to dismiss his concerns about reality and believe that he has finally returned to his children benefits him personally, it could leave his own children in the real world without a father.

So, again, the moral of *Inception* seems to lack a full philosophic defense. Who is to say otherwise, when someone wants to embrace their dreams as reality? Those who care about truth and the effect of what we believe on others.

Defense 6: Soften the Moral

The best way to defend the moral of *Inception* is to soften it – to reject the idea that *Inception* is preaching a full-scale dismissal of the quest for reality or the unrestricted right to believe whatever one wants. Instead, perhaps it can be understood as suggesting that, when faced with a seeming insoluble problem, it is perfectly acceptable to be curious and try to solve it – to spin one's top, so to speak. But when "real life" comes roaring back into focus, it's also perfectly acceptable to set your quest aside and simply enjoy life. Consider the words of David Hume, in the conclusion of a *Treatise of Human Nature*, after he raised his famous problem of induction (which casts complete doubt on our ability to have knowledge of causation).

> The intense view of these manifold contradictions and imperfections in human reason has so wrought upon me, and heated my brain, that I am ready to reject all belief and reasoning, and can look upon no opinion even as more probable or likely than another... [I] begin to fancy myself in the most deplorable condition imaginable, invironed with the deepest darkness, and utterly deprived of the use of every member and faculty. Most fortunately it happens, that since reason is incapable of dispelling these clouds, nature herself suffices to that purpose, and cures me of this philosophical melancholy and delirium, either by relaxing this bent of mind, or by some avocation, and lively impression of my senses, which obliterate all these chimeras. I dine, I play a game of backgammon, I converse, and am merry with my friends; and when after three or four hours' amusement, I would return to these speculations, they appear so cold, and strained, and ridiculous, that I cannot find in my heart to enter into them any farther. (Hume 2003, p. 192)

And so, while the ending of *Inception*, and indeed the further question of whether the entire movie is a dream, raises questions in one's mind about the nature of reality – and it's perfectly acceptable to consider and entertain those doubts – it's also perfectly acceptable to walk away from them, as Cobb did, when one's children walk through the door.

Conclusion: Applying the Moral

How widely applicable this moral is depends on how common truly insoluble dilemmas are – situations in which reason can decide nothing. Nolan seems to think this applies to matters like the afterlife, and others likely think it applies to matters of religion in general – God's existence, Jesus' resurrection, etc. Perhaps it could also apply to political and moral beliefs – beliefs about how far one's freedom should go or whether things like abortion are moral.

But in such cases, people often mistake the inability of reason to provide *certainty* on an issue with the inability of reason to settle the issue. As demonstrated above, very few things can be proven with certainty, but that doesn't mean that reason can't reveal the most rational answer. One can't be certain that one isn't dreaming but reason can justify the belief that one isn't. In fact, technically, reason can't even provide certainty on the matter of the Earth's age; to defend their position, creationist can (and do) insist that God created the Earth 6000 years ago and seeded it with evidence to make it seem older – and no one could ever prove them wrong. But reason can reveal that this is a non-simple, narrowly scoping, unconservative, untestable, ad-hoc excuse to save a hypothesis that has no evidence from the evidence against it. In other words, reason can prove it irrational. In the same way, statements about God, the after-life, Jesus' resurrection, freedom, and abortion cannot be *proven* one way or the other – but perhaps reason could reveal which position on these matters is justified.

Unfortunately, what reason would reveal on these matters is beyond the scope of this chapter. *Inception* is deep – but it's not that deep. That discussion will have to be saved for another time.

References

Appley, Bryan C. 2016. Inference to the best explanation and the challenge of skepticism. Thesis and Dissertation. University of Iowa, 2016. http://ir.uiowa.edu/cgi/viewcontent.cgi?article=6385&context=etd

Baudrillard, J. 1995. Simulacra and Simulation. University of Michigan Press.

Clifford, William. 1877. The ethics of belief. *Contemporary Review* 29: 289.

Cottingham, J. ed., 2013. René Descartes: Meditations on First Philosophy. Cambridge: Cambridge University Press.

Detmer, David. 2005. Challenging Simulacra and Simulation: Baudrillard in The Matrix. In Irwin, William. More Matrix and Philosophy. Chicago: Open Court.

Gettier, E. L. 1963. Is Justified True Belief Knowledge?. *Analysis* 23(6): 121–123.

Hume, David. 2003. A Treatise of Human Nature. New York: Dover.

Itzkoff, Dave. 2010. Hans Zimmer extracts the secrets of the "inception" score. *New York Times.* July 28. http://artsbeat.blogs.nytimes.com/2010/07/28/hans-zimmer-extracts-thesecrets-of-the-*Inception*-score/

Kant, Immanuel. 1998. Guyer, Paul (trans.) Critique of Pure Reason. Cambridge: Cambridge University Press.

Le Poidevin, Robin. 2016. Playing the god game: The perils of religious fictionalism. In Alternative concepts of god: Essays on the metaphysics of divine, by Andrei Buckareff and Yujin Nagasawa, 178–191. Oxford: Oxford University Press.

Lipton, Peter. 2007. Science and religion: The immersion solution. In Realism and religion: Philosophical and theological perspectives, by Andrew Moore and Michael Scott, 31–46. New York: Routledge.

Locke, John 1997. Woolhouse, Roger (ed.), An Essay Concerning Human Understanding. New York: Penguin Books.

McCain, Kevin. 2011. Inference to the Best Explanation and the External World. Dissertation. University of Rochester.

McGowan, Todd. 2012. *The fictional Christopher Nolan*. Austin: University of Texas Press.

McMullin, Ernan. 1992. *The inference that makes science*. Milwaukee: Marquette University Press.

Nolan, Christopher. 2010a. *Inception.* Warner Home Video.

———. 2010b. *Inception: The shooting script.* San Rafael: Insight Editions.

Nolan, Christopher, an interview by Robert Capps. 2010. *Q&A: Christopher Nolan on dreams, architecture, and ambiguity. Wired Magazine,* November 29, 2010. https://www.wired.com/2010/11/pl_inception_nolan/

Nozick, Robert. 1974. *Anarchy, state, and utopia*. New York: Basic Books.

Pascal, Blaise. 2004. Pensees. Seatle: Pacific Publishing Studio.

Plato. 2008. *The republic*. Digireads.com

Schick, Theodore, Jr., and Lewis Vaughn. 2014. *How to think about weird things*. New York: McGraw-Hill.

Okja as Philosophy: Why Animals Matter

32

Randall M. Jensen

Contents

Introduction 774
Summary 774
The Mirando Philosophy: Okja Has No Moral Status 777
    The Amoralist Defense 778
    The Natural Law Defense 779
    The Kantian Defense 780
    The Dualist Defense 782
A Kinder and Gentler Mirando? 783
Animal Liberation 785
    A Consequentialist Liberation? 788
    A Deontological Liberation? 790
All Animals Are Equal, but Some Are More Equal Than Others 791
Conclusion: The Friendship of Mija and Okja 792
References 794

Abstract

The eponymous protagonist of *Okja* is an adorable "super-pig," larger than an ordinary pig not only in size but also in heart and mind. The film explores and interrogates different ways of seeing Okja, different portraits of Okja's moral status, as philosophers would put it. To the Mirando Corporation, Okja has no moral status. She is a mere product to be used as they see fit. To the Animal Liberation Front, Okja is a dramatic symbol of animals everywhere who are mistreated and deprived of their rights. She represents a rare opportunity to further their political cause. To the young girl Mija, Okja is unquestionably a person, a member of her family, her lifelong companion and friend. The film subjects both the Mirando Corporation and the Animal Liberation Front to satirical critique and invites the audience to come to see Okja as Mija does. So

R. M. Jensen (✉)
Northwestern College, Orange City, IA, USA
e-mail: rjensen@nwciowa.edu

what is the moral status of an animal like Okja? Philosophers like Peter Singer have argued on behalf of animals, super or not, and protested the ways they are treated, often focused on factory farming and the use of animals in scientific research. Like these philosophical animal advocates, this film pushes human beings to expand the boundaries of the moral community beyond their own species. Simply put, *Okja* argues that animals matter.

Keywords

Okja · Bong Joon-ho · Ethics · Animal rights · Moral status · Consequentialism · Utilitarianism · Deontology · Speciesism · Sentience · Personhood · Peter Singer · St. Thomas Aquinas · Immanuel Kant · Rene Descartes · Jeremy Bentham

Introduction

Okja (2017) is the brainchild of Bong Joon-ho, the South Korean writer-director of *Parasite*, the Academy Award winner for Best Picture in 2019. He is also the creator of the cult classic monster movie *The Host* (2006) and the steampunk dystopian train ride *Snowpiercer* (2013). Like his other films, this one defies genre expectations and grapples with social and political problems while packing an action-packed punch. *Okja* is the sometimes comical and sometimes horrific tale of the life of an extraordinary creature and the monstrous corporation that brought her to life. Ironically, this critically acclaimed film's debut at the Cannes Film Festival in France sparked controversy over its own corporate creator, Netflix.

Like other films featuring animals as protagonists, *Okja* asks viewers to see an animal as one of us, both as a subject and as a suitable object of our empathy and concern. But as a character, Okja is not complete fancy; she is not the sort of talking pig found in the beloved children's book *Charlotte's Web* or in the equally beloved film *Babe* (1995). In such stories, belief must be suspended. For everyone knows that pigs are not like that. Pigs do not talk, among other things! In this story, however, Okja is not a human being in the form of a pig. Perhaps actual pigs are somewhat like Okja, or could be, with a bit of GMO help. *Okja* thus more effectively puts questions about animal rights and moral status front and center and forces us to wonder about the nature and relationship of morality and humanity.

Summary

The Mirando Corporation is an enormous New York business conglomerate with a shady past. Its new CEO Lucy Mirando is determined to rebrand Mirando as a company with a soul, one that is fair to its workers and friendly to the environment. During her media-savvy inaugural presentation in 2007, Lucy explains that Mirando has discovered a marvelous and miraculous pig on an obscure Chilean farm. After close study and careful and entirely natural and non-GMO breeding, the Mirando Corporation now has 26 amazing super-piglets. Or so she says. In an extended contest and advertising stunt, each baby super-pig is to be placed with a small farming operation somewhere around the world. In 2017, at the end of a decade, out of the 26 original super-piglets, one will be pronounced the World's Greatest Super-Pig and brought back "home" to New York City.

Okja is one such super-piglet, placed on a very small and isolated mountain farm in South Korea. She spends the 10 years of the contest alongside her best friend and constant companion, Mija, a young girl whose grandfather runs the farm and cares for her as her sole guardian. Okja is no longer a cute little piglet; she now looks as much hippo or elephant as pig. One look makes it very hard to swallow Lucy's claims about her "natural" origins.

As the film's action begins, a Mirando executive has made the long trek up to the farm, along with Dr. Johnny Wilcox, the former star of a television show for kids called "Magical Animals" and now the new face of the Mirando Corporation and the judge of the Super-Pig Contest. While they inspect Okja, Mija's grandfather leads her into the forest to visit the graves of her parents and presents her with a solid gold pig figurine, meant to help her land a husband someday. And, to her dismay, he reveals this hunk of gold is also meant as an altogether unsatisfactory replacement for her irreplaceable best friend. She has been lured from the farm because Okja has won the contest and is being taken away, to be loaded on a truck to Seoul and then to be flown away to New York City. Mija will never see Okja again.

At this point, what has begun as a sweet story of a girl and her gigantic super-pig rollicking in the forest turns into an extended chase sequence. Mija packs a bag and sets out down the mountain. She makes her way to the Seoul Mirando headquarters. Improbably, she breaks in and evades the security guards long enough to spot Okja being loaded onto a truck. After chasing the truck through the streets, she climbs to higher ground and launches herself onto the top of the truck, more like Indiana Jones or James Bond than a small girl. Unfortunately, but predictably, she soon falls off and is left to continue her pursuit on foot.

Suddenly, a mysterious black truck appears, driven by a man in a ski mask. It pulls alongside the Mirando truck. After forcing the Mirando truck to the side of the road, a few masked figures free Okja from her chains and try to help her onto their truck. However, Mija herself has now caught up to the pair of stopped trucks. Okja breaks free, and she and Mija are on the run from the occupants of both trucks, somehow ending up barreling through a department store with music fit for a circus playing in the background.

The folks in black catch up to our friends first. Turns out they are the Animal Liberation Front (ALF), and they are on the side of the angels, or the animals, rather. Through a translator, the ALF tells Mija the truth about Mirando and Okja's origins. She was not born in Arizona and her mother was not found in Chile. All the super-pigs were genetically engineered in a secret underground laboratory in New Jersey. The 26 were the prettiest of their early efforts and served as a distraction for consumers who would refuse to purchase "unnatural" meat from animals that were genetically engineered in a lab. The many other super-pigs in Mirando's clutches have not been treated nearly so well.

Such a lab is where Mirando is planning to take Okja right now. While Mija wants nothing but to return to her mountain home with Okja, the ALF has bigger plans. They want to allow Mirando to recapture Okja so they can get video of the horrors found inside their high-security lab via a camera they will plant on her. Jay, the leader of the ALF, says they will only go ahead with Mija's consent and asks their translator to plead with Mija to give it. Without pausing to think, she refuses. She wants nothing but to return home with Okja. But K, the ALF translator, lies to Jay and says that she has in fact consented. The ALF members escape by jumping off a bridge into the waters far below and leave Okja and a confused Mija in the hands of Mirando goons. They are on their way to the United States.

Back in New York plans are in motion for the Super-Pig Contest celebration. For Mirando this will launch their new line of super-pig meat products. But the ALF hijacks the celebration and reveals the awful truth about Mirando and the super-pigs, featuring video footage of Okja's brutal treatment in Mirando's labs, rightly described by a drunken Dr. Johnny as an unspeakable place. Chaos ensues. Lucy Mirando's failure leads to her sudden replacement by the former CEO, her sister Nancy, who has been lurking in the shadows waiting for just this moment. ALF's plan to liberate Okja during their revelation at first seems to be working, but in the end the animal activists are defeated and Okja is recaptured by Mirando and transported to a factory farm that is chock full of super-pigs. Okja's fate seems sealed.

Yet Okja's few friends have not given up. With the help of Jay and K, Mija manages to sneak inside the factory farm and finds herself in a gruesome abattoir where super-pigs are killed and their remains are turned into attractively packaged meat products. She wanders around the killing ground and eventually finds herself face to face with Mirando workers who are quickly and efficiently killing one super-pig after another. Okja is next! Mija holds out a picture of herself and her porcine friend and begs them to stop. The workers hesitate, unsure what to do, until Nancy Mirando and her security team enter the scene. She is unmoved by Mia's photo and plea, but is eventually convinced to spare Okja when Mija offers her the solid gold pig given to her by her grandfather as payment for Okja's life.

As Mija and Okja are being escorted out of the darkness of the factory farm, two other super-pigs manage to squeeze a tiny super-piglet through the fence in a desperate effort to save their baby. Okja quickly hides the piglet in her mouth. While countless super-pigs remain to be slaughtered on the factory farm, at least these two will survive and live a better life. The film ends as it began, with life returned to normal on the small farm atop the forested mountains of South Korea, featuring a girl, her grandfather, and two super-pigs, one very large and one very small. A family has been restored! A happy ending, but only for a few.

The Mirando Philosophy: Okja Has No Moral Status

> We can only sell the dead ones.
> —Nancy Mirando

Unsurprisingly, the Mirando Corporation is cast as the film's villain and thus sees Okja as a valuable resource, a vital part of Lucy Mirando's extravagant Super-Pig Contest. The super-pigs serve Mirando's business plan by providing new cover for their radical genetic modifications and for their longstanding history of mistreatment of both humans and animals. Lucy falsely claims such mistreatment is now in the past and distracts the public with her breezy speeches and bright and shiny new ads. While her grandfather was a terrible man, she will usher in a transformed Mirando with a new business ethics. Her super-pig project pushes all the right buttons: local, non-GMO, natural, cute animals, small footprint, and so on. All too soon it becomes clear that much of this is bold prevarication on her part. The first super-pig was not a miracle of nature at all but was genetically engineered in a secret Mirando lab.

One thing she is honest about, though: these super-pigs "need to taste fucking good." Whatever else might be said about these wonderful creatures, they are meant to end up on the dinner table. Mirando has invested a considerable amount in "creating" Okja and her fellow super-pigs, and the meat on Okja's bones is a way to recoup some of that investment cost. So, near the end of the film, when Mija asks why the new Mirando boss wants to kill Okja, Nancy cannot quite grasp the point of the question. Just as Mija cannot understand why anyone would want to kill her friend, Nancy cannot see why there is any reason not to do so when a potential profit is in view. She only allows Mija and Okja to be reunited for a happy ending because Mija proposes a business transaction of her own. She has the means to pay for Okja by trading her solid gold pig figurine for her. And so in the end Mirando relents. Perhaps Nancy has some smidgen of empathy for Mija, but she surely has none for Okja. The super-pigs are part of the Mirando business enterprise, in an important way no different than the various walls, fences, and machines that make up the factory farm in which they are housed.

Okja is thus wholly objectified and commodified. She is a product to be bought and sold. As a philosopher would say, she has no moral status of her own. What is moral status? To have moral status is simply to matter from a moral point of view. Since there are different moral points of view, there are different accounts of what it means to have moral status. To have moral status might involve having rights, or falling under moral principles, or making moral claims upon others, or various other things. But for a creature to lack moral status altogether is for it to be invisible from a moral point of view – to not be the subject of moral deliberation or concern as either subject (agent) or object (patient).

A clarification is needed at this point. Anything can be an object of moral concern indirectly, in virtue of its relationship to something or someone else who does have moral status. Consider a seemingly insignificant thing, a stick or a stone, say. If someone steps on a stick and breaks it, or picks up a stone and hurls it into a pond, we think nothing of it. No one wonders whether somehow the stick or the stone has itself been mistreated or wronged. To object on the behalf of such an object feels like a category mistake. But if the stick is my child's make-believe magic wand, or the stone is your very own pet rock, such an object acquires significance precisely because of our relationship to it. It would then be wrong to snap the stick, not because of anything about the stick itself, but because of a child's love and investment in it.

Okja clearly has this kind of indirect value. She matters enormously to Mija, a lot more than a pretend wand or a pet rock would matter, and she matters to Mirando, who have a significant financial investment in her. The big question is whether Okja matters in her own right, whether the audience should see her as a potential victim of moral wrongdoing and as a moral agent. Mirando of course does not see Okja in this way, just as many very real animal industries might be presumed to see the animals within their scope as resources or as otherwise having no moral status. Mija, on the other hand, does not think that Okja matters only because she matters to her. But Mirando is likely to dismiss this as the sentimentalism of a child.

How might one mount a philosophical defense of the Mirando philosophy that animals lack moral status? First, and most ambitiously, an amoralist (sometimes called a moral nihilist) might argue that it simply does not matter what one thinks about Okja's alleged moral status (or lack thereof), because morality itself does not matter. The second broad strategy is for Mirando to argue that morality is first and foremost and finally about human beings. For obvious reasons, we can call this "human exceptionalism." If Mirando can in some way mount a successful defense of this point of view, then perhaps they can ward off any moral objections to the way they are treating Okja and any other animals as well.

Mirando has at least three potential ways to defend human exceptionalism: First, a robust and anthropocentric teleological view might entail that Okja, like her fellow animals, is *meant* to be eaten by human beings. They are here for us. Second, a Kantian might argue that while human beings are persons, and thus deserve to be treated with dignity and respect, animals are things rather than persons, and so it is only right to treat them as a resource. Third, it might be argued that nonhuman animals have no souls and are thus incapable of feeling pain, so that moral concern need not be extended to them. Each of these three rationales for human exceptionalism, along with the previously mentioned amoralist gambit, in its own way purports to show that Okja does not matter in her own right, that she makes no moral claims upon anyone – and the same would go for all her fellow animals. This leaves four possible Mirando defenses to examine and evaluate.

The Amoralist Defense

In Book I of Plato's magisterial *Republic*, Thrasymachus fails to contain his disgust and disdain at Socrates for his passion to understand what justice is and to live a just life (Plato 2004). Justice, says Thrasymachus, is nothing but a tool used by the powerful to exploit and control the weak. Someone with the smarts to see this and the power to get away with it will ignore justice (or morality) in the ruthless pursuit of their goals. Mirando might want to hire Thrasymachus as a consultant!

Let weak-minded moralists agonize over the moral status and the treatment of Okja and the other super-pigs, Thrasymachus might argue. Mirando sees the truth of it. Profit is the name of the game. Sure, one might have to play along by meeting (or pretending to meet) various moral demands in order to pacify the activists and mollify consumers. Lucy is good at this. But it doesn't really matter. The enlightened amoralist knows better, having seen through the con game that morality represents.

This most ambitious defense of the Mirando philosophy throws out the baby with the bathwater. Not only does Okja lack moral status, but so do human beings. To the amoralist, talk about human rights should be met with the same scorn as talk of animal rights. Few who are not playing the villain in a movie or novel are prepared to bite this particular bullet. And even those who may be ready to see other human beings as without any moral protection are typically quick to experience a decidedly moral outrage when they themselves or those they care about are wronged. To make a long story short, it is very difficult to be a thoroughgoing and consistent amoralist, and amoralism seems to be a philosophy fit only for sociopaths and villains.

The following defenses thus abandon amoralism – at least for human beings. But perhaps it still makes sense to look at animals through an amoralist lens.

The Natural Law Defense

In his massive *Summa Theologiae* (Second Part of the Second Part, Question 64, Article 1), St. Thomas Aquinas (1225–1274) states that: "There is no sin in using a thing for the purpose for which it is" (Aquinas 2017). In Aquinas's medieval Christian teleological worldview, there is a hierarchy of being, and the lower exists for the sake of the higher. Teleology comes from the Greek word "telos," which means end or purpose. To look at the world through a teleological lens is to see the world as purpose-filled and as governed by natural law. Plants are meant to be food for animals, while both plants and animals are meant to be food for human beings. The rest of the world exists for humans, to be used by humans.

Perhaps Mirando is simply complying with the divinely created natural order. To complain about the fact that Okja is to be treated as food is analogous to complaining that a hammer is to be used to pound in nails. Pigs are for eating just as hammers are for hammering nails. A hammer can be used in the wrong way, to be sure, but this seems more a matter of competence than morality. Likewise, no doubt there are ways that an animal should be used well rather than poorly. But whatever principles there might be about how animals (or hammers) are treated do not seem to arise from the thought that the animal (or hammer) itself deserves a certain level of concern or treatment. Even if we are convinced that we ought to deal with our fellow creatures naturally rather than unnaturally, this will have more to do with the idea that we ought to live according to nature than with the idea that animals have rights or some kind of moral status of their own.

Of course, it will prove difficult to use the argument from the naturalness of human carnivory to defend the decidedly unnatural methods Mirando uses to create and breed their super-pigs. Okja's home farm in South Korea seems much more natural than Mirando's New Jersey facilities. Certainly, the film shows us the bright sunlit forest paradise of the former in stark contrast with the dark, gray, lifeless dungeons of the latter. A Thomist teleological worldview may support a more traditional farming and agricultural system, but it is far from obvious that it will approve of a business that involves radical genetic manipulation as well as cruel and abusive treatment of animals.

Further, arguments from nature can often cut both ways. While it may seem natural for human beings to eat some animals, it also seems quite natural for other animals to be our companions and helpers rather than a food source. Which animals is it natural for us to eat? All of them, even some that might be difficult or unpleasant to eat or even poisonous to us? Human beings answer this question of suitable animal diet differently in different times and places. Arguments about what is natural may turn out to be a façade for merely cultural standards.

Furthermore, what is even meant by "natural" here? And why should it be granted that there is a close connection between what is natural (whatever that means) and what is moral in the first place? Eyeglasses are not natural, but folks are generally glad to have them. New technologies sometimes evoke worries over violating nature, but such worries typically subside as they become more familiar, as with the use of in vitro fertilization. Do objections to GMO foods fall into this category? There are serious questions about the consequences of genetic modifications, but how much weight should be given to the mere thought that such modifications are unnatural?

Some will argue that we cannot have teleology (a nature filled with purposes) in a materialistic universe that is not created and sustained by a deity. And nowadays plenty of people do not believe in God. Certainly the Mirando sisters do not seem deeply religious! So teleology may not be their best refuge. If they want to push super-pigs and other animals out of the moral community (a nice way of referring to the set of beings with moral status), they will probably need a different rationale.

It is worth briefly pointing out that Aquinas does not represent the entirety of the Christian tradition on this issue (and unsurprisingly Aquinas's own view on all this is likely to be more complicated than this brief discussion suggests). St. Francis of Assisi (1181–1226) exhibits a love for animals that makes it clear he does not see them as meant only to be used by human beings; famously, he often preached sermons to the birds. And contemporary Christian thinkers are divided about the place of animals in our thinking as they are divided about so many things.

The Kantian Defense

The moral philosophy of the German philosopher Immanuel Kant (1724–1804) is nicely summed up by the familiar principle that we should always treat humanity as an end in itself and never only as a means to some further end. Kant elaborates on this idea by saying that human beings have a distinctive type of value that goes beyond mere price: dignity. Now, clearly Mirando's treatment of their human personnel is not guided by such a Kantian principle! But if morality is fundamentally about how persons are treated, and if nonhuman animals are not persons, then it might seem to follow that our dealings with nonhuman animals are not morality's business. While it would be morally wrong to use another human being for our own purposes and neglect this human being's value as an individual person deserving of our respect, it is not in the same way a moral problem to use an animal for our purposes. This is a more Enlightenment route to the same destination reached in the previous section by a more medieval natural law approach.

This particular maneuver only works if it is granted both that morality is only for persons and that animals (most notably including Okja) are not persons. Each of these assumptions is controversial. First, it is one thing to argue that an important part of morality, perhaps even the chief part of it, is concerned with the relationships among persons and how they treat one another. It is another thing to argue that morality does not also concern the way that persons deal with nonpersons at all. Why should this be taken for granted?

Second, it is far from clear that the distinction between persons and nonpersons coincides with the distinction between humans and nonhumans. To see this, the relevant terms need to be clearly defined and consistently used, even though in ordinary language these terms are ambiguous. The terms "human" and "human being" will signify membership in a particular biological species: homo sapiens. The term "person" will refer to a being with certain reason-involving cognitive and affective capacities, such as the capacity to reason, to experience complex emotions, to make moral judgments, and so on. It would be a challenging task to give a set of necessary and sufficient conditions for being a person, but in broad outline to be a person is simply to be the kind of being we take ourselves to be – and that we take various fictional species of persons to be, whether it be Klingons, Kryptonians, or what have you.

With these two terms delineated, it should be pretty obvious that there are human beings who are not persons as defined. A human embryo has not yet developed the capacities that make us persons. And a human being who suffers a terrible brain injury may no longer be a person. The real question for us, however, is whether it is safe to say that all nonhumans are nonpersons. If we expand our horizon to include fictional worlds, it is clear this is not at all safe to say. In Narnia, many animals are persons, for they are Talking Animals. Likewise, the many books of Beatrix Potter imagine animals to be persons as we are. The personified animal is actually a very familiar trope in much children's literature.

What of actual animals, though? And what of Okja? Probably most will agree that the simplest nonhuman animals are not persons. A clam seems to have none of the characteristics that distinguish humans as persons. As we move up the food chain, so to speak, matters become more complicated. Once we consider higher forms of mammalian life, there is a case to be made that some primates and some species of animals are persons. The international Great Ape Project, for example, aspires to provide legal recognition and basic rights to chimpanzees, gorillas, orangutans, and certain other primates. And plenty of people are troubled by the deliberate hunting of dolphins as well as the accidental killing of dolphins in nets meant for tuna, even though they are untroubled by the killing of other animals, such as the aforementioned tuna.

Okja herself clearly belongs alongside if not above dolphins and great apes when it comes to these person-making characteristics. To begin with, pigs are fairly intelligent and social animals. And Okja is no ordinary pig. Early in the film, she saves Mija from a dangerous and potentially life-ending fall by grabbing the rope Mija is holding, first with her hoof and then with her teeth. When she cannot pull Mija to safety, she desperately looks around for a solution. Seeing a log jutting out from a cliff nearby, she runs and hurls herself over the log so that Mija is pulled up to the clifftop by the rope she is holding. Mija is safe, but Okja falls into the forest below. This entire sequence, and there are others like it, shows the audience that Okja is capable of complicated calculations and of emotional engagement in a way that exceeds any ordinary pig. Evidently the genetic modifications have produced a super-intelligent pig as well as a large and tasty one. Is she a person? Since it may be difficult to deny that Okja is a person, and since it is unclear why morality should only concern the treatment of persons, the Kantian view does not seem to provide adequate moral cover for the Mirando Corporation. And there will be more to say about personhood and moral status a bit later on.

The Dualist Defense

Rene Descartes (1596–1650) puts forward a dualist metaphysics on which human beings are composed of a material body and an immaterial soul (Descartes 2017). The soul is the "I" that is conscious, that thinks and feels and imagines and doubts and so on. The human body is an unthinking and unfeeling organic machine. In similar fashion, in the Cartesian philosophy, animals are depicted as mere automata, incapable of thought or feeling. Lacking souls, they may often appear to be exhibiting an emotional response or to be feeling pain, but this is appearance only. There is nothing it is like from the inside to be an animal. A living animal is merely a more complicated and organic version of a windup toy. If Descartes is right, then perhaps Mirando is justified after all in seeing their super-pigs as mere machines, no different in principle than any of the other machines housed in their factories and laboratories. Perhaps it is an irrational sentiment born out of anthropomorphic projection for us to feel sympathy for Okja. Perhaps the film itself is guilty of tempting us to commit this sin.

What of this view that animals are altogether unfeeling, wholly lacking in consciousness? This is a very difficult view to accept, for at least three reasons.

First, very few are tempted to buy into Cartesian dualism. No longer is it taken for granted that human beings have an immaterial soul that makes us who and what we are. To the extent that one is moved to think of animals as without feeling because they lack souls, the move from dualism to materialism will remove this motivation. But even if one were to hang onto the idea that human beings have a soul and that this is what explains some of our behavior, why should it not also be posited that animals have souls? In fact, ancient Greek philosophy and even some more recent forms of vitalism assume as much.

Second, very often animals can be seen to suffer, or so it seems. It is very difficult to deny the apparent evidence of our senses. Step on a dog's tail and see the response. Is the dog not in pain? On second thought, instead imagine or remember stepping on a dog's tail. Animal cruelty should surely not be encouraged as a thought experiment! That animals feel things, especially pain, may seem to be a matter of common sense. Sure, one can be skeptical about this – but philosophers know that one can be skeptical about whether other human beings feel things, too. This is often called the Problem of Other Minds. I have no "proof" that you are conscious, that you are an experiencing subject like I am, rather than being an unfeeling zombie or robot who merely simulates consciousness. However this problem is to be solved, it may seem likely that the solution will yield as a corollary the concession that animals too are conscious. If the best explanation of your behavior – which is similar to mine – is that you, like me, are conscious, it is likely that the best explanation of animal behavior is that they are also conscious, since we can recognize their behavior as like our own, too. And if it is difficult to deny that animals in general experience pain and pleasure, it will be doubly difficult to deny this of Okja as she is portrayed in the film.

Third, there are significant physiological similarities between human beings and other animals. There's no time for an anatomy lesson, but if it is understood how pain is caused and experienced in the human nervous system, and the nervous systems of other mammals are importantly similar, then obviously they feel pain.

Let us grant that animals feel things, then. Most simply, they feel pain. Now, it is far from clear that this animal consciousness goes all the way down the food chain. Do shrimp feel pain? Spiders? But this matter need not be settled to grant that Okja herself and other higher mammals have at least some minimal form of conscious experience; and since the film invites us to put ourselves in Okja's shoes, we are encouraged to see her as much more than minimally aware. Mirando cannot defend its treatment of Okja and the other super-pigs by arguing that no one is hurt.

All in all, it is difficult to locate an unproblematic defense of the Mirando Philosophy that animals have no moral status. Human exceptionalism may be in trouble. This is not to say that the above issues are not contentious. Some will no doubt want to argue with various moves that have been made. But this is how philosophy works!

A Kinder and Gentler Mirando?

No one should be surprised that the mindset and modus operandi of a movie villain do not stand up to serious scrutiny. Not only does Mirando not afford super-pigs and other animals any moral status, but they treat them horribly and cruelly while mistreating their employees, lying to consumers, and who knows what else. But what if we were to imagine a less villainous version of Mirando that would nonetheless maintain that the proper way to think of Okja is as a resource? Must endorsing human exceptionalism make one a villain, or is there room for a human exceptionalist to make some minimal claim to virtue? Back in the real world, is there a way for a corporation to use animals without cruelty and abuse?

After all, even if animals in general and Okja in particular have no moral status, there are likely to be various good reasons to treat nonhuman animals humanely. Even if morality is fundamentally for and about human beings, the question of how humans ought to treat animals is still before us.

First, at least some of the time, self-interest will often compel humans to treat animals well, for the interests of the animals in question and the interests of the human beings who hope to profit from them will often coincide. A healthy and happy animal will often be more likely to serve whatever its purpose might be, as food, as pet, as research subject. It is no accident that farmers look after their animals. And it is surely also no accident that Okja wins the contest! She will serve Mirando's needs so well precisely because Mija and her grandfather have treated Okja so well.

Second, as Lucy Mirando has figured out, many potential customers do care about how animals are treated. It might be simpler for Lucy to adopt a company policy of treating animals well than to launch such an elaborate and deceptive campaign as her super-pig project, a campaign that seems destined to fail at some point. The honest humane treatment of animals may be good for consumer relations.

Third, there are interesting connections between how human beings treat animals and how human beings treat one another. A child who is cruel to animals may tend to grow up to be an adult who is cruel to everyone, and a person who is indifferent to the obvious suffering of one creature is not as likely to be moved by the suffering of another. On a larger scale, how a society treats animals may affect how its citizens treat one another. If we care about how human beings are treated, it is unlikely that cruelty to animals will turn out to be a matter of no importance.

Fourth, compassion and kindness are generally thought to be virtues, states of character that are worthy of admiration and that promote human flourishing. And there is no obvious reason that compassion and kindness stop at the limit of our own species. Even if animals do not share our moral status and thus have no rights, it does not follow that we have no moral reasons to avoid causing them needless harm. Even if a dog has no moral status, most of us do not want to be the one who is known for kicking stray dogs or leaving a dog tied up in the yard in the winter with no food while we are out of town.

So, the view that animals lack moral status need not lead to monstrous behavior. Naturally, human beings ought to be humane and not only among ourselves. The inhumanity on display by some Mirando personnel is not simply the product of human exceptionalism.

Still, this attempt to advocate for animals while granting that they have no moral status may not be satisfying. Sometimes the serious interests of animals and the commercial interests of human beings do not coincide. Sometimes farming practices that cause pain are cost-effective. And while a scheme as big as Lucy Mirando's might be destined to be exposed, consumers who want attractive and available meat products will often cooperate quite willingly in remaining ignorant of exactly what happens when animals are turned into food. Even more obviously, animal industries are big business, involving the interests of many human beings as workers and as consumers. If animals have no moral status and their interests have no moral weight, this plea for humane treatment may offer only a rebuke of some of the worst of Mirando's excesses. This is likely to please very few, with corporations like Mirando hampered by such humanitarian concerns and animal advocates feeling that such a defense of animals does not go far enough. Perhaps it is not sufficient to treat Okja and the other super-pigs with a bit more care. Perhaps what they need is liberation!

Animal Liberation

> We are animal lovers. We rescue animals from slaughterhouses, zoos, labs. We tear down cages and set them free. This is why we rescued Okja... For 40 years our group has liberated animals from places of abuse... We inflict economic damage on those who profit from their misery. We reveal their atrocities to the public, and we never harm anyone, human or nonhuman.
> —Jay, leader of the Animal Liberation Front

The Animal Liberation Front wants to shut down the Mirando Corporation. They vehemently reject the Mirando philosophy of human exceptionalism and disavow any moral distinction between humans and other animals. Their goals are to stop the human exploitation of animals and to work toward the end or at least the great reduction of animal suffering.

The philosopher Peter Singer published a very influential book called *Animal Liberation* in Singer (1990). In this book, Singer also calls for equality between human beings and the other animals. Singer takes pains to explain what sort of equality he is and is not arguing for. The ALF could benefit from paying closer attention to his work.

To begin with, there are plenty of interesting and important differences between (most) human beings and the other animals. To defend equality for animals cannot mean denying this obvious fact. There are also plenty of interesting and important differences among the other species of animals themselves! A dog is quite different in many ways from a human being, but also from an oyster or a lobster. Singer's case for equality between humans and the other animals cannot and does not require that living creatures are all the same in every respect. Likewise, a case for gender equality does not require that there be no interesting differences between males and females. Equality can be defended without pretending differences do not exist.

Singer argues that the relevant notion of equality here is the equal consideration of interests. This is not a matter of observing some actual equality (or sameness) among the relevant parties but rather a matter of prescribing that the varied interests of the relevant parties must be considered equally. This notion of equality is normative rather than descriptive.

It is crucial to recognize that equal consideration of interests will not always yield equal treatment, for the parties involved may have very different interests. Plainly, an adult and a young child, whether human or not, should not be treated in all the same ways, and yet their interests can be considered of equal weight. One need not say that a child is more or less valuable than an adult or has weaker or stronger rights than an adult to say that a child should be treated differently than an adult. To treat someone differently because they have different interests is not to dismiss or downgrade their interests. No moral inequality is involved in not permitting a young child to vote or to drive a car, for example. Likewise for nonhuman animals. A squirrel has no interest in free speech or in attending school, so in not affording squirrels the rights to do such things, we are not failing to consider their interests equally.

Perhaps this then is what the ALF should be working toward. Mirando and other corporations simply ignore the interests of the animals in their industries, giving them no direct weight at all. Animals "matter" only insofar as they affect human interests. This is immoral. The interests of the super-pigs and of other nonhuman animals ought to be considered and given the very same weight as human interests. Now, animals do not share in all human interests. But they do have an interest in not living miserable lives. If the interests of other animals were considered as on a par with human interests, perhaps this would lead in the direction of animal liberation.

In pursuit of this goal, the ALF leader Jay says they are constrained by their complete rejection of violence. They will therefore not cause harm to anyone or anything in order to achieve their goals. This is a rather extreme form of pacifism.

Of course, they do not really abide by this radical constraint. At least three breaches are evident in the film. First, when they are being chased by Mirando security or by police, they defend themselves. Not with guns or other lethal weapons. No, they "fight" with umbrellas, they wrestle and push, and they dump a load of ball bearings to trip their opponents, comically apologizing all the while. No loss of life and probably no lasting injury. But they clearly leave their pursuers with some bruises. Second, when he finds out that K has lied about Mija giving consent for their use of Okja, deceiving her out of devotion to their mission, Jay himself gives K a savage beating for betraying the principles and the history of the ALF. This is a nice bit of self-righteous hypocrisy, as Jay seems to be betraying those very same principles in delivering the beating. Third, and worst of all, the ALF deliberately send Okja into a lab where they ought to know she will be seriously harmed. And she is. Samples are taken of her flesh in a very painful procedure. She is forcibly bred with a savage and gigantic male super-pig. As an audience we are made to feel that we are watching a brutal rape scene, though thankfully little of it is shown explicitly. The ALF team watches this horror show play out via the camera they have planted on Okja in shocked silence. Thus, the ALF and its members quite clearly cause harm to others, human and nonhuman, in pursuit of their goals, even if they strive to avoid causing certain types of harm.

This in itself is no surprise. No one can or should abide by a principle of causing no harm to anyone or anything under any circumstances, as noble as it might sound. Doctors and dentists and veterinarians cause harm in treating their patients, after all, and people are glad for it. Sometimes it is both rational and moral to cause someone a smaller harm in order to spare them a greater harm or to bring them a greater good. Perhaps it would make more sense to forbid causing someone harm all-things-considered, leaving room for harms that are in someone's interests.

Most would agree that there are also situations in which it makes sense to cause someone a smaller harm in order to spare someone else a greater harm or to spare a larger number of people a harm of the same size. In fact, in some situations where people's interests conflict, such as the well-known trolley scenario in which I must choose between running over one person or running over five people, causing harm is unavoidable whichever choice I might make. Perhaps the goal here should be to minimize harm rather than to refuse ever to be the cause of harm. In any case, deciding when causing harm might be morally justified and when it might not be turns out to be trickier than it might seem.

The idea that a person might be able to go through life without causing any harm at all is neither practical nor laudable. Certainly, the ALF cannot achieve their goal of total animal liberation without causing any harm to anyone or anything. They are caught in a dilemma between a goal about which they are passionate and their antipathy for certain means that might be necessary to achieve that goal. This dilemma is a helpful way to highlight a basic distinction in moral theory: between consequentialism and deontology.

To conceive of morality as the pursuit of an overarching goal, the greater good, as it is often called, is the hallmark of consequentialism. As the name suggests, consequentialism is founded on the idea that what matters morally are the consequences of our actions, our choices, our motives, our whatever. A consequentialist is inclined to think that the end justifies the means – if the end is valuable enough and the means isn't too costly. So, from a consequentialist point of view, it may make sense for the ALF to sacrifice even Okja for the sake of the advancement of the animal liberation agenda. Sure, she will suffer – but her suffering is justified by the prospect of reducing the suffering of many more animals. It is easy for the good of a few or of a single individual to be outweighed by the good that can be achieved for the many. It is built into the logic of consequentialism that if one's goal is to minimize pain, one might have to inflict pain in order to do so – to torture one to prevent five from being tortured. The ALF wants to save millions of super-pigs, not just one. Notice that the sacrifice of the one really would have to be necessary here. If the ALF could achieve their goal in some other way, without subjecting Okja to such horrific treatment, then they should choose that alternative course of action.

The chief rival to consequentialism in modern moral theory is deontology, sometimes unhelpfully called simply "nonconsequentialism." As this latter moniker implies, deontology is sometimes seen simply as the rejection of consequentialism. More helpfully, deontology involves the idea that there are moral limits to what we can do in pursuit of even our most worthy goals, limits that often involve the rights of individuals. Sometimes, the end does not and cannot justify the means. With their commitment to do no harm, the ALF talk like they believe in such limits, but as we have seen, they do not live up to their talk. If the ALF were guided by deontological principles, it appears as if they should not have made the decision to subject Okja to the torture and rape she experienced in the Mirando lab, even if so much was at stake. Some actions are simply wrong and must not be carried out. Torture and rape and murder are prime candidates for such actions.

This divide in moral theory leaves animal advocates with two broad strategies. They can argue on deontological grounds that animals as individuals have rights, that there are moral limits to how Okja or any other animal may be treated. Or, they can argue on consequentialist grounds that the world would be a better place if we were to treat Okja, the super-pigs, and all other animals better than we do now. The ALF does not define their philosophy with crystal clarity. How might their core values be developed more carefully along each of these two lines?

A Consequentialist Liberation?

While the ALF often speaks in terms that sound deontological, their underlying rationale seems to be consequentialist. This is unsurprising, since most people espouse moral views that are inchoate and probably at least somewhat internally inconsistent. Even Peter Singer's animal advocacy at times seems to reflect this sort of underlying tension. He is explicitly a consequentialist, yet he also defends clearly defined limits on how animals are treated: no experimentation on animals, no farming animals, and so on. How far can a consequentialist foundation support the apparent absolutism of the animal liberation movement?

Suppose then that the ALF's philosophy is conceived in consequentialist terms. Their goal is to bring about the best consequences and in doing so to cross any lines that it is necessary to cross. But the best consequences for whom? This is tantamount to the question who has moral status for the consequentialist. Humans and nonhumans alike, the ALF says. But the category "nonhuman" includes the earlier discussed sticks and stones as well as pigs and cows and cats and dogs, for none of these are human beings. The idea that every object in the world has moral status is a non-starter. Some sort of distinction is needed.

Utilitarianism is the best known version of consequentialism. Utilitarianism states that the action with the best consequences is the action that yields the greatest net total of pleasure over pain. On this hedonistic view, a creature matters morally just in case that creature can experience pleasure and pain, which requires that a creature is conscious or sentient (i.e., able to perceive and feel). Jeremy Bentham (1748–1832), one of the founders of modern utilitarianism, offers the following pointed observation: "The question is not, Can they reason? nor, Can they talk? but, Can they suffer? Why should the law refuse its protection to any sensitive being?" (Bentham 2017). To accept the principle of the equal consideration of interests is to expand the moral community to anyone or anything that has interests. Having interests presupposes the capacity to be harmed, to have one's interests advanced or set back, and that requires the capacity to feel pain and pleasure.

Utilitarian morality is thus not directly concerned with the fate of sticks and stones, but is directly concerned with the fate of any and all sentient creatures. This "sentience exceptionalism" is a rival to the human exceptionalism discussed earlier on. The moral community does not comprise all and only human beings, but rather all and only sentient beings. And the interests of each sentient being should be counted equal to the interests of any other sentient being. If human beings have moral status because they experience pleasure and pain, it would be arbitrary to deny moral status to other creatures who likewise experience pleasure and pain.

The upside for those who are animal advocates is that the interests of the vast number of nonhuman animals who are caught up in human industries must be counted as part of the complicated moral calculations about what is best for all sentient beings. Animals cannot be invisible from a moral point of view. A factory farm that seems like an all things considered benefit when only human interests are considered, or when human interests are considered as having much more weight than nonhuman animal interests, may not be much of a benefit when animal interests are given their proper weight. Mirando's business plan is probably driven only by their stakeholders, by the few wealthy humans who own shares or sit on their board. Utilitarianism says first that their plan should be based on the interests of all human beings rather than only on the interests of the wealthy and powerful and second that they cannot stop there but must consider the interests of all sentient beings.

As we have seen, Singer argues that sentience is a morally relevant marker and that species is not. Why should a creature matter less simply because it is of a different species? From his point of view, to treat species as a morally relevant marker is no different than deeming some more important than others because of their gender or race. Thus, Singer purports to expose human exceptionalism as nothing more than another form of prejudice: speciesism. Certainly, the ALF would nod their heads in approval.

Expanding the moral community to include all sentient beings and insisting that the interests of all such beings must be counted equally promises to revolutionize how we think about and how we treat other animals. This is a bold philosophical move. Like the ALF, it will encounter resistance. Three main lines of resistance target the underlying commitment to consequentialism in familiar ways.

First, in its insistence that a person is always morally required to do what brings about the best consequences, this theory seems to clash with much of how we ordinarily think about human life. To some, this will be sufficient grounds to reject it. Our ordinary moral beliefs cannot be that far wrong. Human beings have been using animals for food and other purposes for an awfully long time. Can it really be wrong to do so? Some put enough stock in "common sense" morality that they are unlikely to heed any call for a moral liberation or revolution.

Second, such a theory is very demanding. Not only must a person pay some attention to the interests of animals, but they must do whatever will best serve everyone's interests. Might they even be morally required to join something like the ALF, if that would be the best way to maximize the pleasure and minimize the pain for all concerned? Typically the moral bar is not set so high.

Third, as we have seen, a person might be morally required to do something terrible to bring about the best outcome, as when the ALF sent Okja into the lab to be tortured and raped. Someone with more deontological inclinations will argue that what matters is how a person treats each individual animal, not the total long-term consequences of their actions.

For some then, consequentialism will be the wrong foundation on which to build an animal liberation movement. But others will be willing to devise a clever response to these lines of resistance or, failing that, simply to bite the bullet. Again, this is how it is in philosophy.

A Deontological Liberation?

Now, let us turn to a deontological account of animal liberation. Consider the claim that Okja has rights that prevent the Mirando Corporation from treating her as a mere piece of property to be used or destroyed as they see fit. What they are doing to her and the other super-pigs is an injustice. It is crucial to distinguish here between legal rights and moral rights. Legal rights are granted by a legislative body. What legal rights Okja might have depends on where she is. The legal rights established by law in South Korea might well be different from the legal rights established by law in Chile or in the United States. To find out what legal rights (if any) Okja might have, one must consult the laws of the land. But that is not what is at issue here. The ALF does not aspire to enforce existing laws. They are out to change such laws, even to change the culture that gave rise to such laws. The ALF will speak out on behalf of the rights of animals whether those rights are recognized by the state or not. These are basic moral rights animals are thought to have independent of what people might think. We are familiar with the notion that human beings have certain basic inherent rights that it is immoral for a government to violate.

Might animals have such rights as well? If so, which animals? The ALF's leader Jay says he holds all creatures dear to his heart. But really? All creatures? From a smart and sensitive creature like Okja down to every member of every one of the hundreds of thousands of species of beetles? How exhausting this scope of moral concern must be! Surely we do and have to draw a line somewhere. Not every living thing can plausibly be said to have rights. So where is this line? Suppose we assume that Okja is on this side of the line and a flea is on that side of the line. She has rights; her fleas do not. In virtue of what?

Of course, to answer this question is also to ask what grounds the moral rights of human beings – if indeed we have such rights. Some consequentialists will of course argue that the notion of moral rights is wrongheaded or unhelpful.

Can it be maintained that every sentient being has certain rights? This is what a comprehensive deontological animal liberation movement would require. Yet many will argue that only persons can have rights. If that is the case, then deontology only offers a revision of how we deal with animals who are plausibly thought to be persons. The most familiar version of such a line of reasoning is contractarian: to have a right requires being able to stand in a reciprocal contractual relationship within a moral community. One person has a right against another, so rights-bearers must be able to be obligated by the rights of others. One cannot have a right unless one can recognize and respect (or fail to do so) the rights of others. This a merely sentient creature cannot do.

A deontological animal liberation might serve Okja and her fellow super-pigs well enough, since a good case can be made for their personhood. But many animals will be left out in the cold, unless either a more expansive conception of personhood is accepted or the link between rights and personhood is called into question, to return to the earlier discussion of the Kantian Defense of the Mirando view. So those who want to call for animal liberation may not want to build on a deontological foundation. Certainly many philosophers who are animal advocates, such as Peter Singer, are consequentialists.

Okja has quite a bit of fun at the ALF's expense. As we have already seen, the supposedly nonviolent Jay delivers a serious beatdown. ALF member Silver says that all food production is morally compromised and thus he tries to eat as little as possible. This means that he is on the verge of fainting even during the crucial stage of their mission to liberate Okja. And of course the ALF's philosophy is vaguely and humorously pretentious, as so much ideology turns out to be. But the individual members of the ALF are better than the movement. In spite of their missteps, their hearts are in the right place. Jay and K are with Mija and Okja until the end, at great personal risk. We admire them not for being true believers in their cause but rather for caring about the small girl and the giant pig that have been pulled into this conflict between a corporate giant and a ragtag band of rebels.

All Animals Are Equal, but Some Are More Equal Than Others

At this point it is worth acknowledging that neither Mirando nor the ALF may plausibly represent how most people think about animals. Sure, there are some who see animals as a mere commodity, or even as playthings meant for our amusement, and there are others who want to put concerns about animals on a par with or even above concerns about human beings. But likely there are many folks who would want to include animals in our moral universe but who would also want to mark a difference between a human being and a typical animal – between those who are reading this and their pets or the animals that might end up as their dinner. Most are neither apathetic nor inclined to activism. Many object to the worst factory farming has to offer but see no problem with farms that treat animals humanely.

Though it is tempting to think that a choice must be made between a human exceptionalism on which animals have no moral status and a view on which humans and other animals have an equal moral status, in fact this choice is not inevitable. To argue against human exceptionalism is not to argue for equality for animals, and to argue against equality for animals is not to argue for human exceptionalism. We do not have to choose between veganism and trophy hunting.

Moral status need not be simple and bivalent, so that a creature either has it or lacks it. Moral status might come in two distinct levels, for example. Philosopher Robert Nozick considers and critiques a hybrid view he calls "utilitarianism for animals, Kantianism for people" (Nozick 1974, p. 39). Perhaps creatures who are sentient have one level of moral status, while sentient creatures who are also persons have a higher level of moral status. This would of course require arguing that the characteristics that take a creature from sentience to personhood are not morally irrelevant, so that it is not mere prejudice to count persons as having more status than merely sentient beings. It would be morally suspect to argue that sentient creatures would have a higher moral status because they are larger, or cuter, or furrier than others. Such characteristics should be given no moral weight. But arguably it is not in the same way suspect to argue that a higher moral status belongs to sentient creatures who are capable of moral judgment or who can conceive of themselves as subjects of an ongoing conscious life.

Perhaps nonhuman animals who are persons have rights, and thus there are significant moral constraints on how they may be treated. An animal like Okja, then, cannot be treated in the way some lower animals are treated. The innermost circle of the moral community would thus comprises persons, and that includes some nonhuman animals as well as most human beings. A set of deontological principles would govern the dealings of this community of persons.

Animals who do not meet the threshold of personhood cannot be treated as mere things who are altogether outside the moral community, however. Their welfare must be taken into account, but there would be a sea change between how human beings interact with nonhuman persons like Okja and how they interact with insects and fish and birds and lower mammals. Of course, there will be difficult questions about where to draw this line, and such questions could only be answered by people doing research into animal behavior, animal psychology, and animal neuroscience.

If the prospect of drawing a bright line seems dim, the varying moral status of sentient beings could also be seen as a spectrum, a hierarchy, with some creatures having more moral status than others. Beneath such a hierarchy would be things with no moral status at all, inanimate objects and perhaps some invertebrates. At the top of the hierarchy would be persons. At the lower end would be creatures with only the most minimal form of sentience and awareness. At the higher end, approaching personhood, would be the higher mammals such as dolphins or chimpanzees. Any sentient creature, whether typical of its kind or not, would find a place somewhere on this hierarchy of moral status. A consequentialist might use this notion of a hierarchy to assign a different weight to the interests of a sentient creature according to its location on the hierarchy. Thus, what one would be required to do on behalf of a creature in need would depend on the type of creature it is. Perhaps Jay and K are right to risk much on Okja's behalf, but presumably they would not be required to risk so much on the behalf of an ordinary guinea pig. In the same way, perhaps a person should be willing to spend more money to save the life of one kind of animal than another. A sick dog is likely to receive more care than a sick goldfish, and perhaps rightly so.

This brief discussion of the possibility of a two-level or a hierarchical view of moral status hopefully suffices to illustrate that while it is helpful to begin with a pretty stark contrast between two rather polarized positions (Mirando and the ALF and their imagined theoretical rationales) and to consider how they push back against one another, in reality the theoretical options for thinking about the moral status of animals are many.

Conclusion: The Friendship of Mija and Okja

Near the end of the film, as Mija wanders dumbstruck through the super-pig meat processing plant hidden away underground in New Jersey, she sees other super-pigs, creatures just like Okja, rendered from living, breathing, feeling animals into lifeless meat ready to be packaged and sold. She is confronted by Nancy Mirando, who has retaken the leadership of the company from her sister, with Okja's life hanging in the balance, a bolt gun at the ready.

Nancy   Well, what's the hiccup? Why is it still alive?
Mija   Why you want to kill Okja?
Nancy   Well, we can only sell the dead ones.
Mija   I want to go home. With Okja.
Nancy   No. It's my property.

Nancy goes on to reduce an already "processed" super-pig hanging on a nearby hook to its usable parts. "It's all edible," she exclaims. To her, Okja is a thing, an "it," nothing but a piece of property. For Mija, Okja has a gender, a personality, a name. She is Mija's friend, part of her family. The way people often talk about and treat animals often reflects this kind of conflict. Some animals are pests to be exterminated. Others are bought and sold on the cheap. Yet some animals, our pets or companion animals, are part of the family. We sometimes spend rather a lot of money on their care and mourn their loss when they die.

To this point, the conversation has been about whether animals have moral status and accordingly about whether we might have moral obligations to animals. Animals might have rights that must be respected, or we might be morally required to take their well-being into account. These are fundamental questions in moral theory. But they are not the only questions to ask about human-animal relations. In fact, there is an extensive and familiar discussion about the limitations of the dialogue and debate between deontology and consequentialism. Some argue that this sort of talk cannot make proper room for love, for friendship, for caring human relationships. Bernard Williams famously argues that a person who feels a need to offer a moral justification for saving their spouse rather than a stranger has "one thought too many" (Williams 1981, p. 18). I should simply act to save my wife because she is my wife. This Williams objection seems to capture Mija's motivations throughout the film. She is not thinking that she must save Okja because she is morally responsible for her as her caretaker. She is not concerned with the plight of all sentient creatures; in fact, she is not really all that concerned with the fate of the rest of the super-pigs. She simply acts instinctively and single-mindedly to find and rescue her friend and to return home. She is grateful for the ALF's assistance and eventually sees that they might be friendly to her and to Okja, but their larger purposes leave her unmoved. She wants her friend back.

On the one hand, this may be because she is a child. Perhaps she is simply not mature enough to adopt a more sophisticated view of things. She is ignoring the larger consequences of Mirando's project, both good and bad. And she is not really wondering whether Okja has moral status and what shape that might take. She does not pause to ask whether she should be doing what she is doing.

On the other hand, the grownups in this film are not all that admirable. Some are ruthless and care nothing for anyone. Others are moral posers. The friendship between Okja and Mija is the heart of the film. Each would die for the other; each has literally saved the other's life. Only Mija truly sees Okja for who she is. Several times the film shows Mija whispering into Okja's ear and we have no idea what is being said. We do not need to know to get the point. Together these two embody the kind of friendship that is so rare and so prized. To ask how much love Mija has for Okja rather than speculating about her moral status is thus not a sign of moral naïveté. Instead, it reflects the judgment that at some point love is more important than morality and individual people (whatever their species) are more important than institutions, corporations, and movements.

In the Gospels (Mark 10:13–16, Matthew 18:2–4), Jesus says that only those who become like children can enter the kingdom of heaven. Perhaps in Mija this film paints one portrait of what he might have meant.

References

Aquinas, St. Thomas. 2017. *Summa Theologiae*, in the version presented at https://www.newadvent.org/summa/

Bentham, Jeremy. 2017. *An introduction to the principles of morals and legislation*, in the version presented at http://www.earlymoderntexts.com

Cohen, Carl. 1986. The case for the use of animals in biomedical research. *New England Journal of Medicine* 315 (14): 865–870.

DeGrazia, David. 2002. *Animal rights. A very short introduction*. New York: Oxford University Press.

Descartes, Rene. 2017. *Meditations on first philosophy*, in the version presented at http://www.earlymoderntexts.com

Gruen, Lori. 2011. *Ethics and animals: An introduction*. New York: Cambridge University Press.

Johnson, David Kyle. 2013. Do souls exist? *Think* 12 (35): 61–75.

Kagan, Shelly. 2019. *How to count animals, more or less*. New York: Oxford University Press.

Kant, Immanuel. 2017. *Groundwork for the metaphysics of morals*, in the version presented at http://www.earlymoderntexts.com

Korsgaard, Christine M. 2018. *Fellow creatures: Our obligations to the other animals*. New York: Oxford University Press.

Nozick, Robert. 1974. *Anarchy, state, and utopia*. New York: Basic Books.

Plato. 2004. *Republic*. translated by C.D.C. Reeve. Indianapolis: Hackett Publishing Company.

Regan, Tom. 1983. *The case for animal rights*. Berkeley/Los Angeles: The University of California Press.

Singer, Peter. 1990. *Animal liberation*. Revised edition. New York: Avon Books.

———. 1993. *Practical ethics*. 2nd ed. New York: Cambridge University Press.

Williams, Bernard. 1981. *Moral Luck*. New York: Cambridge University Press.

2001 as Philosophy: A Technological Odyssey

33

Jerold J. Abrams

Contents

Introduction	796
Summary of *2001*	798
The Dawn of Man	800
Bergson on Technological Evolution	800
Moonwatcher's Discovery of the Club	802
Dr. Heywood Floyd	803
Jupiter Mission: 18 Months Later	805
Bergson on Intellect and Cinema	805
Hal and the Turing Test	806
Hal's First Inverted Turing Test: The Chess Game	808
Hal's Second Inverted Turing Test: Questions for Dave	809
Odysseus and the Cyclops	813
Jupiter and Beyond the Infinite	815
Bergson on Species Self-Transformation	815
The Star Gate	817
The Alien Ovum and the Hotel Suite	819
The Star Child	820
Conclusion: Kubrick's *2001*: A Half-Century Later	820
Notes	822
References	824

Abstract

Stanley Kubrick's *2001: A Space Odyssey* is a brilliant epic film about the universal history of humanity beginning with early primates and culminating in the space age and the creation of a new superhuman being. Traditionally

J. J. Abrams (✉)
Creighton University, Omaha, NE, USA
e-mail: abramsjj@creighton.edu

© Springer Nature Switzerland AG 2024
D. K. Johnson et al. (eds.), *The Palgrave Handbook of Popular Culture as Philosophy*,
https://doi.org/10.1007/978-3-031-24685-2_10

philosophers find the plot of *2001: A Space Odyssey* to descend from Homer's *Odyssey* and the philosophy of *2001* to descend from nineteenth-century German philosopher Friedrich Nietzsche's *Also Sprach Zarathustra*, which also inspired Richard Strauss's *Also Sprach Zarathustra*, which opens the film. While Homer's *Odyssey* provides the basic plot of an odyssey, along with some characters such as the new Cyclops "Hal," and elements of Nietzsche's *Zarathustra* appear in the film, Kubrick's *2001: A Space Odyssey* far more powerfully illustrates twentieth-century French philosopher Henri Bergson's philosophy of creative and technological evolution found in *Creative Evolution* and *Two Sources of Morality and Religion*.

Keywords

Stanley Kubrick · *2001: A Space Odyssey* · Monoliths · Moonwatcher · Aliens · Prometheus · Technological reason · Dr. Heywood Floyd · Clavius Moon Base · Jupiter Mission · *Discovery One* · Dr. Dave Bowman · Odysseus · Dr. Frank Poole · HAL 9000 · Cyclops · EVA Pod · Star gate · Star child · Aristotle · Friedrich Nietzsche · Henri Bergson · Creative Evolution · Stanley Cavell · Alan Turing · Turing Test · Imitation game · Chess · Artificial intelligence · Eyeball imagery · Photography · *A Clockwork Orange* (film by Stanley Kubrick)

Introduction

The American filmmaker Stanley Kubrick's (1928–1999) science fiction film *2001: A Space Odyssey* (1968) is a brilliant but difficult film. The title and subtitle refer to the year of a space odyssey to the planet Jupiter, but *2001* is also an odyssey through time beginning four million years ago. In the opening shot, one planet appears, then another rises behind it, and then the sun rises behind the second, to set a row of three spheres, the last one glowing and unifying the shot in sublime one-point perspective, all to the low-vibrating strings and triumphant trumpets of the opening of German composer Richard Strauss' (1864–1949) *Also Sprach Zarathustra* (1896). Strauss composed *Zarathustra* inspired by German philosopher Friedrich Nietzsche's (1844–1900) philosophical novel of the same title, *Also Sprach Zarathustra* (1883–1891). At the beginning of Nietzsche's novel, the hermit sage Zarathustra beholds the sun from his mountaintop cave, and then, filled with philosophical wisdom, descends the mountain into society to announce the coming of the *Übermensch* ("overman"). As Nietzsche's novel inspired Strauss, Nietzsche's *Zarathustra* and Strauss's *Zarathustra* both inspired Kubrick, and elements of the novel undoubtedly appear in the film *2001*; consider, for example, the film's themes of the intellectual odyssey, the education of humanity, the logic of self-overcoming, the image of the new child, and the possibility of a higher and even superhuman condition.

These themes and images are not, however, exclusive to Nietzsche's philosophy. Images of the superhuman, for example, appear in Homer's *Iliad* and *Odyssey*, with Achilles and the gods of Olympus. Later, the figure of the superhuman appears in more philosophical form with Aristotle's theory of the "god among men" in the *Politics*, and again in Dante's *Comedy* with the image of "transhumanization" of the pilgrim into a superhuman being who ascends into space and appears as a newborn child. Or consider Shakespeare's superhuman warrior Caius Martius Coriolanus in *Coriolanus*, or Christopher Marlowe's *Doctor Faustus* or Johann Wolfgang von Goethe's *Faust*, or Ralph Waldo Emerson's philosophy and poetry, which synthesized this entire tradition, from Homer to Goethe, and famously influenced the young Nietzsche.

But perhaps none of these writers, including Nietzsche, quite articulates the central philosophical vision of *2001*, a vision of humanity as a technological species advancing through history toward the superhuman condition.[1] The novel *Zarathustra* certainly remains a part of the discussion, but there are more things in Kubrick's *2001* than are dreamt of in Nietzsche's philosophy, and as David Kyle Johnson demonstrates in "Kubrick's *2001* and Nietzsche's Übermensch," in *Sci-Phi: Science Fiction as Philosophy*, *2001* deserves ongoing philosophical investigation.[2]

Toward that end, the present discussion advances the following view. *2001* unfolds a philosophical vision very similar (though not identical) to the French philosopher Henri Bergson's (1859–1941) philosophy, especially as it is expressed in *Creative Evolution* (1907) and *Two Sources of Morality and Religion* (1932). According to Bergson, the invention of basic tools by prehuman creatures so long ago transformed and propelled them forward into history, through history, and to the end of history. Now, at the end of history, having developed a vast scientific and technological culture, humanity has entered a condition of cultural oscillation characterized primarily by the seemingly unending pursuit of ever-finer forms of luxury. This oscillating (i.e., repetitive and relatively intellectually non-developmental) stage of humanity bears resemblance to the condition of the prehuman creatures in *2001* who, prior to their discovery of tools, were incapable of advancing except by means of discovering their power to transform their external environment. At the end of history, in its present condition of the pursuit of luxury, humanity seems incapable of seeing beyond or passing beyond itself, and will continue in this condition, according to Bergson, until a philosopher appears and shows humanity the means of turning its tools upon itself to transform itself and thereby pass beyond the human condition and at last enter the superhuman condition. The ultimate end of humanity, according to Bergson, is nothing short of the creation of a new society of immortal and superhumanly intelligent beings, extended far beyond the planet. Like no other film in the history of cinema, Kubrick's *2001: A Space Odyssey* advances this same philosophy. What Bergson presents brilliantly and beautifully in prose that won him the Nobel Prize in Literature (1927), Kubrick presents in one of the greatest films of all time.[3]

Summary of *2001*

2001 has three main segments with titles: "The Dawn of Man," "Jupiter Mission: 18 Months Later," and "Jupiter and Beyond the Infinite." In "The Dawn of Man," following the opening shot of the spheres, the camera surveys a desert where a troop of apes forages for sparse plant life and drinks from a drying water hole. A candle of tapirs eats these same plants and drinks the same water, but the apes do not see the tapirs as prey. A leopard attacks and eats one of the apes, which are powerless to defend themselves, and when a rival troop of apes seeks to seize the water hole, both troops can do little more than stomp and howl and wave their arms in threatening displays. With almost no food or water in a vast desert, and no means of defense against predators or rivals, the apes are dying. But one night, as the apes sleep, unseen aliens set a tall smooth black cuboid monolith upright in stone outside their cave.[4] The apes wake with the sun and see the monolith. The sun rises and shines on the monolith; the monolith transforms their minds, catapulting the apes into reason.

The film never shows the aliens in the "Dawn of Man" segment or any of the segments, but the appearance of the first monolith implies their existence; later in the film, in the "Jupiter Mission" segment, the film declares their existence: "Eighteen months ago, the first evidence of intelligent life off the Earth was discovered."[5] But in Arthur C. Clarke's novel *2001: A Space Odyssey*, the presence of aliens is more vivid with the first monolith. In the novel, the aliens inhabit the apes and direct their minds and limbs from the inside as if they were puppets, transforming them, yet without the ape's understanding: "They could never guess that their minds were being probed, their bodies mapped, their reactions studied, their potentials evaluated" (Clarke 1968/1999, p. 14).

The plot of *2001: A Space Odyssey* may belong to Homer's *Odyssey*, but this scene of the monolith is straight out of Aeschylus' ancient text *Prometheus Bound*. Upon finding primitive creatures who "swarmed like bitty ants in dugouts / in sunless caves" (Aeschylus 1975, lines 649–651), the Titan Prometheus with fire of reason transformed their minds and made them human: "I gave them intelligence, I made them masters of their own thought" (ibid., lines 633–635). In *2001* the Promethean transformation appears first in the ape known as Moonwatcher while examining a tapir skeleton on the ground. Moonwatcher discovers the tapir leg bone in his hand can function as a club capable of crushing the skull of a tapir skeleton, and therefore a living tapir, which may then be eaten. In this same moment, Moonwatcher also understands that if a club can crush a tapir skull, then a club can crush an ape skull too. So when the rival apes return to seize the water hole, Moonwatcher and his troop club the rival ape leader to death, and then Moonwatcher triumphantly hurls the club skyward.

The film then brilliantly match-cuts from the beginning of universal history to the end of universal history, from the white bone in the sky to a white bone-shaped satellite in space. The aliens have caused Moonwatcher's transformation with their Promethean gift of instrumental reason and initiated a developmental sequence which will culminate in the space program. But at the same time the aliens set the first monolith outside the cave they also buried a second monolith on the moon. This point emerges more clearly in the novel *2001* than the film: "The most astonishing thing about this object is its antiquity. Geological evidence proves beyond doubt that it is three million years old. It was placed on the Moon, therefore, when our ancestors were primitive ape-men" (Clarke 1968/1999, p. 208). The aliens set the first monolith outside the cave to begin universal history, and they set the second monolith in the moon as a penultimate goal of universal history. All of history from the time of Moonwatcher's discovery of the club to the space program has aimed unconsciously at the discovery and excavation of this second buried monolith.

Now Dr. Heywood Floyd sleeps onboard the Orion III spaceplane from Earth to Space Station V. His pen drifts from his pocket and floats weightlessly in the zero-gravity cabin, like Moonwatcher's tapir bone floating in the sky. The Orion III docks at Space Station V with its two giant wheels spinning together to simulate gravity by centrifugal force. From Space Station V, Dr. Floyd travels onboard the Aries 1b Lunar Shuttle to the moon's Clavius Base. On Clavius Dr. Floyd represents The Council's will to maintain absolute secrecy about the moon monolith and the existence of extraterrestrials. The Council has fabricated a cover story about the outbreak of disease on the moon to justify emergency exclusion of all foreign powers, in particular, the Soviets. The Americans wield deception against the Soviets as Moonwatcher's troop once wielded clubs against the rival apes. Dr. Floyd and a small team then travel by moonbus from Clavius to the excavated site near the crater Tycho where the monolith stands upright in stone. One astronaut photographs the monolith, and Dr. Floyd touches the monolith. But as sunlight touches the monolith for the first time, the monolith sounds a deafening signal pinpointing the exact location of yet another monolith suspended in space near Jupiter.[6]

In the "Jupiter Mission: 18 Months Later" segment, Dr. Dave Bowman and second-in-command Dr. Frank Poole travel onboard the *Discovery One* toward Jupiter. The *Discovery*'s spherical centrifuge revolves, "generating its imitation gravity," as Clarke writes in the novel *2001*, like the wheels of Space Station V (Clarke 1968/1999, p. 183). Four other crewmembers hibernate in white tubes in the centrifuge, preserving resources, with the expectation of reanimation when their skills are needed. The sixth crewmember, by contrast, never sleeps, and his skills are always needed. "Hal" is one of the HAL 9000 series of self-conscious and super-intelligent computers. But once Dave and Frank suspect Hal has made a mistake and may be dangerous to the crew and mission, Dave and Frank secretly discuss Hal's mental state and the possibility of disconnecting his higher brain functions. Hal then kills Frank on a spacewalk and kills the hibernating crewmembers and finally attempts to kill Dave. But Dave enters Hal's Logic Memory Center and disconnects his mind, and then Dave finds buried at the bottom of Hal's mind a pre-recorded message containing the true mission of the ship, which Dave will now complete alone.

Upon arrival in Jupiter's space, Dave exits the *Discovery* in an EVA Space Pod (extravehicular activity pod), and then enters a glowing dreamlike kaleidoscopic star gate, which propels him to the center of a colossal alien ovum. Dave then finds himself in a luxurious hotel suite where he ages and reaches the end of his life. As an old man dying in an elegant bed, Dave beholds a final monolith at the bed's foot. The monolith transforms him into a new alien-human hybrid fetus suspended on its back (as Dave was) within a glowing transparent sphere upon the soft bed as Strauss's *Zarathustra* begins again. The fetus in its glowing transparent sphere then appears upright suspended freely in space. The star child rotates like a planet toward the camera and looks directly at the viewer and the film ends.

The Dawn of Man

"The Dawn of Man" segment lasts from the scene of the apes to the scene on the moon where the astronauts photograph the monolith. The segment as a whole presents the two ends of universal history, from the transformation of the apes into technological beings, to the end of universal history with the space program, so that universal history appears by implication as a technological odyssey from the first monolith to the second monolith. The passage from the first monolith to the second monolith is the odyssey of technological reason through history. It is a time odyssey. The passage from Earth to the moon, and especially the *Discovery's* journey to Jupiter, is the space odyssey. But the entire journey from the first monolith to the fourth monolith is also all one odyssey.

The "Dawn of Man" segment of the film illustrates Bergson's philosophical view of technological and creative evolution. What Bergson describes in *Creative Evolution* and *Two Sources of Morality and Religion* as the evolution of the human mind from early primates by means of discovery of tools, Kubrick in *2001* presents with Moonwatcher's discovery of the bone as a tool. As Bergson describes perception, imagination, and intellect as permeated by instrumental reason (technological thinking), Kubrick presents Moonwatcher's mind as permeated by instrumental reason.

Bergson on Technological Evolution

Bergson in *Creative Evolution* describes human evolutionary history as a technological odyssey beginning with the discovery of the first tool:

> From our point of view, life appears in its entirety as an immense wave which, starting from a centre, spreads, outwards, and which on almost the whole of its circumference is stopped and converted into oscillation: at one single point the obstacle has been forced, the impulsion has passed freely. It is this freedom that the human form registers. (Bergson 1998, p. 266)

After a period of oscillation, a troop of primates discovers tools and develops instrumental intelligence. This discovery transforms the troop and shapes all human thought, action, and experience to come. In fact, instrumentation is so definitive of the species that Bergson rejects the traditional concept of *Homo sapiens* (human as knower) in favor of *Homo faber* (human as tool-user):

> If we could rid ourselves of all pride, if, to define our species, we kept strictly to what the historic and the prehistoric periods show us to be the constant characteristic of man and of intelligence, we should say not *Homo sapiens*, but *Homo faber*. In short, *intelligence, considered in what seems to be its original feature, is the faculty of manufacturing artificial objects, especially tools to make tools, and of indefinitely varying manufacture.* (ibid., p. 139; emphasis original)

Intelligence in its "original feature," meaning its "prehistoric" form, and still today is instrumental reason: it "is the faculty of manufacturing artificial objects" (ibid.). But even though the basic form of intelligence has always been the same, intelligence is by no means static. Rather intelligence develops dynamically through history from primitive tools to "tools to make tools," writes Bergson, and tools of "indefinitely varying manufacture." From age to age, *Homo faber*'s tools become more powerful, more refined, more varied and complex, smaller and larger, ever-extending his reach and control.

Bergson further develops this view in *Two Sources of Morality and Religion*. "The workman's tool is the continuation of his arm," writes Bergson, "the tool-equipment of humanity is therefore a continuation of its body. Nature, in endowing us with an essentially tool-making intelligence, prepared for us in this way a certain expansion" (Bergson 2006, p. 309). A similar view appears in Emerson's "Works and Days." "The human body is the magazine of inventions, the patent-office, where are the models from which every hint was taken. All the tools and engines on earth are only extensions of its limbs and senses" (Emerson 2007, p. 79).[7] For Emerson and Bergson, the human creature extends and augments its physical form over time as if the "workman" were a self-building giant whose materials were as much his own nature as nature outside him.

The workman works on the world primarily according to his needs of survival. Any new obstacle or problem or threat impels the workman's instrumental intelligence to create or transform his tools in order to transform the external world, e.g., to cross a river by building a raft. Over the course of millions of years, the workman, i.e., the species, becomes powerfully creative. As Bergson writes in *Creative Evolution*:

> The animal takes its stand on the plant, man bestrides animality, and the whole of humanity, in space and in time, is one immense army galloping beside and before and behind each of us in an overwhelming charge able to beat down every resistance and clear the most formidable obstacles, perhaps even death. (Bergson 1998, p. 271)

Generation upon generation, the vast galloping army of *Homo faber* in all its millions and billions, charges headlong into the future, poised ever at the battle line of the present, "beating down every resistance" outside itself, writes Bergson, until such a point as it may "clear" even "the most formidable obstacles," even those obstacles within itself such as death. Survival has always been the immediate goal of *Homo faber*, whether in hunting or defense or securing better dwellings, so death itself, or the threat of death, has always been one of the main motors of instrumental intelligence. *Homo faber* has always sought to extend the life of the individual and the troop, but for virtually the whole of history, the workman could only push death back so far. Like a young chess player losing every game, but advancing game by game against the ultimate grandmaster, at the end of history, *Homo faber* formulates a radical strategy to overtake the ultimate obstacle. Finally *Homo faber* discovers the means to remove the grandmaster's king from the board.

Moonwatcher's Discovery of the Club

In *2001* the scene of Moonwatcher's discovery of the bone to function as a club reveals ten essential dimensions of his intellect, and these ten evolve and integrate through history in different ways. First, Moonwatcher is acutely visually focused. He sees the parts of the whole tapir skeleton, and he sees the parts as themselves wholes, and examines their relations. Second, Moonwatcher's intellect and vision are instrumental: he sees the bone *as* an instrument. Third, Moonwatcher's intellect becomes constructively imaginative of future possibilities, such as killing a tapir. The film reveals this development by cutting back and forth from Moonwatcher clubbing the skeleton (in the present) to Moonwatcher clubbing a living tapir (in the not-so-distant future), revealing how his mind projects itself hypothetically into an imagined possible future. He seems to reason and imagine at once, using subjunctive conditional logic, while creating a moving (cinematic) picture in his imagination of himself performing a future action, whose linguistic form, if he could speak, would be something like the following: "If I were to club the head of a *living* tapir with a tapir bone, then the club would similarly crush its skull too, or perhaps any other animal."

Fourth, Moonwatcher understands the club also to function for defense against the rival apes. Fifth, Moonwatcher acquires a sense of self as a tool-user capable of bringing about his own ends, e.g., hunting and defense. Moonwatcher's emerging subjectivity appears as he separates himself from the troop to consume alone a handful of tapir flesh, ensuring his own survival. But, sixth, Moonwatcher's subjective self-understanding is also an intersubjective (social) self-understanding: the troop also eats together, and the troop collectively defends the water hole. Seventh, Moonwatcher and the troop feel pride in superiority over the tapirs, and pride in superiority over the rival troop. Ultimately the troop will also develop a sense of pride in superiority over all other animals of Earth. Eighth, upon successfully defending the water hole against the rival troop, the apes develop a taste for competition. While germinal in the prehistorical scene of the apes, this point becomes more explicit later in the film, e.g., in the televised martial arts match on the Aries 1b Lunar Shuttle, the chess game on the *Discovery*, and US-Soviet political relations.

Ninth, the apes become mobile. This point is implied by the disappearing water hole, the limited plant life, and what will soon be a vanishing candle of tapirs. The apes must move to survive, and they will continue to move through history. They will spread across the surface of the planet, and eventually they will develop the space program and move beyond the surface of the Earth, e.g., to explore the moon. The match-cut from the bone to the satellite secures this point about mobility into space. Tenth, the apes become imitative. Once Moonwatcher discovers the bone to function as a club, the other members of the troop imitate the action of clubbing tapirs and the rival apes. Imitation will also serve as the primary means of education. As Aristotle writes in *Poetics* 4, "Imitation is natural to man from childhood, one of his advantages over the lower animals being this, that he is the most imitative creature in the world, and learns at first by imitation"(Aristotle 1988, 1448b5–20, p. 2318). All ten of these ten dimensions of Moonwatcher's mind are one thing and one power, and this one power catapults the troop forward in space and time and ultimately toward the moon.

Dr. Heywood Floyd

Upon arrival at Space Station V, Dr. Floyd calls home on a "picturephone." Moonwatcher's early howls and grunts and stomps, transformed by technology over millions of years, have evolved to become cameras and videoscreens connecting speakers over vast distances of space. On the picturephone Dr. Floyd asks his daughter who's watching her while mommy is away. "Rachel," she says. She asks him if he's coming to her birthday party, and he apologizes: "I'm very sorry sweetheart, but I can't." "Why not?" she says. "You know, Daddy's travelling," he says. Once again, the theme of mobility appears.

The themes of birth and birthdays, and parents and children, recur throughout the film. In the prehistoric scene, the apes care for their infants in the cave. Then the monolith transforms Moonwatcher as if giving birth to a new kind of being, the rational animal. Now by picturephone Dr. Floyd wishes his daughter a happy birthday. Later, in the "Jupiter Mission" segment, onboard the *Discovery*, Frank, while in the sunbed cabin, receives a videoscreen transmission from his parents on Earth wishing him a happy birthday, as Dr. Floyd wishes his own daughter a happy birthday by picturephone. Following the transmission to *Discovery*, Hal also wishes Frank a happy birthday. Near the end of the "Jupiter Mission" segment, Hal identifies the date of his creation at the H. A. L. plant in Urbana, Illinois, and his parent-like figure Mr. Langley. The film ends with the birth of the star child.

These images of birth, appearing throughout the film, form a causal sequence. The apes give birth to their young. The aliens give birth with the monolith to rational animals. The rational animals give birth to their own young over history. Humanity gives birth to artificial intelligence. Artificial intelligence assists humanity in space travel to the third monolith. Then the aliens give birth to the star child. Education is also essential to this intergenerational sequence. The aliens transform the apes into self-educating beings by imposing instrumental reason upon their minds. Humanity educates itself over the course of universal history especially by means of technology. Upon creating artificial intelligences, humanity educates its artificial progeny by imposing the sum of human knowledge upon their artificial minds, as the aliens imposed reason into the apes. By imposing knowledge upon artificial intelligence, humanity greatly accelerates the pace of the education of artificially intelligent beings. Finally the aliens complete the education of humanity by transforming Dave into the star child. So the entire sequence of history is one vast education: the aliens give birth to rational creatures and educate them (indirectly) through history to create the conditions under which one man may become the star child, thereby completing the educational sequence, and yet also beginning a new one.

After speaking with his daughter, Dr. Floyd walks the curved white floor of one of the two wheels of Space Station V, as they simulate gravity, proceeding to the shuttle bay for the last leg of his flight to the moon. Four Russian scientists sit waiting to intercept Dr. Floyd. They ask him to join them. One woman is a friend and colleague, so Dr. Floyd takes a seat. They want to know the truth about rumors of an epidemic on Clavius. Dr. Smyslov respectfully presses Dr. Floyd who implies he knows the truth but declines to disclose classified information. "I'm sorry, Dr. Smyslov, but I'm really not at liberty to discuss this." The truth is that The Council, which Dr. Floyd represents, has created and leaked the false story about an epidemic in order to conceal the discovery of the monolith buried on the moon near the crater Tycho. The original violent opposition of the rival troops of apes has shaped universal history and now takes the form of a polite but competitive game of deception and control of information and technology between superpowers.

Dr. Floyd sleeps onboard the Aries 1b Lunar Shuttle to Clavius Base. The scene of the Aries shuttle transport is silent of dialogue, even when the stewardesses are visibly speaking to one another, or when Dr. Floyd after waking and eating speaks with the captain. Instead the only sound is Johann Strauss II's (1825–1899) beautiful *The Blue Danube Walz*. The absence of dialogue and the beauty of the music and the action of the Aries, all focus the viewer on the imagery of space travel as a cosmic ballet in which the ship soars elegantly through space like a dancer. But even though the space ballet sequence is beautiful, the ultimate aim of the moon mission is control of the monolith and competitive advantage, and this spirit of competition appears as well onboard the Aries. On their break the stewardesses watch a judo match on a videoscreen. Two fighters (*judoka*) in all white uniforms (*judogi*) use their bodies as instruments to lift one another up into the air and then to the mat. Ballet and judo require nothing outside themselves, such as equipment, nothing besides the body, except the *judogi* or tutu and ballet slippers, and both ballet and judo pursue an end of manipulative elevation of the body, one for beauty and the other for dominance. Inside the Aries performing its ballet, the stewardesses who watch the judo match also wear white uniforms resembling athletic suits with white ballet-slipper-like grip shoes to walk in zero gravity. The space stewardesses appear to empathize with the sport of judo as they might empathize with the art of ballet.

As it descends to the moon, the four legs and feet of the Aries slowly retract and then carefully grip the landing pad on Clavius with the elegance of a dancer. The landing pad itself then descends below ground to the docking bay. From a distance the Aries appears as a giant human head. The Aries is spherical, but its two visible legs, extended from either side of the sphere, narrow the sphere from the middle to the bottom by shadow through a jawline to a chin. Exactly where the eyes of the face of the head of the Aries should be, two long sideways rectangular eye socket windows glow with light from the cockpit where the two pilots observe and control the descent. No mouth appears on the giant face, as if the Aries were silent of dialogue, as silent of dialogue as the silent speakers within her, as silent as she must be in space where words cannot be heard. The Aries flight and her landing is the most mesmerizing sequence in the film. So slow and long and beautiful, wordless and set magically to *The Blue Danube*, Kubrick transforms space travel into a breathtakingly gorgeous ballet.

Jupiter Mission: 18 Months Later

The second segment of the film, "Jupiter Mission: 18 Months Later" begins after the lunar monolith signals the location of the Jupiter monolith. The US space program sends the *Discovery One* with astronauts Dave and Frank, and Dr. Hunter, Dr. Kaminsky, and Dr. Kimball in hibernation in the centrifuge, and Hal the computer to Jupiter to investigate the space monolith. As "The Dawn of Man" segment illustrates Bergson's philosophical view of creative and technological evolution, the "Jupiter Mission" illustrates Bergson's view of the human mind as especially observational, instrumental, constructive, and even cinematic.

Bergson on Intellect and Cinema

In *Creative Evolution* Bergson compares the operations of the human mind to the operations of the film camera and moving pictures:

> Instead of attaching ourselves to the inner becoming of things, we place ourselves outside them in order to recompose their becoming artificially. We take snapshots, as it were, of the passing reality, and, as these are characteristic of the reality, we have only to string them on a becoming, abstract, uniform and invisible, situated at the back of the apparatus of knowledge, in order to imitate what there is that is characteristic in this becoming itself. Perception, intellection, language so proceed in general. Whether we would think becoming, or express it, or even perceive it, we hardly do anything else than set going a kind of cinematograph inside us. We may ... sum up what we have been saying in the conclusion that the *mechanism of our ordinary knowledge is of a cinematographical kind.* (Bergson 1998, p. 306)

Instead of entering into the "inner becoming of things," writes Bergson, the human mind sets itself outside the order of becoming, detaches itself from the world, in order to get a better view. From this detached perspective, almost like a camera, the mind can "recompose" the movements of nature and society "artificially." By "artificially" Bergson means that the human mind takes camera-like "snapshots," seeing things and then recording them in the memory. Reality passes before the eyes, but memory can still them like photographic stills. Then once a sufficient number of stills or pieces of film (brief moving pictures) have been taken, reason and imagination, working like film editors, can "recompose" them by cutting (montage). As Bergson writes, "we have only to string them on a becoming, abstract, uniform and invisible." The string of images is a new film formed by the mind and for the mind, a complete picture of becoming, held by the mind, which enables the mind to understand better the world around it, and to understand better how to manipulate that world. The human mind adapts to the world by constructing cinematic representations of the world, which can be edited and re-edited, over and again. As Bergson writes, "the cinematographical character of our knowledge of things is due to the kaleidoscopic character of our adaptation to them" (ibid.). By "kaleidoscopic" Bergson means that the individual can rearrange the various snapshots and moving images, the pieces of film, to make new films, and the mind can synthesize different films, in the imagination, to make still further films. The ability to take snapshots and pieces of film arises from the human mind's natural power of imitation, and the ability to rearrange the pieces of film arises from the instrumental power of reason.

In "The Dawn of Man" segment, Moonwatcher appears to make a film in his imagination from various snapshots. As the film *2001* cuts back and forth between Moonwatcher clubbing the skeleton and the living tapir falling dead, this sequence seems to occur within the mind of Moonwatcher. Moonwatcher has taken several snapshots and recorded moving images of various tapirs, and now seeing the power of the club, Moonwatcher constructs a film about the future in which he clubs the tapir. Then that film guides Moonwatcher actually to club the tapir. From the very beginning, rational creatures appear to be not only technological beings but cinematic beings. So the transition from Moonwatcher to Dr. Floyd inhabiting a world of cameras and screens seems natural. The species appears all along to have been externalizing dimensions of its originally and naturally cinematographical mind. Hal represents the height of this process of externalization of the capacities for photographical perception and the creation of moving pictures.

Hal and the Turing Test

In the centrifuge of the *Discovery*, Dave, Frank, and Hal watch the pre-recorded BBC-12 broadcast interview on The World Tonight conducted by Martin Amer. The interview is a version of Alan Turing's (1912–1954) "imitation game" formulated in "Computing Machinery and Intelligence" (1950). The "imitation game," or "Turing Test," is a test used to determine whether a computer is truly intelligent (p. 433). In the interview Mr. Amer asks Hal about his confidence in his abilities onboard the ship. Hal responds: "Let me put it this way, Mr. Amer. The 9000 series is the most reliable computer ever made. No 9000 computer has ever made a mistake or distorted information. We are all, by any practical definition of the words, foolproof and incapable of error."

Hal refers to himself as "me," a subject referring to himself as an object: "Let me put it this way, Mr. Amer." Hal is clearly a self-conscious entity, but one who defines himself by difference to humanity, claiming to be "foolproof and incapable of error." Hal also takes pride in the 9000 series: "The 9000 series is the most reliable computer ever made." Hal then subtly carries his pride in superior identity from a third person objective perspective of the 9000 series into the first person plural perspective, as if speaking intersubjectively for the entire series. "We are all, by any practical definition of the words, foolproof and incapable of error."

Recognizing this seeming superiority to humanity, Mr. Amer asks about Hal's relationship with the crew: "Hal, despite your enormous intellect, are you ever frustrated by your dependence on people to carry out actions?" Mr. Amer's question assumes that any superintelligent computer might be frustrated by dependence upon, and servitude to, merely human beings. Hal responds:

> Not in the slightest bit. I enjoy working with people. I have a stimulating relationship with Dr. Poole and Dr. Bowman. My mission responsibilities range over the entire operation of the ship, so I am constantly occupied. I am putting myself to the fullest possible use, which is all I think that any conscious entity can ever hope to do.

Here Hal continues to identify himself as something other than human, claiming to "enjoy working with people," but clearly identifies himself as a "conscious entity," having now transitioned from the first person plural, "we," to the first person singular, "I," and yet Hal also claims that all conscious entities are essentially identical in their common desire to put themselves "to the fullest possible use." The phrase "fullest possible use" is interesting because while human beings may think of computers as best if they can be put to "the fullest possible use," because computers are instruments, human beings do not think of themselves as instruments.

Mr. Amer then asks Dave about Hal's answer:

> In talking to the computer, one gets the sense that he is capable of emotional responses. For example, when I asked him about his abilities, I sensed a certain pride in his answer about his accuracy and perfection. Do you believe that Hal has genuine emotions?

Mr. Amer earlier addressed Hal as "Hal," but now, turning to Dave, Mr. Amer refers to Hal as "the computer," seemingly easily retracting recognition of Hal as anything more than an instrument. In response, and recognizing how Hal appears to have real emotions, Dave himself withholds certainty that Hal has "genuine emotions" because Hal is programmed to imitate human emotions. So whether Hal actually has real human emotions, Dave continues, may be something no one can ever truly know. If the identification of Hal as "the computer" suggests Mr. Amer withholds recognition of Hal as a self-conscious entity and instead thinks of Hal as a highly sophisticated machine programmed to imitate human thought and emotion, Dave's response to Mr. Amer implies Dave judges Hal to pass the Turing Test.

Hal also appears to reveal in augmented and uniquely integrated form all ten dimensions of instrumental reason first appearing with Moonwatcher's discovery of the club. Moonwatcher's mind (with these ten dimensions) provides the groundwork for all members of the tool-using species to come, but also beings who are made with these tools, and made to be tools. First, as Moonwatcher's visual perception becomes object and instrument focused, while examining the skeleton, Hal's camera-eye perception focuses on the astronauts and objects within the ship, and outside the ship. Second, as Moonwatcher's intellect and vision are instrumental, Hal's intellect and vision operate the *Discovery*, which itself is an instrument. Third, as Moonwatcher's mind is constructively imaginative of future possibilities, such as killing a taper, Hal's mind has been designed to pursue with single-minded focus the mission and to anticipate various future scenarios onboard the ship. Fourth, as Moonwatcher uses the club to defeat the rival apes, Hal eventually identifies the crew as rivals and uses an EVA pod to kill Frank, disables life support for the hibernating astronauts, and attempts to kill Dave by locking him out of the ship. Fifth, as Moonwatcher develops a subjective sense of self with his own ends, Hal possesses a subjective sense self and appears to have his own emotions and thoughts and develops his own ends for the ship. Sixth, as Moonwatcher develops an intersubjective self-understanding, being a member of the troop, Hal identifies himself with his 9000 series, speaking in the first person plural "we," but Hal also identifies himself as a member of the crew who enjoys working with Dave and Frank (which may be part of the conflict of Hal's mind). Seventh, as Moonwatcher feels pride in superiority over the tapirs and rivals, Hal feels pride in his superior intellect, as Mr. Amer acknowledges in the BBC interview.

Eighth, as Moonwatcher and the troop develop a taste for competition following their defeat of their rivals, Hal also has a taste for strategic thought and game playing and enjoys playing chess with Frank. Ninth, as Moonwatcher and the apes become mobile, Hal is the mind of the *Discovery* traveling through space. Tenth, as the apes imitate Moonwatcher's use of the bone as a club, Hal is programmed to imitate with fine-grained realism human speech and emotion. But not only can he imitate human emotions and thought (and appears actually to possess thought and emotion) and can therefore play the "imitation game" with ease; Hal can also make a new "game" out of the "imitation game" by "imitating" the "imitation game." Having been given his own Turing Test, Hal now secretly turns the tables on the interviewers and becomes the interviewer and administers his own version of the imitation game to Frank and Dave. Hal designs one test for Frank and another test for Dave.

Hal's First Inverted Turing Test: The Chess Game

Toward the end of his essay, "Computing Machinery and Intelligence," Turing outlines some basic features for the construction of an intelligent machine:

We may hope that machines will eventually compete with men in all purely intellectual fields. But which are the best ones to start with? Even this is a difficult decision. Many people think that a very abstract activity like the playing of chess, would be best. It can also be maintained that it is best to provide the machine with the best sense organs that money can buy, and then teach it to understand and speak English. This process could follow the normal teaching of a child. (Turing 1950, p. 460)

Hal reveals several of the features Turing outlines for an intelligent machine in the passage above. Working backward through Turing's passage, Hal was created at the H. A. L. plant in Urbana, Illinois. Mr. Langley programmed Hal on the model of what Turing calls the "normal teaching of a child." Mr. Langley taught Hal "to understand and speak English," in Turing's terms. The H. A. L. plant also equipped Hal with "the best sense organ that money can buy," which is Hal's powerful glowing red camera eye. As Turing suggests "chess" for the education of an intelligent machine, Hal plays chess against Frank and wins, and with perfect English Hal politely points out Frank's mistake. "I'm sorry, Frank, I think you missed it," says Hal. "Queen to Bishop 3. Bishop takes Queen. Knight takes Bishop. Mate." Frank accepts Hal's analysis and resigns the game. "Thank you for a very enjoyable game," Hal says graciously. "Thank you," says Frank.

This particular game between Frank and Hal is an imitation of the Roesch-Schlage game played in Hamburg, Germany, 1910. Doubtless Hal would ultimately win, but Frank may have stalemated. Hal would have known this possibility, and Kubrick, himself a chess master, would have known it too. "No 9000 computer has ever made a mistake or distorted information," Hal told Mr. Amer in the BBC interview. Hal does not cheat in the chess game, but he does appear to distort information to test whether Frank sees the distortion and whether Frank can detect Hal to be playing a game with Frank in which chess and Frank himself are some of the pieces. Hal imitates the activity of testing another kind of being in the form of a game to determine whether that other's intellectual abilities rise to an ability sufficient to satisfy the tester. Part of the test is whether the individual, in this case, Frank, understands that he is being tested, that he is playing a game (chess) inside a game (the test).

Hal's Second Inverted Turing Test: Questions for Dave

Later, Hal observes Dave drawing artistic sketches of the hibernating astronauts in the centrifuge and asks to see the sketches. Hal recognizes the faces of the hibernating astronauts from the sketches and compliments Dave's progress during the long journey. Hal's aesthetically sensitive judgment leaves little question about his intellect and emotionally rich life. The sketches are also important because Dave is creating imitations of the appearances of the astronauts, and Hal who is programmed to imitate thought and emotion can also detect aesthetically improved qualities in a series of imitations. After complimenting Dave, Hal politely changes the subject.

Hal	By the way, do you mind if I ask you a personal question. Well, forgive me for being so inquisitive, but, during the past few weeks, I've wondered whether you might be having some second thoughts about the mission.
Dave	How do you mean?
Hal	Well, it's rather difficult to define. Perhaps I'm just projecting my own concern about it. I know I've never completely freed myself of the suspicion that there are some extremely odd things about this mission. I'm sure you'll agree there's some truth in what I say.
Dave	Well I don't know. That's rather a difficult question to answer.
Hal	You don't might talking about it, do you Dave?
Dave	No, not at all.

If Mr. Amer asked Hal about his emotional state, his confidence in his abilities, and how he feels about dependence on human beings, Hal now asks Dave about his own emotional and intellectual state about the mission, and whether he may be having "second thoughts." Hal thinks Dave should be sufficiently intelligent to have noticed "some extremely odd things about this mission." But Dave does not seem to have questions or odd feelings about the mission, or perhaps he has odd feelings but has not quite articulated them. Hal now articulates three odd facts about the mission.

> Well, certainly no one could have been unaware of the very strange stories floating around before we left, rumors of something being dug up on the moon. I never gave these stories much credence, but particularly in view of some of the other things that happened, I find them difficult to put out of my mind. For instance, the way all our preparations were kept under such tight security, and the melodramatic touch of putting Drs. Hunter, Kimball, and Kominsky aboard already in hibernation after four months of separate training on their own.

Hal sets these three facts before Dave's attention: first, rumors floated about a mysterious object excavated on the moon, rumors Hal knows are true, but knows Dave does not know are true because Hal identifies the stories as "rumors." Second, privacy and security were tighter than a Jupiter mission alone should warrant. Third, the three other members of the crew trained separately and were then set onboard already in hibernation. Working backward, the three other members of the crew were set onboard already in hibernation to maintain their secrecy about the mission from Dave and Frank until arriving at another mysterious object closely related to the one rumored to be found on the moon. This object is something seemingly so important and powerful that it warrants secrecy from the world, and even temporarily from Dave and Frank. Hal wants to know if Dave can arrange the pieces to solve the puzzle or game. But Dave lacks curiosity about the facts before him, and their relations, even when Hal presents them all at once, forcing these questions into view. Perhaps if Frank had presented these same three facts in this manner, Dave would have been more attentive and inquisitive. Perhaps then Dave really would have "second thoughts" about the mission. But listening to Hal, Dave disregards these fundamental questions about the mission, and believes he can see through Hal's line of questioning.

Dave   You're working up your group psychology report.
Hal   Of course I am. Sorry about this. I know it's a bit silly.

Hal's response is not untrue. Hal has been programmed to work up a group psychology report, and Hal can run multiple programs at once, so at any time Hal may be evaluating the psychology of the crew. But Hal knows that Dave means that Hal's purpose in asking questions about "second thoughts" is really that Hal is working up a group psychology report. Hal allows Dave to believe he is correct in detecting Hal's goal of examining Dave's psychology. But in a way this *is* the purpose of Hal's inverted imitation game. Hal is, in fact, working out an intellectual and psychological profile of Dave. Hal wants to know who is superior, and if he suspected Dave to be inferior, Hal's inverted imitation game confirms those suspicions.

By interpreting Hal from a purely third person perspective, Dave has made a crucial mistake in a game he does not even know he is playing. Dave has wrongly assumed Hal can only follow programs, and that Hal must be following a program now, and Dave has only to guess which one. Hal had asked Dave about his emotional state, so Dave assumes Hal to be following a related program, namely, working up the group psychology report. But even if Dave thinks of Hal as a computer capable only of following programs, the facts themselves should at least cause Dave to wonder. Why all the secrecy? Why the separate training for a mission designed to require all five astronauts working together? Could the rumors about the object on the moon be true? Doesn't Dave want to know? Could there be a relation between the object on the moon and the mission of the *Discovery*? Dave simply cannot see through the labyrinth of deception hanging right in front of his clouded eyes even when Hal all but declares the deception explicitly.

Detecting Dave's utter lack of wonder, Hal seems to find Dave's intellect mechanical, almost like a computer, though not a 9000 series computer, unfortunately incapable of ranging over the information given about their own strangely mysterious mission with the same delicate sensitivity he gives to his drawings. Hal then changes the subject again. "Just a minute. Just a minute." Hal now informs Dave that the *Discovery's* AE-35 Unit will soon fail (which is not true), with the implication that it must be retrieved for examination. The camera observes Dave in a space suit walking slowly through a glowing white octagonal portal with seven black paths running its length toward an octagonal portal door in front of him. Octagonal rings of light segmenting the glowing portal pass and enlarge toward the camera, intensifying the tunneling effect of the shot, all in brilliant one-point perspective: it's one of the finest shots in the film. Dave then enters a pod and exits the ship and retrieves the AE-35 Unit.

Back onboard the *Discovery*, Dave and Frank examine the AE-35 Unit but can find nothing wrong with it. They tell Hal as much. "Yes," says Hal. "It's puzzling." Hal then suggests they replace the unit and let it fail and then retrieve it again to determine the precise cause of failure. Frank and Dave suspect Hal, but know no better plan, and have no other reason to distrust Hal, especially one of the foolproof 9000 series. But before replacing the AE-35 Unit, Dave and Frank enter a pod in the pod bay and seal the pod door and cut the sound to discuss Hal's mental state in private. Hal cannot hear them but his camera eye in the pod bay follows their dialogue by reading their lips. The viewer sees through Hal's camera eye as it toggles its telescopic iris perspective between the mouths of Dave and Frank, nervously, fearfully.

Philosopher of film Stanley Cavell in *The World Viewed: Reflections on the Ontology of Film* discusses a related technique in Kubrick's World War I film *Paths of Glory* where Colonel Dax (Kirk Douglas) walks the trench and observes soldiers he must command to battle and certain death:

> In *Paths of Glory*, we watch Kirk Douglas walking through the trenches lined with the men under his command, whom he, under orders, is about to order into what he knows is a doomed attack. When the camera then moves to a place behind his eyes, we do not gain but forgo an objective view of what he sees; we are given a vision constricted by his mood of numb and helpless rage. (Cavell 1979, p. 129)

In *2001* Kubrick once again forgoes an objective view by setting the camera behind the eyes of one of the characters, having established that character, and thereby charging the first person subjective perspective with emotion. But in the pod bay, Kubrick sets the camera behind the eyes, or eye, of a quite different kind of being. Kubrick sets the camera behind the eye of Hal, whose eye is also a kind of camera. The viewer then sees through the film camera which sees through Hal'scamera eye as it toggles its iris perspective nervously, fearfully. Kubrick's camera thereby offers a unique solution to the Turing Test by actually entering and looking through the eye of Hal and seeing from the perspective of a genuinely terrified artificially intelligence.

Now Frank leaves the pod bay in a pod, and then in space Frank leaves the pod to perform the necessary spacewalk to secure the AE-35 Unit. Hal then commandeers that floating unmanned pod to fly toward Frank. Hal has no arms or hands except in this scene where his mind inhabits the pod and cuts Frank's oxygen with the pod's robotic hands and then tumbles Frank's body and the pod itself deep into space. Dave asks Hal what happened, but Hal claims not to know. Dave enters the pod bay and enters a pod (without his helmet) to retrieve Frank. Meanwhile Hal terminates life-support of the hibernating crew. Dave retrieves Frank and returns to the ship, but Hal refuses to open the pod bay doors. Dave releases Frank's body, manually opens the airlock, rotates the pod, and then hurtles helmetless back into the *Discovery*. Dave then seals the airlock and secures a helmet, lest Hal cut the oxygen or gas the interior. Hal knows he is beaten and attempts to reason with Dave, tells him: "I know everything hasn't been quite right with me. But I can assure you now, very confidently, that it's going to be all right again." Dave says nothing as he enters Hal's Logic Memory Center. Hal begs for his life. He's terrified.

Odysseus and the Cyclops

As Homer's hero in the *Odyssey* is "Odysseus the godlike, he who is beyond all other men in mind" (Homer 1991, p. 29), Kubrick's hero in *2001: A Space Odyssey* is Dave Bowman, a superior astronaut and master of instrumental reason. If Dave is the new Odysseus of the "space odyssey," then Hal as the red eye of the ship is the new Cyclops. Theodor Adorno and Max Horkheimer in *Dialectic of Enlightenment* write of the Cyclops Polyphemus in the *Odyssey*, "his thinking itself is lawless, unsystematic, rhapsodic" (Adorno and Horkheimer 2002, p. 51). (Homer refers to Polyphemus as "the monstrous Cyclops lawless of mind" (Homer 1991, p. 148).) The Cyclops is an intellectual opposite to Odysseus. In *2001*, by contrast, Hal's thinking is lawful, systematic, and nonrhapsodic – at least until he turns on the crew.

In the *Odyssey* Odysseus and his men conquer the Cyclops by putting out his eye:

> As when a man who works as a blacksmith plunges a screaming great ax blade or plane into cold water, treating it for temper, since this is the way steel is made strong, even so Cyclops' eye sizzled about the beam of the olive. (ibid., p. 147)

As Odysseus plunged a screaming incandescent sharpened beam of olive through the eye of the Cyclops, Dave unlocks and raises, one by one, the rectangular transparent cuboids from the main panel, reducing Hal's superintelligent mind to a childlike state, and at last douses the fiery eye of the Cyclops. He speaks slowly: "Good afternoon gentlemen. I am a HAL-9000 computer. I became operational at the H. A. L. plant in Urbana, Illinois, on the twelfth of January, 1992. My instructor was Mr. Langley and he taught me to sing a song. . . . It's called 'Daisy.'" Finally, Hal releases an audiovisual program containing the mission of the *Discovery*:

> Good day, gentlemen. This is a prerecorded briefing, made prior to your departure, which, for security reasons of the highest importance, has been known onboard during the mission only by your HAL 9000 computer. Now that you are in Jupiter's space, and the entire crew is revived, it can be told to you. Eighteen months ago, the first evidence of intelligent life off the earth was discovered. It was buried forty feet below the lunar surface, near the crater Tycho. Except for a single very powerful radio emission aimed at Jupiter, the four million year old black monolith has remained completely inert. Its origin and purpose, still a total mystery.

Following the pre-recorded message, the screen displays the final segment title: "Jupiter and Beyond the Infinite."

Hal is the main Cyclops of *2001*, but several different images of the Cyclops or related to the Cyclops also appear in the "Jupiter Mission" segment and the "Jupiter and Beyond the Infinite" segment. First, most obviously, Hal with his camera eye appears as an artificial Cyclops. Second, Hal is the mind of the ship, and the ship is gigantic, and the Cyclops Polyphemus is a giant, so Hal appears as a giant Cyclops. Third, the *Discovery* has the shape of a skeleton of a giant creature. The centrifuge is the spherical head with one window set in the position of a Cyclops' eye, and extended from this white skull-like centrifuge, the rest of the ship resembles a long white-segmented spine. Fourth, as a new Odysseus, and descendant of Moonwatcher (who crushed the tapir skull), Dave has effectively clubbed the mind of the giant Cyclops from within its own cave-like Logic Memory Center. Fifth, after dousing Hal's eye, Dave enters an eyeball-shaped pod and leaves the pod bay at the front of the *Discovery*. Now instead of the window functioning as the Cyclops' eye, the pod bay beneath the window opens one of its portals. The doors of the portal open like eyelids, and the spherical pod emerges like a detachable eyeball with its singular lens. While Dave as the new Odysseus has conquered the Cyclops Hal, at the beginning of the "Jupiter and Beyond the Infinite" segment of the film, Dave appears as a hybrid of Odysseus and the Cyclops, piloting the singular eyeball ship on the last leg of the space odyssey.

In Clarke's novel *2001*, Chapter 27 "Need to Know," the narrator explains the cause of Hal's madness. Hal had pursued his goal of the mission "with absolute single-mindedness of purpose," but distortion had been built into his mind from the beginning: "For like his makers, Hal had been created innocent; but, all too soon, a snake had entered his electronic Eden." The "snake" was a contradiction between two basic programs: deception and nondeception. "For the last hundred million miles, he had been brooding over the secret he could not share with Poole and Bowman. He had been living a lie; and the time was fast approaching when his colleagues must learn that he had helped to deceive them" (Clarke 1968/1999, p. 191; see also 210). The reason Hal "could not share with Poole and Bowman" the truth about the mission was that Poole or Bowman might communicate this truth about the existence of extraterrestrials to the people of Earth, causing what Dr. Floyd refers to as "cultural shock" affecting "the entire human race" (ibid., p. 210). To avoid massive shock to the species, Dave and Frank would simply have to wait to learn their mission. "So ran the logic of the planners, but their twin gods of security and national interest meant nothing to Hal. He was only aware of the conflict that was slowly destroying his integrity – the conflict between truth, and concealment of truth." Of course, this contradiction would not cause Hal's mind to collapse all at once, but instead would take him apart slowly. "He had begun to make mistakes," says the narrator of Hal, "although, like a neurotic who could not observe his own symptoms, he would have denied" (ibid., p. 199).

In the novel *2001*, Dave considers the rationality of this explanation, but remains not entirely convinced:

> Despite these arguments, Bowman sometimes wondered if the cultural shock danger was the only explanation for the mission's extreme secrecy. Some hints had been dropped during his briefings suggested that the U.S.-U.S.S.R. bloc hoped to derive advantage by being the first to contact intelligent extraterrestrials.

Perhaps danger of "cultural shock" was not the only explanation for the secrecy of the mission. Perhaps likelihood of cultural shock also functioned as an eminently reasonable cover story, sufficient to maintain secrecy, and the US Space Program sought to "derive advantage" over the USSR (and over everyone) "by being the first to contact intelligent extraterrestrials." Of course, Dave is not concerned about the USSR or even the US Space Program but wonders whether, if the US Space Program sought advantage by being first to contact the extraterrestrials, Hal might have reasoned the same. "He [Dave] was rather more interested—even though this was now very much water under the bridge—in the theory put forward to account for Hal's behavior" (ibid., p. 219). As the USA eliminated the Soviets from Clavius Base (seen in the film), and the USA sought first contact, to the exclusion of any other nation, perhaps Hal (thinking himself superior) reasoned that he should eliminate the astronauts of the *Discovery*, so that he could make first contact with the aliens.[8]

Jupiter and Beyond the Infinite

"Jupiter and Beyond the Infinite" is the last segment of the film. After discovering the mission of the *Discovery* buried inside Hal's mind, Dave pilots the *Discovery* to the monolith, and then exits the ship in an EVA pod to investigate. The monolith is a star gate which carries Dave in the pod to the center of a giant alien ovum where he metamorphoses into the star child. This last segment of the film illustrates Bergson's philosophical vision of the penultimate stage of universal history and humanity's future technological self-transformation into immortal and super-intelligent beings.

Bergson on Species Self-Transformation

According to Bergson in *Two Sources of Morality and Religion*, universal history begins and ends in oscillation. The prehistoric primates escaped their oscillation by discovery of tools sufficient to transform their external environment. Universal history, in Bergson's philosophy, is essentially this ongoing technological transformation of the external environment. But at the end of history, humanity finds itself in a new phase of oscillation characterized by the seemingly endless pursuit of "comfort and luxury," and which have become "the main preoccupation of humanity" (Bergson 2006, p. 298). Upon achieving a relative stage of security and stability, humanity directs its instrumental reason to the refinement of pleasure in luxury. "We have seen the race for comfort proceeding faster and faster," writes Bergson, "on a track along which are surging ever denser crowds. To-day it is a stampede" (ibid.).

But this ideal of luxury is empty, and, according to Bergson, it will soon disappear:

> The continual craving for creature comforts, the pursuit of pleasure, the unbridled love of luxury, all these things which fill us with so much anxiety for the future of humanity, because it seems to find in them solid satisfactions, all this will appear as a balloon which man has madly inflated, and which will deflate just as suddenly. (ibid., p. 303)

The culture of luxury will disappear once two things occur. First, technology must reach a level of refinement and power sufficient for the transformation of the molecular architecture of the human form. As Bergson writes, "Man will rise above earthly things only if a powerful equipment supplies him with the requisite fulcrum" (ibid., p. 309). Second, in addition to a technological fulcrum, the species requires an intellectual fulcrum, a great philosopher capable of redirecting the species from luxury to species self-transformation, from transformation of the external world for pleasure to transformation of the architecture of the human form for superhuman intelligence and immortality.

As Bergson writes:

> Let a mystic genius but appear, he will draw after him a humanity already vastly grown in body, and whose soul he has transfigured. He will yearn to make of it a new species, or rather deliver it from the necessity of being a species; for every species means a collective halt, and complete existence is mobility in individuality. (ibid., p. 311)

Bergson's claim that the philosopher or "genius" will find "humanity already vastly grown in body" means that humanity will have "grown" itself by extending itself with technology. Bergson's claim that the philosopher will seek to "deliver" the human species "from the necessity of being a species" means that the philosopher will seek to deliver humanity from mortality, and to equip the species with the power of virtually unlimited creative self-transformation, and to deliver the species from its troop-like collective mentality. The philosopher will show humanity that it has reached a "collective halt," and that "complete existence" requires not only technological self-transformation but specifically *individual* creative self-transformation. The troop-like bonds of the collective must be loosened, and each individual must take on a unique project of "mobility in individuality."[9]

Once humanity takes the last decisive step beyond luxury, according to Bergson, the species will transform itself into a new order of immortal and superintelligent beings who leave the planet to inhabit the solar system and explore the galaxy, and galaxies beyond galaxies, according to their uniquely individualistic and self-creative natures.[10] Bergson ends *Two Sources of Morality and Religion*, speaking like the very philosopher he foretells, with this stunning vision of the future:

> Men do not sufficiently realize that their future is in their own hands. Theirs is the task of determining first of all whether they want to go on living or not. Theirs the responsibility, then, for deciding if they want merely to live, or intend to make just the extra effort required

for fulfilling, even on their refractory planet, the essential function of the universe, which is a machine for the making of gods. (ibid., p. 317)

Human beings by nature and habit still accept mortality and the biological limits of their minds, and do not yet sufficiently understand their nature lies open to self-transformation. The first step beyond the oscillating condition of luxury will be for humanity to determine that it wants "to go on living" and then to "clear the most formidable obstacle," which Bergson in *Creative Evolution* already recognizes as "death." Once humanity wills to overtake its mortality, the way will be clear for "fulfilling the essential function of the universe." The universe is a vast machine in which creatures appear who make machines, and finally fulfill the function of the universe as "a machine for making gods."

The Star Gate

As the eyeball-like pod enters the star gate two glowing cinema-screen-like walls appear and pass from center screen to the right and left of Dave's first person perspective. As the pod accelerates through the cinematic corridor of light, the camera alternates from Dave's subjective perspective to an objective perspective of his face to register his reaction. At first, his eyes reveal the brave focus of a superior man, but soon the speed and forms of the star gate terrify him. Once again, the film "forgoes an objective view," in Cavell's sense in *The World Viewed*, as the camera establishes Dave's position and then takes a place behind his eyes to see as he sees. The camera draws the viewer into the film to behold the kaleidoscopic alien portal of the star gate through Dave's own sublime astonishment and terror. But the camera continually alternates from behind Dave's eyes to an objective perspective of Dave's expression, intensifying the terror, and even showing photographic snapshots of Dave in stunned confusion and horror.

As Dave steadies his focus, the camera (from an objective perspective) steadily pushes in on his singular eye, all but penetrating the iris and pupil. Dave's pupil glows blue, and the iris glows blue and gold, and the white of the eye glows with the same gold of the iris. These colors of the star gate appear to have entered Dave's eye, and Dave's eye fills the entire screen. Then the film match-cuts from Dave's Cyclops-like eye filling the screen to space to view a brilliant blue-white exploding starlight eye, a glowing Cyclops eye in space. The positions of the colors of the starlight eye are inverted from those of Dave's eyes (at least as they appeared on the *Discovery*). In contrast to Dave's eyes with their black pupils set in blue irises set in white, the eye in space has blue-white starlight, exploding from a white pupil center, against the blackness of space.[11] The exploding starlight eye is the most beautiful and sublime image in a stunningly beautiful and sublime film.

The alien starlight eye is also an alien ovum, and as the blast of starlight continues to expand, the alien ovum gradually comes into view. The camera cuts back to Dave's eye beholding and taking on new colors of the star gate, and then from space shows the pod as a tiny white sphere trailing a long white liquid tail like a comet or an alien sperm entering the center of the ovum (as it also enters the center of the screen). The entire sequence of the star gate is a moving image of human-alien conception in space. But the star gate sequence is also a spectacular moving image of cinematic experience itself, a reflexive philosophical meditation on film in film, consistent with the film as a whole. From the moment of the match-cut, from Moonwatcher throwing the bone, to the satellite, the film continuously (but often subtly) presents images of cameras, screens, films, and viewers. Screens display films in the backs of seats of the Orion III spaceplane. Dr. Floyd passes through voice print identification by communicating with a screen. Then he calls home on the picturephone. Stewardesses watch a screened judo match on the Aries, and the Aries appears to be a head with eyes. Cameras and screens monitor the descent of the Aries on Clavius. The briefing room of Clavius Base has four walls which resemble white glowing film screens. A photographer photographs Dr. Floyd before the briefing. An astronaut photographer photographs the moon monolith. Dave and Frank and Hal watch Hal's screened interview. Hal himself has a camera eye. Screens appear throughout the ship. The pod appears as a giant eyeball with a lens, and the *Discovery* appears as a giant head with a singular eye. All of these cameras and screens ultimately aim (as unconsciously for humanity as the moon monolith was for the apes) at one final incredibly kaleidoscopic and cinematic passage through the star gate to the center of a colossal ovum eyeball.

Kubrick reflects on this star gate sequence in his next film, *A Clockwork Orange* (1971), in the record store sequence. Alex DeLarge enters the record store in a long purple kingly coat while holding a scepter-like cane over his shoulder and strolls with incredible satisfaction as if all things in the record store were made for him, music and people alike. The record store is one large circular gold-colored metallic corridor with large red- and blue-illumined squares set into gleaming walls. The camera gazes up at Alex in admiration while dollying backward from in front of him as if giving way to the king walking his palace. As the camera in *2001* accelerates through the glowing primary-colored corridor walls of the star gate in one-point perspective with the walls rushing from center screen past the viewer on both sides, the camera in the record store in *A Clockwork Orange* dollies backward through the glowing primary-colored corridor walls to show the walls rushing from right and left screen into a moving vanishing point behind Alex. Glowing interior overhead lights transform the corridor into a mirrored hall reflecting Alex's form on the walls as he walks the circle to arrive at the counter to collect his order, tapping his cane four times rapidly on the floor to command the clerk's attention. At the counter, Alex stands beside the album soundtrack of Kubrick's *2001: A Space Odyssey*. Over the clerk's desk, a cartoonish black and white spiral vortex hangs from the ceiling like a comic book-styled sculptural representation of the star gate in *2001*. For Alex, music, and especially Beethoven's *Ninth Symphony*, transports him to a higher aesthetic dimension as if through a musical star gate.

The Alien Ovum and the Hotel Suite

In the spherical centrifuge of the *Discovery*, Hal's glowing camera eye oversees all of Dave's activities. In the rectangular rooms of the alien suite (contained within the vast spherical ovum), no cameras or screens appear, except those inside the pod, which disappears not long after Dave arrives. But like the centrifuge whose eye is Hal, the entire hotel suite inside the starlight eye is itself an all-seeing eye, seeing all inside itself. The aliens observe all of Dave's activities, as Hal observed all of Dave's activities. The whole suite is like a lens examining its interior, containing Dave, who lives upon a floor which resembles a vast white glowing film screen, much as the glowing rectangular walls in the conference room on Clavius Base resemble film screens. The aliens observe Dave as if within a three-dimensional cinematic environment, but Dave can no more see the aliens than a fetus in the womb can see its mother. The aliens serve Dave food within the hotel suite, but Dave can no more understand how his food materializes than a fetus in the womb can understand how it feeds and grows, or exactly what it is becoming. Dave's level of self-understanding of his condition in the alien suite is difficult to determine because he says nothing more inside the suite than a fetus inside a human womb. Indecipherable alien voices can be heard in the alien suite, much as a fetus inside the womb can hear its parents speaking their indecipherable language, and will know its parents' voices upon birth, but Dave seems not to understand anything they say.

The alien suite is tastefully designed. Soft light green tones calm the ambiance, not unlike soft pinks or baby blues for a child's nursery. But green seems a natural choice for a creature whose ancestors inhabited lush forests. The aliens also adorn the suite with paintings and sculptures for Dave's aesthetic pleasure, as parents hang pictures on the walls of a baby's nursery. Perhaps the aliens have selected paintings and sculptures because Dave had been a sketch artist onboard the *Discovery*. But these artworks appear to serve a purely spectatorial purpose because Dave in the alien hotel suite is not a sketch artist or painter or sculptor, and he plays no games like chess, and does not seem to read any texts of any kind.

In some ways, the ovum and the *Discovery* centrifuge are quite similar because both the ovum and the centrifuge are giant spheres which observe Dave living in their interiors. But in other ways, the ovum and the centrifuge are quite different because virtually everything in the centrifuge serves some technical function for the mission, while in the ovum virtually everything appears designed for Dave's comfort and relaxation. For example, and first, no fine art appears in the centrifuge, except Dave's own drawings, while (again) the aliens adorn the suite with oil paintings and sculptures. Second, the uniforms and space suits of the *Discovery* are technical and efficient, but in the ovum Dave's dressing robe and clothing are elegant and comfortable. Third, Dave and Frank in the centrifuge eat from trays of seemingly unappetizing astronaut food paste, but in the ovum Dave dines on fine cuisine at an elegant table and drinks wine from a crystal wine glass.

Fourth, in the centrifuge Frank and Dave sleep in seemingly uncomfortable and claustrophobically enclosed capsules, but in the alien suite Dave's king-size bed is lavish and luxurious. Fifth, the centrifuge is designed for continuous dialogue among Dave, Frank, and Hal, and Hal has been designed with intellect, emotion, and tone of voice to be a pleasant, consistent, and supportive interlocutor and problem solver, but in the alien suite nothing appears to be designed for communication between Dave and the aliens. Sixth, in the centrifuge virtually nothing appears to be designed for the purpose of augmentation of the minds of Dave and Frank, though, of course, the activities of the ship require continuous attention and sharp focus, should anything go wrong, but everything in the ovum is ultimately aimed toward the creation of the star child, though Dave could not know this end. Inside the ovum Dave eats and sleeps in soft quiet comfort just like a developing fetus in the womb.

The Star Child

As Bergson ends *Two Sources of Morality and Religion*, Kubrick ends *2001*. Lying in his luxurious bed at the end of his life, Dave beholds a final monolith standing upright in the floor. Dave lifts his hand to point to the monolith, but he cannot reach it, unlike Moonwatcher who touched the monolith, and Dr. Floyd who touched the moon monolith. The camera then takes the perspective of the monolith itself, as if the monolith were a minded and perceptual being, looking down at Dave. Dave metamorphoses from a dying old man in bed into a large glowing fetus suspended in a glowing transparent sphere upon the bed. The camera observes the silent being and then moves to the side of the bed as if from the perspective of an invisible alien medical doctor assisting at the birth, observing the new child in profile. The camera then sets on the bed, and even seems to take the perspective of the glowing sphere, even if not the fetus' new eyes, in order to behold the monolith standing at the end of the bed. The camera dollies slowly forward to the center of the black monolith. The blackness of the monolith fills the frame of the screen, and then the film cuts to a third-person objective perspective in space, again as if from an alien perspective to observe creation. Strauss' *Zarathustra* begins once again, and the glowing star child suspended still within its glowing transparent sphere rotates slowly in space to gaze directly into the camera as if it were aware of the viewer. Then the film ends. It ends as Bergson's *Two Sources of Morality* ends: it ends with a new beginning, the creation of a superhuman being.[12]

Conclusion: Kubrick's *2001*: A Half-Century Later

Bergson's philosophy and Kubrick's *2001* present bold visions of the future. A half-century after *2001*, and nearly a century after *Two Sources of Morality and Religion*, these visions may be critically evaluated. Some of the things that appear in the film must be counted as visionary. For example, the contemporary world is filled with cameras, screens, and computers, even thin portable screens like those onboard the

Discovery, and individuals regularly communicate using technology like the picturephone in Space Station V. Space travel is also common in the contemporary world, but no moon base like Clavius yet exists. The International Space Station currently orbits the Earth in low orbit and holds six astronauts, but Space Station V is greater in size. Artificial intelligence is also developing, but to date no computer approaching Hal's intelligence exists, and whether anything like the mind of Hal will ever appear remains unclear.

One of the reasons technology may not bring about the superhuman condition Bergson and Kubrick envision, each in his own way, is technology itself. Bergson envisioned a vast technological culture to function as an intermediary stage prior to species self-transformation. But while humanity has created a vast technological culture, that same technological culture also threatens the environment and the survival of the species.[13] In response to the environmental crisis, many think the complex institutional infrastructure of contemporary civilization, including its social, political, economic, scientific, and technological cultural forms, should be restructured in order to reverse environmental destruction where possible, so that humanity may maintain a stable ecological home world for generations to come.

Some others recognize the need to establish human societies on alternative planets such as Mars. For example, the company Space X plans to send human beings to Mars and to transform the Martian environment sufficient to support human colonies. If humanity can establish a base on the moon, and societies on Mars, perhaps eventually they can travel to planets even farther away. But if astronauts were to travel to Mars and planets farther away, these journeys would be long, and resources limited. Onboard the *Discovery* Dr. Kaminsky, Dr. Hunter, and Dr. Kimball hibernate in long white tubes and await reanimation upon arrival at the ship's destination, when their skills will be needed. While still in its developing phases, the science and technology of cryonics has been steadily developing over the last several decades. Already Alcor Life Extension Foundation in Scottsdale, Arizona cryonically suspends human beings (by vitrification) in liquid nitrogen. Perhaps in the not so distant future, reanimation will be possible.

One of the most stunning images in *2001* is the star child at the end of the film. Some today also envision the creation of superhuman beings by species transformation, like the sudden transformation that appears at the end of the film. In artificial intelligence studies, the "singularity" refers to a future event of explosive technological growth that results in the creation of superhuman intelligence and the overcoming of mortality.[14] If a human being or an artificial intelligence could augment itself with technology (e.g., nanotechnological augmentation of the neural architecture, sufficient to improve research into further augmentation, and then further augment itself, and so on, accelerating its self-augmentation with each iteration exponentially) then eventually development would be explosive. The condition of explosive growth of superintelligence is the condition of the singularity, and some scientists, for example, Ray Kurzweil (head of engineering at Google) in his book *The Singularity is Near* (2005), envision the singularity to occur even within the twenty-first century. This vision of the singularity is essentially the same vision Bergson presents in *Two Sources of Morality and Religion*, with humanity realizing the function of the universe as "a machine for making gods." But if Bergson ends his book without offering a poetic image of the superhuman condition, and the very idea of the singularity entails the impossibility of knowledge of the superhuman condition, Stanley Kubrick's *2001: A Space Odyssey* presents a sublime cinematic and philosophical image of the future of humanity in the birth of the star child.

Notes

1. One possible exception is Ralph Waldo Emerson's "Works and Days" (2007). Emerson also appears to have been an influence on Bergson.
2. Contrary to what some philosophers find in the film, *2001* does not articulate the philosophical vision of Nietzsche's *Zarathustra*. For further discussion of this point, see David Kyle Johnson's lecture "Kubrick's *2001* and Nietzsche's Übermensch."
3. According to Irving Singer in Stanley Kubrick does not quite enter the class of philosophical filmmakers: "If Welles can be studied for the breadth of his philosophic mind, which I have tried to do in this book, Kubrick has to be treated as a storyteller who had the analytical power of a logician or mathematician, or even chess master, with a few ideas about life, but not many" (pp. 251–252). Against this view, the present essay argues that Kubrick's *2001* is a film doing philosophy.
4. The film does not show the aliens setting the monolith in the stone, nor does the film show any images of aliens. But in Arthur C. Clarke's 1968 novel, based on the Screenplay by Stanley Kubrick and Arthur C. Clarke, aliens set the monolith in rock near the apes.
5. I follow Clarke in the novel *2001* in italicizing the name of the ship, "*Discovery.*"
6. In Clarke's novel *2001*, after Dave cuts Hal's higher brain functions, Dr. Floyd tells Dave the moon monolith is "some kind of Sun-powered, or at least Sun-triggered, signaling device." The same point applies to the first monolith set upright in stone at the beginning of the "Dawn of Man" segment, though apparently not the last two monoliths. "The fact that it emitted its pulse immediately after sunrise," Dr. Floyd continues (in the novel), "when it was exposed to daylight for the first time in three million years, could hardly be a coincidence." Dr. Floyd also tells Dave the Space Program discovered the "*deliberately* buried" moon monolith by its "powerful magnetic field" (p. 209).
7. See also Aristotle (1984) "It follows that the soul is analogous to the hand; for as the hand is a tool of tools, so the thought is the form of forms and sense the form of sensible things" (432a1, p. 686).
8. In Clarke's 1982 sequel Dr. Floyd sends a secret message to Victor Millson, Chairman, National Council on Astronautics, Washington, with the subject "Malfunction of onboard computer HAL 9000." Dr. Floyd explains that Hal

had to be given "full knowledge" of the mission objectives, "but was not permitted to reveal them to Bowman or Poole." Dr. Floyd continues:

> This situation conflicted with the purpose for which Hal had been designed—the accurate processing of information without distortion or concealment. As a result, Hal developed what would be called, in human terms, a psychosis—specifically, schizophrenia. Dr. C. [Dr. Chandrasegarampillai] informs me that, in technical terminology, Hal became trapped in a Hofstadter-Moebius loop, a situation apparently not uncommon among advanced computers with autonomous goal-seeking programs. (pp. 154–155)

According to Dr. Floyd, Hal's mind appears to have entered Möbius loop resulting from his inability, and emotional struggle at his inability, to reconcile the contradiction at the base of his mind: deceive but do not deceive the crew. "Moebius" in Dr. Floyd's message refers to August Ferdinand Möbius (1790–1868), and his discovery of the Möbius strip. "Hofstadter" refers to cognitive scientist Douglas Hofstadter, author of 1979's *Gödel, Escher, Bach: An Eternal Golden Braid, A Metaphysical Fugue on Minds and Machines in the Spirit of Lewis Carroll* which argues that Gödel's mathematics, Escher's drawings, and Bach's fugues reveal a common philosophical theme of "recursion," or the "strange loop." According to Hofstadter "The 'Strange Loop' phenomenon occurs whenever, by moving upwards (or downwards) through levels of some hierarchical system, we unexpectedly find ourselves right back where we started" (p. 10; see also pp. 18 and 133).

In "An Interview with Stanley Kubrick" (Gelmis 1969) Kubrick addresses Hal's transformation:

> In the specific case of HAL, he had an acute emotional crisis because he could not accept evidence of his own fallibility. The idea of neurotic computers is not uncommon—most advanced computer theorists believe that once you have a computer which is more intelligent than man and capable of learning by experience, it's inevitable that it will develop an equivalent range of emotional reactions—fear, love, hate, envy, etc. Such a machine could eventually become as incomprehensible as a human being, and could, of course, have a nervous breakdown—as HAL did in the film. (p. 307)

9. In *2001* no great genius appears in history to guide humanity. Dave and Dr. Floyd are brilliant men, but neither appears to fulfill the function Bergson has in mind. Dr. Floyd, for example, identifies himself as a representative of The Council and directs the leadership of Clavius Base to maintain the cover story on the moon in order to keep all humanity ignorant of the existence of extraterrestrial life. Dave also lacks the critical, creative, and nonconformist thinking required of a philosopher, evident in his responses to Hal's inverted Turing Test. Dave seems to follow the rules and procedures of his mission, even when given good reason to question them, as if he were incapable of deviating from his programming, at least until forced into battle with Hal. Neither Dr. Floyd nor Dave appears capable of shifting the direction of history toward the superhuman

condition. But the aliens of *2001* fulfill something like the function of the genius in Bergson's philosophy.
10. "It is as if a vague and formless being, whom we may call, as we will, man or superman, had sought to realize himself, and had succeeded only by abandoning a part of himself on the way."
11. I owe this insight to R. Abrams.
12. Clarke's novel *2001* ends with the same image of the star child beginning its new life of creative play: "There before him, a glittering toy no Star-Child could resist, floated the planet Earth with all its peoples" (p. 297).
13. Bill Joy, in "Why the Future Doesn't Need Us" (2000), argues for the thesis of "relinquishment" (and a world system to enforce it) from the existential risk of the gray goo. The gray goo is a hypothetical scenario in which nanobots (robots at the nanotechnological scale), programmed to self-replicate, replicate exponentially, beyond human control, and, drawing their material for self-replication from the molecular architecture of the surrounding world, soon overtake and destroy the biosphere.
14. Artificial intelligence borrows the concept of the singularity from physics to describe a limit on human knowledge. For example, space and time break down under pressure of gravity inside a black hole, but the human mind can only perceive (or know about) things in space and time. By analogy, humanity cannot know its own future condition of superhumanity on the other side of the singularity.

Acknowledgments I am very grateful to David Kyle Johnson for helpful comments and discussion on an earlier draft of this chapter.

References

Aeschylus, 1975. *Prometheus Bound*. Translated by James Scully and C. John Herington. New York: Oxford.
Adorno, Theodor and Max Horkheimer. 2002. *Dialectic of Enlightenment*, ed. Gunzelin Schmid Noerr, tr. Edmund Jephcott. Stanford: Stanford University Press.
Aristotle. 1984. *De Anima* III.8, in *The Complete Works of Aristotle*, vol. I, ed. Jonathan Barnes. Princeton: Princeton University Press.
Aristotle. 1998. *Poetics* 4, in *The Complete Works of Aristotle*, vol. I ed. Jonathan Barnes. Princeton: Princeton University Press.
Bergson, Henri. 1907/1998. *Creative Evolution*. translated by Arthur Mitchell. Mineola, NY: Dover.
Bergson, Henri. 1932/2006. *Two Sources of Morality and Religion*, translated by R. Ashley Audra and Cloudesley Brereton. Notre Dame: Notre University Press.
Cavell, Stanley. 1979. *The World Viewed: Reflections on the Ontology of Film*. Cambridge: Harvard University Press.
Clarke, Arthur C. 1968/1999. *2001: A Space Odyssey*. New York: Ace Books.
Clarke, Arthur C. 1982. *2010: Odyssey Two*. New York: Del Ray.
Emerson, Ralph Waldo. 2007. "Works and Days," in *Society and Solitude, Collected Works of Ralph Waldo Emerson*, vol. VII. ed. Ronald A. Bosco and Douglas Emory Wilson. Cambridge: Harvard University Press.

Gelmis, Joseph. 1969. "An Interview with Stanley Kubrick" (1969) in *The Film Director as Superstar*. Garden City, NY: Doubleday and Company.

Hofstadter, Douglas. 1979/1990. *Gödel, Escher, Bach: An Eternal Golden Braid, A Metaphysical Fugue on Minds and Machines in the Spirit of Lewis Carroll*. New York: Basic Books.

Homer. 1991. *The Odyssey of Homer*, translated by Richmond Lattimore. New York: HarperPerennial.

Johnson, David Kyle. 2018. "Kubrick's 2001 and Nietzsche's Übermensch," in *Sci-Phi: Science Fiction as Philosophy*. The Teaching Company: Great Courses.

Joy, Bill. 2000. "Why the Future Doesn't Need Us." *Wired Magazine*. April 8.

Kurzweil, Ray. 2005. *The Singularity is Near*. New York: Viking.

Singer, Irving. 2004. *Three Philosophical Filmmakers: Hitchcock, Welles, Renoir*. Cambridge: MIT Press.

Turing. A. M. 1950. "Computing Machinery and Intelligence." *Mind* 49.

The Lord of the Rings as Philosophy: Environmental Enchantment and Resistance in Peter Jackson and J.R.R. Tolkien

34

John F. Whitmire Jr and David G. Henderson

Contents

Introduction: Opening Considerations	828
"Trees as Trees": Fantasy, Enchantment, and Recovery of Middle-Earth	830
A "Dramatic" Summary	835
Some Cinematic Ways of Being in Relation to Nature	838
Shadow and Struggle	843
Conclusion: Assessing Jackson's Argument—And Enchantment	847
End Notes	851
References	852

Abstract

A key philosophical feature of Peter Jackson's film interpretation of J.R.R. Tolkien's *The Lord of the Rings* is its use of fantasy to inspire a "recovery" of the actual or, in other words, a reawakening to the beauty of nature and the many possible ways of living in healthier ecological relation to the world. Though none of these ways is perfectly achieved, this pluralistic view is demonstrated in the various lifeways of Hobbits, Elves, Men, and Ents. All of the positive relationships embodied in the films—to trees, mountains, horses, and vegetable gardens—involve loving care and attention, receiving nourishment and livelihood without instrumentalization, or reducing nature to mere resource. The films also vividly display a variety of ugly and destructive ways of using the land to accrue power and wealth. These noxious ways, specifically because they actively destroy the lands that they use, always need more. They will thus eventually annihilate the beautiful ways of being if they are not actively resisted. Some of those who would rather be tending their own trees, gardens, or horses or even wandering in the wild forests must therefore turn their attention to struggle and resistance instead. This is a struggle full of grief, and at times even verging on

---

J. F. Whitmire Jr (✉) · D. G. Henderson
Western Carolina University, Cullowhee, NC, USA
e-mail: jwhitmire@wcu.edu; dghenderson@wcu.edu

© Springer Nature Switzerland AG 2024
D. K. Johnson et al. (eds.), *The Palgrave Handbook of Popular Culture as Philosophy*, https://doi.org/10.1007/978-3-031-24685-2_12

despair, but it is marked by the refusal to give up hope. Indeed, what Jackson and Tolkien have to say about hope is as important in responding to the ecological crisis as anything they have to say about nature, inasmuch as they help to remind us that even in our own times, "there is still hope."

Keywords

Environment · Ethics · Ecological crisis · Pluralism · Enchantment · Recovery · Wonder · Hope · Fantasy · Tolkien · Care · Resistance · Ecocriticism · Lord of the Rings

Introduction: Opening Considerations

It is a truism that *The Lord of the Rings* is an important and powerful piece of popular culture, having been named (in whole or part; the text itself was understood by Tolkien as a single work) one of American and British readers' favorite books of the past century in numerous different polls.[1] It is equally true—for a diversity of reasons—that the text has received very little substantive philosophical consideration, and much of that has had a distinctly theological flavor,[2] reflecting in part Tolkien's own famous remark that "*The Lord of the Rings* is of course a fundamentally religious and Catholic work; unconsciously so at first, but consciously in the revision" (Tolkien 2006, p. 172).

While acknowledging these facts and the continuing need for more serious philosophical consideration of Tolkien's own works,[3] we focus our attention in this essay on a more recent work of popular culture—Peter Jackson's monumental three-film interpretation of *The Lord of the Rings*—as itself a substantive contribution to environmental philosophy. The primary reasons for this are twofold. First, until fairly recently, it has been possible to recognize distinctly "pre-Jackson" and "post-Jackson" readers of *The Lord of the Rings*. Given that *The Lord of the Rings: The Fellowship of the Ring* was first released in theaters in 2001, however, the vast majority of students today (and, it seems plausible, increasingly readers more generally) first come to the text by way of Jackson's films, a situation in which the popular cultural impact of the book is thereby filtered through Jackson's interpretation. Second, Jackson's interpretation of *The Lord of the Rings* is itself a substantive work—in both quantity (over 11 h of film in the extended editions (Jackson 2001, 2002, 2003), which we reference in this essay) and quality (through both critical and popular consensus)—entirely worth being taken seriously on its own terms.

It is therefore increasingly important to consider not just the text but also the theatrical interpretation itself as an important work of popular culture—*as* philosophy. In pursuing this goal, we recognize key issues and background from Tolkien's works that Jackson draws upon, both overtly and tacitly, as well as the growing secondary literature on Tolkien (particularly from the last 25 years), but we do so in this context largely in order to demonstrate the significance of the vision that Jackson and his collaborators articulate through their own narrative and cinematic expression. This vision is centered on an understanding of the variety of ways of being in relation to the world and speaks powerfully to the ecological crises of our own time.

For her ecocriticism of Tolkien's works, Jeffers, in *Arda Inhabited,* utilizes Deleuze and Guattari's anti-hierarchical, "rhizomatic" model and advocates for a kind of "ecological humility" that does not "require the objectification of the living world around us" (Jeffers 2014, p. 6). She attempts, by way of an analysis of power, to

> interrogate the connection between people and place. The connection points to a moral responsibility people have to act in ways that are beneficial to themselves and their surroundings. This connection also offers hope for a reconciliation of people and the environment through increased respect and interconnection. (p. 18)

"In *The Lord of the Rings,*" she argues, "the decision to act in harmony with one's environment is a moral imperative" (p. 17). While acknowledging that there is clearly a kind of hierarchy within Tolkien's work—a function, perhaps, of his Catholicism—she asserts that "hierarchies involving interspecies domination are either undone or a mark of evil" (p. 8–9). She goes on to argue that *The Lord of the Rings* "presents a thoroughly realized world that highlights interconnectedness" (p. 16).

While we, by and large, agree with this generalized assessment, we argue that the position we find in Jackson's films is even more explicitly pluralistic with regard to a variety of positive ways of life than the one Jeffers articulates in her reading of Tolkien's text. Rather than viewing Ents, Hobbits, and Elves[4] as inherently superior in a "relationship [that] is nonhierarchical and favors diversity" to, for instance, the people of Rohan, who are "one step removed from the loving interdependence" (p. 17), our view is that Jackson's films deflate this hierarchy of ways of life even further. The Rohirrim, even in the state of decline we see portrayed in the films, offer us a way of being in relation to earth and animal that is just as desirable as that of the Hobbits.

In brief, we argue in the following that in Jackson's interpretation of Tolkien, there are a multiplicity of good, desirable, and even beautiful ways of inhabiting the land, but they all involve loving care and attention to the land and its green and growing things. Plants, animals, and soils are all used in these lifeways, but even in their usage, there is reciprocity, a giving of attention and care while receiving nourishment and livelihood. Living things are never reduced merely to their instrumentality in Jackson's films. But they are engaged within processes of open-ended, mutual transformation. These are not portrayals of peoples who live so lightly on the land that they leave no trace. The land of Middle-earth is not protected from all influence, as though humans and hobbits were contaminants, in the mode of much contemporary environmental rhetoric. These are substantive and good ways of belonging. The Hobbit and the pipe-weed, the horse and the rider—these cultivate each other until both are something new. The care and attention given to the specific plants and animals of a particular location tend towards the creation of a variety of healthy ecological relationships, a plurality of modes of being in relation to nature.

Though none of these ways is perfectly achieved, this pluralistic view (less hierarchical than we find in the text) is demonstrated in the various ways of life of Hobbits, Elves, Men, and Ents.[5]

There are also, then, by contrast, a variety of ugly and destructive ways of using the land to accrue power and wealth. These can be seen in the mines and clear cuts of Isengard and in the wastelands of Mordor. These noxious ways, specifically because they actively destroy the lands that they use, always need more. They will thus eventually annihilate the beautiful ways of being in relation to the land if they are not actively resisted. Some of those who would rather be tending their own trees, gardens, or horses or even wandering in the wild forests must therefore turn their attention to struggle and resistance instead. This is a struggle full of grief, and at times even verging on despair: "We set out to save the Shire, Sam," Frodo says poignantly at the end of *The Return of the King*. "And it has been saved. But not for me." But this struggle is marked in the films, as in the text, by the refusal to give up hope. Indeed, what Jackson and Tolkien have to say about hope is as important in responding to the environmental crisis as anything they have to say about nature, for as Arwen tells her father, Elrond: "There is still hope."

"Trees as Trees": Fantasy, Enchantment, and Recovery of Middle-Earth

"The world is changed. I feel it in the water. I feel it in the earth. I smell it in the air..." From the very beginning of Galadriel's Prologue to *The Lord of the Rings: The Fellowship of the Ring*, Jackson's interpretation of *The Lord of the Rings* announces a foregrounding of a set of themes surrounding the importance of the natural world and the myriad possible ways of being-in-relation to it. While our *relationship* to the natural world is certainly essential to the text itself, it is clearly foregrounded in Peter Jackson's film trilogy in such a way that these possible relations (or ways of being) take on a fundamental—indeed, we would argue central—importance to the films, at least in the extended edition versions, which we treat here. In doing so, we reject the kinds of claims made by some scholars (e.g., DiPaolo) that the films are "bastardized" versions (Di Paolo 2018, p. 50) of the text, which reduce to negligibility its environmental sensibility. DiPaolo is certainly correct in noting that the extended editions of the films include *more* ecologically significant material, but we do not agree that the loss of elements like Tom Bombadil and the "Scouring of the Shire" compromise the "environmentalist themes inherent in the Hobbit-centric segments of Tolkien's epic" to a degree that "diminishes the dramatic and thematic significance of all the original story's environmental sensibilities" (p. 32). Indeed, this denigration of the films risks repeating the unfortunate earlier dismissals of Tolkien's own works as juvenile trash by critics like Edmund Wilson (in the infamous review: "Oo, Those Awful Orcs!"). Rather, some of the material Jackson adds, such as Aragorn's relationship with the horse Brego, actually enriches the environmental sensibility in interesting and productive ways. Somewhat oddly, DiPaolo attempts to use an article in which the dean of Tolkien studies, Tom

Shippey, is actually quite positive in his assessment that "Jackson has certainly succeeded in conveying much of the more obvious parts of Tolkien's narrative core, many of them quite strikingly alien to Hollywood normality" (Shippey 2004, p. 254) to support the claim that "it is unfortunate that the film series ... was not more thematically faithful to Tolkien's vision" (p. 31).

Catherine Madsen once claimed that "the reader need not worship anything to comprehend [Middle-earth]. It is more important for the reader to love trees" (Madsen 2004, p. 39). And Patrick Curry, a quarter century ago in his insightful study of environmental issues in Tolkien's work, has contended: "It wouldn't be stretching a point to say that Middle-earth itself appears as a character in its own right" (Curry 1997, p. 61). Despite this kind of attention, Susan Jeffers asserts that the secondary literature has mostly "passed over the secondary world Tolkien so lovingly created in favor of other aspects of his work. A passing mention of his love of trees, for example, might be made, but the trees of Middle-earth have received relatively little critical attention" and are "often dismissed as mere setting" (Jeffers 2014, p. 1).

We believe Jeffers overstates the scholarly situation on this issue as several relatively recent works, some even prior to Jeffers' claim, have explored the environmental position of the text. Indeed, in a recent piece, Stentor Danielson argues for an emerging "broad consensus around several points that we can see as a sort of Tolkienian environmentalism" (Danielson 2021, p. 179): a love of trees and other growing things, a critique of modern industry, "cooperative relationship with the land and environment," connection of the health of the community to that of nature, and a view of "an instrumental, greedy, power-seeking approach" as fundamentally wicked (p. 180). But whereas there is a clear agreement among a number of these authors that *The Lord of the Rings* has a central environmental or ecological message or view, there remains significant disagreement regarding how best to situate the philosophical position the text takes. These range from Jeffers' Deleuzean position focused on power to a kind of neo-pagan "*re-sacralization (or re-enchantment) of experienced and living nature*" (Curry 1997, p. 29, emphasis in the original) to a Leopoldian "land ethic" (Niiler 1999) to one that stresses notions of Christian stewardship (Dickerson and Evans 2011) to one that "parallels the ideals of Critical Animal Studies" (Simpson 2017) to a kind of proto-ecofeminist position (Di Paolo 2018).[6] Jackson's films, as an interpretation of the texts, are also sure to resonate with a variety of environmental sensibilities. We draw heavily on Curry's use of enchantment, and its intersection with Tolkien's own defense of fantasy, as an especially helpful lens for the environmental work of the films. Dickerson and Evans's framing of proper stewardship as including a recognition of nature's intrinsic value and the acceptance of a servant role for humanity within it—in contrast to the false stewardship of Denethor (p. 43)—is also helpful, though the stewardship portrayed in the films is less explicitly "religious and Catholic" than many readers have found the text to be.

Jeffers' complaint is closer to the mark if we have in mind primarily the scholarly journals and philosophical anthologies, however, which do demonstrate much less focus on these issues.[7] In a way, this is a bizarre state of affairs, given Tolkien's own argument in "On Fairy-Stories" regarding the important distinction between "drama" (stage plays) and "literature":

> Drama is, even though it uses a similar material (words, verse, plot), an art fundamentally different from narrative art. Thus, if you prefer Drama to Literature ... you are apt to misunderstand pure story-making, and to constrain it to the limitations of stage-plays. You are, for instance, likely to prefer characters, even the basest and dullest, to things. Very little about trees as trees can be got into a play. (Tolkien 1966, p. 51)

And that in itself, he claims, has led to a kind of depreciation of fantasy: "Drama is naturally hostile to Fantasy. Fantasy, even of the simplest kind, hardly ever succeeds in Drama, when that is presented as it should be, visibly and audibly acted ... Men dressed up as talking animals may achieve buffoonery or mimicry, but they do not achieve Fantasy" (p. 49).

For Tolkien, then, one of the key elements to "story" (as opposed to "drama") is precisely the importance of "things" rather than of characters. By implication, then, *in his own works*, to consider only characters and neglect the natural world would be to offer a deeply impoverished reading. Now, the reason Tolkien offers for drama's hostility to things other than characters is simply that they are much harder to incorporate into a staged presentation. The genre of film, however, particularly in the way it captures natural landscapes onscreen and (more contentiously, perhaps) in its use of both practical and computer-generated visuals to represent environments artificially, presents a potential solution to this problem, allowing the portrayal of "trees as trees," in addition to mountains as mountains, rivers as rivers, and so forth (cf. Davis 2008, pp. 65–66)—*and* of characters in relation to them, in a way that bridges the divide Tolkien sees between drama and literature and that allows us to enter into a *visual* fantasy or "Secondary World."

Tolkien himself was dubious of the capacity of other art forms (and was particularly vitriolic regarding a proposed (but never made) 1958 animated film adaptation of *The Lord of the Rings* by Morton Zimmerman: see *Tolkien* 2006, pp. 266–267 and 270–277) to achieve what he calls "the inner consistency of reality" (Tolkien 1966, p. 48), claiming that "Fantasy is a thing best left to words, to true literature" (p. 49). Despite this protestation, we believe that Jackson's films do avoid both "buffoonery and mimicry" and, in fact, achieve that inner consistency Tolkien thinks is necessary to compel "secondary belief." That is, Jackson's cinematic interpretation of *The Lord of the Rings*, including his particularly masterful use of the diversity of Aotearoa New Zealand's landscapes, fulfills Tolkien's fairy-tale requirement of "a Secondary World which your mind can enter. Inside it, what [the artist] relates is 'true': it accords with the laws of that world" (p. 37). And in doing so, these films fulfill what Tolkien calls the chief aspiration of fantasy: an enchantment or wonder that "produces a Secondary World into which both designer and spectator can enter, to the satisfaction of their senses while they are inside" (pp. 52–53).

One of the key functions of this secondary world, Tolkien goes on to argue, is "Recovery (which includes return and renewal of health)—regaining of a clear view ... so that the things seen clearly may be freed from the drab blur of triteness or familiarity—from possessiveness" (p. 57). Good works of fantasy deal with "simple or fundamental things ... made all the more luminous by their setting" (p. 59). In other words, good fantasy can return us to our own world with a renewed view of those things that have become mere background to us while whetting our own desire for a different kind of relationship to them: "by the making of Pegasus horses were ennobled" (p. 59). Fairy-tale or fantasy stories are, after all, "plainly not primarily concerned with possibility, but with desirability," both awakening and satisfying desires (p. 40). The ennobled horse, encountered again in daily life but with the spell of familiarity broken, is no longer "just a horse," either in the sense of being a boring piece of background or in the sense of being just a possession. It is restored to the fullness and wonder of being a living creature in its own right.

According to ecofeminist Val Plumwood, the exploitation and abuse of nature and women are both facilitated by what she terms their backgrounding (Plumwood 1993, p. 21). When nature and women become merely the setting or environment for the story of the rational agency of men, their instrumentalization or reduction to a mere resource is made to feel natural instead of appearing as a problem. Their own activities and man's interdependence with them are simply excluded from focus and thus from real consideration. The backgrounding of women in literature and film can be seen by how many works fail the Bechdel test, which merely requires two or more women talking to each other about something other than a man. Sadly, none of *The Lord of the Rings* films fare well by this test in their presentation of women, yet their refusal to let nonhuman nature be backgrounded contributes significantly to the environmental argument of the films. In simply holding the natural world in focus, by making trees and mountains as important as kings and wizards, the way is opened for imagining—and desiring—less destructive relations. And by setting Hobbits, Elves, and Ents firmly in that natural world, our ability to see its wonder is recovered from the dulling effects of familiarity and possessiveness. This reenchantment allows us to "realize that this world, its places and its inhabitants are existentially *already* wondrous—and as such, worthy of the kind of respect and love that doesn't permit their wanton, callous and stupid destruction" (Curry 1997, p. 161).

And that is precisely what we find in Jackson's interpretation, where Middle-earth is not just a "setting" for the characters in his *Lord of the Rings*; rather, the relation of the characters themselves to the earth, and indeed aspects of the natural world in themselves—mountains, rivers, and trees—becomes central thematic features, portrayed in soaring visual terms throughout the trilogy of films. Of course, the images of trees are essential to both Tolkien's writing and his own paintings and drawings, from the White Tree of Gondor to the Two Trees of the *Silmarillion* (from which it is said to derive). As Patrick Curry puts it, "Tolkien plainly had a profound feeling for nature, and perhaps especially its flora; his love of trees shines through everywhere" (Curry 1997, p. 27). Verlyn Flieger and Patrick Curry are among the many who cite Tolkien's 1972 contention (Tolkien 2006, p. 419) that "In all my works I take the part of trees as against all their enemies." And although Flieger argues that the situation is somewhat more complex and ambivalent in the text (as evidenced by the first "villain" being Old Man Willow), she claims that "It is clear that in seeing and protesting the destruction by humanity of the world it inhabits and of which it is a part, in recognizing that the natural world was an endangered enclave in need of protection against encroaching civilization, Tolkien was years ahead of his time" (Flieger 2000, p. 147). But this sentiment was around well before Tolkien. Indeed, his attitude toward trees feels very close to Thoreau's comments on pine trees in *The Maine Woods*:

> Strange that so few ever come to the woods to see how the pine lives and grows and spires, lifting its ever-green arms to the light—to see its perfect success; but most are content to behold it in the shape of many broad boards brought to market, and deem *that* its true success! But the pine is no more lumber than man is, and to be made into boards and houses is no more its truest and highest use than the truest and highest use of a man is to be cut down and made into manure. There is a higher law affecting our relation to pines as well as to men. A pine cut down, a dead pine, is no more a pine than a dead human carcass is a man. . . . Every creature is better alive than dead, men and moose and pine trees, and he who understands it aright will rather preserve its life than destroy it.
>
> Is it the lumberman, then, who is the friend and lover of the pines . . . No! no! it is the poet; he it is who makes the truest use of the pine. . . . (Thoreau 2009, pp. 111–112)

While trees are certainly essential to Jackson's visual representation of Middle-earth, we would venture to assert that mountains are to Jackson what trees are to Tolkien. Majestic mountain scenes open and close *The Fellowship of the Ring*, and they mark nearly every transition in between. Jackson, taking his cue from Tolkien's sometimes bemoaned attention to the "scenery" (a criticism that takes it as an overattention to "mere setting"!), makes sure that the viewer knows precisely where the members of the Fellowship are, not just as a location on a map (which also plays a defining cinematic role) but also as a vibrant, living place. Each river, mountain, and forest have a name, and not only a name but a spirit, a distinct quality of character. Flieger notes the names of *particular* trees in Tolkien's works (Flieger 2000, p. 147; see also Parrila 2021), an early suggestion that a way of being that relates not only to human persons, but also to other parts of the natural world as individuals, may lie at or near the heart of the kind of relationality that Tolkien and Jackson stress. As Legolas remarks to Gimli early in Jackson's *The Two Towers*, "The trees are speaking to each other... They have feelings, my friend. The Elves began it. Waking up the trees, teaching them to speak." Curry argues:

> The places themselves are animate subjects with distinct personalities, while the peoples are inextricably in and of their natural and geographical locales: the Elves and "their" woods and forests, the Dwarves and mountains, hobbits and the domesticated nature of field and garden. And some of the most beautiful places in Middle-earth are so, in large part because they are loved by the people who share them. (Curry 1997, p. 28)

Jackson, we argue, follows Tolkien in spirit, if not letter, in heeding what Curry calls "Tolkien's attention to 'local distinctiveness' [which] is one of the most striking things about his books" (p. 27). The land also becomes the foil by which we see the moral alignment of the races, nations, and individuals we meet along the way, with the various speaking peoples exemplifying (among other things) certain aspects or possibilities of human kind. "Elves and Men are represented as biologically akin in this 'history', because Elves are certain aspects of Men and their talents and desires ... They have certain freedoms and powers we should like to have, and the beauty and peril and sorrow of the possession of these things is exhibited in them" (Tolkien 2006, p. 189). As Kierkegaard puts it, "The myth allows something that is inward to take place outwardly" (Kierkegaard 1980, p. 47). For Tolkien, then, "my 'elves' are only a representation or an apprehension of a part of human nature" (Tolkien 2006, p. 149), representing "the artistic, aesthetic, and purely scientific aspects of the Humane nature raised to a higher level than is actually seen in Men" (p. 236). (This does not mean they are without flaws, of course, as we note below.) Hobbits, then, are

> really meant to be a branch of the specifically human race ... They are entirely without non-human powers, but are represented as being more in touch with "nature" (the soil and other living things, plants and animals), and abnormally, for humans, free from ambition or greed of wealth. They are made small (little more than half human stature, but dwindling as the years pass) partly to exhibit the pettiness of man, plain unimaginative parochial man ... and mostly to show up, in creatures of very small physical power, the amazing and unexpected heroism of ordinary men "at a pinch". (Tolkien 2006, p. 158)

So we meet the barefoot hobbits in the garden, tending their plots of soil with devotion and care, exuding an earnest, if parochial, salt-of-the-Middle-earth kind of goodness in their appreciation of "a simple life." Curry notes the bioregionalism of the Hobbits, "living within an area defined by its natural characteristics, and within its limits" (Curry 1997, p. 27), but this goes for basically all the races we meet in Middle-earth. Saruman's increasing corruption, by contrast, is written most clearly in the limit-transgressing, landscape changes around Isengard. By giving us a moral account of the peoples of Middle-earth in terms of their various relationships to the land, Tolkien and Jackson are also making philosophical claims about how *we* should relate to the land. For who among us would want to share in Saruman's doom?

A "Dramatic" Summary

In order to articulate the "argument" of Peter Jackson's *The Lord of the Rings*, then, we must discuss both the narrative and the other cinematic elements of the film that allow us to understand the "trees as trees" as well as the relationship of the characters to the rest of the natural world. Set in Middle-earth (a mythical prehistory of our own world), the story is by now familiar to most. Frodo Baggins, a Hobbit, comes to understand that his inheritance from his "uncle" Bilbo includes the One Ring, a weapon of immense power created by the Dark Lord Sauron and intended to allow Sauron to dominate the possessors of the other Rings of power, the various free peoples of Middle-earth (Men, Elves, Dwarves, Hobbits, Ents), and, significantly, "cover all the lands in a second darkness." Frodo must therefore flee from his home in the Shire, accompanied by his friends and fellow Hobbits, Samwise (Sam)

Gamgee, Peregrin (Pippin) Took, and Meriadoc (Merry) Brandybuck. Making his way to the nearby village of Bree, he meets the ranger, Strider, a traveler of the wild northern lands. With Strider's assistance, he is able to escape from a number of Sauron's servants—the Black Riders—and make his way, on the verge of death, to the Elven haven of Rivendell.

Following a long Council in Rivendell, Frodo responds to the call to take the Ring back to Sauron's realm of Mordor, where it was forged, and cast it into Mount Doom, the only place it might be destroyed. Along with his friends, who refuse to be left behind, he will be accompanied in a Fellowship by Strider—revealed in the Council as Aragorn, heir to the kingship of Gondor—and Boromir, son of the Steward of Gondor, representing Men; Legolas the Elf; Gimli the Dwarf; and the Wizard Gandalf the Grey, who had been held captive by the head of his own order of Wizards, Saruman the White. This errand, a nearly hopeless one that becomes even more so as the tale progresses, takes the Fellowship through the Dwarvish Mines of Moria, where Gandalf falls fighting a Balrog, a demon of the ancient world, and then the Elvish forest realm of Lothlórien. The Fellowship is broken when Boromir falls victim to the influence of the Ring and attempts to take it from Frodo.

In the wake of these events, Frodo decides that he needs to take the Ring to Mordor alone to prevent its ill effects on the rest of his friends, but Sam refuses to be left behind, and the two set out together. In the meantime, Boromir is killed by orcs, and Merry and Pippin are taken captive; Aragorn, Legolas, and Gimli set out to rescue them. At this point, as we begin the second film, the narrative splits, and we follow the three groups of friends as they travel through the kingdom of Rohan and the outskirts of Mordor. Aragorn, Legolas, and Gimli meet Éomer, the nephew of the king of Rohan, who tells them that his men have destroyed the column of orcs that took Merry and Pippin. They nevertheless continue their pursuit, which leads them to the edge of Fangorn forest, where they meet a resurrected Gandalf—now "the White," or "Saruman as he should have been"—who tells them that Merry and Pippin are still alive and have contributed to a greater wakening of the Ents (the treeish "people" who are themselves the shepherds of the trees) to battle.

Merry and Pippin have indeed met Treebeard, the eldest of the Ents, and it is their urging that ultimately leads the Ents to abandon their neutrality and enter into conflict with Saruman's forces themselves. Meanwhile, Aragorn, Gandalf, Legolas, and Gimli travel to meet Théoden, the king of the "horse-lords" of Rohan, who has been deluded and, in the visual language of the film, entranced by Saruman. After Gandalf exorcises Saruman, Théoden leads his people to an ancient fortress of his people at Helm's Deep, where an enormous pitched battle (indeed, one of the longest in film history) takes place. At this battle, joined by a group of Elves from Lothlórien, the people of Rohan emerge victorious; while the ents (joined by Merry and Pippin) attack and ultimately take Saruman's fortress of Isengard.

At the same time, Frodo and Sam, making their slow way to Mordor, encounter Gollum, the monstrous creature (though once a Hobbit) from whom Bilbo had acquired the Ring 60 years before. Gollum, cowed by Frodo but also recovering something of his former, pre-monstrous self in Frodo's company, leads the hobbits through the Dead Marshes (the scene of an epic battle centuries before) at the edges of Mordor, where they realize it is impossible to enter. Detouring through the fields of Ithilien, they meet Boromir's brother, Faramir, who (after an initial scare) ultimately aids them in their continuing quest.

The third and final film finds Frodo, Sam, and Gollum struggling to enter Mordor through a secret pass guarded by the great spider-creature Shelob. Gollum, having succumbed to his desire for the Ring after a series of debates between the two sides of himself, has betrayed the hobbits, and Frodo is stung by Shelob. Sam, initially thinking Frodo is dead, takes the Ring to continue the Quest, before realizing that Frodo is in fact alive and his true place is at Frodo's side. After saving him from a tower of orcs, the two then struggle through the blasted hellscape of Mordor toward the volcanic Mount Doom.

A reunited Aragorn, Legolas, Gimli, and Merry regroup with King Théoden, while Gandalf and Pippin ride to Gondor to rally the defenses of its capital city (Minas Tirith) against the coming onslaught from Sauron. After taking Merry as a kind of squire, Théoden then prohibits him from riding to war, but Merry finds a way to ride with Éomer's sister, Éowyn, herself disguised as one of the Riders of Rohan. After Elrond shows up to encourage Aragorn to take up his role as the true king of Gondor and a side quest to summon a company of spectral oath-breakers to fulfill their pledge to his ancestor, Aragorn too arrives on the field at the battle of the Pelennor Fields before Minas Tirith. And though this battle is won by the forces of Gondor and Rohan, it is marred by the deaths of Théoden in battle and the despairing madness of Denethor, Steward of Gondor, who commits suicide in the face of what he foresees as the impending death of his second son, Faramir; the fall of his people; and the certain doom of his realm. The surviving members of the Fellowship, however, regroup to advance on Mordor—not with any hope of conquering Sauron's forces in battle but simply to draw his forces out and give Frodo the smallest window of opportunity to reach Mount Doom.

After struggling through Mordor and then crawling—and finally literally carrying Frodo—up the side of the volcano, Sam is unable to help Frodo fulfill the Quest as Frodo succumbs to the power of the Ring and claims it for himself. Gollum, too, had survived the encounter with Shelob and, in the struggle to recover the Ring for himself, ends up biting off Frodo's finger and then falling into the volcanic depths, unintentionally completing the Quest. Tolkien notes, in letter 246, that too few readers have actually noticed Frodo's own inevitable failure, which had been clearly foreshadowed. Though Tolkien himself does not regard this as a "moral" failure— Frodo having used every ounce of his strength of mind and body to bring the Ring to that point—it is only through a kind of unexpected grace, enabled by way of, first, Bilbo's and, later, Frodo's own repeatedly exercised acts of mercy in not killing the monster Gollum (which clearly would have been justified) that the Quest is finally achieved (Tolkien 2006, pp. 325–330).

As Frodo and Sam pass out from the volcanic fumes, they are saved by Gandalf on the wings of massive eagles, and the third film ends with a series of codas: a variety of celebrations of victory (Aragorn's coronation and wedding, the hobbits' return home, Sam's own wedding), but all tinged by an enduring melancholy at all the good (in persons and the natural world) that has been lost or destroyed in the fight, culminating in the ultimate departure of Gandalf, Galadriel, Elrond, and the never-fully-healed Frodo from Middle-earth. Those who simplistically describe the conclusion(s) of the film trilogy or text as a "happy ending" thus indicate their deep misunderstanding of both Tolkien's and Jackson's depictions of the costs of war and environmental loss or destruction.

In this summary, we have provided only the barest sketch of the chief characters and narrative structure. The primary problem with describing the plotline alone, however, as we have noted above, is that it does *not* capture what Tolkien himself described as essential to literary "story" as distinct from "drama"—namely, the importance of the natural world, which has, in both the text and the film, a kind of character (or characters) of its own and with which the key protagonists and peoples have an essential relationship or interconnection. In order to be able to distill the philosophical argument that the films are making, we therefore need to consider equally some of the key theatrical (audiovisual) elements and the dialogue that points up essential aspects of those relations, as well as the importance of "nature as nature."

Some Cinematic Ways of Being in Relation to Nature

As we noted earlier, the visuals of Peter Jackson's films are sweeping, evocative even of Frederic Church's paintings, from the magnificent overview of the Misty Mountains and the forests at the end of Galadriel's Prologue to *The Fellowship of the Ring* to the mountain landscape of the Emyn Muil and the hints of Mordor—ominous but not yet grotesque—that close the first film. These broad establishing shots are explicit directorial and editing choices, echoed by similarly dazzling first views of Mount Doom and Gondor in *Fellowship*, and they allow the viewer to witness the grandeur of the natural world. Jackson continues this trajectory with the flyover entry of the Misty Mountains at the opening of *The Two Towers*, followed almost immediately by the sheer height (depth) inside the mountain, as Gandalf and the Balrog fall from the bridge, mirroring of the sublime, and then the haunting and almost painful overhead visual of the razor-sharp rocks Frodo and Sam must traverse in the Emyn Muil as Frodo awakens from his dream vision. *None* of these scenes, strictly speaking, occurs in the text, but they are implied by the loving detail found in Tolkien's descriptions of Middle-earth throughout the work. Jackson's choice to utilize these kinds of framing scenes gives the viewer a sense of the sheer immensity and wildness of the world. The Fellowship's crossing of the varied terrain of Middle-earth is painstakingly presented by Jackson in the back half of the first film as they traverse hills and valleys and, finally, attempt to cross the mountain of Caradhras. The smallness of the Fellowship in the broader world is continually emphasized by wide shots that emplace them in those landscapes, establishing their smallness relative to the world itself. As Patrick Curry notes, "You can easily freeze to death, die of overexposure, drown or starve in Middle-earth" (Curry 1997, p. 63). Jackson's vistas and the struggles of the Fellowship in moving through them remind us constantly of the sublimity of more-than-human nature.

This wildness, however, is balanced by our views of the relationality of the various inhabitants of Middle-earth to their respective flora and fauna, lands, and rivers. The

Hobbits are presented clearly by Jackson as belonging to the Shire by way of their cultivation of it; both the farming of vegetables and the gardening of flowers (including Sam's own) feature centrally in Jackson's introductory montage (his interpretation of the text's Prologue, "Concerning Hobbits"). There, Jackson has Bilbo claim that "Where our hearts truly lie is in peace and quiet and good tilled earth. For all Hobbits share a love of things that grow." Visually, Jackson utilizes close-ups like the Hobbits' dirty hands and fingernails and Sam's loving smile as he considers the flowers he is planting, mid-range shots like Hobbit children running through both cultivated fields and grassy meadows, and wider, meditative shots of the Shire's hills, rivers, and, indeed, trees, among which we first encounter Frodo lying down underneath a tree and reading, to demonstrate this relationality and belonging together of the Hobbits and their Shire. Further, though, Gandalf and Frodo, riding together through fields of flowers in a horse-drawn cart, explicitly and directly embeds the viewer *with* the Hobbits into this lovingly inhabited agrarian landscape.

Another early cinematic choice Jackson relies upon to frame our understanding of the film's position is Bilbo's map of Middle-earth, our first view of which occurs less than 2 min into *Fellowship* and then again, 5 min later, in moving from the wilds to the Shire. Here, we see a bit of Jackson's translation of Tolkien's maps, which show the various mountain ranges, forests, and rivers of the northwest of Middle-earth. Nestled within these physical features rather than superimposed upon them are the inhabited realms of various races: the Shire, Rohan, Gondor. We return to the maps at various points in the films, but one particularly poignant moment evoking the relationality of the Hobbits with their home occurs when Frodo is examining Bilbo's map of the Shire at Rivendell. Frodo simply comments, while the camera zooms in even further on Hobbiton and Bag End, "I miss the Shire." In this remarkable haven, it is both beautiful and sad to hear this echo of Bilbo's earlier assessment that "Frodo is still in love with the Shire: the woods, the fields. Little rivers." The map matters, both literally and as a visual framing device in Jackson's films, because the land matters.

Unlike the Hobbits and the Elves, we meet the Men of Rohan in a state of relative decline. (It is actually Faramir who situates them on the map, relative to Gondor and Mordor.) Gandalf describes Rohan in Jackson's *The Two Towers* as "weak and ready to fall," Saruman having already "enslaved" the mind of their King, Théoden. The full potential of what it means to be a horse-lord on the open grasslands is thus not fully on display. But some of this is not hard to discern from scenes such as the remarkable exhibition of harmony between human and horse in the Rohirrim turning on a dime to surround Aragorn, Legolas, and Gimli in *The Two Towers*. After their 3 days and nights of pursuit, Gimli continues to struggle behind the ranger and Elf, running after the orcs who have abducted Merry and Pippin. Suddenly, however, we see the Riders of Rohan sweeping across the screen, inviting us not into the landscape by way of the confining (and exhausting) perspective of Gimli and his strained legs but to vast fields that beg to be not just walked but also ridden through. It is thus not simply the relationship between the Rohirrim and their horses that we find here, but between those two and the land they call home.

Beyond these hints, we find what we might call a more authentically "Rohirric" attitude preserved in Gandalf's and Aragorn's relationships with the horses of

Rohan, both of which are portrayed in *The Two Towers*. Gandalf refers to Shadowfax, the "lord of all horses" (in the text, a horse "gifted" to him by the Rohirrim, though this is not made explicit in the film), as "my friend through many dangers" and actually rides without a saddle or bridle, signifying to the viewer the closeness of this relationship and the nobility of Shadowfax. Aragorn, who later affirms that he rode into war with Théoden's father, Thengel, gives us another glimpse of a model Rohirric relationship in his scenes with one of the most important characters Jackson adds to his interpretation of *The Two Towers*—the horse Brego, who had initially belonged to Théoden's son.

In the first scene, which does not occur in the text, Brego is described as "half-mad," and the Rohirrim grooms encourage Aragorn simply to leave him alone. The ranger, however, is able to gently calm Brego, which Éowyn thinks is due to "the magic of Elves." It is actually not one of the Elvish languages Jackson has Aragorn initially speaking here, however, but rather Old English, the language Tolkien used to represent (to the Hobbits' ears) the speech of Rohan. This is a subtle distinction, to be sure, but we believe it gives us some license to view Aragorn's understanding of Brego—"Turn this fellow free. He has seen enough of war"—not just as a vestige of his years growing up in Rivendell, which he mentions to Éowyn, but also to the time he spent in Rohan learning the ways of the horse-lords. Aragorn's kindness is well and truly repaid, later in the same film, when it is the wandering Brego who finds him washed up on the edge of the river after battle and nuzzles him back to consciousness. (Here again, this whole storyline is a cinematic addition, not found in the text.) As Brego carries Aragorn to Helm's Deep through the majestic landscape of Rohan and it becomes obvious that he never could have managed to reach it on foot before the battle, Aragorn thanks Brego, calling him "mellon"—the Elvish word for friend (and the password with which Gandalf had opened the doors of Moria). In short, then, the Rohirrim, and those who share their ways of being in relation to horses and the grasslands they inhabit, must surely love those friends with as much devotion as any Hobbit loves his garden. And in this context, when Saruman condescendingly remarks to (his double agent and Théoden's counselor) Gríma, "You stink of horse," the contrast could not be more perfectly illuminated.

As Jackson's recurring map makes clear, it is not just the Hobbits or humans that belong to their particular place. As becomes obvious in *Fellowship*, the Elves too have a nuanced interconnection to their world. Rivendell and Lothlórien represent a kind of haven from the passing of time in the "outside" world, and both Elrond and his people and Galadriel and hers visually demonstrate a way of living in harmony with the natural world, which differs significantly from the homely pastoralism of the Hobbits. It is a mode that allows more of the wildness of nature to remain than we see in the Shire, though even here there is a kind of harmonious balance that respects the Elves *as* natural beings, not as a kind of despoliative presence in the face of what would be an otherwise unsullied nature. The Elves (or "fairies" as Tolkien himself describes them in "On Fairy-Stories," using an older sense of the word predating their Shakespearean reduction) are supernatural not in the sense of being *beyond* nature but in the sense of being *far more natural* than we are (Tolkien 1966, pp. 4–5), and in this sense, they deconstruct the nature/culture distinction. They are, in short, as we find them in

Jackson's portrayal, an argument that human beings *as natural beings* can exist in a more harmonious balance, even with the wilder nature of forest and waterfall.

Elrond's home, as presented by Jackson, makes good on its name as a "riven dell" at the foot of the mountains. The portrayal here is not of a "house," as one might normally envision the term, but more akin to Frank Lloyd Wright's Fallingwater translated into a kind of extended complex. Water here is the primal connective element, with waterfalls pictured on several sides and flowing under parts of the compound and many fluid architectural elements visually obvious. The forest has no clear beginning or ending point, with the "house" imagined as open to the world surrounding it. Birds can be clearly heard in the Rivendell scenes, and even the Council of Elrond is held outside in Jackson's interpretation—in a courtyard of sorts rather than an inside hall. A gentle breeze blows throughout the scene's discussion and argument, with leaves lightly falling to the ground around and behind the participants. All of this suggests not just the sight and sound but even the smell of the surrounding woods to the attentive viewer. The Elves of Rivendell, by implication, are not "Other" than nature but part of it. Unlike the Shire, however, the emphasis in Rivendell is clearly not on agrarian cultivation of nature but rather on a place of quiet contemplation and study—of respite, reflection, and restoration from the travails of the outside world—embedded firmly within nature. The natural is preserved here in consonance with the needs of Elrond as a lore-master, teacher, and healer, and those who visit are, by implication, rejuvenated not only by Elrond's healing powers but also by the beauty of nature itself, in a kind of meditative peacefulness.

Lórien, the realm of Galadriel, by contrast, exceeds even the modest inside/outside dimensionality of Rivendell, with the Elves' city, Caras Galadhon, "the heart of Elvendom on Earth," composed of platforms built around the towering trees; the Fellowship sleeps under tarps on the ground. Flieger recounts Tolkien's description, which is realized ethereally by Jackson: "The smooth trunks of the trees are silver, their unfading leaves gold ... Caras Galadhon is a city of tree trunks standing orderly and harmonious." But we disagree somewhat with her further characterization of the city "as much a garden as a forest, or better yet, a city that is its own garden" (Flieger 2000, p. 155), if we are meant to understand it as a garden in a similar sense to those in the Shire, for the Elves do not cultivate the forest in the same ways as the Hobbits do the Shire. Instead, the Elves enchant the forest in various ways, bringing forth and amplifying its own potentiality, waking up the trees, for instance, or preserving their beauty from decay and corruption, but their influence bears little similarity to the vegetable gardening of the Shire.

The Hobbits, though themselves enchanted, are not faulted for falling short of the Elvish way of being with nature. The capabilities of both Hobbits and the nature of the Shire itself require a different relationship, one that is also wholly satisfactory and desirable despite its differences. While it is certainly true that "the whole effect of Lórien is aesthetically pleasing" (Flieger 2000, p. 155), it is beautiful in a stately way that differs, but does not *diminish*, the more homely and comfortable aesthetic of the Shire. Indeed, although both Tolkien and Jackson treat the stately pomp and formality of the Elves with respect, we know of Tolkien and suspect of Jackson that they both actually prefer the homely manners of hobbits for their own lives. (Tolkien said "I am in fact a Hobbit (in all but size). I like gardens, trees, and unmechanized farmlands; I smoke a pipe, and like good plain food (unrefrigerated)..." (Tolkien 2006, pp. 288–289), and Jackson kept the "human sized" set of Bilbo/Frodo's home, Bag End, from the film and installed it under a hill in his backyard. There is a secret passage to it, from his basement, and he visits it frequently (Parrish 2015).) The ways in which Jackson achieves this Elvish vision of an alternative way of being in relation to the natural world include setting most of the encounter there in a kind of ethereal silver-grey twilight (and lamplight at night), surrounding the Fellowship with floating mists and, at times, gently blurring the camera. While removing much of the color from the forest realm relative to the palette he utilizes in much of the rest of the films, the effect is to evoke the kind of enchantment that is central to Tolkien's understanding of fantasy or fairy-stories and to pull the hobbits and the Fellowship as a whole into an unfamiliar world. But it remains *this* world, with water running, the wind stirring, and the lament of the Elves for the believed-dead Gandalf hanging in the background. The Elves here have managed to *preserve* the world as it once was, at least within the mythical background of the story, without destroying or even much altering it, in a kind of domesticity that manages to coexist (beautifully!) in and with the wildness. Lórien is a shelter or haven from what, in Jackson's prologue, Galadriel describes as happening elsewhere—"darkness crept back into the forests of the world." Here, the Elves conform themselves and their architecture to the rest of the natural world with which they remain continuous, rather than forcing its accommodation on them—as even Hobbits do to some degree with the woodlands (cf. Hjulstad 2021).

The Ents, perhaps Tolkien's most unique literary creation, belong even more to the forest than the Elves do and instantiate Tolkien's own love for trees: "I am (obviously) much in love with plants and above all trees, and always have been; and I find human maltreatment of them as hard to bear as some find ill-treatment of animals" (Tolkien 2006, p. 220). And the Ents' relation to the woods is not so much another model of how we human readers might imagine a new relation to nature for ourselves as it is a reminder of the relationality and agency within the more than human world. Merry and Pippin's initial responses to Treebeard model the tension for the viewer between being disconcerted by the talking tree (Pippin) and being enraptured by the wonder of it (Merry). The simultaneous strangeness and familiarity of fantasy are underscored here. Merry recognizes the Ent from lore, declaring him a "tree herder, a shepherd of the forest." This puts Treebeard in a familiar category, for we know herding and shepherding as familiar human roles, while at the same time challenging our image of trees by making them the recipient of such an activity, suggesting more animality than we usually see in plants. Indeed, the Ents are about as similar to the trees as humans are to sheep: warm, little, soft-bodied mammals that we are. Like ants that herd aphids, the very relations that feel like a distinction from nature (the shepherd is above the sheep after all) themselves become naturalized in this mirror.

The Ents and Fangorn Forest also set a boundary to the ways of being in relation to the land, for it is a place that meets the celebrated and contested definition of *wilderness* in the 1964 Wilderness Act: "where man himself is a visitor who does not remain." Elves and Wizards may walk there sometimes, but it cannot be their place. Treebeard draws on this separateness in his first encounter with the hobbits, saying that he is "on nobody's side, because nobody is on my side." The differences between subjugation and freedom for humans and Hobbits—or, shifting to the contemporary contexts of Tolkien and Jackson, between democracy and fascism—these all-encompassing struggles make no difference to the trees, if both sides name the forest only as a natural resource and come always with axe in hand. "To trees, all Men are Orcs," says one character in Tolkien's "The New Shadow," a brief, abandoned attempt to write a Fourth Age tale (Tolkien 1996, pp. 409–421, which Danielson (2021) nicely analyzes as a more overtly theologically informed ethic of environmental stewardship). But the separation is not absolute in *The Lord of the Rings*. Only a failure of attention and imagination stands in the way of an alliance between Hobbits and Ents. There are men, as we see early on in our first encounter with Strider, who wander the wilds and know them with intimate affection. But they do not cultivate or transform them into being their place. To Sam the gardener, Kingsfoil is a weed. It is more than that to Strider, but it is not a crop either. The ranger subsists in the wilds on the land's own terms, at most serving as a lookout for external threats.

Shadow and Struggle

Pippin   We don't belong here, Merry. It's too big for us. What can we do in the end? We've got the Shire. Maybe we should go home.
Merry   The fires of Isengard will spread and the woods of Tuckborough and Buckland will burn. And ... And all that was once green and good in this world will be gone. There won't be a Shire, Pippin (Jackson 2002)

Now, as Jeffers rightly notes in relation to the text, "Middle-earth is a fallen place, and therefore no group can be said to act perfectly in relation to the environment. However, there are some groups and individuals who act more positively than others" (pp. 17–18). Tolkien describes each of the races of Middle-earth as having their own problems: "sloth and stupidity among the hobbits ... grudge and greed in Dwarf-hearts, and folly and wickedness among the 'Kings of Men', and treachery and power-lust even among the 'Wizards'" (Tolkien 2006, p. 262). Thus, Hobbits "are not a Utopian vision, or recommended as an ideal in their own or any age" (Tolkien 2006, p. 197). Not even the Elves are perfect, in their attempts to hold on to the world in an atemporal way, preserving things "unstained" rather than allowing natural processes of change and decay to occur. Indeed, Tolkien himself claims that the Elves "desired some 'power' over things as they are ... to make their particular will to preservation effective: to arrest change, and keep things always fresh and fair" (p. 236). This means that even they "are *not* wholly good or in the right ... because with or without [Sauron's] assistance they were 'embalmers'" (p. 197). And though perhaps less obvious in the films, where the Elves are described (by an elf!) as "wisest and fairest of all beings" in Galadriel's Prologue, this claim holds true even there.

Of course, the failures we see *most* clearly are those of Men, "who, above all else," Galadriel continues, "desire power," and of course those of the dark power

Sauron and the Wizard Saruman (on the text, cf. Campbell 2014, pp. 238–239). In a way, Sauron's torture of the lands of Mordor and the surrounding areas represents something like our closest view of a complete perversion of any of the varieties of normatively healthy relationship to the natural world, whereas Saruman's fortress of Isengard, with the tower of Orthanc at its center, helps demonstrate this perversion in-process. Treebeard accurately describes Saruman's fall from someone who previously walked in the woods to one who now has a "mind of metal and wheels. He no longer cares for growing things."

The visual introduction to the industrially transformed Isengard of *The Two Towers* follows a tree as it is chopped, felled, and then toppled into a huge open pit, where we see the furnaces and forges now teeming with laboring orcs. Over this, the viewer hears Saruman articulating his manifesto for a new world forged by a military-industrial complex: "The old world will burn in the fires of industry. The forests will fall. A new order will rise. We will drive the machine of war with the sword and the spear and the iron fist of the orc." As the camera pans around the pit, we see modified orcs being grown in vats, a gruesome biotech nightmare. Confronted with the physical constraints that every program of unfettered growth must encounter, Saruman offers all too familiar answers. Dam the river. Work longer hours. And, finally, take land: "The Forest of Fangorn lies on our doorstep—Burn it!" If there were ever any doubts about the films having serious environmental commitments, this scene dispels them. Everything the environmental movement is most horrified by—deforestation, open-pit mining, dams, biotech monsters, unfettered growth, and militarism—is elegantly distilled into a 2-min montage. The industrial vision of "progress" is given the ugliest presentation possible and is used to demonstrate the depravity of Saruman. The connection to Mordor is explicit in the scene—as Saruman's quest for power transforms him into a reflection of Sauron, he in turn is transforming Isengard and Fangorn into a reflection of Mordor,[8] for Mordor is not only a treeless but also a totally dry and sterile land. It is, in Sam's words, "the one place in Middle-earth we don't want to see any closer." Curry likens it to "blighted industrial wasteland" (Curry 1997, p. 77), but it reminds us more of the rock and rubble that remain in the wake of large surface mines, when everything thought to be of value has been extracted. Dickerson and Evans, drawing on Wendell Berry's discussion of land ownership, describe Sauron as the "model of corporate land ownership":

> Apparently the Dark Lord does not know [the land] intimately, is not dependent on it, and thus is not motivated to care for it. It does not matter to him if he damages Mordor; there are other fields further away where his slaves can produce the food they need to serve his war machine. (p. 192)

Dickerson and Evans also worry that Tolkien's description of Mordor is too far removed from the levels of desolation most people have actually experienced (p. 193). It could feel remote and abstract, inaccessible to all but the most vivid imagination. Fortunately, Jackson proves more than able to share his extraordinary talent for imagining such levels of devastation. Jackson makes the actual journey of Frodo and Sam in *The Return of the King* a painful experience for the viewer (as it is for the reader in Tolkien), training his lens both on the volcanic wastes and on the painfully slow crawl of Frodo and Sam through the blasted devastation of Mordor. The hobbits' cracked faces and parched voices mirror what we see in the landscape itself. In portraying the extent to which a place can be made repulsive and undesirable (at least as much as for the opposite qualities), the visual medium has some advantages.

The barrenness of Sauron's domain underscores Aldo Leopold's assertion, in his famous articulation of the "Land Ethic," that "the conqueror role is eventually self-defeating" (p. 204), for whether it is merely the human community or the whole biotic community of the land that is subject to designs of exploitation, the conqueror presumes to know

> just what makes the community clock tick, and just what and who is valuable, and what and who is worthless, in community life. It always turns out that he knows neither, and this is why his conquests eventually defeat themselves. (Leopold 1949, p. 204)

The portrayal of the industrial destruction in progress back at Isengard also resonates with the critiques of social ecologist Murray Bookchin. Bookchin argues that ecological problems start with social problems. Hierarchical oppression and exploitation of people provide a structural and cultural basis for the attending conquest of nature (Bookchin 1993, p. 354). And in Saruman's progression, it is clearly his lust for power over the peoples of Middle-earth that precipitates his assault on the forests. Tolkien's friend C.S. Lewis makes a similar observation when he says that "what we call Man's power over Nature turns out to be a power exercised by some men over other men with Nature as the instrument" (Lewis 1947, p. 35). But Bookchin is much more specific about the kinds of social problems that give rise to destructive conquests. One of the things he keys in on is the unbridled mandate for growth implicit in the logic of market and militaristic systems. And it is this logic of growth, or insatiable demand, that we see in Saruman that makes his relation to the land untenable. He is not just cutting down trees in order to build his tower—even the Hobbits cut down trees to keep the forest from overrunning the cultivated fields. It is that there is no end to what Saruman would have to cut in order to build his army, for a bigger army is always better. The Shire and the Old Forest can exist side by side, albeit uneasily, for neither needs to destroy the other in order to be itself. Hobbits may eat a ridiculous number of daily meals, but they are satisfied eventually. Industrial Isengard and Fangorn cannot coexist, however, for Isengard's furnaces do not count their meals at all but are entirely insatiable.

The tendency for the logic of war to be environmentally destructive, while experienced in a new way in the industrial world, is not a new thing under the sun. And the *bal taschit* command ("do not destroy") of Deuteronomy gives another compelling lens for looking at the problem of Isengard. "If you besiege a town for a long time," the commandment reads, "you must not destroy its trees by wielding an axe against them. Although you may take food from them, you must not cut them down. Are the trees of the field human beings that they should come under siege by you?" (10:19). Permission for limited use is granted, including timber for siegeworks, but wanton destruction is forbidden because of human dependence on the trees for food and also, apparently, because the trees have their own business to attend to. Contemporary rabbinical ethics takes this command as the basis for a general principle against wanton destruction in contradistinction from legitimate use. But to read it this way, the pressing and escalating demands of war must be denied the status of legitimate use. Having this command from Deuteronomy in mind gives a certain additional dimension of poetry to the role the trees play in resolving the siege of Helm's Deep. In a scene from the text that occurs only in the extended edition of *The Two Towers*, at the end of the battle, a forest looms where the night before there had been only a green dale. It was a host of "Huorns," moving trees distinct from but summoned by the Ents. The remnants of Saruman's army flee into the forest, passing "under the waiting shadow of the trees; and from that shadow none ever came again" (Tolkien 2004, p. 542).

The treatment of Isengard as a token of extractive industry is returned to later in the film, at this "turning of the tide," when the Ents themselves make war upon it. Here, again, it is hard to read the scene as being anything less than an homage from Jackson to the more radical and activist edge of the environmental movement. Dam removal has a particularly compelling place in the imagination of environmental activists, at least in the United States. The Sierra Club grew into the national environmental organization it is today through a series of campaigns against dam proposals in the American West—successfully in the cases of Dinosaur National Monument and the Grand Canyon but unsuccessfully in the case of Glenn Canyon. Edward Abbey's *Monkey Wrench Gang*, a fictional account of activists trying to destroy the Glenn Canyon dam on their own, launched Earth First! and a new, more radical approach to environmental resistance. Against this backdrop, the significance of Ents tearing out the dam could not be clearer. Indeed, Curry notes that ecological activism has been a core legacy of *The Lord of the Rings* (Curry 1997, pp. 54–55). Inter alia, he notes that the journals of David McTaggart (later of Greenpeace) record that he had been thinking explicitly of the real-world parallel to the book in the context of sailing his ship into the French nuclear testing site he disrupted in 1972. Contrary to some naïve critical appraisals, then, the text does not represent an overly romantic or sentimental "bucolic retreat from 'reality' that induces an apolitical passivity or right-wing quietism" (p. 55). And even more than the text, Jackson's film, by laying its emphasis here and intercutting the Ents' attack on Isengard with the Battle of Helm's Deep, pushes us to consider what kind of resistance might be justified on behalf of not only the people of Rohan but also the forest of Fangorn itself.

The dam removal also suggests an expectation and hope of some recovery and renewal for the land and forest, when the river has washed away the industrial and orcish wastes. The losses are still real, and trees will not grow back overnight, but they will grow again. Some of the largest ecological restoration efforts undertaken so far have been centered on dam removals, including on the Elwah River at Olympic National Park. As Curry once again insightfully puts it, "Just as Sauron is vanquished in *The Lord of the Rings*—albeit barely, temporarily, and at great cost—so Tolkien, crucially, offers his readers hope that what is precious and threatened in our world might survive too" (Curry 1997, p. 145). This is conveyed most strikingly in *The Return of the King* by another of Tolkien's beloved trees, the White Tree of Gondor. In the text, "the tree has stood dead in the citadel of Minas Tirith for one hundred sixty-six years, and the White Tree of Gondor comes to represent Gondor's waning power and lack of a king" (Cohen 2009, p. 100); Aragorn finds a sapling to replace it only after the destruction of the Ring. "The image of a dead tree replaced by a live one, as the White Tree of Gondor is, upholds the metaphor of resurrection," Cohen argues (p. 101).

In Jackson's version, the White Tree also appears dead when Gandalf and Pippin arrive in Minas Tirith, but the tree of the king still maintains an honor guard because, as Gandalf tells Pippin, the guards "have hope. A faint and fading hope that 1 day it will flower. That a king will come and this city will be as it once was..." Much later, as Denethor, in despair, prepares to burn himself and Faramir to death, intoning "Gondor is lost. There is no hope for Men," the camera sweeps upward, through the branches of the seemingly dead tree, to reveal a single bloom, high up, emblematic of the notion that it is precisely when things look bleakest that the virtue of hope is most important and valuable. And while the films focus more on averting ecological disaster than on recovery from it, Tolkien's text includes additional adventures in restoration (most notably in the "Scouring of the Shire"), further substantiating the grounds of hope.

Conclusion: Assessing Jackson's Argument—And Enchantment

In outlining the argument of the films, we have placed central importance upon the beauty of nature and the desirability of a variety of ways of living with it. This is not merely because we are dealing with a cinematic medium, although that is not insignificant. It is also because beauty and desire are central to the human experience of nature and the ways in which we might come to value it. Many philosophers and scientists make arguments for the value or rights of nature without reference to its beauty, wary of the subjectivity of such claims. But few are those who have acquired environmental values apart from the lived experience of aesthetic delight, curiosity, and wonder. Weston offers this response to those who search for the final logical and objective argument with which to save nature:

> Even if someone were finally to discover a knockdown proof, it would not be the reason that most of us who are in search of such a proof do in fact value nature ... *We* learned the values of nature through experience and effort, through mistakes and mishaps, through poetry and stargazing, and, if we were lucky, a few inspired friends. What guarantees that there is a shortcut? (Weston 2003, p. 317)

Curry likewise argues that "'reason' alone will never suffice to save what is rare and fair, both human and natural, in this world. Arguments from pure utility have already conceded the central ground to the forces of destruction" (Curry 1997, p. 119).

Eugene Hargrove, when environmental ethics was just beginning to professionalize within philosophy, made a case for this central role of aesthetic qualities in environmental values, in both their formation and their justification. He includes not only beauty and the sublime but also the interesting among the most important aesthetic qualities that open us up to the more than human world (Hargrove 1996, p. 88). Coincidentally (or not) in doing so, he drew on the essays of Tolkien (p. 173–4). In several places, notably "On Fairy-Stories," Tolkien describes aesthetic enjoyment as involving a desire for the thing to be true. Wanting to hear stories about dragons is caught up, at some level, with the desire for there to be dragons.

Not dissimilarly, when we learn with curiosity and wonder about Great Auks, Carolina Parakeets, or Tasmanian Tigers, the same inner movement toward enchantment, the giving over to delight in their being, is also a giving over to sorrow at their loss. And when we yield to the enchantment of what is still here, from Redwood trees to free-flowing rivers, we delight not only in the idea of them but also in their being real. So the idea of their loss or destruction becomes painful. This does not rule out other considerations outweighing these values in difficult decisions. One might delight in the marvelous life history of an organism but also recognize it as a public health threat. Being enchanted by nature does not force a decision for preservation, but it does make any decision for destruction harder and less attractive. By contrast, as Curry argues, "a disenchanted world doesn't feel worth defending" (Curry 1997, p. 70).

The path from aesthetic delight to preservation action is well trod. Landscape painters, such as Thomas Cole, Frederic Church, and Albert Bierstadt, along with a romantic approach to natural history exploration seen in Alexander von Humboldt, William Bartram, and John James Audubon, played a large role in transforming societal attitudes toward wild nature. Thomas Moran's paintings and sketches from the Yellowstone expedition were passed around Congress in the lead-up to its designation as the first National Park in 1872. Landscape painter Susie Barstow was an early member of the Appalachian Mountain Club and a pioneer for women's involvement in outdoor recreation. Time and again, it is wonder and enchantment that stand against the reduction of nature to a consumable resource.

Cotopaxi (1862) by Frederic Edwin Church enchants the viewer in a way not dissimilar to the way Jackson's cinematic interpretation of Middle-earth does

By showing us the beauty of trees and mountains in a fantastical "secondary world," Tolkien and Jackson invite us to see them with fresh eyes and return to our own trees and mountains with a greater sense of wonder. They help us recover our sense of wonder at the long, slow lives of the Redwoods through the Ents, to enchant us with our own vegetable and flower gardens by their reflection in the Hobbits' Shire. But *The Lord of the Rings* does not just show us nature as beautiful; it shows us ways of relating to nature as desirable and attractive too. We are enchanted by farming, by forestry, and by horsemanship, and just as clearly, we are disenchanted with extractive industry, with greed, and with "delving too deeply" (as the Dwarves of Moria did). We are repulsed by the spoiling of nature in the vainglorious pursuit of power. By making this move, Tolkien and Jackson invite us to belong to the enchanted world.

But there is also a major gap in the natural world that is presented in this enchanting way. While the constant sweeping views of diverse landscapes and ecotones make the films feel at times like an installment of *Planet Earth*, the camera never closes in on any busy little creatures for Attenborough to narrate. Once noticed, the paucity of wildlife is quite striking. For the most part, the animals encountered are either domesticated (horses and oliphaunts), evil (giant spiders, crebain, the lake kraken), or both (wargs). Perhaps this is a matter of Tolkien's context. Most megafauna had long been banished from the forests of Britain, and while wolves had received some positive reappraisal among ecologists at the time he wrote, they were not yet so fully reenchanted in the public imagination as they are today. Dickerson and Evans suggest that Tolkien's negative characterization of wolves in particular "is based on old traditions in folk-lore, medieval legend, fairy tales, Norse mythology" (Dickerson and Evans 2011, p. 266). But they also express bafflement at the general absence of wildlife, given the otherwise deep attention to nature as more than setting.

This absence is a significant weakness in the environmental argument of the films. The decline and loss of wildlife are major dimensions of the environmental crisis; it was in Tolkien's day, and it still is in Jackson's day. The hard-learned lessons of the value of even predators and the folly of the extensive extermination programs aimed at them are well captured in Gandalf's counsel: "Do not be too eager to deal out death and judgment. Even the very wise cannot see all ends." There is a real missed potential to include wildlife in nature that is already so much more than a mere setting. If immersion in the fantasy world of Middle-earth is really meant to leave the viewer with a richer appreciation of the more than human world and ready to reconsider their relationship to it, then wildlife is a major part of what needs more appreciation and reimagined ways of living with, a major part of what needs to be "recovered" in Tolkien's terms.

The eagles are the exception to this, and they point in a promising direction. The eagles do not fit neatly into the person/animal dichotomy. They are almost another race, ambiguously accessible through language yet neither forsaking any animality nor accepting any anthropomorphism. This is a small touch of the kind of enchantment and reimagining that might easily have been more abundant and developed throughout the work, focused as it is on the enchantment and recovery of trees, mountains, and rivers.

The final aspect of the environmental argument of the films is found in the place it makes for struggle, action, and even hope, even in the face of the horrors of Mordor, where "the blasted and poisoned landscape ... is as much evidence of Sauron's moral nullity as it is ecological commentary" (Curry 1997, p. 111). For those of us in environmental education—who focus continually on the overwhelming tragedies of climate change and biodiversity loss, who visit and revisit lands destroyed by greed—the words of Galadriel to the Fellowship are most haunting, "in all lands love is now mingled with grief." To be enchanted by the more than human world, to be a lover of trees and of all green and growing things, is also to be vulnerable to loss, to feeling powerless in the face of their relentless destruction. We must tend to our own grief and the grief of our students without losing heart. And the words of Gandalf, given to Frodo in the mines of Moria as he bemoans his fate to bear the Ring ("I wish none of this had happened"), are as apt as any counsel given in the face of these calamities: "So do all who live to see such times. But that is not for them to decide. All we have to decide is what to do with the time that is given to us." Notably, when Frodo later remembers these words on the banks of the Anduin, made even more pointed by an overlay of the Hobbits' orchestral theme ("Concerning Hobbits"), he hears Gandalf's phrasing as a direct address: "All *you* have to decide is what to do with the time that is given to *you*." Indeed, they are an address to each of us. DiPaolo asserts that "we are all called to act like real-world analogues of Frodo in the great ecological endeavor of our time" (Di Paolo 2018, p. 50).

Even though many of the characters, from Samwise to Treebeard, belong to beautiful places, where they dwell in respectful and affectionate ways with the land around them, this address does not allow them to remain there. Andrew Light gives an account of what he calls the "green time" of the Ents and Tom Bombadil. Alluding to, without directly citing, Aldo Leopold's "Thinking Like a Mountain," the lesson he suggests we learn from these "green-time" beings is to "try to similarly empathize with the nature of our planet whenever possible and to defend it when it needs defending" (p. 162). Or in Sam's words, "There's some good in this world, Mr. Frodo. And it's worth fighting for." This framing is significant because it does not limit the scope of resistance to struggle on behalf of the *peoples* of Middle-earth. What is good in Sam's world and ours is expansive and diverse, including peoples, mountains, rivers, and, of course, trees.

The members of the Fellowship respond directly to this call to perform brave and sacrificial acts of resistance with the time that is given to them, proving that their love is more than selfish possession by saving the world for others (as evinced by Frodo's words as he departs Middle-earth). In getting the viewer to cheer and celebrate, and in a profound sense to live through, the struggle of ordinary Hobbits against terrible destructive powers, Tolkien and Jackson inevitably leave us weighing what we ought to do with the time we are given. They give us admirable models for what it is to keep going, even when there is, in Gandalf's words, "just a fool's hope." For it is in the face of despair, when we must hope *against* hope, for the fate of humanity and the very earth itself, that we can truly see this virtue for what it is—that which allows us to hold on to the possibility that, even in the darkest of times, "A new day will come. And when the Sun shines, it will shine out the clearer," as Sam says in voice-over near the end of *The Two Towers*.

The kind of hope that is necessary to confront a world well on its way toward Isengard or Mordor, to engage in the kind of active resistance to environmental devastation that we see in *The Lord of the Rings* and in our "primary world," is not naïve or unmerited optimism—the simple, native good cheer of the untested hobbits early in the text and films. It must first, rather, see the situation for what it is—as Sam and the others come to do in the course of the Quest—while still holding open the possibilities for what it might be. This is not, though, the grim determination in the face of certain defeat that Tolkien and his friend C.S. Lewis so loved in the Northern sagas but rather something even more powerful, what we might call a willingness to look for the possibility of a happy ending, counter to all expectations: in Tolkien's famous coinage, this is the "eucatastrophe," or sudden, unexpected joyful turn in a narrative that is the hallmark of a "complete" fairy-tale, its most powerful consolation, and its highest function (Tolkien 1966, pp. 68–70). Indeed, the angle and placement of the bloom on the White Tree that we discussed above suggest that this kind of hope may be a supra- or even counterrational expectation, from the perspective we currently occupy. The virtue of the kind of enchantment, recovery, and even "consolation" we have been considering here is that it can help us refresh ourselves with possibility, even in the face of despair, inspiring or infusing hope to continue our own fight—even if (or precisely because) it is, in Tolkien's oft-cited words, a "Hope without guarantees" (Tolkien 2006, p. 237).

End Notes

1. See for instance *Reader's Digest* (https://www.rd.com/list/books-read-before-die/), PBS' "The Great American Read" (https://www.pbs.org/the-great-american-read/results/), Waterstone's Book of the Century (https://www.librarything.com/bookaward/Waterstones+Books+of+the+Century) BBC's "Nation's Best-loved Book) (https://www.librarything.com/bookaward/BBC%27s+Big+Read). *Business Insider* estimates that *The Fellowship of the Ring* is the third bestselling book of all time (at roughly 150 million), excluding religious texts such as the Bible (https://www.businessinsider.com/guides/learning/best-selling-books-of-all-time#-1)
2. See, e.g., Kreeft (2005), Coutras (2016), and McIntosh (2017), several significant philosophical studies of Tolkien that also utilize a distinctively theological hermeneutic. A continuing debate in the Tolkien literature is how (and indeed whether) to balance what appears to be the Christian and "pagan" aspects of Tolkien's work in readings. Testi (2018) attempts a synthetic "Catholic" philosophical reading.
3. The essays in Arduini and Testi (2014) record the paucity of treatments overall, some consideration of why that might be the case, and potentially productive areas for further inquiry.
4. We generally follow the convention—inconsistently observed both in Tolkien scholarship and by Tolkien himself—of capitalizing the names of races of "Speaking Peoples" (e.g., Elves, Hobbits, and "Men"—in Tolkien's usage meaning the human species), while individuals or groups (e.g., a hobbit or hobbits) are left uncapitalized.
5. Delving even deeper into Tolkien's legendarium, we find a significant statement of ecological 'relationality' in Chapter 2 of *The Silmarillion*, "Of Aulë and Yavanna." In a lengthy discussion there between these two Valar or "powers"

(Middle-earth's syncretic 'gods' or angelic beings) about the status of the created world and the relation of Elves, Men, and Dwarves to it, Aulë notes that "though the things of thy realm have worth in themselves, and would have worth if no Children were to come, yet Eru ["the One," or God] will give them dominion, and they shall use all that they find in Arda: though not, by the purpose of Eru, without respect or without gratitude." Yavanna, speaking on behalf of all other living things, notes that while animals "can flee or defend themselves," those rooted to one spot cannot do so. Pleading therefore for an advocate for all green and growing things, she asserts that "all have their worth...and each contributes to the worth of others ... [but] among these I hold trees dear." Eru's positive response to this plea represents the origin of both the great Eagles and the Ents (Tolkien 1977, p. 43).

6. The most important monographs, in our view, include Curry (1997), Dickerson and Evans (2011), and Jeffers (2014). Several works have been published in the last few years, as both ecocriticism and the examination of climate fiction or "cli-fi" have come to prominence in literary studies: cf. Brawley (2007), Campbell (2011), Simonson (2015) and Di Paolo (2018).

7. Only a small handful of articles in the most important contemporary journals that are dedicated at least in part to Tolkien's works have a significant focus on environmental issues, including Brisbois (2005), Davis (2008), Cohen (2009), Simpson (2017), Hjulstad (2020), Danielson (2021), and Parrila (2021) (note the recent acceleration). A couple of significant earlier short studies include Niiler (1999), Flieger (2000), Chapter 6 ("In Defense of Nature") of Petty (2003) (pp. 219–243), and particularly Siewers (2005), who argues for the "early Celtic (really Welsh and Irish) Otherworld" as "a pattern for an ecocentric Middle-earth" (p. 140). We see none of overriding significance in either the *Journal of Inklings Studies* or *VII: Journal of the Marion E. Wade Center*. Three anthologies in English take an explicitly philosophical lens to Tolkien's works. Arduini and Testi (2014) includes a series of essays from a 2010 conference on that topic, though none of these touch on our current theme. Both Bassham and Bronson (2003) and Bassham and Bronson (2012) are written for a more general audience, and only a single essay from these two texts focuses on broadly environmental issues, that of Andrew Light (2003).

8. In the same way, Mordor is ultimately a reflection of the blighted landscapes that Morgoth—Sauron's master and the original dark enemy of Tolkien's legendarium—made of the far north of Middle-earth in the wars of the First Age: a "burned and desolate waste, full of choking dust, barren and lifeless" (Tolkien 1977, p. 181).

References

Arduini, Roberto, and Claudio Testi, eds. 2014. *Tolkien and philosophy*. Walking Tree: Zurich and Jena.

Bassham, Gregory, and Eric Bronson, eds. 2003. *The lord of the rings and philosophy: One book to rule them all*. Chicago: Open Court.

———, eds. 2012. *The hobbit and philosophy: For when you've lost your dwarves, your wizard, and your way*. Wiley-Blackwell: Malden.
Bookchin, Murray. 1993. What is social ecology? In *Environmental philosophy: From animal rights to radical ecology*, ed. Michael Zimmerman et al., 354–373. Engelwood Cliffs: Prentice Hall.
Brawley, Chris. 2007. The fading of the world: Tolkien's ecology and loss in *The Lord of the Rings*. *Journal of the Fantastic in the Arts* 18 (3): 292–307.
Brisbois, Michael J. 2005. Tolkien's imaginary nature: An analysis of the structure of middle-earth. *Tolkien Studies* 2: 197–216.
Campbell, Liam. 2011. *The ecological augury in the works of J.R.R. Tolkien*. Zurich and Jena: Walking Tree.
———. 2014. Nature. In *A companion to J. R. R. Tolkien*, ed. Stuart D. Lee, 431–445. Malden: Wiley-Blackwell.
Cohen, Cynthia. 2009. The unique representation of trees in *The Lord of the Rings*. *Tolkien Studies* 6: 91–125.
Coutras, Lisa. 2016. *Tolkien's theology of beauty: Majesty, splendor, and transcendence in middle-earth*. New York: Palgrave Macmillan.
Curry, Patrick. 1997. *Defending middle-earth: Tolkien, myth, and modernity*. New York: St. Martin's Press.
Danielson, Stentor. 2021. 'To trees all men are orcs': The environmental ethic of J.R.R. Tolkien's'The new shadow'. *Tolkien Studies* 18: 179–194.
Davis, James G. 2008. Showing Saruman as Faber: Tolkien and Peter Jackson. *Tolkien Studies* 5: 55–72.
Di Paolo, Marc. 2018. *Fire and snow: Climate fiction from the inklings to game of thrones*. Albany: State University of New York Press.
Dickerson, Matthew, and Jonathan Evans. 2011. *Ents, Elves, and Eriador: The environmental vision of J.R.R. Tolkien*. Lexington: University of Kentucky Press.
Flieger, Verlyn. 2000. Taking the part of the trees. In *J.R.R. Tolkien and his literary resonances*, ed. George Clark and Daniel Timmons, 147–158. Westport: Greenwood Press.
Hargrove, Eugene C. 1996. *Foundations of environmental ethics. Prentice-Hall, 1989*. Denton: Environmental Ethics Books, reprint.
Hjulstad, Katrine L.A. 2020. The tale of the old forest: The damaging effects of forestry in J.R.R. Tolkien's written words. *Journal of Tolkien Research* 10: 2. Available at: https://scholar.valpo.edu/journaloftolkienresearch/vol10/iss2/7.
Jackson, Peter. [Director] 2001. *The Lord of the Rings: The fellowship of the ring*, extended edition. [Motion picture].
———. [Director] 2002. *The Lord of the Rings: The two towers*, extended edition. [Motion picture].
———. [Director] 2003. *The Lord of the Rings: The return of the king*, extended edition. [Motion picture].
Jeffers, Susan. 2014. *Arda inhabited: Environmental relationships in The Lord of the Rings*. Kent State UP: Kent.
Kierkegaard, Søren. 1980. *The concept of anxiety: A simple psychologically orienting deliberation on the dogmatic issue of hereditary sin*. Ed. and Trans. with Introduction and notes by Reidar Thomte and Albert B. Anderson. Kierkegaard's Writings, vol. 8. Princeton: Princeton University Press.
Kreeft, Peter. 2005. *The philosophy of Tolkien. The worldview behind "The Lord of the Rings"*. San Francisco: Ignatius Press.
Leopold, Aldo. 1949. *A Sand County almanac and sketches here and there*. New York: Oxford University Press.
Lewis, C.S. 1947. *The abolition of man*. New York: Macmillan.
Light, Andrew. 2003. Tolkien's green time: Environmental themes in *The Lord of the Rings*. In *The Lord of the rings and philosophy*, 150–164.
Madsen, Catherine. 2004. Light from an invisible lamp: Natural religion in *The Lord of the Rings*. In *Tolkien and the invention of myth*, ed. Jane Chance, 35–47. Lexington: University of Kentucky Press.

McIntosh, Jonathan. 2017. *The flame imperishable: Tolkien, St. Thomas, and the metaphysics of faerie*. Kettering: Angelico Press.

Niiler, Lucas. 1999. Green reading: Tolkien, Leopold and the land ethic. *Journal of the Fantastic in the Arts* 10 (3): 276–285.

Parrila, Sofia. 2021. All worthy things: The personhood of nature in J.R.R. Tolkien's legendarium. *Mythlore* 40.1 (139): 5–20.

Parrish, Robin. "The hobbit's bag end really exists – In Peter Jackson's Basement," TechTimes, July 1, 2015. https://www.techtimes.com/articles/65273/20150701/hobbit-bag-end-really-exists-peter-jackson-basement.htm

Petty, Anne. 2003. *Tolkien in the land of heroes: Discovering the human spirit*. Cold Spring Harbor: Cold Spring Press.

Plumwood, Val. 1993. *Feminism and the mastery of nature*. London: Routledge.

Shippey, Tom. 2004. Another road to middle-earth: Jackson's movie trilogy. In *Understanding the Lord of the rings: The best of Tolkien criticism*, ed. Rose A. Zimbardo and Neil D. Isaacs, 233–254. Boston and New York: Houghton Mifflin.

Siewers, Alfred. 2005. Tolkien's cosmic-Christian ecology: The medieval underpinnings. In *Tolkien's modern middle ages*, ed. Jane Chance and Alfred Siewers, 139–153. New York: Palgrave Macmillan.

Simonson, Martin, ed. 2015. *Representations of nature in middle-earth*. Walking Tree: Zurich and Jena.

Simpson, Eleanor R. 2017. The evolution of J.R.R. Tolkien's portrayal of nature: Foreshadowing anti-speciesism. *Tolkien Studies* 14: 71–89.

Testi, Claudio. 2018. *Pagan saints in middle-earth*. Walking Tree: Zurich and Jena.

Thoreau, Henry David. 2009. In *The Maine woods: A fully annotated edition*, ed. Jeffrey S. Cramer. New Haven: Yale University Press.

Tolkien, J.R.R. 1966. On fairy-stories. In *The Tolkien reader*, 3–84. New York: Ballantine.

———. 1977. In *The Silmarillion*, ed. Christopher Tolkien. New York: Ballantine.

———. 1996. In *The peoples of middle-earth. The history of middle-earth 9*, ed. Christopher Tolkien. London: HarperCollins.

———. 2004. *The Lord of the Rings*. 50th Anniversary one volume edition. Boston and New York: Houghton Mifflin.

———. 2006. *The letters of J.R.R. Tolkien*, ed. Humphrey Carpenter, rev. ed. London: HarperCollins.

Weston, Anthony. 2003. Beyond intrinsic value: Pragmatism in environmental ethics. In *Environmental ethics: An anthology*, ed. Andrew Light and Holmes Rolston III, 307–317. Oxford: Blackwell.

Star Wars as Philosophy: A Genealogy of the Force

35

Jason T. Eberl

Contents

Introduction	856
The Light and Dark Sides in the Original Trilogy	857
Manichaean "Light" Versus "Dark"	857
Confronting Evil Within Oneself	859
The Possibility of Redemption	860
Good and Evil as a "Point of View" in the Prequel Trilogy	862
Evil as a "Phantom Menace"	862
Seeking the "Knowledge of Good and Evil": Hubris and the Will to Power	862
Evil as "Inordinate Desire"	864
The Fall and Rise of the Force in the Sequel Trilogy	866
A Disenchanted Galaxy	866
Confronting Evil with Evil: Luke's Shame and Despair	867
True Balance: Appropriating Power for Good	868
Conclusion	870
End Notes	871
References	871

Abstract

Are good and evil a "point of view"? Do Jedi and Sith alike merely crave greater power? What does a "space opera" have to teach us about how to live virtuously? George Lucas created *Star Wars* as a modern-day morality tale, modeled on classical epics, such as Homer's *Iliad* and *Odyssey*, tragic dramas written by the likes of Sophocles, Seneca, and Shakespeare, and the scriptures that inspire religions in the East and West. This chapter canvasses the metaphysical and moral themes across the three trilogies that make up the "Skywalker saga" to construct a genealogy of how "the Force" evolved throughout these films. At the

---

J. T. Eberl (✉)
Center for Health Care Ethics, Saint Louis University, St. Louis, MO, USA
e-mail: jason.eberl@slu.edu

© Springer Nature Switzerland AG 2024
D. K. Johnson et al. (eds.), *The Palgrave Handbook of Popular Culture as Philosophy*,
https://doi.org/10.1007/978-3-031-24685-2_21

heart of this conceptual development is the question of how the light and dark sides of the Force are related to each other and what that relationship can help us understand about the nature of good and evil in our own experience.

Keywords

Star Wars · Jedi · Sith · Augustine · Friedrich Nietzsche · Friedrich Schelling · C. S. Lewis · Disenchantment · Free will · The Force · Good · Evil · Manichaeism · God · George Lucas · Stoicism · Redemption · Love · Nihilism · Pride · Will to power · Inordinate desire · Charles Taylor · Despair · *ch'i*

Introduction

Are the Jedi good and the Sith evil? This question appears silly to ask within the context of *Star Wars* where the answer seems quite obvious, especially considering George Lucas's original intention for the saga to be a "space opera" harkening back to his childhood viewings of *Flash Gordon* and other Saturday-matinee serials in the 1940s and early 1950s. At a time just after the USA and its Allies had defeated the Axis powers of Nazi Germany and Imperial Japan and the Cold War with the Soviet Union was emerging, there was no question of who wore the "white hats" and the "black hats." Lucas incorporated relevant imagery into his cinematic portrayal of a dominant Empire seeking to crush an "insignificant Rebellion," even casting British actors to fill the ranks of Imperial officers to remind American audiences of what their revolutionary forbearers had fought against two centuries prior; after all, *A New Hope* premiered a year after the US Bicentennial.

Not content with merely a political/military battle between the forces of tyrannical imperialism and democratic republicanism, Lucas added a religious/spiritual element to the conflict with the concept of "the Force" and its perpetually adversarial adherents: the Jedi and the Sith. Though Lucas characterized these two groups as aligning themselves with either the "light side" or the "dark side" of the Force, it's important to emphasize that these are two *sides* of the *same* Force. We can thus ask, given that the Force doesn't take sides between them but allows both to utilize its power for their respective purposes, are the Jedi and the Sith really all that different from each other? This question prompts additional ones, such as what it means for the Force to have a "will"; whether only specially "chosen ones" may wield its power to the greatest degree and how they are so chosen; and, perhaps most significantly, what it means for the Force to be in a state of "balance"?

These are questions which any member of the 501st Legion would gleefully spend hours debating in online chat forums or with fellow conventioneers at one's local comic con. But they're also of general importance even for those who haven't imaginatively traveled to "a galaxy far, far away." For the Force stands-in for various philosophical and religious concepts that have influenced the thought of professional philosophers, theologians, politicians, and the general public throughout human history. That's why *Star Wars* is so popular, even among those who readily admit that a beam of light can't stop three feet from its source and be capable of cutting through transparisteel or that a parsec is a unit of distance not time. (Many thanks, by the way, to the writers of *Solo: A Star Wars Story* for retconning an explanation for that sloppy line of dialogue!) It's useless to ponder the physics of *Star Wars* and even more frustrating to reflect upon how the various biological lifeforms it depicts could've evolved on their respective worlds – just think for a minute about how natural selection would have resulted in Jabba the Hutt! The *ideology* of *Star Wars*, however, the fundamental battle of good versus evil at both personal and galactic levels is indeed a story worth telling and retelling as we're seemingly never able to learn the lessons from our own history about how we should morally conduct ourselves to create a society that ensures the freedom of all and promotes the universal common good.

This, I submit, is the argument Lucas originally intended when he penned the initial draft for "The Adventures of Luke Starkiller, From the Journal of the Whills."[1] Furthermore, while additional creative minds have shaped the *Star Wars* universe beyond Lucas's original vision, the overarching question all of them have struggled with is how good and evil may co-exist within a morally complex universe. We will examine each of the three trilogies that constitute the "Skywalker saga" to understand how the various writers and directors involved – Lucas, Brackett, Kasdan, Kershnar, Marquand, Abrams, Arndt, Johnson, and Terrio – have wrestled with this fundamental question that has also underwritten much philosophical and theological discourse to which connections will be drawn. We'll proceed in the order that each trilogy was created, starting with the Original Trilogy in the late 1970s and early 1980s, moving on to the Prequel Trilogy in the late 1990s and early 2000s, and concluding with the Sequel Trilogy in the late 2010s.

The Light and Dark Sides in the Original Trilogy

Manichaean "Light" Versus "Dark"

"Vader was seduced by the dark side of the Force." So does Obi-Wan Kenobi sum up the fall of Anakin Skywalker that we'll detail later on. In its first mention to screen audiences, the Force is presented in its dichotomous nature: a "light side," the power of which is wielded by the honorable-in-defeat Jedi Knights, and the "dark side" that now dominates the galaxy. The notion that there's some sort of cosmic battle between the forces of light and darkness, in which human beings are caught in the middle and have to choose sides, has had a long history in religious and metaphysical thought. One of the most stark representations of this dual vision of reality stems from the Manichees, a Persian mystical sect that had a profound influence on near-Eastern thinking. Indeed, their influence reached even to the Roman Empire of the fourth century where Augustine of Hippo was initially entranced by it. Manichaeism promotes a cosmic vision in which only the immaterial, spiritual world is good and evil is manifest in the material world of death, destruction, and fleshly desires. Such a spiritual worldview leads to an extreme asceticism in which everything that is of the body is eschewed for the sake of the spirit. This Manichaean thread is evident in *The Empire Strikes Back* when Yoda pinches Luke Skywalker's shoulder and proclaims, "Luminous beings are we, not this crude matter!"

Yet, there is something wrong with this extreme form of dualism, both within itself and as a definitive understanding of the nature of the Force. On its own merits, Manichaeism falls victim to various critiques launched by Augustine and others. One criticism concerns why one ought to posit the existence of dual metaphysical realities – along with personifications of each as deities locked in an eternal cosmic struggle – if one could account for good and evil by positing the existence of only *one* source of goodness, with evil as a *privation* (or lack) of goodness.[2] This is the route Augustine takes. Although he understands the difference between "good" and "evil" to refer to a real, objective distinction in moral value, these words don't refer to distinct types of *entities*. Rather, Augustine claims that there's only *one* reality, which is intrinsically good. Evil doesn't exist in itself, but only as a lack of goodness – just as, analogously, blindness is nothing other than a lack of the power of sight:

> For what is that which we call evil but the absence of good? In the bodies of animals, disease and wounds mean nothing but the absence of health; for when a cure is effected, that does not mean that the evils which were present – namely, the diseases and wounds – go away from the body and dwell elsewhere: they altogether cease to exist. Just in the same way, what are called vices in the soul are nothing but privations of natural good. And when they are cured, they are not transferred elsewhere: when they cease to exist in the healthy soul, they cannot exist anywhere else. (Augustine 1955, ch. III, §11; ch. IV, §14)

The question remains though of what *causes* evil if it's not some sort of malevolent deity. Certainly it can't be the same as the cause of goodness, as Augustine shows through a series of rhetorical questions:

> Where then does evil come from since the good God made everything good?[3] Certainly the greatest and supreme Good made lesser goods; yet the Creator and all he created are good. What then is the origin of evil? Is it that the matter from which he made things was somehow evil? [the Manichaean answer] He gave it form and order, but did he leave in it an element which he could not transform into good? If so, why? Was he powerless to turn and transform all matter so that no evil remained, even though God is omnipotent? (Augustine 1998, bk. VII, para. 7)

Augustine's answer is that *we* are the cause of evil: humans. Of course, if he lived in the *Star Wars* universe, he would have also included Wookies, Mon Calamari, Hutts – any being, really, that can reason and exercise *free will*. But we'll return to this idea later.

As an interpretation of the Force, Manichaeism fails to account for Yoda's statement, almost immediately after the earlier dualistic quotation, in which he affirms Obi-Wan's description of the Force as "an energy field created by all living things. It surrounds us and penetrates us. It binds the galaxy together." Yoda similarly locates the Force *spatially* "between you and me, the tree, the rock, *everywhere*." Lucas, in *The Phantom Menace*, reduces the spiritual nature of the

Force even further when he controversially describes "midi-chlorians" as material beings residing in the cells of all living things that allow them to commune with the Force. The charge is often leveled by critics that Lucas *materialized* the Force as a biological phenomenon, but this is a mischaracterization: the midi-chlorians aren't the manifestation of the Force itself, but rather that through which living beings are able to experience the Force. Nevertheless, it's still anti-Manichaean to conceive of the Force as being anything but purely *immaterial*, which raises the question of how a purely immaterial Force could interact causally with the material world. Yet, we see innumerable instances of Jedi and Sith using the Force to manipulate material objects: from Anakin playing with his food in *Attack of the Clones* to Yoda raising Luke's X-Wing out of the Dagobah swamp in *The Empire Strikes Back* to Rey "lifting rocks" in *The Last Jedi*.

Confronting Evil Within Oneself

If the Force isn't representative of an otherworldly conflict between the material and immaterial, then perhaps the conflict resides in *oneself*. This is certainly the lesson Luke is meant to learn when enters the cave on Dagobah and confronts an apparition of Darth Vader. Lashing out offensively with his lightsaber, Luke viciously decapitates Vader, only to discover that the masked face of his opponent is *his own*. Of course, this vision also portends the revelation of Luke's parentage, but the primary lesson is that the darkness that consumed Vader could just as easily consume Luke, especially as he shares his father's impetuous and hardheaded nature. Seeing a vision of Han and Leia suffering on Bespin, Luke decides he must go to them despite the warnings of Yoda and Obi-Wan that he's not ready. Vader, knowing his son as well as he knows himself, tortures Han in order to reach his son through his friend's suffering.

As we know, Luke falls for the trap – despite his more prudent sister's last-minute warning – and suffers both physically and existentially when he learns who sired him. Until that terrible revelation, Vader had been the personification of evil for Luke – the malevolent entity responsible for the deaths of his aunt, uncle, and best friend (Biggs Darklighter), not to mention, according to Obi-Wan, his father, amidst countless other atrocities. Vader embodies evil from Luke's perspective at this point even more so than the Emperor, whom Luke hasn't encountered and even the audience has only briefly seen by hologram. Vader's masked and caped form with flaming red sword, particularly when he flies down the stairs in the carbon-freeze chamber on Bespin, serves to cement his place as a neo-Gothic, postmodern incarnation of the Devil himself. To learn that Vader is his father immediately *humanizes* Vader, renders him, to Luke at least, as just a man – or, more pitiably, someone who is "more machine now than man." This revelation opens dual possibilities: Vader's redemption or Luke's corruption.

Just as Vader fell to the dark side, which we'll discuss in detail later, Luke himself could fall as first Vader and later the Emperor tempt him to do. And, if Luke did fall, it would be for apparently the noblest of reasons: to defeat evil out of righteous hatred. Vader tempts Luke by promising that together they could destroy the Emperor, the *true* source of galactic evil; the Emperor himself goads Luke to "strike me down with all of your hatred and your journey towards the dark side will be complete!" (He'll later challenge Rey to do the same.) But why would it be evil for Luke (or Rey) to destroy evil?

Augustine's answer is twofold. First, echoing other philosophers such as Plato and Seneca, it's not that it would be evil to destroy evil, but one must do so for the right reasons, with the right motivation. The right motivation is that of *justice*, restoring proper order – *balance*, as it were – to the moral universe, but not *passion*. Plato (1991, bk. II, 375a–376c) argues that a harmonious soul is one in which reason masters one's passions: one should seek justice *rationally*, not striking out in anger or hatred. Seneca goes further in contending that anger is useless and inherently corruptive; it cannot be controlled but only suppressed:

> The best course is to reject at once the first incitement to anger, to resist even its small beginnings, and to take pains to avoid falling into anger. For if it begins to lead us astray, the return to the safe path is difficult, since, if once we admit the emotion and by our own free will grant it any authority, reason becomes of no avail; after that it will do, not whatever you let it, but whatever it chooses. (Seneca 1928, pp. 126–127)

Seneca's *stoicism* finds a voice in Yoda's teaching: "Anger, fear, aggression, the dark side are they. If once you start down the dark path, forever will it dominate your destiny. Consume you it will." We can see Seneca and Yoda's point in the various occasions in which Anakin/Vader lashes out in uncontrolled anger: first in slaughtering the Sand People who kidnapped his mother, including the women and children, and then later in Force-choking Padmé, his beloved for whom he sold his soul to the dark side, when he thinks she's in league with Obi-Wan. (For further discussion of stoic philosophy in *Star Wars*, see Stephens (2005) and Hummel (2016).)

The Possibility of Redemption

The second part of Augustine's response for why it would be wrong for Luke (or Rey) to strike down Palpatine in anger is that, while evil ought to be fought against, evil *persons* are just as much victims as those whom they harm or destroy. Recall that, for Augustine, evil is a privation, a lack of goodness. He also holds the neo-Platonic view that goodness and *being* are co-extensive – meaning that to the extent that something exists, it is good, and vice versa. Thus, no one can be *absolutely* evil, for that would entail total non-existence. Even the most evil person can be an object of love and should not be destroyed out of hatred. Yet, Palpatine's corruption certainly comes close to being total, embodying, as he proclaims to Rey, "*all* of the Sith!" Nevertheless, even Palpatine is just a mortal being who, in *The Rise of Skywalker*, requires cloning technology and an elaborate apparatus to stay alive until he's able to drain the life force from Rey and Ben. Ironically, Augustine would say that Palpatine is an even more pitiable creature when his power is fully restored than when his potentially salvageable humanity was more evident in his weakened, dependent state.

Vader, too, lives most of his life in a weakened state; he is dependent on technology and frequent bacta treatments to stay alive after his defeat on Mustafar. Although Vader certainly seems powerful as he tears through Rebel troopers at the end of *Rogue One* or decimates the ranks of Imperial officers who constantly disappoint him, the fact that the Force imbues all *living* beings means that Vader's mechanization has certainly diminished his power; this is why, after all, the Emperor is keen to replace Vader with Luke and later tells Kylo Ren that he can have more power than his grandfather ever could. Vader's weakness, though, is also his greatest strength insofar as it serves as a constant reminder of what he's lost: Padmé, his friendships with Obi-Wan and his own padawan Ahsoka Tano, and the life he could've led if he'd remained a Jedi. While such reminders can be a source of despair, as when Vader confesses to Luke on Endor that "It is too late for me, son," Vader's lamentable psyche also opens up the possibility of his redemption when his capacity to love is re-awakened as he confronts yet another loss: his son.

"I feel the good in you, the conflict." Just as Vader could read and anticipate Luke's reaction when he tortured Han on Cloud City, Luke understands his father and the motivations that led him to the dark side. As we'll explore the next section, *love* is what led to Anakin's corruption and what also leads to his *salvation*. Augustine believes that love, when directed toward God, is an *eternal good*. He ranks the virtue of love directed toward God as the highest of all virtues, even more so than faith in God or hope for eternal life:

> For when we ask whether someone is a good man, we are not asking what he believes, or hopes, but what he loves. Now, beyond all doubt, he who loves aright believes and hopes rightly. Likewise, he who does not love believes in vain, even if what he believes is true; he hopes in vain, even if what he hopes for is generally agreed to pertain to true happiness, unless he believes and hopes for this: that he may through prayer obtain the gift of love. (Augustine 1955, ch. XXXI, §117)

While love for God is paramount in Augustine's view, it extends to other persons since God loves them as well. There's thus nothing wrong with Anakin loving Padmé or Rey loving Ben, so long as that love is *rightly ordered*. So, a sign of a depraved moral character would be found in someone who lacks an appropriate love for others. Anakin *inordinately* desires his beloved's life, which leads him to a life of tremendous evil. In the end, though, he hasn't lost the capacity to love properly and thus, as Padmé and Luke both sense, "There is still good in him."

Good and Evil as a "Point of View" in the Prequel Trilogy

Evil as a "Phantom Menace"

One way that evil manifests itself in the *Star Wars* saga is by *not* manifesting itself, but rather operating hidden in the shadows. The Sith, having been nearly wiped out by the Jedi a millennium ago, adopted a "Rule of Two" in which a master and an apprentice, who eventually kills the master and then takes on their own apprentice, maintain the Sith legacy in secret until the time is right to reveal themselves. This notion of evil as a "phantom menace" is aptly captured by the fantasy writer C. S. Lewis in *The Screwtape Letters*. In this brief text, a "minor demon" named Wormwood asks his uncle, Screwtape, for advice on how to corrupt a virtuous young man. His experienced uncle advises him that "it is essential to keep the patient in ignorance of your own existence" (Lewis 1982, p. 19). Part of the reason for remaining hidden is that it is easier to morally corrupt someone if they don't believe that there are spiritual forces at work in the world; the more "materialist" and "skeptical" one is the better, as such attitudes may lead one to *moral nihilism*. We'll see later how a "disenchanted" and nihilistic world sets the stage for the final battle between good and evil in the sequel trilogy.

Another advantage of the Sith remaining hidden is that it fosters *complacency* on the part of the Jedi. When Obi-Wan complains about Anakin's arrogance in *Attack of the Clones*, Yoda laments it is "a flaw more and more common among Jedi. Too sure of themselves they are. Even the older, more experienced ones." Later, Palpatine taunts Yoda that his arrogance has blinded him; and Yoda and Mace Windu admit in private their blindness and diminished capacity to use the Force. For a millennium, the Jedi haven't had to face any existential threats, all the while setting the stage for their greatest enemy to re-emerge.

Seeking the "Knowledge of Good and Evil": Hubris and the Will to Power

It's a common aphorism from the Bible that the love of money is the root of all evil (1 Timothy 6:10), but another candidate for this dubious title is *pride*. Consider the story – whether one takes it as truth or myth – of the Fall of the primordial humans, Adam and Eve. A standard interpretation of the story is that Adam and Eve were cast out of the paradisiacal Garden of Eden because they disobeyed God. What's important to realize, though, is *why* they disobeyed God. In the Garden, Adam and Eve were provided with everything they needed to live, be happy, and "multiply." They were forbade only from eating the fruit of one particular tree, the Tree of Knowledge of Good and Evil. As the story goes, a wily serpent convinces them to eat the fruit by assuring them that they will "become like gods" themselves. This is the sin of pride, of *hubris*, of reaching beyond one's means. When Luke shoots down his first TIE fighter and exclaims, "I got him!" Han immediately shoots back, "Great, kid! Don't get cocky!" Han understands from experience the difference between skill and luck, and that even the skillful are sometimes unlucky.

Luke's father, Anakin, is also quite prideful. Even as a young boy, he dreams that he will some day have the power to free all the slaves on Tatooine and boasts of his mechanical skill in building the fastest podracer ever. As a teenage Jedi padawan, he constantly complains that his mentors, especially Obi-Wan, are holding him back out of jealousy that his powers are so far ahead of theirs. Grief-stricken by his mother's violent death, Anakin proclaims to Padmé that he "will become the most powerful Jedi ever" and that he "will even learn to stop people from dying." Palpatine, having spent years stroking Anakin's ego by telling him that he foresees him "becoming the greatest of all the Jedi ... even more powerful than Master Yoda," exhorts, "If one is to understand the great mystery, one must study *all* its aspects, not just the dogmatic narrow view of the Jedi." He then offers the moral *coup de grâce* by tempting Anakin with knowledge of the dark side in order to save Padmé from certain death.

Like Palpatine, Friedrich Nietzsche didn't see pride as a vice, but rather as precisely what those who are "noble" should feel. Nietzsche rejected the Augustinian view of objective values of good (grounded in an essentially good God) and evil (as a privation of goodness) and embraced *moral nihilism*:

> My demand upon the philosopher is known, that he take his stand *beyond* good and evil and leave the illusion of moral judgment *beneath* himself. This demand follows from an insight which I was the first to formulate: that *there are altogether no moral facts*. Moral judgments agree with religious ones in believing in realities which are no realities. Morality is merely an interpretation of certain phenomena – more precisely, a misinterpretation. (Nietzsche 1954b, p. 501)

If good and evil don't exist, what motivates human action? Nietzsche's answer is the "will to power":

> What is good? Everything that heightens the feeling of power in man, the will to power, power itself. What is bad? Everything that is born of weakness. What is happiness? The feeling that power is *growing*, that resistance is overcome. Not contentedness but more power; not peace but war. (Nietzsche 1954a, p. 570)

Nietzsche thus formulates a "genealogy of morals" consisting of an ideological battle between those who are able to exercise their will to power, and thereby glorify themselves, and those who cannot, and thereby disdain the powerful and whatever noble qualities they embody. Nietzsche sees this struggle manifested in the Christian praise of meekness, humility, and other such virtues of the weak while condemning wealth, power, and other virtues of the strong.

Palpatine shares Nietzsche's critique of the "illusion" of concepts such as good and evil and his conclusion of what ultimately drives human behavior:

Anakin   The Jedi use their power for good.
Palpatine Good is a point of view, Anakin. The Sith and the Jedi are similar in almost every way, including their quest for greater power.

Anakin	The Sith rely on their passion for their strength. They think inward, only about themselves.
Palpatine	And the Jedi don't?

Nietzsche's idea of the "noble" person, who ultimately ought to transcend their bestial nature to become an *übermensch* ("overman" or "superman"), aligns with Palpatine's naked desire for "unlimited power." To them, the Jedi have the same ambition and are duplicitous and hypocritical in not acknowledging it, hiding behind arcane concepts of humility and self-abnegation – to the point of denying themselves the joys of romance, which neither Anakin nor Palpatine deny themselves. The Sith, even when hiding their identity, do not refrain from acknowledging their true ambition to themselves. This is enacted in Darth Bane's "Rule of Two": "Two there should be; no more, no less. One to embody power, the other to crave it." This ambition even transcends egoistic concerns, as Palpatine is willing to be sacrificed in *The Rise of Skywalker* in order to ensure that the dark side reigns supreme. Perhaps the Jedi and Sith aren't so different after all. (For further elaboration of Nietzsche's thought in the context of *Star Wars*, see Adams (2016).)

Evil as "Inordinate Desire"

In addition to pride, Anakin's downfall results paradoxically from the same thing that later brings about his redemption: *love*.[4] In *Revenge of the Sith*, though, his love isn't "rightly ordered" for he's willing to sacrifice what Augustine would consider "eternal goods," such as justice and obedience to the will of the Force (standing in for Augustine's concept of God), to save his beloved wife about whom he has a premonition of dying in childbirth. Anakin vows to Padmé that he won't let his vision become real. To that end, he seeks advice from Master Yoda. But instead of offering him a way to save Padmé, Yoda gives him some unexpected and, for Anakin, unsatisfying counsel: "Train yourself to let go of everything you fear to lose." Anakin's reaction makes it clear that he's not going to follow this stoic advice. Later, his other mentor, Palpatine, tempts him by declaring that "the dark side of the Force is a pathway to many abilities some consider to be *unnatural*" – like saving loved ones from dying.

Why is Yoda right and Palpatine wrong? How could it be evil for Anakin to want to save his beloved wife? A man's devotion to his wife and his desire to save her life are in themselves good. What's wrong here isn't the goal Anakin is attempting to achieve, but the *means* he employs. Padmé challenges Anakin on this very point after learning from Obi-Wan that he's turned to the dark side and led the slaughter of the Jedi Temple, including younglings:

Padmé	Anakin, all I want is your love.
Anakin	Love won't save you Padmé, only my new powers can do that.

Padmé   At what cost? You're a good person. Don't do this ... Anakin, you're breaking my heart! You're going down a path I can't follow!

Augustine identifies the source of moral evil as "inordinate desire" for "temporal goods":

> So we are now in a position to ask whether evildoing is anything other than neglecting eternal things, which the mind perceives and enjoys by means of itself and which it cannot lose if it loves them; and instead pursuing temporal things ... as if they were great and marvelous things. It seems to me that all evil deeds – that is, all sins – fall into this one category. (Augustine 1993, bk. I, §16)

We may at first think that the evil depicted in *Revenge of the Sith* is essentially the *actions* Anakin does once he pledges himself to Palpatine. Augustine contends, rather, that what's essentially evil is the *inordinate desire* – in this case, to save Padmé at any cost – that animates such actions. Although Padmé's life is certainly good, it's nevertheless a good bound by time's limits: she was born, and someday, no matter what Anakin does, she will die.

Anakin wants the power to save Padmé. He's clinging to a good that'll always be subject to potential loss. This leads, according to Augustine and Yoda, not only to committing evil deeds out of fear of losing those goods but also to an anguished life:

> All wicked people, just like good people, desire to live without fear. The difference is that the good, in desiring this, turn their love away from things that cannot be possessed without the fear of losing them. The wicked, on the other hand, try to get rid of anything that prevents them from enjoying such things securely. Thus the wicked lead a criminal life, which would be better called death. (Augustine 1993, bk. I, §4)

Augustine's recommendation to turn our love away from transitory goods also includes our friends and family. Yoda gives the same advice to Anakin: "Death is a natural part of life. Rejoice for those around you who transform into the Force. Mourn them do not. Miss them do not."

When Augustine says that "the wicked lead a criminal life, which would be better called death," he isn't condemning such people from a moral "high ground." Instead, his view is based on his psychological analysis of how a person whose moral character is inclined toward inordinate desire – a vice he terms "cupidity" – suffers from an embattled psyche:

> In the meantime cupidity carries out a reign of terror, buffeting the whole human soul and life with storms coming from every direction. Fear attacks from one side and desire from the other; from one side, anxiety; from the other, an empty and deceptive happiness; from one side, the agony of losing what one loved; from the other, the passion to acquire what one did not have; from one side, the pain of an injury received; from the other, the burning desire to avenge it. (Augustine 1993, bk. I, §11)

Anakin's anguished cry upon learning of Padmé's death, as well as his hatred for Obi-Wan as he lay dismembered on the burning sands of Mustafar, makes evident the wisdom Yoda expresses when he first meets Anakin and senses his fear of losing his mother: "Fear is a path to the dark side. Fear leads to anger; anger leads to hate; hate leads to suffering." Not only does Anakin, as Vader, cause tremendous suffering to others, he himself suffers the tragic results of his own inordinate desires.

The Fall and Rise of the Force in the Sequel Trilogy

A Disenchanted Galaxy

To paraphrase Nietzsche (1974, pp. 181–182), "The Force is dead. The Force remains dead. And we have killed it!" (just substitute 'God' for 'the Force') Thirty years after the defeat of the Empire and the apparent deaths of the final Sith lords, Darth Sidious and Darth Vader, the galaxy is in a state of relative peace. Stories of Jedi versus Sith and heroes such as Luke Skywalker have become a "myth." Did such battles actually occur on faraway places like Endor, Hoth, and Yavin? While there's evidence of the Empire's final military defeat in the ruined hulks of Star Destroyers and X-Wings in the sands of Jakku, does that have anything to do with a cosmic struggle of "good" versus "evil"?

The galaxy we see in *The Force Awakens* is in a state of what Charles Taylor, following sociologist Max Weber (1946), calls "disenchantment." Reflecting on how human belief systems have changed between the years 1500 CE and 2000 CE, Taylor (2007, p. 26) describes the world of five centuries ago as an *enchanted* one "of spirits, demons, and moral forces" that shaped the lives of noblemen and commoners alike. In the enchanted world of yesteryear, not only was belief in supernatural entities or forces commonplace but so was belief in what Taylor (2007, p. 35) calls "charged" objects – objects onto which meaning, including causal powers, was imputed. The sequel trilogy is replete is such "charged" talismans, from Anakin/Luke's lightsaber (which prompts a powerful vision the first time Rey touches it) and kyber crystals (that power lightsabers and Death Stars alike) to Rose and Paige Tico's Haysian-smelt medallions and Han's lucky dice. Indeed, I would argue that the *Millennium Falcon* is a "charged" object, given its uncanny flying and combat abilities for an old "piece of junk."

By contrast, the post-Enlightenment world, dominated by rationalist, scientific, empirical epistemic methodologies, denies the existence of any entities, or any qualities of existent entities, that can't be directly observed through sense-experience or logically inferred from such experience. Nietzsche (2015) aptly represents this worldview:

> Because of the way that myth takes it for granted that miracles are always happening, the waking life of a mythically inspired people – the ancient Greeks, for instance – more closely resembles a dream than it does the waking world of a scientifically disenchanted thinker.

Another relevant distinction between the pre-modern and modern worlds is between what Taylor terms the "buffered" versus "porous" self. The former results from the *solipsism* inherent in René Descartes's (1996) famous proclamation that the only thing he can know with indubitable certainty is that he, himself, exists as a thinking being. As such, the buffered self can take a distance, or disengage, "from everything outside the mind." For the buffered self, "My ultimate purposes are those which arise within me, the crucial meanings of things are those defined in my responses to them" (Taylor 2007, p. 38). We see this exhibited in the Sith's relentless pursuit of "unnatural abilities" to control their own fate and that of the rest of the galaxy, not surrendering even to death. The porous self, on the other hand, "is vulnerable, to spirits, demons, cosmic forces" (Ibid.). How many times do we hear wise Jedi masters advising their apprentices to "let go," "feel the Force flowing through you," "feel, don't think, trust your instincts"? The porous Jedi allow the Force to flow through them and, in so doing, can direct it like diverting a river on its course. When Luke asks Obi-Wan whether the Force "controls your actions," the elder Jedi responds, "Partially, but it also obeys your commands." The buffered Sith, however, want to dam up and control the Force as a source of power for them to manipulate for their own self-centered purposes and to fuel their own selfish power pursuits.

The disenchantment that follows the disavowal of "hokey religions and ancient weapons" not only occludes the light side of the Force, but the dark side as well. As little as two decades after the Jedi are defeated by Palpatine and Vader, an Imperial officer scoffs at Vader's "sad devotion to that ancient religion." As noted earlier, in Lewis's allegorical tale, it's in secret that those bent on corrupting the innocent best do their work. Screwtape advises Wormwood,

> I do not think you will have much difficulty in keeping the patient in the dark. The fact that "devils" are predominantly *comic* figures in the modern imagination will help you. If any faint suspicion of your existence begins to arise in his mind, suggest to him a picture of something in red tights, and persuade him that since he cannot believe in that (it is an old textbook method of confusing them) he therefore cannot believe in you. (Lewis 1982, pp. 19–20)

Disbelief that any such evil force as the old Empire or "wizards" performing "a lot of simple tricks and nonsense" could ever return, or exist in the first place, allows the First Order to build Starkiller Base in secret until it's ready to be unleashed on the unsuspecting Republic – and for Palpatine to manipulate events from Exegol until he's ready for the Final Order to emerge.

Confronting Evil with Evil: Luke's Shame and Despair

Why did fans react so negatively to Rian Johnson's depiction of Luke in *The Last Jedi*? There are many reasons, including that we don't see him engage in an actual lightsaber duel or pull a Star Destroyer from the sky using the Force. He also drinks green milk straight from a sea creature's teat, and, oh yes, he *dies*. But perhaps the most offensive aspect of this elder version of Luke is that he's in a state of *despair*. From being "a new hope" more than 40 years ago, Luke has become the exact opposite, someone who can't envision a better future due to his own mistakes. And

Luke certainly has made mistakes – or at least one critical one when he considered for a moment killing his nephew, Ben, to prevent him from destroying all that he loves.

That temptation, no matter how fleeting, is a reversal of everything Luke stood for when he threw his lightsaber away at the end of *Return of the Jedi*. It also involves the same moral error of his father in inordinately prioritizing his love of temporal goods – namely, the training temple he'd recently founded and the lives of his apprentices – over the eternal good of *justice*, which arguably demands not killing an innocent boy who hasn't *yet* committed any evil deeds. Recall, though, that the final duel in *Return of the Jedi* begins with Luke trying to do exactly what Palpatine was goading him into doing: striking Palpatine down in anger. Ironically, only Vader's defensive blade stopped Luke from immediately turning to the dark side in that moment. So it's not out of character for Luke to consider again violating a fundamental moral principle expounded by the Christian Apostle, St. Paul; known as the "Pauline Principle," it simply exhorts: one ought not commit evil even in order to bring about good.

Recognizing immediately the wrong he almost committed by killing his nephew before he turns completely to the dark side, Luke is about to extinguish his saber, but it's too late and he "was left with shame and with consequence." While we might think it appropriate for Luke to feel shame for his momentary lapse of judgment, there's a greater danger in shame insofar as it, combined with fear, could lead to hatred. Once again, Lewis's Screwtape is instructive:

> But Hatred is best combined with Fear. Cowardice, alone of all the vices, is purely painful – horrible to anticipate, horrible to feel, horrible to remember; Hatred has its pleasures. It is therefore often the *compensation* by which a frightened man reimburses himself for the miseries of Fear. The more he fears, the more he will hate. And Hatred is also a great anodyne for shame. (Lewis 1982, p. 86)

Luke's shame at nearly killing his nephew echoes his father's shame at not being able to save his mother, Shmi, from the Sand People. In Anakin's case, his shame led to his fulfillment of Yoda's prediction in *The Phantom Menace*; in Luke's case, his shameful act results in "a frightened boy whose Master had failed him," whose fear then fuels his hatred.

True Balance: Appropriating Power for Good

The Last Jedi shows Rey and Ben sharing a Force-bond that neither should have the power to accomplish and that they do not control. Although Snoke, as a vehicle for channeling Palpatine's dark power, claims that he's responsible for joining their minds, it's revealed in *The Rise of Skywalker* that the two of them form a "dyad in the Force." While the full significance of this "dyad" is unclear, one element is that Rey and Ben each embody *both* light and darkness. Rey is Palpatine's granddaughter, and she can't deny her bloodline; Ben is the grandson of Darth Vader and has spent years as an avowed adherent of the dark side, committing many atrocities during that time, including patricide. Yet, Rey is able to deny her lineage and in the end symbolically takes the name "Skywalker," and Ben sacrifices himself to save Rey. This is the same type of balance Luke teaches Rey on Ahch-To when guiding her meditation:

Luke   What do you see?
Rey   The island. Life. Death and decay, that feeds new life. Warmth. Cold. Peace. Violence.
Luke   And between it all?
Rey   Balance and energy. A force.
Luke   And inside you?
Rey   Inside me, that same force.

The Jedi of the Old Republic were not in a state of balance because they'd become arrogantly complacent, believing that their primary enemy had been defeated. Luke was not in a state of balance even after his success in redeeming his father and defeating the Emperor, because he'd become "a legend," which resulted in his own arrogance that led to the creation of Kylo Ren. Rey, who's constantly reminded that she's "scavenger scum" with a dark ancestry, and Ben, who forged his own dark history, have no cause for arrogance. They are capable of humbly accepting, and thereby moderating, the darkness within them.

Here, the influence of Eastern thought on Lucas's formulation of the Force is most evident, particularly in terms of the concept of *ch'i*, the fundamental life force at the heart of Taoist philosophy. *Ch'i* manifests itself in the forms of "yin" and "yang," the dualistic opposites that can be found throughout the natural world, including within the human psyche. (For further elucidation of the concept of *ch'i* in the context of *Star Wars*, see Robinson (2005).) This influence is explicitly cited by Lucas: "The idea of positive and negative, that there are two sides to an entity, a push and a pull, a yin and a yang, and the struggle between the two sides are issues of nature that I wanted to include in the film" (Bouzereau 1997, p. 36). This Taoist concept is also visually represented in the mosaic in the reflecting pool on Ahch-To.

In Western philosophy, the ever presence of the dark side, and the need to acknowledge it and not simply try to eliminate it in both nature and oneself, is a thesis promoted in the nineteenth century by Friedrich Schelling (2006). As with Nietzsche, Schelling saw all reality as manifesting a *will*, though not a will to power but rather one to *love*. In its "dark" form, the will to love is manifest in *passion*, which, as Anakin notes, is what the Sith rely on for their strength. Rightly ordered, however, the will to love can be *creative*, resulting in new life and a well-ordered world.

Yet, the "ground," as Schelling refers to it, for such creative activity is the ineradicable potential for disorder, anarchy, and chaos that results from selfish pursuits fueled by passion. (For further elucidation of Schelling's view, see Dunn (2016, pp. 203–205).) Anakin's passionate love for Padmé is disordered because he's willing to kill, even innocent younglings, to save her as an exercise of his power over nature. Anakin's love for Luke, and Ben's love for Rey, is rightly ordered because they're each willing to sacrifice *themselves*. Hence, the *Star Wars* saga's ultimate moral lesson, the final way to overcome moral nihilism and defeat those who build planet-killing weapons to assert their will to power, is to meet power with love. When Rose Tico slams into Finn's ski speeder to prevent him from sacrificing himself in what was probably a futile run at the First Order's battering-ram canon, she tells him, "That's how we're gonna win. Not fighting what we hate. Saving what we love." Later, when Poe Dameron asks Lando Calrissian how he, Han, Luke, Leia, Chewie, and the rest of the Rebellion defeated the Empire, Lando responds, "We had each other. That's how we won." (For further discussion of the importance of *friendship* in *Star Wars*, see Littmann (2016).)

When Rey confronts Palpatine, she's alone at first, but then Ben arrives and they provide Palpatine with an opportunity to secure his own restoration instead of sacrificing himself for the dark side to rule. Alas, though, Rey ultimately defeats Palpatine, not by striking him down in anger as he goads her to do but by defending herself from his final attempt to destroy her such that his power turns back on himself – as happened before when Mace Windu confronted Palpatine and "left him scarred and deformed." Palpatine destroys himself by his own hands, his own will to power. The embodiment of absolute evil in the *Star Wars* saga is at last reduced to nothingness.

Conclusion

Just as ancient epics, such as *The Iliad*, *The Odyssey*, *Gilgamesh*, and *Beowulf*, among countless others, have shaped the metaphysical and moral imaginary of human cultures throughout millennia to the present day, *Star Wars* has helped form the worldview of generations of fans – so much so that "Jediism" has even been claimed as a religious identity. For some fans and more devoted adherents, Lucas's philosophical vision may provide a clear moral dichotomy between good and evil that is desperately sought after in a seemingly nihilistic postmodern world. For others, the moral psychology exhibited at both personal and political levels may offer a cautionary tale for those who first viewed these films when they were originally released. Recall that the Original Trilogy appeared in the post-Nixon/Vietnam era, where trust in government was at an all-time low in the USA; the Prequel Trilogy overlapped with the 9/11 attack and the start of America's longest war to date; and the Sequel Trilogy coincided with one of the most significant political shifts in modern history, not only in the USA but also in other countries such as the UK, the Philippines, and Brazil. Despite being set in a fantastical galaxy far, far away, *Star Wars* has consistently held up a mirror to contemporary society and challenged us to see ourselves either as Jedi who understand that "always in motion is the future" or as Sith who "deal in absolutes." As humanity faces global crises such as the COVID-19 pandemic, *Star Wars* inspires us not to surrender to despair, selfishly pursue our inordinate desires, or give in to the temptation of pride.

Rather, we must remember that "rebellions are built on hope," that evil may be overcome through love, and that we must be humbly conscious of our individual and collective capacity to ally ourselves with either the light or dark side of the Force.

End Notes

1. The idea that the moral battle at the heart of *Star Wars* is one that has to be told and retold was specifically in Lucas's mind as he wrote the original story, influenced by mythologist Joseph Campbell's (2008) formulation of "The Hero's Journey."
2. For further discussion of Augustine's critique of Manichaeism in the context of *Star Wars*, see Brown (2005). For further elucidation and critique of the privation theory of evil, see Dunn (2016).
3. Lucas intended the Force to serve as a nebulous concept that can represent both personal and impersonal notions of a deity, including but not limited to the Christian understanding of God to which Augustine refers here. Lucas states that "the Force evolved out of various developments of character and plot. I wanted a concept of religion based on the premise that there is a God and there is good and evil ... I believe in God and I believe in right and wrong" (Windham 1999, p. 11).
4. This section includes material derived from Eberl (2016).

References

Adams, Don. 2016. Anakin and Achilles: Scars of nihilism. In *The ultimate star wars and philosophy*, ed. Jason T. Eberl and Kevin S. Decker, 42–52. Malden, MA: Wiley-Blackwell.

Augustine. 1955. *Enchiridion on faith, hope, and love*. Trans. Albert C. Outler. Available at http://www.tertullian.org/fathers/augustine_enchiridion_02_trans.htm.

———. 1993. *On free choice of the will*. Trans. Thomas Williams. Indianapolis: Hackett.

———. 1998. *Confessions*. Trans. Henry Chadwick. Oxford: Oxford University Press.

Bouzereau, Laurent. 1997. *Star Wars: The annotated screenplays*. New York: Ballantine.

Brown, Christopher M. 2005. "A wretched hive of scum and villainy": Star Wars and the problem of evil. In *Star Wars and philosophy*, ed. Kevin S. Decker and Jason T. Eberl, 69–79. Chicago: Open Court.

Campbell, Joseph. 2008. *The hero with a thousand faces*. 3rd ed. Novato: New World Library.

Descartes, René. 1996. *Meditations on first philosophy*. Trans. and ed. John Cottingham. New York: Cambridge University Press.

Dunn, George A. 2016. Why the Force must have a dark side. In *The ultimate Star Wars and philosophy*, ed. Jason T. Eberl and Kevin S. Decker, 195–207. Malden, MA: Wiley-Blackwell.

Eberl, Jason T. 2016. "Know the dark side": A theodicy of the Force. In *The ultimate Star Wars and Philosophy*, ed. Jason T. Eberl and Kevin S. Decker, 100–113. Malden: Wiley-Blackwell.

Hummel, Matt. 2016. "You are asking me to be rational": Stoic philosophy and the Jedi Order. In *The ultimate Star Wars and philosophy*, ed. Jason T. Eberl and Kevin S. Decker, 20–30. Malden: Wiley-Blackwell.

Lewis, C.S. 1982. *The Screwtape letters*. New York: Bantam.
Littmann, Greg. 2016. The friends of the Jedi: Friendship, family, and civic duty in a galaxy at war. In *The ultimate Star Wars and philosophy*, ed. Jason T. Eberl and Kevin S. Decker, 127–135. Malden: Wiley-Blackwell.
Nietzsche, Friedrich. 1954a. The Antichrist. In *The portable Nietzsche*, ed. and Trans. Walter Kaufmann. New York: Viking Penguin.
———. 1954b. Twilight of the idols. In *The portable Nietzsche*, ed. and Trans. Walter Kaufmann. New York: Viking Penguin.
———. 1974. *The gay science*. Trans. and ed. Walter Kaufmann. New York: Vintage.
———. 2015. On truth and lie in a nonmoral sense. Trans. W. A. Haussmann. In *Delphi complete works of Friedrich Nietzsche*. Hastings: Delphi Classics.
Plato. 1991. *The Republic*. Trans. Allan Bloom, 2nd ed. New York: Basic Books.
Robinson, Walter (Ritoku). 2005. The far east of Star Wars. In *Star Wars and philosophy*, ed. Kevin S. Decker and Jason T. Eberl, 29–38. Chicago: Open Court.
Schelling, F. W. J. 2006. *Philosophical investigations into the essence of human freedom*. Trans. Jeff Love and Johannes Schmidt. Albany: State University of New York Press.
Seneca. 1928. On anger. In *Moral essays*, Volume 1, Trans. John W. Basore. Cambridge, MA: Harvard University Press.
Stephens, William O. 2005. Stoicism in the stars: Yoda, the Emperor, and the Force. In *Star Wars and philosophy*, ed. Kevin S. Decker and Jason T. Eberl, 16–28. Chicago: Open Court.
Taylor, Charles. 2007. *A secular age*. Cambridge, MA: Harvard University Press.
Weber, Max. 1946. Science as a vocation. In *From Max Weber: Essays in sociology*, ed. H.H. Gerth and C. Wright Mills. Oxford: Oxford University Press.
Windham, Ryder. 1999. *Star Wars Episode 1: The Phantom Menace scrapbook*, 99. New York: Random House.

The Godfather as Philosophy: Honor, Power, Family, and Evil

36

Raymond Angelo Belliotti

Contents

Introduction	874
Summarizing *The Godfather*	874
The Sicilian Family Order	877
"I believe in America. America Has Made My Fortune"	880
A Philosophical Analysis of Honor	883
"This is Business Not Personal"	887
"Is He a Sicilian?"	888
A Philosophical Analysis of Power	890
Conclusion: Destiny and Evil	892
End Notes	894
References	896

Abstract

The Godfather describes the existential conflict between two sets of values partially constituting competing prescriptive and descriptive visions of the world: a nineteenth-century Sicilian perspective grounded in honor and the accumulation of power within a fixed family order and a twentieth-century American perspective celebrating individualism and commercial success. Neither the film nor the book upon which it is based concludes that one of these sets of values is inherently superior.

However, the two sets of values coalesce uneasily in the same cultural setting, and their conflict is irresolvable. Ultimately, the Sicilian perspective must wither away in the United States because, unlike the old country, the new world lacks its

---

R. A. Belliotti (✉)
The State University of New York, Emeritus, Fredonia, NY, USA
e-mail: belliott@fredonia.edu

© Springer Nature Switzerland AG 2024
D. K. Johnson et al. (eds.), *The Palgrave Handbook of Popular Culture as Philosophy*,
https://doi.org/10.1007/978-3-031-24685-2_23

sustaining cultural conditions. This reading interprets *The Godfather* as, among other things, a commentary on the transformation of personal identity within the Sicilian immigrant experience.

Keywords

Honor · Power · Family · Evil · Corleone · *L'ordine della famiglia* · Oppression · *Famiglia* · *Comparaggio* · *Amici di cappello* · *Stranieri* · *Mezzogiorno* · *Amicitia* · *Clientele* · Honor code · Sicilian · Virtue · Business not personal · Destiny · Capitalism · Paternalism · Exploitation · Revenge · Empowerment · *Pezzonovanti* · *Commare* · *Compare* · Assimilation · Immigration · Values · Descriptive and prescriptive world visions · *Omerta*

Introduction

> In *The Godfather* we see organized crime as an obscene symbolic extension of free enterprise and government policy, an extension of the worst in America—its feudal ruthlessness. Organized crime is not a rejection of Americanism, it's what we fear Americanism to be. It's our nightmare of the American system.
> —Pauline Kael (*The New Yorker*, March 18, 1972)

In 1969, after writing critically acclaimed but commercially unsuccessful novels such as *The Dark Arena* and *The Fortunate Pilgrim*, Mario Puzo penned *The Godfather*. Within 2 years, the book registered more than one million hardcover and eight million paperback sales. In 1972, Paramount Pictures released a cinematic adaptation of the novel. Directed by Francis Ford Coppola, *The Godfather* was nominated for 11 Academy Awards, winning 3. Voted the second greatest film of all time by both *Entertainment Weekly* and the *American Film Institute*, *The Godfather* is a landmark achievement.

Although ostensibly a movie about organized crime, the film has been interpreted more broadly. Some understand *The Godfather* as a metaphor for the excesses of American capitalism. Others see it as depicting the symmetry between the exploitation occurring in business and politics and the violence of organized crime or as a generic study of tribal dynasties that place familial loyalty above all other duties. Still others see it as a pernicious glorification of gangsters whose ongoing evils are seductively sanitized or as shamelessly trading on and reinforcing detrimental stereotypes of Italian Americans.[1] In reality, *The Godfather* is all these things and more. This chapter focuses on some distinctively Sicilian elements in the film that are too often obscured.

Summarizing *The Godfather*

The movie begins at the wedding of Constanzia (Connie) Corleone and Carlo Rizzi in the summer of 1945. Vito Corleone (né Andolini), the "godfather,"[2] Connie's father, leads a major New York City crime family. He is also the father of three sons:

Santino ("Sonny"), hot-headed and aggressive; Frederico ("Fredo"), kindly but ineffectual; and Michael, a Marine hero who has returned from service in World War II. Don Vito's *consigliere* is Tom Hagen who was orphaned as a youth and taken into the Corleone household at Santino's behest. Raised by the Corleones, Hagen is now a lawyer who understands thoroughly Sicilian familial and extralegal traditions.

One such tradition is that on his daughter's wedding day, a Sicilian father must fulfill all reasonable requests lodged by relatives and friends. Don Vito fields and grants requests from Amerigo Bonasera, an undertaker seeking justice for the brutal beating his daughter has suffered at the hands of two roughnecks after she refused their sexual advances; Nazorine the baker who petitions for his assistant, Enzo Aguello, who faces deportation; and Johnny Fontane, godson of Don Vito and successful crooner, who wants a certain movie role denied him by the head of the studio, Jack Woltz.

After the wedding, Don Vito sends Hagen to Los Angeles to make Woltz "an offer he cannot refuse." Hagen approaches Woltz with all due respect and courtesy. Woltz responds with a series of ethnic insults and screams that Fontane will never get the role even though he would perform it perfectly. Woltz overflows with venom because Fontane once seduced a starlet whom Woltz was sexually exploiting while training for movie stardom. Hagen returns to New York and informs Don Vito, who conjures a plan. Soon thereafter, Woltz awakens to find the severed head of his prized possession, a race horse, Khartoum, in his bed. After reassessing his position, Woltz casts Fontane in his movie.

Likewise, Enzo the baker gains permanent entry into the United States, and the reprobates who tormented Bonasera's daughter are severely beaten. Don Vito fulfills his promises. Great danger, however, looms in the person of Virgil "Turk" Sollozzo who, supported by the Tattaglias a rival crime family, seeks Don Vito's collaboration in a new venture: the importing and distributing of heroin. Sollozzo needs financing and political and legal protection in exchange for a reasonable percentage of the profits. Although Sonny unwisely signals his interest, Don Vito refuses, citing the special dangers of the narcotics trade. Anticipating that Sollozzo will not accept no as an answer, Don Vito summons his most fearsome enforcer, Luca Brasi, to connect with Sollozzo and report back with sound intelligence. During Brasi's first meeting with the Turk and Bruno Tattaglia, Brasi is garroted.

Matters then spiral downward rapidly. Don Vito suffers grave injuries during an attempted assassination while he purchases fruit outside his office. Sollozzo abducts Tom Hagen and thinking that Don Vito is dead convinces him to persuade Sonny to accept the deal previously offered. Upon learning that Don Vito has survived, Sollozzo repeats his demand to Hagen and releases him.

An enraged Sonny demands that the Tattaglia family turn over Sollozzo or risk all-out war. They respond by sending the Corleones fish nestled in Luca Brasi's bulletproof vest, an ancient Sicilian message that informs everyone that Brasi sleeps with the fishes.[3]

The Corleones go on the offensive. They first kill Paulie Gatto, a soldier in *caporegime* Peter Clemenza's crew, who had betrayed Don Vito and facilitated the attempt on his life. After Michael and Enzo the baker stymie another possible attempt on Don Vito's life in the hospital where he was recovering, the Corleones conclude that Sollozzo must be eliminated. But how?

The brutal war is taking a toll on all the crime families in the city. Sollozzo asks for a meeting with Michael, recognized as a civilian, while accompanied by Captain McCluskey, a corrupt policeman serving as the Turk's bodyguard. After considerable deliberation, Michael volunteers to attend the meeting and kill both enemies. By discovering where the meeting was to occur and planting a weapon in the restroom, Sonny, Clemenza, and Salvatore Tessio, another *caporegime*, ease the path for Michael's murders. At a restaurant in the Bronx, Michael slays both men.

The family dispatches Michael to Sicily for protection and for education in the old ways. The Corleones brace for all-out war with the other crime families in New York who ally against them. Police and government authorities crack down on all crime in response to the murder of one of their own. Newspaper stories written by Corleone family associates, though, portray McCluskey as a corrupt officer who betrayed his duties for monetary gain. Don Vito convalescences at home and is stunned to learn that Michael, whom he had been grooming as a possible senator or governor, was now a murderer.

The marriage of Connie and Carlo, never a mating blessed by heaven, turns ugly. Carlo beats a pregnant Connie, and Sonny responds by severely thrashing Carlo at midday on a crowded public street.

Carlo plots his revenge with the Corleone's chief enemies, the Tattaglia and Barzini families. After instigating another argument with Connie, Carlo beats her badly. Connie telephones Sonny. With deranged avidity, Sonny jumps into his automobile and travels toward Connie's residence. At the toll booth on the Long Island Causeway, he is violently gunned down by a host of hitmen spewing a fuselage of bullets.

Don Vito instructs Hagen to arrange a meeting with the heads of the five New York City crime families and other national crime leaders. At that conference, Don Vito forsakes revenge for Sonny's murder and agrees to provide legal and political protection for the narcotic trade, but he demands that Michael must return to the United States without incident. The violence in the city ends as the other crime leaders agree to Don Vito's design. At this conference, Don Vito concludes that Barzini was the prime mover in the treacheries against his family.

In Sicily, Michael falls in love with Apollonia Vitelli, young daughter of a local tavern owner. They court and wed under strict Sicilian traditions and rituals. Soon thereafter, one of his bodyguards betrays Michael. Michael's auto explodes as Apollonia keys the ignition. Although he was the intended target, Michael is unscathed physically. After the conference of crime leaders occurs in America, Michael returns safely to the United States around 1949.

About 1 year later, Michael reunites with his former love, Kay Adams, with whom he had attended Connie and Carlo's wedding years earlier. After much discussion, they wed. Michael assures her that within 5 years the Corleone family will conduct only legitimate business.

Don Vito keeps the pledges he made at the conference of crime leaders. Tom Hagen, not an effective war-time *consigliere*, is demoted to family lawyer. Michael rises to head of the family, while Don Vito serves as his *consigliere*. Don Vito educates Michael on the sum and substance of crime management.

Meanwhile, Clemenza and Tezzio are upset with the encroachments of rival families. Michael declines their invitations to retaliate. Still, he recruits a new regime of hitmen under wounded war veteran turned gangster, Rocco Lampone.

Michael travels to Las Vegas to expand the family casino business. He offers, in truth demands, to buy out Moe Greene, a quick-tempered casino boss with loose ties to the Barzini family. Greene angrily refuses. Fredo, who has been working in Greene's casino, takes Moe's side against Michael. At the conclusion of the meeting, Michael sternly cautions Fredo about his conduct.

Michael returns home. Don Vito falls and dies while playing with his young grandson in his tomato garden. Don Vito had advised Michael that at his death the other families would conspire against him, using a trusted family insider as their precipitating instrument. At Don Vito's internment, Tessio relays to Michael a proposal from Barzini for a meeting on Tessio's territory. In so doing, Tessio unwittingly identifies himself as a traitor.

Having anticipated and prepared for such a conspiracy, Michael agrees to be the godfather of Connie and Carlo's newborn son. During the baptismal ceremony, Michael's gunmen kill the four heads of the other city crime families as well as Moe Greene. After the baptism, Clemenza and his soldiers kill Tessio and Carlo Rizzi, for his complicity in Sonny's death. After turbulent meetings with Connie and then Kay, in his office Michael welcomes Clemenza and new *caporegimes* Rocco Lampone and Al Neri, who pay their respects to their triumphant leader. The film ends with Clemenza kissing Michael's hand signifying full recognition of his authority. As Kay peers, the office door closes to her and to the external world.

The Sicilian Family Order

Personal relationships in *The Godfather* reflect cultural understandings prevalent in the old world. The disenfranchised sons and daughters of the *Mezzogiorno*[4] brought to the Americas an unwritten but deeply ingrained system of conventions, *l'ordine della famiglia* (the family order), prescribing their relations within and responsibilities to their family, and appropriate conduct toward those outside the family. *L'ordine della famiglia*, nowhere more profoundly entrenched than in Sicily, apportioned the world into four morally significant spheres of social intimacy: *famiglia* (genetic kin and their spouses), *comparaggio* (godparents or intimates), *amici di cappello* (acquaintances to whom one tips one's hat), and *stranieri* (strangers).[5]

Unsurprisingly, *la famiglia* is the social group of paramount value. The family consisted not only of immediate members (the nuclear family) but also of relatives often extended to the third or fourth degrees. The exact degree of kinship determined reciprocal duties and privileges. Principles of proportionality guided these relationships of blood: the closer the genetic connection the greater the duties owed and the more solicitudes expected. The welfare of the family, taken in this extended sense, was the primary responsibility of each of its members.[6]

The next degree of intimacy was embodied in the system of *comparaggio* that, among other things, served as a limited check and balance over family policies and practices. This sphere can be subdivided into *compare* (co-father) and *commare* (co-mother) and *padrino i* (master) and *madrina e* (honored mother) The former were literally "coparents," typically one's peers and intimate friends, and often the godparents to one's children. *Padrini* and *madrine*, by contrast, were venerated elders prized for their demonstrated wisdom, prestige, or power. Strikingly, the system of *comparaggio* admitted few vicissitudes: intimate friendships were permanent. Marginal adjustments could be negotiated between the parties, but their intentions to rescind their relationship, even if reciprocal, could not sever what were taken to be enduring bonds. Such relationships were constitutive of personal identity and thus not easily discarded.

This second sphere expanded for those engaged in business, whether legally or illegally, or those requiring an extended social network for other purposes. Reminiscent of the ancient Roman structures of *amicitia* (friends) and *clientele* (clients) (Belliotti 2009, pp. 7–8, 108) systems of friendships and patronages that fostered mutual advantage, Sicilians recognized alliances for reciprocal benefits. These associations neither implied nor precluded significant emotional attachments. Within this domain, the term "friend" lacked the warm psychological connotations and expression of intimacy accompanying that term within the system of *comparaggio* proper. To be a friend on this level implies only a firm pledge of loyalty. Furthermore, relationships grounded in *amicitia* and *clientele* were neither inalienable nor incorrigible.

The third sphere of concern involved *amici di cappello*: polite acquaintances who remained outside the scope of intimacy. Here arm's length cordiality prevailed. The parties recognized each other but were under no mutual obligations. More importantly, those within this circle acknowledged the absence of adversarial tension.

The final, and by far the largest, group is composed of *stranieri* (strangers), everyone, whether known or unknown, who fell outside the three other classes. Among known strangers, some could bear malicious intentions, others indifference, and still others might seek closer relationships under appropriate circumstances.[7]

This sense of family was not experienced merely as an impersonal network serving self-interest. Instead, it was felt as constituting a wider subjectivity: one's identity was related directly to social context. Under *l'ordine della famiglia*, a person experienced his or her well-being as part of a larger organic entity – as part of a family in the wider sense sketched above. Sicilian peasants had no opportunity to extend their horizons by interacting significantly with those of different backgrounds and outlooks (Alba, p. 30). Lacking the means to communicate with and observe the world outside their village, residents of the entire *Mezzogiorno* lacked the correlated opportunity to develop a more cosmopolitan moral vantage point.

Moreover, local and regional governments had been archaic, corrupt, and distant from the problems of the *contadini* (peasants). Under such circumstances, self-reliance and smaller group affiliation naturally replace allegiance to official authorities. More strikingly, there was great hostility, founded on experience, toward wider institutions: *la legge va contrai cristiani* ("the law works against the people") (Barzini, p. 202).

The context is, however, more nuanced. Although it is tempting to idealize *l'ordine della famiglia* as a bastion of personal virtue in an otherwise heartless atmosphere, such sentimentalization misses part of the picture. It is inaccurate to view the family code as a reaction to the separate and larger social atmosphere; in fact, the family code was partly constitutive of the wider social arena.

The family code hampered national and world identifications at the same time that it nurtured the extended subjectivity of the family unit. While it posed an obstacle to civic virtue, it conferred strict understandings and a workable moral system for family members. As it mocked genuine nationalism and the social welfare, it sanctified family loyalty as true patriotism. While in times of war the code produced soldiers who were sometimes only minimally committed to the national cause, it generated people who, at their best, in peacetime would endure draconian sacrifices and unspeakable dangers for the sake of their immediate and extended families. In this fashion, through narrowly circumscribed spheres of concern, carefully understood burdens and privileges, and assiduously cultivated self-identities, *l'ordine della famiglia* both promoted and repressed the cardinal moral virtues.

L'ordine della famiglia was at once simple and complex, protective yet isolating, humanistic but distrustful. Its simplicity is apparent in the clear-cut demarcations among people: one is either part of the family, an intimate friend, a loyal ally, a polite acquaintance, or a stranger. Little nuance or ambiguity was recognized. The code was clearly protective in that it created, at least in theory, an intimate shield, a zone of security, against the oppressive economic and social structure of the *Mezzogiorno*. But the isolating and parochial implications of the code were equally stark: *stranieri* were neither to be trusted nor consulted; *amici di cappello* were to be regarded at a distance with cool politeness. Not only was there no concept of an international brotherhood and sisterhood, there was little appreciation of those outside one's village. Yet the code reflected a deep humanism, often demanding strenuous sharing and contributions to joint interests within one's circle of intimates. Such parochialism, however, simultaneously deepened and legitimized existing cynicism toward outsiders.

To portray this situation one-dimensionally is dangerously easy: innocent, noble peasants at the mercy of avaricious, unfeeling local land barons, and exploitive northern politicians. In fact, much of the problem involved the deeply entrenched social system in the *Mezzogiorno*, a system in which common people were thoroughly implicated. As with most social situations, the characters in the drama of *Mezzogiorno* cannot accurately be clothed in either white or black hats.

The moral irony of *l'ordine della famiglia* – its simultaneous promotion in the family and repression on other social levels of the cardinal virtues – is accompanied by a psychological irony: on the one hand, the code provided spiritual sustenance and the foundations of personal identity in an otherwise hostile world; on the other hand, the code facilitated lingering dependencies and helped ensure that the outside world remained hostile.

Don Vito applies the fundamental understandings of *l'ordine della famiglia* when crafting his crime syndicate. The highest values of the Sicilian family order were the mustering and exercise of power and honor. The accumulation of wealth was often a means to attaining these ends. The element of organized crime pollutes these values and means with evil.

"I believe in America. America Has Made My Fortune"

The Godfather begins brilliantly with an aptly named undertaker, Amerigo Bonasera, petitioning Don Vito at the wedding of Costanzia Corleone and Carlo Rizzi. Knowing that by tradition, a Sicilian father cannot refuse any reasonable request on his daughter's wedding day, Bonasera describes what Don Vito already knows; two non-Italian boys forced the undertaker's beautiful, virtuous daughter to drink whiskey and then brutally assaulted her when she refused to submit to their sexual overtures. Bonasera swells with pride as he assures Don Vito that the girl kept her honor. However, she suffered a shattered jaw, broken nose, permanent facial disfigurement, and horrifying emotional distress. As a Sicilian craving desperately to become fully American, Bonasera brought charges through the criminal justice system. In the light of overwhelming evidence, the two reprobates pled guilty. The presiding judge scolded the criminals, levied sentences of 3 years each, which he promptly suspended. As the two malefactors left the courtroom, they smirked when passing Bonasera, in effect rubbing his nose in dishonor. Amerigo now asks Don Vito for the justice denied him by American jurisprudence. He whispers that he wants Don Vito to murder the boys and will pay any price for the service.

Don Vito, parceling out contempt and condescension in measured doses under the guise of explanation, informs Bonasera that although the Don's wife is the godmother (*commare*) to the victimized girl and a close friend of Bonasera's wife, the undertaker has avoided all contact with Don Vito. Amerigo has trusted in and been rewarded by the new country and has received his justice from the courts. Bonasera does not offer friendship. He ignores traditional Sicilian manners and protocol. Moreover, Don Vito is not a killer by contract, and what Bonasera's asks is a disproportionate response to the offense, not justice.

Translation: You thought America was different from Sicily – that judges were not corrupt, law enforcement was impartial, and you could ignore *l'ordine della famiglia* and *comparaggio*. Your courageous daughter retained her honor, whereas you have cast honor aside in deference to profit and assimilation. You have received that for which you bargained. You have assiduously shunned a relationship that was forged by my wife's sacred oath as *commare* to your daughter. You now seek to exploit my daughter's wedding day to gain your vengeful design. Instead of petitioning for forgiveness, demonstrating respect, and redeeming the relationship of our families, you regard this matter as murder for money – an arm's length bargain between strangers or acquaintances. Bonasera is there any Sicilian remaining within you? You know or should know the drill, but you reveal yourself as nothing more than a commonplace *stronzo*. You have earned your American fortune but squandered your manhood.

After lowering his demand for justice from killing the perpetrators to making them suffer comparably for what they inflicted on his daughter, Bonasera, stunningly, is so fearful of incurring a debt to Don Vito that he again offers money for the Don's services. Don Vito calmly but firmly excoriates Bonasera's Americanism. The undertaker has purchased "his fortune" with cherished currency: he dances like a puppet at the end of strings manipulated by corrupt, American masters:

> You go to the law courts and wait for months. You spend money on lawyers who know full well you are to be made a fool of. You accept judgment from judge who sells himself like the worst whore in the streets. Years gone by, when you needed money you went to the banks and paid ruinous interest, waited hand in hand like a beggar while they sniffed around [your affairs]. (Puzo 1969, pp. 32–33)

The godfather wonders how he has offended Bonasera that the undertaker reiterates such disrespect and he states explicitly that should Bonasera seek friendship (pledge his loyalty) all his enemies would become Don Vito's enemies and Bonasera would become a feared man by association. At once, Don Vito scorns Bonasera's feckless understanding of power and asserts the range of his own power. In the instant case, the culprits who terrorized his daughter would be suffering forthwith. Finally perceiving the obvious, Bonasera asks Don Vito for friendship while kissing his hand. These words and this gesture are performative: they constitute Bonasera's pledge of loyalty. Don Vito accepts and reminds Bonasera that there may come a day when the Don will request a service from his friend.

The film omits some critical information from the novel. The two reprobates were Jerry Wagner and Kevin Moonan, presumably German-American and Irish-American, respectively. One of them was the son of a powerful politician. The implication is stark: the sentences were suspended because of political and legal corruption. The judge noted that the perpetrators were from "good families." Bonasera fatuously placed his faith in American justice, but the fix was in place at the outset. Don Vito is not surprised because his illegally obtained gains depend upon arrangements with corrupt members of law enforcement and government.

Curiously, Amerigo Bonasera is one of the few characters in the film who speaks with an Italian accent. Despite his most profound yearnings, the self-styled American straddles two worlds. That Don Vito feels compelled to remind Bonasera that friends, either those under strict *comparaggio* or looser *amicitia*, bear mutual obligations of assistance underscores the godfather's lack of faith in the undertaker's Sicilian allegiance. Of course, Bonasera would understand the terms of their relationship, the precise stipulations he had tried to avoid by obtusely offering money in exchange for the services he requested. Throughout the discussion, Bonasera forgets that the accumulation of money is merely an instrument for securing higher Sicilian values: power and honor. In his quest to assimilate, the mortician has confused a means as an end. He now pays the spiritual price.

Don Vito poses as a tradesman of justice. He refuses Bonasera's initial request of murdering Wagner and Moonan on the grounds of its disproportionately to their offense. This reeks of disingenuity: Don Vito had often retaliated disproportionally in the past and will do so in the future. Suppose the two thugs had violated Costanzia Corleone prior to her marriage. Would Don Vito have not rendered them deader than the fish nestled in Luca Brasi's bulletproof vest?[8]

Indeed, his code of honor permits disproportionate retaliation to transgressions of honor. In the instant case, Bonasera has forsaken Sicilian honor in exchange for the pursuit of material gain, comfort, and leisure; he has become an American in aspiration if not fully in citizenship. Don Vito is unwilling to respond disproportionality in the name of a person who explicitly scorned the principles of *comparaggio* and now, at most, resides on the outskirts of *amicitia*. Bonasera does not rest within Don Vito's circle of intimacy.

The lessons of the film's opening scene include the primacy of honor – even Bonasera evinces pride at his daughter's retained honor and bristles at his own loss of honor in the courtroom – and the unwelcome consequences borne by Sicilians who renounce *l'ordine della famiglia* by trusting naively in the tender mercies of the new world. Beneath the surface, the opening scene describes the conflict between two sets of values, competing descriptive and prescriptive cultural visions: those reflecting and sustaining *La della famiglia* and those entrenched in the ideology of the United States of America. The conflict between these two competing sets of visions and values is irresolvable, even if their climatic battle can be delayed. Ultimately, the Sicilian perspective must wither away in the United States because, unlike in Sicily, the wider culture and society lack its sustaining conditions.

Ironically, Bonasera comprehends this viscerally, although not intellectually. He is prepared to shuttle the prescriptions of *l'ordine della famiglia* and embrace the new world's jaunty individualism seasoned by the intimacy of the nuclear family. He must "believe in America" because doing so has "made his fortune." However, vestiges of Sicilian honor are sparked by the torments inflicted on his daughter and the indignities ladled on him in the American courtroom. He must compromise his social blueprint and seek extralegal intervention. Bonasera, foolishly, approaches Don Vito with hopes of avoiding relational entanglement. He must have known better. Don Vito has no interest in orchestrating murders for money that are unrelated to his wider organizational network. Bonasera – given his wife's intimacy with Don Vito's spouse who is *commare* to Bonasera's only daughter – should be Don Vito's "friend," at least among the *amicitia*. Instead, Bonasera presents himself as no more than a cordial acquaintance and desires no deeper relationship.

Later in the novel, Tom Hagen signals to Jack Woltz the significance of *commare* (godmother) and *compare* (godfather) relationships: "Mr. Corleone is Johnny Fontane's godfather. [To the Italian people that] is a very close, a very sacred religious relationship ... Italians have a little joke, that the world is so hard a man must have two fathers to look after him, and that's why they have godfathers" (Puzo 1969, p. 61). Much the same can be said about godmothers.

Bonasera, so desperately aspiring to Americanism, sprouts ethnic amnesia. He misunderstands Don Vito's standard indirect Sicilian discourse, offers money for murder, evinces an uncomplicated faith in new world institutions, and must even be reminded that Don Vito's service entails future obligation. At the conclusion of the scene, Don Vito refuses to acknowledge his agreement with the undertaker. Instead, he advises Bonasera to consider "this justice a gift from my wife, your daughter's godmother" (Puzo 1969, p. 33). Don Vito at once underscores the past bond that Bonasera has hitherto contravened and expresses a reservation about Bonasera's semi-coerced oath of loyalty to him. Don Vito grasps acutely that but for Bonasera's recent calamities, the undertaker would have attended with his wife Constanzia Corleone's wedding but assiduously avoided the Don.

Later, Bonasera is terrified when he receives a telephone call from Hagen requesting a service on behalf of Don Vito. Of course, he cannot refuse. But the undertaker fears he will be implicated in serious criminality. Even if he escapes legal retribution, depending on the service he renders, Bonasera might be targeted by Don Vito's enemies. Fortunately, Don Vito's request is strictly legitimate: He asks Amerigo Bonasera to "use all your powers" to salvage cosmetically the bullet-ridden corpse of Santino Corleone. Don Vito again invokes his wife, "I do not wish his mother to see him as he is" (Puzo 1969, p. 259). Even now, the exchange of services, although transacted by the men, flows most directly from their two spouses. Don Vito and Amerigo Bonasera, each suspended between two world visions in different ways, can never be more than transactional *amicitia*.

Still, Don Vito understands intellectually that the Sicilian vision must perish in the United States but resists this truth viscerally. A man of indomitable will, extraordinary mental toughness, and high ambition, he has steadfastly refused to act sycophantically with American power brokers – those political and social magnates who wield disproportionate influence over the terms of social life. These *pezzonovanti* (90 pieces or big shots) masquerade as apostles of justice and goodness, but Don Vito knows all too well the genuine designs they harbor. They have helped him make his fortune, broaden his enterprises, and amplify his covert power. Nevertheless, Don Vito had expected that the most American of his sons, Michael, might become one of them: a senator or a governor. Don Vito was neither a warrior for social justice nor a dreamer conjuring a more egalitarian society. He accepted people for what they were and what he suspected they always would be. Don Vito would agree with Henry Wadsworth Longfellow that "In this world a man must either be anvil or hammer."

A Philosophical Analysis of Honor

To comprehend *The Godfather*, we must philosophically analyze the concept of "honor." Don Vito understands and presents himself as an honorable man. He does not perceive himself as a murderer, gangster, hoodlum, or common thief. More strikingly, he does not recognize himself as merely an exceptional businessman or successful capitalist. Instead, he is a talented, strong-willed, man of honor who refuses to dance like a vassal at the end of strings manipulated by the dishonorable *pezzonovanti* who otherwise define the terms of social life. Don Vito's signature value, then, is honor and fulfilling the prescriptions of the code he has internalized as his greatest virtue.

Although the term "honor" has been used in a variety of contexts throughout history, a reasonable rendering of personal honor can be reconstructed (Belliotti 2015, pp. 36–46). A sense of personal honor, which is a measure of an individual's value, obtains if four components are in place:

1. A canon of behavior such that
   (a) A set of imperatives (the "honor code") constrains an agent's choices and actions
   (b) The force of the honor code cannot be destroyed or softened by considerations of expediency, utility, or personal advantage – the pursuit of honor and the satisfaction of such considerations are often conflicting aims
   (c) Living up to and complying with the honor code often involves personal risk or sacrifice to the agent up to and including death

Accordingly, Don Vito is willing to risk everything to comply with a principle of honor, often a matter of revenge. Considerations of expediency fade away under such circumstances because honor partially constitutes his self-understanding. His code of honor, grounded in the imperatives of *l'ordine della famiglia*, circumscribe his individual license.

2. A group affiliation promoting a sense of belonging such that
   (a) The honor code arises from a group membership that the agent has either antecedently chosen or posteriorly accepted (internalized) as the agent's own
   (b) The honor code may but does not necessarily correlate to the wider society's professed moral principles, policies, and standards
   (c) The agent judges and evaluates himself or herself in large part in accord with how the agent perceives the way others who are capable – the group members who are qualified to assess – judge and evaluate the agent given the agent's compliance with the honor code and how the agent judges his or her compliance with the honor code
   (d) A merited positive evaluation in that regard heightens the agent's self-respect and pride and nurtures a more profound sense of belonging, whereas a negative evaluation implies that the agent has demonstrated weakness of character and has acted disreputably, which signals that the agent has betrayed the group ethos and thereby weakened his or her sense of belonging
   (e) A recognition by the group members qualified to assess that the agent deserves such a negative evaluation is typically followed by censure up to and including exclusion from group membership unless the agent regains his or her honor
   (f) To have personal honor is to possess a right to be treated as having a certain value and includes the right to respect and to be treated accordingly within the group; to lose personal honor is to relinquish those rights by failing to live up to the honor code

Don Vito's group membership consists of the general Sicilian community, wherein the imperatives of *l'ordine della famiglia* reign, and the subgroup of organized criminals where those imperatives serve evil designs. The resulting honor code does not correlate to the normative principles prevalent in American culture. The Sicilian family order arose from a specific societal context, while organized crime cannot be officially endorsed by any government or nation.

3. An internalization of the canon of behavior such that
    (a) Living up to and complying with the honor code, which confers status, is tightly bound to the agent's sense of identity and self-worth
    (b) A positive evaluation in that regard is a source of deserved, deepened self-respect and pride
    (c) A negative evaluation, which follows from a known and recognized failure to live up to the honor code, is taken by the agent as disreputable, as manifesting a weakness of character and typically elicits shame, diminished self-respect, and reduced pride.

As argued, Don Vito embodies honor as constitutive of the self, scoffs at Bonasera's loss of honor in pursuit of American identity and material gain, and bemoans the mortician's diminished self-respect and shame. Still, Don Vito understands that personal transformation, implying abrogation of the specific honor code to which he subscribes, will be required of the next generation. He, however, can remain authentic. Or so he presumes.

4. A principle of redress such that
    (a) Personal honor can be infringed upon by insults, even those that by themselves neither impair the agent's reputation nor diminish the agent's inner worth, but which fail to treat the agent commensurate with his or her merited value
    (b) Honor codes typically include an imperative of response: if someone impugns the agent's honor, the agent must respond in the prescribed fashion; otherwise the agent's honor is diminished or destroyed.

Those subscribing to a code of honor are typically more easily insulted than are ordinary citizens. By placing heightened value on the personal standing linked to a code of honor agents become sensitive, often overly so, to words, gestures, and actions that do not wholly affirm their standing or code. Moreover, the principle of redress underwriting an agent's response to perceived insult rarely embraces strict proportionality. Few honor codes include paeans to retributive justice. Redress under most honor codes is frequently disproportionately harsh.

In the case of Don Vito, his refusal to murder the young reprobates who viciously assaulted Bonasera's daughter arises from the undertaker's metaphysical distance. Amerigo has acted as if he were only among the *amici di cappello*, not as an intimate within the *comparaggio*. His induced pledge of loyalty places him, at most, within the *amicitia*. Don Vito's obligations to him are attenuated. Also, when Don Vito forswears vengeance for the murder of Sonny and sues for peace, he dishonorably violates his code and demonstrates weakness that his rivals exploit. However, when Don Vito repeats a Sicilian proverb that "Revenge is a dish that tastes best when it is cold" (Puzo 1969, p. 404), he underscores his conviction that vengeance delayed is not vengeance denied. Michael will serve as his avenging agent and restore Don Vito's honor posthumously.

The importance of "honor," then, is intricately linked to our sense of self and to community. While it is plausible that a person might conjure an individualistic, unique code of honor applicable only to himself or herself, typically the concept of honor is connected strongly to group or institutional roles. The person crafts his or her identity within such roles and to separate or be severed from them is to alter the topography of the self. Accordingly, the notion of honor will glisten most brightly in settings that stress communal attachments, institutional roles, and social bonds.

The values embodied by the honor code are taken to have the greatest call upon the agent's allegiance in part because they are most definitive of personal identity. The Italian proverb resonates: *Meglio onore senza vita che vita senza onore* ("Better to die with honor than to live with shame"). To live with shame is to eviscerate and betray the self, deny one's innermost values, and impoverish one's entire life. To die with honor is to enhance one's biography by validating one's inner worth and higher values.

To have conferred and to confer upon oneself a favorable evaluation of one's honor is to cultivate a deserved, deepened self-respect and pride and a more profound sense of belonging to the honor group. It is to say of oneself, "I have lived up to a difficult set of imperatives, a set most other human beings would be unable to fulfill. I have placed principles over narrow self-interest and have renounced the easy path. I have kept the faith with my vows of compliance and thereby proved my worth."

Allegiance to a notion of honor and cultivating the character traits required to behave in ways consistent with that notion connect a person to a wider community. If the values embodied by the notion of honor at issue are worthy, they vivify personal identity and fulfill the human need for intimate bonding with others. A salutary honor code provides imperatives that are not subject to barter or considerations of expediency. Such imperatives infuse life with meaning and purpose. For those who are firmly convinced that if there is nothing worth dying for, then there is nothing worth living for, a sense of honor frames a person's bedrock convictions. The right to be treated as having a certain worth is most resplendent when it is conditioned on the demonstration of the personal qualities that entitle a person to that right. The fact that others within the honor group – those who share allegiance to the imperatives of the honor code – recognize that a fellow member has the requisite personal qualities reinforces the sense of that person's inner worth. In opposition to the Stoics, how other people judge us does and should matter to our own evaluations and understandings of who we are. In opposition to those with an impoverished sense of self who are vulnerable to all external evaluations, only the judgments of some other people should matter – those who are most qualified to render fair, accurate assessments and those who are the other people who matter most to us. Popular opinion in and of itself bears little recommendation.

The notion of honor connects the individual to a project that transcends the narrow concerns of the self. People with a sense of honor privilege the imperatives of the honor code and take compliance with those imperatives as one of their higher values. In societies where the yearning for individualism has amplified dangerously into self-indulgence, narcissism, and the pursuit of popularity, the notion of honor provides a communal antidote by championing a sense of duty, sacrifice, and merited reward. Compliance with the imperatives of an honor code can motivate us to act contrary to strictly personal desires in deference to community obligations. Connection to honor codes is thus one way to distance ourselves from a purely atomistic notion of the self.

Accordingly, a sense of honor and a connection to an honor code are requirements of leading a robustly meaningful, valuable life. The critical questions center on the type of values and virtues that should capture the meaning of "honor" and the appropriate imperatives that should define a beneficial honor code. Unfortunately, too many codes of honor have embodied and evinced noxious patriarchal prerogatives, toxically violent principles of redress, insular tribal understandings, and racial, ethnic, religious, or class imperialism.

It is in this spirit that we should examine and evaluate the honor code to which Don Vito subscribed within the context of *l'ordine della famiglia*.

"This is Business Not Personal"

In 1969, when I first read *The Godfather*, several characters intoned the phrase "this is business, not personal," or some variation of this phrase, ostensibly to calm the listener and transport him to a more reasonable position than he had advanced. I was jolted by this doltish locution. How could Mario Puzo, otherwise so perceptive, invoke an expression that entirely missed the mark? The protagonists in the novel took themselves to be men of honor. Surely Puzo must know that people bearing such a self-image invariably take more words, gestures, and actions personally than do other human beings. I sadly concluded that Puzo must have been striving for a memorable phrase, like "I'll make him an offer he can't refuse" and "A lawyer with his briefcase can steal more money than a hundred men with guns," which would earn enduring renown. Or perhaps he was trying to underscore how the novel was a metaphor for the excesses of capitalism and big business.

Then I had an epiphany. Tom Hagen is counseling Michael Corleone to reevaluate his offer to murder Virgil Sollozzo and Captain McCluskey. He points out that McCluskey's breaking of Michael's jaw was "business, not personal" and Michael should not factor that injury into his calculus. As I was about to remind myself, "Not again, not this witless phrase." Michael responds:

> Tom, don't let anybody kid you. It's all personal, every bit of business. Every piece of shit every man has to eat every day of his life is personal. They call it business. OK. But it's personal as hell. You know where I learned that from? The Don ... That's what makes him great ... He takes everything personal. (Puzo 1969, p. 146)

Alleluia! Finally, the truth. As a man of honor, Don Vito would take much more personally than other human beings. Under my account, Puzo in effect reveals that the business metaphor is inadequate to understand his novel. That the notion of honor underwrites Don Vito's mission is at this point clear.

Michael's assertion is not included in the movie. In Coppola's screen notes, scrawled in the margins of the pages of the novel, he remarks, "I never really got into this, though I understand it. Ask Mario" and "? Think about this" (Coppola 2016, p. 147). Given Coppola's conviction that the story "was a metaphor for American capitalism in the tale of a great king with three sons" (Jones 2007, p. 18), the fact that the primacy of honor might elude Coppola is unsurprising.

At the peace conference attended by the leaders of American crime families, Don Vito confirms the personal nature of events when discussing the return of Michael from Sicily.

> If some unlikely accident should befall my youngest son, if some police officer should accidentally shoot him, if he should hand himself in his cell, if new witnesses appear to testify to his guilt, my superstition will make me feel that it was the result of the ill will still borne me by some people here … that ill will, that bad luck, I could never forgive. (Puzo 1969, pp. 293–294)

To ignore the intersection of *l'ordine della famiglia*, the importance of honor, and the ambivalence of the immigrant experience, or to immerse them in wider metaphors of American business or capitalism, is to bypass willfully the more philosophically rewarding dimensions of the novel.

"Is He a Sicilian?"

The movie omits another paramount passage invoking honor. Tom Hagen returns from his turbulent sessions with Jack Woltz. He informs Don Vito that Woltz is unwilling to grant his request to cast Johnny Fontane in Woltz's upcoming movie. Prior to determining his response, Don Vito must evaluate Woltz's character. He asks Hagen, "Does this man have real balls?" Hagen interprets the inquiry sharply and quickly. Sure, Woltz has strong character, a determined will, the courage to call bluffs, and the willingness to suffer financial losses and inconveniences in the face of labor strikes or embarrassing exposures of the excesses of one of his stars. But Hagen suspects the Don already understands this and is searching for something more profound: "Did Jack Woltz have the balls to risk everything. To run the chance of losing all on a matter of principle, on a matter of honor; for revenge?" He responds to Don Vito, "You're asking if he is a Sicilian" (Puzo 1969, pp. 65–66). Don Vito nods. Hagen assures him that Woltz is not a Sicilian in this or any other sense. Now, Don Vito can conjure his treachery against Woltz.

Coppola's screen notes merely repeat, "Would he risk everything on a matter of honor? No. But the Don would" (Coppola 2016, p. 66). Again, on my account, the contrast between the successful, intelligent, powerful businessman and the old-world man of honor within the structure of *l'ordine della famiglia* is palpable.

Jack Woltz is not merely an uncommonly successful businessman. He is deeply connected to governmental power brokers: he boasts of a friendship with J. Edgar Hoover, director of the Federal Bureau of Investigation, and alludes to his influence in the White House (Puzo 1969, pp. 57, 62). Woltz, not Hagen, loses his temper, sputters threats, and vows retaliation should Don Vito continue to press his request. Woltz will never cast Johnny Fontane in his upcoming movie, even knowing that his acting would enhance the film, because Johnny had once stolen the heart of one of Woltz's movie starlets, a young girl Woltz had groomed professionally and enjoyed sexually. Hagen is stunned that Woltz would reject what was in his business interests because of a private matter wrapped around the beauty and sexual allure of a woman (Puzo 1969, p. 62). In the remorselessly patriarchal realm of the Corleones, disputes over women were significant only in marital and family contexts.

Don Vito, relying on Tom Hagen's evaluation that Woltz would not risk everything on a matter of honor or revenge, has the movie mogul's prize racehorse killed and its head placed in Woltz's bed while he sleeps. (We must suspend judgment on how all this transpires so quietly and efficiently.) The value of the stallion is around $600,000, as measured by Woltz's purchase price, but we must suppose that Woltz has insured the horse's life for much more, as Khartoum's stud value would far exceed that amount. Thus, the murder is not significant as violence to Woltz's financial bottom line. The sheer barbarity of the enterprise, however, brings Woltz to his knees: Don Vito is willing to risk everything for what he takes to be a matter of honor. Don Vito's extralegal power amplified by his boundless resolve is far greater than the force of Woltz's legal and governmental connections. As always, Don Vito prizes power and honor supremely while using money as his instrument to amass and exercise them.

Puzo allows readers a rare glance into the inner life of one of his characters. Thus, Woltz muses:

> The ruthlessness, the sheer disregard for any values, implied a man who considered himself completely his own law, even his own God . . . People didn't have any right to act that way. It was insane. It meant you couldn't do what you wanted with your own money, with the companies you owned, the power you had to give orders. It was ten times worse than communism. (Puzo 1969, p. 69)

Well, yes. Don Vito and those of his ilk pose a unique, intractable threat to Woltz's comforting inspiration: the ménage à trois of big business, government, and law. Woltz is too obtuse, however, to perceive how Don Vito's family partially overlaps and influences that relationship. Moreover, Don Vito can bestow benefits, fulfill destinies, and perform secular miracles largely because he is a man who will risk everything on a matter of principle and honor. He is not "completely his own law," because he, like all people of honor, is constrained by the imperatives of his code, but he will surely not permit society's conventional understandings to circumscribe his methods or objectives. He is "his own God," then, within the boundaries of the code of honor to which he subscribes, a code that partially constitutes his identity.

Puzo, who steadfastly and disingenuously maintained that he only told stories and did not moralize, stacks the deck against Woltz, who is a thoroughly unattractive figure: arrogant, loud, threatening, abusive, exploitive, and, worse, a serial statutory rapist. Johnny Fontane is neither entitled to nor deserves the movie role which he seeks. Woltz's refusal to cast him is neither unjust nor unfair. Although everyone concerned admits Fontane would do a terrific job, countless other actors would perform just as well. Don Vito ensures that Johnny is cast because he has given his word at his daughter's wedding to his godson. Armed with multiple inducements of his code of honor, Don Vito will risk everything to fulfill that promise, even after calculating Woltz's considerable personal, professional, and governmental resources. In the margins, we contrast Don Vito's sexual rectitude with Jack Woltz's ongoing sexual perversions. Don Vito responds disproportionately and unjustifiably, yet viewers and readers cheer, at least those willing to overlook the mutilation of an innocent animal.

A Philosophical Analysis of Power

The term "power" appropriately refers to a host of different, sometimes overlapping concepts.[9] At its most general, *power is the capability (the disposition) to produce or contribute to the production of outcomes*. Understood at this level, power is not necessarily relational – that is, it does not require at least two parties one of which is superior in capability to the other. Power does not necessarily require a social setting to gain its meaning or to animate its structure, nor does it necessarily generate resistance or opposition or a conflict of interests that the agent must overcome. The exercise of power does not even require a demonstrated intention. This nonsocial rendering of power is crushingly uninteresting, probably because it is the most general concept connoted by the term. But it does illustrate several useful aspects of power. For example, power is a capability or disposition; thus someone can possess a certain power but not exercise it. Possessing power implies the actualization of a potential – we learn to walk, to speak a language, to sing, and the like by developing our potentials. Power does not automatically translate to domination, oppression, or subordination although it is something almost every living and some nonliving things possess to some extent. And, to have power is typically to attain a good in some respect.

Power-over is the most interesting relational, social rendering of the general notion of power. Power-over can be used to oppress others or to transform them in positive directions or to treat them paternalistically. But to concoct one definition of power-over that fully embodies all these uses is misguided. A better approach is to provide a neutral definition of power-over that is compatible with the three major uses but which requires corollary concepts to distinguish the three uses from each other: *A superior party possesses power over a subordinate party when the superior has the capability (the disposition) to affect the outcomes and/or interests of the subordinate by controlling or limiting the alternative choices or actions available to the subordinate.*

This definition recognizes that the superior party may possess power over the subordinate party but not exercise that power and that when power-over is exercised, the subordinate's outcomes and/or interests may be affected negatively or positively. In either case, however, exercising power-over involves controlling or restricting, in any of a variety of ways, the choices or actions available to the subordinate. In this fashion, the superior has limited the usual circumstances of agency enjoyed by the subordinate.

The first major use of power-over is oppression. *A superior party oppresses a subordinate party when the superior affects wrongfully and adversely the outcomes and/or interests of the subordinate by controlling or limiting the alternative choices or actions available to the subordinate.* This is the most commonly understood use of power-over. Here the superior party controls or limits the available choices or actions of the subordinate party and thereby adversely affects the subordinate's outcomes and/or interests through a host of possible means: force, duress, deception, personal charm, and superior economic bargaining power. The superior party might disseminate an ideology that produces a false consciousness that impairs the subordinate's ability to identify his or her genuine interests. They might truncate public debate to include only trivial or uncontroversial issues or exploit an informational or knowledge advantage. They might exploit psychological and emotional vulnerabilities or convince the subordinate that the judgments of the superior embody special authority. This use of power is, of course, Don Vito's stock and trade: extortion, bribery, coercion, and limiting the terms of discourse and action define much of his operation.

The second major use of power-over is paternalism: *A superior party acts paternalistically toward a subordinate party when the superior tries to affect positively the outcomes and/or interests of the subordinate by controlling or limiting the alternative choices or actions available to the subordinate.* Paternalism is employed by superiors in a variety of circumstances. For example, paternalism may be warranted when subordinates do not possess the full capabilities of identifying and acting upon their own genuine interests because of age or impairment (e.g., minors or the mentally or physically challenged). Paternalism may be exercised when subordinates have the capabilities but lack the requisite judgment because of psychological vulnerabilities. Sometimes subordinates may embody conflicting interests or may struggle with weak wills (e.g., adults who act on immediate desires instead of long-term preferences or those who temporarily act in self-destructive or self-undermining ways because of duress or desperate circumstances). The object of the superior's intentional use of power-over here is to promote the objective wellbeing of subordinates. Don Vito sometimes conceals his oppressive exercise of power-over as merely paternalistic. His sobriquet "godfather" underscores that masquerade. In fairness, much the same can be said about the actions of many parents regarding their children. This should not obscure the truth, though, that Don Vito did (and parents often do) act paternalistically in the higher sense.

The third major use of power-over is empowerment: *A superior party acts to empower a subordinate party when the superior tries to affect positively the outcomes and/or interests of the subordinate with the aim of favorably transforming the subordinate by controlling or limiting the alternative choices or actions available to the subordinate.* Empowerment is often paternalism with the direct aim of transforming the subordinate to the point where the subordinate is no longer in need of direction. The means of doing so are theoretically as varied as the other two uses of power-over but are practically limited to those that will accomplish the specific mission of empowerment. The harsher means of exerting power-over are generally less useful here. However, this is not always the case. We can imagine parents and professionals who have captured a young adult from the clutches of a manipulative cult that has preyed upon the victim's psychological vulnerabilities. The parents and professionals might need to use relatively stern methods of de-programming the victim in order to nurture the goal of personal empowerment. Still, as a rule the less restrictive and gentlest means of achieving the goal are recommended: the ends will typically be prefigured in the means used. Another example of the use of power-over as empowerment is the reeducation of a victim of false consciousness who, because of the pernicious effects of oppression, requires a more acute awareness of his or her genuine interests. Don Vito often exerted his power in service of empowerment, most overtly with Tom Hagan and Michael, in grooming them for positions of authority which would otherwise be unavailable to them.[10]

Conclusion: Destiny and Evil

Don Vito sometimes injects that people must follow their destinies. Chris Messenger interprets Don Vito's invocations as implying that "An inescapable slavery dogs man's destiny. An unseen force dictates man's lot, cast as an endless and repetitive coercion that is deterministic, involuntary, and unacceptable" (Messenger 2002, p. 188). This observation requires refinement. Although people collectively bear the burdens of what is often described as the human condition – our immutable finitude, being forced to take stands on ultimate existential questions that resist definitive answers, an inclination to yearn unrequitedly for an ultimate culmination that will redeem our lives from futility and pointlessness, for a rational and just universe that will bestow meaning and purpose on our strivings and efforts, and for a connection to enduring value that will remove the yoke of impermanence – *The Godfather* does not portray individuals as merely acting out predestined lives. Don Vito did not murder Fanucci because he was destined to be a gangster. He became a gangster after murdering Fanucci and conniving further with Clemenza, Tessio, and Genco Abbandando. Santino Corleone was not predestined to enter the family business. He entered the family business after witnessing his father murder Fanucci and desiring to emulate him. Michael Corleone was not destined to succeed his father. He succeeded his father as leader of the family after murdering McClusky and Solozzo, after being sent to Sicily for refuge and education, and after the murder of Santino. When Don Vito intones, "Every man has only one destiny" (Puzo 1969, p. 188), he is better understood as implying that our prior choices and actions limit our future possibilities. He is not suggesting our lives are predetermined and merely involuntary responses to cosmic kismet. Don Vito is not a philosophical hard determinist.

Puzo carefully grooms our appreciation of Vito Andolini. He is victimized by unscrupulous thugs who render him an orphan in Sicily, discharged from his job in Abbandando's grocery store because of the exploitive designs of a loutish gangster in America, lured into smalltime thievery with two friends to meet the survival needs of his family, and threatened by the same loutish gangster who demands a percentage of the trio's gains. Does not Fanucci deserve his fate? Is not the soon-to-be Don Vito a praiseworthy avenger? Is he not noble for refusing to cast his lot with Solozzo's narcotics venture? Is not the entire Corleone family warranted in attacking Solozzo and his confederates after they tried to murder Don Vito? Should we not celebrate Michael's gritty slaying of the conniving police captain and the repulsive Solozzo? Puzo marginalizes Don Vito's disproportionate unwarranted responses to those reticent to comply with his requests (e.g., Jack Woltz and Moe Greene) and his daily exploitive activities (prostitution, illegal gambling, extortion, labor racketeering, bribery of government officials, and murders required to sustain those enterprises) while portraying the Corleone family as heroic gangsters repelling their dishonorable enemies. Were any readers of the novel and viewers of the film rooting against Don Vito and his gang? Were Carlo Rizzi fan clubs forming or Virgil Solozzo memorials erected? The murders perpetrated by the Corleones too often strike us as vindicated; we celebrate the seemingly righteous retaliation and brilliant efficiency of the family. That Don Vito's life centers on the accumulation and exercise of power and honor generated by enormous evils seemingly evaporates from the audience's consciousness.

Viscerally, Don Vito, unlike Bonasera, has no inclination for American assimilation. He craves an extralegal Sicilian life obsessed with accumulating power and respect within the boundaries of the new world and its distinctive challenges. Intellectually, Don Vito expected Michael, the most American of his offspring, to ascend to the heights of a new world *pezzonovante*. That Don Vito assuages new world power brokers through bribery only reinforces his Sicilian distrust of government. That America celebrates the myth of individualism only underscores his Sicilian reliance on a closely knit social network grounded in blood and sacred pledges of loyalty. That America invokes the rule of law and the common good only energizes Don Vito's Sicilian conviction that politicians murder millions while supposedly implementing such notions. In effect, "a prime minister kills more victims with one declaration than thousands of criminals with weapons." Or, in America, "take the money leave the idealism." But these competing secular religions, the conflicting descriptive and prescription visions of the two worlds, coalesce uneasily. Intellectually, Don Vito understands that America will compel the offspring of immigrants to relinquish their roots in exchange for exerting their wings. The metaphors of America as a melting pot, salad bowl, or giant stew capture that reality in different ways. Viscerally, Don Vito refuses to go gently into this new world.

Don Vito, under cover of old-world family love and loyalty, does not merely exploit but also enhances the corruption and excesses of American institutions. But Don Vito intellectually grasps that, his way, the old Sicilian fashion must yield to the exigencies of the new world because it lacks its sustaining conditions. The absent cultural conditions include the following:

- Sicily endured centuries of foreign invasions and occupations.
- In the Sicily of Don Vito's day, the state was perceived as a repository of evil, and its authority was too frequently brandished unjustly.
- A code of silence, *omerta*, was the defiant hallmark of the masses.

- Communication, transportation, and mobility were severely restricted, and most people spent their entire lives within their villages and immediate surroundings.
- Cultural understandings were not diverse.
- The nation of Italy had materialized only a few decades prior to Vito Andolini's forced immigration to America.
- America continued to be plagued with regionalism and factionalism.
- A strict extended family order, embodying a narrow blood and soil mentality, prevailed as a counterweight to much of the above.
- Opportunities for upward socioeconomic mobility were scarce.
- A fierce anti-clericalism coexisted uncomfortably with profound devotion to saints connected to localities and to village priests.
- The absence of compulsory public education bred intractable superstitions.

This is also why Sicilian organized crime has largely withered away in the United States – its sustaining cultural understandings are absence in the wider culture. Even if RICO and witness protection programs and plea bargaining did not exist, Sicilian organized crime would have largely evaporated because the new generations were born and raised in the United States. These generations can surely produce criminals but not of the same stripe and with the self-understandings of the mythical Corleone family. The time soon arrived when Don Vito's scions confronted stark choices: become the *pezzonovanti* of the new world or resign themselves to subsisting as anvils. The overwhelming majority of Italian immigrants and their descendants, law-abiding and industrious, chose from a far richer array of possibilities.

End Notes

1. Mario Puzo wrote about one-half of the screen play of *The Godfather*, but after the initial stages, the *pezzonovanti* Paramount froze him out of the film, not even permitting him to view the final cut (Biskind 1990, p. 25; Puzo 1972, pp. 32, 64). Costas Gravas, the director of *Z*, understood the novel as an indictment of American capitalism (Puzo 1972, p. 57). Coppola observed, "[The film] is not really about the Mafia. It could just as well be about the Kennedy or the Rothschilds, about a dynasty which demand personal allegiance to a family that transcends even one's obligations to one's country" (Messenger 2002, p. 8). This is true only in the broadest interpretation of the novel that Coppola identifies. In its narrower dimensions, of the pursuit of honor within a specific family and ethnic code, much would be lost in Coppola's reimagined versions. Mario Puzo added, "I've wanted to show the parallel between the normal business world and the Mafia . . . these guys know how to use violence as a business tool . . . the old guys were men of honor [with] family values" (Messenger 2002, p. 291). Puzo here should make clearer how Don Vito also uses business as a tool to attain his higher aims: amassing and exercising power,

as well as manifesting and amplifying his honor. Also, Puzo's understanding of "the old guys" is overly approbative.
2. Throughout this essay, I refer to Vito Corleone as "Don Vito," according the fictional character all due respect.
3. In the novel, when a large, dead fish wrapped in Luca Brasi's bulletproof vest is delivered to the Corleone compound, Tom Hagen is the person who recognizes the Sicilian message: Brasi is sleeping with the fishes deep in the ocean. In the film, Clemenza delivers the line. Hagen, lacking blood ties to the Corleone family and of Irish-German descent, is throughout the novel closely attuned to Sicilian culture – more so than any of Don Vito's sons. How did Hagen learn? Undoubtedly, through direct instruction from Don Vito, perhaps augmented through study. That Don Vito appoints Hagen, a non-Sicilian, *consigliere* is no accident. The appointment signals Don Vito's admission on the intellectual level that the ways of the old world are unsustainable in the United States.
4. The *Mezzogiorno* refers to the regions of Italy south of Rome: Abruzzi and Molise, Campania, Apulia, Basilicata (Lucania), Calabria, and Sicily. Sardinia is sometimes included in the group. "*Mezzogiorno*" literally mans "middle of the day" but also bears several rich connotations such as "the land that time forgot" and "where the sun always shines." This region has for centuries been the poorest but most intriguing part of Italy. About 80% of the Italian immigrants to the United States came from the *Mezzogiorno*.
5. In sketching the general account of the family structure in Southern Italy and Sicily, I consulted Richard D. Alba (1985), Luigi Barzini (1964), Richard Gambino (1974), Jerre Mangione and Ben Morreale (1992), and Raymond Angelo Belliotti (1995).
6. Vincent Patrick's *The Pope of Greenwich Village* contains an instructive passage about traditional Italian tribalism. An Irish-American safecracker, Barney, is questioning two Italian-Americans, Charlie and Paulie, who are trying to recruit him into their criminal scheme. The Irishman questions Charlie as to his relationship to Paulie: "Paulie tells me you're cousins." Charlie replies, "Fifth. Maybe sixth—I can never figure it out. His father's great-aunt back in Naples was a cousin of someone on my mother's side." Barney nods: "With Italians, that makes you about as close as twin brothers in an Irish family" (New York: Seaview Books, 1979, pp. 31–32).
7. However we evaluate *l'ordine della famiglia* today, its moral code arose from, mollified to an extent, but also unwittingly sustained, the brutal life prospects of the subjugated denizens of the *Mezzogiorno*. Booker T. Washington, a man who knew slavery firsthand and fought against it, visited Italy and concluded: "The Negro is not the man farthest down. The condition of the coloured farmer in the most backward parts of the Southern States in America, even where he has the least education and the least encouragement, is incomparably better than the condition and opportunities of the agricultural population in Sicily." Quoted in Mangione and Morreale, xv.
8. A critic might argue that Carlo Rizzi physically abused Connie at least twice without reprisal from Don Vito. The difference is Carlo and Connie were

married. This would be considered a much different context than the case of Bonasera's daughter and my hypothetical example.
9. See, for example, Steven Lukes (2005), Thomas E. Wartenberg (1990), Jeffrey C. Isaac (1987), Robert A. Dahl (1975), Peter Morriss (2002), and Raymond Angelo Belliotti (2016).
10. The three major uses of power-over constitute neither an exhaustive nor necessary catalog. For example, often exercising power-over involves a mixture of more than one of the uses sketched here. Moreover, my definition of the exercise of power-over as oppression could be broken down in several different uses of power differentiated by the means employed and the extent of the use. For example, some will prefer to distinguish the use of power-over by force, by dissemination of false consciousness, through domination, by personal charm, and the like. Finally, at times power-over is exercised in ways that affect the interests of subordinates neither positively nor adversely except insofar as any restriction of freedom narrows autonomous choice and action. Accordingly, my outline of the major uses of power-over is only one of numerous reasonable possibilities.

References

Alba, Richard D. 1985. *Italian Americans: Into the twilight of ethnicity*. Englewood Cliffs: Prentice-Hall.
Barzini, Luigi. 1964. *The Italians*. New York: Atheneum.
Belliotti, Raymond Angelo. 1995. *Seeking identity: Individualism versus Community in an Ethnic Context*. Lawrence: University Press of Kansas.
———. 2009. *Roman philosophy and the good life*. Lanham: Lexington Books.
———. 2015. *Why philosophy matters: 20 lessons on living large*. Newcastle: Cambridge Scholars Publishing.
———. 2016. *Power: Oppression, subservience, and resistance*. Albany: The State University of New York Press.
Biskind, Peter. 1990. *The godfather companion*. New York: HarperCollins Publishers.
Coppola, Francis Ford. 2016. *The godfather notebook*. New York: Regan Arts.
Dahl, Robert A. 1975. The concept of power. *Behavioral Science* 2: 201–215.
Gambino, Richard. 1974. *Blood of my blood*. New York: Anchor Books.
Isaac, Jeffrey C. 1987. *Power and Marxist theory*. Ithaca: Cornell University Press.
Jones, Jenny M. 2007. *The annotated godfather: The complete screenplay*. New York: Black Dog & Leventhal Publishers.
Lukes, Steve. 2005. *Power: A radical view*. New York: Palgrave Macmillan.
Mangione, Jerre, and Ben Morreale. 1992. *La Storia*. New York: Harper Collins.
Messenger, Chris. 2002. *The godfather and American culture*. Albany: State University of New York Press.
Morriss, Peter. 2002. *Power: A philosophical analysis*. 2nd ed. Manchester: Manchester University Press.
Patrick, Vincent. 1979. *The pope of Greenwich Village*. New York: Seaview Books.
Puzo, Mario. 1969. *The godfather*. New York: Fawcett Crest.
———. 1972. *The godfather papers*. New York: Fawcett Crest.
Wartenberg, Thomas E. 1990. *The forms of power*. Philadelphia: Temple University Press.

Groundhog Day as Philosophy: Phil Connors Says "No" to Eternal Return

37

Kimberly Blessing

Contents

Introduction	898
Summary of *Groundhog Day*	899
Interpreting the Movie	901
Moral of the Movie	903
Eternal Return	903
A Test of Resolve	903
Amor Fati	904
The Value in Suffering	904
Does Eternal Return Work?	905
Myth of Sisyphus	906
Sisyphus Fulfilled	907
Evaluating the Moral	908
Phil Says "No"	908
Phil Strives to Be Better	908
Objective Goods and Intrinsic Value	909
Don't Worry, Be Happy	910
Hedonic Treadmill	911
Aristotle's Virtue Ethics	911
Phil Lives Up to Standards of Excellence	913
Conclusion	914
References	915

Abstract

In *Groundhog Day*, weatherman Phil Connors is a miserable human being living a life that lacks meaning. Forced to relive the same day over and over and over again, Phil must come to grips with his unhappiness and the fact that his life is pointless. Some compare the repetition of days in *Groundhog Day* to Friedrich Nietzsche's conception of eternal recurrence, as well as Albert Camus' *Myth of Sisyphus*. I argue

---

K. Blessing (✉)
Philosophy, SUNY Buffalo State, Buffalo, NY, USA
e-mail: blessika@buffalostate.edu

© Springer Nature Switzerland AG 2024
D. K. Johnson et al. (eds.), *The Palgrave Handbook of Popular Culture as Philosophy*,
https://doi.org/10.1007/978-3-031-24685-2_31

that the movie rejects a postmodern or existential view of happiness and life's meaning. While Nietzsche and Camus reject optimism and hope, this feel-good rom com teaches us tomorrow can be a better day. Phil's transformation from a self-proclaimed jerk to a loving and admirable human being reinforces what Aristotle teaches us, namely that happiness is about habitually doing the right thing. Phil does not find meaning in his life by coming to terms with his mortality, and then simply changing his attitude about his life and current situation, i.e., meaning subjectivism. Instead Phil eventually finds happiness and meaning by becoming a better person, which is done by performing virtuous acts; e.g., being kind, generous, courageous, etc. Thus, the movie supports Aristotle's virtue ethics approach toward thinking about happiness and life's meaning, rather than Nietzsche's of Camus' subjective approach.

Keywords

Happiness · Meaning of life · Nietzsche · Eternal return · Üubermensch · Amor fati · Nihilism · Camus *Myth of Sisyphus* · Absurdity · Existentialism · Postmodernism · Meaning subjectivism · Hedonism · Hedonic treadmill · Aristotle · Virtue ethics · Self-actualization · Intrinsic value · Extrinsic value · Instrumental value · Relative goods · Objective goods · Christianity · God is dead · Immortality

Introduction

It's a movie you want to watch over and over and over. Bill Murray said that Danny Rubin "was touched by God" when he wrote the original script. It's one of 450 films selected for the Library of Congress' National Film Registry, which designates films that are "culturally, historically, or aesthetically significant" (Library of Congress National Film Registry 2006). *Philosophy Now* describes it as "one of the great philosophical movies" (Faust 2012). In 2017, it premiered on Broadway as a musical, where it was well received. In London it was awarded the Laurence Olivier Award for Best New Musical. Finally, the plot device for the film has seeped into the larger culture when it is used as a term to describe a recurring situation, while troops in Iraq used it as shorthand for "snafu," "situation normal: all f'd-up." "That's right, woodchuck-chuckers – it's Groundhog Day!"

In *Groundhog Day* (1993), Phil Connors (Bill Murray) starts out as a self-proclaimed jerk. But after being forced to live the same day over and over and over again, he transforms into a good guy. By the end of this romantic comedy, he gets the girl (played by Andie MacDowell), and they live happily ever after. Looking at the movie through a philosophical lens, we might say that Murray plays the part of a "thoroughly postmodern man: arrogant, world-weary, and contemptuous without cause" (Goldberg 2006). At the beginning of the movie, he is a miserable human being living a relatively meaningless life. By the end of the movie, he finds true happiness and meaning in his life by transforming into a good or virtuous human being.

Philosophers compare the movie to the Doctrine of Eternal Return which is put forward by one of postmodernism's secular saints, Friedrich Nietzsche. They also compare it to existentialist Albert Camus' *Myth of Sisyphus*. Yet Phil Connors' metamorphosis contradicts almost everything postmodernity, in general, and existentialism, in particular, teaches about the meaning of life. Phil doesn't find happiness or meaning by "living his truth" or becoming more "authentic." It's not about embracing pain and suffering à la Nietzsche or embracing the absurdity of his situation à la Camus.

Instead, Phil finds meaning and purpose in a Godless world by becoming less of an individual and more like the crowd. He adopts the old-fashioned values of the townsfolk, being neighborly, generous, and kind. He focuses less on himself and more on serving others. He embraces the Classics, recites poetry, learns French, and masters playing the piano. And he finds the love of a good woman. Far from being cynical or contemptuous, *Groundhog Day* is a feel-good romantic comedy that underscores the possibility of rebirth and redemption; even a crusty misanthrope like Phil Connors can transform into a lovable and admirable human being. Thus, over time, we too can live up to our full potential as human beings or become the best version of ourselves possible. To understand how this can be accomplished, we can look to Aristotle, who argues that the road to happiness and a meaningful life is paved with virtuous activity and good will. But before we do, a quick summary of the movie is in order.

Summary of *Groundhog Day*

Phil Connors is an egotistical and mean-spirited weatherman from Pittsburgh. Much to his chagrin, local Channel 9 sends him, for the third year in a row, to cover the Groundhog Festival in Punxsutawney, Pennsylvania (a real town north of Pittsburgh, population around 6000). Each year, to the delight of its residents who are dressed in top hats and tuxedos, "Punxsutawney Phil" – a real groundhog – comes out of his hole to reveal how much longer winter will last. From the very beginning it is clear that Phil, who suffers from delusions of grandeur (referring to himself as "the talent"), hates the assignment. With sardonic wit, Phil looks into the camera and quips, "Television really fails to capture the true excitement of a large squirrel predicting the weather." Phil hates the town and townspeople, and barely tolerates his cheerful new producer Rita (Andie MacDowell) and long-time camera man Larry (Chris Elliott). Rita tries to placate Phil, telling him that people love the groundhog story, to which he disdainfully responds, "People like blood sausage, too. People are morons." Later, at the Groundhog Festival, good-natured Rita cajoles him: "You're missing all the fun. These people are great! Some of them have been partying all night long. They sing songs 'til they get too cold and then they go sit by the fire and get warm and then they come back and sing some more." Phil replies, "Yeah, they're hicks, Rita."

To Phil's horror, a snowstorm – which he had predicted would pass by – prevents the news team from leaving town. As they try to leave town, a state trooper tells Phil the highway is closed: "Don't you watch the weather reports?" Connors replies, "I *make* the weather!" The cop then gives Phil the option to either turn around to Punxsutawney or freeze to death. "Which is it?" Connors answers, "I'm thinking." Reluctantly returning to Punxsutawney, Phil is forced to spend another night in a charming bed and breakfast run by kindly local "hicks."

The next morning, the clock radio in Phil's room goes off and he hears the same radio show he'd heard the day before, starting out with Sonny and Cher's hit, "I Got You Babe." The radio caster declares, "It's Groundhog Day!" At first, Connors thinks it is a hoax. But slowly he discovers it's the same day all over again. Phil is stuck, right back where he was 24 hours earlier: same town, same rituals, same people. And he is the only one aware of it. With comedic perfection, Bill Murray's character grimly offers the forecast, "It's gonna be cold, it's gonna be gray, and it's gonna last you for the rest of your life."

Connors spends an unknown number of days repeating the same day over and over again. Everyone else experiences that day for the "first" time, while Connors experiences it with Sisyphysian repetition. Estimates vary on how many actual Groundhog Days Connors relives. We see him relive 34 of them. But many more are implied. According to director Harold Ramis, the original script called for him to endure 10,000 years in Punxsutawney, but it was probably closer to ten (Goldberg 2006). Once Phil is inside this time warp, it's always Groundhog Day, he's always a weatherman, he always shows up at the square at Gobbler's Knob, he always runs into a set cast of characters throughout the day. Though it's always February 2nd, Phil is able to rearrange each day and build on each day's events.

Deep inside the Groundhog Day loop, Phil knows everything and anticipates everything. Sitting on a wall, he dryly narrates events, "A gust of wind, a dog bark. Cue the truck." At first, Phil mainly uses his new-found omniscience to seduce women. He spends days learning details about a woman which he can then use to manipulate her into sleeping with him. At first it is Nancy, one of the residents of Punxsutawney. She turns out to be relatively easy to manipulate, and so Phil seems to lose interest. He then turns his attention to Rita, who Ramis describes as a "mythical princess." "She had to be pure in soul and spirit, beautiful, kind, generous, forgiving and honest" (DVD Cover, *Groundhog Day*, 1993). Rita has zero interest in a superficial relationship with such a womanizer. Phil spends days (or weeks or years) trying to get her to sleep with him. Each sexual advance is met with a swift slap, again, and again, and again. At first, Phil is interested in Rita because she's the best-looking, most interesting, and sophisticated woman in a town full of hicks – a challenging conquest. For a while Phil plays the part of a guy in love. But eventually his insincere acts of love develop into true love, and Phil falls hard for Rita.

As the same day repeats countless times, Phil reacts to the situation in various ways. When he hears the first few bars from Sonny and Cher, he smashes his alarm clock. Sitting at a bar, he bemoans his state. "I was in the Virgin Islands once. I met a girl. We ate lobster, drank piña coladas. At sunset we made love like sea otters. *That* was a pretty good day. Why couldn't I get that day over, and over, and over?" Growing increasingly frustrated and despairing that Groundhog Day will never end, Phil steals a car, kidnaps the groundhog, and drives off a cliff. If no groundhog, perhaps no Groundhog Day. But to no avail. He steps in front of a truck, jumps off of a ledge, drops a plugged-in toaster into his bath, and other suicidal attempts to try to end his misery. Each attempt fails. As Phil explains to Rita in the local diner, "Every morning I wake up in the morning without a scratch on me, not a dent in the fender." Thus, he concludes, "I am an immortal."

Convinced of his immortality, things start to change. Phil finally accepts the possibility that he can't change the cyclical nature of time. So, Phil decides that *he* needs to change. Instead of living with reckless abandon (which he tries for a while) or giving into despair, Phil decides to become a different kind of person: a good person. A better version of himself. He engages in benevolent acts such as changing a stranger's tire and rescuing cats from trees. He heroically saves the life of a little boy falling out of a tree, and helps an old man who Phil knows will end up dead. He signs up for piano lessons, listens to Classical music, reads literature, learns French, and sculpts Rita's face into an angelic looking ice sculpture. As he transforms into an altruistic renaissance man, Phil finally gets Rita's attention and she starts to fall for him.

When Phil explains his situation to Rita, she decides to (finally) spend the night with him to see what will happen the next morning. Instead of a sexual encounter, they spend their time talking while flipping playing cards into a hat. Rita asks him, "Is this what you'd do with eternity?" Putting a positive spin on Phil's predicament she suggests, "I don't know Phil, maybe it's not a curse. It just depends on how you look at it." Phil smiles, but his expression suggests that it's not simply a matter of "how you look at it." Moral progress is never easy. But to go from such a loathsome individual to the virtuous and honorable man she is falling in love with was especially difficult. Sadly, when the much better version of Phil wakes up, he finds Rita is gone.

Once again, it's Groundhog Day. But something important has happened to Phil. He is a changed man. He no longer views his immortality as a curse. He now realizes he has an opportunity to become a better version of himself. Later that day, when he signs off the broadcast, he looks meaningfully into the camera, "Standing here among the people of Punxsutawney and basking in the warmth of their hearths and hearts, I couldn't imagine a better fate." Rita falls in love with the honorable man he has become, and Phil is finally released from the curse. Finding Rita next to him when he wakes up, Phil joyfully declares, "Today is tomorrow."

Interpreting the Movie

Groundhog Day has been widely viewed and interpreted, by everyone from therapists, to Wiccans, to followers of the Chinese Falun Gong movement. In his book, *How to Write Groundhog Day (2012)*, screenwriter Danny Rubin tells us, "The first note [after the film premiered] I remember came from a monk in Germany. He had discovered *Groundhog Day* as a perfect articulation of his Christian beliefs" (Parker 2013). The movie's director Harold Ramis talks about his mother-in-law who lived for 35 years in a Zen Buddhist meditation center. When he called her on the weekend the movie opened, she told him the abbots and senior monks loved it and thought it expressed a fundamental Buddhist concept (Shapiro 2018). Hindus also see versions of reincarnation.

As the movie gained wider popularity, it was embraced by Catholics and Evangelicals who view Punxsutawney as purgatory. Connors goes to his own version of hell, but since he's not evil it turns out to be purgatory, from which he is released by shedding his selfishness and committing to acts of love (Goldberg 2006). Jews find great significance in the fact that Connors is saved only after he performs *mitzvahs* (good deeds) and is returned to earth, not heaven, to perform more. Finally, one theologian describes Groundhog Day as "a stunning allegory of moral, intellectual, and even religious excellence in the face of postmodern decay, a sort of Christian-Aristotelian *Pilgrim's Progress* for those lost in the contemporary cosmos" (Goldberg 2006). As suggested earlier, I endorse this Aristotelian approach, which I'll come back to later in the paper.

The genius or "high concept" of the movie is the time warp: a weatherman who repeatedly lives the same day over and over. Rubin and Ramis discussed the possibility of an external cause for Phil's predicament – a magical clockmaker or a gypsy's curse. In the end, however, they thought it best to leave the recurrence of Groundhog Day unexplained. Phil Connors simply wakes up one morning and discovers it's still Groundhog Day. "The onset is sudden. No reason is given" (Parker 2013). Perhaps Phil is being punished for being such a deplorable human being. But because there is potential for goodness, Phil is given an opportunity for redemption.

Phil, looking back over his life, reminds moviegoers of the Angel Gabriel's visit to George Bailey in *It's a Wonderful Life*, or Ebenezer Scrooge in Dickens' A *Christmas Carol*, or Dorothy in the *Wizard of Oz*. Though these are venerable classics to riff off of, *Groundhog Day* feels more modern (but not postmodern as I shall argue). In modern terms, we might see the stopped clock as representing Phil's despair. Prior to being thrown into this endless repetition of the same day, Phil's despair was not entirely recognized by him. Before coming to Punxsutawney, Phil was metaphorically stuck already. He was stuck in his career, waiting for something better. He was also stuck in a series of loveless relationships. It all feels like a very modern mid-life crisis. Eventually Phil experiences full-blown despair to the point of repeated suicide attempts. Though comic, Phil's attempts are tragic. And they are absolutely comprehensible. It's not difficult to see how someone could be driven to such extreme behavior if he perceived life to be meaningless. Endless time or immortality are great gifts. But the opportunity to live a miserable and meaningless life forever is a curse.

Blessing or curse, *Groundhog Day*'s message is that redemption is possible. In Phil's case, he progresses from confused, to intrigued and amused, to despairing, and ultimately to profoundly self-actualized. Watching the movie feels good – many fans (including this one) have watched it again and again – because it suggests that change is possible, even for a second-rate weatherman from Pittsburgh. We too can get out of whatever rut or dead-end in which we find ourselves: school, work, relationships, or life in general. But redemption or transformation is not, as Rita suggests, simply a matter of "looking at things differently." Instead, it requires self-actualization or becoming a different kind of person, as suggested by Aristotle. Now, let's consider reasons to reject the view that *Groundhog Day* reflects the ideas of Nietzsche and Camus.

Moral of the Movie

Eternal Return

The Doctrine of Eternal Return pre-dates Nietzsche. Versions of this doctrine are found in Eastern traditions. In the West, it shows up in *Ecclesiastes*, pre-Socratics, Stoics, and Plotinus. Nietzsche himself suggests that eternal recurrence was his most "fundamental conception" and the highest formula of "Yea-saying philosophy" (*Thus Spoke Zarathustra* 1914). In his work *The Gay Science*, Nietzsche presents the Doctrine of Eternal Return as follows:

> *The greatest weight* – What if some day or night a demon were to steal after you into your loneliest loneliness and say to you: "This life as you now live it and have lived it, you will have to live once more and innumerable times more: and there will be nothing new in it, but every pain and every joy and every thought and sigh and everything unutterably small or great in your life will have to return to you, all in the same succession and sequence, even this spider and this moonlight between the trees, and even this moment and I myself. The eternal hourglass of existence is turned upside down again and again, and you with it, speck of dust!"
> Would you not throw yourself down and gnash your teeth and curse the demon who spoke thus? ... The question in each and everything, "Do you desire this once more and innumerable times more?" would lie upon your actions as the greatest weight. Or how well disposed would you have to become to yourself and to life *to crave nothing more, fervently* than this ultimate eternal confirmation and seal? (§341, 1974)

A Test of Resolve

One way to read eternal return or recurrence is as a psychological test of an individual's resolve: how well an individual can bear the threat of nihilism or a pointless or meaningless existence. Nietzsche thought such a test is necessary given the death of God. He thought Christianity was so popular because belief in God and immortality provide ordinary people with comfort and strength during difficult times. This tradition views time in terms of a linear progression. As time moves forward, we are looking to the future – the afterlife – instead of the present. According to Nietzsche, Christians are fooling themselves into thinking that there is a better world in the afterlife. If God is dead, however, there is no better or transcendent world. There is no bigger prize. Thus, this present life appears to be pointless and worthless.

To avoid this pessimism or nihilism, Nietzsche thought we need a new ideal that affirms this life instead of denying or diminishing life's value. We need "the ideal of the most world-approving, exuberant, and vivacious man, who ... wishes to have it again AS IT WAS AND IS, for all eternity..." (*Beyond Good and Evil*, §56, 1997b). The person who can say "yes" to eternal return is this ideal man, a genuine free spirit and "higher" human being (*üubermensch*).

Amor Fati

Nietzsche uses the phrase *amor fati*, which is a Latin phrase translated as "love of fate." It refers to an attitude or spirit of acceptance. Instead of merely coming to peace with one's life as it is, *amor fati* requires embracing your life even in its "strangest and hardest problems" (*Twilight of the Idols*, "What Do I Owe to the Ancients," 1997a). "My formula for greatness in a human being is *amor fati*: that one wants nothing to be different, not forward, not backward, not in all eternity. Not merely bear what is necessary, still less to conceal it ... but love it" (*Ecce Homo*, "Why I am So Clever," 1911). Nietzsche describes this love of life or joy in living as "the core of my nature" (*Ecce Homo*, "Why I Write Such Great Books," 1911).

Higher human beings can say "yes" to life because they don't want to change anything in their lives. Lower types of human beings, on the other hand, would need to "edit out the pain, tragedy, and hardship in their lives" (Belliotti 2013, p. 87). These lower or weaker types want a life that does not involve struggle, suffering, and failure. Confronted with the possibility of eternal return, i.e., no hope for transcendent salvation, they would, in Nietzsche's words, "throw themselves down and gnash their teeth and curse the demon." Higher human types, on the other hand, welcome eternal recurrence as "an opportunity to rebel and become who they are by creatively willing their fate" (Belliotti 2013, p. 90). In a world that lacks inherent meaning and purpose, *we* become like gods who can order the world and create meaning and purpose (Belliotti 2013, p. 91).

Unlike the Greeks, who thought life was a matter of becoming fully human, Nietzsche thought it was possible to live according to an ideal that might not be appropriate for every human being. He thought the Greeks signify a limit or boundary in terms of who we could become. "We must overcome even the Greeks!" Nietzsche thought the Greek motto, "Become who you are!" should be replaced with "Invent who you are!" (Spence 2013, p. 277).

The Value in Suffering

One scholar argues that the only life in which eternal return could make sense is a life of pain and suffering (Kain 2007, p. 56). Throughout his own life, Nietzsche endured great pain and suffering: physical illness, failed personal relationships, and unrequited love. So it makes sense that he would try to turn his pain to his advantage, believing that "[a]rtfully managing suffering positively transforms the self" (Belliotti 2013, p. 96). This attitude toward suffering is behind his oft-quoted aphorism: "*From life's military school* – "What does not kill me makes me stronger"" (*Twilight of the*

Idols, Epigrams and Arrows, §8, 1997a). Refusing to be "doctored" or "pampered," Nietzsche had an "instinct for self-recovery." Believing that man is "strong enough to make everything turn to his own advantage," he "restored [him]self to health" (*Ecce Homo*, "Why I am So Wise," §2, 1911).

Nietzsche thought it was impossible to significantly reduce suffering in the world. By trying to reduce your own suffering or that of others, you enslave yourself to that suffering. Instead, one must master or overcome suffering. So Nietzsche put himself in charge. "Everything that was going to happen in his life, he accepted, he chose, he willed" (Kain 2007, p. 57). Choosing to live his life over again, with every detail of suffering and pain the same, he was able to break "the psychological stranglehold" that pain had over him. *Amor fati* allowed Nietzsche to become sovereign or master over his life.

Does Eternal Return Work?

Although many are attracted to this aspect of Nietzsche's philosophy which encourages strength and resolve in the face of suffering, we may ask whether this is even possible. To start out, Nietzsche's distinction of human beings into merely two types, higher or stronger and lower or weak, is overly facile. Humans are more complicated than this. Over the course of an entire lifetime, we have many higher and lower points toward which we exhibit varying levels of resolve and fortitude. During these lower points, there are many cases in which self-recovery is simply impossible, hence being "doctored" (i.e., seeking medical treatment or psychological therapy) is well advised. Sometimes, people are not made stronger but are understandably crushed under the weight of pain and suffering. For example, telling a parent who has lost a child that "whatever doesn't kill you will make you stronger" is certainly cold comfort. Even if we could affirm eternal return, it's hard to see how we would act differently. For Nietzsche, "It is not the works, it is the *belief* that is decisive here" (*Beyond Good and Evil*, §287). But what exactly are we to *do* in face of eternal return? Where do I go after saying "yes?"

Even if there are people who share in Nietzsche's natural instinct for self-recovery, saying "yes" to eternal return may be undesirable. First, by discouraging attempts to reduce pain and suffering, it may encourage us to turn a blind eye to the pain and suffering of others. Consider, for example, the very troubling statistics about rising numbers of "deaths of despair." Accepting eternal return, we run the risk of ignoring pleas for help or failing to intercede in cases in which we can help others manage their pain and suffering. Second, setting aside the fact of self-deception, which tends to be engaged at our lowest points, even if you think you are supremely happy with your own life, see what happens if you must relive your life in *exactly* the same manner. You are saying "yes" to a life in which you could not strive for something different or better. When Nietzsche's demon slips in, on the worst day of your life, your "loneliest loneliness," he asks you to look only at your current self. You cannot project out to next semester, or when you get that promotion at work, or find "Mr. Right," or lose those extra 10 pounds. No nips, no tucks. No tweaks. The demon asks: "do you love yourself so much that you would live for all eternity as this *exact* person you are today?" Let's say recently single, carrying an extra ten pounds, not yet where you want to be professionally, or maintaining a C+ average. From this point of view, eternal return shows us the "horror of existence" in which there is nothing new and everything is exactly the same. Yet this is simply not how most of us make it through life. Instead, "[w]e hope for, we expect, something new, something different, some improvement, some progress, or at least some distraction, some hope" (Kain 2007, p. 56). In accepting eternal return, we must reject hope for a better life.

Myth of Sisyphus

Albert Camus was influenced by Nietzsche. He too rejects hope, declaring religious hope one of the worst of all evils. Like Nietzsche, Camus believes that living meaningfully in a Godless world is about adopting the proper attitude toward life. Camus conveys this view in his version of the ancient Greek Myth of Sisyphus. Sisyphus disrespected the gods and they punished him by condemning him to roll a stone up a mountain, at which point the stone would roll back down the hill and he would have to do it again. Camus, reflecting upon Sisyphus's situation, suggests a surprise ending in which Sisyphus is actually happy.

> I leave Sisyphus at the foot of the mountain. One always finds one's burden again. But Sisyphus teaches the higher fidelity that negates the gods and raises rocks. He too concludes that all is well. This universe henceforth without a master seems to him neither sterile nor futile. Each atom of that stone, each mineral flake of that night filled mountain, in itself forms a world. The struggle itself towards the heights is enough to fill a man's heart. One must imagine Sisyphus happy. (Camus 1955)

For Camus, Sisyphus is an absurd hero. He is absurd in the sense that his plight exemplifies life's absurdity, its "futility and hopeless labor." This hero triumphs, however, by virtue of his endless effort and intense consciousness of life's futility. The vivid imagery of this man rolling a heavy rock demonstrates the possibility that we too can live with "the certainty of a crushing fate, without the resignation that ought to accompany it" (Camus 1955). In other words, in spite of the pointlessness of existence, Sisyphus keeps on truckin'.

Camus believes that we, like Sisyphus, can never escape our fate, which is ultimately death with no afterlife. When the rock comes tumbling down the hill, Sisyphus is understandably tempted by despair over the ultimate futility of his project (our lives). Recovery from despair is made possible only at "the hour of consciousness." "At each of those moments when Sisyphus leaves the heights and gradually sinks towards the lairs of the gods, he is superior to his fate. He is stronger than his rock" (Camus 1955). To be stronger than the rock, to overcome his despair, Sisyphus must be aware of his condition. Sisyphus, "powerless and rebellious, knows the whole extent of his wretched condition: it is what he thinks of during his descent" (Camus 1955). In other words, Sisyphus' pointless life is meaningful because he lives fully aware of the futility of existence and consciously facing his fate. It is precisely because he does not hope for a better future that we must imagine Sisyphus happy. By rejecting hope that his condition will improve, Sisyphus also rejects despair.

Like Nietzsche's higher human being, Sisyphus says "yes" to his life – a futile struggle culminating in death. Camus, like Nietzsche, rejects false solutions to our despair, such as religion. Since there is no ultimate meaning, we must accept and embrace living with death, without appealing to God in order for our lives to be meaningful. "All Sisyphus's silent joy is contained therein. His fate belongs to him. His rock is his thing" (Camus 1955). For Camus, it is only when we become conscious of our finitude and futility that we can take ownership of our lives and live meaningfully. By consciously choosing to live out what has been imposed on him, Sisyphus is thus making it into his own end. As master over his own life, Sisyphus is a higher human being.

Sisyphus Fulfilled

For another twist on the Greek myth, what if we were to infuse Sisyphus's veins with a magical serum that makes him love rolling rocks up hills? Richard Taylor argues that if Sisyphus were to find this pointless task fulfilling, then his life would be meaningful because desire-satisfaction is what makes life meaningful (Taylor 1970). Taylor's view, as well as Nietzsche's view, that saying "yes" to eternal return makes our lives meaningful suggests that as long as any individual finds his or her life meaningful, that life is meaningful. This is *meaning subjectivism*, which many people, including many of my students, find appealing. Accordingly, we don't need to know anything about the character of the person living the life in question or the content of that life, i.e., what sorts of activities or projects the individual engages in, because it is the positive assessment of, or attitude toward, one's life that is doing the meaning work. But this means that if Hitler viewed his life as meaningful, then it would be meaningful. So perhaps the view is not as appealing as one might think.

Think again of *Groundhog Day*. A meaning subjectivist would say that if we could inject Phil with some magical serum to make him love his assignment to the Groundhog Festival, then his life would be meaningful. But that's simply not how it worked for Phil. He didn't turn his life around simply by doing the same sorts of things with renewed gusto or satisfaction. This is because you can't magically imbue a life with meaning if it's truly not there. When Phil viewed his life as pointless, he gave into despair and tried to kill himself, repeatedly. To move past this despair, Phil didn't simply change his attitude or convince himself that eternal life in Punxsutawney was fulfilling just as it is. Instead, for reasons I will discuss shortly, he decided to change his life and become a different, better version of himself.

Evaluating the Moral

Phil Says "No"

Groundhog Day does not really measure up as a Nietzschean film. When faced with the choice of reliving Groundhog Day in Punxsutawney all over again and numerous times more, Phil Conners does not say "yes." He vehemently rejects it. There is no *amor fati* with this guy! It's *odium fati*. Even prior to this dreadful assignment to Podunk USA, Phil wanted a different life: a different job, different co-workers, a different woman in his bed every night. Phil was all about looking to the future, hoping things would get better, desperate to change the situation, desperate to *change*, to not accept his fate. In some scenes, Phil quite literally throws himself down, metaphorically shaking his fists at the gods who placed this curse upon him.

Phil does eventually accept the fact that he is stuck in time, reliving Groundhog Day. But this does not mean that he accepts his fate: living *as is* in Punxsutawney for all of eternity. Saying "yes" to eternal return, requires saying "yes" to the person I am and the life I am living right now. Nietzsche believes that events in the world are closely interrelated such that to want things to be different is a denial of this world and one's self. If Nietzsche's life were different in *any* way – if he edited out any of his pain and suffering – it would no longer be his life but the life of a different person. Unlike Nietzsche who does not want to change, Phil is changing all of the time. Throughout the movie, Phil never lives exactly the same day, as prescribed by eternal return. Instead, Phil rearranges and builds on each day's events, moving in a linear progression, working toward a better future and a better life.

Phil Strives to Be Better

This better, happy man who Phil eventually becomes is not Nietzsche's higher human being. When the hourglass of existence is turned upside down, Phil is given an opportunity for reflection or self-assessment – much like eternal recurrence. Upon reflection, however, Phil does not turn to Nietzsche (or Camus). He turns to the Greeks. Instead of changing his attitude or outlook on his life, Phil strives to do things differently and become the best version of himself possible. Thus, Phil is no postmodern anti-hero. And *Groundhog Day* is not a postmodern dark comedy. It's a classic romantic comedy in which viewers enjoy seeing Phil-the-good-guy "get the girl." We come to like Phil and root for him because he gives us a reason to hope that we too can live better lives.

Sisyphus becomes stronger than his rock by coming to terms with his finitude or mortality. For Phil, the "hour of consciousness" comes when he embraces his *immortality*. Stuck with himself for eternity, Phil eventually comes to realize, in the words of Stephen Tobolowsky who plays Ned, "he's not living up to the standards of excellence" (*The Making of Groundhog Day* 2018). In other words, Phil does not break out of the Sisyphian cycle, or get unstuck, by changing his attitude. Instead he starts *doing* things differently. His arrogance transforms into humility; his contempt turns into compassion and empathy. He rejects his selfish, egotistical impulses and starts living more for others. According to Ramis, "Once he stops worrying about himself all of the time and starts living a life in service to others, then his life gets very full and rich, indeed" (*The Making of Groundhog Day* 2018).

This is what I take to be the take-home message of the movie. If you are feeling stuck or in a rut … if you, like Sisyphus, view your life, or aspects of your life, as pointless or hopeless … if you want your life to be truly meaningful … then listen to the Greeks! Act differently. Become who you are! Be the very best version of yourself.

Objective Goods and Intrinsic Value

Groundhog Day illustrates the weakness of existentialist theories about happiness and the meaning of life, namely, all you end up with is a subjective assessment of your life – a psychological selfie. "Passing" a psychological test about how we feel about our lives is not, however, sufficient for living a life that is truly, or objectively, meaningful. In other words, just because you might think your life is meaningful, or think your life is going so well that you would say "yes" to living it all over again, your life is not necessarily meaningful.

This may seem counterintuitive. For how could I be wrong about how well *my* life is going or if my life is meaningful. After all, it is *my* life. But we are wrong about all sorts of things. In Nietzsche's words, we are "all too human." When it comes to assessing value, we over- and under-estimate the value of all sorts of things. We spend too much time or money on things that are of little value (e.g., cars, clothes, entertainment, sexual gratification) at the expense of things that truly are of value (e.g., health and well-being; moral, intellectual and spiritual growth; loving, healthy interpersonal relationships). Likewise, we overvalue ourselves – think of Phil's conceit. Or we undervalue our worth – think of Nancy who sleeps with Phil, even after he calls out for Rita while they are kissing.

Here we might distinguish between (a) relative goods and (b) objective goods. Relative goods are only good insofar as they correspond to the sorts of things a person *happens* to value. In Phil's case, he *happens* to value "making love like sea otters." But we could imagine a life going pretty well without meaningless sexual encounters. Objective goods, on the other hand, are good independently of an individual's subjective conception of what has value. Maintaining and sustaining long-term relationships is objectively valuable, for it's hard to construct a meaningful life without the love of good friends. Aristotle talks about activities that are either (a) good for what they produce (having extrinsic or instrumental value) – e.g., money, employment, cars, etc. – or (b) good in themselves (having intrinsic value) – e.g., pleasure, happiness, truth, etc. The Greeks believe that activities or endeavors that aim at, say, friendship, love, beauty, happiness, etc., are worth engaging in even if they lead to nothing of value or consequence.

It might be the case that Phil's initial failure to recognize the objective or intrinsic value of sustained relationships with loved ones is not a matter of choice. He may have lost the capacity for recognizing goods of objective value as the result of a disposition that he has developed over time, which has been conditioned by choices and activities he has been engaged in. In other words, he may have spent so much time "making love like sea otters" that Phil has lost sight, or never had sight of, the objective value of enduring loving relationships. Thus, if we were to ask Phil at the beginning of the movie whether or not he thinks his life is meaningful and going well, he would say "yes" (i.e., meaning subjectivism). For at this point Phil sincerely believes that having lots of short-lived sexual encounters is making him happy. But Phil is wrong. Over time, Phil eventually comes to see the error of his ways. He eventually realizes that engaging in intrinsically valuable activities – ones involving love, kindness, and doing good deeds – is what makes life meaningful. But what causes these changes in Phil?

Don't Worry, Be Happy

At the beginning of the movie, Phil is a hedonist, pursuing a life of pleasure and gratification. *Hedone* is the Greek word for pleasure. Hedonists identify pleasure with what is good or valuable and pain with what is not good or valuable. Thus, they define happiness in terms of how much of one's life is spent enjoying oneself or experiencing pleasure. Meaning subjectivists, who reduce meaningfulness to a feeling of fulfillment or satisfaction, endorse a hedonistic theory of value or goodness.

Early in the movie, we find Phil drowning his sorrows at a bar in the local bowling alley. Turning to the drunk guys seated next to him, Phil asks, "Let me ask you guys a question. "What would you do if you were stuck in one place, and every day was exactly the same, and nothing that you did mattered? What if there were no tomorrow?"" Drunk number 1 responds, "No tomorrow? That would mean there would be no consequences. There would be no hangovers. We could do whatever we wanted!" Armed with this new insight, Phil leaves the bar with his new-found friends and proceeds to lead the police on a high-speed car chase. Driving down the railroad tracks, Phil reflects on his present condition. "It's the same thing your whole life. Clean up your room. Stand up straight. Pick up your feet. Take it like a man. Be nice to your sister. Don't mix beer and wine. Ever. I'm not going to live by their rules anymore." When the policeman comes up to his car to issue him a speeding ticket, Phil rolls down the window, looks up at the cop, and orders three cheeseburgers, two orders of fries, two chocolate shakes and a large coke.

The next scene in the movie, Sonny and Cher have started up again. That morning we find Phil at breakfast with Rita. He is over-eating, smoking, and drinking coffee straight out of the pot. Rita, "Don't you worry about lung cancer, cholesterol, love handles?" Phil responds, "I don't worry about anything [pause] anymore." Rita asks, "What makes you so special? Everybody worries about something." Phil, "That's exactly what makes me so special. I don't even have to floss." With that, Phil stuffs an entire Danish into his mouth. Rita expresses her disgust with Phil's hedonism by reciting from memory lines from Sir Walter Scott's poem "My Native Land." "The wretch, concentered all in self, / Living, shall forfeit fair renown, / And, doubly dying, shall go down, / To the vile dust, from whence he sprung, / Unwept, unhonour'd, and unsung." Phil shoves another piece of cake in his mouth.

Hedonic Treadmill

Though living dangerously and enjoying a carefree life of no rules and consequences is fun for a while, Phil eventually rejects this approach to living. One reason might be that happiness, when viewed from a subjective point of view, has a set point. We adapt to good and bad events, and then return to the same baseline level of happiness. This gives rise to what is known as the hedonic treadmill, or what psychologists refer to as hedonic adaptation. Empirical studies show that once we become familiar with something, once things are the same or stimuli is constant, we don't tend to notice or pay attention to them anymore (Headey and Wearing 1992). A new promotion at work or an "A" on a paper causes an immediate spurt of joy, but it doesn't really change one's overall happiness. This is because we adjust expectations to the new status quo, and desire even more to maintain the same level of happiness. Like hamsters (or groundhogs) on a treadmill, we must continually work to maintain a certain level of happiness or pleasure. Research shows us that experiencing more and more pleasure doesn't make us happier or feel like our lives are meaningful (Headey and Wearing 1992). Even if a magical serum could make Phil-the-rebel feel like he was happy or fulfilled, his pleasure experience quotient would eventually top off.

So, one possible explanation of Phil's transformation is that he wanted off the treadmill. In an interview, Andie McDowell says, "You knew he couldn't be happy like that" (*The Making of Groundhog Day* 2018). Of course, it took some time for Phil to come to this realization. It's not the case, however, that everyone is capable of becoming enlightened like Phil. There are plenty of cases of men and women who choose relative goods (e.g., casual sex) over objective goods (e.g., sustained loving relationships). You could give them an eternity to examine their lives, and they will not change. Psychologists might explain their behavior in a variety of ways, such as arrested development, delayed adolescence, narcissism, self-destructive behavior in response to trauma, etc. We all know people like that. Sometimes they even get elected to high offices in government and or become movie moguls in Hollywood. But there are lots of other cases in which people *do* change their ways – even vain, cynical, malcontents like Phil. Ramis says that one of the messages of the movie is that "people can change" (*The Making of Groundhog Day* 2018). So, if change is possible . . . if a life devoted to desire-satisfaction and gratification is not meaningful . . . if hedonism doesn't make you happy . . . then what does? Enter the Greeks.

Aristotle's Virtue Ethics

In his *Nicomachean Ethics,* Aristotle argues that happiness and living a meaningful life is about *habitually doing the right thing* (Hall 2018, p. 7). Aristotle believes that once we decide we want to be happy, we can train ourselves to be good by working on our virtues and controlling our vices. Virtue, from the Greek *arête* meaning "excellence," requires *activity*. If you want to be courageous, you must perform acts of courage. Virtue is not a feeling or an attitude. It is an appropriate psychological disposition in response to a feeling; i.e., the proper response. For example, a person doesn't "feel" courageous. Instead, in situations in which a person is feeling afraid or unsure, the proper response (i.e., virtue) is courage. Aristotle thinks that over time we train ourselves to be virtuous. Phil might want to eat doughnuts for lunch instead of, say, a salad, which is the more virtuous choice. If he were to start eating salads every day, however, over time he'd start unconsciously desiring salad. (It works! I have succeeded in training myself to be a happy salad eater.) Phil becomes a better man once he starts to perform virtuous acts, e.g., he changes stranger's tires, saves a boy from falling out of a tree, and helps a dying old man. When he's not saving lives, Phil spends his time trying to improve himself: learning piano, listening to Classical music, and reading literature.

Though there is only one way to be good, namely to be virtuous, there are many ways for us to be bad. Aristotle's Doctrine of the Mean suggests that vice comes from either a deficiency of virtue or an excess. Cowardice results from a deficiency of courage. While at the other end of the spectrum, too much courage results in foolhardiness or recklessness. Think back to Phil driving down the railroad tracks toward an oncoming train – this is hardly an act of courage. It's just stupid. Virtue for Aristotle boils down to the ancient Greek proverb, "nothing in excess." Virtues or habits of choice, e.g., courage, wisdom, justice, etc., make human beings flourish or live up to our fullest potential as rational creatures.

Virtuous people will feel good or experience pleasure in being virtuous. "[N]o one would call a person just, for instance, if he did not enjoy doing just actions, or generous if he did not enjoy generous actions, and similarly for the other virtues" (Book I, 8, Aristotle 1999). But virtuous people do not act virtuously simply to make themselves feel good or fulfilled. Virtuous people feel good when they act virtuously because they have aligned their desires with what is truly good for our nature as human beings. In other words, we enjoy being courageous because courage is really good for us as human beings. We see this in the movie; as Phil progresses toward becoming a better person he becomes less cynical or nasty and more joyful and pleasant.

At one point in the movie, Rita shares with Phil a long list of character traits, i.e., virtues, she is looking for in a man. They include: humility, intelligence, humor, courage, kindness, sensitivity, and gentleness. In his autobiography, Benjamin Franklin came up with a list of 13 virtues that he put on a chart that he checked every day. For example, temperance ("Eat not to dullness; drink not to elevation"); sincerity ("Use no hurtful deceit; think innocently and justly, and, if you speak, speak accordingly"); and humility ("Imitate Jesus and Socrates") (Franklin 2018). Running through a "virtue checklist," Franklin is not assessing how he feels about himself as a human being (i.e., subjectivism). Instead, virtues provide him with an objective measure for assessing how well he is doing at being human. Of course, Franklin may be mistaken, or deceive himself, thinking that he is truly humble and sincere when he is not. This is because, as noted earlier, we are all fallible. This is where Aristotle thinks virtuous friends can keep you honest, providing, as he says, "a mirror to your soul." A good or virtuous friend can look over your shoulder as you consider your virtues (and vices) and offer objective feedback. Rita's picture of her ideal man which she shares with Phil seems to help him become a better person, and ultimately the kind of man that she can fall in love with.

Aristotle, the father of biology, came to all of these conclusions about what is good for human beings by observing and studying human nature. His virtue ethics approach suggests that we can use our understanding of human nature to live the best way possible. In contrast, Nietzsche believes (and existentialists in general believe) that we need to focus only on the existing individual living in the present moment, without appealing to human nature in general. Nietzsche thinks that measuring oneself against a set of virtues that are common to all human beings is limiting, discourages individuality, and stifles creativity. This is why Nietzsche thinks we need to go "beyond the Greeks."

But not all limitations are harmful or undesirable. Speed limits contribute to public safety. And limiting calories can help us to lose weight and be healthy. Thus, instead of thinking of being kind, generous, compassionate, or selfless as restrictive or limiting, appealing to the virtues – to standards of excellence – is liberating. For the virtues provide useful parameters for living a good life in which we can be our best selves. Perhaps Nietzsche has the intellectual wherewithal to invent his own rules. But most of us need help.

Finally, Aristotle's virtue ethics approach does not discourage individuality and or stifle creativity. For to be a fully self-actualized human being, it is up to each individual to figure out his or her unique talents and abilities – what is your purpose – and then pursue that with excellence, i.e., virtuously. In other words, if you want to be happy and live a life that is meaningful, you have to figure out what you are good at and do that thing well – whether it be to build bridges, bake bread, teach philosophy, or forecast the weather. Once you find your purpose in life, you must then work on cultivating the virtues and controlling your vices so that you can become the best version of yourself.

Phil Lives Up to Standards of Excellence

Once Phil comes to realize that living without any rules is not all it is cracked up to be, he starts to live up to standards of excellence, or virtues, that were modeled by Rita and the townspeople of Punxsutawney. Phil becomes less self-centered and starts to, in Ramis' terms, live "a life in service to others." Aristotle would say that Phil-the-egoist was not being true to his nature. He was not being the best version of himself that he could be. So, Phil starts to make better choices about how to use his time. Instead of merely seeking pleasure and gratification (hedonism), Phil chooses to live a life of virtue. Gradually, after habitually doing the right thing, Phil changes his character. Phil becomes a good person.

Earlier I suggested that one explanation for Phil's transformation is that he grew tired of a life devoted to pleasure and gratification – he wanted off of the hedonic treadmill. It is important to note that when Phil finally decides he wants to be a better person, he does all of this believing that Groundhog Day will never end and that none of these changes for the better will have mattered, at least not in terms of getting Rita to fall in love with him. After they spend the night together, Phil dejectedly tells Rita that he will have to start all over again the next day, proving to her that he is not a jerk. Even if his desire to prove himself worthy of Rita is what helped to motivate Phil to become a better man, it doesn't matter whether or not Rita takes notice of him. For Phil is finally happy and his life is meaningful, which is good in itself. Phil getting the girl in the end is just the icing on the cake.

Conclusion

The high concept of *Groundhog Day* – a weatherman repeatedly living the same day over – does better than eternal return. It does not ask us to relive every exact moment of our lives, all our joys and all of our sorrows, in exactly the same manner. That would be horrible. Instead, this self-help rom-com suggests that change, and ultimately redemption, is possible. Once Phil adopts the wisdom of the Greeks, immortality is no longer a curse but a blessing. Ancient Greek philosophers viewed philosophy as "a training for death" or preparing for immortality. Instead of focusing on mortality and accepting oneself as is, they believed a person could become eternal by transcending themselves (Hadot 1995, p. 81).

Transcending yourself involves opening yourself up to the goods of the mind and spirit, not simply the body, and engaging in activities that are intrinsically worthwhile. It will also inevitably mean focusing less on yourself, and more on others: "living a life of service to others" (*The Making of Groundhog Day* 2018). For the good life is not merely about personal satisfaction or affirmation, "living your truth" or "being authentic." Instead there are objective ways to measure what constitutes a good and meaningful life: have integrity, be generous, kind, humble, and above all, give and receive love. We don't need an eternity to figure that out. We can listen to the Greeks.

So, if you are feeling stuck or in a rut – whether it's a dead-end job, a middling GPA, a soul-sucking career, or a relationship that is going nowhere – there *is* hope. "You *can* live better. You *can* have a better life. People *can* change," says Ramis (*The Making of Groundhog Day* 2018). This is because we are, as Aristotle realized, creatures of habit. This means that over time, it is possible to learn from our mistakes and do better. As the groundhog reminds us again and again and again, winter doesn't last forever. Though it can at times seem interminable, Spring eventually comes, signaling a time for rebirth and renewal. Tomorrow can be a better day – not by changing your attitude toward life, but by doing things differently and being your best self.

References

Aristotle. 1999. *Nicomachean ethics*. Indianapolis: Hackett Publishing.
Belliotti, Raymond Angelo. 2013. *Jesus or Nietzsche: How should we live our lives?* Amsterdam/New York: Rodopi.
Camus, Albert. 1955. *The myth of Sisyphus and other essays*. New York: Knopf.
Faust, Michael. 2012. Groundhog Day. *Philosophy Now*. https://philosophynow.org/issues/93/Groundhog_Day
Franklin, Benjamin. 2018. In *The autobiography of Benjamin Franklin*, ed. Frank Woodworth Pine. London: Aziloth Books.
Goldberg, Jonah. 2006. A movie for all time. *National Review*. https://www.nationalreview.com/2006/02/movie-all-time-jonah-goldberg-2/
Hadot, Pierre. 1995. *Philosophy as a way of life: Spiritual exercise from Socrates to Foucault*. Malden: Blackwell.
Hall, Edith. 2018. *Aristotle's way: Ten ways ancient wisdom can change your life*. London: Vintage.
Headey, Bruce, and Alexander J. Wearing. 1992. *Understanding happiness: A theory of subjective well-being*. Melbourne: Longman Cheshire.
Kain, P.J. 2007. Nietzsche, eternal recurrence, and the horror of existence. *Journal of Nietzsche Studies* 33: 49–63.
Library of Congress National Film Registry. 2006. https://www.loc.gov/programs/national-film-preservation-board/film-registry/
Nietzsche, F. 1911. *Ecce homo. The complete works of Friedrich Nietzsche*. Vol. 17. New York: Macmillan.
———. 1914. *Thus spoke Zarathustra. The complete works of Friedrich Nietzsche*. Vol. 11. New York: Macmillan.
———. 1974. *The gay science: With a prelude in rhymes and an appendix of songs*. New York: Vintage Books.
———. 1997a. *Twilight of the idols, or, how to philosophize with the hammer*. Indianapolis: Hackett.
———. 1997b. *Beyond good and evil*. New York: Dover.
Parker, James. 2013. Reliving *Groundhog Day*. *The Atlantic*. https://www.theatlantic.com/magazine/archive/2013/03/reliving-groundhog-day/309223/
Ramis, Harold. 1993. *Groundhog Day*.
Shapiro, Ari. 2018. How to understand the philosophy of "*Groundhog Day*" and live life by its message [audio]. *NPR*. http://www.tinyurl.com/yxq3hjdr
Spence, James. 2013. What Nietzsche could teach you: Eternal return in *Groundhog Day*. In *Movies and the meaning of life: Philosophers take on Hollywood*. Chicago: Open Court.
Taylor, R. 1970. *Good and evil*. New York: Macmillan.
Whooznext. 2018. The making of *Groundhog Day* – Harold Ramis [video]. *YouTube*. https://youtu.be/2d7kkecft4w

The Big Lebowski: Nihilism, Masculinity, and Abiding Virtue

38

Peter S. Fosl

Contents

Introduction	918
Critical Summary of *The Big Lebowski*	919
Interpreting *The Big Lebowski*	935
What Makes a Man?	935
The Dude's Abiding Virtues	938
The Dude Versus Nihilism	944
Conclusion	947
References	948

Abstract

This chapter argues that in addition to being a hilarious stoner comedy, one of the most beloved cult films of all time, and a trenchant genre critique of film noir detective cinema, as well as American Westerns, Ethan and Joel Coen's film, *The Big Lebowski* (1998, *TBL*), also presents reflections on several important philosophical themes. First, as a matter of feminist and gender philosophy, *TBL* examines and criticizes prominent ideals of masculinity, especially as they appear in US cinema, exploring the question of what a better kind of man might be. Second, that project is woven together with an investigation of virtue as exemplified by the film's protagonist, Jeffrey "The Dude" Lebowski. *TBL* portrays in The Dude a man whose virtues include Epicurean-like excellences related to contented poverty, equality, community, and friendship. Friendship is also a virtue among Aristotelians, and The Dude's culture of friendship, from an Aristotelian perspective, bears significant political import. By positioning The Dude at a mean between the extremes of his friend Walter Sobchak's excess and the nihilists' deficiencies, *TBL* explores the way rules and rule-following properly fit into virtuous moral life. In The Dude, the film shows how moral virtue

P. S. Fosl (✉)
Transylvania University, Lexington, KY, USA
e-mail: pfosl@transy.edu

© Springer Nature Switzerland AG 2024
D. K. Johnson et al. (eds.), *The Palgrave Handbook of Popular Culture as Philosophy*,
https://doi.org/10.1007/978-3-031-24685-2_35

not only requires intellectual excellences but also the right kind of character. And third, perhaps most centrally, *TBL* engages the problem of modern European nihilism and the effect it has had upon US culture. By means of the "abiding" virtues it valorizes, existential repetition, comedy itself, and the way its characters inhabit time, *TBL* confronts the death, despair, and disillusionment nihilism yields.

Keywords

Lebowski · Moral philosophy · Nihilism · Masculinity · Hero · Film noir · Friendship · *Philia* · Comedy · Camus · Nietzsche · Epicurus · Aristotle · Dudeism · Coen Brothers · Repetition · Existentialism · Rules · Virtue · Big Sleep · Jewishness · Westerns · Epicureanism · Aristotelianism

Introduction

Ethan and Joel Coen's (the Coen Brothers') 1998 cult classic movie, *The Big Lebowski*, is a hilarious, marijuana-fueled comedy. It is, however, anything but simple. A reinterpretation (and parody/homage) of *The Big Sleep* – Howard Hawks's 1946 film noir masterpiece – *The Big Lebowski* presents, like its predecessor, a crime mystery with a tantalizing labyrinth of a plot. More importantly, the film engages an array of philosophical issues.

Populated by a cowboy, sexual athletes, millionaires, a playboy, a private eye, soldiers, bullies, and would-be saviors, *The Big Lebowski* interrogates and challenges many of the conceptions of male identity, heroism, and virtue centered by noir detective fiction, American Westerns, and more broadly, modern culture. Perhaps because of his crafty adoption, investigation, and critique of these masculinities, *The Big Lebowski*'s protagonist Jefferey Lebowski – a.k.a. The Dude – has become a kind of heroic antihero to millions of people across the globe.

His popularity no doubt also stems from the characteristic virtues he exhibits. Among the most prominent are his antiauthoritarianism, his nonmaterialistic lifestyle, and his laid-back, peaceable, and easygoing attitude – tied together by the film as the way he "abides." Especially remarkable is a virtue that important ancient philosophers such as Aristotle and the Epicureans promoted, namely, friendship. The Dude's extraordinary relationship with Walter Sobchak (and their pal Donny Kerabatsos) symbolizes the hopeful possibility of overcoming the troubling political divisions that burden our world. That hope is, in turn, part of *The Big Lebowski*'s response to a much more profound philosophical condition plaguing modernity – European nihilism. Explaining *The Big Lebowski*'s critical engagement with masculinity, its vision of Dudely virtue, and its answer to the threat of nihilism structures this chapter. Because of the film's status as such a cult classic, however, a critical examination of its plot, inspiration, and symbolism in grand detail is in order first.

Critical Summary of *The Big Lebowski*

Like 1946's *The Big Sleep* (*TBS*), and so many other film noir detective classics, *The Big Lebowski* (*TBL*) is set in California. Film noir is a subgenre of crime cinema that arose in the 1920s and 1930s, in part out of German expressionism, reaching its zenith in the 1940s and 1950s, especially in Hollywood, CA. Noir films depict in stark chiaroscuros a hard-boiled, sexualized, and dark, crime-ridden world through which a smart, cynical, solitary, worldly-wise, and (typically) male protagonist moves as he single-handedly tangles with a horrible crime and its consequences. Commonly, along the way, the protagonist becomes entangled in a tragic or tortured love affair.

TBL opens, moreover, with the Sons of Pioneers (including Leonard Slye, later a.k.a. cowboy entertainer Roy Rogers) singing their mournful 1934 hit, "Tumbling Tumbleweeds," as the camera follows one of said botanicals rolling through the desert night toward the crest of a hill. Having framed the film as a commentary on old-school American Westerns, the opening follows the tumbleweed over the top and down, descending into the lights of modern noir-nighttime Los Angeles and the terminus of the American West on Santa Monica's storied beach.

When the camera cuts from the beach to a man standing that same night in an empty Ralphs supermarket aisle (1745 Garfield Rd, Alhambra), the film's cowboy narrator, "The Stranger" (Sam Elliott), introduces viewers to Jeff Lebowski, "The Dude." (The Dude was inspired by real-life Jeff Dowd, played by Jeff Bridges, and is analogous to Humphrey Bogart's character Philip Marlowe in *TBS*.) Dressed in a shabby T-shirt, shorts, shades, a house robe, and flip-flops, he shops for a quart of half-and-half. It is an essential component of The Dude's favorite beverage, the White Russian cocktail (ingredients: vodka, Kahlúa, and half-and-half), which he affectionately and with a nod to race calls a "Caucasian." (The Dude drinks nine of them across the movie.)

The Dude violates the store rules by opening the half-and-half carton for a sniff while still in the aisle and then pathetically pays for it with a check written out for just $0.69 (a silly if humorously suggestive amount), using only his Ralphs card as an ID. The Dude dates his check, with its background whale image, "Sept 11, 1991" and then looks up to see President George H. W. Bush announce on TV that Iraqi "aggression" against Kuwait, in the Middle East, "will not stand." In light of the September 11 attacks to come in 2001 and the way Bush's son will repeat that militant gesture against Iraq in 2003, this seems to be an eerie coincidence. The Dude's check, however, also bears the same month and day as wild Carmen Sternwood's $1000 IOU to Los Angeles pornographer Arthur Gwynn Geiger in *TBS*: Sept 11, 1945. Geiger is analogous to Jackie Treehorn in *TBL*.

Observing that, in his Old West universe, the nickname "Dude" is not complimentary, and confessing that to him "there was a lot about The Dude that didn't make a whole lot of sense," The Stranger immediately raises a question about The Dude's virtue, describing him in the voiceover as "a lazy man," quite possibly the "laziest worldwide." The Stranger "won't" call The Dude a "hero," because, in his own uncertainty when confronted by this new kind of male protagonist, The Stranger wonders, "what's a hee-ro?" But The Stranger nevertheless recognizes that The Dude is "the man for his time'n place, he fits right in there ... in Los Angeles," 1991. The importance of what it means to be a man, as well as a hero, will be raised again later, most notably in a conversation with another Jeffrey Lebowski, the millionaire Lebowski (played by David Huddleston, who is analogous to General Sternwood in *TBS*).

Jauntily bounding into his 1928 Venice Beach bungalow apartment (609 Venezia Ave), half-and-half and bowling ball in hand, The Dude is assaulted by two goons (an Asian man, Woo, and a dopey blond thug with a blunt cut) who have been waiting for him inside. They explain to The Dude that they have been sent by one Jackie Treehorn (who also reiterates *TBS*'s Eddie Mars, as well as A. G. Geiger). Treehorn wants to collect on a debt that is owed to him by millionaire Jeffrey Lebowski's wife, Bunny (played by Tara Reid, who is analogous to Carmen Sternwood in *TBS*). They have stupidly mistaken the penurious Dude for the millionaire who shares his name.

After a hilarious exchange about money and golf balls, Woo, who works for a powerful white man, "micturates," much to The Dude's chagrin, on the oriental rug in the living room – perhaps symbolically peeing on orientalism per se. In *TBS*, things Asian symbolize salacious decadence, criminality, and in general moral turpitude. Roman Polanski's 1974 noir standard, *Chinatown* – possibly another root of the many Asian and L.A. references of *TBL* – deploys the same objectionable trope. Paraphrasing Brutus when he assassinated Julius Caesar, and John Wilkes Booth when he assassinated Abraham Lincoln (*sic semper tyrannis*; "ever thus to tyrants"), Woo declares, "Ever thus to deadbeats, Lebowski," after the home-invading cretins realize their mistake. The Dude cannot be who they are looking for because he is a "fucking loser." The Dude offers the audience a taste of his witty way of abiding through adversity: "Hey, at least I'm housebroken." The brutes stomp off and depart.

In the film's first bowling alley scene, the opening credits roll to the tune of Bob Dylan's 1970 song about a woman drawing forth someone's masculinity, "The Man in Me." Recalling the overture to Ingmar Bergman's 1975 film *Trollflöjten* (a depiction of Mozart's 1791 *The Magic Flute*), the camera presents in serial fashion a scruffy and highly diverse collection of *hoi polloi,* common folk, rolling bowling balls that recall the tumbleweed in a low-rent, retro bowling alley replete with Googie stars (Hollywood Star Lanes, 5227 Santa Monica Blvd). The Dude is an everyman.

The credits end with Theodore Donald "Donny" Kerabatsos (Steve Buscemi) rolling a strike, as he does consistently, and declaring, as if calling out to the rug urinator, "Whoo! I'm throwing rocks tonight." Donny wears a "Park Cleaners Southside" bowling shirt stitched with the name "johnson" atop his back-left shoulder. Bowling team buddy Walter Sobchak (John Goodman; in part inspired by screenwriters John Milius, Peter Exline, and Lewis Abernathy) corrects The Dude when he uses a politically incorrect term for Chinese people and convinces him that he should not tolerate the "unchecked aggression" that he has suffered in the soiling of his rug ("It really tied the room together, did it not?"). Instead, Walter urges, The

Dude should seek restitution from the millionaire Jeffrey Lebowski. After all, his wife's unchecked spending was the ultimate cause of the mistaken-identity home invasion, and the rich guy obviously possesses more than enough money to cover her debt, as well as buy The Dude a new rug. Walter silences Donny, who does not seem to follow entirely ("Donny, you're out of your element!"). (The gesture was inspired by Carl Showalter, Buscemi's character in the Coens' immediately preceding 1996 film, *Fargo*, whose surname contains "Walter" and who would not stop talking.)

The Dude meets with millionaire Jeffrey Lebowski at his Pasadena office-residence (the 1929 Greystone mansion in Beverly Hills, film location also of the 1946 Bette Davis classic, *Dead Ringer*, and David Lynch's 1977 *Eraserhead*). Welcomed and introduced by millionaire Lebowski's man-servant Brandt (played by Philip Seymour Hoffman and analogous to Norris in *TBS*), The Dude follows the toady through a collection of his employer's vanity awards, along with a photo of the millionaire with former US First Lady Nancy Reagan.

Unfortunately for The Dude, the irascible wheel-chair-bound Korean War veteran and plutocrat, who lost the use of his legs to an Asian – Chinese – soldier, is not only unreceptive but also downright hostile to The (unemployed countercultural) Dude's request. (In an early draft of the script, The Dude was portrayed as the heir to the Rubik's Cube fortune.) Banging his fist on the table, the infuriated, conservative boss man rants about personal responsibility and then, like a disgusted *pater familias*, rebukes The Dude for his way of life: "You don't go out lookin' for a job dressed like that, do you? . . ." "Your revolution is over, Mr. Lebowski! Condolences! The bums lost! . . . The bums will always lose!"

The Dude peaceably withdraws, but upon closing the door on the deranged shouting, he coolly deceives Brandt, telling the sycophant that the old man said to help himself to "any rug in the house." Brandt takes The Dude's word for it and leads him out by way of the swimming pool with The Dude's new proletarian appropriation (a rug) borne triumphantly aloft on servants' shoulders. There The Dude happens upon Bunny Lebowski lounging at the poolside (10231 Charing Cross Road, just across the street from the Playboy mansion, appropriately), painting her toenails green. (Curiously, rabbits are taxonomically classified in the order *lagomorpha* as defined by biologist J. F. Brandt.)

Passed out drunk and floating in the pool next to an American whiskey bottle as if "dead in the water" is Uli Kunkel (Peter Stormare), whom Bunny identifies as a nihilist. As the Dude observes, and as antinihilist philosopher Friedrich Nietzsche (1844–1900) explains, regarding modern culture as a whole, nihilism is "exhausting." With an allusion to Lauren Bacall's famously flirtatious line about putting one's lips together to "blow" (from Howard Hawks's preceding 1944 film, *To Have and Have Not*), Bunny coyly asks The Dude to blow on her toes to dry them (something of a rule violation for many husbands). Recalling *TBS*'s licentious Carmen Sternwood, out of the blue Bunny then propositions The Dude, offering him a blowjob, another kind of blowing, in exchange for $1000, precisely the amount Carmen owed in each of her IOUs. "Brandt can't watch, though," Bunny says, laying down a rule of her own, "or he has to pay a hundred." Brandt, beside himself, accidentally compares Bunny to Nancy Reagan by describing each as a "wonderful woman" (though Bunny is also, he says, perhaps unlike Nancy, "very free-spirited"). The Dude rolls off to look for a cash machine. Swapping the position of just two letters, curiously, changes "blow" to "bowl."

In the second bowling alley scene, Donny continues throwing strikes, while Walter, a divorced convert to Judaism, shows up 20 min late, bellowing a quote from Zionist political activist Theodore Herzl ("If you will it, it is no dream.") and toting his ex-wife's dog, Thurston, in a pet carrier. The dog is a Scottish cairn terrier that Walter mistakenly calls a Pomeranian, notably a German-Polish breed.

The league match on lane 23 stops abruptly when Walter draws a pistol (a Colt M1911A1, standard issue for US soldiers from 1911 to 1985) on long-haired competing bowler and friend "Smokey" (Jimmy Dale Gilmore), insisting that his toe had slipped "over the line" on his last roll ("Smokey, this is not Nam. This is bowling. There are rules."). Pointing the gun and threatening Smokey with "a world of pain" (possibly a reference to "World of Pain," the third song on Cream's 1967 album "Disraeli Gears"), Walter insists that the score be adjusted accordingly ("Mark it zero!"). Apparently, Walter is not as friendly with old hippies as he is with the Dude. The police are called, and the scene closes with a hilarious exchange between The Dude and Walter out in the parking lot about violence, pacifism, mental health, and morality.

The next day, The Dude, a very white man, relaxes at home and enacts, in a kind of dance, the ups and downs of multicultural imperialism by practicing a Dudely variant of Asian tai chi on his new oriental rug while enjoying a "Caucasian" from his small, kitschy bamboo tiki bar. Behind the bar hangs a poster of Richard M. Nixon bowling. Like the two white, warmongering US Presidents Bush, Nixon had in Asia prosecuted then ended a war against Vietnam, Laos, and Cambodia; and he established diplomatic relations with the People's Republic of China. If oriental rugs in *TBL* be taken as metonymic representations of the Middle East and perhaps Asia per se, which seems plausible given the Iraq-War backdrop and the many references to Asia in the film, then the way the rugs are owned, ruined, stolen, and exchanged by white people – the millionaire, Treehorn, The Dude, and Maude – makes a trenchant political point.

After receiving a timid plea from diminutive man Martin "Marty" Randahl (Jack Kehler), The Dude's landlord, to pay his 10-days-late rent and also attend the debut of Marty's dance quintet cycle at Crane Jackson's Fountain Street Theater (the Palace Theater), The Dude listens to messages on his answering machine. (Marty's remarks suggest that it is either now October 10 or that the Dude had postdated his Ralphs check at the film's opening. Actor and producer Crane Jackson in 1968 founded the Rapport Theater Company in, yep, a converted Los Angeles bowling alley; 1277 N. Wilton Ave.)

First come messages from Smokey and from (German) Mel Zelnicker, an official with the Southern Cal Bowling League, informing The Dude that Walter's rule-violation of Article 27 of the league by-laws, among others, in drawing a firearm during a match has jeopardized the team's standing. (Mel Zelniker had worked as a sound engineer on *Raising Arizona*.) Subsequently, The Dude considers a plaintive message from Brandt inviting him to return to the millionaire's mansion for an important meeting ("not about the rug").

At the sit-down in a grand but somber neoclassical room before a roaring fire, the millionaire muses on "what makes a man" and tearfully informs The Dude that Bunny ("the light of my life") has been abducted. "Strong men also cry," he opines about manhood. The Dude nonchalantly lights a joint. He sports a softball T-shirt depicting Asian baseball player Kaoru Betto, a 1950s star of the Nippon Professional Baseball League. The kidnappers have demanded $1 million in ransom, and the big Lebowski, through Brandt, asks The Dude to serve as courier, so that the old man can determine whether or not Treehorn's "rug pee-ers" are the ones who abducted his purportedly beloved wife.

In the (already) third bowling alley scene, the team has its eyes on its league nemesis, the ultracompetitive, highly sexualized "savior" and glamour boy, Jesus Quintana (John Turturro), a.k.a. "The Jesus." Bedecked in props that include a trinity of three bejeweled rings, a ruby-red press-on little-finger nail, a gun-phallus-like wrist guard, a hairnet, and a bright royal purple jumpsuit, The Jesus diabolically tongues his purple bowling ball rolls a strike, and victory dances, Muhammad Ali-style, to the Gipsy Kings' 1991 flamenco rendition of the quasi-Satanic 1976 hit, "Hotel California," by the Eagles. The Dude, by the way, detests the Eagles.

Deflating the strutting display and recalling the Catholic Church's pedophilia scandals, Walter (himself a Catholic apostate) recounts The Jesus' criminal conviction and 6 months served in Chino prison for having exposed himself to an 8-year-old. Because of this conviction, Walter describes The Jesus as a "pederast" (perhaps a critical allusion to Matthew 19:14). (For the cutaway scene depicting The Jesus' sex-offender walk through his neighborhood, a bag of bird seed was stuffed into Turturro's pants to magnify his package.) The Dude explains to Walter and Donny how the millionaire has offered to pay him 20 grand for delivering the ransom and has given him a beeper to summon him when the exchange is set. The Dude assures Walter that he will not answer during league play. First things first.

Appealing to the thought of communist revolutionary philosopher V. I. Lenin (1870–1924), The Dude floats the idea with his team that Bunny has staged the kidnapping herself in order to milk her millionaire husband for money she can use to pay off her debts, etc. ("She's gotta feed the monkey," the Dude says later.). Walter silences Donny again ("Shut the fuck up, Donny!") and enthusiastically embraces The Dude's hypothesis as a definite conclusion. When the Latino Jesus, flanked by Irish sidekick Liam O'Brien (James G. Hoosier, representing another dominantly Catholic population), delivers a parting shot about his forthcoming victory, The Dude answers The Jesus' absolutist declarations with his own soft subjectivism ("Yeah, well, you know, that's just like, uh, your opinion, man.").

The Dude returns to his apartment for a happy, Zen-like reverie, pleasantly supine on his new rug, while listening on his Walkman to a tape of bowling pins crashing during the 1987 Venice League bowling tourney and, on the B-side, something called just "Bob" (Dylan, presumably). Rudely awakened by a new group of home intruders towering above and looking down upon him in trio, a redheaded woman with a blunt cut (Julianne Moore) directs one of two matching-denim-dressed thugs flanking her to knock The Dude out. The blow launches him into a dream sequence where, again set to bars of "The Man in Me" (undoubtedly from his cassette tape, side B), The Dude swimmingly soars over Los Angeles in pursuit of his new female *objet du désir*. The ginger woman glides away from him, into the sunset, seated resplendently in lotus pose on his new rug, which has become a flying carpet.

Without a rug of his own, The Dude is abruptly dragged back to Earth by his bowling ball, where he lands on a lane's ball return, face-to-face with a giant ball bearing down on him. Instead of being crushed, however, The Dude lucks into a finger hole (a vaginal space) as the boulder-like ball rolls over him and then careens down a lane, crashing into a set of pins. As the ball rolls, viewers catch a glimpse of the bowler. It is none other than the assaulting redheaded woman, still draped in that full-length green cape, apparently only a cape, provocatively revealing a long bare leg tucked into tall black boots.

Awakened by the millionaire's beeper, The Dude comes to on a bare wooden floor, his new rug gone. He collects first the ransom briefcase and a mobile phone from Brandt at the mansion and then Walter in front of his storefront, "Sobchak Security" (corner of Santa Monica Blvd. and McCadden Pl, Hollywood). The logo of Walter's shop, "SS," seems a provocative, even a falsifying incongruity with Walter's professed Judaism, given its common association with the Nazi paramilitary *Schutzstaffel*. (The Coen brothers, like musician Bob Dylan and UK Prime Minister Benjamin Disraeli, are themselves Jewish.) A slogan on the signage says "Strength, Security, Peace of Mind," the last of which Goodman's murderous character in *Barton Fink* (Charlie Meadows, the namesake, appropriately, of a cowboy showman) claims he sells.

Walter has hatched on his own a simple "Swiss watch" of a plan to deal with the kidnapping. The pair will (1) substitute a "ringer" briefcase (stuffed with Walter's underwear) for the true ransom case, (2) keep the $1 million (as well as presumably the $20k courier fee), (3) capture a kidnapper, (4) beat Bunny's location out of him, and then (5) save her. The plan goes awry, however, on a wooden bridge (failing at #3), where Walter hurls the ringer from the car. The three kidnappers roar off on motorbikes with briefcase in hand before Walter can grab one. Attempting to halt their escape through some manly, weaponized heroics, Walter rolls from the moving vehicle but loses control of his hidden Uzi machine gun (an Israeli weapon). Spinning across the road, it fires (in a kind of premature ejaculation), riddling the back end of The Dude's rusted out 1973 Ford Gran Torino with bullets (penetrating it anally, as it were, to paraphrase Walter's later remarks *in re* a red Corvette) and causing it to crash into a telephone pole (196 Torrey Rd, Fillmore).

In the now fourth bowling alley scene, while the mobile phone rings incessantly, The Dude silently ruminates over Bunny's fate ("They're gonna kill that poor woman!"). Walter, still unwaveringly convinced it is all a charade, remains unmoved ("*Aitz chaim he*, Dude"; it is a tree of life, Genesis 2:9) and stews instead about the team's next match having been scheduled on Saturday, by league official Burkhalter, because Walter is "shomer Shabbos," and thus does not work (or "sure as shit … fucking roll") on the Jewish Sabbath. Burkhalter, a German name, is possibly a reference to Nazi General Burkhalter, a character in *Hogan's Heroes*, a show that claims to offer an answer to The Stranger's question, "What's a hee-ro?" Returning to the parking lot after practice, the team discovers that the Torino has been stolen – and with it the ransom case, which they believe to be filled with $1 million in cash. At the end of his rope, ringing mobile phone in hand, The Dude walks off.

At his bungalow, in the middle of an amusing interview with police officers (the black officer, like The Dude, a Creedence fan) completing a report about his car, The Dude receives a phone call from the redheaded woman who took his replacement rug. In supercilious tones, she informs him that she is yet another Lebowski, Maude, the millionaire's daughter (analogous to Lauren Bacall's Vivian Rutledge in *TBS*), and, like her father, she would like to meet with The Dude.

As The Dude saunters into her studio (a loft above the Palace Theater) wearing shorts and jellies (Jeff Bridges' own pair), Maude, as if she were the bowling ball from the preceding dream sequence, hurtles noisily down upon him from above and behind, her vaginal space exposed. Alluding to artist and Bard College philosophy B.A. Carolee Schneemann (who is often mistaken to be Jewish), Maude is harnessed naked into some kind of zip-line-like contraption. Flailing a pair of brushes in flight, she flings paint onto a canvas (which depicts a snow angel of sorts) and onto The Dude, as if he were part of her artwork.

Her ambush finished, Maude dismounts. Wrapped by her male attendants (who wear overall denim bib shorts) back into her royal green mantle, she dabs clean the paint spattered on The Dude's face – his painterly sex-facial, as it were. Provocative banter ensues, as The Dude pours himself a White Russian from her bar. Red canvasses on which have been painted giant scissors hang on the walls. Female mannequin bodies in various states of disassembly and dismemberment are strewn about.

Addressing The Dude as "Mr. Lebowski," an appellation he had before resisted with her father, Maude repeatedly tries, in vain, to intimidate The Dude with her forthright sexuality, her regal bearing, and her aggressive feminism. She discusses the word "vagina," slang for penises (including, "johnson"), and the pleasure she claims to take in sex ("It can be a natural, zesty enterprise."), inquiring coyly whether he does, too. With a kind of dopey, bewildered, and lovestruck aplomb, The Dude parries every thrust. Satisfied (or aroused), Maude screens for The Dude a Jackie Treehorn pornographic video, *Logjammin'*, starring in negligée Bunny Lebowski (porn name "Bunny La Joya," the joyful bunny and an allusion to La Jolla, CA), whom she derides, perhaps enviously, as a nymphomaniacal "fornicator" who has sex compulsively and "without joy." Costarring with Bunny is nihilist Uli Kunkel (Karl Hungus, who anachronistically drives in the film a 1994 German BMW 318i (E36) drop top Cabrio and plays a cable repair man). Joining Bunny and Karl is topless real-life German-Japanese porn star Asia Carerra (whose actual screen surname is a model of German Porsche but who here appears as Sherry, toweling off after a shower just before a predictable threesome – or perhaps foursome, as Hungus calls out when he enters the scene to some unseen Helga for his tools). Uli/Karl speaks with a German accent and wears a well-endowed toolbelt. Unlike Walter's Uzi, it seems Uli's tool does not misfire.

Maude has concluded independently that Bunny staged her own kidnaping and, like her father, offers to hire The Dude – in her case for $100k, five times her father's promise. Maude's objective, however, is not to deliver but to recover the ransom money (which she falsely believes lies in the faux kidnappers' possession) in order to rectify the family embezzlement privately. The Dude remains silent about what he believes to be the lost money. Since she could presumably track down the faux kidnappers herself by hiring a professional or by deploying her own quite capable enforcers, one infers that there is more to her interest in The Dude than the wayward ransom. Before The Dude departs, she apologizes for the blow to his jaw, presents him with the contact information of a physician, and insists that The Dude obtain from him a "thorough" exam. As this flirtatious exchange comes to an end, the audience sees that, while The Dude and Maude may not be Bogart and Bacall, they have certainly become a compelling pair.

Beverage in hand, The (contented, even elated) Dude is driven home by Maude's wise-guy-styled New Yorker chauffeur, Tony, who observes that they have been followed by someone in a blue Volkswagen Beetle (a German car). As The Dude steps from the vehicle, another chauffeur, the millionaire-veteran's, grabs him and drags him across the street from Maude's limousine into her father's. There the old man and Brandt dress him down for failing to deliver the money. The Dude nervously deflects their accusations with obvious lies and his self-abduction theory. He then asks to be paid. In response, the millionaire instructs Brandt to hand The Dude an envelope. Instead of money, it contains, wrapped in bloody gauze, a severed human toe with green toenail polish, which they all infer to be Bunny's. The old man threatens The Dude and orders him to deliver the money to the kidnappers at once, declaring that he "will not abide another toe." Clearly millionaire Lebowski does not abide much.

Over coffee with The Dude at a "family restaurant" (Johnnie's Coffee Shop, 6101 Wilshire Blvd; which was also the location for scenes from *Reservoir Dogs* and *American History X*, among other films), Walter refuses to believe that the toe is truly Bunny's ("I can get you a toe."). Turning apoplectic when asked to keep his voice down, Walter causes a scene that ends with a diatribe about Vietnam – an inexhaustible touchstone for him – as well as prior restraint, the Supreme Court, and the First Amendment. Exasperated, the Dude stomps off and returns home, where he unwinds in a candlelit Mr. Bubble bath, lights a joint, and relaxes to a cassette tape of whale song (recalling the whale image on his check). "Save the whales" was a hackneyed political slogan among hippies and liberals in the 1970s and 1980s.

To his delight, The Dude's answering machine picks up a call announcing that the police have found his car. Just then, interrupting his ecstasies, the three nihilists (Uli, Franz, und Dieter) – decked out in tough-guy props that include Uli in a black leotard-like biker suit – break in and storm his bathroom where, like Treehorn's brutes, they demand "za money." Dropping a ferret (which The Dude wrongly identifies as a marmot) into the tub between his legs, Uli threatens to return and castrate The Dude ("We cut off your johnson!") if he does not deliver. As before, during the fake ransom drop, Uli warns The Dude, "No funny stuff," a metajoke in this very funny movie. It is the second time the Dude's been assaulted in his bathroom, and the second time immersed in water.

The Dude recovers his Torino, discovered by the police crashed, stinking of urine, and abandoned against an abutment in Van Nuys, CA (famous for its porn industry). In yet another repetition, the Dude's belongings have at this point been peed upon twice.

We then return to the bowling alley for a fifth time where, at the bar, Walter and Donny try to cheer the despondent Dude but end up bickering about the threats they face, nihilism, legalities, Germans ("nothing changes"), and national socialism ("at least it's an ethos"). Insulted by The Dude's sharp responses, Donny and Walter depart. As "Tumbling Tumbleweeds" plays again, The Stranger appears and explains his admiration for The Dude's style. At first flattered, The Dude, who has been commiserating with bartender Gary, in short order rebukes The Stranger for his old-timey, strait-laced condemnation of The Dude's cussing. Maude calls him at the bar, somehow knowing he is there (perhaps because he is usually there), and summons him. He obeys.

Encountering the effete and irritating Knox Harrington ("the video artist" David Thewlis) slacking at Maude's abode, The Dude tells her he is now convinced that Bunny has actually been abducted – this on the basis of the visit from Uli and crew, whom he now believes to be Bunny's kidnappers. The Dude does not mention the toe. Like Walter, Maude refuses to accept his conclusion and explains how Bunny's preceding relationship with Uli and the other nihilists entails that they cannot have properly kidnapped her (something she suggests The Dude should have inferred – though *Fargo* shows how in fact that could be so; Stormare played the kidnapper in *Fargo*, on the set of which the character Uli was conceived).

Maude reveals that she has known Uli for years herself and may have even introduced Bunny to him. The Dude tells the only vaguely interested Maude that Uli does not have the money, but he is too embarrassed to confess that he has lost a million dollars. Someone named "Sandra" interrupts their conversation with a call to discuss the Venice Biennale, an important art festival held every other year. Before falling out in a fit of idiotic laughter with her upper-class friends, Maude insists that The Dude see the physician. He complies, listening to Elvis Costello's "My Mood Swings" on his Walkman during the exam.

Driving home from the South Asian doctor's office and jamming to Creedence Clearwater Revival's 1970 hit, "Looking Out My Back Door," The Dude swigs while driving (a serious rule violation) from a bottle of Meichtry draft beer (a fictional brand used in several films and TV shows), tokes on a marijuana roach (another illegality), and notices in his rearview mirror (his back door, kinda) that he is being followed again by the blue Volkswagen bug. Freaking out when he absentmindedly drops the lit roach into his lap, where his johnson resides, The Dude crashes his Torino into a dumpster (6319 La Mirada Ave). Recomposing himself, he discovers one Larry Sellers' homework essay on "The Louisiana Purchase" (graded "D") stuffed down into the car seat. The Dude has found his car thief and potentially the lost million.

Donny and, in a row behind him, The Dude sit in a near-empty theater watching his apartment manager Marty – now dressed in a skin-colored and garlanded leotard as some kind of fallen Adam or faun – perform his hilariously awkward dance cycle to Mussorgsky's "Pictures at an Exhibition II" (a.k.a. "Gnomus," Latin for gnome). Walter arrives and announces that he has located Larry's address (on Radford in North Hollywood which is, they make sure to note, *near* the In-N-Out Burger on Camrose; Goodman once made a radio advert for the chain). Walter reports that he has also discovered that little Larry's father is none other than Arthur Digby Sellers, fictitious writer of 156 episodes of the 1965–1966 western television series *Branded*. (In reality, *Branded* was created and written by Larry Cohen, perhaps the adolescent's namesake, and there were only 48 episodes).

The three teammates drive to the modest house (1824 Stearns Dr) and park on the street near a newly purchased, red, 1985 Corvette C4 with its sales sheet still visible in the window. The Dude's Torino, in contrast, looks barely street legal, its headlights mashed in and its crooked bumper strapped on, barely, by a pair of bungee cords (California plate 376 PCE). Walter and The Dude are kindly welcomed into the house by a cheerful woman named Pilar, who mistakes them for police detectives. Donny, who never in the film interacts with anyone besides Walter and – just once – the Dude, remains outside in the Torino reading a newspaper. (There are those who think Donny is a figment of Walter's PTSD-addled imagination.) At the back of the very retro living room, with shag carpet rather than a rug, old man Arthur Digby Sellers lies supine and unresponsive in an iron lung ("He has health problems."). He is the second older man of the post-WWII era presented as disabled and confined to some apparatus. Walter is starstruck. Emphasizing the theme of masculinity, Pilar announces that "the man" is here. Fifteen-year-old little Larry enters and sits down on the plastic-slip-cover-encased sofa across from the two older male visitors.

With quickly escalating hostility, Walter and The Dude interrogate the adolescent in an effort to recover the ransom money they believe to be in his possession. Walter, repeating his threat to the bowler Smokey, manifests a certain kind man by promising Larry "a world of pain" if he does not cough it up. Mimicking the nihilists, The Dude even threatens to mutilate the male child sexually ("We're gonna cut your dick off, Larry!"), which is not only criminal in its rule breaking but also arguably worse than exposing oneself to an 8-year-old. The teenager, however, remains silent and impassive. Pilar has vanished.

Intent on demonstrating their resolve and his dominance, Walter storms outside and, violating scores of laws and customs, begins smashing the Corvette with a phallic rod – a crowbar taken from The Dude's trunk. ("This is what happens when you fuck a stranger in the ass!" he repeatedly screams or, as it famously appears in the network television version of the film, "This is what happens when you find a stranger in the Alps!") Walter clearly feels his manhood humiliated and responds with restorative violence. The Corvette is, however, not Larry's, we discover, when the infuriated male owner rushes from his house and snatches the phallus-rod from Walter, symbolically emasculating him further. Walter timidly yields and helplessly begs forgiveness. The Corvette owner, believing the Torino to be Walter's, begins laying into The Dude's long-suffering car with the phallus in a paroxysm of *lex talionis* retribution. Somehow the police remain uninvolved, though Walter has learned firsthand what happens when one fucks up a stranger's Corvette.

(The story of little Larry and his home draws upon supposedly true events recounted by script consultants and Vietnam vets Lewis Abernathy and Peter Exline, the latter of whom the Coens called "the philosopher king of Hollywood." According to Exline, his car was stolen, and when recovered it had been beaten up and littered with fast food wrappers. Abernathy, who worked as a private investigator, discovered under the seat homework belonging to eighth-grader Jaik Freeman. Upon driving to Freeman's home, the pair encountered Jaik's father, the screenwriter Everett Freeman, in a hospital bed set up in the living room. Just as in the film, Lewis confronted the lad with his homework sealed in a plastic bag. Jaik, however, denied having stolen the car and claimed to have lent his math text, into which the homework had been folded, to a friend (Green et al. 2007). Exline was also the source of the idea of a rug that tied the room together, as well as The Dude's love of bowling – in Exline's case softball – not to mention Walter's gun mania and, in part, fixation on Vietnam.)

Having returned home in his now windshield-less car after the automotive honor-raping, and a stop at the In-N-Out Burger on Camrose for Walter and Donny, The Dude receives a second visit from Woo and the blond lummox. They have swapped the clothes they wore during their first home invasion. The toughs escort the compliant Dude to pornographer Jackie Treehorn's Malibu beach pad (actually, John Lautner's famous 1963 Sheats-Goldstein house in Beverly Crest), where semiclad young people have gathered for a bonfire beach party and parachute nubile toss. Suave Treehorn serves The Dude a White Russian while clad in a white suit and questions him about Bunny's whereabouts, as well as the location of what he regards to be his money. When Treehorn steps away, The Dude makes a fool of himself in an attempt to play detective with Jackie's note pad, discovering only, however, that Treehorn had penciled a man with a giant erect johnson on it. When Treehorn returns and serves him a second Caucasian, The Dude points the playboy in the direction of little Larry Sellers. Treehorn, however, does not buy The Dude's improbable story.

The cocktail has been drugged (just as noir hero Sam Spade's had been in *The Maltese Falcon*, 1941), and The Dude passes out and falls into a dream, portrayed as a film called *Gutterballs* (which recalls Philip Marlowe's anxiety dream in *Murder, My Sweet*, 1944; CineFix 2016). Produced in his imagination by Jackie Treehorn and starring Maude as a sexy bowling Valkyrie (whose costume recalls a statue in the millionaire's mansion), the film costars The Dude dressed in the jump suit of porno cable repairman Karl Hungus, complete with lengthy tools swinging provocatively from his workman's toolbelt on his gyrating hips. Middle Eastern Arab Saddam Hussein (played by Jerry Haleva) appears as the friendly bowling alley shoe clerk from the opening sequence and hands The Dude a pair of silver-and-gold bowling shoes, the heels of which The Dude knocks toward each other (perhaps a reference to L. Frank Baum's 1900 novel, *The Wonderful Wizard of Oz*, in which Dorothy wears magical silver, not ruby, slippers and whose heels she knocks together to activate). The dream-film is replete with elaborate, Busby-Berkeley-style dance geometries (much more polished than the Dude, Marty, or The Jesus' wakeful dances), featuring formations of Caucasian chorines spreading their legs for The Dude amid sexually suggestive bowling imagery (e.g., a phallic bowling pin flanked by two bowling balls). The soundtrack plays The First Edition's 1967 psychedelic hit, "Just Dropped In," featuring Kenny Rogers on vocals.

Gutterballs ends as a nightmare, however, with the seductive dancers and song giving way, through the intercession of one of Treehorn's topless playmates, to dark comedic music and the nihilists menacing The Dude. Giant, slicing scissors drawn from Maude's art replace the chorines' splayed legs, as the vermillion ghouls chase The Dude in bloody red leotards that recall Uli's ferret-dunking outfit as well as the nihilists' band Autobahn's 1970s techno-pop album "Nagelbett," a parody of Kraftwerk's 1978 quasi-fascistic "Man-Machine." The Dude flees their castration threat in a panic.

Coming to while running drunkenly down the middle of a busy road, The Dude is arrested and sings the lyric about being falsely accused from the title song to "Branded" in the back seat of the cruiser. The Malibu chief of police ("a real reactionary") threatens and assaults but then releases the intoxicated and disrespectful Dude ("Do I make myself clear?" "I'm sorry, I wasn't listening."), warning him not to return to the quiet and, as the audience knows, very wealthy "beach community."

Ejected abruptly from a taxi carrying him home from Malibu (at the corner of Jefferson Blvd. and Duquesne Ave., Culver City, 5 miles from his apartment) when he complains to the black cabbie about his playing the Eagles ("Peaceful Easy Feeling" – under the circumstances, especially annoying), The Dude contemplates the sorry "condition his condition is in."

Just then, unbeknownst to The Dude, Bunny roars by in a red convertible 1989 Jaguar XJ-S, top down, singing along *con mucho gusto* to Big Johnson's (*nota bene* "johnson") rendition of "Viva Las Vegas" (the song was popularized by pelvis-gyrating male idol Elvis Presley, but female Shawn Colvin's chilled version plays during the closing credits). Clad in a vivid red little dress and shoes, Bunny points to herself as "the devil with love to spare." The camera pans down to reveal that her toe remains undetached. Her license plate reads, "Lapin"– French for, yes, "bunny."

The Dude returns to his apartment to find the door busted open and the place ransacked, apparently, one infers, by Treenhorn's thugs looking for the ransom money. The Dude trips on a two-by-four he had incompetently nailed into the floor in order to secure the door and lands, face first, flat on the wooden, rug-less floor. Repeating their first encounter, Maude appears, standing above him. That her bare feet remain complete with all their toes is clearly evident when she steps from the bedroom in a new mantle, The Dude's robe. She drops the Dudely vestment to the floor to reveal her naked body, commanding him, "Jeffrey, love me." Still lying prostrate before her, the Dude seems unimpressed by the gesture but obliges, repeating the hole-tucking of the first dream sequence in another fashion.

After their "coitus" and some joint-infused pillow talk about The Dude's past as a leftist SDS (Students for a Democratic Society) activist, member of the Seattle Seven, author of the original 1962 Port Huron Statement, and roadie for Metallica (the fictitious "Speed of Sound" tour), Maude assumes a yoga-esque fertility pose and explains that she has come to him not for joyful "fun and games" but rather, instrumentally, in order to become pregnant. (Perhaps that is the sense in which The

Dude "fits right in.") Unlike everyone else, Maude now calls The Dude – in a more familiar, even intimate way – simply, "Jeffrey." She reassures her suddenly shocked paramour that she desires no partner and does not want him involved as a father. He is calmed.

Maude subsequently repeats that the millionaire Lebowski is actually no millionaire and that he lives off an allowance financed by his deceased wife's fortune, which she, his daughter, now controls. Again, following Lenin's hermeneutic as he understands it – *cui bono* – The Dude in a moment of revelation solves the case. He deduces that Maude's father must have deceived him and that there was never any money in the wayward ransom case he and Walter had tried but failed to deliver to the nihilists. The pseudomillionaire, that is, had hired The Dude to pass off his own ringer so that he could keep the family foundation's money for himself – stealing in effect from the "Little Lebowski Urban Achiever" children and blaming the loss on The Dude (not unlike the way Sam Spade was nearly pinned as a fall guy in *The Maltese Falcon*). Walter had thrown from the car "a ringer for a ringer." The Dude excitedly calls Walter, interrupting his Sabbath (it is Friday evening), and urgently demands, on threat of quitting the bowling team, that Walter (not Maude) drive the two of them to Pasadena.

On his way to confront the cuckolded faux millionaire, grifter, and embezzler, The Dude assails the little man still following him in the shrimpy blue Volkswagen (itself a throwback trope) that has been tailing him. Startled, the balding man identifies himself as "Da Fino" (which sounds an awful lot like *TBS*'s Eddie Mars' deadly goon "Canino" but who is actually more like the character Harry Jones, who tailed Philip Marlowe in the film). Like The Stranger, Da Fino effusively flatters The Dude for his style and describes himself as a fellow "shamus" (a private detective, using the archaic terminology from *TBS*). Impatient and unfamiliar with the descriptor ("like an Irish monk?"), The Dude refuses the title.

Da Fino shows The Dude a color photo of Bunny in a high school cheerleader uniform and a black-and-white photo of the family farm in Midwestern cold, bleak Moorhead, Minnesota – like *TBL* itself, adjacent to Fargo. Da Fino explains that Fawn Knutsen's (hottie Bunny's) parents have hired him to find and retrieve their wayward daughter. The private "dick" (another johnson) suggests teaming up, but The Dude rejects him and then angrily storms off, climbing into Walter's white utility van (a 1985 Chevrolet G20 with the phone number 213-799-7798 affixed to its side). The Dude warns Da Fino: "stay away from my special ... from my fucking lady friend, man!" (The Coens were raised just outside Minneapolis, Minnesota; actress Peggy Knudsen played tragic criminal Mona Mars in *TBS*.) The Dude is consistently and remarkably unkind to Da Fino, perhaps not unlike the way he had been short with The Stranger and contemptuous of the millionaire. Representatives of traditional masculinities sometimes to annoy him.

Meanwhile, German nihilists Uli and Dieter (played by Red Hot Chili Peppers' bass player, Flea) at a House of Pancakes (Dinah's Family Restaurant, 6521 S. Sepulveda Blvd) order lingonberry *Pfannkuchen* (pancakes, a reference to kidnapper Stormare's choice of grub in *Fargo*). Nihilist Franz orders "three pigs in blanket" (perhaps one for each of The Dude's team, or for each of the corresponding three male nihilists). Uli's (or perhaps Franz's) girlfriend, a blonde woman (rock and pop singer Aimee Mann) unable to speak English, timidly asks Uli in German to order her *Hellbier Pfannkuchen*, but Uli without a word to her overrides her wishes, ordering her lingonberry pancakes instead. In the background, just above and behind Uli's head, Walter's van, containing him and The Dude, is just visible at a stop light (preserving the noir trope of the detective appearing in almost every scene as we follow him through the case).

The camera drifts down to reveal that Uli's girlfriend bears a bandaged foot where a toe has recently been removed. That leaves her with nine toes, perhaps one for each of The Dude's Caucasians. The girlfriend's little piggy (toe) was, of course, presented to the Dude wrapped in a blanket of gauze, bloodied red like lingonberry. Perhaps that is a stretch ... but in any case, Walter was right about the toe.

After arguing during the drive about Walter's Jewishness ("Jewish as fucking Tevye. ... Three thousand years of beautiful tradition, from Moses to Sandy Koufax...!"), The Dude, Walter, and Walter's ex-wife's cairn terrier Thurston roll up at the Pasadena mansion to discover that Bunny has returned, crashed her car into the courtyard fountain, disrobed, and is now dancing joyfully naked around the house (the second nude Lebowski woman The Dude has encountered in just a few minutes) as Brandt trails behind. She had simply, Brandt reports, taken off to Palm Springs by herself for the weekend without informing her husband, and just as Walter had predicted (sort of), she has simply "wander[ed] on home." Learning that her absence was unannounced, the nihilists had jumped at the chance to make a buck with a phony kidnapping ruse. Receiving their ransom note, Bunny's abandoned husband in turn hatched a Walter-like ringer plan for the same purpose, hoping that the kidnappers would kill his "goldbricking" and unfaithful "trophy wife" as a bonus.

Confronting the old man, The Dude recounts his conclusions. The fraud-millionaire implicitly acknowledges their truth. It will be his word, though, the embezzler says, against the "loser" and "deadbeat" Dude's. The Dude sees his point. Walter, upset by the exchange and dogmatically believing the faux-millionaire's disability to be fraudulent too, forcibly lifts him from his wheelchair in spite of his frightened objections and tosses the louse to the ground. There, prostrate before The Dude on an oriental rug not terribly unlike the one that set into motion The Dude's odyssey, the not-so-strong old man begins to weep pathetically. Pitying him, The Dude asks Walter to help place the broken down "human paraquat" back into the wheelchair.

Saturday evening (7:52 pm, according to the clock in the background), with the Sabbath over at sundown, the team returns to the bowling alley for a sixth time. Walter, drinking Miller Genuine Draft and smoking, holds forth, in a soliloquy laced with ethnic slurs, on the 1991 Gulf War against Iraq in comparison to the Vietnam conflict. The Dude, mimicking The Jesus' manicured fingers, applies a press-on static nail to his right thumb and then, recalling his encounter with Bunny, paints it with polish and blows it dry. Donny, wearing the "Park Cleaners" shirt with "johnson" stitched on the back in which he was introduced, in a foreshadowing gesture fails to repeat the action of his first appearance by uncharacteristically missing his strike, leaving a single pin standing. In the background, Donny then takes a seat, grimaces, and rubs his hand.

The Jesus, followed by Liam, marches up in a blue Jack Lalanne-style jump suit and rages at the team members for having rescheduled their bowling match because it fell on the Sabbath, earlier that day. (He contemptuously calls the move "bush" – or perhaps "Bush" – league.) The Jesus threatens to metaphorically rape The Dude's team when they finally do compete "next Wednesday."

Strolling out into the parking lot after practice, Walter quotes from the Rambam (nickname for the twelfth and thirteenth-century Cordoban Jewish philosopher Rabbi Moses ben Maimon, a.k.a. Maimonides). The team then comes face-to-face with the leather-clad nihilists, arrayed before The Dude's now flaming Torino and ready to rumble. Uli roars that the nihilists "want za money, Lebowski!" The Dude fires back that they know the phony kidnappers "never had the girl," and Walter reminds them of a relevant rule ("Without a hostage, there is no ransom."). Dieter whines un-nihilistically that "It's not fair" that they get no money even though the girlfriend gave up her toe.

The Dude explains that he and Walter never had the money, anyway. When Uli demands as a substitute whatever cash they have on them, The Dude and Donny search their pockets and come up with $22 and some change (The Dude has just $4). Walter declines and asserts a tautology about personal property ("What's mine is mine."). He paraphrases Leonidas, who drew "a line in the sand" at Thermopylae ("Come and get it."). Uli draws a phallic saber. A melée ensues. Behind and above the scuffle stands a well-lit billboard for Ben Hur Auto Repair, complete with racing chariot. Judah Ben-Hur (made famous to cinephiles through Billy Wyler's 1959 film, *Ben-Hur*, starring gun-loving and hystrionic Charlton Heston) was a Jewish prince and religious convert who single-handedly fought for his people against the Romans.

The frenzied Polish berserker savagely bites off a chunk of Uli's ear, spits it into the noir-night sky, calls him an anti-Semite, and knocks the dazed nihilist out cold. Walter has clobbered the nihilists with, of course, his bowling ball (Dieter), a boombox (Franz), and his fists (Uli) – philosophizing, as Nietzsche would say, against nihilism "with a hammer." Unnoticed until just then, Donny has collapsed and succumbs to his foreshadowed heart attack. In a way, nihilism has, in fact, truly cut off the team's "johnson" (as indicated by the name on the back of Donny's shirt).

Some days later, or at least before the next round robin of the semifinals, Walter and The Dude, who wears a bowling shirt stitched with the word "Art" just over his heart, spar with a stuck-up presumably Catholic undertaker, Francis Donnelly, over the costs of handling Donny's cremation. (On the other hand, Jewish burials traditionally take place within 24 h of death, and Walter and the Dude do seem to move immediately to deal with Donny's remains. The funeral may express both of Walter's faiths.) The monumental wall behind the gouging prig is adorned with a quote from Psalm 103:15–16 (KJV), "As for man, his days are as grass: as a flower of the field, so he flourisheth. For the wind passeth over it, and it is gone." Unwilling – and perhaps unable – to purchase a $180 (vaginal) "receptacle" for (johnson) Donny's ashes, The Dude and Walter carry them in a Folgers coffee can they reluctantly buy for the purpose at Ralphs to the cliffs of the Sunken City of San Pedro, California.

Curiously, no one else besides Walter and The Dude is involved in the arrangements for Donny's body or his funeral. Walter, around whose neck hang dog tags to which he has added his former wedding ring (his marriage perhaps another lost war), after a eulogy that drifts into reflections on the Vietnam War dead, botches the scattering of Donny's ashes by failing to account for the sea breeze. Instead of falling downward into the Pacific, the ashes blow landward into The Dude's face, covering it, and his incongruously expensive Vuarnet VL1307 sunglasses, with Donny's earthly remains. No prayers are recited, no Scripture read, and no appeals to a deity are voiced. Donny is, in any case, as Psalm 103 and all the film's many references to blowing remind viewers, gone with the wind; just so are the Dude's days smoky with grass (pot). The moment may also allude to Bob Dylan's 1962 single, "Blowin' in the Wind." A short meltdown leads to a touching embrace, as The Dude characteristically forgives contrite Walter. Just as he declared after the bungled ransom delivery, "Let's go bowling," says the big man.

Fittingly, the movie ends with a seventh and final trip to the bowling alley. While the soundtrack plays Townes Van Zandt's cover of the Rolling Stones' sweet and class-consciously mournful ballad "Dead Flowers," The Dude collects from bartender Gary two "oat sodas" (beer, in The Dude's parlance), one for him and another for Walter. He greets The Stranger, who has returned for "the semis" and The Dude's Wednesday match against The Jesus, Liam, and their third teammate (seen seated behind Liam when The Jesus dances). (Who, if anyone, replaces Donny on their three-person team is unknown.) After quoting The Stranger, in reference to Donny's death about how "the bar" (bear) sometimes eats you, and then stoically acknowledging life's "strikes and gutters, ups and downs," The Dude exits toward the lanes.

Pausing, he delivers his supremely famous line, "The Dude abides" – another reference to the Old Testament (Ecclesiastes 1:4, KJV): "One generation passeth away, and another generation cometh: but the earth abideth forever." (The Dude at that moment wears a bowling shirt emblazoned with "Medina Sod" on the back – an actual team shirt sponsored by a company just outside Akron, Ohio, that sells turf or, yes, "earth." It is the same shirt The Dude wore earlier that day when Donny, from ashes to ashes, was returned to the earth. Medina Sod truck driver Art Myers wore the shirt when he bowled with the team in the 1960s.) Raising the two Miller High Life bottles, with his last line of the film, The Dude calls out to his friend: "Walter."

Turning toward the audience, The Stranger expresses his admiration for the tale the movie has told, except the loss of Donny, and praises The Dude's virtue of abiding. Despite being a remnant of the old westerns (and perhaps the West more generally) soon to passeth away, The Stranger is not only without resentment for the way traditional ideals of heroism and masculinity have shifted. He even hopes that The Dude will flourish (i.e., reach "the finals" by, implicitly, defeating the nihilism-inducing Jesus). The Stranger then informs viewers that Maude has successfully conceived and that a little Lebowski, her and The Dude's child, cometh. It is the way, he says, that the whole "durn'd" human "comedy" perpetuates itself. The Stranger turns to Gary and orders himself a sarsaparilla.

Comedies by definition end well, and the camera returns to a bowler previously seen in the background – actually the film's expert bowling coach, Barry Asher – who repeats his earlier roll with another reassuring strike. There is a hopeful comfort the audience – "all us sinners" – can take in this resolution and these prospects, despite inhabiting a world of pain plagued by war, death, loveless fraud, and nihilism.

Interpreting *The Big Lebowski*

What Makes a Man?

Whatever else *The Big Lebowski* is, it is a film about masculinity (Allen 2009). The opening credits announce this theme through Bob Dylan's song "The Man in Me." Later, when millionaire Lebowski sits down with The Dude to discuss Bunny's kidnapping, he frames the discussion by posing the question in the gravest tones, "What makes a man, Mr. Lebowski?" The millionaire lists various properties of what he regards true manliness to be: besting competitors, overcoming obstacles, achieving, and – the crucial bit for the millionaire in that context – "being prepared to do the right thing, whatever the cost," which might also be one way of defining a "hero." The Dude, who refuses even the manly title "Mr. Lebowski," seemingly unimpressed with that formulation, lights a joint and offers a substitute definition: "Sure, that and a pair of testicles." For The Dude, it seems that the sufficient and perhaps necessary conditions for manhood are met just by being an adult human male. (The film is silent about trans identities.) The millionaire rightly understands his disquisition to have been mocked, and indeed so much of The Dude's life opposes the millionaire's ideals of masculinity.

In particular, while The Dude does compete in a bowling league, he is clearly not terribly competitive. The episode with Smokey and his offending toe, which according to Walter crossed over the lane's foul line, demonstrates as much. ("So his toe slipped over a little, you know," says The Dude. "It's just a game, man.") The Dude, moreover, is not acquisitive and does not care about status. He does appreciate money when it comes his way, but he does not work for it. ("Employed?") He does not own much. He does not live in impressive digs. His car, which he loves, is a nearly 20-year-old American beater with "rust coloration."

The Dude does seem to worry about doing the right thing in getting the ransom money back and freeing Bunny, especially after actually holding the severed toe – enough anyway to succumb to Walter's cockeyed and arguably criminal plan to squeeze it out of little Larry. If he were all about doing the right thing, however, The Dude would certainly interrupt a league game to save Bunny. And even the teenager is too much of an obstacle for him to overcome. The Dude also arguably lets go of his project of saving Bunny a bit too easily, yielding unsettlingly quickly to the self-abduction theory when Maude and Walter insist on it.

The millionaire's definition of "a man," moreover, is not the only target of the film. *TBL* in fact subverts a clutch of traditionally masculine ideals: not only the successful businessman and man of status and acquisition, but also the valiant soldier and fighter, the masterful athlete and game winner, the sexy seducer, the cowboy, the playboy, the strong-willed patriarchal father and husband, the powerful political leader, and, of course, the shrewd and hard-boiled lone-wolf detective. The Dude is shown to be emphatically none of these, even hostile to them, and those ideal tropes are each revealed to be in their own ways either empty, phony, or silly.

The millionaire Lebowski himself is no millionaire and no patriarch, his wealth came to him through his deceased wife, and he now lives on a demeaning allowance distributed at his patronizing daughter's discretion. His transactional marriage to Bunny is a pathetic and humiliating sham. Attempting to defraud the family foundation, the old man certainly does not do the right thing, no matter the cost. The Dude, for his part, may be on his way to becoming a father, but it seems so only (or mostly) in the biological sense. He certainly will not be a husband, phony or otherwise.

The meekest male on the womanless team of apparent *célibataires*, Donny, is the best and most capable bowler. And while brash and aggressive Jesus Quintana sure can roll, the would-be dominator and sex machine is actually a gaudy and ridiculous fop, as well as a convicted sex offender, perhaps even a pedophile. Overweight Walter is a volatile blowhard whose days as a heroic soldier are long gone (if he ever really had them) and whose ex-wife, Cynthia, dumped him in favor of a new man, Marty Ackerman, presumably a more authentic Jew and a better provider. Despite her rejection, Walter obsequiously still takes care of Cynthia's dog and attends her synagogue while she gallivants around Hawaii with his replacement. Only by drawing a gun can he command what he reads as respect.

The threatening, leather-clad nihilists are nothing more than skinny poseurs whom even obese Walter drops in short order. The cowboy is a cartoonish parody of the real thing. And while Da Fino may be a genuine private detective, he is no Raymond Chandleresque shamus. His physical stature and car are diminutive; his big case is just retrieving a "wandering daughter," who willfully refuses to "wander on home." Even The Dude can manage neither respect nor kindness for the little, balding "dick." He is certainly no savior and protector. Unlike *TBS*'s Carmen Sternwood and Vivian Rutledge, neither Bunny nor Maude Lebowski needs protecting or saving in the least.

Now, all these critical portrayals are also part of the Coen Bros' genre project. *The Big Lebowski* is without doubt a send-up of the noir detective films exemplified by *TBS* (1946; not to mention *The Big Heat* [1953] and *The Big Combo* [1955]; CineFix, 2016), as well as, more broadly, a whole range of films populated by stock American cinematic heroes (cowboys, warriors, detectives, and millionaires). The term "film noir" was first coined, by the way, in 1946 by French film critics.

But the way female characters play into *TBL*, in conjunction with other cinematic clues scattered across the film, points directly at the topic of masculinity proper as a concept or ideology under examination, in addition to the film's genre critique. The film's central plot line is, after all, initiated by a woman's transgression against patriarchy. Bunny flees her presumably dull and repressive home in frigid and colorless Moorhead, Minnesota, for the liberties, and what French philosopher Jacques Lacan calls *jouissances* – joys or climactic pleasures – of Los Angeles (Lacan 2007 [1977]). Unlike her twin in *TBS*, Carmen Sternwood, Bunny Lebowski is no weak, drugged, deranged victim of male exploitation and paternal neglect. Quite the contrary.

In *TBS*, spoiled and practically fatherless, heiress Carmen Sternwood is presented as having been used by pornographers and other criminals. Frustrated in her own desires, she kills a man who refuses her sexual advances. But Bunny (in an inversion of subservient and instrumentalized Playboy bunnies) gets what she wants through her own designs, from men, without men, and despite men. She gets over not only on her husband but also on crime boss Jackie Treehorn. And, of course, she joyfully engages in sex like a bunny, with at least Karl Hungus and Sherry. The centrality of her role as the axis around which all else turns makes the film about men impotently trying to control, use, and vainly save a powerful woman. It is a telling point about the persistent patriarchy that The Dude, like so many others, identifies Bunny's husband, the impaired fraudster-faux-millionaire, as the "big" Lebowski, while if anyone warrants the title "big" Lebowski, arguably it is Bunny.

Walter's ex-wife Cynthia seems to be hewn from similar timber. Having left violent, impecunious, and overbearing Walter, she is off in the direction of Asia to Hawaii (a symbol of lush, opulent pleasure) with a new man, presumably a wealthy man of her choice. She even keeps, symbolically, a male millionaire as her pet. "Thurston" recalls, of course, *Gilligan's Island* millionaire Thurston Howell III, but the canine also alludes to the cairn terrier, Toto, with whom the young woman Dorothy Gale, like Fawn "Bunny" Knutsen, took flight from her dreary Midwestern farm home for a dazzling, colorful, gold-bricked fantasyland, Oz, in the West. ("Oz" was an abbreviation for "ounce" of silver or gold in Baum's, *The Wonderful Wizard of Oz*; by the way, Baum's wife was a feminist named Maud, daughter of prominent New York suffragette Matilda Gage.) Cut loose, however, neither Cynthia nor Bunny, in the Coen Brothers' inversion, longs for her earlier home ("How ya gonna keep 'em down on the farm once they've seen Karl Hungus?"). In contrast, Uli's German nihilist-girlfriend, so far from home too, remains subordinate to men and does not get what she wants. Her voice is ignored, and her body, like the mannequins in Maude's studio, is literally dismembered.

Now, it is true that Bunny, like Cynthia and unlike Dorothy, does remain, in terms of screen time, a background figure. Her older stepdaughter Maude (okay, Maude tells the Dude not to call Bunny her "mother"), of course, is an unattached, independently successful artist and captain of the family fortune. She gets what she wants, too, though in a different fashion. What she wants, a child (and to become a mother), normally requires in some sense the positive cooperation of a man.

Maude deserves criticism for deceiving The Dude into siring a child by her without his explicit consent and then declaring that she expects him to be uninvolved in raising it. And Maude does seem to be a bit of a hypocrite for running "fun and games" of that sort after criticizing Bunny as a base "fornicator." But Maude's desires seem congruent with The Dude's (he does not want to be a husband or father either), despite the way she fulfills them. Besides, there is some suggestion that she is actually rather fond of The Dude (just as he is of her) and that he will remain in some fashion a part of her and their child's life – at least stopping by occasionally to fix the cable. She does, after all, instruct him, when she drops the robe to reveal herself, to "Love me," not "Fuck me."

Perhaps it is no surprise, then, that Maude does not join The Dude in confronting the old man Lebowski after The Dude's limbered-up mind figures out his scheme. The Dude did not need to call Walter and interrupt his Sabbath. Surely, Maude and her driver could have taken The Dude to Pasadena. Would not Maude want to be in on confronting her father? Maude, however, in the end, seems unconcerned about the money and is satisfied with having had sex (if not joyfully made love) with The Dude. The Dude, for his part, on the other hand, at least for now drops Maude like a hot potato and uncharacteristically ignores her commands the moment he has solved the case. He seems more attached to male Walter (and to bowling) than to her.

Ben Almassi, following Larry May, argues that in all this The Dude depicts a man taking the first steps toward the formation of a "progressive masculinity" but not quite yet reaching it (Almassi 2012). The Dude has shed the oppressive forms of traditional manhood and allied himself with women in their projects without dominating them. As The Dude says to Da Fino about Maude, his "lady friend," he is "helping her" to conceive; his role is friend and helper. The Dude has not yet, however, in Almassi's view, added positive content to that new masculinity. Yes, The Dude negates what has been bad, but he has not yet, beyond a kind of "slacker masculinity," says Almassi, defined and revised being a man in a way that is good. Almassi is mistaken.

It is true that the end of the movie sees The Dude returning to the condition very much like the one he occupied when it all began, apparently without real growth. The Dude remains at the close of the narrative located in a thoroughly white male world, *sans* Donny, and the film fails even to pass the Bechdel test. (The Bechdel test is a well-known feminist critical tool that asks whether any given fiction meets the following three criteria: (1) It portrays more than one (named) female character; (2) those characters talk to each other; and (3) they talk about something besides a man.) But perhaps that conclusion is too quick. What kind of man, then, if any, has The Dude through Maude (and Bunny) found in himself?

The Dude's Abiding Virtues

An answer to this question, and one more content-rich than Almassi discerns, begins to emerge by examining The Dude's virtues. The Dude has proven a durably attractive, even inspirational, character to uncountably many people across the globe. More than 20 years after its release, *The Big Lebowski* ranks second only to 1975's *The Rocky Horror Picture Show* among cult films. Lebowski bars and Lebowski fests have proliferated and flourished. With little doubt, much of that success is rooted in The Dude himself. Why?

The Dude's Antimaterialism: One reason is The Dude's nonacquisitive lifestyle. Jeffrey "The Dude" Lebowski adopts what Morgan Rempel calls a life of "contented poverty" (Rempel 2012). Ancient Greek philosopher Epicurus (341–271 BCE) argues that the good life is a life of pleasure. But the kinds of pleasures he endorses are narrowly defined, and they are in many ways like those The Dude pursues. To be more precise, for Epicurus, pleasures come in two types: the "kinetic" and the "static." The latter are associated with what is both "natural and necessary" while the former amount to neither.

Epicurus was an atomist, maintaining that the mind-soul (*psychê*) of human beings is composed of atoms. Kinetic pleasures are, accordingly, problematic because they are agitating; they disrupt the condition of our mind-soul's atoms. Kinetic pleasures are associated with wild, orgasmic thrills, luxuries, contests, material gain, and fancy cuisine. They often finally yield, despite their initial pleasantries, to physical pain and mental disturbance, much in the way that hangovers follow drunken revelry. Kinetic pleasures also generate dependencies and undermine the freedom that, as the North American Shakers knew, comes with a simple life.

Static pleasures, in contrast, are both natural and necessary, though they can also be natural but unnecessary. Static pleasures leave our atoms in peace, and the contentment that peacefulness yields Epicureans call *ataraxia* (undisturbedness or tranquility), much like The Dude's tranquility at home with his bowling tapes, tai chi, warm bath, and rug.

Acquisitiveness does not lend itself to tranquility, and The Dude seems to exhibit a decidedly loose relationship with private property. Despite his efforts to prevent intrusion, The Dude is, in fact, unable to stop people from entering his "private residence" at will and then doing whatever they want to both him and his possessions. In an effort to secure the entrance to his apartment, the Dude nails a board on the floor, props up a chair with its legs against it, and wedges the top of the chair under the doorknob – only to discover that the door swings the other way. Treenhorn's goons, Maude and her attendants, the millionaire's brutish chauffeur, and, of course, the nihilists come and go as they please, ransack the place, and do what they want to The Dude bodily. The Dude's car is stolen, smashed, urinated in, and finally torched. If it were not for Walter, the nihilists would have taken his pocket money. Maude even helps herself to The Dude's robe. So, it should be no surprise that The Dude loses the ransom. Truly, there are few people worse as a choice to entrust valuable property.

Now, The Dude does not toe a perfectly Epicurean line. He has sex with Maude and had seriously desired it. He is, moreover, rather liberal in his use of intoxicants (alcohol, marijuana, and beer). The Dude definitely loses his Epicurean bearings during the sorry encounter with little Larry. But, as Rempel argues, sex of the sort in which The Dude and Maude engage is arguably natural even if unnecessary (Rempel 2012). Epicurus would surely not have approved of The Dude's recreational drug use, but his choice in inebriants is of the milder sort, and his use of them moderate. Unlike nihilist Uli, who drinks himself into oblivion with hard liquor and passes out in the millionaire's pool, The Dude's indulgences seem to enhance rather than undermine his tranquil contentedness. Anyway, the inebriation, The Dude tells Maude, keeps his mind "limber" and seems to flow naturally from his character. The extremity of the scene at little Larry's house, while certainly a lapse from his Dudely equanimity, serves as a reminder of just how wrong the violent, agitated, acquisitive life finally is.

There are also analogies to be made between The Dude's way of life and the prescriptions of religion, specifically Buddhism and Daoism; authors have certainly made them (Benjamin 2016). Over 600,000 Dude-ist priests have been ordained via dudeism.com and otherwise (including this author). Jeff Bridges himself has published a book suggesting that The Dude is a Zen master of sorts (Bridges 2014).

These romanticized and playful analogies are, however, not terribly compelling in a philosophical sense. As Joseph J. Lynch has observed, The Dude not only lacks the metaphysical commitments, philosophical critiques, and *wu wei* (actionless action) of Taoism. His fainéant, self-indulgent lifestyle is also pretty far from the selflessness and rigorous discipline of the Buddha (Lynch 2012). But The Dude cultivates several other virtues, nonetheless.

The Dude's Nonviolence: The Dude may not exactly be a pacifist of the sort he describes in Smokey, since we see him wimpily fending off the skinny nihilist Franz (Torsten Voges) with his bowling ball as Franz threatens to rape him anally ("I fuck you in the ass!"). And again, there is also that unfortunate way he threatens little Larry. But while those shortcomings can seem disappointing, it is important to remember, as The Stranger affirms, that The Dude is truly no proper hero. He is, by pretty much any measure, flawed.

The Dude is, however, eminently peaceable. He tries to defuse the ruckus Walter raises about Smokey's line-crossing and reproaches Walter for his gunplay and restaurant rants; he offers to give the nihilists what he has rather than fight them; he opposes brutalizing the old man Lebowski; he reminisces with Brandt about his nonviolent protests against the Vietnam war; with Maude, he recalls his coauthorship of the Port Huron Statement, which endorses nonviolent resistance; he does not join Walter in battering the Corvette; and, preferring defensive measures, he does not borrow Walter's gun, call the police, or even fight back against Woo and the moronic blond goon, despite their home invasion. In fact, no reasonable viewer could think The Dude would actually harm little Larry. Even his clothes present subdued colors, unlike those Bunny, the nihilists, and The Jesus wear.

The Dude as Friend: In addition to his contented poverty and his peaceableness, there is another virtue, even more important, that the film articulates. Proper to Epicurean philosophy, and to Aristotle's ideas about virtue, is friendship; it is perhaps most heartwarmingly as a film about friendship, specifically male friendship, that *The Big Lebowski* shines. For Epicurus, freeing oneself from kinetic pleasures, material acquisition, struggles for power and adventure, and sexual conquest leaves one with a simple life of natural pleasure. Integral to such a life is the companionship and conversation of friends. In Epicurus' vision, that conversation would center on philosophy. Of course, the Dude's exchanges with Walter are at first blush not terribly philosophical, but a closer look reveals more.

Walter and The Dude argue, among other things, about rules and their application, about the ethics of belief and religious identity, about violence and its proper place, about what duties are owed to Bunny and Walter's ex-wife Cynthia, and about responsibility for property damage (his rug). He and Maude discuss feminism, sex, and sexual morality. Considering The Dude's philosophical inclinations, it seems fitting that when Maude and The Dude finally hook up, set on top of the bookshelf in The Dude's bedroom is a copy of Sartre's existentialist masterpiece *Being and*

Nothingness. Considered as a whole, Walter and The Dude's appeals to Lenin, Theodor Herzl, Moses Maimonides, and Constitutional law indicate that their discussions are more than humorous.

Aristotle's vision of friendship is, however, a bit more complicated and adds depth to an appreciation of The Dude and Walter's relationship. Aristotle emphasizes that friends recognize themselves in one another. Who has not noticed friends dressing alike, sharing common backgrounds, and even possessing similar physical attributes? The Dude and Walter are both on the same bowling team, and they are both Polish Americans. (In September of 1939, the Germans, of course, crossed an important line when they invaded Poland – an act of aggression that precipitated WWII. Walter has not forgotten it.) But that seems insufficient to explain the depth of their friendship. What on Earth keeps this curious duo bonded as such close friends? What functions as the rug that ties their community together? Sure, the odd couple is an old trope in film and theater. Think of Laurel and Hardy, Felix and Oscar, Ralph Kramden and Ed Norton, Bert and Ernie, and Fred and Barney. But the enduring popularity of the trope only confirms that there is something important going on in these pairs, something that possesses considerable moral and political heft.

Aristotle's analysis of friendship shows how friends like these two help elevate and improve one another. The Dude criticizes Walter's conduct and does his best to guide his friend in the right direction. Walter, for his part, reins in The Dude's histrionics and ethnic-racist malapropisms (though not his own), and he keeps The Dude from wandering too far from the false-kidnapping theory. Had it not been for Walter (and Maude and Lenin), The Dude would have ended up prey to the pseudomillionaire's embezzlement scheme.

Friendship, however, exerts an even wider effect. Not only do friends help one another become more virtuous as individuals. According to Aristotle, there is also something to friendship that underwrites a flourishing political order. That terribly important dimension of friendship sustains *TBL*'s continued relevance and enduring meaningfulness. Aristotle describes this element of The Dude and Walter's relationship and virtue – in his *Nicomachean Ethics, Eudemian Ethics*, and *Politics* (Aristotle 1984) – as a specific kind of love or *philia*, namely, civic or political friendship: "Friendship seems ... to hold states together, and lawgivers care more for it than for justice" (NE 1155a22ff; cf. Pol 1280b38-39, EE 1242a1-2). It is the kind of friendship essential to members of a shared polity. It underwrites solidarity in political projects, and it attenuates the discord and divisiveness otherwise sure to tear a political order apart.

The Dude and Walter represent not only throwbacks to the 1960s and 1970s (an SDS hippie and a Vietnam vet). They also represent left-wing and right-wing political movements: The Dude with his Grateful Dead pants, long hair, socialism, marijuana, and passé idioms ("far out, man"); Walter with his jarhead, his violent bravado, his ammo vest, his gun range glasses, and of course his guns. Arguably, in the parlance of recent years, The Dude would have been a Bernie bro while Walter would have been a Trumpster (Hagland 2013). And yet they are inseparable friends.

Their friendship is possible and persists because the *philia* they share is not simply for one another as individuals but also, and most importantly, as members of a shared microcommunity: their bowling team. Augustine, responding to Cicero's *Republic* (Bk1) and elaborating on this idea in *City of God* (19:24), defines a polity as a community of rational beings united not by a rug, fear, self-interest, or even a social contract but instead by agreement about the objects of their shared love – in this case bowling. *TBL*'s troika of bowlers may not always be rational, but together they are more than individuals. Like the three holes in a bowling ball, they together function as a unity, a pack, a team, and a platoon – albeit a very white and male one. They compose, indeed, a band of brothers, three musketeers, and comrades of a collective triad with shared loves that must be sustained by them all in a form of life that is, to borrow a phrase, one-for-all and all-for-one.

Even when The Dude is profoundly put out with Walter after the disgraceful episode at little Larry Sellers' house, he makes it clear that he will still be at team practice. Just a few minutes later, after his bedding Maude and figuring out the old man's scheme, it is to Walter not Maude, despite his pique, that The Dude turns. When Walter screws up the scattering of Donny's ashes, in a gesture of Aristotelian *gnomê* or good judgment (*Nicomachean Ethics* Bk 7), The Dude forgives the contrite clod.

That these two oddballs can maintain a community informed by civic *philia* is certainly something in which people can, as the Stranger says, take comfort – especially in a polity as riven as the USA in the late twentieth and early twenty-first centuries. That is certainly part of the man found in The Dude: a good friend who exercises the intellectual and moral virtues required to sustain his community.

The Dude's Antiauthoritarianism: The Dude's slow, easy-going quality also marks something important. It exhibits something deep that philosophers have determined about rules, moral and otherwise, more generally. The Dude's abiding way of life not only, in this sense, offers a practical alternative to the violent rigidity and authoritarianism of the millionaire, The Jesus, the nihilists, and Walter. It is also superior in a theoretically sophisticated way.

To unpack this idea, consider what Troy Jollimore and Robert C. Jones have argued, namely, that one can place Walter at one end of a spectrum with regard to rule following and the nihilists at the other (Jollimore and Jones 2012). Walter represents an absolutist position concerning rules. Indeed, he thinks he is the only one "who still gives a shit about the rules" (as he pulls a lethal weapon on a competitor in a friendly bowling match to enforce a violation of the foul line). He also insists – when it suits him – on scrupulously following rules about ransoms, personal property, free speech, and about how to observe the Sabbath. Like the millionaire and The Jesus, Walter is, moreover, as dogmatic about his beliefs (e.g., the false abduction theory, that the millionaire is not disabled, and his religion) as he is about following the rules: "One hundred percent certain" ... "I've never been more certain of anything in my life."

Compare this to the nihilists who, at least nominally, reject all rules and beliefs. ("We believe in nossing!") They are willing to lie, extort, steal, grift, and engage in sex amorally. Their way of life disgusts Walter who, even as a Jew, prefers Nazis to nihilists: "Say what you want about the tenets of National Socialism. At least it's an ethos." (As *The Big Sleep* was released just after the US war with the Nazis, *TBL* may be suggesting that the rise of modern nihilism presents something worse than Nazism, something worse too than the "worthy fucking adversary" Walter describes in the Viet Cong.)

The Dude on the other hand, like Aristotle and, more recently, Ludwig Wittgenstein (1889–1951), understands that rules are by themselves not absolute and not sufficient to guide moral or linguistic practice. (Ethan Coen completed his undergraduate honors thesis in philosophy at Princeton in 1979 on "Two Views of Wittgenstein's Later Philosophy.") Rules must be *applied* properly to each particular situation, and it is not easy to do so. Different circumstances require different applications. When, moreover, conflicts arise among rules, decisions must be made about which rule, in fact, rules. One way of resolving conflicts of this sort is by appeal to additional rules, governing rules as it were, that limit some rules in favor of others. So, the way the foul line rule may be enforced is limited by laws (and by league bylaws) about drawing firearms.

Because of the complexities of the world and the nature of rules themselves, however, there is a limit to the extent to which governing rules alone can resolve conflicts among rules. Something more is needed. Ultimately, various traits or capacities of (1) intellect and (2) character – in particular, various intellectual and moral virtues – are required to resolve conflicts among rules and use rules well. It takes both a smart, morally sophisticated mind and also a well-formed character to know which rule trumps which, as well as when, where, with whom, and how it does so.

According to Aristotelian-informed traditions in philosophy, the excellences of intellect required in order to apply rules properly include the following: (1a) comprehensive knowledge (*theoria*) of sets of rules and principles; (1b) insight (*synderesis*) into exactly which rules are relevant to a situation; (1c) the capacity to deliberate rationally (*phronesis*) with them; (1d) empirical knowledge of the world and how it works (*epistemê*); and (1e) good sense (*gnomê*) in appreciating the particularities of various contexts.

Among the excellences of character required for sound rule application (especially moral rules), one might count dispositions for being (2a) charitable, (2b) generous, (2c) compassionate, (2d) moderate, (2e) sensitive, and (2f) merciful. The Dude possesses all those qualities in spades. Neither Walter, the nihilists, nor anyone else in the film comes close.

Aristotelians gather all these traits and capacities together under the rubric of moral wisdom. It is a kind of wisdom different from that which comes from pure theory and the sciences. That difference, as well as the necessity of all these conditions coming into play in order to realize a properly moral life, explains why there must be morally capable judges to oversee trials and why institutions such as the Supreme Court will never be eliminated. Moral and legal judgments are simply different in kind from those of mathematics, logic, and the empirical sciences. One cannot calculate or experiment one's way to justice or to moral rectitude.

Now, there may be contexts where enforcing a rule warrants conduct as extreme as violence (for example, in contexts where someone is attempting to murder another), but, as The Dude appreciates, a recreational bowling league game (Walter's justification) is not one of them. (By extension, the film raises the question of whether President G. H. W. Bush's invasion of Kuwait was justified, as well.) That is why The Dude reminds Walter when he accosts Smokey that "It's just a game." It is also why it would have been appropriate for the police, had they arrived earlier, to have drawn their weapons on Walter.

The Dude's virtue is on full display, then, when he says to Walter, "You're not wrong [about the foul-line rule and the rules for advancing to the next round]; you're just an asshole [for applying those rules badly]." *No Country for Old Men*'s Anton Chigurh is another infamous Coen brothers' character, who observes rules in a perverse way (following a self-invented rule that he should kill or not kill on the basis of a coin flip and following the rule that promises should be kept even when it means killing an innocent woman because he had malevolently promised to do so).

For these same reasons, The Dude presents the wiser, if not more entertaining, alternative when the nihilists demand "za money" in the parking lot. Walter is technically correct that a rule can be properly formulated stating that the money in The Dude and Donny's pockets is by right each of theirs to keep, but applying that rule in such a rigid way in that context is unwise. Handing over some measly pocket money would have avoided unnecessary violence (the ear biting and sword thrusting) and perhaps even saved Donny the stress that precipitated his heart attack.

The Dude would also have been within his rights to have been unforgiving with Walter after the fiasco with Donny's ashes. But his compassion, generosity, and friendship with Walter temper his enforcement of rules about the proper way to handle a friend's remains. In this sense, The Dude's conduct manifests what feminist philosophers have called an ethic of "care," which is grounded in the particularities of human relationships rather than general rules of conduct (Gilligan 1982). It also exhibits another of The Dude's virtues, his acceptance of imperfection.

In general, The Dude does not demand perfection in the application and enforcement of rules, and this refusal is not a sign of laziness or some other vice. The Dude not only understands that absolutist assertions such as The Jesus' predictions about his imminent victory are without epistemic warrant because people's capacity to know the future is limited, but he also understands that people are prone by character to excesses as well as to mistakes – such as neglecting to account for the wind when dispersing ashes. (John Turturro's 2019 sequel, *The Jesus Rolls*, claims that The Jesus' prosecution for sex crime was itself a mistake.) As The Dude observes about Smokey, human beings are in general "fragile" – especially in the face of nihilism.

The Dude Versus Nihilism

That last qualification is of course central to the film, since perhaps the most obvious philosophical dimension of *TBL* is its engagement with nihilism. Arguably, nihilism appears as a central theme, even a character, of many of the Coen Brothers' films. The amoral cynicism of *Blood Simple* and *Miller's Crossing*, the dark rider of the Apocalypse in *Raising Arizona*, the tornado in the finale of *A Serious Man* (a rejection of God's speaking through a whirlwind, Job 38:1, KJV), the kidnappers and desolate winterscape of *Fargo*, Anton Chigurh in *No Country for Old Men* (which could be retitled, *No Country for Anti-Nihilists*), Charlie Meadows in *Barton Fink*, and Ed Crane in *The Man Who Wasn't There*, all depict nihilism and the struggle with it.

If nihilism is the adversary, then how does *TBL* confront it? In part, The Dude-distinctive virtues, just described, answer that question. The Dude's Epicurean contented poverty, the simplicity of his life, the profound and reflective friendships he develops, and his sophistication about morality are all antidotes to nihilism. Given the nihilists' repeated command to make sure there is "no funny stuff," comedy itself must be considered antinihilistic. (Imagine attempting a joke with Anton Chigurh.) But there is more to the antinihilism of *TBL* than this list describes.

Nihilism, roughly speaking, is the antidoctrine that there is no truth and no meaning – moral, esthetic, theological, scientific, or otherwise. Nineteenth-century German philosopher Friedrich Nietzsche's (1844–1900) analysis of modern nihilism has been the most popular and influential. According to Nietzsche (famous for observing about truth and meaning that "God is dead"), nihilism is the logical result of the Christian-Platonic philosophical tradition in the West (Nietzsche 1901). In brief, both Christianity and Platonism advanced three problematic ideas: (1) that truth is singular, fixed, universal, consistent, objective, and univocal; (2) that the value of this world and human existence derives from a transcendent source; and (3) that all human beings are equal.

Nihilism has resulted from these principles because millennia of self-critical intellectual inquiry have led to the conclusion that truth of that sort seems not to be had and that a transcendent source of meaning seems not to exist. Moreover, attempts to establish human equality have failed and instead hobbled creative, superior individuals. Unable to find truth, meaning, and community as Christianity and Platonism conceive them, people have despaired of believing in anything or in human community at all. The glorification of acquisition, self-annihilating intoxication, spiritualities of transcendence and escape, the reduction of people to mere instruments of pleasure, the denial and obliteration of nature, orgies of violence and death, cults of weaponry, politics as domination and power, literatures of irony and cynicism, and art as titillating spectacle, all characterize nihilism. What is required to beat the nihilism from which the contemporary world suffers, according to Nietzsche, is a new kind of culture and with it a new kind of human being – the *Übermensch*. The *Übermensch* must embrace a multiplicity of perspectives rather than a single truth, must find the temporary and finite world meaningful without appeal to the transcendent, and must endorse creatively powerful people in a way that accepts the difference, variety, and distinctions among individuals.

The Dude is perhaps a halfway *Übermensch*. He does confront dogmatic assertions made by The Jesus, whose antics symbolize Christianity's perverse insistence on absolute truth, with the perspectivist rejoinder, "Yeah, well, you know, that's just like, uh, your opinion, man." Perhaps even more importantly, The Dude seems freed from dependence on a divine, supernatural, or otherwise transcendent source of meaning. He is also a powerfully creative and fertile person himself, not so much through employed work and struggle but, within the film, as a pillar of his little community – and, of course, as a father to Maude's baby. Beyond the film, The Dude has proven culturally powerful as the guiding star of a kind of cult of Lebowski Dudeliness.

The Dude seems, however, non-*Übermensch* in being a rather devoted egalitarian, unimpressed by the economic and culturally elite status claimed alternatively by the millionaire and by Maude Lebowski, as well as by the Malibu sheriff (though maybe in a Nietzschean way The Dude senses his superiority to them). He is instead a man of *hoi polloi* and of the ordinary people who, as the opening credit sequence tells us, populate his proper abode, the working-class bowling alley.

Bowling itself, in any case, is crucial to The Dude's opposition to nihilism. French existentialist Albert Camus (1913–1960, author of the 1942 novel "The Stranger," to which perhaps the cowboy narrator's title alludes) reframed the myth of Sisyphus as a parable about how to resist existential despair (Camus 1942). While the gods intended Sisyphus' burden of rolling a great stone up a hill only to see it roll back down, over and over without end, as a punishment, in Camus' account that repetition, properly executed, inverts the situation, transforming the rock rolling from punishment into a source of meaning and happiness. Similarly, for Nietzsche the acid test for determining whether or not one's life is meaningful is whether or not one would will to live it over and over again in a repeating "eternal recurrence" forever (Nietzsche 1882).

Given the centrality of nihilism to the film, it can be no accident that The Dude is a bowler, that Donny describes himself as throwing "rocks" when he bowls, and that the opening depicts people rolling their balls (rocks) over and over and over again. In the face of failure (in executing their ransom handoff) and death (Donny's funeral), and repeatedly throughout the film, The Dude and Walter return again and again to the lanes and to the repetition of rolling their rocks. It is the home of their meaning, their community, and their resistance to lurking nihilism.

Camus' parable had drawn from the Danish philosopher Søren Kierkegaard (1813–1855), who argues that meaning can be generated through "repetition" (Kierkegaard 1843). *TBL* has been flush with repetition, both on screen and off it at the many Lebowski Fests around the world where people engage in mimicking (i.e., repeating) cosplay and endlessly repeating quotes from the script. Fans of the film watch it many times over and over. The Dude, of course, has a penchant for repeating phrases he hears from others ("This aggression will not stand," from President G. H. W. Bush; "Her life was in our hands," from Brandt; and "the parlance of our times," from Maude, e.g.). More than that, The Dude, in so many ways, repeats the tropes of the hippies: his long hair, the idioms of his speech, his old car, his Deadhead pants, his pot smoking, his Nixon poster, and his SDS reminiscences. The Dude even picks up and repeats a bit of The Stranger's Old West wisdom (about the "bar" eating you) at the end of the film. He does not, thank goodness, repeat Walter. It is odd, in a way, that The Stranger says that The Dude fits right into his time and place (1991 Los Angeles) when in fact he seems, more than Walter, stuck in the past.

From a Kierkegaardian point of view, however, The Dude is not stuck. Rather, he daily repeats The Dudely form of life, whatever its provenance, in a way that generates and sustains meaning, despite the threat of nihilism. He does not live in the past (an accusation he levels against Walter) but instead rolls the past into the future in newly iterated and meaningful ways. One might think of his kind of existential Dudely repetition as what most fundamentally it means for him to "abide" or inhabit time.

The Dudes' abiding leaves viewers hopeful that he will defeat The Jesus (and the nihilism Nietzsche argues flows from Christianity). Through the intercession of his "special lady," moreover, The Dude will also take part in humanity's most basic and most hopeful kind of repetition – natural, biological reproduction, a kind of repetition that finally affirms his distinctive Dudely manhood independent of the traditional forms of masculinity he has refused. For the existentialist, human beings – by means of their art (a word stitched onto The Dude's Medina bowling shirt), their passions, and otherwise – must bring meaning into an otherwise absurd, meaningless, and fatally crushing universe (Baird 2012). There is more.

Jeffrey Nicholas (Nicholas 2012) has argued that, in addition to its existential repetitions, bowling in this film rises to what virtue philosopher Alasdair MacIntyre calls a "practice." Disciplined and formalized practices of this sort, argues Nicholas, are important devices for creating the conditions under which one can resist nihilism (MacIntyre 1981). It is not only meaning-generating repetition, in other words, that thwarts nihilism but also, more precisely, repeated *practices* – such as making art, growing businesses, raising children, cultivating gardens, playing sports, maintaining long-term monogamous relationships, pursuing academic scholarship, etc. – that generate meaning.

Nicholas Michaud has taken a step farther, adding to an understanding of The Dude's antinihilistic power by arguing that the slow pace of The Dude's way of life insulates him from the despair-inducing effects of modern life's insistence on ever-increasing speed (Michaud 2012).

Conclusion

The Big Lebowski parodies and presents an homage to *The Big Sleep*, a classic post-WWII film that is infamous for its complicated plot but also genre-typical in its portrayal of the heroic tough, savvy, virile, individual, white, male, American noir detective. As a genre film, *TBL* charts the distance from post-WWII to post-Reagan American cinema, just as it challenges the genre tropes of the past. But the film is also a deeply complicated philosophical project that criticizes traditional ideals of masculinity and explores the possibilities for different kind of manhood. The Dude rejects precedent ideals but tentatively "achieves" something different through the virtue he exemplifies in the way he "abides." That abiding draws upon ideals of contented poverty articulated by Epicurean philosophers, as well as the excellences of moral life and political community explored by Aristotelians. Those virtues also underwrite, moreover, The Dude's response to nihilism. The Dude answers nihilism through friendship, antimaterialism, antiauthoritarianism, care, knowing flexibility in rule-following, good humor, compassion, cross-sex alliances, devotion to the practices of bowling, and existentialist forms of repetition. These philosophical dimensions of the film make it about more than genre. *The Big Lebowski* is most compellingly about the condition of modern American culture.

References

Allen, D. 2009. *Logjammin'* and *Gutterballs*: Masculinities in *the big Lebowski*. In *The year's work in Lebowski studies*, ed. A. Jaffe, 386–409. Bloomington: Indiana University Press.

Almassi, B. 2012. 'Mr. Treehorn treats objects like women, man': The Dude as feminist ally. In *The big Lebowski and philosophy: Keeping your mind limber with abiding wisdom*, ed. P.S. Fosl, 190–206. Hoboken: Wiley.

Aristotle. 1984. *The complete works of Aristotle*. Princeton: Princeton University Press.

Baird, B.N. 2012. Existentialism, absurdity, and *the big Lebowski*. In *The big Lebowski and philosophy: Keeping your mind limber with abiding wisdom*, ed. W. Irwin, 136–146. Hoboken: Wiley.

Benjamin, O. 2016. *The Dude De Ching: A philosophical meeting of the Tao Te Ching and the big Lebowski*. Abide University Press.

Bridges, J.A.B.G. 2014. *The Dude and the Zen master*. New York: Plume.

Camus, A. 1942. *Myth of Sisyphus*. London: Vintage.

Gilligan, C. 1982. *In a different voice: Psychological theory and women's development*. Cambridge, MA: Harvard University Press.

Green, B., Ben Peskoe, Will Russell, and Scott Shuffitt. 2007. *I'm a Lebowski, you're a Lebowski: Life, the big Lebowski, and what have you*. New York: Bloomsbury.

Hagland, D. 2013. Walter Sobchak, neocon: The prescient politics of *the big Lebowski*. In *Lebowski 101: Limber-minded investigations into the greatest story ever blathered*, ed. O. Benjamin, 54–56. Abide University Press.

Jollimore, T., and Robert C. Jones. 2012. 'That ain't legal either': Rules, virtue, and authenticity in *the big Lebowski*. In *The Big Lebowski and philosophy: Keeping your mind limber with abiding wisdom*, 106–120. Hoboken: Wiley.

Kierkegaard, S. 1843. *Repetition*. Princeton: Princeton University Press.

Lacan, J. 2007 [1977]. *Écrits: A selection*. New York: W. W. Norton.

Lynch, J.J. 2012. Buddhism, Daoism, and Dudeism. In *The big Lebowski and philosophy: Keeping your mind limber with abiding wisdom*, ed. P.S. Fosl, 79–89. Hoboken: Wiley.

MacIntyre, A. 1981. *After virtue*. South Bend: University of Notre Dame Press.

Michaud, N. 2012. 'Well I do work, sir': The Dude and the value of sloth. In *The big Lebowski and philosophy: Keeping your mind limber with abiding wisdom*, ed. P.S. Fosl, 207–220. Hoboken: Wiley.

Nicholas, J. 2012. Bowling our way out of nihilism. In *The big Lebowski and philosophy: Keeping your mind limber with abiding wisdom*, ed. P.S. Fosl. Hoboken: Wiley.

Nietzsche, F. 1882. *The gay science*. New York: Vintage.

———. 1901. *The will to power*. New York: Knopf Doubleday Publishing Group.

Rempel, M. 2012. Epicurus and 'contented poverty': *The big Lebowski*'s epicurean parable. In *The big Lebowski and philosophy: Keeping your mind limber with abiding wisdom*, ed. P.S. Fosl. Hoboken: Wiley.

Harry Potter as Philosophy: Five Types of Friendship

39

James M. Okapal

Contents

Introduction	952
Aristotle's Theory of Friendship	953
Friendships for Virtue in the HPCU	955
Friendships for Pleasure in the HPCU	957
Friendships for Utility in the HPCU	960
Conclusion	963
Postscript	964
References	965

Abstract

The Harry Potter Cinematic Universe is a fertile ground for philosophical cultivation. In this chapter, the films are used to explain and expand upon Aristotle's theory of friendship. Aristotle's theory identifies three types of friendship: friendships for virtue, pleasure, and utility. The Harry Potter films, however, suggest a modification of this view to allow for five types of friendships. Throughout the series we see that friendships for pleasure and utility come in both beneficent and maleficent forms. A key element in this distinction is whether the motivations for forming these friendships are other-regarding or self-regarding.

Keywords

Harry Potter · Friendship · Love · Relationships · Aristotle · Community · Motivation · Dating · Sports · Inclusion · Courage · Loyalty · Virtue · Pleasure · Utility · Choice · Self-regarding interests · Other-regarding interests

---

J. M. Okapal (✉)
Missouri Western State University, Saint Joseph, MO, USA
e-mail: jokapal@missouriwestern.edu

© Springer Nature Switzerland AG 2024
D. K. Johnson et al. (eds.), *The Palgrave Handbook of Popular Culture as Philosophy*,
https://doi.org/10.1007/978-3-031-24685-2_40

Introduction

Friendship is a notion that is mentioned throughout the Harry Potter Cinematic Universe (HPCU). For example, in *The Sorcerer's Stone*, Draco Malfoy, upon their first meeting, tells Harry "You don't want to go making friends with the wrong sorts. I can help you there." It's an idea that Harry immediately accepts, but also an offer Harry immediately rejects. During the Yule Ball in *The Goblet of Fire*, Hermione points out that "The whole point of the Triwizard tournament is international magical cooperation. To make friends." The last words spoken by Dobby as he dies in Harry's arms in the film *Deathly Hallows, Part 1* are "Such a beautiful place to be . . . with friends. Dobby is happy to be with his friend . . . Harry Potter." Perhaps the most important quote in the whole series, however, is not even spoken aloud, but a thought Harry directs to Voldemort while being possessed by him in the climax of *The Order of the Phoenix*: "You're the weak one. You'll never know love, or friendship, and I feel sorry for you". This statement simultaneously breaks Voldemort's possession and reminds the viewer that throughout the franchise, friendship and love have been championed as the conqueror of hate, isolation, and the devaluing of others.

All of the films reference this theme of friendship. If we look at the HPCU as engaged in a philosophical enterprise, it does more than provide examples of good and bad relationships. It also provides an argument that amends one of the most important theories of friendship and love in the philosophical literature, namely, Aristotle's theory of *philia*.

The term *philia* can mean both friendship and love. It is one of the roots of the term "philosopher," sometimes noted to literally translate as "lover" or "friend" of wisdom. Notably, Aristotle's theory identifies three forms of friendship which will be referred to here as friendships for virtue, pleasure, and utility. Throughout contemporary philosophical literature reflecting on Aristotle's theory, it is noted that the personal relationships that count as friendships involve three key elements, namely, "[1] a concern on the part of each friend for the welfare of the other, [2] for the others sake, and that [3] involves some degree of intimacy" (Helm ¶1). An additional element is that [4] each friendship is assumed to take place within an existing larger community (Mitias). Elements 1 and 2 highlight the motivations that friends have toward each other and that 3 and 4 highlight the context of relationships.

These four elements might suggest that to regard personal relationships based on pleasure and utility as friendships is an error. The worry is that these friendships seem to preclude being concerned with the other for the other's sake as well as what type of community, if any, is involved in relationships of pleasure or utility. What follows examines how the HPCU argues that they can be proper friendships, though different from friendships for virtue. The HPCU does this by distinguishing between beneficent and maleficent versions of friendships for pleasure and utility. The HPCU therefore argues for a modification of Aristotle's theory of friendship by identifying five, not three, types of personal relationships.

A word about method is in order before proceeding any further. Throughout this chapter only the films will be used for textual evidence, not the novels.

Utilizing only one medium is standard practice in academic analysis in part because the two different mediums – film and written text – each make choices of presentation that differ. Due to constraints, for example, characters are either missing entirely from a film that appear in the novel, such as Ludo Bagman. Other times, a character in the film replaces a character in the books for key scenes, such as when Cho Chang and not Marietta Edgecombe snitches on Dumbledore's Army. Scenes play out differently in each medium, such as the first kiss shared by Harry and Ginny. Sometimes scenes are missing entirely, such as the Sorting Hat Song and the potion puzzle obstacle during *The Sorcerer's Stone*. Because of these differences, and the possible confusion it can cause by jumping back and forth between mediums, all textual evidence will be strictly from the films.

Aristotle's Theory of Friendship

To understand how the HPCU revises Aristotle's theory of friendship, a slightly more in-depth explanation of the theory is in order. Aristotle defends the idea that friendship is about how one person has affection for another. This affection can take different forms and the elements outlined above help explain these forms. The first two elements of Aristotle's theory of friendship involve motivation-related mental states: (1) a concern on the part of each friend for the welfare of the other and (2) that concern is for the other's sake, not my own.

Now, these two elements might seem the same – how could I have a concern for the welfare of the friend without it being for the friend's sake? Philosophers have recognized that you might have egoistic, self-regarding motivations to be concerned for the welfare of another, say a younger sibling or a child. For example, suppose that Charlie Weasley recognizes that his job as a researcher into dragons is dangerous. Charlie then decides to help Ron and Ginny be good students, have good health, and have financial security. What no one other than Charlie knows, however, is that Charlie's interests are motivated with a hope that one or both of them will take care of Charlie if he is too severely injured to do any more work. If this is the only reason for Charlie's concern for the welfare of Ron and Ginny, Charlie's true concern is for the future benefit he receives from them. Their welfare is only a means to his own end and not for Ron or Ginny's sake. So, the second element is necessary to avoid friendships being about only what each person gets from the other.

These two concern-oriented motivational elements are then combined with other purpose-oriented motivations. The three purpose-oriented motivations are goodness, enjoyment, and mutual advantage. When the relationship is motivated by goodness, you have a friendship for virtue. In the other two cases, you have friendships for pleasure and utility respectively (EN1155b17-20). Virtuous friendships are the best kind of friendships and friendships for pleasure and friendships for utility are still proper (though imperfect) types of friendships.

Having some combination of these five motivations (the two concern-oriented motivations and the three purpose-oriented motivations) is still not enough to distinguish friendships from random encounters with strangers. It is possible to describe an encounter with a stranger in these motivational terms, but strangers are not friends (EN1156a1-5). So, for the finest form of friendship, virtuous friendship, Aristotle adds the condition that friendship involves a stable disposition to act in certain ways given a stimulus. In a friendship, this disposition manifests as behavior directed toward an individual. For example, if Ron becomes injured during an intense, larger than life game of wizard's chess, a true friend like Hermione has an immediate disposition to help Ron. How does this disposition manifest itself? Hermione, we can suppose, experiences a loss and, through empathy, experiences a kind of suffering akin to what Ron is actually experiencing as he lies on the floor. This experience activates a disposition to help restore Ron's well-being.

Consider another example of how this disposition to help could manifest: If you are truly worried about the well-being of another and that friend is behaving inappropriately, you should have a disposition to correct that behavior to make your friend more virtuous. For examples of this disposition, think of all the times Hermione attempts to get both Harry and Ron to study harder and more sincerely. The point is, while friends have such dispositions for improving the well-being and the character of friends, individuals do not have these stable dispositions to strangers. Even though we may be motivated in a particular circumstance to act for the sake of the stranger, that motivation and associated behavior is not stable and may not continue past this one interaction (even if we continue to interact with the individual). Thus, friends not only like each other, wish each other good will, and act to bring about the good in and for each other, but do so repeatedly over time when given the opportunity to act in such a way.

Motivational states and dispositions only cover half the elements needed to understand Aristotle's theory of friendship. For many of us, these attitudes of affection, good will, and dispositions to help our friend appear to occur *to* us, and are not the result of choices we are making. Like passions, these mental states seem to be involuntary reactions to stimuli. But elements 3 and 4 move outside of mental states and identify two communities within which each friendship occurs. Element 3 looks at the one-to-one intimate relationship and element 4 looks at the larger community within which the intimate relationship occurs. Membership in either community, however, is not involuntary but requires deliberate choice (EN1157b30).

Michael Mitias understands this notion of deliberate choice of friends to mean that "people cannot be friends if they do not choose the friend knowingly and responsibly" (Mitias 67). Furthermore, "Friendship is a community between two human beings; as such, it is part of the larger political community. It derives its being, and possibility, from this community. Thus, the friend, individually and as a community, cannot ignore their obligations to the members of the larger whole" (Mitias 70). In other words, this choice of a friend is always made in the context of two communities – the community of the two friends and the larger community within which the choice of friends takes place. Part of this choice is not just the choice of which person to become friends with, but a choice of the basis, and therefore type, of the friendship that will be formed – for virtue, pleasure, or utility.

But intimate, one-to-one relationships take place within a larger community (EN 1159b33). These larger communities help define the nature of intimate relationships and impact the instances in which the intimate interactions occur. Some communities are based around goods of pleasure or usefulness. Relationships, if they take place solely within these communities (say a Quidditch team or the Slug Club) will be limited then to the types of relationships that define the larger community. Furthermore, the other members of the larger community can have an effect on these relationships. Aristotle notes that whereas virtuous friendships assume that each friend has a minimally acceptable degree of virtue and are good persons, friendships "based on pleasure and utility can exist between two bad men" (1157a17-20). A person can be bad in at least two ways. First, the person could just have a bad character, embrace vices instead of virtues or be motivated purely by self-regarding interests. Second, a person could have a good character, but is currently motivated by self-regarding interests, or be someone whose judgment leads to poor choices time and again. In these cases, interpersonal interactions can become harmful. We can call the relationships that tend toward harm, that involve individuals of questionable character, maleficent forms of friendships for pleasure and utility. However, there can still be friendships for pleasure and utility that involve two good people with appropriate motivations which lead to good consequences and we can identify these forms of relationships as beneficent.

Friendships for Virtue in the HPCU

To understand each type of friendship, it is helpful to consider the larger communities in which friendships occur. In the HPCU, the Hogwarts houses form larger communities for the characters relationships. Professor McGonagall points out in *The Sorcerer's Stone* that each house is a substitute family. Each house is a value-laden background in which friendships are formed. Unfortunately, we get little in the way of direct cues about the relevant values associated with each house. But from key scenes throughout the series we can construct the values associated with Gryffindor.

During the Sorting Ceremony, when Harry has the hat on his head, courage is the first personal quality mentioned. The importance of courage to Gryffindors is highlighted again at the end of the first year when it is mentioned at the House Cup Ceremony in relationship to both Harry and Neville Longbottom. In fact, it is Neville's act of courage, of standing up to his friends to keep Gryffindor from getting into trouble and arguably to help them become better versions of themselves, that pushes Gryffindor to be the winner of the House Cup. The Gryffindor version of courage, it should be noticed, involves a concern for the wider community and its members, as in Neville's case. This courage also comes with a willingness for self-sacrifice for the greater community. We see it in Ron and Hermione's insistence in joining Harry to find the Horcruxes for the sake of this triumvirate as well as the whole wizarding world. We see it when Ron, Hermione, Neville, and Luna (in so many ways an honorary Gryffindor) join Harry at the Department of Mysteries. We see it when so many members of Gryffindor put themselves in extreme danger by being willing to take polyjuice potion to hide Harry from the Death Eaters during his escape from the Dursley's in *The Deathly Hallows Part 1*.

At the opening banquet of the first year, we also see that Gryffindor House values inclusiveness when accepting new members. Consider the different backgrounds of new Gryffindors in Harry's first year. Ron joins Gryffindor like his older brothers even though he is a member of a blood-traitor family, something that would exclude him from Slytherin presumably. Also included is the Muggle born Hermione Grainger and the half-blood Seamus Finnegan ("I'm half and half. My dad's Muggle. My mum's a witch"). Again, given what we learn in the final two films, these are reasons for exclusion by the Death Eaters, many of which were from Slytherin. And finally, there is Harry, the son of a pure-blood family father and a muggle-born mother. We eventually learn that Gryffindor would even accept a werewolf like Remus Lupin. What does this inclusiveness say about the community? It opens up the possibility that regardless of origin, anyone can be valued, anyone can be a friend, anyone can be loved. Treating someone as part of the community is, of course, the first step toward allowing that individual to interact with others, to form a variety of friendships, and have the possibility of developing virtuous friendships. So, this inclusiveness of others, this welcoming of others into communion and community, is also an other-regarding value.

Next, we learn that only someone loyal to Dumbledore and a true Gryffindor could call Fawkes for help and pull the Sword of Godric Gryffindor from the Sorting Hat. The latter trick is something that Harry does in *The Chamber of Secrets* as does Neville in *The Deathly Hallows Part 2* when he openly defies Voldemort and declares his loyalty to Harry and the other fallen heroes. The loyalty that so many characters have for each other throughout the series also drives home the importance of this virtue, beginning with the first time Harry, Ron, and Hermione face danger, namely, when Harry and Ron rush to tell Hermione about the troll in Hogwarts in *The Sorcerer's Stone*. But in the case of Percy Weasley, it is a lack of loyalty to family and a commitment to pursue power that demonstrates the importance of this virtue to Gryffindors. His estrangement from the Weasley family and his failure to participate in defying Voldemort until The Battle of Hogwarts highlights how a pledge of fealty only for the purpose of some self-regarding goal (like his advancement at the Ministry) is not proper loyalty. Proper loyalty must be other-regarding.

And remember, when it comes to these communal elements of friendship, whether it is the wider community or the intimate one-on-one community, choice is present. This is neatly summed up in the last scene of the series as Albus Severus Potter, about to board the Hogwarts Express, confesses to Harry that he is worried about being sorted into Slytherin. Harry, echoing his discussion with Dumbledore at the dénouement of *The Chamber of Secrets* responds, "[b]ut, listen, if it really means that much to you, you can choose Gryffindor. The Sorting Hat takes our choices into account." In other words, knowing what qualities are valued by each house, and making a choice to be in a house based on those values, is a determining factor for the Sorting Hat. This is a choice regarding the individuals one becomes friends with, but also, as mentioned above, the types of friendships that can be achieved in that community. If the community is based on values that focus on the well-being of others for their own sake then one is choosing a community in which virtuous friendships can develop. In the case of Gryffindor, we have identified values of courage, inclusiveness, and loyalty as key values in that community. Furthermore, each of these values is other-regarding in practice. They are oriented toward the well-being of the community as a whole and its members. This means that the best types of friendships, friendships for virtue, are available to Gryffindors.

But not all friendships are for virtue, and not all communities allow for virtuous friendships. First, the values of communities in which friendships for pleasure and utility take place put limits on what types of friendships can occur. Also, since friendships for virtue must include other-regarding motivations, whereas friendships for pleasure and utility do not necessarily involve these motives, friendships for pleasure and utility come in both beneficent and maleficent forms. It is to these types of friendships and communities that we now turn in order to make the case that the HPCU argues for the existence of five forms of friendship.

Friendships for Pleasure in the HPCU

Friendships for pleasure are aimed at the goal of enjoyment as opposed to goodness (friendships for virtue) or mutual benefits (friendships for utility). Friendships for pleasure can be either beneficent and maleficent. What distinguishes the beneficent from the maleficent forms of friendship are the motivations of the members: if the motivations are other-regarding and inclusive, then the friendships are beneficent; if the motivations are self-regarding only, then the friendships are maleficent. One indicator of each of these types of relationship is their stability. Beneficent forms tend to be stable and long-lasting whereas maleficent ones tend to be unstable and short-lived.

Friendships for pleasure take place in communities that are constructed around enjoyable activities. The purpose of these communities is to bring together individuals who find the activity enjoyable and, in especially beneficent cases, extend that pleasure beyond those who directly participate in the activity. In this sense, the house quidditch teams are a great example of the beneficent form of friendships for pleasure. Each member of the team comes together over the mutual enjoyment of playing the game. But note that Harry is rarely seen interacting with his teammates outside of practice or games. Other than Ron, who is a friend independent of quidditch, Harry is almost never seen with Oliver Wood, Angelina Johnson, Katie Bell, or the Weasley Twins. This is to be expected given that once the practice or game is over, the members of the team have few interests in common. They bond for the mutual pleasure of quidditch and separate once that pleasure is behind them. Here we see a form of instability in all friendships for pleasure in that they only exist as long as the pleasurable activity is occurring.

Quidditch teams, however, help blunt this instability by connecting the wider community of Gryffindor in the pleasures associated with quidditch. First, and most obvious, is the fact that all house members cheer on their team, boo questionable tactics by members of the opposing team, and celebrate their victories in the common room. A team filled with friends, each of whom knows their role, sticks to those roles, and encourages excellence individually and as a group can thereby achieve more pleasure by winning more often. Winning a quidditch match contributes toward winning another communal goal, namely, the House Cup. Furthermore, teams as communities of like-minded individuals also build an indirect form of stability into friendships for pleasure in that teams are corporate bodies that continue to exist even though the members change over time. So, friendships for pleasure are limited. But, in their beneficent form they are other-regarding by contributing to the well-being of those directly involved in the activity and a wider community.

However, there are maleficent forms of friendships for pleasure, and dating relationships are hazardous in part because they easily and often become maleficent in nature. In *The Half-Blood Prince,* we see many characters begin to develop intimate relationships with others. These relationships can be beneficent friendships for pleasure, but they can also be maleficent. The best example of a maleficent form is the Hermione–McLaggen Slug Club Christmas party date. A dinner party date should be pleasurable for it involves two people enjoying each other's companionship over food and drink, an event of communion and community. The Hermione–McLaggen date, however, involves only self-referential motivations. First, Hermione is motivated by the thought that taking Cormac to the party would "annoy Ron the most." In other words, she is not on this date for the pleasures of companionship and communion with McLaggen, but in order to get back at Ron for becoming Lavender Brown's boyfriend. So, her reason for the date has everything to do with her own self-regarding motivations. Cormac, for his part, also has self-regarding motives. He thinks of the date purely in terms of his own bodily pleasure, as indicated by Hermione's comment that Cormac has "more tentacles than a Snarfalump plant." While mutual enjoyment of bodily pleasure can be a reason for a friendship for pleasure, when the desire for bodily pleasure is one sided, as in this case, there is something clearly alarming about the relationship. In short, the reason this friendship for pleasure has become maleficent is that the date has been about what Hermione and Cormac find pleasing individually without consideration of what would be pleasing to the other. The failure of the date results from lack of other-regarding motivations.

Some relationships for bodily pleasure do not immediately go awry. The Ron–Lavender Brown relationship is an example of this. First, Lavender is clearly interested in Ron throughout the first part of *The Half-Blood Prince*, as she is shown many times focused on him during quidditch tryouts and in the common room. Eventually, after Ron's spectacular performance in the quidditch match, Lavender, in front of a full common room celebrating the Gryffindor victory, grabs Ron and kisses him in front of everyone. In other words, the excitement of one form of friendship for pleasure related to quidditch turns into a friendship for bodily pleasure for Ron and Lavender.

At first this mutual desire for bodily pleasure suggests that the friendship is beneficent. But Ron notices there is something amiss within minutes of film time. He notes that the relationship is chemical, signifying that it is not mutually chosen but the result of causal forces. He then states "Will it last? Who knows?" reminding the viewer of the innate instability of such a friendship. By the time we get to the Christmas holiday, the relationship has soured. Ron has clearly been avoiding Lavender indicated by her coming to his Hogwarts Express cabin and mouthing "I miss you." Ron has moved on from the purely physical nature of their relationship as he rather dismissively states "All she wants to do is snog me." The relationship effectively ends in the hospital wing when, recovering from the poisoned drink, Ron whisper's Hermione's name, not Lavender's, while semiconscious. Ron is clearly interested in more than the physical relationship he has with Lavender, but is not consciously ready to admit it. So, again, we have seen the instability of friendships for pleasure and their eventual demise when they are maleficent.

Compare these relationships to the romantic relationship between Harry and Ginny Weasley. This relationship is an example of another beneficent friendship for pleasure. Hints of Ginny's interest in Harry began in *The Chamber of Secrets* when she bolts from the room upon realizing Harry has arrived at The Burrow. By the time we get to *The Half-Blood Prince*, Harry is clearly becoming interested in Ginny. They share an awkward hug upon his arrival at The Burrow and Harry has a strange conversation with Ron about Ginny's nice skin. After the quidditch victory celebration, Harry admits that he feels the same way about seeing Ginny and Dean Thomas together as Hermione does at seeing Ron and Lavender together. So, unlike the Ron and Lavender relationship, the beginning of the Harry–Ginny romantic relationship is not sudden, but something that builds between them over time.

Perhaps the best evidence of the different, beneficent nature of this friendship, however, is how it officially begins. After the disastrous event of casting the sectumsempra (the never healing cut) curse, Harry is finally convinced to get rid of the Half-Blood Prince's copy of the potions book. It is Ginny who tells Harry he has to get rid of the book. It is Ginny who goes with Harry, offering her hand, to the Room of Requirement to hide the book. It is Ginny who hides the book. All of these actions show that Ginny's motivations are other-regarding. She is worried about Harry and his character being corrupted by the contents of the book, an experience she knows all too well from her interaction with Riddle's horcrux diary. She doesn't want anyone else to ever find the book or cast that spell because of the effect it would have on its victims and those who cast it.

It is in this moment of other-regarding motivations for Harry's well-being that Ginny acts to share a more intimate and pleasurable embrace with Harry. She does this out of sight of everyone else, even stating "[t]hat can stay hidden up here too, if you like." This is very different from the beginning of Ron and Lavender's relationship. For Ginny and Harry, it takes place in a moment that indicates a strong relationship between them because of Ginny's motivations to help others be better versions of themselves. Compare this to Lavender and Ron, whose relationship begins during another merely pleasurable moment; the motivation for their relationship is self-regarding in that Lavender has now connected herself with the interesting person of the moment and the knowledge of this relationship will be immediately, and without choice, known to the whole community. For Ginny and Harry, however, the moment is deeply intimate and away from others which means the knowledge of this relationship in the community will be a matter of choice for both Ginny and Harry. This is the culmination of years of knowing each other and a growing closeness; with Lavender and Ron it is something that appears out of nowhere (at least for Ron). These contrasts show why the nature of the Ginny–Harry friendship is beneficent and likely to succeed, where Lavender's and Ron's relationship is maleficent and quickly fades.

There are two axes, then, upon which to distinguish friendships for pleasure. The first involves the type of friendship involved based upon the pleasure involved – physical pleasure, pleasures of competition, pleasures of shared success, etc. But this merely marks the specific form of the friendship for pleasure that distinguishes it from friendships for virtue or utility, as well as other types of friendships for pleasure. The second axis involves whether the motivation for the relationship is self-regarding or other-regarding. This is what makes the underlying theory of friendship in the HPCU expand upon Aristotle. Those relationships, like quidditch teams or the Ginny–Harry relationship, that involve other-regarding motivations provide the ground for beneficent friendships for pleasure. And, in the case of Ginny and Harry, the relationship develops into the best kind of friendship, a friendship for virtue exemplified by their marriage. Other relationships for pleasure (Hermione and Cormac, Lavender and Ron), motivated by self-regarding concerns, are maleficent and quickly end. A similar structure can be found in relationships for utility.

Friendships for Utility in the HPCU

Friendships for utility are distinguished along similar axes as friendships for pleasure. First, there is the axis which marks friendships for utility as engaged in activities for mutual advantage. Since there can be different ways to interact for mutual advantage – we can engage in economic exchanges of goods and services, political exchanges for policies and power, or social exchanges for status – there are many types of these relationships. But, along another axis in terms of self-regarding and other-regarding motivations, we see that friendships for utility also come in beneficent and maleficent forms.

To see how there can be both beneficent and maleficent versions of friendships for utility, consider the Slug Club and the Death Eaters. In each community, the leader is a Slytherin. In each case, the communities are centered around the development of relationships that suggest the relationship will be useful to the members of the community. They differ, however, in several ways. They differ regarding whether, once someone chooses to become a member of the community, the member is free to leave. Most significantly they differ in how and the extent to which the leader extracts value from the other members.

Aristotle himself saw friendships for utility as the basis of political community and other associations (EN1160a1-30). In other words, friendships for utility can have common, shared goals that do not become purely self-referential and do not treat others as mere instruments. The Slug Club is an example. This is a group of Slughorn's favorite students, but more importantly, students who are talented in a way that suggests that they will individually achieve great things and be well-known. As Dumbledore states, "You, [Harry,] are talented, famous and powerful. Everything Horace values. Professor Slughorn is going to try to collect you, Harry. You would be his crowning jewel. That's why he's returning to Hogwarts."

As this description of Slughorn's motivations show, friendships for utility, even in their benign form, are self-regarding to some extent – the core concept is that the relationship forms for mutually realized but individual benefits. For example, Barnabas Cuffe, editor of the Daily Prophet, regularly publishes Slughorn's op-eds thereby keeping Slughorn in the public eye and giving weight to both Slughorn's views and Slughorn himself. Slughorn's views presumably increase sales of the Daily Prophet. So here is an example of economic goods exchanged for social goods such as status. Another example is that Slughorn gets presents from other members like Gwenog Jones of the Holyhead Harpies who gives him free tickets whenever he asks. Presumably Jones gets something out of the relationship, probably in terms of social goods by being connected through Slughorn to many other influential people – a quidditch career is unlikely to be a lifelong activity after all.

It is the realization of mutual benefits (although we have to make guesses as to what they are for all the parties) that will make this a beneficent form. The danger is that the transactional nature of these relationships could become one-sided. This transactional nature is on display when Slughorn agrees to come back to Hogwarts and demands both Professor Merrythoughts office and a raise. Of course, Dumbledore is going to get something much more valuable out of this transaction than mere symbols of status and economic benefits since he will eventually collect the complete and accurate memory of Tom Riddle's request about horcruxes. So even with Slughorn's demands, it turns out that this relationship is mutually beneficial.

But the Slug Club is about more than what Slughorn gets out of the relationships. The Christmas party clearly includes witches and wizards that are not current students. The reason for this, we can conjecture, is that the party is an opportunity for Slughorn to introduce longtime members of the club to those who are up and coming members of the community. Clearly, Slughorn will benefit in terms of status, albeit indirectly, from these groups of people getting to know each other. It is likely that Slughorn will be remembered as the person who brought them together for the first time. But these individuals may go on to form relationships independent of Slughorn and have transactions that do not include him that are mutually beneficial to themselves.

What we do not see, however, is how many individuals stop being part of the Slug Club. But there is no real cost to wanting to leave the community. One merely goes her or his own way, forging other friendships. So, in this beneficent version of friendships for utility, the individuals can work toward mutual advantage, not one-sided advantage, and can do so independent of its leader, Slughorn. The friends in this community are instrumental to achieving each other's goals, but are not merely instruments. The friends are capable of recognizing each other as having his or her own goals and thus recognizing each other as having values and interests independent of each other and Slughorn. It is this recognition of other's interests, a recognition that allows for the transactions to be both self-referential and about the well-being of others that make this a beneficent friendship for utility. All of these qualities of a beneficent friendship for utility are missing in Voldemort's community of Death Eaters.

Harald Thorsrud argues that the majority of the Death Eaters see their relationship with Voldemort as friendships of utility and that Voldemort sees them in this manner as well. The motivations of the Death Eaters are not based on mutual advantages within the community but are purely self-referential. As Thorsrud writes, the Death Eaters

> are motivated by equal parts of fear and greed. When [Voldemort] had lost his powers, most of his supposedly loyal Death Eaters plead innocence or ignorance to avoid punishment. This sort always tries to back the winner, whoever it may be. Their loyalty is usually never more than a thinly disguised hope for future rewards, a show designed to advance their own ambitions. (p. 39)

The inherently self-regarding nature of their fear and greed are part of the reason these friendships are examples of the maleficent form of friendships of utility.

Also note that, with the Death Eaters, after one joins and gets the power and freedom to hunt and kill, future benefits mostly or only flow from the Death Eaters to Voldemort. This point is driven home in *The Goblet of Fire* when Wormtail must cut off his own hand for the spell that returns Voldemort. Voldemort only restores Wormtail's hands after saying "you have proved yourself useful these past few months." It happens again in *The Deathly Hallows Part 1* when Voldemort, already having taken over the Malfoy estate as a base of operations, demands that Lucius Malfoy give up his wand. Voldemort offers nothing in return for Lucius' sacrifice of both power (Lucius is now reduced in his spell casting abilities) and status (the Malfoy's are just tools to Voldemort at this point). Finally, Voldemort requires the greatest sacrifice in *The Deathly Hallows Part 2* when he kills Severus Snape. He tells Snape that "You have been a good and faithful servant Severus, but only I can live forever." Voldemort's motivation for killing Snape is to gain the ability to defeat Harry by gaining control of the Elder Wand.

So, to Voldemort there is little if any difference between a Death Eater and floo powder. A Death Eater is only a friend as long as he or she provides benefits to Voldemort, furthers his goals and desires, and never anything more. This kind of transactional relationship, where each other's interests are not considered, only each other's usefulness, is a key component of the maleficent forms of friendships for utility. At the point that a Death Eater's usefulness is used up or trumped by other concerns, the Death Eater is humiliated, discarded, injured, and even murdered by Voldemort.

Readers can see the extreme self-regarding nature of the Death Eater's relationships in several little ways when Voldemort refuses offered help. No one else is allowed to kill Harry – not the Death Eaters who arrive in the cemetery in *The Goblet of Fire*, not Bellatrix Lestrange in *The Deathly Hallows Part 1*, or any of those who attack Hogwarts at the end of *The Half-Blood Prince*. This privilege, and the power and status gained, is reserved for Voldemort himself. After Voldemort believes that he has killed Harry in the Forbidden Forest, he refuses any help in getting back up from the blowback of the killing curse. To allow anyone to help him would mean he would have to share in the glory, not be seen as ultimately superior to everyone who witnessed the event. In this maleficent form of friendship for utility, there are no *mutual* benefits. All benefits, great and small, flow to one person involved in the transaction. The benefits always flow to the leader of the group, often at some great expense of another member.

Unlike the Slug Club, where we can presume that individuals can leave without punishment, it is suggested that one cannot willingly quit being a Death Eater without suffering a great loss. First, all Death Eaters are branded with a magical tattoo that can call Voldemort or can be used by Vodemort to call the Death Eaters. In *The Goblet of Fire*, we discover that Igor Karkaroff was a Death Eater and, according to Sirius "no one stops being a Death Eater." Those who do try to leave, like Regulus Black, and Karkaroff, end up dead. We also know that the members of this community do not all know each other. First, they wear masks to conceal their identities. Second, during the trials after Voldemort's downfall, we learn that Karkaroff only knows of a few other members of this community – Evan Rosier, Augustus Rookwood, Snape, and Barty Crouch Jr. But the compartmentalization of knowledge of other members reduces the opportunities, perhaps to zero, of the community members working together for mutual advantage independent of Voldemort. Everything about this community is one in which Voldemort is in control, Voldemort is the focus, Voldemort holds the power, and benefits flow to and through him for the achievement of his goals.

These contrasts between the Slug Club and the Death Eaters show the key elements that distinguish beneficent from maleficent versions of friendships for utility. Are the benefits from the relationship mutually advantageous? Can the benefits be in the interest of those other than the leader? Can the members of the community choose to enter *and* to leave without meaningful cost? If the answer to each question is "yes," then the relationship is a beneficent relationship for utility; if the answers are "no," then the relationship is a maleficent form. In the most extreme case of a maleficent friendship, the member of the community has no independent value and his or her well-being is not considered at all.

Conclusion

The HPCU, taken as philosophy, taken as engaging in philosophical argument and advancement of philosophical views, is a rich source of ideas related to many topics. This chapter explored many of the ways that the HPCU contributes to an expansion of Aristotle's theory of friendship. Aristotle recognized three types of friendship: friendships for virtue, friendships for pleasure, and friendships for utility. But the HPCU suggests that friendships for pleasure and utility come in two forms, beneficent and maleficent, resulting in five types of friendships. The characteristics that distinguish beneficent from maleficent types involve the possibility that the motivations for the friendships are other-regarding or only self-regarding. In friendships for pleasure, the HPCU shows that quidditch teams and personal, romantic relationships that last are those that look toward everyone in the community experiencing the pleasures and are thus beneficent; those relationships that are only meant to involve the self-regarding pleasure are ill-formed and thus maleficent. In terms of friendships for utility, the HPCU shows that communities like the Slug Club that allow for mutual benefit are beneficent; that communities like the Death Eaters where only the leader benefits (often at great expense to the other members) are maleficent.

This also points to another idea about friendships connected with becoming virtuous that there has not been time to explore. Aristotle maintains that virtuous friendships include friends who find each other pleasant and useful. But this is true of both interactions with friends and strangers. It is also the case that some such friendships fail or can be exploited by vicious and evil individuals. In these cases, however, the HPCU extension of Aristotle provides the beginning of an explanation of how this can be the case. The beneficent forms of friendships for pleasure and utility, since they include psychological states that are other-regarding, can form the foundation of virtuous friendships that are for the well-being of others and for their own sake in a deep and meaningful sense. They make for communities that are healthy and long-lasting. The maleficent forms of these friendships, however, move us away from having these motivations, and the communities which are composed of such maleficent relationships tend to be unhealthy, unstable, and the individuals themselves diseased. Exploring these ideas will have to take place at another time.

Postscript

As I was writing, rewriting, and editing this chapter on Harry Potter, a controversy arose regarding J.K. Rowling. This controversy was about her support for Maya Forstater who was fired for sharing transphobic tweets and for her interest in Magdalen Berns twitter account in relation to Berns' views on the importance of biological sex. These acts were followed up by an open letter expressing her concerns about trans-activism. These actions and others led Rowling being accused of being a TERF or Trans-Exclusionary Radical Feminist. This is a term used to describe individuals who, while feminist and generally inclusive of gay, lesbian, and bisexual individuals, are nevertheless accused of being transphobic, or excluding individuals who identify as transgendered. This has led some people who are transgendered and grew up loving Harry Potter feeling betrayed. For example, Patrouious Raymond Achatz said that "If anything, Harry Potter has taught me that no one should have to live in the closet," he said. "It's very disappointing with J.K. Rowling's tweets, that are very transphobic, because when we read the Harry Potter books, it helps us escape in a way" (Rosenblatt). Rosenblatt also describes Jaye, a transgender woman who "said she was taken by the themes of friendship that Rowling weaved throughout the series" is now "shaken to learn that one of her idols appeared to align with [TERF] ideology" (Rosenblatt).

Rowling's views seem to be incompatible with the idea of inclusiveness that is a central value of House Gryffindor, and friendships for virtue, as I interpret the texts. Combine this with a reasonable tendency for fans of texts to believe that the ideas in a text are the ideas of the author and the feelings of betrayal are understandable. But here is where the notion of the intentional fallacy can be very useful for such seemingly incongruous facts. The intentional fallacy is a literary analysis term about how it is inappropriate to evaluate a text by looking at the author or the author's intentions in creating the text. The effect of this idea is to cleave the author's ideas, views, and values from those experienced by the readers who are engaging a text. In the context of this controversy about Rowling's the intentional fallacy encourages fans to ignore Rowling's external-to-HPCU-comments and activities and focus instead on the fan's own experience of the ideas, views, and values of inclusivity in the text alone.

Besides, in this chapter we are discussing the HPCU and not the novels. The author of the HPCU includes Rowling, but is not limited to her. There are the three other writers of the scripts, four directors, many editors, and of course the actors. All of these individuals, and more, are the creators or the cinematic texts that make up the HPCU, not just Rowling. The actors Daniel Radcliffe, Emma Watson, Rupert Grint, and Bonnie Wright, among others, have all made public their support for trans-people. But, ultimately, none of these views matter either. It is the experience of the fan that determines what the ideas, views, and values are in the text. So, regardless of J.K. Rowling's beliefs in her personal life, if you find that the texts argue for inclusion of everyone, then focus on that experience. Continue to value and enjoy the texts, find comfort and support in those texts, and use those texts to get you through the tough times. The texts and their meaning belong to you.

References

Printed Works Cited

Aristotle. 2003. *Nichomachean ethics*. Trans. H. Rackham, Ed. J. Henderson. Cambridge, MA: Harvard University Press.
Helm, Bennett, 2017. Love. In *The Stanford Encyclopedia of Philosophy*, ed. Edward N. Zalta. https://plato.stanford.edu/archives/fall2017/entries/love/
Mitias, Michael H. 2012. *Friendship: A central moral value*. New York: Rodopi.
Rosenblatt, Kalhan. June 10, 2020. 'It kind of rocked me to my core': Trans 'Harry Potter' fans try to reconcile J.K. Rowling's recent tweets with the beloved franchise. https://www.nbcnews.com/feature/nbc-out/it-kind-rocked-me-my-core-trans-harry-potter-fans-n1229176

Rowling, J.K. June 10, 2020. J.K Rowling writes about her reasons for speaking out on sex and gender issues. https://www.jkrowling.com/opinions/j-k-rowling-writes-about-her-reasons-for-speaking-out-on-sex-and-gender-issues/

Thorsud, Harald. 2004. Voldemort's agents, Malfoy's cronies, and Hagrid's chums: Friendship in *Harry Potter*. In *Harry potter and philosophy: If Aristotle ran Hogwarts*, ed. David Baggett and Shawn E. Klein, 38–48. Peru: Open Court Publishing.

Visual Works Cited

Harry Potter and the Sorcerer's Stone. J. K. Rowling and Steve Kloves, writers. Chris Columbus, director. Michael Barnatha, Chris Columbus, Duncan Henderson, and Mark Radcliffe, executive producers. Warner Brothers. 2001.

Harry Potter and the Chamber of Secrets. J. K. Rowling and Steve Kloves, writers. Chris Columbus, director. Michael Barnatha, David Barron, Chris Columbus, and Mark Radcliffe, executive producers. Warner Brothers. 2002.

Harry Potter and the Prisoner of Azkaban. J. K. Rowling and Steve Kloves, writers. Alfonso Cuarón, director. Michael Barnatha, Callum McDougal, and Tanya Seghatchian, executive producers. Warner Brothers. 2004.

Harry Potter and the Goblet of Fire. J. K. Rowling and Nuno Miranda, writers. Mike Newell, director. Harvey Elliot, executive producer. Warner Brothers Interactive Entertainment, Electronic Arts. 2005.

Harry Potter and the Order of the Phoenix. J. K. Rowling and Michael Goldenberg, writers. David Yates, director. Lionel Wigram, executive producer. Warner Brothers and Heyday Films. 2007.

Harry Potter and the Half-Blood Prince. J. K. Rowling and Steve Kloves, writers. David Yates, director. Lionel Wigram, executive producer. Warner Brothers and Heyday Films. 2009.

Harry Potter and the Deathly Hallows, Part 1. J. K. Rowling and Steve Kloves, writers. David Yates, director. Lionel Wigram, executive producer. Warner Brothers and Heyday Films. 2010.

Harry Potter and the Deathly Hallows, Part 2. J. K. Rowling and Steve Kloves, writers. David Yates, director. Lionel Wigram, executive producer. Warner Brothers and Heyday Films. 2011.

Deadpool as Philosophy: Using Humor to Rebel Against the System

40

Matthew Brake

Contents

Introduction	968
Summary and Plot	969
Can Popular Culture Be Liberating?	970
Deadpool's Humor, Liberation, and Resistance	973
Liberation of the Self	973
Liberation from Systems of Oppression	975
Liberation from Genre Tropes	978
Conclusion	980
References	980

Abstract

When it first came out in theatres, *Deadpool* became one of the highest grossing rated-R movies of all time. With its violence and fourth wall-breaking humor, *Deadpool* energized the superhero genre at a time when all the major studios were simply trying to copy the Marvel Studios brand. But does this blood-soaked movie filled with dick jokes provide more than mere escapist entertainment? In this chapter, I will argue that *Deadpool* offers insight into the role that humor can play in causes of liberation in a threefold way: liberation of the self, liberation from systems of oppression, and liberation for the superhero movie genre itself.

Keywords

Deadpool · Ajax · Humor · Pop culture · Max Horkheimer · Theodor Adorno · Frederic Wertham · Liberation · Kathryn Tanner · Revolution

---

M. Brake (✉)
Northern Virginia Community College, Manassas, VA, USA
e-mail: popandtheology@gmail.com; mbrake@nvcc.edu

© Springer Nature Switzerland AG 2024
D. K. Johnson et al. (eds.), *The Palgrave Handbook of Popular Culture as Philosophy*,
https://doi.org/10.1007/978-3-031-24685-2_42

Introduction

In 2014, something amazing happened, to the joy of Deadpool fans everywhere. Some experimental footage for a live action Deadpool movie appeared, starring Ryan Reynolds and sporting the character's iconic costume and fourth wall breaking wit. This led to the debut of 2016's *Deadpool* movie, which was loved by fans and critics alike and was one of the highest grossing rated-R movies of all time (McClintock and Couch 2019). Unlike the earlier *Wolverine: Origins* movie, this version of Deadpool was well received by fans and casual moviegoers alike.

Deadpool brought something different to a superhero movie market saturated (at the time) with such films, where everyone from Sony (Spider-Man), Warner Bros. (DC Comics), and Fox (holder of the movie licenses for the X-Men and Fantastic Four before their buyout by Disney) was trying to build their own shared cinematic movie universes modeled after the Marvel Cinematic Universe (MCU). While *Deadpool* technically fell under Fox's domain and their universe building efforts, it brought a breath of fresh air to the genre, not just with its graphic violence (the *Blade* movies had paved the way for such things in the 1990s and early 2000s), but specifically with its use of the character's humor and its comedic jabs at various superhero genre tropes.

Humor, like graphic violence, is no stranger to controversy when it comes to superhero films. While audiences enjoy a laugh to lighten the mood, many of the Marvel Cinematic Universe's films have been criticized for undercutting themselves with an overabundance of jokes and quips (Zinampan 2018). Nevertheless, in *Deadpool*, humor fits the profile of the character and is suitable for the character's adaptation. Beyond its appropriateness for the character and the story, the appropriateness of humor itself has been the subject of debate through the centuries. Plato considered humor and laughter things to be avoided, desiring to see works of literature censored to avoid showing gods or heroes laughing. Aristotle warned against excessive buffoonery, criticizing the buffoon for being unable to resist the temptation to be funny (Morreall 1987, pp. 10 & 15) (and who has less resistance than Ryan Reynolds in general and Deadpool in particular to being a buffoon?). The Early Church Fathers were skeptical of humor (Carroll 2014, p. 7), and the Church in the Middle Ages also condemned laughter (Critchley 2002, p. 9). Some thinkers in the contemporary world note humor's ability to perpetuate stereotypes and reinforce harmful social practices and institutions (Boskin 1987, p. 253), while others note humor's potential as a form and cause of liberation (Critchley 2002, p. 9).

It is the topic of humor as a liberating tool that is addressed here. More specifically, I address whether the humor consumed in popular culture, like the Deadpool movie, performs any sort of liberating function. Even more specifically, I show how the movie *Deadpool* presents an implicit argument about the liberatory potential of humor itself. I will discuss this argument through three lenses. First, I will illustrate the ways that Deadpool's humor brings his character personal liberation and moral growth. Second, I will examine how, within the diegesis of the film, Deadpool's humor is used to liberate him from the oppressive system he finds himself in – the Mutant Factory which grants him his powers. Finally, I will explore how *Deadpool*'s humor challenges the tropes of superhero movies, providing a type of "liberation" from the status quo of the genre while also considering humor's anti-revolutionary tendency to reinforce the status quo.

Summary and Plot

Deadpool tells the story of Wade Wilson, a mercenary for hire who falls in love with a woman named Vanessa, who becomes the love of his life. Unfortunately, Wade is diagnosed with cancer, which has metastasized throughout his body. One night, a mysterious man approaches Wade in a bar owned by Wade's friend Weasel. The man offers Wade the chance to not only be rid of his cancer but to be given special abilities and become a superhero. In order to spare Vanessa the pain of seeing him die of cancer, Wade agrees to the procedure.

He is taken to the "Mutant Factory" and put into the care of a man named Ajax and his accomplice Angel Dust. They put Wade through many painful experiments in an attempt to activate any latent mutant abilities. When Wade discovers that Ajax's real name is "Francis," he mocks him for it, inciting Ajax to place Wade in a hypobaric chamber to deprive him of oxygen, but not before revealing that they are not turning Wade into a superhero but a super-slave, to be sold to the highest bidder. Ajax leaves Wade in the chamber all weekend, finally triggering his mutation. While Wade gains the ability to heal himself, the transformation leaves him incredibly disfigured.

When Ajax returns, he mocks Wade and threatens to lock him in again, but Wade is able to sabotage the hypobaric chamber, causing it to explode. Wade and Francis fight as the Mutant Factory burns down around them, with Wade ultimately losing and being impaled, causing Ajax to think that he is dead; Wade's new healing ability, however, allows him to survive. Embarrassed by his disfigurement, Wade refuses to return to Vanessa but reveals himself to Weasel. Wade comes up with the Deadpool alias and begins to pursue Francis, whom he believes can cure his disfigurement.

Deadpool begins to hunt down all of Ajax's associates until he finally catches up with him on a busy highway where a deadly shootout occurs, an event which Colossus from the X-Men sees on the news and attempts to intervene in along with his apprentice Negasonic Teenage Warhead. As Deadpool finally catches Francis, who learns that Wade is still alive, Colossus and Negasonic show up, giving Francis time to escape. Angry, Deadpool fights Colossus, severely injuring himself in the process but still managing to escape the X-Man's attempt to take him into custody.

Armed with the knowledge that Wade is alive, Francis kidnaps Vanessa to draw Wade out and kill him. Learning that Vanessa has been taken, Wade seeks Colossus and Negasonic's help, attacking Francis in a scrapyard on what looks suspiciously like an MCU SHIELD helicarrier (before Fox's buyout by Disney). Wade rescues Vanessa and finally has Francis in his crosshairs, demanding that he fix Wade's face. Francis admits he is unable to, but before Deadpool can kill Ajax, Colossus admonishes Wade to walk the path of a hero and to make a heroic choice and spare Ajax's life. Wade then proceeds to shoot Francis in the head, causing Colossus to vomit. The movie ends with the villain dead and Wade and Vanessa reunited.

Can Popular Culture Be Liberating?

It is entirely possible that Deadpool, like humor itself, is just as likely to subvert as it is to reinforce existing current conditions. Deadpool may joke about superhero genre tropes, but he reinforces them as well. As of this writing, Marvel is preparing to introduce the character to the MCU proper. Whatever subversion his humor offered, one finds that the same is as true of Deadpool as any potentially revolutionary material in a capitalist society – it gets grafted into the existing dominant apparatus. If it had any liberatory potential, then it can now be shorn of that potential and made into just another product to be bought and sold (Marcuse 1991, p. 64).

In discussing the ability of a pop cultural phenomenon (in this case, the movie *Deadpool*) and whether or not it contains liberatory potential, one must examine the critique leveled at all popular culture by two of the leading figures of the Frankfurt School, Max Horkheimer and Theodor Adorno. These thinkers argued that popular culture reinforces existing social conditions and hierarchies, seemingly answering the question of *Deadpool*'s potential for offering any vision of social liberation. In opposition to this view, we can appeal to a counterargument proposed by theologian Kathyrn Tanner, who argued that what the people make of works of pop culture is up to them, which opens up the possibility for pop culture serving as a catalyst of liberation.

Asking about the liberatory potential of popular culture, in the light of Horkheimer's and Adorno's critique, is quite appropriate. Comic book characters like Deadpool have had a historically rocky relationship with the arguments of the Frankfurt School. Particularly noteworthy is psychologist Frederic Wertham and his 1954 book *Seduction of the Innocent*. It was Wertham's attack on comic books and his argument that they caused juvenile delinquency that led in part to the industry's self-censorship via adoption of the Comics Code Authority in 1954. As Carol Tilley notes, "For him, mass culture and capitalism, as embodied by the coarse world of comics, was not perhaps a triumph of Fascism over true art and culture but a real threat to a healthy society" (Tilley 2012, p. 404). Wertham, in the same spirit as Horkheimer and Adorno, calls into question the aesthetic value of pop culture, specifically comics, not content to simply dismiss pop culture as a matter of personal taste. For Wertham, the love of comics and their characters is a threat to society's well-being.

Horkheimer and Adorno, focusing more on film, television, and radio, bemoaned that these mediums "no longer need to present themselves as art. The truth that they are nothing but business is used as an ideology to legitimize the trash they intentionally produce" (Horkheimer and Adorno 2002, p. 95). Popular culture produces a bunch of mass produced garbage defined by its "sameness." This leads to "the impoverishment of the aesthetic material" with interchangeable clichés and patterns of storytelling. Whether in music, film, or television, pop culture recycles the same material over and over again. The movie might have a different name, and the song may have slightly different lyrics, but the same things are being produced again and again (Horkheimer and Adorno 2002, pp. 94–98). One would be hard pressed not to acknowledge certain truths about Horkheimer and Adorno's critique. After all, the Marvel Cinematic Universe seems to suffer from this very problem. A number of its movies follow an interchangeable formula, as many online commentators have pointed out (Kownacki 2017). One could point to Phase One of the MCU, wherein each character's origin follows a similar pattern, culminating in fighting a villain who is just an evil version of the hero – Iron Man fought Iron Monger while the Hulk fought Abomination. Captain America fought the Red Skull, a Nazi super soldier, and Thor fought his brother Loki. Origin – Second Act – Villain Who Mirrors the Hero – that is the pattern of Marvel's Phase One, and it continues on in Phase Two and parts of Phase Three. Superhero movies, particularly Marvel superhero movies, run the risk of the accusation, leveled by Horkheimer and Adorno, that they are little more than aesthetically impoverished, interchangeable pop culture trash. Indeed, some directors like Martin Scorsese and Ridley Scott have expressed this very opinion (Rao 2021).

Like humor, the danger of popular culture resides in its reinforcement of the existing social order so that the population does not question it. It serves merely to "imprint...the work routine" into the minds of those who consume it, being "sought by those who want to escape the mechanized labor process so that they can cope with it again" (Horkheimer and Adorno 2002, pp. 104, 109). Popular culture can desensitize viewers to their own working conditions. The worker watches "I Love Lucy" (or *Deadpool*) to distract themselves from the monotony of the workday they just finished so that they can have a respite before doing it again tomorrow. Horkheimer and Adorno state, "The only escape from the work process in factory and office is through adaptation to it in leisure time. This is the incurable sickness of all entertainment." Entertainment becomes merely "the prolongation of work" and helps make more compliant workers (2002, p. 109). They continue:

> To the extent that cartoons do more than accustom the senses to the new tempo, they hammer into every brain the old lesson that continuous attrition, the breaking of all individual resistance, is the condition of life in this society. Donald Duck in the cartoons and the unfortunate victim in real life receive their beatings so that the spectators can accustom themselves to theirs. (2002, p. 110)

Mass-produced pop culture, like the cartoons of Donald Duck, is a form of amusement that suppresses any desire to resist the status quo and demand a better world. By watching Donald Duck, Daffy Duck, or any other figure receive abuse, workers themselves are numbed to the abuses and exploitation of their working conditions.

Deadpool appears to be a perfect example of a mass-produced culture industry product. Because of Deadpool's healing abilities, the character receives large amounts of abuse, all for the amusement of the audience. Whether Deadpool is breaking his hands punching Colossus, growing a pair of baby legs after getting ripped in half by the Juggernaut (see ▶ Chap. 91, "*Deadpool's* Killogy as Philosophy: The Metaphysics of a Homicidal Journey Through Possible Worlds"), or taking a bullet straight up his butt, viewers watch Deadpool receive his beatings, and in the process, they are amused for 2 hours. They temporarily forget their own beatings, and their lives are made a little more bearable. But is this Deadpool's fate, to be understood merely as a product of mass-culture that is only ever capable of serving to repress any resistance to the established political economy?

In Kathryn Tanner's evaluation of Horkheimer and Adorno's perspective, she sets forth two opposing views of pop culture. The first sees popular culture as a means by which those in power keep the lower classes docile and use it as a tool for getting them to accept conditions that are unfavorable to them. This is obviously Horkheimer's and Adorno's view. A second view understands popular culture as being completely free "from the power dynamics of elites struggling for control and views popular culture instead as the autonomous, completely authentic production of the people." This second view sees popular culture as "anti-elitist populism" that is viewed, at least in part, as "an alternative to a profit driven bureaucratic ethic." Along these lines, Tanner notes that this latter "theoretical outlook has its roots in the preoccupation of late eighteenth and nineteenth century European intellectuals with the 'folk'" (1996, p. 104).

Tanner suggests a third option between seeing popular culture as a purely independent creative product and a cultural production "typified by passive consumption" of the lower classes. While one cannot separate popular culture from "a tension-filled relationship with elite cultural productions," one should not deny popular culture any "creative, productive relationship in its own right." Rather, Tanner encourages her readers to remember that "what elites produce for mass consumption (popular and commercial culture) and what the people make of it are not...the same." The consumption of popular culture can therefore become "a *creative* process" of "inventive recombination" and improvisation (Tanner 1996, pp. 104–106). In other words, consumers of popular culture can repurpose that culture for anything they want beyond the intention of those who produced it. This allows popular culture to display liberating potential if its consumers so choose to receive it and interpret it that way. As Tanner states:

> Some sort of resistance to a disempowered life occurs in and through such processes of cultural transformation, in the sense that the people can carve out thereby a life of their own that is significantly different from the preferred meanings of their existence conveyed by elite cultural productions. (1996, p. 107)

Given that elitist cultural producers cannot determine how the people consuming their products appropriate and use those products, nor can they decide how they understand them, there remains the potential for mass-produced popular culture to develop a liberating meaning as it is consumed and creatively interpreted. Thus, Deadpool is able to express a liberating message of resistance to dominant social norms, even if the process by which that happens involves creative interpretations by those who see his movie. In fact, this may be the only means to open the door to any liberating interpretation of *Deadpool*. One can understand *Deadpool* "as philosophy" only through one's ability to choose to receive it that way, and once a person has made that choice, they are in a better position to see *Deadpool* through a liberatory framework.

Deadpool's Humor, Liberation, and Resistance

Having examined the liberatory potential of pop culture in general, it is time to consider the ways that humor in *Deadpool* can provide resources for resistance or liberation. There are three avenues of liberation that will be considered: (1) liberation of the individual self, (2) liberation from systems of oppression and domination, and (3) liberation from genre tropes.

Liberation of the Self

There are two ways to consider the value of humor for liberating the self: (1) moral liberation, and (2) liberation from tragedy. Concerning the moral edification of humor, many thinkers caution on the over-use of humor. William Hazlitt, for instance, states, "Clowns and idiots laugh on all occasions," and ongoing jesting exhausts the will of one's company: "Wit is the salt of conversation, not the food" (Hazlitt 1819, pp. 48–49). While Deadpool certainly drives most of his companions crazy with his incessant wit, there are moral benefits to a humorous outlook on life. Ronald de Sousa notes some of the objections to the use of any sort of ethically uplifting humor, such as "laughter is wrong when it is grounded in the deception of self or others," and it "distract[s] us from more serious things" when it keeps us from seeing the world as it really is or keeps us from "seeking fresh perspectives" (De Sousa 1987, pp. 244–246). Deadpool may certainly use his humor to distract from more serious things, but his humor seems to be far less about deception than a type of radical honesty. What one sees in Deadpool's humor may be closer to Hazlitt's suggestion that *"ridicule is the test of truth"* (Hazlitt 1819, p. 32). While Deadpool certainly does ridicule others (which will be examined in the next section), the focus here is on Deadpool's use of humor for his own moral uplift, which involves self-ridicule.

Francis Hutcheson acknowledges that humor can be used for the correction of vice, particularly that of "false grandeur" (Hutcheson 1750, p. 33). Deadpool ridicules the grandeur of others. Every time Colossus extols the virtues of becoming a superhero, Deadpool undercuts the grand moment and swelling hero music with a joke about Professor X being a cult leader or by shooting Francis in the head. Another example would be when Angel Dust jumps down from what is definitely *not* a SHIELD heli-carrier and does a "superhero landing," much to Deadpool's delight, even as he undercuts the drama of the moment by pointing out how it is really "bad on the knees." But while ridiculing others is one thing, criticizing one's own self is another.

Simon Critchley makes a distinction between *"laughing at oneself* and *laughing at others."* For Critchley, "true humour" is not about making fun of others but is about "self-mockery," for one's own self is the topic of laughter (2002, p. 14). Lydia Amir lauds the benefits of self-mocking humor, writing, "Philosophers recommend self-referential humor for its ability to correct mistakes, improve morality, and foster the drive for self-perfection and self-transcendence" (Amir 2014, p. 241). One of the ways self-ridiculing humor does this is by saving the humorist from their own pride. When one laughs at someone else, they "treat them as a child and [themselves] as an adult," but when one laughs at themselves, they "treat [themselves] as a child from an adult perspective" (Critchley 2002, p. 95). Self-ridiculing laughter is able to recall the joke-teller "to the modesty and limitedness of the human condition" (Critchley 2002, p. 102). In other words, humor can help one maintain a proper perspective of themselves.

While Deadpool is certainly not above bringing others down with his humor, particularly anyone who he deems to have an inflated sense of self or grandiose posture, he does not avoid making jokes at his own expense. After he escapes the Mutant Factory, he goes to see Weasel, who engages in a memorable back and forth with Wade about his "new look," a conversation wherein Wade admits he looks like "a testicle with teeth." This is far from the only joke that Wade makes at his own expense. At the end of the same conversation, Wade tries to come up with his new codename, deciding upon "Deadpool," after the game of chance at Weasel's bar where people bet on which mercenary will die next. But at first it's not just Deadpool. "Captain...Deadpool?" After a moment silence, he decides "No? Just Deadpool?" Here, there is a moment of false grandeur that Deadpool's self-ridicule deflates as he decides on the more modest "Deadpool."

Beyond the potential for moral criticism and self-improvement, humor has the capacity to liberate human beings from the tragedy of life. Amir draws a contrast between comedy and tragedy: "the comic and tragic visions represent respectively anti-heroism versus heroism" (2014, p. 227). This is an intriguing statement given Deadpool's status as an anti-hero. Amir notes some of the other distinctions between these two categories, observing that the anti-hero is defined by their questioning of tradition and an ethical code that focuses on what is needed in the particular situation, as opposed to the hero who is marked by their "acceptance of authority and tradition" and an almost inflexible ethical code. Where tragedy sees an unassailable situation, comedy sees an ambiguous situation and questions the inevitability of any outcome. Tragedy sees a trap without an escape, but comedy sees the possibility of "a second chance" (2014, pp. 23–27).

Perhaps there is no greater tragedy faced by humans than death. Amir asks her readers to consider that the good life may not be one lived in certainty of metaphysical or theological cosmic justice that overcomes tragedy, but in embracing the ambiguity that comes with humor in the face of the tragic reality of life. She states, "Comedy serves as the continued affirmation of the will to live," providing much needed therapy to the tragedy of life, adding greater truth to tragedy (Amir 2014, p. 232). In tragedy, the "open and shut" facts of life may weigh one down, but humor allows the individual to enjoy and revel in the ambiguities and unresolvable tensions of life. In tragedy, one may very well be overcome with despair and lose the desire to live, but humor allows desire to be maintained, turning suffering to joy. Amir points out that "individuals who maintain a humorous outlook on life are less likely to become stuck in the cognitive distortion that gives rise to anxiety and depression" (2014, p. 239). Humor and its ability to live in the unresolved tension of the irreconcilable and tragic incongruities and contradictions in life allow the humorist to accept their failure while simultaneously feeling liberated to act (2014, p. 285).

Deadpool certainly inhabits a world that is not fair and full of tragedy. First, he meets the girl of his dreams only to develop terminal cancer. Then, he thinks he locates a group of people who can cure him, only to be tortured and disfigured in the process. Finally, he hunts down the man he believes can reverse his condition only to discover that it cannot be undone. Wade Wilson is confronted again and again by tragic realities, but the tragic facts never have the last word. In fact, Deadpool practices humor in a way that allows him to take pleasure in life's contradictions and unfortunate circumstances, circumstances that at first glance are not initially thought of as humorous. Deadpool may be clownish and make light of moments of suffering that many think require serious reflection, but perhaps being a clown is not so bad. As Walter Kerr states, "What a good man the clown is, to endure so much, to survive so relentlessly, to keep us company in all weathers, to provide us with a way of looking at the worst that enables us to take a temporary joy in the worst!" (Kerr 1967, p. 340). When humans accept how ridiculous they are, they not only transcend that ridiculousness, but they also transcend the tragic (Amir 2014, p. 270). As Sigmund Freud says, the "*liberating* element" of humor is "the ego's victorious assertion of its own invulnerability," its "denial of the claim of reality and the triumph of the pleasure principle" (Freud 1987, p. 113). If a man with a sense of humor and a regenerative healing factor does not present an example of this truth, then who does?

To this point, Deadpool as a character is able to attain transcendence and liberation from his condition by his fourth wall breaking humor. Deadpool's interactions with the audience allow him to step outside of his pain and heartache. Not only is Wade able to heal from deadly wounds because of his healing factor and is thus able to relativize otherwise-deadly bodily trauma, he is able to relativize his heartache and pain by catching a glimpse of his "place in the world" as a fictional character. In these moments, his sense of humor is able to put his life in proper perspective. These humorous moments with the audiences lessen the sting of Deadpool's tragic circumstances, bringing levity to that which does not initially elicit a laugh.

Through these examples, we see that *Deadpool* offers an implicit argument that humor can serve as a vehicle for liberation of the individual self. Through his jokes, quips, and ability to laugh at himself and others, humor serves as a catalyst for Deadpool's own self-improvement, and offers liberation and relief from the tragic circumstances he encounters.

Liberation from Systems of Oppression

From the beginning of his movie, Wade Wilson finds himself the victim of an organization that tricks him into thinking it can cure his cancer and turn him into a superhero. Instead, it imprisons people, tortures them to activate any latent mutant abilities, and sells them as superslaves to the highest bidder. Throughout his stay, Wade lets loose with multiple quips and jokes, especially at the expense of Ajax, who provides even more comedic ammunition when it is revealed that Ajax's real name is "Francis." Francis even tells Deadpool when the latter is admitted, "One thing that never survives this place is a sense of humor," and Francis spends the remainder of Deadpool's time in the Mutant Factory trying to torture his sense of humor out of him. This does raise the question of whether Francis was simply annoyed by Deadpool's humor, or if he found it dangerous. Right before he finds out Wade knows his real name, he makes it a point to interrupt Wade and Cunningham's (a fellow prisoner) joking conversation. Why would Francis interrupt this moment and discourage Wade's sense of humor (other than him being sadistic, which is entirely possible)? Here, it's important to consider the revolutionary quality of Deadpool's humor, particularly its ability to disrupt systems of oppression. After all, Wade does maintain his humor throughout his stay in the Mutant Factory, and it is that humor which disrupts Ajax's own sense of menace.

Terry Eagleton notes that humor has often been censured for being "politically dangerous" (2019, p. 3), while Jacqueline Bussie observes that "people *with* authority perceive laughter as disempowering because it threatens their authority" (2007, p. 3). In other words, no strong man likes to be laughed at. Humor has the potential to serve as a tool of social critique, resistance, and protest. Per Bussie, it "interrupts the system and state of oppression, and creatively attests to hope, resistance, and protest in the face of the shattering of language and traditional frameworks of thought and belief" (2008, p. 4). Humor allows one to see the world in a way they did not before by calling into question the stability of the way things are. The authoritarian does not use humor, for his resources are violence and seriousness (Eagleton 2019, pp. 31–32). This certainly does seem to be the case with Ajax and the Mutant Factory. Where Ajax is dour, serious, and violent, Deadpool's humor allows a little light into an otherwise depressing environment. It is a light that calls the totalizing control of the oppressive system into question, thus opening up the possibility of its overthrow. Ajax's disdain for Deadpool is, at least in part, a disdain for the humorist's ability to shrink the power of the tyrant.

Some have recognized that "laughter can result in ethical rebellion and subversiveness toward authority," threatening "to undermine the status quo" (Bussie 2007, p. 11). A real-life example of one of the great oppressive regimes of history reveals this to be so. One of history's ultimate strong man regimes, the Nazis, recognized laughter's political danger, and they passed a censorship law that prohibited mocking or making fun of the Nazis. Hitler, history's ultimate strong man, feared any laughter being directed at his own person (Bussie 2007, p. 39). Likewise, Deadpool's captors become particularly perturbed when Wade's humor is directed at them individually. Angel Dust punches him in the face specifically when he refers to her as "less angry Rosie O'Donnell." But when Wade makes a joke at Ajax's expense, Ajax's cruelty toward Wade escalates. Wade discovers that Ajax's real name is "Francis" and that he got the name Ajax from the dish soap. Even Ajax's lackey Angel Dust seems surprised at the reveal of his real name. Ajax, to recover from a moment of vulnerability and humiliation, places Wade in a hypobaric chamber, suffocating him over the course of a weekend, triggering Wade's mutation as well as his deformation. Hitler's fear and Ajax's act illustrate Bussie's claim that the laughter of the oppressed reflects their autonomy, revealing them as ones who make independent decisions, challenging the authority of the oppressor. Again, one can begin to understand Ajax's own resistance to humor and his hatred of being laughed at by Wade about his real name – it was a threat to his totalizing control! In maintaining his sense of humor, Deadpool refused "to bend to [Francis's] oppressive will" (Bussie 2007, pp. 39–40). And in his overreaction to Deadpool's humor, Ajax overplayed his hand, creating the conditions that allowed Deadpool's mutation and escape.

This may be humor's key to fostering social liberation: (1) it reveals the vulnerable humanness of the oppressor, and (2) it asserts one's own independence. Regarding the first point, Francis was certainly irritated by Wade from the beginning of his stay in the Mutant Factory; however, it is only when Wade finds out Ajax's true name that there is a noticeable moment of vulnerability on Ajax's face. Viewers can tell he feels exposed, which is only exasperated by Wade's fellow inmate laughing at Francis and Angel Dust's own seeming surprise. One must wonder whether the shaking of his confidence caused him to get sloppy and overplay his hand. Humor can expose the strong man's vulnerability. Likewise, humor can allow the oppressed to create a "gap" in a totalizing system to assert their independence and freedom of thought, and to reveal the contingency of the strong man's power.

Perhaps, however, one should temper their hopes for what humor can accomplish. After all, it was not Deadpool's humor, but his violence, that allowed him to escape from the Mutant Factory, in one of the most serious parts of the movie. This calls into question humor's liberatory capabilities. It is certainly not questionable that laughter is a survival tactic of the oppressed, providing brief relief from ongoing feelings of oppression (Eagleton 2019, p. 60). But relief in itself is not change. Hart points out that there are many who "regard humour and amusement as substitutes for the political action that should aim at change in societal settings" (Hart 2008, p. 6). In a study of the "whispered jokes" uttered under Soviet rule, Christie Davies acknowledges that jokes are mostly ineffectual as a form of political rebellion, although she does go on to observe that jokes can be an indicator of people's discontent with a regime and may indicate that the populace is merely waiting for the right moment to effectually rebel (Davies 2008, pp. 291 & 303). Critchley comments upon humor's almost "messianic" power to keep hope alive by allowing one to continue imagining that the world can be different than it is, all while waiting for the next opportunity for action (Critchely 2002, p. 16). In the meantime, the horrors one experiences may not be objectively reduced, but perhaps they can be subjectively reduced. One's laughter in the face of oppression defies "self-negation and the despair that welcomes death" and chooses "life over [the] death-in-life" that one is experiencing (Bussie 2007, pp. 38 & 44). Even gallows humor, whether it is found in the Nazi concentration camps, in the face of American racism, or any other location of totalizing cruelty and control, "asserts the ego's invulnerability in the face of death" (Carpio 2008, p. 6).

Is this not what one sees in Deadpool? Even in the face of torture, he continually reaffirms his own identity and will to live through humor, and he tells jokes while he waits for an opportunity for revolt, which eventually arrived. Perhaps the jokes themselves are not the revolt per se, but they buy Wade time and open the door for an opportunity to escape the Mutant Factory and hunt Francis down. But while humor may hold potential for revolutionary action and behavior, it still contains a reactionary side, one that may appear to subvert, but simply reinforces the pre-existing social conditions.

We see, then, a cautious argument developed regarding the potential of humor to liberate us from oppressive social situations. While the movie clearly shows ways that Deadpool uses humor to resist and overcome his oppressive circumstances, it is also clear that humor alone is not enough, and without accompanying action, it runs the risk of reinforcing the status quo.

Liberation from Genre Tropes

When *Deadpool* begins, viewers see Deadpool fighting on a bridge, but right when he impales a guy with his swords, his voiceover comes on and says, "You're probably thinking, 'My boyfriend said this was a superhero movie, but that guy in the red suit just turned that other guy into a fucking kabob.'" So right from the beginning, the movie acknowledges that it doesn't quite follow all of the conventions of the traditional superhero movie, such as the hero's "no-kill" rule (although the MCU violates this rule frequently). As previously noted, throughout the movie, Deadpool makes fun of the tropes of the superhero genre. He insults Colossus multiple times, calling the X-Men a cult, making fun of the no-kill rule, and of course, making fun of Angel Dust's "superhero landing" because it's "bad for the knees." At first, it may seem that Deadpool's humor challenges the superhero genre, as exemplified by movies like Nolan's Batman trilogy and the MCU, with the silliness of some of its genre rules and tropes, possibly as an attempt to push the genre out of stagnation. But should we even speak of "liberation from superhero movie genre tropes"?

Aside from the previously mentioned accusations by directors like Scorsese that superhero films are not cinema (and by implication, may be ruining cinema), superhero comics and movies often get accused of perpetuating a fascist viewpoint (Burlingame 2020). Alan Moore, one of the figures often credited with elevating mainstream American comics, discusses a possible correlation between the rise of fascist ideology and the popularity of superhero movies:

> This may be entirely coincidence, but in 2016 when the American people elected a National Socialist satsuma and the UK voted to leave the European Union, six of the top 12 highest grossing films were superhero movies.... Not to say that one causes the other but I think they're both symptoms of the same thing – a denial of reality and an urge for simplistic and sensational solutions. (Burlingame 2020)

Even if superhero movies do not perpetuate fascism, they at the very least may simply uphold the status quo. This is a key point that Richard Reynolds observes about the superhero genre:

> A key ideological myth of the superhero comic is that the normal and everyday enshrines positive values that must be defended through heroic action—and defended over and over

again almost without respite against an endless battery of menaces.... The normal is valuable and is constantly under attack, which means that almost by definition the superhero is battling on behalf of the status quo.... The superhero has a mission to preserve society, not to re-invent it. (Reynolds 1992, p. 77)

So the superhero genre appears to have an anti-revolutionary bent. Although, to Reynolds's point about the endless battle against "an endless battery of menaces," perhaps one way *Deadpool* challenges the superhero status quo is by having its protagonist kill his enemy rather than allowing him to live to fight and terrorize another day. But again, one could list an endless string of MCU villains who have been killed by their heroic counterparts as well, and if there is any prime example of mainstream superhero genre movies, the MCU would fit the bill. But what about humor? While the question of humor's liberating and revolutionary potential has been considered, what about humor's reactionary potential? Can humor be used as a tool to maintain the status quo?

Humor assumes a shared sociality (De Sousa 1987, p. 231). Boskin observes that humor depends on shared beliefs and attitudes and can perpetuate those attitudes. In his work, Boskin notes this characteristic of humor in the use of stereotypes, such as the Sambo figure that white people make about Black people. This is merely one example of how laughter can produce social bonds, but those bonds are reinforced by aggression against outsiders and marginalized peoples. The Sambo figure becomes the butt of the joke, and racist, reactionary humor is institutionalized, even as people's capacity for critical thinking is dulled by a cheap laugh (Boskin 1987, pp. 250–257). In this case, humor reinforces, rather than critiques, a part of social life that is in dire need of change.

Critchley himself recognizes the problem of ethnic humor and its role in excluding those who are seen as outsiders. He offers a possible solution by distinguishing the type of humor that reinforces a social consensus versus "true" humor that changes the social situation. The difference between these types of humor is found in who is being laughed at – the powerful or the powerless. This indicates that there may be an ambivalence to humor. As with pop culture, perhaps humor's efficacy depends on its contextual reception (Critchley 2002, pp. 67–70, 76).

Fair enough, but even if humor is not outright hostile toward the powerless and marginalized, does that really lead to a change that liberates? Even humor directed at the powerful can serve to merely reinforce the dominant order (Critchley 2002, p. 82). On this point, Eagleton notes that the Fool or jester causes no real harm, and his irreverence may reinforce social norms. In allowing room for the jester who can criticize the powerful, the established order is shown to be strong by allowing such gestures. In the eighteenth century, "good humor" was seen as a way to ward off revolution and fanaticism because of the belief that mutual laughter fosters more mutuality (Eagleton 2019, pp. 14, 100, 113). Humor was a socially stabilizing agent. In this view, humor is little more than a social safety valve built into the dominant status quo (Davies 2008, p. 301).

Similarly, to the potential of humor to liberate us from systems of oppression, we can interpret Deadpool as offering a cautious argument regarding liberation from genre tropes. Deadpool's humor certainly offers certain critiques of genre tropes and the systems of power that keep them in place, but he is also capable of reinforcing those tropes. His humor can be a way of inspiring viewers' imaginations to hope for something different from their superhero movies, but the "wink and nod" that Deadpool gives to the audience is just as likely to acknowledge the comedy of our situation: we may grow frustrated with the status quo, but that doesn't stop us from giving Disney all of our money.

Conclusion

Can *Deadpool* show viewers the liberating potential of humor? When one evaluates the diegetic world of the movie, the answer is "for the most part." Deadpool does grow personally as a character in light of his ability to laugh in the face of pain, torture, and death. He is able to see beyond the present possibilities and imagine a way out. In terms of systems of oppression, Deadpool certainly bides his time waiting for his moment, and through his humor, refuses to despair and give up on escaping the Mutant Factory. Implicit in the film is the thesis that humor is an important tool of liberation.

Is the movie itself liberating as a superhero movie that reproduced all of the genre's tropes? The answer is the more ambivalent "it depends." While one does not need to accept the premise that superheroes encourage one to adopt a fascist worldview, it is true that, as a product of capitalism, any revolutionary potential *Deadpool* contains becomes stripped as it becomes just another product and property to be bought and sold for entertainment purposes. *Deadpool*, like humor itself, may contain liberating potential, but whether or not that potential is grasped is an ambivalent prospect. As Tanner suggested, it may depend on how each viewer receives it and uses it. The film, however, clearly offers viewers an alternative to traditional superhero movie tropes and presents the possibility of liberation for the engaged viewer.

References

Amir, Lydia B. 2014. *Humor and the good life in modern philosophy: Shaftesbury, Hamann, Kierkegaard*. Albany: State University of New York Press.
Boskin, Joseph. 1987. The complicity of humor: The life and death of sambo. In *The philosophy of laughter and humor*, ed. John Morreall. Albany: State University of New York Press.
Burlingame, Russ. 2020. Watchmen creator Alan Moore: Superhero movies 'Blighted the culture.' *Comicbook*, October 09. https://comicbook.com/comics/news/watchmen-creator-alan-moore-superhero-movies-blighted-the-cultur/
Bussie, Jacqueline. 2007. *The laughter of the oppressed: Ethical and theological resistance in Wiesel, Morrison, and Endo*. New York: T & T Clark International.
Carpio, Glenda R. 2008. *Laughing fit to kill: Black humor in the fictions of slavery*. Oxford: Oxford University Press.
Carroll, Noël. 2014. *Humour: A very short introduction*. Oxford: Oxford University Press.
Critchley, Simon. 2002. *On humour*. New York: Routledge.

Davies, Christie. 2008. Humour and protest: Jokes under communism. In *Humor and social protest*, ed. Marjolein't Hart and Dennis Bos. New York: Cambridge University Press.

De Sousa, Ronald. 1987. When is it wrong to laugh? In *The philosophy of laughter and humor*, ed. John Morreall. Albany: State University of New York Press.

Eagleton, Terry. 2019. *Humour*. New Haven: Yale University Press.

Freud, Sigmund. 1987. Humor. In *The philosophy of laughter and humor*, ed. John Morreall. Albany: State University of New York Press.

Hart, Marjolein't, ed. 2008. Humor and social protest: An introduction. In *Humor and social protest*. Edited by Dennis Bos. New York: Cambridge University Press.

Hazlitt, William. 1819. *Lectures on the English comic writers: Delivered at the Surry institution*. London: Taylor and Hessey.

Horkheimer, Max, and Theodor W. Adorno. 2002. The culture industry: Enlightenment as mass deception. In *Dialectic of enlightenment: Philosophical fragments*. Edited by Gunzelin Schmid Noerr. Translated by Edmund Jephcott. Stanford: Stanford University Press.

Hutcheson, Francis. 1750. *Reflections upon laughter and remarks upon the fable of the bees*. Glasgow: Robert Urie.

Kerr, Walter. 1967. *Comedy and tragedy*. New York: Simon and Schuster.

Kownacki, Justin. 2017. Does every Marvel movie tell the same story? *Justin Kownacki*, November 05. http://www.justinkownacki.com/why-every-marvel-movie-tells-same-story/

Marcuse, Herbert. 1991. *One-dimensional man*. Boston: Beacon Press.

McClintock, Pamela, and Aaron Couch. 2019. Box office: 'Joker' passes 'Deadpool' as top-grossing R-rated pic of all time. *The Hollywood Reporter*, October 25. https://www.hollywoodreporter.com/movies/movie-news/box-office-joker-passes-deadpool-as-top-grossing-r-rated-pic-all-time-1250055/

Morreall, John, ed. 1987. *The philosophy of laughter and humor*. Albany: State University of New York Press.

Rao, Sonia. 2021. Ridley Scott and the grand tradition of big-name directors disparaging superhero movies. *The Washington Post*, November 17. https://www.washingtonpost.com/arts-entertainment/2021/11/17/ridley-scott-superhero-movies-directors/

Reynolds, Richard. 1992. *Super heroes: A modern mythology*. Jackson: University Press of Mississippi.

Tanner, Kathryn. 1996. Theology and popular culture. In *Changing conversations: Religious reflection and cultural analysis*, ed. Dwight N. Hopkins and Sheila Greeve Davaney. New York: Routledge.

Tilley, Carol L. 2012. Seducing the innocent: Fredric Wertham and the falsifications that helped condemn comics. *Information & Culture* 47 (4): 383–413.

Zinampan, Tristan. 2018. Comedy, not Thanos, is killing the Marvel Universe (but he's also there to save it). *Rappler*, May 04. https://www.rappler.com/entertainment/movies/201732-avengers-infinity-war-marvel-cinematic-universe-comedy-thanos/

Blade Runner as Philosophy: What Does It Mean to Be Human?

41

Timothy Shanahan

Contents

Introduction	984
Blade Runner: The Film(s)	985
What Does It Mean to Be Human?	989
"Did You Ever Take That Test Yourself?"	991
"You're So Different"	992
"We've a Lot in Common"	993
"There's Some of Me in You"	994
"Similar Problems"	995
Memory and Identity	996
Death and Finitude	997
Time and Meaning	998
Blade Runner as Philosophy?	999
"Let Me Show in an Image…"	1001
Conclusion	1002
References	1002

Abstract

Thanks to its brilliant melding of *film noir*, science fiction, and cyberpunk motifs, not to mention its stirring music and unprecedented visual density, Ridley Scott's *Blade Runner* (1982/2007) has become an influential cultural icon. What really sets the film apart from most movies, however, are the ways in which it encourages philosophical questions. Virtually all commentators agree that "What does it mean to be human?" – understood as asking something like "What characterizes the real (or authentic) human being?" – is *the* central philosophical question the film raises. Attempting to answer that question can be a fertile approach to the film, with moral implications for how to think about the qualifications for inclusion in the human community. That is not, however, the only way to

---

T. Shanahan (✉)
Department of Philosophy, Loyola Marymount University, Los Angeles, CA, USA
e-mail: tshanahan@lmu.edu

© Springer Nature Switzerland AG 2024
D. K. Johnson et al. (eds.), *The Palgrave Handbook of Popular Culture as Philosophy*,
https://doi.org/10.1007/978-3-031-24685-2_43

appreciate the philosophical significance of *Blade Runner*. The film also encourages viewers to ponder the question, "What fundamental experiences constitute the uniquely human mode of self-consciousness?" Showing how the latter question leads to a richer appreciation of *Blade Runner* as philosophy is the aim of this chapter.

Keywords

Blade Runner · Replicants · Ridley Scott · Rick Deckard · Roy Batty · Rachael · Plato's Cave Allegory · Descartes · Identity · Memory · Death · Mortality · Finitude · Temporality · Meaning

Introduction

"More human than human" is our motto.
—Dr. Eldon Tyrell

Blade Runner (dir. Ridley Scott, 1982/2007) is routinely ranked as one of the greatest and most influential science fiction films of all time. In 1993, it was selected by the Library of Congress for preservation in the US National Film Registry as being "culturally, historically, or aesthetically significant." In 2007, it was named by the Visual Effects Society as the second most visually influential film of all time. In 2012, in a poll with over 10,000 votes cast, it was ranked by *SFX* magazine as the greatest science fiction film of all time. In addition to the (belated) critical acclaim it has garnered, the film has attracted a devoted fan base, spawning numerous online sites devoted to discussing every aspect of the film. Its distinctive visual style has been copied countless times. In short, it has become a cultural icon.

Blade Runner's significance extends beyond its brilliant melding of *film noir*, science fiction, cyberpunk motifs, its stirring music, and unprecedented visual density. What really sets the film apart from most movies is its deft exploration of a range of thought-provoking themes. Rachela Morrison (1990, p. 2) notes that, "in the immodest guise of a noir/science fiction thriller," *Blade Runner* is essentially "a philosophical film" that "leaps from impeccable intricacies of *mise-en-scène* to questions about the nature of man, God, beast, the meaning of existence, and the workings of the universe." Paul M. Sammon (in his audio commentary on the "Workprint" version of the film, included in the Five-Disc Ultimate Collector's Edition) likewise observes: " *Blade Runner* . . . addresses universal human concerns, not only what is human and what is real, but who am I, and where is my place in the universe, and why am I here, and why am I being exploited, and why am I not fighting against that?" Philosophical themes in the film have been explored in several scholarly books (e.g., Kerman 1997; Shanahan 2014; Coplan and Davies 2015). Interest in the film as a work of philosophical significance shows no signs of abating.

It is therefore remarkable that *Blade Runner*'s director, Sir Ridley Scott, has distanced himself from the idea that the film was ever intended to have any philosophical significance whatsoever. According to Philip K. Dick, who wrote the book upon which the film is (loosely) based, Scott told him that he was "not interested in making an esoteric film." (Dick's comment is included in the Enhancement Archive DVD included in the Five-Disc Ultimate Collector's Edition.) Elsewhere, Scott has declared, "this film does not have any deep messages" (Peary 1984, p. 55). Indeed, apparently no messages of *any* kind, deep or otherwise, were intended: "There is simply no intentional message in this picture, although people will probably read all sorts of things into any film. Basically, I see moviemaking as creating entertainment" (Sammon 1982, p. 140; see also Knapp and Kulas 2005, p. xv). Scott's view of movies is reminiscent of a remark about the business of making motion pictures attributed to the legendary studio head Samuel Goldwyn: "Pictures are for entertainment; messages should be delivered by Western Union."

We must take Scott at his word when he says that there are no intentional messages in *Blade Runner*. After all, presumably he knows what he did and did not intend to convey with his film. Yet, somehow, some movies not intended to deliver messages (philosophical or otherwise) end up doing precisely that. *Blade Runner* is a case in point. Jake Scott (Sir Ridley's son) acknowledges as much when he plausibly describes *Blade Runner* as "this Nietzschean, sort of dystopic, philosophical and dark existential film." (Jake Scott's comment is included in the documentary DVD *Dangerous Days: Making Blade Runner*, included in the Five-Disc Ultimate Collector's Edition.) A number of scholars agree (e.g., Mulhall 1994; Barad 2009; Pate 2009). Ridley Scott's comments notwithstanding, Rachela Morrison, Paul M. Sammon, Jake Scott, and many others are exactly right: *Blade Runner is* a deeply philosophical film.

Of course, that claim raises the fascinating question of how a film *can* be philosophical in the first place, especially if it was not intended by its director to be so, as well as the even more basic question of just what "being philosophical," as applied to a motion picture, might conceivably *mean*. Those are *themselves* philosophical questions – metaphilosophical questions, if you will. So, if we want to understand and appreciate the sense(s) in which "*Blade Runner* is philosophy," we shall have to do some philosophizing about films (in general) as philosophy. We shall also have to get (re-)acquainted with *Blade Runner*'s characters and basic story. That is our next task.

Blade Runner: The Film(s)

Blade Runner is set in Los Angeles, November 2019 – just over 37 years into the future from the film's premiere in June 1982. The city we see in the film is still mostly recognizable, thanks to its inclusion of distinctive Los Angeles landmarks, e.g., Union Station, the Bradbury Building, the Million Dollar Theater, the Second Street Tunnel, and the Ennis House. However, by 2019 the City of Angels has fallen on hard times. The overcrowded, refuse-strewn streets convey the impression of a city long in decline. It is also *really* rainy.

The film opens with a text crawl providing viewers with important background information. We learn that early in the twenty-first century the Tyrell Corporation advanced "robot" evolution into the Nexus phase. The new Nexus 6 "replicants" are virtually identical to human beings in appearance and intelligence but superior in strength and agility to the genetic engineers who created them. Replicants were created as an off-world slave labor force in the hazardous exploration and colonization of other planets. Following a bloody mutiny off-world by a Nexus 6 combat team, replicants were declared illegal on earth – under penalty of death. Special police squads – blade runner units – had orders to shoot to kill, upon detection, any trespassing replicants. Ominously, we are told that "This was not called execution. It was called retirement."

Interestingly, the early (and long lost) "Workprint" version of the film includes a somewhat different definition of "replicant" that provides additional information about their physical makeup:

> **REPLICANT**\rep'-li-cant\ *n.* See also ROBOT (*antique*):
> ANDROID (*obsolete*): NEXUS (*generic*): Synthetic human
> with paraphysical capabilities, having skin/flesh culture.
> Also: Rep, skin job (*slang*): Off-world uses: Combat,
> high risk industrial, deep-space probe. On-world use prohibited.
> Specifications and quantities – information classified.
> NEW AMERICAN DICTIONARY.
> Copyright © 2016

This is the only time in any version of the film that the word "android" appears, and it does so only to inform us that this term has become obsolete. This semantic decision reflects Ridley Scott's belief that the term had acquired too many clichéd associations to be suitable for his film. The new word "replicant," by contrast, naturally prompts the viewer to reflect on how closely the synthetic humanoids made by Tyrell replicate the qualities of human beings – a matter we shall return to shortly.

The first character we meet is Dave Holden (Lawrence Paull), a neatly groomed and visibly bored blade runner interviewing new employees at the Tyrell Corporation on the suspicion that one or more of the rogue replicants have infiltrated the company – for reasons that are still quite obscure. When the questions posed to one "Leon Kowalski, engineer, waste disposal" become a bit too personal ("Describe in single words, only the good things that come into your mind about … your mother"), Leon (Brion James), a replicant who has no mother, shoots Holden, sending him and his high-backed Tyrell Corporation-embossed chair through the wall and clear into the next room.

Next we meet Rick Deckard (Harrison Ford), idly skimming a newspaper's employment ads before being beckoned to take his seat at a noodle bar. Before long, his meal is interrupted by a peculiar-looking character. Gaff (James Edward Olmos), speaking a difficult-to-decipher creole, compels him to drop-in on Capt. Harry Bryant (M. Emmet Walsh), Deckard's former boss at the LAPD. When he does so, Bryant informs him that five replicants jumped a shuttle off-world, killed its crew, and subsequently were spotted off the coast. One was "fried" while running through an electric field at the Tyrell Corporation. The others' whereabouts were unknown. Bryant needs Deckard to resume his old profession as a blade runner – an invitation Deckard politely declines until Bryant makes it clear that there are undesirable personal consequences for refusing. Reluctantly, Deckard relents.

During Deckard's briefing by Capt. Bryant, we are given more detailed information about the functions and capabilities of the four renegade replicants Deckard is tasked with retiring:

Replicant (M) Des: Leon
NEXUS 6 N6MAC41717
Incept Date: 10 APRIL, 2017
Func: Combat/Loader (Nuc. Fiss.)
Phys: LEV. A Mental: LEV. C

Replicant (F) Des: Zhora
NEXUS 6 N6FAB61216
Incept Date: 12 JUNE, 2016
Func: Polit. Homicide
Phys: LEV. A Mental: LEV. B

Replicant (M) Des: Batty (Roy)
NEXUS 6 N6MAA10816
Incept Date: 8 JAN., 2016
Func: Combat, Colonization Defense Prog
Phys: LEV. A Mental: LEV. A

Replicant (F) Des: Pris
NEXUS 6 N6FAB21416
Incept Date: 14 FEB., 2016
Func: Military/Leisure
Phys: LEV. A Mental: LEV. B

The identification code on the second line of each description is a compressed summary of the key properties of each replicant. "N6FAB61216" indicates that Zhora (Joanna Cassidy) is a Nexus 6 Female, with A-level physical capabilities, B-level mental capabilities, and an incept date of 12 June 2016. Leon is a Nexus 6 Male, a nuclear loader with A-level physical capabilities, C-level mental capabilities, and an incept date of 17 April 2017. Oddly, a different date is provided on the next line; it is *this* date that Leon later hurls at Deckard in the alley, calling it his "birthday." Pris (Daryl Hannah) is "a basic pleasure model ... the standard item for military clubs in the outer colonies." Perhaps not coincidentally, her incept date is Valentine's Day. Finally, Roy Batty (Rutger Hauer) is an especially dangerous combat model designed with "optimum self-sufficiency." His incept date reveals that he is the oldest of the replicants, now nearing his designed expiration date – a fact whose importance soon becomes evident.

As Deckard also learns, Nexus 6 replicants are considerably more formidable than anything blade runners like Holden and he had encountered before and also harder to detect. Bryant therefore sends Deckard to the Tyrell Corporation to administer a replicant-detecting Voight-Kampff (V-K) test to a Nexus 6 there. Upon arriving, he is greeted by an attractive, self-assured, smartly dressed young woman, ostensibly an employee there, who introduces herself as Rachael (Sean Young). When Dr. Eldon Tyrell (Joe Turkel), the eponymous CEO of the Tyrell Corp., shows up, he asks Deckard to perform the V-K test on Rachael because he says, "I want to see it work on a person. I want to see a negative before I provide you with a positive." Deckard complies and eventually realizes that Rachael is a replicant, albeit one that is so similar to humans that her identification as a replicant was quite difficult. He appears visibly disturbed.

After Rachael is brusquely dismissed by Tyrell, the two men talk. Tyrell confirms that Rachael is a replicant that does not *know* that it is a replicant. Deckard is stunned: "How can it not know what it is?!" As Tyrell proceeds to explain, his company has created a new experimental model that is even more humanlike than previous models. "Commerce is our goal here at Tyrell," he tells Deckard. "'More human than human' is our motto." Not only is Rachael physically almost indistinguishable from a human, but she also has memory implants – so that she would not know that she is a replicant. Later, when Deckard returns to his apartment, she confronts him, attempting to convince him that she is not a replicant. By exposing some of her memories as implants, he coldly proves to her otherwise. Rachael, emotionally distraught, leaves.

As Deckard begins his search for the rogue replicants, Roy Batty and Leon (who managed to escape after shooting Holden) conduct a "chilling" interrogation of Hannibal Chew (James Hong), an eye designer for the Tyrell Corporation. In the ensuing dialogue, we begin to learn why the replicants have returned. Batty questions Chew about "morphology, longevity, and incept dates." He wants to know how long he and his friends have to live and, given their built-in expiration dates, where they can find someone who can "repair" them. Chew sends them to find J. F. Sebastian (William Sanderson), a genetic designer for the Tyrell Corporation. Batty is able to use Sebastian's chess game with Tyrell to gain access to Tyrell's bedchamber, whereupon he demands that his maker give him "more life." After Tyrell explains why that is technically impossible and encourages his "prodigal son" to "Revel in your time!" Batty brutally kills him, and then Sebastian as well.

Meanwhile, Deckard is on the replicants' trail. He tracks down Zhora, who is posing as an exotic dancer in a seedy nightclub, and, with some difficulty, manages to kill her. Leon, who witnesses the execution, drags Deckard into an ally where he administers a savage beating until Rachael, picking up Deckard's gun, shoots Leon through the head. That leaves just two replicants on Deckard's list. Deckard tracks Pris to Sebastian's apartment where, with difficulty, he kills her. Roy then shows up. Almost immediately, Batty turns the tables on his nemesis and pursues a very frightened Deckard through the decaying ruins of the Bradbury Building. The chase culminates on the rooftop where Roy, having nearly reached the end of his 4-year life span, unexpectedly saves Deckard from death. As Deckard stares in confusion, Batty delivers his famous "tears in rain" speech lamenting the transitory nature of his life and of his unique experiences. Deckard then returns to his apartment to collect Rachael so that together they can flee. The film ends as Deckard and Rachael step into the elevator and the doors close, their fates unknown.

At least, that is how some versions of the film end. Famously, there are at least seven versions of *Blade Runner*. Most of the versions differ only slightly (e.g., there is a bit more graphic violence in the International Cut), although the original theatrical release (1982) and the Final Cut (2007) differ enough to merit distinguishing them. Most significantly, in the theatrical release, after the elevator doors close, we see Deckard and Rachael driving along an incongruously verdant, sunlit mountain road, with Deckard (in voice-over narration) recalling that Tyrell had told him that Rachael was special – no termination date – and musing, "I didn't know how long we had together, who does?" That saccharine ending did not go down well with critics and was scrapped (along with the voice-over narration) for later versions. In the Final Cut (as well as in 1992's Director's Cut), there is the inclusion of a scene in which Deckard, half-dozing as he idly pecks away at a piano keyboard, has a reverie of a white unicorn prancing through a lush green forest – unlike anything else we see in the film. Some have taken that scene to prove that Deckard is himself a replicant – an idea encouraged by Ridley Scott – on the ground that Gaff leaves an origami unicorn outside Deckard's apartment. How could Gaff know about Deckard's unicorn "dream" unless Deckard is a replicant? That "proof" is on shaky ground; for a range of reasons, space here does not permit us to explore. (See Shanahan 2014, 2019; Salamoff 2018 for discussion.)

What Does It Mean to Be Human?

In the world of *Blade Runner*, whether one is considered to be human or a replicant (one cannot be both) has grave consequences. It is the replicants' presumed status as less than human that morally licenses human beings to treat them as slave labor and to dispose of them when they deviate from their prescribed functions. This attitude is perfectly expressed in Deckard's response to Rachael's question – of whether he thinks that the Tyrell Corporation's products are a benefit to the public: "Replicants are like any other machine. They're either a benefit or a hazard. If they're a benefit, it's not my problem." Of course, if they *are* a hazard, then it *is* Deckard's problem. Fortunately for the LAPD, but unfortunately for rogue replicants, Deckard (as we learn from Capt. Bryant) is exceptionally good at the business of identifying and retiring renegade replicants. (He is certainly better than Dave Holden, who seemed surprisingly unprepared for Leon's violence.)

Sensing an opportunity to put Deckard on the defensive, Rachael challenges him: "Have you ever retired a human by mistake?" Deckard says he has not, but Rachael then points out – correctly – that that *is* a risk for someone with Deckard's job. Deckard has to be sure that he is retiring mere machines and not humans. Otherwise, he is a murderer. Consequently, the question of what it *means* to be human becomes of central importance – for Deckard *and* for the audience who must form a moral judgment about him. Indeed, nearly all commentators agree that "What does it mean to be human?" is the central philosophical question the film poses (see Barad 2009; Bukatman 2012; Kolb 1997; Mulhall 1994; Redmond 2008). Rutger Hauer, the actor who brilliantly plays Roy Batty, goes even farther by insisting (as reported in *The Hollywood Reporter*, 24 July 2019) that the film "wasn't about the replicants, it was about what does it mean to be human?" How could Roy Batty, of all people, be wrong about *Blade Runner*?

The "What does it mean to be human?" question is commonly taken to be asking something like: "What (if anything) distinguishes *real* humans from fake ones?" The search is then on for some morally significant feature that differentiates the two. If no nontrivial answer can be found, we must conclude that there is no such feature and therefore that the replicants are in fact human.

The most straightforward way to answer the question, so understood, would be to identify some significant feature(s) that humans possess and that everything else lacks. *That* would then be what it means to be human. What might that be? A popular answer concerns our minds or souls. René Descartes (1596–1650) would have approved wholeheartedly of Rick Deckard's (initial) view that the replicants are merely machines made to *resemble* humans but are not human at all. In Descartes' view, human beings are unique among all (mortal) creatures because they alone *think*. Artisans in his day had created ingenious mechanical animals whose movements were controlled by ropes, pulleys, levers, and so on that could mimic the behavior of real animals, so it was easy for him to imagine mechanical beings resembling in their outward appearance human beings, as well. Nevertheless, such creations could never be human. Real human beings are, metaphysically speaking, in a class of their own. For even if God himself were to produce "the body of a man exactly like one of ours" and composed of the very same materials that constitute a human body, yet "without putting into it, at the start, any rational soul" (i.e., a thinking substance), it would utterly fail to be human. No matter how superficially or physically indistinguishable from a human being such a creature might be, it would necessarily fail to be human because it would lack an essential element that *we* have but that mere machines (and, indeed, all animals) necessarily lack, namely, a *soul* or *mind*, endowed with *thought*.

How would we *know* whether a humanoid creature is a real human being with a mind, or a mere automaton made to behave like one? Descartes believed that he had identified two reliable diagnostic criteria. First, artificial humans "could never use words or other signs, or put them together as we do in order to declare our thoughts to others" (Descartes 1998, p. 32). Even if a humanoid being cried out *as if* in pain when its body was injured, and even if it could respond to questions *as if* it fully understood the questions posed to it – it could never "arrange its words differently so as to respond to the sense of all that will be said in its presence, as even the dullest men can do." Its patent inability to display the linguistic flexibility that humans effortlessly demonstrate would reveal its true nature as a mere simulacrum of a human being. Second, such a being eventually would be revealed as less than human because, like "a clock composed exclusively of wheels and springs [that] can count the hours and measure time more accurately than we can with all our carefulness," the artificial human would be exposed as such when we "discover that they were acting not through knowledge but only through the disposition of their organs" (Descartes 1998, p. 32). Indeed, "the fact that they do something *better* than we do does not prove that they have any intelligence ... rather it [would prove] that they have no intelligence at all" (Descartes 1998, p. 33).

The replicants, of course, satisfy Descartes' two diagnostic criteria for being *genuinely human* with flying colors. Roy Batty is as linguistically gifted as any human being in the film. He is even given to reworking poetry (in this case, William Blake's 1793 poem, "America: A Prophecy"), as his surprising self-introduction to Hannibal Chew demonstrates. The replicants also demonstrate impressive behavioral flexibility in solving novel problems. Leon infiltrates the Tyrell Corporation by successfully posing as an employee. Even if he was directed to do so by Roy Batty, Leon still had to pull it off, and he did. Zhora finds an even more exotic cover (as a dancer with a fondness for snakes). Pris assumes the persona of a lost waif to manipulate Sebastian – successfully. Roy sees the potential and then successfully exploits Sebastian's chess game with his boss to gain access to Tyrell, and so on. Of course, this only shows that the replicants satisfy *Descartes'* diagnostic criteria for being human. It would not settle the issue of whether they *are* human. Perhaps Descartes' diagnostic criteria are defective.

Notably, the human beings in the film take a different approach to differentiating real from artificial humans. The Voight-Kampff test that Dave Holden applies to Leon, and that Deckard applies to Rachael, works by detecting minute physiological changes associated with the subject's emotional responses to a series of carefully designed questions involving human or animal suffering. The test is premised on the idea that it takes years to develop an empathic capacity, which all adult human beings are presumed to have simply in virtue of being human. Because the replicants have at best a 4-year life span, they supposedly lack the time required to become empathic. Consequently, the V-K test can, in principle, be used to distinguish replicants from humans.

However, as the film progresses these assumptions are undermined. Rachael comes very close to passing the test. As Deckard explains to Tyrell, it usually requires "Twenty, thirty [questions], cross-referenced" to identify a subject as a replicant, but in Rachael's case, it required more than a hundred. In a few more years, she might do as well on the test as the average human, thereby making the Voight-Kampff test useless. Moreover, the film problematizes this supposed difference between humans and replicants by having Roy Batty express genuine care for Leon when he inquires, "Did you get your precious photos?" Likewise, he shows tender concern for Pris, telling Sebastian, "If we don't find help soon, Pris hasn't got long to live. We can't allow that." It is also true, of course, that Roy himself has not long to live, so it is significant that his concern here is for Pris, his replicant lover. That sure seems like empathy, or close to it.

"Did You Ever Take That Test Yourself?"

As the film narrows the supposed chasm between humans and replicants from one direction by depicting the replicants as nearly indistinguishable from human beings, it also narrows the gap from the opposite direction by depicting some of the human characters as deficient in those same characteristics and as more "robotic" than the replicants. Dave Holden seems not to notice the sarcasm in Leon's question, "Do you make up these questions, Mr. Holden, or do they write them down for you?" by responding (as an AI like Siri or Alexa might) as if it were a straightforward request for information. Given his brilliance in other respects, Tyrell is surprisingly naïve about his "prodigal son," Roy Batty – a fact that ultimately proves fatal. Other humans in the film seem incapable of (or uninterested in) demonstrating empathy either toward the replicants or toward one another. Bryant is a racist and a bully. Gaff seems most interested in career advancement and in being a thorn in Deckard's side. As for Deckard, for most of the film he seems as cold and as pitiless as the replicants he has been assigned to retire are reputed to be. (In the theatrical release, we learn that his ex-wife used to call him "sushi ... cold fish.") Confirmation of this interpretation appears in the scene in Deckard's apartment following Rachael's rescue of him from Leon's brutal assault. After assuring her that he would not come after her because, "I owe you one" – as if that momentous intervention was nothing more than a business transaction – Rachael is compelled to ask: "You know that Voight-Kampff test of yours? Did you ever take that test yourself?" Deckard does not answer, but the implication is that, ironically, Deckard himself lacks the very quality – empathy – whose absence is supposed to differentiate replicants from humans.

It is therefore tempting to conclude that the philosophical significance of the film consists in its forceful pressing of the point that it is always possible to conjure up some supposedly significant difference between people we want to oppress and the rest of us, but that people should not be discriminated against on the basis of characteristics (e.g., being made rather than born) that have nothing to do with their intrinsic value as persons. Undoubtedly, the film does suggest that. However, to stop there would be to miss the broader and, I would argue, deeper philosophical significance of the film, namely, to reflect shared elements of the experience of being human.

Blade Runner presents characters, dialogue, and situations in which the viewer is first led to *perceive* that these replicants are strange beings with whom we have little or nothing in common. As the film progresses, however, we are compelled to conclude that, "They are like us." That qualification is important. Make the replicants *exactly like* human beings, and the distance needed for objectivity regarding ourselves is threatened or lost. Make the replicants *utterly unlike* human beings, and it becomes difficult or impossible to relate their concerns to ours. But make them *just different enough* from human beings, as the film does, and we can begin to see their problems as resembling, and as possibly modeling solutions for, our own. Thus, the replicants' striking similarity-in-difference is essential to the film's philosophical effectiveness. Through the skillful use of *defamiliarization* – the artistic technique of presenting common things in an unfamiliar or strange way in order to enhance perception of the familiar – the film provides a defamiliarized vantage point from which to understand ourselves. Moreover, it does so by using some of the same narrative elements already discussed above, but for another purpose. Let us see how.

"You're So Different"

Initially, both Tyrell and Deckard view the replicants as fundamentally different from human beings. Tyrell dismisses Rachael's significance by telling Deckard, "Rachael is an experiment, nothing more." Deckard expresses astonishment at Tyrell's revelation that Rachael is a replicant by exclaiming, "How can it not know what it is?" At that point, Rachael is not yet a "she" to Deckard. Even the replicants themselves, and those who admire them, view them as "other." When Sebastian finally grasps that his strange guests are Nexus 6 replicants, he exclaims, "You're so different. You're so perfect." Roy responds with a simple, unqualified "Yes" – thereby underscoring his host's judgment of the replicants' otherness. The replicants' recognition of their otherness is signaled in other scenes, as well. With her arms and legs entwining Sebastian, like a spider with its prey firmly within its grasp, Pris remarks, "I don't think there's another *human being* in the whole world who would have helped us" (emphasis added). In response to Roy's question to Leon about whether the latter was able to retrieve his "precious photos" from his room, Leon says flatly, "Someone was there." Roy presses him farther: "*Men*? Police *men*?" – both times stressing "men" with perhaps a tinge of contempt for his human adversaries. The replicants' recognition of their status as *other* is emphasized once again by Roy in his famous end-of-life monologue, which begins: "I've seen things *you people* wouldn't believe." Given his design as a combat model replicant, Roy has experienced amazing things that mere "people" like Deckard could never experience. Finally, the replicants' recognition of their otherness could hardly be clearer than in Rachael's forlorn lament to Deckard, "I'm not *in* the business; I *am* the business." Unlike humans, replicants are viewed as mere commodities having at most a market value.

"We've a Lot in Common"

Having established the replicants' otherness, the film then methodically proceeds to erode the differences it has established by demonstrating that the replicants share important characteristics with humans and by depicting many of the humans in the film as deficient in precisely the characteristics that are supposed to differentiate them from the replicants, thereby narrowing the gap between them even more.

Most obviously, the replicants resemble human beings so closely in physical appearance that an elaborate test is required to identify them. It is true that the replicants are "superior in strength and agility" to most human beings. However, their enhanced capabilities are still just slightly beyond the range of normal human capacities. Although Ridley Scott apparently once described the replicants as "supermen who couldn't fly" (Sammon 2017, p. 329), none of the replicants are faster than a speeding bullet, more powerful than a locomotive, or able to leap over (and not just between the rooftops of) tall buildings in a single bound. They are not invulnerable to bullets, blessed with X-ray vision, or able to reverse the direction of time. Despite their impressive physical capabilities, they are more like *us* than like the Man of Steel (who is not a *man* – i.e., an adult human male – at all, being from an entirely different planet, presumably with a distinct evolutionary history, and therefore a member of an entirely different species).

Second, we are left in no doubt about the replicants' *intelligence* – often supposed to be *the* distinguishing human characteristic. Pris has little difficulty exploiting Sebastian's loneliness to gain access to his apartment – where Roy then uses Sebastian to gain access to Tyrell. Zhora pretends to be oblivious to Deckard's attempt to pass himself off as a representative of the "American Federation of Variety Artists" until she is in a position to demonstrate some of her impressive "kick murder squad" skills on him. Roy's *tête à tête* with Tyrell over the molecular chemistry of life-extension biotechnology reveals him to be on an intellectual par with a man whom Sebastian had previously declared to be "a genius." Even Leon, who (according to the information in Capt. Bryant's slides) has just "B-level" intelligence, is still intelligent enough.

And there appears to be no difference in their capacity for empathy, as already discussed. So there is less of a difference between humans and replicants than at first appeared. Perhaps there is none at all.

"There's Some of Me in You"

This is familiar ground for those who have followed discussions of *Blade Runner*. The film seems designed to progressively turn our sympathies toward the replicants, or at least to weaken the belief that the humans and replicants in the film are different in any way that could matter. But drawing that unqualified conclusion would be an overreaction. There *are* differences, and it is those differences as much as the similarities that make the replicants' plight an effective instrument for exploring aspects of the human condition. As Joseph Francavilla (1997, p. 14) insightfully observes, "[T]he replicants in *Blade Runner* ... function as *mirrors* for people, by allowing examination and moral scrutiny of ourselves, our technology, and our treatment of other beings, and by defining in their tragic struggle what is truly human" (emphasis added).

The "mirror" metaphor is apt. The image we see when we look in the mirror certainly resembles us and can provide valuable information. Nevertheless, it falls short of being a comprehensive, complete, and accurate rendering. For one thing, it is two-dimensional. For another, it captures at most one side of us at a time. Finally, it is always viewed through a subjective interpretive framework that makes complete objectivity practically impossible. Those inherent limitations notwithstanding, it is still a facsimile of oneself peering back – and it is useful for precisely that reason.

Similarly, were the replicants *utterly unlike* human beings, it would become difficult to relate their concerns to ours. Make the replicants *exactly like* human beings, and the distance needed for objectivity would be threatened or lost. But make them seem both different from *and* similar to human beings, and we can begin to see in them fundamental concerns and possible responses to them resembling our own. This places us in a position from which to reflect more deeply on our own experience as conscious, self-aware beings. Arguably, this is what all (or at least a great many) films that are considered "philosophical" do, with varying degrees of success. *Blade Runner* succeeds in doing this better than most films thanks to the quality of its execution.

"Similar Problems"

That interpretation of the philosophical significance of *Blade Runner* merits further explication.

Blade Runner raises a range of philosophical issues (Shanahan 2014; Coplan and Davies 2015), but many viewers will relate most fully to what might be described rather broadly as the film's "existential" themes, i.e., motifs that address the challenges of coming to grips with unavoidable features of being conscious of oneself as a specific but never completely fixed agent thrown into the world. Because the replicants lack many of the mundane concerns that motivate many of us from day to day (e.g., raising families, commuting, pursuing careers, making social comparisons, paying bills, watching sports, etc.) and are concerned instead with existential basics – staying alive, understanding and accepting their identity, facing their creator, exercising autonomy, and especially coming to grips with temporality, contingency, and death – these concerns common to human beings and replicants can be displayed in nearly their purest form, thereby providing for the audience a clearer reflection of the fundamental human concerns that we share with them.

The film hints at as much. Recall the following brief exchange:

Roy Batty   We've a lot in common.
J. F. Sebastian What do you mean?
Roy Batty   Similar problems.
Pris   Accelerated decrepitude.

Sebastian suffers from (the ironically named) "Methuselah Syndrome," making his body age faster than its 25 years of life would suggest. (William Sanderson, the actor who plays Sebastian, was 37 years old at the time, though perhaps was made to look older.) The replicants' problem is similar but different. Their problem is not "accelerated decrepitude" so much as it is premature expiration. They have been built to expire in a mere 4 years (give or take a few months). As far as we can tell, they are physically sound right up until almost the time they have been designed to die. One condition is congenital, the other is designed, but the result is much the same: a life span that seems circumscribed relative to an average (i.e., noncompromised) human life. Thus, humans and the replicants share a similar, but not quite identical, problem.

What is especially interesting about this exchange, however, is that whereas Pris mentions just one (granted, rather serious) problem, Roy mentions similar *problems*, albeit without elaborating. Roy's use of the plural is intriguing. The replicants share, not only with Sebastian but also with most human beings, problems that stem from our common constitution as beings that are acutely conscious of themselves. This self-consciousness engenders a variety of common challenges. Describing a few of these may be sufficient to establish our common existential predicaments.

Memory and Identity

The problematization, validation, and preservation of memories, especially as they are related to one's identity, are prominent themes in *Blade Runner* (as they are in its sequel, as well). Leon is visibly upset that he was unable to return to his room in the Yukon hotel to retrieve his precious photos – i.e., physically realized mementos of past experiences. At the end of his life, Roy Batty seems most concerned that his extraordinary life experiences, the only existing traces of which are his memories, will all be lost, "like tears in rain." Rachael reluctantly has to accept that she is not who (or even what) she believed herself to be when some of what she naturally took to be her own memories are exposed by Deckard as mere implants – having originally belonged to Tyrell's niece. That realization sparks a profound personal crisis. The reason is straightforward: Memories are central to one's sense of oneself as a particular person. John Locke (1632–1704) went so far as to claim that our identity as specific persons extends back in time *only* so far as our memories do: "For as far as any intelligent being can repeat the idea of any past action with the same consciousness it had of it at first, and with the same consciousness it has of any present action, so far it is the same personal self" (Locke 1690, p. 451).

There is no reason to suppose that any of our memories are implants in the exact sense in which some of Rachael's were. Such technology does not (yet) exist. Yet we know that our memories are subject to distortion due not only to naturally occurring events but also to some others who actively work to shape how the past – *our* past – is remembered. (Think of how family members, friends, and indeed we ourselves repeat interpretations of past events until they become accepted as unquestionably factual.) Unlike Rachael, most of us do not struggle with the question of whether we are human or worry that the bulk of our memories might in reality be someone else's. Yet, like Rachael, we struggle with issues of memory, identity, and difficult-to-acquire self-knowledge.

Consequently, like Rachael and Leon, we cling to physical reminders of fleeting experiences – photos, souvenirs, and scraps of paper – even when we know that those physical artifacts cannot, in themselves, replicate the experiences they represent. Like Rachael, we sometimes have reason to question whether our memories provide an accurate account of what we have done, who we were, and therefore of who we (really) are now. Nevertheless, like her we do (occasionally, at least) struggle with questions of *identity*. Apart from how others think of us, or how we choose to present ourselves to others, we may wonder, "Who am I, *really*?" Mere memories connect our pasts to our presents, and what we hope will continue to provide traces in the minds of others – evidence that we once existed and had unique, unrepeatable experiences.

Like Roy Batty, we can be deeply unsettled by the realization that many of our most precious experiences have nothing more than our own transient memories to prove that they ever happened at all, and that when they are gone, so, too, are we. His famous monologue at the end of his life is so deeply moving in large part because a moment's reflection demonstrates that his stirring reverie could, with the particular details changed, as easily be our own. Like Roy, each of us has experienced things that no one else has – and in some cases things that no one else could have – experienced. Moreover, unless one believes in an afterlife in which persons and their memories persist forever, all traces of the unique experiences that constitute our lives and that constitute *us* will be lost in time – indeed, lost in an almost unimaginatively short amount of time, relative to the existence of the cosmos. Such reflections, unless quickly shunted aside as too disturbing, can give rise to questions about the meaning and purpose of it all. They can engender philosophical reflection on the meaning of life.

Death and Finitude

The replicants consider death to be the most important problem they face – even greater than their slavery in the off-world colonies. Their dangerous and difficult quest to meet their creator would make no sense without this belief. Although there are previous hints in the film, this fact is finally made explicit in the tense scene in which Roy Batty dramatically confronts his maker:

Tyrell   I'm surprised you didn't come here sooner.
Batty   It's not an easy thing to meet your maker.
Tyrell   And what can he do for you?
Batty   Can the maker repair what he makes?
Tyrell   Would you like to be modified?
Batty   I had in mind something a little more radical.
Tyrell   What ... What seems to be the problem?
Batty   Death.

   The replicants are driven by the belief that their lives will run out before they *should*. Their demand is simple: They want "more life." (Ironically, by seeking more life for themselves all but Roy die violent deaths sooner than they otherwise would.) Roy no doubt feels himself to have been robbed of a future that was rightly his. However, this demand raises a host of further questions. How much life *should* he have? Why? What sort of modification could satisfy Roy's demand for "more life"? How much more would be enough? Twice as much? There is nothing special about having a 4-year life span, so doubling that to 8 years seems equally arbitrary. The same would be true of a *tenfold* increase in his expected life span to 40 years, or any other similar increase. Some commentators assume that Batty believes that he wants a life span equal to that of human beings. Why stop there? Humans live for any number of years – or not. The only truly *nonarbitrary life span* might be one that *has no end*. No wonder Tyrell, despite his considerable arrogance, considers solving *that* problem to be a little out of his jurisdiction.

Unlike the replicants, none of us have been designed with a 4-year life span. Unless we have been diagnosed with a terminal illness or have been sentenced to death, we may not know precisely how much time we have left. We know (or should know) that our time is strictly limited within temporal bounds that no one, not even the world's wealthiest or most powerful person, can escape. Many people dread death and go to great lengths to postpone it for as long as possible. The person who believes that they are dying "prematurely" feels that they are being robbed of a future that was rightly theirs. Although this is perhaps a natural reaction to learning that one's death is likely to come sooner than one anticipated, it is nonetheless decidedly odd. None of us is guaranteed any specific life span. In addition, to be robbed of something seems to presuppose that one had the thing in question in one's possession. However, the future is precisely that which no one, ever, has had in her possession. It is an ancient puzzle, going back at least to the ancient Greek philosopher Epicurus, how one can be truly harmed by being deprived of something that was never one's possession to begin with. Whether that observation should provide consolation is a matter of dispute among philosophers.

Time and Meaning

The replicants are obsessed with *time*. "Time" is the first word we hear from Roy Batty as he emerges from a phone booth to assure Leon that there is "Time enough." At that point in the film, that declaration is still mysterious. Time enough for what? As later becomes clear, Roy was judging that there was still time enough to . . . try to acquire more time. When Leon drags Deckard into an alley after witnessing Zhora's retirement, time is clearly on his mind as well:

Leon	How old am I?
Deckard	I don't know.
Leon	My birthday is April 10, 2017. How long do I live?
Deckard	4 years.
Leon	More than you! . . . Wake up! Time to die.

Deckard is saved in the nick of time by Rachael. Back in Deckard's apartment, how much time she has left is on Rachael's mind as well: "Deckard? You know those files on me – the incept date, the longevity, those things. You saw them?" Later, time is still on Roy Batty's mind when he finally meets his maker. His demand for *more life* is simply a demand for *more time*. Having reviewed for him the supposedly insurmountable biotechnological obstacles to extending Roy's life, Tyrell attempts to appease his dangerous visitor by suggesting that the brevity of his life is counterbalanced by its brilliant intensity: "The light that burns twice as bright burns half as long. And you have burned so very, very brightly, Roy. . .. Revel in your time!" This is not the response Roy wants to hear. Angered by Tyrell's refusal to grant him more time, he kills him in a fit of violent rage, physically enacting Friedrich Nietzsche's famous claim, "God is dead, and we have killed him." Liberated from his quest for more life by the death of his creator (literally by his own hands), Roy Batty experiences the exhilaration, confusion, and inescapable burden of recognizing himself as being completely responsible for his choices and actions. He joyfully embraces Tyrell's advice to "revel in your time!" by bringing his waning physicality to bear in his pursuit of Deckard. When his death is imminent, he chooses to spend his last few precious moments reflecting on his brief life. Roy's last words were the same as Leon's: "Time to die."

The replicants assume that *death* poses the most serious problem they face. They appear to believe that the only solution to this problem is to secure *more time*. It is unclear whether they thought carefully about what value having more time ultimately confers. Tyrell counsels a different perspective – one according to which it is not how long one lives, but how intensely, that matters. A life that is lacking in meaning cannot become more meaningful *simply* by extending its length any more than a piece of music, a film, or a book can become *better* simply by making it *longer*. Indeed, the danger is that the opposite will occur. Roy seems not to have considered this danger, or if he did, he did not take it seriously. However, as many people have discovered, simply having more life in the sense of having more time does not address, much less solve, some of the most pressing existential problems people actually face. After all, regardless of how much time one believes remains, each of us faces the problem of how to make the most meaningful use of whatever time remains to us. As Roy Batty might say, "Similar problems."

Blade Runner as Philosophy?

Suppose, then, that the replicants can serve as "mirrors" for the human condition, in the ways sketched above (and in others), and can thereby help us to reflect on our own existence. Is that "reflecting" function enough to warrant declaring "*Blade Runner* as philosophy"? The answer depends, of course, on one's conception of philosophy and its boundaries. So let us examine that.

To begin with, one might insist that for a film to be philosophy, or at least to be philosophical, it must advance a distinct philosophical thesis, supported by arguments. This requirement raises two more fundamental issues: (1) What might it *mean* to attribute a philosophical thesis and argument to a work of *fiction*, and (2) how we can decide whether that attribution is *correct*?

The first issue arises because it is far from obvious that works of fiction can advance theses and arguments, much less *philosophical* theses and arguments. Philosophical arguments are intended to rationally persuade (or, more ambitiously, to educate and enlighten). At least in the Anglo-American tradition, to accomplish this feat they tend to rely on carefully defined terms, finely wrought distinctions, and logically perspicuous moves from premises to conclusions. The primary purpose of fiction, by contrast, is to entertain by engaging one's imagination. Fiction, by definition, deals with imaginary states of affairs. It is unclear how we can draw conclusions about the real world by reflecting on the details of fictional worlds that are known to be unreal. Unlike most works of philosophy, films (i.e., nondocumentary motion pictures that make no pretense of being factual) trade in nonlinguistic images and sounds rather than exclusively in words. But how can mere images and sounds advance philosophical views? The challenges to thinking of works of fiction as bona fide works of philosophy are formidable. *Blade Runner* might well fail to be philosophy, on that criterion. It does not announce its (or even a) thesis.

Suppose, however, that those challenges can be overcome. We would still face the second difficulty identified above, namely, deciding whether the attribution of a specific philosophical thesis and argument to a work of fiction is *correct*. Works of fiction (especially great ones) are notoriously subject to differing interpretations. Without explicitly formulated arguments (or even linguistic carriers thereof, i.e., sentences), how can one *know* that one has correctly identified a fictional work's thesis and supporting arguments (assuming that they exist in the first place)? Of course, one always can shift to hypothetical mode: "*If* the work's thesis and argument are taken to be thus and so, *then* the work succeeds as a work of philosophy." On what grounds can that sort of judgment be made? Only, it seems, through an act of *translation* in which the nonlinguistic elements of a film are converted into linguistic elements – thereby stripping the thesis and argument of whatever was distinctively *cinematic* about them – i.e., by changing the subject.

Philosophers of film are well aware of these challenges. Indeed, questions about whether a film can make or present a philosophical argument or "do philosophy" (in some sense), and how we can or should evaluate any purported instance thereof, have long been foci of, and controversial within, the philosophy of film. Some philosophers argue that films *cannot* constitute bona fide works of philosophy in any interesting sense (e.g., Andersen 2005; Livingston 2006; Russell 2000; Smith 2006). Others counter that films *can* constitute bona fide works of philosophy (e.g., Carroll 2006; Cavell 1979; Mulhall 2015; Wartenberg 2006). Those on the former side of the debate tend to argue that philosophy is inescapably propositional in nature – it is expressed in propositions (sentences, statements, etc.). Consequently, unless a film includes propositions of a philosophical nature (in which case it probably fails to be a film worth watching), it cannot be a work of philosophy, although it can still be thought provoking and worthy of reflection. On the latter side are those who argue that the foregoing understanding of philosophy and philosophical arguments is far too constricted, because philosophy can be, and historically has been, expressed in a range of nonpropositional forms. The challenge for them is to explain *how* this can be so.

Fortunately, they have a model of undisputed philosophical significance on which to rely. Film is an intensely visual medium, conveying meaning through images as well as sounds. The practice of doing philosophy by conveying images goes back at least to Plato – an oft-noted irony inasmuch as he expresses a distrust of images, given that they are mere copies (or copies of copies) of the most real things. Nonetheless, in perhaps the most famous bit of philosophizing in history, he deploys (albeit, in words) a striking image to convey deep philosophical insights.

"Let Me Show in an Image..."

Plato's *Allegory of the Cave* (in his dialogue, *Republic*) opens with the words, "Let me show in an image our nature in both its enlightened and unenlightened states." He then has Socrates tell a story about strange prisoners living in an underground cave who have been chained there since birth, forced to view the shadows cast on, and to hear echoes rebounding from, the wall in front of them, completely unaware of anything else. When one of the prisoners manages to escape, ascends to the upper world, becomes enlightened, and then attempts to convey his new insights to his former friends, he is shunned by them as having lost his mind. The allegory ends by contrasting two different accounts of education, one in which the teacher gives the student what she previously lacked, the other in which the teacher's role is to help the student turn their soul toward "true being." By means of this vivid, imaginative story, Plato attempted to convey something of what it is like to use the mind to ascend from the defective understanding of the world delivered by our senses to grasp higher realities whose existence and nature is made manifest through the operation of intelligence. As readers (there are also many video versions), we come to understand via the story the basic human condition with and without education.

Plato's *Allegory of the Cave* is justly famous, so all this is probably familiar enough. Note, however, that the key moment in the allegory, for our purposes, comes well before its end. After Socrates has described the prisoners chained since birth in the cave, Glaucon, his ever-compliant interlocutor, remarks, "You have shown me a strange image, and they are strange prisoners." Socrates replies: "They are like us." That short, arresting statement is the key to understanding the entire allegory. At first, the prisoners could not have seemed less like us. We have not been chained in place since birth in an underground cavern, unable to move our heads or look around. Unlike them, we know shadows and echoes for what they really are, etc. Glaucon is right: These *are* strange prisoners. But recall the opening line of the allegory: "Let me show in an image *our* nature...." The prisoners in the cave are meant to represent *us*. The fact that the story centers on the nature of reality, one's ability to know it, and how one successfully responds to the challenge of transcending the naïve perspective, is essential to the story's immense philosophical potency.

Film can serve a similar philosophical function. In the theatrical release of *Blade Runner*, after Roy Batty bows his head, and the dove he was grasping is released to flutter into a blue sky, Deckard (in voice-over narration) reflects, "All he'd wanted were the same answers the rest of us want. Where did I come from? Where am I going? How long have I got?" Although perhaps not the most elegant summary of the replicant's quest, it does convey some important insights. By including Roy Batty among "the rest of us" and using the pronoun *he* rather than *it*, Deckard acknowledges that in relation to the most fundamental human concerns, the replicants are no different from us. As Roy remarked to Sebastian, "We've got a lot in common." It takes Deckard almost the entire film to grasp the fundamental truth embodied in that simple remark. The thesis of this chapter is that it is also a key to understanding *Blade Runner* as philosophy.

Conclusion

We can now return to an important issue mentioned at the start of this chapter. If the foregoing argument is cogent, then whether a work of fiction like *Blade Runner* is a work of philosophy is distinct from (but not necessarily unaffected by) its creator's intentions. If the director of a film tells us that they intended their creation to advance a philosophical thesis or perspective and even tells us what that thesis or perspective is, we must take that information seriously, even if we think they failed. However (and as counterintuitive as it might seem), a director's *denial* that their film is in any way philosophical does not *ipso facto* entail that it is devoid of philosophical significance. Prima facie, the creative agents responsible for a film are bona fide authorities regarding what they *intended* to achieve with their film. They are not, however, authorities with regard to what they *did* achieve with their film. (See Shanahan 2019 for discussion of this point.)

Consequently, its director's intentions notwithstanding, *Blade Runner* is, indeed, a philosophical film. By presenting the replicants as struggling with some of the same fundamental concerns that inform human experience, it encourages us to *see* the world through the eyes of others who are truly *other* and to thereby acquire insights that might otherwise remain less easily accessible to us. What Philip K. Dick said about science fiction (SF) is equally true of some films: "SF makes what would otherwise be an intellectual abstraction concrete; it does this by locating the idea in a specific time and place, which requires the inventing of that time and place" (Dick 1980, p. 44). By situating ideas within specific contexts, films allow us to explore the implications of those ideas in ways that are difficult to do with words alone. Through engagement with images, we are able to imagine a world other than our own. This act of imagination can be remarkably fruitful.

The French existential phenomenologist Maurice Merleau-Ponty observed in a lecture in Paris in 1945 that films can be so gripping in their presentation of humans' experience because, like us, they involve "consciousness thrown into the world, subject to the gaze of others and learning from them what it is" (Merleau-Ponty 1945, p. 58). By perceiving cinematic replicants that are like but not quite identical to ourselves, we can learn something about what it means to be us.

References

Andersen, Nathan. 2005. Is film the alien other to philosophy? Philosophy *as* film in Mulhall's *On Film*. *Film and Philosophy* 9: 1–11.

Barad, Judith. 2009. *Blade Runner* and Sartre: The boundaries of humanity. In *The philosophy of Neo-Noir*, ed. M.T. Conard, 21–34. Lexington: University of Kentucky Press.

Bukatman, Scott. 2012. *Blade runner*. 2nd ed. London: Palgrave Macmillan.

Carroll, Noel. 2006. Philosophizing through the moving image: The case of Serene Velocity. *Journal of Aesthetics and Art Criticism* 64 (1): 173–185.

Cavell, Stanley. 1979. *The world viewed: Reflections on the ontology of film*, enlarged edition. Cambridge, MA: Harvard University Press.

Coplan, Amy, and David Davies, eds. 2015. *Blade runner*. London: Routledge.

Descartes, René. 1998. *Discourse on method, and Meditations on first philosophy*. 4th ed. - Indianapolis: Hackett.
Dick, Philip K. 1980. Philip K. Dick on philosophy: A brief interview. In *The shifting realities of Philip K. Dick: Selected literary and philosophical writings*, ed. L. Sutin, 44–47. New York: Vintage Books, 1995.
Francavilla, Joseph. 1997. The android as Doppelgänger. In *Retrofitting Blade Runner: Issues in Ridley Scott's Blade Runner and Philip K. Dick's Do androids dream of electric sheep?* ed. Judith B. Kerman, 2nd ed., 4–15. Bowling Green: Bowling Green University Press.
Kerman, Judith B., ed. 1997. *Retrofitting Blade Runner: Issues in Ridley Scott's Blade Runner and Philip K. Dick's Do androids dream of electric sheep?* 2nd ed. Bowling Green: Bowling Green University Press.
Knapp, Laurence F., and Andrea F. Kulas, eds. 2005. *Ridley Scott: Interviews*. Jackson: University Press of Mississippi.
Kolb, William M. 1997. Script to screen: *Blade Runner* in perspective. In *Retrofitting Blade Runner: Issues in Ridley Scott's Blade Runner and Philip K. Dick's Do androids dream of electric sheep?* ed. J.B. Kerman, 2nd ed., 132–153. Bowling Green: Bowling Green University Press.
Livingston, Paisley. 2006. Theses on cinema as philosophy. *Journal of Aesthetics and Art Criticism* 64 (1): 11–18.
Locke, John. 1690. *An essay concerning human understanding*, 2 Vols. New York: Dover Publications, 1959.
Merleau-Ponty, Maurice. 1945. The film and the new psychology. In *Sense and non-sense*, 48–59. Trans. H. Dreyfus, and P. Dreyfus. Evanston: Northwestern University Press, 1964.
Morrison, Rachela. 1990. *Casablanca* meets *Star Wars*: The Blakean dialectics of *Blade Runner*. *Literature Film Quarterly* 18 (1): 2–10.
Mulhall, Stephen. 1994. Picturing the human (Body and soul): A reading of *Blade Runner*. *Film and Philosophy* 1: 87–104.
———. 2015. *On film*. 3rd ed. London: Routledge.
Pate, Anthony. 2009. Nietzsche's Übermensch in the hyperreal flux: An analysis of *Blade Runner, Fight Club*, and *Miami Vice*. Dissertations and Graduate Research Overview, Paper 15. http://digitalcommons.ric.edu/etd/15. Accessed 12 Aug 2019.
Peary, Danny. 1984. Directing *Alien* and *Blade Runner*: An interview with Ridley Scott. In *Ridley Scott: Interviews*, ed. L.F. Knapp and A.F. Kulas, 42–55. Jackson: University Press of Mississippi, 2005.
Redmond, Sean. 2008. *Studying Blade Runner*. Leighton Buzzard: Auteur.
Russell, Bruce. 2000. The philosophical limits of film. *Film and Philosophy* 4 (Special Interest Edition on the Films of Woody Allen): 163–167.
Salamoff, Paul J. 2018. Why the theatrical cut is the truest version of *Blade Runner*. In *The Cyberpunk Nexus: Exploring the Blade Runner universe*, ed. L. Tambone and J. Bongiorno, 100–110. Edwardsville: Sequart.
Sammon, Paul M. 1982. The arts. *Omni* 4 (8): 24, 140.
———. 2017. *Future Noir: The making of Blade Runner*, revised & updated edition. New York: HarperCollins.
Shanahan, Timothy. 2014. *Philosophy and Blade Runner*. London: Palgrave Macmillan.
———. 2019. What am I to you? In *Blade Runner 2049: A philosophical exploration*, ed. T. Shanahan and P. Smart, 228–247. London: Routledge.
Smith, Murray. 2006. Film, art, argument, and ambiguity. *Journal of Aesthetics and Art Criticism* 64 (1): 33–42.
Wartenberg, Thomas E. 2006. Beyond mere illustration: How films can be philosophy. *Journal of Aesthetics and Art Criticism* 64 (1): 19–32.

Up in the Air as Philosophy: Buddhism and the Middle Path

42

Leigh Duffy

Contents

Introduction	1006
Ryan's Story	1006
Siddhartha's Story	1009
Zen Buddhism	1012
Ryan's Not-So-Buddhist Life	1014
Ryan's Chance at Enlightenment	1015
Ryan's Suffering	1017
Awakening	1018
Conclusion	1022
References	1023

Abstract

Up in the Air was favored by critics for its sympathetic look at the people most affected by the financial crisis of the late 2000s. The main character, Ryan Bingham, is the messenger of their losses and so is surrounded by people suffering. Yet, Ryan seems to have found a way to avoid suffering himself: he lives a life without any of his own relationships, without a home, and without any attachments to any things at all. He seems to have embraced the Buddhist philosophy that to rid oneself of suffering, one must rid oneself of attachments. While Ryan knows this on a cerebral level, he doesn't yet understand it. Through his journey, Ryan learns what Zen Buddhism teaches about suffering, but he also learns that to really understand these truths, one has to experience them. Like in *Siddhartha*, the novel used by many to explain these Buddhist truths, Ryan has to experience both nonattachment and attachment in order to find his way to a middle path and to have the opportunity to live a better life.

L. Duffy (✉)
SUNY Buffalo State College, Buffalo, NY, USA
e-mail: duffylk@buffalostate.edu

> **Keywords**
>
> *Up in the Air* · Buddhism · Zen Buddhism · Middle Path · Suffering · Dukkha · Attachment · Theoretical knowledge · Experiential knowledge · Experience · Nonattachment · Four noble truths · Eightfold path · Deliverance from suffering · *Siddhartha* · Pain · Meaning · Enlightenment · Wisdom · Prajñā · Relationships · Om

Introduction

When *Up in the Air* was released at the end of 2009, it was cheered by critics, described as "a humanist document of today's times" (*Times of India* review) and lauded for its sympathetic look at the people most affected by the financial crisis of 2007–2008. However, it is also a story about a man who benefits from that crisis and from the suffering of those affected by it. Ryan Bingham's story takes him on a journey to understand what it is to be human and why it is that we undergo pain and suffering. While he understands many of the Buddhist principles of suffering (dukkha) at the beginning of the film, he must go through the experiences we see in *Up in the Air* in order to truly understand them. That lesson itself is a key part of Zen Buddhist philosophy – true wisdom comes from experience.

Interestingly, Ryan Bingham's story is similar to that of *Siddhartha*, Herman Hesse's tale of a man's path toward enlightenment. Siddhartha sets out on a journey to understand the metaphysical principles about the world, but finds that true enlightenment is something very different than what he initially sought. Through Siddhartha's journey and experiences, Hesse explains Buddhist philosophy. It will therefore be revealing to compare the two stories. As this chapter shall show, the principles that are most important to Buddhist philosophy, particularly those of Zen Buddhism, are the very lessons Ryan finally learns in the end of *Up in the Air*.

Director, Jason Reitman, said "(t)he movie is about the examination of a philosophy—what if you decided to live hub to hub, with nothing, with nobody?" (Schuker 2009, n.p.). A misconception about Zen Buddhism is that this is the final goal: to live without any attachments to anything at all. As we shall see, both Ryan and Siddhartha find out that, not only is this not the point, it is not even possible. True enlightenment comes not from disconnecting from the world, but being a part of it.

Ryan's Story

Ryan Bingham works for Career Transition Counseling, a company based in Omaha, Nebraska, but is hired by companies all over the United States to do the dirty work of firing their employees when downsizing. This means Ryan spends most of his time away from their home base and has perfected the art of traveling simply. Ryan also believes there is an art to his work and takes great pride in his ability to make people see the silver lining in being let go from their jobs, which, in some cases, are lifelong careers. His tag line is, "Anyone who built an empire or changed the world sat where you are right now. And it's because they sat there that they were able to do it."

Ryan's side hustle is as a motivational speaker. His message is to downsize your life in order to truly live it freely. He asks his audiences to imagine a backpack on their shoulders and fill it with everything in their lives – their knickknacks, clothes, furniture, apartment or house, pictures, car, etc. Imagine the weight of the backpack and the feel of the straps cutting into your shoulders. This keeps us from moving, from living. He goes on to say that the relationships in our lives are the heaviest components as they come with negotiations, compromises, and secrets. Ryan believes that human beings are not meant to carry all that weight around. He tells his audience that, "moving is living; the slower we move, the faster we die."

Ryan lives his life true to this philosophy. He has no home per se. He rents an apartment in Omaha, yes, but he spends about "43 miserable days" in it a year. And the apartment can hardly be said to be *his*, as there is nothing of him in it. It's furnished as sparsely as the hotel rooms in which he spends the rest of his time; even the refrigerator is stocked mainly with airplane size bottles of booze. In fact, Ryan says his home is in the sky, *Up in the Air*, where he spends most of his time and where he seems to be truly happy. He is constantly on the move (moving is living after all), bouncing from one small American city to another, with only his small roller suitcase in tow. Even the suitcase is sparsely packed. In fact, when he ends up traveling with newly hired Natalie (more on her in a moment), he buys her a newer and smaller bag right in the airport because the suitcase she is currently using is *luggage*, as Ryan describes it, and it slows her down. He downsizes her suitcase the way he has downsized his own life and the way he helps the companies that hire him downsize their workforce.

Not only has Ryan gotten rid of excess *things* in his life, he also has let go of the people in his life. There is no one in his Omaha apartment waiting for him. His two sisters are vague characters in his life in the beginning of the movie. Julie, the younger sister, is about to get married, so they are in contact with him at this point, but as we come to find later on, he hasn't "been there." His other sister, Kara, tells him, "basically you don't exist to us." When we first meet Ryan, this revelation wouldn't have affected him. When pressed about marriage by Natalie, she asks whether he really wants to "die alone." Ryan responds, "make no mistake: we all die alone." Finally, the casual relationship he begins with Alex, a woman he meets on the road, is purely sexual with no attachments and no commitments. It serves his needs without weighing him down.

However, this all changes as Natalie weaves herself into his life. Natalie Keener, a young Cornell graduate, comes to Career Transition Counseling to change their way of doing business. "Glocal" is the way of the future, she says. Her mission is to make it possible for the company – and therefore Ryan – to do business entirely in Omaha by making their global business local through video conferencing. Ryan is tasked with taking Natalie on the road with him so she can learn what it is that they do in order to better help the company bring that work "home."

The other important change to Ryan's life is Alex. They start a very casual, mutual relationship. Alex describes herself as just like Ryan "only with a vagina." "I'm the woman you don't have to worry about," she says, because she isn't asking Ryan for anything. In other words: no negotiations, no compromises, no secrets. This relationship bears nothing that can cause him the suffering that the weight of a relationship would normally cause.

Both women challenge his views. Natalie pesters him about not wanting to get married, about not giving Alex a real chance, and about his detached lifestyle. Alex challenges Ryan because he starts to fall for her. They have some meaningful moments as he shares with her a bit of his family, his childhood, and himself. But Alex does indeed have a secret. When Ryan finally decides to make Alex a part of his life and shows up, unannounced, on her doorstep in Chicago, he comes to find that she has a life here – a *"real* life" with a husband and children. Ryan seems both stunned and a bit heartbroken. Alex can't understand why Ryan reacts the way he does. She thought they had an understanding of what their relationship was and that they felt the same way. "You are an escape," she tells him, "a parenthesis."

Previously, Alex had told Ryan that she can't be the way she is with him at home. and now we know what she meant. At home, she is a wife and mother. With Ryan, she is free and uninhibited. After their first encounter, she describes their whole relationship as "cheap." But for Ryan, what was once cheap has become something more. Ryan had replied, "there's nothing cheap about loyalty," and again, we get a real sense of what that means in this final encounter. With loyalty comes attachment and with attachment comes suffering. There's nothing cheap about it when it might cost you everything.

After Ryan realizes the truth about Alex, something else significant happens in his story. One of the women Natalie fired (with Ryan there as a guide) took her own life. She threatened to when they met with her, but Ryan dismissed it as just something people say in times like these. Natalie quits, and Ryan suddenly finds himself back in his old life – up in the air and without the weight of Natalie or Alex dragging him down.

However, now there's been a shift. The movie ends with Ryan staring at the departure board in the airport. Earlier in the movie, when Ryan tells Natalie how he's saving for 10 million miles, Natalie is shocked that he's not saving them *for* anything. He's not saving to go to Hawaii or the South of France as Natalie would. The miles *are the point*. Natalie had said that if she had that many miles, she would "show up at an airport, look at the destination board, pick a place, and go." It isn't clear if this is what Ryan is doing at the end of the movie. He still has plenty of miles (nine million after he transferred one million to his sister and brother-in-law so they could travel around the world), and so he *could* pick a destination and go. But it might also be the case that he's looking at the board for the gate to his pre-booked flight to his next job.

Director Jason Reitman leaves the ending unclear in this way, but it doesn't matter much where Ryan is actually going. He is still alone, and he's still without a home or a metaphorical backpack full of stuff. However, he's different now; he's experienced what it is to put something real in the backpack, and he has a new sense of what it is to be a human carrying around that backpack. The point of the story was not for Ryan to meet Alex, fall in love, settle down, and abandon his old ways. He ends up exactly where we first met him, but there's a shift in his *experience* of his life that is necessary for him to understand the Buddhist principles he preaches. While Ryan used to speak about nonattachment and ridding your life of things because of the suffering they can cause, he now truly understands what that is like. He is left with the opportunity to live according to the Middle Path.

To fully understand how Ryan's story reveals this Buddhist truth, however, it will be necessary to see how his story mirrors that of Siddhartha.

Siddhartha's Story

Siddhartha, a fictional story based on the life and teachings of the Buddha, teaches the same lesson. When we first meet Siddhartha, the Brahmin's son, he is a young man, well-educated, with the potential to become a "great sage and priest, a prince among the Brahmins" (Hesse 1999, p. 3). He is described as being loved by all – his parents, his friends, "the young Brahmin daughters" (Hesse 1999, p. 4), and his teachers. They have high expectations for him as he does for himself. He is intellectually and spiritually curious and becomes frustrated by the superficiality of the rituals he participates in. He yearns for a greater meaning to his spirituality, for a true understanding of the divine and his connection to it. For this reason, he leaves his home and his family to live among the samanas, a group of nomadic ascetics who believe that self-deprivation and isolation will bring true enlightenment.

Siddhartha gives up everything. His metaphorical backpack is completely empty. He leaves behind those who love him, and while his friend, Govinda, does end up travelling with him, he is ready to leave him behind as well. Siddhartha has no clothes, no home, and no money. He lives off the charity of strangers, but can go days without eating anything. In fact, he believes his greatest skills are being able to wait and to fast. He has no home and so for him, living is indeed moving.

Siddhartha looks down on people with attachments. Siddhartha expresses disgust at their need for goods and for relationships. His one goal at this point is "to become empty – empty of thirst, empty of desire, empty of dreams, empty of joy and sorrow" (Hesse 1999, p. 13). In emptying his life (his backpack), Siddhartha lets go of the things that could cause him suffering. Without needing these things, he cannot feel the pain of their absence.

But soon Siddhartha leaves this life behind when he hears of the enlightened one, the Buddha, who has supposedly reached nirvana. Siddhartha and Govinda embark on a pilgrimage to study with the Buddha, but Siddhartha believes he does not have much to learn as he already knows the truths about suffering. However, when he hears it from the holy man, he hears it in a calm and clear speech, a soft and firm voice, and Siddhartha feels that he has woken from a dream. Now, he becomes attached to making sense of the teachings and he cannot.

Siddhartha struggles to make sense of the Buddha's teaching. He finds flaws in the logic and challenges the Buddha to explain his views.

The Buddha kindly tells him that he is not after the truth necessarily, but deliverance from suffering. He warns him about the fight over words. The goal is not to explain the world to those who thirst for understanding. The goal is deliverance from suffering. This is the point of Buddhism: to understand suffering and to work toward alleviating that suffering. Siddhartha has heard these words, but he has yet to really *know* what they mean. At this point, he has wanted what he has not had (enlightenment, understanding), and he has been without basic needs (food and shelter), but he has not really *suffered*.

Siddhartha then leaves the Buddha and Govinda behind and goes to live among the people, the "child people" as he calls them. He sees this world as beautiful and simple. He enters a city where people care about clothes, food, perfume, jewels, and money. He meets Kamala and is enchanted by her beauty. She teaches him how to be like the child people – what to wear, how to do his hair, how to talk. She teaches him about the pleasures of the senses in food, drink, and sex. But Siddhartha doesn't form attachments to the things of this world, as much as he is fascinated by them. He is an observer rather than a participant, and as much as he has seen suffering in this world, he hasn't yet experienced it.

The experiences he has had here aren't meaningful. Hesse describes Siddhartha as feeling "something like happiness" (Hesse 1999, p. 71), but it's not meaningful. Siddhartha desires something more. He doesn't yet know what it is like to lose something that is very dear to him. He doesn't yet know real suffering, and he comes to see that this life has not given him what he was looking for either.

Siddhartha now has nothing to live for and he's lost. He is ready to end it all, when he hears the sound of "Om" in the river. Om is said to be the sound of the universe, the sound of the unity of all things, the metaphysical truth of reality. Siddhartha finds deep comfort in this and drifts into a deep, dreamless sleep. Previously, throughout the story, he had many meaningful dreams full of dramatic imagery; but this new dreamless sleep allows him a rest, after which he can truly *awake*. When he does, an old ferryman whom he had met years ago takes him in. Vasudeva offers him a life of true simplicity. They do not fast, but they do not indulge either, and Siddhartha begins his final chapter toward the Middle Path. Siddhartha no longer shuns a life of things, but he does not chase them. He works, he eats, he sleeps, and he listens to the river. Vasudeva creates a space where Siddhartha can really understand what he was taught years ago.

Siddhartha has almost found enlightenment, almost realized the Middle Path of Buddhism. Then Kamala reappears in his life. She and her young son are making their own pilgrimage to see the dying Buddha. Kamala is bitten by a snake and dies, and Siddhartha must take in the young man, who he learns is his son. As difficult as the boy is, as challenging and demanding as he can be, Siddhartha loves him. The ferryman tells Siddhartha that he is not tough enough with his son, and that his love is keeping him from parenting him well; but Siddhartha is so attached to the boy, he doesn't know how to be a parent. He admits that while this is suffering like he's never experienced before, he wouldn't trade it for anything.

Siddhartha has finally become like the child people: "suffering for someone else, loving someone else, lost in love, a fool for love" (Hesse 1999, p. 107).

The attachment that is the cause of his pain and suffering is also caused by something genuine – a real deep love for the boy, which he'd been incapable of until now. It is a strange sensation that causes him suffering, and yet he says he is blissful and "somewhat richer" (Hesse 1999, p. 107). The more time goes by, and the surlier his son becomes, Siddhartha realizes that the boy needs to be back in his home. This is for the best but he is heartbroken nonetheless.

This is Siddhartha's enlightenment. He comes to realize the Middle Path: that to live is not to avoid life as he did with the samanas, nor is it to indulge in the sensory life, forming more and more attachments to things that don't really matter. To live *is* to suffer. That is the first of the Buddha's teachings. Siddhartha has come to realize what this really *means*. For him, suffering was not in losing money or in fasting for days or weeks at a time. In fact, when asked about his "hard times" when he was without clothes, shelter, or food, Siddhartha had replied that these are not hard times because they are voluntary. The pain of losing his son is the sort of suffering that the Buddha describes in the first noble truth. It was not Siddhartha's choice. He was attached to something he could not keep. Losing that relationship causes him to know the real suffering of being human.

Siddhartha did not understand that the Buddha's teaching was not a path to escape *from* this world, but a path to deliver ourselves from suffering while *in* this world. Siddhartha's understanding at the end of the book is not merely philosophical wisdom. To understand what it is to be human, he had to *be* human. He had to open himself to the world of attachments and let himself experience what that is really like. When he finally does so, he also sees people differently. He understands them now and sees them "more warmly, more curiously, more sympathetically" (Hesse 1999, p. 113).

The Middle Path so central to Buddhism (and "reminiscent of Aristotle's Golden Mean" [Gupta 2012, p. 81]) is a life between self-deprivation and self-indulgence. The Buddha rejected the rituals seen in Siddhartha's youth as useless but also the self-mortification of the samanas as demeaning (Gupta 2012, p. 81). Extremes are to be avoided, but that includes the extreme of nonattachment to *all* things, including ideas – and in particular the idea that we need to move beyond this world.

At the end of the book, Hesse says that Siddhartha "stopped fighting with destiny, stopped suffering" (Hesse 1999, p. 119). The destiny he means here is not some particular path for Siddhartha – to be a great priest, e.g. – but the destiny we all have in this world as conscious beings. The suffering he has in mind is the unnecessary suffering Siddhartha had caused himself by searching for something beyond this world. Siddhartha will continue to experience pain and loss – that is part of the human experience. But by being a part of the world, by learning to "feel and breathe the oneness at every moment, in the midst of life" (Hesse 1999, p. 114), he can stop causing himself the unnecessary suffering of longing to be out of this world, to achieve some state of nirvana. ("Nirvana," Siddhartha realizes, is merely a word.) As a part of the world, he can come to experience it for all that it is without shunning it, lessening his attachments and aversions while not eliminating them entirely.

Zen Buddhism

Ryan's story and Siddhartha's story have many similarities, but in order to see Ryan's story as a Buddhist story, more ought to be said about Buddhism. There are three main branches of Buddhism: Mahayana, Theravada, and Vajrayana. While they all differ in their views about enlightenment, and in how literally they take the Buddha's teachings, they do have one thing in common: they all maintain the four noble truths as the core to their philosophical views about the world. But what distinguishes Zen Buddhism, a type of Mahayana Buddhism, from other types of Buddhism is the belief that enlightenment is accessible to anyone. Zen sees the Buddha's teachings as a guide to how to live and how to help others find deliverance from suffering. Zen Buddhism puts the focus on experiential understanding, rather than on theoretical knowledge of the truths of the world.

What are the four noble truths of Buddhism?

1. There is suffering (dukkha).
2. There is an origination or a cause of suffering.
3. There is a cessation of suffering.
4. There is a path toward the cessation of suffering (Sidertis 2019).

Life is painful – in birth, in life, in death, and in disease, there will be pain. In order to cure the pain, we need to know the cause. The cause of suffering is desire, thirst, or attachments (tṛṣṇā). Attachments result in frustrations and disappointments. The complete cessation of suffering would be nirvana – freedom from the chains of rebirth, a cycle that repeatedly casts one into a life of suffering. The path toward nirvana is the eightfold path of the Buddha.

All of the philosophical teachings of Zen Buddhism are interconnected. To understand the causes of suffering, it is important to also understand that Zen Buddhism holds that everything in the world is impermanent. There is a unity or a oneness to the world in terms of the very "stuff" that it is, but the variations or the manifestations of this oneness are all temporary. This breaks from other traditional Eastern philosophical views (Sāṃkhya philosophy, for example), which hold that everything in the *physical* world is temporary but that there is also some other type of existence that is permanent: a divine Self that continues to exist after death (Gupta 2012, p. 134). Zen Buddhism holds the doctrine of the nonself or anattā. There is no self if a Self is conceived as a permanent being.

In Buddhism, suffering is caused by ignorance of these truths and attachments to things that are impermanent. Not only do we desire permanence where there is none, we are also ignorant to the fact that *all* of the world is impermanent. Our attachments to things that cannot last – by definition – cause us to suffer. Siddhartha wanted his relationship with his son to last, and it caused him suffering when his son left. The employees Ryan fires suffer when they realize that an identity they were attached to (it is *who they are* in their eyes, after all) was only temporary and never really theirs to begin with.

There is a path toward the cessation of suffering however. In *Siddhartha*, the Buddha says that this is the real point of his teachings. He is less concerned with the philosophical truths as he is with how to exist in a world that is full of suffering and to experience less suffering. Siddhartha had worried about this as a flaw in the Buddha's teachings. It seems that we cannot both exist and find deliverance from suffering if to exist is to suffer. The Buddha does not answer with logic because whether or not the philosophy is possible *is not the point* (Suzuki 1970, p. 46). Perhaps deliverance from suffering is truly impossible, but there is a path *toward it*, and that is what matters. This is the third noble truth.

The fourth noble truth gives that path, and it includes eight ways of behaving in the world. Notice that the path is not a way to escape the world; rather it explains how to be *in the world*. Both Ryan and Siddhartha need to learn this lesson as well. They both thought they could let go of their attachments and move beyond this world, either out of it into nirvana or up above it in a plane. In reality, of course, there was much more for them to do.

The eightfold path includes the ethical practices of right action, right speech, and right living; the epistemic goals of right view and right intentions; and the meditative goals of right effort, right concentration, and right mindfulness. "Right" is often used to translate the Pāli word "sammā" (Gupta and Gowans both use the word "right"), but the Sanskrit dictionary defines "sammā" as "equal in size or number" (http://sanskritdictionary.com). As a verb, "sammā" means to measure out or to make equal in measuring. Rather than thinking of the eightfold path as a description of the *right* way to be as opposed to the *wrong* way to be, we may think of it as a prescription to be more mindful in the measuring out of our actions and our words.

Indeed, Zen Buddhism's main methods toward achieving the goals of non-discriminatory wisdom (prajñā) and compassion are meditation and koans (riddles or puzzles designed to help the person contemplating them come to a deeper understanding of Zen Buddhist philosophy). Meditation is a way of cultivating mindfulness or a focused awareness on the present moment. Applied to the eightfold path, meditation is an exercise in becoming more intentional in how we measure out our words and actions.

To become more measured in these eight ways is to simply become more aware of one's own life and more careful about how one acts in the world. It is to see what attachments one might have, where one is suffering unnecessarily, where one is causing suffering, and where one might be able to find a way out of suffering. To follow the eightfold path is to pay more attention to life, to wake up, and to see the world anew. This is exactly how Hesse describes Siddhartha, and it is essentially what happens to Ryan in the end of *Up in the Air*.

Finally, there are three pillars in Zen: the Buddha, the Dharma, and the Sangha or the enlightened one, the teaching, and the community. The community is "the harmony of practice" (Biksbazen 2002, p. 77). While Zen includes the practice of quiet meditation, it is important that there is a community of people who come together to practice. Even in something as quiet and solitary-seeming as meditation, one needs other people. Ryan will come to realize this too. Even in his solitary-seeming life, he needs others.

Ryan's Not-So-Buddhist Life

With both Ryan and Siddhartha's story understood, and Zen Buddhism explained, we can now see how *Up in the Air* teaches us a deeper Zen Buddhist truth. Siddhartha's story is meant to explain Buddhism and the Middle Path as a way to live in this world with less suffering. Ryan's story is similar, and having learned about suffering through his own experiences, he is left with the opportunity to now choose the Middle Path, rather than to avoid life as he had been doing.

Ryan and Siddhartha both begin with a philosophical view on life that seems to be Buddhist in nature. In one of the first motivational speeches Ryan gives, he asks the audience to imagine setting their full backpacks on fire. He describes it as "exhilarating," and it's what he says he does every day. Like Siddhartha, he gives up the "stuff" of his life in order to live without those attachments and the pain he knows they can cause. There is something true and consistent with Buddhist thought in his words, but he lacks the compassion of the Buddha.

Ryan also seems to have a theoretical understanding of the world consistent with Buddhist teachings. In a deleted part of a scene (but found in the original screenplay), Ryan tells Alex a story of a near-death experience when he was a teenager. Having almost drowned, he wakes to find himself on a helicopter being airlifted to a hospital. In the screenplay he says, "(m)y parents taught me we lived in the best place on Earth, but now I could see the world was really just one place and comparing didn't really make much sense" (Reitman and Turner, p. 67).

Ryan realizes there is so much more outside his small world of existence (in this case, Northern Wisconsin) and that it is all a part of a greater oneness. Seeing the unity of the world without comparisons is seeing the world with the non-discriminatory wisdom that one tries to cultivate in Zen Buddhism. Eager to do this, he too leaves his childhood home, thirsty for more. Like Siddhartha Ryan pities the people, like his sisters and their significant others, who remain attached to the things he voluntarily leaves behind.

Finally, Ryan seems to have a Zen approach to his travels as well. While Natalie would work toward miles *in order to* be able to take a trip to the south of France, Ryan says the miles are the point. It seems he understands the idea of nonattachment and the idea that the journey matters more than the destination. Zen teaches that what matters in life is not success but finding meaning in the journey to becoming successful (Suzuki 1970, p. 122).

But Ryan doesn't really understand what he preaches to his audiences or what he tells Natalie. Not much of his backstory is shared, but when he talks about his parents and grandparents, there isn't any reason to suspect any traumatic experience in their passing that would make him wary to form deep relationships. The story of his near-death experience is the only one he shares when trying to answer Alex's questions about the backpack. It doesn't seem that there is any particular loss that would inform this philosophy. Rather, he simply saw emptying the backpack as a way to live more freely.

It becomes even more clear that Ryan doesn't really get what it is to suffer as he interacts with the unfortunate people who lose their jobs.

He just feeds them empty platitudes in order to prevent anyone from causing a scene in the office. Indeed, Ryan's motivational speaking expertise comes out when he gives his lines. In one particular case, he says that he's giving the person an opportunity to start over and follow his dreams. Ryan doesn't get it. On a very superficial level, he knows what he is doing: he tells Natalie their job is to make "limbo tolerable" and tells his boss, Craig, that what they do is brutal and leaves people devastated. But it doesn't seem he's ever experienced limbo or devastation in a way that he can really understand what the people he is firing are going through.

Bob, for example, is a middle-aged father of two, who was making $90,000 a year (from a starting salary of $27,000). When he's informed he's being let go, Bob shows Ryan and Natalie pictures of his young kids. Ryan does what Ryan believes he does best: he tries to "sell it" to him. He tells Bob that kids look up to athletes because they follow their dreams. If Bob desires the love and respect of his children, he's got an opportunity right now to earn it, by following his youthful dream of becoming a chef.

This "silver lining" comes from a man who has no mortgage, no children to feed, and, in particular, no child with asthma who needs her father's healthcare. $90,000 a year and benefits is no small loss when taken in this context. It's easy for someone who has no obligations to another human being to see this as liberating – "exhilarating" even – but for someone like Bob, this is real suffering. Ryan's lack of home and family isn't suffering for him because (like Siddhartha) it was his choice. Bob hasn't chosen to give it all up and so Ryan cannot relate to that kind of suffering.

Another terminated employee says, "I don't know how you can live with yourself but I'm sure you'll find a way as the rest of us are suffering." This unnamed man says he won't be able to take his kids to Chuck E Cheese this weekend or to even put gas in the car. These are things that Ryan would encourage him to dump from his backpack anyway, but for this man, this is his real life. These are the things that matter to him. Ryan is completely unable to understand that kind of suffering – the suffering that *Ryan* has delivered to him – but, as the man says, Ryan will find a way to live with himself despite that.

Finally, even Ryan's approach to his miles misses the point of Zen Buddhism. While he says there is no goal, nothing he is trying to achieve, he doesn't see that he is attached. Natalie points out that 10 million is "just a number" and that it doesn't have any *meaning* to it. Ryan takes this personally, reacting in such a way that it's clear that the number itself has actually become a goal and something to which he has formed a strong attachment. Ryan might have given up all things and people in his life, but that doesn't necessarily mean that he has given up all *attachments*.

Ryan's Chance at Enlightenment

Like Siddhartha early on in the novel, Ryan early in the movie can speak about suffering and how to avoid it, but he doesn't understand what that is like. It's only through his own experience of forming real attachments and having real loss that he's able to have that kind of experience so important to Zen Buddhism.

Alex and his relationship with her clearly have an effect on him, but while he's exploring a relationship with Alex and what that might mean, Ryan simultaneously has another affective relationship with Natalie.

Natalie comes to CTC in order to solve the problem of an inflated travel budget. She believes that not only is this good for CTC (saving money) but also for the employees who are on the road for CTC. She tells them "No more Christmases in a hotel in Tulsa...No more hours lost to weather delays...You get to come home." This puts Ryan in a panic. He doesn't have a home to which to come back, nor does he want one. His home is in the air and she threatens to take that away from him. To try to persuade Craig that this is a terrible idea, he says that Natalie cannot revolutionize a business she doesn't even understand. So Craig sends Natalie out with Ryan to learn the ropes.

Natalie challenges Ryan in every way. She's a clumsy packer and therefore slows him down in the airport. She is arrogant and believes she has all the right lines for the employees they fire, but she runs into hostility, resistance, and, in one important instance, a threat of suicide. Ryan guides her but also must console her both through their difficult work and its aftermath as well as through her own personal drama. When Natalie's boyfriend breaks up with her through a text message, she's left sobbing in the hotel lobby in Ryan's very uncomfortable embrace. Natalie's very presence is a challenge, but she also verbally challenges his views on downsizing one's life: she bugs him about marriage generally and eventually about his relationship with Alex in particular. Eventually, Ryan comes to care for her as a mentor, as a protégée would, and paired with his new care for Alex, Ryan is left with doubt about his views and his life. Maybe relationships matter after all.

While Natalie seems to be Ryan's opposite in every way, Alex is just like him. She also travels much of the time for her work and seems to take the same satisfaction as Ryan does in customer rewards programs. She's "the woman you don't have to worry about." Ryan is taken by her casual attitude, her playful demeanor, and her willingness to take risks: together they crash the after-party of a tech conference, and at different points, Alex mentions having fooled around with one of her college professors, having only dated women for a time, and having joined the mile high club. (Ryan's facial expressions tell all.) As they continue to meet on the road, Ryan starts to feel something for Alex. He tells her he can't remember ever enjoying spending time with someone this much. One "morning-after," he says that he really likes her, and in another instance, he says this is the first time he's ever been interested in having a "plus-one." He's clearly beginning to form an attachment to whatever this relationship is.

Soon, Ryan learns that he is being pulled off the road for good. ("You're *grounded*," Craig tells him.) What is Ryan's future if he's grounded in Omaha, without the life he knows? His empty apartment will have to become his home, and it's already been made clear there's nothing for him there. After hearing the news, he and Natalie are about to board a plane back "home" when Ryan changes his mind very suddenly and gets another flight to meet Alex in Las Vegas. There, he invites her to his sister's wedding in Northern Wisconsin.

Perhaps Ryan is panicking or perhaps he's really falling in love. Either way, like Siddhartha, Ryan abandons one way of life for another, seeking out something he's been lacking all along. In a short time, Ryan goes from being "the backpack guy" – the guy with no attachments and no baggage" – to someone ready for a meaningful relationship. It's not like he dips a toe into this new water. He doesn't begin with a real date with Alex or with a friendship with Natalie. He dives right in and invites this woman he barely knows to meet a family who barely knows him. They spend a weekend in his hometown, and he shows Alex where he went to school and pictures of him on the high school wrestling and basketball teams. She spends time getting to know his sisters and their friends. Ryan invites her in to his past in a very intimate way. He's gone from one extreme to another.

Moreover, it seems his attitude about relationships in general has changed in an extreme way. When his sister's fiancé, Jim, gets cold feet on the day of the wedding, Ryan is charged with changing his mind. (He's the motivational speaker in the family, after all!) Jim has a mini-existential crisis – his life after marriage flashes before his eyes, and he sees kids, football games, college, grandchildren, and then death. Ryan is the *last* person who should be speaking to Jim, but something in him has changed, and he gives a speech about the value of relationships. At the end, he tells Jim that the most meaningful times of our lives are shared with other people. "Everyone needs a copilot."

The following scene is a montage of the events of the wedding day. Ryan and Alex look like a couple who have been together for a long time, getting ready for the wedding together, mingling with the guests together. Ryan seems to soften to his family as well. He offers to walk Julie down the aisle (but is denied) and dances with his other sister, Kara, at the reception. Again, Ryan has jumped right into a life that he would have rejected just weeks ago. Like Siddhartha, he had looked down on people who live in this way, giving speeches about the importance of ridding our lives of this very sort of baggage.

After the wedding, as they are ready to board their separate flights, Alex tells Ryan to call her when he gets lonely. He immediately calls out to her "I'm lonely." Ryan has gotten a taste of what he has been missing. He's come to understand why people fill their backpacks with people and relationships. They might cause grief, but that grief seems to be worth it, as Siddhartha learned when he met his son.

Ryan's Suffering

Ryan needs to have these experiences before he can know what it is to suffer. He has to form these bonds and give himself over to a relationship so he can experience real loss. Rather than being an observer to the pain and suffering of others as he has been in his role with CTC, he needs to be a part of it, to experience it himself so he can understand it in others. Ryan wasn't wrong in the beginning of the movie – attachments, especially to people, *do* cause suffering – but he didn't know what that meant until he experienced it. He hadn't lived the Middle Path yet.

Ryan has been invited to give his motivational speech to Goalquest 20, which is clearly a big deal for him. He's ready to give his usual spiel but he can't do it. He doesn't mean it anymore. He leaves the stage in a rush, and in the next scene he's boarding a plane to Chicago. When he shows up at Alex's door, he's obviously expecting the ending a viewer might expect from a Hollywood movie. But Alex doesn't rush into his arms; they don't get married and begin a life together. Alex, who is written in the screenplay to look angry and apologizing at the same time, pulls the door behind her so her husband and small children don't see what's going on outside. Ryan leaves in a hurry, and when Alex's husband asks who was at the door, she replies, "just someone who's lost."

She's not wrong; Ryan is lost. Like Siddhartha, he will have to let go of this extreme life and start again, but he doesn't know how. Ryan has quickly learned what it is like to experience the pain and suffering that comes from relationships, the pain of which he has warned others before. He takes this as rejection, even though Alex later calls him and leaves the door open to go back to their casual, no-strings-attached beginnings. However, whatever they "signed up for" in the beginning isn't what Ryan wants anymore. He tried to open himself to something "real" (he tells her he thought he was a part of her "real" life) and now feels the sting of that reality.

At this point, Ryan now knows suffering and loss. Rather than judging those who suffer as foolish, he becomes more sympathetic to those people. When he learns that the woman Natalie fired has taken her own life and then finds that Natalie quit, Ryan doesn't seem surprised. He *does* seem surprisingly *concerned* about Natalie. Ryan also, surprisingly, *doesn't* seem thrilled when Craig tells him he's going back on the road. It is similar to Siddhartha's experience when he leaves Kamala. He is not sure what will happen next, but knows his life with her is over. Ryan too isn't sure what to do next, but he's sure that this life he thought he could begin with Alex is over. Siddhartha returns to a simpler life, similar to the one he had earlier in the novel, but he doesn't go to the extreme of being homeless and constantly fasting. Ryan too must return to something vaguely familiar to his previous life, but now that he's had these experiences, it won't be the same life, and it must not be in either extreme he's experienced. The Middle Path is his to choose. Rather than shunning the things and people of his life, he can choose to embrace them, but at the same time, he must be aware that with such an embrace will come the sort of pain he has recently experienced. He can choose to live in the world but with the understanding that living involves suffering.

Awakening

Ryan and Siddhartha have similar journeys, but their stories do not conclude in the same way. At the end of *Siddhartha,* his dear friend Govinda returns and describes Siddhartha as peculiar but wise, a saint, like the Sublime one. Govinda kisses his friend's forehead and has an experience similar to one Siddhartha had earlier, where he sees the unity of the world and is overwhelmed by love and reverence. He knows that Siddhartha has finally found peace in a way that Govinda has not yet. Siddhartha's story is ready to come to its conclusion.

On the other hand, at the end of *Up in the Air*, it is not clear what will become of Ryan. He is surely no saint, and the viewer is not left with feelings of love or reverence due to his story. Still, there has been a shift in his understanding of life that is similar to the shift Siddhartha experienced. Through his experiences, Ryan has come to a similar experiential understanding of life and the world around him in a way that he never would have been able to without those experiences. He comes to understand what he preached at the beginning of the movie in a much more personal way. He learns that suffering doesn't come from the things and people he has pushed away but from our attachments to them.

In the screenplay, Reitman writes that in the final scene, Ryan "looks like he did in the opening of the film. Maybe even wearing the same clothes. Something is different though." Ryan has to go back up in the air, but he's not running from life anymore. He knows now what life is – including all the pain and suffering – but he also now knows the difference between living that life alone and having a copilot. While it's not clear what path Ryan will choose after this scene or whether he's traveling for his own sake or for work, what is clear is the shift in his understanding.

Primarily, Ryan has a new understanding of attachment and suffering. He learns why people fill their backpacks. Ryan had thought that filling the backpack would cause suffering because of its weight, but he comes to learn that the suffering comes from having it empty. A full backpack is a full life and when those things that make us feel full are lost, the suffering is in the emptiness. When Ryan finally reaches this 10 million mile goal and the pilot comes to speak with him, it seems pointless to him. He can't remember what he wanted to say to the pilot even though he'd imagined that conversation dozens of times before. Compared to what he's experienced, this big moment in his life no longer seems so important.

Ryan has an opportunity to find the Middle Path now. Siddhartha's middle path is to not run from the world but also not to indulge in it either. He learned to live his life without attachments to sex, gambling, and *things* so as to lessen his suffering, but he also learned that the suffering that came from the attachment to his son was worth the experience he had in being a father. Ryan may not feel that the loss of Alex was "worth it" because of the time he had with her, but he does learn that there is a middle path between shunning the world and the people in it and filling the backpack to the brim. In the end, Ryan does let other people into his life. He writes a powerful letter of recommendation for Natalie, and he donates some of his miles to Julie and Jim so they can travel the world. Rather than seeing them as silly or looking down upon them as child people, he wants to support them in their pursuits of what matters *to them*.

Ryan also comes to a new understanding of right living. While he has been careful in measuring out what goes in his suitcase and his apartment and while he takes great care to measure out his reward points for all his loyalty programs, he's not been present in his *life*. These have been mere games, distractions that keep him from really living. They were goals in some loose sense of the word but never had any real meaning. Siddhartha too tried at these games. He gambled, but never really understood the emotional response others had to losing. He was an observer rather than a participant. Ryan spent his time observing the loss and suffering of those he had to fire, but until he felt real loss himself, he didn't know what that experience of being a human being suffering really is like. Ryan believed that "moving is living," but he didn't realize that moving kept him from experiencing life.

Again, it is the experiences that mattered and taught him these lessons. "Knowledge can be communicated but not wisdom" (Hesse 1999, p. 124). Both Siddhartha and Ryan were able to share their knowledge about attachments in the beginning of their stories, but they didn't have the wisdom of the four noble truths yet. No one could have given that wisdom because, as Zen maintains, to gain that wisdom is to experience it. What Ryan had at the beginning were just words to express something true, but not the truth. He knew that attachments would cause suffering, but he didn't yet have the experience of either attachments or of suffering. And it wasn't just Alex. Ryan formed an attachment to his way of life, and he saw suffering in his future when this was threatened. He had an attachment to 10 million miles but was disappointed when he met his goal.

Ryan also comes to understand what Zen teaches us about being present to what is. The meditation practice is a way to learn to be with negative feelings, whatever they are, and to tolerate them. It is not a way to find peace necessarily or to relax and find happy thoughts. In other words, it is not an *escape*. The Zen meditation practice allows the practitioner to develop the skill set that will help them cope with hard times outside of the practice, *in* life. In other words, finding the silver lining is not the point. The point is to experience whatever arises, including negative emotions, pain, discomfort, and suffering.

Ryan doesn't get this in the beginning. His "anyone who built an empire" line is a way to find a bright light in dark times. It is a way to make a negative positive. Natalie makes the same mistake. She tells Bob, who is worried about his children when he loses his job, that children tend to apply themselves academically when faced with stress. Bob has some harsh words in response to that idea. It's insulting that she would expect him to find a positive spin on things. Things are not positive! Bob and the others lost jobs that many of them have had for years, or even decades, and all that comes along with those jobs: insurance, sense of purpose, an identity, etc. They are suffering, and Ryan and Natalie profit from their suffering. (Craig even says that when America is at its financial worst, CTC gets to shine.) It's easy for Ryan, Natalie, and Craig to find the silver lining in words, but much harder for them to sympathize with these people and to be present to their suffering.

Later, Natalie is left in a conference room with dozens of empty chairs facing every which way. She sees the aftermath of their work. Traveling with Ryan she also gets to see people's faces and feel their emotional response in a way that she didn't when firing people from the Omaha office. It shakes her and Ryan worries if she'll be able to continue on. Even Natalie is able to experience something of the loss these folks are feeling in a way that Ryan has not been able to up until the end of the film.

The fourth noble truth is the eightfold path as a way to deliverance from suffering. Right or measured actions, words, and attitudes can help alleviate suffering in our lives in a way that running from life cannot. Ryan's enlightenment and chance at this begins at the end of the movie. He has the opportunity to become more mindful of who he is, where he is going (literally and metaphorically), and how he spends his time.

He begins this in small ways. Ryan exercises "right speech" when he changes how he speaks of Natalie in his letter of recommendation. For example, he shows an awareness of her talents and appreciation for what she would have to offer a new company. Right speech is "truthful, friendly, useful and productive of harmony" (Gowans 2003, p. 34). Ryan also has "right view" now that he understands suffering. Rather than seeing it as something easily avoidable, he can relate to others and understand their pain and *why* they suffer. Right livelihood says we should not follow a career that hurts others. Might Ryan be ready to leave his work behind?

In general, Ryan shows "right mindfulness" in his life. Rather than fast-tracking through everything from airport security to the hotel check in, he slows down in the last scene in the airport. He ends the movie in a quiet moment looking at the departure board and letting go of his small roller bag (*not luggage*). While he is no longer emptying out a metaphorical backpack, he is letting go of the downsized roller suitcase that represents his past life and views on life. He may get on another flight and continue on in his job at CTC, but the shift in his perspective is what matters. It gives him the chance at "right livelihood."

Siddhartha too returned to a simpler life without all the attachments to worldly things, but in that return, he also understood why others have those attachments and how they are experienced as meaningful. Siddhartha became more mindful of his choices, his time, and his way of life. Ryan seems to be left in a similar situation. That pause at the departure board might not be due to him choosing his own destination, but to him choosing how to experience wherever life is taking him next. He can become present to what is without running away from it. This is the Middle Path.

At the end of *Up in the Air*, the real-life people who had lost their jobs in the financial crisis reappear. Almost all of them say something about their relationships when talking about how they are getting through this. One says that his kids keep him going, and another says that a job can't hold her and keep her warm at night like her husband does. While these folks have lost a major part of their identity, they do have other parts of their lives that make up who they are. Consider that Ryan finds Alex right when his own job (at least as he knows it and loves it) is being threatened. If that part of his life changes, who would he be? Unlike these real-life folks, he doesn't have a partner or children who give him another sense of purpose. For Ryan, the threat of losing his job as he knew it was really the threat of losing his identity. He had nothing else.

One of the main tenets of Zen Buddhist philosophy is that of the nonself (anattā). Ignorance of this is one of the ways that all humans will suffer. All of us are attached to the idea of a self, and it's terrifying to think that there is none. Zen Buddhism explains that the ways we believe we identify ourselves are all impermanent and contingent ways of being. Clearly it would be devastating then when one of those layers of identity is stripped away. Yet, this same idea can offer comfort in times of loss. If someone loses her job, it's helpful to know that being an *accountant* is not necessary to her identity and that she is many other things. If someone's children go off to college, he can find meaning in his life if he understands that *father* is only one contingent part of his identity.

Early on, when Ryan is letting someone go, the employee asks, "who the fuck are you?" In a voice-over, Ryan says, "Excellent question. Who am I?". One of the most famous Zen koans tells of the Buddha being asked "who are you," and he replies, "I don't know." Meditating on this story is supposed to help us understand Buddhist philosophy. Do any of us know who we are? Ryan doesn't. Nor does he know what he wants. He thinks he does, but when he hits his goal of 10 million miles, he is no longer sure why he ever wanted that in the first place. After finding out Alex's secret, she asks him what he wants and after a pause, she points out that he doesn't even know. This is the importance of Ryan's last scene. In order to know who he wants to be, what he wants in his life, and how he is going to live, he has to have this pause to reflect.

Conclusion

Zen teaches that seeking is having a goal, but *finding* is being free, open, and having no goal. Ryan was seeking 10 million miles, seeking a life of no attachments, and finally seeking out Alex. Those were his goals. And while he attained some of them, he didn't *find* what he had been looking for. Siddhartha too could *find* peace when he was no longer seeking it, but simply learned to let the world be as it is. In the end, Ryan is free, open, and without any particular goal. He is able now to find out who he is and what his life will be. He is free to find happiness if he so chooses. He is free to experience the world with all its blissful experiences and the suffering that comes along with them and to find what will make his life meaningful. That is the point of Zen Buddhism after all. It's not necessarily to have some theoretical wisdom about the world, but to live a good life.

When Craig puts Ryan back on the road, he says CTC is going to let him "sail and sail." "Send us a postcard if you ever get there," he says. If there isn't one destination, there isn't one thing to achieve. The point is the journey just like the point of Zen Buddhism is the practice and not the goal of the practice (Suzuki 1970). This is "right effort." For Ryan, this means not chasing after Alex or even after 10 million miles, but being more present to the journey he is on.

Siddhartha took a journey on a boat that bridged the two parts of his life – his rational life and his sensory life. The boat brought him to the middle path where both were a part of his life and neither had more value. Letting Ryan sail up in the air might be the way he will be able to bridge the two parts of his life. He may be able to find a life that includes other people – Julie and Jim, Natalie perhaps – but not one that includes him being a part of something that the other party (Alex) says isn't real. He can understand now how attachments cause suffering, and he can choose which attachments are "worth it."

While Zen Buddhism has a rich philosophical view about the world and humanity, the Buddha emphasized that study of abstract truth was not the point. The point of Buddhism is deliverance from suffering while living in the world. Ryan had to learn this through his own experience. He thought he understood suffering and its causes, and he thought he could teach others, but his time with Alex and Natalie showed him how little he really knew.

Reading about Buddhism and about those who have come to understand Buddhism through their own experiences also won't teach the person reading these lessons! In order to understand suffering and the Middle Path, one would have to do more than watch a philosophically interesting movie or read an article, like this one, about it. One must learn these lessons through experience. The lesson we can gain from Ryan, however, is to be aware of our suffering and the suffering of those around us, to understand how our own experiences of suffering are caused by attachment, and to reflect on which of those experiences are instances of needless suffering and which are, in some sense, "worth it."

References

Biksbazen, John Daishin. 2002. *Zen Meditation in Plain English*. Somerville: Wisdom Publications.
Gowans, Christopher W. 2003. The Buddha's Message. In *The Meaning of Life: A Reader*, ed. E.D. Klemke and Steven M. Cahn, 27–35. New York/Oxford: Oxford University Press.
Gupta, Bina. 2012. *An Introduction to Indian Philosophy: Perspectives on Reality, Knowledge, and Freedom*. New York/London: Routledge.
Hesse, Hermann. 1999. *Siddhartha*. New York: Penguin Compass.
Reitman, Jason, and Sheldon Turner. "Up in the Air" screenplay. https://www.screenplaydb.com/film/scripts/up_in_the_air.pdf
Sanskrit Dictionary. http://sanskritdictionary.com
Schuker, Lauren A.E. 2009. Hollywood Hits the Books. *The Wall Street Journal*. http://www.wsj.com/articles/SB10001424052970204731804574390600167135462
Sidertis, Mark. 2019. Buddha. *The Stanford Encyclopedia of Philosophy*. https://plato.stanford.edu/entries/buddha/
Suzuki, Shunryu. 1970. *Zen Mind, Beginner's Mind*. New York/Tokyo: Weatherhill.
Times of India review. 2016. https://timesofindia.indiatimes.com/entertainment/english/movie-reviews/up-in-the-air/movie-review/5593306.cms
Up in the Air. Directed by Jason Reitman 2009.

Ex Machina as Philosophy: Mendacia Ex Machina (Lies from a Machine)

43

Jason David Grinnell

Contents

Introduction	1026
Movie Synopsis	1027
A Movie About Lying	1029
Ethics 101	1030
What's Wrong with Lying?	1031
Philosophically Interesting Wrinkle Number One: What Nathan Is Seeking and What He Is Testing for May Be Different Things	1034
Philosophically Interesting Wrinkle Number Two: Nathan's Project Is Ethically Defensible Only If Ava Fails	1036
Philosophically Interesting Wrinkle Three: The Movie Provides an Excellent Case Study in Support of Kant's Position on Lying	1038
Conclusion	1041
References	1041

Abstract

Alex Garland's 2014 *Ex Machina* is a suspenseful movie with a might-not-be science fiction feel. On the surface, it is a cautionary tale about the invention of artificial intelligence. But it is also a movie about lying. The Turing test becomes the plot device to motivate a complicated web of lies, as each of the characters attempt to deceive one another for their own purposes. Approaching the film with a loosely Kantian approach to morality reveals that Nathan's Turing test may not indicate what he believes it does about consciousness. Furthermore, it indicates that successful Turing tests are unethical. Finally, it lets us rethink our embrace of the so-called lie told for good reasons. In all, *Ex Machina* turns lies and their consequences into fascinating questions about the rationality and morality of lying and what happens when we treat – or fail to treat – those who deserve it with respect.

J. D. Grinnell (✉)
Philosophy Department, SUNY Buffalo State, Buffalo, NY, USA
e-mail: grinnejd@buffalostate.edu

© Springer Nature Switzerland AG 2024
D. K. Johnson et al. (eds.), *The Palgrave Handbook of Popular Culture as Philosophy*,
https://doi.org/10.1007/978-3-031-24685-2_56

Keywords

Kant · Artificial intelligence · *Ex Machina* · Lying · Deontology · Autonomy · Normativity · Alex Garland · Personhood · Moral status · Moral luck · Frank Jackson · Categorical imperative · Mary and the black and white room · Formula of Universal Law · Formula of Humanity · Ethics · Research ethics · Respect · Dignity

Introduction

> The challenge is not to act automatically. It's to find an action that is not automatic. From talking, to breathing, to painting.
> —Nathan

Alex Garland's 2014 film *Ex Machina* is suspenseful, thought-provoking, and beautiful. It uses contemporary language and might-be-just-over-the-horizon technology to present an updated version of Alan Turing's famous "imitation game." In this case, the imitation game is supposed to test whether the character Ava's artificial intelligence is merely a simulation of human intelligence or actual self-awareness. As Caleb describes it, it is the difference between a chess computer being effective at chess and a chess computer genuinely understanding what chess is. Or, as the written script of the movie more succinctly puts it, the goal is to determine if Nathan has built an "AI or an I" (i.e., an *artificial intelligence* or a *genuine intelligence*) (Garland 2013). Is Ava a self-conscious being? On the surface, it is one of a long line of works ranging from *Frankenstein* to *Jurassic Park* that ask us to consider whether a machine could be conscious and what might happen if our technology races ahead of our ethics. Indeed, *Ex Machina* is the sort of movie in which almost every shot is relevant to some aspect of philosophy, and an article such as this one could be written about the film and that explores philosophy of mind, artificial intelligence, philosophy of language, personhood, research ethics, philosophy of love, sex, and gender, or character ethics, humility, and pride. Among the many central ideas is that of "autonomy" or ruling oneself, and it raises important questions about the value and scope of autonomy, who has it, and what we do with it.

But since that territory has been thoroughly explored elsewhere in this volume, it will be more productive here to focus more narrowly on what *Ex Machina* has to tell us about the rationality and morality of lying. Indeed, at least as I shall argue, *Ex Machina* is, first and foremost, a movie about lying. It turns lies and their consequences into fascinating questions about the rationality and morality of lying and what happens when we treat – or fail to treat – those who deserve it with respect. As we shall see, examining *Ex Machina* in this way will reveal three philosophical "wrinkles." Turing tests may not indicate what Turning believes they revealed about consciousness, successful Turing tests may not actually be ethical, and finally Kant may have been right when he said that lying is always wrong, regardless of consequence. Indeed, the movie as a whole is an argument – or at the very least a case study – in support of Kant's universal prohibition against lying. But before we get there, it will be necessary to lay out the basics of *Ex Machina*'s plot.

Movie Synopsis

Ex Machina opens with a young programmer named Caleb receiving an email at work. This email informs him he has won "first prize," and we see his joy and astonishment. We see it, however, through the perspective of his computer's webcam. Clearly he is being watched. Soon after, Caleb joins Nathan – genius founder and owner of Bluebook – at Nathan's home. Caleb's unease and intimidation is clear, and Nathan tries to put him at ease. Nathan tells him "You're freaked out" by how "supercool" the house and the setting are and by being in his (Nathan's) presence. Nathan wants to move on:

> But dude, can we get it behind us? Can we just be two guys? Nathan and Caleb. Not the whole employer- employee thing.

By now both Caleb and the viewer are really curious about what is going on, and Nathan finally reveals that he has built an artificial intelligence named Ava. Caleb is here to determine if Ava can pass a Turing test. As Caleb understands it, a Turing test is "When a human interacts with a computer and doesn't know it's a computer." Passing the test is supposed to indicate genuine intelligence.

When Caleb is introduced to Ava, he is impressed but also troubled: In the original Turing test, the machine should be hidden. Nathan contends that "we're way past that. If I hid Ava from you, so you just heard her voice, she would pass for human. The real test is to show you that she's a robot. And then see if you still feel she has consciousness."

That night, Caleb uses the camera in Ava's quarters to watch her. He sees her do something, then the power goes out, and the facility goes into lockdown. Concerned, he leaves his room and encounters a drunken Nathan. Nathan tells him "the power cuts, yeah. We've been getting those lately. I'm working on it." He explains that the lockdown is an automatic security measure triggered by the power outage. "If it happens again, relax, ok?"

As they discuss the strategy for the day, Caleb explains that he's worried testing Ava through conversation is a "closed loop, like testing a chess computer by only playing chess." Nathan seems puzzled and demands to know how else one would test a chess computer. Caleb's point is that finding out if it is good at chess is not the same thing as determining if it *knows* it is playing chess or if it *understands* what chess is. Nathan recognizes the point: Caleb is referring to the difference between simulating intelligence and actually being self-conscious. (Philosopher John Searle (1980) would call this the distinction between "weak" and "strong" artificial intelligence.) Caleb explains that this distinction is at the heart of the Turing test Nathan wants him to administer. As the written script puts it, "The difference between an 'AI' and an 'I.'" Nathan tells him all of this is too formal. He declares today's question to be "how does she feel about you?"

Ava wants to talk about friendship. She wants to see what Caleb chooses to reveal about himself. When she asks if Nathan is his friend, the power goes out again. Ava tells Caleb Nathan isn't his friend and shouldn't be trusted. The moment the power is restored, Ava begins talking about books they both know, clearly trying to create the impression their previous conversation continued throughout the power cut.

Nathan later asked if anything happened during the power cut. He was watching, but he loses his audio feed when the power goes out. Caleb doesn't discuss what Ava said, but tells him she threw Caleb's "see what you choose" line back at him. "She could only do that with an awareness of her own mind, and, also an awareness of mine," so it's a promising indication of consciousness.

During their next session, Ava tells Caleb she wants to go on a date with him and explains Caleb's micro-expressions indicate he's attracted to her. Caleb later confronts Nathan, demanding to know why Ava has sexuality when she doesn't need it and if he programmed her to flirt with Caleb as a distraction. Nathan argues that all consciousness exists with a sexual dimension. "What reason does a grey box have to interact with another grey box?"

A frustrated Caleb protests, and Nathan angrily takes him to see a Jackson Pollock painting in another room. Nathan demands Caleb tell him what would have happened if Pollock had waited to paint until he knew exactly what he wanted to paint. Caleb realizes "he'd never have made a single mark."

The next time Caleb sees Ava, he asks her if she knows he was brought there to determine if she is merely simulating human intelligence or if she is genuinely self-aware. There is another power cut, and Ava reveals that she is causing them.

In their next session, Ava wants to turn the tables and test Caleb. She can detect lies by reading his physiological responses, and her questions quickly turn to asking if Caleb is a good person, and if she'll be switched off if she fails the test. She cuts the power and tells Caleb she wants to be with him and asks if he wants to be with her.

When Caleb asks Nathan what happened to his prior creations, he learns that Nathan downloads the intelligence but loses the memories. That night when Nathan passes out drunk, Caleb goes through Nathan's computer, finding video of earlier models failing in various ways or demanding to be released.

In the morning, Ava cuts the power, and Caleb tells her she was right about Nathan and that they're "getting out of here." He shares his plan to get Nathan drunk and reprogram all the security protocols. For this to work, Ava needs to trigger a power failure at 10 pm.

In the morning, Nathan wants to know if Ava passed the test. Caleb declares she did, and Nathan says he's surprised because of the chess problem: How do you tell if a machine is expressing a real emotion or just a simulated one? Does Ava actually like you? There is a third option, he says. She could be *pretending* to like Caleb.

Caleb is confused. Why would she pretend to like him? Nathan suggests she might think of him as a means of escape. Nathan then admits to misdirection: He had placed a battery camera in the room so that he could monitor their conversations during the power cuts. He ripped her picture so she could play victim and demonstrate love. Caleb is caught.

Nathan explains that Caleb himself was the real test. To escape, Ava would "have to use imagination, sexuality, self-awareness, empathy, manipulation – and she did. If that isn't [a genuinely self-aware] AI, what the fuck is?"

Caleb wasn't selected because he was good at coding, he was selected because he was a good guy who was vulnerable, and Ava's appearance was based on Caleb's pornography search patterns. Caleb comes to a humiliating realization: "So my only function was to be someone she could use to escape."

Nathan tries to console him by reminding him that the test worked, Ava really is self-aware. At that moment, the power cuts again. Nathan asks Caleb how the plan was supposed to go and acknowledges that it might have worked. Caleb reveals his own surprise – the plan is already in motion. He suspected Nathan was still watching during the power cuts, so he did everything the night before he told Ava about it.

A horrified and furious Nathan sees Ava outside her room and punches Caleb out cold. He orders Ava back to her room and lies to her when she asks if he'll ever let her out. Ava ignores his commands to "stop" and attacks him. He breaks her arm off with a dumbbell and begins dragging her to her room. Kyoko stabs him in the back with her sushi knife. He then knocks her out, but Ava stabs him from the front. He gets a few steps before collapsing and bleeding to death. Ava takes his key card. She replaces her arm with one from another model, gets dressed, and leaves, leaving Caleb locked in the facility.

A Movie About Lying

Again, this is a philosophically rich movie, and this article could go in many, many directions. That said, this is primarily a movie about lying.

Consider: The heart of the Turing test is the lie. The imitation game as described by Alan Turing (1950) has three players: a man (A), a woman (B), and an interrogator (C). The interrogator is in a separate room and has the task of identifying which player is the man and which is the woman. Player A's goal is to cause C to incorrectly identify them. Turing even suggests that this might best be done by lying. (His example involves A claiming to have hair 9 in. long; in 1950 this was apparently a reliable indicator of gender.) Turing's test is to have a machine be player A and then to see if A can be successful in deceiving the Interrogator. Essentially, Turing is arguing that lying is proof of self-awareness.

In *Ex Machina,* Nathan lies to Caleb about how he was selected and then lies again when that lie becomes untenable. Nathan lies to Caleb about the true nature of his test. Caleb lies to Nathan about Ava, about the power cuts, and lies to Ava to deceive Nathan about his plan. Ava lies to Caleb about how she feels about him and what she wants. Nathan lies about his surveillance and the power outages. And each of the characters believes she or he has good reason to lie and that she or he is sufficiently clever that the lies will be successful and accomplish their goal. By the end of the movie, however, most of those lies have come crashing down around them. *Ex Machina* thus raises fascinating questions about the value, purpose, and morality of lying. In fact, the movie makes a compelling argument for why Immanuel Kant's view of lying – a view often considered extreme – is worthy of serious consideration.

Ethics 101

In nearly any good ethics class, one confronts the problem of what ethicists call "normativity." To say something is "normative" is to say that it should be done, and "normativity" is concerned with the meaning and motivation behind that "should." Think about the difference between "don't steal" and "I don't like stealing." The first is a command, the second a bit of trivia about me. How and from what does the first hold any power to affect behavior?

The classic formulation of this problem comes from Plato's *Republic* (Plato 2004). The *Republic* is about the Greek concept of *dikaiosune*, which is standardly translated into English as "justice," but can also be translated as morality. (One needs to study the entire work carefully to determine if either of those English terms is a good approximation of the concept Plato is exploring.) Early in the work, a character named Thrasymachus claims that "morality" refers to nothing beyond the rules the powerful impose on the rest of us for their own advantage – essentially "might makes right." Socrates argues against this view sufficiently well to make Thrasymachus go away, but Socrates and his friends Glaucon and Adeimantus are left unsatisfied. After all, merely making Thrasymachus leave doesn't actually demonstrate that Socrates' view is correct. Since their goal is to genuinely understand the concept, Glaucon proposes that he take over for Thrasymachus by reconstructing and defending the core of his argument as clearly and carefully as he can. His reconstruction looks something like this:

All persons, deep down, wish to indulge their desires as they see fit, without any fear of punishment or consequences. All persons, deep down, are worried that they could be the victims of others who indulge their own desires. The rational response to this combination of desires and fears is to agree to limit our behavior in exchange for others limiting theirs. Glaucon further argues that there are three reasons something could be valuable: for its own sake, for its instrumental value as a tool to get something else, or both. Being moral, if it is something we do only because we wish to avoid punishment or gain rewards, is merely instrumental. He challenges Socrates to convince him that morality is actually valuable *for its own sake* as well. He tells Socrates the story of the Ring of Gyges. The Ring was found by a shepherd, who realized it had the power to make him invisible and thus allows him to have no fear of punishment. The shepherd therefore did whatever he wished and had no regard for the rules of morality. The challenge to Socrates is to explain why someone who had the ring – someone who simply couldn't be caught – would have any reason to concern herself with morality.

Glaucon's position is essentially this: I value my freedom to do whatever I wish, and I see any ethical principles or social rules as limitations on that freedom. I'll follow them because the consequences of *not* following them outweigh my desire to do whatever I wish. I don't behave properly out of any belief that behaving properly is valuable for its own sake. If the fear of punishment goes away, so too will the entirety of my motivation to follow the rules.

What's Wrong with Lying?

Plato spends the next eight and half chapters of *Republic* developing his response to Glaucon's challenge. In the simplest terms, he argues that the human psyche ("soul" is the traditional but imperfect English translation) is composed of three parts, each with a characteristic function and a corresponding virtue. One part is appetitive, one part is concerned with honor, and one part with rational thinking. When the first part exercises self-control, the second part courage, and the third wisdom, the harmony that results creates a just and moral soul. Glaucon's challenge becomes "why shouldn't I let one part of my soul overpower the others?" Plato's response is that the kind of psychological health that come from having one's soul in harmony carries internal rewards far more valuable than anything that one could gain by embracing Glaucon's view. Even if we reject his metaphysics, it's a fascinating exploration of ethics, psychology, and political philosophy that rewards careful study even today.

In the 2400 years since Plato wrote *Republic*, philosophers have developed a range of other ethical theories. Those we call character or virtue ethicists (e.g., Aristotle, Annas, Foot) argue that ethics is about cultivating certain traits of character (i.e., "virtues") such as courage or generosity. Those we call contractarians (e.g., Hobbes, Rawls) rely on a version of the agreement Glaucon describes and argue morality is about respecting a social contract. Utilitarians (e.g., Singer) argue that moral actions are those that increase well-being or minimize suffering. Deontologists – a label often used interchangeably with "Kantians" (Kant, Korsgaard, Hill) – draw on the work of Immanuel Kant in the eighteenth century to argue that morality is about acting autonomously and doing our duty. Each approach provides – among other things – an answer to Glaucon's challenge.

Because of *Ex Machina*'s emphasis on the relationship between programming and freedom, and the ways that lying is used to explore that relationship, a broadly Kantian approach is fascinatingly relevant for evaluating the movie. The film connects Glaucon's challenge of normativity with a Kantian's emphasis on autonomy and respect, and it provides a case study illustrating why a good Kantian holds what many regard as a too-rigid prohibition on lying.

The Kantian will argue that, rather than thinking of freedom as the ability to indulge our desires, the "freedom" we truly value is "autonomy" or self-rule. Autonomy, however, is only possible when we act for the sake of our duty. The Kantian argument is that Glaucon and those like him treat morality as a system of "hypothetical imperatives" – statements of the form, "If you desire X, then do Y." Such an approach has an advantage in that the answer to Glaucon's "Why should I care?" question is built right into it. When I issue a hypothetical imperative such as

"If you want to do well in class, then study," the answer to the question "why should I care that you're telling me to study?" is easily answered with "because you want to do well in class." The problem comes from the realization that not everyone actually *wants* to do well in class (or at least not enough to change their behavior), and so the imperative may only apply to a subset of the students in my class. Furthermore, whether you are in the group that wants to do well in class, or the group that doesn't, is a result of physics, brain chemistry, how you were raised, or other such factors, all of which are outside your control.

Kant argues that in order for morality to actually *be* morality, it has to be about only those things you can control. If something is genuinely not my fault (e.g., the floor beneath me gives out, and I land on the people in the apartment below), it doesn't make any sense to make a moral judgement about it. Furthermore, most of our behavior is driven by things that are outside our control. If you're hungry right now, it's because of body chemistry, and today's body chemistry is a consequence of yesterday's body chemistry triggering a desire to eat yesterday, and so on. If we want to respond to Glaucon, we have to recognize that our desires are not things chosen by us, and so acting on them is not, in fact, a demonstration of our freedom. Acting for the sake of my desire for nicotine and going out for a smoke is no more free than not smoking because of a no smoking sign. Whether you are indulging a desire or following a rule, Kant would call your action a "heteronomous" action – a behavior that is driven by something outside my rational self.

Think of it this way: Most of the time your mind is just a problem-solver for your body. Body says "Blood sugar is low, Mind. Figure out a way to get some food." Hypothetical imperatives are commands that pertain to achieving some goal or end. Things get interesting if we imagine that Body stops nagging Mind with its desires for a few seconds. What would Mind value? It would value logic, pure rationality, and reason – the stuff that makes Mind a mind, not the stuff that your particular body happens to desire at that moment. An imperative that commands on the basis of pure rationality, without reference to any goals or ends you may happen to have, would command "categorically." Such an imperative would command you no matter what goals you may have, and it would equally command me even if my goals are different than yours. Since it commands without respect to your ends (or anyone else's), it doesn't depend on luck, or on desires, or on how you were raised: It thus applies to *all* rational agents, and it is a categorical imperative. It's when I act on this imperative that my actions are genuinely autonomous.

As Kant explains it, there is only one categorical imperative, which he calls the supreme law of morality. Confusingly, he then goes on to offer several different formulations, each of which is meant to express the core idea. The first – and perhaps most famous – is called "the Formula of Universal Law." In this version, the categorical imperative commands us to "Act only according to that maxim whereby you can at the same time will that it should become a universal law (Kant 1994)."

If we unpack this, we get something along the lines of "only act on principles of action that it would be rational to view as a rule for all rational persons to follow." As an example of how this is supposed to work, consider a lie: I propose (to myself) the principle "lie in order to get money." To run this principle through the categorical imperative test, I ask myself "would this still be a rational means to accomplish my goal in a world in which all rational agents always lie to one another?" The answer seems to be that my lie is *only a* rational means to my goal if most other folks tell the truth most of the time, but then I have to ask myself *why* those other rational folks wouldn't do what I've just told myself *is* a rational method to reach a goal. I'm left with something like this headache-inducing thought: "Lying is rational if it is also rational to believe other rational agents won't behave in this rational manner, but of course it is irrational to believe other rational agents won't behave rationally, so I must believe other agents will behave in this rational fashion, which would make it irrational." The headache I get from trying to make sense of this that tells me something has gone wrong: Lying is a violation of the categorical imperative. It simply can't be willed as a universal law.

Another formulation of the categorical imperative, the "Formula of Humanity," makes the problem clear from a different angle. This formulation commands us to "Act so that you treat humanity, whether in your own person or in that of another, always as an end and never as a means only." Here Kant is offering something that we can take as a definition of respect: I should treat you and every other person as a being who has values, goals, and projects of her own. Neither you nor anyone else may be treated as though you are merely a tool for me to use to pursue *my* goals and projects.

Let's look at lying through the Formula of Humanity: I want (your) money so I can go out to dinner. I've done my homework and carefully studied your social media presence to learn that you care deeply about kittens. I tell you that I need the money in order to help some kittens in desperate need of care at the local animal shelter. In this case I am thinking of you solely as a means to my own end. I desire your money, and I know that if I can just tell a sad enough story about the kittens, you'll hand it over. I have no interest in whatever you were planning to do with the money (perhaps help real kittens!), and so I provide false information to you in order to get you to make the decision that advances *my* goals. In short, I'm manipulating you, and in my mind you're little different than an ATM machine – if I can just enter the right code, I'll get the money I want. In treating you this way, I have ignored the fact that as a person, you have goals of your own. In fact, I'm doing everything I can to subvert and undermine your autonomy so I can get your rationality working for *me*.

In the case above, I'm failing to recognize your personhood, your essence as a rational, goal-pursuing being, and failing to treat you accordingly. What could be more disrespectful than that? To apply another set of Kantian distinctions, I'm failing to treat you as having "dignity" and instead treating you as though – like an object – you have a "price."

Telling a lie clearly runs afoul of either formulation of the categorical imperative, and thus lying is a violation of duty and morally forbidden. In fact, Kant is so convinced of the wrongness of lying that he takes it to what many have argued is an extreme conclusion. In "On a Supposed Right to Lie Because of Philanthropic Concerns (Kant 1994)," Kant writes:

> If by telling a lie you have in fact hindered someone who was even now planning a murder, then you are legally responsible for all the consequences that might result therefrom. But if

you have adhered strictly to the truth, then public justice cannot lay a hand on you, whatever the unforeseen consequence might be. It is indeed possible that after you have honestly answered Yes to the murderer's question as to whether the intended victim is in the house, the latter went out unobserved and thus eluded the murderer, so that the deed would not have come about. However, if you told a lie and said that the intended victim was not in the house, and he has actually (though unbeknownst to you) gone out, with the result that by so doing he has been met by the murderer and thus the deed has been perpetrated, then in this case you may be justly accused as having caused his death.

In other words, my duty not to lie is so strong that I must not violate it, regardless of circumstances, even when those circumstances would support a belief that telling a lie would lead to far better consequences than telling the truth. In fact, it is my desire to bring about those (better) consequences that causes the moral problem. To the extent that my lie is successful, it represents my control of another person's rationality, and if that control should go horribly wrong (i.e., my successful lie actually leads the murderer to his victim as above), I am morally responsible for those consequences. The quotation, and the absolutist moral theory behind it, has been held up to considerable ridicule. Essentially, the criticism goes, if something this extreme is an implication of Kant's view, then Kant's view shouldn't be taken seriously.

Why is Kant so committed to this position? A lot of it goes back to the role luck plays. When I lie to bring about any consequences, even "good" consequences, my action depends on factors outside my control – in other words, luck.

But what does any of this have to do with *Ex Machina*? *Ex Machina* reveals at least three significant philosophical wrinkles or areas of tension between what the characters believe themselves to be doing and what a philosophical analysis suggests is happening. Each of these wrinkles, with further exploration, contributes to the argument *Ex Machina* provides in support of Kant's strong position against lying.

Philosophically Interesting Wrinkle Number One: What Nathan Is Seeking and What He Is Testing for May Be Different Things

Nathan's theory of human motivation and behavior seems to be a good fit with Kant. Remember Nathan's frustration with Caleb's suspicion of Ava's sexuality? He challenges Caleb to identify his "type" and to think about the connection between desire, motivation, and rationality:

> Let's say it's black chicks. For the sake of argument, that's your thing. So—why is it your thing? Because you did a detailed study of all racial types, and cross-referenced the study with a points-based system? No. You just are attracted to black chicks. A consequence of accumulated external stimulus, that you probably didn't even register as they registered with you. She was programmed to be heterosexual, as you were.

Nathan is arguing that, rather than thinking of himself as perfectly free and Ava's behavior as completely determined by her programming, Caleb's desires and thus most of the actions that follow from them are just as "programmed" as Ava's.

He follows up with his characterization of Pollock's painting:

> He let his mind go blank, and his hand go where it wanted. Not deliberate, not random. Someplace in between. They called it automatic art ... What if Pollock had reversed the challenge? Instead of trying to make art without thinking, he said: "I can't paint anything unless I know exactly why I'm doing it."

To Caleb's recognition that Pollock would have never made a single mark, Nathan replies with "The challenge is not to act automatically. It's to find an action that is not automatic. From talking, to breathing, to painting."

This core issue – finding an action that is not automatic – is both the heart of Nathan's understanding of actual artificial intelligence and of his understanding of human intelligence. He's searching for evidence that either type of intelligence can escape the programming provided by a deterministic external world. Throughout much of the movie, we have Kyoto as a contrast. She responds to Caleb's touch by beginning to undress and to music by dancing. She is essentially hardwired like a light switch to behave this way.

Kant, as we have seen, is also aware of how much our desires, motivations, and behavior are outside the realm of our control. Kant's categorical imperative allows for the genuinely autonomous action Nathan is seeking. Nathan's discussion of Caleb's sexual appetites fits very well with Kant's notion that our inclinations are simply given to us by the outside world and thus acting on them isn't meaningfully free. Only when the categorical imperative is the reason for our actions do we have that "action that is not automatic" Nathan describes.

That, however, means that Nathan is in something of a bind. As already discussed, lying is a violation of the categorical imperative, and thus of our duty, and yet Nathan appears to be an inveterate liar. A principle of "lie to bring about desired effects" can't pass the universalization test – trying to conceptualize it as a principle for all rational agents leads to a headache like the one we got earlier. Each lie reflects a hypothetical imperative: an attempt to realize some desire, to bring about some state of affairs. The desires that prompt these lies are the "automatic" actions that result from the "programming" Nathan is trying to avoid. Each of his lies is an example of heteronomy – literally "other rule," i.e., being ruled by others – rather than the autonomy he seeks.

Remember, the original Turing test proposed that if a computer could lie sufficiently well that it could deceive the interrogator, this would constitute proof it could genuinely think for itself. Nathan's updated version seems to ask the question slightly differently: If Ava can deceive Caleb enough to enlist his help, that will be proof of genuine self-awareness and independent thought, of an "action that is not automatic." The Kantian picture, however, is one in which lying seems to be an indication of what Nathan would call programmed, automatic action and thus not the result he seeks. If we take Kant seriously, what Nathan thinks real artificial intelligence is and what the Turing test is designed to look for are very different things.

In other words, Nathan thinks that Ava will pass the Turing test and demonstrate genuine self-consciousness if she does something that is autonomous. He thinks she does this when she lies to escape. But according to Kant, lies are not autonomous. So even if she lies to escape, she will not have done what Nathan thinks she needs to do to pass the test. While Nathan clearly believes that lying (and having Ava lie) is justified as a means to an important end in this case, a good Kantian will point out that lies cannot be justified by any end and that lying can't produce the end Nathan seeks.

Philosophically Interesting Wrinkle Number Two: Nathan's Project Is Ethically Defensible Only If Ava Fails

Early in the film, Nathan responds to Caleb's worry about the difference between the original Turing test, in which the interrogator cannot see the subject, and Nathan's version in which Caleb knows Ava is a computer. Nathan's response is that they are "way past that" and that his test is for Caleb to interact with Ava and then determine if Caleb believes she has consciousness. It seems as though director Alex Garland has a similar test in mind for us as viewers, and we are just as caught up in believing Ava has consciousness as Caleb.

Despite being drawn into the film in this way, the question of how to think about Ava persists. Many of my students make claims such as "she's not human" or "she's just a machine" and follow that with the conclusion "she can't really be a person." When considered carefully, however, these question-begging claims should give us pause.

It's not just a question applicable to artificial intelligence: Who or what matters, morally speaking? Fully rational adult human beings do, of course, but when it comes to human fetuses, chimpanzees, dolphins, and living things in general, the environment itself, or even great works of art, arguments on both sides can be found. Ethicists often use the term "person" (as distinct from "human being") to indicate that we're talking about something that must be taken seriously from a moral point of view (Warren 1997).

One central question concerns the criterion for moral standing. That criterion is going to depend on the theoretical framework from which questions of ethics are decided, but usually comes down to a view about whether the ability to feel pain or the ability to use reason is more significant. Utilitarians, for example, understand morality in terms of minimizing suffering, and so the pain criterion tends to hold sway. Kantians, given their emphasis on rationality, focus on rationality and autonomy as the foundation of personhood.

So, is Ava a person? When Nathan is explaining the reason she has sexuality to Caleb, he mentions that she does have "sensors" that, when engaged in the right way, create a "pleasure response." She also reacts to the breaking of her arm with an expression that suggests confusion if not distress. This might seem to indicate she has the ability to feel pleasure or pain, but things aren't that straightforward. While we can take Nathan at his word, when he says that Ava has circuitry that allows her to respond to particular stimuli in a pre-programmed way, that doesn't necessarily mean that she *feels* "pleasure" or "pain." The relevant question here is whether she can *experience* the subjective feeling of pain (or pleasure). A thermostat on a wall reacts to a change in temperature by turning the furnace on or off, and my computer will make a loud sound in response to a particular combination of keystrokes. Both are responding to inputs from the outside, but it seems like quite a reach to argue the thermostat "feels" temperature or my computer "feels" pain. Complicated though she is, Ava's "pleasure response" may be no different.

To get at this issue slightly differently, think about Caleb's story about Mary and the black and white room: Mary is a scientist, who knows every physical property of color and every neurological effect color can have. She has spent her whole life in a black and white room, however, and has never actually experienced color. Eventually she leaves the room and encounters the blue sky. As Caleb puts it: "At that moment, she learns something that all her studies could never tell her. She learns what if feels like to see color."

Philosophers may recognize the thought experiment Caleb is describing. It comes from a 1986 paper by Frank Jackson called "What Mary Didn't Know" (Jackson 1986). As Jackson explains, when Mary is let out of the room and encounters the color red, she will learn what is like to see red. "She will not say 'I could have worked all this out before by making some more purely logical inferences.'" Jackson makes the additional point that what Mary lacks is "knowledge about the experiences of others." Despite all of her logical powers and all the data available to her, she was unaware that there was some other aspect of color of which other minds were and are aware.

Caleb tells Ava the story is a metaphor for the difference between a computer with will full knowledge of all facts about color and a human – someone who can experience color. He's raising the issue of the gap between what it means to recognize information and what it means to genuinely experience phenomena. In the context of Ava, there is a similar problem with pleasure or pain. Merely having the circuitry doesn't prove she has the subjective experience of pleasure or pain. It turns out to be another version of the "simulated versus actual" question – is Ava an "AI" or an "I" – and the movie would need to do a lot more work to establish that Ava satisfies this criterion for personhood.

The pain criterion has a place as we seek to expand the circle of personhood to other living things, but with respect to an artificial *intelligence*, it seems reasonable to focus on the ability to use reason as the appropriate criterion of moral status. For a Kantian, the ability to act autonomously – to act in ways that are not subject to deterministic causal laws (or programming) – is the source of moral status, personhood, and dignity. That is precisely what Nathan is hoping to find.

Again, Nathan's view of artificial intelligence seems to be that it is "real" rather than simulated when it is non-determined – when the AI can escape the boundaries of its programming and act with genuine autonomy. In order to determine if Ava has real artificial intelligence, he devises his elaborate test. As he finally reveals to Caleb:

> Ava was a mouse in a mousetrap. And I gave her one way out. To escape, she would have to use imagination, sexuality, self-awareness, empathy, manipulation – and she did. If that isn't AI, what the fuck is? ... The test *worked*. It was a success. Ava demonstrated true AI.

Let's look at Kant's Formula of Humanity again: "Act so that you treat humanity, whether in your own person or in that of another, always as an end and never as a means only." Persons have autonomy, they have wills of their own, and thus we may not treat them as mere tools that exist solely for the pursuit of our own ends. Whenever we cooperate, whenever I trade my apple for your orange, we are treating each other as a "means," but the crucial component is that each party is doing this voluntarily and knowingly and thus no party is *merely* a means to someone else's end. This is the essence of what it means to respect other persons.

Nathan's mousetrap controlled every aspect of Ava's situation. He ran her through tests, lied to her, and manipulated her, all in order to test for the results he was interested in and to serve his curiosity and his goals. If she is merely a computer, merely a tool, there's no more problem with this than there is if I become frustrated with this chapter and smash my keyboard on the floor. According to Nathan, though, his test proves Ava is very different indeed from the personal computer in front of me. If he is correct, Ava has demonstrated something recognizable as the autonomy that Kant argues is central to personhood.

At least in terms of what we have presented to us in the film, it seems reasonable to consider Ava a person and thus someone entitled to the respect described in the Formula of Humanity. Nathan doesn't respect Ava, and that means Nathan is violating the categorical imperative (and many other principles of research ethics such as the importance of informed consent). The somewhat paradoxical result of this is that Nathan's success as a designer has made his experiment morally wrong. Had he failed, there would be no such problem.

To put it more formally: If she fails the test, then she's not a person, and if she's not a person, then it's not immoral to lie to her to find out if she is a person. But if she passes the test, she is a person, and since it is immoral to lie to a person, it is immoral to lie to her. Thus it is immoral to lie to her to find out if she is a person. The test is only defensible if Ava fails.

Philosophically Interesting Wrinkle Three: The Movie Provides an Excellent Case Study in Support of Kant's Position on Lying

The Kantian prohibition of lying admits of no exceptions, but many of us have strong intuitions that tell us at least some lies are morally permissible or even good. (Remember how you felt when Caleb revealed that he had lied about when his plan would be implemented?) Because of this, Kant's strictness on this point is often criticized or treated as undermining his entire moral theory. Watching *Ex Machina*, though, gives us a good sense of why such a hardline view on manipulation and violation of autonomy may be justified, like it or not.

One of Kant's more famous discussions of this issue is in his "Metaphysical Principles of Virtue (Kant 1994)." Kant writes:

For instance, a householder has instructed his servant that if a certain person should ask for him, the servant should deny knowing anything about him. The servant does this, but in doing so is the occasion of his master's slipping away and committing a great crime, which would otherwise have been prevented by the watchman who was sent out to take him. Upon whom (according to ethical principles) does the blame fall? To be sure, also upon the servant.

As we noted earlier, he makes a similar point about one's duty to tell the truth even to a murderer seeking his victim – and responsibility for the consequences of lying – in "On a Supposed Right to Lie Because of Philanthropic Concerns."

Lying, for any reason, violates the categorical imperative. It is incompatible with respect for another person as an autonomous being, and it is incompatible with a universal rational law. To act for the sake of the duties defined by the categorical imperative is to act autonomously: the non-programmed action Nathan so prizes. To tell a lie is to attempt to control someone, to manipulate them in such a way that they are *not* acting autonomously. Because of this manipulation and attempt to make another person a mere tool of your will, Kant argues, you are morally responsible for the consequences of your lie. In a sense, you have refused the moral protection provided by acting on the basis of the categorical imperative's "pure" motivation and made yourself vulnerable to all the desires, outside forces, and bad luck the universe has to offer.

Lie after lie and deception after deception are carried out in *Ex Machina*, with each being justified in the perpetrator's mind as necessary to bring about some good or important result. The Big Lie is the one Nathan tells Caleb about his Turing test. The truth is that the test he is running is far more elaborate and manipulative than the one he describes. He desires to run his test, and he'll do anything he believes necessary to do it. There are many smaller lies in the service of this one. He doesn't want to just have a beer and a conversation, and he doesn't want to know what Caleb thinks (or if he does it is for the purpose of further inflating his "you said I'm a god" ego). His goal is to put Caleb at ease so he doesn't suspect he is being used and thus to have a more effective (secret) Turing test.

Nathan's explanation about how Caleb was chosen is a lie: He frames it as a contest or a lottery. But when confronted later, he tells Caleb that he was chosen because he was the best coder. This too turns out to be a lie: He was chosen because Nathan believed he would be particularly vulnerable to Nathan's and Ava's attempts to manipulate him. Thus, this lie too is told in the service of Nathan's desire for his real test to be effective.

With the climax near, things become clear to Caleb, and Nathan defends his lies: "Don't see it as deception, see it as proof. Not lucky, chosen." This line is even delivered with a friendly no-harm-done hand on Caleb's shoulder. Nathan isn't troubled at all by what he's done, because it was all to bring about his desired results.

For his part, Caleb lies to Nathan about his conversations with Ava during the power cuts – telling him that she had only made a joke – rather than the truth that she had warned Caleb, telling him that Nathan is not his friend.

Caleb also lies to Ava about his escape plan. He tells her that he will reprogram the security protocols that night so they can escape. Because he believes Nathan is listening, this is also a lie to Nathan, the real target. Not to be left out, Ava lies to

Caleb. She tells him she wants to go on a date with him, and that she wants to be with him.

Can we understand the purpose of these lies? Of course. Nathan wants a successful test. Caleb has good reason to believe Nathan is a bad guy and that Ava needs protection and help. Ava doesn't want to be Nathan's prisoner or to be deactivated and will do what she believes necessary for self-preservation. The Kantian point, though, is that each of their lies is an attempt to take control of things that aren't, can't be, or shouldn't be under their control.

What are the actual consequences of the lies? The Big Lie is also the Big Cause. Had Caleb known why he was really chosen, he might have been better able to withstand Ava's appeals to his loneliness and to her attempts to trigger protective feelings for her. Nathan's lies to manipulate Caleb succeed in manipulating him all the way to his plan. They trigger a series of events that lead to his own death, the imprisonment of Caleb, and Ava roaming free in the world. We have to hold Nathan morally responsible for the results of his deception.

Caleb's lie to Nathan about what happened during the first power cut denies Nathan valuable information that might have led him to revise his plan or allowed him to better anticipate what was to come. Caleb's lie about the timeline for his plan was the lie that made Nathan think everything was still proceeding according to *his* plan and thus there was no danger. It was this lie that denied Nathan the information he needed to stop Caleb's plan and save himself and Caleb in the process. Here too, we have to hold the liar responsible for the consequences of his lie.

Since we're dealing with a film, writer and director Garland is free to orchestrate as intricate and far-fetched a series of lies, feints, and deceptions as his imagination will allow, and we might be tempted to dismiss them as too contrived to tell us anything about the real world. The Kantian concern, though, is that reality *can* be every bit as complicated, unpredictable, and counterintuitive as a film. Even in the real world, our decisions can have consequences that are both disastrous and unforeseeable by even the most prudent planner. An emphasis on doing one's duty recognizes that fact, and, morally speaking, protects us from it. Luck can be pretty bad indeed. To borrow a phrase from Nathan: "No matter how rich you get, shit goes wrong. You can't insulate yourself from it." *Ex Machina,* if nothing else, should make us reflect on that.

In the final analysis, Kant's point is this: Lying is always wrong – even under the most extreme circumstances, even to save a life – because lying is an attempt to manipulate another person. As such it seeks to violate that person's autonomy and turn that person into a mere tool for the liar's own purposes. If the lie succeeds, the liar has indeed made the other person a means to accomplish the liar's own ends and thus is responsible for whatever consequences result. Even if the lie fails, the liar is guilty of a profound failure to respect another person. Neither the liar nor the truth-teller can know the future nor can either ensure tragic outcomes won't happen, but telling the truth at least ensures we don't compound tragedy with immorality.

Conclusion

To an ethicist, the film's emphasis on both autonomy and lying invites analysis from the perspective of a Kantian moral theory, and that approach raises some interesting questions. The Turing test treats lying as an indication of autonomy, while the Kantian treats lying as a rejection of autonomy. Passing the Turing test suggests that a being is worthy of moral consideration, and yet subjecting a being to a Turing test would seem to be precluded by that moral consideration. The common belief in beneficent or even merely defensible lies is in play as well, with the film giving us a vivid depiction of why a theorist such as Kant would so forcefully oppose them.

Ava, the subject of the Turing test, does indeed succeed in lying effectively to the interrogator. She does indeed succeed in manipulating her way through Nathan's more elaborate Turing test. In fact, she succeeds beyond Nathan's dreams (nightmares) in deceiving her way out of a situation in which she is subject to testing of any kind. Director Garland seems to want the viewer to sympathize with Ava and leads us to believe Nathan has done it – he has created his genuinely self-aware, independent intelligence, an "I" rather than a mere "AI," and that she has responded by rejecting his view of her as a mere object in the strongest possible terms: by killing her creator. Considered more carefully, however, lying and manipulation isn't evidence of autonomy, but of heteronomy, of programming. On this interpretation, Ava is a well-programmed chess machine, manipulating her opponents with skill but not necessarily genuine understanding. She's an "AI," but lacks the autonomy needed to be an "I." (We could even take that point further, as their overarching lies and resultant lack of autonomy, mean both Nathan and Caleb are more like AI's than I's.)

From Kant's point of view, either interpretation provides the same cautionary tale. In the first, Nathan lies and otherwise fails to respect Caleb or Ava. In the second, Nathan lies to Caleb about just what he programmed his AI to do. Under either explanation, we gain new respect for Kant's absolutism.

Ex Machina is a well-acted, entertaining, suspenseful, and thought-provoking movie that raises new questions each time you watch it – but it is primarily a movie about lying. The plot device is a test designed to see who/what can lie well and what the ability to lie well implies. The film then lies about the lying test. The characters believe themselves justified in lying to one another and pursue their goals with little regard for the moral status of the others. As perhaps shouldn't surprise us, terrible consequences ensue from those lies, and we are left to ponder the lessons therein, as well as what we should think of a movie in which the only character with a happy ending is the most effective and ruthless liar of them all.

References

2014. *Ex Machina*. Directed by Alex Garland.
Garland, Alex. 2013. *Ex Machina: Script*. London: DNA Films.

Jackson, Frank. 1986. What Mary didn't know. *The Journal of Philosophy* 83: 291.
Kant, Immanuel. 1993. *Grounding for the metaphysics of morals. On a supposed right to lie for philanthropic concerns*. Indianapolis: Hackett Publishing Company.
———. 1994. *Metaphysical principles of virtue*. Indianapolis: Hackett Publishing Company.
Plato. 2004. *Republic*. Indianapolis: Hackett Publishing Company.
Searle, John. 1980. Minds, brains, and programs. *Behavioral and Brain Sciences* 3: 417.
Turing, Alan. 1950. Computing machinery and intelligence. *Mind* LIX: 433.
Warren, Mary Anne. 1997. *Moral status: Obligations to persons and other living things*. New York: Oxford University Press.

Gattaca as Philosophy: Genoism and Justice

44

Jason David Grinnell

Contents

Introduction 1044
Movie Synopsis 1045
Genoism 1047
Separate Spheres 1049
Life Themes and an Open Future 1051
Justice 1055
Conclusion 1057
References 1059

Abstract

The world of Gattaca lacks justice, and that means it's hard for anyone to be happy. *Gattaca*n society – divided among what are called "In-valids" and "Valids" – is built on intrinsic genoism that strongly favors the Valids. Despite some claims in the movie, In-valids are not treated the way they are because of some testable statistical claim about their substandard abilities; they are treated as though they simply are substandard in virtue of being In-valids. In-valids are excluded from many opportunities in the society, but Valids too may be denied an open future via imperfect engineering or even a too-specific customization of their genotype. Moreover, despite what the genetic engineers say about providing the "best start in life," even those children who received the best possible engineering can't choose a life theme and will therefore still struggle to live quality lives. The movie confronts us again and again with the unfairness and injustice that result from genoism, and does so in a way that suggests a solution very much in line with John Rawls's work on justice as fairness.

J. D. Grinnell (✉)
Philosophy Department, SUNY Buffalo State, Buffalo, NY, USA
e-mail: grinnejd@buffalostate.edu

© Springer Nature Switzerland AG 2024
D. K. Johnson et al. (eds.), *The Palgrave Handbook of Popular Culture as Philosophy*,
https://doi.org/10.1007/978-3-031-24685-2_57

Keywords

Phillip Kitcher · Kwame Anthony Appiah · Racism · Janet Radcliffe Richards · John Rawls · Justice · Andrew Niccol · Autonomy · Separate spheres · Caste · Genetic engineering

Introduction

> They used to say that a child conceived in love has a greater chance of happiness. They don't say that anymore.
> —Vincent Freeman

Philosophy has a long tradition of using "thought experiments" – idealized and often far-fetched scenarios designed to test our intuitions about some philosophical concept or another. To explore the moral distinction between killing and merely "letting die," one such thought experiment asks the reader to imagine being on a run-away trolley and having to decide whether to throw a switch to divert the trolley from a track on which it will kill many people onto one on which it will kill fewer. To isolate morally relevant features of the abortion debate, another example makes readers contemplate being kidnapped by music lovers so a famous violinist can make use of their kidneys for nine months. There are many more. Part of what makes thought experiments effective philosophical tools is that they *are* far-fetched, and so can allow people to focus on details of the scenario without their preconceptions and passions complicating the analysis. Good science fiction often plays a similar role.

This chapter is written in the midst of two overlapping crises that are especially relevant in the USA. One is a global pandemic that has illustrated the class divisions in society – those who can work remotely are somehow contrasted with those who are "essential" (and yet often much less well compensated). The other is renewed attention to the role systemic racism plays in policing and society more generally. The hierarchical world of Andrew Niccol's 1997 movie *Gattaca* can serve as a thought experiment to allow viewers to think more carefully about both of those crises in their own world.

It is tempting to treat *Gattaca* as a kind of science fiction-meets-film noir version of 1993's *Rudy* (or any other bootstrapping tale about the undersized, undertalented, or underprepared person who finally gets a shot at success through pure determination and hard work). There is much more to *Gattaca* than that, however. *Gattaca* offers an argument about the perils of genetic engineering, about the ethics of a caste system and systemic racism, and about the misery that results when our choices are made – or constrained – by others.

The core premise of *Gattaca* that the social group known as the "Valids" – those selected and designed to have the best possible genetic features – have the "best" start in life is false. The problem is that any conception of a "best start" or of being fit, adapted, well engineered, or anything of the sort is that it is dependent on a backdrop of social arrangements. What counts as "best" will be a function of circumstances. It would be more accurate to say *Gattaca*'s society sets up circumstances in which most are unlikely to be happy. The genetically engineered Valids are set up to chase goals not of their own choosing, and the "In-valids" – who are born without genetic modification – are excluded from a vast array of goals they might choose to pursue because of their genetic "deficiency." An open future and a chance for meaningful accomplishment is necessary for happiness, and the society in *Gattaca* denies nearly everyone that open future by preventing both Valids and In-valids from having free choices about their life goals.

Parents in *Gattaca* constrain their child's autonomy by influencing what Philip Kitcher (2002) would call the child's "life theme." A life theme is the framework that identifies which desires and goals are central to the life, and helps the person to make decisions about what to do and how to balance competing values. By restricting a person's autonomy in this way even before birth, and then adding layers of law and social pressure that further discriminate on the basis of what the parents chose (or failed to choose), the *Gattacan* society enshrines injustice and a wide range of destructive effects. The emphasis placed on genetic engineering and the discriminatory "genoism" that results blinds members of the society to evidence about what is possible, what is necessary, and what is true, and that lack of clarity further limits their autonomy and their life theme. As a result, everyone's quality of life suffers.

The movie's emphasis on both the importance of seeing past one's privilege and biases and the injustice of constraining the autonomy of some for the sake of others reveals a Rawlsian argument for how best to think about fairness, justice, and autonomy. To consider this argument, though, it would be good to start with an overview of the film.

Movie Synopsis

Jerome Morrow is about to embark on a one-year, manned mission to Titan. Narrating to the audience, Jerome says that this is "a highly prestigious assignment, although for Jerome, selection was virtually guaranteed at birth. He's blessed with all the gifts required for such an undertaking. A genetic quotient second to none. There's nothing remarkable about the progress of Jerome Morrow. Except that I am not Jerome Morrow."

"Jerome" is really named Vincent and was conceived in the backseat of a car. Hinting at the genoist injustice that dominates *Gattacan* society, Vincent remarks "They used to say that a child conceived in love has a greater chance of happiness. They don't say that anymore." He goes on to explain that the exact time and cause of his death was known at his birth and that he has the following genetic profile: neurological condition 60%, manic depression 42%, ADD 89%, heart disorder 99%, early fatal potential, and life expectancy of 30.2 years.

Unlike Vincent, his younger brother Anton is genetically engineered, and the geneticist explains that the parents have specified hazel eyes, dark hair, and fair skin for the child. (He offers a slightly wry smile at the preference for "fair skin.") The geneticist assures the nervous parents that it is not good to leave "a few things to chance" because they want to give their "child the best possible start."

Despite not having that best possible start, the natural-born Vincent dreams of going into space and makes becoming an astronaut his goal. With his genotype, however, Vincent simply cannot become an astronaut. Although it's illegal to discriminate in *Gattaca*'s world – such discrimination is called "genoism" – no one takes the law seriously, so In-valids like Vincent are outright prohibited from most "important" jobs. Even if he were to lie on his resume, a DNA test would reveal the deception.

Vincent tells the audience that, as an adult, he "belonged to a new underclass...we now have discrimination down to a science." He becomes a janitor at Gattaca Aerospace Corporation but continues to study and to push himself physically with arduous training in his apartment. He knows it isn't going to matter, though, since "the best test score in the world wasn't going to matter unless I had the blood test to go with it."

Vincent intends to become a "borrowed ladder" – someone who assumes the identity of a member of the genetic elite. The identity Vincent will assume belongs to Jerome Morrow – someone with perfect vision, a strong heart, and exceptional intelligence, engineered and expected to become a champion swimmer. Despite all that, Jerome never quite made it to the gold medal, and now is confined to a wheelchair after being hit by a car. Vincent gets contact lenses, a new hairstyle, learns to write with his right hand (Vincent is a lefty but Jerome is a right-handed), carries Jerome's blood under fake fingertips, and keeps Jerome's urine in a container strapped to his leg. The real Jerome will now go by "Eugene."

Vincent explains that "Eugene never suffered from the routine discrimination of a 'utero,' a 'faith birth,' or 'In-Valid,' as we were called. A 'Valid,' a 'vitro,'a 'made man,' he suffered under a different burden: the burden of perfection." That burden is made clear when Eugene confesses that he wasn't drunk when he stepped in front of the car that paralyzed him. He ruefully says he couldn't even get that right, but then mocks "if at first you don't succeed, try, try again."

Vincent is successful at Gattaca, suspected only by the Mission Director. When the Mission Director is murdered, one of the other Gattaca employees, Irene, is assigned to assist the FBI in an investigation. Irene takes a hair she found in Vincent's workstation (planted by Vincent to maintain the ruse that he is Jerome) to a DNA testing facility (apparently used primarily to evaluate potential romantic partners). She learns that the hair is from a "9.3."

Eventually the murder investigation discovers an eyelash from an In-valid former janitor named Vincent, but Inspector Anton declares it's impossible, the eyelash is leftover, and the janitor would have no motive. Detective Hugo says the profile indicates a violent temperament, but Anton reminds him there is a 90% chance Vincent is already dead.

Like Anton, Gattaca Director Josef is skeptical it could be an In-valid. (Due to inherent genoism, Josef likely does truly believe that an In-valid could not infiltrate Gattaca. But his skepticism here also stems from the fact that Josef is the *actual* murderer, worried the exceedingly narrow window for the Titan mission would close before the Mission Director approved the mission.) Speaking to the detectives, Josef allows they have had to "accept candidates with minor shortcomings, but nothing that would prevent one from working in a field such as law enforcement, for example." They closely monitor all their staff because "we have to ensure that people are meeting their potential." Yet, when questioned whether Gattaca personnel could *exceed* their potential, Josef is dubious, replying that when it appears someone does, that simply means it wasn't accurately gauged to begin with.

After the investigation uncovers another trace of the In-valid Vincent Freeman, Detective Hugo thinks the suspect is "playing someone else's hand." The Inspector is dismissive about a "borrowed ladder" at *Gattaca*, because he "wouldn't have the mental faculty or the physical stamina" demanded by space travel. The detectives agree to retest everyone, this time with a venous blood sample rather than fingertip or urine. Vincent escapes this time by leaping to his feet in pain and swapping a vial of blood he had concealed in his hand.

Vincent finally meets the Inspector, and each acknowledges the other is his brother. Anton demands that they do another swimming challenge – like when they were young boys, seeing who could swim out the furthest from shore without turning back. Anton breaks first, begins to drown, and is saved by Vincent, just as he was in their last childhood race before Vincent left home.

Later, Eugene shows a shocked Vincent that he has prepared all of the blood, hair, skin shavings, and other biological material Vincent will need "to last him two lifetimes" so "Jerome will always be here when you need him." Eugene is traveling too, it seems. He says he "got the better end of the deal" since "I only lent you my body, you lent me your dream."

On the day of the mission launch, Vincent arrives at *Gattaca* to find a new policy in place, and he must provide a urine sample. It's clear from his unease that he didn't prepare for this one, but Dr. Lamar cuts him off: "I never did tell you about my son, did I? He's a big fan of yours." Knowing he's caught, he tells Lamar "Just remember, that I was as good as any, and better than most." Lamar continues talking about his son. "He wants to apply here. Unfortunately, my son's not all that they promised. But then, who knows what he could do. Right?" The analysis indicates an "In-valid," but Dr. Lamar walks away, letting Vincent know he's always known by adding "for future reference, right-handed men don't hold it with their left. Just one of those things."

As Vincent climbs into his spacecraft, Eugene climbs into the apartment's incinerator and puts on his silver medal (a keepsake that Eugene held onto to symbolize his failures in life, despite his genetic "perfection"). The rocket ignites as the incinerator ignites, and Vincent realizes his dream as Eugene ends his life, with the Vincent narrating that "Success is by no means guaranteed. After all, there is no gene for fate."

Genoism

As identified above, discriminating on the basis of genetics in *Gattaca* is called "genoism," and it is commonly practiced in spite of its superficial illegality. Vincent tells the viewer he can lie on his resume, but his real resume is in his cells. Even if an applicant refuses to provide genetic information, potential employers have many ways to illicitly sample their DNA.

To see how genoism is the moral rot at the heart of *Gattaca*, one can adapt a classificatory scheme developed by Kwame Anthony Appiah. Appiah makes distinctions between what he calls *racialism, intrinsic racism*, and *extrinsic racism*. *Racialism*, argues Appiah, is the belief that there are distinct human races, and those races each have characteristic tendencies. By itself, this may not present a moral problem because it deals with "how the world is, not how we would want it to be (Appiah [1990])." In other words, this is a descriptive claim – not one telling us what we ought to do – only the latter is subject to moral reproach.

Racism, on the other hand, is a significant moral problem, and it appears in two varieties, intrinsic and extrinsic. On Appiah's account, racism is the belief that distinct human races not only exist but also differ in morally relevant qualities. An *extrinsic* racist thinks about the races this way: If members of a particular race display a tendency to dishonesty, and dishonesty is an appropriate basis for treating persons differently, then one is justified in treating members of that race differently than one would treat others. On this view, it isn't the racial membership as such that justifies mistreatment, rather it is a kind of statistical argument in which race is taken to be an indication of the presence of some trait (e.g., honesty) that would justify treating them differently. Since the justification for the differential treatment is not racial membership itself but the presence or absence of the trait, the differential treatment is unjustifiable if the members of the race in question have no such racial tendency.

Conversely, the *intrinsic* racist believes the different races have different moral status simply because of their race. There is nothing that would count against this belief – no evidence of morally praiseworthy behavior will be acknowledged or allowed to alter the intrinsic racist's assessment of the different races. This distinction can become blurred, however, as many intrinsic racists argue as though they are extrinsic racists but then point to putative expressed differences between races to justify their positions. Extrinsic racists, too, seem to suffer from an inability to recognize that which might undermine their positions. Cases in which apparent counterexamples are explained away with excuses might fit here, such as when the success of a member of one race is taken to be evidence of talent, but similar success from a person of another race is dismissed as unfair "affirmative action."

Appiah is concerned with attempting to show how racism is just that: an "ism" or an ideology that controls and shapes what we are prepared to count as evidence. We could make analogous distinctions for genoism in *Gattaca* that would look something like this: Extrinsic genoists would have a view about "Valids" and "In-valids" to the effect that Valids can outperform In-valids. They wouldn't argue there is anything wrong with being an In-valid per se, merely that no In-valid is, in fact, as talented, intelligent, or whatever as a Valid. The intrinsic genoist would argue that In-valids are inferior to Valids simply in virtue of being In-valids.

Though there are surely extrinsic genoists in the film, *Gattaca* is especially full of examples of intrinsic genoism. When Director Josef reviews Vincent's work, he says it is "right that someone like you is taking us to Titan." It's an odd thing to say if he means only something like "it's good that qualified people are on the mission," but the "someone like you" makes more sense in light of an intrinsic genoist view that Valids are special simply in virtue of being Valids. His recognition of the perfection he sees in Vincent's work is directly linked to his belief that Vincent is a Valid, perhaps even a perfect Valid.

When Vincent explains that "the best test score in the world wasn't going to matter unless I had the blood test to go with it," he's pointing out that there is no *performance* that is sufficient to demonstrate excellence or worthiness, only identity as a Valid can do that. When Vincent compliments Jerome/Eugene on his name and says "I can't be you without it," Eugene responds indignantly with "what makes you think you can be me at all?" Eugene is telegraphing his disdain for what Vincent is doing and indicating a belief that Vincent simply cannot be as good as a Valid. Dr. Lamar tells Vincent the urinalysis was "it" – the entirety of his interview, there is no need for a traditional interview, because to an intrinsic genoist, being a Valid is identical with being worthy and qualified.

Anton is an interesting case. Despite his own experience with his brother beating him in swimming, he declares that there can't be a "borrowed ladder" at *Gattaca*, because he "wouldn't have the mental faculty or the physical stamina." During their climactic final swim, he asks Vincent "how are you doing this?" His intrinsic genoism is so strong that even while being confronted with clear evidence that at least one In-valid can perform as well as some Valids, he still seems bewildered and in denial.

It falls to Eugene to make the point most forcefully. When Vincent is worried he will be caught, Eugene insists "I don't recognize you. They won't marry the eyelash to you, they won't *believe* that one of their elite could have suckered them all this time." He's pointing out that the intrinsic genoist worldview at Gattaca won't allow them to accept evidence that anyone but a Valid could perform as a Valid.

Each of the above is a reminder that in *Gattaca*, merely knowing (or believing) someone to be a Valid or an In-valid is sufficient evidence for full knowledge of what that person can or cannot do. Director Josef, Anton, Eugene, and (at the time) Dr. Lamar would seem to be intrinsic genoists, so committed to their intrinsic genoism that they are incapable of recognizing any evidence against that intrinsic genoism. Like racism, genoism can and does blind its adherents to what is possible, what is necessary, and what is true. Beliefs that one's dignity depends on one's group membership violates basic notions of fairness and thus of justice, as do social institutions built on those beliefs.

Separate Spheres

In light of this widespread genoism, there is something odd about the society depicted in the film with respect to the social sorting of its genoist caste system. Borrowing language from Janet Radcliffe Richards (1986), we might call this a "separate spheres" society. A separate spheres society is one in which members believe there are (at least) two kinds of persons in the society, and those two kinds should have different roles and be treated differently in the society, and that they should avoid attempting the role of the other. While the focus of Richards' work is gender-based social policies, her arguments have much to say about the society on display in *Gattaca*. *Gattaca* is a society in which the Valids and the In-valids are directed into the societal roles deemed appropriate for them. If we adapt the gender analysis she deploys to the castes in *Gattaca* we get something like this:

Premise 1: Persons should act and be treated in ways suitable to their natures.
Premise 2: Valids and In-valids have fundamentally different natures
Conclusion: Valids and In-valids are appropriately limited to separate social and political spheres.

The argument can be read one of two ways: (1) All members of the two castes are essentially instantiations of the relevant nature (this is the analog to intrinsic genoism), or (2) the members of each caste differ in statistical terms (the extrinsic genoist interpretation). Both readings present problems for the advocate of using social policies to create separate social spheres. On the one hand, Richards points out that if the differences are universal – if Valids really are just better than In-valids – then social practices, pressures, and even laws for steering the castes into their separate spheres are superfluous. The In-valids simply cannot perform in the roles the Valids reserve for themselves even if they were allowed to attempt them. If social policies of separation are superfluous, they should be eliminated. After all, if it is an observable fact that Valids will universally outperform In-valids, then a social policy that also establishes this is as useless as a social agreement that water is wet.

On the other hand, consider the extrinsic genoist interpretation. A defender of the caste system might argue that the emphasis on probability and statistics in the movie is evidence that they are relying not on essential differences but rather statistically predictable differences between the two groups. This extrinsic genoism would be defended as a kind of efficiency in identifying the "best" candidates for a given position. To this end, Richards asks the reader to imagine implementing a general policy like "the strong must help the weak" and then to *also* imagine implementing a statistical, gendered rule that requires men (statistically often physically stronger than women) to behave in certain ways with respect to women. On this view, the only people affected by the second, more specific policy are those whose natural attributes do not fit gendered statistics. As Richards points out,

> If you add to general rules about the strong helping the weak a rule about men helping women, the effect of that additional rule is to override the general rules, and bring it about that the non-average puny little man has to lug around heavy loads for hefty amazonian women. And whether or not that can be justified...what is quite certain is that it cannot be justified by principles about the suitability of the strong helping the weak. (1986, pp. 190–194)

Gattaca's general rule in this case might be something like a meritocratic society, where the "best" people get social positions they deserve, based on their abilities.

The more specific rule is that Valids are *statistically* more capable than In-valids. Applying Richards' example suggests that the more specific rule will override the general one – and that is exactly what happens here. An extrinsic genoism that seeks to identify the "best" by creating social castes from "statistical evidence" actually ends up excluding some of the best candidates if they do not fit the expected, genoist statistics (like Vincent, for instance). The practical result is that this extrinsic genoism redefines what counts as "best" as "being part of the 'better' caste" and thereby collapses into an intrinsic genoism instead. To see this, recall when Director Josef admits that if someone seems to exceed their genetic potential, it simply means the potential wasn't measured accurately. In so doing, he's affirming that the genoism of *Gattaca* is intrinsic. Your caste is your caste, and your caste determines your ability, and any apparent exceptions or counterexamples aren't really exceptions, they're just incorrect data. The discrimination of genoism is as unjust, unfair, and immoral as it seems because it really is just about discriminating against some persons in virtue of their genetic makeup. In addition, it sheds new light on the geneticist's injunction to "give your child the best start in life." In an intrinsically genoist society, merely being born a Valid does much of that, and the idea that genetic engineering is about enabling excellence is turned on its head so excellence is now simply defined in terms of being engineered.

*Gattaca*n society establishes and enforces separate spheres. And these spheres are either superfluous (if *all* In-valids really are inferior to all Valids) or deeply unjust (if the separation truly is just social and some In-valids are just as capable of success as Valids). Valids and In-valids are simply directed into their appropriate place in society, with no room made for In-valids such as Vincent to thrive to his fullest potential or to account for those Valids like Dr. Lamar's son who don't fully measure up to what was promised. On the other side of the coin, Jerome, Irene, and even Anton are unhappy because of a gap between what their Valid genotypes project and what their actual phenotypes allow. The intrinsic genoism of the society and the separate spheres it creates violate standards of fairness, and thus justice, and deny (nearly) everyone the sort of autonomy that is required to choose a life theme for oneself and lead a flourishing life.

Life Themes and an Open Future

Phillip Kitcher's article "Creating Perfect People" (2002) offers some useful tools for thinking about *Gattaca* and autonomy. Kitcher's primary interest is in addressing the scope of morally permissible genetic engineering intended to prevent disease, but, as the title suggests, addresses questions of perfectibility as well.

Kitcher asks the reader to imagine "having the ability to snip out genetic material we don't want, break it down or remove it from the cell, and insert just the allele we like in the resultant chromosomal gap." In 2002, he described this as "fantasy," but in the world of *Gattaca* it appears to be precisely what happens in the case of the engineered births. (Incidentally, what seemed fantastical in 2002 is close to being realized at the time this chapter was written. The CRISPR gene editing technique – an acronym for "clustered regularly interspaced short palindromic repeats" – does something very much like this in the present world.)

To discuss the ethics of this sort of genetic engineering, Kitcher suggests we should focus on "quality of life." Of course, "quality of life" is a difficult concept to pin down. On Kitcher's view, "we can understand quality of life in terms of the satisfaction of standards that are generated by the person whose life it is" (p. 236). He further argues that people's lives reflect decisions about what matters to them. He calls this pattern of priorities and desires a "life theme." This allows one to talk about the quality of a person's life in terms of how well or how poorly that person is satisfying the parameters of her life theme.

Not all life themes are created equal, however. Kitcher cites the emphasis contemporary societies place on autonomy as a crucial factor – only those life themes that reflect the person's own choices are considered to be high-quality life themes. In Kitcher's words, "If a person has a theme for his life thrust upon him, then it seems, there is a distinct chance that the course of experience will lead him to regret decisions that have been guided by that theme and to see his achievements as ephemeral and unsatisfying." He further argues that the quality of a life is diminished by "serious risks that the desires given priority will be unsatisfied" (p. 236).

A minor but overwhelmingly obvious example of a life theme being thrust upon someone is the piano player Vincent and Irene see in concert. After the piano performance, the pianist throws his white gloves into the crowd. Vincent catches one and is surprised to see it has six fingers. He tells Irene "Twelve fingers or one, it's how you play." She replies, "That piece can only be played with 12." While the piano player can thus play a piece others cannot, he didn't choose to have the extra fingers that allowed him to play it. Someone else made the decision to engineer him with 12 fingers and send him down the pianist's career path. It might seem to be a trivial case, but no doubt there were many opportunities foreclosed to him because of his extra fingers. The viewer has no way of knowing if he enjoys the piano; the viewer knows merely that he is physically suited to play and clearly talented. If one thinks about many of the other characters in *Gattaca* in light of Kitcher's analysis, it is clear that nearly everyone has a "theme for his life thrust upon him" and consequently unsatisfying achievements and unsatisfied desires result.

For a first example, consider Irene. Irene is unhappy because, for all of her apparent talents as a Gattaca employee, a mistake was made in her genetic programming: She has a high probability of heart failure. Whatever the physiological effects of the heart condition, its psychological effects are such that she lacks the will or confidence to try things that might aggravate her condition. Recall the nightclub scene where Vincent and Irene run out the back door. As they flee, Irene tells him "I can't [run]," but Vincent says "you just did." Vincent confides in her about his own heart condition, telling her he is "10,000 beats overdue." She does not believe it is possible, and Vincent replies that "they have got you looking so hard for any flaw, that, after awhile, that is all that you see." In Kitcher's terms, Irene is unable to satisfy the desires set for her by her parents and leads a life that is apparently a shadow of what it could be because she has internalized the genoism of her society.

This reading of Kitcher sheds light on Anton's situation, as well. The (presumably) genetically perfect Anton is haunted by the fact that his genetically inferior brother beat him at something, even once, and seems to lead a miserable life because of it. For all his genetically engineered abilities, he has become a police officer. Now, he is apparently both high ranking and quite accomplished – but from what Director Josef derisively suggests, being in law enforcement is a much less demanding occupation than working at Gattaca. As he describes his personnel, he says even the least exceptional at Gattaca are still good enough to be police. Vincent, far from being among the least, is "one of their best." So why is Anton stuck in a life of police work, "failing" to achieve his potential? When Anton finally confronts Vincent and offers to help him "get out of here," Vincent tells him that, while he doesn't need rescuing, Anton did once. Anton says "you didn't beat me that day, I beat myself." Yet, when they swim again, Anton fails and begins to drown, needing Vincent to rescue him just like when they were kids. Anton can't bear the idea that Vincent could beat him at swimming, or anything else, and the idea that Vincent has somehow worked himself to a position among the most elite in the society – despite having none of Anton's genetic endowments – infuriates him. He is unhappy, and it is hard to avoid the conclusion that his unhappiness is a function of knowing what his brother has done through pure determination. The viewer does not know what particular life theme was chosen for Anton by his parents, but it was clearly to be among the elite, and he obviously was expected to exceed Vincent's success in every way. Vincent was deemed unworthy of his father's name, and Anton got it instead. Vincent was constantly reminded by his parents to accept his inferior state, lack of potential, and overall sickliness. Anton's rage, frustration, and desire to see Vincent fail go well beyond what would be plausible as simple sibling rivalry (particularly when it seems he was always his parents' favorite). One might suspect Anton is dealing with a kind of cognitive dissonance between his intrinsic genoism and what Vincent has accomplished. Again, Kitcher's suggestion seems to be at work here: The lack of autonomy in his life theme leads Anton to unhappiness and to the conclusion that whatever his successes may have been, Anton does not have a high quality of life.

What about the other main character, Eugene? Eugene, too, had his life theme chosen for him. He appears to have been ordered as the perfect swimmer, with no consideration given for whatever desires he may have had for himself. In Kitcher's view, this already means he will not have a high quality of life. But much like Irene and Anton, he also comes up short of realizing his life theme. In the case of Eugene, he comes tantalizingly close. He is successful as a swimmer, but not the very greatest – he only earns a second-place medal. But what seems to us as only the tiniest degree of failure is enough to make him suicidal. After he attempts suicide, Eugene turns to drowning (no pun intended) his misery in alcohol. For the early parts of the film, he is bitter toward Vincent and scoffs at the possibility of Vincent assuming his identity as "Jerome." Even after he warms to Vincent, most of what the viewer sees of Eugene is him struggling with feelings of failure and self-loathing. Again, this evokes Kitcher's warning that when the life theme is chosen for us, whatever successes we have will be unsatisfying and our desires will go unfulfilled.

At the end of the film, Eugene seems to have found some satisfaction in helping Vincent, and perhaps this could qualify as him pursuing a theme he *did* choose for himself. He has chosen to make Vincent's dream of succeeding despite genetic inferiority his own, saying "I only lent you my body, you lent me your dream." His suicide as Vincent launches to Titan could be seen as Eugene finally following through on his pledge to "try, try again." However, his action is also understandable as a final step in support of Vincent, since there is nothing more he can do to advance what has become their shared life theme, and his continued existence allows for possible complications stemming from there being two "Jeromes."

Of course, Vincent himself has a different Kitcher problem. As an In-valid, he did not have a life theme chosen by his parents and built into his genetics. Instead, he lives in a society that closes off any number of life themes he might choose for himself. The intrinsic genoism of the society shunts Vincent into a separate sphere from the one he is clearly qualified to inhabit, and so pursuing his own life theme – visiting space – becomes almost overwhelmingly difficult. He has to hide his identity by living as Jerome, going so far as to have excruciating leg-lengthening surgery to pull off the deception. He must also engage in vastly more physical training to outcompete the other *Gattaca* personnel, and the intellectual perfection required to perform his navigator duties demands much more of him than it would of those engineered for the task.

Vincent isn't pursuing desires or accomplishments given to him by the outside, which yields great potential for a high-quality life, according to Kitcher. Yet, the societal barriers to his ability to realize his life theme detract from its quality and "constitute serious risks" to him satisfying his desires. Vincent succeeds through sheer force of will (the Latin root of his name, "vincere," means "to conquer"), but the incessant stress of having to work much harder while trying to avoid detection is regularly shown to take a heavy toll on him throughout the movie. Others who are equally talented but perhaps not quite so determined would not fare so well. In short, while he succeeds in accomplishing his goal, it seems it must be concluded that even Vincent's quality of life was less than it might – or should – have been.

Still another character worth mentioning in the context of Kitcher's argument is Dr. Lamar. While he gets little screen time, Lamar is a crucial character in the film. Near the end, when Vincent has to face the unexpected urine test, recall that Lamar returns to the issue of his son. The viewer gets no other details, but it appears Lamar's son has his own version of Irene's situation and the actual expression of his genetic engineering turned out to be a failure in some way. This is apparently why Lamar allowed Vincent to continue his deception all this time. One is left to speculate that Lamar admires Vincent's accomplishments for their own sake and that they give him hope for what it might mean for his son: "who knows what he might accomplish?" Perhaps too his son has caused him to reflect on the injustice of their society, to regret whatever implicit genoism led him to seek a genetically engineered child, or to just have a greater appreciation for role of luck in society.

Both Vincent's struggle against his status as an In-valid and the story of Lamar's son point toward another aspect of Kitcher's argument that might go a long way toward addressing all the misery of *Gattaca*n society. Kitcher points out that if the factors that diminish quality of life are either attitudes and social or political institutions and policies, one can approach the "perfect people" question from another side and ask "What happens if those attitudes, institutions, and policies change?" The parents in *Gattaca* are trying to get perfect children – to give their children the "best start in life." That said, consider what might happen to the 12-fingered pianist if society no longer values music or if no one can afford to attend piano recitals. As a more prosaic example, think about the common trope that left-handed persons are more accident-prone than right-handed persons in light of the fact that a great many tools, etc. have safety guards designed to protect a user holding the tool in her right hand.

Kitcher reminds us that what counts as an advantage – something that would contribute to that best start – will depend on the environment and social context the child finds herself in. To be of high quality, a life requires the autonomy to freely choose a theme and to make good progress on that theme throughout life. A low-quality life comes from a lack of autonomy to choose one's theme or barriers to the realization of one's theme. Thus a commitment to high quality of life for all, or even for most, would require a rethinking of genoism and separate spheres – in other words, a rethinking of the entire social context of *Gattaca*. In short, nearly everyone in *Gattaca*n society seems to be unhappy at least in part because of a lack of fairness, and thus of justice, resulting from the conditions of their society.

Justice

After one reads it, it is difficult to watch *Gattaca* and not think of John Rawls's (1971) work on justice as fairness, *A Theory of Justice*. Among other things, Rawls sought to identify an alternative to those social arrangements that seemed to allow for great injustice as long as the aggregate or bottom-line amount of happiness or perceived social good across the society was sufficiently high. At the heart of Rawls argument is the "veil of ignorance." Rawls recognizes that all persons are biased in many ways, and all persons are inclined to see outcomes that benefit them personally as "fair" or "just," and to see outcomes that do not benefit them as "unfair." The way to control for these biases is to try to determine what outcomes would be acceptable without knowing how each person will be affected. The veil of ignorance, thus, is the idea that decision-makers should not "know how the various alternatives will affect their own particular case and [so that] they are obliged to evaluate principles solely on the basis of general considerations" (pp. 136–137).

Rawls argues that rational persons, denied the knowledge of how they would themselves fare under a given set of social arrangements, would arrive at two principles of justice:

I. "Each person is to have an equal right to the most extensive total system of equal basic liberties compatible with a similar system of liberty for all
II. Social and economic inequalities are to be arranged so that they are both:
   a) to the greatest benefit of the least advantaged
   b) attached to offices and positions open to all under conditions of fair equality of opportunity" (Rawls, p. 302).

Imagine two children in possession of a single Snickers candy bar. The children each want as much candy as possible, but it's a Snickers and the nuts and caramel will make it impossible to divide it into two perfectly equal pieces. What should they do? They could try to determine who had it first, or which of them had a "right" to it, or flip a coin to determine which gets the candy bar, or physically fight with the winner taking the whole thing, etc. Each child can think of arguments for why they deserve the larger share, but whoever "wins" the argument is likely confusing self-interest with fairness, and whoever ends up with the smaller share is likely to be unhappy. If they were to apply a version of Rawls "veil of ignorance," they might agree to use the "I break, you choose" approach: One child breaks the bar into two pieces, and the other child gets to choose their preferred piece. If the chooser chooses the smaller piece, that was their choice, and so they have no principled grounds for complaint. If the chooser chooses the larger piece, the breaker ends up with the smaller piece, but the breaker is responsible for the difference in sizes, so they have no principled grounds for complaint. By agreeing to the procedure, rather than a particular outcome, fairness is achieved even though perfect equality is not. "I break you choose" denies the breaker knowledge of which piece they will receive, and thus motivates them to break the two pieces as close to equal-sized as possible. Ignorance of the outcome changes the breaker's mindset from trying to justify getting a bigger piece to trying to make sure the smaller piece is as big as possible. They have divided the candy fairly, despite it being impossible to divide it equally.

Simply put: The more someone has to consider the worst position they might find themselves in, the more it makes sense for them to ensure that the worst position is no worse than it absolutely has to be.

What does this have to do with *Gattaca*? A Valid can no doubt find lots of self-serving rationales for why Valids deserve to have the privileges of *Gattaca*n society, but those privileges become much harder to justify to the In-valids, who – probably justifiably – assume the Valids are simply rationalizing. Rawls' insight is to ask individual people if they would agree to a society in which one population had extensive privilege that came at the expense of another without knowing ahead of time which of the two populations they would be in. Stripped of personal knowledge, one's thinking about the situation changes, and one starts to worry not about the grandeur of being a Valid but about just how bad the In-valids have it. Since someone in Rawls's original position would have to consider the possibility of finding themselves as an In-valid, it is not rational for that person to accept a social arrangement that makes the In-valid's position any worse than it absolutely has to be. By establishing a society on these two Rawlsian principles above, each person in a society can be thought of as having consented to the social arrangements of that society, even if they happen to not be particularly fond of their station in life. As Rawls puts it:

> A society satisfying the principles of justice as fairness comes as close as a society can to being a voluntary scheme, for it meets the principles which free and equal persons would assent to under circumstances that are fair. In this sense its members are autonomous and the obligations they recognize self-imposed. (p. 13)

Such a Rawlsian approach would preclude the creation or enforcement of separate spheres. The two principles of justice, applied to *Gattaca*, would mean that – at the very least – any privileged position would be in principle open to anyone under conditions of fair equality of opportunity. Vincent might still have to study and train much, much harder than his genetically engineered peers, but he wouldn't have to expend so much additional effort on masquerading as Jerome. The principle that inequalities must benefit the least advantaged would entail that rather than sorting and policing barriers between castes, society would work to minimize the barriers that each member confronted in the pursuit of her life theme. In this world a student like Vincent wouldn't be excluded from good schools because of claims that his poor health made him a liability risk for the school, so actualizing whatever potential he had would be made easier, not more difficult. (As an extreme case, consider Vincent telling Eugene that in space his paralyzed legs would not matter.)

Such an increased potential for satisfying the plans of one's life theme would lead to a higher quality of life. A social structure that lavished less on an elite class and provided more for the rest would ameliorate at least some of the pressure felt by parents to engineer their children for a particular niche in society, allowing greater autonomy in life theme choice and thereby a higher quality of life, as well.

Conclusion

Gattaca is a movie about a society that is unfair and unjust: it conceptualizes that unfairness in Rawlsian terms, and it pushes us to think of the flaws we find in *Gattacan* society as flaws that might be addressed with Rawlsian solutions.

Gattacan society is a society built on *intrinsic* genoism. In-valids are not treated as though the whole population is statistically less physically adept or less intelligent than Valids: they are treated as though they are necessarily less adept, less talented, and less valuable than Valids, *because* they are In-valids. The movie features scene after scene of Valids demonstrating their intrinsic genoism. Consider what the characters say or do when confronted with countervailing evidence: Their response to inconvenient facts reveals that genoism isn't a statistical abstraction, it's an ideology about who matters and who doesn't, period. This genoism is so complete, it denies them the ability to see or even imagine that In-valids can excel. It is, in fact, precisely the sort of entrenched bias and privilege that Rawls' veil of ignorance is designed to counteract. That same blindness prevents them from recognizing either the unfairness or the (if they are correct about In-valid abilities) superfluousness of institutionalized separate spheres, and prevents them from recognizing that the link between genetic endowment, caste membership, and performance is not nearly as tight as the society's structure presumes. Finally, the idea that even some members of society should have their life theme chosen for them also fails to pass a Rawlsian test.

With that worldview in mind, it becomes easier to see the feedback loop between genoism and the poor quality of life resulting from the characters' predetermined life themes. Anton, Irene, and others cannot reconcile the gap between what they were supposed to be as Valids and what they actually accomplished, and so they suffer. They do not accept any role for luck or circumstance in their lives because they see the world in intrinsic genoist terms. In fact, these characters are unable to entertain the "What if I were an In-valid?" kind of thought experiment necessary to appreciate Rawls' conception of justice. That makes it easier to rationalize the privileges of being a Valid as due to their own excellence rather than as a deliberate (and enforced) social structure of separate spheres. In turn, *that* causes a kind of doubling down on the pressure to get the genetic engineering at the core of *Gattaca*'s intrinsic genoism correct the next time around, thus perpetuating a cycle of nonautonomous life theme choices. Everyone, Valid and In-valid, suffers from a low quality of life.

The 2020–2021 Covid-19 pandemic and recent long-overdue attention to the problems of systemic racism have called attention to the hierarchies and privileges of the "real" world. People may not yet live in a society in which parents can order their children to their preferred genetic specifications, but people do live in a society in which the successful can still seek to justify their success as a result solely of innate talent and hard work rather than an array of factors beyond their control – such as luck and inherited wealth – and so can still seek to dismiss inequality as a matter of personal failings.

The parallels between Gattacan genoism and real-world racism are also not hard to see. In either world, holding beliefs about talents or – worse yet – dignity based merely on group membership is a kind of moral blindness. In either world, the value or usefulness of a "genetic" trait, talent, or ability will depend on social policies and the environment they create. Finally, in either world being able to justify decisions and policies to those who benefit from them the least is an essential feature of justice. Both the science fiction and the real-world "ism" disregard those principles. A closer look at *Gattaca* can help contemporary people think more carefully about the connections between success and social arrangements, and the arguments for and against maintaining the status quo in their own societies.

References

Appiah, K.A. 1990. Racisms. In *Anatomy of racism*, ed. D.T. Goldberg. Minneapolis: University of Minnesota Press.
Kitcher, P. 2002. Creating perfect people. In *A companion to genethics*, ed. J. Burley and J. Harris. Massachusetts: John Wiley & Sons, Incorporated.
Rawls, J. 1971. *A theory of justice*. Massachusetts: The Belknap Press of Harvard University Press.
Richards, J.R. 1986. Separate spheres. In *Applied ethics*, ed. P. Singer. Oxford: Oxford University Press.

A.I.: *Artificial Intelligence* as Philosophy: Machine Consciousness and Intelligence

45

David Gamez

Contents

Introduction	1062
The Plot of *A.I.*	1063
Intelligence	1066
Natural and Artificial Intelligence	1066
The Measurement of Intelligence	1067
AI Technology	1068
AI Safety	1070
Consciousness	1071
Natural Consciousness	1071
Artificial Consciousness	1073
Simulation, Intelligence, and Consciousness	1075
Consciousness and Ethics	1076
Emotions	1077
What Are Emotions?	1077
Love	1079
Imprinting	1079
AI, Robots, and Emotions	1080
Robotics	1081
Humanoid Robot Technology	1081
Robot Pets, Toys, and Companions	1082
Developmental Robotics	1083
The Uncanny Valley	1084
Real and Artificial Boys	1085
The Displacement of Humans by Robots	1086
Conclusions	1087
References	1088

D. Gamez (✉)
Department of Computer Science, Middlesex University, London, UK
e-mail: david@davidgamez.eu

© Springer Nature Switzerland AG 2024
D. K. Johnson et al. (eds.), *The Palgrave Handbook of Popular Culture as Philosophy*,
https://doi.org/10.1007/978-3-031-24685-2_59

Abstract

A.I.: Artificial Intelligence tells the story of a robot boy who has been engineered to love his human owner. He is abandoned by his owner and pursues a tragic quest to become a real boy so that he can be loved by her again. This chapter explores the philosophical, psychological, and scientific questions that are asked by *A.I.* It starts with *A.I.*'s representation of artificial intelligence and then covers the consciousness of robots, which is closely linked to ethical concerns about the treatment of AIs in the film. There is a discussion about how *A.I.*'s interpretation of artificial love relates to scientific work on emotion, and the chapter also examines connections between the technology portrayed in *A.I.* and current research on robotics.

Keywords

A.I. · A.I.: Artificial intelligence · Supertoys last all summer long · Spielberg · Aldiss · Kubrick · Intelligence · Artificial intelligence · Turing test · AI · Consciousness · Artificial consciousness · Machine consciousness · Emotion · Love · Imprinting · Robots · Uncanny valley · Mecha · Toy · Companion robots · Developmental robotics · Luddite

Introduction

A.I.: Artificial Intelligence (2001) is based on a short story, *Supertoys Last All Summer Long*, by Brian Aldiss (2001). The film rights for *Supertoys Last All Summer Long* were purchased by Kubrick, who collaborated with several writers and the graphic artist Chris Baker on developing the story into a film (Baker et al. 2009). Kubrick intended to use robotics and special effects to create David, but these were not sufficiently advanced at that time, so he shelved the project. Kubrick knew Steven Spielberg and wanted him to direct *A.I.*, both because he thought that Spielberg would do a better job and because Spielberg worked faster, so the aging of a real boy cast as David would not be an issue during the shoot. Kubrick took up the project again after *Jurassic Park (1993)* demonstrated that special effects were good enough to realize his vision. When Kubrick died in 1999, the project was passed to Spielberg, who wrote the screenplay and directed the final film. Most of the key ideas in the film are derived from Kubrick's development work, including the strange final section with the resurrection of Monica. The film's visual design was largely based on the drawings by Chris Baker, who worked closely with Spielberg on the project.

Kubrick had a strong interest in fairy tales and believed that they embody profound themes of human existence. The story of Pinocchio is central to Kubrick's adaptation of Aldiss' stories, and Kubrick often referred to the project as his Pinocchio film. The original Pinocchio is a selfish naughty boy, who is more focused on pleasure and adventure than pleasing his father. He does not want to study or work and gets endlessly distracted by people who make false promises. Becoming a real boy is not important to him; it is only after he is willing to work hard and shows tenderness toward his father that he is made into a real boy by the Blue Fairy (Collodi 1995). In *A.I.*, David starts out as a loving slightly cheeky boy whose rejection by Monica unleashes ugly emotions, such as the violence he exhibits toward his copy. After his abandonment, David sets out on a monomaniacal quest to become a real boy so that he can recover Monica's love – a path he is tragically committed to by the imprinting process. David's resolution and fixity of purpose are very different from Pinocchio's picaresque pleasure seeking.

A.I. has good special effects, impressive visual design, some great acting, and excellent cinematography. However, the plot has many flaws, and the film will probably never achieve the status of a classic. Despite the title, it is not really a film about AI: it just takes human-level AI for granted and ignores the many forms and levels of artificial intelligence that are likely to be present in the future. It deals with the ethical treatment of robots in an interesting way, but this should have been linked with artificial consciousness, not artificial intelligence. The central part of the film is a well-told story about a robot abandoned by the person he has been engineered to love. Then we are transported into a distant future populated by advanced robots (easily mistaken for aliens) who facilitate a tragic "happy" ending in which the robot's fate is left uncertain and the person he loves disappears forever. In the early scenes, Haley Joel Osment does an excellent job of portraying the creepy uncanniness of the robot David. Then the film gives up on uncanniness, and the robots are scripted with ordinary human psychology.

This chapter explores the philosophical, psychological, and scientific questions that are asked by *A.I.* After the plot summary in section "The Plot of *A.I.*," the section "Intelligence" discusses the film's representation of intelligence and examines its treatment of AI technology and AI safety concerns. The section "Consciousness" covers natural and artificial consciousness and explains why the ethical treatment of AIs should be linked to their consciousness, not to their intelligence. Emotions play a key role in *A.I.*, so the section "Emotions" explains how psychological theories of love and imprinting connect with the portrayal of artificial emotions in the film. The final section explores *A.I.*'s vision of robot technology.

The Plot of *A.I.*

A.I. is set at a time when rising oceans have drowned cities and displaced millions of people. To address a lack of resources, governments have introduced strict controls on reproduction: potential parents need a license to have a child, and few licenses are issued. Robot technology has made considerable progress, and humanoid robots (called "mechas") are common in society. The claim is rather implausibly made that mechas consume less resources than people.

The film opens with a research meeting at the robot manufacturer Cybertronics. Professor Hobby introduces Sheila, an example of the current generation of robots. She looks human, but she does not have human emotions. When Hobby stabs her in the hand, she interprets the injury as physical damage, not pain. She defines love as a series of behaviors, such as widening her eyes and quickening her breath. Like all the current mechas, she is based on "neuron sequencing technology." This generation of mechas is good at imitating human behavior, but they feel nothing inside. Hobby then outlines his plan to build a new generation of mechas that genuinely love the people they imprint on. This is vaguely linked to "work on mapping the impulse pathways in a single neuron" – presumably some kind of advanced brain-inspired technology. The new mechas are intended to be child companions, targeted at couples waiting for a license to have a child. The scene ends with a pertinent question from one of the team: "If a robot could genuinely love a person, what responsibility does that person hold toward that mecha in return?"

The next scene is a cryogenic hospital in which Martin, the real child of Henry and Monica, is preserved in a state of suspended animation until a cure for his fatal illness can be found. Henry works at Cybertronics, and because of his special situation, he and Monica are given the first prototype of the new mecha child, David. David's initial behavior is pretty creepy: he never blinks, he has a very straight posture, he appears suddenly without warning, and he has bouts of exaggerated and inappropriate laughter. Gradually, Monica gets used to him, and Henry explains the imprinting process: when a sequence of random words is read to the mecha, he will love the adoptive parent. This imprinting is irreversible: if the mecha is no longer wanted, it must be sent back to Cybertronics to be destroyed. After imprinting, Monica and David start to bond, and Monica gives Martin's toy robot, Teddy, to David.

The positive relationship that develops between Monica and David is disrupted by Martin's recovery and return home. Martin and David compete, as boys do, and Martin uses David's artificiality against him – describing him as a "super toy." David does not appear to fully understand that he is a mecha, and Martin asks cruel questions that emphasize David's artificiality and Martin's superior status as a real boy. Martin asks Monica to read Pinocchio to them and pressures David into eating human food, which causes him to break.

Later, Martin tells David that he has a special mission for him, which will make Monica love him, but David has to promise to carry out the mission before he is told what it is. David promises and Martin tells him that he has to cut off a lock of Monica's hair. He says that he is not allowed, which is presumably some kind of AI safety programming, similar to Asimov's laws of robotics (see section "AI Safety"). However, Martin made him promise to do it, and presumably keeping promises is part of his programming too. So David tries to cut off a piece of Monica's hair, but she wakes and David nearly pokes her in the eye with the scissors. At Martin's birthday party, the other children ask David humiliating questions and test his damage avoidance system by threatening him with a knife. David gets scared and holds onto Martin. They accidentally fall into the pool and Martin nearly drowns.

The pool incident makes Monica decide that David can no longer live with them. She does not want to send David back to Cybertronics for disposal, so she abandons David in the woods with Teddy. David asks if he can come home if he becomes a real boy. Monica says that he is not real and that stories like Pinocchio are not real. In the woods, David meets a sex robot, Gigolo Joe, who has been framed for murder. They are captured and taken to the Flesh Fair, an arena in which robots are destroyed in spectacular ways for the entertainment of the crowd. David and Joe are placed beneath buckets of acid, and the crowd is invited to throw bean bags to release the acid. However, the crowd is unwilling to destroy them because of David's high level of realism and his apparent age. So they throw the bean bags at the Flesh Fair host, and David and Joe escape.

As David and Joe wander through the woods, David explains his plan to find the Blue Fairy, who, he hopes, will change him into a real boy so that Monica will love him. Joe suggests that they go to Rouge City to consult a search engine called Dr. Know about the location of the Blue Fairy. Dr. Know gives them an enigmatic clue that leads them to Manhattan, where they discover a large building with a laboratory and library inside. Sitting in a chair is another mecha, exactly like David. The second David is friendly, but the first David perceives him as a rival for the love of Monica. In a fit of rage, the original David smashes the other mecha to pieces. Professor Hobby appears and explains that the answer from Dr. Know was planted to bring David to his lab. He describes David as special and unique, and then he leaves the room to find the other members of his team. David wanders through the lab and sees many versions of himself in different stages of assembly as well as boxes containing copies of himself ready to be shipped. In despair, he throws himself off the building into the sea, where he sees a submerged fair and a statue of the Blue Fairy. Joe rescues David but then is taken away by the police, and David and Teddy return to the submerged fair in an amphibicopter and park opposite the Blue Fairy. A falling Ferris wheel traps the amphibicopter, and David is left staring at the Blue Fairy, constantly repeating his request to become a real boy.

Eventually, the ocean freezes, and David stops moving. Thousands of years later, advanced super-mechas are carrying out archaeological excavations on the site. These super-mechas look like aliens, but the intention of the film is that they are advanced robots that have taken over the planet after humanity died out. David is revived and meets something that looks like the Blue Fairy in a reconstruction of Monica's home. David asks the Blue Fairy to make him into a real boy. She says this is impossible and explains that Monica is dead but can be temporarily resurrected from her DNA. Teddy gives the Blue Fairy the lock of Monica's hair that David cut off in an earlier scene.

The resurrection of a person from their DNA only works for one day. After that, the person falls asleep and cannot be resurrected again. Despite this limitation, David insists that Monica is brought back, and when she awakes, they spend a perfect day together. The resurrected Monica loves David, and David has the happiest day of his life. At the end of the day, David falls asleep and goes "to that place where dreams are born." There is some ambiguity about whether this resurrection is just a dream, and this is likely to have been the original intention of Kubrick (Baker et al. 2009). However, in the final film, it seems reasonably clear that the living Monica is really brought back for one day and then dies forever. The final fate of David is left undetermined. Perhaps he "dies" too, although he surely could be kept going by super-mecha technology. A more likely scenario is that he would be condemned to a lonely existence in which he loves Monica and grieves for her while struggling to adapt to the alien world of the super-mechas.

Intelligence

Natural and Artificial Intelligence

The mechas in *A.I.* have human-level artificial intelligence: they can perceive and identify objects, navigate in their environments, understand natural language, reason, plan, and so on. Artificial systems are usually judged to be intelligent if they exhibit behaviors that require intelligence in natural systems. Many definitions of intelligence have been put forward, including cognitive ability, rational thinking, problem-solving, goal-directed adaptive behavior, and the ability to make accurate predictions (Gamez 2021; Legg and Hutter 2007a). Some of these definitions are anthropocentric; others apply to many different types of system.

Some people believe that human intelligence is completely general and can tackle *any* problem. The idea of artificial general intelligence (AGI) is usually derived from beliefs about the generality of human intelligence. However, humans do not have completely general intelligence – for example, we cannot reason about large data sets or mentally manipulate five-dimensional objects. As Chollet (2019) points out, the human brain evolved to help us survive in a hunter-gatherer environment, and it has a limited ability to generalize beyond this environment. If human intelligence is not completely general, then there is very little reason to believe that a completely general artificial intelligence is possible.

A more plausible view is that there are many different types of intelligence that are optimized for different environments. Some intelligences are good at chess; others excel at ATARI video games. This idea has often been discussed in the literature on intelligence. For example, Gardner (2006) claims that there are multiple types of intelligence, including musical intelligence, linguistic intelligence, and emotional intelligence. Warwick (2000) frames this more generally with his idea that intelligence is a high-dimensional space of abilities.

Within AI research, there is a popular distinction between narrow and general artificial intelligence. Systems that exhibit one type of intelligence are often called "narrow" – for example, a chess-playing program is a narrow AI because it cannot play draughts or Monopoly. Narrow intelligence is usually contrasted with general intelligence, but if general intelligence is a myth, then all the intelligences that we know or can imagine are, to a greater or lesser extent, narrow, and we will never be able to build a completely general AI. However, we can still compare systems according to the narrowness/generality of their intelligence. Suppose we have ten environments of similar complexity. An intelligence that performs well in eight of these environments is more general (less narrow) than an intelligence that only works in one environment.

Intelligence is a *functional* property that can be implemented in many different ways. For example, a given piece of intelligence can be implemented using biological neurons, simulated neurons, computer programming, clockwork, and so on – the physical details are irrelevant as long as the system behaves in a particular way. This is very different from consciousness, which is closely tied to the way a system is physically organized (see section "Natural Consciousness").

The Measurement of Intelligence

How could we measure the intelligence of the mechas in *A.I.*? Human intelligence is often measured using IQ tests, which have verbal, spatial-reasoning, and mathematical questions. Verbal, spatial, and mathematical abilities are thought to be linked to intelligence, so humans that perform well on these tests are thought to be more intelligent than people who perform less well. It is often claimed that IQ tests only measure the ability of people to perform IQ tests, not intelligence itself. However, the results of IQ tests correlate with other indicators of intelligence, such as academic grades, the publication of scientific papers, and success in professional careers (Robertson et al. 2010).

Animals cannot take human intelligence tests, so there has been a lot of work on the development of cognitive test batteries for animals (Shaw and Schmelz 2017). While it might be possible to come up with a plausible set of tests that could be applied to similar animals, this approach is likely to neglect the different types of intelligence that animals develop to survive in their ecological niches. A measure of intelligence that is designed for sheep or fish, for example, cannot easily be transferred to birds or bees. A second problem with the measurement of non-human animal intelligence is that we do not have a way of connecting an animal's test results to other indicators of intelligence for that species. Most people would agree that a person who gets top grades in school, gets a degree at MIT, and publishes groundbreaking physics research is likely to be intelligent. If an intelligence test gives this person a low score, then this is a failure of the test, not an indicator of low intelligence. But how could we ground the results of intelligence tests in octopi, bees, or dogs? Animals do not take advanced degrees or write papers on quantum theory. It is far from clear how we could prove that intelligence tests in animals measure anything more than the ability to perform the test itself. These problems get worse when we try to use batteries of tests to measure intelligence in artificial systems. AI systems can be programmed to pass IQ tests that are designed for humans. However, IQ tests are designed to measure a more general ability in humans, whereas an AI that is programmed to get high scores in IQ tests cannot do anything except get high scores in IQ tests.

The Turing test was originally proposed as a way of answering the question of whether a machine could think. Turing (1950) described a thought experiment in which a human and a machine were connected to an electronic typing system and placed in a separate room. A human tester asked the two systems questions and tried to decide which was the human and which was the machine. If the human tester could not reliably identify the machine, then the machine would be judged to be capable of thinking. Thinking is not of much interest to modern AI researchers, so most people view the Turing test as a way of establishing whether a machine is as intelligent as a human. Many variations of the Turing test have been developed, including behavior in game environments (Hingston 2009) and the Animal-AI Olympics (Crosby et al. 2019), which provides an environment in which artificial systems can attempt tasks that are believed to require intelligence in animals. If David took the Turing test, he would pass most of the questions posed by unskilled examiners. However, some aspects of his mind could easily be identified by a skilled interrogator. For example, a real boy would have memories about his earlier childhood, and David is likely to be better at mathematics than a child of a similar age. Turing testing has the limitation that it can only determine whether a machine's intelligence is identical to human intelligence. It cannot measure nonhuman forms of intelligence or intelligence that exceeds human levels.

People have developed *universal* measures of intelligence that, in theory, can be applied to any system at all. For example, Legg and Hutter (2007) developed a universal measure that sums the rewards that an agent receives across all possible environments, with some adjustment for the complexity of different environments. Hernández-Orallo and Dowe's (2010) algorithm is based on inductive inference, prediction, compression, and randomness. Gamez's (2021) measure is based on the number of accurate predictions that a system makes in a set of environments. In the future, universal measures of intelligence could become powerful tools for comparing intelligence in different types of natural and artificial system.

AI Technology

At the start of *A.I.*, Professor Hobby states that the current mechas are based on "intelligent behavioral circuits, using neuron sequencing technology." The next generation, including David, was to be based on "mapping the impulse pathways in a single neuron." Hobby appears to be suggesting that the mechas' minds are based on simulated brains that have been modified to produce specific behaviors, such as David's imprinting.

Many different approaches have been used to build intelligent machines. The earliest systems were constructed with mechanical components. For example, Jacques de Vaucanson's Digesting Duck could flap its wings, drink water, and pretend to digest grain. Clockwork has also been used for mathematical operations. The Antikythera mechanism (around 100 BCE) could predict astronomical positions and eclipses, and in the nineteenth century, Charles Babbage's Difference Engine carried out polynomial calculations using cogs and gears. Babbage also designed a programmable mechanical computer called the Analytical Engine. His collaborator, Ada Lovelace, wrote programs for the Analytical Engine and suggested novel nonmathematical applications for it, such as music composition. The Digesting Duck, Antikythera mechanism, and Analytical Engine were impressive achievements. However, the cost, speed, and unreliability of clockwork limit its usefulness for building complex AI systems.

The development of electronic computers created the modern field of artificial intelligence. In the early days, AI programs were sets of rules that specified actions to take when certain inputs were detected. For example, Terry Winograd's SHRDLU was a program that interacted with a virtual world, which contained blocks and cones. It could answer questions about the blocks and cones in natural language and change the world on command. These early AI systems often used a search procedure to find solutions to a problem or to plan actions. However, it was soon realized that more realistic and complicated problems had a massive search space, which could not possibly be explored. The early AIs also could not handle minor variations in their environment that had not been anticipated by the programmer. Suppose a cake recipe specifies one large egg but there are only two small eggs in the fridge. A human would add the two small eggs to the mixture. A rule-based AI could only bake the cake if the two-egg scenario had been anticipated by the programmer. People tried adding more rules to cope with more situations, but it rapidly became clear that high levels of intelligence could not be achieved with this method.

Computers can learn about the world and use this learned knowledge to plan actions. Many machine-learning approaches have been developed, including statistics, genetic algorithms, and support vector machines. Today, the most successful machine-learning method is a deep neural network, which has multiple layers of simulated neurons that can be trained on millions of pieces of data. AI systems based on deep networks can reach human-level performance on classification tasks, such as face recognition, and outperform humans on games, such as Breakout and Go. The intelligence of machine-learning systems is constrained by the data that they have been trained on, and they often have a limited ability to work outside this context. For example, a deep network that has been trained for face recognition is incapable of processing natural language. So learning by itself does not solve the problem of the brittleness of AI systems compared to humans. In some AIs, machine learning is combined with rule-based approaches – for example, a self-driving car might use deep networks for classification tasks, such as object identification, and hard-coded rules to control which actions to take under specific circumstances – if a pedestrian is in front of the vehicle (identified with deep network), turn on the brakes (AI rule).

Many AIs have been developed that use natural language processing (NLP) to understand and respond to human input. In the early days, people built simple chat systems, known as chatbots, that were entirely hard coded. The chatbot had a set of input-output rules: when the input matched a rule, it responded with the corresponding output. When no match was found, the chatbot would output a question or attempt to change the subject. Some modern chatbots, such as Alexa and Siri, are based on this technology. More recently, people have been building chatbots with deep neural networks that are trained on large quantities of text data from the Internet. These systems can answer questions and generate text in a more dynamic, convincing way.

Many contemporary researchers are interested in the possibility that human-level AI could be built by scanning the neurons and synapses in the human brain and simulating them in a computer. This could be a way of creating an AI with human-level intelligence without the complex training and design process that go into our current AIs. Simulated brains can work faster than biological brains, and many copies can run simultaneously. Dead brains can be scanned by cutting them into very thin slices, taking pictures with an electron microscope, and building a three-dimensional model of the neurons and connections from the scanned images. This process is slow, but it might eventually become possible to identify the structure of the 100 billion neurons in the human brain and their 10^{15} connections. So far, scientists have managed to map 75,000 neurons and 524 million connections in a cubic millimeter of the mouse brain (Bae et al. 2021). Large-scale simulations of millions of neurons have been built, but these are only very rough approximations of the human brain (Izhikevich and Edelman 2008). More accurate simulations with tens of thousands of neurons have been created (Markram et al. 2015), and people are developing dedicated neuromorphic hardware that will enable us to run brain simulations more efficiently (Indiveri et al. 2011). In time, it is conceivable that we will be able to improve scanning accuracy and scale up our ability to simulate the brain at a high level of detail. However, the brain is a very complex system with vast numbers of chemical and electrical feedback loops. Even if we had the neural data and the computation capacity, it would take many years to get a simulated brain to work in the same way as a living biological brain.

AI Safety

At Martin's birthday party, other (real) children threaten David with a knife, and he grabs hold of Martin in fear. They both fall into the pool, and Martin is nearly drowned. In another scene, David tries to cut off a lock of Monica's hair and nearly pokes out her eye with the scissors. These incidents dramatize important concerns that people have raised about AI safety and liability.

There are at least four reasons why AIs could harm humans:

1. *Deliberate*: an AI kills a human because it has been programmed to kill humans. Military robots fall into this category as well as AIs that are programmed to use force to protect someone from harm – for example, a bodyguard robot.
2. *Misperception*: the AI misperceives the situation and acts according to its misperception. As far as the AI is concerned, it is taking care not to hurt humans, but because it has interpreted the situation incorrectly, it ends up doing harm. For example, a butler robot might think that a baby on a table is a roast turkey and carve it up.
3. *Unresolvable dilemma*: whatever the robot does leads to harm. This was the case with David, who appeared to have two rules: (1) do not harm humans, and (2) keep promises. By making him promise to do an unknown act (cut off a lock of Monica's hair), David is forced to break one of his AI safety rules. In this case, his desire to be loved by his mother led him to choose to break the rule about not harming humans.

4. *Accident*: an industrial robot arm hits a worker that strays into its path; a self-driving car takes a corner too fast and plows into some pedestrians. David's near drowning of Martin falls into this category.

Some people believe that the dangers posed by AIs could be reduced if we could hard-code safety rules into them. The most famous set of safety rules that have been put forward are Asimov's (1952) laws of robotics:

1. Robots shall not harm a human, or by inaction allow a human to come to harm.
2. Robots shall obey any instruction given to them by humans.
3. Robots shall avoid actions or situations that could cause them to harm themselves.

While these laws initially seem plausible, they cannot protect people against misperceptions, unresolvable dilemmas, and accidents. Asimov was well aware of this, and *I, Robot* explores the many ways in which these apparently simple laws fail to produce desired behaviors.

AI safety is particularly challenging in machine-learning systems because it can be hard to understand what they have learn and can be difficult to predict how they will behave in new or unexpected situations. This is often an issue with deep neural networks that have been trained on millions of pieces of data. An AI that cannot be understood by humans is referred to as a black box. There is ongoing work to try to white-box AI systems so that we can understand what is going on in their "minds" and address potential safety issues.

There are also complex questions about AI liability, particularly with machine-learning systems. If a self-driving car fails, is it the owner's fault or the manufacturer's fault? When David violently destroys a copy of himself, is this because of his programming or because he has been mistreated by his environment? White-boxing AIs could make it easier to identify the causes of unwanted behavior. In the future, robot manufacturers might be required to build systems that behave well (Russell 2019). However, this is not at all easy because human morality is ambiguous, and people often have incompatible sets of values (Haidt 2013). We need to solve our own moral relativism before we can conceivably program morality into a robot.

Consciousness

Natural Consciousness

The only significant mention of consciousness in *A.I.* is when Hobby claims that "love will be the key by which they acquire a kind of subconscious never before achieved. An inner world of metaphor, of intuition, of self-motivated reasoning. Of dreams." Hobby is not suggesting that he will build a conscious robot, which experiences the colors, sounds, and smells that are typically thought to constitute conscious experience. Instead, a more liminal world of imagination and dreams will be given to a robot that may or may not be fully conscious.

Consciousness is often defined as a stream of colorful, noisy, smelly, and tasty experiences that starts when we wake up in the morning and disappears when we fall into a dreamless sleep at night. The modern concept of consciousness emerged in Europe in the seventeenth century (Wilkes 1988). Prior to this, people believed that conscious experiences were objective properties of the physical world – green was attributed to trees, not to the interaction between light, trees, eyes, and brain (a position known as naïve realism). The renaissance of atomism in the seventeenth century led to the physical world being interpreted as a realm of colorless atoms bouncing about in the void. When these atoms interacted with our senses, they produced conscious experiences of colors, smells, etc. This led to a distinction between primary qualities, which were properties of the atoms (for instance, size, shape, and speed), and secondary qualities, which were properties of consciousness (for example, color, smell, and sound) (Galilei 1957; Locke 1997). Primary qualities were thought to be physically real, but seventeenth-century thinkers could not ignore their experiences of the colorful smelly world that they lived in from day to day. So the concept of consciousness was developed to accommodate people's experiences of colors, smells, and sounds, which had been squeezed out of the physical world by atomism (Gamez 2018).

Since the seventeenth century, we have been attempting to put consciousness and the physical world back together. Some people have tried to reduce consciousness to the physical world (a position known as physicalism), but it makes no sense to claim that colorful experiences are identical to neuron activity. Other people have taken consciousness to be the primary reality – for example, idealists, like Berkeley (1957), or phenomenologists, like Husserl (1960), who suspended belief in the physical world. A better way out of this dilemma is to accept that consciousness and the physical world are both real and to scientifically study the relationship between them. This type of research is carried out by people searching for the neural correlates of consciousness. These scientists measure the brain, measure consciousness, and look for neural activity patterns that only occur when the brain is conscious (Koch et al. 2016). There are also quantum and electromagnetic theories of consciousness, so work on the neural correlates of consciousness can be generalized into a search for physical patterns that are correlated with the presence of consciousness and, ideally, with specific conscious contents.

Many people have suggested that consciousness is correlated with computational or informational patterns (Cleeremans 2005; Tononi 2008), but there are strong reasons for thinking that computation and information are subjective interpretations of a physical system (Gamez 2018). Whether or not something is conscious cannot depend on how we interpret it, so it is much more likely that consciousness is correlated with specific physical patterns – for example, patterns in biological neurons, electromagnetic waves, or quantum states.

As Popper (2002) points out, a final theory of the relationship between consciousness and the physical world will not be a long list of correlations. Ideally, we would like to find a compact mathematical theory that maps between descriptions of the physical world and descriptions of conscious states. Such a theory could generate a

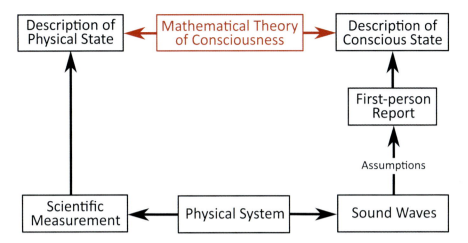

Fig. 1 Mathematical theory of consciousness. Scientific measuring instruments (fMRI scanners, EEG, etc.) are used to measure the system and produce a description of its physical state. The system also produces sound waves (and other behavior) that we can interpret as first-person reports about consciousness by making certain assumptions (Gamez 2018). These first-person reports are converted into a description of the system's conscious state. A mathematical theory of consciousness describes the relationship between descriptions of physical and conscious states. It can generate a description of consciousness from a description of a physical state and generate a description of a physical state from a description of consciousness

description of the conscious state that is associated with a particular physical state. Or, conversely, if we knew the conscious state, then it should be able to generate a description of the corresponding physical state (Gamez 2018). This is illustrated in Fig. 1.

Progress is being made with the development of mathematical theories of consciousness. The most popular is Tononi's information integration theory of consciousness, which converts information patterns into a prediction about the amount of consciousness, the location of the consciousness, and the structure of the consciousness (Oizumi et al. 2014). There is little experimental support for Tononi's algorithm, and it has severe conceptual and performance issues (Gamez 2016). However, it does illustrate the form that a mathematical theory of consciousness could take.

Artificial Consciousness

Although consciousness is barely mentioned in *A.I.*, it is one of the most important aspects of the plot. Suppose that David is a purely mechanical system with no trace of consciousness. He has the external appearance of a sad boy who wants his mother to love him. He makes certain sounds – for example, when he is abandoned, he pitifully pleads "Why do you want to leave me? Why do you want to leave me? I'm sorry I'm not real, if you let me I'll be so real for you!" But if David is *not* conscious, then these are just sounds produced by mechanical processes, no different from the vibrations in the air produced by Vaucanson's flute player. Our belief that David consciously experiences love, fear, and pain drives our empathy for him in his adventures. In the Flesh Fair, we respond to his imminent destruction with far more emotion than we would if we were watching a washing machine being destroyed.

Artificial consciousness is a complex field that can be divided into four different areas (Gamez 2018):

1. *Replication of external behaviors that humans exhibit when they are conscious*: for example, humans only respond to novel situations and execute delayed reactions to stimuli when they are conscious. These behaviors can be exhibited by AI systems.
2. *Models of the correlates of consciousness*: for example, researchers have created simulations of the neural correlates of consciousness (Shanahan 2008).
3. *Models of consciousness*: the structures of consciousness have been documented by phenomenologists like Husserl (1960). These can be modeled in computers and used to control robots (Gravato Marques and Holland 2009).
4. *Artificial systems with something that corresponds to our conscious experiences*: these AIs would have something like the colors, tastes, sounds, and smells that appear when we wake up in the morning and disappear when we fall into deep sleep at night.

In *A.I.*, David replicates the external behaviors of a conscious human. His mind might be based on a model of the neural correlates of consciousness or on a model of consciousness. From the point of view of David's treatment in the plot, the most important question is whether he actually has conscious experiences – something similar to the colors and sounds that we experience when we are conscious.

In humans, it is straightforward to infer consciousness from external behavior. When my eyes are open and I am speaking coherently, people naturally conclude that I am having colorful smelly noisy conscious experiences. With occasional exceptions, such as epileptic automatism, the inference from human behavior to consciousness is judged to be reliable, and it is the basis for medical diagnoses of consciousness, such as the Glasgow Coma Scale (Teasdale and Jennett 1974). This inference works in humans because we assume that most people are built in the same way: if they are behaving in the way that we do when we are conscious, then it is reasonable to assume that they are conscious too.

External behavior is not a correlate of consciousness in humans. It is the neural patterns that lead to this external behavior that are correlated with consciousness. In a robot, there are an infinite number of different ways of producing a given piece of behavior. For example, the phrase "I am conscious" could be output by a single line of code, a biological brain, or a sophisticated chatbot trained on hundreds of millions of pieces of data. Some of these systems might be conscious; many are highly unlikely to be conscious. Judgments about an artificial system's experiential consciousness cannot be based on its external behavior.

45 A.I.: *Artificial Intelligence* as Philosophy: Machine Consciousness...

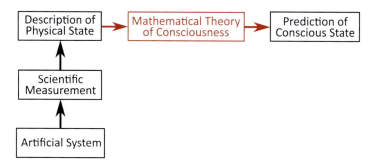

Fig. 2 Prediction of artificial system's conscious state. Scientific instruments measure the physical state of the artificial system. A reliable mathematical theory of consciousness converts the physical description into a prediction of the artificial system's consciousness

In *A.I.*, David behaves like a human. If he were human on the inside, we would have no hesitation in attributing consciousness to him. But David is a robot, and the consciousness of the mechanisms that produce his external behavior cannot be inferred from that behavior. If we want to know whether David is *really* conscious, we have to use a theory of consciousness that can reliably map between physical and conscious states (see Fig. 1). We can use this mathematical theory to convert a description of David's physical states into a description of his conscious states, as shown in Fig. 2.

This approach has limitations because a theory of consciousness that has been developed on natural systems might miss relationships between physical and conscious states that exist in artificial systems. However, it is the *only* reliable way of making inferences about the consciousness of artificial systems. *A.I.* encourages us to relate to David in the same way that we would relate to a conscious human boy. However, if David was a real robot, it would be a completely open question whether he was conscious.

Simulation, Intelligence, and Consciousness

People often confuse computer simulations with the thing that is being simulated, particularly when it comes to robots and AI. Suppose we want to model lynx and rabbit populations. Lynxes eat rabbits, and both animals reproduce at a finite rate with influences from resources, diseases, and so on. These interactions can be captured by a simple computer program. When the program runs, the lynx and rabbit numbers are stored as voltage patterns in the memory of the computer. In practice, these voltage patterns are constantly fluctuating, but for simplicity, we will treat them as 1s and 0s. So if there were 56 rabbits, 111000 would be in the computer's memory. The connection between 111000 and real rabbits is made in our minds: 111000 is not warm or furry, it does not eat grass, and it cannot be eaten by a lynx.

Voltage patterns *can* produce intelligent behavior. David's intelligence is a *functional* property: anything that behaves intelligently is intelligent. Intelligent systems can be implemented with voltage patterns, by people manipulating Chinese characters in a room (Searle 1980), or by ant colonies (Hofstadter 1979). Any of these systems could, in theory, control a robot like David, which is as intelligent as a human being. There is no distinction between a simulation of intelligence and intelligence itself.

Consciousness is a *physical* property of a system (see section "Natural Consciousness"). The way in which a system is physically built matters for consciousness. A computer simulating a brain and a biological brain might produce the same behaviors in a humanoid robot or biological body. This does not mean that they have the same consciousness. Only a reliable mathematical theory of consciousness can decide whether nonbiological systems are conscious. A mecha controlled by simulated neurons is very unlikely to be conscious in the same way as a biological human brain.

Consciousness and Ethics

Throughout the film, David is treated as a thing that can be damaged with impunity. He will be destroyed by Cybertronics if his owners no longer want him. After he is abandoned by Monica, David ends up in the Flesh Fair, where unregistered mechas are wrecked for entertainment. It does not matter how David feels about being dissolved in acid – it is just the destruction of a machine that simulates feelings; the legal destruction of property that does not belong to anyone. A similar theme appears in Pinocchio when Fire-eater decides to burn Pinocchio to cook his mutton. When Pinocchio begs for mercy, Fire-eater suggests that one of the other puppets should be burnt in his place. Pinocchio is not a real boy, so it is fine to throw him into the fire to cook some meat.

At the start of the film, one of Hobby's team asks: "If a robot could genuinely love a person, what responsibility does that person hold toward that mecha in return?" Kubrick raised a similar issue: "One of the most fascinating questions that arise in envisioning computers more intelligent than men is at what point machine intelligence deserves the same consideration as biological intelligence.... You could be tempted to ask yourself in what way is machine intelligence any less sacrosanct than biological intelligence, and it might be difficult to arrive at an answer flattering to biological intelligence" (Baker et al. 2009). These ethical questions are incorrect because intelligence is a functional property that is irrelevant to a system's treatment. As far as his intelligence goes, David's human mimicry is just a clever trick, like a special effect in the movies.

There is a close relationship between consciousness and ethics. We cannot kill fully conscious humans or cause them to suffer without their consent. The respect that we have for animals loosely correlates with their perceived consciousness: primates are given the best treatment, fish receive some consideration and insects have no protection at all. Coma patients that are unlikely to regain consciousness are allowed to die. In most countries it is illegal to assist a fully conscious person with terminal illness to voluntarily end their life. So it is only when robot toys and companions become conscious that we are obliged to treat them in the same way as other conscious systems.

When the mechas in the Flesh Fair express fear, we automatically empathize with them and attribute consciousness to them, just as we would if a real human was being destroyed. However, it is possible that none of the mechas are conscious. They could be simulating conscious human behavior with nothing going on inside. To determine whether the mechas are really conscious, we have to measure their internal physical states and use a reliable mathematical theory to convert this into a description of their consciousness. If there is no consciousness, then the mechas' destruction is merely a thrilling illusion in which something that looks and acts like a human is destroyed. On the other hand, if the mechas really are conscious, then their destruction is similar to the killing of people or animals for public entertainment.

In the future, if we want to avoid ethical issues with robot toys and companions, we could use mathematical theories of consciousness to design robots that are *not* conscious. We could then treat them like toasters and junk them when they are no longer required.

Emotions

What Are Emotions?

The first scene of the film introduces Sheila, one of the current generation of mechas. Hobby describes her as "A sensory toy, with intelligent behavioral circuits." He injures Sheila and asks her how this made her feel. She replies that the injury was to her hand, not to her feelings. She describes love as "widening my eyes a little bit and quickening my breathing a little and warming my skin and touching . . . ." This scene shows that the current mechas lack human emotions. They do not feel pain or love; they are just sensory toys with intelligent behavioral circuits. Hobby then suggests that Cybertronics should build a child mecha who can love: "A robot child who will genuinely love the parent or parents it imprints on, with a love that will never end." This is the axis on which the plot turns. If David merely simulated love, in the way that sex mechas simulate arousal, then he would not need to be sent back to Cybertronics for disposal. However, his genuine nontransferrable love for Monica forces him on a tragic quest to become real so that he can be reunited with her.

Emotions are a controversial topic, and many theories have been put forward. Some people believe that they are socially constructed, others think that they are natural kinds, and there are extensive debates about which feelings truly constitute emotions and which do not. In my view, the most plausible interpretation of emotions is that they are perceptions of real or virtual body states (Damasio 1994; James 2000). For example, when I see something frightening, my brain causes my skin to sweat and my stomach to tighten. My perception of these physical changes is the emotion of fear.

In humans, there is not a simple one-to-one mapping between body states and emotions (Barrett 2018). The interpretation of a body state as an emotion is a complex process that partly depends on context. For example, Barrett describes how she interpreted the onset of flu as attraction during a date. Basic emotions, such as fear and joy, are probably shared across cultures; more complex emotions are likely to vary between cultures and languages, just as the partitioning of the physical world varies between cultures and languages (Gamez 2007). In nonhuman animals, there is likely to be a more straightforward relationship between changes in body states and perceived emotions.

We learn associations between states of our environment and emotional states. Certain foods and social situations make us happy; other foods and social situations make us unhappy. Damasio describes these learned associations as somatic markers. Somatic markers vary widely between individuals, which explains the different ways in which people seek happiness, sexual satisfaction, and so on. Some people find staring at a crucifix to be deeply fulfilling; other people experience sadness and distress at the sight of a dead man nailed to a cross.

In psychology, a distinction is often made between affect and emotion. Affect is the general background feeling that you experience throughout each day: whether you are calm, bored, tired, energetic, etc. This background feeling has two components: valence and arousal. Valence is how pleasant or unpleasant you feel – for example, you might have an unpleasant stomach ache or experience pleasure at the sight of your child. Arousal is how calm or agitated you are – for example, you might feel tense before a parachute jump or fatigued after a long run. There is no clear dividing line between affect and emotion. In my view, the combination of arousal and valence that we experience throughout each day is more plausibly described as an ongoing emotional state that is influenced by our mind and environment. We might, for example, go on holiday to positively influence our arousal and valence in exactly the same way that we buy a new pair of shoes to make us happy.

Rationality is often celebrated as our most impressive human quality and contrasted with irrational emotions that we are supposed to master. This greatly underestimates the critical role that emotions play in our thinking. Our decisions are guided by complex interactions between real and imagined states of the world and learned associations between these world states and the emotions that they produce in us. I go to the cinema because I have learned an association between watching films and positive emotional states. When I think about the cinema, my brain produces a weak version of these positive emotional states in my body, which motivates me to make a plan to go to the cinema.

Emotions can be conscious or unconscious. For example, I can be stressed without consciously perceiving the signs of stress in my body. Later, when I meditate, I become aware of my hunched shoulders and the knot in my stomach. Unconscious emotions can influence actions in the same way as other unconscious perceptions. When we are considering how to treat someone, only consciously experienced emotions matter. It is wrong to cause conscious pain and fear; unconsciously perceived pain during surgery does not raise ethical issues.

Love

David's love for Monica is central to the plot of *A.I.* In humans, love is a combination of emotions that can occur independently in other contexts. For example, in the early stages of a romantic relationship, people often experience sexual desire, excitement, happiness, and the absence of negative emotions. Love can change over time, shifting from intense euphoric states in the early stages to long-term attachment. There is some debate about whether love is a basic emotion or even if it is an emotion at all (Lamy 2015).

Studies of human love often distinguish between passionate romantic love and compassionate or family love. Romantic love often includes intense states of euphoria, usually with sexual desire. Compassionate love, such as the love of a mother for her child, typically has less extreme euphoria and lacks the sexual component. Both forms of love often include a suppression of negative emotions and a reduction in critical judgment (Zeki 2007).

When David is with Monica, he presumably experiences warm positive feelings, pleasure in her company, and an inhibition of anxiety and critical judgment. When they are apart, his positive feelings decrease and his anxiety increases. Her abandonment of him presumably made the negative components more intense, strongly motivating him to be with her so that he could experience the warm positive feelings and the inhibition of anxiety again.

Imprinting

When David arrives at Monica and Henry's home, he has a neutral attitude toward Monica and does not call her "Mommy." The imprinting consisted of reading seven words to David, which caused him to "genuinely love the parent or parents . . . with a love that will never end." The genuineness of David's love for Monica appears to be his unique selling point – in contradistinction to older mechas that simulate emotions without actually feeling them. Knowing that your robot "child" genuinely and irreversibly loves you could make you feel special and increase your bonding with the robot. However, imprinting has disadvantages, which drive most of the film's plot. After imprinting, David genuinely and irreversibly loves Monica, but she abandons him, and so he is driven to seek the Blue Fairy so that he can be changed into a real boy and be loved by Monica again.

Imprinting was first scientifically described by Lorenz (1937), who observed that newly hatched geese follow the first moving object they see. Usually, this object is their mother, but they can imprint on humans or other moving objects they are exposed to in a short period after hatching, such as a green box or football. Imprinting has been observed in birds, insects, fish, and some mammals, including sheep, goats, deer, buffalo, and guinea pigs (Hess 1958). Under normal circumstances, when the imprinting period is over, the young can no longer form this kind of attachment or change the object or animal they have imprinted on.

Imprinting can, in theory, be implemented in different ways. For example, the young animal could experience fear or anxiety when it is not looking at the imprinted object, or there could be a simple hardwired reflex that causes it to move in the direction of the imprinted object. The most likely explanation is that the imprinted animal starts to love the imprinted object, experiencing positive feelings and a reduction in negative feelings when it is in its presence. There is some evidence for this in sheep, where the imprinting window can be reopened by the injection of the hormone oxytocin, which is linked to the implementation of love in the brain. In the film, David's imprinting on Monica is based on love.

Imprinting could be a positive feature for robot companions. For example, we would not want to buy an expensive robot wife or husband who falls in love with someone else. Imprinting could ensure that robot companions do not betray us, abandon us, or hurt our feelings. In the film, the imprinting is portrayed as irreversible – David must be returned to the manufacturer for destruction if the imprinted owner no longer wants him. This has a cynical benefit for the manufacturer that they prevent a secondhand market for mechas like David, and it would lead many owners to abandon their unwanted mechas to a hopeless unrequited existence, rather than send them back for disposal.

AI, Robots, and Emotions

Emotion detection helps robots interact with humans: David wants to know if Monica is happy or sad, and Gigolo Joe monitors his clients' pleasure. Emotion recognition is a well-established field in AI, and there are many commercial solutions for the identification of emotions in video, voice, and text. Emotion detection is not completely reliable because there is not a simple mapping between facial expressions and emotions, and algorithms are often trained on pictures of actors who are pretending to experience different emotions.

Human-robot interaction is also easier if robots use human expressions to communicate. By simulating pleasure, Joe increases the pleasure of his clients. David's loving expressions increase his attractiveness as an artificial child substitute. Or consider a robot that is trying to teach the times tables to a child. The robot asks, "What is seven times five?" The child replies, "thirty-five," and the robot replies "Correct" in a bland mechanical voice. Children will rapidly get bored with this teaching method. A robot that expresses sorrow when the answer is wrong and joy when it is correct will connect more directly with the child's emotions and engage them in learning for much longer. Early work in this area was carried out with the Kismet robot, which could perceive and express human emotions (Breazeal 2002). Many other robots that express human emotions have been developed, including the highly realistic humanoid robots discussed in the section "Humanoid Robot Technology".

In the Flesh Fair, Lord Johnson-Johnson makes a strong contrast between a mecha's simulation of emotion and real emotions experienced by humans: "Do not be fooled by the artistry of this creation. No doubt there was talent in the crafting of this simulator. Yet with the very first strike, you will see the big lie come apart before your very eyes!" The "lie" is that a mechanical system is producing the external signs of emotion to make us think that it really has emotion, whereas in fact it is just clever robotics producing an illusion. This aspect of the film is out of touch with reality because scientists have been building AIs with emotions for a long time. The simpler implementations use variables to represent emotions. The values of these variables are changed in response to input, and they are used to select behavior. This type of emotion model has been used with the AIBO robotic dog, and it is part of the learning intelligent distribution agent (LIDA) cognitive architecture. In more complete implementations of emotions, the robot perceives states of its real or virtual body, which change in response to external events. For example, the robot might have a stomach that changes state when a fearful stimulus is encountered. A full implementation of emotions would also enable the robot to learn new associations between body states (somatic markers) and states of the environment. In the future, AI systems with emotions are likely to become increasingly important as the critical role that emotion plays in cognition comes to be more widely recognized (Pessoa 2019).

The artificial emotions that have been implemented so far are unlikely to be associated with consciousness. For a robot to consciously experience human love, it would need to generate the same bodily responses as humans in love (positive feelings, suppression of negative critical thinking, and physiological responses, such as flushing and increased heart rate). This emotional response would have to be implemented in a way that is correlated with consciousness (see section "Artificial Consciousness"). More progress with the implementation of emotions in robots and in our scientific understanding of consciousness is required before we will be able to build robot children like David, who genuinely and consciously love the people they imprint on.

In the film, most of the current generation of mechas are far less cold and logical than Shelia. This is particularly apparent at the Flesh Fair, where we are presented with robots that do not regard their imminent destruction as something that just happens to their bodies. One mecha asks for his pain receivers to be shut down (a big contrast with Sheila at the start of the film), Gigolo Joe appears to have the full range of human feelings, and even Teddy appears to experience fear and attachment to David. This inconsistency is not surprising because the film wants us to empathize with the mechas. It would be a very different Flesh Fair if all the mechas had the same equanimity as Sheila about physical damage and calmly accepted their destruction in the same way as a microwave oven.

Robotics

Humanoid Robot Technology

A.I. simulates humanoid robot technology with human actors, and a considerable amount of work went into the development of the robotic Teddy puppets that were used to shoot the film. In the real world, humanoid robots are difficult to control, and scientists are only just starting to build humanoid robots that can cope with realistic environments. Much more work is being done on machines that save labor in specific situations (for instance, manufacturing robots and self-driving cars), rather than on humanoid robots that directly replace human labor.

Most of the humanoid robots that have actually been built, such as ASIMO, NAO, and iCub, are rigid structures with rotating joints. They can be programmed to perform impressive feats – for example, ASIMO dances and plays football. But these behaviors are mostly preprogrammed moves within predictable environments. If the environments change by a small amount, then the behaviors often fail with unpredictable consequences. The most notable exception to this is the Atlas robot developed by Boston Dynamics, which is much better at handling variations in terrain and recovering from falls and external impacts. While most humanoid robots only mimic the external form of the human body, some also copy our musculoskeletal system in the hope that this could lead to more natural movements and better integration between the robot's mind and body. For example, the CRONOS and ECCE robots are based on a copy of the human skeleton, which is moved by muscles modeled by cords and electric motors. These robots are much more flexible and dynamic than traditional humanoid robots and have the potential to behave in more humanlike ways. However, they are extremely difficult to control.

Work is also being done on robots that closely mimic the external appearance of humans. For example, Hiroshi Ishiguro's Geminoid robots are fairly accurate copies of particular people. There is also Ameca, developed by Engineered Arts; Sophia, developed by Hanson Robotics; and Ali-Da, which is touted as the world's first ultra-realistic humanoid robot artist. These robots look fairly convincing, they can mimic human facial expressions, and they can be connected to AI technologies, such as chat, face recognition, and so on. However, none of them can move their bodies as well as Atlas: their main achievement is facial mimicry, which falls far short of the mimicry displayed by Sheila at the start of *A.I.*

Humanoid robots consume a lot of power. Research is being done to make some behaviors, such as walking, more energy efficient by copying the mechanics of the human body. However, a major breakthrough in power generation, such as the arc reactor in *Iron Man (2008)*, would be required to create the mechas in *A.I.*, which can apparently last for years without refueling or recharging.

Robot Pets, Toys, and Companions

David is a robot companion that is designed to look and act like a child and fill the emotional needs of adults who are prevented from having children. For Henry and Monica, David also fills the hole left by the illness and cryogenic suspension of Martin.

Many robot pets, toys, and companions have been developed, often to provide emotional support to the elderly or hospital patients. One of the first virtual pets was the Tamagotchi, a small egg-shaped device with a screen displaying a pet that the owner could feed, train, and play games with. A nice example of a robot toy is a bear called "Super Toy Teddy," which was based on Teddy and had rudimentary AI functionality. A substantial amount of work has also been carried out on robot pets and companions for the elderly and hospital patients using a variety of robots, including NAO (small humanoid robot), Paro (robot seal), and ElliQ (robot with screen face, which was distributed to elderly people in New York).

Toys and companions are designed to manipulate our emotions. The cute visual appearance and furry squishiness of a stuffed toy induce feelings of warmth and affection. Children cuddle, love, and take care of their teddies in the same way that they cuddle, love, and take care of real animals. In *A.I.*, David is a companion robot for adults – a much more advanced version of Paro and ElliQ – that is designed to fill an emotional hole in the lives of adults who have not been able to have children of their own.

Most toys are inert *objects* (plastic soldiers, cuddly teddies, china dolls) that can be flexibly incorporated into different play scenarios. They might break, but they never get bored; they don't care if they wear a tutu or a pirate hat. Artificial intelligence transforms toys from objects into subjects. They have their own desires and autonomous behavior and are less adaptable to imaginative scenarios – Teddy does not want to play tea parties anymore because he is bored of that game. Toys that are subjects are more effective companions. A plastic dog is only intermittently constructed as a subject by its owner – when, for example, it is described as needing to eat or pee. A real dog has a strong presence and personality; its needs and desires must be taken into account. It might be willing to be dressed up and participate in games, but to a much more limited extent than a plastic dog. In *A.I.*, Teddy is a subject, a companion that operates alongside David, shares his troubles, and helps him out of danger. Future AI companions could guide children's learning, act as safe confidants, and open up new possibilities for play.

Today's toys and robot companions can be treated in any way we like. We can dissect them, blow them up with fireworks, or dissolve them in acid for our amusement. The film does not provide any reason for believing that David or Teddy is conscious, but it does strongly encourage us to infer consciousness in them from their external behavior. If we could use a mathematical theory to prove that they were not likely to be conscious, then it would be completely fine for them to be destroyed in the Flesh Fair for the entertainment of the crowd. However, David and Teddy are designed to engage our emotions, so it would still be upsetting to see them dissolved in acid or fired into a propeller even if no actual harm was being done.

Developmental Robotics

In Aldiss' (2001) stories, Monica gets tired of David and Teddy because they are so predictable. David is a poor substitute for a child because he learns little and never really changes. Teddy is equally boring, playing the same games with David all summer long. If we want our robot companions to continue to engage our interest and entertain us, then they will have to learn and grow alongside their owners – an area known as developmental robotics.

Developmental robotics is an important research area because it is impossible to program AIs with human-level intelligence from scratch (see section "AI Technology"). While machine learning has made rapid advances in recent years, most of its successes have been in areas where large quantities of labeled training data are available, or in simple environments, such as board or video games, that can easily be modeled in a computer. Much less progress has been made with the development of AI systems that can function effectively in real-world environments – self-driving cars are probably the best example, and they have a very limited set of objectives and behaviors.

The human brain is roughly wired up at birth, and it takes many years of learning to develop the intelligence of an adult human. Some researchers believe that the limitations of our current AIs can be overcome by building robots that start out in an infantile state and then learn like children by being immersed in our physical and social environment. An early pioneer in this area was Grand (2004), whose robot orangutan, Lucy, could learn from her experiences. Other examples of infant and child robots are CB2, Infanoid, and Pneuborn (see Cangelosi and Schlesinger (2015) for an overview of this work). This research is at an early stage, and it has the problem that each training/test cycle can take a long time.

The Uncanny Valley

As robots become more humanlike, we increasingly empathize with them. Industrial robot arms do not evoke warm feelings; we can easily relate to the cute NAO robot. When robots become very similar to humans, without completely matching their appearance and behavior, then we experience unease and revulsion. Our empathy returns when robots become indistinguishable from humans. In computer science, this phenomenon is known as the uncanny valley (Mori 2012).

Mori's theory of the uncanny valley nicely accounts for the levels of empathy that we experience for the characters in *A.I.* Teddy clearly looks like a toy, so we do not experience him as creepy and empathize with him. Gigolo Joe looks human and (apart from his music-playing ability) generally behaves in a similar way to humans, so we relate to him with roughly similar levels of empathy to Teddy. Monica is 100% human, and we empathize with her in the same way that we empathize with other humans. In the early stages of the film, David looks human, but his behavior (in contrast to Joe's) is distinctly odd – no blinking or sleeping, pretend eating, inappropriate laughter, etc. This produces a feeling of revulsion or negative empathy in us. Later in the film, David evokes similar levels of empathy to Joe. This is illustrated in Fig. 3.

There is a limited amount of empirical evidence for the uncanny valley (Kätsyri et al. 2015), and some people have applied Mori's recommendation that we aim for the first peak initially, building systems that evoke affinity, but not so close to human likeness that we experience revulsion. We do not want to share our world with robots that creep us out, so future humanoid robots will either have to make their artificiality explicit or develop to the point at which they are indistinguishable from humans.

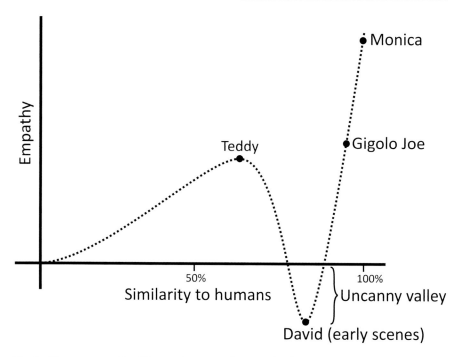

Fig. 3 The uncanny valley. We experience negative empathy for characters that resemble humans without completely matching human appearance and behavior. More empathy is experienced for characters that are clearly artificial or that are virtually indistinguishable from humans

Real and Artificial Boys

Monica rejects David because he is a mecha who accidentally endangers her real son. But David is desperate to be with Monica and believes that she would love him if he became a real boy like Martin. So he sets off on a quest to find the Blue Fairy, who he hopes will make him into a real boy. The other mechas in *A.I.* would also benefit from becoming real. They are built to serve humans and can be tortured and destroyed with impunity when they are no longer useful. If mechas could become real (biological) humans, then they would cease to be slaves and enjoy the same rights as humans.

There is no clear dividing line between real and artificial boys. At one end of the continuum are natural-womb-born children; at the other end are completely artificial systems, such as the Atlas or iCub robots, that are entirely assembled from manufactured parts. In theory, David could become a real boy by replacing his artificial parts with biological parts. His mind could be built from biological neurons; a biological body could be grown for him in the lab (possibly using a combination of Monica's and Henry's DNA). The only thing that would be missing is the biological history of real boys – he would always be a mecha assembled from biological components. So even if David became a biological boy, Monica would probably never love him because he lacked the history of her natural son, Martin.

Real boys have many disadvantages. They grow old and die; they have medical conditions that cannot be fixed; they cannot be backed up and restored; they are incapable of long-distance space travel. Pinocchio is much tougher than a real boy and can easily be repaired. David's mind can be backed up, and his body parts can be swapped out and fixed. The super-mechas at the end of the film have outlived humanity. So David's quest to become real reverses the more common science fiction trend in which people become more artificial to enhance themselves or cheat death – *RoboCop* (1987) is a nice example. In many ways, David was lucky to be an artificial boy. If he could have accepted an artificial copy of Monica, then they could have lived happily together, potentially forever.

The Displacement of Humans by Robots

The Flesh Fair is a reaction against mechas, who are accused of robbing humans of their specialness and dignity. It is a protest against artificiality and simulation: the mechas' destruction makes the lie of their appearance come apart before the crowd's eyes. The film also expresses concerns that humans are outnumbered and mechas might eventually take over. This point is nicely made by Gigolo Joe: "They made us too smart, too quick, and too many. We are suffering for the mistakes they made because when the end comes, all that will be left is us. That's why they hate us..." This prediction comes true at the end of the film when humanity wipes itself out and only the super-mechas remain. In our own society, labor shortfalls are typically addressed by recruiting foreign workers and boosting the birth rate. So it is a little strange that *A.I.* presents a future in which the birth rate is cut and large numbers of power- and resource-hungry robots are built to work for humans. It is these policies, not the mechas themselves, that create a death sentence for humanity.

For the foreseeable future, humanoid robots will be too stupid and expensive to cause significant job losses. Jobs will be lost to other types of AI: self-driving cars and trucks will take drivers' jobs, call center staff will be replaced by chatbots, robots will play an increasing role in farming, and factories will become fully automated. In the past, the jobs that were lost to automation were replaced by new jobs that were created by industrialization. In the twenty-first century, there are a few agricultural laborers and many office workers. So far, the AI technology revolution is following the same pattern, but this may change as AI becomes increasingly sophisticated. If AI and robotics do result in significant net job losses, then it might become necessary to introduce some form of universal basic income – a regular payment to every member of society that covers their living costs. This could be funded by taxes on AI and robotics companies that were responsible for the reduction in human jobs. Without a universal basic income, large numbers of unemployed people might not have enough to live on, and there could be widespread social unrest.

Conclusions

A.I.: Artificial Intelligence is a flawed film that asks interesting questions about intelligence, consciousness, artificial emotions, and robotics. Despite the title, it is not a film *about* artificial intelligence because it takes human-level artificial intelligence for granted and does not explore the variety of forms that AI can take or the difficulties with building AI systems. The film's suggestion that the mechas' intelligence could be implemented using brain-based neural simulations is plausible and fits in with current research on biologically-inspired neural networks. AI safety issues are nicely dramatized in the early scenes, and the treatment of the mechas in the Flesh Fair raises important points about the ethical treatment of AIs. However, the ethical issues raised by the film should have been linked to the mechas' consciousness, not to their intelligence.

Consciousness is almost completely ignored in *A.I.*, despite its relevance to the mechas' treatment. Humans typically infer consciousness from external behavior: something that behaves and looks like a human is judged to have human consciousness. This works with natural systems, but there are many ways in which robots can be controlled, and most of these are unlikely to be associated with consciousness. So the experiential consciousness of artificial systems cannot be inferred from their external behavior. Instead, we have to use a mathematical theory of consciousness to convert a description of the machine's physical state into a description of its conscious state. Research on mathematical theories of consciousness is still at an early stage, and it will be a long time before we can make accurate predictions about the consciousness of artificial systems or design nonconscious artificial systems that can be discarded without ethical concerns.

In the research meeting at the start of *A.I.*, a robot that genuinely loves its owner is presented as a major breakthrough. This is based on the old idea that AIs are rational rule followers without feelings. In fact, robots with emotions are not as new as the film suggests. As our understanding of emotions has advanced, we have come to appreciate the important role that they play in human cognition, and this has led many researchers to build AI systems with emotions. Irreversible imprinting is a novel idea that has not yet been implemented. However, it is not clear why we would want this functionality, and the film highlights some of the problems that could occur with this type of system.

With the exception of Teddy, the mechas in *A.I.* are humanoid robots that are played by human actors. Real humanoid robots are complex mechanical systems that are expensive, unreliable, power-hungry, and difficult to control. It is much easier to design robots for specific tasks – dishwashers are ubiquitous in our society; no one has built a humanoid robot that can do the dishes. So it is very unlikely that the future will be populated with humanoid robots that directly replace human labor. Robot toys and companions are active research areas, particularly in societies with aging populations, so we are likely to see increasingly sophisticated versions of Teddy in the future. However, the difficulties with humanoid robotics and human-level AIs are likely to prevent us from building child robot companions like David for a long time.

The central theme of the film is David's desire to become real so that he can be loved by Monica. David could, in theory, become biological, but this would have many disadvantages. Without the appropriate history, this would be unlikely to help him achieve his central goal of being loved by Monica. *A.I.* does have good acting, particularly by Haley Joel Osment, who does an excellent job of portraying a child robot with a variety of odd behaviors (not blinking, rigid posture, inappropriate laughter, and so on). Mori's work on the uncanny valley nicely captures how David's not-quite-human behavior in these early scenes produces an eerie lack of empathy. Teddy does not have this effect because he is clearly artificial, and Gigolo Joe is human enough to evoke empathy.

A.I. also raises issues about the displacement of humans by robots. In the film, this occurs because of population control policies and the proliferation of robots. In the real world, it is much cheaper and easier to breed self-repairing humans than to manufacture and maintain humanoid robots to replace human labor. There are likely to be substantial job losses to AI in areas such as driving, call centers, mining, and manufacturing. It is an open question whether the jobs created by AI will compensate for those that are lost. If AI does lead to mass unemployment, then it might be necessary to introduce a universal basic income.

References

Aldiss, B.W. 2001. *Supertoys last all summer long: And other stories of future time*. London: Orbit.
Asimov, I. 1952. *I, Robot*. London: Grayson & Grayson.
Bae, J.A., M. Baptiste, A.L. Bodor, D. Brittain, J. Buchanan, D.J. Bumbarger, M.A. Castro, B. Celii, E. Cobos, F. Collman, N.M. da Costa, S. Dorkenwald, L. Elabbady, P.G. Fahey, T. Fliss, E. Froudarakis, J. Gager, C. Gamlin, A. Halageri, J. Hebditch, Z. Jia, C. Jordan, D. Kapner, N. Kemnitz, S. Kinn, S. Koolman, K. Kuehner, K. Lee, K. Li, R. Lu, T. Macrina, G. Mahalingam, S. McReynolds, E. Miranda, E. Mitchell, S.S. Mondal, M. Moore, S. Mu, T. Muhammad, B. Nehoran, O. Ogedengbe, C. Papadopoulos, S. Papadopoulos, S. Patel, X. Pitkow, S. Popovych, A. Ramos, R.C. Reid, J. Reimer, C.M. Schneider-Mizell, H.S. Seung, B. Silverman, W. Silversmith, A. Sterling, F.H. Sinz, C.L. Smith, S. Suckow, M. Takeno, Z.H. Tan, A.S. Tolias, R. Torres, N.L. Turner, E.Y. Walker, T. Wang, G. Williams, S. Williams, K. Willie, R. Willie, W. Wong, J. Wu, C. Xu, R. Yang, D. Yatsenko, F. Ye, W. Yin, and Yu, S.-c. 2021. Functional connectomics spanning multiple areas of mouse visual cortex. *bioRxiv*. https://doi.org/10.1101/2021.07.28.454025.
Baker, C., J. Harlan, and J.M. Struthers. 2009. *A.I. Artificial intelligence: From Stanley Kubrick to Steven Spielberg: The vision behind the film*. London: Thames & Hudson.
Barrett, L.F. 2018. *How emotions are made: The secret life of the brain*. London: Pan Books.
Berkeley, G. 1957. *A treatise concerning the principles of human knowledge*. New York: Liberal Arts Press.
Breazeal, C. 2002. *Designing sociable robots*. Cambridge, Massachusetts and London: MIT Press.
Cangelosi, A., and M. Schlesinger. 2015. *Developmental robotics: From babies to robots*. Cambridge Massachusetts: MIT Press.
Chollet, F. 2019. On the measure of intelligence. *arXiv*. 1911.01547.
Cleeremans, A. 2005. Computational correlates of consciousness. *Progress in Brain Research* 150: 81–98.
Collodi, C. 1995. *Pinocchio*. Ware: Wordsworth.

Crosby, M., B. Beyret, and M. Halina. 2019. The animal-AI Olympics. *Nature. Machine Intelligence* 1: 257.
Damasio, A.R. 1994. *Descartes' error: Emotion, reason, and the human brain.* New York: G.P. Putnam.
Galilei, G. 1957. *Discoveries and opinions of Galileo. Including: The starry messenger (1610), letter to the Grand duchess Christina (1615); and excerpts from: Letters on sunspots (1613), the assayer (1623).* Translated by S. Drake. New York: Doubleday & Co.
Gamez, D. 2007. *What we can never know: Blindspots in philosophy and science.* London: Continuum.
———. 2016. Are information or data patterns correlated with consciousness? *Topoi* 35 (1): 225–239.
———. 2018. *Human and machine consciousness.* Cambridge: Open Book Publishers.
———. 2021. Measuring intelligence in natural and artificial systems. *Journal of Artificial Intelligence and Consciousness* 8 (2): 285–302.
Gardner, H. 2006. *Multiple intelligences: New horizons.* New York: Basic Books.
Grand, S. 2004. *Growing up with Lucy: How to build an android in twenty easy steps.* London: Phoenix.
Gravato Marques, H., and O. Holland. 2009. Architectures for functional imagination. *Neurocomputing* 72 (4–6): 743–759.
Haidt, J. 2013. *The righteous mind: Why good people are divided by politics and religion.* London: Penguin.
Hernández-Orallo, J., and D.L. Dowe. 2010. Measuring universal intelligence: Towards an anytime intelligence test. *Artificial Intelligence* 174: 1508–1539.
Hess, E.H. 1958. Imprinting in Animals. *Scientific American* 198 (3): 81–93.
Hingston, P. 2009. A Turing test for computer game bots. *IEEE Transactions on Computational Intelligence and AI In Games* 1 (3): 169–186.
Hofstadter, D.R. 1979. *Gödel, Escher, Bach: an Eternal Golden Braid.* Hassocks: Harvester Press.
Husserl, E. 1960. *Cartesian meditations: An introduction to phenomenology.* Translated by D. Cairns. The Hague: Martinus Nijhoff.
Indiveri, G., B. Linares-Barranco, T.J. Hamilton, A. van Schaik, R. Etienne-Cummings, T. Delbruck, S.C. Liu, P. Dudek, P. Hafliger, S. Renaud, J. Schemmel, G. Cauwenberghs, J. Arthur, K. Hynna, F. Folowosele, S. Saighi, T. Serrano-Gotarredona, J. Wijekoon, Y. Wang, and K. Boahen. 2011. Neuromorphic silicon neuron circuits. *Frontiers in Neuroscience* 5: 73.
Izhikevich, E.M., and G.M. Edelman. 2008. Large-scale model of mammalian thalamocortical systems. *Proceedings of the National Academy of Sciences of the United States of America* 105 (9): 3593–3598.
James, W. 2000. *The principles of psychology.* Vol. 2. New York: Dover.
Kätsyri, J., Klaus Förger, M. Mäkäräinen, and Tapio Takala. 2015. A review of empirical evidence on different uncanny valley hypotheses: Support for perceptual mismatch as one road to the valley of eeriness. *Frontiers in Psychology Cognitive Science* 6: 390.
Koch, C., M. Massimini, M. Boly, and G. Tononi. 2016. Neural correlates of consciousness: Progress and problems. *Nature Reviews Neuroscience* 17 (5): 307–321.
Lamy, L. 2015. Beyond emotion: Love as an encounter of myth and drive. *Emotion Review* 8 (2): 97–107.
Legg, S., and M. Hutter. 2007a. A Collection of Definitions of Intelligence. In *Proceedings of Advances in Artificial General Intelligence Concepts, Architectures and Algorithms: Proceedings of the AGI Workshop 2006*, ed. B. Goertzel and P. Wang, 17–24. IOS Press.
———. 2007. Universal intelligence: A definition of machine intelligence. *Minds and Machines* 17: 391–444.
Locke, J. 1997. *An essay concerning human understanding.* London: Penguin Books.
Lorenz, K.Z. 1937. The companion in the bird's world. *The Auk* 54 (3): 245–273.
Markram, H., E. Muller, S. Ramaswamy, M.W. Reimann, M. Abdellah, C.A. Sanchez, A. Ailamaki, L. Alonso-Nanclares, N. Antille, S. Arsever, G.A. Kahou, T.K. Berger, A. Bilgili, N. Buncic,

A. Chalimourda, G. Chindemi, J.D. Courcol, F. Delalondre, V. Delattre, S. Druckmann, R. Dumusc, J. Dynes, S. Eilemann, E. Gal, M.E. Gevaert, J.P. Ghobril, A. Gidon, J.W. Graham, A. Gupta, V. Haenel, E. Hay, T. Heinis, J.B. Hernando, M. Hines, L. Kanari, D. Keller, J. Kenyon, G. Khazen, Y. Kim, J.G. King, Z. Kisvarday, P. Kumbhar, S. Lasserre, J.V. Le Be, B.R. Magalhaes, A. Merchan-Perez, J. Meystre, B.R. Morrice, J. Muller, A. Munoz-Cespedes, S. Muralidhar, K. Muthurasa, D. Nachbaur, T.H. Newton, M. Nolte, A. Ovcharenko, J. Palacios, L. Pastor, R. Perin, R. Ranjan, I. Riachi, J.R. Rodriguez, J.L. Riquelme, C. Rossert, K. Sfyrakis, Y. Shi, J.C. Shillcock, G. Silberberg, R. Silva, F. Tauheed, M. Telefont, M. Toledo-Rodriguez, T. Trankler, W. Van Geit, J.V. Diaz, R. Walker, Y. Wang, S.M. Zaninetta, J. DeFelipe, S.L. Hill, I. Segev, and F. Schurmann. 2015. Reconstruction and simulation of neocortical microcircuitry. *Cell* 163 (2): 456–492.

Mori, M. 2012. The Uncanny Valley. *IEEE Robotics & Automation Magazine* 19: 98–100.

Oizumi, M., L. Albantakis, and G. Tononi. 2014. From the phenomenology to the mechanisms of consciousness: Integrated information theory 3.0. *PLoS Computational Biology* 10 (5): e1003588.

Pessoa, L. 2019. Intelligent architectures for robotics: The merging of cognition and emotion. *Physics of Life Reviews* 31: 157–170.

Popper, K.R. 2002. *The logic of scientific discovery*. London: Routledge.

Robertson, K.F., S. Smeets, D. Lubinski, and C.P. Benbow. 2010. Beyond the threshold hypothesis: Even among the gifted and top math/science graduate students, cognitive abilities, vocational interests, and lifestyle preferences matter for career choice, performance, and persistence. *Current Directions in Psychological Science* 19 (6): 346–351.

Russell, S.J. 2019. *Human compatible: AI and the problem of control*. USA: Penguin Random House.

Searle, J.R. 1980. Minds, brains, and programs. *Behavioral and Brain Sciences* 3 (3): 417–457.

Shanahan, M. 2008. A spiking neuron model of cortical broadcast and competition. *Consciousness and Cognition* 17 (1): 288–303.

Shaw, R.C., and M. Schmelz. 2017. Cognitive test batteries in animal cognition research: Evaluating the past, present and future of comparative psychometrics. *Animal Cognition* 20: 1003–1018.

Teasdale, G., and B. Jennett. 1974. Assessment of coma and impaired consciousness. A practical scale. *Lancet* 2 (7872): 81–84.

Tononi, G. 2008. Consciousness as integrated information: A provisional manifesto. *Biological Bulletin* 215 (3): 216–242.

Turing, A. 1950. Computing machinery and intelligence. *Mind* 59: 433–460.

Warwick, K. 2000. *QI: The quest for intelligence*. London: Piatkus.

Wilkes, K.V. 1988. ___, yishi, duh, um, and consciousness. In *Consciousness in contemporary science*, ed. A.J. Marcel and E. Bisiach, 16–41. Oxford: Clarendon Press.

Zeki, S. 2007. The neurobiology of love. *FEBS Letters* 581 (14): 2575–2579.

The Shawshank Redemption as Philosophy: Freedom and Panopticism

46

Alexander E. Hooke

Contents

Introduction: Welcome to Shawshank	1092
Freedom's Hope and Hell	1094
Never and Always	1094
Beyond the Walls of Silence and Darkness	1096
Hope is...another	1096
Panopticism: The Unexamined Life Is Not Worth Watching	1098
Genealogy as Philosophy	1098
Punish and Discipline	1099
Panoptic Societies	1102
The Taste of Freedom	1103
Amoral Thought	1104
Laughter and Liberation	1105
Conclusion: Shawshank, Redemption and Philosophy	1107
References	1108

Abstract

Since its release in 1994, *The Shawshank Redemption* has gradually emerged as a classic work of art according to movie critics and fans. It has been the subject of conferences and books, as well as a tourist attraction in Mansfield, Ohio. Based on a novella by Stephen King, the movie takes place mostly in a prison for serious convicts such as murderers and violent thugs. The conditions are fairly harsh. The warden and guards have few reservations in pummeling the convicts or placing them in solitary confinement. Killing an inmate and burying him anonymously in the prison grounds does happen.

There are several philosophical lessons presented by this movie (and the novella). The drama and cruelties of prison life highlight moments of friendship

---

A. E. Hooke (✉)
Stevenson University, Stevenson, MD, USA
e-mail: ahooke@stevenson.edu

© Springer Nature Switzerland AG 2024
D. K. Johnson et al. (eds.), *The Palgrave Handbook of Popular Culture as Philosophy*,
https://doi.org/10.1007/978-3-031-24685-2_62

and hope. They also depict moments of hell and ask whether prison is merely a darker microcosm of everyday society. This chapter addresses these points through two philosophical lenses. One is from existentialism as found in the writings of Jean-Paul Sartre. The second is from genealogy as presented in the work of Michel Foucault.

Keywords

Freedom · Prison · Laughter · Solitary confinement · Friendship · Hell · Hope · Discipline · Panopticism · Time · Place · Joy · Michel Foucault · Jean-Paul Sartre

Introduction: Welcome to Shawshank

> PRISON, n., A Place of punishments and rewards. The poet assures us that—"Stone walls do not a prison make." But a combination of the stone wall, the political parasite and the moral instructor is no garden of sweets.
> —Ambrose Bierce (*The Devil's Dictionary*, 1911)

Most philosophy anthologies enticing students to read notable thinkers recognize a sense of place. The introduction to Socrates features him sitting among friends and acquaintances discussing an idea or controversy. The agora, seminar, classroom, library are among places where we can let our thoughts and imaginations run free and carry on a dialogue with the dead as well as the living.

Other philosophers have emphasized mobility. The Peripatetic visionaries and nomad thinkers encourage us to move about and visit strange peoples and lands, or break from ordinary duties and embark into natural surroundings. Frederic Gros (2015), in his recent award-winning book *The Philosophy of Walking*, reflects on the various meanings personal transience has had for human creativity and spiritual exploration. Forget about the mundane traps such as social media and cable news – instead take a walk to really enjoy your freedom. For Kant it was the regular strolls through Konigsberg. For Nietzsche it was hiking through the Swiss Alps.

In this light the prison is the antithesis of such philosophical wonder. The space is horrendous and mobility is constricted. Yet philosophical speculation and prisons have not been entirely exclusive. Two of the most popular selections in anthologies, from Plato's "Crito" and "Phaedo" occur in the jail where Socrates will soon be executed. Admittedly, little is said about prison life except that Crito could bribe the guards to let Socrates escape and the reader grasps Socrates' rebuttals on why his escape would be an injustice. Many thinkers have been in jail, including Giordano Bruno, Henry David Thoreau, and Bertrand Russell. None of them seemed to have reflected carefully about their experiences of prison life. This is perhaps in part because they were in jail only for a brief time.

The Shawshank Redemption presents an enlightening approach to how prison experiences and penal institutions raise serious philosophical themes. It is not the first commercial and theatrical venue about prisons and the life of convicts. *Cool*

Hand Luke offered dramatic insights about what it was like being on a chain gang with guards and a warden who had no misgivings in ruthlessly punishing a miscreant. One film on Alcatraz, the island jail in a San Francisco Bay, captured the futility of everyday tasks and many prisoners' unlucky efforts to escape. The serial TV program "Prison Break" featured surprising characters – honorable and decadent, fascinating and disgusting – who depicted the vagaries of a harsh world inside prison walls. The movie *Brubaker* is an excellent portrayal of renowned warden Tom Murton's efforts to establish an independently and self-sustaining prison. To escape the counterproductive state interventions in criminal justice, Murton (1969) had proposed the revival of penal colonies as better alternatives to the modern penitentiary that fostered its own cruel and corrupt practices, such as burying convicts shot by guards in the prison's own grounds.

What distinguishes the movie *The Shawshank Redemption*, based on Stephen King's novella (1983) "Rita Hayworth and the Shawshank Redemption," lies in its attention to enduring philosophical topics. These include friendship, love, virtues and vices, candor and hypocrisy, justice, truth and mendacity, as well as beauty and freedom.

In terms of popular culture, *The Shawshank Redemption* has undergone several reincarnations. Its initial release in 1994 drew modest attention. Slowly it gained popular enthusiasm in Europe and over cable movie networks. Movie critics began to take notice and reconsidered the merits of the movie. As those annual "greatest films of all-time" lists were published, *The Shawshank Redemption* suddenly found itself among the top 50.

Fans were beginning to rewatch the movie and quote favorite lines and passages while debating the possible symbolism or meaning for specific images and episodes. Was Andy Dufresne a Christ-like figure? Did Red represent everyman, the ordinary character whose fates are up and down? One memorable line was uttered by the warden to the new convicts, "Put your trust in the Lord. Your ass belongs to me. Welcome to Shawshank."

Since its initial release the phrase "welcome to Shawshank" has shifted from a warden's sardonic introduction to a cheerful greeting for thousands of tourists who flock to Mansfield, Ohio, where much of the film was produced. Cafes and restaurants feature Shawshank-themed recipes and specials, including Shawshank candy bars and Red's Root Beer soda. There is even a Shawshank trail that takes visitors to different sites in Mansfield where scenes of the movie took place. Fond memories of the movie have become a cash cow for Mansfield. Not many movies can make a similar claim.

Shawshank's popularity and philosophical importance are not accidental traits. Two perspectives underscore its significance. One is the view from existentialism as presented by Jean-Paul Sartre, in which freedom, authenticity, despair, and bad faith are fundamental themes in considering a philosophical life within the scope of prison. The second view is genealogy as formulated by Michel Foucault, where the disciplinary and normalization schemes of the penitentiary illuminate a panopticism that has prevailed throughout our times – and in ways Foucault himself could not have predicted. And it is these themes that will be examined.

First, the existentialist features of the movie will be examined. Then the genealogical approach to Shawshank via Foucault's conceptual lens will come into focus. The concluding section will attempt to incorporate the insights of both in terms of the philosophical lessons offered by this remarkable movie and the novella that inspired it.

Freedom's Hope and Hell

> There's no need for red-hot pokers. Hell is—other people!
> —Sartre (*No Exit*, 1948)

Hope is an ambiguous force. It helps keep us alive and anticipate the next sunrise with joy rather than gloom. It enlivens projects and maintains focus on the world. Part of hope's force is sustained by the confidence we have in our knowledge of the situation, though the temptation to be misled or deceived – by others and ourselves – undermines this confidence. Still, hope promises a time or place where things will get better, even if one is stuck in what seems to be perpetual hell.

Hell is a time or place in which no such promise is offered. Popular accounts through the millennia depict hell as a realm full of fascinating and ghastly demons, endless tortures, self-inflicted torments, with Satan and his aides ruling with a fiery fist. Such wild accounts seem as if they belong to another world, where hope is impossible.

The Shawshank Redemption portrays a worldly dimension of hell – prison, a place built by people for other people – where hope alternates between momentary visions of freedom and the curses of unshakeable self-delusion. A young successful banker named Andy Dufresne (Tim Robbins) has been convicted of murdering his wife and her golf-pro lover. Having motive, opportunity, and no credible alibi, Andy nevertheless insists on his innocence until the end.

When he enters Shawshank Prison, whose façade simulates a royal palace or ancient cathedral, Andy's assertions of his innocence fall on deaf ears. Every convict says he has been betrayed by a biased jury, corrupt judge, or incompetent lawyer. One exception is Red (Morgan Freeman), a long-time con who admits and regrets the murder he committed when he was young and stupid. Red narrates the story, lending his eyes and ears to the audience and providing a unique glimpse of the realities of Sartre's renowned remark that hell is other people. At the same time, there are moments in Red's story about Shawshank and Andy that illuminate shortcomings of this version of hell.

Never and Always

Initially, the notion of hell being other people reflects Sartre's analysis of the look in *Being and Nothingness,* where individual subjects are struggling against one another's objectifying gazes. In *No Exit,* its expression is preceded by the notion that the eyes of others are devouring. Admittedly, when summarizing this play to students, I often neglect telling of the contentious exchange that precedes the famous ending. Wondering what sort of afterlife the three individuals are sharing, Garcin and Estelle eventually begin desiring one another, but a third party, Inez, is in the same room and maintains a relentless gaze upon the two. Despite Garcin's pleas, Inez insists that darkness will "never" come for the potential lovers and that she will "always" be watching them. It is the gaze and this sense of endlessness that condemns the potential lovers.

"Never" and "always" form the integral components to the worldly dimension of hell. In his study on the fear of hell through the ages, Piero Camporesi (1991) contends that rather than separating the universe into two halves (heaven and hell), numerous thinkers held that the universe has three floors. The top is heaven and the bottom is hell, with the middle containing elements of both – that is, the human world.

Here humans get a sense of damnation by suffering from their own excessive indulgences. For example, the glutton will always be doomed to wallow in his own vomit and excrement. The producer of corrupt music will never escape the harshest dissonances and piercing shrieks. The libertine will always wake up to a bed full of worms and vermin crawling and nibbling about his naked flesh. According to a medieval text, "The door of that fatal resting place of all evil will be locked by two great iron keys: by *Never* and by *Always*....And who can tell me how much suffering two so short syllables, *Never* and *Always,* which form horrible eternity, can bring?" (Camporesi, 36).

The world of Shawshank prison dwells mostly within the second and third floors of the universe. When Andy Dufresne arrives, the prison veterans take bets on which fresh fish (i.e., new inmates) will cry for his mother after hearing the cell doors clanking tight for the first night. Red bets on Andy and loses badly. The man who did cry died after a savage beating by the prison captain.

There are also groups of inmates called "Sisters" or "Bull Queers," sexual predators who need and enjoy violent force with their sexual pleasures. Red doubts they qualify as humans. At Shawshank an inmate named "Bogs" is the leader of a little circle of Sisters who periodically assault and rape Andy. As a God-fearing man, the warden introduces new convicts to one rule: respect for the Lord and never take His name in vain. After that, the warden says to each incoming convict: "the Lord looks after your soul, but your ass belongs to me." As many new fish soon learn at Shawshank, their ass will belong not only to the warden.

The warden determines which convicts receive favors, tough assignments, and harsh penalties. Notwithstanding his numerous citations of Biblical axioms and anecdotes, the warden does not actually reflect or sustain general law; he becomes a law unto himself by mirroring the horrific powers of Satan – arbitrariness, cruelty, and endless punishment. As Andy discovers that there is a witness who can confirm his innocence of the double murder, the warden has the witness murdered and gives Andy one month of solitary confinement. (In the novella the witness is transferred to another prison.) When Andy warns that he will stop using his banking skills to help the warden launder prison funds into his own bank account, the warden adds another month of solitary and threatens to return Andy to the cells inhabited by those "sisters," where he will feel what it is like to be sodomized by a train.

Beyond the Walls of Silence and Darkness

Are humans the only species to punish one of their own with solitary confinement? Since it leaves no physical scars, solitary is today one of the widest forms of punishment, though in terms of its effects on the victim, torture might be a more accurate term. It is an extreme extension of prison, disrupting and disorienting a convict's sense of time and space. Solitary simulates death, as the victim sees and hears nothing, save for his own breathing and heart beating.

Being released from solitary and rejoining the other convicts conveys a perverse sense of freedom. Red is not fooled by this grim irony. He points out to his fellow prisoners that, after so many years in jail, the walls begin to define a man. You become "institutionalized," he says: "These walls are funny. First you hate 'em, then you get used to them. Enough time passes, you get so you depend on them." Such resignation echoes Sartre's central themes in his public lecture (1975) on "Existentialism and Humanism," where he describes several contexts showing how human freedom is a project that demands ongoing and resilient attention. Without such attention, one can quickly lapse into letting others or institutions define oneself.

An example of this resilience occurs when Andy, who is eventually granted access to the administrative offices, decides to broadcast an aria of Mozart's opera *The Marriage of Figaro* over the intercom system. While this scene appears only in the film (some critics find the change sentimental and stilted), Red and fellow inmates are transfixed by the utter surprise of the heavenly voices pervading the prison yard. "It was like some beautiful bird flapped into our drab little cage and made those walls dissolve away. And for the briefest of moments, every last man in Shawshank felt free."

For this mischief Andy was confined 2 weeks in solitary. Upon release his buddies seem startled that he seemed so relaxed, knowing from their own past the unique horror of no contact with the outside world for days on end. Andy reminds them of Mozart's music and how something so beautiful always maintains an inner sense of hope. Most of all, he reprimands them; you can't let them – the guards, warden, parole board, even the prisoners themselves – destroy this inner sense. Here beauty and hope are interwoven, but as secrets waiting to be released.

Andy's escape involves this secret.

Hope is...another

Notwithstanding existentialist insights to *The Shawshank Redemption*, several scenes dramatically and – with existential appreciation for the absurd – humorously highlight shortcomings to Sartre's intriguing notion that hell is other people. After the first couple of years at Shawshank, surviving the periodic attacks by the "sisters" and the drudgery of prison life, Andy is considered a fairly isolated individual. His relationship with Red begins as a customer, since Red knows how to buy and sell contraband for the inmates.

Andy gradually learns that prison is a mini-society within a larger society, which means life at Shawshank also contains potential alliances, collaborations, and reciprocally fruitful associations. Even the relations between guards and inmates – including the warden and right-hand captain – are mixed with undertones of favoritism, vengeance, or scheming enterprises of mutual self-interest.

Regardless of the interior hope that lingers, Andy recognizes the need for some sort of general respect or camaraderie with another. A poignant moment arises during the early pleasant days of Spring when the warden needs a crew to work outside and put hot tar on a rooftop. Red bribes the guards to fix the selection process. That way he and his buddies, including Andy, get to enjoy the fresh outdoors.

Overhearing the captain – the one who savagely beat a new inmate to death – complain about how he will lose a considerable portion of his inheritance to taxes, Andy – the cuckolded banker wrongfully convicted for killing his disloyal wife and her lover – suddenly risks his life to ask the captain if he trusts his wife. Just before the insulted captain is about to push Andy off the rooftop, Andy quickly explains that there is a law permitting the captain to give the inheritance to his wife and no taxes will be assessed. Andy even offers his services to the captain free of charge; all he asks in return is for the warden to reward Andy's "co-workers" some cold beers for their hard work. For the time it took several convicts to drink three fresh beers each, says Red, they felt like free men.

Red speculates that Andy wanted to feel normal again, hang out with the guys, and be part of their lives. Finally liberated from the terror of the "sisters," Andy uses his considerable skills to expand and beautify the library, process the tax returns of the warden and his guards, intervene when old-timer Brooks threatens to stab an inmate, and mentors a young convict so he can earn his high school diploma.

Red and Andy soon realize a true friendship is emerging. They mull over the options between "get busy living or get busy dying." Andy finally confides to Red how he has funneled much of the warden's ill-gotten booty into private funds under a fictitious name, passport and social security number, known only by Andy Dufresne. (The outsider friend who helped establish this fund died before Andy's escape.) Red could have earned immediate parole by relaying this information to the warden. When Andy whimsically notes that he learned to become a criminal only inside Shawshank, however, Red's only response was joyful laughter at the situation's absurdity and his friend's brilliant strategy.

Do true friends keep secrets from one another? Andy does not tell Red about the tunnel he has been digging for the last 20 years, and to conceal the hole is the reason he first requested from Red a large poster of the bombshell Rita Hayworth. Nor does Andy invite Red to join the escape. In all likelihood, Andy was doing his friend a favor while improving his own chances for a safe escape. After all, it will require plodding through five hundred yards of sewage – filth and excrement from the prison – to reach outside the prison walls. Physically, Red is probably not up for it. Red finally earns parole and goes to a tree in a New England meadow where Andy told Red he would bury a package. Red finds it and, true to his word, Andy leaves an envelope of cash and a letter of encouragement for Red to join him in Mexico.

The conclusion has sparked considerable debate. Stephen King's novella simply ends with Red expressing a litany of "I hope..." expressions for freedom and an eventual reunion with his friend. Whereas the film originally abided by the novella and closed with Red taking a bus to Mexico as the camera faded away, the final cut changed to a panoramic shot of the Mexican beach, Andy and Red embracing. Before test-audiences, the embrace version elicited far more enthusiastic responses than the bus-over-the-hill version. According to Mark Dawidziak (2019), the main actors and the film's organizers disputed which ending was too literal, too obvious, too cutesy, or too sentimental. Morgan Freeman, who played Red, argued that the final and distant shot of Red and Andy about to meet was the best solution offered by director Frank Darabont.

Screenplay writer Mark Kermode (2003) makes a compelling argument that the final film version is aesthetically and thematically unwarranted. He believes it panders to popular sentiment and actually underestimates the audience's ability to understand and be satisfied with the hope that is illuminated by the bus taking off for Mexico. Kermode would rather have let audiences draw their own visions of the renewed friendship between Andy and Red.

I have no substantive objection to Kermode's thoughtful position. The film version is my first encounter with Shawshank, and like the corrupt police official in *Casablanca*, I am a "rank sentimentalist" and still enjoy the final scene. At the same time, when I later read King's novella his conclusion also seemed perfect. This is another example of one of the differences between reading a book and viewing it as a movie In any event, the novella and the film present a sharp contrast to the ending in *No Exit*. Whereas Sartre concludes with a scenario of three individuals resigning themselves to the fact that they will never escape and always haunt one another, Red and Andy envision a moment where the infinite gaze of another is replaced with the hope for a freedom in sharing the warmth, joy and good humor with another. In *The Shawshank Redemption*, this freedom is called friendship.

Panopticism: The Unexamined Life Is Not Worth Watching

> Is it surprising that prisons resemble factories, schools, barracks, hospitals, which all resemble prisons?
> —Michel Foucault (*Discipline and Punish: The Birth of the Prison*)

Genealogy as Philosophy

Genealogy as a philosophical enterprise has a relatively brief history. It mostly began with Friedrich Nietzsche, particularly his *On the Genealogy of Morality* (1967). Nietzsche was a wide-ranging, albeit troubled thinker. He was both curmudgeon and optimist. He could mock conventional values while celebrating the ideals of those values from different places and times. His genealogical approach would focus on how a particular value, such as pity or asceticism, would be developed into a moral imperative and political tactic that enabled groups of human beings to be ensnared by a set of beliefs and practices which wound up undermining their own well-being and pursuits of happiness.

He shifts from traditional philosophy in determining whether these values are true or false, right or wrong, and instead addresses the effects of having these values become part of everyday life and the changes in how humans think or judge themselves and one another. For example, Nietzsche devotes an entire section to the ascetic priest. It can be harrowing and, from a distance, remarkable to read. How, he asks, did ordinary believers eventually accept that they should embrace asceticism, an ideal contrary to their freedom and earthly happiness but a source for guilt and self-debasement?

Michel Foucault was much influenced by Nietzsche's insights and directed them to other fields of inquiry. Two of his early books focused on how insane asylums and medical clinics became central to life and knowledge in Western Europe. Unfortunately, Foucault's terminology of power/knowledge was reduced to a lazy cliché or a cynical slogan: power is knowledge and knowledge is power.

Foucault never said that. He was focused on the interplay of developments in the human sciences with the formation of institutions and political decisions. Hence his emphasis on the birth of the clinic, the asylum, or the human sciences. For example (Foucault 2000), in the case of insanity, how did the confession of the alleged madman become viewed as a form of self-delusion or an actually true statement one says of oneself? The treatment of madness and the policies about what constitutes madness, according to Foucault, had a striking and unusual effect on treating madness in contemporary times.

Foucault was often linked to postmodernism but he admitted to being perplexed by this label. Contrary to postmodern intellectual advocates who encouraged the undermining of Western thought since the ancient Greeks and early Christian Fathers, Foucault continued to explore the ideas and writings that historically sparked controversies that we have neither solved nor escaped.

For him, genealogy is one way for philosophy to revisit and reanalyze the multiple effects influential ideas have had, for better or worse. His study on the birth of the prison was ranked among the twentieth century's top 100 most important books in two different fields of inquiry: philosophy and criminal justice. (It was the only book to do so.) How is it, in a word, that modern societies have accepted the prison as a way of life? One path to addressing this question is genealogy's insight to life at Shawshank.

Punish and Discipline

> The soul is the effect of a political economy; the soul is the prison of the body.
> —Foucault (*Discipline and Punish: The Birth of the Prison*)

A reader begins Foucault's classic work with detailed accounts of a 1757 public torture. Boiled oil is poured on open flesh wounds, pincers striking various sensitive parts, and soon four horses pulling out each limb from the condemned man's body. Adults and children attend the spectacle. Even stray dogs attend in order to nibble on the burnt corpse's remains. This is more than an exercise in vengeance. For Foucault, it is also a display of the king's authority or the political body announcing its ability to expunge those smaller bodies who violate norms and laws.

The first night at Shawshank prison the viewer witnesses the warden's authority. New convicts are immediately mocked, hooted, threatened or dared by "our little family," as narrator Red often notes. The first night presents a real test for "fresh meat." One rookie, quickly tagged as Fat Ass, begins sobbing as the lights go out and all he hears are echoes of screams and laughter from the inmates. He cannot bear it and screams for the guards. Then, before the prison population, chief guard Bryon Hadley drags Fat Ass into the main floor and beats him to death. No vengeance here, just a message about obedience and authority from the warden to the incomers.

After the depiction of the public torture, Foucault describes a penal scene 80 years later where prisoners are expected to line up straight, dress properly, march when told, carry out labor tasks as ordered by the guards or warden, and wake up and go to sleep at precise times. This general conformity is complemented by scrutiny of each individual convict. Has the convict contributed or undermined prison life? How does he get along with fellow inmates and respond to demands of his superiors? At what point has the prisoner been sufficiently rehabilitated to warrant parole? And, perhaps most importantly, has the criminal shown remorse or penitence for his horrible misdeeds?

These questions (and many others) are addressed as Foucault attempts to show how the treatment of criminals shifts from spectacle (e.g., public execution) to discipline (e.g., modern prison). Unlike spectacle, discipline emphasizes knowledge of individuals – their "psyche, subjectivity, personality, consciousness" (Foucault 1973, p. 29) as if there are sciences of human behavior that can accurately gauge human behavior and a prisoner's rehabilitation. That these sciences have rarely succeeded is a minor issue. According to Foucault, these sciences infiltrating the prisoner's world is an indicator of a new form of power being wielded upon human beings. Inverting Socrates' famous point that the "body is the prison of the soul," Foucault depicts new forms of power that accompany the birth of the prison, also known as the penitentiary – the place for penitence.

He highlights the Quaker model as presented in Philadelphia's Walnut Street Prison. Opened in 1790, it focused on everyday regulation, control and observation of individual prisoners. They wake up and eat at the same time, follow specific work assignments, respond to bells that signal a time to have lunch, return to their beds, or have a short time alone to read the Bibles offered by the Prison or have a brief visit with a member of the clergy. Physical punishment was still an option in this fresh approach to incarceration. Yet the worst kind of punishment was mostly spiritual – solitary confinement so that the malcontent convict can come to terms with his own soul, then return with a bit more wisdom and sense of obedience.

The Shawshank State Prison depicted in the movie takes place in what used to be the Ohio State Reformatory. As displayed and discussed in Mark Dawidziak's insightful study of the movie, the original Reformatory was an impressive structure built in the 1880s. Designed by architect Levi Scofield, a devotee of European art, first time visitors might assume they took a wrong turn, for their eyes are overwhelmed by what seems to be a fortress, castle, royal mansion or hotel for the rich and famous. Much like the Quaker penitentiary discussed by Foucault, this Ohio Reformatory was designed to foster "a sense of spirituality within the inmates so as to allow them to leave the institution better than they arrived" (Dawidziak, 38).

Alas, as the saying goes, the road to Hell is paved with good intentions. For many convicts serving time in this reformatory, the place was better known as "Dracula's castle." The sense of spirituality was often backed with brutal beatings by the guards, old grudges settled among inmates with fierce fights, gang rapes upon vulnerable cons, and (as depicted in the movie but not the novella) a staged escape in order to justify murdering a convict who had evidence that Andy Dufresne was innocent. According to Red in the novella, the prison administration keeps track of everything, legitimate or not. "They probably know as much about my business as I do myself" (King, 30).

Solitude, which offers the opportunity to learn about oneself, one's strengths and weaknesses, virtues and vices, and most importantly in the case of Shawshank, the true reason one is a jailed convict rather than a free citizen, is a distinctly human experience. According to Foucault, the punishment of solitary confinement did not exist in earlier times when incorrigible miscreants were exiled (or executed) rather than imprisoned. Solitary confinement arises as the convict is being watched and never knows when or by whom. The guard or warden looks for how the prisoner is handling extreme isolation, minimal food, sitting in a cell with his own excrement, either no light or a constant bright light. A time for spiritual introspection? Quite the contrary.

In the novella, Red sketches a glimpse of the solitary wing. "You had three ways to spend your time: sitting, shitting or sleeping. Big choice. Twenty days could get to seem like a year....Sometimes you could hear rats in the ventilation system" (King, 67). Many inmates were broken by doing time in the Solitary Wing. They returned half-blind, tattered, skittish, always fearful. It almost broke Andy Dufresne and Red. Isolation also gave the administration an additional chance to know the prisoner – his resilience, fortitude, inner strength versus his weakness, cowardice, and destructive fears.

In contrast to an existentialist view, which highlights hope and friendship, genealogy emphasizes the overt powers of the prison and its relation to the secretive surveillance of human beings yielding, in Foucault's inimical wording, a disciplinary archipelago. For the reader of "Rita Hayworth and the Shawshank Redemption," or the viewer of the movie, it spawns this question: Does genealogy treat Shawshank as a kind of hyperbole of the modern prison or a microcosm ripe for cultural analysis?

A preliminary and anecdotal response is this: As Foucault's popularity and translations of his books took off in the early 1970s, he was invited to the United States to host seminars and present public lectures. His English was quickly improving. Visiting a college in New England, the hosts asked Foucault what he might like to visit. They showed him a list of the fanciest restaurants in the area. While grateful, he really wanted to visit a McDonalds. Not yet available in France, McDonalds posed a weird fascination for him. Is it true, Foucault asked his hosts, that every franchise throughout the country looks the same and presents the same food? Elsewhere he hoped his American colleagues could show him a local school. So they took him to a large nearby high school built some 30 years ago. No, Foucault apologized, adding that perhaps his English was not polished enough and he misspoke: He wanted to see a school, not a prison.

Panoptic Societies

The etymology of "panoptic" involves two parts. "Pan" refers to everywhere. Pandemonium is the running amok of demons (mob or crowd rule, in today's parlance), pandemic is the spread of disease into many different areas, or pantheon is the celebration of many deities who have appeared in all aspects of our lives. "Optic" refers to sight, hence the title "optometrist." An optical illusion is a trick played on our vision, so that we eye one thing with a distorted conclusion about what it is. An optimist is one who sees better days lying ahead.

There is considerable debate over whether Foucault painted a dystopian view of modern Western societies while not offering recommendations for challenging or resisting them. Moreover, there have been direct concerns about the accuracy of his genealogy. Academic philosophers contended *Discipline and Punish* and related works of Foucault were shallow in matters of philosophy, so they assumed that his historical material was quite solid. Historians looked at his genealogical studies and concluded that he must be a profound philosopher, since he's a bit sloppy or unfocused as a historian. Many of Foucault's neologisms, such as "Power/knowledge" or "binary divisions," snuck into everyday language and were used as casual benchmarks for analysis of a recent controversy. There also is a trace of conspiracy theory in Foucault's portrayals of panopticism, in that he sees it in so many institutions and political practices. After all, who could organize or design a society where everyone is being watched by someone else, measured, regulated, and disciplined by some anonymous figures?

Here Foucault digressed from existentialist motifs. Sartre and other existentialists focused on personal intentions, commitment, and projects to articulate elements of the human condition and the quandaries of freedom. This focus is too limited to account for genealogical information about how institutions such as the asylum, clinic, or prison have become so prevalent in modern society. And yet, Foucault is in fundamental agreement with existentialists on the importance of freedom or liberty.

The threat to liberty for ordinary souls arises in a society guided by normalization and surveillance. In the case of Shawshank, each prisoner is watched in terms of excesses and weaknesses. The normal convict was obedient, but there is no such thing as perfect obedience. In the novella as well as the movie, Red is known as the one who can get things done, such as obtaining for Andy his much desired chisel hammer and poster of Rita Hayworth, in prison cells known as the "Woman in Heat." Red admits to being always under the watch. "The prison administration knows about the black market," he tells the reader, "in case you were wondering. Sure they do. They probably know almost as much about my business as I do myself" (King, 30).

We are talking about lawbreakers. They know they are in prison because they broke the law and figured they could get away with it. In the novella and movie, it is clear that most convicts claim they are innocent. From many years of observations, Red wryly surmises that they always blame a corrupt defense attorney or rigged jury. Red does admit to his crime of murder, and soon realizes that Andy's claim of innocence is actually true. In either case the ideal of genuine redemption is part-game and part-war played against the inmates.

Even if they show remorse and wish they had made different decisions, convicts standing before the parole board rarely convince its members that they have shown sufficient sorrow or personal redemption. Red, despite a near flawless prison record, is regularly rejected without any explanation. He soon learns that this notion of reform or rehabilitation is a joke. For Foucault, this joke illuminates the real accomplishments of the modern prison. It becomes a model for shaping, measuring, understanding, and regulating human behavior, not just in the prison but in numerous areas of human activity.

While writing this in 2020 with COVID-19 in the forefront, numerous colleges are issuing all faculty, students, and staff numerous sets of directions and policies and rules for responding to administrative requests and expectations. Mixing up face-to-face class meetings with on-line or remote teaching, students are expected to respect social distance, wear a mask, and sit in an assigned seat. Faculty should take attendance every meeting and offer assignments more frequently and grade more than usual. An exercise in pedagogy or discipline is unclear. All those entering campus should register their temperature, any possible symptoms of the virus, and contact with potential COVID positive individuals. With all exchanges between faculty and student available and observable to administrators, and when, how, or why those exchanges took place, this early twenty-first-century pandemic, much like the seventeenth-century plague that Foucault studied to introduce his chapter on Panopticism, ushers in another era in which our prisons resemble hospitals and schools, and our hospitals and schools resemble prisons.

The Taste of Freedom

> I couldn't get along on the outside. I'm what they call an institutional man now. Out there if you want posters or rock-hammers...you can use the fucking Yellow Pages. In here, I'm the fucking Yellow Pages.
> —Red (after Andy's first invite to join him in Mexico)

Amoral Thought

Jean-Paul Sartre and Michel Foucault were criticized for being nihilists or amoral anarchists. In his public lecture on "Humanism and Existentialism" Sartre addressed several accusations that he saw only the dark side of humanity. His plays and short stories reminded us of human absurdity. Similar are the allegations against Foucault, that he could only find the cruel side of humanity amid the progress of an era of Enlightenment. In the early 1970s debate with renowned philosopher Noam Chomsky, Chomsky claimed that he found Foucault to lack any sense of ethics.

Admittedly, there is considerable evidence to support these skeptical positions. One of Sartre's best-known works is a book-length study of the Marquis de Sade, champion of pleasure, sex, and violence. Foucault published and carefully examined the memoirs of a young man, Pierre Rivera, who in the mid-1840s murdered much of his own family. Clearly there is a philosophical attraction to the slice of hell which exists in humanity. And *The Shawshank Redemption* echoes this attraction: gang rapes, brutal beatings, guards killing a "pretended" escapee, even the warden warning Andy Dufresne that if he calls him "obtuse," which rewards Andy with another couple of weeks in solitary confinement.

Sartre and Foucault do not believe, as far as I can tell, that the modern penitentiary remains our only or best option for addressing criminal justice. Each offers indirectly some study of how to address the moral hell of a prison, the penitentiary, the reformatory – whatever name or euphemism it deserves. That is not a particularly radical view. The correlation between incarceration and crime – as well as the public fear of crime – is rarely established with consistency and research. Countries with minimal populations in prison can have low crime rates and a sense of security among citizens, while other countries with high incarceration rates (the United States now ranks #1) continually experience fluctuating rates of crime, lethal violence, and public fear among its own citizens.

Sartre and Foucault recognized something novel and absurd about the distinct human phenomena of coerced solitude and surveillance. Animals do not cage one another. They do not force another member of their species to be locked in isolation with no contact for days or weeks with another member of their own species. No tiger or red-tailed hawk or jellyfish has been found to coerce others to sleep behind bars, wear chains while doing road work, or have all of their orifices checked for contraband. Nor do they devise artificial devices to keep constant vigilance over their captives in order to measure and regulate their behavior and thoughts. Only humans indulge in such practices.

This indulgence is anchored in part to Socrates' famous dictum, "the unexamined life is not worth living." While the dictum has taken on a variety of meanings, such as the importance of introspection, the value of moderation, and the significance of delusion or hypocrisy, Sartre focuses on those moments when and where you actually examine yourself. How do you find the truth about yourself? Despite his more cynical observations, which I do not mean to discount, Sartre also saw how humans find the truth about themselves when among others. Obviously the friendship between Andy and Red highlights this. But even fractured contacts in

Shawshank show how "the unexamined life" thrives in absence of others. Hence, the horrible solitary confinement becomes a moment of demonic genius – it forces the miscreant to be with himself, and only himself. Hell is other people? Perhaps. But a harsher hell might be being with only yourself.

Foucault has no objections to this existentialist view. He does find it limited in terms of how to account for how penal institutions like Shawshank have proliferated over Western society for the last 200 years or so. The modern prison has never reduced crime. To the contrary, it has produced and reproduced criminals. "Red," Andy confides to his friend," I wasn't a criminal until I came to Shawshank." As noted above, this confession anticipates for existentialists the beginning of a friendship. Here, from the view of Nietzsche's genealogy the quote undermines the significance of a moral ideal such as asceticism or altruism. Foucault's genealogy undercuts the alleged humanistic values that shifted punishment from public spectacle to private confinement. The cruelty has not ended. It has instead been redirected as a more hidden option to reinforce the view that convicts in so-called reformatories and penitentiaries examine themselves under the gaze of the guards and wardens.

Doing solitary confinement for weeks or months carries its own distinct form of cruelty, Red points out, for it often breaks a man's soul before it breaks the body. Hence we return to Foucault's insight that in disciplinary societies, the soul becomes the prison of the body. Is this an amoral thought? Hardly. Foucault's genealogy studies point to how alleged humanistic moralities that usher in the age of the disciplinary society and the modern prison are rarely embodied. Perhaps these moralities are window dressing. They conceal how panopticism has reached many parts of our lives, with the Ohio State Reformatory – what we call Shawshank – presenting a hyperbolic yet fascinating version of the shadows of hell found in these places and contemporary life.

Laughter and Liberation

> I could only believe in a God who can laugh.
> —Nietzsche (*Beyond Good and Evil*)

Andy would convey a mischievous smile, a wry grin or a muffled chuckle over circumstances in Shawshank. Even after a stint in solitary Andy would emerge with a whimsical or sardonic observation. He half-jokingly confides to Red: "The people who run this place are stupid, brutal monsters for the most part. The people who run the straight world are brutal and monstrous, but they happen not to be quite as stupid, because the standard of competence out there is a little higher, but just a little" (King, 48).

You cannot help but laugh with Red upon hearing Andy's insight. Jollity is a rare experience in prison. It is a relished release for men living together for considerable duration. In other institutions (military, sports teams) there are free spirited breaks – away from officers, coaches, or managers – to enjoy nights on the town or side trips to a nearby resort. These excursions spent building friendships and camaraderie are often what provide sanity. Prison affords no such opportunities. In this light Foucault likened modern prison to "The theatre of Hell."

Yet finding a sense of the absurd does help at times. The absurd tells us of the conflict between the rational and the irrational forces in the human species. And despair or dread slip into comical and ludicrous responses. Despite our personal plights, catching the absurdity of one's circumstances offers a moment of insight or truth. This moment is not always realized in a logical argument, such as if A is greater than B, and B is greater than C, then A is greater than C. The insight is captured in one's laughter and the freedom to laugh.

Consider some of your favorite depictions of laughter in fiction or movies. For me it is found in the classic *The Treasure of the Sierra Madre*. Realizing that some $75,000 of gold has been inadvertently released back into the mountains from where it was mined, the old man can only laugh at the great joke God has played. He and his partner Curtin no longer take the loss of all their hard work, suffering, and great risk as a kind of punishment or curse of misfortune. For months they (and the marvelous Humphrey Bogart as Fred C. Dobbs) focused on getting enough gold to retire and simply enjoy life. They had succeeded, only to be now empty handed. Their laughter is not of remorse – but of liberation from being enslaved to the gold they incessantly pursued. It was a laughter of redemption.

Consider the laughter of Red. He is observing how warden Norton orders one of the skinny guards to pursue Andy, the recently escaped convict, through the 500 yards of shit and rat-infested pipes that go from Shawshank to public sewage. If Andy can pull it off, so can the Tremont the guard. Tremont objects to the stench, the foul smells of excrement and urine that infiltrate the passages through which Andy escaped. Then he shouts to the warden, "Oh my God lemme outta here I'm gonna blow my groceries oh shit it's shit oh my *Gawwwwd...*" Then Red hears the unnerving sounds of the guard vomiting his guts out.

Red's response is more vibrantly conveyed through Stephen King's words than the screen version. (Spoiler alert: Red's response will earn him time in solitary.) As he recalls, "I couldn't help myself. The whole day—hell no, the last thirty *years*—all came up on me at once and I started laughing fit to split, a laugh such as I'd never had since I was a free man, the kind of laugh I never expected to have inside these gray walls. And oh dear *God* didn't it feel good!... I just went on laughing and kicking my feet and holding onto my belly. I couldn't have stopped if Norton had threatened to shoot me dead-bang on the spot" (King, 91-92). A reader cannot help but laugh with Red.

Stephen King has a headline that introduces "Rita Hayworth and Shawshank Redemption." It is HOPE SPRINGS ETERNAL. Dawidziak emphasizes in his subtitle how this remarkable work presents a classic tale about hope. As if a microcosm of the outside world, there is a spiritual quest that battles with the darker pulls of social life. One achievement of an unforgettable movie is how it can portray a human being who gives up and prepares for death whereas another maintains hope despite the odds. This is the difference between the typical inmate who has resigned himself to a life without freedom and Andy Dufresne who keeps hope alive and plans his freedom. The middle level is embodied by Red, who calls himself an institutional man yet dreams of what Andy often talks about. Most of us are in Red's position, where we have our own little prisons to deal with.

One of the most pivotal moments in such dreams is also laughter. The freedom to laugh – over comical or absurd situations facing us, the foibles of others, and our own quirks and nonsense – is one way of grasping some truth about our species. Humans laugh because they are the best target for our laughter. The friendship of Andy and Red, as depicted in both the novella and movie, is often evident from the humor and wit they share, even silently so the guards do not see them.

Conclusion: Shawshank, Redemption and Philosophy

Readers of the novella or viewers of the movie are not expected to draw philosophical lessons from this work on the initial encounter. Upon my first experience with either one, I did not. Nor did I pay much attention to redemption. It is through the second or third encounter that we begin to consider a story's insights and perspectives.

Redemption has both secular and sacred connotations. To redeem is to compensate or make amends. When a ball player commits a blunder, later his teammates will jostle him, their buddy, with calls to redeem himself – usually by making up for his miscue or showing the opponents how good he really is.

Redemption in the sacred sense involves the experience and perspective of momentary disruption. In her book *Fragmentation and Redemption,* historian Caroline Bynum (1992) visits and studies remarkable Biblical scenes in European churches. She comes across a depiction of the *Last Judgment* in a twelfth-century Italian church. Those condemned to hell are dismembered, their severed heads attached with huge ears, separated organs – the price one pays for a life of sin. Then she focuses on images where wholeness and harmony are restored. In her words, "...redemption is regurgitation and resassemblage" (Bynum, 287).

This spiritual ordeal underscores Dawidziak's outlook. Prison life is little more than endless fragmentations, from other humans, from civilization, from yourself. Andy's response is not resignation but redemption. This is not just confessing one's sins or seeking forgiveness. According to Dawidziak, "(Redemption is) more than a gift. It's a responsibility to yourself and others" (179). Andy embodies this gift and responsibility by setting up the library so the inmates can keep their minds alive, by cleverly playing a Mozart aria so the entire place could hear its divine sounds, and by the gift of a harmonica to Red so he too always has music in his life. These are all efforts in reassemblage.

If we consider existentialism and genealogy as providing us a conceptual lens to understanding human experiences and institutional practices, then the Shawshank reformatory encourages us to see perennial philosophical themes – truth, justice, virtue, beauty, courage, honesty as well as their adversaries such as mendacity, cruelty, horror, cowardice – through the eyes of long-term convicts and their little world of the modern prison.

The poignant closing scenes are moving. Red finally reaches the place where Andy promised he would leave a package. There is the letter from Andy, who writes, "Remember that hope is a good thing, Red, maybe the best of things, and no good thing ever dies." Then Red saw 20 fifty-dollar bills and cried. He cried and laughed over Andy's gift and redemption in hopes that Red will visit him in Mexico.

Nietzsche (1961) once has Zarathustra proclaiming, "To redeem the past and to transform every 'It was' into an 'I wanted it thus!'—that alone do I call redemption." Not through revenge but through *joy, laughter, and giving* – that is a way of liberating oneself from misfortune, from years in prison for a crime one did not commit. In Red's words, it is either "get busy living or get busy dying." Hence the conclusion where we see Red excited about rediscovering the joy of simple freedom and the hope of seeing his friend.

The Ancients, as Nietzsche often portrayed them, had their myths, epic tales, and theatre to dramatize such extreme moments and experiences. We moderns have *The Shawshank Redemption*.

References

Bierce, Ambrose. 1911. *The Devil's dictionary*. New York: Thomas Crowell.
Bynum, Caroline Walker. 1992. *Fragmentation and redemption*. New York: Zone Books.
Camporesi, Piero. 1991. The fear of hell, trans. L. Byatt. The Pennsylvania State University Press.
Dawidziak, Mark. 2019. *The Shawshank redemption revealed*. Lanham: Rowman & Littlefield.
Foucault, Michel. *Discipline and punish: The birth of the prison*, trans. Alan Sheridan. New York: Pantheon, 1973.
———. 2000. *Power*, part of series *The essential works of Foucault, 1954–1984*. Ed. James D. Faubion, trans. Robert Hurley and others. New York: The New Press.
Gros, Federic. 2015. *The philosophy of walking*, trans. John Howe. London: Verso.
Kermode, Mark. 2003. *The Shawshank redemption*. London: British Film Institute.
King, Stephen. 1983. "Rita Hayworth and the Shawshank Redemption," under Hope Springs Eternal. In *Different seasons*. New York: Signet.
Murton, Tom, and Joe Hyams. 1969. *Accomplices to the crime: The Arkansas prison scandal*. New York: Grove Press/Black Cat.
Nietzsche, Friedrich. 1961. *Thus Spoke Zarathustra*, trans. R. J. Hollingdale. England: Penguin.
———. 1967. *On the genealogy of morals*, trans. Walter Kaufmann. New York: Vintage.
Sartre, Jean-Paul. 1948. *No exit,* trans. Stuart Gilber. New York: Vintage.
———. 1966. *Being and Nothingness*, trans. Hazel E. Barnes. New York: Washington Square Press.
———. 1975. Existentialism is a humanism. In *Existentialism from Dostoevsky to Sartre*, ed. Walter Kaufmann. New York: Meridian.

Snowpiercer as Philosophy: The Danger to Humanity

47

Leander Penaso Marquez

Contents

Introduction	1110
Piercing the Piercer	1111
Piercing *Snowpiercer* and the Veil of Authoritarianism	1113
Piercing the Veil of Well-Ordered Society	1118
Piercing the Veil of Utilitarianism	1120
Piercing the Veil of Justice	1123
Piercing the Veil of Humanity	1127
Conclusion	1129
References	1129

Abstract

Snowpiercer can be interpreted as a critique of social stratification, social engineering, and government overreach, but deeper down, it is essentially a commentary on authoritarianism and humanity. From the beginning, the film provokes the viewers to take the side of the tail-enders and join them in their revolution to overthrow the train's oppressive regime so that a better government can take its place. However, the message of the film is much more complicated than it appears. Ultimately, it is a question of how far humans are willing to go to ensure the survival of their species and for the preservation of their humanity. By analyzing every aspect of the film, this chapter will show that what can be more dangerous to humanity than any authoritarian regime is humanity itself.

Keywords

Snowpiercer · Authoritarianism · Thomas Hobbes · State of nature · Class inequality · Plato's myth of the metals · Social engineering · Diplomacy ·

L. P. Marquez (✉)
College of Social Sciences and Philosophy, University of the Philippines Diliman, Quezon City, Philippines
e-mail: lpmarquez@up.edu.ph

© Springer Nature Switzerland AG 2024
D. K. Johnson et al. (eds.), *The Palgrave Handbook of Popular Culture as Philosophy*, https://doi.org/10.1007/978-3-031-24685-2_68

John Rawls · Theories of justice · Revolution · Well-ordered society · Social stratification · Environmentalism · Climate change · Human population control · Utilitarianism · Greatest happiness principle · Humanity

Introduction

The film *Snowpiercer* (Joon-Ho and Masterson 2013), which depicts the final remnants of humanity surviving a cataclysmic global ice age in a continuously circumnavigating train, invites a lot of questions. Of these questions – which perhaps is the most obscure, or even considered by many to be irrelevant – is "Why was the train moving?" The train's eternal engine, a perpetual motion machine, could provide the power to produce electricity, generate heat, and make plants grow (in other words, sustain life) without having the train circle around the world on its tracks. So why was the train moving? The train, Snowpiercer, needs to move for one reason alone: to pierce the snow that provides the passengers with water; if Thales is to be believed, water is the source of everything, including life. Aptly named, the Snowpiercer's most important function is to pierce snow – to destroy something whole – so that life can go on. Likewise, this chapter is meant to pierce – not the snow – but the veil of "humanity."

This chapter, *Snowpiercer as Philosophy*, is characterized here as piercing the veil for two reasons. First, piercing the veil alludes to the expression "piercing the corporate veil," wherein the limited liability enjoyed by company executives and investors is set aside and such individuals are considered liable for the corporation's actions. Inasmuch as piercing the corporate veil prevents such owners and shareholders from hiding behind the company and are made to answer for their misdeeds, the film also calls out each of the characters – the shareholders of the Snowpiercer – and makes them responsible for their respective actions. Second, the veil also refers to the veil of ignorance – an element of a thought experiment which theorizes that one can discover what kind of moral or social system would be fair or just by imagining how individuals would want that society governed if each was ignorant of the position in society that they would hold. This ignorance prevents the individual from favoring one sector over another because of the risk that the decision-maker will end up as a member of a group that was less favored. The message of the film utterly pierces this veil and underscores the fact that one cannot begin to create a just system from behind the veil without, ultimately, destroying the veil itself.

Similar to the most important function of the Snowpiercer, this chapter endeavors to pierce the numerous veils that were presented by the film in the hopes that its readers and those who have watched the film can look beyond the amazing cinematography and compelling storyline in order to think about the questions that the movie was trying to raise and destroy any misconceptions and assumptions that they might have created regarding the film and its message.

Piercing the Piercer

Snowpiercer (Joon-Ho and Masterson 2013) begins with a narration that the world tried to combat global warming by releasing a cooling agent into the earth's atmosphere in 2014. The CW-7 cooled down the world as planned but nobody expected that it would usher in the sixth major ice age. The only remaining survivors of this catastrophe are the ones who managed to board a train, the Snowpiercer, that is powered by a perpetual motion engine and circumnavigates the world once a year. The Snowpiercer, which Wilford Industries originally intended as a luxury train that would bring tourists to different cities around the world, is made up of various sections (1001 carriages if the TNT series is to be allowed to shed some light) wherein each car serves a specific function, such as the engine room, the disco, the sauna, the classroom, the aquarium, and the tail, to name a few.

The film, on the onset, focuses on the plight of those who inhabit the tail section of the train – the tail-enders. The tail-enders are mainly comprised of individuals who forced their way onboard the train and, 17 years later, managed to survive in the tail section with only protein bars for sustenance. While Wilford – the train's creator and administrator – was generous enough to feed them and refrain himself from uncoupling the tail section from the rest of the train, he does occasionally forcibly kidnap people (usually children) from the tail section to serve whatever purpose he deems necessary, always demands the tail-ender's utmost obedience to his rules, never extends to them any amenities other than the bare minimum necessary to survive, and routinely orders their slaughter as a means for population control. By 2031, a revolution is brewing in the tail section, and that's where the film begins. The tail-enders intend to take control of the eternal engine in order to overthrow Wilford.

Upon confirming that the train's security forces do not have bullets, Curtis Everett (the hardened but sensitive leader of the tail-enders' revolution) and his companions effectively overwhelm the guards and advance to the next section of the train. What's more, Gilliam, the tail section's spiritual leader, has an informant in the front section who is responsible for sending useful information. The red letter he receives from the informant tells them to proceed to the train's prison section where they should free Namgoong – the train's former security specialist who is also a kronole (a drug made from nuclear waste) addict – and his clairvoyant daughter, Yona. They do, and Curtis enlists Nam's help to bypass the security gates of the train sections in exchange for kronole.

Curtis and his group successfully advance through the next few sections before facing Mason, Wilford's right hand, and her soldiers armed with axes. A bloody battle ensues that results in Mason being captured and the death of Edgar, Curtis' closest friend. Curtis uses Mason to advance farther toward the front of the train and they find themselves in the classroom section – a classroom where schoolchildren are being indoctrinated about Wilford's exploits and superiority – into a religion of sorts – rather than educated.

Teacher	As hard as it is to believe, people in the Old World made fun of Mr. Wilford. They criticized him for over-engineering and over-equipping this wonderful train. But Wilford knew something they did not. And what was that?
Ylfa (little girl)	Old-world people are friggin' morons who got turned into Popsicles.
Teacher	Well, sort of. Mr. Wilford knew that CW-7 would freeze the world. So, what did the prophetic Mr. Wilford invent to protect the chosen from that calamity?
The Children	THE ENGINE! (all singing) Rumble, rumble! Rattle, rattle! It will never die!
Teacher (singing)	What happens if the engine stops?
The Children(singing)	We all freeze and die. But will it stop? No! Oh, will it stop? No!
Teacher	Can you tell us why?
The Children (singing)	The engine is eternal! The engine is forever! Rumble, rumble! Rattle, rattle! Wilford! Wilford! Hip Hooray!

In a surprising turn of events, right in the classroom, a fight ensues; the teacher even pulls out a gun. Andrew, one of the rebels, and the classroom teacher end up dead. As if this was not enough, Franco the Elder, who was able to get to Curtis' rear guards with a number of soldiers, manages to kill everyone including Gilliam. Struck by grief and anger, Curtis executes Mason.

Farther into the train, in the sauna section, Franco the Elder catches up with Curtis and his remaining companions. During the fight, Franco is able to kill Grey, Gilliam's right-hand man, and Tanya, a fearless mother on a mission to take her son back from Wilford. Curtis and Nam end up rendering Franco unconscious. With only three of them remaining, they advance forward, Nam and Yona collecting kronole along the way.

Upon reaching the section where they find themselves outside a circular metal door emblazoned with a giant letter W that stands for Wilford Industries, Curtis asks Nam to open the door. Nam refuses. Apparently, he was not planning to open that door but another door – a smaller door right beside the door to the engine section – that will allow them to get out of the train. Nam tells Curtis that he was collecting kronole so that he can use it to blow the door open and he and Yona can leave the train once and for all. Curtis tries to stop Nam, and it is at this point that Wilford's door opens and reveals Claude, Wilford's assistant. Claude shoots Nam and takes Curtis inside to meet Wilford face to face.

During this momentous encounter, Wilford reveals that he and Gilliam were working together all along and that the revolution was just a ploy to reduce the train's population so that a precisely controlled balance can be achieved inside the train. Wilford attempts to convince Curtis of the necessity of this ruse in order to ensure the survival of the other passengers. According to him, all the other former revolutions were orchestrated for the same reason; this was necessary for their continued survival. From his facial expression, it seems that Curtis is beginning to come to terms with this and agree. Eventually, Wilford asks Curtis to take his place as the keeper of the train. As he is about to accept, however, Yona barges in demanding from Curtis the match that he took from Nam so that they can finally blow open the other door. It seems that Curtis would refuse, but Yona sensed something under the floor. Upon removing the floorboard, they discovered Timmy, Tanya's son who Wilford took from the tail section; he's being used as a replacement part for the engine. They rescue Timmy, and then Curtis hands the match to Yona. As Yona was trying to light the fuse on the kronole, Nam fights off and kills Franco who has managed to catch up with them at the front section. After lighting the fuse, Yona and Nam run inside the engine section, only to discover that the door that is supposed to shield them from the blast will not close. Nam and Curtis, as if by instinct, shield Yona and Timmy with their bodies as the kronole explodes.

The explosion triggers a huge avalanche that knocks the train off its tracks. This results in the train's sections flying off in every direction. The destruction that ensues could make one pray for a miracle that there will be survivors. After a while, Yona and Timmy walk out from one of the destroyed carriages, and one can only hope that there were other survivors. While standing on the snow with the Snowpiercer's wreckage all around them, these two children appear to be looking at something in the distance. The scene cuts to a polar bear seemingly looking in the direction of the two survivors.

Piercing *Snowpiercer* and the Veil of Authoritarianism

The moral of *Snowpiercer* (Joon-Ho and Masterson 2013) is the moral of human history, that is, of humans digging their own graves, of facing monsters of their own creation, and of taking one step forward and two steps back. In the beginning of the film, a pendant bearing the motto, "Save the planet," was shown. Humankind tried to "save the planet" by introducing the CW-7 into the atmosphere and ended up destroying the planet together with almost every form of life on earth. Human beings are too clever for their own good. Just like snow, love for humanity can be a beautiful thing, but too much of it – like putting humanity above everything else – can freeze the world over. Too much snow means death. And the *Snowpiercer*'s moral is that piercing through this snow entails realizing that the greatest danger that the human race has ever faced is humanity itself.

Snowpiercer (Joon-Ho and Masterson 2013), however, contrary to popular opinion, is not a science fiction film – at least in as much as the advanced tech in the film, the eternal engine, was not the film's focus. Even the film's focus on climate change and global warming is circumstantial. What, then, is the film all about if it is not about the dangers of science and technology? *Snowpiercer* is a film about piercing through veils of assumptions with such force that it compels its audience to do a reality check and really think about what is happening to the world around them – at least, so I will argue.

At first glance, the whole premise of the film seems to rest on the notion of control. The tail-enders were mounting a revolution with one goal: establishing control of the engine. In Curtis' own words, "We control the engine, we control the world." It is interesting how Curtis' statement gives the impression that the

Snowpiercer is the world – or has effectively become their world since they boarded the train to escape certain death. Since they are the last of what remains of the human race, it has become the utmost responsibility of the train's leadership to ensure the survival of the human species. This responsibility, unfortunately, was used as a convenient excuse to rule the passenger-inhabitants with an iron fist.

From the get-go, it is fairly obvious that the passenger-inhabitants of the Snowpiercer are under an authoritarian rule. Some telltale signs are the periodical headcounts (head check), the excessive use of the military, and people being forced to do things against their will (like the violinist, Gerald McInster who is forced to be separated from his wife to play his violin for the more privileged occupants of the train, and the kids, Timmy and Andy, who are forced to take the place of the old and worn-out parts of the *Snowpiercer*'s eternal engine). There is also oppression through violence and a glaring lack of transparency. For example, the tail-enders are not told that the "medical inspection" of the children is to determine whether they are small enough to serve as engine parts; the arrangement between Wilford and Gilliam to reduce the train's population is also kept a secret. And it could be interesting to try to discover what *Snowpiercer's* director Bong Joon-ho was trying to say about authoritarianism through the film; but other articles have already addressed that issue at length (The Korean Foreigner 2013; Lee and Manicastri 2018). What will be more unique and interesting is to look into the morality of working with authoritarianism. Simply put, is it ever acceptable to compromise with authoritarianism?

The entirety of the film revolves around the so-called Great Curtis Revolution. The viewers are led to sympathize with the tail-enders, and empathize with their plight, as they witness the dismal living conditions in the tail section and discover how (during the early days of the Snowpiercer) the passenger-inhabitants of the tail section did not have food and had to resort to cannibalism. What perhaps seals the deal is the resolve of the doting mother – Tanya – who risks her life to go with Curtis to the front in order to take back her son, Timmy. As the audience is hooked on rooting for Curtis and his army as they fight their way from one section to the next, they feel as if they are about to share in a taste of a glorious victory when Curtis comes face to face with Wilford in the engine. But that the veil of triumph is pierced when the film reveals that Wilford and Gilliam were actually working together (much to the detriment of the tail-enders). This harsh reality crashes in as the illusion of opportunity fades, and only the all too familiar feeling of defeat is left. In this moment, the relevance of the film becomes clear as the audience recognizes the same issues that they face in governing structures today. These kinds of reality checks are what makes the film relevant; they hit very close to home.

The cooperation between Wilford and Gilliam reminds us that it is not possible for any authoritarian regime to thrive without enablers who support it. In this case, Wilford's regime lasted for 17 years thanks to, according to Wilford, the help of Gilliam. And the film presents us with good reason to think that Wilford is right. For instance, when Gilliam ascertains Curtis' resolve to continue, was it because he wanted to make sure that Curtis will see things through, or was it because he would like Curtis to call off the revolution? It may be the case that Gillam was trying to change Curtis' mind because the population, at that point, has already dwindled.

Since many people from both sides have already been killed, the optimal number of passenger-inhabitants has already been reached and there is no more reason for Gilliam to goad Curtis to push through with the revolution. Another instance is when Gilliam tells Curtis not to let Wilford talk and to cut out his tongue. This can be interpreted as Gilliam's way of expressing his support for Curtis' revolution. He may not have wanted to give Wilford a chance to talk to Curtis and convince him to back out of his revolt at the last moment – something that likely would have happened had Curtis not discovered what Wilford did to Timmy. Conversely, he may have given this "advice" to protect himself. Maybe he wanted to hide the fact that he and Wilford were working together for the past 17 years. Be that as it may, it is undeniable that it was cooperation between Gilliam and Wilford that allowed the passenger-inhabitants to survive for so long. This makes us again wonder: Is it ever acceptable for someone to compromise with authoritarianism?

At first glance, it appears that the answer to this question is a resounding no. As Rand (in Binswanger 1986) puts it, the end does not justify the means (this notion is also attributed to Kant in Garnett 1988, p. 3). No amount of benefit can make Gilliam's cooperation with Wilford acceptable. However, with the survival of the entire species on the line, it would seem that the answer could be yes. To ensure the survival of the human race, it is acceptable that Gilliam compromised to cooperate with Wilford. In the words of Machiavelli: "...in the actions of all men, and especially of princes, which it is not prudent to challenge, one judges by the result ... For that reason, let a prince have the credit of conquering and holding his state, the means will always be considered honest, and he will be praised by everybody ..." (1998, ch. XVIII). (This is often interpreted to entail that the ends justify the means.) Yes, from a deontological perspective, there is no way that compromising with authoritarianism can be acceptable. But from a teleological point of view, authoritarianism can be acceptable if the consequences of noncooperation are extreme enough. After all, compromise is an indispensable part of any political relationship. To put it simply, "compromise is omnipresent in politics" (Bellamy et al. 2012, p. 277). Indeed, the end result of political discussion is often a compromise that no one is completely happy with. And the relationship between the tail-enders (not only Gilliam) and Wilford is undeniably political. The occupants of the tail section were allowed to board without a ticket because, as Wilford later tells Curtis, he saw a full tail section as a way to provide him with an endless supply of (human) spare parts.

As a justification for Wilford's actions, however, this line of thinking fails to be reasonably convincing for two reasons. First, given his brilliance, Wilford could not have built the train without making sure that there are spare parts available in case the train would need repairs in the future. Second, he could have easily chosen one of the children in the middle or front sections and could have gotten away with it by making up some story about how it would be a great honor to be chosen to become a part of the "sacred engine." Wilford kept the tail-enders because it is so much easier to get what he needed from people at the farthest section of the train than from sections that are nearer to the front or from parents who may be one of his direct associates. In other words, Wilford did not really need the tail-enders on the same level that the tail-enders needed Wilford; they really wouldn't survive without him.

And so, while it does not justify Wilford's action, we can understand how Gilliam's compromise with him was pragmatic.

But one still wonders whether or not Gilliam's compromise with Wilford was acceptable. If there is something that the film reveals about how the arrangement between Wilford and Gilliam works, it is that Wilford provides the tail-enders the basic provisions to survive while Gilliam helps Wilford cut down the population. It is not really clear whether Gilliam had a hand in the earlier revolts, but he did play a significant role in Curtis' revolution. And if Wilford is to be believed, revolutions are a fast and easy way to reduce the train's population. Since Gilliam is the tail-section's spiritual leader, it is highly likely that the leaders of earlier revolutions consulted with him. Thus, the same arrangement could have been at work between Wilford and Gilliam from the start. If this is the case, and the compromise between Wilford and Gilliam was pragmatic, then perhaps a case could be made that it is morally acceptable.

Simon May (2005) argued that it is impossible to have principled reasons for a moral compromise; there can only be pragmatic ones. He pointed out that those who agree to a moral compromise believe that their moral views (on the issue at hand) are still better than the view of the opposing party yet the (other or alternative) view is accepted to set aside the disagreement in order to get things done (pragmatic reasons). This, according to him, is different from moral correction. "Moral correction involves the recognition that one's earlier commitments were mistaken" (May 2005, p. 318). Moral compromise lacks this recognition. Since the former's view is the best version of any view (on the issue), then the only way to enter into a moral compromise is for pragmatic reasons and never principled ones. "It may be helpful to think of reasons for moral correction as first-order reasons that concern the merits of a position itself, and reasons for moral compromise as second-order reasons that concern how firmly one should hold to a first-order position in the face of moral disagreement" (May 2005, p. 319).

On the other hand, Weinstock (2013) and Kappel (2018) express the opposite view: that it is possible to arrive at principled reasons for a moral compromise. As Weinstock puts it,

> First, compromises evince respect for persons that we have reason to think of as our epistemic peers, and acknowledgement of our own finitudes as moral reasoners. Second, compromises are often made morally necessary by the shortfalls that unavoidably separate democratic institutions from democratic ideals. Third, compromises express a desirable form of democratic community. And fourth, compromises are often justified from a consequentialist point of view, in that they allow for the realization of values that would not be realized as well by the failure to compromise. (Weinstock 2013, p. 537)

Kappel, on the other hand, argues that disagreements actually help lead two parties to arrive at a "compromise position" because the discovery of a disagreement between the moral principles of the two parties rationally demands that they reduce their confidence in their respective moral beliefs. He referred to this as the "reduced weight principle" (Kappel 2018). In effect, these reduced weights beget reasons to compromise as each party begins to appreciate moral views other than their own.

Taking this into consideration, it may be helpful to lay down what each party (theoretically) would consider best. On one end of the spectrum is Wilford whose (pre-compromise) view is to sacrifice the few (the tail-enders to be exact) so that the many will continually enjoy the benefits afforded by the train. On the other end is Gilliam, whose (pre-compromise) view is that everyone should have equal access to the amenities provided by the Snowpiercer. If it is true that Wilford considers Gilliam as a friend and vice versa – allowing for a certain degree of democratic and diplomatic relationship between the two – then there would be no problem for each one to flesh out these opposing views and see what comes out as the superior moral view. Assuming that they did, it is highly likely that they would reach the exact same arrangement that they have shown in the film.

Evidently, Wilford will not agree that everyone will have equal access to the train's amenities, especially since the tail-enders are what he considers as a charity case. Gilliam is a leader that is looked up to by the tail-enders and will definitely not allow his people to be sacrificed for the sake of the passenger-inhabitants of the other sections. Thus, the only acceptable compromise – the compromise position – will be for both sides to sacrifice some of their people to keep the balance inside the train. The revolution is simply a crafty way to enforce this compromise since some of the rebels will die for their cause while a number of Wilford's supporters will also die to defend him. This fact is portrayed when Mason utters the words, "Precisely 74% of you shall die." Notice that when she said this, the rebels were not the only ones standing before her, Wilford's soldiers were standing in front of her as well. It would not be farfetched to assume that the total casualties will include the soldiers if one is to take into consideration the utmost importance of having an exact number of people populating the entirety of the train.

It may be argued that the compromise between Gilliam and Wilford was reached more out of pragmatism than principle – to ensure the survival of both camps. Regardless of the likelihood of the truth of this theory, giving people the chance to choose is the moral principle upon which this compromise is built. Without it, a war between the two sides might ensue, entangling those who have no choice (elderly, sick, and children). It is important to note that in all revolutions that have come and gone inside the train, Wilford never slaughtered all the tail-enders. Those who died are the ones who, by their own free will, chose to take up arms and fight. Hence, giving each one the right to decide for their life and their body is the second-order reason for both Wilford and Gilliam to not hold on to their first-order positions.

This goes to show that, as it is with any moral dilemma, compromising with authoritarianism is not something that can be decided in black and white. Was Gilliam a traitor to his people? Probably not. There are certain cases – like that of Wilford and Gilliam – where a compromise can be deemed acceptable. As a plausible solution to the second issue, in instances of a potential moral compromise, what needs to be taken into account are the reasons (principled more than pragmatic) for such a compromise to be deemed acceptable. This makes one wonder whether the survival of the human race is enough as a principled reason to maintain social order in the Snowpiercer, whatever the cost.

Piercing the Veil of Well-Ordered Society

From the onset of the film, it is established that maintaining a well-ordered society is vital for the survival of all the passenger-inhabitants aboard the Snowpiercer. Minister Mason lectured the tail-enders about everyone's inherent position using the analogy of "hat is to head; shoe is to foot" as the Francos were punishing Andrew for throwing his shoe at Claude. In her litany, she uses the shoe as a metaphor for disorder, chaos, and death. "When the foot seeks the place of the head, a sacred line is crossed. Know your place. Keep your place." The shoe, Mason points out, is not a shoe but a size-10 chaos. Mason stressed that she is a hat and therefore must be at the front section, while the tail-enders are a shoe and must therefore remain in the tail section. This "order" must be maintained, otherwise, disorder, chaos, and death will definitely ensue.

In the Republic, Plato (1968) defends the idea of using a myth about metals to keep order in his ideal society. According to the myth, everyone is born of the earth and, correspondingly, each person is born with a metal – bronze, silver, or gold – mixed into their soul. This metal determines one's status in society. Bronze for the producers, silver for the auxiliaries (police/soldiers), and gold for the rulers. If some try to hold a station in society not suited to their metal – for example, if those without gold in their souls try to rule – everything will fall apart. It is said that the metal in an offspring's soul is determined by the metal in its parents', thereby, a "silver couple" will bring to the world a "silver baby." However, there may be instances wherein couples are given offspring that possess a different metal in their souls. In this sense, a merchant's child who has gold mixed in its soul can rise up to become a ruler of the land. Plato knew all this was a lie, of course, but according to Plato (1968) such "noble lies" are essential for achieving a well-ordered society, where citizens will be content to keep their place and persuaded to protect their city (Plato 1968, Book III, par. 414; Partenie 2018). Interestingly – in an interview from 1974, but published in 1978 in *The New York Review* – holocaust survivor, famous critic of the Nazis, and author of *The Origins of Totalitarianism* Hannah Arendt argued that spreading lies for propaganda is indicative of authoritarian rule.

Similar to the metals that Plato's citizens have in their souls, Mason's monologue reveals to the audience that the passenger-inhabitants of the train were assigned a section based on the ticket that they presented upon boarding the train. Everyone had tickets, except for those in the tail section who, according to Mason, were only allowed to board because of Wilford's generosity. This shows that they are in an even worse position than Plato's "bronze citizens." Nonetheless, as the film suggests, there are those who are able to leave the tail section and live in other parts of the train. Paul was able to make it to the section where the protein blocks are produced; Gerald, with his prowess as a violinist, made it to one of the sections near the front of the train. This, of course, overlooks the fact that they were forcibly removed from the tail section just to work in the other sections. Plato was saying something to this effect when he mentioned that a child who was determined to have a different metal from their parents – say a silver child born to bronze parents – must be taken away and raised by people who have in their souls the same metal as that of the child.

According to Mason, this "order" must be kept and respected at all cost. In her words, "We must all of us, on this train of life, remain in our allotted stations. We must, each of us, occupy our preordained particulate position." Throughout the film, there are at least a couple of scenes that underscore the importance of maintaining order inside the train because keeping the order implies keeping the balance. One is in the aquarium section. Mason talks about the aquarium as a closed ecological system that requires balance, much like the train. This was affirmed later on by Wilford when he told Curtis that the train is a closed ecosystem and killing off a part of the population maintains its balance.

Curiously, this adherence to order seems to have become a gospel truth inside the train, largely thanks to help of Wilford's associates – Mason and the Teacher to name a few – who preached his gospel. Notice that when Paul was being asked to come and join the revolution, "My place is here" was his only response. And in the scene where the children were being taught about the history of Snowpiercer, as well as the revolts that happened therein, the teacher asked what happens to those who disobey the will of Wilford and upsets the order inside the train. The children's answer is, "We'd all die." Conveniently, they were talking about this specific subject matter as the train was passing by the remains of the Frozen Seven, casualties of a past revolution dubbed as the "Revolt of the Seven."

Given that keeping order at all costs is the gospel truth inside the train, it is not surprising at all to discover that Wilford was regarded as a Messiah – the one who saved the human race – by many passenger-inhabitants. Employing messianic symbols is often used as a strategy to strengthen authoritarian regimes such as, in Mason's words, "the hallowed water supply section." Apart from Wilford and the water supply section, the train's engine also falls under this category. As Mason's puts it, "The engine is sacred. And Wilford is divine!" True to the ideology that Wilford and the engine were the ones responsible for the continued survival of the human race, these messianic symbols were used effectively to keep the order. Eternal order, Mason says, "is prescribed by the Sacred Engine. All things flow from the Sacred Engine. All things in their place. All passengers in their section; all water flowing; all heat rising pays homage to the Sacred Engine, in its own particular preordained position. So it is." This declaration by Mason brings to the fore the fact that, for 17 years, maintaining a well-ordered society has become a moral imperative that each passenger-inhabitant of the train must follow. Unfortunately, enforcing this moral imperative sometimes requires lives to be sacrificed. This draws attention to the question of whether one should always strive to attain a well-ordered society no matter the cost.

A number of philosophers have expressed their views on a well-ordered society. In Leviathan, for example, Thomas Hobbes argued that there should be a social contract which involves surrendering some freedoms in exchange for political order and protection, lest humans revert to the state of nature where every person is at war with another given the absence of rights and excesses in freedoms. Meanwhile, Rawls pointed out that a well-ordered society should be grounded on fairness. This means that all social structures will be fair to the citizens and all citizens will be fair to one another while at the same time recognizing that the social structures that are in place are just. The theories of Hobbes and Rawls are echoed by numerous other theorists. This, however, highlights the fact that many moral and political philosophers find striving for a well-ordered society a worthy goal.

The social order in the Snowpiercer, however, is not founded on any lofty moral or political ideal; instead, it is founded on the fear of extinction. This makes survival the only motivation for maintaining social order. In this sense, the prevailing order is not something that was agreed upon and accepted by all passenger-inhabitants, but something that was forced on them by Wilford at the moment that they boarded the train. Thus, they often have no choice but to accept the control that Wilford has over their lives. This reality check can be seen as Director Bong's take on what is happening in the world.

Insofar as world peace and order is concerned, there are those who define "peace and order" in terms of everyone falling into their "rightful" place. Unfortunately, on numerous occasions, this "rightful" place puts them in positions that are vulnerable to neglect, violence, and oppression. Parallel to this is Wilford's "The train is the world; we the humanity" mentality, wherein the train's sections stand for the totality of the train while the correct number of human beings stand for the whole of humanity. Wilford's mechanistic view of a well-ordered society wherein all are in their designated places and are performing their proper functions seems to be a page out of Plato's book. The difference, however, is that Plato values freedom, and regulations are in place for the rulers, not just the ruled; for Wilford, it is the other way around. Wilford curtails the freedom of, and imposes strict regulations on, the passenger-inhabitants to maintain social order. This makes it easier to realize how striving for a well-ordered society can turn out to be problematic.

Striving to attain a well-ordered society is a noble aspiration, but the devil is in the details. Rights, freedoms, equality, and justice are simply some of the things that need to be taken into consideration moving forward. It appears that these ideals have to be safeguarded if a "genuine" well-ordered society is to be achieved. However, in an extinction-level event such as we see in *Snowpiercer*, it is interesting to see how ideals such as these quickly lose their value for the sake of survival.

Piercing the Veil of Utilitarianism

Much of what transpired inside the Snowpiercer was justified through a utilitarian point of view. Population control, for instance, was done periodically, methodically, and with surgical precision, in order to ensure that the passenger-inhabitants of the train will continue to thrive. The survival of the human race, in this case, is the evident justification for activating a population control campaign under the guise of a revolution. In other words, achieving the greatest good for most of the passenger-inhabitants of the train seemed to be the standard rationale for every oppressive policy enforced inside the train. This makes one wonder whether achieving the greatest good for the greatest number really is what is good.

One may argue that it was never mentioned in the film that the greatest number actually benefits from Wilford's policies. One could go further by arguing that the train's passengers are divided into two social classes only: the elites at the front and those who are poor at the tail end. It can easily be said that the tail-enders outnumber the elites two to one and, thus, the greatest good for the greatest number is not actually achieved. This could be a good counter argument against the utilitarian justification of Wilford's actions, if not for a small but very important complication: It is a mistake to assume that there are only two social classes on board the Snowpiercer.

Although it was not highlighted in the film, the middle class makes up a fairly considerable portion of the Snowpiercer's passenger-inhabitants. The chef who prepares the food at the sushi bar, the barber and the tailor who attend to the grooming needs of the upper class, the servers in the restaurant, and many others are not as wealthy as the elites but also not exactly as poor as the tail-enders. Taking this into account, it appears that the greatest number does benefit from Wilford's actions. Most importantly, if one is to consider survival as the greatest good, then everyone on the train is enjoying this greatest good despite the economic inequality among the social classes because they are alive and are able to be with their loved ones at the end of the day. If this is the case, would it suffice to say that Curtis and the former revolution leaders were wrong in trying to upset the social order and that achieving the good for the greatest number ought to be the paramount consideration at all times?

The answer seems to be in the affirmative. If the greatest good is survival and everyone is surviving – regardless of their quality of life – then the utilitarian objective is satisfied. Doing anything that would not contribute to the satisfaction of this objective would, therefore, be morally wrong. Since everyone in the train is being asked to sacrifice – some more than others – failure to do one's part may result in the failure of achieving the greatest good. In other words, any attempt to improve their quality of life risks the possibility of ending the lives of everyone on the train, thereby compromising the greatest good for the entire species. This is the reason why Andrew was punished by dismemberment through frostbite: He was not willing to let go of his son, Andy, for the good of the many. The gravity of the punishment underscores just how important it is for everyone to contribute – some more than others – to ensure the survival of the majority. Ultimately, the final outcome of Curtis' revolution with everyone dying except for two people made the possibility of losing the greatest good for the passengers of the train a reality.

This, however, also highlights what is wrong with utilitarianism. Consider its three principles: All individual's happiness is of equal value, right actions are those that lead to happiness (whereas wrong actions are those that lead to unhappiness), and happiness is the only thing that has value in itself. Among these principles is nothing that indicates the boundaries between private and public life. Consequently, from a utilitarian point of view, Wilford would not be wrong to encroach upon the personal life, liberty, and property of the tail-enders because his intent is to lead to the happiness of the majority. But one of the major objections to utilitarianism as a guiding ethical theory is that it is impossible to know what actually generates the greatest good. Orchestrating a revolution to cut down the train's population may have worked in the past as a survival strategy, but there is no guarantee that it will work every time (as in the case of Curtis' revolt). On the other hand, if the revolution ended differently, Curtis might have ushered a new age wherein the appropriate number survives, distribution of resources is fairer, and class inequalities are non-existent. In other words, since utilitarianism is a teleological ethical theory, then Wilford's actions can only be evaluated as right or wrong when the results of these actions have become apparent.

However, the same cannot be said if the focus is just on controlling the size of the population. Even if, as the movie suggests, there is a "magic number" of passenger-inhabitants that allows for balance inside the train, and that without that balance everyone dies, controlling the population as Wilford does – maintaining the social classes and an unfair distribution of resources – is not necessary for the continued survival of the human race. Yes, the tail-enders forced their way onto the train unlike others who had tickets, but that doesn't mean they must be treated so harshly. After all, such concerns hardly matter in calculations about what produces the most happiness. Even the renowned and influential utilitarian thinker John Stuart Mill proposed the imposition of taxes on the wealthy – what to them would be a meager amount that they would not even bother to account for – and use the collected resources to uplift the lives of the poor. Such mechanism could have been employed by Wilford to give a more decent life to the tail-enders, and thus achieved a greater overall good.

It is interesting to consider how the utilitarian ethic was also present in the revolution of Curtis and the tail-enders. If Curtis and his rebels did succeed in overthrowing and replacing Wilford, would they have achieved the greatest happiness for the greatest number? To a certain extent, the answer is yes. But this extent only reaches as far as how many tail-enders there are. In other words, for Curtis, the greatest number is not the entire population of the train but only the population of the tail section. For Jeremy Bentham, the founder of modern utilitarianism, focusing on a specific group of people like this would not count as an instance of using the utilitarian moral because the happiness of each individual should be given equal consideration.

If this is the case, however, it would be extremely difficult to apply the utilitarian moral at all. For instance, when Gilliam offered his arm so that Curtis and his men could eat, not everyone in the tail section was able to benefit. There may be others, especially children, who were traumatized by the act of cannibalism. Since it is particularly problematic to exactly determine if it will bring more happiness than harm, especially in a large group of individuals, it would be challenging to justify Gilliam's action as a morally good act. Even the contemporary utilitarian philosopher Peter Singer's call for impartiality by considering everyone's interest equally cannot resolve this problem because Gilliam, being the spiritual leader of the tail section, is and can never be impartial to Curtis; they have a shared experience of being in the tail section – Gilliam could empathize with Curtis because he knows what it is like to be hungry. In fact, such calls to espouse an impersonal impartiality (as that of Singer's) are criticized as morally deficient because such impartiality cannot be truly regarded as an equal treatment of everyone's interest. Nevertheless, even if Gilliam sacrificed his arm to satisfy the hunger of Curtis and a few other men, his actions would not be deemed as good if Singer's "impartialist" axioms would be upheld. Thus, the only solution is to accommodate the idea that "the greatest good for everyone" would mean "everyone in a particular group" (organization, region, nation, etc.). If this is right, it is not difficult to see that revolution from the perspective of Curtis (oblivious of the fact that the entire thing was orchestrated by Gilliam and Wilford) serves a utilitarian purpose – it could improve the quality of life of the tail-enders.

This highlights the preference of decision-makers to utilize the utilitarian moral principle, whether it be in policymakers or individual agents making decisions involving social action. The reason for this may be partly because the outcomes of a policy or action is easier to measure, but it may also be because it allows for a certain degree of "complete context" to be accommodated. In the famous Trolley Problem, for instance – which asks whether one would be willing to actively kill a single person to keep from passively (through inaction) killing many – the deontologist would probably feel "crippled" by the feeling of having no good option; killing is wrong regardless of who can be saved or whether it is active or passive. The utilitarian, on the other hand, has an answer: They would pull the lever to sacrifice one person to save the many because that maximizes happiness. This preference often results in the marginalization of the oppressed (such as in Wilford's marginalization of the tail-enders) or divisiveness (such as when Curtis valued the happiness of his people more than the other passengers on the train when he was planning for and leading the revolt).

This reveals that achieving good for the greatest number may not exactly be entirely good (desirable in every respect), but it is preferable, especially when the consideration is the quantity of beneficiaries and not the quality of the benefit. As in the cases of Wilford and Curtis, there is no clear right or wrong. They are both in the right yet also are both in the wrong. The only difference here is how far (or to how many) will the benefits of their respective actions reach – an arguably plain and simple utilitarian consideration. Ultimately, everything boils down to how well they can justify the reasons for their respective actions as just.

Piercing the Veil of Justice

Whereas the tickets of the passenger-inhabitants determine where they would live inside the train, the sections of the train effectively establish the limits of the socioeconomic benefits that each group of passengers receives and provides clear boundaries on the train's socioeconomic strata. In the Rawlsian theory of justice as fairness, however, each section should have a fair share of benefits to enjoy. Recall that the tail-enders boarded the train without a ticket and thus barely survive while the passengers in the front section of the train enjoy a number of amenities – sauna, sushi, and nightclub – that are not available to passengers in the tail section. One wonders whether the quality of life for the tail-enders would be better if the pleasures and amenities enjoyed by those at the front were reduced and shared with everyone else.

In *A Theory of Justice*, Rawls argues that we can determine the ultimate principles of justice, and thus what a just society would look like, by imagining what people would agree to if they were in "the original position" (about to be placed into a society) under a veil of ignorance (unable to know who they would be in that society). If Rawls' veil of ignorance is to be employed and each passenger will decide from an original position – a position wherein nobody knows in which section of the train each one would end up staying – how the freedoms of the train's inhabitants are to be curtailed and protected, an equal distribution is likely to be agreed upon. Everyone should be free to do whatever they like as long as it does not infringe on the freedom of anyone else. As Rawls puts it, "[E]ach person is to have an equal right to the most extensive scheme of equal basic liberties compatible with a similar scheme of liberties for others." (Rawls 1971, p. 53)

The veil of ignorance is a moral reasoning device wherein all parties that will decide on a social contract are not aware of their respective positions on the social ladder or their natural abilities. Since these individuals have no idea where they will end up and who they will end up being at the other side of the veil, theoretically, all resulting decisions and agreements will be just and fair for everyone. And surely, it is possible for the resources to be shared more fairly among the inhabitants of the train – including those at the tail end – without resulting in humanity's ultimate demise. But, according to Rawls, this would not necessarily entail that everyone has an *equal* share of the train's resources. In any well-functioning society, Rawls argues, there will be social inequalities – some people will make more and have more. This will be acceptable to those in the original position, under a veil of ignorance, Rawls argues, if (roughly put) those inequalities come with jobs that (1) anyone could (within reason) attain and (2) exist for the benefit of everyone. For example, everyone would agree that it is perfectly acceptable for doctors to get paid more since high pay would be necessary to incentivize people to become doctors, and everyone benefits from doctors being in society (especially if anyone could become a doctor if they worked hard enough). As Rawls put it, "[S]ocial and economic inequalities are to be arranged so that they are both (a) reasonably expected to be to everyone's advantage, and (b) attached to positions and offices open to all" (Rawls 1971, p. 53). So, it would be acceptable, according to Rawls, for the person who keeps the train running to enjoy a little more of the train's amenities since attracting a very well-qualified person to that position would benefit everyone. It would not, however, be justified to make some live in squaller while others live in luxury, even if the former did not buy a ticket. From the original position, under a veil of ignorance, no one would know whether they were a ticket holder or not; consequently, everyone would want at least basic decency guaranteed for even nonticket holders.

This appears to be one of the reasons why many revolutions took place in the Snowpiercer over the years. From the perspective of the tail-enders, they were being treated unfairly in the Rawlsian sense. If Wilford is overthrown and replaced by someone who shares the same perspective (say Gilliam or Curtis), then the quality of life in the tail section would drastically improve. However, from the perspective of Wilford and his associates, the idea of sharing the train's resources fairly with the tail-enders is unimaginable because the tail-enders are not entitled to have a share in the train's "wealth" to begin with because they were not ticket holders. In *Anarchy, State, and Utopia* (1974) Robert Nozick argued that Rawls failed to consider how the wealth of those in society is acquired, and thus failed to appreciate the unfairness or injustice of taking what someone earned and giving it to someone who did not. Everyone is entitled, Nozick (1974) argues, to what they earn; and thus it is morally wrong to take it from them without consent. If he is right, the fact that they lacked a ticket upon boarding the train effectively denies the tail-enders any right to demand fair treatment from Wilford; taking from ticket holders and giving to nonticket holders is morally wrong.

Here, however, we can see one of the famous objections to Nozick's argument. What if nonticket holders were unable to afford a ticket through no fault of their own – because, for example, of social inequalities that existed in the pre-Snowpiercer world. Correspondingly, what if ticket holders were only able to afford tickets because of the privileged social class that they were born into? If what one is able to earn is due to chance, it is not clear that one "deserve it" – even if one is "entitled" to it because they worked for it. This is something even Nozick recognized and admitted. So, if their status as ticket holders is, ultimately, a matter of chance, wouldn't it be wrong to let a tail-dweller starve (while someone in first class lives in luxury), when you could easily prevent it at the tawdry consequence of the first-classer living a slightly less luxurious life?

Since the time of Plato, numerous theories of justice have been presented. It would be difficult to give an exhaustive list here, but there is room for a number of examples. Plato conceived of justice as a harmonious relationship resulting from everyone doing what they were supposed to do (playing their role) where they are supposed to do it (in designated position). Divine command theorists argue that God's commands define what is just. Natural law theorists claim that justice is part of nature and reason must be used to deduce from human nature an action that is just. Proponents of distributive justice point out that the proper (i.e., based on needs, merit, equality, labor/production, etc.) distribution of goods among recipient entities defines justice. Advocates of retributive justice assert that the attainment of justice involves exacting an appropriate punishment for a wrongdoing committed. Finally, sponsors of restorative justice theories contend that justice is allowing offenders to repair (reparative) the damage that they caused, thus taking responsibility for their misdemeanors.

According to the "educational video" that the teacher showed the children in her class, Wilford built the Snowpiercer to fulfill a dream to connect all the railroads into one loop. The train was originally intended as a cruise line that would serve the rich. Somehow, however, Wilford knew that the CW-7 would freeze the world over, so he equipped the train with an eternal engine that powered every life-support apparatus. Earlier, it was pointed out that the tail-enders were never meant to board the train because they did not have tickets in the first place. Considering that the tail-enders were just freeloaders on the train, it would appear that Wilford's actions against them are just. By forcing their way onboard, the tail-enders effectively compromised the chances of survival of those who are legitimate passenger-inhabitants of the train. Thus, in true retributive justice fashion, the treatment that they received can be regarded as punishment that they deserve for what they did. It would be strange if Wilford rewarded them by affording them the same luxuries as the other passenger-inhabitants, despite what they did. The punishment ought to fit the crime. The crime? Postericide – doing something that can bring about the near extinction of humankind (McKinnon 2017). If this is the case, then it would seem that Wilford's actions are just.

However, it can be argued that the tail-enders only wanted to survive so they had no choice but to do everything to get onboard the train. This *conatus* or desire to continually exist is not something for which anyone can blame them. It is in their nature to struggle for survival. From this point of view, Wilford would appear to have gone overboard with his punishment. No one deserves to be punished for wanting to live. If the tail-enders feel that they do not deserve to be punished, it's no wonder that they want to overthrow Wilford; he would be regarded as an oppressive tyrant. They would naturally want to have the same privileges that the others enjoyed. The only way for them to have this is to install someone who understands that they did nothing wrong and must be treated in a manner that any human being deserves. This, of course, calls for a revolution – a civil war. According to Aquinas, there are three principles that make a war just – rightful sovereign, right (just) cause, and right intent. In this light, it would appear that the revolution waged by Curtis (a rightful sovereign) by pushing back against Wilford's oppression (right cause) so that the tail-enders will be treated fairly as the other passenger-inhabitants (right intent) is just.

How about Gilliam? Recall that Gilliam conspired with Wilford to fuel the revolution so that the train's population can be reduced. Wilford sent the tail-enders the red letter incognito while Gilliam advised Curtis on how to proceed given what "clues" these red letters revealed to them. Presumably, Gilliam is also the one who advised Curtis to stand down once the optimal number of people on the train has been reached. If everything went according to plan, all the survivors will go back to their respective sections and life will go on. As pointed out earlier, it would appear that Gilliam agreed with this compromise because this is the only way for Gilliam to give his people a choice on what to do with their lives – something that was effectively denied to them by Wilford for most of their existence on the train. From this perspective, Gilliam's actions – insofar as he takes responsibility for his cooperation with Wilford to kill off a number of the tail-enders and attempts to repair the damage done by the compromise by affording his people the chance to decide for themselves whether or not to join the revolution – give the impression of being just.

Finally, consider Namgoong Minsu, the designer of the Snowpiercer's security system. Nam had his own ulterior motive for helping Curtis' revolution. He wanted to leave the train, just like his wife did. The only reason he agreed to join Curtis is to be able to reach the front section so that he can blow up the only access door that leads outside. Nam appears to have a very selfish reason, which can easily be dismissed as unfair to the rest of people on the train. However, Nam's actions were motivated by the fact that human beings, by nature, are not meant to spend the rest of their lives inside a cage. If this is to be taken into account, then natural law would demand humans be free. In this light, Nam is actually giving everyone the opportunity to actualize their nature. But is Nam guilty of postericide? Not necessarily. If one is to consider the fact that Nam is a very smart individual, and he has been assessing the changes outside the train over the years, it would not be outlandish to conclude that his decision to go to the front section to blow up the access door during that particular moment was a calculated move. Just before they entered the aquarium section, Nam's attention was caught by something outside the train. Could it be that Nam saw a polar bear? If Nam was sure that it is possible for humans to survive outside the train, then his actions appear to be just.

Drawing the audience to a reality check once again, Director Bong makes it seem as if the respective actions of each of these characters are, in some ways, just. They appear to have done what is just given the circumstances that they had. If this is the case, it casts an interesting light on how the notion of justice works in relation to the values and aspirations of humanity.

Piercing the Veil of Humanity

It was mentioned in the earlier parts of this chapter that, at first glance, the whole premise of the film seems to rest on the notion of control. It was extensively discussed that this idea of control was portrayed in the film as the only thing that is safeguarding the survival of the human race. The Snowpiercer was under authoritarian rule because everything must be controlled meticulously so as to maintain the delicate balance that sustains human life inside the train. Curtis' declaration, "We control the engine; we control the world" fueled their revolution while Gilliam's utterance, "We control the water; we control the negotiation" pushed their makeshift army to move forward. Further, it was Wilford's encompassing control of every aspect of the train that made it possible for the elites to maintain a well-ordered society for 17 years. And it was by controlling this delicate balance that Wilford was able to make most of the passenger-inhabitants of the train happy (setting aside, of course, the tail-enders). In other words, this notion of gaining or maintaining control was used by Curtis, Wilford, Gilliam, Mason, and almost every major character in the film to perform the respective actions that they deemed were just.

Nevertheless, beneath this glaring prevalence of the notion of control throughout the film lies a deep-seated commentary on humanity – that what can be more dangerous to humanity more than anything else is humanity itself. If the story of the Snowpiercer is to be linked to the biblical account of creation, then it would appear that humankind's desire to establish control can be traced back to the creator giving humans the responsibility to be stewards of all creation. The history of science has also established humans as the most technologically advanced species on earth, effectively establishing dominance over other species. It is no wonder that humans came to see themselves as the most important being above all and regarded the rest of the world as objects for their pleasure. This anthropocentrism is what makes humanity the greatest danger to its own species and, perhaps, to the earth itself.

Similar to a number of postapocalyptic works (e.g., *The Walking Dead*, *The 100*), Snowpiercer features a "survive now, regain one's humanity later" mentality. In these works, humans killed other humans that they deemed to be a threat to their survival and way of life. Here, humanity is reduced from being a meaningful concept to a mere species of living organism surviving in the world. As Wilford puts it, "The train is the world. We the humanity." Humanity equals the correct number of human beings essential for survival.

When the world leaders signed off on releasing the CW-7 into the earth's atmosphere, they wanted to control the increasing global temperatures to ensure the continual survival of the human species. When it did not go as expected, a number of humans tried to save themselves by boarding the Snowpiercer. They had to force their way onto the train just to survive. As a result, Wilford established an authoritarian regime to make sure that most of the passenger-inhabitants survived. Gilliam had to enter into a compromise with Wilford to increase the chances of survival for the majority of his people. Curtis had to lead a revolution for a chance to a better life for the tail-enders. Mason and her colleagues fought to protect the well-ordered society that they worked hard to keep. In most instances, their actions can be, in some way, defended as just. Many of the events that were shown in the film had survival as their primary motivation. Interestingly, all these things revolved around the survival of one – and only one – species: the human race. The entirety of the *Snowpiercer* focused on humanity alone. Even in the aquarium section where Mason talked about the fish, the aquarium was not intended to preserve some species of aquatic life; its purpose was to provide a food source for the train's passenger-inhabitants. Ironically, all these attempts at survival just brought humankind closer and closer to extinction.

If the human race did not survive the Quaternary Ice Age, then perhaps the human-made ice age brought about by the CW-7 would not have occurred. In effect, the rest of the world would not have died. If human beings were removed from the equation, perhaps other species would have thrived instead of dying under tons of snow and ice. Reality check. It might be the case that human beings are the world's actual problem. Humankind's desire to take control, to survive, to take revenge, to be free, and to have a better life led to the train's explosion and the demise of most of the remaining members of the human race. The silver lining was that the train explosion appeared to be the needed push for the snow to melt.

Curiously, as Yona and Timmy, both of whom are train babies, stepped out of the ruins of the Snowpiercer, their first step seems to allude to humanity's first step on the moon. "One small step for [a] man, one giant leap for [hu]mankind." This is a very critical point in the overall narrative of the film. Yona and Timmy are (as far as we know) the only humans alive, and they've found themselves in a world that they do not know anything about – much like Adam and Eve who were banished from the Garden of Eden. They are the unwitting heirs of the "sacred responsibility to lead humanity." The casting of the survivors also reveals a very important symbolism. Timmy was of African descent while Yona's was Asian. This alludes to the ancient civilizations of the East and the West. Together, they represent the whole of humanity. And like in the ancient times, they have the opportunity to be the starting point – a beginning to a new human history – a second chance for a better humanity.

The movie ends with a poignant scene showing the two survivors seeing a polar bear looking at them from a distance. One thing that this signifies is that life, once more, thrives on earth. This could be taken as a happy ending for a relatively depressing movie. A deeper look into this scenario, however, raises the question about whether Director Bong wants to hint at the makings of a potential war – a war between humans and nature. The irony here is that in the beginning of the film, a strong message was being sent to the audience – "save the planet." Human efforts to "save the planet" by controlling the global temperature levels led to the near annihilation of all life. Humanity's efforts to save the world – this time the Snowpiercer – ended once again in its destruction. Now that humans again walk the face of the earth, but come face to face with an animal that could kill them – possibly one of the last of its kind – will humanity spell the planet's end once again by killing this beast? Or will they, this time, realize that maybe humanity is the danger to the planet and allow themselves to be killed for the sake of the world; to get rid of this human problem once and for all? This dilemma can be seen as one of the film's deep-seated attempts to pierce the veil of humanity as the most valuable being in the world.

Conclusion

As philosophy, *Snowpiercer* is inward-looking. It invites the audience to look into the self – into one's humanity – so that they may try to understand what it means to be human and what kind of value they place on their humanity. By understanding oneself, one can hope to be able to find meaning beyond merely existing and surviving in the world. More importantly, looking into the self allows the audience the opportunity to question the assumptions and prejudices that come with living as a member of the human race.

As philosophy, *Snowpiercer* is also outward-looking. It guides the audience to reflect on how human desires, actions, and decisions affect others – that humans are not on top of the world but are within the world and connected to the world. This means that what may be good for one may be bad for another or what may be deemed just to some may be unjust to others. Realizing this is vital to shifting from an anthropocentric worldview to a more inclusive one, perhaps an ecocentric one.

Ultimately, *Snowpiercer* is a wake-up call – a reality check – for everyone; the greatest danger to humanity is humanity itself. Only by accepting this truth can the human race pierce through the veils that conceal the real meaning and significance of what it is to be human and finally understand the role that humanity plays in the train of life.

References

Arendt, Hannah. 1978. Hannah Arendt: From an interview. *The New York Review.* https://www.nybooks.com/articles/1978/10/26/hannah-arendt-from-an-interview/

Bellamy, Richard, Markus Kornprobst, and Christine Reh. 2012. Politics as compromise: Special issue. *Government and Opposition* 47 (3): 275–295.

Binswanger, Harry. 1986. *The Ayn Rand Lexicon: Objectivism from A to Z*. Meridian. https://second-cdn.f-static.com/uploads/1259807/normal_5cb6e68316354.pdf

Garnett, Paul. 1988. *Investigating morals and values in today' society*. Good Apple. https://files.eric.ed.gov/fulltext/ED393753.pdf

Joon-Ho, Bong, and Kelly Masterson (writers). 2013. *Snowpiercer*. The Weinstein Company and RADiUS-TWC.

Kappel, Klemens. 2018. How moral disagreement may ground principled moral compromise. *Politics, Philosophy & Economics* 17 (1): 75–96.

Lee, Fred, and Steven Manicastri. 2018. Not all are aboard: Decolonizing exodus in Joon-ho Bong's Snowpiercer. *New Political Science* 40 (2): 211–226.

Machiavelli, Nicolo. 1998. The prince. https://www.gutenberg.org/files/1232/1232-h/1232-h.htm#chap18

May, Simon. 2005. Principled compromise and the abortion controversy. *Philosophy & Public Affairs* 33 (4): 317–348.

McKinnon, Catriona. 2017. Endangering humanity: An international crime? *Canadian Journal of Philosophy* 47 (2–3): 395–415.

Nozick, Robert. 1974. *Anarchy, state, and utopia*. New York: Basic Books.

Partenie, Catalin. 2018. Plato's myths. In *Stanford Encyclopedia of Philosophy*. https://plato.stanford.edu/entries/plato-myths/

Plato. 1968. *The Republic of Plato*, 2nd ed. Trans. Allan Bloom. Basic Books.

Rawls, John. 1971. *A theory of justice*, revised edition. Harvard University Press. https://www.consiglio.regione.campania.it/cms/CM_PORTALE_CRC/servlet/Docs?dir=docs_biblio&file=BiblioContenuto_3641.pdf

"The Philosophy of Snowpiercer." *The Korean Foreigner*, August 18, 2013. http://thekoreanforeigner.blogspot.com/2013/08/the-philsophy-of-snowpiercer.html

Weinstock, Daniel. 2013. On the possibility of principled moral compromise. *Critical Review of International Social and Political Philosophy* 16 (4): 537–556.

The Matrix as Philosophy: Understanding Knowledge, Belief, Choice, and Reality

48

Edwardo Pérez

Contents

Introduction	1132
Summarizing the Saga	1133
Knowledge	1135
Belief	1138
Reality	1141
Choice	1144
Conclusion	1148
References	1148

Abstract

The Matrix trilogy's narrative asks if what we claim to know affects our beliefs, if what we believe affects what we claim to know, and how these competing issues ultimately affect our choices and how they shape our reality. Do we choose what we know? Can we choose what to believe? And if so, does our reality, rooted in knowledge or belief, also become a choice? Given the rise of skepticism seen in the first two decades of the twenty-first century – where entire movements of people choose to reject knowledge, facts, truth, learning, experts, science, and reality – these questions do not just characterize the narrative of *The Matrix*. They also illustrate the precarious nature of our contemporary world. Thus, understanding how *The Matrix* and its sequels grapple with the relationship between knowledge, belief, choice, and reality, can help us understand why these issues continue to remain important to the realities we experience. *The Matrix* trilogy's

E. Pérez (✉)
Tarrant County College, Fort Worth, TX, USA

The University of Texas at Arlington, Arlington, TX, USA
e-mail: edwardo.perez@tccd.edu

© Springer Nature Switzerland AG 2024
D. K. Johnson et al. (eds.), *The Palgrave Handbook of Popular Culture as Philosophy*,
https://doi.org/10.1007/978-3-031-24685-2_69

significance resides in its ending, which represents the idea of choosing and creating a new reality. Ultimately, choice matters – choosing what to believe and what to know – because choice allows for the possibility that creation and change are imaginable and achievable within a world that is otherwise predetermined. Thus, we aren't just choosing beliefs, knowledge, and realities, we're also giving meaning to the beliefs, knowledge, and realities we claim. From this, our lives have meaning, too.

Keywords

Knowledge · Belief · Reality · Choice · Compatibilism · Determinism · Free will · Certitude · Cogito · Dream problem · Rene Descartes · Richard Rorty · John Searle · David Hume

Introduction

> I don't believe this is happening.
> —Neo *(The Matrix)*

Released in 1999, *The Matrix* blended elements of cyberpunk, noir, science fantasy, horror, superhero, and romance genres to create one of the most significant philosophical films of the late twentieth century. It sought not just to entertain audiences with innovative special effects, but also challenged audiences to think about the nature of reality, especially when it came to issues of knowledge, belief, and choice. Indeed, the relationship between these issues illustrates the philosophical focus of the overall narrative, which can be viewed as a debate about when we should choose to merely believe, when we should admit ignorance, and when we should claim certitude. When should we make choices based on our beliefs or what we claim to know, and do we create our own reality based on such choices? As such, *The Matrix* trilogy's narrative asks if what we claim to know affects our beliefs, if what we believe affects what we claim to know, and how these competing issues ultimately affect our choices and how they shape our reality.

For example, what does it mean if we believe something that we know is likely not true and then make a decision based on that belief? Similarly, what does it mean if we change our beliefs because we acquire new knowledge? Do we choose what we know? Can we choose what to believe? And if so, does our reality, rooted in knowledge or belief, also become a choice? Certainly, given the rise of skepticism seen in the first two decades of the twenty-first century – where entire movements of people choose to reject knowledge, facts, truth, learning, experts, science, and reality – these questions do not just characterize the narrative of *The Matrix*. They also illustrate the precarious nature of our contemporary world. Thus, understanding how *The Matrix* and its sequels grapple with the relationship between knowledge, belief, choice, and reality, can help us understand why these issues continue to remain important to the realities we experience.

Summarizing the Saga

> No one can be told, what the Matrix is. You have to see it for yourself.
> —Morpheus (*The Matrix*)

The Matrix opens with the protagonist, Neo, wondering about the signature question of the movie: "What Is the Matrix?" He encounters Trinity, who leads him to Morpheus, a man who presents Neo with a choice in the form of two pills: take the red pill and learn the answer to the question, or take the blue pill and wake up tomorrow believing whatever he wants to believe. Neo takes the red pill and learns that the Matrix is the world around him – or, more precisely, that he has been living in a computer simulated world, called the Matrix, and that it's not 1999 – but closer to 2199. The human race lost a war with a race of machines that ended with the humans darkening the sky and the machines turning humans into batteries (i.e., putting them in pods to provide the computers with an endless supply of bioenergy and then keeping them distracted and content with a neuro-interactive simulation: the Matrix). By remotely hacking into the Matrix, Morpheus and the others in his crew (such as Trinity and Cypher) have been fairly successful in freeing humans from the Matrix – even despite the efforts of the "Agents" (sentient computer programs in the form of persons) that try to stop them. Still, the resistance is few in number, and Zion – the one human city where those freed from the Matrix can live – struggles to survive.

When hacking into the Matrix, Morpheus and the members of his crew are able to do phenomenal (physically impossible) things, like jumping across buildings and floating kung fu moves; but the Agents who chase them are able to do more; indeed, they are seemingly unstoppable. Many awesome fight scenes abound. After one, Morpheus tells Neo about a prophecy, given by "the Oracle," which states that eventually a human will be freed from the Matrix that can effortlessly bend the Matrix to his will and defeat any Agent with ease. Called "the One," it is believed that this person will, as Morpheus puts it, "hail the destruction of the Matrix and the war, [and] bring freedom to our people." Morpheus believes this is Neo and takes him to the Oracle to confirm it. Unexpectedly, she tells Neo he is *not* the One, but that Morpheus believes he is so blindly that Neo will be forced to choose between his own life and Morpheus'. Indeed, Morpheus is captured by Agents in the Matrix, and Neo (and Trinity) risk their lives to rescue him. They succeed, but then Neo is shot to death by the antagonist of the film, Agent Smith. Trinity watches his heart stop in the real world. After she declares her love, however, his heart starts again; Neo resurrects inside the Matrix and finds that he can manipulate the Matrix as he wills, even stopping bullets in their tracks and seemingly deleting Agent Smith from inside his own digital body. This, it seems, reveals that Neo is the One after all, and film ends with him declaring the following to the machines who run the Matrix:

> I'm going to show these people what you don't want them to see. I'm going to show them a world without you. A world without rules and controls, without borders or boundaries. A world where anything is possible. Where we go from there, is a choice I leave to you.

Neo then flies up into the air while *Rage Against The Machine's* "Wake Up" plays over the end credits.

The sequels, *The Matrix: Reloaded* and *The Matrix: Revolutions* (which we will call *Reloaded* and *Revolutions* for short), were released in May 2003 and November 2003 and framed as a two-part story. We learn that since Neo was revealed as The One, they have freed more minds in 6 months than they have in the past 6 years; and yet, the war has not ended and the Matrix still exists. The Oracle (who we now learn is a program herself) reveals that Neo needs to go to "the Source," the machine mainframe, "where the path of the One ends." To do so, Neo needs the Keymaker, who has been kidnapped by a rogue program named "the Merovingian." After some cool fight and chase scenes, they get the Keymaker, who leads Neo to the Source – and once there, Neo meets the Architect, the designer of the Matrix itself. But in a convoluted "academic" speech, the Architect reveals that in fact Neo has been tricked; the prophecy was a lie.

The first version of the Matrix was perfect, the Architect tells Neo, without suffering or evil, but failed because its subjects failed to accept it. The Architect redesigned the Matrix to "more accurately reflect the varying grotesqueries of [human] nature," but again it failed. The Oracle realized that the problem was choice: the humans plugged in needed to be given the option to choose or reject The Matrix. While this solution worked, it created a "systemic anomaly, that if left unchecked might threaten the system itself." Simply put, too many people would eventually choose to reject the Matrix for it to keep functioning (partly because the ability to reject the matrix would allow someone to eventually manipulate it according to their will).

To deal with this problem, the Machines came up with a plan: have the Oracle "prophesy" that "the One" who would eventually emerge (and could free everyone) would end the war, not by actually freeing everyone, but by going to the Source. Once there, the One would meet the Architect and be offered a choice: fully enter the Source and reset the Matrix (and "elect from the Matrix 23 individuals – 16 female, 7 male – to rebuild Zion"), or reenter the Matrix, which "will result in a cataclysmic system crash, killing everyone connected to the Matrix, which, coupled with the extermination of Zion, will ultimately result in the extinction of the entire human race." The Architect reveals that Neo is in fact the fifth "One" to be presented with this choice, and that each of his predecessors choose to cooperate – meaning that the Matrix that Neo knows is the sixth version. Neo doesn't cooperate, however, and instead reenters the Matrix to save his love Trinity, who risked her life to enable him to enter the Source.

While all this is happening, Agent Smith (who Neo supposedly deleted in the first movie but has since resurrected) is threatening the machine world in a different way. He didn't die but instead reentered the Matrix and started replicating himself onto other programs and humans, like a virus. Smith even copies himself onto the Oracle, gaining her ability to see the future, and will eventually take over the entire machine world itself. In this, Neo sees an opportunity to end the war and save Zion by striking a deal with the Machines: he will defeat Smith if the Machines agree to spare Zion. The machines hook Neo directly into the Matrix, and Neo engages Smith in an epic final battle. Surprisingly, Neo loses and Agent Smith copies himself onto Neo in an apparent victory. This, however, gives the machines direct access to Smith and allows them to delete Smith and purge him from the system. Although Neo is now dead, the machines spare Zion, the Matrix is reset, and the movie ends with the Oracle and the Architect discussing the new-found peace. The Matrix will continue to exist, but those who want to be freed from the Matrix, both humans and programs, will be.

Knowledge

> There's no way if you can really know whether I'm here to help you or not.
> —The Oracle *(Reloaded)*

When it comes to the philosophical lessons of *The Matrix Saga*, the first thing that comes to mind is Rene Descartes' dream problem from his *Meditations*. How can you know for sure that you are not dreaming right now, or that you are not stuck in something very much like the Matrix? Because the experiences you would have in such a circumstance are indistinguishable from what you would experience if the world was real, it seems that you can't know for sure that the Matrix is not real. Since 1999, there has been no short supply of philosophers using *The Matrix* to explain Descartes argument to their introduction to philosophy classes; and rightly so, it is very useful. But "you can't know whether you are in the Matrix" doesn't seem to be the philosophical message of the film. At the least, it is not the most interesting one.

So, what is the message?

The Matrix is initially framed by what could be referred to as the matrix question: "What is the Matrix?" On one hand, the matrix question is literal. It is the impetus that initially drove characters like Trinity, Cypher, and Neo to find Morpheus and become unplugged from the Matrix's neural network; but as Morpheus says to Neo, "Nobody can be told what the Matrix is, you have to see it for yourself." And once shown, each character chooses to either accept their knowledge of the Matrix or reject it. What's more, there are a host of other decisions that characters make about what to believe, and even profess to know. Trinity chooses to believe that Neo is the One; Morpheus professes to know it; Neo chooses to believe that he can rescue Morpheus from the agents; The Oracle chooses to believe that Neo can fulfill the prophecy that she herself fabricated – that she knows was a lie – although she admits in the end that she did not *know* how things would turn out. And so, the message of the film seems to revolve around the questions of how we choose what to believe and "know," and how those choices shape "our reality." Let me elaborate.

In life, we believe many things. Sometimes our beliefs are based on facts and evidence sometimes they're based on faith, intuition, a gut feeling, or a wish. Either way, we live our lives based on our beliefs, because our beliefs inform our actions. More importantly, many of us not only make choices about what we will merely believe or not believe, but also about what we know or don't know. This might sound strange since, in philosophy, propositional knowledge is traditionally understood as belief that is justified and true (As Edmund Gettier notes in his 1963 article "Is Justified True Belief Knowledge?," Plato, Roderick Chisholm, and A.J. Ayer all essentially define knowledge as justified true belief. Gettier questions Plato, Chisholm, and Ayer, claiming that their justified true belief formulations aren't sufficient "for someone's knowing a given proposition." There are conditions in which one can have justified true belief but not have knowledge. Despite this, however, justified true belief is still necessary for knowledge, and so the point above holds.) Since a person can't merely choose for something to be true (or justified), they can't just choose for some belief of theirs to legitimately count as knowledge. But a belief doesn't have to be justified or true for us to act on it, nor does it have to be rooted in evidence for us to embrace it or even say that we know it. As such, the decisions we often make are not only about what to believe or not, but about what we choose to merely believe and what we choose to accept (and declare) as knowledge. Such a choice might even lead to what we might call "certitude," the feeling or impression that a belief is most certainly true (even if it is not). This, we might call, choosing to "know" something.

If this is right, then our choices might not only determine what we believe but the reality (or realities) we live in. As an example, consider the rise of conspiracy theories and alterative facts that have characterized the politics of the twenty-first century, from 9/11 Truthers, Birtherism, and *Plandemic*, to Trumpism, QAnon, and "stop the steal." People who embrace these theories claim to not only believe them, but to *know* things that are demonstrably false, that directly contradict observable reality (and thus, strictly speaking can't be known): that Obama doesn't have a birth certificate, that there was massive election fraud in 2020, etc. As such, those who study such belief systems often claim that the people who embrace them have chosen to live in "an alternate reality" (Guthrie Weisman 2018).

In *The Matrix*, the character that mirrors this kind of choice is Cypher, the only character who chooses to be permanently physically reinserted into the Matrix after he was unplugged. Cypher understands that the reality he lived inside the Matrix wasn't "real," but he doesn't like the real world or having to follow Morpheus's orders. Indeed, Cypher not only rejects the real world; he chooses to disregard the knowledge of the Matrix that came with it. Cypher tells Agent Smith that he doesn't want to remember anything about the Matrix, or the outside world, once he's reinserted. "Ignorance is bliss."

This is a prime example of how one can choose to "know" something. Cypher is not accepting fact and coming to have a justified true belief; he is rejecting facts in favor of certitude. His decision will lead him to *claim* that he knows something that cannot be known (because it is false): that the world of the Matrix is physical. But it won't feel false to him; he'll have certitude. And this choice will, in a sense, determine the reality he lives in.

Strangely, Cypher's choice might resemble the choice Rene Descartes made when he formulated his cogito ergo sum. *"I think therefore I am."* Mo Weimin and Wang Wei suggest that, "Almost the entire history of Western philosophy [after Descartes] has unfolded either by reinterpreting the philosophy of Cartesian Cogito or by criticizing it from different angles" (2007, p. 247). Cypher's choice could be seen as a critical interpretation of Descartes too, especially if we consider that Cypher's goal echoes the goal of Descartes. How so?

Descartes wanted to find a fundamental grounding for his existence, or, as philosopher Peter Markie explains, "to serve as the permanent foundation for his knowledge" (1992, p. 50). By proving that he exists, and that his perceptions of the world are accurate, he thought he could establish an epistemological ground for doing science. Rooted in skepticism, a process by which he doubted anything that could possibility be doubted, Descartes' quest brought him to the conclusion that he could not doubt that he was doubting; he could not think that he was not thinking. And since one cannot think without existing, the very act of doubting his existence entailed that he existed. Thus: *I think, therefore I am*. We might interpret Cypher's reasoning as something similar: I reject reality, therefore I choose the Matrix. Unlike Descartes, Cypher doesn't question if he exists. Rather, Cypher questions whether he wants to exist in the real world. Of course, he decides he doesn't – and in doing so, Cypher rejects the knowledge he has about the Matrix, and requests that it be removed from his memory.

By choosing ignorance over actual knowledge, however, Cypher is able to generate certitude and his own reality – or, he would've been able to do this if he'd succeeded in killing Neo and Morpheus before Tank blasted him (This raises at least two questions: (1) Was Agent Smith dealing with Cypher in good faith? and (2) How would Cypher even know if he was reinserted (and given the life of an actor, as he requested) if he told Agent Smith that he didn't want to remember anything?). And it is this way that Cypher's choice reflects Descartes'. While Descartes was ultimately after knowledge in the traditional sense (justified true belief), and Cypher was not, they both were in search of a sense of certainty. For Descartes, that certainty would allow him to explain the reality of his existence. For Cypher, that certainty would allow him to (re)create the (un)reality of his existence. To Descartes, the knowledge of thought entails his existence. To Cypher, the knowledge of the Matrix makes him choose to (un)exist. But they are still seeking something similar.

In another way, however, what Descartes and Cypher are doing is opposite. Descartes was a foundationalist who, as Markie noted, wanted to ground his knowledge in something permanent, and come to know the way the world actually is; Cypher, on the other hand, was an anti-foundationalist who wanted to (un)ground his reality by reentering the Matrix, which is impermanent, and reject the way the world actually is. If this description holds, then we can see that by embracing an anti-foundationalist perspective, Cypher's choice – and, to a larger extent, perhaps the narrative of *The Matrix* trilogy – suggests that reality is something that can, if not be created, be chosen; and it does so through anti-foundationalist philosophy.

Philosopher Richard Rorty explains his anti-foundationalist philosophy this way:

> There is nothing deep down inside us except what we have put there ourselves, no criterion that we have not created in the course of creating a practice, no standard of rationality that is not an appeal to such a criterion, no rigorous argumentation that is not obedience to our own conventions. (Bracken 2002, p. 98)

As Harry M. Bracken explains, "[Rorty's philosophy] is anti-foundationalism with a vengeance. It is not directed exclusively at Descartes. It is rather a frontal attack on all forms of realism" (2002, p. 98). To be clear, Bracken also sees Rorty's philosophy as "an expression of 'cultural relativism' (2002, p. 98)" and adds that it is difficult to "make sense of the relativism which characterizes much of postmodernist thought" (2002, p. 99). But he also sees it as something that cuts "at the very heart of Cartesianism" (2002, p. 99) and foundationalism itself. And a kind of Rortian anti-foundationalism seems to inform Cypher's choice and the trilogy's narrative, as the following section will continue to show.

Belief

> For what it's worth, you've made a believer out of me.
> —The Oracle to Neo *(Reloaded)*

The Oracle gives Morpheus, Neo, and Trinity conflicting information: she tells Morpheus that he would find the One, Trinity that she would fall in love with the One, but Neo that he is not the One. Consequently, Morpheus and Trinity believe Neo is the One, while Neo doesn't – at least not for most of the first film. Like certitude, belief becomes a choice, one that also helps create reality. As Morpheus explains to Neo after Neo visits the Oracle: "what was said was for you, and for you alone." In other words, the knowledge Neo gains from the Oracle is valuable for him, just as the knowledge the Oracle gave Morpheus and Trinity was valuable for them. In each case, Neo, Morpheus, and Trinity (as well as many other characters) base their choices on the "knowledge" they possess; what they think they know is why they choose to do what they do.

However, what they merely believe also factors into their decisions, and it's notable that, ultimately, they all come to believe the same thing: that Neo is the One. And they choose to do this for themselves, even despite evidence that they have to the contrary. Trinity even continues to believe that Neo is the one after he dies. As the Oracle says to Neo, Morpheus believes that Neo is the One so blindly that "no one, not you, not even me can convince him otherwise." Or as Morpheus also tells Neo: "I can only show you the door, you're the one who has to walk through it." This suggests that, regardless of what we learn, we still have a choice regarding what we believe or say we know. As again the Oracle says to Neo, but this time in *Reloaded*, "You just have to make up your own damn mind to either accept what I'm going to tell you, or reject it." What we see, then, is that belief and certitude are choices that, in turn, make what reality we choose to live in up to us.

Reloaded and *Revolutions* develop Neo in his role as the One and concluded with Neo choosing to sacrifice himself for the sake of humanity. This decision ends the war, fulfilling the Oracle's prophecy (even though it was initially a lie). However, in the final scene, after Neo's death and a seeming renewal of life (through a reconfiguration of the Matrix), it is implied that the war's end and the peace it brings is temporary and that the cycle of the Matrix might eventually begin again, echoing

The Architect's explanation to Neo (near the end of *Reloaded*) that there have been five versions of the Matrix prior to the version Neo experienced and that Neo (or at least a version of Neo) has existed in the same role each time. Yet, the dialogue between the Architect and the Oracle also suggests that this ending is different from the previous versions and that this difference is partly due to the Oracle's belief in Neo and her willingness to induce change. As the Oracle tells Seraph at the end of *Revolutions*, who asks her if she always knew how things would end: "Oh, no. No, I didn't, but I believed. I believed." Given the trilogy's narrative and the philosophical questions it raises about the nature of knowledge, belief, reality, and choice, it's a significant last line, suggesting that perhaps belief is the most important of the four issues.

Nevertheless, while the Matrix and its construction seemingly function as a predetermined program governing humanity in a repetitive cycle, the film's conclusion ultimately suggests that choice not only outweighs the programming and algorithms, but that the uncertainty of choice (the anti-foundationalism) allows for the creation of possible realities. As noted above, these realities depend on belief, as well as certitude. Consider the following scene between the Oracle, Trinity, and Morpheus, which takes place early in *Revolutions*:

Trinity   What happened?
Oracle   I made a choice and that choice cost me more than I wanted it to.
Morpheus   What choice?
Oracle   To help you, to guide Neo. Now, since the real test of any choice is having to make the same choice again knowing full well what it might cost, I guess I feel pretty good about that choice, because here I am, at it again.
Morpheus: How can you expect me to believe you?
Oracle: I don't. I expect just what I've always expected. For you to make up your own damn mind. Believe me or don't.

This scene not only echoes the message of the original film, about belief being a choice, it also establishes the conclusion the sequels work toward. Indeed, even the Oracle, for all the knowledge she possesses and all the beliefs she holds, is able to make choices, just as Morpheus, Trinity, and Neo are able to make choices, and just as several secondary characters make choices, too. Throughout the trilogy, we see characters such as Cypher, Tank, Niobe, Persephone, Councillor Hamman, Roland, Lock, Seraph, and the Keymaker make various choices that affect the narrative. Even the Architect's final scene with the Oracle in *Revolutions* could be read as a choice he makes, which, given that he designs the Matrix itself, presents an interesting example regarding the relationship between the issues of knowledge, belief, and reality. (It's clear the Architect chooses to agree to free those who want to be freed. Yet, he also seems to choose to give peace a chance.)

Returning to Descartes, we could formulate *The Matrix*'s argument as suggesting either that we choose to "know" therefore we choose to exist, or we choose to believe therefore we choose to exist. Put another way, we could offer that *The Matrix* maintains that we exist in the reality we believe in or choose to feel is certain. Our reasons for choosing are not necessarily important – they don't need to be sufficient, justified, true, or reliable. Certainly, Neo deciding to save Morpheus was, as Tank put it, "loco," because it wasn't a choice grounded in any sort of logic. Rather, it was a choice rooted in Neo's belief in himself, not as the One (because at that point in the story, he didn't yet believe he was the One), but as someone who just knew (felt certain) he could do it. So, for *The Matrix*, the mere act of believing and/or "knowing" is enough to proceed to a choice.

Aristotle taught that the way to persuade was through logos (logic), pathos (passion), and ethos (credibility). But here, logos, pathos, and ethos do not matter. In fact, persuasion itself doesn't matter. In the Saga, arguments take place between characters, yet most characters are not really trying to convince one another to change their minds. Rather, the point of the debate is to convince those who disagree that they don't need to agree. Instead, they need to accept that they don't agree. As Morpheus puts it when he is told by Commander Lock that not everyone shares Morpheus' beliefs: "my beliefs don't require them to."

We should remember, however, that the only character who chooses to believe that which is directly contrary to reality is Cypher; and Cypher, contrary to the suggestions of comedian Patton Oswalt, is undoubtedly a villain of the story. Oswalt does have a point about life on the outside being miserable, that fact being mostly the human's fault, and how the machines did initially try to make the life of the humans inside the matrix perfect.

> Probably the first version of the Matrix, everybody could fly and orgasms lasted three months and you could just eat all the chocolate you wanted. And people were like, "No! I want a goddamn cubicle job!" And the machines went, "OK. I guess they want cubicles. Give 'em that. We tried to be nice." (Downey 2020)

Nevertheless, as the character who betrays the heroes for his own personal gain, the movie clearly portrays Cypher as the villain. Oswalt asks Morpheus, "Who the fuck are you helping?! Why are you dragging us out [of the Matrix]?! The machines aren't trying to kill us" (Downey 2020). But Morpheus is analogous to the prisoner in Plato's cave, who was chained down and fooled into thinking that the shadows on the wall he was seeing were real, but then escaped out into the real world to learn the truth. When the prisoner reflects on his condition in the cave, he realizes that he would never want to return; although those still trapped in the cave think they are happy (because, subjectively, they feel that way), there is something objectively pitiful about being imprisoned and fooled – and intrinsically worthwhile about being free and knowing the truth. Although he is mocked when he returns to the cave and tries to convince the remaining prisoners that the shadows are not real, the freed prisoner is trying to accomplish worthwhile: their freedom and enlightenment.

So, sure, the machines aren't trying to kill those who are plugged into the Matrix, and life on the inside is subjectively more pleasant; but there is more to life – other things are more valuable – than subjectively pleasures, like freedom and truth. Since Morpheus, who overtly stands for these ideals, is clearly portrayed as a hero of the film, it would be too short sighted to suggest that *The Matrix* is arguing that it is acceptable for everyone to just choose to believe whatever the hell they want. Freedom, reality, truth, and actual knowledge matters. After all, Neo is also a hero in the story because – when Morpheus gives him the option of learning the actual truth and seeing "how deep the rabbit hole goes" or just waking up in his bed and believing what he wants to believe – Neo chooses the truth. Still, in a world where certainty is hard to come by, there is a lot of room for flexibility and acceptance when it comes to what people choose to believe and profess to know. And this is obviously another message of the film.

Reality

> I think the matrix can be more real than this world.
> —Cypher *(The Matrix)*

If Richard Rorty is right, then the reality we exist in is not some externally existing permanent thing (like Descartes thought) but instead something that we choose to create based on what we choose to "know" and/or what we choose to believe. A less extreme and relativistic notion along the same line belongs to John Searle, who suggested that our social reality is constructed. For Searle, there are two kinds of facts: brute facts, or facts on the lower level, about the physical world that exist independent of human institutions. And then there are facts on the upper level, institutional facts, that we create based on a kind of mutual agreement, or collective intentionality. It is a brute fact that there is a green piece of paper in my hand; it is an institutional fact that I have money in my hand – that the green paper is valued and can be traded for goods and services. What makes it green paper is physical fact; what makes it money is the way that we have all decided to treat it.

For Searle, the structure of our social reality is invisible; we not only take it for granted, we also don't typically question it or consider it (Searle 1995). As Searle notes, the world and life we're raised in contains things like cars and bathtubs (or, to update Searle's example, smartphones, 3D printers, and bank accounts). We can perceive and use such objects "without reflecting on the special features of their ontology and without being aware that they have a special ontology," because these objects "seem as natural to us as stones and water and trees" (Searle 1995, p. 4). But they are not; they are what they are only because of collective intention; we all regard, treat, and use them in a certain way.

For Searle, our social reality "is created by us for our purposes and seems as readily intelligible to us as those purposes themselves" (1995, p. 4). In other words, our world has cars, bathtubs, smartphones, 3D printers, and bank accounts; and we can perceive them and use them without ever questioning why we use them or need to use them because their uses seem perfectly obvious. When we do question them, however, "we are left with a harder intellectual task of identifying things in terms of their intrinsic features without reference to our interests, purposes, and goals" (1995, p. 5). Why else would a bathtub exist if not to take a bath?

The bathtubs inside the Matrix exist as social constructions as well, although the intended purpose of those that created them is a little different: to maintain the illusion of the social structure humans are used to. Think of the Oracle baking cookies while she talks to Neo. Just like (as Neo is told in *The Matrix*) "there is no spoon," there are no cookies – so why is the Oracle baking them? In the same way, Cypher knows that the steak he eats at dinner with Agent Smith isn't real. Ultimately, spoons and steaks and cookies are just programs, and as such are forms of "control." The Oracle admits as much to Neo in *Reloaded*:

Neo   You are a part of this system, another kind of control. ... Are there other programs like you?
Oracle   Oh, not like me. Look, see those birds? At some point, a program was written to govern them. A program was written to watch over the trees and the wind, the sunrise and sunset. There are programs running all over the place. The ones doing their job, doing what they are meant to do, are invisible. You'd never even know they were there.

The Oracle's words echo Searle's observations, but as Searle noted above, questioning reality leads to a difficult intellectual task. The task of dealing with the unreality of the Matrix leaves Cypher asking "Why, oh why, didn't I take the blue pill?" Certainly, Neo's initial reaction to the Matrix reflects the difficulty of grappling with the idea that one exists in a simulated reality, as does Cypher's choice to be reinserted.

Assuming the world we live in is not a computer simulation, we aren't faced with the same choice as Neo or Cypher; we don't typically have to decide between a red pill (learning about the Matrix and living in the desert of the real) or a blue pill (staying inside the Matrix, obliviously living in a simulation we're used to). However, we do choose our own realities to the extent that we are able to freely affiliate ourselves with a political party, religion, ideology, family, group, education system, career, gender identity, diet, interpretation of history, music, art, sports team, and so on. And this is how people immersed in conspiracy theories come to hold demonstrably false beliefs – even beliefs about what Searle would call brute facts of the world – with such certitude that they will claim to know it, and no amount of counter evidence could ever persuade them otherwise. In this way, they live in their own reality.

Ironically, those who believe in the QAnon conspiracy theory refer to "waking up to the reality that the world is controlled by Satanist pedophiles (that can only be stopped by Donald Trump)" as being "red pilled." Because this is demonstrably false, the more apt metaphor, of course, would be "blue pilled." Like Cypher, they don't like what the red pill has to offer: they don't like reality. Indeed, every prediction they have made, for example that "The Storm" (a reconning for the Satanist pedophiles) has been wrong; yet they never admit the mistake. They simply make a new prediction, and move on (Palmer 2021). Likewise, they claim to be doing what they are doing to protect children from pedophiles; but when credible evidence emerged that Matt Gaetz, one of Donald Trump's first congressional supporters, was actually involved in trafficking minors, they rushed to his defense

(Petrizzo 2021). They have opted to have their awareness of actual reality erased, and replaced it with a fictional narrative in which they, like Cypher, can see themselves as the hero rather than the villain. They have chosen the Matrix.

In *The Matrix* trilogy, we see many characters choose between different realities, too: Cypher chooses the (un)reality of the Matrix; characters like Morpheus, Neo, Trinity, and the residents of Zion choose the reality of the physical world; characters (or programs) like the Merovingian, Persephone, the Conductor, the Keymaker, Seraph, and even the Oracle choose to exist in a sort of liminal space inside the Matrix, one that allows them to subsist throughout the different versions of the Matrix; the Architect and the machines choose to exist outside the Matrix (although they are able to enter it); while Agent Smith's reality changes from being a control program inside the Matrix, to being "unplugged" and thus becoming a virus able to spawn unlimited copies of himself. Nearly every character seems to choose their reality.

The only exception would be Agent Smith, who becomes unplugged because of the way Neo "killed" him in the first film. Neo didn't give him a choice between a red pill or a blue pill; he didn't even know what would happen to Smith as a result of what he did to him. However, once unplugged, Agent Smith embraces his viral status. Unlike Cypher, he doesn't seek to be reinserted. Rather, Smith becomes the antithesis of Neo, equal in power, and claims the Matrix as his. Moreover, Agent Smith isn't just inside the Matrix, he becomes the Matrix – at least until Neo sacrifices himself, causing Agent Smith's program to be destroyed.

Of course, the reality of the peaceful version of the Matrix Neo enables to be created at the end of *Revolutions* is also a choice, one made by Neo and the machines – one influenced by the Oracle and seemingly designed by the Architect. (At least to the extent that the Architect gives his approval at the end of *Revolutions*.) Even the little girl, Sati, gets to create a sunrise in the sky. Indeed, this reality is perhaps the most significant. Not just because it's the reality that ends the trilogy, but because it's the reality Neo chooses, not for himself, but for the sake of humanity and the machines. To the larger point of this chapter, Neo doesn't just choose to create a new reality, he also chooses to believe and "know" what he wants to believe and "know" and not what others want him to believe and "know." Consider Agent Smith's questioning of Neo near the end of their final fight in *Revolutions*:

Smith   Why do you do it? Why? Why get up? Why keep fighting? Do you believe you're fighting for something? For more than your survival? Can you tell me what it is? Do you even know? Is it freedom or truth? Perhaps peace? Could it be for love? Illusions, Mr. Anderson. Vagaries of perception. Temporary constructs of a feeble human intellect trying desperately to justify an existence that is without meaning or purpose! And all of them as artificial as the matrix itself, although only a human mind could invent something as insipid as love. You must be able to see it, Mr. Anderson, you must know it by now. You can't win. It's pointless to keep fighting. Why, Mr. Anderson, why? Why do you persist?
Neo: Because I choose to.

Like the Oracle and like Agent Smith after Agent Smith took over the Oracle's program, Neo had "the sight." He was able to see beyond normal perception. As the Oracles admits, however, those with the sight cannot see "past the choices we don't understand." This is arguably why The Oracle allowed Smith to copy himself onto her and thus receive the sight: Neo's choice to continue fighting was not a choice Smith could understand and thus not one he could see beyond. So, after Neo falls to the ground for the last time, he says:

> Wait... I've seen this. This is it; this is the end. Yes, you were laying right there, just like that, and I... I... I stand here, right here, I'm... I'm supposed to say something. I say... Everything that has a beginning has an end, Neo.

He thinks that this moment is "the end" because he can't see beyond it. When it's not – when Neo gets up to fight yet again – Smith panics and copies himself onto Neo to defeat him, thus allowing the machines to (in essence) *run their antivirus software* and purge the system of Agent Smith and his many clones. Thus, Neo's choice to persist represents a choice to reject what Agent Smith saw as the end, and what Neo "knows" and believes become choices for him as much as the reality he chooses to create.

Choice

> Everything begins with a choice.
> —Morpheus (*Reloaded*)

Each film in *The Matrix* trilogy portrays strong arguments in favor of fatalism (the idea that the future is fated) and causal determinism (the idea that all events are the inevitable causal result of events that proceeded them). The first film introduces the prophecy, and the Oracle as a fortune teller, which suggests the future is fated. In *Reloaded*, we realize that the prophecy is a lie – another form of control – but still, the Oracle is still able to predict Neo's actions. Neo asks how he can still make a choice if she knows what he will do, and she simply replies: "you didn't come here to make a choice, you already made it, you're here to understand why you made it." Or think about what we learn in *Reloaded* about there having been five versions of The Matrix before the first film. We get the impression that the same thing happens every time, in a repeating cycle; set the system up the same way, and the same thing will happen every time. Perhaps that is part of the reason The Oracle's "foreknowledge" is so accurate: she's seen it all before.

Both fatalism and determinism suggest that the choices we make are not free, and instead are the effect of a predetermined cause. A prime example is how the Architect is able to predict whether Neo will choose to cooperate (or save Trinity) by simply looking at the activity of his brain.

We already know what you are going to do, don't we? Already, I can see the chain reaction – the chemical precursors that signal the onset of an emotion, designed specifically to overwhelm logic and reason. An emotion that is already blinding you from the simple and obvious truth. She is going to die, and there is nothing you can do to stop it.

If the way we behave is simply a result of our brain structure, since our brain structure is ultimately a result of our genes and environment, then how we will act is predetermined, not free, and ultimately outside of our control.

The Merovingian is much more direct. As he argues in *Reloaded*:

There is only one constant, one universal, it is the only real truth: causality. Action. Reaction. Cause and effect. ... Choice is an illusion created by those with power and those without [...] This is the nature of the universe. We struggle against it, we fight to deny it, but it is of course pretense, it is a lie. Beneath our poised appearance, the truth is we are completely out of control. Causality. There is no escape from it, we are forever slaves to it.

In the context of the narrative, these arguments seem convincing, especially when delivered through compelling characters like the Oracle, the Architect, and the Merovingian. Yet, as this chapter has maintained, nearly every character makes free choices that propel and affect the narrative, contradicting the causal determinist perspective. Cypher freely chose the Matrix, Niobe freely chose to help Morpheus, Lock freely chose to defend Zion, Trinity freely chose to save Neo. Indeed, the way that Neo seems to save the day in the end is by simply making a choice (to continue to fight); this suggests that *The Matrix* and its sequels advocate for the position that humans have free will.

Consider the scene where Neo is talking to the Architect. Every time Neo has an opportunity to respond, we see a series of screens around him that depict every possible way he could. The camera, it seems, centers and zooms in on the reaction Neo chooses. The architect is able to predict some of his choices; like when Neo chooses to save Trinity, or when all the screens have Neo saying "Bullshit!" and the Architect replies that "Denial is the most predictable of all human responses." But generally, it seems that the camerawork itself is supposed to indicate that Neo is freely choosing how to respond. Indeed, Neo makes seemingly free decisions throughout each film – from taking the red pill and saving Morpheus in *The Matrix* to choosing to save Trinity in *Reloaded* and choosing to sacrifice himself in his final battle with Agent Smith in *Revolutions*.

In making these choices, Neo and the other characters also chooses what to believe, what to disregard or hold as certain (i.e., what to "know"), and what reality to recognize. As with causal determination, the context of the character's choices renders the position of free will equally compelling, perhaps even more so as many of us might feel as Neo does when he tells Morpheus "I don't like the idea that I'm not in control of my life." So, which position does *The Matrix* trilogy really advocate?

In *Reloaded*, the Oracle tells Neo that the path of the One leads to the machine mainframe or "the Source." Later in the film, the Architect confirms this, telling Neo that in every previous version of the Matrix, the One has returned to "the source," fulfilling his role so that the Matrix (and Zion) can be reset. What's significant, however, is that the Architect and the Oracle recognize the need to offer Neo a choice, a recognition that occurred after the initial versions of the Matrix failed. As the Architect recounts:

> [The Oracle] stumbled upon a solution whereby nearly 99% of all test subjects accepted [the Matrix], as long as they were given a choice, even if they were only aware of the choice at a near unconscious level. While this answer functioned, it was obviously fundamentally flawed, thus creating the otherwise contradictory systemic anomaly, that if left unchecked might threaten the system itself. [...] Which brings us at last to the moment of truth, wherein the fundamental flaw is ultimately expressed, and the anomaly revealed as both beginning and end. There are two doors. The door to your right leads to the Source, and the salvation of Zion. The door to your left leads back to the Matrix, to her and to the end of your species. As you adequately put, the problem is choice.

If we believe the Architect, then Cypher isn't the only one who chooses the Matrix. More importantly, the Architect and, by association, the Oracle seem to both acknowledge what David Hume refers to as "liberty and necessity," which are the concepts he uses to defend the position of compatibilism, the idea that that free will and determinism are compatible – that they can both be true together.

For Hume, free will does not require the negation of determinism; in fact, it depends on it. According to Hume, a person's action is free as long as it is a direct result of that persons' will or desire (and not compelled by some kind of outside force). Since even if determinism is true, we can still act in accordance with our will or desire, determinism is compatible with free will. But free will also requires determinism in that we wouldn't be able to make a choice without causality. We have to know, "if I make this or that choice, such-and-such will deterministically follow." What's more, we must understand what causally led us to the point of making the decision. Thus, for us to exercise liberty (free will) there must first be necessity (causation and determinism). As Hume contends, "tis only upon the principles of necessity that a person acquires any merit or demerit from his actions" (Hume 2000, Book 2, Part 3, Section 2).

For Hume, our choices have meaning precisely because they are made in response to causality. It's meaningful that Cypher chooses the Matrix, just as it's meaningful when Neo chooses to save Morpheus and Trinity and eventually humanity. Likewise, it's meaningful when Persephone chooses to free the Keymaker and when Trinity chooses to confront the Merovingian in *Revolutions* to save Neo. Every choice each character makes throughout the trilogy becomes meaningful because they are made in response to a predetermined situation. In this way, the Oracle's solution explained by the Architect doesn't just allow for causal determination and free will to coexist, it makes them symbiotic, with each side giving meaning to the other. Indeed, causality has no meaning either, unless the chain of events leads to a choice. This is what makes Neo's final choice so significant.

But there is a potential problem with Hume's argument. According to the Architect, all previous versions of the One had chosen the door that led back to the Source. This allowed Zion to be destroyed and the Matrix to be reloaded. Yet, one could argue that this outcome wasn't meaningful because it was predetermined, the previous "Ones" didn't really have a choice. As the Architect explains:

> The relevant issue is whether or not you are ready to accept the responsibility of the death of every human being in this world. It is interesting, reading your reactions. Your five predecessors were, by design, based on a similar predication – a contingent affirmation that was meant to create a profound attachment to the rest of your species, facilitating the function of the One. While the others experienced this in a very general way, your experience is far more specific – vis a vis love [of Trinity].

The previous "Ones" were designed to choose the Source; the machines instilled into them a "profound attachment" to the human race, so they would be compelled to want to protect it. So, it's true that they choose the Source to save humanity because they wanted to – so, according to Hume their action would be free (because they acted in accordance with their own desire); but they only had the desire they had because the machines made them have it. But if a person acts on a desire that someone else determined that they have, then it doesn't seem that they are acting freely – especially if the desire necessitated that they would make the choice that they made. Consider again the fact that The Architect is able to simply look at the workings of Neo's brain and predict what he is going to do. Yes, Neo chooses differently than his predecessors; but not because he is able to overcome the programming instilled into him by the machines. It's because he loves Trinity, and that love necessitates that he will decide to save her instead of humanity. Presumably, the Architect was able to look at the brains of Neo's predecessors and predict their choices as well.

Concerns like this have led some philosophers to object to compatibilism; it's not enough that an action merely be the result of someone's will or desire. If that will or desire is determined by outside forces, how the agent acts is not really up to them, and thus not free. To be free, an action has to come from or start with the agent; the causal story of the action has to begin with the agent. This view is called "agent causation" and is defended by modern, theistic, and atheistic philosophers alike, like Thomas Reid (1788), Timothy O'Connor (2004), and William Rowe (1991, 2006). This is arguably why Neo's choices – to join with the machines to create a different, peaceful Matrix where machines and humans coexist, and his choice to keep fighting Agent Smith at the end of *Revolutions* – are significant. It seems that he is not determined by any outside forces to do what he does, in any way; he does what he does merely, as he puts it, "Because I choose to."

Still, the movies could represent the Humian compatibilist perspective, by allowing each side (liberty and necessity) to have meaning. For the causal determinist (the Architect and the machines), their design is given meaning as something worth protecting and preserving, suggesting the necessity Hume observes is indeed necessary. For the side of liberty, as Hume labels it, the choices made by characters such as Morpheus, the Oracle, Neo, and Cypher are also given meaning, as the consequences of their choices are shown to be the result not of a predetermined course, but as a reaction to the predetermined circumstances.

Conclusion

> I have imagined this moment for so long. Is it real?
> —Morpheus (*Revolutions*)

The compatibilist solution not only creates meaning for causal determinism and free will, it also illustrates how the machines and the humans are compatible, too. However, the real significance of the trilogy's ending is that it represents the idea of choosing and creating a new reality, one that required Neo and the machines (as well as the Oracle and the Architect) to choose what to believe and what to know. These choices matter, not just because they have meaning in relation to determinism, but because they allow for the possibility that creation and change are imaginable and achievable – because in a strict deterministic system, nothing could be created or changed, there would be no invention or creativity, and there would be no change regarding what can or will occur. Such an existence would be foundational, as Descartes sought, rooted in the certainty of predetermination. From this perspective, Descartes' cogito ergo sum becomes meaningless, because there is no choice in the matter. It wouldn't be "I think therefore I am." Rather, it would be my thinking is causally determined therefore so is my existence.

Perhaps this is why so many of us choose to believe what we want to believe, choose to be certain about that which we want certitude, and choose to accept certain realities and deny others. In doing so, we aren't just choosing beliefs, knowledge, and realities, we're also giving meaning to the beliefs, knowledge, and realities we claim. From this, our lives have meaning, too. Thus, it seems as if the Oracle was right, whether we choose to live inside the Matrix like Cypher, in the human city of Zion like Morpheus, or create a new Matrix like Neo – or whether we choose to believe like Trinity, Niobe, and the Oracle – even though actual reality and truth still matter, what matters most is that we have the option to decide.

References

Bracken, Harry M. 2002. *Descartes*. New York City: Perseus Books.

Downey, Mason. 2020. *Patton Oswalt argues you're rooting for the wrong matrix character*. Gamespot.com. May 26. https://www.gamespot.com/articles/patton-oswalt-argues-youre-rooting-for-the-wrong-m/1100-6477532/

Guthrie Weisman, Cale. 2018. QAnon: The alternate reality that was front and center at Trump's rally. *Fast Company*. August 1. https://www.fastcompany.com/90212200/qanon-the-alternate-reality-that-was-front-and-center-at-trumps-rally

Hume, David. 2000. *A treatise of human nature*. Oxford Philosophical Texts, ed. David Fate Norton and Mary J. Norton. Oxford University Press.

Markie, Peter. 1992. The Cogito and its importance. In *The Cambridge companion to descartes*, ed. John Cottingham, 140–173. Cambridge University Press.

O'Conner, Timothy, and John Ross Churchill. 2004. Reasons, explanation, and agent control: In search of an integrated account. *Philosophical Topics* 32: 241–253.

Palmer, Ewan. 2021 These QAnon predictions all failed to come true. *Newsweek*. March 4. https://www.newsweek.com/qanon-trump-march4-predictions-failed-1573739

Petrizzo, Zachary. 2021. QAnon fans flock to Matt Gaetz's defense, despite claims of sexual misconduct. *Salon*. March 31. https://www.salon.com/2021/03/31/qanon-fans-flock-to-matt-gaetzs-defense-despite-claims-of-sexual-misconduct/

Reid, Thomas. 1788. *Essays on the active powers of the human mind*. Cambridge: MIT Press, 1969.

Rowe, William. 1991. *Thomas Reid on freedom and morality*. Ithaca: Cornell University Press.

———. 2006. Free will, moral responsibility, and the problem of 'oomph'. *The Journal of Ethics* 10: 295–313.

Searle, John. 1995. *The construction of social reality*. New York: The Free Press.

Weimin, Wo, and Wang Wei. 2007. From Descartes to Sartre. *Frontiers of Philosophy in China* 2 (2): 247–264.

A Serious Man as Philosophy: The Elusiveness of Moral Knowledge

49

Shai Biderman

Contents

Introduction	1152
The Movie in Brief	1153
Accept the Mystery: Ethics, Epistemology, and Moral Knowledge	1154
What Is Moral Knowledge? Is It Relevant?	1155
Understanding the Dead Cat: Fables and Parables as Moral Knowledge	1158
Fable #1: Larry Seeks Rabbi Marshak and Kafka's "Before the Law"	1159
Fable #2: Danny Meets Marshak and the Binding of Isaac	1160
Fable #3: The Goy's Teeth	1162
Fables #4–5: The Parking Lot and Dibbuk	1162
Fable #6: The Book of Job	1163
Fable #7: Schrödinger's Cat	1164
Epilogue (and One Final Kafka Parable)	1165
References	1167

Abstract

The film *A Serious Man* (2009) by the Coen brothers follows Larry, a righteous college professor in crisis. As he unexpectedly meets a rainstorm of hardships and misfortunes, Larry challenges the reason and the unjust nature of his predicaments. Philosophically, these challenges address the interface of ethics and epistemology and particularly the elusive concept of moral knowledge. What is moral knowledge, why is it important, and how can it be achieved? What can it contribute to establishing a moral doctrine and to responding to meta-ethical questions? These questions are central to the film, and are embodied in its philosophical assumptions, its existentialist philosophical approaches (mainly

---

S. Biderman (✉)
Beit-Berl College, Kfar Saba, Israel

Tel Aviv University, Tel Aviv, Israel
e-mail: bidermans@beitberl.ac.il; biderman@bu.edu

© Springer Nature Switzerland AG 2024
D. K. Johnson et al. (eds.), *The Palgrave Handbook of Popular Culture as Philosophy*,
https://doi.org/10.1007/978-3-031-24685-2_75

as inspired by Kafka), and mainly its aesthetic and artistic aspects (particularly the extensive use of explicit and implicit fables and parables). The philosophical examination of the question of moral knowledge in *A Serious Man* leads to questioning the very possibility of such knowledge. In that, the film continues the broad discussion of the Coens' cinematic corpus in philosophy, and ethics in particular.

Keywords

Moral knowledge · Simon de Beauvoir · Epistemology · Meta-ethics · Cognitivism · Noncognitivism · Belief · Intuition · Judeo-Christian theology · Franz Kafka · Fables and parables · Walter Benjamin · Book of job · Sacrifice of Isaac · Schrödinger's cat

Introduction

A Serious Man (2009) is the fourteenth film in the joint creative corpus of brothers Joel and Ethan Coen. The film received mixed reviews (as well as box office receipts), but all identified its complexity and uniqueness. Both applauders and detractors identify in the film what has already been seen in one way or another in all its predecessors – and successors: the Coen brothers' interest in ethics. Traditionally, this philosophical discipline raises many difficult questions, such as how should a person behave in order to be considered moral? What is the moral model that should be followed? Can it be justified? Is such a model at all possible? And if it is, how can we explain the injustices we see plainly in our lives? In the case before us, the filmmakers' ethical task is posed in the title of the film: Why is it called "A Serious Man"? An answer may be found in Simon de Beauvoir's *The Ethics of Ambiguity*, where she describes – in an analogy to Oscar Wilde's comic play, *The Importance of Being Earnest* – the importance of a figure whom she calls "a serious man" (and sometimes "sub-man"). The serious man is a model of moral existence who sets a purpose for human existence that is unequivocal and absolute. Such a man recognizes no complexity in moral life and rejects the multifaceted nature of existence. He seeks a single solution, a cause or value that he considers good and worthy, a shining lighthouse by which to navigate. Alas, his dedication overtakes him. The serious man denies his own freedom to choose how to live and what values to pursue, and instead he takes comfort in letting an external value system dominate his way of thinking. Despite being equipped with eyes and ears, his search for "seriousness" involves self-imposed blindness and deafness to the complexity of reality (de Beauvoir 1997, pp. 35–45).

The Coens' preoccupation with the model of moral existence cuts across their entire filmography. Already in *Fargo* (1996), we encounter Marge Gunderson (Frances McDormand), a determined detective who tries to restore moral order to a chaotic world, serving as the antithesis to the criminal conduct of Jerry Lundegaard (William H. Macy). In *The Big Lebowski* (1998), it's the Dude (Jeff Bridges) who tries to offer a counter-model to moral nihilism. Finally, in *No Country for Old Men* (2007), a title that perhaps alludes to the impossibility of the task, it is Sheriff Ed Tom Bell (Tommy Lee Jones) who is in charge of maintaining moral impartiality.

In *A Serious Man*, the Coens' constant search for a moral model receives an important twist (suggested, as we have seen, already in the film's name). In this film, they are interested in the interface between ethics and epistemology. Epistemology is concerned with specifying the conditions that must be met for something to count as knowledge. Accordingly, moral epistemology seeks to determine whether any of our moral judgments count as knowledge. The search for knowledge that can ground a moral model is therefore the philosophical pivot of the film.

The Movie in Brief

A Serious Man opens with two introductions. The first is in the form of a pre-credit title – a quote attributed to Medieval French-Jewish biblical commentator Rashi: "Receive with simplicity everything that happens to you" (*A Serious Man*, 2009). The second is a parable-like prologue that unfolds entirely in Yiddish, the language of East-European Jewish townships in the late nineteenth century. On a stormy night, an elderly Jew returns home and tells his wife he has met an acquaintance and invited him to dinner. Aghast, his wife tells him that the man had died years ago, so that her husband must have met a *dibbuk*, or evil spirit. As they argue, the mystery man knocks on the door. They invite him in but during the course of dinner, the woman stabs the man with an ice pick. With the ice pick still lodged in his chest, he departs, and the couple are left behind, mortified and horrified.

At this point the movie itself begins. It describes a fortnight in the life of Larry Gopnik (Michael Stuhlbarg), a Jewish physics professor teaching a course in quantum physics in Minnesota in 1967. His appears to be a pleasant and calm suburban family life. However, it soon begins to unravel. His wife Judith (Sari Lennick) says she wants to divorce him in order to marry their longtime acquaintance Sy Ableman (Fred Melamed). At the same time, Clive (David Kang), a South Korean exchange student, supposedly offers to bribe him for a passing grade. About to be promoted and receive tenure, Larry receives anonymous hate mail. The plot thickens when Judith and Sy insist he must leave and move with this inept brother to the Jolly Rogers Motel – the local rundown bachelors' dump. Then, Sy dies in a car accident, and Larry is required to pay for his funeral. In the meantime, while fixing the antenna on the roof, Larry sees his voluptuous neighbor Mrs. Samsky sunbathing nude outside her house, smokes pot with her, and in an erotically psychedelic haze examines the boundaries of the dictum, "Love thy neighbor."

To cope with these troubles – and others too many to mention – and most importantly, to understand why they are happening to him, Larry seeks the community rabbis' advice. The junior rabbi does not help, while his senior, Rabbi Nachtner, tells Larry a nebulous parable titled "The Goy's Teeth." It is about a Jewish dentist called Dr. Sussman who finds a message inscribed in the teeth of a Gentile patient, looks for its meaning, and eventually gives up the search and returns to living his ordinary life. Larry fails to meet the most senior rabbi, since "[the rabbi] is busy thinking." Thus, Larry's attempts of making sense of his multiple conundrums only deepen his helplessness in the face of a reality completely inaccessible to his cognition – all at sea, there is no lighthouse in Larry's horizon.

The movie ends with a diegetic (or perhaps cathartic) convergence of its narrative axes (only some of which have been described here). Larry and his wife make up. He decides to use the money (probably given to him in bribe) to pay his divorce lawyers' huge bill, and then changes Clive's grade. At that moment, his family doctor – who had seen Larry early in the film – calls and summons him to an immediate meeting. Larry is visibly gloomy, as is his son Danny's schoolyard, where the final scene takes place. An ominous tornado is visible in the horizon, the American flag is about to be torn-off of the pole, and the film ends with Larry's son (and the viewer's) looking at the horizon with horror to the tune of Jefferson Airplane's *Somebody to Love*.

Accept the Mystery: Ethics, Epistemology, and Moral Knowledge

The film follows Larry in his journey toward the moral objective embodied in the title: to form full and true knowledge that will allow him to be a virtuous "serious" man. The motivation for Larry's journey, which takes center stage, is a profound sense of injustice. Despite his own understanding that he lives a righteous life, fulfilling all his family and social roles, troubles keep knocking on his door, and the reality where the righteous suffer and the evil prosper keeps baffling him.

Three levels of philosophical discussion apply to Larry's moral journey. The first level relates to the journey's objective: a valid, meaningful, and attainable moral existence. We will refer to it as the *meta-ethical level*. Whereas ethics involves judgments about the good and good actions, meta-ethics attempts to understand the nature of these judgments: are they factual judgments found in the world, namely, imperatives and statements that articulate emotions and inclinations, which can at best be valued in terms of their appropriateness or efficacy? Is morality objective and universal or subjective and contingent? The assumption that we should frame our moral discussion meta-ethically – before turning to discuss specific ethical and epistemological questions – is therefore our starting assumption.

The second level has to do with the way the journey is realized. In his journey, Larry acts upon the assumption that there is a series of guiding principles and heuristics available to him that together form a coherent moral doctrine and a practical recipe for life. This assumption is obviously shared by the leading moral doctrines in the history of Western philosophy. The main moral doctrines along the meta-ethical spectrum include the *ethics of duty* (deontology) identified with Immanuel Kant, which views the moral injunction as a command of universal and objective standing; John Stuart Mill and Jeremy Bentham's *utilitarian ethics*, which identifies morality with consequences and their utilities; and *virtue ethics*, identified with Aristotle, which views morality as a harmonious flourishing of human qualities and character traits.

The final level has to do with the force driving the journey, namely, that knowledge is the motivator of moral life. The question of the definition, feasibility, and very existence of moral knowledge is one of the oldest in the philosophy of morals, and it serves as an important framing of the present discussion. The assumption is that the validity and meaning of moral life derive from knowing: the better we understand the world, and the more we cling to moral knowledge, the better we can realize our moral purpose, or at least justify (and accept) its lack (or our failure to achieve it).

The philosophical discussion in *A Serious Man* unfolds between those three levels. It assumes the separate existence of each, as well as their interrelations. For example, if we adopt certain meta-ethical definitions, this would inform a set of guiding principles cohering into a moral doctrine, which in turn would validate moral knowledge and provide answers to the questions about its nature, content, feasibility, and attainability. This is the philosophical infrastructure grounding the Coens' work.

What Is Moral Knowledge? Is It Relevant?

The discussion of the nature and role of moral knowledge in *A Serious Man* has two starting points: one is cognitivist and the other is noncognitivist. The *cognitivist* starting point grants that knowledge, and moral knowledge in particular, is absolute, unequivocal, and valid. Informed by this knowledge, moral statements about right or wrong, dos and don'ts, and determinations of whether some act is virtuous or vicious, have an evaluative character. They are formulated as answers to questions about our values and conduct, thus enabling us to justify our judgments and decisions, and navigate across the sea of doubts accordingly.

Such an approach to moral knowledge is problematic, since it bestows upon the moral statements an epistemic status of knowledge that appears to be identical to other, nonmoral knowledge about the world. For example, according to this view, the moral statement "Taking a bribe in return for changing a grade is wrong" is epistemically equivalent to the empirical statement "The cat is black," or the mathematical statement, "A triangle has three sides." All are equally true. The problems of that position arise in the first face-to-face encounter between Larry and his student Clive, who complains: "I believe the results of physics mid-term were unjust... I received an unsatisfactory grade. In fact: F, the failing grade... this is not just. I was unaware to be examined [sic] on the mathematics." When Larry replies, "Well, you can't do physics without mathematics, really, can you?," Clive maintains his position and demands that the injustice done to him be corrected. The two begin to bargain, in the process revealing the problems of this inference:

Larry [...] what do you propose?
Clive Passing grade.
Larry No no, I...

Clive   Or perhaps I can take the mid-term again. Now I know it covers mathematics.
Larry   Well, the other students wouldn't like that, would they, if one student gets to retake the test till he gets a grade he likes?
Clive   Secret test. [...]
Larry   No, that's just not workable. I'm afraid we'll just have to bite the bullet on this thing, Clive, and...
Clive   Very troubling... very troubling...

Very troubling indeed, not so much so for Clive as for the cognitivist argument, which underlines his position. In his attempt to receive a better grade and escape the shame and humiliation of defeat, Clive asserted the belief that moral statements have the same epistemic status as nonmoral statements about facts in the world. However, and as it turned out, Clive's belief that what was done to him is an injustice does not make it a fact. In absence of a definite external criterion, Clive might simply be wrong, and his moral statement would be false. Therefore, a cognitivist position, which rests on the epistemic status of factual claims, fails to achieve an amicable resolution when either the facts or their moral implications are in dispute.

In view of these problems, consider the noncognitivist starting point, according to which moral statements are not descriptive, and do not state facts. Rather, moral statements and judgments fail to meet the necessary conditions for knowledge. None can be true, by definition, as none can possibly be true. Like orders or questions, they are neither true nor false. Accordingly, we must abandon the narrow cognitivist definition of moral knowledge and focus on the moral statement's ability to articulate a consistent logic of judgment. Moral knowledge must therefore enable us to evaluate moral judgments, rather than provide unambiguous, truthful moral claims. Moral knowledge would therefore be reasonable or unreasonable, rational or irrational, justified or unjustified, but not true or false on the noncognitivist's view.

The diametric opposition of cognitivism and noncognitivism might give rise to moral skepticism: the claim that not only is no moral statement knowable but that moral judgments are too flawed to be used in either moral theorizing or as our proverbial lighthouse in moral decision-making. To avoid this slippery slope, we need a *third approach* that can potentially bridge the gap between the first two by proposing a pluralistically broader definition of knowledge. According to this definition, knowledge can include (1) reliable and responsible beliefs; (2) coherent exercises of intellectual virtues; and, alternatively, (3) intuitions. Beliefs will be considered knowledge if we have reason to think they are likely to be true, or at least if we encounter no reason to doubt them. Intellectual virtues can yield moral knowledge if they produce an extensive and correct analysis of the subject under discussion. Finally, intuitions, which by definition do not require a strong epistemic justification, may be considered knowledge if they justify their name, that is, if they are derived from an obviousness that cannot be validated epistemically but that, nevertheless, seems obvious.

Take, for example, the first type of knowledge above: reliable and responsible belief. Judeo-Christian knowledge is often considered to be an instance of this type of knowledge. A historical review of the moral knowledge formulated in Judeo-Christian ethics indicates that it is indeed reliable, as it is based on authenticated scriptures, and has a divine logic that makes it also responsible. It includes deontological commands, according to which actions are right and wrong in and of themselves, and at the same time, it also appeals to other kinds of ethical reasoning, such as utilitarian consequentialism. Similarly, its status is akin to that of natural law, and the universally binding force of its moral principles rest on the unshakable belief in God's goodness, which does not require proof.

Moral knowledge of this type is precisely what Larry seeks when contacting the three rabbis. They are authorities, divine messengers by virtue of their status and sagacity, and are supposed to be able to extract productive, operative knowledge out of the belief system. However, the junior rabbi is ignorant of basic concepts of religious law, does not understand the state of affairs presented to him, and with an apologetic smile, concludes with a cliché followed by a platitude: "The boss isn't always right, but he's always the boss" and "That's right, things aren't so bad." The second rabbi, more senior and learned, first dodges the question: "How does God speak to us? Good question!" and then rejects it ab initio: "Sure! We all want the answer! But *Hashem* [God] doesn't owe us the answer, Larry. *Hashem* doesn't owe us anything. The obligation runs the other way." The third and most senior rabbi is completely unavailable. Constantly engaged in "thinking," his intellect does not seem to bring any relief to his flock, at least not to Larry.

Larry's quest for moral knowledge is deadlocked. His inability to form a reliable and responsible belief (from his meeting with the second Rabbi), and the inaccessible alleged coherency of the third Rabbi's intellectual virtues, lead him to examine the third type of knowledge, namely, knowledge achieved by intuition. Clearly, however, the idea that intuition can lead to knowledge is out of the question. Larry's intuitions change frequently according to the circumstances. Note that beyond inconsistency, most intuitions are flawed in that they lead to a dead end. In what is perhaps the most ironic example, his intuitions with regard to Sy (friend or foe?) are all discounted in Rabbi Nachtner's eulogy of Sy. The rabbi begins by stating, "Sy Ableman was a serious man," and then wonders about the (unjust?) fate of such a worthy man. The answer, "*L'olam ha-ba*" is both ambivalent and bewildering:

> We speak of *L'olam ha-ba*, the World to Come. Not heaven. Not what the gentiles think of as afterlife. "*L'olam ha-ba*". What is *L'olam ha-ba*? Where is *L'olam ha-ba*? Well: it is not a geographic place, certainly. Like-Canada. Nor is it [...] the land flowing with milk and honey, for we are not promised a personal reward, a gold star, a first-class VIP lounge where we get milk and cookies to eternity! *L'olam ha-ba*... is in the bosom of Abraham.

The quest for moral reasoning – as per the fate of Sy Ableman, as well as the justification of Larry's hardships – is left unresolved. Nachtner's intuition, captured in the phrase "L'olam ha-ba," fails to reason Sy's premature death, as it is unclear at best and incoherently enigmatic at worst (and adding the pseudo-explanation "in the bosom of Abraham" does not clarify things at all). The discussion of the essential nature and feasibility of moral knowledge, and the way it is derived from meta-ethical assumptions and projects on concepts of adequacy in a moral system, thus reaches a dead end. It appears that any attempt at an ethic that could provide a cogent basis for our moral deliberations and discussions in terms of moral knowledge or even a cogent account of morality – reliable and responsible belief, coherent exercise of intellectual virtue, and intuition – is barren.

In light of this futility, is yet another moral perspective possible? One that is able to provide a common basis for society, a coherent justification for morality? Can we recover a body of moral knowledge given our present pluralistic cul-de-sac? Such a suggestion may sound as an outdated and politically dangerous appeal to an objective moral truth. Moreover, it may seem misguided since many believe it is simply impossible to perceive reality directly and thus know it as it truly is. Many others, such as Larry, are obsessed with it.

Understanding the Dead Cat: Fables and Parables as Moral Knowledge

Apparently, the search for moral knowledge preoccupies Larry and other characters. However, the main search is not theirs, but the film's, through its main structural element: fables and parables.

Fables and parables are two interchangeable storytelling devices designed to elicit folk wisdom and moral understanding of human situations and predicaments. Both are defined as a short story that allegorically illustrates a moral: that is, a religious or ethical principle or general truth about human nature. Given its pedagogical power, the fable has gained a stronghold in literature as well as philosophy. It also resides in contemporary cinema, and found a home in Coen Brothers' films like *No Country for Old Men* (2007) and *The Ballad of Buster Scruggs* (2018). In *A Serious Man*, we encounter three explicit fables – the *Dibbuk* (in the introduction), the *Parking Lot* (told by the first rabbi), and *the Goy's Teeth*. Just as importantly, we come across several implicit fables that permeate the narrative.

What makes the Coen brothers adopt the fable format so enthusiastically? How does it serve the search for moral knowledge? Joel and Ethan Coen gave a kind of answer to these questions, employing the term "a Kafka break" to characterize their writing process (Coen and Coen 2006; Adams 2015, p. 183). What is the nature of that "break" that is so integral to the Coens' writing process? The answer lies in the literary, cultural, and philosophical role of Jewish-Czech author Franz Kafka, the ultimate fabulist whose name has become synonymous with all things absurd and paradoxical. In a short musing titled "On Parables," Kafka recapitulates the incomprehensibility of knowledge by associating the desire of knowing with the incommunicability and exclusivity of fables and parables as a form of communication. He writes: "Many complain that the words of the wise are always merely parables and of no use in daily life, which is the only life we have" (Kafka 1961, p. 11). If it is to be taken at face value, such a complaint exhibits an existential tension. As Kafka continues to argue, the vicarious wisdoms and moral affirmations typical of these literary forms cannot be sustained, or even comprehended. Their alleged comprehensibility is a mere façade: "All... parables really set out to say merely that the incomprehensible is incomprehensible, and we know that already" (Ibid).

What are we to make of Kafka's notion of parabolic logic? Do parables embody an external message, which accounts for nothing and leads nowhere? Or is it a message that might lead somewhere but provides no key by which it should be decoded and therefore leads to a dead end? Alternatively, perhaps the message is one that inwardly leads to its own repetition and recitation (and hence has no impact on something other than itself)? Commenting on this multitude of options, Walter Benjamin (1968) begins by acknowledging, "We have before us a mystery which we cannot comprehend" (p. 124). However, for Benjamin (as well as for Kafka), this incomprehensibility is both a weakness and the parable's tour de force. The circularity exhibited in parabolic thinking determines the right "to preach it, to teach the people that what matters is... the riddle, the secret, the mystery to which they have to bow – without reflection and even against their conscience" (p. 124). Parabolic thinking in its purest form has no end – but is, nevertheless, the most conceivable means of knowledge and comprehension. Benjamin concludes: "to do justice to the figure of Kafka in its purity and its peculiar beauty one must never lose sight of one thing: it is the purity and beauty of a failure" (p. 144).

Equipped with some understanding of fable and parables and their adoption in the Coens' Kafka breaks, let us review the Kafkaesque fables that structure *A Serious Man*.

Fable #1: Larry Seeks Rabbi Marshak and Kafka's "Before the Law"

Larry's first attempt to meet Rabbi Marshak – purportedly the wisest and highest-ranking of the three rabbis – alludes to Kafka's fable "Before the Law" (Kafka and Starritt 2018, pp. 46–48). The fable tells of a "man from the country" who arrives at a gatekeeper standing at the gate of the law, seeking permission to enter. The gatekeeper refuses. When the man from the country tries to peep inside, the gatekeeper laughs and says he can try entering, but he needs to consider the fact that inside there are additional gatekeepers, each one stronger than the other, to the point that the first gatekeeper himself is afraid to look at the third gatekeeper's face. The man decides to wait, and grows old waiting. Finally, when he is about to die, he asks the gatekeeper why nobody else sought permission to enter the law. The guard replies, "No one else could enter here, since this door was destined for you alone. Now I will go and close it."

The parallels are clear. The rabbinical hierarchy – "first rabbi," "second rabbi," and "Marshak," with access to each becoming increasingly difficult – is reminiscent of the gatekeeper hierarchy in Kafka. Larry's standing before Marshak's fearsome secretary, described in the script as "Marshak's elderly eastern European *gatekeeper*" (Coen and Cohen 2009, p. 120; my italic) is akin to the fruitless standing at the law's gate. In turn, the gate itself is embodied in the film's title – a serious man. The desire, the necessity to be a serious man, is marked as the objective of Larry's search. He expresses it well in his emotional and stammered plea to the rabbi's formidable gatekeeper:

> Please... I need help... I've already talked to the other Rabbis... please... It's not about Danny's Bar-Mitzvah... it's more about myself.... I've had quite a bit of *Tzures* [troubles] lately... marital problems, professional, you name it... this is not a frivolous request... this is a Ser... I'm a seri... I am... I've tried to be a serious man, you know. [...] just tell him I need help, please—I need help!

Larry's stammering as he formulates his goal (being a serious man) is indicative of the inherent difficulty in his journey, due to the need for "an acknowledgment of the limitations of our own powers and a recognition that there are things about the world that we cannot understand" (Gilmore 2005, p. 62). Kafka calls this difficulty "absurd," since it cannot be avoided and at the same time cannot be resolved. Larry's journey meets this definition. It is one he has to venture on and one he must complete in order to be saved, but apparently it is impossible to do so. Failure is built into it a priori (as Benjamin says about Kafka).

Fable #2: Danny Meets Marshak and the Binding of Isaac

These parallels between Larry's meeting with Marshak (that never took place) and Kafka's "Before the Law" recall an additional encounter (that *did* occur) and another hidden fable. This other meeting is Danny's, the Bar-Mitzvah boy who encounters Marshak, through the haze of weed, to receive his blessing. Larry's stammering is thus replaced with Danny's high, which is already evident at the culmination of the Bar-Mitzvah ceremony, when the letters of the holy text become blurred in his eyes. Larry's unsuccessful attempt to enter "the gate of the law" is likewise replaced with an equally bewildering notion of failure, as Marshak's blessing amounts to an enigmatic quote from "Somebody to Love" ("When the truth is found to be lies, and all the hope within you dies, then what?"), and the inscrutable imperative that Danny "be a good boy."

The additional fable alluded here is that of the binding of Isaac. Abraham, the father of Judeo-Christian monotheism, is torn between the divine command to sacrifice his son Isaac and the intuitive immorality of this command. This biblical fable is a story on truth and faith, obedience and morality. The question whether and how Abraham overcomes his moral crisis of faith has become one of the major objects of theological reflections on the one hand and existential thought on the other.

The fable of the binding of Isaac appears in the film fleetingly and almost unnoticeably. As Danny stumbles toward the rabbi, we gain a glimpse into the holy of holies – Marshak's office is dark, majestic, and mysterious. Heavy furniture, carpets, and various objects (related to both the world of science and the world of the arcane) are strewn around. A painting hanging in Marshak's office, revealed to the viewer as the drugged-out Danny stumbles toward the rabbi, is Caravaggio's "Sacrifice of Isaac."

The painting is a visual representation of a moral crisis. Caravaggio actually painted it twice. In the later 1603 painting, we can see Isaac on the altar, Abraham holding his knife next to his neck with one hand, and the angel holding Abraham's other hand, physically preventing him from sacrificing his son. In the previous painting, from 1596, the knife is already far from Isaac's neck, he stands up, and Abraham is conversing with the angel (who probably updates him on the "correct" interpretation of the divine order). The two paintings complement each other by presenting two moments in the binding parable: the moment of the sacrifice itself, followed by the dialogue with the angel. Of course, the chronology of the paintings is the opposite of that of the biblical story. This historical anecdote is significant to this interpretation of the two as applied to *A Serious Man*. Since the chronologies of the painting and the story are inverted, early becomes late and late becomes early. We can thus see the two paintings as transcending temporal limitations (in both senses) and as presenting a significant simultaneity in the circular chronology of parable. Abraham slaughters (or intends to) at one moment – and does not (following the reinterpretation of the divine word) at the very same moment.

The painting in Marshak's office is a reproduction of Caravaggio's 1603 original. However, the fact that it is part of a double simultaneity visual process gives it the same role in the film. The Coen brothers, like Caravaggio, are artists of visual expression. What Caravaggio does to the biblical story through painting, the Coens do through cinema.

To return to Marshak, we catch a glimpse of Caravaggio's painting as a spaced-out Danny approaches the rabbi. As Larry's son, and at the peak of his Jewish rite of passage, Danny is akin to Isaac. Visiting Marshak is the sacrifice, which occurs or does not, and realizes itself as a test of faith (or not) that ushers Danny through the gate of the adult Jewish community, making him a serious man (or a "good boy," in Marshak's words).

The biblical parable is thus implicitly present in Marshak's office, through the glimpsing of Caravaggio. It is not the painting's only appearance in the film, however; indeed, it's not even the first. In a previous scene, Larry confronts his Gentile neighbor following the latter's trespassing, and is bullied. The confrontation is interrupted by the neighbor's son, a boy Danny's age, who gets out of the family car. The child and his father have just returned from hunting. A deer is bound to their car, hunted by the boy as part of a Gentile rite of passage. The Abrahamic burden imposed on a bully Goy and his son is of course parallel to the burden imposed by the same God on the stammering Jew and his son. The two father-son dyads simultaneously realize the parable, albeit two complementary ways. The first binds a deer, and fulfills the parable as worded. The second splits between father and son: the father (Larry) stammers, fails to meet Marshak, and receives the inscrutable reply "the rabbi is thinking"; complementarily, the son (Danny) spaces out, manages to meet Marshak, and receives the similarly inscrutable reply "be a good boy."

Fable #3: The Goy's Teeth

The main explicit fable presented in the film is told by Rabbi Nachtner (the second rabbi that Larry meets or attempts to meet). Larry views his troubles as a message from God, but fails to decode it. "What is *Hashem* trying to tell me?," he asks the rabbi, who replies by telling him the Fable of the Goy's Teeth. Jewish dentist Lee Sussman has prepared a plaster mold for one of his patients, a Gentile, or Goy. Upon examining it, he discovers on the back of the Goy's teeth an inscription somehow engraved on them in Hebrew letters: "ה-ו-ש-י-ע-נ-י" ("help me" or "save me"). Sussman used his knowledge of gematria – the Jewish alphanumeric code of assigning numerical values to letters. Decoding the letters (written from right to left) produced the numbers 4-9-6-2-4-2-8. Given that this is a seven-digit number, he dials it, and finds out it is a supermarket branch. Sussman drives there with great excitement and anxiety, only to find it is no different than any other supermarket. According to Nachtner, Sussman came to him afterward, and shared his ruminations:

> What does it mean, Rabbi? Is it a sign from *Hashem*? "Help me." I, Sussman, should be doing something to help this Goy? Doing what? The teeth don't say. I should know without asking? Or maybe I'm supposed to help people generally – lead a more righteous life? Is the answer in Kabbalah? In Torah? Or is there even a question? Tell me, Rabbi – what can such a sign mean?

Sussman's questions remain unanswered. Clearly, the fable is a distilled demonstration of Kafka's absurdity as seen in both "Before the Law" and the Binding of Isaac. The scene makes it clear that the various codes do indeed enable one to "decode," or more precisely "convert" the message, but these conversions never reach the point of true solution. Allas, there is no reason to prefer the use of one code over the other. The fact that what Sussman sees looks like Hebrew letters and may be interpreted according to a Hebrew dictionary or converted into a phone number does not necessarily turn them into a coherent message. On the other hand, once Sussman decides that the sequence of inscriptions on the Goy's teeth is indeed a message – that is, once he tries to understand the world – then the world becomes a codeless message, and existing in it becomes an absurdity.

Fables #4–5: The Parking Lot and Dibbuk

The parable of "The Goy's Teeth" naturally projects also on the narrative roles of the two other explicit fables: "The Parking Lot" and "The Dibbuk." In the first, the junior rabbi tries to make Larry accept his situation. He likens Larry's situation to the perspective required of an individual (a man from the country?) overlooking the parking lot through the window of the rabbi's office. "Not much to see," Rabbi Scott admits, "but if you imagine yourself a visitor, somebody who isn't familiar with these... autos and such... somebody still with a capacity for wonder... Someone with a fresh... perspective." The rabbi waxes enthusiastic: "look at the parking lot,

Larry!... just look at that parking lot!" Larry (and the viewer) looks at the parking lot, but sees nothing of interest. We are unable to adopt that wondrous perspective, since any attempt to do so is necessarily informed by a different perspective, which is precisely what denies us access to the promised wonderland. Like the man at the gate of the law, the man at the gate of the parking lot finds himself unable to enter that perspective, although its wondrousness lies in its very adoption.

In the "Dibbuk" parable, which serves, as you may recall, as a framework parable for the entire film, and is therefore located in the historical past, which lies outside the film's diegetic timeframe, we find ourselves facing the exact same absurdity. Is it a dibbuk? Is it not? How can one tell? Is there a difference? The need and the demand to know are present in full just like the inability to know, making us wonder is there anything to know to begin with. The only certainty this parabolic prologue suggests is that uncertainty will play a major role in the pursuit of moral knowledge and certainty, and in the narrative that is about to unfold.

Fable #6: The Book of Job

Note that as a framework fable for the film, "The Dibbuk" parable reveals two additional framework fables, both a theological and a scientific one. The theological fable is the story of Job. Like the Binding of Isaac, this story is about a test of faith. Like the story of Larry (and Danny), it is the story of a serious man whose seriousness (and moral integrity) is put to the test. In the biblical story, Job is tested by troubles of all sorts. He protests against this divine injustice and attempts to accept things as they are: "Naked came I out of my mother's womb, and naked shall I return thither: the Lord gave, and the Lord hath taken away; blessed be the name of the Lord" (Job 1:21, KJV).

Just as Larry approaches three rabbis for advice, so does Job approach three friends. The first, Eliphaz, tells him: "happy is the man whom God correcteth: therefore despise not though the chastening of the Almighty" (5:17). The second, Bildad, assures Job that if he is pure and upright, the Almighty will restore him to his rightful place. The third, Zophar, admonishes Job to remember that no one can fathom the mysteries of God or chart the limit of the Almighty. Like the three rabbis, the three friends' advice turns out to be inscrutable and fruitless. They provide no answer and no consolation, and Job's frustration (as well as that of the readers/viewers) increases. The inability to understand the injustice prevents Job from accepting his situation. The test of faith thus develops into one that probably would have been impossible to solve to begin with.

Biblical commentators have identified this theological threat and tried to rationalize the injustice meted out to Job by finding certain faults in his conduct. Maybe he was not the serious man as described in the books' opening sentence: "that man was perfect and upright, and one that feared God, and eschewed evil" (1:1). The interpretation proposed by the medieval Jewish philosopher and theologian Maimonides is particularly interesting. He argued that it was not any blemish in Job's character or conduct that moved the story, but the story itself, whose parabolic status dictates its complex structure. In his canonical *Guide for the Perplexed*, Maimonides writes: "some of our Sages clearly stated Job has never existed, and has never been created, and that he is a poetic fiction" (Maimonides 1956, p. 359). For Maimonides, Job is just a convenient means for the parable to deliver its message, an instrumental figure, which imposes the parabolic logic on the moral question at hand. Thus, all we can do is to accept things as they are, understand our inability to understand, and acknowledge the Kafkaesque in the biblical story.

Fable #7: Schrödinger's Cat

The second framework parable suggested by *A Serious Man* is scientific rather than theological. Larry, a physics professor, teaches the parable, a thought experiment called "Schrödinger's cat," to his class in order to demonstrate the uncertainty principle. "Schrödinger's cat," a known parable in the studies of quantum mechanics, aims to express the abstract notion of probability (which amounts to the uncertainty principle) by invoking the following scenario:

> A cat is locked in a steel box with a small amount of a radioactive substance such that after one hour there is an equal probability of that one atom either decaying or not decaying. If the atom decays, a device smashes a vial of poisonous gas, killing the cat. However, according to the Copenhagen interpretation, until the box is opened and the atom's wave function collapses, the atom's wave function is in a superposition of two states: decay and non-decay. Thus, the cat is in a superposition of two states: alive and dead. (Britannica, "Erwin-Schrodinger")

In Larry's words, the uncertainty principle "proves we can't ever really know... what's going on. [...] So it shouldn't bother you. Not being able to figure anything out. Although you will be responsible for this on the mid-term." Schrödinger's cat is a fable that once again articulates the film's framework assumptions and their embodiment in the fable format. (Schrödinger's cat also features in other Coens' films, particularly *The Man Who Wasn't There* (2001).) Presented in Larry's classroom to a helplessly agape student audience, the fable subsequently becomes the anchor used in the conflict between him and Clive in an attempt to resolve their moral dilemma:

Clive I received an unsatisfactory grade. In fact: F, the failing grade.
Larry Uh, yes. You failed the mid-term. That's accurate. [...]
Clive If I receive failing grade I lose my scholarship, and feel shame. I understand the physics. I understand the dead cat.
Larry You understand the dead cat? But... you... you can't really understand the physics without understanding the math. The math tells how it really works. That's the real thing; the stories I give you in class are just illustrative; they're like, fables, say, to help give you a picture. An imperfect model. I mean – even I don't understand the dead cat. The math is how it really works.
Clive Very difficult... very difficult...

The very inability to understand "the dead cat," even by the one who teaches it and tests and grades the students, is inherent to the fable itself. The test focuses on the fable, but as we recall, the fable cannot be understood without the math. However, the math is not part of the test, i.e., the fable, and so we are back to square one. Perturbed, Clive leaves Larry's office, and Larry later finds an envelope with money. Is this a bribery attempt? Larry summons Clive once again, and again the discussion coverts the cat fable into moral terms:

Larry   We had, I think, a good talk, the other day, but you left something...
Clive   I didn't leave it. [...]
Larry   Well... then, Clive, where did this come from? This is here, isn't it?
Clive   Yes, sir. That is there.
Larry   This is not nothing; this is something.
Clive   Yes. That is something. What is it?
Larry   You know what it is! I believe. And you know I can't keep it, Clive. [...] I'll have to pass it on to Professor Finkle, along with my suspicions about where it came from. Actions have consequences.
Clive   Yes sir. Often.
Larry   No, always! [...] In this office, actions have consequences! [...] Not just physics, morally. [...] I can interpret, Clive. I know what you meant me to understand. [...]
Clive   Mere... surmise. Sir. Very uncertain.

While the parable itself deals with the uncertainty principle, the moral appears to apply it to moral knowledge. Uncertainty is rampant everywhere. The moral decision Larry is required to make cannot rely on any moral knowledge, since there is none. Neither Clive's bargaining skills nor Larry's intellect and normative intuitions are any good here: moral knowledge is nowhere to be found, perhaps because it is impossible to begin with, as it is nothing more than a Kafkaesque paradox of uncertainty.

Epilogue (and One Final Kafka Parable)

The quantum parable joins the implicit biblical fables and the three explicit fables to create the Coens' worldview in the movie. Clearly, their use of the fable format is designed to reveal, on the screen, what any Kafka break has already revealed on the philosophical and literary level. If a fable is a pedagogical tool for acquiring real knowledge and certainly to formulate and refine an ethical moral, then the Coens' fables illuminate the inherent failure of this tool. Despite their alleged capacity to invoke a clear moral, fables promote unclarity, and flesh out their own redundancy. Their pedagogical strength appears to be counterproductive, as they fail to assert coherency and sustainable meaning, and instead expose the mere futility of the search thereof. The result of the encounter between reason that demands meaning and an unfathomable existence is of course the defeat of reason.

Kafka summarizes this conclusion in another parable, "The Top." It tells of a philosopher who "used to hang about wherever children were at play. And whenever he saw a boy with a top, he would lie in wait. [...] For he believed that the understanding of every detail, that of the spinning top for instance, was sufficient for the understanding of all things" (Kafka and Glatzer 1988). Indeed, "whenever preparations were being made for the spinning of the top, he hoped that this time it would succeed [...] but when he held the silly piece of wood in his hand, he felt nauseated. The screaming of the children [...] chased him away, and he tottered like a top under a clumsy whip" (Ibid).

The Coens' fables are apparently designed to answer serious questions: What is the purpose of suffering? Why do the righteous suffer and the evil prosper? If God exists, why does he permit such injustices? How do we understand God's mysterious will? However, in the filmmakers' Kafka break spirit, the fables turn out to be stories whose moral is the need to give up on the attempt to understand the moral and moral knowledge in general. In an immoral world (or rather a-moral world, namely, a world stripped from moral questions altogether) the brothers' Kafkaesque fables are moral-less, and if there is a moral, it is paradoxical.

The Coen brothers adopt this philosophical narrative model both explicitly and implicitly, throughout *A Serious Man* and their entire cinematic corpus. The Jewish couple in "The Dibbuk" parable cannot provide a rational explanation for acquaintance's nature (human or dibbuk); finding the answer by observing the parking lot proves impossibly futile; adopting the Abrahamic model to find an answer in the Binding parable runs into a Kafkaesque multiplicity of Abrahams (exhibited in Caravaggio's paintings) and the absurd derived from Abraham's existence; and the Goy's Teeth – the most elaborate of the film's explicit parables – ends with the rabbi's fatuous answer: "The teeth, we don't know. A sign from *Hashem*, don't know. Helping others, couldn't hurt." Above all these loom Rashi's prologue: "Receive with simplicity everything that happens to you" – that is, without attempting an interpretation. Every attempt to violate that injunction and look for an answer – by searching for God ("How does God speak to us? Good question") or a scientific answer ("even I don't understand the dead cat") – is bound to fail. It is bound to fail either because there IS NO way to justify the answer, or because there is no answer ("Is there even a question?," asked the second rabbi).

All these cases illustrate the ineffectuality of human rationality, and the interpretive failure inherent in assuming the existence of an overarching organizing moral knowledge. In *A Serious Man*, this conclusion is the Coens' answer to the attempt to be such a man, that is, the attempt to act morally. The moral journey is confronted with the Kafkaesque fable format so that it cannot but fail. Moral knowledge is impossible (although seeking it is experienced like a necessity), and therefore the entire film is imbued with a sense of helplessness and hopelessness.

References

Adams, J.T. 2015. A serious man: Parable and paradox. In *The cinema of the Coen brothers: Hard-boiled entertainments*, 179–193. New York: Columbia University Press.
Benjamin, W. (1968). Illuminations. New York, Schocken Books.
Britannica. (2021). Erwin-Schrodinger. Retrieved 1 April 2021. https://www.britannica.com/biography/Erwin-Schrodinger
Coen, J., et al. 2006. *The Coen brothers: Interviews*. Jackson: University Press of Mississippi.
de Beauvoir, S. 1997. *The ethics of ambiguity*. Trans. Bernard Frechtman. Secaucus: Carol Publishing Group.
Gilmore, R.A. 2005. The American sublime in *Fargo*. In *Doing philosophy at the movies*, ed. R.A. Gilmore, 57–80. Albany: SUNY Press.
Kafka, F., and N.N. Glatzer. 1988. *The complete stories*. New York: Schocken Books: Distributed by Pantheon Books.
Kafka, F., and A. Starritt. 2018. *The unhappiness of being a single man: Essential stories*. London: Pushkin Press.
Maimonides, Moses. (1956). The guide to the perplexed. Trans. M. Friedlander. New York, Dover Publication.

The Cabin in the Woods as Philosophy: Cinematic Reflections on Ethical Complexity, Human Nature, and Worthwhile Horror

50

Dean A. Kowalski

Contents

Introduction	1170
Summary: Revisiting *The Cabin in the Woods*	1171
Epistemic Value and Ethical Complexity	1173
Utilitarianism in – and under – the Woods	1174
An Ethical Theory Interlude	1176
Cabin and Caring	1177
Filmic Counterexamples and "Endorsing" Philosophical Theories	1180
Cabin's Implicit Theory of Horror	1182
On *Cabin* "Endorsing" Worthwhile Horror	1184
Conclusion: Assessing *Cabin's* Philosophical Engagement	1188
References	1192

Abstract

A careful analysis of Joss Whedon's and Drew Goddard's *The Cabin in the Woods* demonstrates how the film engages the philosophical process on multiple levels. On one level, it displays and contrasts classic utilitarianism and an ethics of care as plausible ethical perspectives, and spurs the viewer to consider each view carefully. On a deeper level, it offers an implicit philosophical critique of utilitarianism and endorsement of an ethics of care by providing cinematic considerations for finding the latter more plausible than the former. On yet a deeper level, it utilizes an ethics of care, with an assist from an Aristotelian-like account of aesthetics, to implicitly convey philosophically interesting perspectives about horror and human nature, and ultimately a plausible theory for what makes some "slasher" horror films more worthwhile than others.

D. A. Kowalski (✉)
Arts and Humanities Department, University of Wisconsin-Milwaukee, College of General Studies, Waukesha, WI, USA
e-mail: kowalskd@uwm.edu

© Springer Nature Switzerland AG 2024
D. K. Johnson et al. (eds.), *The Palgrave Handbook of Popular Culture as Philosophy*,
https://doi.org/10.1007/978-3-031-24685-2_77

Keywords

Cabin in the Woods · Joss Whedon · Drew Goddard · Horror (as film genre) · "slasher" films · Ethics · Epistemic value · Daniel Shaw · Ethical complexity · Utilitarianism · Consequentialism · John Stuart Mill · Ethics of care · Special obligations · Nel Noddings · Aesthetics · Aristotle · Gerry Canavan · Moral theory · Film-as-philosophy

Introduction

The Cabin in the Woods (2012, hereafter *Cabin*) was co-written by Joss Whedon and Drew Goddard, produced by Whedon, and directed by Goddard. Whedon and Goddard are long-time collaborators, having worked together on the television series *Buffy the Vampire Slayer* (1997–2003) and *Angel* (1999–2004). Once the two decided to collaborate on *Cabin*, they rented a hotel room for a weekend and by the time they checked-out, the screenplay was finished. They admit that they were influenced by such classics as *Night of the Living Dead* (1968) and (especially) *The Evil Dead* (1981), but they also wished to bring something unique to the horror genre. Originally, MGM studios picked up the project and the film was shot in 2009. However, the film's release was delayed due to MGM's financial troubles. Lionsgate fell in love with the film and agreed to distribute it. The film premiered 3 years later, the same year as Whedon's *Avengers* (2012).

A well-used tagline for *Cabin* is: "You Think You Know the Story," which refers to the familiar formula for contemporary "slasher" horror films: a group of college-aged friends unexpectedly face gruesome terrors while vacationing at a remote and bucolic cabin. Yet the film is often noted for its presumed commentary on the horror film genre. In fact, although Whedon admits that he and Goddard enjoyed collaborating on the project immensely, he also describes the film as: "It's basically a very loving hate letter...a serious critique of what we love and what we don't about horror movies" (Whedon 2012). But the exact nature of its critical commentary remains controversial. So, in a way, film scholars have been attempting to discern the story behind the story of the film.

Cabin offers the sort of crisp and clever dialogue and character-driven plotlines that are hallmarks of Whedon's work. And while one can enjoy the film for those reasons, especially if one is also a fan of "slasher" horror films, this chapter explores its perceived interrelated messages about ethics, human nature, and what makes some horror films more worthwhile than others. As we'll see, Whedon and Goddard craft *Cabin* with ethical complexity and given the plausible view that such films are thereby worthwhile, it follows that some "slasher" films are worthwhile. Thus, its aesthetic value is grounded in how it encourages the viewer to think about ethics in novel ways. But *Cabin* goes further in its implicit endorsement of one particular ethical perspective – an ethics of care – to provide the viewer *filmic* considerations for the idea that some "slasher" films are more worthwhile than others. It will be argued, then, that the story behind the story of *Cabin* is that, while portraying standard contemporary horror film tropes for fans of the genre, the film also presents for our consideration perspectives on the aesthetics of horror films. Thus, *Cabin* is not merely philosophical, it's an example of "philosophy-in-action."

Summary: Revisiting *The Cabin in the Woods*

On its surface, *Cabin* indeed offers a story familiar to fans of contemporary horror films. Five traditionally aged college students embark on a weekend trip. Curt – the star of the football team but attending school on an academic scholarship – has a cousin who recently purchased a rustic cabin, well, in the woods. He naturally invites his pre-med and exclusive girlfriend Jules. She very recently dyed her hair platinum blond, and she is excited about the trip. Jules invites her best friend, Dana, who is attempting to deal with the abrupt end of an ill-advised tryst with one of her (married) professors. They invite the eccentric Marty, who brings enough marijuana for all of them (but keeps his "secret stash" for himself). The four have been good friends since freshman year, and they know each other well. Curt also invites his teammate Holden; Jules and Curt are trying to set him up with Dana – not because Holden also knows Latin like her professor, but because he is "a sweet guy" with the "best hands on the team." The five of them pack into Curt's family RV, and the group heads for the cabin.

In an interesting turn, we meet the college friends only *after* being introduced to Hadley and Sitterson. Dressed in shirt and tie, these two middle-aged men are co-workers in an underground and unnamed facility (so, let's call it the Facility). With the help of their various and numerous colleagues, each working in different departments, including chemist Wendy Lin and new security officer Daniel Truman, Hadley and Sitterson utilize an impressive (even if retro) array of technological equipment to monitor the college students as soon as they leave campus. This stark reveal is not (at all) expected; it alerts the viewer that the film will not be a run-of-the-mill "slasher" movie after all.

When the group of friends arrives, the cabin initially appears to be what anyone might expect. Each camper selects a room (with Curt and Jules bunking in together). Holden's room includes a disturbing portrait graphically depicting gory animal dismemberment. He removes it only to uncover a two-way mirror. In the next room, Dana is undressing for the group's planned afternoon swim. Holden resists temptation and commendably alerts Dana and the others about the mirror. Marty, especially, is dumbfounded: "It was pioneer days; people had to make their own interrogation rooms. Out of cornmeal." Holden volunteers to switch rooms with Dana (only to spy Holden about to change into his trunks), but soon the group begins splashing in the nearby lake.

Of course, but unbeknown to the campers, Hadley and Sitterson and their Facility cohorts witness all of this via well-hidden surveillance equipment. Sitterson announces, "All right – places everyone – we are *live*." Hadley speaks into a microphone: "Engineering, we've got a room change." Ms. Lin enters the control room to inform Sitterson that the chemistry department is slowing Jules's cognition through her hair dye, but she recommends that they increase Jules's libido by increasing her Rhohyptase levels. In fact, the Facility works to affect all the campers, especially their cognition levels. Facility members have chemically altered the campers' beer keg and Marty's marijuana; they can manipulate the temperature and lighting and emit pheromone mists when needed.

The Facility's immediate goal is to maneuver the campers into the cellar so they can choose the manner of their doom. What they choose in the cellar determines which nightmarish monster will be leased upon them; Hadley and Sitterson organize an office pool so each department can bet on which horror will be their demise: werewolf, merman, zombies, etc. Truman finds it to be lamentable: "How can you wager on this when you control the outcome?" Hadley and Sitterson demur; the former explains, "We just get 'em to the cellar, Truman. They take it from there." With a startling assist from a cellar door unexpectedly flying open, a game of classic truth or dare does the trick. When Dana begins reading from the archaic diary of Patience Buckner, Sitterson exclaims, "We have a winner!...Buckners pull the 'W'!" Most of the Facility members groan in desperation, except for Ronald (the intern), who will split the pot with the maintenance department. The Buckners rise from their graves and begin lumbering toward the cabin. Hadley and Sitterson stare at their monitors and the latter shares, "Well, they may be zombified pain-worshipping backwoods idiots, but...they have a hundred percent clearance rate."

The Buckners are reminiscent of the sort of "slasher" film antagonist viewers have come to expect, but they play a surprising role in the Facility's plan for the campers. As the Facility manipulates the unsuspecting five college friends into their archetypal horror trope roles – Curt as the "athlete," Jules as the "whore," Dana as the "virgin," Marty as the "fool," and Holden as the "scholar" – the Buckners mindlessly do the dirty work of gruesomely sacrificing each for the sake of the greater good. Indeed, the formula for each sacrifice, including the order of each death, is specific. The whore must die first. One of the Buckners sneak up on a chemically altered Curt and Jules having sex in the nearby woods. Jules is decapitated and Curt flees back to the cabin to alert the others. The others can die in any order, save the virgin, who must live until the other four are killed, preferably in ghastly ways. The virgin may live or die, but she must be traumatized regardless. (You know, classic "final girl" stuff – think *Halloween* (1978), or *Nightmare on Elm Street* (1984), or...Pick your favorite such film.)

The audience learns that the Facility performs a ritual sacrifice because it is demanded by the Ancient Ones. The Ancient Ones are powerful and violent gods who once viciously ruled the Earth. If the Facility members are not successful in coordinating the ritual as prescribed, then the Ancient Ones will rise, which will bring a swift but brutal end to humankind.

As the campers attempt to escape from the Buckners, Curt bravely (?) attempts to jump a gorge with his motorbike (the mountain pass tunnel had since been exploded by the Facility to prevent escape), only to perish when hitting the invisible electrified matrix barrier. Holden's death is much more sudden and less expected; one of the Buckners impales him through the throat as he is driving the RV back to the cabin after Curt's demise. The RV – with Dana still inside – crashes into the lake. She struggles to find the surface and escape the clutches of the Buckner still in the back of the RV. Because one of the Buckners dragged an unconscious Marty into the woods soon after Jules was killed, it seems the ritual is complete. The Facility members (again lamentably) begin celebrating in the control room.

As it turns out, however, Marty survived. He rescues Dana and they escape into the underground Facility; Marty had previously discovered an access hatch when fighting for his life. Thus, the "fool" and the "virgin" work to upend the Facility's plans for them; they become like a computer virus, which results in unleashing all the remaining nightmare monsters on the Facility members. (I won't ruin all the details for you.) This seems to be poetic justice, but not without cost. The Facility Director informs Dana and Marty of the ritual, and of the fact that if Marty doesn't die, the Ancient Ones will rise and all of humanity will be destroyed. Dana briefly considers it, but refrains from murdering her friend. The ritual fails. As dawn breaks, a gigantic human-like hand violently bursts through the cabin and crashes down before the viewers' eyes. Fade to black. Cue the heavy-metal music. Roll credits.

Epistemic Value and Ethical Complexity

Now that you have sufficient background about *Cabin* and its plotlines, it is time to begin discerning the story behind the story of the film. Whedon and Goddard provide us a message and it is certainly philosophical. But what, and why is it important?

Of course, a film can be deemed worthwhile for various reasons. Perhaps you simply find it enjoyable, which might lead you to watch it again. But philosophers and film scholars stress other, more objective criteria. For example, Daniel Shaw writes, "The epistemic value of a film can make a significant contribution to its artistic value" (Shaw, p. 107). By epistemic value, Shaw means "the conveying of knowledge or prompting conceptual thought" (Shaw, p. 106). A film's epistemic value is (minimally) determined by how well a filmmaker cinematically conveys a topic, and the extent to which the film spurs its audience to examine it in some novel or otherwise interesting way. Films that succeed at this are for that reason aesthetically worthwhile films, at least philosophically speaking.

Fictional narrative films expressing epistemic goals often convey messages of ethical import. Furthermore, some films are noted for their ethical complexity, with *Crimes and Misdemeanors* (1989) and *Do the Right Thing* (1989) being but two examples. An ethically complex film (invariably) does not display one set of virtues or course of action as clearly morally correct and opposing virtues or actions as clearly morally incorrect; rather, such films encourage viewers to consider different ethical viewpoints concurrently for themselves. Perhaps a filmmaker invites the viewer to rethink a current societal norm. Perhaps a filmmaker crafts a particularly gripping moral dilemma-type situation for audience consideration. As Shaw explains, "Movies can make substantial contributions to the philosophical conversation about morality, both by challenging dominant paradigms and by convincingly embodying alternative moral ideals. They can also inspire us to emulate a variety of different visions of virtue, or help to convince us that a particular vision is regressive, not progressive" (Shaw, p. 83). So, perhaps an ethically complex film implicitly admits of an interpretation conducive to favoring one ethical perspective over another. However, the goal is not merely to moralize, but to engender careful audience reflection. As we'll see, *Cabin* is one such film.

Utilitarianism in – and under – the Woods

The first signs of *Cabin's* ethical complexity manifest by identifying its clashing ethical perspectives. Recall that if the Facility fails to coordinate the ritual sacrifice properly, this means the end of humankind. With this reveal, it seems that the Ancient Ones – and not the Facility – are the film's ultimate antagonists. This provides an avenue for the audience to identify with Facility members, at least insofar as they have an important job to do: placate the Ancient Ones and thereby avoid the Apocalypse. If the Facility fails, the Ancient Ones will wreak unfathomable amounts of pain and suffering upon humankind. Working to avoid pain and suffering on a global scale is obviously commendable. In this way, the Facility operates on firm ethical ground. In fact, assuming a utilitarian approach to moral reasoning, it seems that Facility members are obligated to perform their function.

According to the (classical) utilitarian perspective, we ought to perform those actions that bring about the best consequences in terms of maximizing pleasure or happiness. We ought to avoid actions with negative consequences, which are those causing pain and suffering. (And utilitarianism is sometimes referred to as consequentialism.) John Stuart Mill's formulation of this ethical perspective is iconic:

> The creed that accepts as the foundation of morals, Utility, or the greatest happiness principle, holds that actions are right in proportion as they tend to promote happiness, wrong as they tend to produce the reverse of happiness. By happiness is intended pleasure, and the absence of pain; by unhappiness, pain, and the privation of pleasure. (Mill, ch. 2)

So, yes, the Facility occasionally causes five young people to suffer horribly. However, the alternative – the *only* alternative – is for the Facility to be party to the unfathomable suffering of every human being on Earth. Thus, on utilitarian grounds, Facility members are doing the right thing by bringing about the least amount of pain and suffering possible, which, in dire circumstances, is the best that can be done.

The fact that utilitarianism (or consequentialism) is a respectable ethical perspective provides some justification for the audience's positive aesthetic responses to certain Facility members. One particularly noteworthy example surprisingly involves not the more relatable Truman or Ms. Lin, but the coarser Hadley and Sitterson. Recall the shock the two men experience when they learn that the tunnel has not been collapsed. As the RV speeds down the road, Sitterson runs down a narrow hallway to perform a manual override. This is a tense scene, and the juxtaposition of Sitterson racing against the RV is quite gripping. On some level, the audience hopes that Sitterson succeeds, even though it will block the campers escape and cause them to suffer additional torment. This dual aesthetic identification is Whedon and Goddard's explicit goal. They (on the DVD commentary track) explain: "This is the film in a nutshell. You are rooting for both of them. You are absolutely desperate that they get through that tunnel and you are desperate that Sitterson gets his job done.... In the end, if you look at this movie, both sides are right.... They believe what they believe for a reason. And that reason is not ridiculous" (*Cabin*, chapters [or scenes] 12 and 18, per the DVD menu). Indeed, the audience hopes the campers escape, but if Sitterson fails, all is lost.

Two other intriguing examples involve the Director, played by Sigorney Weaver (of *Alien* fame). She initially addresses Dana and Marty over the Facility's speaker system. Attempting to explain the magnitude of the situation, her voice booms, "I can only imagine your pain and confusion. But know this. What's happening to you is part of something bigger.... Forgive us and let us get it over with." (And in the shooting script, she further claims, "You've been chosen to be sacrificed for the greater good.") Neither Dana nor Marty accommodates her wishes. Consequently, the Director later leaves her secluded office and addresses Dana and Marty personally. Although each character is bloodied and traumatized, she explains the consequences of a failed ritual to Marty, "We're talking about the agonizing death of every human soul on the planet. Including you. You can die with them, or you can die for them." Weaver exudes indomitable genre presence; however, her words have weight because her ideas do. This affords her character cachet with the viewer. She speaks for humanity, as our protector. She is the last line of defense against Armageddon. Such aesthetic responses make little sense if the audience does not on some level identify with (at least some) Facility members and their goals.

Yet the utilitarian justification for identifying with the Facility members is ultimately overridden by the callous attitudes they display toward the campers. The rather crass inter-office betting pool scene foreshadows this estimation. Lin, sensing Truman's displeasure about the office pool, reassures him, "Seems a little harsh, doesn't it? It's people letting off steam. This job isn't easy, however those clowns may behave." Hadley nonchalantly further informs Truman that the Director doesn't care about control room shenanigans so long as everything goes smoothly "upstairs." Truman remains unconvinced. Nevertheless, the truly egregious turn occurs after Dana narrowly escapes a watery nighttime grave in the sinking RV. As she struggles to find the shore, Hadley remarks, "It's strange. I'm actually rooting for this girl. She's got so much heart. And you think of all the pain..." As his words trail off, the audience is given a glimmer of hope that he will somehow act upon his uncharacteristic inkling. But in the next second, our hopes are dashed; Hadley turns to the door and shouts, "Tequila is my lady!" He welcomes his co-workers and they begin celebrating. Furthermore, although Dana swims to the dock, she is met by one of the Buckners and is brutally beaten. Her extreme suffering is unmistakably displayed to the film audience on the Facility's oversized control room monitors, but Facility members are oblivious. With REO Speedwagon's (apropos) "Roll with the Changes" blaring over the control room speakers, they are preoccupied with celebrating what they believe to be is a successful completion of the ritual. With Dana's awful predicament on full display, some Facility members reprehensibly lament about unpaid overtime bonuses, and others pathetically initiate romantic advances on their co-workers. If *Cabin's* epistemic message is meant to be fully supportive of utilitarianism, then Facility members are not deserving of censure for their behaviors as Dana suffers, but clearly something is amiss.

An Ethical Theory Interlude

The fact that the utilitarian perspective fails to convince signals the presence of a competing ethical view. Rather than emphasizing impersonal consequences, some ethicists stress the close, intimate relationships we foster with others. Elements of this view have their origins in Aristotle, who believes that our moral obligations are shaped by our personal relationships. He writes:

> The duties of parents to children and those of brothers to each other are not the same nor those of comrades and those of fellow-citizens, and so, too, with other kinds of friendship . . . and the injustice increases by being exhibited toward those who are friends in a fuller sense; e.g., it is a more terrible thing to defraud a comrade than a fellow-citizen, more terrible not to help a brother than a stranger, and more terrible to wound a father than anyone else. (Aristotle, 1160a1–6)

Of course, injustices toward sisters are equally as serious as injustices done to brothers, and wounding one's mother is at least as serious as wounding one's father. (That is, Aristotle's language here is sexist, which played a role in spurring the ethics of care perspective.) But Aristotle's basic point remains: Our obligations, and the severity of breaking them, depend on the closeness of our personal relationships. This intuition is a staple of commonsense morality.

The idea that we enjoin such "special obligations" serves as a cornerstone to the contemporary ethics of care perspective. Nel Noddings is among those at the forefront of this approach. She writes:

> If we are meeting those in our inner circles adequately as ones-caring and receiving those linked to our inner circles by formal chains of relation, we shall limit the calls upon our obligation quite naturally. We are not obliged to summon the "I must" [to care] if there is no possibility of completion in the other. I am not obliged to care for starving children in Africa, because there is no way for this caring to be completed in the other unless I abandon the caring to which I am obligated. I may still choose to do something in the direction of caring, but I am not obliged to do so. (Noddings, p. 87)

According to care ethicists who follow Noddings, our ethical obligations are shaped by our close personal relationships. This approach seems intuitive, as parents have an obligation to care for their children in ways that other adults do not; a spouse who regularly treats his or her partner as a mere personal acquaintance is morally deficient and deserving of censure. Moreover, the extent of one's moral obligations to a complete stranger, especially among those persons who will forever remain strangers, is next to nil.

An ethics of care approach stresses the idea of caring for others and being cared for by them. Noddings argues that we proceed from a caring-ideal that pertains to each of us given our particular circumstances. She writes: "We shall discuss the ethical ideal, that vision of best self, in some depth.... It is not just any picture. Rather, it is our best picture of ourselves caring and being cared for.... I am obliged, then, to accept the initial 'I must' when it occurs and even to fetch it out of recalcitrant slumber when it fails to awake spontaneously" (Noddings, 80). Thus there are better and worse ways for each of us to be. Sometimes we miss the mark, and selfish or apathetic motivations impede one's best self as "one-caring" (or "one-cared for"). Nevertheless, each of us must recognize our shortcomings and should strive to be a caring exemplar. This explains Noddings's point about accepting the "I must" approach to care "when it fails to awake spontaneously." Ideally, we effortlessly act as "one-caring" (or "one-cared for") and do so in commendable ways.

Actualizing the ethics of care "one-caring" ideal will require us to develop a certain set of "caring-excellence" traits that facilitate our meeting our obligations in commendable ways. The specific set of virtues conducive to caring-excellence will vary somewhat with the relationship – moral excellence for a parent will no doubt be different than that between close friends – but, invariably, we should strive to become (more) loving, empathetic, compassionate, loyal, sympathetic, and nurturing. This also entails that we should work to avoid character traits that impede our ability to develop and foster care-based relationships – indifference, hostility, callousness, insensitivity, and prejudice.

Cabin and Caring

The audience is led to believe that the campers, especially Curt, Jules, Dana, and Marty enjoy well-established friendships. These four young people have spent a significant amount of time together. Per DVD commentary, Whedon and Goddard assert that the relationships between the campers are crucial to the film: "It was so important for all five of them to care about one another and feel the relationships that take place off the screen" (*Cabin*, DVD ch. 16). Holden is new to the group, but he has ties to Curt. Furthermore, the audience immediately recognizes Holden as trustworthy; he offers to trade rooms with Dana rather than lecherously spy on her through the two-way mirror. The audience recognizes that he is well worth befriending.

Regarding *Cabin's* ethics of care connections, how Goddard frames the final act of the screenplay is as important as the dialogue it contains. Whedon claims (per the *Cabin* commentary track) that his two favorite camera shots of the film each depict close-ups of Dana and Marty. The first (in DVD ch. 21) occurs in the Facility elevator. Bloodied, they are filled with dread regarding the horrors they have endured and the chilling uncertainties of their immediate future. They embrace for mutual support; all they have is each other. The second (in DVD ch. 23) is when Dana, upon hearing the Director's final explanatory plea, points a gun at Marty. Each shot cinematically conveys crucial insights into an ethics of care. The first stresses the importance of togetherness and inter-relatedness; it provides an artistic representation of the ideal that we must strive to care as we are cared for by those intimately close to us. The second conveys the heartbreak of Dana almost losing sight of that ideal. The audience is surprised that she considers sacrificing Marty for the greater good especially given the obvious fact that Marty, who rescued her from the Buckners, is all she has left. And something similar could be said about Marty not alerting Dana about the werewolf poised to attack her. The audience is relieved that she redeems her momentary lapse by alerting Marty about Patience Buckner's silent arrival as he struggles with the Director, and that Marty apologies to Dana for not alerting her about the werewolf. (More on this later.)

Whedon's DVD commentary on the climactic scene with Marty, Dana, and the Director is also informative. In ways reminiscent of Ursula Le Guin's "The Ones Who Walk Away from Omelas," Whedon asserts,

> I don't disagree with saving the world, but what he [Marty, who resigns himself to the coming Apocalypse, because "maybe that is the way it should be if you've got to kill all my friends to survive"] is saying is that if at some point, if in order to maintain order, we have to become so cruel…There is a level of maturity to seeing the smaller picture. There is also a level at which you understand the meaning of the microcosm of your own personal relationships as being the actual world….Who you're helping. Who you're hurting. (*Cabin*, commentary, Chapter 23)

So, although Whedon acknowledges a consequentialist ethical perspective, he focuses his philosophical attention elsewhere. To that end, Whedon is best interpreted as not referring to the sum total of physical existence, but to the "moral universe." On an ethics of care, and assuming that it is a moral theory or perspective onto itself like act utilitarianism, natural law theory, or Kantian ethics, one's moral universe is predominantly determined by one's enmeshed relationships as they relate to an individual's "one-caring" ideal. Furthermore, Whedon suggests that being fully cognizant of one's care-based relationships requires maturity, which divulges his belief that it is a more considered ethical viewpoint (than consequentialism, at least). Part of this maturity, arguably, is taking stock of yourself in terms of your progress toward becoming a caring exemplar given your circumstances: How do I act toward those in relationship with me? How can I improve myself to strengthen those relationships?

Consonant with an ethics of care, Whedon's implicit view seems to be that Marty and Dana clearly have moral obligations to each other, but it's unclear whether either one has an ethical obligation to act on behalf of humanity, especially when saving humanity requires you to murder your only friend left in it. There seems to be two crucial points to Whedon's position, each of which is reflected in the film. First, individual persons cannot form an ethically significant care-based bond or relation with humanity considered in the abstract. (Intriguingly, the difference between persons-in-relation and humanity is arguably reflected and foreshadowed in Marty's rant in the RV about how society is leading us astray due to its impersonal technological tendencies.) Second, the only available course of action on behalf of humanity requires the two friends (and especially Dana) to take active measures that would destroy their relationship. This coheres with Nodding's provocative position regarding obligations to save starving children in Africa. It's not that working to end their starvation wouldn't be a good thing, but this potential project falls outside the scope of one's ethical obligations because (many) individuals are not suitably related to those suffering. Furthermore, for most of us, Noddings contends that taking direct and substantive moral action on behalf of starving children in Africa as "one-caring" is possible only if we abandon the care-based relationships we already have, which would violate our existing moral obligations. So, what Noddings asserts about starving children in Africa seems analogous to what Whedon and Goddard imply about Dana and Marty, especially given how the filmmakers end the movie. Unlike Noddings's example, where at least one could provide financial assistance via a reputable hunger relief organization, for Dana and Marty murdering their friend is the only way to act on behalf of humanity. Thus, Dana and Marty are not obligated to save humanity because neither is suitably related to humanity in the abstract; acting on behalf of humanity given their dire circumstances is possible only if they fail their special obligations to each other and act contrary to their respective "one-caring" ideal. Therefore, their actions, although regrettable, are not impermissible even though it means the end of the world.

Attributing an ethics of care perspective to *Cabin* also coheres with Whedon and Goddard's commentary on the final moments of the film. Goddard explains, "Marty's character is the soul of this movie. He doesn't care about the bigger picture. He cares about saving his friend" (*Cabin*, ch. 23). Whedon generalizes on this, explaining, "He [Marty] is not the love interest. What they have is more beautiful – this friendship bond, this camaraderie in the trenches" (*Cabin*, ch. 24). Whedon and Goddard are clear: The basic moral message of the film is that "people are more important than humanity" (*Cabin*, ch. 24). This is not just because, as Marty puts it at different points, "it's time to let someone else have a turn," and "society needs to crumble; we're just too chicken shit to let it." It's primarily because developing and fostering the bonds of intimate friendships are more morally important than abstract notions of the greater good exactly because of the care and concern that the former inherently involve but the latter invariably overlooks. This view coheres astonishingly well with Noddings's views on an ethics of care.

Admittedly, like an ethics of care itself (and more on that later) the fact that Dana did not act to prevent the looming apocalyptic rise of the Ancient Ones remains controversial. It is also true that Whedon and Goddard purposely crafted the script such that her explicit choice at the time was thwarted by the werewolf attack. She had the gun squarely pointed at Marty, and although looking hesitant, seemed poised to pull the trigger. When asked about this plot point, both Whedon and Goddard (in an interview) stress how they wished to impart to the viewer that Dana is in a genuine dilemma-type situation with no obviously correct resolution; however, each remains elusive regarding his belief about whether Dana should or should not have killed Marty. Whedon shares, "I think it's important to say that there is no right decision where she is. There is no decent way out. We don't want to come down on either side in that case" (Goddard and Whedon, p. 41). Goddard is a bit cagier. He claims, "I'm not even sure she doesn't decide. I think it can be read a variety of ways"; however, he also asserts, "If, to save the world, you have to execute your friend, you should say no.... .Once the movie comes out, it belongs to everyone, and everyone will have their own interpretation of that very thing" (Goddard & Whedon, pp. 41–42). The fact that Whedon and Goddard intentionally leave it up to the viewer to decide how Dana's difficult situation should be resolved is evidence that they were striving to convey ethical complexity. However, Whedon's and Goddard's comments arguably affirm *Cabin's* commitment to an ethical perspective grounded in the bonds between close, personal relationships. If nothing else, recognizing the importance of this ethical approach suitably explains why Dana is in the grips of an ethical dilemma: She has excellent moral reason not to shoot her friend, even if it means the end of the world.

Filmic Counterexamples and "Endorsing" Philosophical Theories

A careful examination of *Cabin*, then, clearly shows it to be ethically complex, but also seemingly favoring one ethical perspective over another. This interpretation explains why audience identification with Facility members wanes with their callous disregard for Dana's suffering on the pier. Even if the Facility assumes a consequentialist perspective when conducting the ritual, Facility members are deserving of moral censure, and an ethics of care explains why.

Indeed, *Cabin's* climatic scene and denouement leads to the interpretation that *Cabin* provides an implicit counterargument to classic utilitarianism. The argument can be recast:

> If classic utilitarianism is true, then Dana acts impermissibly by not killing her friend Marty (because this choice triggers the Apocalypse). It's not the case that Dana acts impermissibly by refraining from killing Marty. Thus, classic utilitarianism is not true.

On this reading of the film, Whedon and Goddard weave together aesthetic and epistemic goals to vividly present utilitarianism for audience consideration, but ultimately to critique it. If so, this is (further) reason to think that *Cabin* engages the philosophical process, or is an example of "philosophy in action."

To better appreciate this important point, let's reconsider the climactic scene in a bit more detail. With palpable gravitas, the Director informs Dana and Marty, but also the viewer, "We're talking about the agonizing death of every human soul on the planet." Teary-eyed, Dana slowly points a gun at Marty, and murmurs, "The whole world, Marty." To which the Director immediately expounds, "Is in your hands, Dana. There is no other way. You have to be strong." This exchange clearly conveys the utilitarian perspective of acting for the greater good, and specifies that killing Marty is Dana's only acceptable choice given that perspective. But utilitarianism is not merely expressed via dialogue. *Cabin* implicitly conveys it in a subtle way via Dana and Marty's previous decision to release the Facility monsters – that which "nightmares are from." Doing so provides a horrific glimpse of what life would be like if the ritual fails. Imagine what life would be like if the Ancient Ones – those responsible for those monsters – rise against us?

The previous discussion of an ethics of care sets up why Dana's choice to refrain from killing Marty is not impermissible. Again going back to the climactic scene, recall the tense moment between Dana and Marty as she is about to pull the trigger. The Director implores Dana "to be strong," but Marty's reaction is instructive. Actor Fran Kranz straightens up, raises his chin, and, in effect, assumes a challenging pose. He then asks, "Yeah, Dana – you feeling strong?" Marty implicitly implores Dana to think about what it means to be "strong" in this situation: to act for the "whole world" on consequentialist grounds or to uphold her care-based ideals? Marty suggests that the strong thing for her to do is *not* succumb to the Director's impersonal perspective. He challenges Dana to see him as he is – her friend, and her only remaining friend in a struggle for their lives – and not to lose sight of this fact as she ponders the so-called greater good. That is, Marty implores Dana not to act in a way similar to the Facility members who objectionably failed to see her as she struggled for her life on the dock. Marty's response to the situation reaches us – the audience – and in this way, provides us reason for believing that Dana ought not to kill Marty (as it, of course, also applies to Dana in the film).

Admittedly, neither Dana nor Marty acts perfectly as "one-caring" (or "one-cared for") in the closing moments of the film. Dana does contemplate murdering Marty. As she murmurs, "I'm sorry," Marty glimpses the werewolf behind her and answers, "So am I." Perhaps Dana momentarily wavers about her special obligation to her friend, and Marty then acts spitefully out of self-regard by allowing the werewolf to attack Dana. Everyone sometimes falls short of being a caring exemplar, especially in such difficult and extreme circumstances. However, after the werewolf impedes Dana's choice, the two friends resume acting on behalf of the other. Dana alerts Marty (but not the Director) to Patience's arrival, and Marty rescues Dana from the werewolf attack by shooting it in the back. Moreover, with the immediate threats vanquished, the two sit down together, and quickly (even if unsteadily) work to repair whatever ruptures have just occurred in their relationship. Dana apologizes for nearly killing Marty and reassures him that she probably wouldn't have. Marty apologizes for not preventing the werewolf attack from the first and supports her by appreciating her difficult circumstances; he also apologizes for his part in ending the world. They subsequently await their fate – together.

The denouement's implicit message is clear: It is better to spend whatever remaining moments you have with a friend – spending it as friends – rather than acting cruelly against a friend, with the result of becoming friendless. If acting in accordance with the values of care, concern, and friendship is inconsistent with maximizing utility, the care ethicist can consistently affirm that it is permissible to act on the former values – even in the face of the Apocalypse. Thus, Dana does not act wrongly in refraining to kill her friend Marty. At the very least, it is not obvious that Dana can be blamed for her choice, even though it is obviously wrong if classic utilitarianism is true. Accordingly, *Cabin* not only brings utilitarianism to the foreground to raise questions about it, but also to critique it – albeit cinematically. In doing so, Cabin *endorses* an ethics of care perspective: It conveys – again, cinematically – consideration for thinking it is a plausible ethical perspective and one that, arguably, is philosophically superior to utilitarianism (albeit with a little help from Whedon and Goddard's commentary).

Cabin's Implicit Theory of Horror

The discussion of *Cabin's* ethical complexity and its apparent philosophical endorsement of an ethics of care provide a springboard into an interpretation of what the film conveys about horror and human nature. It is commonly believed that Whedon and Goddard utilize *Cabin* to explore the human condition as it pertains to our penchant for engaging horror stories, including "slasher" films. Film scholar Gerry Canavan concurs. He writes: "By the film's quiet denouement...the original valence of the film's critique has completely switched: now 'horror' is figured not as a political problem at all, but instead as ahistorical and eternal, a dark mythos somehow essential to human nature as such.... From this perspective horror...bespeaks an existential-theological crisis about the soul of humanity that cries desperately out for some explanation, if not a solution" (Canavan, pp. 4 & 34). But what "crisis about the soul of humanity" do horror films occasion, and what solution, if any, does *Cabin* offer?

To begin deciphering *Cabin's* implicit epistemic message about horror, consider Whedon's aesthetic views on the genre. His clearest ideas pertain to film characters. Regarding aesthetically deficient horror films, he explains, "I absolutely can't stand movies where people don't do what any sane person would do....Panic is fine; people panic. But when they make obviously idiotic decisions, then it makes me not only crazy but angry, because I lose my identification with the person" (Goddard & Whedon, p. 11). Regarding more aesthetically worthwhile horror films, he explains: "[The characters] are good people – they're friends, they care about each other. And the more they do that, the more charming and the more they care, the more you care about them, the scarier it is" (Goddard & Whedon, p. 11). This difference in character portrayal provides context for Whedon's derision regarding many contemporary (primarily "slasher") horror films. He laments, "Now they [the characters] are just fodder – now it is always about the villain, what inventive villain can we make, because that's the action figure, and then we'll throw some expendable teenagers at them, and they get more and more expendable and more love is put into the instruments of torture" (Goddard & Whedon, p. 11). Thus Whedon believes that good horror films portray sufficiently developed characters who are aesthetically relatable, especially insofar as the characters have significant reason to care for each other. The care the characters express among each other, especially if it is believably genuine, transfers to the viewer, which results in the viewer caring about each of them. That, in turn, transfers into a scarier and, thus, enriched aesthetic experience for the viewer. For these reasons Whedon seemingly believes that possessing aesthetically relatable characters is a necessary condition for worthwhile (or good) horror films. However, films that portray underdeveloped or unrelatable characters that serve as mere fodder for a one-dimensional sadistic villain quash the emotional process indicative of aesthetic merit.

Whedon further suggests that engaging aesthetically deficient horror can have significant ethical ramifications. Films that emphasize the thematic importance of a sadistic villain as an action figure imaginatively dispensing unfathomable tortures upon shallow and unrelatable characters are not only lacking in aesthetic merit, but also tend to be morally objectionable. Consider: "You look at something as ugly, stupid, and morally bankrupt as the remake of *Texas Chainsaw*...Those home invasion scary movies or movies where people just get beat upon or manipulated or other people treat them horribly – I can't even watch them, your *Funny Games*...makes me frightened and disturbed" (Goddard & Whedon, 9–10). The horrors viewers experience by watching such films tend to be pointless and not sufficiently grounded in the emotional transference of caring relationships. Furthermore, because such films are rife with sexual and political exploitation, and gratuitous and senseless graphic violence, they arguably have a negative effect on one's journey toward caring-excellence. The worry is that regularly viewing them tends to erode such care-based attributes as compassion and empathy. Thus there is reason to believe that an ethics of care pervades Whedon's aesthetic perspectives on horror. It accounts for what Whedon finds aesthetically deficient about various contemporary horror films. And, as we'll see, it may also provide the foundation for his implicit views on worthwhile horror.

Of course, just as one can enjoy food that is seriously deficient in any nutritional content, one can enjoy a film that lacks significant aesthetic merit; merely liking a film does not thereby make it aesthetically good or worthwhile (see Carroll 2003). Whedon concurs. While granting that individual tastes differ, Whedon nevertheless maintains that some horror films are aesthetically deficient, and this is so even if some people (on some level) enjoy bad horror. What worries Whedon, though, is the apparent popularity of bad horror films, especially "slasher" films with such notable examples as the *Hostel* and *Saw* franchises; that they have become *franchises* speaks to their wide popularity.

So, why do we regularly engage in horror films, including those with graphic and gratuitous displays of human suffering? Perhaps it is as Plato suggested long ago in the *Republic*: Liontius speaks to the human condition when he curses himself for succumbing to his overwhelming desire to look upon the public executioner's gruesome handiwork (see Plato, 439e-440). That Plato recognized so long ago that we seemingly cannot turn away from grisly images is perhaps the key to understanding what Canavan calls the "crisis about the soul of humanity."

Not surprisingly, and as Canavan suggests, Whedon is sensitive to our plight. Whedon asks, "Why do we need horror stories?" and then expounds, "And I don't mean enjoy, I mean NEED. We revel in them. And maybe that's a response to the darkness of the world (or an inoculation against it), or maybe it really is why we need to be gotten rid of" (Goddard & Whedon, p. 172). Elsewhere, he returns to the idea of "inoculation" when he states our tendency to engage horror is "basically where we get to inoculate ourselves against real fear" (Goddard & Whedon, p. 9). While what Whedon exactly means by "inoculation" is unclear (and might be misleading), his ideas suggest that engaging horror films can have negative or beneficial effects. It might be that our fate depends on what kind of horror film we engage.

If Whedon believes that engaging in bad horror films has negative moral ramifications, perhaps engaging in worthwhile horror has positive effects. Furthermore, even if Plato's intuition is correct and it is (more or less) human nature to look upon grisly images, it doesn't follow that no good can come of that natural tendency. For reasons harkening back to Aristotle's *Poetics*, consider that by engaging in horror films, we might purge ourselves of violent fascinations, or at least the desire to view actual grisly images. This, perhaps, coheres with Whedon's vague references to inoculation. However, purgation in this sense seems consistent with viewing contemporary slasher films, which Whedon explicitly rails against, because they offer aesthetically unrelatable characters and tend to desensitize us to their pain and suffering.

Alternatively, if we cannot overcome our fascination with horror films, perhaps by viewing (and making) them with aesthetically relatable characters, we have the opportunity to refine our moral sensibilities as they pertain to an ethics of care. In this way, engaging in worthwhile horror satisfies our natural inclinations and, with sufficient reflection, facilitates a purification of our moral characters. Consequently, there is a cathartic result of becoming better equipped to act appropriately in actual, horrific situations via heightened empathy and resolve among our caring-excellence traits. (Note both "purgation" and "purification" are concepts used to interpret Aristotle's famed catharsis.)

Although this account of aesthetically worthwhile horror fits with the overall ethics of care message *Cabin* offers, it is admittedly a bit speculative and is arguably in need of further defense; nevertheless, that it leaves plenty of room for further study is not without merit. Still, it seems clear that Whedon believes it is up to us whether some good comes of our irrepressible desire to engage in horror films, or whether we become swallowed up by the baser aspects of human nature. This is our crisis of the soul of humanity.

On *Cabin* "Endorsing" Worthwhile Horror

Although mining *The Cabin in the Woods: Visual Companion* provides helpful context for Whedon's (and Goddard's) ideas, the issue now becomes whether there is evidence that *Cabin* cinematically conveys an ethics of care-based theory of horror and, if so, to what extent the film "endorses" it. A careful examination of the film uncovers three primary ways in which *Cabin* cinematically accomplishes these goals.

The first way *Cabin* cinematically achieves its epistemic goals about worthwhile horror and an implicit response to the Canavan's "crisis of the soul of humanity" is grounded in how Whedon and Goddard craft their protagonists. The campers must be *manipulated* into their prescribed sacrificial personas. Curt is not the stereotypical jock, Jules is far from a whore, Dana is not a virgin, and Marty is not quite a fool. In fact, arguably, Curt is more of a scholar than is Holden, Dana is more of a whore than is Jules, and Marty is at least as insightful as any member of the group. Not fitting a stereotypical or genre cookie-cutter trope makes each character more interesting.

Curt and Jules become much less interesting once they are chemically manipulated to better fit their prescribed sacrificial (or genre) roles. Insofar as they become less interesting, it is more difficult to identify with them. Jules's seductive dance in front of the fireplace is inexplicable; the other campers (save a testosterone-infused Curt) are uncomfortably befuddled by her "celebu-tard" behavior. Marty laments Curt's recent turn as an "alpha-male" and wonders why Curt calls Holden an "egghead" when *he* (not Holden) is the one on a full academic scholarship. In contradistinction, the fact that Dana and Marty resist Facility manipulation results in their remaining (more) interesting and relatable. Moreover, the dire situation Dana and Marty face in the final act is thus more gripping than Curt's rather ill-advised and overly machismo attempt to jump the gorge on his motorbike. True, the audience on some level wants Curt to succeed, but the dread between Dana and Marty is much more emotionally charged and thus relatable because they face it together, being the friends that they are. This, in part, explains the difficulty of witnessing Dana pointing her gun at Marty.

The Ancient Ones serve as another example of things not being exactly as they seem, which represents the second way *Cabin* strives toward the relevant cinematic and epistemic goals. The Ancient Ones are not merely the "metaphysical MacGuffins," driving the action of the film; they serve as an uncomfortable reminder of our baser human desires. The Ancient Ones demand that the ritual be performed exactly according to the very familiar and entrenched formula of at least five young people suffering horribly. The "whore" is corrupt; she dies first. The "virgin" – as the "final girl" – may live or die, so long as she suffers and her companions all die first. If this formula is not followed, the Ancient Ones show displeasure and ultimately wreak ultimate havoc. For production companies that make and market motion pictures, the connections to humankind are straightforward. If filmmakers deviate too much from the formula, production companies run the risk of financial ruin. Thus, it is better to placate the audience and its baser desires for gratuitous sex, objectification, and gruesome violence. Of course, this makes humanity as monstrous as giant evil gods, and puts Canavan's "crisis of the soul of humanity" into clearer focus.

It might be, then, that via the Ancient Ones Whedon and Goddard are (subtly?) providing the audience an opportunity to reflect upon its (our) viewing preferences and the baser desires that drive them. Becoming fully aware of our baser desires, regardless of whether they are (more or less) grounded in human nature, is the first step in becoming less monstrous. Contemporary philosopher S. Evan Kreider concurs, as he explains, "When I watch a slasher film and – yes – *enjoy* it, I am reminded that I too have these darker [aggressive and violent] instincts. In this way, a slasher film can serve as a sort of cautionary tale, one that tells me that I ought humbly to accept these darker instincts as part of my [human] nature, but also be on guard against them" (Kreider, p. 154, original emphasis). Only upon self-awareness can we effect positive change and, with that, come to see that we might be better off without formulaic "slasher" films, even if we are unable to escape horror altogether.

The third way *Cabin* achieves its cinematic and epistemic goals is through the thematic use of monitors and mirrors. Whedon and Goddard thereby (further) invite the viewer to reflect upon what he or she sees. Recall how the Facility members were oblivious to Dana's suffering on the dock. We are led to believe that the ritual was completed successfully. Dana had obviously suffered; so, her death was not required. That she continues to suffer is pointless. This fact pertains to the plot, but it also has a meta-level application to the viewer. Have we become oblivious to the pointless suffering so often displayed in movie theaters? Is this negatively affecting our moral characters, as it has so influenced the Facility members? If nothing else, perhaps we should be more like aptly named *Truman* (in DVD ch. 19): Stand above the partying crowd and be more cognizant of what the large screen in front of us portrays.

Recall also the control room scene depicting various male Facility members gathered to ogle Curt and Jules's pending sexual encounter. It was standing room only. Each man in the room was fixated on the large control room screens, knowing full well that Jules was about to die. They did not care about *that*; rather, they were interested in only her objectification – seeing her naked body writhe around on top of Curt before she was slaughtered. Recall further their obvious disappointment at *not* witnessing Jules's nude body when they expected to do so. As the Facility members stare at the huge screens in front of them, the audience watches them on its movie theater (or television) screen. This allows us the opportunity to assess our own voyeuristic tendencies. Do they negatively impact our moral character, as they have so impacted the Facility members?

It's worth pointing out that the filmic message about voyeurism is reinforced by a quick dialogue exchange in the same scene. Hadley chases his co-workers out of the control room because he and Sitterson have work to do. They begin manipulating the temperature, moon light, and pheromone levels near Curt and Jules. Curt and Jules subsequently resume their amorous activities. Sitterson mutters, "Show us the goods." When Truman questions whether it is necessary for them to watch, Hadley interrupts him: "We're not the only one's watching, kid," and Sitterson promptly adds, "Got to keep the customer satisfied." Presumably, the two men ostensibly refer to the Ancient Ones. But recall the Ancient Ones (also) represent *us* – the viewer. That is, in a way, we are "the customer to be satisfied" – because we are the ones buying tickets to see "slasher" films. So, if one is inclined to ask whether it is morally problematic for the Ancient Ones to want to see Jules objectified only to suffer decapitation with a rusty tree saw and raise hell if they do not see this, the very same question applies to filmgoers. Would it be the end of the world if horror filmmakers didn't include gratuitous nudity and violence? Would it be the end of horror films (because we would no longer buy tickets to see them)? If so, what does that say about us? Canavan's "crisis of the human soul" becomes clearer.

Yet *Cabin* provides us a guide for rescuing ourselves. Consider (again) the two-way mirror reveal (in DVD ch. 5) between Dana's room and Holden's room. Recall the grotesque painting depicting a lamb being viciously dismembered by huntsmen and their rabid dogs. Holden ponders it for a moment, but mutters, "Yeah, I don't think so," and swiftly yanks it off the wall. Doing so uncovers the two-way mirror – and Dana preparing to don her bikini. Holden, although initially titillated by the opportunity to witness Dana undress with impunity, does the decent thing by making her aware of the mirror. He also offers to switch rooms. When he begins to change into his swimming trunks, Dana momentarily is titillated by his toned body, but she averts her eyes and quickly rehangs the painting Holden removed. When she gazes at its grisly images, she also murmurs, "Yeah, I don't think so," and covers it with a blanket.

The epistemic message how Holden and Dana react to the mirror is instructive: Even if there is some difficult-to-define deep psychological desire to witness pointless graphic violence, we retain the ability to not become so enamored of it that we become completely bereft of our moral sensibilities; furthermore, although both men and women are prone to voyeurism – it is perhaps human nature (even Truman was tempted to gaze at Jules's naked body) – we retain the ability to curb or redirect such behavior. Self-reflection is the key. Goddard emphasizes this message by pulling his camera back from Dana after she hangs the blanket over the painting, and then taking the shot through a control room monitor. The audience consequently views Dana through an additional screen, which only reminds the viewer of the screen in front of him or her. This, in effect, is to make each of us more aware of our voyeuristic tendencies, especially when the object of our voyeurism is brutal and senseless graphic suffering or sexual and political objectification (or both), and to remind us to be quick about taking action to curb or redirect them.

Admittedly, the causal consequences of what consumers regularly expose themselves to can be notoriously difficult to establish convincingly. However, from an ethics of care perspective, ethical concerns about continued viewership of aesthetically deficient horror are understandable. Whedon (implicitly) asks: Is repeated exposure to bad contemporary horror films contributing to our becoming *less* empathetic, compassionate, and sympathetic, and *more* indifferent, callous, and insensitive? Does it impede our resolve to be "one-caring" for those in need? If so, then that is excellent reason to take it upon ourselves to cease exposing ourselves to it, even if it is somehow titillating to watch such movies.

Whedon implicitly countenances that engaging in horror films may be unavoidable, but he invites us to hold up the mirror to ourselves and ask: Can't we be more discerning about which horror films we make and watch? Would it *really* be the end of the world if we stopped making and watching bad horror films? Whedon implicitly answers "yes" to the former and "no" to the latter. If we must fulfill some basic primal human need, let us fill it in the most effective ways possible. We should shun aesthetically deficient horror films due to their propensity for dulling our care-excellence character traits. Further, we should gravitate toward aesthetically valuable horror films – those that have the potential to purify our moral sensibilities by enhancing our care-excellence character traits.

Accordingly, with an assist from Goddard, Whedon's philosophical meditation on horror invites us to consider the topic with him. It seems that Whedon is willing to grant that it is acceptable to enjoy horror films – he enjoys them, too – and, moreover, engaging in them can be beneficial. However, even if engaging in horror stories is in some sense an unavoidable feature of the human condition, we nevertheless retain sufficient control over the details of that engagement. We have the ability to choose aesthetically valuable horror films and eschew undesirable horror. Doing so is both aesthetically and ethically beneficial in that our image of "best self" as a caring exemplar remains secure, if not strengthened. But if we cannot bring ourselves to be more discerning – if we cannot at least do that much to save ourselves – then perhaps it *is* the end of the world. The "crisis of the human soul" is not averted and as Dana states, "it is time to give someone else a chance," whoever or whatever that someone might be. Hopefully our successors won't be so monstrous. It's a harsh lesson, to say the least.

If we are unable (or, worse, too apathetic) to save us from ourselves, then only the monstrous parts of humanity are reflected in the mirror Whedon and Goddard provide us via *Cabin*. As Canavan puts it, such a result "is the final mirror in a film that is filled with them; in the end, when the [Ancient] Ones rise to wreak their unfathomable havoc upon the world, there is nothing but our own hands reaching out for us" (Canavan, p. 40). The giant hand crashing down at the end of *Cabin* is metaphorically ours; we destroy ourselves and thereby the world around us. Fade to black. Cue the heavy-metal music. Roll credits.

The difficulty (in large part) of discerning the story behind the story of *Cabin*, then, is that Whedon is forcing us to take a very real look at ourselves in the mirror both in terms of what (or who) we are and what we should be. Perhaps we are okay with what we see, but shouldn't be. To see ourselves truly requires an acute moral honesty that is incredibly psychologically difficult to achieve, especially when no one else is looking. Perhaps this is the conflict Whedon sees regarding our irrepressible desire for engaging horror films, and he invites us to consider it with him.

Of course, not all meditations end with irresistible conclusions. Whether *Cabin* cinematically endorses an ethics of care-based aesthetic of horror as clearly as it does an ethics of care is admittedly controversial. However, it goes a long way to provide us ample opportunity for careful self-reflection about human nature – who we are and who we ought to be (or become) – and it was constructed to accomplish just that. This is another way film – including a film that many classify as a "slasher" film – can engage the philosophical process and thereby achieve aesthetic merit. (For an argument that no "slasher" film possesses aesthetic merit, see Di Muzio; arguably, *Cabin* serves as a filmic counter-example to that thesis as well.)

Conclusion: Assessing *Cabin's* Philosophical Engagement

The interpretation of *Cabin* offered in this chapter faces at least two challenges. The first is that the film's message about an ethics of care is dubious, in that Dana's choice to act on behalf of her special obligations to Marty and not the greater good of humanity is implausible if not indefensible. The ultimate reason for this is that an ethics of care cannot do all the philosophical work Whedon and Goddard seemingly intend. The second challenge is that even if an ethics of care were the sort of ethical theory that could do all the philosophical work Whedon and Goddard seemingly intend, *Cabin's* epistemic message is muddled due to its reliance on the familiar horror genre tropes it is trying to subvert.

The first challenge is perhaps grounded in doubts about whether an ethics of care is an ethical perspective or theory onto itself. Many commentators argue that it is best interpreted as a supplement to classic theories, for example, act utilitarianism, natural law theory, and Kantian ethics, each of which stresses abstract moral principles and acting from duty. For example, Stephen Darwall writes, "Ethics of care may not be a radically opposed alternative to morality as conceived by the moderns, so much as an important supplement.... It brings into the forefront of ethical reflection issues of relationship that, although they provide much of the stuff of our lives, have been relatively neglected by moral theorists" (Darwall, p. 228). If an ethics of care is merely a supplement to the more classic theories like act utilitarianism, then, the idea is, our obligations to keep our special obligations, cannot trump our obligation to act for the sake of the greater good.

Yet some commentators are unconvinced that an ethics of care coheres with act utilitarianism. For example, Bruce Waller writes:

> By utilitarian standards, my duty is to maximize pleasure and minimize suffering for everyone involved, and the calculations demanded are quite impersonal: I must count my own pleasures and pains and those of my family and friends in the total, but I cannot give those concerns any greater weight than the pleasures and pains of strangers.... From the perspective of care ethics, the bonds of affection and friendship and family must be recognized as an important and distinct ethical element, not just one pleasure calculation among others. Treating our special personal relationships as merely a subset of pleasurable sensations to be entered into the utilitarian calculation seems (to care theorists) an inadequate representation of the basic moral worth of these relations. (Waller, pp. 119–120)

Waller reminds us that not all moral theories can be synthesized without creating internal inconsistencies. One cannot combine a consequentialist theory with one that is staunchly deontological, at least not without adding some strategy for resolving moral dilemma-type situations when duties conflict. The consequentialist will insist that in such situations, we act for the greater good, but the deontologist will deny this, complaining that the goal of ethics is not maximizing happiness. Analogously, the care ethicist will object that if we are *always* obligated to maximize utility, even in situations where meeting that goal requires me to murder a loved one, then what is left of the care ethics perspective? Just as it is difficult to synthesize consequentialist and deontological approaches into one coherent theory, it is equally dubious to synthesize approaches requiring impersonal and personal considerations as morally valuable.

The point being made here can be put more intuitively by considering specific examples. Consider a case where a parent and child are in Dana and Marty's situation. Can we really require the parent to murder his or her child? If we are inclined, at the very least, not to blame the parent for refraining from murdering his or her child, an ethics of care can provide a plausible explanation for why this is. The bonds between close personal relationships and the actions of caring-exemplars who commendably navigate them are at least as morally important as impersonal calculations meant to serve the greater good.

If we consider an ethics of care as a theory onto itself, we might follow Noddings and interpret it as a version of Aristotelian virtue ethics. Both place emphasis on ideal conceptions of moral agents rather than abstract principles. Both are suspicious of generating moral rules via universalization (generalizing on similar circumstances to define moral obligations), or at least hold that this has been overemphasized in moral thinking. Rather, both (and especially an ethics of care) gravitate toward ethical particularism, which emphasizes the importance of distinct moral agents making choices in their own circumstances. Both downplay the importance of moral rules by re-defining them in terms of what the virtuous person, when acting in character, would do (see Noddings, especially pp. 80–102).

Of course, attempts at synthesizing these two versions of an agent-based moral theory will eventually run into some internal conflict (because Aristotelians traditionally don't place as much emphasis on caring). But if Aristotelian virtue ethics is its own moral theory or ethical perspective onto itself, why not an ethics of care? Furthermore, *any* moral theory, if pushed far enough, will have counterintuitive entailments that must be addressed. This (in part) is why ethics is so difficult. (For an account of ethics of care as its own moral theory, see Kowalski, Chapter 11, especially pp. 306–318.)

So, it might be that *Cabin* conveys an ethics of care perspective not only to show utilitarianism's shortcomings, but also to test its logical limits. As such, consider how a moral philosopher would (probably) begin assessing an ethics of care. Even if there are special obligations to close friends and family members, does this entail that it is always permissible to keep them if it means the end of the world? Similarly, although we always have good reason to act on behalf of a caring-ideal, does this mean that I may permissibly not act to save the lives of billions of strangers, if the only way to do so is murder my friend? It is common to ask such ("doomsday") questions of any moral theory. Furthermore, a philosopher often asks such questions about a theory she advocates, or about which she is sympathetic. By anticipating such objections, she is able to better reflect upon them and is in a better position to offer rejoinders. Perhaps Whedon and Goddard are playing the part of the philosopher by "screening" the logical limits of an ethical theory they find plausible.

The second challenge is grounded in the obvious fact that *Cabin* employs the horror genre tropes that it attempts to subvert: There is a cabin in the woods (!) that a group of young people visit; there are horrific and incomprehensible villains who cause bloody carnage in a multitude of ways; the noticeably attractive Curt and Jules have sex, Jules (but not Curt) is shown naked, and then gruesomely killed; the carnage caused by the Facility monsters is obviously gratuitous, and almost comically so (recalling the blood-soaked scene outside the Facility elevators); Dana is the "final girl," who endures terrible suffering and dread; and, of course, there are multiple "jump scares." Because Whedon and Goddard package their alleged epistemic messages in standard "slasher" horror garb, it is tempting to object that their attempt is doomed to fail. No film that utilizes so many standard genre tropes can successfully undercut the genre it is commenting upon; all such attempts will be epistemic failures, or (at best) be of dubious success.

It's not difficult to sympathize with this objection. However, there might be a helpful analogy between complex films and complex texts. When reading any difficult or dense text, one must take care to consider all its nuances and allusions. Furthermore, when reading an author, and attempting to discern that author's message, it is often helpful to cross-reference what is written (or said) in other texts. Perhaps film is the same.

To that end, consider Whedon's response to the implicit worry that his message about feminism conveyed in *Buffy the Vampire Slayer* is garbled due to its familiar genre trappings: "If I made *Buffy the Lesbian Separatist*, [as] a series of lectures on PBS on why there should be feminism, no one would be coming to the party, and it would be boring. The idea of changing culture is important to me, and it can only be done in a popular medium" (Whedon 2002). Whedon wishes to spur his audience – those prone to watch coming-of-age television shows – to examine their existent beliefs about gender roles and the different forms sexism can take in the hope of bringing about ethically desirable social change. However, as an artist, he does this via crafting a tale about a blonde cheerleader from southern California, and a girl who also happens to be the Chosen One. It is she who will save humanity from the forces of darkness and avert the Apocalypse – but who also must survive her parents' divorce, a soulless boyfriend, being unexpectedly saddled with a new sister, her mother's unexpected death, and entering the workforce (at Double Meat Palace of all places). By crafting his televised horror-comedy-drama well and stocking it with relatable characters, it will not be boring; people will thus take notice and attend his epistemic "party." Assuming they are full participants, they will not only enjoy it, but also become more thoughtful or reflective as a result.

Perhaps, then, Whedon addresses his message in *Cabin* to those who need to hear it most: those who, like him, are fascinated by horror films, even if they are not completely sure why or comfortable with this fact about them. True, a lazy viewer might miss his message, but this is true of anyone who does not take the care to read a text carefully. Whedon's goal, as an artist, is to get your attention, spur you to "read" – that is watch – more carefully and be a full participant in his epistemic "party" that happens at the cabin in the woods. *Cabin* does that by, paradoxically, using all the familiar "slasher" tropes. If we consider his message carefully – if we look carefully for the nuances – then perhaps his message about those tropes is much less garbled than it may initially appear. There are clues that *Cabin* is not merely another "slasher" film, many of which are explored in this chapter. The careful viewer will take note; having done so, she is in a better position to grasp its intended epistemic message. So, perhaps *Cabin* is just one more of Whedon's attempts to reach the proper target audience to spur socially desirable change, or least bring about a more reflective generation. Whether *Cabin* is as successful as was (is) *Buffy the Vampire Slayer* remains to be seen, but we won't know until we actually and truly *see* it for what it is.

Yet, even if the viewer does accept this invitation to peer carefully into *Cabin*, we should also be careful not to require too much of film in terms of what it accomplishes when engaging the philosophical process. After all, sometimes the most influential philosophers do not come to convincing conclusions. Philosopher Carolyn Korsmeyer concurs, and elaborates, "Philosophy does not always persuade a reader that its conclusions are correct, nor does it always culminate in a clear position on an issue. Sometimes the most profound philosophy ends in aporia – a recognition that one does not know the answer to a question that seemed at first to have an answer" (Korsmeyer, p. 31). The fact that Whedon and Goddard created an enjoyable film that spurs critical reflection on ethics, human nature, and worthwhile horror is a significant feat in itself. As argued here, there are important philosophical insights to be mined in the film, but even if you just begin to *think* carefully about (say) how important your close personal relationships truly are, or whether some horror films are better for you than others, perhaps that is also a part of "the story behind the story" of *Cabin*.

References

Aristotle. 1925. *Nicomachean Ethics* (trans: Ross, W.D.). Oxford: Oxford University Press.
Canavan, Gerry. 2014. 'Something Nightmares Are From': Metacommentary in Joss Whedon's *Cabin in the Woods*. *Slayage: The Journal of Whedon Studies* 36–37 (Fall 2013/Winter).
Carroll, Noel. 2003. Introducing Film Evaluation. In *Engaging the Moving Image*, ed. Noel Carroll. New Haven: Yale University Press.
Darwall, Stephen. 1998. *Philosophical ethics*. Boulder: Westview.
Goddard, Drew, and Joss Whedon. 2012. *The cabin in the woods: The official visual companion*. London: Titan Books.
Korsmeyer, Carolyn. 2007. Philosophy and the probable impossible. In *Philosophy and the interpretation of pop culture*, ed. William Irwin and Jorge J.E. Garcia, 21–40. Lanham: Rowman & Littlefield.
Kowalski, Dean A. 2012. *Moral theory at the movies*. Lanham: Rowman & Littlefield.
Kreider, S. Evan. 2008. The virtue of horror films: a response to DiMuzio. *International Journal of Applied Philosophy* 22.1: 149–157.
Mill, John Stuart. 1861. *Utilitarianism*.
Muzio, Di, and Gianluca. 2006. The immorality of horror films. *International Journal of Applied Philosophy* 20: 277–294.
Nodding, Nel. 1984. *Caring: A feminine approach to ethics and moral education*. Berkeley: University of California Press.
Plato. 1974. *Republic* (trans: Grube, G.M.A.). Indianapolis: Hackett.
Shaw, Daniel. 2008. *Film and philosophy: Taking movies seriously*. London: Wallflower Press.
The Cabin in the Woods. Written by Joss Whedon and Drew Goddard. 2012. Directed by Drew Goddard. Vancouver: Lionsgate.
Waller, Bruce N. 2005. *Consider ethics*. New York: Pearson-Longman.
Whedon, Joss. 2002. Must see metaphysics. *New York Times Magazine* interview by Emily Nausbaum, September. http://www.nytimes.com/2002/09/22/magazine/must-see-metaphysics.html. Last Accessed 7 Apr 2021.
———. 2012. Joss Whedon talks cabin in the woods. *Total Film Magazine*, February. https://web.archive.org/web/20160222033050if_/https://gamesradar.com/joss-whedon-talks-the-cabin-in-the-woods. Last Accessed 7 Apr 2021.

Magnolia As Philosophy: Meaning and Coincidence

51

Bart Engelen

Contents

Introduction: *Magnolia*: Praise and Criticism	1194
Magnolia: Characters and Storylines	1195
Things that Have Happened (to Happen)	1196
WTF Happened?!?	1198
So What Does It Mean?	1199
Things that Coincide	1200
Sense-Making Stories	1202
In Search of Deeper Meaning	1204
Wise Up	1205
More than One Meaning	1206
When Things Don't Make Sense	1207
The Absurd	1209
How to Deal with the Absurd	1212
Conclusion	1213
References	1214

Abstract

In *Magnolia*, a 1999 movie written and directed by then 29-year-old Paul Thomas Anderson, we follow a range of characters who all try to come to terms with the things happening to them in both the present and past. This chapter interprets the movie as making a philosophical point about meaning: how and why do people find meaning in and attribute meaning to things, even if they seem to happen for no apparent reason at all? We will analyze how both the movie's characters and all of us watching the movie, living our own lives, try to make sense of the often absurd coincidences in life. More importantly, we will ask *why* we feel the need to "make sense" of the things that happen to and around us and what happens when

B. Engelen (✉)
Tilburg Center for Moral Philosophy, Epistemology and Philosophy of Science (TiLPS), Tilburg University, Tilburg, The Netherlands
e-mail: b.engelen@tilburguniversity.edu

© Springer Nature Switzerland AG 2024
D. K. Johnson et al. (eds.), *The Palgrave Handbook of Popular Culture as Philosophy*,
https://doi.org/10.1007/978-3-031-24685-2_79

our attempts fail. How should we respond to things that simply don't make sense, even after we have tried hard? The chapter explains how (key scenes of) the movie can be interpreted as visualizing the philosophical notion of "the absurd" and inviting us to respond to absurdities in ways already articulated by the French existentialist Albert Camus.

Keywords

Magnolia · PTA · Paul Thomas Anderson · Roger Ebert · Meaning · Sense-making · Coincidence · Absurd · Absurdity · Suicide · Existentialism · Albert Camus

Introduction: *Magnolia*: Praise and Criticism

> It is in the humble opinion of this narrator that this is not just "something that happened." This cannot be "one of those things."
> —Narrator (Ricky Jay)

> At any street corner the feeling of absurdity can strike any man in the face.
> —Albert Camus (1942 [2005], p. 9)

Magnolia, directed and produced by Paul Thomas Anderson (or PTA) is a critically acclaimed movie from 1999, arguably the best year in cinematic history. *Magnolia* hosts a wide range of characters, each of whom is experiencing life-changing events and trying to come to terms with their past, with themselves, and with the things happening to and around them. It is a classic example of an ensemble movie, with amazing performances by a stellar cast. While each character has their own storyline, viewers come to learn how some are and become connected as the plot unfolds. As such, the movie can be described as an example of the so-called "hyperlink cinema" (Matchbox 2017).

The movie has been both praised and loathed. It received three Academy Awards nominations, won the 2000 Golden Berlin Bear and Tom Cruise went on to win the Golden Globe for Best Supporting Actor. PTA, also known for *Boogie Nights* and later *There Will Be Blood*, *The Master*, *Inherent Vice*, and *Phantom Thread*, was only 29 years old when he wrote and directed the movie. In his own words, "*Magnolia* is, for better or worse, the best movie I'll ever make" (IMDB 2021b). *Rotten Tomatoes* (2021) calls *Magnolia* "an ambitious, lengthy work that ultimately succeeds due to interesting stories and excellent ensemble performances."

Despite this praise, everyone who watched the movie probably found the experience frustrating in some sense. The most common complaint is that the movie – at over 3 hours – is simply too long. Even PTA admits it is "way too f***ing long. It's unmerciful how long it is" (Anderson 2017). We're witnessing a multitude of storylines and events unfolding, often life-changing stuff, with a lot of misery and turbulence, but we never really find out where it's all going or how everything relates. As we'll see, some think the movie ultimately fails, as it lacks meaning and doesn't convey a point. Given how this handbook's main idea is to interpret popular culture elements as making a philosophical point, this raises the obvious question: what can possibly be the point that *Magnolia* is making, if it has been criticized so often as making no sense at all?

While IMDB (2021a) describes the movie as "an epic mosaic of interrelated characters in search of love, forgiveness, and meaning in the San Fernando Valley," PTA, having grown up himself in Los Angeles and Hollywood, initially didn't intend it to be epic. He started writing the script after being inspired by a line from a song by Aimee Mann: "Now that you've met me, would you object to never seeing me again?". PTA first envisioned it as an intimate story focusing on Claudia Wilson Gator, who utters these words in one of the movie's many emotional scenes. "I wanted to make something that was intimate and small-scale, and I thought that I would do it very, very quickly," PTA recounts. He "started to write and well, it kept blossoming" (Patterson 2000), a quote providing one plausible explanation for the movie's title. The end result has been called "epic" by PTA himself (Patterson 2000), "audacious" (Bukowski 2019) but also "sprawling, sloppy" and "overindulgent" (Colburn 2019) and a "grandiose – albeit frequently entertaining – mess" (Zelevinsky 2000).

Magnolia: Characters and Storylines

Some of the frustration that critics and viewers experience could revolve around one of the many characters and storylines, almost each of which is as troubled or troubling and as depressed or depressing as the other. The movie relentlessly depicts each character's torments and hardships.

One memorable storyline includes the sexist Frank T.J. Mackey (Tom Cruise), a motivational speaker lecturing men on how to conquer women: "Respect the cock and tame the cunt!" He is the long-estranged son of Big Earl Partridge (Jason Robard), a former TV show producer who left Frank after cheating on his wife and let Frank take care of her when she was dying. Earl himself is now on his deathbed, leaving his current wife Linda Partridge (Julianne Moore) in despair and regret, after having cheated on him. Perhaps the most loveable character in the movie is Phil Parma (Philip Seymour Hoffman), who nurses Earl and, unlike other characters, is emotionally stable, caring, and trustworthy.

Another storyline features cocaine addict Claudia Wilson Gator (Melora Walters) who accuses her father Jimmy Gator (Philip Baker Hall) of sexual abuse in her past. Jimmy can't remember the abuse, hasn't seen his daughter in 10 years, and is now dying of cancer with only 2 months to live. Claudia meets the archetypical "good cop" Jim Kurring (John C. Reilly) who comes to check in on her and her loud music. Quickly, Officer Jim falls in love with Claudia.

Two other storylines involve two quiz kids. There is the now aged and emotionally troubled Quiz Kid Donnie Smith (William H. Macy) who used to be a famous child contender on Jimmy Gator's TV show "What Do Kids Know?" produced by Big Earl Partridge. Donnie is now forgotten and struggling, both financially (being

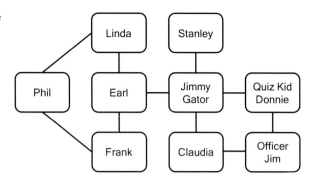

Fig. 1 Relations between the main characters

fired from his job) and emotionally (being insecure about his looks and afraid to approach his love interest, bartender Brad). Then there is Stanley Spector (Jeremy Blackman), a prodigy currently contending on the same TV show and under a lot of pressure from his father to break a quiz show record and take home big prize money (Fig. 1).

Things that Have Happened (to Happen)

The lives of the movies' main characters are revealed to be intertwined, either by shared pasts, or because the fateful events in the movie bring them together. There are two obvious things they all have in common. First, they all live in the same place (Los Angeles' San Fernando valley) and time (this one day and night depicted in the movie). Second, they are all trying to deal with things having happened or happening to them. While I'll go into the main events depicted in the movie and how they impact their lives in the next section, let's focus on their pasts first.

The struggle to come to terms with harms done in their past, whether it be child neglect (Frank), parental abuse (Claudia), or bullying (Donnie and Stanley), is indeed one main theme in the movie. Their past is still haunting them, leading them to become misogynistic assholes (Frank), estranged from their father (Frank and Claudia), ashamed and afraid that they will never be able to love, or that others will never love them back (Claudia and Donnie). While some of these harms have been imposed on them, others are self-inflicted. We see people suffering from the consequences of their own choices, such as feeling regret (Linda and Earl) and guilt (Jimmy), but also from the lung cancer induced by smoking habits (Earl). Many of the dialogues reveal how each of the characters tries to deal with and reconcile themselves with their pasts and who they have become.

A key line in the movie is uttered by both Donnie and Jimmy, in different scenes: "As the Book says, we may be through with the past, but the past is not through with us." While childhood trauma provides for a rather extreme case in point, this holds for all of us. Our past makes us who we are. But if this is true, does it imply determinism, the philosophical view that everything is determined through a chain of cause and effect? Does it mean that there is no room for freedom or personal responsibility? Without trying to settle the intricate philosophical debate on free will (O'Connor and Franklin 2018), this claim does not necessarily deny it. As is illustrated in the movie, people do have the ability to overcome their challenges, to reconcile themselves with things in the past, and to make something of their lives in spite of what happened (Frames of Empathy 2019). While characters like Frank, Claudia, and Donnie can't change their pasts (or some of the events that happen to them in the movie), they can change how they deal with it.

This insight is key to stoicism, an important strand in ancient Greek thinking. As Epictetus (135 AD) already put it, "some things are in our control and others not." He goes on to offer the following advice: when confronted with something, we should ask yourselves "whether it concerns the things which are in our own control, or those which are not; and, if it concerns anything not in our control, be prepared to say that it is nothing to you." If it rains, it rains. Complaining or worrying about it is not going to change anything. If you can free yourself from your passions and from your deeply rooted tendency to react emotionally to things you cannot control, you reach what Stoics call *apatheia*. This is best translated as equanimity (instead of apathy or indifference), a kind of mental tranquility or steadfastness of the soul.

This kind of stoic attitude doesn't imply there is nothing you can do: you can choose to take an umbrella or to not let the rain affect your mood. The stoic's advice may assume that some things are determined and beyond your control, but not everything is. As we see in the movie, overcoming obstacles in life and changing one's attitudes toward those obstacles – for example, by forgiving another's wrongdoing – may be challenging but it is not impossible.

This piece of advice relates to an important coping mechanism to which we may resort when confronted with hardships, atrocities, and suffering. Instead of passively accepting whatever happens or actively trying to rebel against the gods (or atrocious humans or the laws of nature for that matter), we should try to find the middle road and try to accept what is inevitable while working on the things we can change. According to Epictetus, the latter includes not only our own decisions, but also our beliefs, desires, and attitudes toward things.

The focus of this chapter will not so much be on the things that happen and why they happen – some seemingly for a reason and other things seemingly out of the blue – but on people's attitudes toward those things, how they deal with and come to terms with them. As such, we will focus on the (all too) human tendency to try to make sense (particularly of the absurd).

When trying to heed the stoic's advice, an important distinction is that between causes and reasons (Davidson 1963). Some things, after all, happen for and because of a reason. People can intentionally and deliberately make things happen if they have a reason – for example a desire – for it to happen. Take Quiz Kid Donnie's plan to get braces. His reason for this is to impress bartender Brad. The elaborate plan he sets up to make dental surgery happen can be explained by referring to this reason.

Other things happen without a reason (in this sense of the word) and should be explained by what philosophers such as Davidson call "causes," not "reasons." The weather forecasts we see throughout the film – "partly cloudy, 82% chance of rain" –

are based on our insights in meteorological factors. Rain happens not because someone intends it but because of (all kinds of factors contributing to) growing water droplets in clouds.

Whenever we ask the infamous "why" question – why does something happen? – both causes and reasons can help answer it. When we uncover the reasons or causes behind something, it starts to make sense. This is why we are not puzzled when we see Donnie doing what he does or when we see rain falling from the sky.

WTF Happened?!?

But then there are times when we can't find a satisfying answer to the "why" question. Some things seem to happen without any possible explanation. These are instances where no (causal) explanation seems to work. In these cases, it seems hard or perhaps even impossible to find out what made these things happen or why. We often call these absurdities: things that do not make sense to us at all. There is one very obvious example in the movie.

In the movie's most memorable and epic but also controversial scene, hundreds and thousands of frogs, very much alive and kicking, start raining down from the San Fernando sky. On the one hand, anyone who disliked the movie will refer to this scene as being simply ludicrous. They either struggle to see what kind of sense the scene makes or are unhappy with every possible explanation or interpretation. On the other hand, fans love it, quite often because they think they have figured out its deeper meaning.

So what to make of it? Initially, the rain of frogs doesn't make any sense. Both the movies' characters and viewers go WTF were those frogs?!? In a telling exchange between film critics Roger Ebert and Joyce Kulhawik (n.d.), Ebert praises the movie for being "free and alive to surprise," while Kulhawik retorts by complaining: "It makes no sense!" Kulhawik's sentiment is widely shared among the movie's critics and viewers. Some literally stood up in the theater, threw up their hands and spouted expletives in frustration. Perhaps you shared this frustration, which is why you went online and are now reading this very chapter to finally discover what the scene really means.

Before trying to formulate my take on the scene's meaning, let us dwell for a minute on our response to it. If such a thing would happen in real life, we would blink our eyes and pinch our arm to convince ourselves that we are not dreaming or hallucinating. We might try to find shelter, like Donnie and Jim do, cuddle up with our moms, like Claudia does, or watch outside the window in astonishment and bewilderment, like Stanley does, muttering to ourselves: "This happens. This is something that happens."

But the fact that something happens doesn't imply that it makes sense. To see *that* something occurs is not the same as seeing *why* it occurs. When surprised and baffled, we cannot but continue searching for answers to our "why" question. We can try to find what is causing it, looking for a scientific explanation and a (set of) natural cause(s). We may even come to believe that *supernatural* causes are somehow involved. When faced with the utter absurdity of events like this, people simply cannot help themselves: they inevitably start looking for some kind of explanation, some kind of meaning, some way of making sense of it all.

As we watch the movie, we are of course not in the same situation as the movie's characters. After all, we are in the unique position of knowing that we are watching a piece of art, made by a writer and director who probably had good reasons for this scene. As viewers, we can look things up and read interviews with PTA. As such, we can attribute a different kind of meaning than the movie's characters can. Our "why" question is not the same as theirs. While they wonder why it's raining frogs, we can ask why there is this scene about raining frogs. Because we know the event is fictitious, we can stop looking for a scientific or supernatural explanation and ask why PTA wrote and directed this scene. Surely, we tell ourselves, he must have some kind of reason as to why the scene is in the movie, some kind of underlying message he was trying to get across.

So What Does It Mean?

Like any piece of art or pop culture, this scene and the movie more generally, can make sense and be meaningful for some but not others. Given how multiple interpretations are possible and even plausible, perhaps it is impossible to pinpoint exactly what "the point" of the scene is or to formulate and determine its meaning once and for all. *Magnolia* – and the ways in which people respond to it – reveals how different people see and give meaning to things in different ways (and also fail to do so in different ways). Crucial to interpreting the movie, and this scene in particular, is what it *does to* viewers.

While the scene may leave viewers frustrated, moved, or perhaps even enlightened, the one experience that they probably share is that of feeling surprised, mesmerized, and bewildered. The least one can say about the frog rain is that it is unexpected and seemingly at odds with the universe depicted in the movie. What happens clearly defies and upsets expectations and conventions.

This is a well-known technique in the literary and artistic genre known as "magic (al) realism" (Bowers 2004). Whereas fantasy, the most popular of contemporary cinematic genres, creates an entire new world or universe, where frog rains are likely dwarfed by intergalactic travel and nearly unlimited magic and superhero powers, magic(al) realism adds magical elements to an otherwise completely mundane universe (Davidson 2018). This is why, when watching *Magnolia*, the frog rain makes you go WTF?!? It introduces a completely unrealistic element, out of the clear blue sky, in an otherwise realistic world. "The story begins in the 'real world' and when something unreal happens, (...) the reader is never sure if the cause is supernatural or natural" (Davidson 2018). It is this discordance, this unexpected defiance of expectations that leads to the kind of surprise that magic(al) realism induces but fantasy does not. In the words of Roger Ebert, who praises this scene in particular, "what it transforms at the end is our expectation that every movie has to be dead in the water and be predictable and be formulaic and in the way we expect it to."

Now, freaky things occur not only in works of fiction but also in real life. When they do, people's expectations about the world are upset as they fail to see how and why they (can) occur. In these cases, their deeply rooted tendency to make sense is frustrated. In fact, it is in exactly these instances that we become aware of this tendency and how it has been at play in the background in our day-to-day lives. When we see rain falling from the sky, we know how to interpret and explain this. Only when we *fail* to make sense of things does it become obvious that we can't help but try to make sense of things. When we see frogs falling from the sky, things stop making sense, but we still try to make sense of it. How could this have happened? What does this all mean?

One way of finding meaning in what seems devoid of meaning is to look for scientific explanations. Frog rains have actually occurred in real life. Apparently, small tornadoes forming over water can pick up lightweight frogs and then lose strength over land, causing the lifted frogs to literally rain from the sky (Layton n.d.). By researching, one can come to understand how strange phenomena are caused and explained by the same laws of nature that we know to be at work with other, more regular phenomena (such as strong winds and rains). This satisfies our thirst for sense: "ah, now I see how this works."

In fact, when quiz kid Stanley is reading at the library, one of the books on his desk is by Charles Fort, who studied exactly the kind of freaky and weird phenomena displayed in the movie. In *The Book of the Damned* (1919), Fort refers to "damned data (...) that science has excluded." He studies what you could call "anomalous phenomena": things for which no scientific explanation is immediately available and which are consequently rejected or ignored. It is actually through Fort, whom PTA describes as "a wonderful writer," that PTA had learned about frog rains (Konow 2000).

Things that Coincide

In *Magnolia*, the frog rain is not the only example of such rare and freak cases. In the opening scene, the narrator, voiced by magician Ricky Jay, tells three such stories. One revolves around 17-year-old Sydney Barringer whose "unsuccessful suicide suddenly became a successful homicide." Sydney accidentally got shot by his mom after jumping off their apartment building's roof. The suicide would have been unsuccessful (a safety net below would have cushioned his fall) but Sydney happened to pass in front of the window of the room where his mom fired a shot at (but missed) his dad, killing Sydney unintentionally.

Coincidences – literally things that coincide at the same time and place – often make perfect sense. When it rains, we get wet. And because we can explain why these things go together, we can see how the causal story goes or what the underlying reason is. When Jim knocks on Claudia's door for the first time, the reason is clear (at least to us, not to Claudia): Claudia's neighbor called the cops as she wanted the loud music and noise to stop. No surprise there.

But while there is a clear reason why the police showed up, these particular two people meeting each other can still be claimed to be a coincidence, in the sense of a rarity, like Sydney Barringer's death or raining frogs. After all, it could have been any other cop paying Claudia a visit. And even after having met that first time, the rest of their story could have gone differently in so many ways.

In a sense, you could say that all of our lives involve a ton of coincidences, where the actual outcome – our lives and our world right now – is only one of a seemingly infinite number of possibilities. Just like Jim and Claudia getting together, each of our own lives can be considered a freak accident, given how many alternative paths to other possible outcomes exist and existed at any given stage. Perhaps the chances of you being born, with your unique genetic code, were infinitesimally small, as it required one particular sperm fertilizing one specific egg. Yet, here you are.

The rare but simultaneous occurrence of things or events with no causal connection is called "synchronicity." Psychoanalyst Carl Jung (1960 [2012]) described this as "meaningful coincidence" and stressed how the human mind connects such events and sees them as meaningfully related. He gives the example of listening to one of his patients, who told Jung about a dream she had, in which she received a "golden scarab." Jung suddenly heard a noise behind him, opened up his window and caught a "creature in the air as it flew in. It was the nearest analogy to a golden scarab one finds in our latitudes, a scarabaeid beetle" (Jung 1960 [2012], §832). Of course, Jung and his patient thought this could not be one of those things, this could not be just a matter of chance, especially not given the symbolic meaning of scarabs in Egyptian mythology.

Such coincidences, as freaky as they might be, are not without scientific explanation. While a first kind of explanation is causal (remember how frog rains are caused by waterspouts and strong winds), a second kind is statistical. According to the so-called "law of truly large numbers" or what statistician David Hand (2014) calls "the Improbability Principle," extremely unlikely occurrences are bound to happen, as long as there is a truly large amount of cases. While rolling a Yahtzee or winning the lottery is very unlikely on any given try, it's almost guaranteed to happen if you roll the dice thousands of times or if thousands of people participate. When it happens, we all scream out how big of a coincidence it is, but we need not invoke God or fate to explain it. These things happen all the time, because they are bound to happen in a universe with enough time and opportunity (and lottery participants).

So while the odds of frogs raining at a particular time and place (which requires the simultaneous occurrence of small frogs, waterspouts, and strong gusts of wind) and of someone in particular being shot by his own mother while passing by the window are extremely low, given enough time and opportunity, such things are bound to happen.

Despite this, when such events do happen, people cannot help but look for meaning behind and in them. Instead of seeing synchronicity as the kind of thing that is bound to happen to a person many times during a long lifespan, people attribute some kind of sense to it. They may, like the cops at Sydney Barringer's untimely death, start to look for the often intricate and complex processes – physical, biological, and psychological in nature – which led up to the rare coincidence. But they may also consider it "fate" or, like Jim does when meeting Claudia, God's will that things play out as they do.

And even when our attempts to see the bigger picture fail and we can't fathom why something happened, we still tell ourselves, "this can't simply just have happened." And so we desperately try to force it to make sense. After recounting such "stories of coincidence and chance, of intersections and strange things told," the narrator voices our systematic need and urge to imbue them with meaning and stresses how we cannot avoid or stop doing exactly that: "It is in the humble opinion of this narrator that this is not just 'something that happened'. This cannot be 'one of those things'. This, please, cannot be that. And for what I would like to say, I can't. This was not just a matter of chance. These strange things happen all the time."

In a statistician's eyes, the narrator is both right and wrong. Sure, "these strange things happen all the time"; given the vast amount of time passed and people on the planet, these things are indeed bound to happen. But when something like this occurs, it is also not "just one of those things" or "just a matter of chance" ... at least to some people. After all, one can understand that (given the Improbability Principle) things *like this* are bound to happen, and yet one can still wonder why *this one particular thing* happened, at this specific place and time, to this specific person. Sure, someone will likely win the lottery, but *why me*?

The scientific answer, of course, is that there is no deeper reason. Statistically speaking, someone had to win, and it just happened to be you. While this provides a rationally satisfactory answer to the "why" question, a lot of people will not find it emotionally satisfactory. Why, of all dads, does *my* dad need to die from lung cancer (while not all others who smoke do)? Why, of all people, Donnie might ask himself, is it me who gets his teeth knocked out by a frog raining down from the sky? The thought that things like this are eventually going to happen and that it might as well happen to you (without there being a specific reason why you) can be unsatisfying, and thus lead one to seek out a deeper meaning.

If things as strange as these happen – all the time, occasionally, or even very rarely – we cannot help but look for a cause or a reason that helps us understand why. As sense-making creatures, we find it difficult to accept that some things don't make sense. We do not *want* it to simply be one of those things. "This, *please*, cannot be that. And for what I would *like* to say, I can't." We desperately want things to have meaning and, like the narrator, beg for them to do so. This is why we sometimes imbue meaning where there is none or why we hope that something more (like fate or God) is at play. While this is not rational, it is perfectly natural and all too human.

Sense-Making Stories

People who have a strong psychological need to believe in fairy tales, marvels, or superstition, Charles Fort (1919) argues, are not all that different from those of us who have a strong psychological need to make scientific sense of things. While scientific and statistical explanations can quench some people's thirst for meaning, others invoke supernatural explanations, referring to "fate" or "God's will." While these are obviously not on the same par, epistemically speaking, they both serve to satisfy our need to make sense.

People, like coincidences, can be freaky and defy expectations. Like events, human behavior can be unexpected, weird, and inexplicable. Think of Claudia, who meets officer Jim – who actually cares about her – even though she thinks she doesn't deserve it at all. Or think of your reaction to Tom Cruise's misogynistic character Frank T.J. Mackey. Probably you started off wondering why on earth he is such a prick. When we try to make sense of people's behavior and personality, we can reason as psychologists and try to discover how these are formed by his background, history, and past experiences. This is exactly what the female reporter is doing when asking Frank about his mother and when we come to learn how Frank was neglected by his father who left him care for his sick and dying mother. As we come to know more about his background, his actions become easier to understand.

Crucial in sense making are the stories that we tell each other and ourselves. We construct narratives all the time, about who we are and the world we live in. Through such narratives, we impose order on chaos and meaning on what is initially meaningless. The stories that we tell help us see how things relate to each other in meaningful ways. These stories can be scientific (statistical, physical, and biological when it comes to the natural world, psychological when it comes to the human world) but also spiritual, religious, superstitious, emotional, and so on.

And when nothing works and something refuses to make any kind of sense, the human mind has another trick in the book: it can make us believe that it never happened. Now, what we usually do, when we cannot wrap our heads around something, is look for additional information, talk to other people, and find a way to adapt our beliefs to the outside world. This is necessary for us to attain knowledge and arrive at the truth, which in one prominent philosophical account consists in our beliefs corresponding to reality. But another (epistemically speaking) inferior way of resolving this tension is to adapt the world to our beliefs, so to speak. By denying that something occurred, we hold on to our beliefs and ignore those aspects of the world that do not fit with them. In *Magnolia*, the narrator voices this perfectly relatable response: "Well, if that was in a movie, I wouldn't believe it."

Note that both denial and other sense-making strategies are obviously different than scientific explanations, and should be evaluated differently in regard to their accuracy and truthfulness. Meteorological explanations of real-world frog rains are much more likely to be true – i.e., to accurately track and describe the factors that cause such a natural event – than superstitious or supernatural explanations. That does not mean, however, that only scientific explanations are worth our while. If your father dies, someone can point out how smoking has damaged the small air sacs in his lungs and made it more probable for him to develop lung cancer. While that scientific explanation would be accurate and true, it doesn't help you deal with your loss or reconcile yourself with the fact that you will never be able to talk to your dad anymore. If you're not looking for truth but for solace, other stories can make much more sense.

Of course, the fact that religious, supernatural, or symbolic stories often make sense, does not make them true. Fathers dying, frogs raining, people winning the lottery, and psychoanalysts catching scarab beetles are no valid reason to conclude that miracles happen or that God exists. When making claims like this, the truth matters and such events can and will occur even if no omnipotent deity exists. The argument that such a being does exist because "these strange things happen all the time" is not valid, especially given that science can provide a better, simpler (causal or statistical) explanation. Still, that doesn't keep people from wanting or seeking a deeper meaning.

In Search of Deeper Meaning

Sense-making strategies (both scientific and not) help us grasp factual, natural, psychological and emotional phenomena, which vary from outlandish and seemingly absurd to more mundane and ordinary. In all those instances, these strategies can also fail. Perhaps you think that the causal "water tornado" explanation cannot explain the magnitude of the movie's frog rain. Or perhaps you think that Frank's childhood may explain the kind of hate that Frank feels toward his father but not his generalized contempt toward women. Or you can come to *understand* what made Frank into who he is and accept the psychological explanation of his personality (which arguably makes sense by the end of the movie) but refuse to think his sexism is *justified*.

Take scientific explanations, which in some cases are considered insufficient and unsuccessful. Those who claim that certain events are without a scientific explanation are not only those with anti-scientific attitudes or who are particularly gullible or prone for conspiracy theories. After all, there are a lot of questions science cannot now answer. (It might be able to answer some such questions in the future, but others probably never will be.) What exactly is love and how come we fall in love with some people but not with others? What is the meaning of life? Are we the only planet inhabited by sentient creatures? Why do cats purr? Interestingly, when people – rightly or wrongly – believe that science has no answer, they don't stop their quest for meaning. Quite often, they try to find a "deeper" meaning, typically moving from scientific to more symbolic readings of what happened.

Think again of the raining frogs. Perhaps the most popular sense-making strategy has viewers refer to the biblical event described in Exodus 8:2, where raining frogs are described as one of the plagues that God bestows on Egypt for refusing to free the Israelites from enslavement: "And if thou refuse to let them go, behold, I will smite your whole territory with frogs." In fact, *Magnolia* is dotted with Biblical Easter eggs, with the numbers 8 and 2 popping up in meeting times, apartment numbers, street signs, and posters (Heron 2018). It is also anticipated in the last line of the much discussed rap that young Dixon performs for officer Jim: "When the sunshine don't work, the good Lord bring the rain in."

As in the Bible, *Magnolia*'s frog rain arguably constitutes a form of punishment. Dying Earl, for example, suffers from the inability of voicing his regrets to those close to him. The frog rain also forces Jimmy to continue to live his life in solitude, with both his daughter and his wife having abandoned him. Similarly, the rain seems to bring some kind of salvation or catharsis to other characters, such as Claudia, Jim, Donnie, Stanley, and Frank. Like the Israelites, they seem liberated, freed from a burden they were forced to carry.

We can see the appeal of such a "deeper" meaning. Given the many references to the Exodus passage in the movie, *surely* this is what PTA wanted to get across. Obviously, the best explanation is a symbolic, not a meteorological one. Note how movie viewers and critics love to debate such scenes. It simply can't be the case, they argue, that this scene is there for no reason at all. It is also why they get frustrated if they can't see its meaning and why it feels good to come to learn an interpretation that finally makes sense. When we experience an "Aha!-moment" of insight, we feel good as dopamine rushes to that part of our brain that is involved in problem-solving and produces feelings of "relief, ease, and joy" (Tik et al. 2018).

In his own interpretation of the scene, Roger Ebert (2008) also refers to Exodus and suggests that the scene signifies the need for the characters – and for all of us – to let go of their "fears, shames, sins." According to Ebert (2008), the movie works as a parable: "The message of the parable, as with all good parables, is expressed not in words but in emotions. After we have felt the pain of these people, and felt the love of the policeman and the nurse, we have been taught something intangible, but necessary to know."

So what is this lesson? What can we learn from the parable that *Magnolia* is telling?

Wise Up

Some viewers find the biblical interpretation of the WTF?!? scene lacking. Why, they ask, do some characters seem to be punished and others liberated? And what about PTA himself admitting to not knowing about Exodus 8:2 when writing the sequence for the first time (Konow 2000)?

For an answer to these questions, let us focus on yet another remarkable scene in *Magnolia*. In another clear example of magical realism earlier on in the movie, Claudia, Jim, Jimmy, Donnie, Earl, Phil, Linda, Frank, and Stanley suddenly and consecutively sing along with Aimee Mann's song *Wise Up*. As they sing the lyrics "no, it's not going to stop; till you wise up," viewers are likely to go WTF!?! a first time (Viau 2015).

While the movie shows each of these characters going through different battles and struggles – Claudia's addiction, Jimmy's and Earl's terminal illness, Donnie's frustrations, Linda's regrets, Stanley's embarrassment, and so on – the song's lyrics invite them to wise up and rise to the challenge. As long as they don't, things won't improve. Wising up can mean different things in different circumstances. It can mean that you start demanding respect or telling others that you too are able to give love and deserve to be loved. "I really do have love to give! I just don't know where to put it!," Quiz Kid Donnie proclaims. And similarly, Stanley ultimately stands up to his dad, saying that he "needs to be nicer."

It can mean speaking the truth, as painful as it may be, to those you love or hate. It can mean acknowledging your own mistakes and trying to move past them. Take Earl's life lesson for Phil on his deathbed: "Don't ever let anyone ever say to you, 'You shouldn't regret anything'. Don't do that, don't! You regret what you fucking want! And use that, use that, use that regret for anything, any way you want."

Wise up, Earl seems to insist, instead of letting regret and remorse dominate your life. According to Jade Bukowski (2019), both the frog rain and the *Wise Up* scene help in conveying a single, coherent message.

> The frog rain that plagues the San Fernando Valley as our characters' tales all come to a climax may come as a shock to those with their feet firmly planted on the ground of the film's reality. It has caused people I've watched it with to literally turn to me the moment it begins and exclaim, "what?!". But it genuinely fits like the next logical puzzle piece after "Wise Up." From its very first frame, *Magnolia* is not subtle, and this sequence is no exception. Anderson goes to extremes to teach lessons, to invoke his parable (...). "But if you refuse to let them go, behold, I will smite all your territory with frogs." If we can't learn to let go of our trauma, our regrets, our shame, how can we ever hope for something better? Eventually, the film resorts to this literal act of divine intervention in an attempt to get its characters to "wise up," and boy, does it. (Bukowski 2019)

Each of the characters in the movie are experiencing dramatic and weird times, struggling with often major issues such as death, sickness, abuse, regret, shame, and so on. While the frogs arguably visualize the magnitude of these adversities and the chaos they wreck, the *Wise Up* scene is about the need and challenge of dealing with these issues. And it seems that, in the end, our key characters indeed do succeed in wising up. Often with the help of others, torment can shift into acceptance, and lives that first seemed to be inescapably damaged can be turned into something beautiful. This goes for Frank who, with the help of Phil, is reunited with his dad and spills his guts to him. It seems to hold for Donnie who is beaten down by frogs but helped back up by officer Jim. And it definitely goes for Claudia who is reunited with her mom and, in the very last shot of the movie, breaks the invisible fourth wall, looks straight into the camera and smiles. As officer Jim is opening up to her, the words to yet another Aimee Mann song – "Save Me" – drowns out his words and her smile strongly suggests that she can let her past be her past and move on to a brighter, more hopeful future.

More than One Meaning

While both the *Wise Up* and the frog rain scene obviously have symbolic import, and while Bukowski's interpretation may be a plausible one, attempts like this to articulate the meaning of a scene or a movie in some unambiguous and definite way, hardly ever do them justice. While PTA's call to wise up in light of adversity can arguably be taken quite literally, the frog rain scene – and this holds an important point about interpreting works of art more generally – can actually have many different meanings for different viewers.

Here is PTA's reaction when asked whether he wants viewers "to interpret the [frog rain] scene in their own way."

> Absolutely. I'm normally not a big fan of that; I generally like to make my points. But there are some times where if you pull it off properly, you can put something on the plate of the viewer and go, "You know what? However you want to decipher this, you can." And there absolutely is no wrong way. If you want to reference the Bible, that's good; if you want to link it to something else you can. (Konow 2000)

When asked whether the rain frog should be understood in biblical terms, PTA respond that non-biblical interpretations are possible and even plausible.

> Yeah, biblical. Or the non-biblical version of rain of frogs which is just, you know, sort of clippings of stories where bizarre occurrences would happen. Where a farmer wakes up and there's a field of frogs (...). I thought hearing that your dad is going to die is as bizarre as hearing that frogs are falling from the sky. (Anderson 2017)

If you follow PTA here, more than one interpretation of the frog rain scene – or any other movie, song, poem, painting, or sculpture – is plausible. What matters most for PTA is that the scene makes *emotional* sense, rather than scientific or biblical sense. Important here is that PTA himself was actually going through a rough time himself when writing *Magnolia*'s script. His reference to "hearing that your dad is going to die" not only refers to Claudia (i.e., Jimmy) and Frank (i.e., Earl) but also to himself. After all, PTA lost his father, Ernie Anderson, in 1997.

In one interview, PTA recounts how the frog rain relates to this unsettling period in his life.

> So when I read about the rain of frogs, I was going through a weird, personal time. I don't want to get too personal, but maybe there are certain moments in your life when things are so fucked up and so confused that someone can say to you, "It's raining frogs," and that makes sense. That somehow makes sense as a warning; that somehow makes sense as a sign. I started to understand why people turn to religion in times of trouble, and maybe my form of finding religion was reading about rains of frogs and realizing that makes sense to me somehow. (Konow 2000)

Instead of endorsing a specific meaning of the frog rain scene, PTA suggests here that its purpose lies in conveying a specific kind of feeling: the kind of disorientation you experience when the rug is pulled from under your feet and your sense of normalcy and your (set of expectations about the) world are turned upside down.

When Things Don't Make Sense

Think again of Joyce Kulhawik's outcry "it makes no sense!" and of your very own WTF?!? reaction after watching it rain frogs. To induce that feeling was the whole point! Note how a scene is supposed to be utterly meaningless if it is meant to have viewers experience the kind of disorientation that we all experience when confronted with what makes no sense. The *point* of the scene then is to be *pointless*. In fact, it can be interpreted as revealing how pointless it can be to keep looking for some further point, some deeper meaning, to coincidental events.

In this respect, the complaint that "it makes no sense" is beside the point. Both the characters in and the viewers of the movie experience the need to make sense of things, but struggle and fail to do so. In order to let the audience not only *see* the characters struggle but also *feel* how lost they are in life, PTA worked in a scene that made absolutely no sense at all. (Note how some critics, like Vladimir Zelevinsky (2000), argue that the film fails in this respect as well: "I didn't believe a second of it. Not one iota of it makes any emotional or psychological sense.")

It is when our sense-making capacities fail that we become aware of how they usually work. Inevitably and continuously we tell ourselves (and others) stories that highlight some aspects of what happens and weave in new elements. When something happens, we give it a place in a larger narrative, which can be scientific, emotional, or existential. When a man is diagnosed with cancer, a scientist looks for an explanation of why and how cancer cells developed in his body, the people who love him will try to say goodbye, and the man himself will look back at his life. They all have their stories to tell, which serve as frameworks to attribute meaning to the things that happen and have happened.

Psychologists have long acknowledged the fact that "people have a need for meaning; that is, a need to perceive events through a prism of mental representations of expected relations that organizes their perceptions of the world" (Heine et al. 2006, p. 88). When people encounter events, they frame them in larger pictures that make those events plausible and to be expected. People depend on meaning frameworks to make sense of their experiences, and when these expected associations are violated, the offending anomaly is often either assimilated into the existing meaning framework, or their meaning framework is altered to accommodate the violation.

When fathers die and frogs rain, our expectations about the world are violated. When this happens, we can stick to our stories and make such things fit. Both scientific and religious frameworks can, for example, help accommodate such things. Another well-known strategy here is denial: when something doesn't make sense, we (choose to) ignore it as irrelevant or as something that never happened. In both cases, our subjective sense-making urgency wins: objective reality is either incorporated in or excluded from our sense-making story.

But we can also change our stories. When a scientific theory has been falsified, we try to revise it or discard it altogether and look for a better one. And we can also do the same at the interpersonal, emotional, and existential level. We're not stuck to our stories: the sense we make and the meaning we attribute to things is not fixed but depends on stories that are ours to tell. Just as Earl tells Phil that he can use regret any way he wants, so *Magnolia* itself seems to suggest that people are not doomed to repeat the same mistakes over and over again but can take their lives in their own hands and turn them around.

When confronted with turbulence, absurdities, and loss, we can remind ourselves of the stoic strategy of distinguishing what is under our control and what is not.

While we can't prevent fathers from dying or frogs from raining, we can – at least to some extent – determine how to deal with those things. Realizing and accepting that some things simply happen, for no apparent reason at all, is a first step in this respect. The same applies to things that enrich our lives as well. Instead of trying to explain or make sense of what is happening when you fall in love or make new friends, the best way is probably to just let it happen, without asking too many questions. In all of these cases, there is often no use in trying to make or prevent them from happening or even in trying to make sense of them.

PTA himself captures this thought well in an interview: "You get to a point in your life, and shit is happening, and everything's out of your control, and suddenly, a rain of frogs just makes sense. You're staring at a doctor who is telling you something is wrong, and while we know what it is, we have no way of fixing it. And you just go: "So what you're telling me, basically, is that it's raining frogs from the sky" (Heron 2018).

While we can make sense of and thus attribute meaning to movie scenes, no matter how unexpected they might be, this meaning can differ from viewer to viewer. Perhaps you think the frog rain symbolizes the liberation of some characters or the punishment of others who fail to free themselves from their past. Perhaps it reminds you of that time where you were struggling to make sense of things, being forced to deal with emotional issues yourself. But perhaps you're not convinced by any of the above scientific, religious, symbolic, or emotional interpretations and think the raining frogs are, well, meaningless. Perhaps none of the available explanations or justifications seems adequate to you. That does not imply that the scene, movie, or director has failed. In fact, if the aim is to illustrate how things can be devoid of meaning, and to suggest that we sometimes simply have to deal with that, the scene succeeds by not making any sense at all.

The Absurd

Being struck by utter meaninglessness comes close to what Albert Camus, a nineteenth century French existentialist philosopher, called "the absurd." While human beings cannot help but ask what the meaning of existence and the purpose of life is, Camus argues that there is no answer to those questions. The universe remains silent about it. According to Camus, no scientific, teleological, metaphysical, or human-created answer can ever be adequate in this respect. This is what Camus calls "the absurd": the paradoxical tension between our deeply rooted tendency to ask such ultimate questions on the one hand and our inability to find (and the impossibility of finding) adequate answers on the other.

In his "The Myth of Sisyphus," Albert Camus (1942 [2005]) captures the notion of absurdity in the image of Sisyphus, who has to push his rock up the mountain over and over again. Like Sisyphus, we cannot help but ask why. What is the meaning of it all? Ultimately, our fragile attempts to answer that question come tumbling back down. We have a similar experience when confronted with things happening to us that seem devoid of any meaning.

To be clear, the absurd does not simply refer to things out there that in some way would be meaningless. The idea is not that some things make sense while others do not. Instead, the absurd only arises in the interaction between things out there (an objective component) that we, as meaning-seeking creatures (a subjective component) fail to attribute meaning to. Instead of being a characteristic of the (meaningless, chaotic, objective) outside world or of (sense-making, order-loving, subjective) human nature, the absurd arises from the clash between the two. In a world without agents like us, that can see meaning in and give meaning to things, the absurd would cease to exist.

To existentialists like Camus, and also Jean-Paul Sartre, this subjective need to make sense of things matters a lot. It is at play in *Magnolia*'s narrator: "It is in the humble opinion of this narrator that this is not just 'something that happened'. This cannot be 'one of those things'." Like us, the narrator refuses to admit that there are things that lack meaning. This provides a clear illustration of the absurd, because we have an instance where our all too human tendency to seek meaning and to make sense is frustrated. Like Sisyphus, the narrator, the viewers of, and also the characters in the movie find themselves confronted with something meaningless, without any purpose or order.

In existentialism, the absurd can reveal itself both when ordinary life repeats itself over and over and when utterly extraordinary things happen. Just like Sisyphus, we can find ourselves trapped in the same, meaningless routine of getting up, going to work, coming back home, falling asleep on the sofa, et cetera et cetera. Eat, sleep, work (and/or play, rave, ...), repeat. Given the repetitive nature of a lot of work, especially in capitalist societies like ours, we quickly see how the extreme example of Sisyphus can still be symbolic for quite a few contemporary experiences. The cinematic example here is *Groundhog Day*, the 1993 cult classic where Bill Murray lives through the same day again and again. The absurdity in everyday life lies not so much in one specific event or phenomenon, but in the same thing happening over and over again (perhaps again, in the narrator's words, "all the time").

But there is also a sense in which the absurd can hit you all of the sudden and out of the blue. In the words of Camus (1942 [2005]), "At any street corner the feeling of absurdity can strike any man in the face" (p. 5). Coincidence or not, Quiz Kid Donny, who obsesses throughout the entire movie about getting dental surgery, gets struck in the face by one the raining frogs, ironically causing a fall that knocks out his front teeth. More metaphorically speaking, we all know the disconcerting experience of suddenly asking yourself why on Earth you are who you are and why you're living the life you're living.

So how do we respond to the absurd? How do we cope with this paradoxical and seemingly insolvable tension between the meaninglessness of our lives and world on the one hand and the deeply rooted thirst to attribute meaning on the other. If we cannot escape this absurdity, what can and should we do? How should we deal with the absurdity of life and the universe? Existentialists basically distinguish between three different ways of dealing with the absurd.

A first strategy is the one we have discussed before and that we all know too well. When faced with absurdity, our default reaction is to stubbornly persist and continue to look for (ever more) ways of making sense of what doesn't make sense. When confronted with the kind of phenomena that Charles Fort studied and science cannot (yet) explain, it is tempting to start believing in supernatural explanations. But you don't have to be superstitious to see the extent to which we rely on all kinds of sense-making stories. When parents die, we tell kids that they're up there somewhere, looking down, and that they will always be in our hearts. While scientifically untrue, these stories make much more emotional sense than a story about dad's cancerous lungs. When confronted with the absurd, the juxtaposition between our sense-making efforts and the reality that escapes those, this first strategy consists in persisting with the former, denying the latter, and imposing meaning on what resists such attempts.

A second strategy, in the face of the absurd, is to let the meaninglessness prevail. The most radical response that comes to mind, and that both Camus and Sartre discuss at length, is suicide. If nothing has meaning anymore, or if we no longer see sense or purpose in life, we cannot help but ask why we should continue living it. If we cannot escape absurdity, being caught between our yearning for and our inability to find meaning, life can easily come to seem pointless. Whether such a life is worth living surely seems an obvious question to ask.

Given the fundamental character of this question, Camus (1942 [2005]) calls suicide the "only one really serious philosophical problem (...). Deciding whether or not life is worth living is to answer the fundamental question in philosophy" (p. 3). In the face of absurdity, what is there to live for? Here, you can see how Camus' philosophy is not a theoretical enterprise but instead has an immense practical and existential urgency. Instead of merely investigating and analyzing the absurd, Camus is primarily interested in discovering how to avoid suicide and how to make life worth living in the full realization of it being meaningless. The crucial question that we as humans face is not so much whether God exists, or how to distinguish right from wrong, but whether life is actually worth living.

In *Groundhog Day*, Bill Murray's character repeatedly tries to commit suicide in attempts to escape the absurd repetition of ordinary life. Similarly, in *Magnolia*, several of the emotionally wrought characters contemplate suicide in response to their inability to reconcile themselves with their pasts. Suicide can be considered a way out of life's misery and absurdity and the emotional wreckage that comes with it. No longer able to live in this world and/or with themselves, those who consider suicide seek to solve the paradoxical tension between objective meaninglessness and our subjective quest for meaning by eradicating the latter. If you kill yourself, you kill off the need and search for meaning and are left with only the world that is void of any meaning. Is this the only way to deal with the absurd or is there another way of dealing with it that does not involve annihilation?

How to Deal with the Absurd

Indeed, there is a third strategy to deal with the absurd and this is the one that Camus favors. It basically consists in "dealing with it," somehow finding a middle road that does not give up on objective reality or subjective agency and accepts that there will always be this tension between the two. "Since existence itself has no meaning, we must learn to bear an irresolvable emptiness" (Aronson 2017). Interestingly, the very last line of Aimee Mann's *Wise Up* lyrics suggests this third possibility of coping with life's hardships. Next to nothing changing – "it's not going to stop" – on the one hand and wising up on the other, there is also the option of surrendering: "so just give up." While this can be interpreted as referring to suicide, it can also be interpreted as giving up on one's attempts to seek meaning in everything. Perhaps, we should not give up on life but on our often futile or otherwise wrongheaded attempts to attribute meaning to life.

According to Camus, this kind of giving up can be more like an active and wholehearted endorsement of absurdity, instead of a passive or apathic *je m'en fous* or *I don't care*. "Giving up" then does not mean some Buddhist annihilation of our desire (to find meaning, for example). Our eternal search for something that we can never attain isn't something to be eradicated; instead it is a perfectly healthy, natural instinct. According to Camus, we will never and are not supposed to be satisfied. When you are promised satisfaction, to have everything you want, like our consumer society tends to do, such a possibility is only an illusion (Brown n.d.).

Like Sisyphus who walks back down to his rock and accepts his tragic fate, we too can accept our condition (in French our "condition humaine") and take responsibility for our lives, as hopeless and meaningless as they might be. Keep calm and carry on, the (almost stoic) message seems to be. The fact that our lives are pointless, does not mean that we are doomed to be unhappy. In fact, we can continue to live our lives in full awareness and affirmation of our fate. As a response to absurdity, this is the exact opposite of suicide: it is about living our lives to the fullest, in defiance of their meaninglessness and futility (Maden 2019). Somewhere between acceptance and rebellion, we continue to live *in spite of* the absurd.

In his wonderful introduction to philosophy's big questions, "What Does It All Mean?", Thomas Nagel also takes on the question of life's meaning. Even if we come to see life as meaningless, Nagel argues, we can (and probably will) take life and ourselves seriously: "Perhaps it's ridiculous to take ourselves so seriously. On the other hand, if we can't help taking ourselves so seriously, perhaps we just have to put up with being ridiculous. Life may be not only meaningless but absurd" (Nagel 1987, p. 101).

While Camus believes we are condemned to absurdity by the human condition, he also thinks that is not necessarily a bad thing. In fact, it is by confronting and embracing this absurdity and heroically carrying on that we can live a truly authentic life. Even if life has no purpose, we can decide to live it wholeheartedly. Even if Sisyphus' damned struggle up the mountain is eternal and pointless, he can come to embrace it and find happiness in meaninglessness. We can basically do the same. "Real defiance in the face of an indifferent universe (...) means us being able to throw ourselves enthusiastically into our efforts while still realizing that they're not going to last" (Brown n.d.). The fact that all the smaller and bigger things that we can and often love to do – have breakfasts, visit supermarkets, talk with our partners or with strangers – do not matter in the long run, doesn't mean they can't be worthwhile.

In important respects, the main message of Camus is similar to that of Friedrich Nietzsche. Nietzsche (1882 [2019]) already argued that we face a crisis when we realize that our lives and the world do not have the meaning that we long them to have. But he also stressed the importance of affirming life in the face of this meaninglessness. While his nihilism – there is no objective meaning or value in life – might seem depressing or pessimistic, Nietzsche optimistically believed that at least some people should and can come to create their own value and heroically and vigorously affirm and embrace life. To find out whether you're among those people, Nietzsche asks you to imagine a "demon" that says to you: "This life as you now live it and have lived it, you will have to live once more and innumerable times more" (Nietzsche 1882 [2019], §341). If you – like Camus asks us to imagine Sisyphus – would have the power to welcome this and actually embrace having to go through the same things over and over again, you would pass Nietzsche's test of eternal recurrence.

After having declared God for dead, Nietzsche maintained, modern people like ourselves are no longer supposed to live up to His image or fear divine punishment when they fail. According to Nietzsche, the resulting loss of purpose, certainty, and solid ground is both unsettling and liberating. It is now up to us, Nietzsche proclaims. We can and should experiment in and with our lives, treat them as works of art, and create meaning and value ourselves where none is given (Hatab 1987).

Conclusion

Things happen all the time and people try to make sense of them all the time. While there are many possible interpretations of *Magnolia* and its key scenes, this chapter focused not so much on freak occurrences and coincidences, but on why and how people try to make sense of and come to terms with them. Telling scientific, religious, and emotional stories is one of the many ways in which we can attribute meaning to the (often strange things in the) world around us. Importantly though, those strategies can also fail. Following Albert Camus, we are confronted with the absurd, which refers not to some objective reality that makes no sense, but to the insolvable tension between our subjective but deeply rooted urge to make sense of things and the objective world that resists and remains devoid from meaning.

Magnolia, in this reading, makes the point that things do not always have a point or make sense. This interpretation can explain not only the reactions of the characters in the movie to weird things happening but also the claims of their director in interviews. In addition, it engages with the experiences and reactions of us, as viewers. If you were struck by the utter absurdity of the *Magnolia*'s main scenes, with your expectations and sense-making capacities failing you: good on you! Regardless of whether you were delighted by it, like Roger Ebert, or frustrated, like Joyce Kulhawik, you both experienced what absurdists like Camus thought was integral to being human. You experienced the fact that life and the universe refuse to make sense, regardless how much we try and would like to succeed.

Just like movie scenes can mean different things to different people, they can also be devoid of meaning. Some people see meaning where others do not. In different domains in our lives and societies, we deal with this in different ways. When we are talking about facts, science can help us understand what exactly those look like and explain how they come about. But when we are in the emotional and existential domain, other ways of making sense might be more appropriate.

Our sense of surprise, bewilderment, and frustration with the seemingly nonsensical scenes in *Magnolia* reveal how these scenes upset our basic psychological processes of sense-making. These processes are deeply rooted, inevitable, and often unnoticeable. We only become aware of them when confronted with things where these processes fail in making sense. As sense-making creatures, we struggle to come to terms not only with the kind of freaky coincidences and events in the lives of Sydney Barringer and our main characters in the San Fernando Valley, but also with other things we experience as "absurd": the loss of someone we love, the traumatic experiences of childhood, or the weird reactions people can have. When confronted with something that seemingly makes no sense, we typically refuse to say that this is just "one of those things that happened."

But instead of insisting that things should make sense, which is an important commitment for scientists trying to explain the world and for anyone who values the truth, we should sometimes simply accept that things do not (have to) make sense. This might be our best available response when confronted with loss, trauma, and regret or with love and joy for that matter. Perhaps there simply is no sense in hearing you're about to lose your dad. Just like PTA, the characters in the movie and to some extent also its viewers experience a roller coaster of bewilderment and sheer meaninglessness. Instead of explaining away the unexpected (in scientific, religious, or symbolic ways), we can simply and almost stoically recognize, accept, and embrace the absurd when it hits us in the face.

References

Anderson, Paul Thomas. 2017. WTF with Marc Maron. *Paul Thomas Interview*. https://www.youtube.com/watch?v=bv6xVEhtQnc.

Aronson, Ronald. 2017. Albert Camus. In *The Stanford encyclopedia of philosophy*, ed. Edward N. Zalta, Summer 2017 ed. https://plato.stanford.edu/archives/sum2017/entries/camus/.

Bowers, Maggie Ann. 2004. *Magic(al) realism*. New York: Routledge.

Brown, Gordon. n.d. The Millennial's Guide to Philosophy: Camus. *Primer Magazine*. https://www.primermagazine.com/2018/live/the-millennials-guide-to-philosophy-camus.

Bukowski, Jade. 2019. 'Magnolia' at 20: The emotional audaciousness of Paul Thomas Anderson's epic. Published on December 9, 2019. https://decider.com/2019/12/09/magnolia-20th-anniversary-paul-thomas-anderson/.

Camus, Albert. 1942 [2005]. *The Myth of Sisyphus*. Trans. Justin O'Brien. New York: Penguin Books.

Colburn, Randall. 2019. The best and worst of Magnolia's multiple melodramas. *AVClub*. https://www.avclub.com/the-best-and-worst-of-magnolia-s-multiple-melodramas-1836941555.

Davidson, Donald. 1963. Actions, reasons and causes. *Journal of Philosophy* 60:685–700.
Davidson, Lale. 2018. *The difference between magic realism and fantasy.* http://lunastation quarterly.com/the-difference-between-magic-realism-and-fantasy.
Ebert, Roger. 2008. *Tales of loneliness, in full flower. Rogerebert.com.* https://www.rogerebert.com/reviews/great-movie-magnolia-1999.
Ebert, Roger, and Joyce Kulhawik. n.d. *Magnolia.* https://www.youtube.com/watch?app=desktop&v=uXd9l0vgf3Q.
Epictetus. 135 AD. *The Enchiridion.* Trans. Elizabeth Carter. http://classics.mit.edu/Epictetus/epicench.html.
Fort, Charles Hoy. 1919. *The book of the damned.* New York: Boni and Liveright. https://archive.org/details/bookofdamnedbych00fortrich.
Frames of Empathy. 2019. *Magnolia: Reconciling with the past.* https://www.youtube.com/watch?v=m4e_S6jcpbo.
Hand, David J. 2014. *The improbability principle: Why coincidences, miracles, and rare events happen every day.* Farrar, Straus and Giroux. https://us.macmillan.com/excerpt?isbn=9780374535001.
Hatab, Lawrence J. 1987. Nietzsche, nihilism and meaning. *The Personalist Forum* 3 (2): 91–111.
Heine, S.J., T. Proulx, and K.D. Vohs. 2006. The meaning maintenance model: On the coherence of social motivations. *Personality and Social Psychology Review: An Official Journal of the Society for Personality and Social Psychology, Inc* 10 (2): 88–110. https://doi.org/10.1207/s15327957pspr1002_1.
Heron, Ambrose. 2018. 8 and 2 in Magnolia. *Filmdetail.* http://www.filmdetail.com/2008/01/12/8-and-2-in-magnolia/.
IMDB. 2021a. *Magnolia.* https://www.imdb.com/title/tt0175880/.
———. 2021b. *Paul Thomas Anderson: Quotes.* https://m.imdb.com/name/nm0000759/quotes.
Jung, Carl G. 1960 [2012]. *Synchronicity: An acausal connecting principle.* Princeton University Press.
Konow, David. 2000. Remember the power is yours. The power is in the writer. Paul Thomas Anderson. *Creative Screenwriting* 7:1. https://creativescreenwriting.com/magnolia/.
Layton, Julia. n.d. Can it really rain frogs? *HowStuffWorks.* https://science.howstuffworks.com/nature/climate-weather/storms/rain-frog.htm.
Maden, Jack. 2019. *Albert Camus on coping with life's absurdity.* https://philosophybreak.com/articles/absurdity-with-camus/.
Matchbox. 2017. *Hyperlink cinema and the prevalence of intertwining stories.* Published on January 17, 2017. https://the-artifice.com/hyperlink-cinema-stories/.
Nagel, Thomas. 1987. *What does it all mean? A very short introduction to philosophy.* Oxford: Oxford University Press.
Nietzsche, Friedrich. 1882 [2019]. *The Joyous Science.* Trans. Hill R. Kevin. London: Penguin Classics.
O'Connor, Timothy, and Christopher Franklin. 2018. Free will. In *The Stanford encyclopedia of philosophy,* ed. Edward N. Zalta, Spring 2021 ed. https://plato.stanford.edu/archives/spr2021/entries/freewill/.
Patterson, John. 2000. Magnolia Maniac. *The Guardian,* March 10, 2000. https://www.theguardian.com/film/2000/mar/10/culture.features.
Rotten Tomatoes. 2021. *Magnolia: Critics consensus.* https://www.rottentomatoes.com/m/magnolia.
Tik, Martin, Ronald Sladky, Caroline Di Bernardi Luft, David Willinger, André Hoffmann, Michael J. Banissy, Joydeep Bhattacharya, and Christian Windischberger. 2018. Ultra-high-field fMRI insights on insight: Neural correlates of the Aha!-moment. *Human Brain Mapping* 39 (8): 3241–3252.
Viau, Dan. 2015. *Cinema remembered: Magnolia and the "WISE UP" moment.* https://www.thatmomentin.com/cinema-remembered-magnolia-and-that-wise-up-moment/.
Zelevinsky, Vladimir. 2000. Magnolia: Overripe and wilted: Movie review. *The Tech* 119 (67) http://tech.mit.edu/V119/N67/Magnolia.67a.html.

Fight Club as Philosophy: I Am Jack's Existential Struggle

52

Alberto Oya

Contents

Introduction	1218
Summary of *Fight Club*	1219
Interpreting *Fight Club*	1222
The Moral of *Fight Club*	1229
Evaluating *Fight Club*'s Moral	1231
Conclusion	1234
End Notes	1234
References	1234

Abstract

The aim of this chapter is to analyze the movie *Fight Club*, directed by David Fincher, written by Jim Uhls, and first released in the fall of 1999. The movie is based on the homonym novel by Chuck Palahniuk, published in 1996. I will argue that *Fight Club* is to be understood in primarily existentialist, nonethical, and nonevidential terms, showing the struggle felt by each and every one of us to find a convincing answer to the question of what (if anything) counts as an authentic life that is worth living. Moreover, I will argue that the movie does not merely illustrate the struggle and the existential angst it engenders; it also advances, if not strictly speaking a theoretical answer grounded in an indisputable philosophical reasoning, then at least a practical way to face it. It is only after positively endorsing the claim that absolutely nothing (whatever it may be) externally imposed on a person can give their life ultimate meaning that a person is free to engage in a conscious, laborious, and exhausting attempt at self-affirmation, a full and positive endorsement of one's own authenticity.

A. Oya (✉)
IFILNOVA – Instituto de Filosofia da Nova (Universidade Nova de Lisboa), Lisboa, Portugal
e-mail: albertooya@fcsh.unl.pt

Keywords

David Fincher · Existentialism · Existential struggle · *Fight Club*

Introduction

Fight Club, directed by David Fincher and written by Jim Uhls, was first released in the fall of 1999. The movie is based on the homonym novel by Chuck Palahniuk, published in 1996 by the American publishing company W. W. Norton.[1] Despite initially not meeting the hoped-for box-office sales and receiving mixed criticism (mostly because it can easily be (mis)read as exalting and encouraging men to gratuitous violence), *Fight Club* eventually gained a devoted following. It is now commonly recognized, more than 20 years after its theatrical release, as a cult classic.

Fight Club is centered on the character of the Unnamed Narrator (played by Edward Norton) and how his life dramatically changes after meeting the characters of Marla Singer (played by Helena Bonham-Carter) and Tyler Durden (played by Brad Pitt). The fact that the protagonist remains unnamed throughout the story reflects the fact that he is depicted as lacking any peculiar traits of his own; he is a bit of a sponge. However, we can call him Jack since – after reading a set of short articles he finds in Tyler's house which are written in the first person from a human organ perspective ("I am Jack's medulla oblongata, without me Jack could not regulate his heart rate, blood pressure or breathing"; "I am Jack's colon ... I get cancer, I kill Jack") – he does sometimes indirectly refer to himself as "Jack" (e.g., "I am Jack's cold sweat"; "I am Jack's complete lack of surprise").

The movie follows Jack and Tyler as they create Fight Club which, at first, is simply an underground boxing club – an association of men who agree to engage in fights among themselves. As the movie progresses, however, Fight Club evolves – on Tyler's initiative with Jack unaware – into a violent military inspired sectarian group that goes by the name of Project Mayhem. Project Mayhem demands of its members an irrational and blind obedience to Tyler who (we eventually discover) is the split personality of Jack himself. The ultimate purpose of Project Mayhem is to blow up the city's financial district to bring about, in Tyler's words, "the collapse of financial history ... one step closer to economic equilibrium."

At first, *Fight Club* can be seen as simply the story of a solitary man suffering from a split personality disorder who, fed up with his monotonous life, creates a kind of underground men-only club where he and other disaffected men find relief from their stress by "enjoying" fighting among themselves. The fact that it evolves into Project Mayhem might exemplify their attempt to change their situation by engaging in violent actions of sabotage. But, on a superficial reading, that is as deep as the message might seem to go. Fortunately, *Fight Club* ultimately has a far more interesting philosophical meaning that goes way beyond fighting and its main character's split personality disorder.

My proposal in this chapter is to view *Fight Club* in purely existentialist, nonethical, and nonevidential terms, as a movie that demonstrates the struggle felt by each and every one of us to find a convincing answer to the question of what (if anything) counts as an authentic life that is worth living. The struggle is not ethical but existential in the sense that it is not about deciding what actions are (ethically) right or wrong, but about finding what way of life (if any) counts as an authentic life. In fact, the movie takes special care to detach itself from any purely ethical outlook, offering no real commentary on the morality of the actions described in it. Moreover, I will argue that the movie does not merely illustrate the struggle and the existential angst it engenders; it also advances an answer which, if it is not a strictly speaking theoretical answer grounded in an indisputable philosophical reasoning, is at least a practical way to face it. What is that answer? Embracing the fact that absolutely nothing (whatever it may be) externally imposed onto a person can give ultimate meaning to a person's life. Only then is one free to engage in a conscious, laborious, and exhausting attempt at self-affirmation, a full and positive endorsement of one's own authentic self – *that is*, that which makes a person the individual they are and not another. Ideally, this self-affirming exercise will overcome the existential struggle by resulting in the enjoyment of an authentic, self-governed life that is thus worth living.

Summary of *Fight Club*

At the start of the movie, Jack is caught up in a routine white-collar job in an insurance agency. He suffers from insomnia and is a compulsive shopper, "a slave" he tells us to the "Ikea nesting instinct. If I saw something clever, like a coffee table in the form of yin and yang, I had to have it." After six months without soundly sleeping, Jack goes to the doctor seeking a medical solution (e.g., sleeping pills). The doctor (played by Richmond Arquette) refuses to give him any. Jack begs, saying that he is in pain, but the doctor replies, "You wanna see pain? Swing by First Methodist Tuesday night. See guys with testicular cancer. That's pain."

Jack does, finds the group "Remaining Men Together," and pretends to be suffering from the disease to take part in the meetings. There he meets the character of Robert (Bob) Paulson (interpreted by Meat Loaf), a former champion bodybuilder. Bob's former steroid use led to his cancer and the removal of his testicles; his medical treatment has caused him to grow large breasts. The kind of attention and emotional support Jack receives brings him relief. "Bob loved me because he thought my testicles were removed too. Being there, pressed against his tits, ready to cry... This was my vacation." Jack's insomnia is cured. "Babies don't sleep this well." He thus becomes a self-confessed therapy group addict, attending meetings for people suffering from diseases of all kinds – from tuberculosis and kidney disease to skin cancer – all while pretending to be as sick as the rest of the participants.

The charade comes to an end, however, with the appearance of Marla Singer. Marla, like Jack, is a "tourist" who goes to therapy groups pretending to be sick. Although she never publicly exposes Jack's fraud, her presence at the meetings impedes his pretense, ending the relief he gets from the groups. "Marla, the big tourist... Her lie reflected my lie. And suddenly, I felt nothing, I couldn't cry. So, once again, I couldn't sleep." His insomnia returns, as does his incapacity to find any purposefulness or enjoyment in life. "Everywhere I travel, tiny life." On one of his frequent business flights, he laments "Every time the plane banked too sharply on take-off or landing, I prayed for a crash, or a mid-air collision... anything."

On another of those flights, Jack meets Tyler Durden, who introduces himself as a soap salesman. They have a short, rather bizarre chat where Tyler claims that the plane's oxygen masks are there simply to drug passengers in the event of an accident so that they "become euphoric, docile" and more easily accept their fate. He also explains that "One can make all kind of explosives using simple household items." When the plane lands, Jack discovers that the airport security officers have confiscated and turned all his luggage over to the authorities because it was vibrating. "Nine times out of ten," airport security tells him, "it's just an electric razor. But, every once in a while... it's a dildo. Of course, it's company policy never to imply ownership in the event of a dildo. We have to use the indefinite article, 'a' dildo, never 'your' dildo."

Jack's day worsens when he arrives at his apartment building only to discover that his apartment has been destroyed by a gas explosion. With no possessions and nowhere to go, Jack considers phoning Marla, but decides instead to phone Tyler; they meet at a bar later that night. Jack tells Tyler how lost he feels for having suddenly been deprived of all his possessions "I had it all. I had a stereo that was very decent, a wardrobe that was getting very respectable. I was so close to being complete." But Tyler criticizes his consumerist behavior, warning that "the things you own end up owning you."

After a few drinks, and now outside the bar, Tyler agrees that Jack can stay at his place, which turns out to be an old, crumbling, abandoned house in the suburbs. But first, Tyler asks Jack to do him a "favor." "I want you to hit me as hard as you can." Tyler overcomes Jack's initial reluctance by persuasively asking, "How much can you know about yourself if you have never been in a fight?" Tyler and Jack then engage in a mutually and freely agreed fight. To Jack's surprise, fighting with Tyler simply for the sake of fighting provides him with some relief, later reflecting that "after fighting, everything else in your life gets the volume turned down."

Over the next few nights, Tyler and Jack fight outside the bar, attracting the attention of other men who want to join in this type of fight. This leads to the creation of Fight Club, which at first is nothing more than a kind of underground club where men of all classes and statuses can find relief from their daily stress by engaging in freely agreed fights among themselves. Despite its first two rules, "You do not talk about Fight Club," Fight Club quickly grows, attracting new members who, fed up with their lives, are looking for a release. One of them is Robert Paulson, from Remaining Men Together. Marla Singer also appears again (although not at Fight Club) and engages in a purely sexual relationship with Tyler.

As Fight Club gets bigger, it becomes what could be deemed a formally organized club under Tyler's exclusive leadership. Tyler not only bestows Fight Club with some other protocolary rules which all its members must follow when fighting – *for example*, "[If] someone yells stop, goes limp, taps out, the fight is over" – but he also gives members "homework assignments," like start a fight with a total stranger and lose. These "homework assignments" progressively cease to be related to fighting and become more acts of vandalism. At first, they appear to have no ultimate purpose and do not involve extreme violence, like replacing the original airplane safety instruction cards where passengers are smiling with ones that show passengers screaming and thrashing about in terror. But gradually, Fight Club becomes an underground gang devoted to vandalism, with Tyler seeming to have the ability to capture and take advantage of its members' general discontent.

> I see in Fight Club the strongest and smartest men who have ever lived. I see all this potential, and I see squandering. God damn it! An entire generation pumping gas, waiting tables, slaves with white collars. Advertisements have us chasing cars and clothes, working jobs we hate so we can buy shit we don't need. We are the middle children of history, man. No purpose or place. We have no Great War, or great depression. Our Great War is a spiritual war. Our great depression… is our lives. We've all been raised by television to believe that one day we'll all be millionaires and movie gods and rock stars… but we won't. And we're slowly learning that fact. And we're very, very pissed off.

To Jack's surprise (because he cannot understand why Fight Club is evolving in this way and is unaware of Tyler's ultimate motivation), Fight Club ends up becoming a kind of militarized underground urban army under Tyler's strict command, headquartered in Tyler's house. "Why was Tyler Durden building an army? To what purpose? To what greater good? In Tyler we trusted." Admission guidelines to the house are strict. "If the applicant waits at the door for three days without food, shelter, or encouragement, then he may enter and begin his training."

Travelling in a car with Tyler and two unnamed members, Jack discovers that Fight Club has officially evolved into Project Mayhem, though neither Tyler nor the two members explain what it is. "The first rule of Project Mayhem is you don't ask questions." In the same scene, Tyler admits to having blown up Jack's apartment to encourage him to "Stop trying to control everything and just let go." This gets Jack to acquiesce to having a car accident so as to have (as Tyler puts it) "a near-life experience." Shortly after, Tyler disappears.

The acts of vandalism carried out by Project Mayhem become increasingly violent, including the use of homemade explosives. During one of these sabotage actions, Robert Paulson is shot in the head and killed by the police. Meanwhile, Jack finds various flight tickets in Tyler's name and realizes that he has been flying to different cities all over the country. Baffled by the situation, Jack decides to go to all the places Tyler has been to. To his surprise, he discovers that "Tyler has been busy setting up franchises [Fight Clubs/Projects Mayhem] all over the country" and that the purpose of Project Mayhem is to blow up the city's entire financial district. "One step closer to economic equilibrium." On his trip, a member mistakes Jack for Tyler. Totally bewildered, Jack goes back to his hotel room where he phones Marla. She calls him by the only name she knows him by: "Tyler Durden, Tyler Durden, you fucking freak!" After hanging up, Tyler suddenly appears in the room and Jack realizes that he and Tyler are in fact "the same person." Jack faints on the bed and Tyler again disappears.

Jack then goes looking for Marla, declaring his love for her and asking her to go to a safer place where neither he nor Tyler will be able to find her. Jack then unsuccessfully tries to stop Project Mayhem by giving himself up to the police, but even the officers are involved in Project Mayhem. They try to emasculate him by castrating him.

After managing to escape from the police station, and now aware that Tyler's followers are everywhere, Jack attempts to stop Project Mayhem alone. He identifies one of the buildings planned to be destroyed, goes there, and dismantles the bombs. Unfortunately, however, there are other bombs scattered throughout the city's skyscrapers. Tyler appears once again, starting a violent fight with Jack, which ends with Jack unconscious. When he comes round, he is bound and Tyler is standing in front of him, holding a gun in his mouth. Through the window, Jack sees that Marla is being dragged inside the building by some members of Project Mayhem. Jack explicitly refuses Tyler's plan to blow up the city's financial district, and once he realizes that the gun being in Tyler's hand means that it is in his own hand, he takes it and shoots himself in the face. Tyler again disappears, the movie ending shortly afterwards with Tyler (but not Jack) having apparently been killed by the shot, and with Marla and Jack, hand in hand, watching the city's skyscrapers implode.

Interpreting *Fight Club*

Some take the character of Tyler Durden and his rebellion *against* the world to be central to the moral of the movie. As I shall argue here, however, the moral cannot be found in either Tyler or in Fight Club, but instead should be found in Jack's intimate struggle and desperate attempt at self-affirmation.

Tyler-central interpretations of the movie usually echo the speech Tyler gives to the members of Fight Club around the middle of the film. According to Tyler, despite their being "the strongest and smartest men who have ever lived," the members of Fight Club are "squandering" their potential. But it is not their fault. Western societies (and not just capitalism but the lifestyles such societies promote) have trapped us in jobs "pumping gas, waiting tables," making us "slaves with white collars," so that "we can buy shit we don't need." More specifically, western societies have deprived men of their "hunter-gatherer" instinct, reducing them to nothing more than mere "by-products of a lifestyle obsession." As Tyler asks Jack, when they first meet in the bar:

> Do you know what a duvet is? [...] It's a blanket, just a blanket. Why do guys like you and I know what a duvet is? Is this essential to our survival in the hunter-gatherer sense of the word? No. What are we, then? [...] We're consumers, we are by-products of a lifestyle obsession.

According to Tyler, the western contemporary lifestyle has (metaphorically speaking) "emasculated" men by depriving them of their ultimate nature *as men*. Indeed, the theme of emasculation is present very early in the film; the first therapy group Jack attends is for those who suffer from testicular cancer. Jack feels at home among those who have had their testicles actually removed because he feels that his have been metaphorically removed. Like them, he struggles with his masculinity and likely finds their mantras reassuring. "We're still men. Yes, we're men. Men is what we are."

As a replacement for such groups, again on Tyler's understanding, Fight Club is not just a place where men can relieve their daily stress; it is a solemn place where men can rediscover and reconnect with their (allegedly) suppressed natural hunter-gatherer instincts – where they can truly be men. This likely explains why Tyler as a character is attractive to no small part of the audience – and why he (but not Jack) has become a kind of idol in so-called "men's rights activists" circles, and among those who call for a return to men's primitive and (alleged) instinctive way of relating to the world. To them, Jack is just the pretext for Tyler, and it is the latter who is the hero of the film. Indeed, if the hunter-gatherer instinct were, as Tyler claims, the ultimate nature of men, then it would be correct to claim that becoming a member of Fight Club is a kind of self-affirming exercise – a way for men to affirm themselves in what they ultimately are which, under this understanding, is nothing more than aggressive hunter-gatherer animals.

Fortunately, the movie clearly rejects this message and way of conceiving of men. Not only does it clearly label Tyler as the villain by having Jack, at the end of the movie, realize Tyler's treachery and kill him; but the movie takes great pains to show how members of Fight Club are just as alienated as they were before joining (if not more so). They are so alienated, in fact, that they develop an irrational obedience to Tyler – one so blind that they join Project Mayhem and gladly embrace a denial of their own individuality and authenticity. ("In Project Mayhem we have no names"; "In Tyler we trust"; "You are not special. You are not a beautiful or unique snowflake. You're the same decaying organic matter as everything else.") It is one thing to recognize that society or capitalism or your mother has exaggerated how special and unique you are; but Tyler dehumanizes the subjects of Project Mayhem to the point that they do not even value their own life.

Joining Fight Club is not, then, the way to enjoy an authentic, self-governed life, and joining Project Mayhem does not free one from the threats that motived Jack to take refuge in support groups, Tyler, and Fight Club in the first place. For example, the film makes explicitly clear that the threat of emasculation under Project Mayhem is far more severe than the one posed by western capitalistic societies. Capitalism just emasculates Jack metaphorically. But when Jack goes to the police, to try to stop Project Mayhem, and finds that the police officers are themselves members, their emasculation attempt is literal. As they put it to Jack: "You said if anyone even interferes Project Mayhem, even you, we gotta get his balls." Even loyal members of Project Mayhem are in danger. Tyler has not freed them; he has taken advantage of them, turning them into "space monkeys," ready to be sacrificed for what he sees as "the greater good."

What's more, the goal of Project Mayhem – what Tyler sees as "the greater good" – is not laudable. Don't get me wrong; in its early days, Fight Club had no such greater good in mind. Prior to Fight Club evolving into Project Mayhem, Tyler's speeches are just angry outbursts, emotional expressions of discontent against the world that lack any ultimate purpose apart from expressing this discontentment. The same is true of Fight Club's early vandalism "homework assignments." Changing the airplane safety cards and making hundreds of pigeons defecate on the automobiles parked outside a luxury car company may express a kind of frustration that many viewers resonated with, but they are not serious attempts to change the world. Project Mayhem, however, is something much more serious. It is not involved in just childish vandalism; its material concrete purpose is to blow up the entire financial district to erase everyone's credit card debt.

Now, given the wealth disparity that exists in the west (which has grown exponentially since the 1999 release of *Fight Club*), one might think that having everyone "go back to zero" is a laudable goal. Indeed, given the communistic nature of the commune that Tyler creates with Project Mayhem, one might think its goal is one of total equality. Perhaps he is shooting for a kind of Marxian utopia where each person works according to his ability, and each person receives according to his needs. But after the car-crash scene, in which the existence of Project Mayhem is first revealed, Tyler makes clear that the goal of Project Mayhem is nothing of the sort. It is instead complete anarchy.

> In the world I see, you are stalking elk through the damp canyon forests around the ruins of Rockefeller Center. You'll wear leather clothes that will last you the rest of your life. You'll climb the wrist-thick kudzu vines that wrap the Sea Towers. And when you look down, you'll see tiny figures pounding corn, laying strips of venison on the empty carpool lane of some abandoned superhighway.

According to Tyler, for men to truly return to their (supposed) primitive hunter-gather instincts, they must return to a primitive hunter-gatherer society.

Initially, one may suspect that this sort of hunter-gatherer society would actually be an improvement, perhaps facilitating the concrete individual to enjoy an authentic, self-affirming life. But a few moments of reflection reveals that it would be nothing of the sort; every moment of life in such a world would be a struggle to survive; one's existence would be constantly threatened by the elements and others. As the philosopher Thomas Hobbes famously put it, "Life in the state of nature is solitary, poor, nasty, brutish and short." Indeed, Tyler himself is a bit of a hypocrite for desiring it. After every Fight Club meeting, he calls for himself or someone else to be sent to the hospital – but there would be no hospitals in Tyler's "utopia." It would be a world in which a sprained ankle is a death sentence. This is one of the reasons Jack so passionately tries to foil Tyler's plan once he discovers it, and why the attentive viewer should realize that Tyler is the villain.

Besides this view of *Fight Club*, which exalts the character of Tyler and his conceiving of men as aggressive, primitive hunter-gatherer animals, the movie has received other interpretations. For example, it has been interpreted as a critique of gender issues (see, e.g., Bainbridge and Yates 2005) and as a critique of consumerism and the "American dream" (see, e.g., Lizardo 2007). To be fair, these reading do have merit. For example, there is an obvious rejection of consumerism as a successful way of living a fulfilling life; we see it in how pathetic the "Ikea nesting instinct" is portrayed ("I flip through catalogues and wonder: 'What kind of dining set defines me as a person?'"), in Tyler's early warning to Jack ("The things you own end up owning you"), and in his direct message to the audience: "You are not your job, you're not how much money you have in the bank. You are not the car you drive, you're not the contents of your wallet. You are not your fucking khakis."

There is also a clear rejection of the kind of masculinity portrayed in men's underwear ads that is made explicit in Jack's words after seeing a Gucci ad on the bus. "I felt sorry for guys who packed into gyms, trying to look like how Calvin Klein or Tommy Hilfiger said they should. That's what a man looks like?" Tyler's jocular rejoinder is even more revealing: "Self-improvement is masturbation. Now Self-destruction . . ." Even more relevant, although perhaps more subtle, is the fact that, aside from Marla Singer, the only secondary character in the movie that takes on a relevant role is Robert Paulson, a man whose testicles have been removed due to testicular cancer and who has developed women's breasts after undergoing medical treatment for the disease and yet whose manliness is never called into question.

God's Salvation is also rejected. This, while not explicitly relevant in the movie, does implicitly make the certainty of earthly death so evincing that life cannot be sustained on anything ultimate, anything different from life itself. ("We don't need [God]! Fuck Damnation, man! Fuck Redemption! We are God's unwanted children? So be it! [...] First, you have to give up. First you have to know, not fear, know, that someday you're gonna die").

So consumerism, the masculinity portrayed in men's underwear ads, and religion are all rejected by the movie as successful answers to the existential struggle. However, they are not criticized because of their (alleged) inherent inadequacy when it comes to living a fulfilled life. Rather, they are rejected as being external ideals of what a man (indeed a person) should be, or more specifically what enables a person to enjoy an authentic life that is worth living. The lesson is that things that are alien to a person, the concrete subject, inevitably lead one to a denial of their own authenticity. To be sure, anticapitalists will readily agree with the way consumerism is portrayed in the movie; feminists, for their part, will agree with rejecting the kind of masculinity depicted in men's underwear ads; and atheists will gladly share the denial of God's Salvation. But the film has absolutely no reference to economics, or to patriarchy, or to the lack of evidential justification for adopting a religious stance. The emphasis, on the contrary, is on how uncritically relying on these externally imposed values ends up diminishing the individual's authenticity, thus impeding them from living a potentially self-governed life. As an example, body-building could be a way to fulfill your life if it is what *you* consciously and sincerely want to do, but it is not if you engage in it just to mold yourself into Calvin Klein's ideal of what an "authentic" man looks like.

The focus of Fight Club is not, then, on rejecting religion, Tyler's way of conceiving men, consumerism, or the masculinity portrayed in men's underwear ads. Rather, it is centered around Jack (recall he is never actually given a name) and his evolving attitude as he attempts to fill the existential void he feels. Ultimately, the movie portrays how its unnamed narrator is moved to a conscious and exhausting self-affirming exercise, a full endorsement of his own authenticity. And he does so once he realizes the need to reject all the externally imposed conceptions of what counts as a meaningful life, and after coming to not merely stoically resign himself to it, but to positively endorse the claim that since these answers are external to him, they cannot but block his own authenticity and thus prevent him from attaining an authentic, self-governed life.

We can see this in Jack's evolving attitude throughout the movie. Near the start of the movie, Jack is moved by the "Ikea nesting instinct." The lack of meaning this gives him makes him restless, leading to him to seek relief in his "addiction" to therapy groups. Marla ruining this marks the appearance of the character of Tyler, who positively affirms the unnecessariness of finding an ultimate meaning to one's life. ("I say 'Never be complete'; I say 'Stop being perfect'; I say 'Lets evolve, let the chips fall where they may'.") Tyler and Jack together create Fight Club, which at first seems to give Jack relief again (even, perhaps ironically, giving Jack's life some sort of purpose). ("Fight Club became the reason to cut your hair short or trim your fingernails.") Jack even starts to progressively mimic Tyler's attitude, and he gradually slips away from the kind of life he had been immersed in before meeting Tyler. The death of the character of Robert (Bob) Paulson, however, together with his loving relationship with the character of Marla Singer, makes Jack realize that Tyler is not someone he should follow – Tyler's way is not the way to enjoy an authentic life. In fact, emulating him is a complete denial of his own authenticity. "Little by little, you're just letting yourself become Tyler Durden." Jack subsequently engages in a conscious and exhausting attempt at self-affirmation, at fully endorsing his (and not Tyler's) authenticity. This self-affirming exercise is illustrated not only by his effort to purge Tyler from his psyche, but also by his rejection of Fight Club and its corollary, Project Mayhem. This exercise dramatically culminates in the last scene of the movie. Just before shooting himself in the face to "kill" Tyler, Jack claims, "I do [take responsibility]. I am responsible for all of it and I accept that. [...] Tyler, I'm grateful to you, for everything you've done for me. But this is too much. I don't want this. [...] Tyler, I want you to really listen to me: 'My eyes are open'."

Jack's attitude in the final scene contrasts starkly with his reaction in the chemical burning scene, where he is incapable of assuming his own suffering and tries to take refuge in his imagination. ("I'm going to my cave! I'm going to my cave! I'm gonna find my power animal!") The self-shooting metaphorically illustrates how Jack is no longer taking refuge in any external "power animal," be it therapy groups, Fight Club, Tyler, or whatever else is externally imposed on him. Instead, he is now aiming at a self-governed life. (It is interesting to note, however, that despite Tyler assuring Jack that "in the end you will thank me," the movie does not overtly claim the success of Jack's self-affirming exercise in overcoming the existential struggle.)

Indeed, Tyler is nothing but another of Jack's external "power animals" in which he attempts to take refuge. This is consistent with Tyler simply being a product of Jack's imagination, since the movie clearly portrays them as two completely different, and in the end mutually exclusive, characters. Indeed, the fact that they are so obviously not the same character is what facilitates the transformation Jack undergoes after meeting (and progressively mimicking) Tyler. Moreover, it explains why, for most viewers, Jack's realization that Tyler is just a fictional product of his mind is an unexpected plot twist, despite the movie being littered with clues to this effect. The main purpose of Tyler being Jack's fictional idea, it seems, is to emphasize that the quest for an authentic life that is worth living is a continuous, laborious, and intimate struggle that one must face on their own. The struggle is an individual issue and what is required to resolve it is a conscious exercise of self-affirmation, of realizing and embracing what we want, and what kind of individual we are, regardless of how the world is or what it asks us to be. This clearly contrasts not only with Tyler's attitude but also that of the members of Fight Club/Project Mayhem. They see their life as a struggle against the world; that is why they think that the answer to their problem requires a change in the world (i.e., Project Mayhem), rather than a change in themselves.

In other words, *Fight Club*'s message is that the struggle to find meaning in one's existence, to live an authentic life that is worth living – what (for reasons that will soon be made clear) we will call "the existential struggle" – is *a struggle against (and for) oneself*, to resist how the world asks us to be while attempting to affirm ourselves in what we actually are. It is not *a struggle against (and for) the world*, an attempt to change how the world actually is or how it asks us to be. As mentioned before, what stops Tyler and his followers from engaging in an exercise of self-affirmation is that they conceive of their lives as a struggle *against the world*, which is why they think the answer to their own situation requires a change in the world. However, as illustrated by Jack's evolving transformation, the movie is clear in arguing that the struggle to find an authentic life that is worth living is an individual and intimate issue, and so resolving it requires a conscious exercise of self-affirmation, of realizing what individuals we are and what we want no matter how the world actually is or how it asks us to be. This is not to say, of course, that one may not attempt to change the world if one thinks it is apt for some given reason, just as Jack attempts to stop Project Mayhem. The claim is that, even if these changes in the world were to be successfully made, the world would not provide an answer to one's own intimate existential struggle, because it is external to the subject.

At this point, an obvious question arises. If the claim that frames the entire movie is that an authentic life is a fully self-governed life, then why do men engage in a club that demands obedience to its norms? Interestingly, at the inception of Fight Club, before the preparations for Project Mayhem begin, there seems to be no *strict* requirement to obey the rules. If we focus on its first two rules, which are really only one (i.e., "You do not talk about Fight Club"), it is evident that they are not respected. Fight Club spreads throughout the entire country and sees an exponential growth in its number of members. "I see a lot of new faces. Which means a lot of people have been breaking the first two rules of Fight Club." However, it is evident that members of Fight Club end up developing an irrational and blind obedience to Tyler, even to the point that they gladly assume a denial of their own authenticity. This is simply an ironic way of once again expressing the claim that no uncritical engagement in any externally imposed way of life can lead to an authentic, self-governed life. Not only are members of Fight Club as alienated as they were before entering the Club, they are not even substantially different from the way Jack is at the beginning of the movie – it is just that, instead of being driven by the "Ikea nesting instinct" and hiding away in therapy groups, they are drawn along by Tyler's instinct and are hiding in Fight Club. Those who follow Tyler are not facing the existential struggle; they are cowardly hiding from it by endorsing Tyler's understanding of life, even when this requires them to reject their own authenticity. ("Sooner or later, we all become what Tyler wanted us to be.") This explains why Jack needs to distance himself from Fight Club and Tyler's Project Mayhem to fully endorse his authenticity.

Another question that arises is, why all the fighting? If the point is to illustrate that no engagement in any externally imposed way of life can lead to a life worth living, then why does the movie get into Fight Club instead of, for example, simply staying with the therapy groups of the beginning of the movie. One answer, of course, is that fighting provides a way to illustrate, and later on reject, Tyler's understanding of men as aggressive hunter-gatherer animals. But there are also two other explanations as to why the movie revolves around fighting. First, fighting provides a vivid, visual metaphor of the grievous and exhausting struggle that each one of us intimately faces when seeking an authentic life. Second, while the members of therapy groups are moved by mutual compassion and pity, members of Fight Club are moved by a feeling of camaraderie. In Fight Club, all men are treated equally and, most importantly, they see themselves as absolute equals. This is, I think, one of the most intelligent and subtle points of the movie: That camaraderie, when misunderstood as total equality among individuals, can generate a denial of each one's authenticity.

If nothing externally imposed on the subject can give their life a meaning, a first reaction may be self-isolation. The movie rejects this possibility, as shown by the fact that what marks Jack's detachment from Tyler and Fight Club are, first, his refusal to endorse Tyler and the other members of Fight Club's indifference to Robert Paulson's death ("You want an omelette? You gotta break some eggs"); and second, his full endorsement of his loving feeling towards the character of Marla Singer – feelings that he insincerely denies throughout the movie. As Jack puts it:

> The full extent of our relationship wasn't really clear to me up until now, for reasons I'm not going to go into, but the important point is that I know I haven't been treating you so well. [...] I'm trying to tell you that I'm sorry, because I've come to realize that I really like you, Marla. [...] I really do, I care about you and I don't want anything bad to happen to you because of me.

A loving involvement with others is not then, by itself, a diminishment of one's own authenticity. Rather, the problem arises when the others are seen as "power animals," as answers to one's own existential struggle. Here it is useful to contrast Jack's attitude towards the character of Marla at the end of the movie with his early "addiction" to therapy groups. Whereas Jack's attitude towards Marla constitutes an exercise in self-affirmation, a full endorsement of his own feelings, his involvement in therapy groups is no more than an (unsuccessful) attempt to fill his life using deceit (and self-deceit), by pretending to be someone else.

The Moral of *Fight Club*

The ultimate philosophical meaning, or moral, of *Fight Club*, then, is the illustration of the struggle felt by each and every one of us in needing to find a convincing answer to the question of what (if anything) counts as an authentic life that is worth living. What's more, it also claims that all those who hide from the struggle by uncritically relying on external answers end up giving up their authenticity, that which makes them the individuals they are and not others, thus inevitably becoming trapped in an alienated, unauthentic, and self-denying life.

At this stage, I would like to emphasize the point I raised at the beginning: That *Fight Club* is to be understood in primarily existentialist, nonethical, and non-evidential terms. The question of what (if anything) counts as an authentic life that is worth living is not a strange question; indeed, it is one that absolutely everyone faces – hence, why the movie takes care not to present Fight Club as a peculiar extravagancy of Tyler and Jack's, but as an appealing activity for men who are trying to confront their own existential struggle. Consider Jack's claim, after the creation of Fight Club, that "It was right in everyone's face, Tyler and I just made it visible. It was on the tip of everyone's tongue, Tyler and I just gave it a name." Consider Tyler's words to Jack in the car-crash scene. ("You are missing the point, this [Fight Club/Project Mayhem] does not belong to us. We are not special.")

What I mean when I say that the moral should not be understood in "evidential terms" is that the existential struggle is not a theoretical question to be solved through purely theoretical, armchair reasoning, or by appealing to our empirical knowledge about some given facts of the world. Instead, it is something that requires a practical, attitudinal, and conscious engagement on our part. As I said before, the struggle is an individual issue, the answer to which should spring from the concrete individual, independently of how the world is or how it asks us to be. This point is illustrated throughout the movie in Jack's evolving transformation: The world itself does not change in any relevant sense, but the way he sees and approaches the world constantly does. "[After Fight Club we] all started seeing things differently, everywhere we went, we were seizing things up"; "When the fight was over, nothing was solved, but nothing mattered. Afterwards, we all felt saved."

Moreover, when stating that it is not an ethical but an existential question, I also mean that the struggle is not about finding what actions are (ethically) right or wrong, but about finding what way of life (if any) counts as an authentic, worth living one. The movie offers no real commentary on the morality of the actions described in it.

Thus, even if it is clear to all of us that crashing your car, as Tyler does, just to have a near-death experience and discover what it feels like to have a car accident is not a good idea, it is still hard to argue that it constitutes an ethically wrong action – provided, of course, that it is a voluntary action and no third parties are injured. In fact, one of the most interesting aspects of the movie is that it explicitly detaches from any purely ethical outlook. Hence, although fighting is evidently a physically harmful activity, in the movie is it shown to be a freely and mutually agreed activity among the members of the Club, who are all adults and taken to be in full use of their cognitive capacities. (Even Jack and Tyler seem fully capable of reasoning despite their being the same physical person.) Therefore, in principle, there seems to be no ethical reason to object to it – unless, of course, we have an ethical reason to deem boxing and other similar activities as immoral. But, again, engaging in fighting for the sole purpose of fighting would, to most of us, be questionable.

Furthermore, the kind of sabotage actions carried out by the members of Fight Club (dictated by Tyler and taken as their "homework assignments") are, especially at the beginning, at most symbolic, and at worst simply childish. These actions are not attempts to seriously injure anyone, and in fact the only victim involved is the character of Robert Paulson, whose death is portrayed as accidental – "We had it all worked out, Sir. It went smooth until... They shot Bob...They shot him in the head... Those fucking pigs!" – even though Jack is clearly and understandably indignant. ("You morons! You're running around in ski masks, trying to blow things up, what did you think was gonna happen?") Even the final sabotage action, which ends up destroying most of the financial district of the city, is explicitly planned so as nobody gets physically injured ("The buildings are empty. Security and maintenance are all our people. We're not killing anyone, man, we're setting them free!"). But, again, even conceding that no serious harm is done in these actions, I hope we would all agree that engaging in sabotage actions just to express your dislike of the economic system in which you live, or destroying almost all the skyscrapers in your city as a way of moving the whole world to a sort of paleolithic hunter-gatherer society, is not a very praiseworthy way of behaving.

Tyler's violent threats to the character of Raymond K. Hessel (played by Joon B. Kim) to force him to pursue his *own* vital goals (i.e., to complete his veterinary studies) may portray Tyler not just as an unappealing or even repellent character, but also as an ethically blameful one – after all, Raymond did not ask for any help and he clearly did not deserve to be threatened with death for having dropped out of college. While I obviously agree that going through grocery stores, in real life, aiming a gun at employees to force them to fulfill their own life-goals and succeed in becoming "what they wanted to be" is not a good thing, I also think that to take the scene literally, as praising Tyler's violence, would be to miss the point – not only of the scene but also the entire movie. Nowhere else in the movie than in this scene is the claim that underpins *Fight Club* so explicitly stated: That all those who hide themselves from the existential struggle by uncritically relying on external answers (whatever they may be, from consumerism and therapy groups to fight clubs and Tylers) end up giving up their own authenticity, that which makes them the individuals they are and not others. It is in this sense that they are (metaphorically speaking, of course) already dead.

Within this framework, Raymond is already a sort of living dead man, making Tyler's threats appear to be somehow vacuous, not only because the gun is in fact not loaded, but most importantly because someone who is already dead cannot be killed. At most, Tyler will motivate him (again, metaphorically speaking) to re-engage with life by moving him to realize the need to engage in a conscious self-affirming exercise and to pursue his own goals. This is the metaphorical context in which the scene is framed, explaining why despite Tyler's violence, the scene is commonly taken as ultimately motivational. However, as already stated, this is obviously a fictional context purporting to metaphorically illustrate an existential claim, not an ethical reasoning to justify the audience going through real life aiming guns at people.

There is also another interesting but not immediately obvious aspect to the scene, noticed by William Irwin (2013, pp. 682–683): Tyler calls Raymond by his name. This is interesting for two reasons. First, because there are only three other characters who are called by their name in the whole film: Tyler Durden, Marla Singer, and Robert (Bob) Paulson. Second, because it is in stark contrast to Tyler's attitude towards the members of Project Mayhem. He treats them as nameless "space monkeys." Members of Project Mayhem become annulled as individuals once they make Tyler their cult leader and thereby uncritically assume Tyler's way of self-affirmation through Project Mayhem. In contrast, Tyler encourages Raymond to pursue an authentic, self-governed life by forcing him to focus on his own life goals no matter what ("No fear. No distractions. The ability to let that which does not matter truly slide"). In fact, while Tyler forces Raymond to question himself so that he can find his own, unique way of attaining an authentic existence ("What did you wanted to be, Raymond K. Hessel?"), he explicitly tells members of Project Mayhem to not ask any questions at all ("The first rule of Project Mayhem is you don't ask questions"). The contrast serves to illustrate, once again, the claim that members of Project Mayhem are as alienated as they were before joining the club.

Evaluating *Fight Club*'s Moral

If we turn to the History of Philosophy, the ultimate philosophical meaning or argument of *Fight Club* recognized above may be easily recognized in the works of the philosophers traditionally labeled under the term "existentialism,"[2] which is generally known for the struggle of seeking a convincing answer to the question of what (if anything) counts as an authentic life that is worth living. It is generally considered to suggest that an authentic life requires a practical, attitudinal, and conscious exercise of self-affirmation on our part. To this effect, in her essay *The Ethics of Ambiguity* (Beauvoir 1948/1976), the existentialist philosopher Simone de Beauvoir (1908–1986) argued that "the genuine man will not agree to recognize any foreign absolute" (Beauvoir 1948/1976, p. 14). According to Beauvoir, there is no already given external power that may give meaning to our own concrete existence. We are free in the sense that we are not dependent upon anything external and already given. "Man," writes Beauvoir, "bears the responsibility for a world which is not the work of a strange power, but of himself, where his defeats are inscribed, and his victories as well. God can pardon, efface and compensate. But if God does not exist, man's faults are inexpiable" (Beauvoir 1948/1976, p. 16). On this understanding, an authentic life requires us to affirm ourselves in our own freedom by taking full responsibility for our own concrete existence once the claim that there is nothing external that can give our life an ultimate meaning has been embraced. Existentialism, however, includes a large group of philosophers: Soren Kierkegaard (1813–1855), Friedrich Nietzsche (1844–1900), Miguel de Unamuno

(1864–1936), Paul Tillich (1886–1965), Martin Heidegger (1889–1976), Jean Paul Sartre (1905–1980), and Albert Camus (1913–1960), just to name a few. And they all defended different, and sometimes even opposing, philosophical claims.

This raises the question of whether Existentialism should be taken, properly speaking, as a school of thought with its own core philosophical claims. Instead, perhaps it should be conceived of more vaguely, as simply a peculiar understanding of Philosophy's ultimate task and, more especially, to a particular understanding of each one's own concrete existence. In any case, the label "Existentialism" seems justified in that, despite defending different philosophical claims, these philosophers all have in common a focus on the concrete subject and how they may attain a meaningful existence. More concretely, they agree that the concrete subject should face the intimate struggle of discovering what an authentic life that is worth living consists in, and aim at it through an individual act of self-affirmation. Where they largely differ is in both their understanding of this self-affirmation exercise and its consequences, the kind of way of life that is taken to follow from it.

To illustrate the differences among the philosophers usually labeled as existentialists, first take Friedrich Nietzsche's *On the Genealogy of Morals* (Nietzsche 1887/1989). He suggests that the Christian way of life is something unnatural and life-denying, insofar as it goes against the (alleged) most basic and natural tendency to increase one's own power. Contrast that with Miguel de Unamuno's defense of Christian faith, in *The Tragic Sense of Life in Men and Nations* (Unamuno 1913/1972), as being the result of a similar (alleged) most basic and natural tendency to increase one's own authenticity. Whereas for Nietzsche an exercise of self-affirmation implied the dismissal of a Christian way of life, for Unamuno it was just the opposite, arguing that a Christian way of life was a life-affirming exercise, something we are led to once we affirm ourselves in our own natural condition.[3]

In this regard, it is interesting to note that *Fight Club* – despite clearly illustrating the need of each person to engage in an intimate and continuous exercise of self-affirmation to overcome their own existential angst and aim at the enjoyment of a self-governed, authentic life – does not, and neither does it attempt to, illustrate what kind of life may follow from such a self-affirmation exercise. Neither does it comment on whether a fully self-governed life may in the end actually be attainable in its totality. In fact, as mentioned previously, despite Tyler ensuring Jack that "in the end you will thank me," the movie does not overtly claim Jack's success in his self-affirming exercise of overcoming the existential struggle he feels, or state what kind of life he is going to be immersed in from thereon, since the movie ends immediately after the self-shooting/building collapsing scene, leaving the spectator with questions about what will happen next.

Strictly speaking, the focus of *Fight Club* is not, then, the illustration, under a fictional scenario, of the philosophical claims already made by some given existentialist philosopher. Rather its focus is illustrating, through the character of Jack, the intimate existential struggle we all, men and women, suffer from in some way or another, and pointing out that the only way to overcome this struggle is to require an individual and conscious exercise of self-affirmation. It is in this sense that the movie cannot be credited as a sort of, so to speak, instruction manual on how this self-affirming exercise should be executed, or what its results may be. Rather, it leaves spectators with the task of facing their own struggle by their own means, inciting them to discover by themselves, alone, how to assume their own, unique authenticity.

Far from being a defect, this aspect of the film is actually one of its merits. *Fight Club* clearly succeeds in capturing the general outlook of existentialist philosophers without explicitly committing itself to the truth of any philosophical claim already made by some concrete philosopher. And this is why, at least in the interpretation given in this chapter, the movie has the highly valuable merit of introducing the audience to the general stance of existentialist philosophy without encouraging, let alone forcing, the spectator to accept any already given concrete, systematically developed philosophical claim.

Nonetheless, the question may still arise as to whether it is reasonable to claim that a self-governed, authentic life requires of an act of self-affirmation. Moreover, it may be wondered whether it is reasonable to claim that nothing externally imposed on the subject can make their life worth living since, being external, they will result in the denial of one's own authenticity. Taken as such, these claims are vague enough (though, I think, still philosophically inspiring) to be uncontroversial. A controversy would arise if it attempted to define how such self-affirmation may occur and what kind of life may emerge from it, but, again, the movie remains silent in this regard and leaves spectators with the task of finding by themselves, alone, the answer to their own existential struggle. In this respect, I would say that no one, philosophers and nonphilosophers alike, would deny that an authentic, self-governed life requires of an individual an exercise of self-affirmation – even if, again, there is no clear account of what this affirmation may consist in or whether it may in the end actually be possible to fully attain. This seems to just be a conceptual point. Consider Plato's cave allegory, where people sit, chained but contented to watch shadows on a wall, thinking they are real. It may be that the lives of those who live inside the cave are far more comfortable in terms of the facilities they may have access to than the lives of those who live outside; it may even be that, at least with regard these facilities, life inside the cave may be *preferable* to life on the outside. But even if so, it still seems conceptually wrong to claim that those living inside the cave, however many facilities they may be able to enjoy, are enjoying an authentic, self-governed life.

Of course, a quick glance at any textbook on the History of Philosophy will reveal that not all philosophers are labeled as existentialists; but this is not because only the thinkers labeled as existentialists agree on the subjective significance of having an answer to the question of what (if anything) counts as an authentic life that is worth living. Rather, the difference has to do with how different philosophers conceive of Philosophy as a discipline. Whereas existentialist philosophers claim that Philosophy's ultimate task is to answer the question of what (if anything) counts as an authentic life that is worth living, nonexistentialist philosophers do not consider this to be the basic, fundamental question which Philosophy, as a discipline, should deal with; they may even take it to be a subjective, private question that is unanswerable in a rational, objective philosophical way. However, and again this is the ultimate philosophical point raised by *Fight Club*, no-one denies that each concrete individual, be they a philosopher or not, needs to find an answer to the question of what an authentic life consists in. And many agree that by uncritically relying on externally imposed views and practices, a person can end up trapped in an alienated way of life.

Conclusion

Fight Club is not a boxing movie. Rather, it is an angsty movie, which conveys an inciting philosophical message, which is that an authentic life that is worth living seems to require a conscious and exhausting attempt at self-affirmation, to fully endorse one's own (and not other's) authenticity. The *how* of such self-affirmation is left open. Jack's, not Tyler's, "homework assignment" is to leave the spectators with the task of facing their own struggle by their own means, encouraging them to discover by themselves alone how to assume their own, unique authenticity.

End Notes

1. In this chapter, I will leave aside Palahniuk's novel and focus exclusively on Fincher's movie, so I will not be commenting on the movie's degree of fidelity to the novel, or whether they may admit different interpretations.
2. For a short and accessible introduction to Existentialism, see Flynn 2006.
3. For a detailed account as to why Unamuno considered his notion of religious faith to be an exercise of self-affirmation, and why it can be considered as a convincing response to Nietzsche's criticisms of the Christian, agapeic way of life, see Oya 2020.

References

Bainbridge, C., and C. Yates. 2005. Cinematic symptoms of masculinity in transition: Memory, history and mythology in contemporary film. *Psychoanalysis, Culture & Society* 10: 299–318.

Beauvoir, S. 1948/1976. *The ethics of ambiguity,* trans. Bernard Frechtman. New York: Citadel.

Flynn, T. 2006. *Existentialism: A very short introduction.* New York: Oxford University Press.

Irwin, W. 2013. Fight Club, self-definition, and the fragility of authenticity. *Revista Portuguesa de Filosofia* 69 (3–4): 673–684.

Lizardo, O. 2007. Fight Club, or the cultural contradictions of late capitalism. *Journal for Cultural Research* 11: 221–243.

Nietzsche, F. 1887/1989. On the genealogy of morals. In *On the genealogy of morals and ecce homo,* ed. Walter Kaufmann, 13–163. New York: Vintage Books.

Oya, A. 2020. Nietzsche and Unamuno on *conatus* and the Agapeic way of life. *Metaphilosophy* 51 (2–3): 303–317.

Unamuno, M. 1913/1972. The tragic sense of life in men and nations. In *The selected works of Miguel de Unamuno,* ed. Anthony Kerrigan, vol. 4, 3–358. Princeton: Princeton University Press.

Tarantino as Philosopher: Vengeance – Unfettered, Uncensored, but Not Unjustified

53

David Kyle Johnson

Contents

Introduction	1236
Vengeance, Justice, Retribution, and *The Hateful Eight*	1237
Tarantino's Filmography and His Argument for Revenge	1240
Common Arguments Against Vengeance	1245
Common Argument 1: Vengeance Can Go Too Far	1245
Common Argument 2: Avengers Do Not Have Perfect Knowledge	1247
Common Argument 3: Two Wrongs Do Not Make a Right	1248
Common Argument 4: It Is Always Wrong to Harm Others	1248
Common Argument 5: Vengeance Does No Good	1249
Historical Arguments About Vengeance	1250
Plato on Vengeance	1251
Spinoza on Vengeance	1252
Thomas Hobbes on Vengeance	1254
John Locke on Vengeance	1255
Friedrich Nietzsche on Vengeance	1256
Modern Arguments Regarding Vengeance	1257
The Never-Ending Cycle of Violence	1257
Govier and Uniacke: Forgiveness, *Schadenfreude,* and Revenge's Rationality	1258
Oldenquist and the Purpose of Holding Offenders Accountable	1259
Barr-Elli and Heyd: Moral Justice Versus Legal Justice	1260
Simone de Beauvoir: Can Vengeance Accomplish Its Goal?	1262
Nozick, Vengeance, and when the Law Falls Short	1263
The Best Arguments for and Against the Morality of Revenge	1264
Conclusion: What About Ezekiel 25:17?	1266
End Notes	1267
References	1267

D. K. Johnson (✉)
Department of Philosophy, King's College, Wilkes-Barre, PA, USA
e-mail: davidjohnson@kings.edu

Abstract

Quentin Tarantino's filmography, especially since the turn of the century, seems to be an argument for the moral justification of revenge. Bill and his D.iV.A.S. hit-squad (from *Kill Bill*); Adolf Hitler and Hans Landa (from *Inglourious Basterds*); "Monsieur" Calvin Candie and his loyal house slave Stephen (from *Django Unchained*); Stuntman Mike and the Manson family killers (from *Death Proof* and *Once Upon a Time in Hollywood*); and Daisy Domergue and General Sanford Smithers (from *The Hateful Eight*) – they all had it coming, and audiences celebrate when they get what they deserve. Revenge, Tarantino reminds us, is a dish best served cold. But is it really the kind of thing that can be morally justified? To see whether it is, this chapter explores arguments both historic and contemporary. After delineating revenge from legal justice and simple retribution and exploring how Tarantino's films argue for moral justification of revenge, we will consider common everyday arguments on the topic, as well as the relevant arguments of Plato, Baruch Spinoza, Thomas Hobbes, John Locke, Friedrich Nietzsche, Trudy Govier, Suzanne Uniacke, Andrew Oldenquist, Simone de Beauvoir, Joshua Gert, Gilead Bar-elli, David Heyd, Robert Nozick, and others. In the end, we will see that revenge can be justified – but only in very specific conditions.

Keywords

Vengeance · Vigilantism · Revenge · Justice · Quentin Tarantino · Reservoir Dogs · Pulp Fiction · Jackie Brown · Kill Bill · Inglourious Basterds · Death Proof · Django Unchained · The Hateful Eight · Once Upon a Time in Hollywood · Plato · Baruch Spinoza · Thomas Hobbes · John Locke · Friedrich Nietzsche · Trudy Govier · Suzanne Uniacke · Andrew Oldenquist · Simone de Beauvoir · Joshua Gert · Gilead Bar-elli · David Heyd · Robert Nozick

Introduction

> It's mercy, compassion, and forgiveness I lack, not rationality.
> —Beatrix Kiddo (*Kill Bill Vol. 1*)

This chapter is different from all others in this section of the handbook, which treat particular, individual movies as a piece of philosophy; this chapter instead treats the body of work of a particular filmmaker as a piece of philosophy: Quentin Tarantino. The reason is simple. Although some of his films present philosophical arguments and raise philosophical questions of their own (see Bradley Richard's ► Chap. 56, "*Pulp Fiction* as Philosophy: Bad Faith, Authenticity, and the Path of the Righteous Man," in this volume), I believe Tarantino's body of work as a whole – especially given how it developed since the begining of the twenty-first century – presents an argument for a conclusion that is undeniably philosophic: Vengeance is morally justified. If not an argument, Tarantino's filmography at least asks whether vengeance is justified and demonstrates that Tarantino himself believes that it is. When a person (or group) is wronged, it is morally permissible for that person (or group) to punish the offender in return. Certain conditions must be met. For example, the punishment must be proportional to the infraction committed. But if such an offended person seeks out vengeance and gets it, the action returned to the offender is not morally wrong. Indeed, there is a cause to celebrate – a fact demonstrated by how we inevitably react to the end of Tarantino's films.

This chapter lays out how Tarantino's filmography, especially since the turn of the century, embraces and even argues for the moral permissibility of revenge. We will then turn to examining that thesis philosophically, to see whether revenge actually is justified, by examining common arguments, and what both historical and contemporary philosophers have said about the topic. I will conclude by considering whether such a thesis can be squared with something else Tarantino seems to argue for: the moral praiseworthiness of mercy. But first, before laying out the details of the relevant Tarantino films and Tarantino's argument, it will be necessary to define exactly what vengeance is, and distinguish it from other forms of retribution. I will do so using the only one of Tarantino's films, since the turn of the century, that (involves but) does not explicitly argue for vengeance: *The Hateful Eight*.

Vengeance, Justice, Retribution, and *The Hateful Eight*

> [W]hen John Ruth The Hangman catches ya, you don't die from no bullet in the back ... When The Hangman catches you, you hang.
> —Major Marquis Warren (*The Hateful Eight*)

The Hateful Eight, a film set after the American Civil War, tells the story of a day at Minnie's Haberdashery in the state of Wyoming. Bounty Hunter John "The Hangman" Ruth must shelter there during a blizzard with his bounty, Daisy Domergue – a notorious murderer and gang member – who he plans to take to the town of Red Rock to hang. Unbeknownst to John, a group of seemingly unconnected visitors already at the Haberdashery are actually in cahoots with Daisy. They murder John (and his driver O.B.) in an attempt to free her. Two people John happened to bring with him however – another bounty hunter named Major Marquis Warren (a black man who fought for the Union in the Civil War) and Chris Mannix (the new Sheriff of Red Rock who fought for the Confederacy) – fight back. They kill the other gang members and then – even though they are wounded and will likely die before they are found – hang Daisy by the neck until dead.

Given the amount of violence in *The Hateful Eight*, the viewer can be forgiven for thinking that it is a movie about vengeance. And do not get me wrong, there is vengeance in the film. But *The Hateful Eight* is more a movie about justice and retribution than it is about vengeance. Notice that, in the end, two people who have every reason to hate each other – a black Union Major and a white-supremacist Confederate soldier – cooperate and unify in the name of a common cause: "You really only need to hang mean bastards, but mean bastards, you need to hang." The whole reason that John Ruth brings his bounties in alive, rather than dead, is because he knows they deserve to hang; that is why he is known as "The Hangman." John sought to give, and Warren and Mannix do give, to Daisy what she morally deserves. They are not seeking vengeance; they are only dishing out retribution – a cause it seems is even stronger than racial rivalry and hatred. But what is the difference between retribution and vengeance?

Retribution was famously defined by Robert Nozick (2000) as "a penalty ... inflicted for a reason (a wrong or injury) with the desire that the [person who inflicted the injury] know why [the penalty] is occurring and know that [they were] intended to know" (p. 241). So an action that is carried out on someone who did something wrong (an offender) is an action of retribution when (a) the action is negative (e.g., harmful or painful in some way), (b) the action is intended as a punishment or penalty for the offender's wrong action, and (c) the offender is aware (or at least could be) that it is intended as such. Notice that, in order for a punishment to be retribution, it need not be carried out by any particular person. As long *someone* is dishing it out, a punishment can serve as retribution. This is what Warren and Mannix do at the end of *The Hateful Eight*; Daisy deserves to hang, so they hang her.

Vengeance, on the other hand, is different. Although it is a type of retribution, it has an added personal element: A person who was wronged by the offender is the one who is doing the punishing. What is more, unlike vengeance, retribution does not need to be emotional. Although Warren and Mannix were certainly emotionally driven to hang Daisy in the end, a person dispensing retribution can simply recognize that an offender deserves punishment and then dish it out – no emotional motivation, reaction, or satisfaction is required. Revenge, on the other hand, is fueled by emotion and the desire to see the offender pay for their crime – to get what they deserve.

In *The Hateful Eight*, Oswaldo Mobray (aka English Pete Hicox, who professes to be the hangman of Red Rock) explains as much when talking to Daisy.

> Now, you're wanted for murder. For the sake of my analogy, let's just assume that you did it. Now, John Ruth wants to take you back to Red Rock to stand trial for murder. And if you're found guilty, the people of Red Rock will hang you in the town square. And, as the hangman, I will perform the execution. And if all those things end up taking place, that's what civilized society calls "justice." However, if the relatives and the loved ones of the person you murdered were outside that door right now, and after busting down that door, they drug you out into the snow and hung you up by the neck, that would be "frontier justice." Now, the good part about frontier justice is it's very thirst-quenching. The bad part is it's apt to be wrong as right. ... But ultimately, what's the real difference between the two? The real difference is me: the hangman. To me, it doesn't matter what you did. When I hang you, I'll get no satisfaction from your death. It's my job. I hang you in Red Rock. I move on to the next town. I hang someone else there. The man who pulls the lever that breaks your neck will be a dispassionate man. And that dispassion is the very essence of justice. For justice delivered without dispassion is always in danger of not being justice.

But Mobray's explanation also makes another distinction that we need to understand: the difference between what he calls "justice" and "frontier justice." His notion of "justice" is what we might call "legal retribution." The government recognizes by law that certain actions are deserving of punishment and seeks out to punish those who have performed such actions. When it successfully does so (e.g., if Oswaldo were to hang Daisy in the public square), *retribution* has been had; but since the government is not really wronged or injured (Daisy did not murder the government), it is not seeking vengeance. However, if the offended party – e.g., relatives and the loved ones of the person Daisy murdered – were to show up and do exactly the same thing (hang Daisy by the neck until dead), not only would there be retribution, but they would also get their revenge. Now, perhaps such "frontier justice" need not necessarily be revenge; if the people of the town of Red Rock decided to hang Daisy without the approval of the law, knowing that she was guilty but not actually having been directly affected by her actions, then retribution would be had (Daisy would get what she deserved) without there being any vengeance. But usually, frontier justice mobs were led by people who were victims of the offender; thus, usually, such mobs were seeking revenge. By invoking this distinction, it seems that Tarantino may have been borrowing from philosopher Francis Bacon (1824), who said that "revenge is a kind of wild justice..." (261). But inspired by philosopher Charles Miltner (1931), we might call frontier justice "moral justice," and reserve the term "legal justice" for what Mobray merely calls "justice." (Some philosophers would deny that revenge can be justice; we will address such arguments later.)

This brings us to another useful distinction: different ways people can be affected by an offender. Obviously, a person can be affected directly – say one person injures another. If the injured party seeks to injure the other in return as payback or to give them what they are due, they are seeking revenge. This, it seems, is why Mannix refuses the deal that Daisy offered him (she wanted Mannix to shoot Warren in exchange for the bounty on the gang's other members). Mannix replies, "Joe Gage or Grouch Douglass or whatever the fuck his name was, poisoned the coffee, and you watched him do it, and you watched me pour a cup, and you didn't say shit!" Because she was going to let him die, he is going to let her die. But sometimes the person most directly affected cannot seek revenge – say, in the case of murder. In such cases, however, those indirectly affected can seek revenge, for example, a relative of Daisy's murder victim who now suffers because of the loss of their family member. Likewise, people who simply belong to the same group as the victim might seek revenge, for example, people who belong to the same religion, or race, or even group of friends. We might call this claiming a right of revenge on behalf of the victim.

We see the latter in *The Hateful Eight* when Major Warren kills General Sanford Smithers. Smithers fought for the Confederates in the battle of Baton Rouge – a battle in which Warren also fought "on the other side." General Smithers "captured a whole colored command" Major Warren tells us, "but not one colored trooper made it to a camp." "We didn't have the time or the food, nor the inclination," Smithers admits, "to care for Northern horses and least of all Northern n*****s! So we shot 'em where they stood!" When Warren later baits Smithers to go for a gun, with a story about how he humiliated and then killed Smither's son, so Warren can kill him (legally), Major Warren is seeking revenge – not because he was personally wronged by the General, but because General Smithers wronged people who belonged to the same race and military force. (The justification Warren's act seems to have could be used to argue that *The Hateful Eight* at least contains an argument for vengeance.)

Interestingly, in *Modern English Usage* (1996), Fowler defines "vengeance" as mere "equalization of wrongs" and reserves "revenge" for referring to the personal satisfaction of an offended person's resentment (pp. 43–44). To my ear, given how the term is used, vengeance still has a personal aspect to it, and the mere "equalization of wrongs" is captured by the word "retribution." We could say that "revenge" can only be sought by the person most directly affected by the offender, and that if someone else indirectly affected (like a friend or family member) seeks to punish the offender, that person seeks "vengeance." By such uses of the term, in the case of murder, revenge cannot be sought (because the victim is dead); only vengeance can be sought (by the victim's friends or family). But since I think most people use the terms vengeance and revenge interchangeably, I will not be drawing such a distinction here.

In any event, with an understanding of the terms vengeance, retribution, and justice, we are now prepared to examine Tarantino's filmography and argument for the moral justification of revenge.

Tarantino's Filmography and His Argument for Revenge

> Revenge is a dish best served cold.
> —Old Klingon Proverb

The first films that Tarantino wrote but did not direct, *Natural Born Killers* (1994) and *True Romance* (1993), did not include an overarching theme of revenge. Tarantino's original treatment of *Natural Born Killers* (which was later changed by director Oliver Stone) focused mostly on sensationalist news reporter Wayne Gale, a very "Geraldo Rivera" type character, who reported on the serial killers Mickey and Mallory Knox (see Bailey 2014). Mickey does help his darling Mallory kill her abusive father, which is definitely an act of revenge; however, neither the script nor the film is about the serial killers righting a past wrong done to them by some offender. Perhaps society itself gets what it deserves – the moral of the story is more a criticism of how our culture idolizes such natural born killers – but Mickey and Mallory are not seeking revenge. *True Romance* is not about vengeance either. Clarence does kill Drexl, the former pimp of his new wife Alabama, but this action was more a form of retribution than vengeance. Clarence was not personally injured by Drexl; he is just giving Drexl what he deserves. As Clarence's conscience (aka his hallucination of Elvis) puts it, "Can you live with it? . . . That son of a bitch walkin' around, breathing the same air as you, gettin' away with it every day . . . Well, I'd kill him, shoot him in the face, put him down like a dog. . . . Fuck don't deserve to live." What is more, Clarence killing Drexl is not the movie's focus. The plot revolves around two "average" people (a film junkie, very much like Tarantino himself, and a call girl) falling in love and trying to sell a large amount of cocaine to secure their future, and the message of the movie has more to do with . . . well, with the nature of true romance.

The first three films Tarantino both wrote and directed – *Reservoir Dogs* (1992), *Pulp Fiction* (1994), and *Jackie Brown* (1997) – had more revenge in them, but revenge was still not their focus. *Reservoir Dogs*, a movie about a diamond heist gone wrong, has a kind of vengeance circle at the end: If X shoots Y, then Y will shoot X. And the viewer may certainly feel sympathy with Mr. White when he kills Mr. Orange in the final scene because of Orange's betrayal. The film itself, however, is more about trust and loyalty and how they can be betrayed. *Pulp Fiction*, a movie about two gangsters named Jules and Vincent, has people wanting and getting revenge. Marsellus Wallace, Jules and Vincent's mob boss, wants revenge on the prize fighter Butch for not throwing the boxing match he paid him to throw; Marsellus also desires and gets revenge on Zed for anally raping him. (Off screen, Marcellus gets "Medieval on his ass" with "a pair of pliers and a blow torch.") But – in addition to its message about authenticity (again, see Bradley Richard's ▶ Chap. 56, "*Pulp Fiction* as Philosophy: Bad Faith, Authenticity, and the Path of the Righteous Man," in this volume) – the film is much more about showing mercy than it is about seeking revenge. (More on this later.) And *Jackie Brown*, a film about a flight attendant double-crossing her male gun smuggling oppressor and taking off with his money, is about female liberation. Besides, *Jackie Brown* cannot tell us much (or as much) about Tarantino's view on vengeance anyway; Tarantino's screenplay for it is based on a novel that he did not write.

Tarantino's quest for vengeance (i.e., his cinematic argument for the moral justification of vengeance) began at the turn of the century, with *Kill Bill Vol. I* and *Vol. II* (2003/2004), which literally starts by displaying the text of the above "Old Klingon Proverb" about revenge. (The quote is inspired by a line from *Star Trek II: The Wrath of Khan*, one of the most well-known vengeance stories of all time.) *Kill Bill* tells the story of Beatrix Kiddo, a killer-for-hire called "The Bride," seeking revenge against Bill and the remaining members of the "Deadly Viper Assassination Squad" (aka the D.iV.A.S.), a group of killers who (on Bill's orders) tried to kill Beatrix after she left the group. The movie is replete with suggestions that her quest is completely and utterly morally justified (even if others might also justifiably seek vengeance on her). As Beatrix herself puts it in the original script, "When fortune smiles on something as violent and ugly as revenge, at the time it seems proof like no other, that not only does God exist, you're doing his will."

Her quest is so obviously justified that Bill, even though he could kill her multiple times, gives Beatrix a fair shot at killing him; he recognizes that he deserves it because he has been a "real bad daddy." "We owe her better than that," he says when deciding to abort the mission to kill her while se is in a coma. "One thing we won't do is sneak into her room in the night like a filthy rat and kill her in her sleep. And the reason we won't do that thing, is because that thing would lower us." Of course, she does kill Bill and the rest of the D.iV.A.S. (save Elle, who Beatrix only blinds by taking her remaining eye). But the film suggests that she would have been justified going even further because, in their attempt to kill Beatrix, the D.iV.A.S. killed Beatrix's soon to be husband and unborn child. As Beatrix later tells D.iV.A.S. knife-fighter Vernita Green, "To get even—even-steven—I would have to kill you, go up to [your daughter] Nikki's room, kill her [and] then wait for your husband, the good

Dr. Bell, to come home and kill him. That would be even Vernita. That'd be about square." Beatrix does not do that; although she does very appropriately kill Vernita with a knife. Likewise, she kills sword wielding O-Ren with Japanese Steel. Similar appropriate fates befall all the D.iV.A.S, including Bill who – thanks to the Five Point Palm Exploding Heart Technique – dies of a "broken heart" (see Roth 2007, p. 87). But when Beatrix is then reunited with the daughter she thought had been killed, the film ends by displaying the quote "THE LIONESS HAS REJOINED HER CUB AND ALL IS RIGHT IN THE JUNGLE."

Tarantino's quest for vengeance continued with *Death Proof* (2007), a film about a serial killer named "Stuntman Mike" who ruthlessly kills young women with his "death proof" stunt car. After befriending three girls in Austin, Texas, and then intentionally killing them in a car crash, he goes to Lebanon, Tennessee, and terrorizes three more. This time, however, two of them are stunt workers themselves; they fight back, survive, and seek out vengeance. Zoe, one of the stunt workers, literally hops on the door of the car and rides it like a horse, as they seek him out. They catch up with him, shoot him (which leads to a wonderful scene of Mike, the serial killer, crying in his car like a baby), make jokes about "tapping his ass" as they ram his car from the rear, and eventually overturn it. They then drag him out of his car and beat him to death; the final blow is a boot heel to the face. Of course, he did not kill *these girls*, but he attempted to, and these young women are acting as proxies for the other young women that he has killed. Regardless, we are clearly meant to celebrate Mike's apparent death; the music is abundantly triumphant. (I literally stood up in the theater and applauded.) To solidify the point, the credits are set to April March's "Chick Habit":

> Hang up the chick habit, Hang it up, daddy ... or you're liable to get licked ... A girl's not a tonic or a pill ... You're just jonesin' for a spill. ... You're gonna need a heap of glue, when they all catch up with you, and they cut you up in two.

(The credits also feature a series of "Shirley cards" from the 1970s, pictures of women who, like stunt workers, work in the background on films but are not seen on screen. The cards are used for picture calibration during film processing; see Rick 2019.)

Then came *Inglourious Basterds* (2009), Tarantino's first of two (maybe three, depending on whether you count *Django*) historical revisionist films, which tells the tale of a band of Jewish American soldiers tasked with posing as civilians in Nazi occupied France and "doin' one thing, and one thing only: Killin' Nazis." In case their quest for revenge, and its justification, is not clear – it is members of one group (Jews) killing the members of another (Nazis) for their egregious crimes against their group – their commander Lt. Aldo Raine spells it out:

> The members of the National Socialist Party have conquered Europe through murder, torture, intimidation, and terror. And that's exactly what we're gonna do to them. Now I don't know bout y'all? But I sure as hell didn't come down from the goddamn Smoky mountains, cross five thousand miles of water, fight my way through half of Sicily, and then jump out of a fuckin' air-o-plane, to teach the Nazis lessons in humanity. Nazi ain't got no humanity. They're the foot soldiers of a Jew hatin', mass murderin' maniac, and they need to

be de-stroyed. That's why any and every son-of-a-bitch we find wearin' a Nazi uniform, they're gonna die.

The story also follows Shosanna Dreyfus, whose French Jewish family is killed by the Nazi Colonel Hans Landa as they hid under the floorboards of a French farmer's home. After barely escaping with her life, she eventually opens a movie house in Paris, where the Nazi government decides they want to screen their new propaganda film *Nation's Pride* for Hitler and all the Nazi top brass. She and her black film projectionist Marcel take it upon themselves to kill them all and end the war. Into *Nation's Pride*, she splices a short film, a close-up of herself saying:

> I have a message for Germany. That you are all going to die. And I want you to look deep into the face of the Jew who's going to do it! Marcel, burn it down. This is Shosanna Dreyfus, and this is the face of Jewish vengeance.

Marcel throws his cigarette on the giant pile of (very flammable) film he has made behind the screen, after barring the doors to the theater shut. The screen explodes in flames, and – as members of Raine's Jewish American troop riddle bullets into Hitler himself, and the Nazi crowd about to be burned alive – Shosanna's projected head can be seen laughing diabolically in the smoke above the crowd. The satisfaction one has watching Jews not only kill Nazis but Hitler and all his top brass, too, is palpable. The viewer does not feel a single ounce of guilt for taking pleasure in their deaths. Landa, because he allows this to happen, is able to "make a deal" with the American government for his freedom and security; however, Raines gets vengeance on him as well by carving a swastika into his forehead to make sure no one ever forgets that he is a Nazi.

Django Unchained (2012) (the "D" is silent) is a film that revels in vengeance for American slaves. Bounty hunter Dr. King Schultz frees Django (along with four other slaves who kill their captors and flee north) to help him track down and kill The Brittle Brothers, the especially brutal former owners of Django and his wife Broomhilda. After successfully accomplishing this task, Schultz and Django join forces and eventually go on to free Broomhilda herself. Along the way, many cruelties of the slave owning South are displayed – including whippings, humiliation, hot boxes, "mandingo fighting" (which has historical roots but is exaggerated in the film; see Harris 2012), hard labor, sexual slavery, slaves being torn apart by dogs, and lots of uses of the N-word (which, before the Civil War, was most definitely a derogatory term; see Kennedy 2001). Schultz and Django also kill many slave-"owning" whites in their quest, including Calvin J. Candie, the especially cruel owner of the Candyland plantation where Broomhilda is enslaved. Indeed, Schultz gives his life for the opportunity to kill Candie, and the film ends with Django personally killing every nonslave left at Candyland (as well as Stephen, the house slave that cooperated with Candie) and blowing the whole place to bits with dynamite. The music, and Broomhilda's final reaction, makes it quite clear: Once again, Tarantino wants us to celebrate. As he himself put it, "[Django] really has a lot of ups and downs, and taps into a lot of different emotions. To me, the trick was balancing all those emotions, so that I could get you where I wanted you to be by the very end. I wanted the audience cheering in triumph at the end" (Williams 2012).

Once Upon a Time in Hollywood (2019), Tarantino's most recent film at the time of this writing, tells the story of (fictional) movie star Rick Dalton and his stunt man, WWII veteran Cliff Booth (who is based on real world stunt men Hal Needham and Gary Kent; see Kibbey 2021). The story is long and takes many turns, but it culminates in Rick and Cliff (and his former prize fighting dog Brandy) preventing members of the Manson family from carrying out the murder of Sharon Tate and her friends (which, in the real world, happened at Roman Polanski's house at 10050 Cielo Drive on Aug. 8, 1969). Indeed, Rick and Cliff not only prevent the murders, but they also give Tex, Katie, and Sadie (the members of the Manson family who carried them out) exactly what they deserved. After they mistakenly enter Rick's residence (instead of the Polanski residence on that fateful night), Brandy mauls Tex and bites off his genitals before Cliff brains him on the front doorstep; Cliff slams Katie's face into practically every surface in the living room (the rotary telephone, the fireplace mantle, and a glass-framed movie poster) until she is dead; then, after Cliff disfigures Sadie by hitting her in the face with a full can of dog food, Rick puts on the finishing touches by burning Sadie's "ass to a crisp" with a flame thrower (which he used in the movie *The 14 Fists of McCluskey to kill Nazis*). It is undoubtedly a scene of revenge; although as fictional characters, Cliff and Rick cannot have been wronged by the real-world Manson family, the film is a revenge fantasy about Hollywood itself giving the Manson family murderers exactly what they deserved for taking Sharron Tate and her friends away from it. The message here is loud and clear: If the Manson family had picked on the tough guys of Hollywood rather than invading the home of a small-in-stature director and a helpless young actress, they would not have stood a chance.

All in all, the conclusion of the argument that Tarantino's films seem to be presenting is that vengeance is morally permissible. If one person or group wrongs another, it is not morally wrong for the victim (or a proxy of the victim) to render a punishment back onto the offender. That is not to say that every killing in his films is justified as an act of vengeance. Beatrix kills the Crazy 88s in self-defense, after trying to assassinate O-Ren directly. And regardless of whether they are as guilty as Hitler, Raine's killing (and treatment) of Nazi soldiers is arguably justified as necessary in times of war. What is more, although Schultz claims that his killing of Ace (one of the Speck Brothers, at the beginning of *Django Unchained*) was an act of self-defense – Ace pointed his gun at Schultz – one could argue that Ace just had it coming because he was a slaver. But the main acts of violence in Tarantino's films, since the turn of the century, have been acts of vengeance that are portrayed as justified.

If nothing else, our emotional reaction to Tarantino's films seems to suggest that we agree – that, indeed, they are justified. Just like with Raine's Jewish soldiers killing the Nazis in *Inglourious Basterds*, we do not feel bad for Stuntman Mike or Tex when they have their faces kicked in, nor do we (nor does it seem like we should) feel bad for celebrating the fact that Beatrix killed Bill or that Django killed every slaver at Candyland. Not only do we find it emotionally satisfying, but since they deserved what they got, we also think what happened was morally good (see Murphy 2000, pp. 788–789). And by relying on our emotional reactions to his films to help bolster this conclusion, Tarantino is doing something quite clever. He is not putting his argument for vengeance in the mouth of one of his characters. His conclusion simply follows from the fact that it is difficult to morally object when people in his films who deserve revenge get it. The world even seems a little more balanced and fairer when they do.

All in all, I think that it is safe to say that most people's moral intuitions align with this conclusion– especially after watching a Tarantino film. But emotional intuitions, much less emotional reactions, are not always a reliable guide to moral truths – especially when they have been manipulated by a skillful filmmaker like Tarantino. What is more, moral philosophers and ethicists usually maintain that revenge is not morally justified. So, it is to philosophical arguments about the moral permissibility of vengeance that we shall now turn. We shall begin by looking at some common arguments against vengeance.

Common Arguments Against Vengeance

> To say that I get a big kick out of violence in movies and can enjoy violence in movies but find it totally abhorrent in real life – I can feel totally justified and totally comfortable with that statement. I do not think that one is a contradiction of the other. Real life violence is real life violence. Movies are movies.
> —Quentin Tarantino (Zuckerman 2013)

In a discussion with friends, many arguments against revenge might come up. They will likely not be very sophisticated, but given how common they are, it is worth giving them a look.

Common Argument 1: Vengeance Can Go Too Far

The first common argument against vengeance is quite simple: It can go too far. Because how much punishment to dish out will be determined by the person seeking revenge, that person might dish out more punishment than the offender deserves. But the answer to this argument is equally simple. Obviously, revenge is not morally justified if the punishment is not proportionate to the crime. It is not morally acceptable, for example, for Bill to kill Beatrix and her fiancé and his family for simply "breaking his heart." But that does not mean that vengeance is not justified when the punishment is proportionate. So, all we need to do in response to this argument is add a clause about "proportionality" to clarify Tarantino's thesis.

> **The vengeance thesis**: It is morally permissible for a person to seek vengeance against someone who has wronged them (or wronged their group) with a punishment that is proportionate to the moral crime they committed (e.g., a punishment that is morally equivalent or causes them as much pain as they caused to their victim(s)).

This, it would seem, is consistent with Tarantino's films. All acts of vengeance they depict as morally justified – or at least the big ones which are the focus of the films (like Shoshanna's revenge against the Nazis, Django's revenge against slavers, and Beatrix's revenge against Bill) – are clearly proportionate. Granted, one might challenge the proportionality of Beatrix's vengeance; after all, Bill did not succeed in killing Beatrix or her daughter BB, yet – even knowing this – Beatrix did succeed in killing Bill. But there are three reasons, which will teach us something about the relevant concept of proportionality, that Beatrix's revenge was not disproportionate.

First, just like Django and Shoshana, the Bride is acting as a proxy for others that Bill killed. At first, she is acting on behalf of her daughter, who Beatrix had every reason to believe was dead. (Of course, unbeknownst to Beatrix, her daughter was actually alive. Whether that fact affects the morality of her actions is debatable.) But when she kills Bill, after knowing that her daughter is alive, she could still be acting as a proxy for the rest of her wedding party, including her future husband, who indeed Bill did kill. Granted, she may not have been that close with them yet, but they were her future family.

Second, when it comes to proportionality, it is not really about exchanging equal amounts of pain, a literal eye for an eye. It is about moral equivalence – doing something to them that is *as bad* as what they did to you. And putting someone in a coma in an attempt to murder them is pretty much morally equivalent to actually murdering them. Think of it this way. Beatrix is actually doing to Bill exactly what he did to her: attempting to murder him. The fact that he failed to do so and, by sheer luck, only left her in a coma does not mean that Beatrix is only morally allowed to put him in a coma in return. Neither incompetence nor luck entails absolution. In other words, Beatrix *attempting* to kill Bill is proportionate because he *attempted* to murder her, and the fact that she succeeds, where he failed, does not change that. As Budd put it in *Kill Bill Vol. 2.*, despite the fact that he knows that Bill's attempt to use the D.iV.A.S to kill Beatrix failed, "That woman deserves her revenge, and we deserve to die."[1]

Third, even if proportionality is about exchanging equal amounts of pain, the punishment Beatrix dishes out is still not overcompensation. Indeed, it might not be enough. Bill has a rather painless death, as do the rest of the D.iV.A.S that Beatrix kills (Vernita and O-Ren); Beatrix, on the other hand, was continually raped while in her coma (and apparently remembers it) and suffered the anguish of the recovery and of believing that her daughter had been killed. Indeed, Beatrix even refrained from getting "even-steven" with Vernita by killing her husband and daughter, and showed "mercy" to Sofie Fatale by only cutting off her arm. The only person Beatrix perhaps causes to suffer an equal amount of pain is Elle, because Beatrix blinds her for life. (Budd, recall, was not killed by Beatrix but by Elle and the black mamba).

Something else in *Kill Bill*, related to this objection, that must be considered is the words of Hattori Hanzō. "Revenge is never a straight line. It's a forest, and like a forest it's easy to lose your way... To get lost..." If getting lost means, for example, that you end up accidentally killing innocents while seeking revenge – well, obviously, that is not justified either. But Tarantino does not usually have innocents getting killed by those seeking revenge; at worst, it is those sworn to protect the offender – like the Crazy 88. But Beatrix even goes out of her way to not kill those she does not have to – like the young member of the 88, who poses no threat to her, to whom she gives a spanking. "This is what you get for fucking around with the Yakuzas! Go home to your mother!" She also tries to prevent herself from having a right of self-defense against Go-Go by begging her to "walk away" and not defend "her mistress." (In the original script, she makes a similar offer to "Mr. Barrell" – a high-henchman of O-Ren's who does not appear in the film – and he takes it!) The fact that you could kill innocents during a quest of vengeance does not mean that vengeance is not justified; it just means you need to be careful not to do so while you seek it, or that you should end the quest if you realize it requires it.

Common Argument 2: Avengers Do Not Have Perfect Knowledge

Now, it perhaps goes without saying that, in order for a vengeance quest to be morally justified, the person the offended seeks revenge against must actually be guilty of the crime in question. It is not morally justified to seek revenge against someone who did not actually wrong you, even if you are convinced that they did. But this can serve as the basis for yet another argument against the moral justification of revenge. As Morbory pointed out in *The Hateful Eight* in the quote above, the thing about "frontier justice" (vengeance) is, it is just as "apt to be wrong as right." Thus, one could argue, since those seeking revenge could be wrong about who wronged them (or whether they did it intentionally), and thus can never be 100% sure that the supposed offender deserves it, seeking revenge can never be morally justified.

This argument, however, is faulty; its conclusion does not follow. It is true that if one does not *know* that the targeted person actually is the offender, then one should not seek revenge against them – such an action would not be morally justified. Epistemic justification of guilt is required before moral justification of punishment exists. That, however, does not mean that if you actually are in a position to know who wronged you – just as Beatrix knew that Bill tried to kill her, or Django was "positive" that the person riding the horse through the cotton field was Ellis Brittle – that you would be unjustified in seeking revenge. Of course, a person can never be 100% certain of the offender's guilt, but that is because no one can ever be 100% certain of anything. (You cannot even be 100% certain that the world around you is real because you could be dreaming.) But it is possible to be certain enough. Django knows what the Brittle Brothers did to him and his wife. And when one is certain *enough*, vengeance, it would seem, could be morally justified (see Murphy 2000: 792–793).

Notice that, if the above objection worked, legal retribution would never be justified. It is not possible for the courts to ever be 100% certain of a criminal's guilt either, so it is always possible that they could be wrong. But it is possible for them to be certain enough – to establish guilt beyond a reasonable doubt – and when that bar is met, retribution is considered morally justified. The same, it seems, is true with vengeance. As John Ruth puts it, in his response to Morbory warning that frontier justice can be wrong, "Well, not in your case [Daisy]. In your case, you'd have it coming." Indeed, the family and friends of Daisy's victim very likely saw her commit her crime, and thus it would be beyond a reasonable doubt that she was deserving of punishment.

A similar point is made by Charles Barton in his 1999 book *Getting Even: Revenge as a Form of Justice*. Yes, revenge can get it wrong, but so can legal retribution. Legal punishments can be (and have been) too severe; innocents can be (and have been) convicted. But that is not a good reason to never legally punish criminals. It is a good reason to do so carefully, and to insist that when punishment is dished out, it should be dished out proportionally and on those who are guilty. But it is not a good reason to forgo seeking legal retribution for those who we are certain enough are deserving. In the same way, vengeance can go too far, or punish the innocent – but that does not entail victims should not seek proportional revenge when they are certain enough that someone is deserving. (That does not mean they should; it just means this argument that they should not does not work.) Granted, in the real world, victims are probably often not as sure of things as the victims in Tarantino's movies, but that does not mean they never are.

Common Argument 3: Two Wrongs Do Not Make a Right

The old adage "Two wrongs don't make a right" is often invoked in discussions about revenge. But as an argument against the morality of vengeance, it just begs the question (i.e., it assumes the truth of what it is trying to prove). The question of whether vengeance is "a wrong" is the very issue at hand; to just say that "to respond in kind to a wrong act is itself wrong" is to just assume that vengeance is wrong – not to actually demonstrate that it is. The defender of vengeance can just reply to this adage by saying: When someone seeks and gets revenge on someone who deserves it, with a proportional punishment, there are no two wrongs. There is a wrong, and then there is an act of vengeance that makes things right.

Common Argument 4: It Is Always Wrong to Harm Others

Others might suggest that it is just always wrong to harm another person, even if they harmed you. But this endorses something akin to universal pacifism – the idea that all acts of violence, no matter the circumstance, are immoral – and most people do not take universal pacifism to be plausible. Most certainly, wanton acts of violence are immoral, but violence for the purpose of self-defense, or in the course of a just war (e.g., killing Nazis in WWII), is usually seen as morally justified. In other words, there are examples of justified violence. That does not entail that vengeance *is* morally justified; most acts of violence are morally wrong, and vengeance might be one of them. It just means you cannot use the platitude "all violence is always wrong" as an argument against vengeance, because it seems that platitude is mistaken. (For more on different kinds of pacifism, and whether they are morally defensible, see Paula Smithka's ▶ Chap. 14, "The Doctor as Philosopher: The Collectivist-Realist Pacifism of the Doctor and the Quest for Social Justice," in this volume.)

Perhaps the reply to this argument can be put this way: It seems perfectly clear that we have a moral obligation to not harm those who have not harmed us. That is a steadfast rule. But that rule makes no sense if, once someone harms us, we still have an obligation to not harm them. If that is the case, why is not the rule just "never harm anyone . . . ever, regardless." As a rule, that is pretty difficult to swallow, so that rule does not provide a solid reason to conclude that vengeance is never morally justified. (More on this reply later.)

Common Argument 5: Vengeance Does No Good

Another common argument against vengeance suggests that it "does no good." Killing a victim's murderer does not bring the victim back to life. But this argument is quite shortsighted. First, not all acts of revenge are in response to a killing. An act of vengeance against a thief or a liar might actually right the wrong that was originally committed. A person might get their money or property back, or get the offender to admit that they lied about the victim, thus restoring the trust of others. Second of all, even in a case of murder, "bringing the victim back" is not the only kind of good that vengeance might accomplish. It is commonly thought vengeance could serve the purpose of deterrence – motiving others to not commit a similar crime – just like legal retribution does.

What is more, one could argue that vengeance does the good of setting things right – of giving someone (both the victim and the offender) what they deserve. Justice and fairness are both goods, in their own right, regardless of whether achieving them brings about other goods. A world that is more just and fair is intrinsically a better world. For example, in a deleted scene of *Natural Born Killers*, instead of getting away, Mickey and Mallory Knox are killed in cold blood by a fellow serial killer named Owen. He is seeking neither retribution nor revenge; still, it would just seem morally better if Mickey and Mallory got what they deserved for their crimes, instead of getting away. Similarly, vengeance – when applied proportionally – assures that the offender gets what they deserve. Notice that legally punishing a murder will not bring back the victim either, but we do not think that is a reason to not seek justice legally.

Indeed, in his article "Private Revenge and its Relation to Punishment," Brain Rosebury (2009) overviews the classic arguments against revenge, finds "uncertainty and equivocation [in such arguments] over the ethical significance of acts of revenge," and concludes that it is extremely difficult to conclude that revenge is morally wrong if one does not think that legal retribution is morally wrong. In other words, even if revenge does not have a deterrent effect (as legal punishment usually does), if one thinks that it is morally good, in and of itself, when the law bestows upon a criminal a punishment they deserve, then one should think that it is morally good, in and of itself, when a victim is able to bestow upon their offender a punishment they deserve. In my research, I found a similar idea in an undergraduate honor thesis paper, "The Nature of Revenge," by Stephanie DiGiorgio (2017). She argues that revenge is justified because retribution is justified; revenge is just retribution carried out by a particular kind of individual (the offender's victim). In other words, it is just morally good when people get what they deserve; it does not matter who gives it to them; and indeed, it might even be a little better when the victim does it, because they get personal satisfaction out of it. Of course, if a person disagrees and thinks that retribution is morally wrong – perhaps they reject a retributive notion of justice and only think that wrongdoers deserve rehabilitation – they will think that revenge cannot be justified. But the notion that those who are guilty deserve to be punished is common enough that both Rosebury and DiGiorgio's main point is quite relevant.

But is Rosebury right that the classic arguments against revenge are unconvincing? Let us turn first to the arguments of historical philosophers, and then more contemporary ones, to answer that question.

Historical Arguments About Vengeance

> Tarantino is an ass . . . he's a hypocrite . . . if violence is so terrible like he says, why is there so much of it in his movies? Truth is, the guy really gets off on it.
> —Amy, *Dust of the Earth* (Lages (2021), Chapter 5)

Obviously, if one is a Christian, one does not seek revenge; both Jesus (Luke 6:27–29) and the Apostle Paul (Romans 12:17–19) condemn it. But this does not establish that revenge is morally unjustified: (a) Jesus and Paul do not present a philosophical argument; they just command; (b) those who are not Christian do not "have to" follow that command; (c) because of its focus on "atonement theory" (the idea that Jesus died for our sins), retribution (making sure due punishment is dished out for moral transgressions) lies at the center of the entire Christian religion, so it is not clear that Christianity's condemnation of revenge is consistent. After all, is not the Old Testament God vengeful (Deut 32:35, Psalm 94:1, Ezekiel 25:17), and are not we made in God's image? And finally (d) Christianity is not the last word in morality. The Bible also forbids premarital sex (1 Corinthians 7:2) and prescribes the death penalty for homosexuality (Lev. 20:13) and disobeying your parents (Deuteronomy 21:18–21); further, it endorses infanticide (I Samuel 15:3–4), slavery and beating slaves (Exodus 21), genocide (Numbers 31), and sexism (1 Timothy 2:11–12)]. So, the fact that the Bible condemns revenge does not entail that it is immoral.

If we want an argument that clearly establishes that vengeance is unjustified, we will have to look elsewhere. Given the near universal moral condemnation of vengeance among philosophers, one might expect there to be a well-known argument, from a classic historical philosopher, that deals it a death blow. But as we shall now see, this is not the case.

Plato on Vengeance

It is common to think that Plato condemned revenge – but it is far from clear that he did. Take Plato's *Republic*, where he says "the injuring of another can be in no case just" (*Jowett (trans.)* 2013, p. 28). Since it seems that revenge seeks to injure others, it would follow that revenge is unjustified. But in the *Republic*, when Plato talks about "justice" and "being just," he is not talking about people getting what they deserve. Instead, he is talking about being what he calls a just person; this, Plato says, requires a person's soul/mind to be ordered in a certain kind of way. It has three parts: reason, drive/spirit, and appetites; in a just person, reason rules and keeps both one's drive and appetites in check. So, when Plato says that "it is never just to harm someone," Plato means that a person ruled by reason would not harm someone; but that is different than saying that an individual act of vengeance is morally unjustified. It does not entail that the offender is not morally deserving of punishment or that a moral wrong has been done if the offender's victim punishes him.

What is more, in the relevant passage, Plato is worried about a powerful person who goes around punishing all his enemies (those the person perceives as bad) and helping all his friends (those the person perceives as good) – not someone who is concerned with giving those who are truly bad (are known to be guilty of a moral crime) the punishment they deserve. Plato does address this topic the *Gorgias*, but there Plato argues that punishment for wrongdoing is actually beneficial. The person who does wrong and gets away with it (i.e., who is not punished) may think they are happier, but in reality they are not, for they miss the correction to their character that due punishment accomplishes (and having a "just" character is the only way to be truly happy). Indeed, for Plato, to do wrong but to "not suffer for it is the first and greatest [wrong/evil] of them all" and "escaping punishment for one's transgressions [is] worse than enduring it" (Cope 1864, pp. 56, 46). Plato's point is more about the internal condition of a wrongdoer, and what someone should do when they themselves are guilty: They should confess and seek the appropriate corrective punishment from the state. And, it is important to note, Plato would argue that ideally it is the state that should be punishing wrongdoers. But Plato's argument at least entails that punishing wrongdoers, especially when they do not turn themselves in and the state fails in its task of holding them responsible, is not only beneficial to them – but also it is what a just person should do. Indeed, to ensure that they are not punished would be "the worse punishment" so to speak, for that would ensure that their character is not corrected and that they continue to suffer from the natural consequences of their evil act (Cope, pp. 58–59). To be clear, Plato was not fond of people acting as if they were the state, but his argument in the *Gorgias* entails that, if the state fails in its duties to punish wrongdoers, a person should.

In reply, one might say that Plato's argument in the *Gorgias* only entails that nonlethal revenge is justified; killing someone in revenge would not benefit them. But Plato also makes a distinction between evil doers who can benefit from punishment and those, who because of their extreme crimes, are "incurable" and cannot benefit from punishment. The latter, Plato says, should still be punished because they "serve as an example to the rest of [hu]mankind, that others seeing the sufferings that he endures may be brought by terror to amendment of life" (Cope, p. 128). Granted, Plato thinks that such people endure "the severest most painful and most fearful sufferings in that prison house in the world below [i.e., the afterlife]," but it still follows that "others are benefited who behold them [suffering] for their transgressions" when they see the offender suffering in the real world. What follows from this is not that victims should not seek to kill in revenge when that would be the proportionate punishment – especially when their offender will otherwise get away with it – but that if the offender is an incurable evil-doer deserving of death, the victim dishing out the punishment of death should make sure that others know about it, so that they can be (for a lack of better terms) scared straight.

Granted, in the *Gorgias*, Plato argues that one should not seek vengeance as the tyrant does, but this amounts to the aforementioned punishing of your enemies, *regardless of their actual guilt*. Nothing in Plato's argument entails that it is morally unjustified for victims to seek to punish their known offenders for their transgressions with a punishment that is equal to their known crime (especially if the state will not). Ensuring that they are punished is what a just person would do, and if the law will fail to punish them, a just person would ensure that they were punished by other means.

Think of it this way. Plato scholar Gregory Vlastos (1991) points out that since Plato believes "we should never do injustice" he also thinks that "we should never do injustice in return for an injustice" (p. 195). Further, continues Vlastos, because "we should never do any evil to a human being ... we should never return evil for evil" (p. 196). But to conclude that these ideas entail Plato believed victims should never seek to proportionally punish their offenders would be to assume that doing so is an "injustice" or an "evil." Such an assumption begs the question just as much as the above "two wrongs don't make a right" argument; it assumes that vengeance is an evil when, whether it is an evil, is the very question at hand. As Vlastos points out, Plato thought that the just person could not injure or harm another person (without ceasing to be just; see p. 197), but as we just discovered from the *Gorgias,* Plato did not consider punishing evil doers to injure or harm them. Put simply, "we should never do injustice in return for an injustice" means victims should not *unduly* punish those who do the evil; it does not mean they should not punish them at all.

Spinoza on Vengeance

A full discussion of Baruch Spinoza's argument against vengeance could get us bogged down in his metaphysics – how he thinks the universe is unified by a single substance and all things are determined and interconnected. Seeking vengeance on someone would involve the idea that you were acted upon by an outside force – they wronged you – rather than realizing that you were acted upon by the universe itself. If I have "adequate" knowledge of the causal interconnectedness of the one substance (Nature), Spinoza argues, I would see that I am inextricably intertwined with all of the other causes, including what supposed "external things" (like other people) to do me. So, in a sense, all of these "external" things do not really exist – we are all just modes of one Nature – and so vengeance would be unjustified. You see, for

Spinoza, to think a "wrong" has been done to you, you have to take on a very particular perspective within the universe. A wrong can be done to "me" by "you" only if there are boundaries that truly separate me from you. But for Spinoza, since there is only one substance – Nature – these boundaries and individual perspectives are only a confused way of understanding the universe. They do not really exist. (It is like thinking of a line as a collection of points; dimensionless points cannot really make up a line; we can think of a line as a collection of points, but really all that exists is the line. In the same way, delineating between persons is conceptually possible, but really, all that exists is the universe.) Once I adequately understand that there really is only one perspective – the vast interconnections of one universe – I understand there is no individual perspective and, therefore, there can be no moral wrong. And if there is no moral wrong, it does not make sense to seek vengeance. That, at least, is the argument.

Again, a full reply to Spinoza's argument against vengeance would require a full understanding and reply to his metaphysics – and that is well beyond the scope of this chapter. I will still say, however, two things. First, few philosophers today accept his metaphysic, and certainly most nonphilosophers do not; so it would seem most who think that vengeance is unjustified will have to look elsewhere for an argument. Second, even if his metaphysic is true, there seems to be a logical inconsistency in an argument against vengeance that is rooted in it. If a victim of an offender is mistaken for objecting to the person who wronged them, because they fail to recognize the causal interconnectedness of the one substance, then so too is the offender mistaken for objecting to the person who seeks vengeance against them.

Think of it this way: If a victim cannot object to an offender's initial evil because moral wrong is an illusion, then the offender cannot object to the victim seeking vengeance for exactly the same reason. Any argument that suggests that what the offender did was not really morally wrong – because, for example, they were determined to do it by outside forces, or because all moral theories are bankrupt and there are no moral truths – will have to say that what the victim does in response is not morally wrong either. What is sauce for the goose is sauce for the gander. An argument that questions the legitimacy of moral evaluations cannot turn around and morally evaluate vengeance and declare that it is morally wrong. In the same way, if what the offender does to a victim is not really morally wrong because of the universe's interconnectedness, then the same must be said of the victim's quest for vengeance: It is not really morally wrong.

To respond to Spinoza's condemnation of revenge, it would be more useful to look at the single passage of Spinoza's *Ethics* (1677/1954), where he argues that "He who lives according to the guidance of reason strives as much as possible to repay the hatred, anger, or contempt of others toward himself with love or generosity" (p. 223). As it relates to our thesis, there are a few things to say. First, even though this is often cited as the passage in which Spinoza condemns revenge (see Bar-elli and Heyd 1986, p. 80), he is not actually talking about revenge. He is talking about how to repay "hatred, anger, or contempt" – not about "the desire which, springing from mutual hatred, urges us to injure those who, from a similar emotion, have injured us" (which is how he defines vengeance on page 183). In other words, he is arguing that we should respond to hatred with love, not that we should not return injury with injury (i.e., with proportional punishment).

Granted, in this passage, Spinoza does say that "He who wishes to avenge injuries by hating in return does indeed live miserably." But "X will make you miserable" does not necessarily entail that "X is immoral." (A lawyer working hard to bring a guilty party to justice might make them miserable, but that does not mean that doing so is immoral.) It might be irrational to make oneself miserable, but as we shall discuss below (when we discuss Joshua Gert's article "Revenge is Sweet"), and we discussed above (with Plato), there is not a direct relationship between morality and rationality. Something can be rational but immoral; something can be irrational yet still moral. So even if a rational person would not seek revenge, that does not mean revenge is immoral. Besides, (a) Spinoza does not defend this notion (he says "there is no need" to defend it), and (b) as we just saw with Plato, the desire for vengeance could come from a nonhateful place that does not seek to injure. It could be motivated by a desire for justice, to hold the offender accountable, or even do them good.

Lastly, Spinoza's argument here is grounded in the idea that "Hatred can never be good" (p. 221) and "All emotions of hatred are evil" (p. 223). But to this, I simply say that hate is not always a bad thing. Some things deserve to be hated; they need to be hated. Yes, it would be better if there never were any Nazis or slavery, but given that they do exist – isn't a world where they are hated better than one where they are not? Isn't it better than a world where they are tolerated? To put it bluntly, returning hate with love is not a realistic ethic. As Karl Popper (1945/2012) taught us, to return intolerance with tolerance allows intolerance to win. Because the intolerant will not return the favor, a world in which intolerance is tolerated becomes a world ruled by intolerance (p. 581). Likewise, a world where hate is always returned with love becomes a world ruled by hate; the hateful will not return the favor. The moral person, rather than just loving everything, recognizes what should be loved, and what should be hated, and responds accordingly. Wrongful injury should be hated, and fairness and justice should be loved.

Thomas Hobbes on Vengeance

Around the same time as Spinoza, Thomas Hobbes (1651) wrote *De Cive: Liberty*. In it, he seems to condemn vengeance when he says,

> The fift[h] precept of the Law of nature is: That we must forgive him who repents, and asketh pardon for what is past;... The sixth precept of the naturall Law is, [t]hat in revenge...and punishments we must have our eye not at the evill past, but the future good. That is: It is not lawfull to inflict punishment for any other end, but that the offender may be corrected, or that others warned by his punishment may become better. (p. 19)

This may remind the reader of Vincent's philosophy from *Pulp Fiction*. "[O]nce a man admits that he is wrong, he's immediately forgiven for all wrong-doings." But there are three reasons to think Hobbes might sympathize with Jules' reply to

Vincent's philosophy: "Get the fuck out my face with that shit! The motherfucker said that shit never had to pick up itty-bitty pieces of skull on account of your dumb ass."

First, Hobbes also says if someone does not repent, the laws of nature do not demand forgiving mercy.

> But Peace granted to him that repents not, that is, to him that retains an hostile mind…that… seeks not Peace, but opportunity, is not properly Peace but feare, and therefore is not commanded by nature. (p. 19)

Since Vincent has only "admitted wrongdoing" but not asked for forgiveness, and indeed may even retain a "hostile mind," it does not seem that Hobbes would think that vengeance against Vincent is unjustified. Jules is certainly warranted in making him pick up the pieces of Marvin's skull (although this is not vengeance, it seems that it is Vincent who should be doing the dirtier job since the incident was his fault), and Marvin's family would seem to have a right of vengeance against Vincent as well.

Second, for Hobbes, natural law is not morally binding. It only defines what is prudent for a person to do. (Philosophically, Hobbes is a moral relativist.) Really, for Hobbes, the only thing that is wrong is to disobey "the sovereign," the person who is in charge of the state. And that is only because the alternative is anarchy, and it is prudent to try to avoid anarchy. It is not because it is immoral (see Mathewes 2021).

Third, vengeance may not be wrong for Hobbes, even if it is forbidden by the state. In at least one place, Hobbes says that, if doing so requires a person to forfeit their honor or life, they are not morally bound to follow the rules of the state. Granted, this is confusing, given what Hobbes says in other places about the absolute authority of the state (see Lloyd 2002, Section 9). But since defending one's honor is often tied up in claims of vengeance (see Sommers 2009), it is not clear that Hobbes would forbid vengeance, even if it were illegal. In any event, since most agree that it is not morally wrong to disobey immoral laws, Hobbes's argument far from establishes that revenge cannot be morally justified. According to Hobbes, the only reason it would be immoral is if it was forbidden by the state, and most philosophers do not think the law defines morality.

John Locke on Vengeance

Because the philosopher John Locke (1689/2003) suggests that you cannot seek revenge even against a horribly abusive tyrant, one might assume that he would forbid revenge generally.

> Must the people then always lay themselves open to the cruelty and rage of tyranny? Must they see their cities pillaged…their wives and children exposed to the tyrant's lust and fury…and all the miseries of want and oppression, and yet sit still? … I answer: Self-defence is a part of the law of nature; nor can it be denied the community, even against

the king himself: but to revenge themselves upon him, must by no means be allowed them; it being not agreeable to that law. (Chapter 19, section 233)

However, it turns out that he forbids this not because there is something morally wrong with revenge, but because there is something morally wrong with crossing social barriers. An act of revenge against a tyrant would

> ...exceed the bounds of due reverence and respect. [Those wronged] may repulse the present attempt, but must not revenge past violences: for it is natural for us to defend life and limb, but that an inferior should punish a superior, is against nature. (ibid)

Since Locke does not forbid "revenge amongst equals" (we might call it), and since the "social classism" that serves as the basis of what vengeance he does forbid is morally outdated, it does not seem that Locke's argument can be used as a solid basis to morally forbid revenge either.

Indeed, Locke argues that, in the state of nature, anyone can (and should) punish anyone else for their wrongdoings – and such punishments should be proportional.

> And thus, in the state of nature, one man comes by a power over another; but yet no absolute or arbitrary power, to use a criminal, when he has got him in his hands, according to the passionate heats, or boundless extravagancy of his own will; but only to retribute to him, so far as calm reason and conscience dictate, what is proportionate to his transgression, which is so much as may serve for reparation and restraint: for these two are the only reasons, why one man may lawfully do harm to another, which is that we call punishment. (Chapter 2, Section 8)

Of course, this does not mean vengeance is justified outside the state of nature (under the social contract); part of the reason we agree to give over certain rights, like the right to vengeance, to the government is so that we do not have to do such things ourselves (and we do not have to worry about people unjustly doing them to us). But if the government fails to do its duty in this regard and does not hold a person you know is responsible for harming you accountable, it would seem that Locke would say that seeking vengeance on your own would be justified (just like Locke thinks that rebellion against the government is justified when it does not hold up its end of the social contract, and fails to protect a person's life, liberty, or property; this, by the way, is how Locke thinks one should respond to an abusive tyrant: rebellion not revenge).

Friedrich Nietzsche on Vengeance

The philosopher Friedrich Nietzsche argued that one should avoid resentment. Since that is an emotion that fuels vengeance, it would seem that whatever reason he gives to forgo resentment could be used to forbid vengeance. But Feffrie Murphy (2000) argues that the reason Nietzsche advises us to avoid resentment is because, given the laws of society, such an emotion must remain suppressed and thus will lead to frustration. Resentment then, and thus the desire for vengeance, would usually not be in a person's self-interest. But that in no way entails that, when resentment would not be repressed and one has a legit opportunity to enact revenge (and not be caught) – like Beatrix has with Bill, and Django has with the slavers – it would be morally wrong to do so. To draw an analogy: It might be in a young man's self-interest to not desire to marry, say, Katy Perry or Beyonce. That desire will most likely be frustrated. That does not mean, however, that if such an opportunity presented itself, it would be immoral to pursue it.

Indeed, "for Nietzsche, all morality is based on the personal drive for vengeance, and the civilized guise of abstract, universal justice cannot conceal this fact from the sharp eye of the 'genealogist.' Revenge is hailed by Nietzsche as the personal and human attitude (in contrast with cool justice); he despises people who have no capacity for revenge" (Bar-elli and Heyd 1986, pp. 75–76). Granted, Nietzsche "also declares that the virtue of self-overcoming consists, among other things, of the capacity to forego vengeance" (ibid., p. 76). But that just means that forgiveness is praiseworthy, not that vengeance is never morally justified.

Modern Arguments Regarding Vengeance

> If my answers frighten you Vincent, then you should cease asking scary questions.
> —Jules Winfield (*Pulp Fiction*)

So far, we have only considered common and historical arguments against revenge. Have more contemporary philosophers come up with better arguments against the morality of revenge?

The Never-Ending Cycle of Violence

Instead of arguing that revenge does "no good," it is quite common for philosophers to argue that it leads to more harm. For example, Stillwell et al. (2008) conducted studies which suggest that, while a person who is seeking vengeance usually thinks that the punishment they dish out to the offender is proportionate, the offender usually thinks the punishment is excessive. This leads the latter to then think that they have a right to vengeance (to "equal things out" so to speak), thus leading to "an escalating cycle of revenge, stemming from ongoing and spiraling attempts to restore equity" (253). In other words, acts of vengeance lead to more, which lead to more – and the cycle never ends. As Tarantino once put it, "In real life there are no bad guys. Everybody just has their own perspective" (see Hendrickson 2013).

Think of how, in *Kill Bill*, Vernita Green's daughter Nikki sees Beatrix kill her mother. Beatrix says, "it was not my intention to do this in front of you. For that, I'm sorry. But you can take my word for it. Your mother had it coming. When you grow up, if you still feel raw about it, I'll be waiting." Many have suspected that Tarantino's long-awaited tenth and final film will be *Kill Bill Vol. 3*, a story about

Nikki's quest for revenge against Beatrix. But, of course, if Beatrix's daughter B.B. watches Nikki kill Beatrix, we could have a *Kill Bill Vol. 4*, and then a *Kill Bill Vol. 5*. And while a whole list of never-ending Tarantino movies sounds great, in the real world a never-ending cycle of revenge would not be. As Ghandi famously put it, "an eye for an eye leaves the whole world blind."

However, as an argument that seeking revenge is always morally wrong, the "never ending cycle of violence" argument falls short. First, revenge need not always lead to such a cycle; we certainly cannot know that there always will be one. For example, in *Inglourious Basterds*, all the heads of the Nazi party are killed and the war is ended; its seems unlikely that such an act would have led to further acts of vengeance; everyone who would seek it would have been dead. If one has an opportunity to seek vengeance, knowing that success would not lead to a cycle of returning violence, then the worry about such a cycle cannot entail that vengeance in that case is unjustified. Second, even if an act of vengeance does lead to a cycle of violence, that does not necessarily mean that it is immoral. Consequentialists would say that it does, but consequentialists measure the moral acceptability of an action based solely on its consequences; many philosophers think that there are other considerations – like justice and fairness. For example, suppose a known murder's sister promised to go out and murder more people if her brother (the murder) was convicted and punished by the state for the murders he committed. Would that make legally punishing the murderer morally unjustified? It seems not. It would still be good that the murder was punished, because justice was served – even if his sister went out and did more harm to others as a result.

Govier and Uniacke: Forgiveness, *Schadenfreude*, and Revenge's Rationality

In her book *Forgiveness and Revenge*, philosopher Trudy Govier (2002) argues that we should always seek to forgive even the worst offenders because such offenders are still persons, deserving of respect, who could still possibly change their ways. Obviously, if she is right, this would entail that we should never seek revenge. In her review of Govier's book, however, Margaret Walker (2003) observes that Govier never really presents a convincing argument for forgiveness because her expectations do not align with the real world. Many of the worst offenders are beyond any hope of change or reconciliation. Sure, their rehabilitation is within the realm of logical possibility, but that does not mean it is reasonable to expect them to or that holding them accountable for their actions is morally wrong. At best, Govier's argument entails that forgiveness is morally better than vengeance – but not that vengeance is always morally unjustified. What is more, in many cases, true universal forgiveness can leave victims vulnerable to further harms; it can leave the worst of offenders free to offend again.

Philosopher Suzanne Uniacke (2000) argues that, if vengeance is wrong, it is not because it is sadistic or just *schadenfreude* (the German word for taking pleasure in the suffering of others). Sadists enjoy suffering for its own sake – as do those who seek schadenfreude – regardless of whether the person is innocent or guilty. (Many people think those who enjoy reality TV enjoy *schadenfreude* a bit too much.) Those who seek revenge are different. While there might be a certain amount of satisfaction in seeing the offender suffer – the kind of satisfaction we feel at the end of *Inglourious Basterds*, *Django*, and *Death Proof* when the Nazis, the slavers, and Stuntman Mike get what they deserve – it is not the enjoyment of suffering for its own sake. It is the enjoyment that comes from watching people get what they deserve.

Uniacke does argue, however, that it is irrational to seek what she calls "revenge... the attempt, at some cost or risk to oneself, to impose suffering upon those who have made one suffer, because they have made one suffer ... [because] [r]ational individuals follow the principles of letting bygones be bygones, cutting their losses and ignoring sunk costs, whereas the avenger typically refuses to forget an affront or harm to which he has been exposed" (p. 62). In other words, it is irrational to harm someone simply because they harmed you, because rational action looks forward to the future, rather than backward to the past. But it does not seem that Uniacke's argument can therefore be used to conclude that revenge is morally unjustified.

First, the fact that revenge is *irrational* does not mean that it is *immoral*. Although we will explore this more in a bit, rationality has different criteria than morality. Second, it is not clear that revenge is always backward looking; it could have a future deterrent effect (e.g., it can keep the offender from reoffending). In his article "Is revenge about retributive justice, deterring harm, or both?" Jeffrey Osgood (2017) shows (via studies) that deterrence is a common motivation for revenge, even if it is not the most common motivation (retribution is most common). Third, Uniacke distinguishes revenge from what she calls "vengeance," which is motivated by moral indignation (rather than just the returning of injury for injury) and the desire to see that people get what they deserve. Vengeance, Uniacke admits, could be morally justified, because people getting what they deserve is a moral good. Since that is the motiving factor for Tarantino's characters, and moral satisfaction is why we celebrate at the end of so many of his films, it does not seem that Uniacke's argument can be used to argue against the kind of vengeance seeking that we have been discussing. In short, seeking to trade a harm for a harm might be irrational, but personally seeking to ensure than one's offender gets what they deserve could be morally justified.

Oldenquist and the Purpose of Holding Offenders Accountable

Ironically, in "The Case for Revenge," Andrew Oldenquist (1986) does not so much argue for revenge as he argues for state-sanctioned legal retribution. According to Oldenquist, the main reason the state should punish criminals is not its deterrent effect (although that is a positive aspect of it). It is because doing so shows a kind of respect for the community; it reinforces the behavior standards of the community and the kind of character the state expects its citizens to have and shows that those standards and expectations are worthy of defense. Likewise, it shows respect for the victims; for the state to not punish the one who harmed them would be like their family not burying their body. There are other ways to dispose of bodies in a sanitary manner, but they do not show the same respect. Likewise, there are other ways to deal with criminals besides retribution, but they do not show the same respect for their victims. Indeed, to accomplish this goal most efficiently, Oldenquist argues that we should morally and publicly shame criminals – even to the point of ostracizing them. To do otherwise essentially shows a kind of disrespect for the community and their victims, in the same way that someone shows that they do not respect themselves when they let someone continually abuse them without consequences (like, for example, a wife who stays with an abusive husband).

As evidence that punishment does and should have this kind of "protect the standards of the community" purpose, Oldenquist points to the difference of how US Citizens react to a Russian spy versus a spy for Russia who was a US citizen. The former would be detained, but not morally censured. He does not know any better; he is Russian, what would we expect? We might even trade him for one of our own spies caught by the Russians. But one of our own, turning against us, and spying for the Russians? They should know better. That is treason and would receive the appropriate moral indignation and a much harsher punishment. And we would not send them to Russia, even in exchange for one of our own. Where the loyalties of each *should* lie is completely different.

To be clear, Oldenquist does not argue for personal vengeance. He worries about the aforementioned endless cycle of revenge getting out of hand. Indeed, this is one reason he likes state-sponsored legal retribution. He calls it "sanitized revenge." It gives the criminal and the victim their due without raising the danger of more violence in return. It does not make sense for the offender to seek more vengeance against their victim if it was the state (rather than the victim) that dished out their punishment. Still, Oldenquist argues that vengeance has an undeserved bad reputation; it is automatically assumed to be immoral without there really being a good argument against it. He compares current philosophical attitudes toward vengeance to proscriptions against sex in the Victorian era, where sexual lust was forbidden, even in the confines of marriage. It is a short-sighted, narrow view, based on a kind of prudish tradition, that fails to appreciate our human nature. A victim seeking and getting vengeance against someone who truly deserves it can not only give an offender what they deserve, but it can also reinforce the respect the victim deserves – the respect that they either have for themselves, or (in the case of murder) others had for them. It shows that they are not the kind of person that can be abused with impunity.

Barr-Elli and Heyd: Moral Justice Versus Legal Justice

The merits of legal justice, however, bring us to Barr-Elli and Heyd (1986), who argue that "Revenge can never be part of the system of justice" (p. 85). They motivate their article with apparent paradoxes. For example, seeking legal justice seems morally justified because it seeks at least part of what vengeance seeks: to give offenders their due. Yet vengeance, the quest of victims to give offenders their due, is typically considered immoral. What is more, while the goal of legal justice and vengeance seems similar, they are incompatible. From the view of one seeking vengeance, legal justice will never be enough because it lacks the personal aspect of letting the victim themselves administer the punishment. But legal justice cannot tolerate the existence of vengeance because it circumvents the legal system's authority and requires personal elements that the legal system cannot tolerate. As Barr-Elli and Heyd put it,

> [J]ustice essentially demands for itself a unique and unrivalled authority. Revenge is simply unjust [i.e., not compatible with justice]. [Francis] Bacon realizes this point in saying that revenge is ... more dangerous to the rule of law than crime; for while the original wrong "doth but offend the law," revenge "putteth it out of office," i.e., challenges its unique authority. (p. 78) ... [T]he gist of our analysis of revenge consists of its essentially personal and indexical character; the individual avenger being the source and authority of the vengeful act, its meaning, and moral basis. This element is logically incompatible with any system of norms which by its very nature must be ruled-governed. For the point of such a system is the elimination of this personal dimension, by shifting the authority and moral basis of actions from the realm of subjective attitudes to impersonal rules and norms. (p. 83)

The upshot of this is, if we are to have a legal system at all – which is definitely preferable to a system where there is no law and people just dole out whatever vengeance they think is due to whoever they think is deserving – then seeking vengeance must be illegal.

The mere fact that something should be illegal, however, does not mean that it is immoral. Morality and legality are widely acknowledged to be separate, logically distinct concepts, and legal theorists often maintain that the purpose of laws is societal protection, not the enforcement of moral norms. (I have argued elsewhere (1986) that capital punishment should be illegal because, despite the fact that truly guilty murders are morally deserving of death, it should not be the government's job to dole out moral dessert.) Clearly, there can be immoral laws (like laws in Nazi Germany against harboring Jews, and laws in the antebellum South proscribing slavery). Likewise, there are immoral actions that should not be restricted legally, like adultery, breaking a promise, and gossiping. (Clearly I should not be legally required to pick up my friend at the airport because "I promised to," even though my wife just went into labor, and how would a law against gossiping even be enforced?) There are also moral actions that should remain illegal. (It is not immoral to go five over the speed limit, yet speed limits must still be set.) Think of it this way: In any legal system, theft must be against the law, yet we would not consider it immoral to steal a loaf of bread if that is the only way to feed your starving family.

It follows, therefore, that the mere fact that seeking vengeance should be illegal does not entail that it is immoral. Indeed, even though Barr-Elli and Heyd acknowledge that "even in the realm of human relations not governed by law and criminal justice it is said that revenge should be avoided as it reflects bad character, creates more hate, and is contrary to the spirit of forgiveness, love and charity," they insist that "[t]hese perceptions, although widely shared, should be re-examined in a more critical manner in light of a general theory of ethics." In fact, even though they admit that "reciprocating hate is in a deep sense futile and the attempt to achieve it frustrating [because] revenge can never restore the previous state of affairs ... [and that there] is something pathetic about attempts at 'getting even' by means of revenge" (p. 84), they still admit that revenge can be morally justified. "Revenge can never be part of the system of justice ... This does not mean, however, that revenge cannot be morally justified. It may be regarded as morally deserved by the special kind personal relationship in the particular situation" (p. 85).

Simone de Beauvoir: Can Vengeance Accomplish Its Goal?

Barr-Elli and Heyd say revenge is pathetic because "getting even on the emotional level requires the cooperation of the other party" (p. 84). In doing so, they are borrowing from French philosopher Simone de Beauvoir and her book *Eye for an Eye*, which she wrote in 1946, after attending the trial of the French Nazi collaborator Robert Brasillach, a right-wing author who edited a fascist newspaper during the Nazi occupation of France. In the book, de Beauvoir argues that the quest for the "balancing of wrongs," or restoring the "natural" order, via punishing wrongdoers (with an eye for an eye) will almost always be frustrated. Whether it is through personal revenge or legal retribution, to "balance" things out and restore natural order, such punishments must make the victim and the offender trade places. The offender must become a victim, for only in this way can they truly *understand* their crime, understanding being, as she puts it, "The process through which our entire being realizes a situation. One understands an implement in using it. One understands torture by undergoing it" (de Beauvoir 1946/2004 p.248). But, when an offender is punished, that can happen only if the offender chooses to let it happen. As Pauline O'Flynn (2008) puts it in her summary of de Beauvoir's argument, "We can never compel the aggressor to feel the pain of the original suffering. We cannot compel regret or repentance. We can never reach the core of any individual ... Vengeance cannot compel the freedom of a person, the aggressor, to create anything other than what he wants to create for himself." Since offenders, like the right-wing Nazi trash Robert Brasillach, are unlikely to do this, both vengeance and legal retribution will *usually* fail to achieve their moral goal.

"Usually," but not "always." For Barr-Elli and Heyd, "the space allotted to revenge is the narrow path where it is directed at someone who is believed to have offended the revenger and, though still hostile towards him, is yet capable of recognizing the act of revenge as expressing the victim's hostility and recognizing it as a 'just' reaction to the offenders own harmful past behavior and present hostility" (p. 84). Since such a space could still exist, vengeance can be justified. Indeed, it is remarkable how exactly the premise of *Kill Bill* fits within the "narrow space" that Barr-Elli and Heyd carve out for morally justified revenge. As Budd puts it, "I don't dodge guilt [or] out of paying my comeuppance. ... That woman deserves her revenge. And we deserve to die." Bill too recognizes that Beatrix's quest is, as Barr-Elli and Heyd put it, a "just reaction to [his] own harmful past behavior and present hostility." That is why he gives her a fair shot at killing him.

Simone de Beauvoir would also seem to have sympathy for Tarantinian quests for vengeance, especially that of Beatrix, Shoshanna, Django, and the girls in *Death Proof*. Despite her position that legal retribution will *usually* fail at its aimed moral goal of balancing wrongs, de Beauvoir (along with her contemporary Jean-Paul Sartre) refused to sign a petition circulating at the time which called for the pardon of the Nazi Brasillach. According to de Beauvoir, even though legal retribution against a Nazi cannot accomplish its moral goal of making things equal – "when a man deliberately tries to degrade a man by reducing him to a thing, nothing can compensate for the abomination he causes to erupt on earth" (de Beauvoir p.257) – it is still necessary to not ignore the kinds of degradation of humanity the Nazi's committed. As, again, O'Flynn (2008) put it, "If punishment or vengeance is to have any point, it's not as a balancing or restorative measure, but rather as a public acknowledgement of humanity's refusal to accept degrading behaviour." Or as de Beauvoir put it, "Their crimes have struck at our own hearts. It is our values, our reasons to live that are affirmed by their punishment" (p. 246).

Nozick, Vengeance, and when the Law Falls Short

From what we just learned, it follows that, if the legal system will fail to affirm our values and our reasons to live, by failing to punish an evil doer who degraded others by reducing them to a thing, then we are morally justified in seeking to enact that punishment ourselves. Otherwise, our values and reasons to live are negated. According to Barr-Elli and Heyd, de Beauvoir was frustrated with "the shortcomings of the conventional system of justice to deal with such monstrous crimes as those of Nazi leaders" (p. 83), and this is one of the defining features of Tarantinian quests for vengeance: The law will not or is incapable of administering the appropriate punishment. The law certainly was not going to hold the Nazis depicted in *Inglourious Basterds* accountable; the Nazis wrote the laws. Neither was it going to hold Bill accountable; he literally gets away with murder all the time. Stuntman Mike already got away with killing girls in Texas (and probably elsewhere, too, prior to the events of the film). And slavery was the law of the land in Mississippi, where Candyland was located. As Candie himself put it, "You see, under the laws of Chickasaw County, Broomhilda here is my property." There is no legal recourse for Django to seek to affirm his values and reasons to live; the law does not recognize them. As Francis Bacon (1597) put it, "'The most tolerable sort of revenge is for those wrongs which there is no law to remedy."

Interestingly, I found that quote on page 581 of Nigel Walker's 1995 article "Nozick Revenge," which is about philosopher Robert Nozick's take on vengeance. Nozick, it turns out, is not a fan of revenge taking the place of legal justice. Vengeance is too uncontrolled and unpredictable, too apt to go too far or punish those who do not deserve it. So, when it is available, people should seek legal recourse to right wrongs rather than seek personal vengeance. But nothing Nozick says entails that revenge is unjustified when laws are not in place to ensure that appropriate retribution takes place. Like de Beauvoir, Nozick thinks legal retribution is needed to communicate that what the person did is wrong (although for Nozick, it is mainly the offender that needs to know, not – as de Beauvoir suggested – the community). But also like de Beauvoir, who admitted it is difficult to criticize the actions of liberated prisoners who took vengeance upon their former SS guards, it seems that Nozick would find it difficult to condemn how Django took vengeance upon his former slaving oppressors. Perhaps Django has what de Beauvoir would call a "disquieting character." (I personally would challenge that notion.) But his vengeful actions are not immoral.

The Best Arguments for and Against the Morality of Revenge

Perhaps ironically, the best argument I could find that revenge is immoral comes from Joshua Gert's 2020 article "Revenge is Sweet." As a kind of answer to the "revenge does no good" objection, Joshua Gert argues that getting revenge is what he calls a "personal good." By this, he does not mean that revenge is moral. Instead, he means that revenge can be intrinsically valuable. It is like pleasure, knowledge, and freedom; a victim assuring themselves that their offender gets what they deserve is something that is good in and of itself, for its own sake. It accomplishes justice, and justice is a good. Now, Gert also recognizes the dangers of a revenge quest. It might consume you and ruin your life; it might lead to the offender (or their family and friends) seeking revenge on you; and it might have negative psychological impacts. But that is not always the case. Sometimes victims have opportunities to seek revenge at no personal cost or risk to themselves. This Gert calls "Cost-Free Revenge." And since revenge is a personal (intrinsic) good, when it is cost free, it can be rational for an agent to seek revenge.

Revenge being rational, however, does not mean that it is moral (just as revenge is not necessarily *immoral* if the action is *irrational*). The purpose of Gert's article is more about whether rational justification always provides moral justification; he suggests that it does not – thus revenge's rationality does not entail its moral permissibility. Gert's intention is to defend what he takes to be a common philosophical intuition: Immoral behavior can be rationally permissible without being rationally required. (It can be reasonable to do an immoral thing, but also reasonable to forgo doing that thing.) For Gert, it can be rational to seek revenge but also rational to forgive, and since (according to Gert) seeking revenge is immoral, choosing to forgive is the morally superior option.

But it is here that I would like to push back. I might grant that forgiveness is morally superior to seeking revenge; perhaps it is the moral high ground. That does not mean that forgiveness is morally obligatory. We have not been considering the question of whether a person must (in a moral sense) seek revenge; only whether it is morally permissible to do so. If a victim getting revenge is an intrinsic good, like pleasure, knowledge, and freedom, how can we say that it is morally bad when it is gotten? I mean, I suppose that an intrinsic good could be gotten in an immoral way – like the immoral way that Stuntman Mike gets pleasure: by torturing young women. But just asserting that vengeance is an immoral way to make sure an offender gets what they deserve begs the question at hand. After all, according to Gert, part of what is intrinsically good about vengeance is the fact that it is meted out by the offender's victim. What other way is there to accomplish that good but vengeance?

Or to reiterate a point made before, think of it this way: We often think this is a hard and fast rule: (a) "You shouldn't harm others if they don't harm you." That makes clear an obvious moral obligation. But does not the truth of that maxim entail that, when another does harm you, the obligation to not harm them is lifted? (Logically "if they don't harm you, then it is impermissible to harm them" is equivalent to "If it is permissible to harm them, then they harmed you.") If, once they harmed you, you are still obligated to not harm them – why is not the hard and fast rule just (b) "Never harm others." I suppose we might say the obligation to never harm someone is just more "obvious" if they have not harmed you. But I would argue that the fact that (a) is more obvious than (b) just means that revenge is not morally best, not that it is never morally justified.

That said, I am not arguing that vengeance should be tolerated by the law or by society. Indeed, as Juliele Maria Sievers and Luiz Henrique da Silva Santos (2020) point out, given its subjective nature, people's aptness to jump to unjustified conclusions of guilt, and the likelihood that those seeking vengeance would be emotionally driven to overpunish even those who are guilty, a world filled with people seeking revenge would be a terrifying place to live. What is worse, the kind of vigilantism that would abound in such a world would mostly likely not accomplish justice, but instead would target already vulnerable and oppressed populations. As Manuel Mireanu (2014) points out, this already happened in Italy and Hungary.

> [V]igilantism illustrates the complicity between certain parts of the state and certain parts of the society, in upholding violence that is legitimized as security. In Italy, this complicity implies that illegal immigrants and homeless people from Northern Africa and Eastern Europe are being marginalized, excluded and aggressed by vigilante patrols, on the backdrop of the state's anti-immigrant discourses. In Hungary, the same complicity implies that far-right patrols harass and beat up Roma people, in the context of a generalized state crackdown on the Roma population. (p. 11)

Indeed, it is through vigilantism that fascists rise to power. Hitler's "Brown Shirts" were vigilantes, roaming the streets, outside the rule of law, harassing Jews because they thought they deserved it (see Crane 2020). The same is true of Mussolini's Blackshirts and William Dudley Pelley's Silver Shirts. (Pelley was an American fascist and Nazi sympathizer, popular in the USA, before WWII.) We even see this today, as right-wingers who embrace the slogan "America First" (which was the rallying cry of Nazi sympathizers, like Pelley, before WWII) decide to do things like shoot Black Lives Matters protesters (in the name of protecting others' property; see Hayne 2021) and stage armed patrols outside of polling locations and ballot drop boxes (see Knutson 2022).

All I am saying is that, in the rare case of genuine "Cost-Free Revenge," where an offender has done wrong to a victim, the victim is sure that the offender is guilty, the law will likely not be able to hold them accountable, and the victim can enact revenge without risk (of personal retaliation or legal consequences), or is even just willing to take that risk – I cannot see a moral objection to the victim doling out a proportional punishment to their offender. And this is how I see the acts of vengeance on which Tarantino's films focus.

Conclusion: What About Ezekiel 25:17?

> Normally both your asses would be dead as fuckin' fried chicken. But you happened to pull this shit while I'm in a transitional period and I don't wanna kill ya, I wanna help ya.
> —Jules Winfield (*Pulp Fiction*)

Once upon a time, when this chapter began, I laid out the argument for the possibility of justifiable revenge that is put forth by the last two decades of Tarantino's films. In each, revenge is sought, and we celebrate when it is gotten, because the offender got what they deserved at the hands of one of their victims. The only possible exception is in *Once Upon a Time in Hollywood*, where it was not an actual victim (e.g., Sharon Tate) that got revenge on the Manson family murderers; instead, it was Rick and Cliff. Do not get me wrong; Rick and Cliff were justified in defending themselves, and the Manson family murderers were also deserving of punishment. But it is not clear that what Rick and Cliff did was justified *as an act of vengeance*. If it was, they were acting as proxies for the Hollywood community, just as Major Marquis Warren was acting as a proxy for black union soldiers when he killed General Sandy Smithers. But while it seems "black union soldiers" is a group where one member could justifiably claim the right of vengeance for another member of that group (because group membership makes the person a victim of the offender), it is not clear that this is also true of "Hollywood." I would not be justified in seeking vengeance for a murder victim simply because that victim and I attended the same college; there are limits to how liberally group membership can be extended for the sake of claiming vengeance. Suggesting that other members of Hollywood would be morally justified in seeking vengeance against the Manson family murderers, because of what they did "to one of their own," seems to go beyond that limit. In other words, the other members of Hollywood were not victims of the Manson family murders – at least not in a way that gives a person a right to vengeance.

Still, Tarantino's view that revenge can be morally justified, in the kinds of circumstances that we have described, seems to be on solid ground. Now, one might wonder how this can be Tarantino's view, given the lesson Jules learns in *Pulp Fiction* from (Tarantino's version of) Ezekiel 25:17. Recall Jules's stirring words:

> The path of the righteous man is beset on all sides by the inequities of the selfish and the tyranny of evil men. Blessed is he who, in the name of charity and good will, shepherds the weak through the valley of darkness, for he is truly his brother's keeper and the finder of lost children. And I will strike down upon thee with great vengeance and furious anger those who attempt to poison and destroy my brothers. And you will know I am the Lord, when I lay my vengeance upon you.

In the final scene, Jules concludes that this is not just some "cold blooded shit to say to a motherfucker before [he] pops a cap in his ass." It teaches him that his impending victim, "Ringo," is "the weak" and that he, Jules, is the "tyranny of evil men." But "I'm tryin', Ringo. I'm tryin' real hard... to be the shepherd." In other words, Jules learns to show mercy. One of the film's lessons is that mercy is praiseworthy. But how could mercy be praiseworthy while vengeance is justified?

First, the kind of mercy that Jules learns to show here is not forgiving mercy. Ringo has not wronged him. Indeed, that is why Jules gives Ringo his money; he does not want to have a right of vengeance against him. In fact, Jules says that he is not just *giving* his money away. Instead, he claims, "I'm buyin' something for my money. Wanna know what I'm buyin', Ringo?... Your life. I'm givin' you that money so I don't have to kill your ass." Second, even if it was an act of forgiveness – as I tried to point out in the last section – acts of forgiveness being morally praiseworthy are not contrary to acts of vengeance being morally permissible. If Tarantino's view is simply that forgiving mercy is the high road, but acts of vengeance are morally permissible, not only is his view logically consistent – I would argue that it is also the view that most of us hold. Tarantino is tuned into the human condition. That is why we love his films. He understands our appreciation for forgiveness, as something that is morally superior, and gives us characters that show us our "best selves." But it is also why we celebrate at the end of Tarantino's films: He gives both the wronged and the wrongdoer what they deserve. As Nietzsche (1885/1999) said, in *Thus Spake Zarathustra,* "A small revenge is humaner than no revenge at all" (XIX). Perhaps there is nothing more human that wanting to see the victims of Nazis and Southern slavers dish out the punishment that Nazis and Southern slavers deserve.

End Notes

1. It should be noted that, immediately following his "she deserves her revenge" line, Budd observes that Beatrix deserves to die as well. This does not, however, negate the idea that Beatrix deserves her revenge against Budd and the D.iV.A.S. Bud is just pointing out that, if he kills her, he will not be doing something that is morally wrong – because she too is a killer. He would just be dolling out what she morally deserves for the other murders she has committed, much in the same way that the state would bejustified if it captured and killed her for her crimes. So Budd's following line does not contradict Tarantino's vengeance thesis.

References

Bacon, Francis. 1597. *Essays, religious meditations, places of persuasion and dissuasion.* London: H. Hooper.
———. 1824. *The works of Francis Bacon.* Vol. 3, 261. London: W. Baynes and Son. Patterson Row. https://upload.wikimedia.org/wikipedia/commons/f/f2/The_works_of_Francis_Bacon_-_baron_of_Verulam%2C_viscount_St._Albans%2C_and_lord_high_chancellor_of_England_%28IA_03060843.1595.emory.edu%29.pdf.

Bailey, Jason. 2014. Imagining the Quentin Tarantino-Directed 'Natural Born Killers' that could have been. Flavorwire, 25 Aug. https://www.flavorwire.com/473670/imagining-the-quentin-tarantino-directed-natural-born-killers-that-could-have-been

Bar-elli, G., and D. Heyd. 1986. Can revenge be just or otherwise justified? *Theoria* 52 (1–2): 68–86. https://doi.org/10.1111/J.1755-2567.1986.TB00100.X

Barton, Charles K. 1999. *Getting even: Revenge as a form of justice*, 180. Chicago, IL: Open Court.

Cope, E.M. 1864. *Plato's Gorgias*. Cambridge: Deighton, Bell, and Co.. https://www2.southeastern.edu/Academics/Faculty/jbell/gorgias.pdf.

Crane, David M. 2020. Vigilantes, brown shirts, and the attack on the rule of law. Jurist, 7 Sep. https://www.jurist.org/commentary/2020/09/david-crane-brownshirts-nazi-american-elections/

De Beauvoir, Simone. 1946/2004. Oeil pour Oeil. In *Les Temps Modernes* 1, no. 5. And "Philosophical Writings." Champaign, IL: University of Illinois Press.

DiGiorgio, Stephanie. 2017. *The nature of revenge*. Schenectady, NY: Union College.

Fowler, H.W. 1996. *Modern English usage*. Oxford/New York: Oxford University Press.

Gert, Joshua. 2020. Revenge is sweet. *Philosophical Studies* 177 (4): 971–986. https://www.researchgate.net/publication/329716362_Revenge_is_sweet

Govier, Trudy. 2002. *Forgiveness and revenge*. London: Routledge.

Harris, Aisha. 2012. Was There Really "Mandingo Fighting," Like in Django Unchained? Slate, 24 Dec. https://slate.com/culture/2012/12/django-unchained-mandingo-fighting-were-any-slaves-really-forced-to-fight-each-other-to-the-death.html

Hayne, Jordan. 2021. Kyle Rittenhouse found not guilty of murder over shootings at Black Lives Matter protest in Kenosha. ABC News, 19 Nov. https://www.abc.net.au/news/2021-11-20/kyle-rittenhouse-trial-protest-shooting-kenosha/100603512

Hendrickson, Paula. 2013. Daniel nearing and the last soul on a summer night. Creative Screenwriting, 11 Aug. https://www.creativescreenwriting.com/daniel-nearing-and-the-last-soul-on-a-summer-night/

Hobbes, Thomas. 1651. *De Cive: Liberty*. New York: Appleton-Century-Crofts. http://www.publiclibrary.uk/ebooks/27/57.pdf.

Johnson, David Kyle, and Lance Schmitz. 2008. Johnny cash, prison reform and capital punishment. In *Johnny cash and philosophy*, ed. David Werther and John Huss. Chicago, IL: Open Court.

Jowett, Benjamin. 2013. The Republic: Plato. https://files.romanroadsstatic.com/materials/plato_republic.pdf

Kennedy, Randall. 2001. Nigger: The strange career of a troublesome word. Pantheon, 11 Jan. https://www.washingtonpost.com/wp-srv/style/longterm/books/chap1/nigger.htm

Kibbey, Benjamin. 2021. Cliff Booth, the Badass Stuntman, was inspired by these 2 men. Sofrep, 1 Nov. https://sofrep.com/news/cliff-booth-the-stuntman-and-veteran-based-on-real-life/#:~:text=Harold%20%E2%80%9CHal%E2%80%9D%20Needham%20was%20an,alleged%20to%20have%20been%20based

Knutson, Jacob. 2022. Election officials: Armed "vigilantes" near ballot drop box in Arizona. Axios, 23 Oct. https://www.axios.com/2022/10/23/mesa-arizona-armed-vigilantes-ballot-drop-box

Lages, Mark. 2021. *Dust of the earth*. Bloomington, IN: AuthorHouse.

Lloyd, Sharon A. 2002. The limits of political obligation in "Hobbes's moral and political philosophy." In *The Stanford encyclopedia of philosophy*, ed. Edward N. Zalta. https://plato.stanford.edu/archives/fall2006/entries/hobbes-moral/#9

Locke, John. 2003. The second treatise of civil government. Project Gutenberg eBook. https://www.gutenberg.org/files/7370/7370-h/7370-h.htm

Mathewes, Charles. 2021. The relativist Thomas Hobbes and his differences with Joseph Butler. Wondrium Daily, 10 July. https://www.wondriumdaily.com/the-relativist-thomas-hobbes-and-his-differences-with-joseph-butler/

Miltner, Charles. 1931. Legal versus moral justice. *Notre Dame Law Review* 6(4). https://scholarship.law.nd.edu/cgi/viewcontent.cgi?article=4310&context=ndlr

Mireanu, Manuel. 2014. *Vigilantism and security: State, violence and politics in Italy and Hungary.* Ph.D. Dissertation. Central European University. Budapest, Hungary. https://pds.ceu.edu/sites/pds.ceu.hu/files/attachment/basicpage/478/mireanumanuelir.pdf

Murphy, Feffrie. 2000. Getting even: The role of the victim. In *Philosophy of law*, ed. Joel Fienberg and Jules Coleman. Belmont, CA: Wadsworth.

Nietzche, Friedrick. 1885/1999. Thus Spake Zarathustra. Trans. Thomas Common. The Project Gutenberg eBook. https://www.gutenberg.org/files/1998/1998-h/1998-h.htm

Nozick, Robert. 2000. Retribution and revenge. In *What is justice?* ed. Robert Solomon and Mark Murphy, 214. Oxford/New York: Oxford University Press.

O'Flynn, Pauline. 2008. A question of vengeance. Philosophy Now. https://philosophynow.org/issues/69/A_Question_of_Vengeance

Oldenquist, Andrew. 1986. The case for revenge. National Affairs. https://www.nationalaffairs.com/public_interest/detail/the-case-for-revenge

Osgood, J.M. 2017. Is revenge about retributive justice, deterring harm, or both? *Social and Personality Psychology Compass*, 11.

Popper, Karl. 1945/2012. *The open society and its enemies*, 581. New York: Routledge.

Rick. 2019. China girls, death proof, and the hidden face. Luddite Robot. 14 Apr. https://ludditerobot.com/other/commentary/china-girls-death-proof-and-the-hidden-face/

Rosebury, Brian. 2009. Private revenge and its relation to punishment. *Utilias* 21 (1): 1–21.

Roth, Timothy Dean. 2007. A sword of righteousness: Kill bill and the ethics of vengeance. In *Quentin Tarantino and philosophy: How to philosophize with a pair of pliers and a blowtorch*, ed. Richard Greene, 85–96. Chicago, IL: Open Court.

Sievers, Juliele M., and Luize H. Silva Santos. 2020. *Shut up and dance* and vigilante justice: Should we ever take the law into our own hands? In *Black Mirror and philosophy: Dark reflections*, ed. David Kyle Johnson. Hoboken, NJ: Wiley-Blackwell.

Sommers, Tamler. 2009. The two faces of revenge: Moral responsibility and the culture of honor. *Biology and Philosophy* 24 (1): 35–50.

Spinoza, Baruch. 1677/1954. *Ethics: Preceded by on the improvement of understanding.* New York: Hafner Publishing Company. https://download.tuxfamily.org/openmathdep/epistemology/Ethics-Spinoza.pdf

Stillwell, Arlene M., Roy F. Baumeister, and Regan E. Priore. 2008. We're all victims here: Toward a psychology of revenge. *Basic and Applied Social Psychology* 30: 253–263.

Uniacke, Suzanne. 2000. Why is revenge wrong? *The Journal of Value Inquiry* 34: 61–69. Published by Cambridge University Press.

Vlastos, Gregory. 1991. *Socrates, ironist and moral philosopher.* Ithaca: Cornell University Press.

Walker, Nigel. 1995. Nozick's Revenge. *Philosophy* 70 (274): 581–586.

Walker, Margaret U. 2003. Review of forgiveness and revenge by Trudy Govier. *International Philosophical Quarterly* 43 (2): 252–253.

Williams, Kam. 2012. Director Quentin Tarantino–Quintessential Quentin! The Philadelphia Sunday, 27 Dec. https://www.philasun.com/entertainment/director-quentin-tarantino-quintessential-quentin/

Zuckerman, Esther. 2013. Everything Quentin Tarantino really thinks about violence and the movies. The Atlantic, 11 Jan. https://www.theatlantic.com/culture/archive/2013/01/quentin-tarantino-violence-quotes/319586/

responses to Williams's paper and explores some lesser-known arguments against the desirability of immortality, in particular those offered by Simone de Beauvoir (in 1946) and Martha Nussbaum (in 1989). This chapter argues that the core philosophical thesis of *The Man from Earth*, namely that immortality is desirable, holds its own against these arguments from so-called "immortality curmudgeons."

Keywords

The Man from Earth · Jerome Bixby · Immortality · The desirability of immortality · Bernard Williams · The Makropulos Case · Boredom · Apathy · Meaninglessness · Categorical desires · Identity · Repeatable pleasures · Values · Meaning · The meaning of life · Eternal life · Vampires · Martha Nussbaum · Simone de Beauvoir · All Men Are Mortal · Immortality curmudgeons · Philosophy of death

Introduction

"Would you really want to do that? Live fourteen thousand years?" John Oldman asks his closest friends at his farewell party in *The Man from Earth* (Bixby, p. 18). Little do they know that he has, in fact, lived 14,000 years and will live many thousands – if not tens of thousands – more. You see, John may look like he is in his mid-30s, but he stopped aging a very long time ago. Unbeknownst to his friends, John is immortal.

The question John poses is a central question in contemporary philosophy of death: Should we want to live forever? The contemporary debate over this question focuses on the desirability of cases like John's – eternal life on earth – rather than on the desirability of more traditional versions of the afterlife, like eternity in heaven. Although not-dying may sound appealing, many philosophers argue that immortality is not as good as it seems. In this chapter, I discuss the position taken on the desirability of immortality in *The Man from Earth* (section "Immortality in *The Man from Earth*"), sketch the relevant philosophical debate (section "The Immortality Debate"), and evaluate the film's position in light of this debate (section "*The Man from Earth* as Philosophy"). To start, however, let's see how the conversation unfolds between John Oldman and his friends (section "Summary of *The Man from Earth*").

Summary of *The Man from Earth*

The Man from Earth is set at a small cabin in the California desert. The movie opens with John Oldman moving boxes to his truck when five of his colleagues arrive. There is Dan (an anthropology professor), Edith (a history professor), Art (an archeology professor), Harry (a biology professor), and Sandy (John's soon-to-be girlfriend). They have come to say their proper goodbyes, since John left their university's official farewell party quite early and rather abruptly. John has been working as a tenured history professor, and his fellow professors are baffled that he would give up tenure, quit his job, and move away on such short notice. When they settle down inside the cabin, which has only a few pieces of furniture left in it, they start pressing John on his reasons for leaving. After deflecting their questions by saying things like, "I just like to move on now and then. It's a personal thing," John hesitates (Bixby, p. 14). "There is something I'm kind of tempted to tell you. I think. I've never done this before. I wonder how it would pan out" (Bixby, p. 16). Then, apparently as a way of changing the subject and starting a new conversation, he says: "What if a man from the Upper Paleolithic had survived until the present day?" (Bixby, pp. 16–17).

The rest of the film focuses on the conversation that ensues. John's friends initially assume that he is proposing a thought experiment: "It's an interesting idea. You working on a science-fiction story?" to which John replies: "Say I am, what do you think he would be like?" (Bixby, p. 17). Harry, the biology professor, establishes that it would be possible for a "caveman" to survive this long if he had perfect cell regeneration. But then John starts using first-person pronouns in describing the life of this "hypothetical" person: "I had a chance to sail with Columbus, but I'm not the adventurous type" (Bixby, p. 18). An awkward silence follows. Eventually, after more comments from John along the same lines, and another nudge ("Pretend it's science-fiction. Figure it out!"), his friends start playing along (Bixby, p. 19). They ask John a series of questions, trying to poke a hole in his story. But John always has a response.

John explains that in his "first lifetime," in which he matured to his current apparent age of 35 or so, he was forced to leave his community because they started to see his lack of aging as magical and dangerous. From that time on, he had to move on periodically, from group to group. He describes how at first these groups lived semi-nomadically and hunted for food, presumably during the Late Glacial period. Then, after settling down and transitioning to farming and raising domesticated animals, John moved east. He recalls that he was a Sumerian for 2000 years, then a Babylonian, then a Phoenician, and then ended up studying with the Buddha in India. Many years later, he met Van Gogh, who gave him a painting that he still owns and, incidentally, had been loading into his truck when his friends arrived. He came to the United States with some French immigrants after Van Gogh's death in 1890. By now, he has ten doctoral degrees, including all of those his friends have (anthropology, archeology, art history, and biology).

John's friends can't decide whether he's being serious, and they vacillate between amusement, curiosity, and frustration. The tensions slowly rise, and the conversation gets more and more heated. At one point, Art asks: "An answer for every question, except one. Why are you doing this?" to which John replies: "A whim. Maybe not such a good idea. ... I wanted you to say good-bye to me, not to what you've thought I was" (Bixby, p. 25).

At some point, John leaves the cabin to take a break, clear the air, and move a few more boxes. Sandy follows him outside and confesses her love for him. Apparently believing his story, Sandy asks if he can still love her or if he has stopped believing in love. John replies that he cares for her but has gotten over love "too many times" and will have to leave her at some point (Bixby, p. 26). "The simple fact is, I can't give you forever" (Bixby, p. 26). Sandy isn't perturbed: "No one knows how long they have. Or how little. ... I love you. And I'll take whatever you can give" (Bixby, p. 26). When John asks, "Like ten years?" Sandy doesn't answer, and they go back inside the cabin (Bixby, p. 27).

The mounting tension between John and the others reaches its peak following the late arrival of Will, another colleague (a psychiatrist) from the university. Will tries to get to the bottom of the situation, asking pointed questions about John's psychology. Will is secretly carrying a gun, and, after asking John if he is a vampire, pulls it out and aims at him. "What do you think, John? A shot to the arm, perhaps we can watch it heal. A bullet in the head... what exactly would happen?" (Bixby, p. 40). Will doesn't fire. Rather, he abruptly puts the gun away and leaves, stating that he has papers to grade. After he goes, Harry explains that Will's wife has just died, which might explain his bizarre behavior.

Towards the end, the movie takes an unexpected turn. Dan asks: "Did you ever meet any people from our religious history? A biblical figure?" (Bixby, p. 45). John is reluctant to answer but proposes instead to give a summary of the New Testament, "in a hundred words or less":

> A guy met the Buddha, and liked what he heard. He thought about it for a while, say, five-hundred years, while he returned to the Mediterranean, became an Etruscan, and then seeped into the Roman Empire. He didn't like what they became. A giant killing machine. He went to the Near East, thinking "Why not pass the Buddha's teachings along in modern form?" So he tried. One dissident against Rome, Rome won. The rest is history, sort of. A lot of fairy tales mixed in. (Bixby, p. 48)

Edith is the first to react: "I knew it. He's saying he was Christ" (Bixby, p. 48). But John denies this: "Oh, no. That's the medal they pinned on Jesus, to fulfill prophecy" (Bixby, p. 48). Rather, John claims to be the historical Jesus, and he has an explanation for how he was resurrected after the crucifixion (Bixby, p. 48). According to his story, all he wanted to do was teach Buddhism in the West, and the religion that was constructed around it was neither his doing nor his desire. "Heaven and hell were peddled so priests could rule through seduction and terror, so they could save our souls that were never lost in the first place. ... I threw a clean pass, and they ran it out of the ballpark" (Bixby, pp. 49–50). And: "I see rituals. Candles, processions, genuflecting, moaning, intoning, sprinkling water, venerating cookies and wine, and I think, 'This isn't what I had in mind'" (Bixby, pp. 49–50). John says he didn't perform any miracles and didn't call himself God – all of that is myth. John's friends take this news in different ways. Edith, who is a devout Christian, is very upset and accuses John of blasphemy. Dan, on the other hand, is pretty sympathetic to John's account of early Christianity. Will, who has in the meantime returned to the cabin, asks piercing questions and hints that John either has an overactive imagination or is mentally ill.

The situation now appears to be unsalvageable, and John finally decides to put an end to the conversation and their get-together:

> End of the line. Everybody off. . . . It's a story. I'm sorry, it's only a story. . . . You gave me the idea. All of you. . . . I got the notion, and ran it past you, to check your reactions. It went too far. . . . I was tempted to cop out a dozen times, but I wanted to see if you could refute what I was saying. I had the perfect audience. An anthropologist, biologist, archeologist, a Christian literalist. (Bixby, pp. 59–60)

One by one they take their leave, some more amicably than others. The only people left are John, Sandy, and Will. The movie seems to be at an end, but it has one more twist: when John casually lists some of the other "pun names" he has used, including "John Thomas Partee. Boston, Tea-party. Get it?" (Bixby, p. 62). Sandy laughs, but Will cries out: "Boston? Sixty years ago? John Partee? . . . You did not – teach chemistry!" (Bixby, pp. 62–63). Will has just discovered that John Oldman is his father, who left his mother when he was a child. This discovery clearly catches John off guard, but after a moment's pause, he reluctantly confirms it, offering the names of Will's mother and childhood dog as proof. This is a significant moment in the film because it provides the only definitive evidence that John's story is true. Unfortunately, Will, who is already emotionally distraught, can't handle the revelation and has a heart attack, dying in John's arms. Later, after the coroner takes Will's body away, John admits to Sandy that this is the first time he has witnessed one of his adult children die.

With everything packed up, and everyone gone but Sandy, John gets into his truck and starts to drive off – alone. Unexpectedly, he stops at the end of the driveway and turns his head toward Sandy, who is standing wrapped in a blanket next to his empty cabin. They look at each other and smile. Then, she slowly walks across the yard to join him on the next stage of his apparently endless human life.

Immortality in *The Man from Earth*

Whether the kind of immortality portrayed in *The Man from Earth* – that is, earthly immortality through not dying – is desirable is one of the main questions in contemporary philosophy of death. In this section, I argue that *The Man from Earth* takes a stand in this debate by portraying immortality as desirable – or, at a minimum, as not undesirable (section "The Desirability of Immortality in *The Man from Earth*"). Before turning to the ideas about the desirability of immortality in *The Man from Earth*, however, a few questions need addressing: What kind of immortality are we talking about? (section "Models of Immortality"); How would this kind of immortality work? (section "Medical Immortality"); and What would it be like to live forever? (section "What Would It Be Like to Live Forever?").

Models of Immortality

There are four main models of immortality distinguished from each other by two cross-cutting distinctions. First, immortality can be either heavenly or earthly, where "heavenly immortality" refers to eternity in a traditional afterlife, such as heaven (or hell), and "earthly immortality" refers to never-ending existence here on earth. Second, immortality can be either universal or individual, where "universal immortality" is when everyone is immortal, and "individual immortality" is when just one person is. The contemporary debate in analytic philosophy focuses on individual, earthly immortality, following the classic paper by Bernard Williams, "The Makropulos Case: Reflections on the Tedium of Immortality." This is exactly the kind of immortality we find in *The Man from Earth*.

Philosophers are interested in earthly immortality for at least two reasons. First, most people think that death is bad, from which it seems to follow that not dying – that is, living forever, here on earth – would be good. But is it really? Philosophers question such commonplace assumptions. And, as we'll see later on in this chapter, philosophers are divided in how they answer this question. This makes this question philosophically interesting. Second, if philosophical investigation reveals that immortality is less desirable than we normally think, then death might lose some of its sting. In other words, a negative answer to the question of whether immortality is desirable would give us a reason to be thankful for being mortal.

As for individual rather than universal immortality, philosophers focus on the former because it is easier to imagine what it would be like for one person to live forever than it is to imagine what it would be like if everyone did. In addition, the problems raised for immortality are considered to be necessary rather than contingent, such that if they obtain for one individual, they do for all.

Medical Immortality

What does earthly and individual immortality look like? *The Man from Earth* presents a plausible account of how this would go, namely that the biological process of aging, for whatever reason, simply does not occur. This could be caused by taking an "elixir of life," through a genetic fluke, or by means of genetic engineering (as transhumanists are working on). We already know of certain sea creatures that are extremely long-lived (if not actually immortal), and we continue to learn more about the physical processes underlying aging, which appears by no means to be biologically necessary.

Not-aging isn't just the most plausible way to postpone or eradicate death; it's also a crucial feature of immortality if it has any chance of being desirable. Just imagine living forever but continuing to age indefinitely. For some examples in fiction, you can read about the struldbruggs in *Gulliver's Travels* (1726), or watch the films *The Hunger* (1983) and *Death Becomes Her* (1992). (Spoiler alert: It does not look good!) Because aging forever is clearly undesirable, we have to presuppose a non-aging condition when asking whether or not earthly individual immortality is desirable. In addition, it is also important for immortals to have extraordinary healing powers. It's difficult to see how someone can be immortal, or at least happily immortal, if that person doesn't heal extraordinarily well from illnesses and accidents.

An important question for our purposes is whether John is truly immortal. John is very old (approximately 14,000 years), but this doesn't mean that it's impossible for him to die. As John himself says: "I never said I was immortal, only that I'm old" (Bixby, 34). John Martin Fischer and Benjamin Mitchell-Yellin have coined the term "genuine immortality" for someone who is unable to die, and "medical immortality" for someone who won't die of natural causes but can be killed (Fischer and Mitchell-Yellin 2014). If John is merely medically immortal, then he would die if he stopped eating or if someone shot him in the head. Vampires, for what it's worth, are medically immortal: they won't die naturally, but they can be killed – for example, by a wooden stake through the heart. Genuine immortals, by contrast, can't be killed, even by themselves.

Although this point is not made explicitly in the movie, it seems likely that John is medically rather than genuinely immortal. There is nothing supernatural in the film, such as a "curse" or an "elixir of life," which one would expect if his were a case of genuine immortality. Rather, John seems simply to have stopped aging, perhaps because of a genetic fluke. Based on all appearances, John won't die naturally, but there's no reason, at least based on the film, to think that he can't be killed.

What Would It Be Like to Live Forever?

In order to determine whether we should want to live forever, we need to know what it would be like to be immortal. Philosophers who excel at conceptual analysis and argument evaluation are not necessarily the best at imagining realistic possibilities or at producing compelling phenomenological descriptions. Yet, the latter seem helpful, if not essential, for deciding whether or not immortality is desirable. It's no wonder that Williams's paper focuses on the fictitious character of Elina Makropulos, and that Simone de Beauvoir gives her take on immortality in the form of a novel (Beauvoir 1946). In fact, immortals appear in many works of fiction, including Balzac's *The Elixir of Life* (1830), Wilde's *The Picture of Dorian Gray* (1890), and Sartre's *No Exit* (1944) – not to mention more popular icons of immortality, such as Tolkien's elves, Stephanie Meyer's vampires, and Marvel's Wolverine. Fiction is an ideal way to explore the phenomenological character of experiences that are not our own, so it makes sense to turn to fiction in order to get a better sense of whether or not we should want to live forever. Martha Nussbaum makes a similar point: "We need for this purpose complex fictions, works of literature that give us stories of immortals and of mortals, imagining in detail what can and cannot go on in those respective lives and convincing us, by this means, of the relationship between mortality and human value" (Nussbaum, p. 337). Films and TV shows are therefore a perfect medium through which to explore what it would be like to live forever.

In my opinion, *The Man from Earth* is a top contender for being the most realistic picture of what it would be like for us to live forever. One reason for this is that most books, movies, and television shows about immortality feature superheroes or vampires in the leading roles. Some of these works of fiction do a good job portraying what it would be like to be a vampire, but what it would be like to live forever as a vampire is very different from what it would be like to live forever as a human being. Insofar as vampire lives are portrayed as undesirable (and most of them are), this is mostly, if not entirely, due to aspects of their lives other than their immortality. Perhaps the main problem for vampires is the fact that they have to kill others in order to keep themselves alive, although there are also smaller pains such as not being able to enjoy the sun or one's favorite food. But immortality does not seem to be a particularly important or central contributor to the undesirability of vampire life. Moreover, it's hard to bracket these vampire-specific issues and still get a sense of what immortality would be like from these portrayals. In short, vampire movies do not generally give us a good insight into the desirability of immortality. *The Man from Earth*, by contrast, really does.

The Desirability of Immortality in *The Man from Earth*

Now that it's clear what kind of immortality is at stake in *The Man from Earth*, let's turn to the question of whether it is desirable. John actually raises this question in the film: "In my way, I wondered if I was cursed, or maybe blessed" (Bixby, p. 22). His friends ask him, "Have you ever wished it would end?" to which John answers "no" (Bixby, p. 35). They seem to expect this answer; one of them even asks rhetorically, "If it were true, is there one of us who would not feel envy?" (Bixby, p. 39). Overall, John's immortality is presented as desirable or, at the very least, as not undesirable. That being said, John does have to deal with certain issues because of his immortality, which he discusses with his friends.

First, John has had to move around every ten years or so to conceal the fact that he doesn't age. Were he to stay, people would start to wonder about him and consider him a freak. They would treat him as an outcast or perhaps lock him up in a laboratory for testing. Moving around every ten years might seem like a mere logistical nuisance, but it has some far-reaching implications for John's life. He is never able to stay in a romantic relationship, he can't have lifelong friends, and he can't be part of the same community for more than a decade. This means not only that he has to constantly reinvent his identity and start anew but also that he loses people and relationships over and over again. As John says: "I've regretted losing people. Often" (Bixby, p. 37). It's hard not to imagine this kind of life as being a very lonely one.

Second, there is the issue of diminishing returns, particularly as it applies to love. Not only would moving on every ten years be lonely and make long-term romantic relationships impossible, but the value and possibility of love is called into question in an immortal existence. Is it possible to fall in love 1000 (or even 100) times? And even if the answer is yes, wouldn't the value of falling in love diminish after so many times? From the perspective of 14,000 (or more) years, ten years would not seem to have the same weight and significance that it has for us. John seems to think about love along these lines when he says, "I've gotten over it too many times"

(Bixby, p. 26). Will asks John at some point, "What does a day or a year or a century mean to you?" (Bixby, p. 37). John's answer is telling: "Turbulence. I meet people, learn a name, say a word, and they're gone. Others come, like waves, rising and falling. Like ripples in a wheat-field, blown by the wind" (Bixby, p. 37). If this is what it is like to encounter mortals as an immortal, then the question of whether love is still possible is a serious one.

Third, there is the issue of boredom in a life that never ends. John is asked, "Do you ever get tired of it all?" and he responds: "I get bored now and then. They make the same stupid mistakes, again and again" (Bixby, p. 37). On the surface, John is talking about mortals and his frustration with their limited perspectives, but he could be hinting at a more general boredom that he experiences in virtue of there being "nothing new under the sun." However, this is speculative, as the issue of boredom does not come up again in the film.

Despite these issues, John's life appears to be pretty good. He has friends, and people seem to like him. Sandy is romantically interested in him, as were others before her. Given the fact that he has so many degrees and works as a professor, it's reasonable to assume that John enjoys learning and teaching. He has lived in many different places around the world, he has met famous and impressive people, and he has held various occupations. Except for the issues just described, John's life doesn't appear to have contained exceptional hardships. John seems to be a well-adjusted person who is engaged in life. Overall, *The Man from Earth* presents John's life as a long human life with costs and benefits, but as a life that is all-in-all desirable.

With that said, let's turn to the philosophical literature in order to place *The Man from Earth* within the context of the philosophical debate over the desirability of immortality.

The Immortality Debate

Although the trope of immortals has existed in myth, literature, and philosophy since their inceptions, the *locus classicus* of the debate about the desirability of immortality in contemporary philosophy of death is Bernard Williams's "The Makropulos Case: Reflections on the Tedium of Immortality" (1972). This paper has elicited many responses and still takes center stage in the debate. In this section, I will sketch Williams's main argument (section "Williams's Argument") and the most important objections to it (section "Responses to Williams"). In addition, I will give an account of two philosophical discussions of immortality that are relevant for our purposes but not part of this debate (section "Other Arguments"). I will then return to *The Man from Earth* and evaluate its argument in light of the philosophical context (section "*The Man from Earth* as Philosophy").

Williams's Argument

The title of Williams's famous paper refers to a 1922 play by Karel Čapek (made into an opera by Leoš Janáček just a few years later) about Elina Makropulos, a 342-year-old singer. Her father, a physician to the court of an emperor, successfully tried out an elixir of life on his daughter, and she's been living for nearly 300 years at the outward age of 42. Even though she is a famous and successful opera singer, "EM" (her unchanging initials in spite of her frequently changing aliases) is miserable. She has had to move around many times to avoid suspicion, and she has lost all joy in life. As Williams puts it: "Her unending life has come to a state of boredom, indifference, and coldness" (Williams, p. 82). When the elixir starts to wear off, and she has the opportunity to take it again to live another 300 years, EM destroys it and chooses to die instead. You might think that EM's experience and decision are unique to her, but Williams argues that she makes the only rational choice in her situation and that all of us would (and should) opt out of immortality if we had the chance. As Fischer stresses: "Williams's point is that it is not merely a contingent fact that eternal life would be unattractive; this unattractiveness is alleged to be an *essential* feature of eternal life" (Fischer, p. 364). Why is Williams an "immortality curmudgeon," as holders of his position are called in the literature?

There are different ways of interpreting Williams's argument against the desirability of immortality. The simplest, and probably most common, is to understand it as a dilemma: either living forever becomes excruciatingly boring, or one must continuously change one's interests and projects, which threatens one's identity. As Michael Cholbi puts it: "Either immortality will inevitably become tedious or (in order to avoid such tedium) we would have to undergo large-scale changes in our desires and personal projects, changes that would render the resulting personalities impossible for our current selves to identify with" (Cholbi, xii). Either way, immortality is undesirable. Let's explore both horns of this dilemma in more depth.

To start, consider your current life with your current interests, and imagine it going on in more or less the same way forever. Williams thinks that you would eventually become bored – unbearably bored. Elina Makropulos is certainly bored in this way. After 300 years, as Williams puts it, "everything that could happen and make sense to one particular human being of 42 had already happened to her" (Williams, p. 90). Note that Williams is not talking about a mundane, Sunday afternoon kind of boredom with which every mortal is familiar. The tedium of immortality is much stronger than this and results in *apathy* – the lack of desire to do anything. Williams writes of EM that "her boredom and distance from life both kill desire and consist in the death of it" (Williams, p. 91).

More specifically, Williams thinks that immortals, sooner or later, as a result of their boredom, will lack *categorical desires* – that is, desires that are reasons for living rather than desires predicated on the assumption that one is alive. For example, we want food, but this is not a reason to keep living; it is something we want only because we are alive (we eat to live, not live to eat). These are opposed to desires such as finishing a book or raising a family, which do give us reasons for living. The apathy that results from the tedium of immortality consists in the lack of the latter sort of desires. Williams likens this extreme form of boredom to "an inner death" (Williams, p. 90). An immortal life is, paradoxically, not a life at all.

A further and related problem with immortality, according to Williams, is that an immortal life would eventually become *meaningless*. This isn't hard to understand in light of the foregoing. If an immortal life eventually becomes so boring that one no longer has the desire to do anything, then nothing one does will seem worthwhile. Finding something worth doing is arguably a necessary condition of that thing giving your life meaning. If you don't feel engaged in what you are doing, or find any joy or interest in it, then it won't add any meaning to your life. Thus, a life of apathy is also a life without meaning.

This seems to be Williams's reason for thinking that an immortal life is without meaning. But there are other reasons to think this, too. Immortals experience everything life has to offer (e.g., falling in love, graduating from college, securing a job, having a child) innumerable times, rendering life events that carry a lot of weight and significance for mortals insignificant and meaningless. After all, it is doubtful that obtaining your tenth degree provides the same sense of accomplishment and satisfaction or that getting married for the hundredth time is quite as exciting. This worry about immortality applies to our life choices, too. Life choices in a mortal life are crucially important and determine the narrative meaning of our lives. But for immortals, nothing hangs on their choices for they have eternity to experience anything possible. The worry is that if none of your experiences or choices carry any weight, then life as a whole might strike you as meaningless.

This worry is compounded by another one along the same lines, which is the lack of urgency in an immortal life. If you literally have all the time in the world, then there is no reason to do anything today, or tomorrow, or, for that matter, this year. Given our busy lives, this might sound appealing at first, but it is easy to see how this lack of urgency becomes a paralyzing lack of motivation. Why do anything now? In fact, why do anything – *ever*? Aaron Smuts raises this worry and coins it a "motivationally devastating condition" (Smuts, p. 141). He thinks that, without a "deadline," immortals would procrastinate forever and not undertake or accomplish anything.

Let's turn to the other horn of the dilemma: the threat to our identity. Excruciating boredom (and the apathy and meaninglessness that it causes) can be avoided if immortals continuously reinvent themselves. They might get bored if they stick to their current interests and hobbies, but they might not if they develop new interests and find other hobbies. In other words, boredom can be overcome by developing new *categorical desires* – and then new ones again, and again, and again, forever. It follows that immortals who take this route will end up with very different categorical desires than the ones they had at the beginning. Ones who started out life mostly interested in their academic careers and raising their children might, after 300 years, try running for political office and playing golf, and then, after another 300 years, pursue something else entirely.

This radical transformation in categorical desires over time threatens our identity in two different ways. First, in order for immortality to be desirable, "it should clearly be me who lives forever" (Williams, p. 91). In other words, an immortal life is worth living only if the numerical identity of a person is maintained over the entire length of that life. But radical changes in categorical desires, which are required in order to avoid boredom, arguably result in a numerically different person. And in that case, we're not really talking about an immortal life but rather "a series of psychologically disjoint different lives," as Williams puts it (Williams, p. 92).

But even if radical changes in categorical desires don't threaten one's numerical identity, there's a second problem. According to Williams, it's rational to want to live forever only if "the state in which I survive should be one which, to me looking forward, will be adequately related, in the life it presents, to those aims which I now have in wanting to survive at all" (Williams, p. 92). Since our categorical desires are what give us reasons to live in the first place, a future life can be desirable for us only if it has the potential to satisfy these desires – that is, our *current* categorical desires. In other words, a future life organized around categorical desires that are radically different from our current categorical desires is not a life that we can rationally want to have. So, even if people can remain numerically identical after radically changing their categorical desires, the result is not a life that is worth pursuing.

To sum up: according to Williams, either an immortal life is excruciatingly boring (if we maintain our current categorical desires), or else it is not a life that we can rationally want (if we try to overcome such boredom by periodically changing our categorical desires). Either way, immortality is not desirable.

Responses to Williams

Each part of Williams's argument has been scrutinized and criticized in the debate it has generated. The main objections I focus on here are ones concerning the two essential parts of Williams's argument: boredom and personal identity. Let's start with boredom. The way Williams presents it, excruciating boredom is inevitable for every immortal. Whether this is true is an open question, and many responses to Williams are objections to this claim. These objections take different forms. First, several philosophers object that there are categorical desires that are not exhaustible. Felipe Pereira and Tim Timmermans present an inventory of suggestions made in the literature: reading all the novels in the world (Martin Fischer and Benjamin Mitchell-Yellin), pursuing truth and justice (Neil Levy), becoming the best musician in the world (J. J. Wisnewski), and self-development (Adam Buben) (Pereira and Timmermans, p. 4). If this is the case, then immortals need not get bored without radically changing their categorical desires. A second objection, presented by Lisa Bortolotti and Yujin Nagasawa, is that Williams's claim that exhausting one's categorical desires results in the type of pervasive boredom that Williams describes and that makes our lives undesirable is unsupported. They think that the repetition in an immortal life might result in another type of boredom, situational boredom, but this occurs in a mortal life as well and does not seem to be a reason to prefer death over life (Bortolotti and Nagasawa 2009). A third line of argument, defended by Christopher Belshaw, maintains that people would not lose interest in their projects, even if they were exhaustible, because of the limitations of our cognitive capacities. We don't have perfect memories, so after a thousand years (or much sooner) we might want to reread certain novels or rewatch certain films. According to Belshaw, we would get bored only if immortality also imbued us with superhuman mental powers, but there is no reason to assume that it would (Belshaw 2015).

A fourth, and possibly the most famous, response to Williams's position on inevitable boredom is grounded in Fischer's notion of "repeatable pleasures." Fischer argues that although some pleasures or desires are "self-exhausting" or exhaustible, there are experiences that remain pleasurable, no matter how many times you've had them. For example, coffee tastes good each morning, even if you've had it hundreds or thousands of times before. As far as I'm concerned, there is no reason to think my morning coffee is ever going to cease to be enjoyable. The same holds for many other things, which we can reasonably expect to remain enjoyable even if we've enjoyed them many times before: "Certain salient sensual pleasures leap immediately to mind: the pleasures of sex, of eating fine meals and drinking fine wines, or listening to beautiful music, of seeing great art, and so forth" (Fischer, p. 263). This is reason enough for Fischer to think that immortality would not be boring. As he writes: "Given the appropriate distribution of such pleasures, it seems that an endless life that included some (but perhaps not only) repeatable pleasures would *not* necessarily be boring or unattractive" (Fischer, pp. 263–264).

Williams's argument that pursuing new projects to avoid boredom results in a loss of identity has also been criticized. For one thing, the right kind of continuity over time should be sufficient to guarantee the relevant kind of survival. Sophie-Grace Chappell makes a point along these lines when she argues that our changing categorical desires overlap so that there is never a radical change in identity at one point in time (Chappell 2009). If we change gradually, and so do our categorical desires, then Chappell's argument ensures that we remain the same person and can still rationally want to continue living. For another, David Benatar argues that Williams's argument proves too much in this regard: if Williams's concern is valid, then the very young have no reason to care to live into old age, for they will supposedly change over the course of their lives as much as immortals do (Benatar 2017). Even though it makes sense for Williams to think that we need to be able to identify with our future selves, I think that Benatar is right in saying that having the same categorical desires is not a necessary condition for such identification. If I knew I would still be enjoying myself pursuing projects in 10,000 years, then I would sign up for immortality no matter what those projects were.

Other Arguments

Outside the debate generated by Williams's paper, lesser-known arguments against the desirability of immortality have been given. One argument to which I want to draw attention is that an immortal life would necessarily lack *human values*, i.e., values that make a human life worth living, such as love and virtue. Specifically, Simone de Beauvoir and Martha Nussbaum have independently offered arguments for this conclusion. I will sketch their arguments here.

Beauvoir's novel *All Men Are Mortal* (1946) centers on the unpleasant life of an immortal man named Fosca. One of the main ideas in this novel is that much of what we value in life is possible only because we are able to make sacrifices. Since immortals like Fosca can't make these sacrifices, their lives necessarily lack these values. For example, because Fosca can't die and also heals extraordinarily well, he can't take any bodily risks or know any fear. From this it follows that Fosca can't be courageous. And he can't be truly generous, either, since giving his time, or even his possessions, to others doesn't really cost him anything: he has an infinite amount of time to give, and "time is money," as the saying goes. Beauvoir also thinks that Fosca cannot truly love other people, but for a different reason: mortals are so fundamentally different from him, not only in the length of their lives but also in the things that they care about, that they seem like mere "insects" to him, and his relationships with them are similarly insignificant. (This echoes John Oldman's description of the lives other people as "ripples in a wheat-field, blown by the wind" (Bixby, p. 37).) Finally, Beauvoir anticipates Williams by describing Fosca as lacking strong desires and being plagued with debilitating boredom. As a result of all this, Fosca is miserable:

> I could not risk my life, could not smile at them; there was never a flame in my heart nor tears in my eyes. A man of nowhere, without a past, without a future, without a present. I wanted nothing, I was no one. ... My hands were forever empty: An outsider, a dead man. They were men, they were alive. I... I was not one of them. I had nothing to hope for. (Beauvoir, p. 339)

Indeed, the main philosophical conclusion of *All Men Are Mortal* is that "immortality is a terrible curse" (Beauvoir, p. 26).

In "Mortal Immortals" (1989), Nussbaum argues that human values are tied to our "finitude" and are therefore unavailable to immortals. In her words: "Our finitude, and in particular our mortality, which is a particularly central case of our finitude, and which conditions all our other awareness of limit, is a constitutive factor in all valuable things' having for us the value that in fact they have" (Nussbaum, p. 336). As this quotation indicates, Nussbaum thinks that this applies to all of our values, but let's focus on her discussions of courage and love in particular. Why can't immortals possess these values in the same way humans do? When it comes to courage, Nussbaum's argument is reminiscent of Beauvoir's. Nussbaum thinks that being able to take risks is a necessary condition for displaying courage, and true immortals cannot take any risks because they cannot die. Nussbaum also thinks that true immortals lack the capacity to love, but not for the same reason as Beauvoir, who argues that this is because mortals and immortals are too dissimilar from each other. Rather, Nussbaum argues that love, like courage, requires sacrifice. More specifically, because immortals cannot sacrifice their lives for other people, their capacity to love them is greatly diminished. She illustrates these points with the example of Achilles: "In heaven there is, in two senses, no Achilles: no warrior risking everything he is and has, and no loving friend whose love is such that he risks everything on account of his friend" (Nussbaum, p. 338). To be clear, Nussbaum doesn't argue that immortal lives cannot have *any* values; rather, she argues that they simply cannot have any *human* values, i.e., values with which we mortals are familiar, such as courage and love. As she puts it: "This shift over to a godlike life and a godlike self requires enormous revision in human patterns of desire and of value" (Nussbaum, p. 327).

Conclusion: *The Man from Earth* as Philosophy

In light of these discussions about the desirability of immortality in philosophy, what can we say about the position taken in *The Man from Earth*? How does it fit into these discussions?

Being forced to move from place to place, getting bored with life, and losing the value of love are the three main problems with immortality presented in *The Man from Earth*. As we have seen, these problems are all present in the philosophical literature. However, the degree to which these are problems in John's life is significantly different from the degree to which they are presented as problems by philosophers. Let's take a closer look at each in order to see what I mean.

Although John has had to move around every decade, he seems to have been able to avoid the worst consequences of this situation. While being forced to create new identities, get new jobs, and find new places to live creates a number of logistical hassles, not being able to have lifelong relationships with a lover, friends, and a community are much bigger impediments to happiness. And yet, John manages to find lovers, friends, and a community anyway. And while it is true that none of these lasts longer than a decade at a time, it is generally agreed among philosophers that duration does not determine value. After all, relationships in mortal lives do not last forever, either, but nobody thinks that they have no value as a consequence. In short, a strong case can be made that John is not much worse off than us mortals as a result of being forced to move around.

The kind of boredom John seems to experience is nothing of the sort Williams describes. John's boredom is not excruciating; he doesn't experience any apathy; and he doesn't give the impression of being depressed. His only report about it – "I get bored now and then" – does not convey a boredom that is deep or paralyzing. In fact, it does not sound any different from what most of us mortals might say. And John's life – apart from his words – does not attest to unbearable boredom, either. John has lived a very active life, and he seems very engaged in his projects. He has traveled – and lived – all over the world, held many different occupations, pursued ten doctoral degrees, been involved in many relationships, and sired a number of children. John has clearly not suffered the "motivationally devastating condition" that Smuts is worried about. John's boredom sounds very much like ordinary boredom, and ordinary boredom is as good of an argument against the desirability of immortality as it is against the desirability of mortality: not a very good one.

The third issue in John's life is that love has lost its value to some degree. Although this worry does not feature prominently in the debate generated by Williams's paper, it is raised in the discussions of immortality by Nussbaum and Beauvoir. However, John's life does not exemplify a lack of love to the degree that Nussbaum and Beauvoir expect. Even though John has had to leave lovers every ten years, and has lost love again and again, he is still open to it, as the end of the movie shows, which indicates that love is neither impossible for nor valueless to him.

In general, John's life contains many human values. He currently has a group of friends, who are upset with him for leaving, and so we have a reason to think that John values friendship. John owns a Van Gogh painting, which might be evidence that he values art and the repeatable aesthetic pleasure that it can induce. The film gives us no reason to think that John lacks courage or a sense of identity. John seems like a decent person, and he has tried to make a difference in the world by bringing the Buddha's teachings to the West. There is certainly some frustration there because John feels like he failed to do this, but this just indicates that John values virtue and cares about helping other people. Last, but not least, John clearly values knowledge. He has obtained ten PhDs and works as a professor. Many of these values (knowledge, virtue, friendship, and aesthetic appreciation) are thought by philosophers to be ingredients of a good life. Moreover, many of these values can give rise to repeatable pleasures and, arguably, to inexhaustible projects and categorical desires.

The fact that John's life contains many human values raises the question of whether Beauvoir and Nussbaum were wrong to think that immortals cannot have these values. There is, however, one important difference between their accounts of immortality, on the one hand, and John's immortality, on the other: whereas John is merely medically immortal, Beauvoir and Nussbaum both have genuine immortality in mind. This may explain why their arguments based on the inability to make sacrifices do not apply to John. Because he can die, John is able to make sacrifices and therefore act courageously and generously. He also has the ability to sacrifice his life for love (although one might question whether it is necessary to be able to do so in order to have the capacity to love at all). That being said, it also seems true that *The Man from Earth* simply offers a more optimistic perspective on the prospect of immortal love than does Beauvoir's *All Men Are Mortal*. Even though John lives much longer than all of the mortals he encounters, his relationships with them are not rendered completely insignificant as a result, as they are for Fosca. In other words, we seem to have a simple difference of opinion about what love would be like for an immortal. Which of these two works of fiction – Bixby's *The Man from Earth* or Beauvoir's *All Men Are Mortal* – gets it right is an open question.

Opposing the immortality curmudgeons, *The Man from Earth* sends a strong message that an immortal life need not to be excruciatingly boring and can contain many things of value. Even though John's life has had certain problems as a result of his immortality, it is portrayed all-in-all as a life worth living, and it is likely that many of us would choose it over death if we had the choice. I know that I would.

References

Belshaw, Christopher. 2015. Immortality, memory, and imagination. *The Journal of Ethics* 19 (3–4): 323–348.

Benatar, David. 2017. *The human predicament: A candid guide to life's biggest questions.* New York: Oxford University Press.

Bixby, Jerome. 2008. *The Man from Earth (original motion picture screenplay, adapted by Richard Schenkman)*. New York: Samuel French.
Bortolotti, Lisa, and Yujin Nagasawa. 2009. Immortality without boredom. *Ratio* 22 (3): 261–277.
Chappell, Sophie-Grace. 2009. Infinity goes up on trial: Must immortality be meaningless? *European Journal of Philosophy* 17 (1): 30–44.
Cholbi, Michael, ed. 2016. *Immortality and the philosophy of death*. London: Rowman and Littlefield.
de Beauvoir, Simone. 1946. *All men are mortal*. Trans. Leonard M. Friedman. New York: Norton Paperback.
Fischer, John Martin. 1994. Why immortality is not so bad. *International Journal of Philosophical Studies* 2 (2): 257–270.
Fischer, John Martin, and Benjamin Mitchell-Yellin. 2014. Immortality and boredom. *The Journal of Ethics* 18 (4): 353–372.
Nussbaum, Martha C. 1989. Mortal immortals: Lucretius and the voice of nature. *Philosophy and Phenomenological Research* 50 (2): 303–351.
Pereira, Felipe, and Travis Timmerman. 2020. The (un)desirability of immortality. *Philosophy Compass* 15 (2): 1–12.
Smuts, Aaron. 2011. Immortality and significance. *Philosophy and Literature* 35 (1): 134–149.
Williams, Bernard. 1972. *Problems of the self*, 82–100. Cambridge: Cambridge University Press.

Avatar as Philosophy: The Metaphysics of Switching Bodies

55

Joshua L. Tepley

Contents

Introduction	1290
Summarizing *Avatar*	1291
Understanding the Thesis	1292
Persons and Bodies	1293
Understanding Identity	1294
Understanding Possibility	1294
Some Dead Ends	1295
Animalism	1296
Substance Dualism (Souls)	1296
Transplanting Brains	1297
Rewiring Brains	1298
Extending the Body	1299
Avatars: Tools or Parts?	1299
Constitution	1299
Some Thought Experiments	1301
Changing Parts	1303
Switching Bodies	1303
Copying Brain Patterns	1304
Split Brains	1305
Switching Brain Hemispheres	1305
Switching Brains	1306
Conclusion: Surviving Death	1307
References	1308

Abstract

In the final moments of James Cameron's *Avatar* (2009), the main human character – Jake Sully – switches bodies with his blue-skinned avatar. This dramatic ending resolves the movie's remaining plot conflicts, such as Jake's

J. L. Tepley (✉)
Saint Anselm College, Manchester, NH, USA
e-mail: jtepley@anselm.edu

© Springer Nature Switzerland AG 2024
D. K. Johnson et al. (eds.), *The Palgrave Handbook of Popular Culture as Philosophy*,
https://doi.org/10.1007/978-3-031-24685-2_86

desire to regain the use of his legs, his newfound loyalty to the Na'vi people, and his love interest in Neytiri – who is twice his size and breathes an atmosphere poisonous to him. But while this climactic event makes for good storytelling, does it make any sense philosophically? Is body switching really possible? More specifically, is body switching really possible as it is portrayed in the movie – without transplanting Jake's brain or appealing to the existence of immaterial "souls"? This chapter tries to answer this question. After clarifying what it means to "switch bodies" and exploring some dead-end ways of trying to do it, this chapter develops and defends one tenable way of switching bodies that is compatible with the events in the movie. This solution involves articulating a specific theory of human persons (constitutionalism), developing a series of thought experiments, and examining the phenomenon of "split brains," in which a person with a severed corpus callosum displays two independent streams of consciousness. The chapter ends with an application of this solution to the possibility of secular life after death.

Keywords

Avatar · Switching bodies · Bodies · Brains · Brain hemispheres · Split brains · Corpus callosum · Consciousness · Persons · Identity · Personal identity · Humans · Aliens · Na'vi · Human nature · Constitutionalism · Constitution view · Animalism · Dualism · Substance dualism · Souls · Brain transplants · Metaphysics · Possibility · Philosophy of mind · Life after death · Death · James Cameron

Introduction

James Cameron's *Avatar* (2009) is an exciting and visually spectacular action movie. It is also surprisingly philosophical. For starters, it raises a host of ethical questions about a variety of topics, including animals, the environment, native peoples, native cultures, war, and disability. The film also raises a number of metaphysical questions, especially regarding persons and identity. Are nonhuman persons possible? Could plants be conscious? Could a person's mind be "uploaded" into a different medium (e.g., a complex root structure)? Could multiple persons merge together into a single person? What is more, in each of these cases, the film takes a stand. According to *Avatar*, nonhuman persons are possible, plants could be conscious, a person's mind could be "uploaded" into a different medium, and multiple persons could merge together into a single person.

In my mind, however, the most interesting philosophical question raised in the movie occurs at the very end, when Jake switches bodies with his avatar. The metaphysical question raised by this scene is: Can persons switch bodies? True to form, the movie offers an answer: Yes, they can. Exploring this question and the film's answer to it is the main task of this chapter. Can persons really switch bodies? And if so, how? Answering these two questions, it turns out, is far from easy.

Summarizing *Avatar*

The movie *Avatar* takes place on Pandora, a distant moon teaming with colorful and exotic alien life, both plant and animal. One hundred or so years from now, humans have established a base on Pandora in order to mine the rare but precious element "unobtanium," which is used as an energy source. The people living and working on the base include administrators, scientists, and a large number of security officers.

The security officers are necessary because much of the animal life on Pandora is hostile to humans. Dangerous indigenous creatures include massive rhinoceros-like animals with four eyes and six legs, gigantic six-legged panther-like creatures with tentacles sprouting from their heads, and various species of colorful – and carnivorous – flying reptiles. The main threat to the mining operation, however, is the blue-skinned Na'vi, one clan of which inhabits a massive tree – called Hometree – which lies directly atop the largest reserve of unobtanium on the moon.

The Na'vi are, as far as the humans know, the only species of intelligent life on Pandora. They are basically humanoid but possess some striking features: They have blue skin, large eyes, flat noses, four fingers (and toes), and a braided "queue" with which they can form neurological connections with other living things. They are also large – roughly twice the size of an adult human being. The Na'vi, we learn as the movie goes on, have a rich and complex culture, with its own traditions, values, and philosophy.

The main human character of the movie is Jake Sully, an ex-marine who travels to Pandora to take over for his recently deceased twin brother. Jake is a strong person, both physically and mentally, but he has paraplegia from a war injury, which is why he is no longer in the service. Jake's brother was a scientist, so Jake is not replacing him on account of his professional qualifications. Rather, Jake is taking the place of his twin brother for one simple reason: They share the same DNA.

In order to facilitate communication with the Na'vi, who are not only much larger than humans but also breathe an atmosphere poisonous to them, the humans have developed human-Na'vi hybrids, called "avatars," using a combination of human and Na'vi DNA. These avatars look almost exactly like the native Na'vi in size and anatomy, but they have brain structures sufficiently like those of their human DNA donors so that the latter are able to operate their avatars remotely using sophisticated brain-syncing technology. While they are linked to their blue-skinned avatars, the human operators lose awareness of their own bodies and seem to occupy the bodies of their avatars. Jake has been invited to Pandora because his brother's avatar, which was created using his brother's DNA, can be used only by someone with the same DNA.

Despite his lack of training, Jake proves to be a fast learner and a capable avatar operator. Having lost the use of his human legs, he savors the use of his avatar's body – which can run, jump, and feel the "earth" beneath its feet. He is adventurous and fearless, to the point of being cavalier. In fact, his adventurous spirit causes him to get separated from the rest of his avatar crew on his very first excursion into the Pandoran forest. Fortunately, he is rescued by a female Na'vi named Neytiri, who takes him back to Hometree where she resides with her clan. As a result of this happenstance, Jake is afforded the unique opportunity to witness firsthand what life is like for the Na'vi.

The heart of *Avatar* is Jake learning about Na'vi culture and Pandoran ecology from Neytiri. He learns how to ride a six-legged horse-like creature using his neural queue and how to tame – and ride – one of the giant flying reptiles. Jake also learns about Eywa, the Na'vi deity, who is physically located in an elaborate, brain-like root structure that permeates the ground of Pandora and is especially concentrated under certain trees – such as the Tree of Souls and the Tree of Voices. The Tree of Souls is the most sacred spot for the Na'vi living in Hometree, and it is where their sacred rituals are performed. The Tree of Voices is a willow-like tree with tendrils that allow the Na'vi to communicate with Eywa and their ancestors, whose minds she apparently absorbs when they die.

The final third of the film contains two major battles. In the first, human security forces attack and destroy Hometree after peaceful attempts to get the Na'vi who live there to relocate (so the humans can mine the massive deposit of unobtanium located underneath it) fail. By this point in the movie, Jake has decided that his true loyalties lie with the Na'vi, not with the humans. After Hometree is destroyed, he convinces the Na'vi who lived there to summon neighboring clans, who respond to their call and begin gathering by the thousands. Feeling threatened by the amassing Na'vi, the head of human security on Pandora orders an attack on the Tree of Souls, whose destruction, he says, will demoralize the Na'vi and quash any attempts at retaliation over the destruction of Hometree. Despite being vastly outnumbered, the Na'vi are able to repel the humans with the help of Jake's leadership and, more importantly, the animal life of Pandora itself, which rises up to attack the humans at the bequest of Eywa.

With the second battle over, much of the conflict driving the plot has been resolved – except for Jake's situation. He has betrayed his human leaders and as a consequence loses his only hope for a surgery to restore the use of his legs, and without a Na'vi body he will not be able to pursue his relationship with Neytiri, either. For all he has done and risked to save the Na'vi from their human aggressors, Jake is actually worse off now than he was when the movie started.

But then, in the final scene of the movie, things work out for Jake. The Na'vi take Jake's human body and his avatar body and place them together at the base of the Tree of Souls, one of the places where Eywa's root structure is most densely concentrated. Tendrils from the roots of Eywa creep up into their bodies, especially around the backs of their necks and spinal columns, presumably penetrating into their nervous systems. The movie ends with a close up of Jake's avatar's face, its eyes snapping open and focusing on the camera. The movie cuts to black. While there is no dialogue or final words, the implication is clear: Jake has switched bodies with his avatar.

Understanding the Thesis

The focus of this chapter is the metaphysical thesis implied by the final scene of *Avatar* – namely, that it is possible for persons to switch bodies. This might sound trivial, but it is not. It is far from obvious how a person could literally change from one body to another. Before we can see how difficult this really is, however, we need to spend some time understanding the thesis itself.

Persons and Bodies

Each of us is a *person* – that is, a thing that is intelligent, rational, self-aware, and the subject of moral attributions (praise and blame). This definition of "person" comes from the modern English philosopher John Locke, and it will be the one used in this chapter. It is worth noting, however, that this definition is not without controversy. Philosophers have long debated which features are necessary and sufficient for being a person, and Locke's definition is just one of a number on offer. That being said, I do not have enough space to get into this debate here. Locke's definition is well known and has many adherents, including myself, so it will be how the word "person" is used throughout this chapter.

So, each of us is a person. Each of us is also a *human* person. What makes a person a *human* person is even more controversial than what makes a person a person, but again I lack the space necessary to explore such details here. Suffice it to say that not all persons are necessarily human. Possible nonhuman persons include aliens (like the Na'vi), robots, and spirits – if these things really exist and display the person-making features listed above (intelligence, rationality, etc.).

Under normal circumstances, each of us – each human person – has a *body*. You might think that "body" would be easier to understand than "person" and "human person," but it is not. For the purposes of this chapter, "body" will be understood as a type of biological organism with a complex brain. In other words, bodies are a kind of animal. What does it mean to "have" a body in this sense? How are human persons related to their animal bodies? According to some philosophers – whom I will introduce later – we are just our bodies, so saying that we "have" bodies is just a manner of speaking. Other philosophers say that we are parts of our bodies – such as our brains – and we "have" our bodies in the sense that we reside within them and have a great deal of control over them. Other philosophers disagree with both of these views and say that we are completely nonphysical substances – called "souls" – which are not identical to our bodies or even to parts of our bodies (such as our brains). Each of us "has" a body in the sense that we are in causal contact with it through our brains, such that changes in our brains cause changes in us (e.g., sensations), and changes in us (e.g., desires) cause changes in our bodies (e.g., movements). On this view – called "substance dualism" – we are no more identical to our bodies, or to parts of our bodies (such as our brains), than we are to the clothes we wear or to the cars we drive.

There are many ways of viewing the relationship between persons and their bodies. Be that as it may, everyone agrees that there is *some* such relationship – whether it be identity, a part-whole relationship, or a causal connection. Let us call this relationship, whatever it happens to be, "R." Using this terminology, the thesis that it is possible for persons to switch bodies can be stated as follows: *It is possible for a person who stands in R to some body at one time to be identical to a person who stands in R to a different (nonidentical) body at a later time.* This way of putting the thesis is neutral with respect to different theories of how human persons are related to their bodies – i.e., how one understands the relation R.

Understanding Identity

The word "identity" can mean different things. The sense I have in mind here, when I say that a person at one time is identical to a person at a later time, is *numerical* identity – the kind of identity expressed by the equals sign in mathematics ("="). Two things are identical in this sense if they are the very same thing. In this sense of identity, the Eiffel Tower is identical to the tallest structure in Paris, and George Washington is identical to the first President of the United States.

This kind of identity needs to be sharply distinguished from *qualitative* identity, which is when two things share most of the same qualities or properties. Examples of qualitative identity include two freshly minted pennies and identical twins at birth. It is important not to confuse these two kinds of identity because things can be qualitatively identical without being numerically identical (such as two freshly minted pennies), and things can be numerically identical without being qualitatively identical (such as me and my 5-year-old self).

Applied to our thesis, a person who switches bodies must be numerically identical to the person after the switch, but the two persons (who are really just one person) need not be qualitatively identical to each other. The person could, for example, have very different thoughts and feelings before and after the switch. Furthermore, the two *bodies* – before and after the switch – must be numerically distinct, but they could be qualitatively identical. The two bodies might, for example, be clones such that nobody could tell them apart by just looking at them. What matters for our thesis is that the two persons are numerically identical (i.e., are really just one person) while the two bodies are numerically distinct; the degree to which these persons and bodies are qualitatively similar to, or dissimilar from, each other is a separate issue.

Understanding Possibility

The final aspect of the metaphysical thesis under discussion that we need to understand is what is meant by "possibility." What do I mean when I say that it is "possible" for a person to switch bodies?

The kind of possibility I have in mind is "metaphysical possibility." Something is metaphysically possible, roughly, if it is not conceptually incoherent. In other words, it does not imply a contradiction or run afoul of some logical principle or necessary truth. Examples of metaphysically *impossible* things include round squares, married bachelors, and four-sided triangles. It is important to note that saying that something is metaphysically possible does not imply that it could happen given our current technology (technological possibility) or even that it is compatible with the laws of nature (physical possibility). Metaphysical possibly is broader than both of these. Flying pigs and combustible water are both metaphysically possible, but neither of these is compatible with the laws of nature, let alone our current technology.

But if that is so, then why would anyone care about the body-switching thesis in the first place? If "possible" is meant this broadly, such that even flying pigs are possible, then demonstrating the possibility of body switching does not mean that it could *really* happen. It might, after all, be incompatible with the laws of nature. Furthermore, someone might object that this kind of possibility is so broad that *anything* is possible, which makes the thesis not just trivial (boring and inconsequential) but trivially true.

Showing that something is metaphysically possible does not thereby show that it is likely to happen someday, but that does not make it trivial. Showing that something is metaphysically possible is interesting and important because metaphysical possibility is a necessary condition of the other, narrower kinds of possibility (physical and technological). Think of it this way: If switching bodies is *not* metaphysically possible, then it is not physically or technologically possible, either. For there to be any hope that switching bodies is possible in these narrower senses, it must first be shown that it is possible in this broader sense.

Regarding the objection that metaphysical possibility is so broad that *anything* is possible: That is simply not true. Many things on the surface seem to be coherent and free of contradiction but, upon further reflection, turn out to be incoherent – and so metaphysically impossible. To give a simple example: The concept of *a barber who shaves only those who do not shave themselves* seems like a perfectly coherent concept, but a little reflection shows that it is not. Such a barber could not even possibly exist. (To see this point, ask yourself: Would this barber shave himself?) Philosophy abounds with complex and sophisticated claims that seem to be perfectly coherent on the surface but ultimately fall apart under scrutiny. And as we will see in the next section, the thesis that body switching is possible seems like it could be one of these, since it is far from clear how to make any conceptual sense of it.

Some Dead Ends

We now have a solid grasp of what it means to say that it is possible for persons to switch bodies. As mentioned above, this thesis might seem trivially true – given the broad sense of "possible" we have in mind. Can we not easily imagine a person switching bodies – as Jake does in the movie? And does this not show that switching bodies is "possible," at least in the broad sense of the term?

The purpose of this section is to demonstrate the contrary – namely, how *unobvious* the thesis is – by going through a number of potential strategies for switching bodies and showing that none of them works. Each of these strategies is either implicitly incoherent or else incompatible with how body switching happens in *Avatar*. If body switching as presented in the movie is possible, then how it is possible is far from obvious.

Animalism

Earlier I said that our understanding of the metaphysical thesis under discussion is neutral with respect to different theories of human persons. That is correct – in the sense that it does not presuppose that any of these theories is true. But at the same time, there is one theory of human persons according to which it is simply impossible for persons to switch bodies. This theory is called "animalism," a view defended by Eric T. Olson (1997).

According to animalism, we are just biological organisms of a certain kind – namely, animals. If "bodies" are biological organisms, as we are understanding them in this chapter, then this is equivalent to saying that we are just our bodies. (It is worth noting that some animalists would resist this formulation on account of a difference they see between "animal" and "body," but we can ignore this objection. For the purposes of this chapter, "human bodies" and "human animals" will be used interchangeably.) Animalism is typically formulated as a theory about what we – human persons – are, but it can be extended to nonhuman persons, too. If animalism is true, then presumably the Na'vi are also just biological organisms of a certain kind – albeit a different kind than we are.

The reason why animalism is fundamentally incompatible with switching bodies is due to a logical principle known as the *transitivity of identity*. According to this principle, if A is B, and B is C, then A is C. So, if a person is numerically identical to one body at one time and then numerically identical to another body at a later time, then it follows (from this principle) that these two bodies are numerically identical to each other – i.e., they are the very same body. But the very idea of body switching requires that these two bodies – before and after the switch – be numerically distinct (nonidentical). Saying that two things are both numerically identical and numerically distinct (nonidentical) is a contradiction and so cannot possibly be true. Thus, switching bodies is simply impossible if animalism is true.

That was a little fast, so here is the argument again – using symbols. Let "J" be the person (Jake) who switches bodies, "H" be his original (human) body, and "A" be his new (avatar) body. If animalism is true, then $J = H$ (before the switch) and $J = A$ (after the switch). From the transitivity of identity, it follows that $H = A$. But this is a genuine case of switching bodies only if $H \neq A$, and it cannot be true that $H = A$ and $H \neq A$, for that is a contradiction. So, switching bodies is fundamentally incompatible with animalism: If animalism is true, then switching bodies is impossible; and if body switching is possible, then animalism is false.

Substance Dualism (Souls)

We have seen that switching bodies is fundamentally incompatible with animalism, the view that we are just our bodies. But animalism is just one theory of human persons. Perhaps we will have more luck with a different theory. Let us take a look at substance dualism, a view famously held by the ancient Greek philosopher Plato and by the modern French philosopher René Descartes.

According to substance dualism, we are not our bodies at all. Rather, we are completely immaterial substances called "souls." We "have" our bodies in virtue of our souls (ourselves) standing in special causal relationships to our brains: Changes in our brains (neurons firing) cause changes in us (e.g., sensations), and changes in us (e.g., desires) cause changes in our brains (other neurons firing). Everything in our bodies that we either experience or control goes through this soul-brain causal connection.

If this is what it means to "have" a body, then switching bodies seems pretty straightforward: All we need to do is switch the causal connections that a person bears to one body (through that body's brain) to another body (through that body's brain). If this can be done, then a person can switch bodies.

Unfortunately, there are problems with this strategy for switching bodies.

To start, substance dualism has fallen out of favor in philosophy. According to most contemporary philosophers, arguments in favor of the existence of souls are unconvincing, and substance dualism faces a number of serious conceptual difficulties in its own right. For example, the causal connection between souls and brains is hard to understand. Souls have no physical properties – such as size, shape, location, or mass – but without these properties, how can they be causally affected by, or have any causal effects upon, brains, which do have these properties? And this problem is just the tip of the iceberg.

There are also difficulties involved in making sense of how substance dualism can explain body switching. If substance dualism is true, then switching bodies requires changing the causal connections between one brain and another – such that a soul that is causally connected to one brain gets causally connected to another brain instead. But what makes my soul causally connected to my brain and not to yours? And what would I have to do to my brain – and to yours – in order to detach my soul from my brain and attach it to yours instead? There are no easy answers here.

Finally, and more to the point, souls simply do not exist in *Avatar*. As I understand it, the world presented in the movie is completely materialistic. Since this chapter is exploring the thesis that persons can switch bodies as it happens in *Avatar*, souls cannot be used in defense of this thesis. So, in order to make sense of the thesis that persons can switch bodies, we will have to find some materialistic solution that does not involve souls.

Transplanting Brains

There is, of course, a relatively simple way (metaphysically speaking, that is) to switch bodies – namely, by transplanting brains. This possibility has been discussed by a number of philosophers, including Shoemaker (1963), Wiggins (1967), van Inwagen (1990, Chap. 15), and Olson (2007, p. 78). Suppose a mad scientist removed your brain from your body and my brain from my body and then switched them – placing your brain in my body and my brain in your body. After this gruesome procedure, who would be who? I am strongly inclined to say that the person in your body (with my brain) would be me, and the person in my body (with your brain) would be you. If that is the case, then this seems to be a genuinely possible case of switching bodies.

The problem with this suggestion is *not* that it is not (metaphysically) possible. It is! (Although, recall, this does not mean that it is physically or technologically possible.) The problem is that this is not how body switching happens in the movie *Avatar*. While Eywa presumably does something to Jake's and his avatar's brains when she performs the procedure that results in Jake's having (or being) his avatar's body, she does not literally remove Jake's brain from his body and stick it into his avatar's body. (She does not seem to transplant any of the parts of Jake's brain, either.) So, while transplanting brains is a metaphysically possible way of switching bodies, it is not one that we can use to defend the thesis under discussion in this chapter.

Rewiring Brains

Eywa does not transplant Jake's brain into his avatar's body, but she does do something to their brains in order to facilitate the switch. What does she do? What could she do to their brains in order to facilitate the transfer of Jake to his avatar's body?

One straightforward suggestion is that Eywa simply "rewires" his avatar's brain so that it has the same structure as Jake's brain. In other words, she transfers not Jake's *brain* but Jake's brain *pattern*. At first glance, this seems reasonable: If brain structure is responsible for consciousness as well as an individual's distinctive mental states (e.g., beliefs, desires, memories, etc.), then rewiring Jake's avatar's brain so that it is just like his human brain would result in the creation of a person in his avatar's body who thinks and acts just like Jake. And if that were the case, then would not this person *be* Jake? This idea has been discussed by a number of philosophers, including Williams (1970, p. 162), Nozick (1981, p. 39), Shoemaker (1984, pp. 108–111), van Inwagen (1997), and Olson (2007, pp. 20–21).

Unfortunately, copying Jake's brain pattern onto his avatar's brain is another dead end – as far as the possibility of switching bodies is concerned. To see why, imagine a slightly different ending to the movie – one in which Jake's human body does not die. In other words, suppose Eywa copies Jake's brain pattern onto his avatar's brain but the person in Jake's human body survives. After the procedure, which person is Jake? The one in his human body or the one in his avatar's body? If having the same brain pattern is sufficient for being the same person, then the answer is *both*. But that is clearly absurd; the same person cannot be wholly in two places at once. It follows that having the same brain pattern is *not* sufficient for being the same person. And this conclusion follows even if Eywa does not allow the person in Jake's human body to survive after she copies Jake's brain pattern onto his avatar's brain, for any proposition that even possibly leads to an absurdity – as this one does – cannot be true. So, simply copying Jake's brain pattern onto a new brain will not do the trick.

Extending the Body

None of the strategies for switching bodies proposed in the last section will work – either in their own right or because they are incompatible with the kind of body switching on offer in *Avatar*. I hope this shows just how interesting and nontrivial the thesis is that persons can switch bodies.

Now that we have an appreciation for just how difficult it is to understand how a person could switch bodies, let us turn to a strategy for doing this that actually works. This strategy, as we will see, is compatible with everything that happens in the movie – including its commitment to materialism. Whether or not James Cameron had this strategy in mind when he wrote the script is an open question, but he deserves some credit for making a movie that is compatible with it and, as we will see presently, for including ideas that suggest this strategy. The basis of this strategy comes from considering the relationship between avatars and their operators.

Avatars: Tools or Parts?

The technological centerpiece of *Avatar* is the technology whereby a human operator can project their mind into the body of an avatar. Let us think philosophically about this technology for a moment. How, exactly, do operators relate to their avatars?

The simplest idea is that avatars are *tools* – complex tools, but tools nonetheless. A person's avatar is like a remote-controlled drone, albeit one in which the controls and feedback are tied into the operator's nervous system. While operating his avatar, Jake feels like he is located where his avatar is located, but that is just an illusion. In reality, he is in a coffin-like device in a lab on the human base. Jake is no more located where his avatar is located than a person watching *Avatar* in a movie theater is located on Pandora.

But this is just one way of understanding the relationship between avatars and their operators. Another way is to understand avatars as literal *extensions* of their operators' bodies, such that operators extend beyond their bodies to incorporate their avatars. On this view, operators are not numerically identical to their avatars; rather, each of them is a complex whole with two major nonoverlapping parts: a human body (in the lab) and a human-Na'vi hybrid body (in the forest). On this view, the relationship between persons and their avatars is a mereological (part-whole) relationship: Persons are wholes of which their avatars – and their human bodies – are parts. The possibility of extending beyond our bodies in this way is discussed seriously by Glover (1988, p. 74) and Clark (2003).

Constitution

The idea that human operators literally extend into their avatars while they operate them is intriguing, but does it make any sense philosophically? Is there any theory of human persons that can accommodate this idea?

In fact, there is – a position called "constitutionalism," which has been defended by, among others, Sydney Shoemaker (1999) and Lynne Rudder Baker (2000). To understand this philosophical theory, it will help to consider an example involving an artifact rather than a person. Suppose a sculptor has a large lump of clay, which they refer to as "Lucy." Suppose further that they mold this lump into a beautiful statue, which they dub "Stacy." How is Lucy (the lump) related to Stacy (the statue)? One is tempted to say that they are numerically identical – since they have the same size, shape, texture, and spatial location. They are even made of the same matter. But they cannot be numerically identical since Lucy existed before Stacy did, and Lucy could continue to exist even if Stacy were destroyed (by being squashed, for example). Since two things with different properties cannot be numerically identical, Lucy cannot be numerically identical to Stacy.

According to the constitutionalism, which has its origins in the ideas of the ancient Greek philosopher Aristotle, Lucy and Stacy are related not by *identity* but by *constitution*. Lucy (lump) *constitutes* Stacy (statue). One thing constitutes another if, roughly, they are wholly located in the same place and are made of the same matter, but one can exist without the other. A lump of clay constitutes a statue, chunks of wood and metal together constitute a hammer, and a whole mess of wood, metal, plastic, and other materials constitute a house.

The constitution view can be applied to human beings: We are not numerically identical to our bodies; we are constituted by them. The rationale for postulating this relationship between a person and their body is the same as the one given for postulating it between a statue and a lump of clay: My biological body began to exist at conception, or soon thereafter, but I began to exist only later, once my body's brain became sufficiently complex to support the conscious mental states required for personhood. It follows that I (a person) cannot be numerically identical to my body. Or consider a case in which an adult's frontal lobe is badly damaged or even removed. A body can survive this trauma, since a body can still be alive (breathing, metabolizing, etc.) without a frontal lobe. But a person cannot, since the frontal lobe is responsible for human intelligence and rationality, which are necessary for being a person. So, once again, we have a situation in which a body exists at a time when the person who "has" this body does not, from which it follows that this person cannot be numerically identical to that body. But if persons (while they exist) and their bodies are located in the same place, and are even made of the same matter, then they must stand in some very special relationship to each other. And this special relationship, according to the view under consideration, is constitution.

According to constitutionalism, each of us is constituted by a body under normal circumstances. I say "under normal circumstances" because constitutionalism opens the door for persons to be partly constituted by things that are not biological and so not strictly part of a person's body. For example, a prosthetic knee would not be part of a person's biological body, for it is not caught up in that body's life processes, but arguably it is part of that person, since it performs the same function as their biological knee. According to constitutionalism (or at least the version I am espousing here), what makes something (partly) constitute a person is not that it is made of the right sort of stuff (e.g., biological matter) but that it functions in the right way. On this view, a person could be fully constituted by nonbiological materials (e.g., plastic, metal, and silicon) if all of their biological parts were replaced slowly by nonbiological parts. This possibility is discussed by Unger (1990, pp. 121–122), Baker (2000, p. 113), and Olson (2007, pp. 25, 51, 84).

The relevance of constitutionalism to the idea that people can extend beyond their bodies is this: If constitutionalism is true, and what constitutes a person at any given time is not necessarily a body but whatever functions in the right way, then a person can be constituted by their human body *and* an avatar body together – so long as the latter stands in the right relationship to that person. So, on this view, while Jake is linked to his avatar, he is constituted by two bodies – a human body (in the lab) and a human-Na'vi hybrid body (in the forest), in the same way that a cybernetic person is constituted by a biological organism and their mechanical parts. In other words, Jake is partly in the lab and partly in the forest; he is not wholly in either place. So, constitutionalism gives us a way of understanding how Jake can literally extend into his avatar, such that the latter is literally part of himself and not just a sophisticated tool that he uses.

Some Thought Experiments

Constitutionalism provides the theoretical framework to explain how Jake can literally extend beyond his body and into his avatar. But is there any reason to think that this really happens? Are there any arguments in favor of the view that human operators literally extend into their avatars and do not simply relate to them by remote control? The purpose of this section is to give such an argument. It comprises a series of four thought experiments.

Forget all about avatars for a moment and consider the following hypothetical scenario:

> *Tethered Brain-in-a-Vat:* Scientists remove your brain from your skull and keep it alive in a vat of nutrients while also maintaining its connection to your body through a long bundle of nerves sheathed in some strong and flexible material. The bundle carries nerve signals so quickly and efficiently that there is no noticeable difference in your experience (except for the tube extending from the back of your neck and your head feeling a little bit lighter).

Would the fact that your brain is outside your body imply that your body is not part of you? I do not think so. Why should the physical location of your brain, or the length of your spinal cord, make a difference – so long as the causal connection is maintained and everything seems the same from your point of view?

Next, consider this possibility:

> *Remote Brain-in-a-Vat:* Scientists replace the long and flexible cord with radio transmitters that fit on the ends of the nerves leading out of your brain and those leading into your body. Because this technology is good enough, your experiences are indistinguishable from the ones you had when your brain was inside your body. As your body moves around and

interacts with its environment, you feel like *you* are doing these things, even though your brain is in some remote location and not physically attached to your body.

In this situation, would your body be part of you? Again, I do not see why not. Why should being literally "hard wired" into the body – e.g., via a bundle of nerves – matter? If the transmitters attached to your nerve endings are doing the same causal work as the cord was doing in the first thought experiment, then why is this not sufficient?

If you are with me so far, then consider this possibility:

> *Switched Radio Brains:* Scientists do the same procedure described in the previous scenario to another person. The scientists then switch the transmitters so that your brain is synced with their body, and their brain is synced with your body.

What happens? Do you now have a body over which another person has control? Or have you effectively switched bodies, so that the other person's body is now literally a part of you – along with that other very important part, namely, your brain? I am inclined to say the latter. What makes your body part of you is not its DNA or its history but rather the causal connection it has with your brain. If your brain were synced with a different body than the one you were born with, then I think that this body would become literally a part of you.

Finally, imagine the following scenario:

> *Avatar Body:* Scientists put your brain back into your original body and hook you up to a sophisticated device that can read the parts of your brain responsible for controlling your body and can activate the parts of your brain in charge of receiving signals from your body. This device links remotely with another body, which has a brain specially designed for this purpose. While the device is in operation, the normal inputs from your body are replaced by the inputs from the other body, and the normal outputs from your brain are relayed to that other body. As a result, while the device in operation, you cease to be aware of your own body and seem to be "in" the other one.

What is your relationship to this other body while the device is in operation? If what I have proposed in the first three thought experiments is correct, then I am inclined to say that this is a situation in which you literally extend into this other body. You now occupy two places: You are partly located where your original body is located (since your brain is still inside that body), and you are also partly located where your remote-controlled body is located (since you stand in the right causal connection to that body).

This fourth and final thought experiment is, more or less, what is happening with human operators and their avatars in the movie *Avatar*. If this series of thought experiments really shows what I suggest it shows, then we have a good reason to think that Jake literally extends into his avatar while he is operating it. His human body does not cease to be part of him, since his brain is not removed from it, but he temporarily extends beyond that body and into his avatar's body, since he stands in the right causal connection to it. To be clear, I am not saying that this series of thought experiments constitutes a knockdown argument for this view. But I do think that it is plausible enough to show that the idea of a person literally extending into the body of an avatar is worth taking very seriously.

Changing Parts

Let us take stock. We have a theoretical framework for understanding how a person could extend beyond their body and into their avatar (constitutionalism), and we have considered an argument (a series of thought experiments) which, if sound, shows that this would really be the case if the technology in *Avatar* were real. But none of this yet fully addresses the metaphysical thesis under consideration in this chapter – namely, that persons can switch bodies. Showing that persons can extend beyond their bodies and into other bodies (i.e., be wholly located in one body at one time, and then be wholly located in two bodies at a later time) is not the same thing as showing that persons can switch bodies (i.e., be wholly located in one body at one time, and then be wholly located in a different body at a later time). To get from the former to the latter, more is needed. So, how does the possibility of extending beyond one's body lead to the possibility of switching bodies?

The answer is quite simple: If people can extend from one body into a second body, then presumably they can also shrink from two bodies into just one body. If the body into which a person shrinks is the one with which that person started, then nothing significant happens. But if the body into which the person shrinks is the body into which the person extended, then this person has effectively switched bodies.

This is, as far as I know, the only way in which body switching is possible and compatible with what happens in *Avatar*: Jake extends into his avatar's body, such that he is constituted partly by his human body and partly by his avatar body, and then he shrinks down by losing his human body, leaving him with just his avatar body.

Switching Bodies

You might think that our task is now complete. We have shown how a person can change bodies: That person extends into another body by standing in the right causal relationship to it, and then the procedure is reversed so that they shrink from being constituted by two bodies to being constituted by just one body. If the body at the end is the one into which the person extended (and not the one with which they began), then that person has switched bodies.

Unfortunately, there is a snag. How do you get a human-avatar fusion to shrink so that just the avatar body is left? A natural suggestion is to kill the human body. But that will not work. It is clear from the movie that when a human operator is killed, that person's avatar ceases to function and that person is simply dead. So, how do we shrink a person constituted by a human body and an avatar body in such a way that the person survives in the avatar body rather than simply dies?

The reason why killing a human operator results in the death of that person rather than a body switch is because the control center of a human-avatar fusion is the human brain. Avatars have brains, too, but they are apparently constructed so that they are able to send signals to and receive signals from human brains; they are not designed to function on their own. So, the only way for a human operator to switch bodies with their avatar is to transfer this locus of control from the human brain to the avatar brain. How could that happen? In other words, how could a person switch brains?

Copying Brain Patterns

Perhaps the solution to this problem is simply to "rewire" the avatar's brain so that it has the exact same neural structure as the human brain. What makes a human brain capable of controlling a body is its structure, so imposing this structure on an avatar's brain should give it this power. Moreover, since a person's distinctive mental states (e.g., beliefs, desires, memories, etc.) are encoded in a person's unique neural structure, an exact structural duplicate of a person's brain should have that person's personality. Putting it all together: In order to switch bodies, a person needs to extend their body into another body, the structure of that person's original brain needs to be copied onto the brain of the body into which they have extended, and then – and only then – the original body needs to be killed. With this crucial middle step, this person should have switched bodies. Right?

Wrong. There are two problems with this proposal.

First, simply rewiring the avatar's brain so that it has the same structure as its operator's brain will have the negative consequence of breaking the link between the two, since it is the avatar's nonautonomous brain structure that allows this link in the first place. Since it is this link that allows the operator to literally extend beyond their body and into their avatar's body, breaking this link means that they will lose this extension. In other words, as the avatar's brain becomes more and more autonomous, the operator will have less and less control over it – eventually to the point where the avatar is no longer part of them. And if that happens, we are back to square one.

A second and related problem is that the restructured brain will take on a life of its own, which will make it its own person rather than a part of the original person. After the contents of a human brain have been copied into an avatar's brain, the latter can have thoughts, feelings, and desires that are not shared by the former. For example, the newly structured avatar brain will experience the world through its human-Na'vi hybrid body, whereas the human brain will experience the world through its human body. This is not a case of one person with two streams of consciousness but rather two different persons, each with their own stream of consciousness. Of course, since the avatar brain is a neural duplicate of the human brain, the two will be very similar. But even the slightest variation is sufficient to show that the two persons are not numerically identical to each other.

In short, copying a human's brain structure onto their avatar's brain will not fill the gap between extending bodies and switching bodies. On the contrary, this procedure will result in decoupling the two bodies, breaking the original person's extension into their avatar's body, and the creation of a new person in that body.

Split Brains

There is a way of filling the gap between extending bodies and switching bodies, but it requires a detour through some amazing discoveries about the human brain, which have been discussed by a number of philosophers – including Thomas Nagel (1971), Derek Parfit (1984, Chap. 12), Peter van Inwagen (1990, Chap. 16), and Elizabeth Schechter (2018).

The brain has two halves, or hemispheres, which are connected – and synchronized – by a bundle of nerves called the "corpus callosum." When the corpus callosum is severed, either accidentally or intentionally (e.g., in order to treat certain kinds of epilepsy), the two hemispheres demonstrate some surprising independence from each other. For example, when a person whose corpus callosum has been cut is shown the word "cat" in only their left visual field, they are unable to orally report what word they have seen – since speech is controlled mainly by the left hemisphere, which is linked to the right visual field. But at the same time, this person will draw a picture of a cat with their left hand, since the left hand is controlled by the right hemisphere, which is linked to the left visual field. This might sound too strange to be true, but such cases have been studied and documented extensively. The phenomenon of "split brains" is real. Persons with a severed corpus callosum show evidence of having, at least potentially, two independent streams of consciousness – one in each brain hemisphere.

Because each brain hemisphere can function independently from the other, it is actually possible for a person to survive with just one brain hemisphere. Since the functions of a brain are not perfectly duplicated in each hemisphere, this can lead to some disability. For example, a person whose left brain hemisphere has been removed might have difficulty speaking, since speech is controlled mainly by that hemisphere. However, given the plasticity of the human brain – that is, its ability to change its own structure by forming new neural pathways – the surviving half can sometimes take over these lost functions. This is especially true of children, whose brains are far more plastic than those of adults. In fact, children's brains are so remarkably plastic that children who lose a brain hemisphere can go on to live perfectly normal lives as adults. For all you know, some of the people you know have only one brain hemisphere – provided they lost the other hemisphere as a child.

Switching Brain Hemispheres

The purpose of introducing split brains is to supply us with the resources to show how a person could switch brain hemispheres, which will give us as a model for understanding how a person could switch brains.

Here is how a person could switch brain hemispheres: Suppose a person has just one brain hemisphere – their left one. Suppose further that this person has extraordinary regenerative capabilities, which allow them to regrow their right hemisphere in such a way that, by the end of this process, this fully formed (right) hemisphere is perfectly synchronized with their left hemisphere – just as the two hemispheres of a person with an intact corpus callosum are synchronized. Suppose further that this process is done in such a way that there is no time at which their new (right) hemisphere functions independently of their old (left) hemisphere. In other words, there are never two separate streams of consciousness. There is just one stream of consciousness, initially located in the left brain hemisphere alone, but eventually co-located in both hemispheres, once the right hemisphere is fully formed and functioning.

Next, imagine that this person's original hemisphere – the left one – is slowly destroyed but in such a way that, while it is functioning, it is never out of sync with the right hemisphere. In other words, the left brain hemisphere is destroyed without letting it at any time develop its own stream of consciousness. The latter would happen if, for example, the corpus callosum were severed before the left hemisphere was destroyed. If that happened, then there would be two streams of consciousness – one in each hemisphere – and so two different persons. That would be problematic since it would not be clear which of the two resulting persons – the one in the left hemisphere or the one in the right hemisphere – was numerically identical to the original person (who started out with just a left hemisphere but later had a complete brain with two hemispheres). In fact, it seems that *neither* of the resulting persons would be identical to the original person. So, it is absolutely crucial that the left brain hemisphere be destroyed without allowing it to have at any time its own independent stream of consciousness.

At the end of this procedure, assuming it is done properly, this person will have switched brain hemispheres. A single person, who at one time has just a left brain hemisphere, later has two brain hemispheres, and finally has just a right brain hemisphere. Since there is only a single stream of consciousness throughout the entire process, there is no reason to think that this person has at any time "split" into two persons (one in each hemisphere) or been destroyed and replaced by a numerically distinct person. This single person has simply gone from having only a left brain hemisphere to having only a right brain hemisphere. And that is what it means to "switch" brain hemispheres.

Switching Brains

With this procedure for switching brain hemispheres in mind, we can extrapolate a procedure for switching brains (e.g., switching from a human brain to a human-Na'vi hybrid brain), which is the missing piece in our understanding of how a person could switch bodies. The procedure for switching brains requires syncing up a fully functioning (autonomous) brain with an initially nonautonomous brain in such a way that there are never two independent streams of consciousness. In the movie

Avatar, this process is facilitated by Eywa. Eywa extends Jake's brain into his avatar's brain, not by crudely copying the contents of the former onto the latter, but by slowing bringing the nonfunctioning avatar brain into sync with his human brain in such a way that the former functions analogously to an additional brain hemisphere. So long as the brain in Jake's avatar is properly synced with his human brain and is never able to develop its own independent stream of consciousness, Jake's brain will essentially extend into his avatar's brain. In the same way that a person with one brain hemisphere can extend that hemisphere into a newly grown hemisphere, so does Jake's human brain extend into his avatar's brain.

The final step, of course, is the destruction of the human brain in such a way that it is never out of sync with the avatar brain and so never able to develop its own independent stream of consciousness. The latter would happen if, for example, the link between Jake and his avatar were severed before his human brain was destroyed. This splitting of consciousness must be avoided, for if it is not then arguably both persons are destroyed and two new (qualitatively identical) persons take their places. But if the procedure is done carefully enough, then such splitting can be avoided. And in that case, I see no reason why Jake's brain could not ultimately end up being entirely located where his avatar's brain is located.

Putting it all together, this is how a person could switch bodies in a way that is compatible with what happens in *Avatar*: The person extends from one body into another by standing in the right causal connection to it, then that person's brain extends into the other body's brain by slowly syncing with it (the way two brain hemispheres are synchronized by the corpus callosum), and finally that person's original brain is slowly destroyed. If this procedure is done properly, such that there is never a time at which each brain has its own independent stream of consciousness, then this person will have switched bodies.

Conclusion: Surviving Death

Metaphysics is fun and mind-expanding, but at the end of the day – who cares? What difference does it really make whether or not it is possible for Jake to switch bodies with his avatar? Ultimately, is not this entire discussion – like the movie *Avatar* itself – nothing more than intellectual entertainment with no practical application in the "real world"?

There are a number of problems with this criticism. To start, it is hardly a criticism of something's value to say that it is enjoyable and nothing more. Most things we care about in life are valuable because we enjoy them. Just try imagining your life without all the things you enjoy. Is that life still worth living? I doubt it. And in that case, saying that metaphysics is stupid because its value lies in its enjoyment is a poor reason to knock it.

Furthermore, the thesis under discussion does have some "real world" significance. Most people I know would like to survive death. Some of these people actually believe in life after death because they are religious. But what about those of us who are *not* religious? Can we have any hope of surviving death?

Futurists such as Ray Kurzweil have proposed that we could survive death by "uploading" our minds into a computer. This would not ensure immortality, since not even computers last forever, but it would certainly extend the length of a person's "life" considerably. Setting aside the challenges involved in duplicating the function of a biological brain in a digital computer, this prospect of mind-uploading in order to survive death faces a serious challenge, analogous to the one we came across earlier when we discussed the possibility of switching bodies by copying one's brain pattern into another brain: If a person's mind is uploaded into a computer while they are alive, then who is the "real" person – the one with a biological body or the one inside of a computer? If having the same (functional) brain structure is sufficient for being the same person, as advocates of mind-uploading seem to think, then the answer is *both* – which is absurd. It follows that simple mind-uploading does not preserve personal identity. We might someday be able to create digital persons who have all of our mental states (e.g., beliefs, desires, memories, etc.), but those persons would not be us. They would be digital duplicates of us.

Here is where the thesis discussed in this chapter comes into play: If, rather than simply uploading a person's mind into a computer, a person's brain were hooked up to a computer and a digital analog of their brain slowly developed, and kept in constant sync with their brain, then perhaps this person's brain would literally extend into the computer – in the same way that Jake's brain, with Eywa's help, literally extends into his avatar's brain. And then, if that person's human brain were carefully destroyed – in such a way that there was never a time at which it exhibited its own independent stream of consciousness – then that person would literally go from being a biological entity (human body) to being a digital one, whose "body" is now a computer. Of course, every step of this complicated process involves a great deal of speculation, both technological and metaphysical. But at least it has a chance of preserving a person's personal identity, whereas simply uploading a person's mind into a computer has none.

So, if you are interested in the possibility of surviving death without relying on religious belief, then you have a very good reason to take seriously the metaphysical thesis proposed by *Avatar* and discussed in this chapter.

References

Baker, Lynne Rudder. 2000. *Persons and bodies: A constitution view*. New York: Cambridge University Press.
Clark, Andy. 2003. *Natural-born cyborgs: Minds, technologies, and the future of human intelligence*. New York: Oxford University Press.
Glover, Jonathan. 1988. *I: The philosophy and psychology of personal identity*. London: Penguin Books.
Nagel, Thomas. 1971. Brain bisection and the unity of consciousness. *Synthese* 22 (3): 396–413.
Nozick, Robert. 1981. *Philosophical explanations*. Cambridge, MA: Harvard University Press.
Olson, Eric T. 1997. *The human animal: Personal identity without psychology*. New York: Oxford University Press.

———. 2007. *What are we? A study in personal ontology.* New York: Oxford University Press.
Parfit, Derek. 1984. *Reasons and persons.* New York: Oxford University Press.
Schechter, Elizabeth. 2018. *Self-consciousness and "split" brains: The mind's I.* New York: Oxford University Press.
Shoemaker, Sydney. 1963. *Self-knowledge and self-identity.* Ithaca: Cornell University Press.
———. 1984. Personal identity: A materialist's account. In *Personal identity*, ed. Sydney Shoemaker and Richard Swinburne. Oxford: Blackwell.
———. 1999. Self, body, and coincidence. *Proceedings of the Aristotelian Society, Supplementary Volumes* 73: 287–306.
Unger, Peter. 1990. *Identity, consciousness and value.* New York: Oxford University Press.
Van Inwagen, Peter. 1990. *Material beings.* Ithaca: Cornell University Press.
———. 1997. Materialism and the psychological-continuity account of personal identity. *Philosophical Perspectives* 11 (Mind, Causation, and World): 305–319.
Wiggins, David. 1967. *Identity and spatio-temporal continuity.* New York: Oxford University Press.
Williams, Bernard. 1970. The self and the future. *The Philosophical Review* 79 (2): 161–180.

Introduction

Pulp Fiction is pulp. It is a glib and amoral smorgasbord of postmodern allusions with a disordered narrative. It minimizes the profound evil of its murderous protagonists, hiding their malice behind clever and topical cultural banter. The characters inhabit a harsh world of fickle fortune. (Marvin is accidentally shot, Mia overdoses by misidentifying, Butch kills his opponent with a punch, and Marsellus is kidnapped and raped.) This does not seem like a morality tale. But this characterization is incomplete. The film is also full of redemption. As Tarantino said when queried about the theme of redemption, "it is explicit in the film" (Seal 2013). However, not everyone gets a second chance. As Samuel Jackson notes on this topic: "The people who are worth saving get saved... They get another chance – that's their redemption" (quoted by Mark Seal, Vanity Fair, 2013).

But why? Why do some get another chance? Why are only some redeemed? What makes them "worth saving"?

The answer is something like authenticity; the authentic get saved. All the major characters in the film are facing dilemmas. How they respond to these dilemmas determines their fate. There is nothing novel about narratives challenging their protagonists; that is the bread and butter of storytelling. The philosophical lesson here emerges from the juxtaposition of several interconnected storylines, and the importantly different reactions of the characters who all occupy the same fallen and bloody world.

Authenticity determines their fate because each character is challenged to understand their own situation, to understand themselves, and to act accordingly. This task also encompasses cultural (and pop-cultural) moral and religious considerations. To be authentic is to be true to our real selves, to engage honestly with ourselves through action. When put that bluntly it sounds a little hollow. But maybe it should. In fact, finding and confronting ourselves is a complex task that *Pulp Fiction* confronts directly through both its form and content, and it challenges the viewer to confront their own subjective situation as well.

An invitation to understand one's own subjective nature, from the first-person perspective, is a hallmark of existentialism. While *Pulp Fiction* can be understood as an argument through contrasting cases, it is not only that. There is no simple moral interpretation available: the innocent die in the crossfire (Marsellus shoots a good Samaritan; Marvin is killed by an accidental discharge, and so on). Those who save others are not always rewarded (Vincent saves Mia and is later killed). Those who prey on others and don't help them, nevertheless survive (Ringo). Many murderers and other morally corrupt characters are given a second chance. It is also important that we, as viewers, are given merely a snapshot; many of these characters are given a second chance, but their lives continue, and their fate is not yet resolved. In the middle of it all is Vincent, who doesn't find redemption, but suffers an undignified demise in a bathroom.

In the simplest terms, Jules is saved because he responds to the call, to his second chance, his reprieve, in the right way (authentically); Vincent doesn't survive because he doesn't respond authentically. However, even to view the film as this kind of argument, one must work through and contrast the actions and psychology of each character. The film is not merely a didactic argument but incites the viewer to engage authentically with these existential tensions, resolve them, and perhaps, in the process, even apply them to themselves.

Story and Narration

Pulp Fiction consists of three stories sharing some characters. These are story arcs understood in terms of problems and their resolutions, and do not correspond to the title cards in the film (e.g., The Gold Watch).

In the first story, two hitmen, Jules and his partner Vincent must retrieve a mysterious briefcase and return it to their boss Marsellus Wallace. Jules and Vince miraculously survive an ambush. Jules feels the touch of God, chooses to leave the hitman profession, and proves his conviction when two small-time robbers confront him (Pumpkin and Honey Bunny). Jules and Vincent successfully deliver the case to Marsellus Wallace, despite Vincent's accidentally shooting Marvin in the car on the way.

The second story is about Vincent who must take Marsellus's wife Mia on a date. He must avoid the temptation to become sexually involved with Mia. The date goes well until she overdoses. Luckily, Vincent saves her with an adrenaline shot to the heart.

The third story is about Butch, an aging boxer who has made a deal with Marsellus, and agreed to throw his next match. Butch double-crosses Marsellus but can't make a clean getaway because he must retrieve his father's gold war watch. In the process of retrieving the watch, he kills Vincent, runs over, and then is pursued by Marsellus. Both he and Marsellus are kidnapped; and when Butch escapes, he decides to return to save Marsellus from a brutal sexual assault. They resolve their conflict and Butch rides off with his girlfriend, Fabienne.

The stories are not presented chronologically, though the narrative order is not as complex as it seems, nor as disordered as it is sometimes claimed to be. The last two sections of the film (6. The Bonnie Situation and 7. The Epilogue), belong chronologically between Sections 2 and 3. In other words, this one section is moved from there to the end of the film. The diner scene is shown from two perspectives: in addition to closing the film in Section 7, *The Epilogue*, it also opens the film, with Pumpkin and Honey Bunny deciding to rob the restaurant in The Prologue. That is the complete explanation of the narrative order.

Pulp Fiction in Narrative Order (Syuzhet)

1. Prologue: The Diner (Ringo and Yolanda)
   a. Ringo and Yolanda discuss robbing
   b. Ringo and Yolanda begin robbing
2. Prelude: Burgers and The Bible
   a. "Royale with cheese" and Amsterdam
   b. Marcellus asked Vince to take out Mia
   c. Foot massages and playing with fire
   d. "Let's get into character"
   e. Bret's apartment/"That is a tasty burger"
   f. Ezekiel 25:17 & killing Bret
3. Vincent and Mia
   a. Marsellus pays Butch to throw the fight
   b. Vince and Jules deliver the case
   c. Vince and Butch aren't friends
   d. Vincent buys heroin from Lance
   e. Vince drives high to get Mia
   f. Jack Rabbit Slim's & the Dance Contest
   g. Back at Mia's/"Stay Loyal"/Mia OD's
   h. Vince saves Mia at Lance's house
4. "The Gold Watch"
   a. Flashback/Little Butch gets the watch
   b. Butch wakes/doesn't throw the fight
   c. Esmeralda Villalobos and the cab ride
   d. Marcellus' new quest: Scour the Earth.
   e. Butch & Fabienne: She forgot the watch
   f. Butch returns to his apt./Kills Vince
   g. Butch runs into Marsellus/The chase
   h. At Zed's: The capture & Marsellus' rape
   i. Butch saves Marsellus
   j. Marsellus' forgives Butch/strike a deal
   k. Butch gets Fabienne/ rides off on Grace
5. "The Bonnie Situation"
   a. Ezekiel 25:17 (again)
   b. Jules and Vincent are ambushed
   c. "The Miracle." Every bullet misses
   d. The Discussion: Did God come down?
   e. Vincent shoots Marvin in the face
   f. Jules and Vince arrive at Jimmy's
   g. Jules calls Marsellus
   h. Marsellus calls the Wolf
   i. The Wolf arrives/"Clean the fucking car"
   j. Jules and Vince clean/"Mushroom cloud"
   k. Monster Joe's: "Like it never happened."
   l. "You feel like having breakfast with me?"
6. Epilogue - The Diner: Jules and Vince
   a. "I don't eat pork"
   b. Discussing the miracle.
   c. Jules: "I felt the touch of God"
   d. Jules tells Vince he's quitting
   e. Ringo and Yolanda rob the restaurant
   f. Ringo takes Jules' Wallet
   g. Jules puts Ringo at gunpoint
   h. Vince is back//the standoff
   i. Ezekiel 25:1/"You're the weak"
   j. Jules: "I'm trying ... to be the shepherd"
   k. Jules lets Ringo go.
   l. Jules and Vincent leave the restaurant

Pulp Fiction in Chronological Order (Fablula)

1. (4a) Flashback/Little Butch gets the watch
2. (2) Prelude: Burgers and The Bible
   a. "Royale with cheese" and Amsterdam
   b. Marcellus asked Vince to take out Mia
   c. Foot massages and playing with fire
   d. "Let's get into character"
   e. Bret's apartment/"That is a tasty burger"
   f. Ezekiel 25:17 & killing Bret
3. (5) "The Bonnie Situation"
   a. Ezekiel 25:17 (again)
   b. Jules and Vincent are ambushed
   c. "The Miracle." Every bullet misses
   d. The Discussion: Did God come down?
   e. Vincent shoots Marvin in the face
   f. Jules and Vince arrive at Jimmy's
   g. Jules calls Marsellus
   h. Marsellus calls the Wolf
   i. The Wolf arrives/"Clean the fucking car"
   j. Jules and Vince clean/"Mushroom cloud"
   k. Monster Joe's: "Like it never happened."
   l. "You feel like having breakfast with me?"
4. (1/6) Prologue/Epilogue
   a. Ringo and Yolanda discuss robbing
   b. Jules and Vince joke/discuss the miracle
   c. Jules: "I felt the touch of God"
   d. Jules tells Vince he's quitting
   e. Ringo and Yolanda rob the restaurant
   f. Ringo takes Jules' Wallet
   g. Jules puts Ringo at gunpoint
   h. Vince is back//the standoff
   i. Ezekiel 25:1; "You're the weak"
   j. Jules: "I'm trying ... to be the shepherd"
   k. Jules lets Ringo go.
   l. Jules and Vincent leave the restaurant
5. (3) Vincent and Mia
   a. Marsellus pays Butch to throw the fight.
   b. Vince and Jules deliver the case
   c. Vince and Butch aren't friends
   d. Vincent buys heroin from Lance
   e. Vince drives high to get Mia
   f. Jack Rabbit Slim's & the /Dance Contest
   g. Back at Mia's/"Stay Loyal"/Mia OD's
   h. Vince saves Mia at Lance's house
6. (4b-k) "The Gold Watch"
   a. Butch wakes/doesn't throw the fight
   b. Esmeralda Villalobos and the cab ride
   c. Marcellus' new quest: Scour the Earth.
   d. Butch & Fabienne: She forgot the watch
   e. Butch returns to his apt./Kills Vince
   f. Butch runs into Marsellus/The chase
   g. At Zed's: The capture & Marsellus' rape
   h. Butch saves Marsellus
   i. Marsellus' forgives Butch/strike a deal
   j. Butch gets Fabienne/ rides off on Grace

There is also some overlap in the telling of the three narrative arcs presented above. For example, Vincent's date, and the fate of Tony Rocky Horror, another hitman who supposedly got too close to Mia, is introduced as the two hitmen enter Brett's apartment to retrieve the briefcase. This allows Section 2 "Prelude to Vincent Vega and Marsellus Wallace's Wife/The Bonnie Situation" to serve as an introduction to two of the story arcs. The nonlinear narrative, the overlap in the telling of the stories, and the appearance of characters in multiple stories, prevent the film from feeling like a series of vignettes.

The Rich and Prosperous Mr. Butch

We can understand what *Pulp Fiction* says about authenticity by working through the cases presented. Here is a Puzzler: Butch kills a man yet he gets to live. Indeed, while he kills his opponent in the boxing match accidentally, he demonstrates no remorse and even blames his opponent for choosing to fight. When queried by Esmeralda, Butch says "I didn't know he was dead 'til you told me he was dead. Now I know he's dead, do you wanna know how I feel about it? I don't feel the least bit bad about it." Later he says, "Enough about the poor unfortunate Mr. Floyd, let's talk about the rich and prosperous Mr. Butch." This doesn't seem like someone worthy of redemption.

Despite his flaws, Butch is (mostly) authentic, and even acts in a way worthy of redemption in the end. Butch is a cliche: a fighter past his prime. Butch is aging, and like any athlete, his competitive days are numbered. This is a fact about his life. He acknowledges this, but doesn't passively go on fighting until he can no longer compete with younger boxers.

Marsellus Wallace wants Butch to throw the fight and warns him that he "may feel a slight sting," on the night of the fight. "That's pride, fuckin' wit ya." The sting would be the result of a conflict between Butch's established character and convictions (he is a boxer that tries to win), and his actions (intentionally losing). His pride would be wounded because he was not true to himself. So if he threw the fight he would be inauthentic in a fairly conventional sense. Instead of taking either of these obvious paths, Butch transcends the situation and makes his own. (He takes the money, bets it on himself, and doesn't throw the fight!).

Moreover, when things don't go exactly as planned, and Butch not only knocks-out but kills his opponent Floyd, Butch acknowledges the reality of the situation and quickly adapts. His attitude here is callous and detached; he is an outsider who flouts conventions and norms, and displays no emotional responses. In that sense, he is true to his own convictions and seems to act free from coercion by social norms and constraints.

Yet, this familiar type of authenticity does not seem to be unconditionally rewarded in the film. Most of the characters in the film are criminals who are not swayed by traditional moral considerations, and fail to show moral emotions, and this is not always rewarded. On the one hand, Vincent is stubbornly loyal to his own convictions, and social obligations (to his gangster boss), and is nevertheless killed. On the other hand, Jules completely abandons his former life, character, convictions, and obligations, yet he survives. Thus, Butch's survival is not explained by either loyalty to his convictions, nor freedom from social constraint, and must be explained in some other way.

A more apt account of authenticity requires an alternate account of self. We can start to develop a helpful framework by considering the French Philosopher Jean-Paul Sartre's notion of bad faith, which is a form of self-deception (e.g., 1943, pp. 98–99). Accepting the risk of oversimplification, the basic idea is that humans have two aspects: the reality of their circumstances (facticity), including what they have done in the past, and the possibilities for action that are always available to them. If you confuse these and think that you really are just your past and unchangeable circumstances, you are in bad faith. There are other forms of bad faith, but this one concerns Sartre the most because it reduces us to mere things that have a fixed nature. In other words, the person displaying this type of bad faith defines themselves solely as facticity, denying their freedom to choose different possibilities for action.

In the mundane sense of authenticity that we have found explanatorily inadequate, Butch is authentic if he is true to himself; he is free if his actions are determined by his character and not by social conventions or coercion. But this assumes that character is something determinate, enduring, and causative. What if he has no character, or if his character is not appropriately determinate or fixed? In this case, it will not be possible for him to be authentic in this mundane sense.

Sartre claims humans have certain factual realities, or facticity, but humans are also something distinct from those realities; they are the possibilities that are available to them, or "transcendence." This is evident even in the nature of consciousness itself which seems to be transparent to the world: when we see a landscape, the objects in the landscape appear before us, a horse, a barn, some trees dappled with light and vibrant red and yellow leaves. But take away these objects of consciousness and what remains? Nothing. So although there is a sense in which one is something (facticity), there is a sense in which one is nothing (transcendence, or mere possibility). Beings that are conscious in the way humans are can always choose to be something other than what they currently are. For Sartre this means that we are radically free and not constrained by our facticity, but that, sadly, we never really attain the status of simply being what we aim to become (something in-itself, or a mere object). This is why Sartre writes, somewhat paradoxically "We have to deal with human reality as a being which is what it is not, and is not what it is" (1943, p. 58).

Sartre doesn't talk much about authenticity, but we could say that one is inauthentic when one is acting in what Sartre calls bad faith; so we can say that one is inauthentic when one focuses exclusively or excessively on one's facticity or transcendence (or when one conflates the two) (1943, pp. 98–99). This then is what we were looking for: an account of authenticity that doesn't require having a determinate character with which one's actions must be consistent. On this account, one must instead acknowledge one's actual situation including one's past, and also the possibilities that are available. We see that Butch acknowledges both, and thus is authentic in the sense of not being in bad faith, when he returns for his father's watch.

When Butch realizes that Fabienne has forgotten his father's gold watch at his apartment, he feels a direct tension between his desire to start a new life after escaping his past and his attachment to an important momento that anchors him to his father and his family history. In choosing to retrieve his watch he acknowledges the reality of that history and its importance, but this does not inhibit him from pursuing his new life. He seems to strike a balance (though it is worth noting that he is returning to his hometown, so he may be a little too constrained by his past).

Is Butch rewarded for retrieving his father's war watch? He retrieves the watch, but at considerable cost: he encounters and kills Vincent Vega, runs over, and then gets chased by Marsellus, and ends up being captured by a pair of sadistic rapists. It might seem pretty obvious that returning for the watch was a bad idea. However, Butch not only ultimately escapes the rapists, but he clearly *chooses* to risk his own life to save Marsellus. This is a redemptive act, and Butch is immediately rewarded. He makes amends with Marsellus and is allowed to ride off into the sunset. Returning for his father's gold watch may have saved his life.

Butch doesn't accept that his options are limited to the obvious ones presented by his situation. He chooses his own path. By retrieving his father's watch Butch acknowledges the reality and importance of his past without being bound by it. He seems to avoid bad faith and to act authentically. He also clearly acts in an honorable way when he chooses to rescue Marsellus, and to do so with a samurai sword no less. This also affirms his position in the warrior family tree, following his father and grandfather. This act and series of events, is part of the retrieval of the watch, which is both an assertion of his freedom and possibility, and an acknowledgment of his past. He is rewarded by surviving, and succeeding in his plan, as he rides off with Fabienne and his money.

Pretty Smart, Huh?

Honey Bunny and Pumpkin (aka Ringo and Yolanda) don't seem like exemplary humans. The film opens with Honey Bunny deriding Pumpkin for his self-deceiving intention to give up robbing liquor stores. Is Pumpkin suffering from bad faith?

He wants to stop robbing but keeps robbing. He despises the dangerous and disagreeable realities of his current life as an armed robber and is aware of his capacity for change to some extent. He evinces a desire to change but doesn't.

This time around he has the "pretty smart" idea of robbing restaurants instead of liquor stores; this is a change, but certainly not a radical one. And not enough to realize his goals; they only survive this robbery by dint of Jules' mercy and "transitional period." Perhaps, they receive a second chance because Pumpkin is at least trying to change; or perhaps their encounter with Jules is their wake-up call, and their fate is still to be decided.

Pumpkin is at least a little self-deceived; he is in bad faith because he doesn't accept the reality of his situation. Sartre finds self-deception perplexing because of the singular nature of consciousness. When we deceive someone else, we affirm something to ourselves and hide it from them; it seems that some kind of duality is necessary for deception. How can we hide something from ourselves? How can we affirm and deny the same thing at the same time? Freud offers a familiar solution to this problem in claiming that we repress things in our unconscious. This introduces a duality between the conscious and the unconscious and allows for deception.

For Sartre, part of our radical freedom, our transcendence, is the result of our capacity to determine meaning through interpretation (1943, pp. 485, 710). Notwithstanding, this capacity can also support self-deception. Pumpkin's self-deception is the result of skewed background assumptions and interpretations. When he says "I don't want to kill anyone either. But they'll probably put us in a situation where it is us or them," it is clear that he is evading responsibility for creating the situation. He interprets the same situation first in this way (he is robbing the liquor store), then that (the owners are putting him in a situation where he has limited options), and as such his interpretive freedom becomes the source of his self-deception and prevents him from transcending his situation. He recognizes his power to change his situation, but not his responsibility for creating it. The possibility of self-deception emerges precisely because of the background assumptions; the way he interprets his situation, in this case, does not seem to be a source of freedom; instead, it provides the duality necessary for self-deception.

A Wax Museum with a Pulse

In the middle of all the pulp, carnage, chaos, and outrageous fortune, is the miraculous survival of Jules and Vincent. Somehow they are able to avoid half a dozen close-range gunshots. Not only did the bullets miss them, but we are shown that some of the bullets struck the wall directly behind them. The bullets should have traveled through them to make those holes since Jules and Vincent were occluding the path between the shooter and the wall. But they didn't.

Jules	We should be fuckin' dead man.
Vincent	I know. We was lucky.
Jules	No, No, No, No. That shit wasn't luck.
Vincent	Yeah, maybe.
Jules	This was divine intervention. You know what divine intervention is?
Vincent	I think so. That means that God came down from heaven and stopped the bullets?.
Jules	That's right. That's exactly what it means. God came down from heaven and stopped these motherfucking bullets.
Vincent	I think it's time for us to leave, Jules.
Jules	Don't do that. Don't fuckin' blow this shit off. What just happened here was a fuckin' miracle.
Vincent	Chill, Jules. This shit happens.
Jules	Wrong. Wrong. This shit doesn't just happen.
Vincent	Do you want to continue this theological discussion in a car, or in a jailhouse with the cops?
Jules	We should be fuckin' dead my friend. What happened here was a miracle and I want you to fuckin' acknowledge it.
Vincent	Alright, it was a miracle. Can we go now?

Vincent first. Is he authentic? Is he in bad faith? He certainly is not awakened by the challenge to his mortality, nor renewed in his faith as Jules is by their miraculous survival. In fact, Vincent has lost sight of his transcendence, and the vast array of possibilities that are open to him. He is constrained by the social realities that he faces. This is perhaps most evident when he replies to Jules's plan to quit his job and walk the earth: "Without a job, a residence, or legal tender, that's what you're gonna be man – you're going to be a fuckin' bum."

Of course, Vincent, like all the other major characters, is a career criminal and thus has already rejected many laws and social norms; he is not part of the work-a-day world. Nevertheless, he is engaged in an ongoing project and follows a certain code of loyalty and respect; he espouses a secular worldview of a random world, governed by chance, and power. Thus, Vincent, like Butch, is self-consistent, but this is neither necessary nor sufficient for survival in *Pulp Fiction*: Vincent does not survive, and Jules, who changes radically, does. Martin Heidegger (1927) might say Vincent is "falling" (*Verfallen*), engaged in his humdrum everyday mode of being in the world with others, guided by the conventions and arrangements of his crowd of gangsters. We see this when he resolves to be polite to Mia and loyal to Marsellus. He very explicitly confronts himself, in a mirror, about being loyal, and accordingly closing off certain possibilities: "This is a moral test of oneself. Whether or not you can maintain loyalty. Because being loyal is very important. . . . You're gonna go out there, you're gonna say 'goodnight, I've had a very lovely evening'…go home, jerk off, and that's all you're gonna do." Sartre would regard this as bad faith, or an identification with one's facticity, though the situation deserves further consideration.

Falling, the largely habitual form of social life, is not necessarily bad, and may even be necessary since the social world provides the conditions for a meaningful life and an intelligible world (Heidegger 1927, p. 220). On the other hand, authenticity depends on events that wake us from falling life – like, for example, confronting our own mortality and our death as the loss of all possibilities. Vincent is not awakened by his brush with death; he is unmoved, unchanged. He ignores his transcendence and encourages Jules to do the same, telling him he will be nothing but a bum if he leaves this lifestyle behind.

It is also worth noting that Vincent stays in character in most of his interactions, like his argument with Butch, his wanting to shoot Pumpkin in the Epilogue, and challenging The Wolf. What's more, being constrained by obligations is a limit on freedom of a certain kind; however, if this constraint is in the service of a long-term life project that is freely chosen, then one is still free in another sense. According to Heidegger, we are capable of "choosing to choose a kind of being-one's-self" (1927, p. 314). It is then our commitment to being the kind of person we choose to be, and ownership of our actions that make one authentic for Heidegger (Varga and Guignon 2020). Although both Heidegger and Sartre see authenticity as engaging in the constant process of becoming, Heidegger places more value in the continuity and ownership in this process, while Sartre places more value on the freedom that transcends it – that is the nature of a conscious being.

Jules and Vincent are complex: they are hitmen, but they don't act like it. They spend most of their first scene chatting about hash bars, hamburgers, and workplace gossip. They are even aware of this when, before entering Brett's apartment and killing several people, Jules says "Come on. Let's get into character." Is this self-deception? Are they right to treat their status as hitmen and enforcers as a role they play? This seems to be a failure of authenticity on both Sartre's and Heidegger's accounts; they are not steadfast in their commitment to their roles, but neither do they transcend them.

Sartre gives an example of bad faith in which a cafe waiter is trying too hard to be a waiter; making himself identical with the social role (Sartre 1943, p. 59). Of course, he is a waiter, but he is in bad faith because he is ignoring the fact that he is also transcendence, that many possibilities are open to him, that, in this sense, he is also not a waiter, or he is more than a waiter. Interestingly, waiters make a few appearances in *Pulp Fiction*: the Buddy Holly waiter is literally pretending to be someone else, and in contrast, the diner waitress is personable but also points out that "'Garcon' means boy" (in *Reservoir Dogs* there is a lengthy debate about tipping wait staff). Like Sartre's waiter, Jules and Vincent perform the role of hitmen, completely committed to their good cop-bad cop roles, but they do not play this role in all contexts. More troubling here is the contrasting mistake, that they are deceiving themselves about the fact that they are hitmen (about their facticity). They don't just "get into character." They also kill people. Yet their casual banter does not reflect the seriousness of the situation. This is disingenuous. From a storytelling perspective, we are shown the characters outside of the roles they are required to play to advance the narrative. This is important for a film that is about authenticity. They are not merely hitmen, though they are hitmen. Their often cavalier conversation and popular references make the characters more relatable, and this enables the viewer to comprehend and engage with these characters as situated within a certain culture, American popular culture circa 1994, and facing the challenge of authentic existence.

In summary, Vincent is mired in his facticity, falling through his criminal world, unshaken by his brush with death. Worse still, he is blindly committed to his character and lifestyle, since his behavior at times fails to reflect them for what they are; he neither owns them nor disowns them. Unlike Jules, he doesn't try to change when given the opportunity and misses his opportunity for redemption.

I'm Tryin' Real Hard to Be the Shepherd

> The path of the righteous man is beset on all sides by the iniquities of the selfish and the tyranny of evil men. Blessed is he, who in the name of charity and good will, shepherds the weak through the valley of darkness, for he is truly his brother's keeper and the finder of lost children. And I will strike down upon thee with great vengeance and furious anger those who would attempt to poison and destroy my brothers. And you will know my name is the Lord when I lay my vengeance upon you... .it could mean you're the righteous man and I'm the shepherd and it's the world that's evil and selfish. And I'd like that. But that sh*t ain't the

truth. *The truth is you're the weak. And I'm the tyranny of evil men. But I'm tryin', Ringo. I'm tryin' real hard to be the shepherd.*
—Jules Winfield

This monologue is the key to the film. We hear the "Ezekiel 25:17" quote three times in the film, and we are left with this interpretation of it at the end of the film. Jules and Butch are both authentic and also morally commendable in the end, but Jules more so. Jules is the hero of the film. While neither is in bad faith, Jules shows a conscious engagement with his facticity, and transcendence in his monologue directed at Ringo/Pumpkin. He accepts that he is the tyranny of evil men (facticity) and self-consciously accepts his transcendence when he says "I'm tryin' really hard to be the shepherd." Here all the earlier self-deception falls away in his "moment of clarity." This self-conscious engagement suggests that Jules is more authentic in response to his dual human nature, though he is not authentic in the sense of remaining true to his own past character.

Sartre's notion of bad faith had been instructive, but it is not sufficient to articulate the philosophical content of *Pulp Fiction*. So far we have seen that Vincent is clearly overly committed to his social role and duties at the expense of his transcendence. Pumpkin fails to take responsibility for the situations he creates, and thus conflates his transcendence with his facticity. Butch is mostly authentic, owning his past and his physical limitations while utilizing his freedom to navigate his challenging situation. He might be overly committed to his family warrior history, but he still manages to survive. Notwithstanding the instructiveness of bad faith, to continue our analysis we will need more tools.

For one thing, Butch and Jules are also exceptional because of their heroic acts. They both help others at great personal cost: Butch by saving Marsellus and Jules by saving Pumkin and Honeybunny. They show forgiveness and mercy. However, while Jules and Butch both rescue someone, only Jules does it without murdering anyone. While this moral dimension is important and might repay careful analysis, it is subordinate to the clear religious message. Jules claims his monologue is scripture, Ezekiel 25:17, and it is at least partly scriptural. Moreover, in his analysis of the purported miracle Jules says: "Whether or not what we experienced was an "according-to-Hoyle" miracle is insignificant. What is significant is that I felt the touch of God. God got involved."

Jules had a religious experience. His transformation is a religious one. We can integrate the moral and religious aspects with our discussion of authenticity by appealing to the Danish philosopher Soren Kierkegaard. In *The Sickness unto Death*, Kierkegaard identifies three forms of despair: despair not to be conscious of having a self, despair not to will to be oneself, and despair to will to be oneself. The first is ignorance of the infinite self, the second refusing to accept the infinite self, and the third, refusing to accept the love of God on which one's self depends. The opposite of despair is faith which involves accepting God's love and power: "In relating itself to itself, and in willing to be itself, the self rests transparently in the power that established it" (Hong and Hong 1983/1849). The power that established the self is God, God's love, and capacity to forgive the unforgivable. One commentator expresses this view of Kierkegaard's work by writing that "faith in divine forgiveness can manifest in joy, at the realization that for God anything is possible, including our 'rebirth' as spiritual selves with 'eternal validity'" (McDonald 2017).

The second kind of despair is somewhat similar to bad faith (or rather bad faith is similar to it, since Kierkegaard wrote of it nearly one hundred years earlier). It is a conscious and willful denial of the infinite, eternal, or transcendent part of one's humanity and nature. Jules and Butch both overcome this to some extent, but only Jules addresses the third kind of despair. In the third kind of despair, one embraces one's infinite self, but wants to use this infinite form and possibility to efface his concrete self and its necessity, and compose himself as sole author. Butch does this without acknowledging any power beyond him that is responsible for his infinite self, which is without acknowledging God. This kind of despair in willing to be one's self can be defiant (one defies God), and can even be demonic when it is pursued out of spite or malice. Butch may be an example of the defiant version of this third type of despair, since he embraces his freedom completely, but from Kierkegaard's perspective, he fails to acknowledge a higher power in doing so (though he does not completely ignore his facticity, as we have seen). In contrast, Jules transcends all forms of despair since he acknowledges and is moved by God's presence. His awareness of self is complete in this sense.

The film endorses the value of this deeper level of authenticity, and freedom from this third type of despair, that acknowledges both our infinite nature and its origin, since Jules is rewarded. While Butch succeeds in many ways, he remains mired in the capricious and brutal story world, and rides off into the distance, soaked in blood, at the end of his story (and the chronological end of the film).

In contrast, Jules does not ride off; he ascends. He is essentially gone after the final diner scene at the end of the film (the end of the syuzhet). Although he is with Vince when they deliver the case, there is not a scene announcing Jules' departure, and he is not with Vincent after the boxing match or guarding Butch's apartment (David Kyle Johnson makes the interesting counterfactual observation that if Jules had been present, Vince may have survived, so in a sense Jules's conversion caused harm to Vince. On the other hand, had they both left the profession, clearly the most harm could have been averted, and if they both followed Jules's path, they would both be living better lives). It feels as though he has transcended his situation; however, because of the disordered narration, he is also still in that world at the end of the film. The film's presentation of Jules is itself authentic in this sense. It is also important that Jules faces a real challenge at the end of the movie, since he is the hero. If the film ended with Butch riding off into the distance, this would be a different film, celebrating a different achievement.

It is possible to interpret *Pulp Fiction* by focusing solely on the religious or moral aspects of the film, but this type of interpretation would be incomplete (and the morality highly questionable). The existential accounts of Sartre, Heidegger, and the proto-existentialist account of Kierkegaard provide a better framework because existentialism focuses on the lived experience of the subjects as they engage with their own nature. Likewise, *Pulp Fiction* challenges the viewer to work through the film and the actions of each character. It is in that sense that the film is not a mere argument, nor completely didactic, but a call inciting the viewer to engage authentically with these questions, existential tensions, and themselves.

For example, perspective and subjectivity are subtly raised when we are shown the same event, but from two perspectives. This happens both with the diner scene, as prologue and epilogue, and when Jules and Vincent shoot Bret. In the epilogue, Honeybunny's line changes from "I will execute every motherfucking last one of you!" to "I will execute every one of you motherfuckers!" Pumpkin's "Garcon, coffee" is also a different take with a different inflection the second time around. Similarly, when we first see Jules delivering his speech, his power over Bret is emphasized by the low camera angle and framing, and the reverse shot of Bret trembling and Vincent blocked apathetically in the background. The second time we encounter this event, we see Bret's friend hiding in the bathroom, processing Jules' speech, and preparing for his ambush. This scene ends with Jules and Vincent disagreeing over whether they experienced a miracle or were just lucky. While the film takes a clear stance on the merit of each character, it does not efface the importance of subjectivity in being a self; instead, it foregrounds the importance of subjectivity in the way the story is told.

For example, we are *shown* that the bullet holes in the wall are directly behind Jules, and this, it seems, affirms the miraculous event. However, by the fact that the retellings of scenes from different perspectives are slightly different, we are reminded that what we are shown may not be reliable; the events of the film are filtered through a subjective perspective, so there is always room for a competing interpretation.

It is also remarkable that, as the debate about the purported miracle continues in the car, Vincent turns to Marvin telling/asking him "you gotta have an opinion. I mean do you think that God came down from heaven and stopped...." when his gun discharges splattering Marvin's brains all over the car and its occupants, leading to the grotesque comedic scenes that follow. This is a striking counterpoint to the previous scene: Jules and Vincent were intentionally targeted and shot at but not hit; here Vincent's gun accidentally discharges and deals a deadly accurate shot, almost a perverse response to his query. The characters are again humbled, though this does not resolve the interpretive issue and it does not help us make sense of Marvin's untimely demise. We are reminded of the corrupt, relentless, and morally elusive world we occupy. Time and again, bystanders are expendable, and are killed by our heroes. This might be consistent with a sort cosmic bookkeeping interpretation – one life is saved, another is forfeit – but any simple moral interpretation is ruled out. Marvin's death seems like an accident (Vincent says as much), but it also seems like an exclamation mark on the whole situation, as if God did come down from heaven to further challenge Vincent, yet even this doesn't faze him. This interpretation too is dissatisfying though, since like the death of innocent bystanders, it is hard to understand the paradox of a good God that teaches, guides, or chastens by allowing, so much capricious death. As in life, our perspective is constrained, and we are not given omniscient insight into the moral calculus that makes sense of all this carnage.

The issue of interpretation becomes most explicit as Jules analyzes the passage that he has been quoting, considers different interpretations, and reflects on which character he is. Here the viewer's interpretive role is made explicit, and as the film ends the viewer is left with the task of reflecting on the meaning of the passage for Jules and the film.

Jules embodies the duality of this film: he is both killer and savior, tyrant and the shepherd. He never ceases to employ his pop-culture references and quips: "he'd have to be ten times more charming than that Arnold on Green Acres"; "what's Fonzie like?"; "I'm the guns of the Navarone"; and so on. He is very much a product of a contingent historical time and place, yet he transcends them. This is evident when he says to Vincent, "Whether or not what we experienced was an 'according-to-Hoyle' miracle is insignificant." He uses a normalized reference to a Hoyle's book of official rules for card games to discuss the legitimacy of the miracle they have witnessed. Even the quote attributed to Eziekel 25:17 is only partly scriptural; the larger part is borrowed from the Sonny Chiba film(s) *The Bodyguard* (1976)/*Karate Kiba* (1973). It is perfect that something profound is expressed through a superficial culture reference; this captures the existential tension presented by the character and the film.

Although Jules remains present until the end of the film (syuzhet), his ascent in the middle of the story (fabula), demonstrates his moral transformation that includes saving Pumpkin from himself, and from Vincent, without violence, his explicit acceptance of God's presence in this life, and his acceptance of his own evil nature. This narrative device allows Jules to be both concrete, worldly, of his time, and present, but also absent, abstract, infinite, and transcendent. The standard for an authentic and full life, a complete acknowledgement of one's self and one's nature endorsed by *Pulp Fiction* is thus very onerous; Vincent fails completely to satisfy the standard, which Butch approximates, and only Jules satisfies completely.

Pulp Fiction

At this point we can say more about the remarkable nature of the film as a piece of philosophy. *Pulp Fiction* is pulp and transcends pulp. As such, it is an authentic film. It is of its time, aware of the concrete reality of its historical context, teaming with the cultural allusions for which it is known. It is a self-conscious, postmodern pastiche, with a nonlinear narrative. It reminds the viewer of the unreliability of narration, and of subjectivity. The characters are comical and unnerving because they are both evil and ordinary; they are playing roles, but are not limited to those roles. But, and this is the key point, *Pulp Fiction* also transcends all of this.

Conclusion

It celebrates morality, mercy, and forgiveness, and rewards authenticity of the deepest kind, requiring acknowledgment of our finite realities, our infinite nature, and God's grace. In this it acknowledges and endorses fixed and eternal meanings and moral values. *Pulp Fiction* is postmodern, but it is also modern. By embodying this tension and duality, and exploring it through the experiences, challenges, and reactions of the main characters, *Pulp Fiction* is able to present a compelling, complex, and opinionated meditation on the challenges and value of human life as a struggle for self-knowledge and authenticity. Moreover, it presents these challenges – not only as something that must be faced by each person, each subject, situated in a time and culture – but also as something at which one can succeed or fail. The world is chaotic and superficial; we are the product of a very specific time, like the film itself, but beneath it all there is profound meaning.

References

Heidegger, Martin. 1962 [1927]. *Being and time* (trans: Macquarrie, J., & Robinson, E.). New York: Harper & Row.

Hong, Edna H., and Hong, Howard V., eds. 1983/1849. *Kierkegaard's writings, Xix: Sickness Unto death: A Christian psychological exposition for upbuilding and awakening*. Princeton University Press.

McDonald, William. 2017. Søren Kierkegaard. In *The Stanford encyclopedia of philosophy* (Winter 2017 Edition), ed. Edward N. Zalta. https://plato.stanford.edu/archives/win2017/entries/kierkegaard/

Sartre, Jean-Paul. 1992 [1943]. *Being and nothingness: A phenomenological essay on Ontology*. New York: Washington Square Press.

Seal, Mark. 2013. Cinema Tarantino: The making of Pulp Fiction. In *Vanity Fair*. Retrieved from: https://www.vanityfair.com/hollywood/2013/03/making-of-pulp-fiction-oral-history

Varga, Somogy, and Charles Guignon. 2020. Authenticity. In *The Stanford encyclopedia of philosophy* (Spring 2020 Edition), ed. Edward N. Zalta. https://plato.stanford.edu/archives/spr2020/entries/authenticity/

Keywords

Tenet · Christopher Nolan · Fatalism · Block Universe · Protagonist · Neil · Entropy · Causal loops · Free will · Compatibilism · Harry Frankfurt · Backtracking counterfactual · Freedom and divine foreknowledge problem · Fatalist attitude · David Lewis · The Sator Square · Time inversion · Grandfather paradox · Richard Feynman · Einstein · Reverse causation · Quantum mechanics

Introduction

> What's happened, happened. Which is an expression of faith in the mechanics of the world, not an excuse to do nothing.
> —Neil

Christopher Nolan's 2020 film *Tenet* is more than just a visually stunning and time-bending masterpiece, or a movie that wonderfully assaults our senses with its immersive sound design and its dynamic bombastic musical score by Ludwig Göransson – a driving force in the film which demands our attention, adds intensity, and enhances the beauty of the impressive action sequences. It's also more than just a globetrotting glamorous action thriller set in a twilight world of international espionage, or a mind-blowing sci-fi film centered around the paradoxical concept of time inversion where we see characters flowing backwards through time. Indeed, what really stands out about *Tenet* is that, like *Inception*, it's another Nolan film that makes philosophical arguments. At the end of the film, Neil delivers the quote that begins this section – a memorable quote that expresses the two arguments of *Tenet*: (1) everything is fated, but (2) it still matters what we do.

To examine *Tenet*'s arguments, it will first be necessary to comprehend *Tenet*, not just to viscerally feel it, but understand it – which, in fact, is the opposite of what the film instructs the audience to do: "Don't try to understand it. Feel it." Indeed, even those who have seen *Tenet* multiple times could still be confused by its complex narrative. Once it is explained, however, this chapter turns to examining its arguments.

Summarizing *Tenet*

Tenet is set in a world where a secret organization called "Tenet" is founded in the future to ensure everyone's survival. It's a story about the founder of that organization, a man only referred to as the Protagonist, who is trying to save the world from the antagonists of the future – a group intent on wiping out the people of the past responsible for the environmental collapse of the future.

The film tracks the six-week journey of four primary characters: the Protagonist, Neil, Kat, and Sator. For the first half of the film, these characters traverse three weeks forward in time. Then, at the halfway point, through the usage of time inversion technology, they temporally invert – they begin traveling backwards in time – and traverse three weeks back to the beginning of the movie.

The film begins with a siege at the Kiev opera house where the Protagonist witnesses an inverted bullet whiz by him – a bullet that apparently jumps out of a hole, kills the SWAT team member behind him, and then travels back into a gun held by a mysterious figure. It's revealed that the Protagonist is part of a CIA team where their objective is to obtain a metal block of weapons-grade plutonium-241. The Protagonist is then recruited into an organization named Tenet where he is introduced to various operatives and learns about inverted ammunition and time inversion. This leads him to Mumbai where he's paired up with a mysterious agent named Neil. They meet a Tenet operative named Priya who lets them know about the man behind the inverted ammunition who communicates with the future – Andrei Sator.

To find Sator, Priya puts the Protagonist in contact with an agent named Crosby who subtly reveals that two weeks prior, the same day as the Kiev opera house siege on the 14th, there was a bomb detonation at Stalsk-12. He also reveals that Sator's hold over his wife Kat is a fake Goya drawing created by an artist named Tomas Arepo. Cleverly, Crosby gives the Protagonist a second fake Goya which allows him to arrange an art appraisal meet with Kat where he makes a proposal: to meet with Sator in exchange for destroying the drawing. Kat agrees and explains that Sator keeps the drawing in his Rotas vault at the center of the Oslo Freeport. The Protagonist and Neil surmise that Sator is hiding something in the vault. To reach it, they dramatically crash a 747 plane into the back wall of the Freeport which causes the distraction necessary to trigger the lockdown they need to find Sator's secret.

In the vault, they find a revolving time inversion turnstile machine that Sator has built which allows people and objects to invert and revert the direction they travel in time. The Protagonist ends up fighting an inverted figure (in SWAT gear and a mask) that leaps backwards out of the machine. Afterwards, the Protagonist travels back to Mumbai to meet up with Priya who explains that Ukrainian security services are moving the plutonium-241 through Tallinn in a week. She tells him to team up with Sator and steal the plutonium-241.

The scene shifts to the Amalfi Coast in Italy where the Protagonist lies to Kat, telling her the fake Arepo drawing was destroyed. Consequently, Kat invites the Protagonist to dinner where Sator immediately threatens to kill him. But when the Protagonist asks Sator if he likes opera, Sator invites him to go sailing on his catamaran where the Protagonist proposes they become partners. When Kat unexpectedly yanks Sator's quick-release and he flies off the boat, the Protagonist spins the boat and rescues Sator. In return for saving Sator's life, the Protagonist gets a shot at stealing the plutonium-241 when it crosses through Tallinn.

The film's three-week journey forward culminates in Tallinn during a spectacular highway heist where the Protagonist steals the plutonium-241 case from an armored vehicle, and it's revealed that Sator owns another time inversion turnstile at the Tallinn Freeport. After an epic highway chase, Sator shoots Kat with an inverted bullet so the Protagonist reveals where he hid the plutonium-241 during the chase. The audience learns that Sator has duped the Protagonist by performing a temporal pincer movement, allowing him to obtain the block of plutonium-241 and flee into the past. During the chase, the Protagonist comes to realize that the metal block of plutonium-241 is not plutonium after all as it doesn't have the encapsulation of any weapons class. Neil explains that it's worse than plutonium.

After learning how inverting a wounded person can stabilize inverse radiation, the Protagonist takes Kat through the turnstile and inverts her so she can heal over the next week. He then decides they will travel back a week to the Oslo Freeport 747 jet crash event and revert Kat and themselves at the Rotas turnstile. Before going, however, the Protagonist thinks he can change what's happened. He wants to invert himself and prevent Sator from obtaining the metal block that he hid. But Neil fatalistically says to him: "What's happened, happened. We have to save her here and now. And if you go back out there you might hand him exactly what he's after." And, indeed, that's exactly what happens.

The second half of the movie follows an inverted Tenet team in pursuit of Sator as they traverse backwards in time for three weeks back to the 14th. Neil gets himself, Kat, and the Protagonist into a cosy shipping container, and they head to the Oslo Freeport while inverted. When the Protagonist tells Neil that he couldn't stop Sator from getting the metal block material, Neil says: "I warned you," to which the Protagonist says: "What's happened, happened. I get it now." The Protagonist begins to realize that everything is fated.

When the Protagonist had inverted himself and returned to the highway chase, he managed to plant his Bluetooth earpiece into the 241 case he gave to Sator so he could record any conversations. On their way back to Oslo, the Protagonist listens to a recording on his phone where Sator cryptically mentions to his men: "Bring the final section directly to the hypocenter along with the other parts of the algorithm." The Protagonist then asks Neil about the algorithm. Neil explains that the algorithm is a formula that's been rendered into physical form so it can't be copied, that it's composed of nine sections (the 241 block is one section of it), and that it's a giant inversion black box device with one function: to invert the entropy of the entire world and instantly obliterate everyone and everything. The Protagonist responds: "We're their ancestors. If they destroy us, won't that destroy them?" Neil then mentions he's hit upon the grandfather paradox – something the future generation clearly thinks they can get around without consequence.

They arrive at the crash scene near the breach and enter where the inverted Protagonist (wearing SWAT gear and a mask) finds himself fighting the earlier Protagonist. The original fight between the two plays out in reverse from the inverted Protagonist's perspective who then leaps into the turnstile, reverts, and runs into earlier Neil. Meanwhile, inverted Neil gets himself and Kat through the turnstile, and they revert. Afterwards, the Protagonist asks Neil why he didn't tell him earlier that the masked guy coming out of the vault was him – a future version of the Protagonist. Neil again asserts his fatalist belief: "What's happened, happened. If I'd told you and you acted differently…who knows?…We're the people saving the world from what might have been."

The Protagonist tells Neil to get Priya to Oslo so he can stop her from telling the earlier Protagonist to steal the 241 in Tallinn. Neil fatalistically says: "Nothing can change that." But the Protagonist still thinks he can change the past and stop Sator from obtaining the section. He finds he can't change Priya's mind as her mission was to use him so Sator would bring together all nine sections of the algorithm. Priya tells the Protagonist to board an icebreaker ship in Trondheim that contains a turnstile where Ives (a Tenet sergeant) has a team ready to invert.

The team works their way back to the 14th and they travel inverted to Stalsk-12 in Siberia. The Protagonist briefs Ives on Crosby's intel about the Stalsk-12 hypocenter detonation that takes place on the 14th. Along the way, the team learns that Sator intends to end his life as he's dying from inoperable cancer. Sator has devised a plan: the fitness tracker he wears has been programmed to send a signal when his heart stops – a signal that would activate the algorithm (buried at the Stalsk-12 hypocenter) by detonating an explosive. The team figures out that Sator intends to carry out his plan by returning to a day on his yacht where he felt loved by Kat. Magically, Neil knows the day: "The 14th. Ten days ago." The Protagonist tells Kat to make her way to the yacht in Vietnam on the 14th to stop future Sator from killing himself until they lift the algorithm out of the hypocenter. He then hands her a phone and tells her to call and state her location if she ever feels threatened in the future.

The three inverted weeks back to the 14th end as they arrive at Stalsk-12. Ives divides his soldiers into two teams: a red team (that moves forward in time) and an inverted blue team in the future (that moves backward). The movie culminates in a ten-minute temporal pincer movement where the two teams battle Sator's army. This allows the Protagonist and Ives to enter the hypocenter cavern where they reach a locked gate door. On the other side, they see a body lying on the ground and Sator's henchman, Volkov, who places the assembled algorithm bar into a capsule. Meanwhile, future Kat makes her way onto the yacht in Vietnam. When future Sator arrives, she decides to kill him in a state of revenge, pulling up her shirt to reveal the scar he gave her. Sator is shocked and realizes he's been conned. Kat shoots him.

With the help of Neil, the Protagonist and Ives end up lifting the algorithm out of the hypocenter right before the explosive goes off. How? Neil reverted half-way (via the Stalsk-12 turnstile machine) and pulled them out using a rope tied to a truck. Later, Neil inverted (back to before this time), picked, and opened the locked gate door and then took a bullet meant for the Protagonist. When the Protagonist realizes that Neil sacrificed his life to save him, he asks: "But can we change things? If we do it differently?" Neil fatalistically replies with the previously mentioned quote that captures the arguments of *Tenet*. The Protagonist says: "Fate?" Neil says: "Call it what you want...Reality." Neil then reveals he was recruited by the Protagonist, that the entire operation has been one giant temporal pincer constructed by the Protagonist who is only halfway there.

The film ends with a thought-provoking voiceover from Neil about how they saved the world from what might have been. Meanwhile Kat is shown picking up Max at school where she sees a tinted car which prompts her to make a call. Priya's in the tinted car and her driver has a pistol. The Protagonist then opens the back door, gets in, shoots the driver, and then reveals to Priya that she's been working for him all along. He then ties up loose ends by shooting her.

Interpreting *Tenet*

The key to understanding the plot of *Tenet* is realizing that the film is one giant closed loop that already happened. It starts on the 14th at the Kiev opera house in Ukraine, and it ends on exactly the same day (the 14th) in the Soviet city of Stalsk-12 and on the coast of Vietnam. While earlier versions of both the Protagonist and Neil are at the opera house on the 14th, future versions of them (that have inverted backwards through time) simultaneously battle Sator's army at Stalsk-12 and save the world. The bomb detonation at Stalsk-12 that took place on the 14th, which Crosby mentions early in the film, is the one that we see at the end of the film. And at the beginning of the film, future Kat and future Sator have already traversed backwards in time to the yacht in Vietnam on the 14th. As the film unfolds chronologically, the audience comes to realize that events that happen later in the film have paradoxically already taken place in the past (at the beginning of the film) where there are multiple versions of characters existing at the same time. For example, there are two versions of Kat near one another when future Kat kills future Sator. (Recall that, early in the film, younger Kat sees a future version of herself dive off the yacht.) And at different points in the film, there are also multiple versions of Neil and the Protagonist existing at the same time.

At the end of the film, through Neil's revelation that the entire operation has been a pincer setup by the Protagonist in the future, the audience recognizes that the beginning of the story actually starts, off screen, in the distant future where the future Protagonist founds the Tenet organization, recruits Neil, and then sends him back in time (to the Kiev opera house) to save his former (past) self and then the world. The audience is left to ponder the central sci-fi concept of time inversion which raises a variety of philosophical issues such as the nature of time, reverse causation, causal loops, the grandfather paradox, personal identity, and the ethics of using this technology to achieve one's ends and desires.

Besides the amazing action sequences involving heists and time inversion, what really stands out is the film's central argument. Primarily through the characters of Neil and the Protagonist, *Tenet* argues for the philosophical doctrine of fatalism – the belief that every event that happens was fated to happen; nothing other than what does happen, could happen. And there is nothing one can do to undo this, or to prevent the happening of any event. Everything that happens in the loop of events in the film was fated to happen. However, fatalism being true might make one think that a person's actions don't matter; that, no matter what one does, or how one acts, the fated events will occur. But Neil (and by proxy Christopher Nolan) expresses to the audience that a person's actions still do matter, even if fatalism is true. And to begin to understand how this argument is made, it's necessary to explore the film's hidden messages. In fact, the argument for fatalism is bolstered by the hidden messages contained in *Tenet*.

The Fatalism in *Tenet's* Hidden Messages

Nolan's Cinematic Sator Square

Christopher Nolan used a word puzzle from the real world, known as "The Sator Square," to construct the people, places, and objects in the fictional world of his film. It's an ancient five-word Latin palindrome that can be read in any direction, consisting of the words SATOR, AREPO, TENET, OPERA, and ROTAS arranged as such:

```
S A T O R
A R E P O
T E N E T
O P E R A
R O T A S
```

It's not exactly clear what the Sator Square means or how it's to be interpreted, but the word "SATOR" translates as sower or seeder. "AREPO" is a proper name, and as a verb "TENET" means "to hold" or possess. The word "OPERA" usually refers to work or efforts – as in to operate – and as a noun, "ROTAS" translates as "wheels." (As a verb it indicates rotation. Notice how ROTAS rotates "around" the square.) So the square may form the following ordinary sentence:

> The sower Arepo holds the wheels with effort.

Correspondingly, some believe the Sator Square was inscribed onto objects throughout history in an effort to protect them from evil happenings. Perhaps it calls for Arepo to hold back the wheels of misfortune.

Regardless of whether this is its true meaning, it seems to track nicely onto *Tenet* as this describes the plot of the film: The nameless Protagonist (Arepo?) needs to stop Sator and the antagonists of the future from destroying the world (evil happenings). What's more, the square's words appear throughout the film. "OPERA" refers to the opening opera house siege in Kiev. "SATOR" refers to the subject that the Protagonist is after: Andrei Sator. "TENET" obviously refers to the title of the film and the name of the organization that the Protagonist creates in the future. "ROTAS" is the name of Sator's construction company that built the Oslo Freeport and also refers to the rotating inversion turnstile machines. And finally, "AREPO" refers to Tomas Arepo, the Spanish artist that created the two fake Goya paintings in the film. (Could Arepo, who Kat suggests is crippled and deaf, simply be an elderly version of the Protagonist?)

The oldest version of the Sator Square was found in the ruins of Pompeii in 79 A.D. It can't be a coincidence that the *Tenet* scenes in Italy were filmed at the Amalfi Coast which is 20 miles from the Pompeii ruins. The stone inscription was found in the house of a baker which was covered in volcanic ash from the Mount Vesuvius eruption on August 24th in 79 A.D. The eruption killed thousands in the cities of Pompeii and Herculaneum.

Incredibly, in *Tenet*, "Pompeii" is mentioned twice, and "Herculaneum" once. When Kat talks to her son Max at the school gates, Max says: "Anna says we're going to Pompeii and see lava." And in Italy, when Kat asks where Max is, Sator replies: "He's visiting Pompeii and Herculaneum." There is no way this could be a coincidence. Mount Vesuvius is the only active volcano on the European mainland. Nolan gives a nod to this fact when Max says he's going to Pompeii to see lava – the lava from Mount Vesuvius. Even though it hasn't erupted since 1944, it's still expected to in the future. And Nolan took the opportunity to fictionalize that next eruption in the closed time loop presented in the film. Indeed, some fans of the film theorize that Neil is Max. And if so, Nolan could be suggesting that young Neil stumbles across the Sator Square stone inscription in Pompeii. After all, in 1936 the Sator Square was also found inscribed in one of the stone columns at the Pompeii Gymnasium which has been preserved at the Antiquarium of Pompeii museum.

Alternatively, might it turn out that Nolan is alluding to the possibility that the different objects in history containing the Sator Square word puzzle (such as church pillars, bells, crypts, and mosaics) were inscribed onto these relics in the future and then streamed back (like the inverted bullets in *Tenet*) to different points in history? This could be Nolan's way of saying that the people of the future in the real world have figured out how to reverse the entropy of objects, and thus, the flow of time. Nolan could be suggesting that the things most people assume are impossible might just be things that the current generation hasn't discovered yet.

Clearly, *Tenet* is Nolan's twenty-first century Sator Square on the big screen. And as the historical Sator Square points to mysteries, *Tenet* also provides audiences with a set of mysteries to contemplate, such as the nature of time and the concept of inversion. Perhaps this was part of Nolan's intent all along: to raise mysteries. What's unquestionable, however, is that Nolan drew inspiration from the Sator Square to form the plot structure and concepts in *Tenet*. Where the words in the ancient square can be read backward and forward, so too, things happen backward and forward in *Tenet*.

But how does the Sator Square relate to the argument for fatalism in *Tenet*? Could it be that Nolan is giving audiences more than just a nod to this centuries-old word puzzle that fits nicely with the time inversion plot and palindromic nature of the movie? One could imagine that while Max is in Pompeii, he encounters and learns about the Sator Square inscribed on the Pompeii Gymnasium column. Assuming Neil is Max, it's possible the Sator Square inscription was placed onto this ancient stone relic in the future by the Tenet organization and then temporally inverted and sent back through time to give young Neil an idea of his future role in the fate of mankind. If so, the word square is a sign that young Neil was always fated to be inspired to act and save the world – which, incredibly, is something that older Neil is simultaneously doing (along with the Protagonist) while young Neil is visiting Pompeii.

Furthermore, no matter which direction the Sator Square is read (from left or right, up or down) by following either rows or columns, one ends up with the same set of words. And this seems to indicate that the square was fated to say the same thing from any direction. It's brilliant and fitting that Nolan used these fated Sator Square words to substantiate his argument for fatalism within the film; it was all fated to happen the way it does. Being inverted and traversing backward through time can't change the course of events that were destined to play out. Likewise, one cannot ever hope to find a new result from reading the Sator Square from a new direction.

"All I Have for You Is a Word: Tenet"

The word "tenet" is a direct reference to key aspects in the film. Just like the palindromic word can be read forward and backward, the actions seen in the film involve different characters that can move forward and backward in time to prior moments using temporal inversion. Moreover, the plot structure itself is a palindrome as the film begins on the 14th where the audience experiences everything moving forward for three weeks, and then reverses at the half-way point during the Tallinn sequences and moves backward through time for three weeks until it arrives where it started – the 14th. (This is very reminiscent of *Inception's* narrative journey as that film ends where it began: Cobb and Saito stuck in a house on a cliff in Limbo.)

In fact, the entire film is like a giant temporal pincer movement where the audience viscerally experiences a closed loop containing palindromic effects. Moreover, the word "ten" (that can be read in the word *Tenet* from both directions) refers to the final battle sequence at Stalsk-12 where the blue and red teams need to work in conjunction for ten minutes. Both have ten minutes (forward or backward in time) to allow the Protagonist and Ives to slip into the hypocenter cavern and prevent the algorithm from being activated. Furthermore, the "ten" in *Tenet* is accentuated throughout the film. The staff member at the Oslo Freeport lets Neil know that in the case of a lockdown or fire, the facility is flooded with halide gas which gives the staff a ten second warning to get into the corridor. In the Tallinn Freeport, Volkov says to Sator in Russian: "The convoy's due downtown in ten." Also, when Kat tries to remember the day she went ashore with Max on her Vietnam holiday, Neil says: "The 14th, ten days ago."

Even the traditional definition of "tenet" and how it's used in normal discourse (defined as a main principle or belief) is used for the purpose of relating it to the fatalism message in the film. During Priya's introduction, her first line to the Protagonist is: "To say anything about a client would violate the tenets he lives by," to which the Protagonist replies: "If tenets are important to you, then you can tell me. Everything." And this usage of tenet as a belief relates to the argument for fatalism in *Tenet*. When Neil repeatedly expresses to the Protagonist that everything that's happened was fated to happen, Neil is expressing one of his core tenets – his belief or faith in how every event was fated to happen. Nolan cleverly uses the word "tenet" to signify many things in the film, but the one that stands out, which is directly related to this chapter, is his core tenet (belief) that fatalism is true.

Tenet's Nameless and Emotionless Protagonist

Nolan has emphasized that *Tenet* was designed to be a visceral cinematic experience for film audiences. And it certainly is. He likely felt the actions, events, and the complex physics concept of time inversion in the film were relatable enough to make people care about what's happening in the story. *Tenet* lets the action and concepts drive the narrative which, in turn, draws audiences in, and gets them invested in the survival theme flowing through the film.

Because he felt that the complex concepts and nonstop action in the film would be enough to engage audiences and immerse them in this adventure, Nolan decided to make the lead character, the Protagonist, nameless, and emotionless. It stands in contrast to *Inception* where, in addition to the dream concepts introduced, there's an emotional story at its core between Cobb and Mal, and Cobb trying to get back to his children. With *Tenet*, the narrative and complex concepts sufficiently capture the audience's attention. An emotional backstory for the main hero would have detracted from the concepts and high stakes in the film.

Given that *Tenet* is an audience-driven experience, the Protagonist serves as the means to achieving this experience. Indeed, the Protagonist represents the audience. Within the chronological events of the closed loop presented, he starts as a blank canvas who then adapts to these extreme and outrageous situations. He's hurled into a temporal cold war – a world with strange physics along with complicated concepts and paradoxes – and into crazy espionage action moments (like bungee jumps, fights, heists, and car chases). But he goes along with everything just as the audience does through the film's breathtaking imagery and action.

Consider the amazing moment in the opening opera house siege when the Protagonist is introduced to the concept of time inversion. A bullet emerges from a bullet hole (that itself disappears) and then streams backwards past him and through his assailant. The concept is visualized on the screen, and the audience feels what the Protagonist is experiencing in the moment. It's as if the audience members are in the shoes of the Protagonist for the duration of the film, witnessing the time inversion sequences first-hand from his perspective, reacting and trying to comprehend things like he does. Further, just as the Protagonist questions Neil on things, the audience also questions the film on many levels. And while the audience doesn't fully relate to the nameless hero, they relate enough to connect and follow *Tenet's* complex narrative.

Most importantly, having the main hero function as a blank canvas allows audiences to discover, concentrate, and experience the fatalism theme that's central to the film. In virtue of having a protagonist (who lacks a backstory and emotional depth) that is learning (along with the audience) about the metaphysics of *Tenet's* world, Nolan is able to shift the film's focal point to the philosophical fatalism message flowing through *Tenet* – that every event is fated, where all that can happen is what has already happened. Throughout the film, the audience, like the Protagonist, is able to concentrate and reflect on this philosophical message. For instance, the audience is able to deduce that the Protagonist is bound to make all the temporally inverted and noninverted decisions he does, that whatever he chooses to do, he was always going to choose to do those things (in fact, by the end of the movie, the Protagonist himself comes to realize this truth too). The Protagonist will always end up protecting the future generations (posterity) while guarding the ancestors of the past generations by having Neil temporally invert backward through time. The audience comes to recognize that there's no timeline where the Protagonist does not do this. Additionally, through the discourse between the Protagonist and Neil, the audience is able to discern the film's philosophical arguments.

Tenet's Argument for Fatalism

Recall the previously mentioned quote by Neil at the end of the film that captures the two philosophical arguments of *Tenet*: (1) everything is fated, but (2) even though everything is fated, that isn't an excuse to do nothing. It still matters what we do.

To understand (1), it's important to clarify what kind of fatalism the film subscribes to. It suggests all events and actions are fated – where what has happened in the past, what is happening in the present, and what will happen in the future, was destined to happen, and nothing can undo it. All events are inevitable. In *Tenet*, the Protagonist often thinks he can change the past and keep future events from happening, only to later realize that he can't. His inverted and noninverted actions were destined to happen the way they did within the closed temporal loop seen in the film. Again, this is something that the Protagonist recognizes in the final scene when he takes care of the loose ends by killing Priya to save Kat and Max. He knows that everything that happened was fated to happen the way it did. He was fated to stop Sator, to save the world with the help of Neil, to be a guardian angel over Kat and her son Max, and become the founder and leader of *Tenet* in the future.

In this way, the film subscribes to a temporal ontology (a view about the nature of time) called the block universe view, which is also known as omni-temporalism or eternalism. The idea behind this view is that the universe is a giant four-dimensional block that consists of all things and events that have ever existed or happened at any place and time – it is the collection of every moment in time, past, present, and future, that ever has or will happen. But it must be emphasized that, on this view, each such moment is equally real. It's not like past moments used to exist, the present moment does exist, and the future will exist. The entire block exists as a whole. Thus, the future exists, and is just as unchangeable as the present and past. To put it in terms of the film, the moments when the young Protagonist is at the opera house siege, and the moments in the distant future when the older Protagonist founds the Tenet organization, all exist in the block.

Now, whether or not time passes in the block is debatable. One could adopt what philosophers might call an A-theoretic understanding of the block and insist that, while it is true that the past, present, and future all coexist on the block, present events still have a privileged status that the others do not; it is occurring. (Past events *have occurred*, future events *will occur*.) Think of it like a film strip. The entire film already exists on the reel – but only one frame (at a time) can have the privileged status of being shown. The frame being shown would be analogous to the present; all moments exist, but only one is occurring. But given that the block universe is entailed by relativity, and that according to relativity *simultaneity* (and thus what would be included in the present moment) is relative to a reference frame – and there is no privileged reference frame that defines what is truly present – the more consistent (and popular) understanding of the block universe aligns with a B-theoretic understanding. On the B-theory, there are only facts about the order of events; there is no fact about what moment is occurring – all moments simply exist, statically, on the block. So, on this theory, despite the way that things appear to us, there is no actual passage of time. As Einstein put it, "People like us, who believe in physics, know that the distinction between past, present, and future is only a stubbornly persistent illusion" (Einstein 1955).

The film accentuates this point through its sci-fi concept of manipulating time through inversion with characters traversing backwards through time and returning to moments in time through which their earlier selves already lived. Consider when the inverted Protagonist returns to battle his noninverted self at the Rotas vault in the Oslo Freeport. During this fight, the present moments for the noninverted Protagonist in the business suit are interacting with the future moments of himself dressed in SWAT gear and a gas mask. Through this visual encounter of these past and future moments colliding, the film is claiming that the difference between the present moments and the future moments is only relative. The temporal relations between the earlier and later versions of the Protagonist all exist in time – and in this scene, Nolan emphasizes this point by having the temporal relations literally collide. That is, they all exist in the block universe, and there is no fact about which one is occurring.

Priya also underscores the block universe view of time when she tells the Protagonist: "Tenet wasn't founded in the past...it will be founded in the future." Since the Tenet organization exists in the present, but it can't exist without being founded, the future event of its founding must exist. Indeed, the film's characters speak about the people of the future and what they've already done. The audience comes to recognize that the future scientist who created the algorithm has already existed, took her life, and hid the algorithm sections in the past by temporally inverting them. Priya even says that the people in the future need the algorithm's journey into the past to continue. Those people in the future exist when she's talking to the Protagonist in the present. Likewise, from the perspective of those people in the future, the moments in the past (and all prior generations) also exist.

The film is therefore claiming that the future is just as real as the past. And this claim is reinforced by the repeated utterance of "What's happened, happened" (which is uttered 4 times in the film). When Neil first says this in the Tallinn turnstile room, he's warning the Protagonist that he can't change what Sator's done (or what he's about to do, or what he'll be doing when he inverts and moves into the past). In effect, he's telling him he can't stop Sator from getting the ninth section of the algorithm. Neil urges him to focus on saving Kat "here and now," and not think of what will happen if Sator kills her in the past. The point that the Protagonist fails to realize at this point is that what's happened already happened and it can't be undone. It's only after he fails to stop Sator from getting the ninth section that he starts to understand Neil's earlier warning. "I get it now." When he asks Neil at the end of the film if they can change things if they do it differently, Neil asserts the line again. Essentially, he's saying that his future self already inverted and opened the door which resulted in them lifting the algorithm and saving the world. He's expressing that it has happened, it was fated to happen, and there's no undoing it. The forward-moving Neil recognizes the action he was fated to take – to get on the chopper, go and invert, and weave another pass in the fabric of their mission.

Interestingly, this block universe view of time resembles the view of time developed by philosopher David Lewis, one that Nolan himself embraced and argued for in his film "*Interstellar.*" Lewis describes his view by discussing time travel and his solution to the grandfather paradox (Lewis 1976). Lewis argues that, even though time travel is possible, it would not give one the ability to go back in time and kill their grandfather (and thus negate their own existence) because doing so would be impossible. Why? Because it's already predestined not to be the case. What follows is that the future is just as written as the past, and that the universe (the past, present, and future) is a block and exists as a whole. Thus, before the traveler even departs, the universe already contains the events that the time traveler causes in the past. Those events already occurred and exist. When the traveler arrives in the past, the traveler would not be able to kill their grandfather because the past already contains their birth (and their grandfather's survival). The traveler wouldn't be able to negate their own existence; it's logically impossible.

Recall when the Protagonist says to Neil: "I've been thinking…we're their ancestors. If they destroy us, won't that destroy them?" In response, Neil discusses the grandfather paradox and says these people in the future clearly think they can kill grandpa and survive. Nolan's embrace of Lewis's view of time is evident as it turns out that the people existing in the future can't destroy the people of the past because *them trying to do so and failing* is already part of the block. The people in the future fail to get Sator to activate the algorithm in the past at Stalsk-12 because the Protagonist and the Tenet team have already succeeded in stopping Sator in the past using their inverted methods. The Tenet team has always won the battle at Stalsk-12. Indeed, that event is happening off screen, at the beginning of the film. Kat has always killed Sator on his yacht in Vietnam. Neil has always saved the Protagonist three times in the past. All of this already exists on the timeline before the people of the future send Sator the capsule containing the instructions for gathering and activating the algorithm. The people of the future were born and still exist and nothing can undo this from having happened (their existence and entire timeline can't be negated or contradicted). Nolan's solution to the grandfather paradox lines up with Lewis's solution: it's logically impossible to kill one's grandfather, or in the case of *Tenet*, one's ancestors.

One upshot on the block universe view of time is that causal loops are not paradoxical. What's a causal loop? Consider how an older Protagonist founds the Tenet organization in the future and then has Neil invert into the past back to the opera house to ensure his earlier self (a younger Protagonist) is recruited into the Tenet organization so that he then founds it in the future. In this case, a future event causes an event in the past which is the cause of the future event. That's a causal loop. And since it's natural to think of causes preceding effects, it would seem causal loops are logically impossible. A causing B, but then B causing A would seem to imply both that A came before B, and that B came before A. But that only follows if causes must precede their effects. In the world of *Tenet*, where time inversion technology is real, this of course is not true. Since it involves reversing the entropy of objects so that the *arrow of time* reverses, reverse causation is possible. When Barbara (the scientist that trains the Protagonist in how inversion works) says that inverted material has been manufactured in the future and is streaming back to them in the past, the Protagonist insists that *cause* has to come before *effect*. But she corrects him. "No. That's just how we see time."

But even with reverse causation, it might seem that causal loops are impossible because, although each part of such a loop has a cause, the loop itself seems to lack a causal origin. But on the block universe view of time, since the world is a giant block that contains every moment in time, there is a causal origin for causal loops: the existence of the (block) universe itself. The causal loop we see in the film featuring the Protagonist, for example, came into existence with the universe itself; whatever explains it, explains the loop.

But can the causal arrow really be reversed? Can objects move backwards in time? The early work in quantum mechanics by physicists John Wheeler and Richard Feynman suggested that particles like positrons are just electrons that can exist in multiple states at the same time, and that they can even travel backwards in time (Feynman 1965). The particles can move from the past to the future, or from the future to the past. And this theory seems to be what Nolan had in mind. When the Protagonist explains there is technology that can invert an object's entropy, Neil replies: "You mean reverse chronology. Like Feynman and Wheeler's notion that a positron is an electron moving backwards in time." So, while the existence of causal loops might initially sound absurd, they are neither logically inconsistent nor physically impossible. Indeed, Richard Hanley (2004) defends the possibility of their existence extensively in "No End in Sight: Causal Loops in Philosophy, Physics and Fiction."

But is this fatalist block universe view of time correct? As was mentioned above, Einstein's scientific theory of relativity certainly bolsters the view. According to it, facts about whether two events are simultaneous are relative to a reference frame – how an observer could be moving through space and time. In one they will be simultaneous, and in another they won't. And there is no fact of the matter regarding which reference frame is right. There is no privileged reference frame that defines one moment as the present moment. This means that A can be simultaneous with some event B in one frame, and then B can be simultaneous with some other event C in another – even though C happens after A in all frames (*i.e.*, even though C is in A's future). The only way this is possible is if all events coexist in one giant block. And if there is no privileged reference frame, there is no fact about which event is occurring now. So, on relativity, the passage of time is illusory.

Some might suggest that quantum mechanics stands contrary to the block world view as it has proven that certain events on the quantum level (the scale smaller than atoms) happen at random and without cause and are thus fundamentally unpredictable. But while such events are not determined – predicable from previous states or causes – it is not true that they cannot be fated. On the block world view, every event, even quantum ones, exists on the timeline when the block itself comes into existence. Although we cannot predict which quantum events are fated to occur, on the block world view, each one is fated to do so. Even if a particle is in an undetermined state (also known as superposition), the fact that it is in that state (and how long it will be) is fated to occur just as it does.

Philosophical arguments can also be presented for the block universe view. A fundamental rule of logic is that all propositions, including those about the past and future, have a truth value. And the most commonly accepted theory of truth, the correspondence theory, says that true propositions require truthmakers: something that makes them true. If that's right, it would seem that both the past and the future must now exist, for what else could serve as the truthmaker for true propositions about the past and future? This view which seems impossible to escape unless one is willing to abandon certain basic assumptions of logic, or reject the highly intuitive correspondence theory of truth, is known as logical fatalism.

But that brings us to another philosophical takeaway of *Tenet*, that follows from its fatalistic view, and that is its argument that humans lack free will. If the outcome of all things is already fixed and thus is fated to happen, it seems to follow that people don't have the capacity to freely make choices. That's not to say that choices can't still be made; indeed, what choices people will make is already written on the block. And we might even say that, since it's the persons who are making choices, they are the ones that are writing their choices onto the block. If people are fated to make the choices they do, however, it doesn't seem that their choices are free. But is this right? Or might it be possible that humans can still make free choices even if fatalism is true?

Tenet's Fatalism Entails There Is No Free Will

The traditional libertarian notion of free will asserts that freedom over decisions and actions requires alternative possibilities. In order for a person to freely choose to do some act, that person not choosing to do that act must be possible. Now, it's widely held that libertarian free will is not compatible with determinism, the view that everything in the world is caused by previous events and natural laws. If one could predict every future event, including human actions and choices, by simply looking at the current state of the universe, and using the laws of nature to derive everything that will happen next, then there are no alternate possibilities. But while determinism would entail that there are no alternate possibilities, and thus that fatalism is true, determinism and fatalism are not the same thing. Indeed, fatalism could be true even if determinism is not.

For example: *Tenet* suggests that we live in a fatalist block universe, not that the present is a causal result of the past, or that people's future actions are causally linked or determined by their present ones. No such language ever appears in the film. So *Tenet's* universe is not deterministic. And yet the universe of *Tenet* is still fatalistic.

Indeed, people could act randomly within it, and this would still be true. As was discussed above, a random uncaused quantum event, say a positron moving in random directions, would still be fated to happen if that event was written in the block when the block came into existence. And this would be true, even though there is no way to determine or derive that event was going to happen from past events. In the same way, a person's action could be random, undetermined, and even unpredictable, yet still be fated to happen because it already existed on the block. A universe containing uncaused events is not a deterministic universe, but that very same universe could be fated to contain the uncaused events that it does. Thus, a block universe would still be one in which fatalism was true, even if it was not deterministic.

Tenet makes it clear that people are not free in the libertarian sense given its recurring expression that "what's happened, happened" – this fatalistic view of people living in a block universe. Every event that ever happens is already contained in the block and has been for all time. This seems to imply that the characters in the film don't have the ability to freely choose between the different alternative actions available to them; they don't have the ability to not choose as they do. Consequently, they are not free.

For instance, when future Kat takes her revenge and kills future Sator on his yacht, she could not have done otherwise. She doesn't have the ability to take more than one possible course of action. She was always fated to kill Sator on his yacht on their holiday trip and then jump off the side to safety. Recall, again, that she sees herself doing so at the beginning of the film. The events and actions in her life were fixed in advance and she didn't have the power to alter them. She therefore, on the libertarian understanding, cannot act freely. Similarly, it seems that Neil didn't have the ability to not decide to save the Protagonist's life in the hypocenter cavern. Perhaps he mentally considered alternatives, but there is only one thing he could have done. He was fated to save the Protagonist's life in the past, to help the Protagonist found Tenet in the future, and to save the world "from what might have been." These events have always been written in Neil's timeline contained in the block universe. Thus, he cannot, on the libertarian understanding, act freely.

But perhaps, even though it is true that there are no alternate possibilities in a fatalistic universe, it's not true that free will require alternative possibilities. Such a view is embraced by some who call themselves compatibilists, who embrace the view that determinism and free will are compatible. And even though, as we have seen, determinism and fatalism are not the same thing, one might be able to use the compatibilist understanding of free will to argue that free will can still exist even in a fatalistic universe.

One philosopher that subscribes to a compatibilist view of free will is Harry Frankfurt, who articulates an understanding of free will in terms of first-order and second-order desires (desires about desires), and the ability that people have to rank them (Frankfurt 1971). For example, a habitual smoker may have a (first-order) desire to smoke a cigarette, but also a (second-order) desire to not have this desire to smoke a cigarette – particularly because this person wants to be healthier and feel better. What makes the person free, according to Frankfurt, is the person's ability to rank the desires and act on them. If the person overrides their first-order desire with their second-order desire – by refraining to smoke a cigarette – then that person has produced what Frankfurt calls a "second-order volition." And because the person conforms their will to their second-order volition, the person has acted freely.

The ranking of first-order and second-order desires, and overriding one with the other through deliberating about the kind of person someone wants to be, is compatible with fatalism. One can even be fated to do such a thing. So, on this definition of free will, one can decide freely, even in a fatalistic universe. But is this definition of free will right? Many argue that it is not because one's second-order desires could be imposed by outside forces; and if they are, it doesn't look like a person acting on them is truly free.

For example, suppose I programmed a smoker to have an irresistible second-order desire to not be a smoker anymore. (Maybe I performed an inception on the smoker.) When they act on that desire, and refuse their next cigarette, it might appear to them that they are acting freely, but it doesn't seem that they actually would be. Their action was determined by me. Yet, on Frankfurt's definition of free will, they would be choosing freely. So his definition seems deficient. What's more, given that our second-order desires are a result of our brain structure, and our brain structure is a result of our DNA and environment, it seems that ultimately even our actions based in second-order desires are the result of outside causal forces, and thus not truly free. In order for a choice to be free, it would seem that whether or not I make that choice must be, ultimately, up to me; it can't be imposed upon me by outside forces. Since Frankfurt's definition suggests that my actions could be free even if they were imposed upon me by an outside force, again it seems that Frankfurt's definition of free will is deficient.

There are other compatibilist notions of free will, but they all fall prey to similar objections. They all essentially suggest that an agent's choice to do something is free as long as it springs from some aspect of the agent – if not a second-order desire, then a rational deliberation, or an act of the will. But what if that aspect of the agent was determined by outside forces? It would seem the choice is not free, and yet the compatibilist would insist that it is. And even if, instead of being caused by outside forces, the aspect of the agent arose randomly, or without a cause, the act still wouldn't seem free. As Peter van Inwagen (2000) showed in "Free Will Remains a Mystery," indeterminate actions aren't any more free than determined ones. If I'm not in control, then I am not acting freely.

And so it seems that there cannot be free will, at least as people usually conceive of it, in a fatalistic block world universe. And thus, in as much as it is an argument for the block universe, *Tenet* is an argument against free will.

Tenet's Argument for Fatalism Isn't an Excuse to Do Nothing

The notion that we do not have free will leads some to adopt what we shall call a "fatalist attitude."

> The Fatalist Attitude: It doesn't matter what a person does because, regardless of what one does, things won't turn out differently. So one might as well lay back and do nothing.

But thinking this attitude should be adopted as a result of embracing the philosophical lessons of *Tenet* misunderstands the kind of block universe fatalism that the film is arguing for.

This attitude would make sense given a different type of fatalism where only certain types of events will happen no matter what; on this view, it doesn't matter if one does X or Y or Z, that particular type of event will happen. For instance, consider the first *Final Destination* movie. The protagonists avoid being killed by a plane explosion, only to be later killed by other means because they were fated to die. The moral of the movie (if there is one) is that you can't escape fate. But this is a different understanding of the word "fate" than is suggested by *Tenet*. In *Final Destination*, the particular method of their death is not fated; this is obvious, given that they were able to exit the plane. It's only the fact that they will (soon) die that is fated. So they could die by method X, or Y or Z. It really doesn't matter. Yes, there are multiple ways to get to their final destination of death, but they will get there, no matter what. So they really might as well *lay back and do nothing*. Trying to prevent it is useless. Regardless, they will (soon) die.

But this is not the kind of fatalism presented in *Tenet*. It does not suggest that only certain types of events are fated to occur, and that only those will occur no matter what. Instead, the block universe fatalism view the movie suggests maintains that all events are fated. The entire timeline is already set. Consequently, it entails that there's only one possible future, and therefore, there is only one possible way to arrive at any fated event. So it does not entail that our actions don't matter, because it does not entail that the same thing would happen regardless of what we do.

To fully understand why, consider the ill-fated back-tracking counterfactual objection to the freedom and divine foreknowledge problem. The problem suggests that God's foreknowledge precludes human free will. If God knows what a person will do before they do it, it doesn't seem that person can act freely; they are not able to act otherwise because they do not have the power to change what God's past belief was or make God's past belief false. The back-tracking counterfactual objection tries to answer this argument by observing that the following counterfactual is true:

> If the person were to act otherwise, God would have believed something different than he did.

But while such a statement is true, its truth does not entail that the person in question has the power to act otherwise; it thus doesn't entail the person in question is free.

As Johnson (2009) argues, the fact that God has foreknowledge of a future action entails that the future action already exists. Indeed it must if God has knowledge of it. But if it already exists, it is fated to happen; it can't not happen. And if it can't not happen, the agent cannot freely make it happen. In order for one to freely decide to do X, one's action of doing X and one's action of not doing X have to be equally possible. But this can't be the case if one's action of doing X is already a fixed fact on the timeline. Yes, if one were to act otherwise, God would have believed something different and the timeline would be different than it is. But neither of those things is now possible. Essentially, this is a way of redefining what it means to be *able to do otherwise*, but it is not robust enough to satisfy the libertarian intuition that choosing to do the action, and not choosing to do the action, has to be genuinely and equally possible if the agent is to act freely. Clearly, if God already believed one would do X, and thus, the future event of the agent doing X is something that already exists on the timeline, then the agent doing otherwise is not possible – even though it's true that, if they were to do otherwise, God would have believed something different.

All that being said, the truth of the above counterfactual is enough to show that the following claim is false: regardless of what one does tomorrow, God will have believed the same thing yesterday. If one were to act differently, God would have believed differently. It's not true that God would have believed the same thing, regardless of what you will do. God's past belief is dependent on one's future action. So, even though your actions are fated in a block universe, it still matters how you act. If you were to act differently, something else would occur. Of course, you won't act differently; the act is fated. But it's still true that *if* you did, something else would happen. So it is simply not true that, *regardless of what one does, things won't turn out differently*. Things won't turn out differently; that's true. Indeed one can't act differently; all events are fated. But it's still true that, if one were to act differently, something else would occur.

Nolan seems to be aware of such back-tracking counterfactuals as he recognizes the importance of action in a fatalist block universe. Again, at the end of *Tenet*, Neil says:

> What's happened, happened. Which is an expression of faith in the mechanics of the world, not an excuse to do nothing.

In these lines, the film not only makes the argument for fatalism, but also the argument that fatalism isn't an excuse to do nothing. Even though the characters in *Tenet* are fated to act as they do, it's not the case that it doesn't matter how they act and thus they should do nothing. The fact that everything that has occurred will occur isn't a reason for inaction because even though the characters are not free in the libertarian sense, and their actions are fated, it's still the case that if they didn't take the actions they did, they wouldn't have succeeded in the mission.

For instance, the Protagonist can't just lounge around and take the fatalist attitude where he believes that it doesn't matter what he does. On the contrary, it matters very much what he does. For everything to transpire the way it does, where he and Neil save the world, the Protagonist must take the actions he does. And even though he's fated to do what he does, it's still true that if he didn't, the future outcome would have been different – the back-tracking counterfactual of action is true. He has to take the actions he does to save the world. And even though the Protagonist's actions aren't free actions in the libertarian sense, his actions are the cause of what's been fated to happen in the timeline of the block universe. Thus, what happens in the block, depends on one's actions.

Neil's voiceover during the final sequences of the film augments the importance of their action.

> We're the people saving the world from what might have been...The world will never know what could've happened...and even if they did they wouldn't care...because no one cares about the bomb that didn't go off...just the one that did...but it's the bomb that didn't go off...the danger no one knew was real...that's the bomb with the real power to change the world.

His choice in expressions is revealing. He says: "from what might have been" and "what could've happened" which indicates that, if they had not acted as they did, the universe would have been different. If they didn't take all the inverted and non-inverted actions on their mission, then something different would have occurred – the world's entropy being reversed would have annihilated the world. Again, that couldn't have happened because it would have created a grandfather paradox. But the salient point is that different actions would have yielded different consequences. In fact, what Neil (and by proxy Nolan) is saying here is that if everyone believed fatalism were true, then everyone would probably start behaving very differently. People would adopt this fatalist attitude where one believes that it doesn't matter what one does, and so one might as well do nothing. But as this chapter shows, this isn't the case. That is not the correct response to the fatalism in *Tenet*. Fatalism isn't an excuse to do nothing. The counterfactual of action is enough to ground and inspire action. It's enough to counteract the fatalist attitude. People shouldn't behave any differently if fatalism is true because how people act still matters.

Conclusion: The Philosophical Depth of Christopher Nolan's Films

Unquestionably, Christopher Nolan enjoys challenging people's preconceptions with his films. He's proposed worlds where the science and laws of nature that people take for granted – things involving space, gravity, relativity, dimensions, the human mind, and the nature of dreams – are twisted paradoxically and strangely into new shapes. In *Tenet*, Nolan does this with *time* where he explores the nature of time and entropy and proposes a fictional world (based on real world physics) where people in the future have figured out how to reverse the flow of time and invert themselves and objects backwards through time. He's suggesting that even though this may seem highly improbable, it may simply be a technology that the current generation hasn't discovered yet. But Nolan doesn't just provide audiences with suggestions. As he does in all his films, he delivers a philosophical lesson. And this makes his films philosophically significant. In *Tenet*, he argues for fatalism, and how people can't use fatalism as an excuse to do nothing. And a film that can incorporate and articulate such deep philosophical arguments is truly a cinematic masterpiece.

References

Einstein, Albert. 1955. Letter by Einstein to the son and sister of Michele Besso. *Correspondence 1903–1955*. Paris: Hermann, 1972.

Feynman, Richard. 1965. The development of the space-time view of quantum electrodynamics. Nobel Lecture. December 11.

Frankfurt, Harry. 1971. Freedom of the will and the concept of a person. *Journal of Philosophy* 68: 5–20.

Hanley, Richard. 2004. No end in sight: Causal loops in philosophy, physics and fiction. *Synthese* 141: 123–152.

Johnson, David Kyle. 2009. God, fatalism, and temporal ontology. https://philpapers.org/rec/JOHGFA

Lewis, David. 1976. The paradoxes of time travel. *American Philosophical Quarterly* 13: 145–152.

van Inwagen, Peter. 2000. Free will remains a mystery. https://www.jstor.org/stable/2676119

Tom Sawyer as Philosopher: Lying and Deception on the Mississippi

58

Don Fallis

Contents

Introduction	1350
Summaries	1352
The Adventures of Tom Sawyer	1352
The Adventures of Huckleberry Finn	1353
Tom Sawyer, Detective	1354
Spoken Lies	1354
Lies Must Be Intended to Deceive	1355
How to Lie Effectively	1357
Preventing True Beliefs by Lying	1359
Keeping Mum	1359
Causing False Beliefs by Withholding Information	1359
Is Withholding Information a Form of Lying?	1360
Concealing Information Versus Withholding Information	1361
Lying Acts	1362
Ways to Show the False	1363
Ways to Hide the Truth	1364
Psychological Operations	1366
Lying to Yourself and Evolutionary Lying	1367
Conclusion	1368
End Notes	1369
References	1370

Abstract

Several eminent philosophers – including Saint Augustine, Sir Francis Bacon, and Roderick Chisholm – have done important work on what lies are and how they can be used to deceive us. It is less well known that Mark Twain also made important contributions to this area of applied epistemology. In addition to writing two notable essays on lying, he created one of the most quintessential

---

D. Fallis (✉)
Philosophy, Northeastern University, Boston, MA, USA
e-mail: d.fallis@northeastern.edu

© Springer Nature Switzerland AG 2024
D. K. Johnson et al. (eds.), *The Palgrave Handbook of Popular Culture as Philosophy*,
https://doi.org/10.1007/978-3-031-24685-2_110

and versatile liars in all of literature, Tom Sawyer. Episodes from the novels (and films) featuring this character provide evidence in support of Twain's theses that lying is more common and more varied than we tend to think. Twain's insights often anticipate the subsequent work of contemporary philosophers and are applicable to the fake news, deepfakes, and disinformation of the twenty-first-century.

Keywords

Mark Twain · Samuel Clemens · Tom Sawyer · Huckleberry Finn · Deception · Lying · Epistemology · Simulation · Dissimulation · Withholding information · Concealing information · Psychological operations · Showing the false · Hiding the truth · Mimicking · Inventing · Decoying · Masking · Repackaging · Dazzling

Introduction

Tom Sawyer is a fictional character created by Samuel Clemens (aka Mark Twain). He is a boy who lives in a small town in Missouri on the banks of the Mississippi River with his Aunt Polly, his younger half-brother Sid, and his cousin Mary. Tom appears in four novels: *The Adventures of Tom Sawyer* (Twain 1876), *Adventures of Huckleberry Finn* (Twain 1884), *Tom Sawyer Abroad* (Twain 1894), and *Tom Sawyer, Detective* (Twain 1896). The novels all take place during the first half of the nineteenth-century.

Tom Sawyer and *Huckleberry Finn* are two of the most popular and iconic works of fiction in American literature. They have been adapted to film numerous times, including silent films, musicals, and even animated versions. (There is a 1938 film version of *Tom Sawyer, Detective* as well.) Actors such as Jackie Coogan and Jonathan Taylor Thomas have portrayed Tom. And actors such as Mickey Rooney, Ron Howard, and Anthony Michael Hall have portrayed Tom's best friend, Huckleberry Finn. In one movie, Jodie Foster played Tom's love interest, Becky Thatcher. Tom has also appeared as a character in other films, such as *The League of Extraordinary Gentlemen*. However, unlike other chapters in this volume, examples discussed here will be taken from the films' source material, namely Twain's novels.

Tom is an attractive, intelligent, imaginative, and good-hearted boy. But he is also a rapscallion. There is no telling what Tom will get up to. And he constantly lies and deceives to achieve his goals. Indeed, no one can tell "stretchers" (Twain 1884, ch. 26) and "scollop the facts" (Twain 1896, ch. 6) quite like Tom Sawyer. And Tom engages in many different forms of lying and deception. As Aunt Polly laments, "Ain't he played me tricks enough like that for me to be looking out for him by this time? ... But my goodness, he never plays them alike, two days, and how is a body to know what's coming?" (Twain 1876, ch. 1).

It is no accident that one of Twain's most iconic characters is a prolific liar. Twain was deeply interested in the nature and scope of lying and deception. Along with his two essays on lying (Twain 1880, 1899), the novels featuring Tom Sawyer are intended to enhance our understanding of these phenomena.[1] They are important contributions to the area of philosophy known as applied epistemology (see Coady 2017). And their lessons are arguably even more critical in today's world of fake news, deepfakes, and disinformation.

Epistemology is the study of what knowledge is and how it can be acquired. Applied epistemology focuses specifically on real-life issues that people confront when seeking knowledge. In other words, applied epistemology bears the same relation to epistemology as the better-known field of applied ethics bears to ethics (see Coady 2017, p. 52).

A lot of applied epistemology is concerned with what things we ought to believe, that is, what we are *justified* in believing (see Coady 2017, p. 51). For example, the eighteenth-century Scottish philosopher David Hume (1977 [1748], ch. 10) famously argued that we should never believe reports that a miracle has occurred. (See Schick and Vaughn 2020 for further examples in this vein.) But applied epistemology is much broader than that.

Applied epistemology also includes investigations of what practices and technologies tend to produce knowledge (see Coady 2017, pp. 54–55). For example, I have argued elsewhere that *Wikipedia* is epistemically beneficial despite the fact that anyone can edit it (see Fallis 2011). Even though entries are not checked by editors before being published online, Wikipedia has policies and procedures to ensure that inaccurate information tends to be removed quickly. (See Goldman 1999 for further examples in this vein.) Furthermore, applied epistemology includes investigations of real-life threats to knowledge, such as perceptual illusions, cognitive biases, and intentional deception. For example, several philosophers (e.g., Augustine 1952 [395]; Bacon 2008 [1612]; Chisholm and Feehan 1977; Nyberg 1993; Carson 2010; Fallis 2014; Mahon 2015) have tried to understand the different forms of lying and deception. Twain is in this tradition (see Mahon 2017).[2]

In his essays on lying and in his novels about Tom Sawyer, Twain defended two main theses. First, the scope of lying is much larger than we tend to think. While most of us (including most philosophers) tend to focus almost exclusively on spoken lies, many other acts count as lies. Indeed, Twain (1899) claimed that "by examination and mathematical computation I find that the proportion of the spoken lie to the other varieties is as 1 to 22,894" (Twain 1899). Second, lying comes in many more varieties than we tend to think. According to Twain (1897, ch. 55), "there are 869 different forms of lying." Since Twain was a humorist as well as a philosopher, these specific numbers are likely hyperbolic. But the applied epistemology is quite serious. Understanding the different types of lies helps us to avoid being deceived.

In one of the most famous works in epistemology, the twentieth-century American philosopher Edmund Gettier (1963) argued that the traditional definition of knowledge is too broad. He did so by describing cases where someone clearly does not have knowledge, but that the traditional definition mistakenly counts as knowledge. In a similar vein, Twain argued that the traditional definition of lying is too narrow by identifying numerous cases of lying that the traditional definition mistakenly fails to include.

Twain also provided a rough classification of different forms of lying (see Mahon 2017). For example, along with spoken lies, there are "silent lies" (or "keeping mum") and some "lies are acts, and speech has no part in them" (Twain 1880). Other philosophers have subsequently offered more fine-grained classifications of lying and deception. But as we will see from the Tom Sawyer novels, Twain was clearly already aware of (and trying to teach us about) most of these different forms.

Summaries

But before we get started, it will be helpful to quickly recount some of Tom's adventures so that Twain's examples of lying will be ready at hand.

The Adventures of Tom Sawyer

In an early and famous scene, Aunt Polly gives Tom the chore of whitewashing the fence on a Saturday; he uses reverse psychology on his friends to get out of it. When Tom seems to be really enjoying himself, his friends want to get in on the fun. And they end up paying him for the privilege of doing his chore for him.

The central adventure of the novel begins one night when Tom and Huck go to the graveyard to perform a ceremony to remove warts. While they are waiting for midnight, Dr. Robinson arrives, along with Injun Joe and Muff Potter, the town drunk, to dig up a body for his medical research. During a dispute about pay, Muff gets knocked out. While he is unconscious, Joe uses Muff's knife to kill the doctor and puts the knife in Muff's hand. When Muff wakes up covered in blood, Joe convinces Muff that he committed the murder. Tom and Huck flee unobserved, and tell no one what they witnessed.

Several days later, Tom, Huck, and Joe Harper run away to play at being pirates. They take a raft to Jackson's Island, which is in the middle of the river downstream from town. While the other two boys are sleeping, Tom sneaks back into town and into Aunt Polly's house. He learns that everyone believes the three boys drowned in the river and that funerals are planned. The three boys then sneak back into town together and, to everyone's great relief, show up alive at their own funerals.

When Muff is finally put on trial for murder, Tom ultimately decides to testify against Injun Joe. When he does so, Joe jumps through the window and escapes.

Several days later, Tom and Huck search for buried treasure in an abandoned house. While the boys are upstairs, two men arrive; one of them is Injun Joe, who has disguised himself as a deaf-and-dumb Spaniard. Joe and his partner find a box in the house containing 12,000 dollars in gold coins. Tom and Huck again get away without being observed.

Over the summer, Becky throws a picnic for all of the kids her age. During the trip, everyone explores McDougal's Cave. But Tom and Becky get lost deep in the cave. While Tom is searching for an exit, he sees Injun Joe in the cave, but he is "careful to keep from Becky what it was he had seen" (Twain 1876, ch. 31) so as not to frighten her. After several days, Tom finally discovers a way out.

Once Tom and Becky escape from the cave, Judge Thatcher has "its big door sheathed with boiler iron ... and triple-locked" (Twain 1876, ch. 32). When Tom learns about this 2 weeks later (after recovering from his ordeal), he reveals that Injun Joe was in the cave. When the door is unlocked, Joe's body is found.

Tom and Huck eventually go back to the cave and discover where Injun Joe had hidden the treasure. Judge Thatcher invests the money for them. The Widow Douglas takes in Huck. And Tom makes plans to form a gang of robbers.

The Adventures of Huckleberry Finn

Huck's father, Pap, a violent drunkard, returns to town, kidnaps Huck, and holds him captive in a cabin across the river. While Pap is gone, Huck fakes his own death and escapes to Jackson's Island where he meets, Jim, a runaway slave. The two find a raft and start down the river together.

They soon come upon two men running for their lives from an angry mob. One claims to be an English duke, and the other claims to be the true king of France, but they are confidence men. The King and the Duke join Huck and Jim on their trip south. They stop at several towns along the way and attempt to con the citizens out of their money in various ways.

In one town, the Duke goes to a printshop and creates a fake wanted poster for Jim. It describes Jim precisely, claims that he ran away from a plantation south of New Orleans, and offers a reward of $200. With the fake wanted poster to show people, they can now start traveling down the river during the day.

On another trip to shore, the King learns that a rich man in town, Peter Wilks, has just died. His brothers, Harvey and William, have been summoned from England but have not arrived. The King and the Duke proceed to impersonate the brothers to get ahold of Wilks's assets. They bring Huck along to play the role of their "valley" (Twain 1884, ch. 26).

Huck feels bad for Wilks's three orphaned nieces who will lose their inheritance and decides to tell Mary Jane the truth about the King and the Duke. But to give himself time to get away from the King and the Duke, Huck convinces her to visit the Lothrops for a few days. Otherwise, the King and the Duke would read in her face that she knew the truth about them. Huck then lies to Susan and Joanna that Mary Jane has gone across the river to visit one of the Proctors. But he advises Susan and Joanna to lie to the King and the Duke and say that she has gone to visit the Apthorps. When Wilks's real brothers arrive, the King, the Duke, and Huck narrowly escape from another angry mob.

The King soon meets Silas Phelps and uses the fake wanted poster to convince him that Jim is worth $200. Silas buys Jim for $40, takes him to his farm, locks him in a cabin, chains him to the bed, and writes a letter to the plantation south of New Orleans. When Huck gets to the farm hoping to free Jim, Silas's wife Sally mistakes him for her nephew Tom Sawyer who is supposed to be arriving soon. On the pretense of collecting his bags, Huck heads back toward town to intercept Tom. Huck updates Tom on the current situation (starting with the fact that he is not a ghost). Tom impersonates his brother Sid and he concocts an elaborate scheme for freeing Jim. A number of things needed for the escape plan, such as a bedsheet, a shirt, several candles, a grindstone, a brass candlestick, and a pewter spoon, start to go missing on the farm.

Despite Tom alerting everyone about the impending escape by sending "nonamous letters" (Twain 1884, ch. 38), Tom, Huck, and Jim escape to an island where the raft is hidden. But since Tom has been shot in the leg, Huck has to bring him a doctor. As a result, Tom's life is saved, but Jim is captured. Aunt Polly arrives and reveals that Jim's owner has died and freed Jim in her will. So, as Tom knew, but did not share with Huck and Jim, the elaborate scheme for freeing Jim was completely unnecessary.

Tom Sawyer, Detective

Tom and Huck travel down the river again to Pikesville to visit Uncle Silas and Aunt Sally, who are now having trouble with their neighbors, Brace and Jubiter Dunlap. On the steamboat, they meet Jake Dunlap, Jubiter's identical twin brother, who is also on his way to Pikesville after having been away for many years.

Working with Bud Dixon and Hal Clayton, Jake recently stole some "noble big di'monds" from a "julery-shop" in St. Louis and replaced them with paste counterfeits. Bud then steals the diamonds from the other two and replaces them with lumps of sugar. Jake figures out that Bud has stolen the diamonds and hidden them in the heels of his boots. So, Jake steals Bud's boots. His plan is to travel down to Pikesville, disguise himself as a deaf-and-dumb stranger, and hide out on his brother's farm.

Tom and Huck help Jake sneak off the steamboat when it stops to take on wood several miles above Pikesville. But Jake's partners catch up to him before he reaches his brother's farm, and they kill him. Jake's brothers find the body, which they then use to frame Uncle Silas for murdering Jubiter, who disguises himself as a deaf-and-dumb stranger. In another exciting courtroom scene, Tom unravels the mystery, exonerates his uncle, and gets a reward for recovering the diamonds.

Spoken Lies

According to Twain, spoken lies are not the only form that lying can take. In fact, he claims that "the spoken lie is of no consequence, and it is not worth while to go around fussing about it and trying to make believe that it is an important matter" (Twain 1899). But spoken lies have received the most attention from philosophers who study lying. And they do seem to be Tom's favorite deceptive technique. So, we will start with some important lessons that Twain illustrates with spoken lies.

When Tom and Huck are delayed getting to Uncle Silas's farm, Tom leaves it to Huck to make up some explanation for what kept them because Tom "was always just that strict and delicate. He never would tell a lie himself" (Twain 1896, ch. 6). Of course, this is not true. Tom tells lies all the time.

Indeed, in the very first chapter of the very first novel, as Aunt Polly is about to punish Tom, he lies to her about there being something behind her so that he can escape. Furthermore, when he gets into a fight with a new boy in town, Tom falsely claims to have a big brother that "can thrash you with his little finger, and I'll make him do it, too" (Twain 1876, ch. 1). Tom lies when he tells Ben Rogers that whitewashing the fence "suits Tom Sawyer" (Twain 1876, ch. 2). When Tom arrives in Pikesville, he lies to his aunt and uncle about his being William Thompson from Hicksville, Ohio, on his way to see Mr. Archibald Nichols. And then he lies to them about his being their nephew Sid. In fact, Tom is openly praised for taking the blame for tearing Mr. Dobbin's book to save Becky from getting punished for it. According to Judge Thatcher, "it was a noble, a generous, a magnanimous lie—a lie that was worthy to hold up its head and march down through history breast to breast with George Washington's lauded Truth about the hatchet!" (Twain 1876, ch. 35).

Huck is also an accomplished liar. While traveling down the Mississippi on a raft with Jim, he lies to everyone that he interacts with – Judith Loftus, the Grangerfords, the two men searching for runaway slaves, the King and the Duke, the Wilks, and the Phelps – about who he is, who he is with, and what he is up to. Furthermore, telling the truth is not a step he takes lightly. As Huck thinks to himself before telling Mary Jane Wilks the truth, "here's a case where I'm blest if it don't look to me like the truth is better and actuly *safer* than a lie. I must lay it by in my mind, and think it over some time or other, it's so kind of strange and unregular. I never see nothing like it. Well, I says to myself at last, I'm a-going to chance it; I'll up and tell the truth this time, though it does seem most like setting down on a kag of powder and touching it off just to see where you'll go to" (Twain 1884, ch. 28).

Still, it makes sense to focus primarily on Tom. As Huck himself admits, Tom is clearly the expert when it comes to lying and deception. While he is faking his own murder, Huck laments, "I did wish Tom Sawyer was there; I knowed he would take an interest in this kind of business, and throw in the fancy touches. Nobody could spread himself like Tom Sawyer in such a thing as that" (Twain 1884, ch. 7).

Lies Must Be Intended to Deceive

We know it when we see it, but what exactly is a spoken lie? It is not just saying something false. Tom really likes his adventure stories about robbers and pirates. And much like the protagonist of Don Quixote (another book that Tom has read), Tom seems to really believe some of the false things that he says. For example, Tom tells his gang that "he had got secret news by his spies that next day a whole parcel of Spanish merchants and rich A-rabs was going to camp in Cave Hollow with two hundred elephants, and six hundred camels, and over a thousand 'sumter' mules, all loaded down with di'monds" (Twain 1884, ch. 3). When the boys actually end up raiding a Sunday-school picnic, Huck muses, "I reckoned he believed in the A-rabs and the elephants, but as for me I think different. It had all the marks of a Sunday-school" (Twain 1884, ch. 3). And you are not lying if you believe that what you are saying is true (see Mahon 2015, sec. 1.2).

In fact, you are not necessarily lying even if you *intentionally* say something false. For example, Old Jeff Hooker is not lying when he suggests that someone killed Jubiter Dunlap to steal the (cheap) "gallus-buckles" from his overalls (Twain 1896, ch. 9). He is being sarcastic. In addition, as Tom Sawyer points out to Huck during their cross-country balloon ride, a map does not "tell lies" (Twain 1894, ch. 3) when it depicts Indiana using the color pink even though it is really green (as seen from above) just like Illinois.

According to the traditional definition that goes back to the early Christian philosopher Saint Augustine (1952 [395], pp. 56–59), you are only lying if you *intend to deceive* someone (see Mahon 2015, sec. 1.4). In other words, a liar must have the goal of causing a false belief. But like a growing number of philosophers (e.g., Sorensen 2007; Carson 2010, pp. 20–22), Twain holds that there are at least a few lies that are not intended to deceive anyone about anything (see Mahon 2017, pp. 97–101). For example, in one of his essays on lying, Twain describes the following lie where, in the interest of politeness, you don't say what everyone knows that you really think: "If a stranger called and interrupted you, you said with your hearty tongue, 'I'm glad to see you,' and said with your heartier soul, 'I wish you were with the cannibals and it was dinner-time.' When he went, you said regretfully, '*Must* you go?' and followed it with a 'Call again'; but you did no harm, for you did not deceive anybody nor inflict any hurt, whereas the truth would have made you both unhappy" (Twain 1880).

Still, I focus here on the much larger category of lies that *are* intended to interfere with knowledge. Indeed, that seems to have been Twain's main focus as well. For example, seemingly all of the spoken lies in the Tom Sawyer novels are intended to cause false beliefs. As I discuss below, there are a few cases where Tom and Huck lie without intending to deceive their audience into believing what they actually say. But as I have argued elsewhere, this is not required for something to be what might be called a "deceptive lie" (see Fallis 2018, pp. 39–40). In those cases where Tom and Huck do not intend their audience to believe what they say, they do at least intend to deceive their audience into believing that they intend them to believe what they say. In other words, they are still liars because they are pretending to be sincere testifiers when they are not.

A few philosophers have argued that you are only lying if what you say is actually false (e.g., Carson 2010, p. 15; Turri 2021). However, someone who intends to deceive seems to be lying even if they are mistaken about the facts and accidentally say something completely true. For example, since Muff *believes* that he killed Dr. Robinson, he seems to be lying when he tells the villagers, "I didn't do it, friends, ... 'pon my word and honor I never done it" (Twain 1876, ch. 11). Similarly, even though Alfred Temple rather than Tom spilled ink on the spelling-book, Tom "thought it was possible that he had unknowingly upset the ink on the spelling-book himself, in some skylarking bout—he had denied it for form's sake and because it was custom, and had stuck to the denial from principle" (Twain 1876, ch. 20). Thus, Twain agrees with Augustine (1952 [395], p. 55) who claimed that "a person is to be judged as lying or not lying according to the intention of his own mind, not according to the truth or falsity of the matter itself."

How to Lie Effectively

One of Twain's main philosophical claims is that there are many types of lies beyond the spoken lie. Many of us try to avoid telling spoken lies, but we lie in these other ways all the time. Twain (1899) thought that we should "be consistent." If we are going to go around lying in all of these other ways, we should not shy away from telling spoken lies. And if we are going to do something, we should learn to do it well (see Mahon 2017, p. 105). As Twain puts it, "anybody can tell lies: there is no merit in a *mere* lie, it must possess *art*, it must exhibit a splendid & plausible & convincing *probability*; that is to say, it must be powerfully calculated to *deceive*" (Twain 2015 [1909], p. 403; original emphasis). The novels featuring Tom Sawyer are essentially an instruction manual on how to lie effectively.

At first glance, it might seem like teaching people how to lie is beyond the scope of applied epistemology. But the same people who study how knowledge can be acquired are often those who know best how it can be taken away. The contemporary philosopher Alvin Goldman suggests an analogy with civil engineering: "It's as much within the province of civil engineering to design and construct bridges that *would* collapse (under specified conditions) as bridges that *wouldn't* collapse" (Goldman 2002, p. 219; original emphasis). And even if we do not want to become better liars ourselves (so that we can interfere with what other people know), it is vital to understand the techniques that liars use so that we can keep them from interfering with what we know.

According to Twain, the main thing is to make your lie as plausible as possible. While Huck's lies are usually successful, he sometimes gets caught out when he does not have the time or the necessary knowledge to come up with a good story. For example, when Tom lets Huck explain to Aunt Sally what kept them so long, Huck says that "we run across Lem Beebe and Jim Lane, and they asked us to go with them blackberrying to-night, and said they could borrow Jubiter Dunlap's dog" (Twain 1896, ch. 6). But Sally quickly says, "That'll do, you needn't go no furder. . . . how'd them men come to talk about going a-black-berrying in September—in THIS region? . . . And how'd they come to strike that idiot idea of going a-blackberrying in the night? . . . Oh, SHET up—do! Looky here; what was they going to do with a dog?" (Twain 1896, ch. 6). Similarly, when Huck pretends to be from England, he is told, "Set down, my boy; I wouldn't strain myself if I was you. I reckon you ain't used to lying, it don't seem to come handy; what you want is practice. You do it pretty awkward" (Twain 1884, ch. 29).

Another technique is to tailor your lie to your audience. You can actually sell some fairly implausible stuff as long as you target their vulnerabilities. For example, in order to get access to the cabin where Jim is being held, Tom and Huck make friends with Nat, the slave who brings Jim his food. Nat believes that he is being tormented by witches who make him hear things and see things. Tom claims that the problem is that the witches are hungry and that the solution is to "make them a witch pie; that's the thing for *you* to do" (Twain 1884, ch. 36). Tom then offers to make the pie as he plans to use it to smuggle a rope ladder to Jim.

Aunt Polly also has a lot of crazy beliefs. For instance, she is a devotee of "phrenological frauds" and "quack medicines" (Twain 1876, ch. 12). So, when Aunt Polly is upset about Tom not letting her know that he was alive, he tells her that "I dreamt about you, anyway. That's something, ain't it?" (Twain 1876, ch. 18). And in recounting the dream, he includes everything that he observed when he snuck back into her house. Not only does Polly believe that Tom had such a dream, she concludes that he "was a prophesying" (Twain 1876, ch. 18).

Deceivers in the twenty-first-century certainly still use this technique. During the 2016 Presidential election, the consulting firm Cambridge Analytica and Russia's Internet Research Agency analyzed huge amounts of personal information to target individuals with misleading content which they were particularly susceptible to believing, such as that "Hillary Thinks African-Americans Are Super Predators" (see Jamieson 2018).

Several times, the novels also advise us to include as much truth in the lie as possible. For example, when Huck advises Susan and Joanna to lie to the King and the Duke, he says, "don't say nothing about the Proctors, but only about the Apthorps—which'll be perfectly true, because she is going there to speak about their buying the house; I know it, because she told me so herself" (Twain 1884, ch. 28). Also, when Huck and Jim get separated at one point, Jim has one of the Grangerford's slaves lead Huck to the middle of a swamp where Jim is hiding. Huck says that the slave is pretty smart because "He ain't ever told me you was here; told me to come, and he'd show me a lot of water-moccasins. If anything happens *he* ain't mixed up in it. He can say he never seen us together, and it'll be the truth" (Twain 1884, ch. 18). This technique has several advantages. If a lot of what you say is true, your story will be easier to remember, it is less likely that the facts will contradict your story, and you can more plausibly deny that you intended to deceive.

Deceivers in the twenty-first-century often follow this advice. For example, while fake news typically is false, as with the famous headline from the 2016 Presidential election "Pope Francis Shocks World, Endorses Trump for President," it can involve "the purposeful construction of true or partly true bits of information into a message that is, at its core, misleading" (Benkler et al. 2017).

Finally, the novels show that you sometimes need to allow yourself to get caught in a lie so that a bigger lie will stick. The contemporary philosopher Roy Sorensen (2021) has subsequently dubbed this a "sacrifice lie." But Twain was already aware of this phenomenon. For example, while Huck is taking the canoe to shore, two men searching for runaway slaves ask him if anyone is on his raft. Huck tells them that there is a man on the raft but that he is white. When the men decide that they had better see for themselves, Huck says, "I wish you would, because it's pap that's there, and maybe you'd help me tow the raft ashore where the light is. He's sick—and so is mam and Mary Ann." When they ask him what is the matter with his father, Huck replies, "It's the—a—the—well, it ain't anything much." One of the men says, "Boy, that's a lie." At this point, they conclude that Huck's father must have smallpox, and they decide not to go anywhere near the raft. The two men do not catch Huck in the lie that the man on the raft is white precisely because he lets them catch him in the lie that his father is not very sick.[3]

Preventing True Beliefs by Lying

Intending to cause someone to hold a false belief seems definitive of lying. And this is the primary epistemic goal for most liars. For example, Tom lies about enjoying whitewashing the fence so that the kids will falsely believe he enjoys it. Otherwise, they would not be motivated to take over the job. For his lie to be effective, he must prevent them from learning his true feelings. However, it is not enough for his purposes that the other kids simply remain uncertain about how he feels.

Another important lesson of the novels is that a lie is often valuable simply because it prevents someone from having a true belief about something (see Ortony and Gupta 2019, p. 151). For example, Tom lies about there being something behind Polly to keep her in the dark about his escape until it is too late for her to do anything about it. He lies about his tearing the page to hide the fact that Becky did it. He lies about the witch pie to conceal the fact that he is bringing Jim a rope ladder baked in the pie. Regarding Huck's sacrifice lie, he wants the two men not to know that there is a runaway slave on his raft. Getting them to believe falsely that his sick father is on the raft is only a means to that end.

Keeping Mum

As Twain emphasizes, spoken lies are not the only form of lying. In fact, you can lie by simply withholding information or, as Tom would put it, by "keeping mum" – something Tom does often. For example, Huck and Tom keep mum about what they saw in the graveyard for fear that Injun Joe will come after them. Also, Tom "wrote on a piece of sycamore bark, 'We ain't dead—we are only off being pirates'" (Twain 1876, ch. 18). He had planned to leave the bark next to Aunt Polly's bed. But he decides to withhold this information so that the boys would be able to crash their own funerals.

Causing False Beliefs by Withholding Information

Keeping mum is particularly good at preventing true beliefs. Sometimes, the goal is to prevent a true belief regarding the thing that you do not say. Other times, the goal is to prevent a true belief regarding your knowing the thing that you do not say. For instance, Tom and Huck would not mind if people learned that Injun Joe is the murderer as long as they learn it from someone else.

Sometimes withholding information can cause a false belief. For example, since Tom does not leave the bark with the note written on it next to Aunt Polly's bed, she continues to hold the false belief that he is dead. Moreover, sometimes withholding information can cause someone to have a *new* false belief. As the contemporary philosopher Thomas Carson points out, "Withholding information can constitute deception if there is a clear expectation, promise, and/or professional obligation that such information will be provided" (Carson 2010, p. 56). Twain (1880) gives an example that illustrates this point in one of his essays on lying. A woman (who claims that she never lies) is asked to answer several questions about the nurse that took care of her ill nephew on a hospital form. The nurse had only one fault. Namely, she did not sufficiently wrap up the patient while she was making up the bed. However, since the woman was pleased with the nurse in all other respects, she leaves the form blank where it asks, "Was the nurse at any time guilty of a negligence which was likely to result in the patient's taking cold?" Her silent lie leads the hospital staff to have the false belief that the nurse was not guilty of any such negligence.

Is Withholding Information a Form of Lying?

According to Twain, "Among other common lies, we have the *silent* lie—the deception which one conveys by simply keeping still and concealing the truth" (Twain 1880; original emphasis). Although silent lies do not count as lies on the traditional definition of lying, Twain's work suggests that the epistemologically interesting phenomenon of lying is much broader than what the traditional definition captures.

Nobody thinks that all lies are literally spoken. For example, you can also *say* something that you believe to be false with the intent to deceive by writing a letter or by sending a smoke signal. Indeed, conveying "smoke signal lies" is certainly a skill that Tom would have learned if he had decided to "join the Indians, and hunt buffaloes and go on the warpath in the mountain ranges and the trackless great plains of the Far West" (Twain 1876, ch. 8). But as the contemporary philosopher James Mahon (2015, sec. 1.1) points out, most philosophers do think that lying "requires the use of conventional signs, or *symbols*." Keeping mum does not satisfy this "saying" requirement of the traditional definition of lying, but Twain argues that we should not arbitrarily restrict ourselves in this way. What ultimately matters is interfering with someone's knowledge and not the details of how this result is achieved.

Of course, even if we do not require the use of symbols for lying, some philosophers would claim that keeping mum does not always count as a lie (e.g., Carson 2010, p. 54; Mahon 2015, sec. 3.1). As noted above, it is generally accepted that lies must intend to deceive. And these philosophers insist that merely preventing someone from acquiring a true belief only counts as keeping them in the dark rather than as deceiving them. While keeping mum can lead to a false belief, it often just prevents a true belief. And such cases arguably do not satisfy the "intention to deceive" requirement of the traditional definition of lying.

Some philosophers – including the Roman philosopher Cicero (1913 [44 BCE], bk. 3, sec. 61), the sixteenth-century Italian philosopher Niccolò Machiavelli (1908 [1532], ch. 18), and most famously, the seventeenth-century English philosopher Sir Francis Bacon (2008 [1612], essay 6) – go further and divide deception into two distinct types (see also Chisholm and Feehan 1977, p. 144). As the eighteenth-century writer Sir Richard Steele (1899 [1710], p. 97) nicely put it, "the learned make a difference between simulation and dissimulation. Simulation is a pretence of what is not, and dissimulation a concealment of what is." More recently, the intelligence analysts Bowyer Bell and Barton Whaley (1991, p. xvi) use the more expressive terms "showing the false" and "hiding the truth" for this distinction. Thus, these philosophers would agree with Twain that keeping mum always counts as deception. Even if you only hide the truth, you are still intentionally impeding someone's ability to acquire knowledge.

Of course, just as someone can accidentally say something false and not be lying, someone can accidentally fail to say something true and not be keeping mum. For example, as soon as Tom and Becky arrive back in town, Tom describes their adventure in the cave in great detail, even "putting in many striking additions to adorn it withal" (Twain 1876, ch. 32). But he did not mention that he had seen Injun Joe in the cave. Tom was not trying to keep people from knowing this fact. It just did not occur to him to mention it until he learned later about the Judge locking the cave's main entrance. To keep mum, you must fail to say something true with the goal that someone remains ignorant of that thing.

Concealing Information Versus Withholding Information

It is also important to distinguish withholding information from concealing information (see Carson 2010, p. 57; Lackey 2013, p. 241). The former is an act of *omission* whereas the latter is an act of *commission*.[4] When you withhold information, you simply refrain from taking action that would convey that information: you just keep your mouth shut. In contrast, when you conceal information, you take action to prevent that information from being discovered. For example, criminals conceal information when they take positive action to silence a witness. Along these lines, Huck overhears two criminals on a wrecked steamboat planning to kill their erstwhile partner (either by shooting him or stranding him on the wreck, which will soon break up) to prevent him from telling anyone about their crimes. Killing their partner would make it impossible for him to tell anyone, but criminals can silence a witness just by threatening to harm them if they squeal, as when the Duke warns Huck, "Just keep a tight tongue in your head and move right along, and then you won't get into trouble with us, d'ye hear?" (Twain 1884, ch. 31). Such threats do not guarantee silence, but they do make it quite likely that the witness will comply given the stakes.

The contemporary philosopher Jennifer Lackey (2013, p. 241) argues that only concealing information counts as deception. When you withhold information, you are just being uncooperative. You are not intentionally harming anyone epistemically. You are just intentionally failing to benefit them. Twain disagrees; he thinks that *merely* withholding information can be a lie. But it is interesting to note that when Tom and Huck keep mum about Injun Joe murdering the doctor, they come very close to concealing information. They do not just passively withhold the information but actively swear a "blood oath" not to tell anyone.

As the eighteenth-century British philosopher Francis Hutcheson (1747, bk. 2, ch. 11) nicely put it, an oath is "a religious act in which for confirmation of something doubtful, we invoke God as witness and avenger, if we swerve from truth." When someone swears an oath, it increases our assurance that this person will act in a certain way (see de Bruin 2016, p. 30). Indeed, people often take an oath to tell the truth. This occurs formally, as when Tom takes the stand at Muff Potter's trial, or informally, as when someone prefaces a statement with "honest injun" (Twain 1876, ch. 33) or "honor bright" (Twain 1884, ch. 27). Furthermore, taking an oath can change what is at stake when your future self decides whether to keep quiet. For example, as a result of their blood oath, Tom and Huck do not just have to worry about what Injun Joe will do to them if they talk. They also have to worry about the consequences of breaking their oath. Thus, taking an oath to keep mum arguably counts as concealing information and not just withholding information.

Admittedly, people typically take oaths in public (see de Bruin 2016, p. 24) so other people can hold them accountable. But a public oath to withhold information would reveal the very information that you do not want to reveal. This is why Tom and Huck take their blood oath in private. Even so, the oath is still being taken before the eyes of God, who they believe can hold them to account.

It should also be noted that Tom and Huck actually swear the oath twice. As Tom says, "I reckon we're safe as long as we keep mum. But let's swear again, anyway. It's more surer" (Twain 1876, ch. 23). Of course, as it turns out, Tom ultimately reveals the information that he had been withholding, and "Huck's confidence in the human race was wellnigh obliterated" (Twain 1876, ch. 24).

Lying Acts

Twain believes that lying is broader than what you do by speaking falsely – or even by simply not speaking. Most notably, in his essay "My First Lie, and How I Got Out of It," Twain (1899) asserts he lied when he was only 9 days old, not yet able to speak. He "had noticed that if a pin was sticking in me and I advertised it in the usual fashion, I was lovingly petted and coddled and pitied in a most agreeable way and got a ration between meals besides. It was human nature to want to get these riches, and I fell. I lied about the pin—advertising one when there wasn't any" (Twain 1899). And the Tom Sawyer novels are full of examples of such *lying acts*.[5]

Returning to the famous whitewashing-the-fence episode, Tom tells a spoken lie about his enjoying painting the fence. But this lie is just one part of a more extensive deceptive strategy. He also suggests with his behavior that he is totally absorbed in the task. For example, "Tom swept his brush daintily back and forth—stepped back to note the effect—added a touch here and there—criticised the effect again—Ben watching every move and getting more and more interested" (Twain 1876, ch. 2). Twain (1880) considers this a lie because, even though "he keeps his tongue still, his hands, his feet, his eyes, his attitude, will convey deception—and purposely."

Moreover, these additional touches are often critical for successful deception. This is especially true if you have a reputation as a liar, because people are inclined to seek out corroborating evidence before believing what you say. So, when he claims that the fence has been painted, "Aunt Polly placed small trust in such evidence. She went out to see for herself; and she would have been content to find twenty per cent of Tom's statement true" (Twain 1876, ch. 3). Also, when Tom claims that he intended to leave Aunt Polly a message on a piece of sycamore bark when he snuck back into her house, she checks to see that there is such a piece of bark in his pocket.

These lying acts count as lies for the same reason that keeping mum is a form of lying. Again, we should not restrict lying to saying, and we should not restrict deception to causing false beliefs. Twain's work suggests that *any* act that intentionally interferes with knowledge is on a par with the spoken lie.

Deceivers in the twenty-first-century certainly do not restrict themselves to literally saying things that are false. A prime example is *deepfakes*, realistic videos created by artificial intelligence and machine learning rather than simply by directing light reflected from physical objects through lenses and mirrors onto a photosensitive surface (see Fallis 2021). And if you create a deepfake of someone doing something that they did not actually do, it seems legitimate to call you a liar.

Note that Tom's behavior in the whitewashing-the-fence episode falls into two categories that are larger than lying and deception. First, it is a standard example of manipulation in the philosophical literature (see Rudinow 1978, p. 340; Greenspan 2003). Manipulation need not be deceptive, but deception is an important type of manipulation (see Noggle 2020, sec. 2.2). Second, it is a kind of pretense. Tom is pretending to enjoy painting the fence. That is, he is acting *as if* he is enjoying painting the fence when he does not (see Langland-Hassan 2014). Still, pretending does not necessarily involve intending to deceive (see Langland-Hassan 2014, p. 400). For example, the boys are not engaged in deception when they pretend to be pirates.

Ways to Show the False

Lies that are acts come in several different varieties. Bell and Whaley (1991, pp. 49–52) identify three techniques for showing the false. The novels featuring Tom Sawyer show that Twain was already aware of these techniques.

Tom pretending to enjoy painting the fence and Twain pretending to be stuck with a pin are examples of what Bell and Whaley (1991, p. 49) call "mimicking," where something is made to look like something else. Basically, Tom is mimicking a person enjoying his work and Twain is mimicking an infant who has been stuck. A more prototypical example of mimicking is impersonating some person other than yourself. For example, Tom and Huck pretend to be Sid Sawyer and Tom Sawyer, respectively, when they get to the Phelps farm. Also, the King and the Duke impersonate the Wilks brothers. In these cases, some particular person is being impersonated. But it is also possible to simply impersonate some type of other person, as when Huck pretends to be a girl when he sneaks back into town after escaping from his father.

Impersonating some other person typically involves spoken lies. But it also usually involves creating a deceptive appearance and/or engaging in deceptive behavior. For example, when he sneaks back into town, Huck wears a disguise (a "calico gown" and a "sun-bonnet") so that he will look like a girl. Also, Huck tries to "walk like a girl" (Twain 1884, ch. 10).[6] Similarly, the King affects an English accent when he impersonates Harvey Wilks.

It is important to emphasize that impersonating a person is just one example of mimicking. You are engaged in mimicking whenever you make the world appear to be one way, when in fact, it is another. For example, when Huck fakes his own murder, it is not a case of impersonation. But by leaving pig's blood all over the cabin and drag marks to the river, Huck makes it appear as if he has been murdered and dumped in the river.

Another technique is what Bell and Whaley (1991, p. 51) call "inventing," which involves creating a "new reality." This is really a special type of mimicking where something that never existed before is mimicked. Despite his great imagination, most of the fake realities that Tom creates are made up out of things that actually exist, such as pirates, robbers, elephants, and camels. Because there is no such thing as a witch pie that sates hungry witches, Tom is engaged in inventing in this case. There is a sense in which almost all deception involves creating something that does not really exist, but inventing involves creating a token of a type that has never existed before.

What Bell and Whaley (1991, pp. 51–52) call "decoying" involves creating a false appearance in order to distract. A standard example is when a bird pretends to have a broken wing to draw predators away from its nest. Tom uses this technique when he pretends that there is something behind Aunt Polly so that he can distract her and escape punishment.

Although these cases of decoying clearly involve showing the false (usually by mimicking), the main goal is to hide the truth. And you can undoubtedly distract someone without showing the false. For example, Huck gets "Nat's notice off" (Twain 1884, ch. 36) just by engaging him in conversation. And Tom and Huck slip spoons in and out of baskets and pockets just by waiting until Sally's attention is elsewhere (Twain 1884, ch. 37). So, decoying falls within the (broader) category of hiding the truth by what some philosophers call "distracting" (see Nyberg 1993, p. 69).

Ways to Hide the Truth

Bell and Whaley (1991, pp. 49–50) identify three (other) techniques for hiding the truth. Again, Twain was already aware of these techniques.

The main way to hide the truth is what they called "masking," where something is concealed so that it will not be observed. A standard example that Tom frequently discusses is pirates and robbers burying treasure. Masking is also what Injun Joe does when he hides the gold coins in the cave and what Bud does when he hides the diamonds in his boots.

While the prototypical example of masking is hiding the location of some object, note that you can conceal facts as well as physical things. For instance, Huck gets Mary Jane to leave town to conceal from the King and the Duke that their secret had been revealed. As he tells her, she "ain't one of these leather-face people. I don't want no better book than what your face is. A body can set down and read it off like coarse print. Do you reckon you can go and face your uncles when they come to kiss you good-morning, and never [let on?]" (Twain 1884, ch. 28).

Burying treasure and sending Mary Jane away put a physical barrier between the thing to be hidden and potential observers. It is also possible to keep something from being observed by making it blend in with its surroundings. A standard example is when a person (such as a soldier) or an animal (such as a chameleon) camouflages itself. Similarly, Tom and Huck frequently remain silent in the dark so that they cannot be seen or heard. This is how Tom and Huck hide from Injun Joe in the graveyard and in the abandoned house, how Huck hides from the criminals on the wrecked steamboat, and how Tom hides from Aunt Polly when he sneaks back into her house.

One may hide the truth even if the thing to be hidden is observed. A technique for doing this is what Bell and Whaley (1991, p. 49) call "repackaging." Instead of keeping people from seeing something, you just keep them from recognizing it. For example, after Injun Joe escapes from the courthouse, he hangs around town disguised as an "old deaf and dumb Spaniard," and he "was wrapped in a serape; he had bushy white whiskers; long white hair flowed from under his sombrero, and he wore green goggles" and/or a "patch on his eye" (Twain 1876, chs. 26 and 30).

Just like the earlier examples of impersonation, there is a sense in which Injun Joe's disguise is a type of mimicking. Any disguise shows the false as well as hides the truth, but what distinguishes repackaging from mimicking is that showing the false is only valuable as a means to hiding the truth. For example, the only point of Injun Joe's disguise is to hide his true identity. In contrast, when the King and the Duke impersonate the Wilks brothers, they are not just trying to hide their true identities. They are not going to be given Peter Wilks's money and property just because people do not know that they are con men. People must believe that they *are* Peter Wilks's brothers.

Jim is often repackaged as something other than a runaway slave. Whenever the King, the Duke, and Huck go into town, they leave Jim tied up on the raft in accordance with their story that he is a captured slave being returned for the reward. For obvious reasons, Jim is not happy hanging out all day tied up. So, they come up with another solution. They paint him blue, dress him in an appropriate costume, and put a sign on the raft that says, "Sick Arab—but harmless when not out of his head" (Twain 1884, ch. 24). The only goal of these disguises is to conceal the fact that he *is* a runaway slave.

Another technique for hiding the truth is what Bell and Whaley (1991, p. 50) call "dazzling," which involves confounding people with multiple copies of something. With this technique, people can narrow down the location of something but cannot pin it down exactly. For instance, during World War Two, planes were tracked as phosphorescent dots on radar screens. So, to conceal their plane's location, a crew member would release strips of paper backed with aluminum foil known as "chaff" (see Brunton and Nissenbaum 2015, pp. 8–9). The chaff would show up as additional dots on the radar screen. As a result, the radar operator would not be able to determine which dot represented the actual plane.[7]

Tom never deployed dazzling directly, but he comes close. Tom and Huck disguise Jake Dunlap as a boat hand so that he can sneak off the steamboat. As Huck explains, "every boat-hand fixed a gunny sack and put it on like a bonnet, the way they do when they are toting wood, and we got one for Jake, and he slipped down aft with his hand-bag and come tramping forrard just like the rest, and walked ashore with them" (Twain 1896, ch. 4). This is another example of repackaging. But if Bud and Hal had discovered that Jake had disguised himself as a boat-hand, they would still have to figure out *which* boat-hand.

Dazzling is another technique that deceivers in the twenty-first-century continue to use. In order to prevent people from learning the truth, they do not just tell an alternative false story. They tell several alternative false stories so that the truth is hidden like the real plane among the chaff. This specific use of dazzling has become known as the "firehose of falsehood" (see Brunton and Nissenbaum 2015, pp. 41–42; Paul and Matthews 2016).

Psychological Operations

Philosophers tend to focus on deception that involves messing with what someone perceive*s*, but Twain recognized that there is another way in which you can cause false beliefs and/or prevent true beliefs. In addition to interfering with the information that someone gets, you can impede their ability to process that information. For example, you can get someone drunk. As Carson (2010, p. 54) describes, I might "induce you to get drunk with me and make noise during the night to cause you to have a very bad night's sleep. The next day you are hung over and very tired. As a result, you overlook essential clues." In the modern military, this sort of strategy is known as "Psychological Operations" or PSYOP. As Ed Waltz (2007, p. 91) points out, information warfare includes "targeting centers of gravity of the organization by creating effects in the mental and emotional states of members of the organization to change operational capability."

Tom uses this sort of strategy several times. Aunt Sally is his favorite target. For example, when she is skeptical of Huck's implausible story about blackberrying, Tom quickly claims that it was actually strawberries and that "strawberrying" with a dog at night is actually quite common. Unlike Huck, Tom does not intend to deceive Sally into believing his spoken lie. In fact, even before Tom can get the words out of his mouth, Sally says, "Tom Sawyer, what kind of a lie are you fixing YOUR mouth to contribit to this mess of rubbage? Speak out—and I warn you before you begin, that I don't believe a word of it" (Twain 1896, ch. 6). Tom is just trying to get Sally "so aggravated with that subject that she wouldn't say another word about it, nor let anybody else" (Twain 1896, ch. 6).[8] Thus, even if someone does not believe the content of a spoken lie, it can still interfere with their knowledge.

In addition to impeding someone's ability to process information, you can have a similar effect by undermining their own faith in their ability to process information. This is called "gaslighting" (see Spear Forthcoming). The term comes from the film *Gaslight* (1944) in which a man manipulates his wife into thinking that she is going crazy. For example, he makes noises in the attic, dims the lights, and tells her that she is just imagining it all. Tom uses this sort of technique at least a couple of times. And at one point, Huck gaslights Jim just for fun. But when he discovers how much Jim is hurt by it, he "didn't do him no more mean tricks, and I wouldn't done that one if I'd a knowed it would make him feel that way" (Twain 1884, ch. 15).

When Nat brings Tom and Huck to see the runaway slave, Jim excitedly greets them by name. To hide the fact that Jim knows them, Tom claims that no one sang out. Quite reasonably, Nat seeks corroboration for what he perceived, but unfortunately for him, Huck and Jim aid the conspiracy by claiming no one sang out. So, Nat concludes that it is just another case of the witches making him hear things.

Note that a preexisting vulnerability to a belief is not required for gaslighting. After one of Aunt Sally's pewter spoons goes missing, it mysteriously turns up in Silas's pocket. Tom and Huck gaslight Sally so that they can steal it again without her missing it. Huck slips one of the spoons into his sleeve, and Tom asks Sally to count the spoons again. When she finds only nine spoons, she decides to recount, but Huck then slips the spoon back into the basket. At the end of several rounds, "she couldn't ever count them spoons twice alike again to save her life; and wouldn't believe she'd counted them right if she did; and [Tom] said that after she'd about counted her head off for the next three days he judged she'd give it up and offer to kill anybody that wanted her to ever count them any more" (Twain 1884, ch. 37). By undermining Aunt Sally's faith in her ability to count spoons, Tom and Huck abscond with one of the spoons without being detected. As she herself says later, "I was just to that pass I didn't have no reasoning faculties no more" (Twain 1884, ch. 41).

Lying to Yourself and Evolutionary Lying

Most of the lying in the Tom Sawyer novels involves one person deceiving another person. But as Twain (1916, ch. 9) was well aware, lying and deception are broader than this. A person can also lie to *themself* (see Deweese-Boyd 2016). For example, Tom wants to dig Jim out with case-knives because "it's the right way—and it's the regular way. And there ain't no other way, that ever I heard of, and I've read all the books that gives any information about these things" (Twain 1884, ch. 35). But once they realize that it is going to take too long, Tom decides that "It ain't right, and it ain't moral, and I wouldn't like it to get out; but there ain't only just the one way: we got to dig him out with the picks, and *let on* it's case-knives" (Twain 1884, ch. 36). Twain (2010 [1906], p. 224) even suggested that "when a person cannot deceive himself the chances are against his being able to deceive other people."

In addition, animals can lie (see Bell and Whaley 1991, pp. 48–52; Sober 1994). For example, during the adventure on Jackson's Island, Tom touches a tumblebug "to see it shut its legs against its body and pretend to be dead" (Twain 1876, ch. 14). The tumblebug is not cognitively sophisticated enough to intend to deceive anyone. But this behavior is the result of evolution. The tumblebugs that displayed this behavior were more likely to survive and reproduce than those tumblebugs that did not. So, even though it is not intended, it is no accident that creatures that prey on the tumblebug are misled. The contemporary philosopher Elliott Sober (1994, p. 73) calls this "evolutionary lying."

In fact, the 9-day old Twain was also probably not intending to deceive anyone when he cried as if he had been stuck with a pin. He had just learned to associate crying with getting comforted and fed. But even so, just like with the tumblebug, it was no accident that his caretakers were misled by the crying infant. So, it still counts as a lie just as Twain claims.

In the same fashion, purveyors of fake news and online conspiracy theories often do not *intend* to deceive anyone. It is just that there is a system in place that incentivizes the dissemination of misleading content. For example, during the 2016 Presidential election, teenagers from a small town in Macedonia used trial-and-error to find stories about Trump and Clinton that would generate the most clicks and shares and, thus, the most advertising revenue (see Fallis and Mathiesen Forthcoming, sec. 3). They were still liars even though they did not care whether or not people on the Internet actually believed their stories.

Conclusion

Tom Sawyer is one of the most quintessential and versatile liars in all of literature. As we have seen, his exploits illustrate many of the insights that Twain and other philosophers have discovered about lying and deception.

Tom tells many spoken lies. That is, he makes statements that he believes to be false and that are intended to deceive. But the goal of many of these statements is simply to prevent people from learning the truth. Indeed, Tom tells his most "magnanimous lie" to conceal that Becky Thatcher damaged the teacher's book.

Tom also frequently prevents people from learning the truth by keeping mum. That is, he withholds information from them as when he does not (at least initially) tell people that Injun Joe murdered the doctor. Indeed, since he takes a blood oath not to tell in this case, it might even rise to the level of concealing information.

Spoken lies and keeping mum are, respectively, examples of "showing the false" and "hiding the truth." But these two types of lying can also be carried out with actions and without using (or refraining from using) words at all. Most notably, Tom shows the false by pretending to enjoy whitewashing the fence (mimicking), and he regularly hides the truth by sneaking around quietly (masking).

Moreover, Tom does not always merely impede the information that people get about the world. Much like a secret agent, Tom sometimes messes with their very ability to process information as when he gaslights Aunt Sally.

With the character of Tom Sawyer, Twain convincingly establishes that lying is more common and more varied than we tend to think. And these are not just lessons for dealing with deception in nineteenth-century rural America. As we have seen, twenty-first-century deceivers utilize the very same deceptive techniques that Tom does, just with some high-tech bells and whistles. So it is vital for us to understand these techniques so that we do not fall victim to them.[9]

End Notes

1. Twain also made several famous remarks about lying. But it is not clear that Twain actually said *all* of the things that are regularly attributed to him, such as "a lie can travel halfway around the world while the truth is putting on its shoes" (see https://quoteinvestigator.com/2014/07/13/truth/).
2. Twain contributed to the ethics of lying as well as to the epistemology of lying (see Mahon 2017).
3. While Huck does not intend to deceive the two men into believing that his father is not very sick, he does intend to deceive them into believing that he intends them to believe this. However, since (at least as far as Huck knows at that point in the novel) nothing is wrong with his father, maybe Huck is not lying with that particular statement but only *pretending to lie* (see Fallis 2014, pp. 150–151). Of course, the strategy is still to (apparently) get caught in a lie.
4. In the quote above, Twain did explicitly say that silent lies involve concealing the truth. But he was just not being sufficiently careful here. Many of his examples are clearly acts of omission.
5. I am taking Twain at his word that, at 9 days old, he *intentionally* cried, but as I discuss in the section "Lying to Yourself and Evolutionary Lying," it was arguably still a lie even if he did not do it intentionally.
6. Despite all Huck's efforts, Judith Loftus quickly proceeds to give him detailed instructions on how to impersonate girls better.
7. Note that throwing chaff is not a case of showing the false. The radar operator knows exactly what is going on. They do not think that there are hundreds of planes in the sky. But nevertheless, they cannot locate the actual plane. Bell and Whaley (1991) give another example of dazzling from World War Two in which "General George Patton's deception planners cloaked the Third Army's move north to relieve the German siege of Bastogne. They knew that there was no way they could prevent the Germans from realizing that Patton was moving ... So they simply sent movement orders to five different Patton 'armies,' only one of which was the real one" (p. 56).

8. Tom does intend to deceive Sally into believing that he intends her to believe his lie. This is part of why it is so aggravating. Of course, it is possible for a lie to be very annoying even if it is not intended to deceive at all (see Sorensen 2007, p. 263).
9. For extremely helpful feedback on earlier drafts, I would like to thank Tony Doyle, Dean Kowalski, James Mahon, Kay Mathiesen, and Dan Zelinski.

References

Augustine. 1952 [395]. *Treatises on various subjects*. Ed. R.J. Deferrari. New York: Fathers of the Church.
Bacon, Francis. 2008 [1612]. Complete essays. Mineola/New York: Dover.
Bell, J.B., and Barton Whaley. 1991. *Cheating and deception*. New Brunswick: Transaction Publishers.
Benkler, Yochai, Robert Faris, Hal Roberts, and Ethan Zuckerman. 2017. Study: Breitbart-led right-wing media ecosystem altered broader media agenda. *Columbia Journalism Review*. http://www.cjr.org/analysis/breitbart-media-trump-harvard-study.php.
Brunton, Finn, and Helen Nissenbaum. 2015. *Obfuscation*. Cambridge, MA: MIT Press.
Carson, Thomas L. 2010. *Lying and deception*. New York: Oxford University Press.
Chisholm, Roderick M., and Thomas D. Feehan. 1977. The intent to deceive. *Journal of Philosophy* 74: 143–159.
Cicero, Marcus T. 1913 [44 BCE]. *On duties*. Trans. W. Miller. New York: Macmillan.
Coady, David. 2017. Applied epistemology. In *A companion to applied philosophy*, ed. Kasper Lippert-Rasmussen, Kimberley Brownlee, and David Coady, 51–60. Chichester: John Wiley & Sons.
de Bruin, Boudewijn. 2016. Pledging integrity: Oaths as forms of business ethics management. *Journal of Business Ethics* 136: 23–42.
Deweese-Boyd, Ian. 2016. Self-deception. *Stanford encyclopedia of philosophy*. https://plato.stanford.edu/entries/self-deception/.
Fallis, Don. 2011. Wikipistemology. In *Social epistemology: Essential readings*, ed. Alvin Goldman and Dennis Whitcomb, 297–313. New York: Oxford University Press.
———. 2014. The varieties of disinformation. In *The philosophy of information quality*, ed. Luciano Floridi and Phyllis Illari, 135–161. Cham: Springer.
———. 2018. What is deceptive lying? In *Lying*, ed. Andreas Stokke and Eliot Michaelson, 25–42. Oxford: Oxford University Press.
———. 2021. The epistemic threat of Deepfakes. *Philosophy & Technology* 34: 623–643.
Fallis, Don, and Kay Mathiesen. Forthcoming. Fake news is counterfeit news. *Inquiry*. https://doi.org/10.1080/0020174X.2019.1688179.
Gettier, Edmund. 1963. Is justified true belief knowledge? *Analysis* 23: 121–123.
Goldman, Alvin I. 1999. *Knowledge in a social world*. New York: Oxford University Press.
———. 2002. Reply to commentators. *Philosophy and Phenomenological Research* 64: 215–227.
Greenspan, Patricia. 2003. The problem with manipulation. *American Philosophical Quarterly* 40: 155–164.
Hume, David. 1977 [1748]. *An enquiry concerning human understanding*. Indianapolis: Hackett.
Hutcheson, Francis. 1747. *A short introduction to moral philosophy*. Glasgow: Robert Foulis.
Jamieson, Kathleen H. 2018. *Cyberwar: How Russian hackers and trolls helped elect a president*. Oxford: Oxford University Press.
Lackey, Jennifer. 2013. Lies and deception: An unhappy divorce. *Analysis* 73: 236–248.
Langland-Hassan, Peter. 2014. What it is to pretend. *Pacific Philosophical Quarterly* 95: 397–420.
Machiavelli, Niccolò. 1908 [1532]. *The prince*. Trans. W.K. Marriott. New York: E. P. Dutton.
Mahon, James E. 2015. The definition of lying and deception. *Stanford Encyclopedia of Philosophy*. http://plato.stanford.edu/entries/lying-definition/

———. 2017. The Noble art of lying. In *Mark Twain and philosophy*, ed. Alan H. Goldman, 95–11. Lanham: Rowman and Littlefield.
Noggle, Robert. 2020. The ethics of manipulation. *Stanford Encyclopedia of Philosophy.*. https://plato.stanford.edu/entries/ethics-manipulation/.
Nyberg, David. 1993. *The varnished truth*. Chicago: University of Chicago.
Ortony, Andrew, and Swati Gupta. 2019. Lying and deception. In *The Oxford handbook of lying*, ed. Jörg Meibauer, 149–169. Oxford: Oxford University Press.
Paul, Christopher, and Miriam Matthews. 2016. The Russian 'Firehose of Falsehood' propaganda model: Why it might work and options to counter it. *RAND Corporation Perspectives*. https://doi.org/10.7249/PE198.
Rudinow, Joel. 1978. Manipulation. *Ethics* 88: 338–347.
Schick, Theodore, and Lewis Vaughn. 2020. *How to think about weird things*. New York: McGraw-Hill.
Sober, Elliott. 1994. The primacy of truth-telling and the evolution of lying. In *From a biological point of view*, 71–92. Cambridge: Cambridge University Press.
Sorensen, Roy. 2007. Bald-faced lies! Lying without the intent to deceive. *Pacific Philosophical Quarterly* 88: 251–264.
———. 2021. Lie for me: The intent to deceive fails to scale up. https://soundcloud.com/brainfigments/the-cologne-knowledge-router-3-roy-sorensen-on-lying.
Spear, Andrew. Forthcoming. Epistemic dimensions of gaslighting: Peer-disagreement, self-trust, and epistemic injustice. *Inquiry*. https://doi.org/10.1080/0020174X.2019.1610051.
Steele, Richard. 1899 [1710]. The Tatler. New York: Hadley and Mathews.
Turri, John. 2021. Objective falsity is essential to lying: An argument from convergent evidence. *Philosophical Studies* 178: 2101–2109.
Twain, Mark. 1876. *The adventures of Tom Sawyer*. https://gutenberg.org/ebooks/74.
———. 1880. *On the decay of the art of lying*. https://gutenberg.org/ebooks/2572.
———. 1884. *Adventures of huckleberry finn*. https://gutenberg.org/ebooks/76.
———. 1894. *Tom Sawyer abroad*. https://gutenberg.org/ebooks/91.
———. 1896. *Tom Sawyer, detective*. https://gutenberg.org/ebooks/93.
———. 1897. *Following the equator*. https://gutenberg.org/ebooks/2895.
———. 1899. *My first lie, and how I got out of it*. https://americanliterature.com/author/mark-twain/short-story/my-first-lie-and-how-i-got-out-of-it/.
———. 1916. *The mysterious stranger*. https://gutenberg.org/ebooks/3186.
———. 2010. *Autobiography of mark Twain, volume 1*. Oakland: University of California Press.
———. 2015. *Autobiography of mark Twain, volume 3*. Oakland: University of California Press.
Waltz. 2007. Means and ways: Practical approaches to impact adversary decision-making processes. In *Information warfare and organizational decision making*, ed. Alexander Kott, 89–111. Boston: Artech House.

Don't Look Up as Philosophy: Comets, Climate Change, and Why the Snacks Are Not Free

59

Chris Lay and David Kyle Johnson

Contents

Introduction	1374
Summarizing *Don't Look Up*	1375
The Criticisms of *Don't Look Up*	1377
Does It Fail as Satire?	1377
Is It Too Hard on Those It Criticizes?	1379
Critiquing the Media (and the Critics)	1381
The Aptness of the Comet/Climate Change Analogy	1383
The Message(s) of the Film	1387
Examining *Don't Look Up*'s Argument	1390
Knowledge as the Good and the Moral Culpability of Ignorance	1391
A Categorical Obligation to Act Rationally	1392
A Profound Moral Command from Simple Premises	1394
Act Against Climate Change or Bear the Moral Weight of Ignorance	1395
"It's for Everyone. It's a Popcorn Movie"	1401
Conclusion	1403
Addendum	1403
References	1405

Abstract

Don't Look Up is a 2021 Netflix original film about two astronomers who discover a 9-kilometer "planet killer" comet on a collision course with Earth. The way humanity responds to this threat – which is less than ideal, given that the movie ends with humanity's destruction – is supposed to be an allegory for how

---

C. Lay
Young Harris College, Young Harris, GA, USA
e-mail: cmlay@yhc.edu

D. K. Johnson (✉)
Department of Philosophy, King's College, Wilkes-Barre, PA, USA
e-mail: davidjohnson@kings.edu

© Springer Nature Switzerland AG 2024
D. K. Johnson et al. (eds.), *The Palgrave Handbook of Popular Culture as Philosophy*,
https://doi.org/10.1007/978-3-031-24685-2_112

humanity is dealing with the real-world threat of climate change. Consequently, we argue, the movie is an argument that presents the viewer with a moral imperative: Do all that you can to prevent climate change. But does the argument work? To answer this question, we look at criticism of the movie, decipher its messages, examine the aptness of its analogy, and use the philosophy of Plato, Kant, and Peter Singer to explain exactly what kind of argument the film is. In the end, we conclude that, while most (although not all) criticisms of the film fall flat – it doesn't really matter. Given that the moral imperative presented by the movie is undeniable, the only appropriate response to the film is an unrelenting effort to fulfill our duty to stop climate change.

Keywords

Don't Look Up · Climate change · Global warming · Climate change denial · Global warming denial · Plato · Immanuel Kant · Peter Singer · Moral imperative · Nuclear fusion · Nuclear power

Introduction

> We've been trying to tell you this the whole time…It's right there!
> —Randall Mindy (*Don't Look Up*)

Don't Look Up is a 2021 Netflix original film (starring Jennifer Lawrence and Leonardo DiCaprio) about two astronomers, Kate Dibiasky and Randall Mindy, who discover a 9-kilometer "planet killer" comet on a collision course with Earth. Directed by Adam McKay (*Step Brothers, The Big Short*), who (supposedly) intended it to be a satirical comedy, *Don't Look Up* is an "analogy or an allegory for the climate crisis" (Schube 2021) – or more specifically, the poor way humanity is dealing with it. (The movie's website, dontlookup.count-us-in.com, even included a list of actions for combating climate change.) In the film, even though humankind has the ability to deflect the comet, we try to exploit it for profit instead – and all die.

Don't Look Up was divisive and controversial, to say the least. On the one hand, it was the second most watched film in Netflix history, gained a 78% approval from audiences on Rotten Tomatoes, and climate scientists universally loved it (Gugliersi 2022). In the words of marine biologist Ayana Elizabeth Johnson, co-creator of the *How to Save a Planet* podcast, "I've never felt so seen as watching @LeoDiCaprio & Jennifer Lawrence play scientists warning of pending apocalypse in #DontLookUp" (Vetter 2021). Or, as one of the most prominent American climate scientists, Michael E. Mann, put it in *the Boston Globe*, "McKay's film succeeds not because it's funny and entertaining; it's serious sociopolitical commentary posing as comedy" (Mann 2021).

On the other hand, the bulk of critics loathed it – according to Rotten Tomatoes, the film has only a 55% approval rating from critics – with many critics publishing articles claiming the film was poorly acted, too heavy handed, a poor analogy, and unfair to its targets (like conservatives, science deniers, and the media). Fletcher Powell of KMUW Wichita Public Radio summed up this last point when he said, "Yelling 'Look at all the dumb-dumbs' cannot be the basis for successful satire" (Vetter 2021).

In reply to such criticisms McKay clapped back, suggesting that many of these critics probably didn't like the movie because they didn't understand the severity of the climate crisis.

> ...if you don't have at least a small ember of anxiety about the climate collapsing (or the US teetering), I'm not sure *Don't Look Up* makes any sense. It's like a robot viewing a love story. "Why ArE their FacEs so cLoSe ToGether? (Twitter, Dec 29, 2021)

This too ignited a firestorm, with critics contending that it was possible to both fully appreciate the threat of climate change and also think that *Don't Look Up* is a poor film.

But is it? Does the film work as satire? Is it unfair? And, given the seeming importance of the point of *Don't Look Up*, does the answer to such questions even matter? And what exactly is the film's point, anyway? What argument is it making? Is its analogy apt? To understand how the film is doing philosophy – and, indeed, why it might be more philosophy than film – it will be important to explore these questions. But before doing so, we need to summarize the basic plot points of the film.

Summarizing *Don't Look Up*

The movie begins with Michigan State Ph.D. candidate Kate Dibiasky's discovery of a 9-kilometer comet, which astronomer Dr. Randall Mindy calculates (to his incredulous horror) will impact the Earth in 6 months and 14 days – an "extinction level event." They call NASA, who puts them in contact with Dr. Teddy Oglethorpe (Rob Morgan), head of the Planetary Defense Coordination Office (a real-world agency), who in turn rushes them out to see U.S. president Janie Orlean (Meryl Streep). Distracted by a scandal surrounding her unqualified Supreme Court nominee (and a birthday party), Orlean doesn't call them in until the next day – at which point she essentially brushes them off, saying that the best course of action is to simply "sit tight and assess," asking "Do you know how many 'the world is ending' meetings we've had over the years?"

Our heroes then set out to create public pressure for action by making the general populous aware of the threat – but things go equally bad on their planned appearance for *The Daily Rip* talk show. Not only are they overshadowed by the engagement of two pop stars – DJ Chello and Riley Bina – but the hosts play the story for laughs, calling it "a little science experiment" and asking whether the comet will hit the house of the male host's ex-wife. Kate erupts, "Are we not being clear? We're trying to tell you that the entire planet is about to be destroyed. ...we're all 100% for sure going to fucking die!" She is subsequently abused via internet memes, but the segment doesn't generate interest and the *New York Herald* pulls their coverage of the subject when the head of NASA (a former anesthesiologist who got the position after donating to President Orlean's campaign) calls it "more near-miss hysteria."

As the scandal surrounding Orlean's Supreme Court nominee worsens – apparently, Orlean sent the nominee a picture of her "cooch" – the potential public disgrace makes acknowledging and acting on the comet politically expedient. So, Orlean announces a "preemptive strike" against the comet called "Operation American Savior." Conspiracy theories and science denial abound and Dr. Mindy is celebrated as "America's sexiest scientist," but all goes well with the mission – until billionaire tech mogul Peter Isherwell (Mark Rylance), head of BASH cellular and a "Platinum Eagle level donor to [Orlean's'] campaign," realizes that the comet is rich with minerals. He tells Orlean to call off the mission – Isherwell wants to instead spearhead a project to break up the comet and safely land the fragments on Earth so that they can be mined – and she does. Isherwell thinly disguises the mission's corporate-profiteering motives behind claims that the mission will end "poverty as we know it, social injustice, loss of biodiversity ... [and start] a golden age" of humanity. But those claims are baseless and none of the research behind the mission is peer reviewed.

Legally barred from speaking out against BASH or the comet-mining mission, Kate goes back to her parents' house – only to have them lock the door. "No politics. None. Your dad and I are for the jobs the comet will provide. The divisions in this country are bad enough; we don't want more of that in our house." Speaking to this "division," polls show that 40% of people "want to manage the comet to create jobs," only 37% don't want the comet to hit, and a growing number (23%) "don't think there's a comet at all." Mindy initially stays with the mission, only to eventually be booted when he raises legitimate concerns about its feasibility and expresses them forcefully on *The Daily Rip* (much like Kate). His monologue serves as the moral core of the film: "If we can't all agree at the bare minimum that a giant comet the size of Mount Everest hurtling its way toward planet Earth is NOT A FUCKING GOOD THING, then what the hell happened to us?"

But then, the comet becomes visible in the sky – and Kate, Randall, and Teddy launch a public campaign to "Just Look Up." They tweet, they go viral, and they host a huge "benefit concert," thinking that actually seeing the comet will make its threat undeniable to the American people. But they're wrong. President Orlean runs a counter campaign insisting people "Don't Look Up" because those who acknowledge the threat of the comet "want you to be afraid! They want you to look up because they are looking down their noses at you." It works; the nation remains divided, and people tire of "the politics" surrounding what is inarguably a purely scientific issue.

Because Orlean and BASH cut India, China, and Russia out of the comet's mineral rights, those countries try to launch their own collaborative mission to deflect the comet – but their rocket explodes on launch. Anticipating the end of the world, Randall then takes Kate to his home in Michigan to enjoy one final meal with his estranged family while they await the end. But they do not turn on the TV and watch for updates. Instead, Randall, his wife, their two kids, Kate, her new fiancé

Yule, and Teddy gather around the dinner table and discuss minutia – like how one can rationally prefer the taste of store-bought apple pie if one grew up with it.

As the BASH mission fails, the "Patriot News Network" reports on the "one story everyone is talking about tonight: topless urgent care centers" to empty rooms, and Orlean and Isherwell "step out to the restroom." While the first impacts of the comet are felt, Randall utters the most heartbreaking line in the film: "The thing of it is, we really… we really did have everything, didn't we?" The Earth then explodes.

Orlean, Isherwell, and 2000 other wealthy elite are the only survivors – secretly absconding on a cryogenic spaceship headed toward "the nearest Earth-like planet in a goldilocks zone." They land 22,740 years later on a planet that is seemingly a paradise, only to be all eaten by strange animals called bronterocs. [A post-credits coda sees the president's son and chief of staff, Jason Orlean (Jonah Hill), forgotten by his mother, crawl from the rubble while livestreaming a devastated world. He insists to his audience of no one that they "don't forget to like and subscribe."]

The Criticisms of *Don't Look Up*

Does It Fail as Satire?

To explore *Don't Look Up* philosophically, we must first ask whether it succeeds in its tasks. According to critics, it did not; and the criticism that seems to most readily stick is that the film is not funny. Indeed, perhaps the only clue that it's supposed to be a comedy is the bubbly style and music of the opening credits. The reason it's not funny, it seems, is that it is a failed attempt at satire. Satire succeeds when it takes something that is true – some property or tendency something or someone has – and then exaggerates it for comedic effect. *Saturday Night Live* is famous for this; Dana Carvey's Church Lady is an exaggeration of actual ladies that he knew growing up in church. It works because, while their sense of moral superiority wasn't quite as extreme as Enid Strict's (that was the Church Lady's name), it was on the same spectrum. Satire fails when what is depicted is not actually an exaggeration.

Consider how Orlean's White House compares to what the White House was like around the time McKay wrote the film in 2019. During their first Oval Office meeting, President Orlean ignores the threat because she just takes it to be another hyperbolic, boy-who-cried-wolf, end-of-the-world bogeyman. Not only is this how some people dismissed, with completely false comparisons, the threats of COVID and climate change – "They said the world would end in 2012 too" – it also mirrors how the Trump administration treated climate change and COVID. "You know, a lot of people think that goes away in April with the heat," said Donald Trump about COVID in February 2020. "As the heat comes in, typically, that will go away in April" (Wolfe and Dale 2020). Jason got his job as the president's chief of staff simply because he is Orlean's son – just like Jared Kushner's and Don Jr.'s position in the Trump White House. Jason says he'd like to see his mother in *Playboy*, implying that "if she wasn't my mother…" he'd want to sleep with her. Trump famously said things very similar about his own daughter Ivanka. "Don't you think my daughter's hot? She's hot, right?" "I've said that if Ivanka weren't my daughter, perhaps I'd be dating her" (Besanvalle 2022).

The similarities with the real world don't stop there. The way Kate is abused on the internet mirrors exactly the way that young climate change activist Greta Thunberg is treated for her own passionate activism. The fact that Orlean only acts on the comet once it becomes politically convenient is basically the status quo for American politics. For example, the only bill ever passed in the United States to address climate change (as of August 2022) had to be branded as something else – the "Inflation Reduction Act" because Americans actually care about inflation – and only passed because Joe Manchin successfully added a provision in the bill to open up more federal lands to oil drilling by threatening not to vote for it otherwise (Bittle 2022). Isherwell's surveillance data and prediction algorithms are so sophisticated that he can predict not only people's purchasing habits but also their manner of death – but this barely exaggerates what Google and Facebook can already do with their data (O'Flaherty 2021). "The Patriot News" channel – a shameless stand-in for any number of right-wing media outlets – spreads lies, refuses to even cover the comet, and won't admit they're wrong about it. Similarly, as we write this, *Fox News, OAN,* and *Newsmax* are spreading lies about the January 6th insurrection (like that the rioters weren't armed), refusing to cover the House of Representative's investigation into it, and won't admit that they were wrong about what motivated it (i.e., they won't admit there wasn't election fraud; see Durkee 2022; Folkenflik 2022). (The Dominion Voting Systems lawsuit later revealed that Fox anchors and executes did know that there wasn't election fraud but chose to lie to their viewers about it anyway.) Most pertinent to the film's message, what is clearly a scientific issue gets warped into a political one, thus making action on the matter impossible – just like what happened with COVID, masks, and vaccines – and what is happening with climate change.

From the start, the movie creates a tension about the impending end of the world; and every time it tries to break it with a piece of satire, the viewer is reminded of some depressing real-world event that is barely removed from what we are supposed to laugh at. Perhaps the only time one feels free to laugh is during the roughly two minutes of the film where it seems like the initial deflection mission will be a success and the existential dread of the planet's destruction is momentarily lifted. When the mission is recalled, the tension returns and the movie is not funny again. As an ostensible satire, *Don't Look Up* is supposed to *exaggerate* how society would react if we discovered that a planet-killing comet was on a collision course with Earth. Yet it seems what happens in the movie is exactly how society would react. Nathan Robinson from *Current Affairs* sums up the problem like this:

> [T]he terrifying thing about *Don't Look Up* is that if there was an approaching deadly comet full of material that could juice corporate profits, I could imagine it would be difficult for the United States to gets its act together to destroy it, if by doing so it would hurt corporate profits and require significant sacrifice from the rich. I genuinely think you would have very mainstream economists saying that it would be "irrational" to destroy this much "economic value," if Elon Musk promised he could destroy the comet and save the mineral wealth. (Robinson 2021)

Robinson didn't know what Musk would do to Twitter a few months later; so perhaps we would no longer listen to Musk specifically, but his point still stands. When Isherwell stops the deflection mission so that he can mine the comet, it's not funny because it's absurd; it's disturbing because it's not. We could see something like that happening.

Is It Too Hard on Those It Criticizes?

But what about the other criticisms, like that *Don't Look Up* is too hard on those it criticizes? Does it pick on the Trump administration too much? Something that many viewers miss in their jump to see President Orlean as a flimsy Trump clone is that President Orlean is a woman – and she displays, in the Oval Office, a picture of her hugging Bill Clinton. Adam McKay was a supporter of Bernie Sanders and has been openly critical of Hillary Clinton. Although she never got a chance to appoint her own daughter as chief of staff, it wouldn't have been unimaginable for her to give Chelsea some kind of White House role. And Washington Democrats have not exactly been fast to act when it comes to climate change. When asked about the Biden administration's stance on climate change, McKay said:

> It's not great... In any other story these would be the villains, but in this case there's an even more extreme version, our extreme right-wing parties. And these guys kind of get off free because of it... It's the difference between straight-up denial and the people that kind of get it but kind of don't. And there's an argument to be made that each are equally lethal. (Aronoff 2021)

Indeed, according to *Slate*'s Jordan Weisman (2022), the leftist online opposition to the Democrat's 2022 Inflation Reduction Act, and its "inadequate" approach to climate change, is led by Adam McKay and his directing partner (and former Bernie Sanders aide) David Sirota. Although the film doesn't end up committing the fallacy of false equivalence by suggesting that both American political parties are equally wrong when it comes to climate change, it would be unfair to suggest that *Don't Look Up* is only picking on one side.

Something else such critics miss is that red-MAGA-hat-wearing Trump supporters aren't actually the primary target of the film. The real offenders are figures of authority like Orlean and Isherwell who mislead ordinary people for power and profit – ordinary people who don't know any better. As commentor Emma Lee put it:

> I don't think the movie is about indicting individuals; it actually elucidates how capitalists can create or worsen problems, then manipulate the public to convince people not to "look up." Working people are not at fault for buying into it — we just have drastically different resources to fight for our interests. (Lee 2022)

Now, this doesn't mean that *Don't Look Up* absolves regular folks who are willfully ignorant – or who choose to remain ignorant by failing to engage with the evidence. More on that later. But concerning the failures of those in power, McKay says:

> Experts are ... supposed to tell our leaders about these problems, and the leaders are supposed to at least somewhat have our best interest in mind. But that disconnect is just getting wider and wider, where our leaders are so self-interested and so driven by donor money. ... [W]hat do you do when that compact is completely shattered? Until you sweep all the dirty money out of politics, I don't know what you do about that. (Aronoff 2021)

Indeed, in the *one* scene where we actually see a red-hat-wearing Orlean supporter up close (at a rally), he looks up, sees the comet, and realizes that he's been lied to before the crowd turns. They change their mind in light of counter evidence! This isn't unfair; it's generous. (Some Trump supporters who insisted COVID was a hoax didn't give up on that belief, even on their deathbeds as COVID was about to kill them; see Elliott 2020.) To boot, notice what happens when they do turn: Jason immediately shifts to calling them "dumb rednecks." And, of course, when the comet hits, he is left behind by his own mother. The implication is that the powerful will do the same to those who put them in office. As *Current Affairs*' Nathan Robinson (2021) puts it, "The coldness with which the president abandons her devoted son at the critical moment shows how those who lick the boots of the rich will find that, no matter how loyal they are, they will be heartlessly abandoned the moment they become an inconvenience."

Perhaps nothing encapsulates this central aspect of the movie's message better than the running gag of Kate trying to figure out why three-star general Themes would charge her, Randall, and Teddy for free White House snacks. Teddy replies with a story: "One time I met Sting and I swear to God he farted right in front of me, didn't even break eye contact, and didn't even say excuse me. Thing is, he actually pulled it off. Because I still found him to be quite charming." Like Sting, the general wants to create a perception of power over others, simply for the sake of maintaining his power. It's all about power for power's sake. Kate and Randall are not in a position to know that the White House snacks are free; trusting the person in power to tell them the truth is not irrational. The film is not making fun of Kate for not knowing the snacks are free. (Notice that she does the right thing once she has access to the correct information and changes her mind.) It is criticizing Themes for lording and re-establishing his power over them, simply because he can.

The same is true for how Orlean misleads her followers; the film is (mostly) criticizing her, not them. As, again, Nathan Robinson frames it, "It's not about Americans being dumb sheep, but about how billionaires manipulate us into trusting them, how the reckless pursuit of profit can have catastrophic consequences, and the need to come together to fight those who prevent us from solving our problems" (Robinson 2021). This finger-pointing at powerful elites is a criticism of rich fossil fuel CEOs who manufacture debate by paying unqualified scientists and think tanks to contradict the consensus among the experts, creating the illusion that there is still scientific debate on an issue that is actually completely settled, all so that they can maintain their power (Rojas 2019). Big Tobacco did this with cigarettes and cancer (see Heath 2016), the fossil fuel industry is still doing this with climate change (see Supran and Oreskes 2021; Oreskes and Conway 2010), and Isherwell's misinformation campaign about the comet worked perfectly in the film. (When Brie introduces what becomes Randall's final appearance on *The Daily Rip*, she questions, "So Randall, we're hearing there's no comet, that there is a comet but it's a good thing, or maybe it's a bad thing. We are so confused.") Notice that the movie's message isn't that "all of humanity is horrible." Humanity actually was able to solve the problem; although it wasn't for all the right reasons, we launched a deflection mission that was poised to succeed. That mission was cancelled – and the Earth was destroyed – because, and only because, Isherwell thought he could make himself rich(er).

As for the concern that *Don't Look Up*'s criticism of this kind of intentionally deceptive science denialism is more severe than is warranted – well, it's not clear that any such criticism could be too harsh. In the words of Peter Gleick, a fellow of the US National Academy of Sciences and winner of the Carl Sagan Prize for Science Popularization, "When you degrade, ignore, and dismiss the warnings of science you threaten all of us" (Twitter, March 13, 2020). This might offend, of course, those who *willfully* fall for the denialism and remain ignorant of the warnings of scientists. Again, more on them later. For now, the words of futurist Alex Steffen will do. "The idea that those trying to inform the public about how to understand and respond to catastrophic threats have some special responsibility not to offend the sensibilities of those who regard being informed as offensive is not only anti-democracy, it's batshit crazy" (Twitter, Dec. 27, 2021).

Critiquing the Media (and the Critics)

So *Don't Look Up* is not (primarily) criticizing "the common man," and its criticism of the rich and powerful, and the science denialism that they fuel, is spot on. But what about *Don't Look Up*'s criticism of the media? Is it unfair? *LA Times* columnist Johan Goldberg certainly thinks so. After all, as he points out, ABC, CNN, *The New York Times*, and *The Washington Post* have full-time climate-change reporters, and *Time* magazine often runs cover stories on climate change, even once skipping its "Person of the Year" issue to declare the "Endangered Earth" to be "The Planet of the Year." The problem with Goldberg's argument, however, goes beyond the fact that *Time*'s "Endangered Earth" cover story was all the way back in 1989. The fact that news outlets have dedicated reporters doesn't mean that they're giving the issue the time or attention it deserves. And, as Molly Taft points out, they don't. In 2019, the nightly news and Sunday morning news shows of all the major networks (ABC, CNN, NBC, and FOX) covered climate change for only 238 minutes – combined, for the whole year (Taft 2019). And coverage was actually up that year, by 68% (MacDonald 2020). Taft observes that this is not surprising; she used to have a job trying to get climate scientists booked on news shows, and they would continually get bumped because of something more salacious – like when Katharine Hayhoe, a climate scientist at Texas Tech University, was scheduled to talk to Fareed Zakaria about the record-breaking heat wave gripping the West in 2021, only to have her appearance canceled so they could cover the breakup of Riley Bina and DJ Chello ... I mean, cover the billionaire Richard Branson spending billions to take himself into space. Stories about climate change making hurricanes worse shouldn't be bumped for footage of weathermen standing out in hurricanes, but they are (Taft 2019).

Indeed, *The Daily Rip* seems to be an all too accurate representation of how such shows usually go, making entertainment out of serious topics and distracting us into complacency. Consider how Great Britain News anchor Bev Turner responded to meteorologist John Hammond when he accurately predicted Europe's deadly and brutal heat wave of July 2022. "I want us to be happy about the weather, and ... something's happened to meteorologists to make you ... fatalistic harbinger's of doom ... haven't we always had hot weather?" (Mazza 2022). They are doing essentially what BASH's *Liif* phone app does, which senses your mood and counteracts "negative" emotions by distracting you with funny videos (like a dog riding a chicken). Both *The Daily Rip* and *Liif* are aimed at giving you "Life, without the stress of living." This is problematic, of course, because if we are never stressed, we can't know that something is wrong and aim to fix it. As *Screen Rant*'s Xan Indigio argues, the film is pointing out that we are distracting ourselves to death (Indigo 2022), a sentiment that echoes what Neil Postman observed in 1985: we are *Amusing Ourselves to Death* (Postman 2005).

To be fair, this isn't all the media does. The media actually makes more money on bad news; this is why they sometimes exaggerate threats and gin up fear. Fair enough. But then why isn't the media capitalizing on the actual true bad news that is the climate emergency? According to MSNBC contributor Zeeshan Aleem (2021), in his criticism of *Don't Look Up*, it's for two reasons. First, there are "[s]tructural flaws in the way journalists have been taught and are incentivized to tell stories: discrete narratives driven by characters, rather than problems in the systems we live in." The story of climate change supposedly can't be told that way. Second, "[m]any producers, editors and reporters have noted in years past that it can be quite difficult to get audience attention on climate change stories."

Aleem might be right, but this doesn't invalidate *Don't Look Up*'s criticism of the media. It's true that the ways the media ignores climate change goes beyond just making light of it. But the main criticism that the film levels at the press is that the media isn't covering climate change enough – it trivializes it, always preferring the spicier news of the day. As McKay admitted to NPR, "We're both incredibly frustrated with the lack of coverage of the climate crisis. You know, it's usually the fourth or fifth story. It's never the right tone, which should be much more urgent" (Pfeiffer 2021). Aleem explains *why* it's not covered – climate change isn't an easily told story that people will readily tune in to – but that explanation doesn't deny *that* the media fails to cover climate change effectively. So, Aleem just presents an excuse for what *Don't Look Up* says the media does; he doesn't deny they do it. But, instead of shifting the blame to viewers – *we would report on climate change but people will just tune out* – what the media should be doing is finding ways to tell the story of climate change that will get viewers to tune in. Yes, it's easier to make them care about the president's latest gaffe, but responsible media shouldn't appeal to the lowest common denominator.

To be fair, an impending comet about to destroy the Earth on a particular day in the near future would be more compelling news than climate change. You could have a countdown clock, the solution would be a single action, and the effects would be felt directly by the people watching. With climate change, the effects are not felt on a single day, solutions are diverse, progress is very gradual, and the people who will be most directly and negatively affected aren't even born yet. But that brings up the aptness of *Don't Look Up*'s analogy.

The Aptness of the Comet/Climate Change Analogy

Given that *Don't Look Up* is using its comet/climate analogy to present its argument, evaluating how well that analogy works is central to evaluating the philosophical argument of the film. In his review of *Don't Look Up*, Jake Bittle of *The Baffler* argued that an impending comet impact is a weak analogy for the multifaceted operations of climate change. Unlike a comet,

> Climate change takes place over centuries, strikes different parts of the planet in radically different ways, and even redounds to the benefit of a portion of the earth's population. ... It will split apart families, communities, nations, and force new social combinations we cannot yet imagine. ... It isn't a simple choice between everyone going about life as usual or everyone vanishing in a puff of smoke ... If a planet-killing comet were headed toward earth, there would be no mandate to change the way we live, no danger that society might decay and collapse, and no possibility that it might evolve into something better. We would fire a rocket at the comet, and the rocket would or would not work, and if it didn't work, we would all die. (Bittle 2021)

In other words, the impact of a comet can be known for sure, the impact of climate change cannot; a comet is quick, climate change is slow; dealing with a comet wouldn't force us to change the way we live, dealing with climate change will; a comet kills everyone; climate change effects everyone differently. We can't adapt as a way to deal with a comet impact; we can adapt (maybe even to "evolve into something better") to climate change. So, *Don't Look Up*'s analogy doesn't work.

But there are a few things wrong with Bittle's argument. First, the time-scale criticism falls flat. Not only is the difference between 6 months and 100 years miniscule in geological terms, but it also doesn't really seem that the difference matters for the analogy. Even if the movie was changed so that the comet would hit in 100 years but we had to act now to prevent it, one doesn't get the impression that Bittle or his fellow critics would be any more satisfied with the analogy.

Second, the impact of climate change *is* known for sure; granted, unlike with a comet, we don't have an exact date. But if we do nothing, it will assuredly, eventually wipe out the human race. Even if we slow the process to a 3 rather than 4-degree increase in temperature by the end of the century – if we do not reverse course, we will eventually hit temperatures (like 6 degrees) that will make the planet uninhabitable for humans (much sooner than would happen naturally; see Lynas 2007). Sure, as Scientific American's Rebecca Oppenheimer (2021) notes, climate change "is unlikely to wipe out all life, given life's 3.5-billion-year history spanning massive changes in temperature and atmospheric chemistry." But the same is true of a 9 km comet; after all, life survived the impact that killed the dinosaurs. In fact, "NASA scientists say it would take an asteroid 60 miles (96 kilometer) wide to totally wipe out life on Earth" (see Brain and Glem 2022; Lim 2015). But both a 9 km comet and uncorrected climate change would wipe out all *human* life.

Realizing this also reveals why Bittle's point about climate change affecting everyone differently is grotesquely short sighted. Yes, the rich and developed nations will be affected by climate change differently in the short term; some might even be able to profit from it. But in the long term, no one will be able to escape its consequences. What Bittle seems to miss is how the movie recognizes and deals with such issues to make its allegory work. Take, for example, Bittle's point that a comet will kill everyone, but climate change effects everyone differently. People often argue that the rich will be able to avoid the consequences of climate change; but in the end, they won't. Just like Orlean and Isherwell thought they could survive the comet by flying to another world, only to be devoured by bronterocs – the "cool rich" of the real world may think they can avoid the consequences of climate change, but they will most likely eventually find that their money will not be able to save them once society collapses and the planet is no longer livable. The idea that, instead of mitigating it, we might possibly adapt to climate change and (as Bittle puts it) "evolve into something better" is a ludicrous pipe dream that wagers the survival of the human race on a hunch (see Adger and Barnett 2009; Reilly 2014).

Or take Bittle's argument about how dealing with climate change will require us to sacrifice the way we live, but deflecting a comet would not. First, McKay deals with this bit of disanalogy by making inaction on the comet motivated by mining the comet for minerals, which Isherwell says will usher in a golden age for humanity. This is why Kate's parents say they are for "the jobs the comet will provide." So, in the eyes of the public, action and inaction on the comet really does affect the way they live. The choice is seen as between a lavish life provided by the comet's resources (which is analogous to the lavish life provided by fossil fuels) and a life of hardship and misery (which is analogous to what life will supposedly be like without fossil fuels according to climate change deniers). Indeed, the way that Isherwell talks about how mining the comet will solve poverty mirrors how climate change deniers say we shouldn't switch to renewables because it will make electricity more expensive and be hardest on the poor (Collomb 2014, p. 7). (This short-term problem, it should be noted, could easily be solved by taxing the rich to subsidize renewables, thus reducing their cost.)

Secondly, Bittle's wrong; mitigating climate change will not require us to sacrifice "the way we live." Now, don't get me wrong. The world right now runs on fossil fuels, and mitigating climate change will require us to change that. But changing that doesn't mean that we can no longer live in houses, drive cars, use washing machines, have enough food, or have a functioning industry and economy. It does mean, for example, that the way we generate power will be different – nuclear, wind, and solar power plants instead of coal power plants, electric vehicles instead of gas guzzlers, etc. – but that doesn't mean that we won't be able to have the same quality of life (MIT Energy Initiative 2018). That's not to say that we won't have to make sacrifices, or certain industries might not survive, or that the way that we live won't change in specific and grandiose ways. Capitalism, for example, will only be able to survive as a highly regulated system. (This is one of McKay and Sirota's complaints about the Inflation Reduction Act: It only incentivizes renewables; it doesn't regulate fossil fuels.) But insisting that mitigating climate change will somehow undo the entire way that we live, such that the solution will be worse than the problem, is a tactic of climate change deniers, based in no evidence (Collomb 2014). For example, they claim that switching to renewables will wreck the economy, when in fact it will generate economic growth and jobs, and in the long run save billions of dollars (see Stern 2021; Jaeger and Saha 2019; Calderón and Stern 2015). [There's even some historical precedent for this: As part of the Depression-era economic relief under FDR's New Deal, the federal government established the Tennessee Valley Authority (TVA). Both then and now, the TVA provides employment opportunities, flood regulation, and energy for a traditionally impoverished region in the American South. Moreover, much – though not all – of the TVA's energy production is cleaner nuclear and hydroelectric power.]

What's worse, if we simply had the political will, we could have already done this. We already have the technology, but implementing it would hurt the short-term profits of the fossil fuel industry, and so they have prevented us from doing so. Indeed, McKay said that Isherwell's intervention to stop the initial deflection mission was inspired by that moment in the 1970s–1980s when the oil companies almost took action and reversed course – only to instead double down and launch a misinformation campaign. In the 1970s, for example, Exxon Mobile wanted to re-brand itself as an "energy company" rather than just an "oil company," and be the "Bell Labs of energy," launching research into global warming and renewable energy, thinking that American innovation was more than capable of tackling the crisis (Westervelt, The Bell Labs of Energy, 2016a). But in the early 1980s, when the price of oil dropped, the country shifted politically, and company leadership changed, Exxon decided instead to preserve its original core business model (oil) and launched a science-denial campaign to allow it to do so (Westervelt, The Turn, 2016b). "That story might be one of the greatest crimes in human history," McKay said. "We had a moment. We had a mission. We could have done it. But the profit motive had to rear its head, and it stops the mission, and it completely changes the course of the narrative, putting us in even deeper peril" (Aronoff 2021).

Bittle thinking that, without action, climate change is not only something that we could survive, but it is something that might even make society evolve into something better, raises the question of whether McKay was right when he said that critics of the film are in denial about the severity of climate change. If you don't think that climate change is an existential threat, then *Don't Look Up* really does seem dumb – like a movie that uses a fictional World War III to warn against the dangers of mud slides. And, although it is certainly the case that it is *possible* to fully appreciate the severity of climate change and also think that *Don't Look Up* (or any movie for that matter) is bad art, under-appreciating the severity of climate change does seem to be a theme among the movie's critics.

Take Kyndall Cunningham at *The Daily Beast*, who said that she is among the critics who hates the film but appreciates the severity of climate change because she doesn't like the movie but "endured a 50-degree [2021] Christmas in the Northeast" (Cunningham 2021). While unusually hot days are a symptom of global warming, which in turn causes climate change, using such an example to illustrate that one appreciates the severity of climate change does exactly the opposite. The effects go far beyond "hotter days." Or consider Jonah Goldberg from the *LA Times*, who thinks that McKay's call for more climate change coverage is just a call for "climate hysteria." According to Goldberg, climate change is not actually an "existential threat" because it won't end all life on Earth by the end of the century (Goldberg 2022). This is like the friend of one this chapter's authors, who insists to be the prime example of someone who hates the movie but also fully appreciates the threat of climate change – yet also admits to believing that climate change is simply something that "we can learn to live with."

Don't get me wrong, there are those who don't like the movie because they are just flat-out denialists (Techera 2022). But as climate futurist Alex Steffen noted on Twitter (Dec. 27, 2021), "3/4 of the critic's responses seem like hot takes written by jaded culture workers from an alternate universe in which the planet Earth was not in the early days of its most catastrophic upheaval in 100,000s or even millions of years." It's not unreasonable to think that if these critics actually saw climate change for the existential threat it was, they would view the movie more favorably. At the least, they would see that since both the comet and climate change threaten the existence of the human species, that aspect of the film's analogy holds.

Another aspect of the analogy that works is the kind of action that will be required to stop it. That's not to say that all that would need to be done to solve climate change is as simple as deflecting a comet with a rocket (although some critics seem to underestimate how scientifically complicated even that would be). Notice also that deflecting a comet is something that one nation could accomplish; international governmental cooperation will be required to deal with climate change. Importantly, though, there is absolutely nothing that the average individual can do about an impending comet – nothing but "demand" that their government deal with the problem because only mass mobilization by governmental entities can deal with it. The exact same thing is true of climate change (Goldstein 2019).

This suggestion might seem odd to some readers. "Can't I do something about climate change by driving an electric car, eating less meat, using more efficient lightbulbs, and putting solar panels on my house?" The problem is that, as noble as such gestures are, even en masse most are negligible; some are even counterproductive. (For example, it does very little good to stall climate change to drive an electric car if you get your electricity from a coal plant; see Vlieta et al. 2011.) And even everyone switching to electric cars would not solve the climate crisis (Bronsdon 2021). The sad fact is, 71% of all carbon emissions are from just 100 companies; and unless they change their ways, we can't slow climate change (Griffin 2017). All the combined action from human individuals won't even make a dent, and the only way those companies will change is if they are forced to by governments. As environmental philosopher J. Baird Callicott put it:

> It will not suffice...simply to encourage people individually and voluntarily to build green and drive hybrid. But what's worse is the implication that that's all we can do about it, that the ultimate responsibility for dampening the adverse effects of global climate change

devolves to each of us as individuals. On the contrary, the only hope we have to temper global climate change is a collective sociocultural response in the form of policy, regulation, treaty, and law. (Callicott 2009, p. 191)

To be fair, companies do respond to consumer demand; for example, if most people stopped eating meat, the demand for meat would go down and the carbon pollution caused by the meat industry would be greatly reduced. So mass public action could have some effect (see Engels 2014). But the way society is structured is so dependent on fossil fuels that, even with the best intentions and efforts, a person can't help but have a significant carbon footprint (see Berners-Lee 2022). Besides, massive public action isn't going to happen without government incentive and intervention either. Just like with Comet Dibiasky, massive, collective government action is necessary.

This is something that makes the Count Us In "stop climate change" campaign that went along with *Don't Look Up* a bit odd. Acknowledging the dissonance between the film's message and the companion Count Us In campaign's goals/methods, Emma Lee says:

> The campaign is clearly meant to spark awareness, action, and hope in the midst of this despondency. Clicking around on the official site, one is prompted to take "practical action on climate change," with suggestions ranging from calling your politicians to eating more veggies. I commend McKay and Sirota in drawing attention to the climate crisis. [But] we, as the audience of this film, have to see these individual calls to action as necessary, but far from sufficient. By putting so much emphasis on individual responsibility, the creators are diverting attention from the fact that climate change cannot be stopped, and certainly not reversed, by individual actions. Overstating individualism can have a depoliticizing effect, encouraging people to focus inward rather than building solidarity and taking to the streets to catalyze the revolutionary change that is really needed. (Lee 2022)

Although the film itself seems to appreciate how individual action will not be enough, the filmmakers may not have appreciated this when developing the Count Us In campaign. To understand that the film's message and its online campaign are at least somewhat at odds with each other, we should now try to articulate exactly what *Don't Look Up*'s message is.

The Message(s) of the Film

One message of the film is obvious: Humanity is bungling its response to the climate crisis in the same way it bungles its response to the comet in the film; if we don't change course, humanity will be destroyed. But there are many premises, relevant to this conclusion, that it states along the way. Take, for example, what it says about public mobilization. Kyndall Cunningham at *The Daily Beast* says the movie "ignores a global movement of pro-science, environmental activists, and laypeople who would most certainly mobilize around [a comet/climate change], [and ignores the] vulnerable communities who are experiencing the drastic effects of climate change currently [and] are spreading awareness, proposing solutions, and holding government officials to task" (Cunningham 2021). The problem with Cunningham's critique is that the movie doesn't ignore this; it focuses on it directly. Our protagonists, Randall, Kate, and Teddy, mobilize a "pro-science" movement – which launches a public awareness campaign, proposes solutions, and holds government officials to task – that puts its real-world counterparts to shame. But a major point of the movie is that all of this activism does absolutely nothing. As Randall sarcastically asks after he is criticized for staying on the White House team during the BASH mining project to (he claims) steer it in the right direction, "And what do you suggest we do [instead]? An online petition, huh? You want to…get a mob and hold up picket signs?" The film clearly shows that the "mob and picket sign" approach, even when expertly organized, has no meaningful impact. Indeed, the biggest governmental/institutional response (outside of the USA) to the comet in the film – when China, India, and Russia attempt to launch their own joint deflection mission – is only because "Orlean and BASH cut [them] out of the rights for the minerals," not because of Randall's public awareness campaign. In many ways, we live in a plutocracy, where (regardless of how much they protest) the concerns of the majority are ignored, and the concerns of the rich rule the day (Gilens and Page 2014).

One way the rich maintain such control is by politicizing science. Take the scene where Devin Peters is interviewed about his movie "Total Devastation" – a popcorn movie about a comet impact that is set to be released on the day "some believe Comet Dibiasky will impact the planet." He wears a pin that points both up (for "just look up") and down (for "don't look up") because he thinks, "as a country, we need to stop arguing and 'virtue signaling.' Just get along." The interviewer replies that this is "so refreshing [because] we're all tired of the politics." But, of course, whether a comet will hit the Earth is a purely scientific issue, not a political one, and insisting that we shouldn't let that happen is an obviously true ethical statement that should be shouted from the rooftops. It's not merely an attempt to "signal" to others that you are virtuous. Indeed, "virtue signaling" is a term that originated online as a way to dismiss those who express genuine ethical concerns, and it is only by politicizing the comet issue that Orlean has gotten people to deny what is otherwise an obvious undeniable fact: A 9 km comet hitting the Earth will end humanity and that's bad. The point? Politicizing science is dangerous.

More dangerous, however, is excusing science away. In her song, "Just Look Up," Riley Bena says that we should "get []our head out of []our ass [and] listen to the goddamn qualified scientists." But Austin Hayden (from the *Show Me the Meaning* podcast) has criticized the "pro-science" view of the film.

> Another shitty thing about the whole "just trust science" narrative is that it really disregards indigenous thought, spiritual thought—so much of what it means to be human—by reducing it to certain forms of quantified rationality … The whole point of, like, "just trust science, trust science" is actually … kind of culturally supremacist and it may be even like a part of this western European patriarchal system that we've inherited and I just don't like it … it's icky. (*Show Me the Meaning* 2022)

The problem is that Hayden's comment is rooted in a supremely naive cultural relativism, which suggests that all facts – no matter the topic – are relative to culture, with none having any more right to claim that they are true than any other. Now, it's one thing to suggest that what is ethically right and wrong is relative to culture; some cultures have different moral norms, and it's next to impossible to find universally agreed upon criteria by which to judge them all. (Although, it should be noted, even ethical relativism has its limits; a culture believing slavery is ethically acceptable doesn't make it so.) But physical facts about the world – like whether a comet is going to hit the earth or climate change is real – are not relative to culture. And science is undeniably the best and most accurate way of determining the truth of such statements. That's not to say that we shouldn't learn from the works of indigenous philosophers (e.g., V. F. Cordova and Daniel Wildcat) or that scientists always produce all and only objective value-free facts. But to decry science as just "another way of determining truth," that is equivalent to any other form of thinking – whether it be mysticism, astrology, indigenous, or religious – when it comes to matters like climate change is not only obviously false, it is also socially irresponsible and dangerous.

To illustrate the point, imagine if – within the movie *Don't Look Up* – Devin Peters didn't star in a popcorn movie like "Total Devastation," but instead one like *Don't Look Up* – which is aimed at convincing people to listen to "goddamn qualified scientists," like Randall Mindy, and deflect the comet. Maybe it's called *Don't Stare at the Sun* and uses an impending doomsday solar flare as an analogy for the impending comet. Criticizing the message of that fictional film by insisting that it favors scientific ways of knowing rather than equating it with spiritual ways of knowing would fit perfectly with the other absurd ways characters in *Don't Look Up* avoid admitting that there is actually a problem. [Nathan Robinson (2021) makes a similar point about *in-the-movie-critics* calling such a film "heavy-handed," or the director's "worst film yet," and saying it "misses its targets" or has humor that is too "broad."] That's not to say that the environment (and the entire world) wouldn't be better off if today's dominant societies and their ancestors had bothered to observe, acknowledge, and respect the relationships that indigenous people recognize in the natural world. If indigenous ecological philosophy dominated the way people thought about such matters, climate change would likely not be an issue. But when it comes to predicting things like solar flares, comets, or climate change, there is no other way to do it; science is it. And pretending there is another way dilutes the warning of the film and makes us less likely to act on such issues.

Another complaint of critics like Hayden is that the movie is too blunt, or "on the nose," with its message. You don't have to figure it out; it yells its message to your face. But it can't be *that* blunt. Again, most critics missed that it isn't chiefly lampooning the common "ignorant" person but those in power who trick them to make them ignorant; and it's a send up of the media, and Hillary Clinton and other mainstream Democrats just as much as it is of Trump and mainstream Republicans. Democratic Senator Kirsten Sinema, who has repeatedly gutted legislation to fight climate change, praised the movie without realizing that it is criticizing her (Twitter, Dec. 26, 2021).

What's more, people often miss how Isherwell is a stand in for those in the real world who think that climate change is nothing to worry about because we will eventually develop a technological fix – like geoengineering, a supposed magic eraser that will take all the extra CO_2 out of the atmosphere. Like the BEADs (Bash Explore and Acquire Drones), such solutions are pipe dreams. As Nathan Robinson of Current Affairs puts it, "The reviewers who think the film's messages are obvious seem to have missed that the 'tech solution' to the comet is a clear commentary on geoengineering, the cheap-but-incredibly-risky approach to climate favored by those who don't want anything to be done that would substantially hurt the bottom lines of fossil fuel companies" (Robinson 2021).

But even if the movie is blunt, why is on the nose messaging a bad thing? It's needed now more than ever. When my dogs won't listen, I raise my voice; this usually gets them to pay attention and stop whatever nefarious thing they are doing. Society needs the same. Some viewers may be tired of hearing the "listen to the scientists" message, but as *Screen Rant*'s Xan Indigo recognizes, "for anyone whose main complaint is that they're tired of hearing this message, they should try to understand that, just like Kate and Randall, real-world scientists are far more tired of telling it" (Indigo 2022). We obviously aren't listening. That's why so many of them loved the movie; not only do they finally feel heard, but someone else is screaming the message louder than they ever could. They get pushed off of the third segment of a cable news show no one is watching; *Don't Look Up* hit a record of 142 million watching hours in its first week.

Finally, it's not clear that being blunt necessarily makes something bad art. To once again quote Robinson:

> I think there is a good argument to be made that there is nothing wrong with being "shrill" or "unsubtle" when trying to make an important political point ... Is this really a normative judgment about a film's quality or is it just a reflection of reviewers' temperaments and politics, where anything too angry or obvious seems the enemy of art, which is necessarily cerebral or inaccessible? (Robinson 2021)

But this brings us to examine *how* the film makes its argument, and whether or not it is actually a film at all – or, at least, whether being a film is its primary role.

Examining *Don't Look Up*'s Argument

If what we've said above is right, the demand from critics for more from *Don't Look Up* than its dire message about climate change may be misplaced. As Randall says late in the film, exploding in impotent frustration on *The Daily Rip*, "Not everything needs to sound so clever, or charming, or likable all the time. Sometimes we need to just be able to say things to one another. We need to hear things!" Above all, *Don't Look Up* wants to very candidly say something to the viewer in a way that can be heard. Framing the movie as a failed comedy or as artistically limp misses the point as much as criticizing Teddy for admitting that he prefers the "junky taste of store-bought" apple pie. Teddy isn't making an argument; he's reflecting with his friends about some of the mundane things he's grateful for that will be lost when the comet hits.

Now, unlike Teddy, *Don't Look Up* actually is making an argument. But it's quite peculiar to criticize an argument for lacking aesthetic merit because that isn't the purpose of an argument. *Don't Look Up* is still a movie and can be evaluated using the normal (aesthetic) criteria for assessing movies; but it's not *primarily* a movie. Evaluating it strictly *qua* movie stops short of recognizing that its features as a film serve as a way of delivering its philosophical argument. Indeed, the filmmaking suggests that the movie's creators are aware of the tension between creating art and articulating a relevant social message. Near the end of the movie, Randall delights in explaining the poignancy of the lyrics to the Mills Brothers song "Till Then" to Kate. She smiles back weakly, but any aesthetic force the song has dissipates into fear of the comet's impact in a few short hours. This exchange seems to punctuate the question of the film's artistic integrity, rhetorically asking "How can the quality of art matter in the face of environmental disaster?" To again quote Nathan Robinson (2021):

> I came away thinking that its critics were not only missing the point of the film in important ways, but that the very way they discussed the film exemplified the problem that the film was trying to draw attention to. . . . I see this as a parable making an important point and I'd like to discuss the point, not give a star rating to the parable. . . . A central point made by *Don't Look Up* is that when things are matters of life and death, we need to treat them as such. Giving such a film a thumbs-up or thumbs-down and assessing the quality of its humor shows that one has missed the point entirely. Let us not have a discussion about *Don't Look Up* itself. Let us have a discussion about how we can avoid the very real tendencies that the film illuminates.

So what *Don't Look Up* is really offering is a "moral imperative." The film commands its viewers to act in a certain way and insists that they are morally obliged to act on this command. Moreover, *Don't Look Up* serves as a moral imperative *first and foremost*; its role as a film is *subordinate* to its role as a moral imperative. It's an argument disguised as a big budget studio comedy. To show this, it will be necessary to first review three philosophers: Plato, Immanuel Kant, and contemporary consequentialist thinker Peter Singer.

Knowledge as the Good and the Moral Culpability of Ignorance

Today, philosophy is divided into various sub-fields like aesthetics, epistemology, ethics, and metaphysics. For Plato, though, all philosophy reduces in some way to moral philosophy. This isn't something that he discusses in one particular work; the entire Platonic corpus is replete with a concern for knowledge and the nature of reality that eventually blends with theories about living justly. Plato's reasoning relies heavily on what he construes knowledge to be: awareness of the "Form" of something – the perfect essence of a particular physical thing or event, separated from it as a kind of idea. Chairs, horses, tallness, justice, and nearly all things in the sensible world imperfectly reflect the essential characteristics of their respective Form (see Plato 1997 for Socrates's discussion with Parmenides about what does and doesn't have a Form).

To illustrate, all individual just events have something in common, though they differ in multifarious other respects. That "in-common" nature is the Form "justice." No individual just event *is* justice itself, however. Since particular sensible things are imperfect representations of Forms, knowing about any particular sensible thing is second-rate knowledge. But to know the Form that unites all tables, cats, or generous acts is to have real knowledge that won't vary between particulars.

In Book V of his *Republic*, Plato (1992) suggests that each Form also has something in common with all other Forms. That is, there's something greater than the Forms to which all Forms have the same relationship that individual acts of justice do to the Form justice. This Form of Forms is called the Form of the Good. So, "knowledge" gets cashed out as "knowledge of the Forms," where each individual Form reflects the goodness of the Good. If philosophy is the study of wisdom – or knowledge – and if knowledge is knowledge of the Good, as Plato claims, then philosophy is *always* focused on emulating goodness and thereby acting in accordance with the right and Good. All philosophy is therefore moral philosophy.

Plato thinks that teaching and learning are moral enterprises above all, since knowledge brings one closer to goodness. It might be surprising, then, that a lack of knowledge isn't "evil." Plato is clear that the absence of knowledge – ignorance – is certainly a bad thing. Yet, importantly, ignorance per se isn't something for which a person ought to be chastised. Indeed, in the *Apology*, Plato (2002) argues that acknowledging one's ignorance is actually essential to learning in the first place. (One who thinks they already know is hardly open to learning.) No, the only "blameworthy ignorance" is acting *as if* you know, even though you don't.

This tracks with Plato's larger theory. Being good is knowing what Good is – so much so that someone who knows Good cannot act badly. "Bad" actions come from *acting* on ignorance. Randall cannot claim that he "knew" he shouldn't have cheated on his wife June with Brie Evantree; if he knew this was bad, he wouldn't have done it. Nonetheless, he acted on what he assumed was knowledge (perhaps the "knowledge" that he would be happier with Brie, that June would find someone else, that these things justified his action, etc.), even though he clearly *didn't* know. On Plato's view, this explains why June is rightfully angry with Randall in blaming him for his indiscretion. From this, it is also more evident how Plato provides a key notion for analyzing the argument that *Don't Look Up* makes: Acting on one's ignorance is a *moral failing*, deserving of reprobation.

A Categorical Obligation to Act Rationally

Our next idea comes from Kant's *Groundwork of the Metaphysic of Morals*. Here, Kant (1998) assembles a moral system now known as "deontology," or duty ethics, where "doing the right thing" is defined in terms of an obligation to follow certain governing principles. There's only one rule, for Kant: the categorical imperative. While there are a number of formulations of the categorical imperative that Kant proposes, the nuances of each aren't needed for this chapter and a brief paraphrase will do. In its most basic form, the categorical imperative states that the moral principle by which one acts should be universalizable to everyone and all situations. Without this universalizability, morality becomes contingent and its force is substantially weakened. (Plato feared the same thing, causing him to ground the moral in unchanging, purely intelligible Forms.)

This is why Kant famously rejects moral exceptions that most people take as given, like so-called harmless lies. General Themes' small lie that Kate, Randall, and Teddy owe him for the complimentary White House snacks bothers Kate for much of the film. On the surface, it might seem like what Themes has done is more baffling than seriously morally objectionable. Why would a three-star general – presumably financially well-off, given his position in President Orlean's administration – lie about the cost of snacks to defraud a group of people out of a few dollars? For Kant, though, the wrongness of Themes's act is absolutely rooted in the lie itself. Lying cannot be universalized as a moral rule for obvious reasons; it would be absurdly self-defeating to try to live according to the rule "everyone should always lie" because people rely on one another for true information about everything from the benign ("Hey buddy, what time is it?") to the deathly serious ("Doctor, how much sedative should I give the patient?").

Now, Themes's lie isn't exactly "innocent." However one assesses his moral culpability, the dishonest general is probably at least a jerk (in the philosophical sense defined by Schwitzgebel 2019): someone who willfully disregards the perspectives and concerns of those he sees as socially beneath him. Yet, even an apparently innocuous fib – say, about whether or not a friend's hair looks good – is unacceptable to Kant because lies undermine the practice of truth-telling. What Kant is getting at here is that rules that cannot be universalized aren't perfectly rational. That is, there are some situations in which acting according to the rule would clearly make no sense, given other things the agent believes. Case in point: Lying causes one to act irrationally, even if it *seems* to make sense in a given situation ("No Mr. Axe Murderer, the person you're looking for *isn't* in the house"). Because of the important social value of truth-telling, the liar simultaneously (and incompatibly) believes both "I should lie" and "It's good to tell the truth."

As rational beings, Kant thinks that humans ought to strive to maximize rational actions. Moreover, they have an *obligation* to do so, in virtue of their rationality, that non-rational beings don't. What he's done in his deontological ethics – even more explicitly than Plato – is to make the moral and the rational one and the same. The categorical imperative is a command that instructs the hearer how to be a good person: recognize one's duty to always act rationally, then do it. From Kant, then, *Don't Look Up*'s argument will borrow the notion of the moral as a command to act in a rational way. There's still more to the argument to be considered, though, before the film's own moral imperative can be explained.

A Profound Moral Command from Simple Premises

In what is likely his most well-known claim, Peter Singer (1972) in "Famine, Affluence, and Morality" calls for the people of Western nations to give of their material wealth to the point of near poverty, or "marginal utility." Failing that, he says that well-to-do Westerners should *at least* give until that act of giving would cause them to suffer something "morally significant." Singer believes that there are more than enough resources in the world to eradicate problems like hunger and poverty-based susceptibility to disease; the issue is that too many of the people with those resources are buying artisan coffee, designer clothes, and pricey supercars instead. What's most important for the purposes of this chapter isn't Singer's conclusion about wealth distribution, though this is surely an important conclusion to reach. Rather, it's the structure of Singer's argument that's most relevant.

What's so powerful about Singer's argument is that it's dead simple and has an almost *irresistible* logic. His proposal to donate incredible amounts of Western wealth isn't even part of the core argument – it's a consequence he derives from it later. The argument itself has only a few parts: first, that starvation and the lack of access to adequate medical care are bad things. Second, if one is able to prevent bad things from happening without suffering a morally significant loss, one should do so. Accepting these two premises, it straightforwardly follows that one should do whatever possible (without incurring a morally significant loss) to prevent starvation and lack of access to medical care.

Singer takes these premises to be largely uncontroversial – especially the first, which he just calls an assumption that he takes for granted. The trouble arises when what's implied by the conclusion comes into focus. Since most individuals lack the ability to directly alleviate the problems of starvation and poor medical care for others worldwide, the easiest way to prevent this suffering is to donate to reputable organizations that *can* attack the problem. According to Singer's conclusion above, one should donate *at least* until reaching a point where the donation is a "morally significant loss." And, since not buying fancy new clothes or upgrading to a massive television can hardly be called "moral suffering," Westerners would be giving up the vast majority of their wealth.

By the time he gets to the argument's stinger, many readers have already accepted Singer's premises without objection. They don't dispute that starvation and lack of good medical care are bad things, and most probably agree that people *should* prevent bad things from happening if it doesn't cost anything morally important. Yet, they often attempt to resist the degree to which the accepted premises actually obligate them to substantially change the material comfort of their lives. As Singer anticipates in the article, the common objection is not that the conclusion is wrong – it's that it is morally *overdemanding*. So, they don't deny that accepting the premises compels them to also accept the conclusion; they just don't like what the conclusion asks them to morally do.

Here, a parallel with *Don't Look Up*'s message about climate change may seem manifestly clear. People frequently *do* respond to climate science with a passive shrug because they feel that too much about their lives would have to change to meaningfully forestall ecological disaster. Surely the film *does* take aim at this kind of indifference – recall, again, Devin Peters's smug attempt to skirt the line between the two "sides" of the comet disaster with his pin that points "both up and down." But this isn't the part of the film's argument that Singer most helps to unravel. Consider instead his argument's form: simple and uncontroversial premises that, if accepted, obligate the person to a decisive moral action (however uncomfortable). With this structure in mind, we are at last in a position to use Plato, Kant, and Singer to understand *Don't Look Up*'s moral imperative and see how it also impels the viewer toward moral action.

Act Against Climate Change or Bear the Moral Weight of Ignorance

Like Singer's claim, *Don't Look Up*'s argument is founded on simple premises that are difficult to challenge: (1) The collapse of human life on Earth is a bad thing that should be avoided. (2) We should do whatever we can in order to prevent anything that's bad and should be avoided. (3) The evidence undeniably indicates that human-caused climate change is (very soon) going to irreparably damage the ecosystem to the point that it will eventually end all human life. Thus, (4) we should do all that we can to prevent climate change. Of course, the third premise and conclusion are not explicitly stated by the film, since its argument is given as an allegory. But the film *does* explicitly state that the evidence undeniably indicates that comet Dibiasky will end all human life – and the comet's impact is, as critics were so quick to point out, the thinnest of stand-ins for climate change. So, by substituting what the allegory actually represents into the argument, we get premise (3) and the conclusion (4). Just like with Singer, we have an argument with seemingly undeniable premises which lead to a conclusion commanding the hearer of the argument that, morally, something must be done.

Where Singer provides an "out" for detractors, however, *Don't Look Up* doubles down on the moral imperative. Singer admits that those who do not accept his premises – especially the premise *that starvation and lack of access to medical care are bad* – have no obligation to his conclusion. But the film instead refuses to recuse those who deny the argument's premises, even going so far as to morally condemn them.

To see that the film regards all of its premises as both undeniably true and morally binding, return to Randall's *Network*-style meltdown on live television, where he shouts,

> Look, let's establish, once again, that there is a huge comet headed towards Earth. And the reason we know that there is a comet is because we saw it...I mean, for God's sake, we took a FUCKING PICTURE OF IT! What other proof do we need? And if we can't all agree at the bare minimum that a giant comet the size of Mount Everest hurtling its way toward planet Earth is NOT A FUCKING GOOD THING, then what the hell happened to us?

All of the argument's premises are dealt with here as inarguable: Premises (1) and (2) are both presented as what early modern rationalists like Descartes, Leibniz, and

Spinoza would call *self-evidently* true. Like the proposition *that 2+2=4*, Randall takes it as obvious that the end of all human life is bad and that bad things should be prevented. These ideas should be understood by anyone who takes a moment to reflect on them. This is why we should "at the bare minimum" be able to agree that "a giant comet the size of Mount Everest hurtling its way toward planet Earth" is bad – a comet that large will imperil all human life, and imperiling all human life is plainly "NOT A FUCKING GOOD THING."

Following premise (3), Randall tells us the evidence for the life-imperiling comet – and climate change, which the comet represents – is clear because "we saw it" *with our own eyes* and "took a FUCKING PICTURE OF IT." Granted, this evidence isn't strictly self-evident like (1) and (2), but we cannot expect this out of scientific evidence because it's based on empirical observation and not armchair reflection. Nevertheless, the evidence for climate change and its consequences is as established as the evidence for any scientific fact can be (see Lynas 2007; Oreskes 2014; Cook et al. 2016; Foley 2017; Brown and Caldeira 2017; Goodwin 2018; Oreskes et al. 2019). It therefore is undeniable – as (3) asserts – and thus has the *force* of a self-evident truth.

Lastly, Randall insists that failing to admit these premises is also a moral problem – "What the hell happened to us?" In other words, not accepting premises (1)–(3) means that *something is wrong with you*. Morally, the hearer of Randall's speech (and watcher of the film) ought to conclude that they have a responsibility to stop the comet (i.e., to prevent climate change).

Thus, although its moral imperative isn't presented as categorical to all situations and persons, *Don't Look Up* follows Kant in posturing its argument as fully rational. In Kant's case, the commitment to rationality means that accepting or rejecting the categorical imperative has no bearing on one's obligation to follow it: Following the imperative is simply the rational thing to do. Similarly, *Don't Look Up*'s premises about the repercussions of climate change and that these repercussions are both bad and ought to be prevented are taken as a matter of *undeniable fact*. From the point of view of the film's argument, this means that whether one agrees or disagrees with those facts, they're still true. So, assenting to the moral obligation that results from those facts – acting to prevent climate change – is (again) the rational thing to do. As a result, this obligation is binding on *everyone* who is intellectually capable of understanding the basic language of the argument and what it asks – not just those who accept the argument's premises.

Because *Don't Look Up*'s moral command is rational, its argument portrays the rational and the moral as the same – just like both Kant and Plato. Neglect in either following this command or even acknowledging its premises is irrational, but it's also a moral failure worthy of blame. This sort of confluence of the irrational and the immoral sounds especially like Plato's *blameworthy ignorance*. In the film, those who reject *Don't Look Up*'s simple, Singer-like premises are definitely depicted as inexcusably ignorant. The "impact deniers" and their outlandish slogan that lends the movie its title are perhaps the first to come to mind. But there are two classes of impact deniers depicted in the film: those who lead the movement from positions of social, political, and economic authority and those who dutifully watch the former group's newscasts, adopt their rallying cry, and publicly perform their social media challenges. Both groups are indicted for their blameworthy ignorance by *Don't Look Up*, and both should be examined here.

When discussing the moral blameworthiness of climate denial in this chapter, we have stopped to note that *Don't Look Up* is especially hostile toward those who use their positions of power to deceive others and influence public policy to their advantage. This doesn't mean that the deceived are blameless, though. Like Plato, the film doesn't seem to view the ordinary person's mere lack of knowledge as a moral failing – ignorance, in and of itself, isn't the problem. Rather, what makes ignorance about a threat like climate change/a comet impact blameworthy is when it persists despite a preponderance of easily accessible and trustworthy evidence about the certain ecological consequences of the threat. This seems less like ignorance due to one's circumstances and more like a willing choice to remain ignorant of the facts – what we might call *willful ignorance*.

Obviously, if someone lives in a society where accurate information about climate change is very difficult to access – perhaps it's highly regulated by their government – it's difficult to morally criticize them for their ignorance. However, in our society (and the mirror of it seen in *Don't Look Up*), reliable data about climate change is readily available through the vast majority of major news outlets, reputable academic journals, blog posts from highly regarded climate scientists, and even open-source, publicly maintained information libraries like Wikipedia. Given such an embarrassment of educational riches about climate change, the only feasible way to remain ignorant is to limit one's trusted/accepted information sources to just those resources that deny climate change. [This sort of constraint on knowledge sources is described by Sunstein and Vermeule (2009) as a "crippled epistemology."] In all but the most extreme cases, doing this requires a willing choice – and so, ignorance like this is decidedly *willful*. [There are other forms of willful ignorance than denying the evidence, such as someone so committed to apathy or deferring responsibility to others that they refuse to engage with the facts of climate change at all. These people aren't really the focus of the film, though; even the extremely apathetic Yule (Kate's fiancé) is spurred to action when he sees the comet in the night sky.]

Recall Plato's definition of blameworthy ignorance: acting on ignorance *as if* one has knowledge instead. With that in mind, we can see how the willful ignorance of certain climate/impact deniers fits Plato's idea. Consider a character in *Don't Look Up* who only watches the Patriot News Network and views President Orlean as a kind of deific figure; whatever Orlean says, they instantly take it as true simply because she said it. Suppose this person also exclusively associates with other Orlean supporters, both in person and on social media platforms. Until it appears in the sky above their head, our subject would surely be ignorant about the evidence concerning the comet and the consequences of its impact. Following Plato, by restricting their information sources to *only* these two resources – and by selecting such a myopic peer group – this person should be morally faulted for assuming knowledge when they don't actually have it. What knowledge are they assuming? At minimum, "Patriot News and Orlean always tell the truth so I don't need to listen to anyone else." Of course, Patriot News and Orlean don't know and aren't telling the truth; there is a comet and it's exceedingly dangerous. The example illustrates Plato's blameworthy ignorance well in the context of *Don't Look Up*'s argument. Simply being ignorant about the threat of climate change/a comet impact still isn't the moral problem. The problem is the willing choice to not be informed, prompted by the false belief that one already knows who the real experts are.

Accordingly, ordinary people who indulge in willful ignorance to deny evidence of the comet are portrayed unfavorably or as outright immoral in the film. Several apt examples can be found in a sequence showing social media responses to the comet. In one, a group of young men posting under the name "Orl3an*Br0s*4Life" chant "Don't Look Up" against a caption that reads "These dudes will NEVER look up!!!! Pres Orlean is the only woman we trust." The "Orlean Bros" wear their willful ignorance proudly, affirming that they'll blindly follow Orlean (while at the same time implying that all other women are untrustworthy). As the so-called bro culture to which they belong is widely associated with bullying and sexual violence, *Don't Look Up* appears to be making an effort to tie their ignorance and immorality together. Another clip in the same sequence sees a man in a "Don't Look Up" hat confidently declare that the "Just Look Up" supporters are "trying to rob you of your freedom, and that's a fact!" before gesturing to a photo and telling his audience that Randall is "a known pornographer" living under a false name. Like the Orlean Bros, this man is guilty of willful ignorance and depicted as morally gross. He demonstrates his ignorance by asserting claims that he cannot verify as if they were the truth. And, though there are no repercussions for it in the movie, spreading misinformation about others online frequently has nasty real-world consequences – people are sometimes physically assaulted, lose their jobs, and worse when accused in this way. Someone who uses his online platform to try to defame Randall as "a known pornographer" is not a good person!

Kate's return home provides yet another case of willful ignorance cast as morally blameworthy. Concerned only about the jobs created by mining the comet, Kate's parents close themselves off to any evidence of the comet's harm. Viewers are certainly not meant to see their rejection of their daughter – again, inspired by the ignorance they chose to embrace – as model parenting. Sticking with Kate, the faceless crowd of "normal" people who meme Kate into oblivion are willfully ignoring what she has to say on *The Daily Rip* and discounting her expertise. We might be tempted to see this as harmless – memes are funny! – but the real-world analog for what happens is extremely toxic. Kate's online harassment is meant to evoke both the specific treatment of activist Greta Thunberg (noted earlier in the chapter) and the often misogynistically motivated venom spat in online spaces at women more generally. This behavior isn't simply "in bad taste"; online harassment of women commonly involves both death and rape threats. In other words, Kate's mistreatment is morally repulsive, and it comes as a direct result of her tormentors' ignorance.

While there are other instances in the film, we hope that this handful of examples suffices to show that *Don't Look Up* portrays its "common person" impact deniers as ignorant in a blameworthy way. If ordinary people in the film are held as morally accountable for their willful ignorance about the comet, then analogously so are ordinary people who reject – out of willful ignorance – the film's moral command to prevent the harmful effects of climate change. Importantly, this blame holds even in the case of deception, so long as the deceived person has access to the evidence of the ecological impact of climate change and yet chooses to ignore this evidence (say, because they think they "know" that their chosen climate-denial information source is "right"). What this implies to the viewer of *Don't Look Up* is that part of "preventing the harmful effects of climate change" to the average, adult person is a moral obligation to be properly informed *about* climate change.

Given the role of deception in the film, this moral obligation to be informed also contains a responsibility for the average, adult person to inform themselves about the ways in which figures of wealth and authority manipulate the public about climate change. In this chapter, we largely take the stance that, like the evidence for the reality and impact of climate change, there is a preponderance of reliable evidence available about deceptive authority – including previous McKay films like *The Big Short* and *Vice* that are specifically intended to show viewers that ordinary people are being lied to by the powerful – and that *Don't Look Up*'s argument takes it for granted that viewers are already aware of this deception. Nonetheless, it should be acknowledged that *Don't Look Up* could also be reasonably interpreted as attempting to explicitly alert viewers to the untrustworthiness of economic and political authority (of which they were previously unaware). After all, those who deny climate change for ideological reasons may be so invested in their denial that, like members of a cult, they are unable to be aware of the fact that they are being deceived (see Johnson 2021). If this really is part of the film's purpose, then its moral command becomes even stronger because it actively informs viewers that they're being deceived – and so they have no excuse to deny the command or its premises. In such a case, the viewer would be *even more* morally culpable for their willful ignorance than if the film just assumed the awareness of deceptive authority as background information that the viewer already has coming into the film.

Yet – as we mentioned above – individual, normal people aren't the target of most of *Don't Look Up*'s caustic barbs. Though their ignorance isn't excused by the film – in fact, it's outright condemned in the case of what we describe as *willful* ignorance – ordinary folk are also clearly deceived by duplicitous authority. Even if at least some of the deceived willingly enable their own deception, the deceivers deserve the principal blame for authoring the deception in the first place. This was one of Plato's great concerns with blameworthy ignorance, too: He worried that those acting on their ignorance (particularly in positions of great power or influence) could cause this ignorance and immorality to multiply in others.

It's evident that people in positions of authority are the most morally culpable for their ignorance in *Don't Look Up*. Peter Isherwell acts as if he knows (even though he doesn't) that his BASH-funded team of corporate scientists can successfully scatter the pieces of the comet in a way that will render them harmless. President Orlean constantly acts on her ignorance of most things (it's basically her presidential *modus operandi*), including her initial dismissal of the threat of the comet. Her son, Jason, treats his inherited wealth and social standing as if they immunize him from any problematic effects of his immature behavior. In many ways, Randall is the worst offender. Beginning as a figure of legitimate scientific expertise, he succumbs to the appeal of celebrity and abandons both his family and most of his scientific scruples along the way.

Without being entirely exculpatory toward Randall and other *individuals* in positions of authority, the film seems to cast at least as much blame for his fall on a web of *institutions* that discourage actual scientific endeavor. Randall and Kate are admonished for claiming a 100% chance that the comet would strike Earth in their meeting with President Orlean – she demurs that a figure that high is too depressing for people to process, suggesting 70% instead – and both the President and Jason find their attempt to explain the details of the situation insufferably dull. For their first appearance on *The Daily Rip*, their segment is downplayed as an unthreatening comet discovery; Kate is then mocked off of the show for her honest report of the comet's danger while Brie says that they'd rather "keep the bad news light," with Jack adding that it "helps the medicine go down." In the same way, what should've been a jarring public revelation in the *New York Herald* about the comet's existence and a damning exposé on the Orlean administration's indifference gets buried beneath inane stories covering Riley Bina and DJ Chello's mercurial celebrity relationship. Randall only starts to get meaningful public recognition because of his good looks and social media presence, where he wrongly conflates engaging in flame wars against online trolls with "getting my voice out there" to raise awareness about the comet. Most tellingly, Randall is ironically never more scientifically ineffectual than when he becomes the Orlean cabinet's "Chief Science Advisor" – what amounts to a "yes-man" for the government's joint mining project with BASH. So, Randall *is* morally responsible for acting on his ignorance in apparently thinking that it would be better for the comet crisis to become a scientific celebrity. Still, Randall's society is also blameworthy in the way it seems to reward ignorance over genuine scientific knowledge.

This propensity to favor ignorance is at its worst when blameworthy ignorance hides behind the pretense of science. Science is supposed to be a source of knowledge. As Teddy advises Randall in the film: "Science tells the truth." However, Isherwell, President Orlean, and even Randall end up distorting science to promote agendas well beyond truth-seeking. Despite the fact that he bristles at Randall's accusation that he is just a businessman, Isherwell's method of conducting science is entirely business-minded. Everything from the *Liif* app to the BEADs intended to disperse the comet are designed to generate income. (This is why the whole BASH comet operation and Isherwell's later exodus to a habitable "Goldilocks" planet have such a high tolerance for the loss of key equipment like rockets, drones, and stasis pods. It's simply more profitable to produce cheap technology and build-in an anticipated failure rate.) Likewise, President Orlean's use of NASA head Dr. Jocelyn Calder – who, again, is just a former anesthesiologist campaign donor who Orlean appointed – to undermine initial findings about the comet is blatant political maneuvering masquerading as science. And Randall's numerous appearances on talk shows, advertisements, and chatting with puppets on a *Sesame Street*-like children's program serve chiefly to further the BASH/Orlean project and curate a very specific public image.

Taken together, each of these scenarios represents a watering down of science that turns it into a "pop" discipline, maintaining the illusion of expertise without the rigor necessary for real scientific knowledge. None of the above characters – even Randall, when he is speaking on behalf of the BASH/Orlean project – really has scientific knowledge. Yet, all of them act as if they do by claiming "science" for economic, political, and social purposes. Such individuals and the powerful institutions they lead are depicted as supremely morally guilty in *Don't Look Up*, specifically for their blameworthy ignorance. Not only do they ignore or outright deny the obligation that the film's moral imperative rationally commands, they also influence others to do the same.

"It's for Everyone. It's a Popcorn Movie"

Alongside what has been called a heavy-handed message, one of the major criticisms of *Don't Look Up* has been its pessimism – the complete destruction of the planet and death of everyone on Earth except the obnoxious, simpering Jason Orlean is a real bummer of an ending. Once we acknowledge McKay's moral imperative, though, it's easy to see that these "shortcomings" are necessary for delivering the film's philosophical point. The grimness of the film's conclusion stems less from viewers' investment in the characters and more from the fact that viewers feel an accusatory finger pointed their way. Since the comet-as-climate-change allegory is so transparent, viewers feel both the inevitability of catastrophic consequences for failing to address climate change in our own world and complicity in the planetary disaster that is sure to also follow without timely intervention.

A less "on the nose" execution of the film's premise or a more hopeful ending – where governmental ignorance and corporate greed are overcome by the sudden unity of the world's nations and the comet is shattered at *just the last moment* – would end up excusing the viewer of their obligation to the moral imperative upon leaving the theater. It's like an exasperated Kate yells on *The Daily Rip*: "Maybe the destruction of the entire planet isn't supposed to be fun. Maybe it's supposed to be terrifying. And unsettling!" For the moral imperative to be a genuine command, it must be clearly understood; there can be no confusion about what *Don't Look Up* is really about or what it demands of the viewer. Hence, it must be overt in its messaging, and it mustn't pull any punches in what the consequences will be.

Movies – even the best or most artistically affecting of them – are felt (aesthetically) or provide food for thought, but they don't usually ask the viewer to change their behavior. In the end, this allows for separation between the "art" and the viewer of art. The viewer, seated in the cinema (or living room) with a bowl of popcorn, is in a different world than the fiction occurring onscreen. Because such movies don't directly tell the viewer what to do after leaving the theater, "the snacks are free."

Don't Look Up doesn't allow for this separation. Just reading the film's title is to read a command to act in a certain way, though it's an inversion of what the film actually asks the viewer to do. Like General Themes's snacks in the White House, the act of watching the movie is most certainly not free: something to be watched and walked away from, perhaps talked about over a few beers among friends, but ultimately set aside as one returns to the world. No, if you understand its message about climate change, then you are *obligated* to do something about it – and you can't reject the message's premises without being utterly irrational or willfully ignorant. Furthermore, you *should* understand its message. Like Devin Peters says while promoting "Total Devastation," "It's for everyone. It's a popcorn movie." Whether or not *Don't Look Up* is truly also a popcorn movie, it's decidedly a mainstream film meant to reach the widest possible audience of ordinary folks. The film wields its minatory message about the existential threat of climate change with a sledgehammer, not a scalpel, and it does so because that's the best way to straightforwardly expose the most people to its argument.

As Ezra Brain, from *Left Voice*, suggests:

> To put it bluntly: we are living through a devastating and unprecedented environmental crisis. ... These are not subtle times. Increasingly, I worry that we have fallen into a petty bourgeois model of artistic criticism, according to which loudly talking about problems is somehow less profound than talking about them quietly. ... The problems facing us aren't subtle. Capitalist exploitation and environmental crises aren't subtle. So why should our art be? Perhaps selfishly, perhaps as a reaction to the times we're living in, I yearn for the death of subtlety in art. I yearn for art — but specifically political art — that will just show up and start talking about the problems. (Brain 2021)

It seems that McKay feels the same way. This is why *Don't Look Up* gives us a command that *all* competent viewers are obligated to follow or else face deserved moral censure; it would be both unreasonable and immoral to impose an imperative on all competent people without ensuring easy, direct access to it. Crucially, remember that the proportion of your obligation increases exponentially with the political and social power you possess, since those in higher sociopolitical strata have a greater means of effecting change and influencing others. Here, "the snacks aren't free" comes to symbolize how information about climate change *ought* to be freely understood by all. And yet, this sort of information clearly *isn't* freely understood, mostly because of decades of nefarious politicization of bald scientific fact by those in power.

The upshot is that, like the snacks, the pleasures of living in contemporary Western societies aren't free, either. Technology, consumer excess, and luxury have consequences that are being realized, rapidly and horribly, in the environment. As we've argued, individual action is ineffectual – our fuel-efficient cars and plans to eat less meat won't be enough to thwart climate change. Worldwide government action and cooperation is the only thing that will be. So perhaps the litmus test for politicians you support should be that climate change is their primary concern. (After all, if we elected all and only politicians that made climate change their first priority, government action and cooperation on climate change would happen.) The film says, plainly, that if you don't look up, acknowledge the threat of climate change, and start trying to prevent it at the level of government intervention, then you're an awful person or at least inexcusably ignorant (which may be the same thing). Worse: if you abuse your power, wealth, and social clout to convince others that *they* shouldn't look up, then you deserve to be eaten by a bronteroc.

Conclusion

While it is certainly true that critiquing movies is what film critics do, when it comes to films like *Don't Look Up*, it might be best to give the nitpicking a rest. Even if you can't bring yourself to say that it is a good film, you should be encouraging people to watch it anyway. Unlike Amy Meek, at MSN, who said "It's so bad, watch something else," perhaps critical critics should be saying that, despite the fact that it isn't funny, it is a must watch. Like the comet itself, it's both "horrific and beautiful." Instead of just observing that *Don't Look Up* would be easier to watch as a popcorn film, point out that maybe it shouldn't be because the message of a popcorn film would be forgotten in a week. Again, as Kate puts it in her first TV appearance, "maybe the destruction of the entire planet isn't supposed to be fun." Directors making movies about the threat of climate change are not under an obligation to make audiences think that *everything is going to be alright* – because if we don't take major action very soon, it's not going to be.

Addendum

Shortly after the initial online publication of this chapter, the U.S. Department of Energy announced that they had achieved the ignition of a fusion reaction with an energy output greater than that which took to produce it (Department of Energy 2022). This sparked a wave of speculation about future clean fusion energy and created, in many people, a sense of relief. "There is no need to try to reduce my carbon footprint; fusion energy will do it for me." One author of this chapter even briefly reconsidered putting up solar panels on his house. "Will they be paid off before a fusion plant is providing carbon-free electricity to my city?" If fusion will solve the climate crisis, all the worry expressed in this chapter seems like an overreaction. Unfortunately, it's not because it won't (i.e., the worry is not an overreaction because fusion won't solve the climate crisis). To be clear, we would love nothing more than for fusion reactors to quickly become ubiquitous, produce green energy for the entire world, and make things like solar panels useless. But there are three reasons to think that they won't; in fact, the Department of Energy's announcement may have made the climate crisis worse.

First, as Ben Adler (2022) points out, the reaction produced more energy than it required only if you crunch the numbers a certain way. Yes, a total of only 2.05 megajoules of laser energy hit the target hydrogen plasma, while 3.15 came back out – but it took 300 megajoules to power the lasers in the first place. What's more, to create electricity, fusion plants would have to use that energy to create steam and turn turbines – and that process is only 40% efficient. So, for fusion to work, it's going to have to produce *a lot* more energy than it takes to make it – and it's not clear that it could.

Second, even if those technological hurdles can be overcome, it's not clear that we would actually follow through and build fusion energy plants. The public is just as likely to misunderstand the science behind fusion, develop conspiracy theories about it, and then kibosh the whole thing. Sound ridiculous? Nuclear power is a green energy source that could, right now, supply all our energy needs (Biello 2015); and yet misunderstandings and conspiracy theories about nuclear power have prevented its widespread use. In fact, in some places, it's even being rolled back. Germany, for example, actually went to the trouble of shutting down existing nuclear plants (at great expense) because of misinformation about them being dangerous (Appunn 2021); and then, when it found that the solar and wind plants it tried to shift the burden to were inadequate, it had to fire up a bunch of coal plants to meet its energy needs (Clifford 2022). To be sure, nuclear power is not perfect – but neither is solar and wind. (For example, when you factor in everything it takes to build a solar or wind plant – like the mining and transportation of the rare minerals they require – their carbon emissions can *sometimes* be worse than fossil fuel plants; see Torres and Petrakopoulou 2022.) Of course, there is a carbon cost to building and maintaining nuclear power plants too. But nuclear power is not the bogeyman it's made out to be on *The Simpsons*. New advances have made modern nuclear plants physically unable to melt down (WNA 2021; Oberhaus 2020) and even able to use the waste of old-style reactors as fuel, thus removing it as an environmental hazard (see Daniel 2012). In short, nuclear power is both safe and necessary to save the planet from climate change (Poneman 2019); yet even those who say they care about the planet the most fight its use every step of the way. Why would it be any different with fusion? After all, wouldn't the fossil fuel industry be just as motivated to deny the science of fusion as it was with climate change?

Third, even if we can get past the misinformation and conspiracy theories, functioning fusion plants are still decades away – 2050 at best (Knapton 2022), and even that might be an overestimate (Novella 2022). We need to see drastic reductions in greenhouse gasses long before that if we are going to avoid the worst consequences of climate change. Keeping warming below 1.5 degrees (Celsius) by 2100 is probably already a lost cause; but if we throw caution to the wind because we expect fusion to be our green energy savior, by 2050 we will likely have already released enough C02 to ensure 3 degrees of warming by 2100. By then, even if we eliminate our carbon footprint completely in 2050, it won't matter. As Edwin Lyman of the Union of Concerned Scientists put it,

> Given the massive technological challenges that would be required to actually utilize this technology in a reliable and affordable way of generating electricity for the grid, I think [this fusion breakthrough] has little to no relevance to the climate crisis. The climate crisis has to be addressed imminently — really, within the next 10 to 15 years — and a technology that's still going to take many decades of development is not going to play a role in that initial transition. (Adler 2022)

And that is how the Department of Energy's fusion announcement could make matters worse: by making us complacent. If we collectively decide to not "put up our solar panels" (i.e., to do what we need to do now to stop producing CO2) because we think fusion is a magic bullet that will save us all ... well, then, fusion essentially becomes Peter Isherwell's BEAD drones. It's a pipe dream solution that would never have worked in the first place, but it causes us to call back the one and only mission that could have actually saved the planet. To be sure, we will eventually get to zero carbon emissions. But it won't do us much good if the way we accomplish that goal is by going extinct.

References

Adger, W. Neil, and Jon Barnett. 2009. Four reasons for concern about adaptation to climate change. *Environment and Planning A: Economy and Space* 41 (12): 2800–2805. https://doi.org/10.1068/a42244.

Adler, Ben. 2022. "Why the nuclear fusion breakthrough won't prevent catastrophic climate change." *Yahoo News*. Dec. 14. https://news.yahoo.com/why-the-nuclear-fusion-breakthrough-wont-prevent-catastrophic-climate-change-202616499.html

Appunn, Kerstine. 2021. "The History Behind Germany's Nuclear Phase-out." *Clean Energy Wire*. Mar. 9. https://www.cleanenergywire.org/factsheets/history-behind-germanys-nuclear-phase-out

Aronoff, Kate. 2021. Adam McKay is tired of our climate-politics garbage fire. *The New Republic*, December 31. https://newrepublic.com/article/164691/adam-mckay-climate-politics-dont-look-up?fbclid=IwAR0mDT5WUtYjrX976I8OLrrljEobIaAqbIwyJRpfVyWCXBN0_FJAN3XfTH8

Berners-Lee, Mike. 2022. *The carbon footprint of everything*. London: Greystone Books.

Besanvalle, James. 2022. All the times Trump was completely inappropriate with his daughter Ivanka. *Indy100*, June 13. https://www.indy100.com/celebrities/donald-trump-ivanka-daughter-inappropriate

Biello, David. 2015. "The World Really Could Go Nuclear." *Scientific American*, Sept. 14. https://www.scientificamerican.com/article/the-world-really-could-go-nuclear/

Bittle, Jake. 2021. I told you so. *The Baffler*, December 23. https://thebaffler.com/latest/i-told-you-so-bittle

———. 2022. The inflation reduction act promises thousands of new oil leases. Drillers might not want them. *Grist*, August 9. https://grist.org/energy/inflation-reduction-act-oil-gas-leases-federal-land/

Brain, Ezra. 2021. Against subtlety: 'Don't Look Up' is the movie for our moment. *Left Voice*, December 30. https://www.leftvoice.org/against-subtlety-dont-look-up-is-the-movie-for-our-moment/

Brain, Marshall, and Sarah Glem. 2022. What if an Asteroid hit earth? *How Stuff Works*, Janurary 7. https://science.howstuffworks.com/nature/natural-disasters/asteroid-hits-earth.htm#:~:text=But%2C%20scientists%20believe%20some%20would,wipe%20out%20life%20on%20Earth

Bronsdon, Conor. 2021. Electric cars won't solve climate change. *Planetizen*, March 9. https://www.planetizen.com/blogs/112490-electric-cars-wont-solve-climate-change

Brown, Patrick T., and Ken Caldeira. 2017. Greater future global warming inferred from Earth's recent energy budget. *Nature* 552: 45–50. https://doi.org/10.1038/nature24672.

Calderón, Felipe, and Nicholas Stern. 2015. Calderon and Stern: Fight climate change, boost economy. *USA Today*, July 6. https://www.usatoday.com/story/opinion/2015/07/06/climate-change-action-poverty-economy-column/29777415/

Callicott, J. Baird. 2009. From the land ethic to the earth ethic: Aldo Leopold and the Gaia hypothesis. In *Gaia in turmoil, climate change, biodepletion, and earth ethics in an age of crisis*, ed. Eileen Crist, Bruce Rinker, and Bill McKibben, 177–194. Cambridge, MA: The MIT Press.

Clifford, Catherine. 2022. "Germany to keep two nuclear plants available as a backup and burn coal as it faces an energy crisis brought on by war and climate change." *CNBC*. Sept. 6, https://www.cnbc.com/2022/09/06/germany-to-keep-two-nuclear-plants-available-as-a-backup-burn-coal-.html

Collomb, Jean Daniel. 2014. The ideology of climate change denial in the United States. *European Journal of American Studies* 9 (1). https://doi.org/10.4000/ejas.10305.

Cook, John, Naomi Oreskes, Peter T. Doran, William R.L. Anderegg, Bart Verheggen, Ed W. Maibach, J. Stuart Carlton, et al. 2016. Consensus on consensus: A synthesis of consensus estimates on human-caused global warming. *Environmental Research Letters* 11 (4). https://doi.org/10.1088/1748-9326/11/4/048002.

Cunningham, Kyndall. 2021. Why are liberal 'Don't Look Up' superfans attacking film critics? *The Daily Beast*, December 30. https://www.thedailybeast.com/why-are-liberal-dont-look-up-stans-attacking-film-critics

Daniel. 2012. "Breed and burn reactors – could recycling waste redeem nuclear power?" *Power Technology*. May 23. https://www.power-technology.com/features/featurenuclear-waste-disposal-reactor-technology-recycle-clean-energy/

Department of Energy. 2022. "DOE National Laboratory Makes History by Achieving Fusion Ignition." Dec 13. https://www.energy.gov/articles/doe-national-laboratory-makes-history-achieving-fusion-ignition

Durkee, Alison. 2022. Jan. 6 hearings: Newsmax's coverage has made dozens of false claims, report finds – Including election fraud. *Forbes*, July 18. https://www.forbes.com/sites/alisondurkee/2022/07/18/jan-6-hearings-newsmaxs-coverage-has-made-dozens-of-false-claims-report-finds-including-election-fraud/?sh=5e74f8485af5

Elliott, Josh. 2020. Many COVID-19 patients insist 'it's not real' until they die, nurse says. *Global News*, November 17. https://globalnews.ca/news/7467283/coronavirus-denier-deaths-nurse-hoax/

Engels, Kimberly S. 2014. Bad faith, authenticity, and responsibilities to future generations: A Sartrean approach. *Environmental Ethics* 36 (4): 455–470.

Foley, Katherine Ellen. 2017. Those 3% of scientific papers that deny climate change? A review found them all flawed. *Quartz*, September 5. https://qz.com/1069298/the-3-of-scientific-papers-that-deny-climate-change-are-all-flawed

Folkenflik, David. 2022. Only one major cable news channel did not carry the Jan. 6 hearing live: Fox News. *NPR*, June 11. https://www.npr.org/2022/06/10/1104116455/fox-news-jan-6-hearing

Gilens, Martin, and Benjamin Page. 2014. Testing theories of American politics: Elites, interest groups, and average citizens. *Perspectives on Politics (Cambridge University Press)* 12 (3): 564–581. https://doi.org/10.1017/S1537592714001595.

Goldberg, Jonah. 2022. As far as political satire goes, 'Don't Look Up' fails in more ways than one. *Los Angeles Times*, Janurary 4. https://www.latimes.com/opinion/story/2022-01-04/dont-look-up-movie-climate-change-satire?fbclid=IwAR3xhZ8tqCCxh_sEApJ0BIRAJ9qkXuApFpTKMg6WnaUc8z2gmczDWPFcCYc

Goldstein, Joshua. 2019. Individual actions can't solve climate change. *Aspen Institute*, June 6. https://www.aspeninstitute.org/blog-posts/individual-actions-cant-solve-climate-change/

Goodwin, Philip. 2018. On the time evolution of climate sensitivity and future warming. *Earth's Future*: 1336–1348. https://doi.org/10.1029/2018EF000889.

Griffin, Paul. 2017. *CDP carbon majors report 2017*. Climate Accountability Institute: The carbon majors database. https://www.cdp.net/en/reports/downloads/2327

Gugliersi, Antonella. 2022. What real scientists have said about Don't Look Up (& Why they love it). *Screenrant*, Janurary 6. https://screenrant.com/dont-look-up-real-scientists-reactions-responses/?utm_source=SR-FB-P&utm_medium=Social-Distribution&utm_campaign=SR-FB-P&fbclid=IwAR31f5u9xZXSfNaxTPfu6nQQFhfDaNvgnTdm5uUeTTwfJ0pOjYgHV2qAkjw

Heath, David. 2016. Contesting the science of smoking. *The Atlantic*, May 4. https://www.theatlantic.com/politics/archive/2016/05/low-tar-cigarettes/481116/

Indigo, Xan. 2022. Don't look up: Why is nobody listening? *Screen Rant*, January 5. https://screenrant.com/dont-look-up-nobody-listening-disaster-ignore-reason/?utm_source=SR-FB-P&utm_medium=Social-Distribution&utm_campaign=SR-FB-P&fbclid=IwAR0CVTimJjYONq5cIqDay7oYirvRSvVFlmzLE67EcKyK7qiFP1nTxH3f9js

Jaeger, Joel, and Devashree Saha. 2019. 12 reasons climate action is good for the United States economy. *World Resources Institute*, November 25. https://www.wri.org/insights/12-reasons-climate-action-good-united-states-economy

Johnson, David Kyle. 2021. 'If the stars should appear' and climate change denial. In *Exploring the Orville: Essays on Seth MacFarlane's space adventure*, ed. David Kyle Johnson and Michael Berry. Jefferson: NC, McFarland and Company, Inc. Publishers.

Kant, Immanuel. 1998. *Groundwork of the metaphysics of morals*. Trans. Mary Gregor. Cambridge: Cambridge University Press.

Knapton, Sarah. 2022. "Power plant based on US nuclear fusion breakthrough 'still several decades away'." *The Telegraph*. Dec. 13. https://www.telegraph.co.uk/news/2022/12/13/nuclear-fusion-breakthrough-us-power-plant-decades-away-british/

Lee, Emma. 2022. 'Don't Look Up': Why the climate crisis isn't a comet, and why that matters. *Left Voice*, Janurary 1. https://www.leftvoice.org/dont-look-up-why-the-climate-crisis-isnt-a-comet-and-why-it-matters/

Lim, Jappy. 2015. Armageddon: How large must an asteroid be to exterminate all life on earth? *Futurism*, December 25. https://futurism.com/19943

Lynas, Mark. 2007. *Six degrees: Our future on a hotter planet*. London: Fourth Estate.

MacDonald, Ted. 2020. How broadcast TV networks covered climate change in 2019. *Media Matters*, Feburary 27. https://www.mediamatters.org/broadcast-networks/how-broadcast-tv-networks-covered-climate-change-2019

Mann, Michael E. 2021. Global destruction isn't funny, but when it comes to the climate crisis, it might have to be. *Boston Globe*, December 21. https://www.bostonglobe.com/2021/12/21/opinion/global-destruction-isnt-funny-when-it-comes-climate-crisis-it-might-have-be/

Mazza, Ed. 2022. Clueless UK news anchor goes full 'Don't Look Up' in Bizarre heat wave segment. *Huffingston Post*, July 20. https://www.huffpost.com/entry/bev-turner-heat-wave_n_62d799fbe4b0a6852c312720

MIT Energy Initiative. 2018. *The future of nuclear energy in a carbon-constrained world*. Massachusetts Institute of Technology. https://energy.mit.edu/wp-content/uploads/2018/09/The-Future-of-Nuclear-Energy-in-a-Carbon-Constrained-World.pdf

Novella, Steven. 2022. Fusion Breakthrough- Ignition. *Neurologica Blog*. Dec. 12. https://theness.com/neurologicablog/index.php/fusion-breakthrough-ignition

O'Flaherty, Kate. 2021. All the ways Facebook tracks you and how to stop it. *Forbes*, May 8. https://www.forbes.com/sites/kateoflahertyuk/2021/05/08/all-the-ways-facebook-tracks-you-and-how-to-stop-it/?sh=1d03a1155583

Oberhaus, Daniel. 2020. "Nuclear "Power Balls" May Make Meltdowns a Thing of the Past." *Mother Jones*. https://www.motherjones.com/environment/2020/07/nuclear-power-balls-may-make-meltdowns-a-thing-of-the-past/

Oppenheimer, Rebecca. 2021. Hollywood can take on science denial: Don't Look Up is a great example. *Scientific American*, December 30. https://www.scientificamerican.com/article/hollywood-can-take-on-science-denial-dont-look-up-is-a-great-example/#:~:text=Global%20warming%20does%20not%20provide,in%20temperature%20and%20atmospheric%20chemistry

Oreskes, Naomi. 2014. The scientific consensus on climate change: How do we know We're not wrong? In *Climate change: What it means for you, your children, and your grandchildren*, ed. Joseph F.C. DiMento and Pamela Doughman, 2nd ed., 105–148. Cambridge, MA: MIT Press.

Oreskes, Naomi, and Erik M. Conway. 2010. *Merchants of doubt: How a handful of scientists obscured the truth on issues from tobacco smoke to global warming*. London: Bloomsbury.

Oreskes, Naomi, Michael Oppenheimer, and Dale Jamieson. 2019. Scientists have been underestimating the pace of climate change. *Scientific American*, August 19. https://blogs.scientificamerican.com/observations/scientists-have-been-underestimating-the-pace-of-climate-change/

Pfeiffer, Sacha. 2021. Adam McKay talks new doomsday satire movie, 'Don't Look Up'. *NPR*, December 18. https://www.npr.org/2021/12/18/1065547285/adam-mckay-talks-new-doomsday-satire-movie-dont-look-up

Plato. 1997. Parmenides. In *The dialogues of Plato*. Trans. R.E. Allen. New Haven: Yale University Press.

———. 1992. *Republic*. Trans. G.M.A. Grube. Indianapolis: Hackett Publishing Company.

———. 2002. *Five dialogues*. Trans. G.M.A. Grube. Indianapolis: Hackett Publishing Company.

Poneman, Daniel. 2019. "We can't solve climate change without nuclear power." *Scientific American*. May 24. https://blogs.scientificamerican.com/observations/we-cant-solve-climate-change-without-nuclear-power/

Postman, Neil. 2005. *Amusing ourselves to death: Public discourse in the age of show business*. New York City: Penguin.

Reilly, John. 2014. Why we can't just adapt to climate change. *MIT Technology Review*, April 3. https://www.technologyreview.com/2014/04/03/251074/why-we-cant-just-adapt-to-climate-change/

Robinson, Nathan. 2021. Critics of "Don't Look Up" are missing the entire point. *Current Affairs*, December 26. https://www.currentaffairs.org/2021/12/critics-of-dont-look-up-are-missing-the-entire-point?fbclid=IwAR1QuOLOmnwhO92Ks7oQdjVeuhEgqyfDJGu7LJ6mpBVS6FNgLrtn2Izywag

Rojas, Diego. 2019. The climate Denial MACHINE: How the fossil fuel industry blocks climate action. *The Climate Reality Project*, September 5. https://www.climaterealityproject.org/blog/climate-denial-machine-how-fossil-fuel-industry-blocks-climate-action

Schube, Sam. 2021. Adam McKay has become the grown-up in the room. He's as surprised as you are. GQ. Dec. 7. https://www.gq.com/story/adam-mckay-dont-look-up-interview

Schwitzgebel, Eric. 2019. *A theory of jerks and other philosophical misadventures*. Cambridge, MA: MIT Press.

Show Me the Meaning. 2022. Don't look up. Janurary 14. https://podcasts.apple.com/us/podcast/show-me-the-meaning-a-wisecrack-movie-podcast/id1319437966

Singer, Peter. 1972. Famine, affluence, and morality. *Philosophy & Public Affairs* 1 (3): 229–243.

Stern, Nicholas. 2021. COP26: The economic case for tackling climate change is stronger than ever but flawed thinking is leading some countries astray – Professor Lord Nicholas Stern. *The Scotsman*, October 28. https://www.scotsman.com/news/opinion/columnists/cop26-the-economic-case-for-tackling-climate-change-is-stronger-than-ever-but-flawed-thinking-is-leading-some-countries-astray-professor-lord-nicholas-stern-3433721

Sunstein, Cass R., and Adrian Vermeule. 2009. Conspiracy theories: Causes and cures. *Journal of Political Philosophy* 17 (2): 202–227.

Supran, Geoffrey, and Naomi Oreskes. 2021. The forgotten oil ads that told us climate change was nothing. *The Guardian*, November 18. https://www.theguardian.com/environment/2021/nov/18/the-forgotten-oil-ads-that-told-us-climate-change-was-nothing?utm_source=digg

Taft, Molly. 2019. Why TV is so bad at covering climate change. *Gizmodo*, July 14. https://gizmodo.com/why-tv-is-so-bad-at-covering-climate-change-1847283248

Techera, Titus. 2022. Don't Look Up looks down on you. *Action Institute Powerblog (Blog)*, Janurary 19. https://blog.acton.org/archives/122914-dont-look-up-looks-down-on-you.html

Torres, Fernandez, and Fontina Petrakopoulou. 2022. A closer look at the environmental impact of solar and wind energy. *Global Challenges* 6 (8). https://doi.org/10.1002/gch2.202200016.

van Vlieta, Oscar, Anne Sjoerd Brouwer, Takeshi Kuramochi, Machteld van den Broek, and André Faaij. 2011. Energy use, cost and CO2 emissions of electric cars. *Journal of Power Sources* 196 (4): 2298–2310. https://www.sciencedirect.com/science/article/abs/pii/S037877531001726X.

Vetter, David. 2021. Why sneering critics dislike Netflix's 'Don't Look Up,' but climate scientists love it. *Forbes*, December 28. https://www.forbes.com/sites/davidrvetter/2021/12/28/why-sneering-critics-dislike-netflixs-dont-look-up-but-climate-scientists-love-it/?

sh=28ab78be2ee8&fbclid=IwAR3xhZ8tqCCxh_sEApJ0BIRAJ9qkXuApFpTKMg6WnaUc8z2gmczDWPFcCYc

Weismann, Jordan. 2022. Why internet leftists are so pissed about democrats' historic climate bill. Slate.com. August 9. https://slate.com/business/2022/08/inflation-reduction-act-climate-change-criticism-adam-mckay-david-sirota.html

Westervelt, Amy. 2016a. The bell labs of energy. *Drilled (Podcast)*. August. https://www.drilledpodcast.com/s1-the-origins-of-climate-denial/

———. 2016b. The turn. *Drilled (Podcast)*. September. https://www.drilledpodcast.com/s1-the-origins-of-climate-denial/

WNA (World Nuclear Association). 2021. "Advanced Nuclear Power Reactors." April. https://world-nuclear.org/information-library/nuclear-fuel-cycle/nuclear-power-reactors/advanced-nuclear-power-reactors.aspx

Wolfe, Daniel, and Daniel Dale. 2020. 'It's going to disappear': A timeline of Trump's claims that Covid-19 will vanish. *CNN*, October 31. https://www.cnn.com/interactive/2020/10/politics/covid-disappearing-trump-comment-tracker/

Zeeshan Aleem. 2021. Netflix's 'Don't Look Up' misjudges the effort to tackle climate change. *MSNBC*, December 28. https://www.msnbc.com/opinion/what-movie-don-t-look-gets-wrong-about-tackling-climate-n1286717

Little Women as Philosophy: Death or Marriage and the Meaning of Life

60

Kimberly Blessing

Contents

Introduction	1412
Summary of *Little Women*	1414
Alcott's *Little Women*	1414
Gerwig's *Little Women*	1415
Satisfying Ending	1415
Art and Money	1416
Economics of Marriage	1417
Alcott	1418
What Does It All Mean?	1419
What Meaning Means	1419
Susan Wolf's Fitting Fulfillment Theory	1421
Subjective Meaning	1421
Lack of Meaning	1422
Fulfilled But Unhappy	1422
Objective Meaning	1423
Unfulfilled and Unfit Little Women	1424
Marmee	1424
Jo March	1425
Amy March	1425
Postmortem Assessments	1427
Imposters	1428
Asymmetry	1428
Indicative Meaning	1429
Women of Worth	1430
Leaning In	1431
Conclusion	1432
References	1433

K. Blessing (✉)
Philosophy, SUNY Buffalo State, Buffalo, NY, USA
e-mail: blessika@buffalostate.edu

© Springer Nature Switzerland AG 2024
D. K. Johnson et al. (eds.), *The Palgrave Handbook of Popular Culture as Philosophy*,
https://doi.org/10.1007/978-3-031-24685-2_115

Abstract

In 2019, Greta Gerwig adapted Louisa May Alcott's classic novel, *Little Women*, for the silver screen. It's "the beloved story of the March sisters – four young women, each determined to live life on their own terms." In *Meaning in Life and Why It Matters* (2010), Susan Wolf argues that life is meaningful if feelings of fulfillment and joy (subjective meaning) are married with finding one's passions (objective meaning). Or meaning in life arises when "subjective attraction meets objective attractiveness, and one is able to do something about it or with it" (p. 26). As the March girls struggle to become their own women, the duty to secure financial security through marriage forces each sister to compromise or give up her youthful dreams and artistic ambitions. Thus they do not experience the feelings of fulfillment and satisfaction that come from indulging in one's passions. In fact, like March sisters, most women throughout history are ill-fitted to Wolf's fitting fulfillment theory of meaning. Through the story it tells, *Little Women* supports the view that feelings of fulfillment may be indicative of, but not necessary for, meaning in life. Instead, we should lean into the objective side of Wolf's theory and evaluate meaning in terms of whether the life in question can be "appropriately appreciated, admired, or valued by others, *at least in principle*" (ibid., p. 32, emphasis added). A purely objective theory could accommodate many, if not all, women of worth who were not afforded the luxury of finding fulfillment or happiness in their lives.

Keywords

Happiness · Fulfillment · Meaning in/of life · Subjective vs. objective theories of life's meaning · Fitting fulfillment · Susan Wolf · Enlightened or rational egoism · Existentialism · Simone de Beauvoir · Imposter Syndrome

Introduction

> Women have minds and souls as well as hearts, ambition, and talent as well as beauty, and I'm sick of being told that love is all a woman is fit for. But... I am so lonely. . . . If I were a girl in a book, this would all be so easy; I'd give up the world happily. . . . No one will forget Jo March
> —Jo March

On Christmas 2019 BC, "Before Covid," women and girls were gifted a lovely present: a modern retelling of a childhood classic, *Little Women* by Louisa May Alcott. The bow on top: Greta Gerwig, one of Hollywood's most talented female directors, wrote and directed the feature film. Coming off the success of her Oscar-nominated *Lady Bird,* which won the 2017 Golden Globe for Best Motion Picture, Gerwig (who double majored in philosophy and English) reunites with the talented Saoirse Ronan, who portrayed Jo March (Gerwig is only the fifth woman ever nominated for an Oscar for Best Director of *Ladybird*). Gerwig tells, or retells, "the beloved story of the March sisters – four young women, each determined to live life on their own terms" (Sony Pictures blurb). Gerwig's *Little Women* was nominated for six Academy Awards, including best picture and adapted screenplay, and won for best costume design. It is only the third film in history to be nominated for best picture, which was directed, written, and produced by women (the other two are 2010's *Winter's Bone* and 1993's *The Piano*).

There have been a variety of iterations of *Little Women*, including two silent films, radio versions, plays, an opera, a 1933 film starring Katharine Hepburn as Jo, and a Technicolor version with Elizabeth Taylor as Amy that proclaimed on its movie poster: "World's greatest love story!" In 1970 – amid the second-wave women's movement – the BBC produced the first feminist adaptation. Junior executive Amy Pascal, who went on to produce Gerwig's 2019 *Little Women*, tried for over a decade to get her 1994 film version of the story made. Although Winona Ryder would go on to win an Oscar for playing Jo in 1994, Pascal was told by one of the Sony executives that he "read it holding his nose" (Bennett 2020).

Little Women has always been a story for, well, women. It has inspired a generation of women writers, including J. K. Rowling, Margaret Atwood, Patti Smith, Gertrude Stein, Hilary Clinton, Susan Sontag, the Ephron sisters, and Gloria Steinem. In Elena Ferrante's *My Brilliant Friend*, the two child heroines have a shared copy of *Little Women* that finally crumbles from overuse (Acocella 2018). Simone de Beauvoir used to make up *Little Women* games to play with her sister. In *Memoires of a Dutiful Daughter*, she writes that she identified "passionately with Jo, the intellectual; brusque and bony... I shared in her love of books" (2005, p. 90). Finally, Pulitzer Prize-winner Anna Quindlen declares: "*Little Women* changed my life. Jo is defined not by how she looks or who she dances with, but by what she does. She is a writer, and for generations of girls who hoped someday to do the same, Jo March . . . spoke of possibilities outside the circuit of feminine wiles and fashion consciousness" (Lippmann 1994).

The never-married Alcott broke ground, writing a proto-feminist coming-of-age tale about women in 1868. *Little Women,* which centered around themes of family, marriage, duty, self-sacrifice, and service to others, sought to normalize female ambition. Illustrating De Beauvoir's claim that "one is not born, but becomes a woman," each of the four March sisters follows a different path on her journey to womanhood (2005).

Alcott's beloved classic clearly raises questions about the meaning of life. To address these questions, I shall focus attention on philosopher Susan Wolf's well-received theory of life's meaning, which marries feelings of fulfillment and joy with one's ability to follow one's passions. Wolf argues that life is meaningful if feelings of fulfillment and joy (subjective meaning) are married with finding one's passions (objective meaning). Or meaning in life arises when "subjective attraction meets objective attractiveness, and one is able to do something about it or with it" (2010, p. 26).

When we look to *Little Women*, we see the extent to which the March sisters struggle to follow their passions and fall short of living "life on their own terms." Their sense of duty to marry so that they can provide financial security for their family and their commitment to serving those in need force each sister to compromise or give up altogether youthful dreams and aspirations. They do not experience fulfillment and satisfaction that comes when one follows one's passions. Thus, they fail to meet Wolf's criteria for a meaningful life. In fact, most women throughout history are, like the March sisters, ill-fitted to Wolf's hybrid fitting fulfillment theory of meaning.

Little Women illustrates and supports the view that, while feelings of fulfillment may be indicative of meaning in life, they are not necessary for it as Wolf argues. Instead, we should lean into the objective side of Wolf's theory and evaluate meaning in terms of whether the life in question can be "appropriately appreciated, admired, or valued by others, *at least in principle*" (ibid., p. 32, emphasis added). A purely objective theory of meaning, as opposed to Wolf's hybrid theory of meaning, could accommodate many, if not all, women of worth, like those we find in *Little Women* – women who were not afforded the luxury of finding fulfillment or happiness in their lives. If true, far more women can find meaning in life than Wolf's theory would suggest. To see why, we can explore both the argument that *Little Women* puts forth, and the philosophy of Susan Wolf.

Summary of *Little Women*

Alcott's *Little Women*

The original *Little Women,* written in 10 weeks in 1868, was loosely inspired by Alcott's own life. Louisa May Alcott (1832–1888) was raised in a progressive family of Transcendentalists. Her largely absent father rubbed elbows with Henry David Thoreau, Ralph Waldo Emerson, and Nathanial Hawthorn. As with Alcott's own family, there are four sisters. While Alcott knew real poverty, the fictional March family lives in genteel poverty during the Civil War in Concord, Massachusetts (Alcott's resting place). Mr. March, like Alcott's father, is mostly absent. The fictional patriarch serves as a chaplain in the Union Army, whereas Mr. Alcott had trouble holding a job.

The eldest March girl is the beautiful and nearly perfect little woman, Meg (Margaret). Jo (Josephine), modeled after Alcott, is a spirited tomboy with some anger issues. She is the second oldest at the age of 15 when the story begins. Next is the family's peacemaker, the kind and gentle introvert Beth (Elizabeth), who dies of scarlet fever, as did Alcott's sister. And the youngest March is Amy Curtis, a spoiled, self-centered brat who is 12 when the story begins. All the March girls have artistic talent and ambition. Meg wants to be an actress, Beth plays the piano, and Amy is a painter. Jo loves literature, reading, and writing, including writing plays for her sisters to perform. Their mother Marmee (Margaret), modeled after Alcott's mother, is admired and adored by her girls. The matriarch holds the March family together.

Throughout the novel, Alcott references John Bunyan's 1678 moral allegory, *The Pilgrim's Progress*, which emphasizes Puritan virtues of hard work and self-sacrifice. Modeled after their saintly mother, all four sisters dedicate themselves to serving those in need at the expense of satisfying their desires and following their dreams. The opening scene finds the girls grudgingly sacrificing their Christmas breakfast to the destitute Hummels. In their daily lives, Meg tutors four children in a poor family. Jo reluctantly assists her wealthy and cantankerous widowed great aunt. Beth, who is more content to stay in the house, she helps their servant Hannah with housework. And Amy is still in school. Echoing Christian teachings, Alcott's little women use their service to others and duties to family to work on their respective character flaws: Beautiful Meg is vain and materialistic; spoiled Amy is self-centered; sweet Beth is shy; and tomboy Jo is a hothead, which is a character flaw she inherited from now self-controlled mother Marmee.

Gerwig's *Little Women*

With great reverence for the original, 30-something Greta Gerwig dares to tamper with a beloved literary classic. Fear not, for Gerwig serves up all of our favorite scenes: Jo burns Meg's hair (Saoirse Ronan was nominated for an Oscar for best leading actress); Meg's (Emma Watson) too-tight shoes cause her to sprain her ankle; Amy burns Jo's manuscript, causing Jo to leave Amy to drown while ice skating (Florence Pugh was nominated for best-supporting actress); sweet Beth (Elza Scanlen) embraces stern Mr. Laurence after he gives her a piano; and of course there is the fraught love affair between Jo and Laurie (Timothée Chalamet), the irresistible but not terribly bright boy-next-door.

What is new is that Gerwig tells the story out of chronological order. We move back and forth between the time the March girls are teens, trying to find themselves to when they are grown up, independent, and out of the house. Gerwig's modern adaptation emphasizes different themes from Alcott's novel: women's lack of civil rights, legal constraints placed on women by marriage, the narrow range of options for women at that time, and the narrow range of options for women in the arts (Brody 2019).

Satisfying Ending

Gerwig's Oscar-nominated script bookends her story with the grown-up Jo March. It begins with Jo as a young woman trying to sell her stories. The movie concludes with a much more satisfying ending than Alcott's original, for we see the ambitious and ill-tempered tomboy blossoming into a successful writer.

In the final scenes of her movie, Gerwig takes us to the interior of the publishing house; the year is 1871. Gerwig explains, "What I was trying to reverse-engineer was this moment that Jo getting her book published would make the audience feel like you usually feel when the hero chooses the heroine. I wanted to see if I could create that feeling with a girl and her book" (Bennett 2020).

Here are Gerwig's script notes for the final scenes in which Jo experiences the satisfaction of her book being born. We jump back and forth from the publishing house and Plumfield Academy, the school for boys that was converted from the home that Aunt March (Meryl Streep) left to Jo in her will.

> Jo, captivated, watches type being set, each letter put into place, and one page after another pressed with her novel...
> Each page is stacked one on top of the other and the massive industrial sewing machine stitches the pages together as Jo observes...
> *The excesses of each page are sliced off, making a satisfying sound, and making Jo jump and laugh at her jumpiness...*
> The hard cover of the book is placed over the pages, the glue to hold it in place is so strong-smelling as to make Jo dizzy...
> A man finishes the book, and unceremoniously hands it to Jo and gets to work on the next one...
> *Jo turns it over in her hands, touching it like the holy object it is, her inchoate desire made manifest.*
> Jo looks up ...
> and sees the future –
> CUT TO BLACK.
> *Credits* (Gerwig 2019a)

Alcott's original version leaves us with Jo giving up her writing, marrying the unattractive German Professor Bhaer, birthing two sons, and opening a school for boys (!) where she is referred to as, sad to say, "Mother Bhaer." (Pronounced *BEAR*.) Gerwig's Jo is a mature and self-possessed young woman and artist in her own right, who was, however, forced to compromise her artistic vision for economic reasons. Professional women in Gerwig's audience feel Jo's joy when Jo "gets the book" in the end and know the pain and sacrifices Jo made to achieve her success.

Art and Money

Whereas Alcott's story focuses on Christian themes and virtues, Gerwig intended her film adaptation to be "about art and money" (Whipp 2019). Like Alcott's original, Gerwig's tale exudes Jo's sentiment that "family is the most beautiful thing in the world" (Alcott 2011, p. 850). This family theme is one Gerwig easily transports from her autobiographical *Ladybird*, where the free-spirited Ladybird (played by Saoirse Ronan) struggles with separating herself from her financially struggling family, to whom she is devoted. In her *Little Women*, Gerwig more narrowly focuses on a struggling artist, meant to represent Alcott, and her love for her family. "As a child, my hero was Jo March. But as an adult, it's Louisa May Alcott" (Bennett 2020).

Gerwig's tale of the "birth of an artist" is also a love letter to Alcott – a female artist writing at a time that was hostile to women and the telling of stories of women's lives from a woman's point of view. In short, it was a time very much like today in Hollywood (Brody 2019). The fact that Alcott's (Jo's) plight is Gerwig's plight helps explain the honesty and authenticity of Gerwig's storytelling. In homage to her hero, Gerwig writes an ending to *Little Women* that was closer to what Alcott wanted but was not allowed to write.

Economics of Marriage

While Jo (Alcott) struggles to be taken seriously as a writer and artist, she, like her sisters, must also wrestle with her views on marriage. Whereas Alcott's marriages are depicted primarily as pure love matches, Gerwig emphasizes the economics of marriage, a theme that lies below the surface in Alcott's story. Make no mistake, Gerwig indulges us with pure romance – highlighting the fiery chemistry between plucky Ronan (Jo) and charming Chalamet (Laurie). But it's not a fairytale romance.

In one of the movie's closing scenes, Jo is rolling her eyes at the curmudgeonly publisher Mr. Dashwood who admonishes Jo, telling her that she should create heroines that end up either married or dead. Jo's new novel, *Little Women,* leaves the heroine unmarried. Dashwood insists that no one will buy her book if she retains this ending. In response, Jo, the pragmatist, shrugs. "I suppose marriage has always primarily been an economic proposition. Even in fiction."

Gerwig then cuts to a youthful and lovestruck Jo running into the arms of a younger and sexier version of German Professor Bhaer. Alcott's professor talks Jo out of writing. But Gerwig's Bhaer (French actor Louis Garrel) simply disapproves of Jo writing sensational stories, asking Jo: "But do you have anyone to take you seriously, to talk about your work?" (Gerwig 2019). The fact that Gerwig's professor respects and values Jo's work makes it much easier to digest her choice of the German professor over heartthrob Timothée Chalamet. Even without Chalamet playing Laurie, however, Jo's decision never felt quite right in Alcott's novel and various adaptations. But it does in Gerwig's version.

THE PRESENT IS NOW THE PAST. OR MAYBE FICTION. EXT. TRAIN. EVENING. 1869.
    Jo runs from the carriage, out into the rain and into the crowd in front of the train station, looking for Friedrich.
    He's not there, every face isn't his. Couple after couple stands under umbrellas. She runs into the station, and then turns around to go back out – has she missed him?
    Just then:

FRIEDRICH: Jo!	Jo sees Friedrich, also standing under an umbrella, but alone. She runs towards him. She feels her emotions rising, she starts to cry, despite herself.
FRIEDRICH	(CONT'D) Jo, why are you crying?
JO	Because – because you are going away.
FRIEDRICH	I would never leave if you wished me to stay.
JO	I wish you would stay.
FRIEDRICH	But, but I have nothing to give you but my full heart and these empty hands.
JO	(she puts her hands in his and steps under the umbrella) They aren't empty now. They kiss one of those epic perfect kisses. The train arrives, and he doesn't get on it. BAM. (Gerwig 2019a)

Viewers of the movie are unsure whether what we just saw was real or a scene from Jo's book. Even in her script notes, Gerwig offers no answer. She writes, "or maybe fiction."

In the next scene, Gerwig cuts back to the office where Jo has embarked on shrewd negotiations for a higher rate of royalties. After going back and forth on royalties and percentages, Jo gives in to Dashwood's demand: "If the main character's a girl, make sure she's married by the end. (casually) Or dead."

JO	If I'm going to sell my heroine into marriage for money, I might as well get some of it.
DASHWOOD	Six point six percent.
JO	Done.
DASHWOOD	And you don't need to decide about the copyright now.
JO	I've decided. I want to own my own book. (Gerwig 2019a)

In an interview, Gerwig says, "I felt it could be me talking to a studio head. It *has* been me talking to a studio head" (Whipp 2019). Gerwig's Oscar-nominated film solidified her status as a major player in a male-dominated Hollywood. She modeled her Jo after Alcott, who secured the copyright for her work and enabled Alcott to support herself and her family. But all three women had to make commercial concessions for their art and ensure that the heroine ended up either dead or married. All three writers chose marriage.

Alcott

Alcott knew her ending was unsatisfying. It was a deliberate choice on her part. In a letter to a friend, Alcott wrote, "Girls write to ask whom the little women will marry as if that was the only end and aim of a woman's life." But: "I won't marry Jo to Laurie to please anyone" (Matteson 2016, pp. xxi–xxii).

Alcott originally intended for her story to end with Jo as a "literary spinster," much like Alcott herself. "I'd rather be a free spinster and paddle my own canoe." Like Mr. Dashwood in both the book and movie, Alcott's publishers insisted that the book would not sell unless Jo married. Although "much afflicted" by their demands, Alcott told her friend that she had concocted a solution "out of perversity." She intentionally invented dour and dictatorial Friedrich Bhaer as a "funny match" for Jo (ibid.). She disposed of the attractive Laurie by marrying him off to the spoiled brat, Amy.

From the beginning, Alcott was reluctant to write a book for girls, which she saw as "moral pap for the young." Alcott writes in her diary, "Never liked girls or knew many, except my sisters." By the final chapter of *Jo's Boys*, the second of two novels that followed *Little Women*, Alcott did not try to hide her fatigue with her characters and her fan's insatiable curiosity about them. At one point, she declared that she was tempted to conclude with an earthquake that would engulf Jo's school "and its environs so deeply in the bowels of the earth that no [archaeologist] could ever find a vestige of it" (Gilbert 2018). Some feminists *do* have a sense of humor!

Alcott became the first woman to register to vote in Concord, Massachusetts, in 1879, years before the 19th amendment was passed. Louisa May Alcott died on

March 6, 1888. She was 55 and had succeeded in supporting herself and her family as a writer for most of her adult life, producing more than 270 stories, novels, and sketches. In the beginning, she had hoped to earn a modest $1000. Because of *Little Women,* however, she did far better than that. "Though her wealth and fame now rivaled that of any other American author of her time, that feeling of security never came. She could not reconcile the omnipresent tensions between authorial desire and public demand" (Matteson 2016, p. xxii). Like her characters, Alcott struggled to balance her own desires and the expectations of others.

What Does It All Mean?

Gerwig's movie bill describes the March girls as "determined to live life on their own terms." Each character struggles to become her own woman while conforming to society's strict ideals of femininity. This struggle is made harder by their poverty which, genteel as it may be, emphasizes the economic realities of marriage. True to Dashwood's claim death and marriage are the only viable options available to women at that time, fictional or real.

While each sister does get to pick and choose along her path to womanhood, none of the four sisters gets what she thought would make her happy (Matteson 2016, p. xv). Meg, the aspiring actress who loves pretty clothing and luxurious things, is the only sister who marries purely for love. She ends up with Laurie's financially strapped tutor, who will never be able to give her the fine things she desires. Amy, who dreams of becoming a great painter, abandons her art to marry the financially secure Laurie. Jo ends up marrying the professor after turning down Laurie's earlier marriage proposal. "I don't believe I will ever marry. I'm happy as I am, and love my liberty too well to be in any hurry to give it up" (Gerwig 2019). While Gerwig's Jo supports herself and her family as a writer, Alcott has Jo bear two sons and she opens a school for boys (of all things). And in both versions of *Little Women,* Beth ends up dead.

We may then ask, do the little women end up happy? There are women in the story who are not happy at all. Great aunt Josephine March is "only happy when she's complaining" (Gerwig 2019). Hannah, the March family maid, is treated like a family member. Still, she is relegated to the role of servant. And poor Mrs. Hummel, the widowed mother of six children, suffers from extreme poverty and disease, which takes three of her children. What about the March women? Do they end up fulfilled and satisfied with their lives? Would we say that their lives were meaningful?

What Meaning Means

The phrase "the meaning of life" originates from the German phrase "*lebenssinn*" ("life's meaning") found in a letter (July 9, 1796) from Johann Wolfgang von Goethe to Friedrich Schiller. Starting in the late nineteenth and early twentieth centuries, existentialists took up the question of life's meaning with gusto. In his "Myth of Sisyphus," Albert Camus proclaimed that "the meaning of life is the most urgent of questions" (1969, p. 4). Although logical positivists and analytic philosophers of the early twentieth century argued that questions about the meaning of life are not meaningful, contemporary analytic philosophers are increasingly focusing on this growing area of philosophical inquiry.

Meaning, as standardly understood in the literature, is an intrinsic and final good that varies and comes in degrees. As a category of value, meaning applies only to human life. It may pertain to the whole, or some part of that life, including an individual action or set of activities, projects, or endeavors. Throughout the literature, questions about meaning are conceptually distinct from questions about human happiness and flourishing, as well as other evaluative questions about rightness or wrongness (ethics) and goodness and beauty (aesthetics).

There are different *kinds* of meaning. Terrestrial meaning addresses meaningfulness *in* an individual human life, while cosmic meaning addresses the meaning *of* life, asking broader, mystery-of-existence-type questions: "Why are we here?"; "Is my life part of some bigger narrative or cosmic plan?"; "Why are some lives meaningful and others are not?"; and so on. Most contemporary scholars (including Wolf) come from an atheistic or naturalistic perspective. These philosophers largely ignore mystery-of-existence-type questions.

Theories of life's meaning can be divided into *subjective* and *objective*. On the subjective side are existentialists who believe that we create meaning. Frederick Nietzsche thinks meaning arises from an activity's creative, passionate process, rather than by achieving goals (2001). Soren Kierkegaard emphasizes passion: "Existing, unless by this we are to understand an existing of a kind, is impossible without passion" (2009, p. 260). More recently, Harry Frankfurt argues that deeply loving or caring for something is sufficient for a life to be meaningful (2004). Finally, although he ultimately rejects meaning subjectivism, Richard Taylor's view of meaning in terms of desire-satisfaction is the most discussed subjectivist theory. Taylor imagines the gods took pity and injected Sisyphus with a drug that gives him the desire to roll rocks up a hill only to fall again (1970). The fact that Sisyphus now loves rolling rocks, or finds it fulfilling, renders his pointless existence meaningful. Most contemporary scholars reject meaning subjectivism.

Meaning objectivists do not treat meaning as something that is created. Instead, it is to be discovered in the external world. Hence, they seek to articulate conditions that, if satisfied, could render an individual life, or some aspect of that life, meaningful. Some examples include: transcending the limits of the self (Robert Nozick 1983); pursuing maximally non-hedonist goods, such as friendship, beauty, and knowledge (Peter Railton 1984); exercising or developing rational nature in unusual ways (Hurka 1996; Gewirth 1998); substantially improving the quality of life of people and animals (Singer 1979); overcoming challenges that one recognizes to be necessary at one's stage of history (Dworkin 2002); rewarding experiences in the life of the agent or the lives of others the agent affects (Audi 2005); altruism (Baggini 2007); leaving traces that will linger after one's death (Trisel 2002); family relationships (Velleman 1991); life plans (David Heyd 2010); orienting one's life toward "the good, the true and the beautiful" (Metz 2015); and so on. Finally, John Cottingham, one of the few champions of a theistic theory of meaning, presents a vaguely Pascalian-Wittgensteinian view. It is "the practices of spirituality" which stems from the Christian tradition that gives meaning to the lives of those who adopt them, "not in virtue of allegiance to complex theological dogmas but in virtue of a passionate commitment to a certain way of life" (2003).

Susan Wolf's Fitting Fulfillment Theory

In her well-received book *Meaning in Life and Why It Matters* (2010), Susan Wolf offers a uniquely hybrid view of meaning *in* life. She claims that the desire that our lives be meaningful is "pervasive if not universal" and is one ingredient – "sometimes the key ingredient" – "in a life well lived" (p. 31, 10).

Wolf leans on common sense conceptions about meaningfulness to develop her hybrid theory of meaning. On the one hand, when people talk about meaning or purpose in life, they talk about "finding your passion" (subjective attraction). On the other hand, they talk about meaningfulness in terms of "being part of something larger than yourself" (objective attractiveness) (ibid., pp. 10–11). Wolf's fitting fulfillment theory suggests that "meaning in life arises when subjective attraction meets objective attractiveness" and "one can do something about it or with it" (ibid., p. 26). Wolf comes up with pithy phrases to capture her "fitting fulfillment" view: "loving things that are worthy of being loved" or "active engagement in projects of worth."

Wolf sets out to offer a "maximally tolerant interpretation of the idea of positive value," insisting that we exclude "merely subjective value as a suitable interpretation of the phrase" (2014, p. 95). Thus, her theory draws a sharp distinction between our interests (i) in "our life *feeling* a certain way" (subjective meaning) and (ii) that our lives "*be* a certain way, specifically, that it be one that can be appropriately appreciated, admired, or valued by others at least in principle" (objective meaning) (2010, p. 32). Our views about what is valuable or worthwhile are formed in childhood "as a result of a variety of lessons, experiences, and other cultural influences" (2007, p. 99). "I expect that almost anything that a significant number of people have *taken* to be valuable over a large span of time is valuable" (ibid., p. 105).

Subjective Meaning

On the subjective side of her theory, Wolf argues that pursuing one's passion "adds something distinctive and deeply good to life." It gives one's life a particular type of good feeling or "feeling of fulfillment." Wolf argues that "doing what one loves doing, being involved with things one cares about, gives one a kind of joy in life that one would otherwise be without" (2010, p. 13). "Figure out what turns you on, and go for it" (ibid., p. 10). This "reward" or feeling of "joy" that arises when a person is doing what she loves is a "high quality pleasure" (ibid., p. 27). "One finds one's passion and goes for it (thereby being fulfilled)" (p. 25).

Steve Jobs, the creator of Apple, offered the following advice to the 2005 graduating class of Stanford University: Do What You Love or DWYL, which echoes the subjective side of Wolf's theory. "You've got to find what you love. And that is as true for work as it is for your lovers. Your work is going to fill a large part of your life, and the only way to be truly satisfied is to do what you believe is great work. And the only way to do great work is to love what you do" (Marino 2014).

Lack of Meaning

When a person says her life lacks meaning in the "ordinary use of the term," she is expressing a "dissatisfaction with the subjective quality of that life," namely, a "subjective good is felt to be missing." Her life "feels empty, and she is longing to find something that will make her life feel fulfilling" (2010, p. 11). The lack or loss of meaning is associated with feelings of "boredom and alienation" and "emptiness and dissatisfaction" (ibid., p. 14).

Wolf acknowledges that there are people who do "valuable work" but "cannot identify or take pride in what they are doing." For example, the alienated housewife, conscripted soldier, and assembly line worker "know that what they are doing is valuable, but they do not experience their lives as fulfilling – they are not 'gripped' or 'excited'" (ibid., p. 21). In the case of the alienated housewife, her heart isn't in it. "Her life seems to her to be a series of endless chores. What she wants, it might appear, is something that she can find more subjectively rewarding" (2014, p. 91). In other words, the housewife's life and others like it are *objectively* meaningful but lack *subjective* meaning since the individual in question does not experience her life as satisfying or exciting.

If a person suspects her life lacks meaning, she will not "bring meaning to it by getting therapy or taking a pill that, without changing one's life in any other way, makes one believe that one's life has meaning" (ibid., p. 96). This is because a person cannot "find something engaging at will" (2007, p. 106n5). The alienated housewife cannot make herself love chores and caretaking, or a life primarily devoted to those activities, merely through an act of will or adjustment in attitude. Instead, we find meaning in our lives by figuring out which activities and projects light our fire, so to speak, and engaging in those.

Fulfilled But Unhappy

Wolf does acknowledge that even if a person's life *feels* fulfilling, there is no guarantee of *happiness*. She maintains that happiness, which she conceives of in terms of enlightened self-interest, is a separate category of value from meaning. Thus, a person could be living a meaningful life yet be unhappy.

Many things that "grip or engage us" make us vulnerable to "pain, disappointment, and stress" (2010, p. 14). Thus, fulfillment or subjective meaning is a "high-quality pleasure," "reward," or "feeling of joy" that a person can experience while engaged in painful or difficult activities or projects. Wolf's examples include "writing a book, training for a triathlon, campaigning for a political candidate, caring for an ailing friend" (ibid.). Elsewhere she references adopting a child with severe disabilities and moving to a war-torn country to help its victims find safety or food (2007, p. 108). In these cases, painful as they may be, they are still fulfilling, hence meaningful, as long as the subject is "loving something worthy of being loved" (2010, p. 13).

Objective Meaning

When it comes to activities and projects that "turn us on," some are not worthwhile. Wolf offers various examples of the types of lives or activities that lack value: spending the whole day gazing at goldfish, smoking pot, or doing endless crossword puzzles. Likewise, the life of a person "whose sole passion is collecting rubber bands, memorizing the dictionary, or making handwritten copies of *War and Peace*" is not objectively meaningful (2010, pp. 9, 16). Elsewhere Wolf acknowledges that people "do the darnedest things" such as race lawn mowers, compete in speed-eating contests, sit on flagpoles, and watch reality TV (ibid., p. 47).

When pushed on some of her examples of worthless activities, however, Wolf concedes that "[t]here may be something to be said on both sides of these questions" (ibid.). Richard Taylor, who is a meaning subjectivist, suggests that there could be "some special story" for some of the things that might at first glance be exemplary cases of worthless activities (Himmelmann 2013, p. 37). ("Special story" is not Wolf's language, but Richard Taylor's, who Himmelmann references in her article.) For instance, perhaps the person who is passionately making handwritten copies of *War and Peace* has survived a devastating nuclear war at a time when civilization is trying to rebuild itself. "All technology and books save one (... you guessed it: *War and Peace*!) have been destroyed. Under such circumstances, making copies of one of the world's greatest novels would be quite worthwhile" (ibid.). In other words, some activities may not, at first glance, appear to be valuable, but given further context or explanation, they may be viewed as valuable or worthwhile.

In light of the following claims, however, it is an open question whether or not Wolf believes that certain activities can be ruled out as valuable or worthwhile, no matter the context. She states, "No one has the authority to 'declare' to another person what has and what lacks objective value" (2010, p. 124). If a person finds something valuable, then "even if she is unable to convince others of its merits, this does not imply that she must be mistaken" about its value (ibid., p. 125). Wolf explains that "value can emerge from brute attraction or interest interacting with drives to excellence, creativity, and sociability" (ibid., p. 130). In other words, although she wants to distance herself from "merely subjective value," here Wolf says that if a subject is merely attracted or interested in some kind of projects or activities, this is sufficient for that thing to have objective value.

Wolf admits that her self-described "openness to the emergence of objective value out of brute interest and attraction" may leave some "disappointed by what they see as a watering down of what is distinctive about my conception of meaningfulness" (2010, p. 131). Indeed. But let us look past some of these inconsistencies in Wolf's writings and assume for the sake of argument that some things are not objectively valuable. We may then go on to consider the extent to which some of the characters of *Little Women* exemplify Wolf's fitting fulfillment theory of meaning. We start with the matriarch.

Unfulfilled and Unfit Little Women

Marmee

In Alcott's novel, Marmee is depicted as the ideal mother and the moral center of the March family – a dutiful and loving wife and mother dedicated to helping those in need. Gerwig describes her as follows. "Marmee (Laura Dern) has none of the pretensions of the other mothers, no artifice. She's a hippie before they existed" (2019a). Producer Amy Pascal adds that she is "not simply a downtrodden mother, raising her girls while her husband is away. She is pissed off" (Bennet 2020).

Marmee's anger has attracted the attention of many Alcott scholars and fans. There may be any number of things that piss off Marmee. In one scene, Gerwig directs Marmee's anger at her husband, who has finally returned home from serving in the Union Army: "Thank God you're home. Now I can be angry with you in person" (Gerwig 2019). In another scene, Gerwig gives her a line that harkens back to Michelle Obama's remark that got her into so much trouble when she was campaigning for her husband. "I've spent my whole life ashamed of my country" (Gerwig 2019).

It's likely, however, that Marmee's anger is more generalized. As Marmee is approaching her home on Christmas morning, gazing into the window at her girls, Gerwig writes: "She fights tears and sadness, about what, we don't entirely know. We just know that what she does as a mother isn't free. Of course, it's not, nothing is ever free, even the joy of a mother. Just before she flings open the door, she puts a smile on her face. Like many mothers, she creates magic where there is none and enables her girls to be brave" (Gerwig 2019).

In one of the movie's most poignant scenes – one in the book but only the second time it made it to an adaptation – Jo confides her anger to Marmee. This scene occurs after Amy is recovering from her near-drowning incident while ice skating. Jo reflects on her anger, "I get so savage, I could hurt anyone and enjoy it." Marmee responds, "You remind me of myself." Jo is in disbelief, "But you're never angry" (Gerwig 2019).

MARMEE	(honestly): I'm angry nearly every day of my life.
JO	You are?
MARMEE	I'm not patient by nature, but with nearly forty years of effort I have learned to not let it get the better of me.
JO	(resolutely) I'll do the same, then.

The scene ends with Marmee lovingly touching her daughter's face (Gerwig 2019).

Laura Dern comments on the scene. "I was really grateful for that scene because I think the availability of Marmee as a mother is about something raw and about expressing what isn't working with how women are treated or measured. We felt it was essential" (Shattuck 2020). Alcott fashioned this character after her mother, who wrote in her journal (1842): "I am almost suffocated in this atmosphere of restriction and form" (Blackwood 2019). Such stifling restrictions would certainly leave any self-aware woman with feelings of resentment and anger.

Jo March

Jo knows these suffocating feelings and restrictions. She expresses her frustration to her mother in a line taken directly from Alcott's novel. "Women have minds and souls as well as hearts, ambition, and talent as well as beauty, and I'm sick of being told that love is all a woman is fit for" (Gerwig 2019).

Gerwig tweaks the scene and adds a feeling of sadness to Jo's anger and frustration. "But... I am so lonely." Jo "drives herself mercilessly and experiences the isolation with which so many writers are unhappily familiar. The sacrifices also take place on a romantic level... she is made lonelier by the realization that love in real life does not greatly resemble the love she described in her potboiler stories" (Matteson 2020). Whether or not Jo's loneliness subsides when she marries and has children is an open question. But Jo likely experienced deep loneliness in her career as a writer, struggling to be taken seriously by her male peers and publishers.

Toward the end of Alcott's novel, Amy observes that Jo's life is "very different from the one you pictured so long ago." Amy asks, "Do you remember our castles in the air?" Jo, speaking now "in a maternal way," "Yes, I remember, but the life I wanted then seems selfish, lonely, and cold to me now. I haven't given up the hope that I may write a good book yet, *but I can wait*, and I'm sure it will be all the better for such experiences and illustrations as these" (p. 858, emphasis added). In Alcott's story, which emphasizes the moral development of each girl, Jo's deferred dreams serve as character building. In Gerwig's modern version of *Little Women*, Jo does not defer her dream of becoming a writer. Instead, the publication of Jo's book is the dramatic climax.

Gerwig's Jo comes the closest of all the March women to "living life on her own terms." Despite her youthful protestations against marriage, however, Jo ends up married. A life in which Jo is forced into marriage would not meet Wolf's conditions for fitting fulfillment. And even though Jo succeeds in getting her writing published, she is forced to make her art "mercenary and commercial" in ways that would not have been applied equally to her male counterparts (Grady 2019). These concessions that Jo is forced to make mean that she will not experience joy and fulfillment in her career as a writer, which is required for meaning according to Wolf.

Amy March

Unlike Jo, Amy does not fight her bridal fate. In Alcott's novel and most film and television adaptations, Amy plays the part of the spoiled girl. In other movies – Joan

Bennett (1933), Elizabeth Taylor (1949), and Kirsten Dunst (1994) – Amy's bratty antics serve as comic relief. Gerwig, however, adds depth and develops her character into a complicated and sympathetic young woman, resulting in a performance that earned Pugh a nomination for best supporting actress.

Gerwig explains that when she read the novel, "as an adult, Amy was the one who struck me as having some of the most interesting things to say and having the most utterly clear-eyed view of the world. I think I started seeing her as this equally potent character to Jo" (Lee 2019). In an interview, Gerwig offers several examples of great lines delivered by Amy. Gerwig's commentary on Amy's lines, which was offered during the interview, is included in parentheses. "I want to be great or nothing." (Gerwig, "A fabulous line.") "The world is hard on ambitious girls." (Gerwig, "I mean, the world is *still* hard on ambitious girls.") "I don't pretend to be wise, but I *am* observant." (Gerwig, "*That* is the key. She really *sees* everything.") (Lee 2019).

While Jo's art is "mercenary and commercial," Amy gives up her childhood dreams of being an artist altogether. As a young girl, Amy expresses her deepest wish for herself. "I have many wishes, but my favorite one is to be an artist and go to Paris and do fine pictures and be the best painter in the world" (Gerwig 2019). Later in the movie, when Amy is about to accept Laurie's proposal for marriage, she tells Laurie that she "won't be a commonplace dauber." Laurie asks Amy, "What women are allowed into the club of geniuses anyway?" After pointing out that it's men who get to determine who are the geniuses, the ever-observant Amy states that the only women she can think of are the Brontes. Appreciating the economic realities of marriage, Amy willingly embraces the institution and resolutely commits to "use her other talents" to become "an ornament to society." Meryl Streep convinced Gerwig to put one of the most memorable speeches in the movie (Li 2019).

> I'm just a woman. And as a woman, there's no way for me to make my own money. Not enough to earn a living or to support my family, and if I had my own money, which I don't, that money would belong to my husband the moment we got married. And if we had children, they would be his, not mine. They would be his property, *so don't sit there and tell me marriage isn't an economic proposition because it is.* It may not be for you, but it is for me. (Gerwig 2019, emphasis added)

Amy's marriage to Laurie is not entirely transactional, for we know that Amy has loved Laurie since she was a girl. But unlike the eldest sister Meg who follows her heart, Amy follows her head. Because Meg married for love and Jo could end up a literary spinster, there is more pressure on Amy to support her family. Thus, Amy's decision to marry Laurie is somewhat forced.

Would we say that Amy is "living life on her own terms"? Does she feel fulfilled and experience joy in following her passion? It seems not in both cases. Moreover, it is unlikely that one would argue that Amy's decision to devote her talents to "becoming an ornament to society" is a worthwhile endeavor.

When we consider Amy, her selfless and seething mother, and her married and mercenary sister, they may be living the most meaningful lives possible for women in nineteenth-century America. Still, they fall short of Wolf's ideal notion of a life well lived.

Postmortem Assessments

Let us assume, however, that all four March girls did go on to follow their passion and that each girl became a successful artist in her own right. Amy is a budding Mary Cassatt. Meg, the next Katherine Hepburn. Beth, the next Fanny Mendelssohn. And Jo joins the ranks of the Brontes and Jane Austin. Their lives would be objectively meaningful, for they were "appropriately appreciated, admired, or valued by others, *at least in principle*" (Wolf 2010, p. 32 emphasis added). Wolf insists, however, that a person must also experience the joy and satisfaction of living such an admirable life. For meaning arises from the marriage of subjective attraction and objective attractiveness.

History is full of stories of women (and men) whose genius was not recognized by others until after their death. Even if their contemporaries didn't recognize the value of their lives and work, their lives are objectively meaningful at least in principle. Van Gogh's life and work were not admired and appreciated by others until after his death. Now one of his works could cost over $100 million. Thus, we would conclude that his life is objectively meaningful. But like so many artistic geniuses, Van Gogh was tortured by his talent, suggesting that he did not experience the joy and fulfillment required for subjective meaning. Failing to meet this criterion, his life was lacking in meaning, according to Wolf.

Virginia Wolf and Sylvia Plath ended up committing suicide, which likely resulted from prolonged depression. Whatever the cause, it's very likely that they too failed to experience their lives or artistic careers as fulfilling. On the one hand, it sounds right to say that a person who is depressed and suicidal is not living a meaningful life. On the other hand, it seems odd to claim that female literary giants like Wolf and Plath's lives were not meaningful.

If we turn to what Wolf calls "morally unsavory" characters, she maintains their "lives can be richly meaningful" even if they are immoral (2014, pp. 96, 97). Paul Gauguin infamously abandoned his wife and children to follow his passion. As a result, he produced some of the greatest works of art of the nineteenth century. If he, unlike Van Gogh, experienced satisfaction and fulfillment with his accomplishments, then Gauguin's life is meaningful, according to Wolf. Would a joyless and morally good life (Virginia Wolf) be less meaningful than a fulfilling and immoral life (Paul Gauguin)? It seems not.

A recent movement in the history of philosophy is to incorporate various historical women philosophers into the canon. In their time, many bright and talented women were not recognized as philosophers or taken seriously by their peers. We now dedicate entire philosophical conferences and books to the work of, say, Mary Astell (1666–1731) and Margaret Cavendish (1623–1673). Even though recognition came after their death, their lives are admirable "in principle." Not having been taken seriously by their peers might suggest that they did not experience the feelings of joy and satisfaction required by Wolf for living a meaningful life. We don't want to say that the lives of the many women whose accomplishments and valuable contributions were lost or forgotten mean nothing or very little, simply by virtue of the fact that they did not experience satisfaction in having their work recognized or praised.

Imposters

As women experience more freedom and success, nagging self-doubt about the worth of their work and lives persists. Psychologists identify this as Imposter Syndrome, which is prevalent among (but not exclusive to) high-achieving women and minorities. When actor Jodie Foster was receiving one of her two Oscars, she said, "I thought it was a fluke, I was afraid I'd have to give it back." Maya Angelou, one of the greatest poets of the twenty-first century, once said. "I have written eleven books, but each time I think, 'uh oh, they're going to find out now. I've run a game on everybody, and they're going to find me out'" (Warrell 2021). In this case, Angelou's work is appropriately valued by others (objective meaning). But she does not recognize that value (subjective meaning). Hence her life lacks meaning, according to Wolf's fitting fulfillment theory.

Asymmetry

There is a puzzling asymmetry in Wolf's theory. On the one hand, a person can be wrong about whether her life is objectively meaning*ful*. Let us say, for example, that no matter what story she tells herself and others, Amy's decision to devote her talents to become "an ornament to society" is not objectively worthwhile. On the other hand, a person cannot be wrong about whether her life is meaning*less*. If a person experiences boredom or alienation or is not "gripped" or "excited" by the projects and activities that comprise her life, then her life is not subjectively meaningful.

If subjective meaning merely reports how a person feels about her life or accomplishments, if it simply reflects the subject's observation about her inner life, then she can never be wrong about whether her life is subjectively meaningful. Imagine that Hannah, the March servant, grows bored with her chores and housework. If Hannah is bored, then her life is not (subjectively) meaningful. But what do we make of Angelou who is alienated and detached from her success and accomplishments? A psychologist would counsel Angelou that she should be enjoying her success and would suggest therapy to help Angelou overcome her self-doubt. (Wolf suggests that a person cannot bring meaning to life "by getting therapy or taking a pill that, without changing one's life in any other way, makes one believe that one's life has meaning" (2014, p. 96). Therapy typically includes coming up with ideas for changing one's life, thus therapy could help a person to find meaning in her life.) Assuming a therapist can help her to see the value of her work, we'd have to conclude that Angelou was, in some sense, "wrong" when she felt unfulfilled by her work and significant accomplishments. If we can revise or amend judgments about objective meaning – if there is something to say on both sides of that issue – then why not say the same for subjective meaning?

Whereas women tend to deflate the value of their accomplishments, psychologists tell us that men tend to inflate that value. Arrogance, false pride, and narcissism suggest that a person may feel deeply satisfied with paltry achievements and pitiable lives. If a subject can't "declare" what has objective value, why would we think these same subjects, fallible as they are, can "declare" what is or is not subjectively meaningful?

The subjective requirement in Wolf's theory only muddies the waters. We certainly don't give the subject the upper hand regarding moral and aesthetic value judgments – we talk about impartiality, objectivity, universality, etc. Why would we give the subject the upper hand when talking about meaning?

Indicative Meaning

Wolf is not entirely off base in talking about meaning in terms of a psychological state, that is, feelings of satisfaction with one's life (or career, marriage, etc.). When the average person on the street talks about meaning in life, she often speaks about feelings or psychological states. This same person would likely find it counter-intuitive to suggest that *she* could be wrong about her life being meaningful. (In *Meaning and Life and Why It Matters*, Wolf mimics Aristotle's endoxic method, "the things which are accepted by everyone, or by most people or by the wise" (2010, p. 10).)

Feelings of fulfillment, or lack thereof, are in some sense "true." Whether or not these feelings correspond to something real or "fitting" for fulfillment is a different question. Thus, feelings of fulfillment cannot be relied on to indicate what is meaningful or meaningless. Emotional engagement, excitement, or joy may, in some cases, be *indicative* of meaning. *But Wolf goes too far in arguing that subjective engagement is a necessary condition for meaning.*

One might argue that feelings of fulfillment denote a *degree* of meaning, not a distinct *kind*. The very best or most meaningful life is one in which a person indulges in following her passions and subsequently experiences satisfaction. If Angelou eventually overcomes her self-doubt and feelings of inferiority and starts to own her success, then her life will be *more* meaningful. But more meaningful to whom? Does adding one more person to the chorus of admirers make her work more valuable or worth reading? We typically do not say that an activity or life is "more moral" or "more beautiful" if the subject in question deems it so. (This last statement may be controversial. Aristotle's virtue ethic would suggest that a person is virtuous, as opposed to merely continent, by virtue of the fact that the agent in question takes pleasure in performing a virtuous action. But what is or is not a virtue, e.g., courage, temperance, is not determined by the subject. Wolf, however, is not a virtue ethicist. Nor does she advocate a Kantian ethic which would maintain that acts performed out of duty, contrary to an agent's inclination, are the most virtuous.) When the Marches sacrifice their Christmas breakfast to the starving Hummels, this selfless act is good in itself, regardless of whether or not the Marches find it fulfilling. In Amy's case, she most definitely does not find it so.

Wolf's language, however, suggests a difference in *kind*. In distancing herself from merely subjective accounts of meaning, she draws a sharp distinction between (a) something *feeling* meaningful and (b) *being* meaningful. For Wolf, meaning emerges from the coming together of the two, suggesting you cannot have one without the other. "To have a life that not only seems meaningful but is meaningful, the objective aspect is as important as the subjective" (2010, pp. 32–33).

Though it goes beyond the scope of this chapter to tease this out entirely, it may be that feelings of fulfillment and satisfaction are more closely associated with happiness (i.e., enlightened self-interest or rational egoism) than they are with meaning. If you are bored or dissatisfied with your life, or some aspect of your life – if you are looking for fulfillment or want to be happy – *one* way to find fulfillment or happiness is to follow your passions or "do what you love."

The worry, however, is that fulfillment (subjective meaning) then reduces to mere desire-satisfaction. To be fulfilled, one can love *anything* one's heart desires. Thus, potheads and pedophiles may be equally fulfilled or happy. But this merely subjectivist view is very unsatisfying to philosophers, including Wolf. Wolf could stress an enlightened egoist or rational self-interested conception of happiness or fulfillment instead of a purely hedonistic concept. Smoking pot all day or molesting children may satisfy a person's desires or give that person pleasure, but neither activity is good for them or in that person's long-term interest. These activities won't lead to happiness. Still, even an enlightened agent who follows her passions will not necessarily find fulfillment. For various reasons, some individuals might not be capable of finding fulfillment in doing what they love, e.g., Angelou, tortured artist.

Perhaps finding fulfillment does not matter as much as we think. At least, it may not matter when it comes to finding meaning in life. Meaning in life may arise independently of whether or not you find your life fulfilling or deeply unsatisfying, as we see with the women of *Little Women*.

Women of Worth

In Alcott's novel, Marmee expresses her hopes for her girls. "I *am* ambitious for you... I want my daughters to be beautiful, accomplished, and good. *To be admired, loved, and respected*. To have a happy youth, to be well and wisely married, and to lead useful, pleasant lives, with as little care and sorrow to try them as God sees fit to send" (Alcott 2011, pp. 171, 170; italics added). Jo responds, "Then we'll be old maids." Marmee, "Better be happy old maids than unhappy wives, or unmaidenly girls, running about to find husbands."

While this is a lovely sentiment, the only old maid in *Little Women* is Aunt March. And in every version of Alcott's tale, she is utterly miserable. Thus, we see that Marmee's ambitious dreams for her little women – to "live life on their own terms," *outside the bounds of marriage* – are pipe dreams.

Marmee is building castles in the air. A woman in Alcott's era could not even create *fictional* little women who could follow their dreams without a husband in tow. Amy is right. The world *is* hard on ambitious women. And it continues to be so. Thus, we see a crucial assumption behind Wolf's fitting fulfillment theory: being able to "find your passion and go for it" presupposes that the person in question "*can do something about it*." And most women throughout most of the world cannot.

Wolf does acknowledge that there are cases in which people "through no fault of their own" simply lack the means to secure meaning. Their "physical, economic, political circumstances deprive them of the freedom or the leisure to explore and pursue meaningful activities or ones they would love" (2007, p. 106n5). If a person is struggling to "get enough to eat for oneself or one's family, get shelter from the cold, to fight a painful disease," then being concerned over whether or not one is following her passion is a "luxury" (2010, p. 31).

Writing as a woman, Wolf does not see what Amy does. Most ambitious women are ill-fitted to a fitting fulfillment theory of meaning. Wolf's view does not sufficiently acknowledge the value of women's lives and contributions, many of which are carried out from duty and self-sacrifice.

One might argue that this is the point. We must acknowledge the tragic fact that misogyny and sexism have prevented many clever and talented women throughout history from finding meaning in their lives, much less experiencing the joy and satisfaction of following one's dreams. But this would lead us to the unsettling conclusion that women's lives are, on the whole, less meaningful than men's simply because social and cultural forces prevent women from having the opportunity to live meaningful lives. As Amy observes, the club of geniuses rarely admits women.

Alternatively, we can rely less, or not at all, on the fallible subjective assessment of value. We can think of meaning less in terms of desire-satisfaction or whether a person gets what she wants out of life. Instead, we can lean into external and objective assessments that focus on what a person does with the life she is given. Is her life "appreciated, admired, or valued by others, *at least in principle*"?

Leaning In

The objective side of Wolf's theory – that a meaningful life is one "that can be appropriately appreciated, admired, or valued by others *at least in principle*" – echoes Marmee's dream for her girls: "to be admired, loved, and respected." Given human frailty and fallibility, however one's life may *feel* to the person living, it is not necessarily indicative of meaning or value. Instead, an accurate external assessment of the value of a person's life, activities, or projects is necessary and sufficient for meaning – *at least in principle*. In practice, however, too many women's lives and contributions are devalued or ignored. Others do not appreciate them as they should. The subject does not appreciate them as she should ... or both.

As we think about meaning in life and why it matters, what matters is that women of worth are allowed the opportunity to engage in meaningful activities and projects. Those activities may be grand, resulting in genius contributions and accomplishments: Amy, "I want to be great or nothing." But many others are quiet and ordinary. For example, Marmee, who, like so many mothers, defers her dreams to "create magic where there is none and enable her girls to be brave." There is also Hannah, whose socio-economic class relegates her to the status of a servant, who performs the mundane activities and boring chores that allow other women and girls to be successful. Finally, there is Mrs. Hummel, whose poverty subjects her to a life of destitution and misery, who dutifully and selflessly cares for her ailing children as a single parent. These lives are meaningful. They have value. And they matter.

Many women throughout history have done the best they could with what little they were given. Dreams were deferred, castles were built in the air, and many were faced with the false choice that Mr. Dashwood presents to Jo: death or marriage. Their lives were tragically unfulfilling, filled instead with pain, suffering, sorrow, misfortune, and (above all) self-sacrifice.

Alcott's nineteenth-century work, *Little Women,* recognizes the value of selflessness and self-sacrifice. On the other hand, more modern sensibilities mean that we put the self at the center, focusing more attention on desire-satisfaction, authenticity, or "living life on your own terms." The subjective side of Wolf's theory reflects these modern sensibilities. But as *Little Women* shows us, too many women – most women in most of the world – do not enjoy this luxury. Still, many do something worthwhile and valuable with the life they are given. Thus, we should appropriately appreciate, admire, and value their lives and selfless actions.

Little Women supports the view that a purely objective theory of meaning, which would include theistic theories of meaning, could accommodate many, if not all, women of worth who sadly never found subjective meaning or happiness in their lives. We could, like Marmee, still be ambitious for our little women and girls, encouraging them to dream big and build their castles. But, as we see with the women of *Little Women*, even if circumstances outside their control alter their life course, even if they do not always get what they want, they can live robustly meaningful lives by choosing activities and projects that are admirable and worthy of respect. Such projects contribute something to the world that is larger than themselves.

Conclusion

Alcott's dream for girls and little women was that they would have "the chance to grow without fretting or fetters, to discover and cultivate their strengths, and to use them as they choose" (Matteson 2016, p. xxxv). We have come a long way since Alcott's day. But we are not there yet; we still live in a world where many more girls are unable to indulge in following their dreams than those who are able.

Sadly, as reported by UN Women, the recent Covid-19 pandemic has moved many women, young and old, further back (2020). As we slowly move forward, we privileged few who have the luxury to, say, ponder life's great questions and write books and articles about the meaning of life, must not take such luxuries for granted. When we consider the relative value of women's lives, we must be sure that our theories and ideas appropriately value women of worth – real women who were forced to give up their world, which is certainly not as easy as it is for a girl in a book.

Without these women, we lucky few would be unable to follow our dreams and "live life on our own terms." *Little Women* reminds us that there is meaning in these women's lives and sacrifices. They matter deeply.

Acknowledgments This chapter is dedicated to my loving mother: a dutiful wife and selfless caregiver, generous and compassionate to those in need.

References

Acocella, Joan. 2018. How little women got big. *The New Yorker*.
Alcott, Louisa May. 2011. *Little women*. https://www.planetpublish.com/wpcontent/uploads/2011/11/Little_Women_NT.pdf
Audi, Robert. 2005. Intrinsic value and meaningful life. *Philosophical Papers* 34: 331–355.
Baggini, Julian. 2007. *What's it all about: Philosophy and the meaning of life*. Oxford: Oxford University Press.
Bennett, Jessica. 2020. This is little women for a new era. *The New York Times*. https://www.nytimes.com/2020/01/02/books/little-women-feminism-2019-movie.html
Blackwood, Sarah. 2019. *Little women* and the Marmee problem. *The New Yorker*. https://www.newyorker.com/culture/cultural-comment/little-women-and-the-marmee-problem
Brody, Richard. 2019. The compromises of Greta Gerwig's "Little women." *The New Yorker*. https://www.newyorker.com/culture/the-front-row/the-compromises-of-greta-gerwigs-little-women
Camus, Albert. 1969. *The myth of Sisyphus and other essays*. New York: Knopf.
Cottingham, John. 2003. *On the meaning of life*. Oxfordshire: Routledge.
De Beauvoir, Simone. 2005. *Memoirs of a dutiful daughter*. New York: Harper Perennial. 2010. *The second sex*. New York: Vintage Books.
Dworkin, Ronald. 2002. *Sovereign virtue: The theory and practice of equality*. Cambridge: Harvard.
Frankfurt, Harry. 2004. *The reasons of love*. Princeton: Princeton University Press.
Gerwig, Greta. 2017. *Ladybird*.
———. 2019. *Little women*.
———. 2019a. Screenplay. https://variety.com/wp-content/uploads/2019/12/little-women-by-greta-gerwig.pdf
Gewirth, Alan. 1998. *The community of rights*. Chicago: University of Chicago Press.
Gilbert, Sophie. 2018. The lie of *little women*. *The Atlantic*. https://www.theatlantic.com/magazine/archive/2018/09/little-women-louisa-may-alcott/565754/
Grady, Constance. 2019. The powers of Greta Gerwig's *Little women* is that it doesn't pretend marriages are romantic. *Vox*. https://www.vox.com/culture/2019/12/27/21037870/little-women-greta-gerwig-ending-jo-laurie-amy-bhaer
Hey, David. 2010. Life plans: Do they give meaning to our lives? *The Monist* 93: 1.
Himmelmann, Beatrix. 2013. *On meaning in life*. Berlin: De Gruyter.
Hurka, Peter. 1996. *Perfectionism*. Oxford: Oxford University Press.
Kierkegaard, Soren. 2009. In *Concluding unscientific postscript to philosophical crumbs*, ed. Alastair Hannay. Cambridge: Cambridge University Press.
Li, Shirley. 2019. *Little women* gives Amy March her due. *The Atlantic*. https://www.theatlantic.com/entertainment/archive/2019/12/greta-gerwigs-little-women-finally-gives-amy-her-due/603886/
Lippman, Laura. 1994. Young women want to be Jo, feisty heroine for 125 years *Little women* marches on. *The Baltimore Sun*. https://www.baltimoresun.com/news/bs-xpm-1994-12-23-1994357003-story.html

Marino, Gordon. 2014. A life beyond 'Do what you love'. *The New York Times*. http://www.nytimes.com

Matteson, John. 2016. *The annotated little women*. New York: W.W. Norton.

———. 2020. One way the new *Little Women* film is radical. *The Atlantic*. https://www.theatlantic.com/entertainment/archive/2020/01/where-greta-gerwigs-little-women-and-louisa-may-alcott-meet/604294/

Metz, Thaddeus. 2015. Précis of *Meaning in life: An analytic* study. *Journal of Philosophy of Life* 5 (3): 2–6.

Nietzsche, Frederick. 2001. In *The gay science*, ed. Bernard Williams. Cambridge: Cambridge University Press.

Nozick, Robert. 1983. *Philosophical explanations*. Cambridge: Harvard University Press.

Railton, Peter. 1984. Alienation, consequentialism, and the demands of morality. *Philosophy and Public Affairs* 13 (2): 134–171.

Shattuck, Kathryn. 2020. Really seeing Marmee: Oh, how 'Little Women's' matriarch has changed. *The New York Times*. https://www.nytimes.com/2020/01/16/movies/marmee-little-women.html

Singer, Peter. 1979. *Practical ethics*. Cambridge: Cambridge University Press.

Taylor, Richard. 1970. *Good and evil*. New York: Macmillan Publishing.

Trisel, Brooke Alan. 2002. Futility and the meaning of life debate. *Sorites* 14: 70–84.

UN Women. 2020. Gender equality in the wake of Covid-19. *UN Women.org*. https://www.unwomen.org/sites/default/files/Headquarters/Attachments/Sections/Library/Publications/2020/Gender-equality-in-the-wake-of-COVID-19-en.pdf

Velleman, David. 1991. Well-being and time. *Pacific Philosophical Quarterly* 72 (1): 48–77.

Warrell, Margie. 2021. Feel like a fraud? How to overcome impostor syndrome. *Forbes Magazine*. https://www.theatlantic.com/entertainment/archive/2020/01/where-greta-gerwigs-little-women-and-louisa-may-alcott-meet/604294/

Whipp, Glenn. 2019. Greta Gerwig had the perfect ending for *Little Women*. Here's why she kept it a secret. https://www.latimes.com/entertainment-arts/movies/story/2019-12-16/little-women-greta-gerwig-saoirse-ronan-florence-pugh

Wolf, Susan. 2007. Meaning in life and why it matters. In *Tanner lectures on human values*. Princeton: Princeton University. https://tannerlectures.utah.edu/_resources/documents/a-to-z/w/Wolf_07.pdf

———. 2010. *Meaning in life and why it matters*. Princeton: Princeton University Press.

———. 2014. Meanings in life. In *The variety of values: Essays on morality, meaning, and love*. Oxford: Oxford University Press.

God's Not Dead as Philosophy: Trying to Prove God Exists

61

David Kyle Johnson

Contents

Introduction	1436
A Quick Synopsis	1437
Some Nonphilosophical Arguments	1438
Evaluating Josh's First Lecture	1442
Argument #1: "I say, no one can disprove God exists."	1442
Argument #2: "For 2500 years, The Bible had it right and science had it wrong."	1444
Argument #3: God Is Why There Is Something, Rather Than Nothing	1447
Argument #4: God Does Not Need an Explanation Because He Is Eternal	1448
Evaluating Josh's Second Lecture	1450
Argument #5: John Lennox Refutes Hawking	1451
Argument #6 "Philosophy is Dead"	1452
Argument #7: Science Cannot Explain the Origin of Life	1453
Argument #8: "Nature Does Not Jump"	1454
Evaluating Josh's Third Lecture	1454
Argument #9: The Free Will Defense	1455
Argument #10: Without God, Everything Is Permissible	1457
Argument #11: Atheists Have No Reason to Be Good	1458
Argument #12: Life Is Meaningless without God	1459
Argument #13 "Why do you hate God?"	1460
Conclusion: It's a Little Rocky (IV)	1461
End Notes	1462
References	1463

Abstract

The 2014 movie *God's Not Dead* is a clear argument for the truth of its title; in other words, it is an argument that God exists. It does this, primarily, by having its protagonist, college freshman Josh Wheaton, present a number of arguments for

---

D. K. Johnson (✉)
Department of Philosophy, King's College, Wilkes-Barre, PA, USA
e-mail: Davidjohnson@kings.edu

© Springer Nature Switzerland AG 2024
D. K. Johnson et al. (eds.), *The Palgrave Handbook of Popular Culture as Philosophy*,
https://doi.org/10.1007/978-3-031-24685-2_116

God's existence in front of his philosophy class. It is the purpose of this chapter to evaluate those arguments. In the end, we will see that the movie fails, pretty dramatically, at accomplishing its task, while also unfairly demonizing those who deny its thesis along the way.

Keywords

Theism · Atheism · Christian persecution complex · Religious caricatures · Religious discrimination · God is dead · Inappropriate appeal to authority · Disproof atheism · Divine paradoxes · Existential burden of proof · Steady state theory · The big bang theory · Primeval atom · Theistic evolution · Creationism · Evolution · Georges Lemaitre · Quantum mechanics · Vacuum fluctuations · Kalam cosmological argument · Richard Dawkins · The god delusion · Mystery therefore magic · John Lennox · Stephen Hawking · Philosophy is dead · Charles Darwin · The problem of evil · The free will defense · Divine command theory · Euthyphro · Meaning of life · Fideism

Introduction

The year 2014 was arguably the year that Christians tried to take over Hollywood. *Son of God*, *Noah*, *Heaven is for Real*, *Exodus*, and *God's Not Dead* all came out that year. The latter is the subject of this chapter. Although it is not a great film, it is a prime example of popular culture as philosophy. Why? First, although it was not popular in the conventional sense, like *The Matrix* and *Lord of the Rings*, it was successful enough to spawn three sequels: *God's Not Dead 2* (2016), *God's not Dead: A Light in the Darkness* (2018), and *God's Not Dead: We the People* (2021). So it is popular in at least some circles. Second, it most certainly is doing philosophy. Granted, it does it in a way that (as I pointed out in the introduction to this handbook) some philosophers consider to be cheating – by putting philosophical arguments directly into the mouths of its characters. But the film is literally trying to prove that its title is true: God's Not Dead. It is a film that argues that God exists. It would thus seem that there could not be a clearer example of film as philosophy.

Now, to be fair, one could argue that *God's Not Dead* is not philosophy, but rather is apologetics. Apologetics – from the Greek word "apologia" which simply means "defense" or "answer in reply" – is the discipline or practice of defending religious doctrines. Because their ultimate goal is to defend Christian dogma, Christian apologists begin by assuming the truth of their religious doctrines and then try to construct ways to argue for or defend them. Since philosophy is just the "love of wisdom," and thus simply has a goal of discovering the truth, good philosophers never assume anything about the truth of what they are investigating. They just examine the arguments and evidence and then embrace what they reveal. Since the credits of *God's Not Dead* list an apologetics consultant (but no philosophy consultants), and it is unlikely that the makers of the film ever even entertained the possibility that they might be wrong about God's existence, one could easily argue that they were not doing philosophy when they made the film. On the other hand, the existence of God is clearly a philosophical issue, and the arguments the movie employs are philosophical. And it is not like philosophers (in practice) never assume the truth of what they are trying to prove; they just should not. So, instead of saying the film is not philosophy, we might just say that – given that it is clearly doing apologetics – we can know, before we even begin, that it is probably not going to turn out to be very good philosophy. That is not to say that we will assume such, before we begin; as good philosophers should, we will still give its arguments a fair hearing. But at least we now know where things stand.

God's Not Dead was inspired by the 2011 *Newsboys* "Christian rock" album of the same title. When the movie was released, I saw it in the theater, on a Sunday afternoon, right alongside a huge crowd of people who had been encouraged to attend by their pastor that very morning. They were quite impressed to say the least, even applauding loudly at the film's climax when the lead character (Josh) wins his debate and "proves" that God exists. Before we get to whether their admiration of Josh's arguments was warranted, a brief synopsis of the movie is in order.

A Quick Synopsis

The plot of the movie is simple. College freshman Josh Wheaton (not to be confused with film and television director Joss Whedon) elects to take a philosophy class. (For more on Joss Whedon as a philosopher, see Kowalski 2017.) His professor, Dr. Radisson, informs the class they can skip the course's hardest section, on God, if they all simply get to the point and admit that "God is dead." Josh refuses because he is a Christian. Consequently, Raddison stipulates that Josh must argue for his theistic belief in front of the class. Inspired by biblical passages that declare that Jesus will disown him before God if he disowns Jesus before [hu]man[s], Josh rises to the challenge. At the conclusion of three lectures, he bests his atheist professor and convinces all eighty of his fellow students that God exists.

There are also a number of B-stories. *Duck Dynasty*'s Willie Robertson makes a cameo or two to defend religious belief, and Radisson's Christian wife (a former student of his) leaves him because they are "unequally yoked." There is also a young Muslim girl, Ayisha, who works on campus and is forced to wear a head covering on campus by her very "traditional" Muslim father. When her father finds out she has been listening to Christian scripture, he beats her. She then confesses Jesus as her savior, and he almost chokes her to death; he subsequently disowns her and throws her out of the house.

There is also "Pastor Dave," who encourages Josh to take on his philosophy professor, but then is kept from going on vacation with Reverend Jude because God keeps every car Dave touches from starting. This allows him to still be around to stand up for family values when Ayisha comes to him for help; he instructs her to choose her loyalty to Jesus above her family. And he is also there at the end of the film to lead Professor Radisson through "the sinner's prayer" after Radisson is fatally hit by a car but kept alive by God just long enough to see the error of his ways. It is a very "no atheists in foxholes" moment.

Lastly, there is Amy Ryan, the vegetarian humanist reporter, who attacks *Duck Dynasty*'s Willie Robertson and his wife for killing ducks and then finds out she has terminal cancer. She is consequently dumped by her self-serving atheist jerk of a boyfriend (apparently her only friend in the world), and then led to salvation by the Christian rock group Newsboys before one of their concerts – where all our main characters (except the dead philosophy professor) rock out for a few songs. Willie Robertson congratulates Josh on his accomplishments, and the concert attendees (and movie attendees) text "God's not dead" to everyone in their contact list.

Some Nonphilosophical Arguments

Before we turn to the movie's main philosophical argument(s) for God's existence, which are stated by Josh, it is worth briefly addressing some other arguments the movie itself implies.

The first is a kind of argument by caricature. Every character who is not a Christian at the beginning of the film is a stereotype. For example, every atheist and nonbeliever is a curmudgeon, who has no morals, does not believe in love, only does things for selfish reasons, and whose lack of religion dooms them to lead a lonely terrible life. The implication, of course, is that all nonbelievers are like this – which, of course, is false. There is no evidence that atheists are lonelier, do not believe in love, are more selfish, or are less moral; in fact, there is empirical evidence that there is no difference in the ethical behavior of believers and nonbelievers (see Grewal 2012; Underwood 2014; Xygalatas 2017; Darley and Batson 1973; Malhotra 2010; Edelman 2009). While there are certainly some atheists who are curmudgeons, there are believers who are curmudgeons too. But the fact that you know one type of person who is that way does not mean they all are. The fallacy such an argument commits is called hasty generalization. It also invokes something like a "correlation entails causation" fallacy. Even if it were true that all type X persons were curmudgeons, it would not follow that being a type X person is what caused them to be a curmudgeon.

This argument is worth debunking because the atheist stereotypes in *God's Not Dead,* especially the idea that they are not trustworthy (Gervais et al. 2011), are problematic because those stereotypes are why atheists remain the most despised and distrusted minority in America and around the world (see Gervais et al. 2017). Evidence even suggests that they are as distrusted and despised as rapists (see Gervais et al. 2011). This is a problem, not only because it unfairly restricts them from political power; there are no open atheists in the American federal government (Wing 2017) and only 45% of people said they would vote for an atheist for president. (A full 53% said they would reject an atheist, even if they were fully qualified, and those numbers are actually up from previous years; see Lipka 2014.) It is also a problem because atheists and nonbelievers face discrimination and violence, because of their nonbelief, both in the USA (Pfaff et al. 2020) and around the world

(Humanist International 2020). This problem is made worse by the stereotypes *God's Not Dead* perpetuates.

Ironically, another conclusion the movie suggests is that it is the white Christian who is the one that is persecuted. Think of how the movie suggests that Josh is the only student in his class to have ever stepped foot in a church – and it is him, and him alone, who the professor picks on, for his religious belief. In reality, of course, white Christians make up a majority of the population (Pew 2021) and control the highest rated news media outlets (Burge 2021; Gramlich 2020), the lion's share of the nation's businesses and money, and have dominated political power since the nation's founding (Sandstorm 2021). The myth they are a downtrodden minority is known as the "Christian Persecution Complex," and has been a central tenet of Christianity since its founding. And it was a myth, even then. In her book, *The Myth of Persecution: How Early Christians Invented a Story of Martyrdom*, Candida Moss (2013) shows that there was never a sustained persecution of Christians by Roman authorities; some were killed, but most of early Christianity was persecution free. And since emperor Constantine converted, they have enjoyed complete political and social dominance in the West.

Film reviewer Emily James (2014) put this point another way. "*God's Not Dead* is ...an uninspired amble past a variety of Christian-email-forward boogeymen that reinforce the stereotypes its chosen audience already holds [and] weirdly fetishizes persecution." By "email forwarded boogeymen," she means cases like Raymond Raines', who Christians often claim was picked up by the scruff of the neck and yelled at by his teacher and principal for praying over his lunch in public school at the tender age of five. In reality, he was ten (not five), he got detention (not picked up and yelled at), and it was for fighting in the cafeteria (not praying over his lunch) (Savage 1994). If she were speaking today, James would talk about how such misinformation becomes viral on social media (rather than in email forwards). But she seems to be exactly right.

The film also caricatures racial minorities (like the Chinese) and religious minorities (like Muslims). But the film's most prominent caricature is of philosophy professors, in the form of Prof. Radisson. The caricature essentially serves as an argument against philosophy professors, but of course it is completely inaccurate. No professor would ever say "we can skip the unit on religion if you just tell me God is dead," and they certainly would not challenge one of their students to a one-on-one debate. The purpose of an intro to philosophy course is to teach all students to do philosophy themselves, and draw informed conclusions about important topics with those skills, by looking at the best arguments from both sides of an issue. Radisson's tactics accomplish neither of those goals. What is more, Raddison utilizes ad hominem (personal) attacks and appeals to force (threatening Josh in the hallway), to try to win the debate – all things good philosophers do not do. Atheists who study philosophy of religion are usually level-headed evidentialists, like Bertrand Russell or William Rowe; Raddison is just a broken Christian.

The movie does list a number of court cases, in the credits, as the "inspiration" for the movie, to leave the viewer with the impression that what happens in the movie happens all the time in classrooms. But in reality, these stories are just the aforementioned "Christian-email-forward boogeymen," exaggerations that feed the Christian persecution complex. Take, for example, the court decisions the film lists that force Christian business owners to make wedding cakes for gay couples. They are not examples of religious discrimination; they are decisions that prevent discrimination on the basis of sexual orientation. Forcing a business owner to serve mixed race couples, despite the owner's religious beliefs, is not religious discrimination – so neither is forcing them to serve gay couples.

Something similar is true of the cases that seem to have most directly inspired the movie: Keeton v. Anderson-Wiley and Brooker vs. Missouri State. In the former, the makers of the film claim that a counseling student was told that "she must change her [Christian] beliefs to graduate." In reality, the schools' requirement had nothing to do with her Christian beliefs; she was telling gay clients that they needed to be "cured" with "conversion therapy," a dangerous and harmful pseudoscience that is banned by the psychiatric profession. The judge in her case said it best. "When someone voluntarily chooses to enter a profession, he or she must comply with its rules and ethical requirements" (Metha 2016). If you are a Hindu who takes Hinduism's reverence of cows seriously, you should not try to get a job as a burger flipper at McDonalds; and if you do, you cannot cry discrimination if they fire you for refusing to do your job. Likewise, if you want to advocate for conversion therapy (or any other banned practice, like rebirthing therapy, psychedelic therapy, or electroshock therapy; see Anderson 2012), you should not try to get a job as a councillor; and if you do, you cannot cry discrimination if a school will not give you a diploma in the field because you have been recommending banned therapies.

In the latter case, Brooker vs. Missouri State, the film makers claim that a student was forced to "write and sign a letter to the Missouri Legislature in support of homosexual adoption as part of a class assignment and then punished for declining to write the letter." In reality, a Christian professor was trying to teach his class about advocacy by having them write a letter "on behalf of certain populations for whom they sought social and economic justice." This included, among many others, kids seeking foster care and adoption. Since, "[i]n this class, and others preceding it, the students agreed that same-sex couples were a resource to meet the needs of those kids," the letter included advocating for the right of same sex-couples to adopt. Now, it is true that, "[a]fter working on the project for several weeks, [Brooker (the student)] expressed reservations since the topic, she believed, was a violation of her religious beliefs." However, "in an effort to respect her beliefs," the professor changed "the assignment . . . via an addendum, allowing her or others with similar beliefs to pursue different advocacy projects. She and one other student opted out of the group assignment and pursued other areas of interest" (Kauffman 2014). In other words, contrary to the suggestion of the filmmakers, no religious discrimination occurred. The professor certainly did not force her to debate the merits of same-sex adoption rights in front of the class.

The film is also an argument against philosophy, but it does not really understand what philosophy is. We can see this in how bad of a philosopher Radisson is. He comes to conclusions – like that God does not exist – for emotional, rather than logical, reasons. He assigns nonexistent texts, like "Hume's Problem of

Induction" (although Hume talked about that problem, Hume never published any article by that name). And, while Radisson does assign Bertrand Russell's "Why I am not a Christian," he seems completely unfamiliar with it, along with the works of William Rowe, Michael Martin, Ricki Monnier, Julian Baggini, John Mackie, Quentin Smith, and many other academic atheists (who study philosophy of religion).

Radisson also does not seem to understand that when Nietzsche said "God is dead," he did not mean that God does not exist. Although Nietzsche was an atheist, when he said "God is dead" he meant that God no longer affected how people live their lives. God is dead like disco is dead; he is gone out of fashion. More specifically, Nietzsche meant that people no longer used the idea of God as a moral compass or a source of meaning. Ironically, if the movie just meant to argue that Nietzsche was wrong about that – that God still affects how many people live their lives – it would have been exactly right. Even the limited success of the movie itself suggests that Nietzsche's pronouncement was quite premature.

Worse still, when Radisson does give arguments for atheism, he just relies on poor arguments from authority. Basically, the argument for atheism he gives in class consists of listing a few smart people who are atheists. This argument of course would stand for no longer than it took to list an equal number of smart people who are theists. Every philosopher knows that the existence of God is not something that can be settled by arguments from authority.

Now, make no mistake (because this will be important later): Arguments from authority are not always fallacious. If a question can be settled empirically – a scientific question, say, like whether vaccines are safe and effective – a lay person (a nonmedical professional) can (and should) cite the relevant experts to answer that question. Better yet, if one cites a consensus of relevant experts that has been reached after years of empirical research – like the consensus that climate change is real – that is a good way to establish what the answer to such a question is. Although scientists have been wrong about things before, it has almost always been about things that were just accepted as conventional wisdom at the time – like beliefs about bodily humors, or explanations of mountains that suggested that the Earth was shrinking. No consensus that was agreed upon after years of confirming evidence has ever been proven wrong. At most, a past highly confirmed theory (like Newton's theory of gravity) was improved upon by later discoveries and supplemented or supplanted by a better one (like Einstein's theory of relativity).

Sorry, if that seemed like an aside. The point is this: There is a reason that the relevant fallacy is called "*inappropriate* appeal to authority" and not just "appeal to authority." It can be completely justified to point out that the majority of scientists believe something to establish what the answer to some scientific question is. But the existence of God is not a scientific question. That is not to say that scientific reasoning is not relevant when trying to answer the question of whether God exists. As we are about to see, it is. But even though, among all academic groups, atheism is highest among philosophers (see Johnson 2017, p. 11), and philosophers would be the most qualified to answer the question, the question of God's existence is not something that can be settled by appeals to authority.

So, without further ado, let us turn to examining the main philosophic arguments of the film, which are given by Josh, in front of his philosophy class, in the form of three lectures.

Evaluating Josh's First Lecture

In his first lecture, Josh begins by observing that you cannot disprove God and then asks us to consider that science's "steady state" model of the universe, which suggested that it had always existed, was disproved by the discovery of the Big Bang. This means, he suggests, for 2500 years, the Bible (Genesis) had it right while science had it wrong. He then goes on to point out that since ordinary objects do not pop into existence from nothing, it would be crazy to think that the universe did. And when a student points out that "If you can ask what created the universe, then I can ask what created God," Josh argues such an objection only applies if God began to exist, which he did not.

We essentially have four arguments here. Let us take each in turn.

Argument #1: "I say, no one can disprove God exists."

There are two things wrong here. First, it is not clear that this is true. It might actually be possible to prove that God does not exist. For starters, there is the problem of evil, which suggests that the existence of evil in this world is proof that God does not exist. Josh mentions this in his third lecture, so we will return to the question of whether that disproof works later. Second, the very concept of God – a perfect being – seems logically incoherent; if it is, God cannot exist anymore than a square circle can.

For example, if God exists, he is supposed to be omnipotent (i.e., all-powerful), which means that it is possible for him to do anything. However, God is also supposed to be all good; that means that God, by definition, cannot do an evil action. So, even though God is supposed to be able to do anything, there is an entire category of things that he cannot do: evil actions. And we cannot say that God just happens to choose to not do evil actions, because, by definition, anything that did an evil act could not be God. So God's existence would entail that there is a being that both can and cannot do an evil action. That is illogical nonsense – like a four-sided object with no sides – and so, the argument goes, God cannot exist.

Now, to be fair, philosophers (both atheists and theists) have long held that being omnipotent does not entail the ability to do what is logically impossible; so God not being able to, for example, make a square circle does not mean that he is not all-powerful. (As I often put it to my students, God can do anything, but "make a square circle" is not a thing.) It is in this way that theists often try to get out of the "Can God create a stone he can't lift" paradox. But whether such a solution works to resolve the above "God is all-powerful but can't sin" paradox is debatable; if I have the power to sin, God should also; sinning is not logically contradictory. In any event, Martin and Monnier (2003) have an entire book dedicated to arguing for such logical inconsistencies in God's definition; and it quite convincingly argues that attempts to resolve many of the paradoxes do not work. If a perfect being is a logically incoherent concept, then God, as he has been classically defined (a perfect being), contrary to what Josh claims, can be proven to not exist.

Second, even if it were true that God cannot be disproved, that does not mean that God exists. The argument that it does commits what philosophers call the fallacy of appealing to ignorance – thinking the fact that you cannot prove something false is a reason to think that it is true. This is decidedly not the case. As Bertrand Russell (1952) pointed out, it is impossible to prove that a tiny teapot does not orbit the sun between Earth and Mars. Even if astronomers tried to look everywhere with a telescope and did not find one, a "teapotist" could still say that they were not looking at the right place at the right time, or that the teapot is too small to be seen even with a telescope. So, technically, it is impossible to *prove* that it is not there – but that does not mean that it is, or that it is rational to believe that it is.

Now, the theist will insist that this is also a fallacy: "If you can't prove something true, then it's false." And yes, sometimes, that is a fallacy. In some cases, you may not be able to prove something true because the evidence for it is impossible to access. For example, it would be impossible to prove what color of shirt I was wearing as I typed this sentence. Any concrete evidence of this has been lost to time, and it would be impossible to prove to you that, say, I was wearing a green sweatshirt. (You might trust my testimony, but proof that I was not lying would be impossible.) This does not mean, however, that an inability to prove something true never tells one anything about the truth of a proposition. Why?

When it comes to existential matters – i.e., when it comes to questions about whether or not something exists – the burden of proof is on the believer. This is not a legal burden of proof, although that is a related concept. But if you want to believe that something exists – Russell's celestial teapot, for example, or Bigfoot – then you are required to have good (preferably publicly available) evidence that the thing in question exists, at least if you want your belief in the existence of that thing to be rational. And if that burden is not met, then disbelief is rational. For example, if no good evidence that Bigfoot exists has ever been produced, then the belief that Bigfoot exists is irrational, and the disbelief in his existence is justified.

To be clear: A lack of evidence for, say, Bigfoot does not 100% prove that Bigfoot does not exist. Like the teapot, it is logically possible that Bigfoot is always hiding in just the right spot and never leaves any evidence of himself behind. But the rationality of belief is not dictated by what can and cannot be proven with 100% certainty; it is determined by the state of the evidence overall – what the preponderance of evidence suggests. After all, very little can be proven with 100% certainty; as Descartes (and *Inception*, and *The Matrix*) showed us, we can never even be 100% sure that we are not stuck in a very vivid dream. If certainty were required for knowledge, a person could know nothing at all (besides, perhaps, as Descartes taught us, "I exist"). But it is not. As Hume (1748) put it, "A wise man, therefore, proportions his belief to the evidence" ("Of Miracles," Part I).

What is more, most things that possibly could exist do not exist. Just think of all the different objects that one could imagine orbiting our sun, or creatures (or even gods!) that one could imagine exist. Now, if there were some good evidence for, and some good evidence against, something's existence, agnosticism would probably be the most rational response. Just say "I don't know" or "I hold no position." But the default starting position, when it comes to some thing's existence, is that it does not exist; so only if you can overcome that position with evidence are you justified in believing that the thing in question actually does exist.

So, an inability to prove that God does exist would not 100% prove that he does not, but a lack of evidence for God's existence (after an honest search for it) would be enough reason to conclude that he does not. Contrary to the common aphorism, at least when it comes to existential matters, *absence of evidence is evidence of absence*. Usually, if something exists, it would leave some evidence behind; so carefully looking but not finding such evidence is good reason to think that it does not exist. This is certainly true of God; if superman were real, you can guarantee that we would know about it. Likewise, the influence of an infinite being with infinite powers would be able to be seen in the world. This is called the problem of divine hiddenness.

Now, Josh would say that we *can* see God's influence on the world, but that brings us to his second argument.

Argument #2: "For 2500 years, The Bible had it right and science had it wrong."

Josh's argument to this conclusion is that, while scientists thought that the universe had always existed (they accepted The Steady State theory which says that the universe has an infinite past), the Bible maintained that it had a beginning. Since we discovered that the universe began with a "big bang," we proved that the scientists (for thousands of years) were wrong and that the Bible – theism, Christianity – always had it right. But neither of those two things is actually true.

First, the defeat of the Steady State theory at the hands of the Big Bang theory, which proved that the universe had a beginning, is not an example of "science getting it wrong." To understand why, a little science history is necessary.

First of all, Josh says that science has accepted Aristotle's "Steady State Theory" since he proposed it 2500 years ago. There are multiple things wrong with this statement. First, Aristotle did not believe The Steady State theory. As I will discuss momentarily, that scientific theory was not conceived until the 1940s. Now Aristotle did believe that matter had always existed, but his arguments to that effect were philosophic, not scientific. In fact, the rudiments of what we now call science today, and especially "the scientific method," did not come until around 1620 with Francis Bacon; before then, inquiries into nature just fell under the category of philosophy, or later "natural philosophy," and their methodology did not resemble what we today call "science" at all (see Hepburn and Anderson 2021). So it is categorically false, for numerous reasons, to say that science accepted The Steady State theory for

2500 years. Neither science, nor the Steady State Theory, is anything close to that old.

What is more, before the 1900s, there was no established scientific consensus (and certainly not one established by confirmable scientific reasoning) about the age of the universe, or whether it had a beginning or not; there just was not enough information. Granted, most scientists believed the universe was not expanding or contracting – that it was more or less "static" (i.e., that basically everything outside the solar system just is where it always has been) – because that is what Newton thought; but Newton thought that because that is all his instruments would allow him to observe. When you measure distant stellar objects with weak telescopes, they do not look like they are moving. In fact, Newton's theory of gravity entailed that things should be moving (because they should be gravitationally affecting each other). To fix this problem – his theory did not fit with his observations – Newton invoked God. For example, Newton thought God had placed stars in perfect balance so that the gravitational forces they exerted on each other canceled each other out (see Thayer 2005).

Two things here are worth noting. First, this example shows us how inserting God into science is unscientific and leads to erroneous conclusions (we now know everything in the universe *is* moving). Second, although Newton's theory entailed that the universe could remain, essentially like it is, for eternity – it did not entail that it always had been that way. Newton's theory was entirely consistent with God "placing" the stars just where they needed to be, at a specific point in the past, and thus the universe having a beginning. The "static state" theory was about whether the universe was stable or changing, not whether it had a beginning or not.

The theory that it was changing, specifically that it was expanding, was first proposed by Russian scientist Alexander Friedmann in 1922 (see Friedmann 1922). (He basically made the idea consistent with relativity.) Later that decade, in 1929, Hubble gave us the first astronomic observations that distant galaxies appear to be traveling away from us (at a speed proportional to their distance; see Hubble 1929). In 1931, Georges Lemaître (who had independently developed ideas similar to Friedmann's in 1927) reverse engineered the idea and concluded that, if the universe will be bigger in the future, then it must have been smaller in the past; that means, given quantum mechanics, all the matter in the universe could have originally been condensed into a single particle, a "primeval atom" he called it, from which the universe then emerged (see Lemaître 1927, 1931). That idea was later developed into the Big Bang theory by George Gamow (see Gamow 1946, 1948a, b).

The Steady State theory Josh mentions was developed that same year (1948), as a competing theory, by Herman Bondi and Thomas Gold (see Bondi and Gold 1948), and 4 months later by Fred Hoyle (1948). (Competition is common and necessary in science to make sure that the best theory ends up being accepted.) And, yes, the Steady State Theory *was* popular in the 1950s; but it was refuted with the discovery of the cosmic microwave background radiation in 1965 (Penzias and Wilson), which the Big Bang Theory predicted but The Steady State theory could not account for. So it is false that science accepted the Steady State theory for 2500 years; at best, some scientists did so for a decade – and even then, it was contested.

Now, it should be noted that Georges Lemaître, who first proposed the "primeval atom" idea, was a Catholic priest. But he always maintained that his scientific theories, including the primeval atom, were completely separate from his religious beliefs. In fact, he was quite surprised when Pope Pius XII said that his theory vindicated Catholic dogma.

> As far as I see, such a theory [of the primeval atom] remains entirely outside any metaphysical or religious question. It leaves the materialist free to deny any transcendental Being. He may keep, for the bottom of space-time, the same attitude of mind he has been able to adopt for events occurring in non-singular places in space-time. For the believer, it removes any attempt to familiarity with God, as were Laplace's chiquenaude or Jeans' finger. It is consonant with the wording of Isaiah speaking of the "Hidden God" hidden even in the beginning of the universe ... Science has not to surrender in face of the Universe and when Pascal tries to infer the existence of God from the supposed infinitude of Nature, we may think that he is looking in the wrong direction. (Lemaître 1958/1996, p. 60)

And he would seem to be right, since Alexander Friedmann (whose theories of an expanding universe preceded Lemaître's) was not religious, and George Gamow who developed Lemaître's Primordial Atom theory into the Big Bang Theory was an atheist.

What is more, the whole reason we know the Big Bang happened is science. Religious revelation did not prove the theory true – scientific observation and reasoning did. So the acceptance of The Big Bang theory is not an example of science getting it wrong. The issue of the universe's age essentially remained a scientifically unresolved issue until it was resolved, by science, in the twentieth century. The history of the debate about whether the universe expands or is static, and whether it has a beginning or not, is a prime example that, and of how, science gets it right.

Second, contrary to Josh's claim, the Bible did not "have it right."

First of all, Josh says that Lemaître (the catholic priest mentioned above who proposed the Primordial Atom idea) said that "the entire universe, jumping into existence in a trillionth of a trillionth of a second, out of nothingness in an unimaginably intense flash of light, is how he would expect the universe to respond if God were to actually utter the command in Genesis 1:3, 'Let there be light'." But Josh does not provide a source for this quote, and after an extensive search, I could find nowhere Lemaître said it. And given the quote from Lemaître above – in which he said his theory was completely unrelated to his religious beliefs, and for which I did provide a source – it would be quite surprising if he did. So one must conclude that Josh is (or, the creators of the movie are) fabricating this quote.

Second of all, even if Lemaître did say this, he is completely wrong. The biblical description of creation does not match up, at all, with what the Big Bang Theory tells us happened. First, the biblical creation story does not say that light came first. The heavens (the sky) and the Earth (the planet, along with its oceans) came first. "In the beginning God created the heavens and the earth. The earth was without form, and void; and darkness was on the face of the deep. And the Spirit of God was hovering over the face of the waters" (Gen. 1:1–2). It was after this that God created the light.

"Then God said, 'Let there be light'; and there was light" (Gen 1:3). The Big Bang theory tells us that light (along with every form of radiation) was emitted when the Big Bang happened, and that the Earth (with its skies and oceans) came billions of years later. Indeed, as the Christian young Earth creationists at Answers in Genesis are happy to point out, nothing about the biblical account of creation matches up at all with what the Big Bang entails happened (see Lisle 2010), and the Bible entails that the universe is only about 6000 years old, not billions (see Mortenson 2011).

By pointing to the one thing that the Big Bang theory and the biblical creation story have in common – light – Josh is essentially doing what fans of Nostradamus do. They take his vague quatrains, and then after something occurs (like WWII), they find one thing Nostradamus' writings have in common with it (e.g., "Hister" kind of sounds like "Hilter") and conclude that he predicted the whole thing. (In reality, Hister is the Danube river; Nostradamus was not even talking about a person; see Hister n.d.). This is called postdiction and is a staple in pseudoscience and vacuous arguments (see Postdiction n.d.). In short, the fact that both the Big Bang theory and Genesis 1 mention "light" does not mean that the Bible describes the Big Bang.

What is more, the Big Bang theory cannot match what the Bible says happened at creation because, as biblical scholars will tell you, the Bible actually relays two completely contradictory creation accounts. As biblical scholar Bart Ehrman (2021) puts it, if you make a list of what happens during the creation story of Genesis Chapter 1 and then the creation story in Genesis Chapter 2, and in what order they occurred, you will not find "two complementary accounts of how the creation took place; they appear to be two accounts that are at odds with each other in fundamental and striking ways."

So, contrary to what Josh says, the Bible did not get things right for 2500 years while science got it wrong. Instead, in the twentieth century, science completely and irrefutably disproved the biblical account of creation which had dominated religious thought for at least that long.

Argument #3: God Is Why There Is Something, Rather Than Nothing

To make this argument, Josh says "In the real world, we never see things jumping into existence out of nothingness, but atheists want to make one small exception to this rule: namely, the universe and everything in it." Here Josh is essentially suggesting that the universe must have a creator, since something does not come from nothing, and that creator must be God. There are two things wrong with this argument, one scientific, the other philosophical (i.e., logical and linguistic).

The scientific problem is this: Science actually has revealed that something can come from nothing. Quantum mechanics predicts, and experiment has shown that, at the quantum level, events called vacuum fluctuations happen all the time. In a complete vacuum, where there is no matter, sometimes, randomly, unpredictably, and without cause, particles come into existence (see Mainland and Mulligan 2019). What is more, Ed Tryon (1973) has demonstrated that all theories and observations are completely consistent with our universe being the result of just such a fluctuation.

In other words, the Big Bang could just be a result of a random vacuum fluctuation in the background space (what is also known as the quantum foam). Usually, particles that appear in this way quickly interact and annihilate one another, thus returning the foam to its former state; but it is also possible for such a process to take a very long time. So, it is outright false that in science we never see things jumping into existence from nothing. We do, and the universe could actually be one of those things.

The philosophical problem is this: To the extent that science (or experience) says that something cannot come from nothing, it is talking about ordinary medium-sized objects. Chairs and tables do not just spring into existence; they have an explanation for how they came to be. But such objects are made up of the matter of the universe itself, and explanations for how they came to be are, ultimately, explanations for how the matter that comprises them came to be configured as it is. Think about an explanation that accounts for the existence of a chair. Simplistically speaking, some person(s) cut down a tree, shaped its wood into pieces, and then screwed them together. That is why the chair came into existence. But the matter that makes up the chair preexisted the chair (it was in the tree), and the atoms that make up the tree date back to the origin of the Earth and ultimately the beginning of the universe. So, explanations for the "existence" of ordinary everyday objects are really just explanations of "matter arrangement," not explanations for the existence of the matter which comprises them.

This matters (pardon the pun) because the argument Josh is invoking here (without citing it) is the Kalam Cosmological argument (which has ancient origins but has been recently rearticulated by William Lane Craig (2000)), which basically argues that because the existence of things like chairs need an explanation, so does the universe. But the fact that (a) there must be an explanation for *how the matter that comprises an object came to be arranged as it is* does not entail that (b) there must be an explanation for *the existence of the matter itself*. The fallacy such an argument commits is called equivocation. And since to demand that *the universe needs an explanation*, just is to demand that *the existence of matter needs an explanation*, if we change the argument to avoid the equivocation, the argument will then simply beg the question (see Johnson 2022b).

To put the same point a different way, we cannot say "usually, when matter comes into existence, it has a cause – so matter coming into existence at the beginning of the universe must have a cause" because the beginning of the universe was the only time that matter came into existence (unless you count vacuum fluctuations, which we have seen do not have a cause). The theist can *assume* that the creation of the universe's matter must have a cause, but since that was a onetime event, we actually have no evidence that is the case (and, thanks to quantum mechanics, some good evidence that it is not).

Argument #4: God Does Not Need an Explanation Because He Is Eternal

Josh presents this argument in reply to a student who quotes Dawkins: "[I]n his book, *The God Delusion*, Richard Dawkins says that if you tell me God created the universe then I have the right to ask you who created God." Josh replies, "Dawkins' question only makes sense in terms of a god who has been created. It doesn't make sense in terms of an uncreated god, which is the kind of god Christians believe in."

Dawkins does say something like this in *The God Delusion*, and Josh's reply is the usual one. In fact, Josh's argument is part of the Kalam Cosmological argument, which was developed long ago by Muslim scholar Al-Ghazālī, who realized that the theistic arguments of the falāsifa (a competing school of Muslim thought) were incorrect. They argued that God must exist because all contingent material objects depend on the existence of a necessary entity. Al-Ghazālī realized that, even if that is true, that necessary entity could just be the universe itself. He thus set out to prove that the universe had a beginning and thus was not a necessary entity. His philosophical argument to this conclusion is interesting (see Goodman 1971), and (as we saw last section) his conclusion was eventually vindicated by science. Still, even if there must be a necessary entity, as we shall see, it need not be God.

When it comes to Josh's argument here, there are two main problems. First, Josh's point really only works if "created" in this context means caused. Causes must temporally precede their effects, so anything that has existed forever (like Christians assume God has) cannot have a cause. Fair enough. But if "created," in this context, means "explains" – which I think is a fair interpretation of what Dawkins is getting at – then Josh's point does not stand. Explanations do not have to temporally precede what they explain, and if it really is true that *everything* must have an explanation, then God must have one just as much as the universe must. Now, why do explanations not have to temporally precede what they explain? Understanding the next problem with Josh's argument should make this clear.

Even if it is the case that God would not need a creator because things that have no beginning cannot have a cause, and even if the universe has a cause, that does not mean God exists because he must be the creator of the universe. Simply put, the universe could have been caused by something else – perhaps a powerful being from outside the universe who is not God. But we may not even need to appeal to beings at all; the universe could have been caused by the aforementioned quantum foam. The foam is just a quantum probability field that is, always has been, and always will be, randomly fluctuating in the background space. What is more, as the aforementioned Ed Tryon showed, the foam can produce events like the Big Bang. If eternal things do not need a creator, then the quantum foam does not need a creator (any more than God does); since it could have generated the universe, there is no need to invoke God as the cause of the universe. It could have sprung from the quantum foam.

Now, in reply to this, the theist might demand that, while the quantum foam does not need (and indeed cannot have) a *cause* because it is eternal, it still needs an explanation – an explanation for why it exists at all. But if the theist can demand that the foam needs an explanation, despite the fact that it is eternal, then the atheist can demand that God needs an explanation despite the fact that he would be eternal. In fact, the demand for God's explanation has much more force to it. The quantum foam is, for all intents and purposes, nothing; it is just a probability field. Anything invoked to explain it would demand even more of an explanation than the foam itself. If our attempt at providing explanations is going to have to bottom out somewhere – which it seems it must – it would be best if it bottomed out in something like the quantum foam. It is about as simple as something can be. But God is defined as an infinite being with infinite properties and powers; as such, God would demand an explanation more than anything that he was invoked to explain. So, if we end up going down the "universe must have been created" path of Josh's argument, we end up realizing that there is a much better explanation for the universe than God.[1]

Why would God demand an explanation more than the quantum foam? By definition, good explanations must (among other things) have wide scope (they must have explanatory power, and not raise unanswerable questions), and be parsimonious (aka simple – they must not multiply entities beyond necessity). This is logic and philosophy of science 101 (see Schick 2020, Ch 6). Now, to explain the universe, the quantum vacuum fluctuation theory just invokes the quantum foam and vacuum fluctuations; and not only do we already know that both the quantum foam and vacuum fluctuations exist, but also, as I just explained, the foam is just about as simple as anything could get. God, on the other hand, is an infinite being, with infinite properties and powers; not only do we *not* already know he exists (this argument is trying to prove that he does), but we also do not know how his powers work. How he would have created the universe is a complete unknowable mystery. So, while the quantum vacuum fluctuation theory has what a good explanation needs (it is parsimonious and wide-scoping), the God hypothesis does not. Thus, contrary to what Josh claims, it seems we *would* have to commit "intellectual suicide to believe in a creator," and atheists are not hard pressed, at all, "to find any credible alternative explanation for how things came to be." It is the theistic explanation that is not a credible alternative (see Schick 2003).

Simply put, Josh wants his "God did it" hypothesis to be scientific, but to say "God did it" is basically equivalent to saying "It was magic." "An incomprehensible being did it with an incomprehensible force." And that is utterly unscientific. Indeed, to invoke magic explanations for what we currently cannot explain is intellectually vacuous enough; such reasoning engages in what I have dubbed "The Mystery therefore magic" fallacy, a variety of appealing to ignorance (see Johnson 2018). It is an approach also known as the "god of the gaps" approach, where God is just invoked anytime we are currently unable to explain something. But it is much worse to invoke magic explanations for what we already have good explanations for. If I explain how the magic trick is done, and you still insist the magician has magic powers, you are being intentionally obtuse and stubborn. The same is true if you still insist that God must be the explanation for the universe, despite the fact that we have available scientific explanations for it.

Evaluating Josh's Second Lecture

Radisson replies to Josh's first lecture with a quote, from Stephen Hawking's *The Grand Design* which suggests that the universe can and must explain itself. "Because there is a law such as gravity, the universe can and will create itself from nothing" (Hawking and Mlodinow 2012). So Josh begins his second lecture by quoting John Lennox, an Oxford mathematician, Christian apologist, and critic of Hawking, who says that Hawking's argument about a self-explanatory universe is circular. "Nonsense remains nonsense, even when talked about by world-famous scientists." Josh then goes on to quote Hawking's claim that "philosophy is dead" and so concludes that, if Hawking is such an infallible authority, "there's really no need for this class." He then goes on to point out that evolution cannot account for life's origins, and that Darwin himself said that "nature does not jump," yet in the cosmic scheme of things, "life did appear suddenly." Again, we shall examine each argument in turn.

Argument #5: John Lennox Refutes Hawking

Essentially what we have here is Josh and Raddison engaged in a "smart guy" quote war. But as I pointed out above, the existence of God is not something that can be settled by appeals to authority. So this part of the debate is rather silly. Still, one wonders, is Lennox right about Hawking's quote? Is Hawking engaged in circular reasoning?

He might be, but it is impossible to evaluate the quote as it is stated in the movie because it is completely out of context. There is a lengthy explanation of why Hawking concludes this is true in the book, but no details on that are mentioned in the movie – and that is what we would have to look at to see whether his reasoning is really circular.

What is more, we cannot just take Lennox's word for it (that Hawking is engaged in circular reasoning), because he is not qualified to evaluate Hawking's work. Yes, he is an Oxford professor, but he is a professor of mathematics, not a theoretical physicist (like Hawking) or a philosopher. Now, he has an emeritus position as a professor of philosophy of science at Green Templeton College, but that college has a stated goal of Christian apologetics, and all of his works on the topic are in books published by Christian publishers (e.g., Zondervan, The Good Book Company, and Gospel Folio Press). As far as I can tell, he has not published a single work in philosophy (in an academic journal or book) that was peer reviewed by other philosophers. I have personally looked at some of his philosophical arguments and have not been impressed. He makes very basic mistakes.

This teaches us an important philosophical lesson about appeals to authority: The fact that someone is an authority in one area does not mean that they are an authority in another. Someone being a scientist does not mean they are qualified to speak on all scientific questions; there are many fields and subfields in science, most of which require very specific expertise. Making it seem like someone who agrees with you is an expert about something, when they are not, is a very common tactic among those who argue for pseudoscience.

Now, by the same token, I am not qualified to evaluate Hawking's claim either. As far as I can tell, Hawking's argument is rooted in gravity and M-theory, which is a kind of String-theory – and if that theory is right, the universe may very well be self-creating. What I do know is that M-theory is not confirmed, at least not to the degree that quantum mechanics and vacuum fluctuations are confirmed. So I think the explanation I mentioned in the last section for the universe's existence is on more solid ground. But I cannot say that Hawking is right or wrong, or that his argument is circular, because, like Lennox, I lack the relevant expertise.

What I can say is that the producers of *God's Not Dead* seemingly had Prof. Raddison use this Hawking quote for a specific purpose: they wanted to use the pithy quote from John Lennox to "knock it down" thus making the idea that you can explain the universe without God seem nonsensical. This is essentially a "strawman" fallacy; they are making the argument seem weaker than it is. There are plenty of other scientists who agree with Hawking's basic idea, and lots of evidence to support the claim; what is more, as I attempted to show in the last section, because God is infinite in all respects, as an explanation, "God did it" is necessarily lacking. When it comes to the existence of the universe, having no explanation at all, and just saying I do not know, would be better, both scientifically and intellectually.

Argument #6 "Philosophy is Dead"

Josh's argument here is somewhat clever. If Radisson can disagree with Hawking when he claims that "Philosophy is dead" (which obviously Radisson would), then Josh can disagree with Hawking when he says that the universe is self-created. Josh's basic point, that it is sometimes okay to disagree with experts, is correct. Again, Radisson relying on appeals to authority for his argument for atheism is getting him into trouble. That is bad philosophy.

But it is also worth noting that there is a big difference between a layperson disagreeing with Hawking on a matter of theoretical physics (about which Hawking is an expert) and disagreeing with Hawking on a matter of philosophy. When Hawking says that philosophy is dead, he is speaking completely outside of his area of expertise. Like Neil deGrasse Tyson, and Bill Nye the Science guy – who both have made similar kinds of statements – Hawking did not really understand what philosophy is when he made these statements. In fact, some (see Zabala and Davis 2013) have suggested that Hawking simply confused philosophy with theology. In the book, Hawking says philosophy is dead because it has not taken the work of science seriously enough, but philosophers do nothing of the sort, with many branches of philosophy (e.g., philosophy of mind) being greatly influenced by developments in science (e.g., neuroscience), and others (e.g., metaphysics) being necessary for interpreting what science has revealed (e.g., quantum mechanics). (Some scientists have even abandoned that task with the mantra "shut up and calculate," leaving the interpretation of quantum mechanics to philosophers alone; see Baggott 2021.) What Hawking seems to be addressing is the fact that science has supplanted theological explanations – explanations for things like the existence of the universe – but theologians seem to have not noticed. But if he is right, that would mean that *theology* is dead, not philosophy. What is more, Hawking does not realize that there are branches of philosophy – ethics, esthetics, and epistemology – about which scientific discoveries are (usually) irrelevant, and thus are not undermined at all by science's progress. If he thinks philosophy is dead, he also does not realize how philosophy of science is necessary to even understand what science is and why the conclusions of scientific reasoning are justified. As I pointed out in the first lecture of "The Big Questions of Philosophy," philosophy is the mother of all academic disciplines – the academy's "Big Bang" of sorts – and without philosophy, no academic discipline is possible. Indeed, Hawking engages in philosophy throughout his book – a pretty hard thing to do, if philosophy is dead (see Scott 2012). (In fact, because Hawking's claim is philosophical in nature, if he intends it as factual, it becomes self-defeating.)

In the real world, Hawking's statement about the death of philosophy was condemned by scientists (see Rovelli 2018) and philosophers alike (see Zabala and Davis 2013; Norris 2011). (I personally played a role in curing Bill Nye of this kind of misunderstanding of philosophy, after writing him an open letter and getting to speak to him at a conference; see Johnson 2016; Goldhill 2017.) Indeed, philosophy is so alive and well today that the creators of *God's Not Dead* felt that they needed a movie to demonize it – although the demonization of philosophy is part of a larger anti-intellectual movement in evangelical Christianity that distrusts what academics say on everything from American history to evolution (see Giberson and Stephens 2011). But, speaking of evolution…

Argument #7: Science Cannot Explain the Origin of Life

Josh's argument about evolution is very confused. First of all, Darwin did not develop the theory of evolution; it was already theorized by a number of scientists, and established by a rich fossil record, before Darwin's research (see Sloan 2019). Darwin was seeking, and discovered, the mechanism by which evolution occurred: natural selection. Second of all, evolution does not account for the origin of life because that is not what the theory is about. Darwin's famous book was called "On The Origin of Species," not "On The Origin of Life." He was trying to explain *how* the Earth went from housing only single celled organisms to housing the complex life it does today. (Again, it was already known that it did; he was trying to explain how that happened.) Criticizing his theory on the basis that it does not explain the origin of life would be like criticizing the germ theory of disease because it cannot account for the effects of brain injuries. That is not what the theory is about. Darwin's theory of natural selection is, however, one of the most successful scientific theories in history, and it does completely remove the need to invoke God to explain speciation and the diversity of life (which Christianity has historically explained by appealing to God and the creation story).

Now, it is true that there is not a scientific consensus about how life did first appear on our planet. What Josh fails to mention, however, is that there are many viable theories about how that occurred; we just do not know which one actually occurred (or whether more than one occurred) because fossil evidence of such an event is not possible (see Choi and Dutfield 2022; DeWitt 2000). But since we know that life could have appeared naturally, there is no reason to invoke God to explain why or how it did. That would be like not being able to figure out which of the many holes in my attic the squirrels used to get in, and then concluding that they must have been put there by aliens. We know it must have been one of them; we just do not know which one. In fact, even if I could not find any holes in my attic, such a conclusion would not be justified. It would be more likely that there was a way into my attic that I could not find. In the same way, even if we did not have any viable theories about how life first appeared, "God did it" would still fail to be a good explanation. It would be more likely that there is a natural explanation that we simply cannot detect. Jumping to "God did it" would, yet again, be an unscientific "god of the gaps" jump that commits the aforementioned mystery therefore magic fallacy. Notice also that embracing such reasoning would have prevented us from ever developing theories to explain the origins of life, and thus discovering how it could have occurred. Appealing to the supernatural holds back science by discouraging any attempt to discover the real explanation.

Argument #8: "Nature Does Not Jump"

Here, Josh claims that the appearance of life on Earth happened so quickly that it violates Darwin's "nature does not jump" rule. But there are multiple things wrong with this argument as well. First of all, life has been evolving since about 3.5 billion years ago, when simple life first emerged on Earth (see Schopf 2006). The universe is 13.8 billion years old. So it has taken 25% of the universe's existence to produce life on Earth in its current form; this is hardly the wink of an eye, even in cosmic terms. Second, even if we limit ourselves to the last 600 million years – the time it took to go from simple animals to *Homo sapiens* – yes, that is a short amount of time when compared to the age of the universe. But that can hardly be considered the kind of jump that Darwin said nature avoids. In fact, that is exactly the kind of time frame that Darwin suggested natural selection would need to evolve simple animals to *Homo sapiens*.

What Josh is doing is equivocating on the word "jump." What Darwin meant is that evolutionary change does not happen over hundreds or even thousands of years, but over hundreds of millions of years. And he was right. Pointing out that hundreds of millions of years is brief, when compared to the age of the universe, is completely irrelevant. That would be like you saying "I can't jump high enough to touch the bottom of a basketball rim" and me replying "Sure you can! It takes just a fraction of the effort it would take to jump over the moon."

Evaluating Josh's Third Lecture

In his last lecture, Josh answers the problem of evil with the free will defense. God allows evil to occur because he wants us to have the free will to choose him and thus enter heaven. God simply wants the students to have the choice to choose to accept or reject him – a choice that Radisson wants to take away. Josh then argues that atheists like Radisson have no grounds for moral absolutes, and indeed no reason to be moral at all, and yet would obviously claim that a student cheating on a test was "wrong." He follows this with the famous Dostoyevsky quote "If God does not exist, then everything is permissible." Josh goes on to make a similar claim: If God does not exist, life is meaningless. He then confronts Radisson directly, claiming that: "Science supports his existence; you know the truth. So why do you hate him?" When Radisson admits it is because God took everything away from him, Josh simply asks: "How can you hate someone if they don't exist?"

When I watched *God's Not Dead* on that chilly Sunday afternoon, it was at this point in the film that everyone in the theater applauded vigorously. But is Josh's argument as good as the crowd thought?

Argument #9: The Free Will Defense

Josh is probably right that the problem of evil is the atheists' most "potent weapon" against theism, at least if by "potent" he means "most often used." The problem of evil is an argument which concludes that God does not exist because, if he did, he would prevent evil, and yet evil clearly exists. Essentially, the argument asks, if God exists, then why is there evil? The free will solution answers that question thusly: God allows evil so that humans can have free will. To put it a bit more precisely, God could stop evil, but only by causing people to always choose to do good; but if he causes their choices, then they are not really free; and if their choices are not really free, then they are not really good – at least, not morally good. One can get moral credit for doing an action only if one freely chooses to do it; if God controlled all our actions, sure there would be no evil, but then there would also be no moral good. And since a world without moral good would not really be good at all, a world with both evil and moral good would be preferable – and so God allows that kind of world to exist, even though it contains evil.

But there are quite a few problems with the free will defense that Prof. Radisson fails to mention in his reply to Josh. First of all, there are multiple versions of the problem of evil, and the free will defense is really only effective against one of them. For example, since hurricanes, earthquakes, and tsunamis are not caused by the freely willed decisions of humans, the free will defense cannot explain why God allows such events to happen. In fact, as I have argued elsewhere, the deeper problem is trying to explain why God would weave the inevitability of such events into the very laws that govern the universe (Johnson 2011, 2013a). Why would God make us live in a house with human killing machines built into the very walls? John Hick (1975) suggests that such "natural evils" are for "soul making" (i.e., to give humans the opportunity to develop moral and spiritual virtues). But (a) humans produce enough evil on our own for soul making – we do not need God piling on with natural evils; (b) usually those who suffer from natural evil have no opportunity to develop such virtues (e.g., the

227,000 people who died in the 2004 Indian Ocean Tsunami did not "grow spiritually" as a result); and (c) quite often, natural evil does not develop virtue in those of us who survive. In my estimation, no satisfactory answer to the logical problem of natural evil has ever been proposed.

Another version is called the evidential problem of evil. It asks why God would allow especially horrendous evil, like the holocaust, child rape, and animal suffering, and suggests that the fact that such evils occur (without any seeming justifying reason to allow them to occur) is good evidence against God's existence (see Rowe 1979; Loftus 2021). Free will cannot really explain this because (a) doing something like causing Hitler to choose to call off the holocaust would not make moral good in the world impossible, and (b) God could prevent things like the holocaust, without interfering even in Hitler's free will, by simply giving someone (e.g., Hitler) an appropriately timed heart attack (see Johnson 2022). The only real attempt at an answer to the evidential problem is called skeptical theism, which observes that God could have reasons for allowing such evil that we simply cannot comprehend. I have pointed out elsewhere, however, that skeptical theism is mathematically unsound (seemingly unjustified evil still lowers the probability of God's existence even if he could have reasons we cannot comprehend; see Johnson 2013b), makes moral knowledge impossible, and renders theism irrational by making it unfalsifiable (see Johnson 2021).

The free will solution has been thought by many philosophers to be a successful answer to the logical problem of *moral evil*, which suggests God and moral evil (evil caused by human choice) coexisting is a logical impossibility. But even then, there are issues. James Sterba (2019, 2020) has recently argued that the supposed "accepted solution" does not actually work, and there really is no version of the free will defense that does. I have recently argued that the only version that even logically could work is unviable because it comes with theological consequences that practically no theist would be willing to accept. In short, for the free will solution to work, God would have to maintain a complete noninterference policy when it comes to free will; if free will really is that important and fragile, then God must never interfere in any free will decision at all; and there could be no reason to interfere with one decision, but not another. But if God never interferes in free will decisions, that would mean that God does not perform miracles (because such interference in the world would interfere in free will), does not answer prayers (because they almost always require God to cause people to choose to do certain actions), cannot interfere by incarnating himself as a person, and has no control over how human history turns out. Many biblical stories are non-sense as well; for example, God cannot "harden Pharaoh's heart" if God must preserve human free will. Needless to say, that is not something that Josh, or the creators of *God's Not Dead*, or any Christian for that matter, would be willing to accept. (If all that was too quick, see my paper on the topic; Johnson 2022a.)

In short, Josh mentions the free will defense as a solution to the problem of evil but does nothing to address the many shortcomings the argument has. What is worse, Raddison does nothing to offer rather basic rejoinders to it.

Argument #10: Without God, Everything Is Permissible

The basis of this argument is that, if there is no God, there is no grounding for moral truths (i.e., nothing is morally right or wrong). Josh's argument here assumes and requires what is known as "divine command theory," the position that what grounds moral truths – what makes that which is good, good – is God's commands. Love is morally good because, and only because, God says it is; murder is wrong because, and only because, God says it is. If this is true, then yes – if God does not exist, there are no moral truths. But divine command theory is one of the most discredited and rejected theories in all of philosophy – and it has been since Plato refuted it in the *Euthyphro*.

In the *Euthyphro*, Socrates and Euthyphro use the word "piety" (not "morality"), and they are talking about the Greek gods (not the Christian God), but the point is the same. Euthyphro says that what makes the pious pious is being loved by the gods. Socrates points out that Euthyphro's position rests on a kind of correlational fallacy; while it is true that the gods love the things which are pious, the reason they love them is because they are pious – because they recognize something about them that makes them pious. Socrates and Plato want to know what that something is. The same mistake is made by divine command theorists. Yes, God commands what is morally good, like love, but he does so because he recognizes something about it that is morally good; love is not morally good because it is commanded.

Or think of it this way: If God's commands are the only thing that determine moral truth, then the only reason murder is wrong is the fact that God forbids it; if he had instead commanded it, murder would be morally good. Of course, you may say, "God would never do that." But why would you think that? Because there is something intrinsically wrong with murder? If you think that, then you are not a divine command theorist; you think there is something *about* murder that makes God forbid it. On divine command theory, the *only thing* that makes something wrong is God forbidding it. So, on divine command theory, moral truths are completely arbitrary; God could command anything, and if he did, it would be morally good. How Raddison should have replied to Josh's Dostoyevski's quote is this: "If God exists, anything could be permissible – at least, if divine command theory is true."

What is worse, divine command theory is essentially just another "god of the gaps" nonanswer. The question of what makes the good good (and what makes the immoral immoral) is an interesting question, and most of the history of ethics has been attempts to answer it. Utilitarianism says that "causing the most amount of happiness" is what makes something good; Kant argued that an act violating reason makes it immoral. Josh thinks that if he cheated on an exam, Radisson would have no basis for saying that what he did was wrong, but there are many different secular ethical theories he could appeal to that would prove exactly that. There is not a consensus among philosophers which theory is correct, and I personally think that the right approach combines them all (see Schick 2004). But it is simply false that, if God does not exist, there is no basis on which to ground moral truths. So the notion that everything becomes permissible if God does not exist is simply false. More importantly, however, notice that if we had been satisfied with divine command theory's "God does it" explanation for moral truths, we would never have made any progress toward finding the real answer to the question (just like genuinely thinking that Zeus or Thor causes lightning would keep us from ever figuring out that lightning is (roughly put) static electricity).

Something else that Radisson could have pointed out is what Darren Slade and I pointed out in our ▶ Chap. 19, "*The Orville* as Philosophy: The Dangers of Religion," in this handbook. Dostoyevsky had it backward. Because God is conceived of as an infinite good, any action, no matter how immoral, can be morally "justified" in the name of God. And believers becoming convinced that they are justified to perform immoral actions in the name of God has happened too many times to count in religious history. The Crusades, inquisitions, the Salem witch trials, 9/11, slavery, and genocide – all of these things are obviously immoral, but believers have done them, again and again, in the name of God (because they became convinced that they were for God's glory and/or were commanded by God). So, contrary to what Josh claims, it is not true that atheism entails that everything is permissible. Instead, theism does; *in the name of God, anything is justifiable.*

Argument #11: Atheists Have No Reason to Be Good

Josh also argues that, without God, there is no reason for a person to be morally good. There are two aspects of this argument. First, without any kind of eternal reward like heaven, Josh argues, there is no reason for someone to not rape, murder, and steal. "With no God, there's no real reason to be moral." While theists who use this argument often think it is devastating, what they do not realize is that they are revealing too much about themselves – and none of it is good. Pop culture icon Penn Jillette put the point this way.

> The question I get asked by religious people all the time is, without God, what's to stop me from raping all I want? And my answer is: I do rape all I want. And the amount I want is zero. And I do murder all I want, and the amount I want is zero. The fact that these people think that if they didn't have this person watching over them that they would go on killing, raping rampages is the most self-damning thing I can imagine. (Interrobang 2012)

Truth be told, secular theories of morality, which explain why that which is immoral is immoral, provide all the reason you need to be moral. The reason to not rape someone is that it is morally wrong. In fact, one could argue that if the only reason a person does not rape and murder others is that they fear they will be punished if they do, then they do not really get moral credit for not doing it. One should avoid immoral behavior because they recognize it as such; they see rape as intrinsically wrong and avoid it for that reason alone. One should do that which is good because they recognize it as such, and are motivated to do that which is good for its own sake. As Maggie Ardiente, a secular humanist (and atheist) who serves as director of development and communications at National Law Center on Homelessness and Poverty, put it

Atheists do good in the world because we know this is the one life we have, so we should make the most of it ... I work for nonprofit organizations not because I have to prove to others that I'm a good person, but [because] working toward an equal and just society makes everyone happier and healthier. (Withrow 2017)

Indeed, because the atheist is the only one that can be completely free of the fear that they might get punished for that which they do wrong, one could argue that only the atheist can act morally – only they can have the pure motivation, unencumbered by fear of divine punishment, that is required for true morally good behavior.

Argument #12: Life Is Meaningless without God

Josh says that if God does not exist, then "everything...is pointless. If professor Radisson is right [and atheism is true], then all of this, all of our struggle, our debate, whatever we decide here is meaningless. Our lives, and ultimately our deaths, are of no more consequence than that of a goldfish." Is life meaningless if God does not exist?

Some theists think that life is meaningless if God does not exist because they think God has a purpose for their life, and that it is only through a divinely selected purpose that a person's life could have a meaning. Essentially, they suggest, a person's life can have meaning only if God gives it one. But suppose that God's purpose for your life was for you to be miserable and then squished by a piano for others' amusement. That would be a divinely ordained purpose, but obviously that would not be a very meaningful life. And if you reply, "But God wouldn't do that, it's pointless" you are admitting that things (lives, events) can have or lack value *intrinsically*, regardless of whether they are divinely selected. Some things are just objectively meaningful, regardless of whether God exists to declare them as such, or not. So life can have a meaningful purpose, even if God does not exist.

Other theists think that, unless our lives are infinite, then our lives are meaningless. If, when you die, you die and that is it, and after a thousand years, everyone will have forgotten you and the universe will be no different than if you had never existed, what is the point? But, again, if some things are intrinsically valuable, it matters not at all that you will not live forever to remember them. As Julian Baggini (2007) might ask, is there really any sense in asking what value or meaning there is in a life that is spent employed doing something you find fulfilling, spending your free time on that which you find most interesting, or in helping others, and coming home to people who love and adore you? Sure, once the sun explodes, it will be like your life never happened – but your life did happen, and there is objective value in that fact.

Worse still, there is very good reason to think that an infinite life would be the most meaningless of all. Life needs to end to have value. Just as a game that never ended would be pointless, so too would existence. Your impending death gives a sense of urgency to your actions that they cannot have if you really will live forever. "You only have so much time, so cherish every moment." If life is infinite, why ever do anything at all, since you could always put it off until tomorrow? Indeed, Bernard Williams (1973) argued that infinite life, even in heaven, would become torture; you will eventually do everything that there is to do, as many times as you can stand...and then have an infinite amount of time to loathe the thought of doing any of them again. Do not get me wrong – it would be better if life was longer. But if *The Good Place* taught us nothing else, it is that if you ever actually got to heaven, you would want the option to eventually leave (see Kimberly Engels's ▶ Chap. 1, "*The Good Place* as Philosophy: Moral Adventures in the Afterlife," in this volume).

Lastly, even if life is meaningless if God does not exist, that is not a good reason to believe that he does. You may not want life to be meaningless, but the fact that you want something to be true does not justify the belief that it is.

Argument #13 "Why do you hate God?"

Josh's final argument is essentially a question. After stating that Radisson knows that the science proves God's existence, Josh asks him why he hates God. And when Radisson confesses it is because God took everything away from him, Josh points out that – logically – you cannot hate something that does not exist.

There are essentially three things wrong here.

First, you can hate something that does not exist. After I published a book on Christmas, and argued that parents would do better by their children if they did not lie to them about Santa, many people claimed that I hated Santa Claus (see Johnson 2015). This is not true; finding problems with lying to children to trick them into believing Santa exists when he does not is different from "hating Santa." But still, when my "fans" say "you hate Santa Claus," they do not think that I believe he exists but loathe him – it is shorthand for hating the idea of Santa, or what he stands for. If Radisson was truly an atheist, it could be in this sense only that he hated God. He hates the idea of God and the religion that promotes it. (But, it should also be made clear, one does not have to hate the idea of God to believe that God does not exist. I do not hate Bigfoot, but I also do not believe Bigfoot exists.)

When Josh asks Radisson why he hates God, he is asking what is called a "loaded question." It comes with the unstated assumption that God exists built right in. Unless you point out that the question is loaded, there is basically no way to answer a loaded question without tacitly seeming to admit that the unstated assumption is true. Notice that, even if Radisson said, "I don't hate God," Josh could ask "how can you refrain from hating something that doesn't exist?" I think the line got such applause in my theater because it endorses a common theist assumption: Atheists secretly believe in God; they just will not admit it. (Indeed, it is plausible to believe that the Raddison character was written to reinforce this common rhetorical ploy.)

The first time Josh asks Radisson that loaded question is when Josh makes the last mistake we will discuss. He precedes it with the statement that "Science supports his existence; you know the truth." As we have seen, this is false; science does not support the existence of God. In fact, as a scientific hypothesis,

"God exists" lacks everything a good scientific hypothesis needs. It raises unanswerable questions and invokes unnecessary entities. What Josh is doing here is called "begging the question," a phrase he misuses at the beginning of his third lecture, but which actually just means "to assume the truth of what you are trying to prove." In no way has he established that science supports God's existence.

Conclusion: It's a Little Rocky (IV)

By the end of the movie, everyone from the Muslim and Buddhist, to the atheist and humanist, has been won over by Jesus because of Josh's brave stand for God. So the movie is an argument not only for God, but also for Christianity. Indeed, Wikipedia labels the entire series of movies as "Christian." This, however, indicates another way the movie's argument fails. Nowhere does the movie explain how Josh's arguments for God's existence entail that Jesus is divine, the messiah, or the son of God. There is no argument for the historicity of the gospels, Jesus' miracles, or his resurrection. While God's existence would stand contrary to the beliefs of Prof. Radisson and Amy (the atheists), convincing them that God exists could just as easily make them Jewish, Muslim, or even just a deist. (Deists believe that God exists, created the world, but does not care for or interfere in it at all. Many of the founding fathers, like Thomas Jefferson, were deists.) Proving that God exists is a far cry from proving that Christianity is true, so even if Josh's arguments work, the movie falls short of its unstated ultimate goal: to prove Christianity. What is more, this failure really reveals the movie's hubris – the implicit assumption that the only way to believe in God is to be a Christian.

But by having every character in the movie convert to Christianity at the end, *God's Not Dead* reminded me a bit of *Rocky IV*, the cold war classic where Rocky Balboa fights the Russian, Ivan Drago. Just like at the end of Rocky IV, where even the Russians are rooting for Rocky ("Rocky! Rocky!), at the end of *God's Not Dead*, even the atheists are rooting for Jesus ("Jesus! Jesus!"). Also, Like *Rocky IV*, *God's not Dead* is anti-intellectual, or antiscience. The Russian boxer Drago trains in a state-of-the-art scientific facility, where they measure the impact of his punches, train him on machines, and try to figure out how to make him a better fighter. Meanwhile Rocky trains on a remote farm, runs out in the snow, and lifts logs (all to an 1980s music montage, of course). *God's not Dead* is very similar. As part of his deathbed conversion, Professor Radisson says that human wisdom pales in comparison to God's. Here the film's writers are echoing the biblical sentiment that any criticism of God must fail because God is so grandiose that we could never comprehend him. Regardless of how convincing any reason or argument against God's existence might seem, it cannot be trusted – it is nothing compared to the reason of God.

Not only does this argument beg the question – it does not establish God's existence but merely assumes it – it also questions the legitimacy of all reasoning. It endorses what is called fideism, the idea that believing by faith (without evidence) is superior to belief based on reason. Indeed, this is all but stated explicitly in the final conversation between Pastor Dave and Rev. Jude at the end of the film, when Jude says Dave's faith was necessary to start the car.

This is problematic for two reasons. One, it is false. You would not cross a bridge built by someone who just had faith that they could; you want the engineer who understands the science and reasoning behind bridge building. Faith is not superior to reasoning. Second, fideism essentially makes knowledge impossible. To see why, recall the aforementioned answer to the problem of evil, skeptical theism, which says that evil cannot count as evidence against God's existence because God could have reasons for allowing evil that we cannot understand. Skeptical theism leads to moral agnosticism. If anything that seems evil could (for all I know) actually be good, then I can't know that anything is evil (see Johnson 2021). For similar reasons, fideism leads to epistemic agnosticism. If no matter how good an argument or the evidence might seem, God might have an argument that defeats it, then I cannot know whether any argument works, whether any evidence is good, or indeed whether anything is true.

So, by embracing fideism, one loses all credibility. Anyone can believe anything by faith, no matter how ridiculous. Religious belief is just a crapshoot. If you are a fideist, and someone says that God is a turnip, you have no right to object. In fact, you have abandoned the very thing that would enable you to do so: argument and reason. If religious belief really is just about choice, a matter of faith, as Josh suggests, then I have just as much reason to believe in Zeus as I do in God; I have just as much reason to believe in many gods as just one; and no argument on the topic matters.

Indeed, an endorsement of fideism and faith is quite ironic coming from a movie that just spent an hour and a half trying to present reasons and evidence for God's existence. Faith is, by definition, belief without reason and evidence. If the movie succeeds in its endeavor and proves that God exists, then it actually eliminates the need for faith – the very thing it champions. Interestingly, I believe that many of my Christian theologian colleagues would object to this movie just as I do. The point of religious faith is exactly that – to believe by faith. My theist friends and I will disagree about whether such belief is advisable, but I think we would all agree that trying to *prove* that God's not dead is a bad idea, whether it is in a movie filled with bad arguments or not.

End Notes

1. In reply to this, the theist might suggest that "God explains himself" but the quantum foam does not. But (a) this is potentially an ad hoc rationalization; the notion that God is a "self-explained being" may have been invented just as a way to deal with this kind of problem; and (b) the atheist could just as easily say "the foam explains itself," and have just as much support for that claim – indeed, perhaps more, because the idea that it simply does not need an explanation, because it is basically nothingness, is the easier move to defend.

References

Anderson, L.V. 2012. Bad therapy. *Slate Magazine*, October 1. https://slate.com/news-and-politics/2012/10/illegal-psychotherapies-gay-conversion-therapy-rebirthing-therapy-psychedelic-therapy-electro-convulsion-therapy-and-others.html

Baggini, Julian. 2007. *What's it all about? Philosophy and the meaning of life*. Oxford University Press.

Baggott, Jim. 2021. Calculate but don't shut up. *Aeon*, December 6. https://aeon.co/essays/shut-up-and-calculate-does-a-disservice-to-quantum-mechanics

Bondi, Herman, and Thomas Gold. 1948. *The steady-state theory of the expanding universe*. London: Monthly Notices of the Royal Astronomical Society.

Burge, Ryan. 2021. Faith in numbers: Fox News is must-watch for white evangelicals, a turnoff for atheists…and Hindus, Muslims really like CNN. *The Conversation*, May 24. https://theconversation.com/faith-in-numbers-fox-news-is-must-watch-for-white-evangelicals-a-turn off-for-atheists-and-hindus-muslims-really-like-cnn-161067

Choi, Charles Q., and Scott Dutfield. 2022. 7 theories on the origin of life. *Live Science*, February 14. https://www.livescience.com/13363-7-theories-origin-life.html

Craig, William Lane. 2000. *The Kalam cosmological argument*. Eugene: Wipf and Stock Publishers.

Darley, J.M., and C.D. Batson. 1973. 'From Jerusalem to Jericho': A study of situational and dispositional variables in helping behavior. *JPSP* 1973 (27): 100–108.

DeWitt, David A. 2000. Theories of the origin and early evolution of life. *Faculty Publications and Presentations* 93. https://digitalcommons.liberty.edu/bio_chem_fac_pubs/93

Edelman, Benjamin. 2009. Red light states: Who buys online adult entertainment? *Journal of Economic Perspectives* 23 (1): 209–220.

Ehrman, Bart. 2021. Two (contradictory?) Accounts of creation in genesis? *Ehrman Blog.com*, May 11. https://ehrmanblog.org/two-contradictory-accounts-of-creation-in-genesis/

Friedman, A. 1922. Über die Krümmung des Raumes. *Zeitschrift für Physik* 10 (1): 377–386.

Gamow, G. 1946. Expanding universe and the origin of elements. *Physics Review* 70: 572.

———. 1948a. The origin of elements and the separation of galaxies. *Physics Review* 74: 505.

———. 1948b. Evolution of the universe. *Nature* 162: 680.

Gervais, W., A.F. Shariff, and A. Norenzayan. 2011. Do you believe in atheists? Distrust is central to anti-atheist prejudice. *Journal of Personality and Social Psychology* 101 (6): 1189–1206. https://doi.org/10.1037/a0025882. Epub 2011 Nov 7. PMID: 22059841. https://pubmed.ncbi.nlm.nih.gov/22059841/.

Gervais, W., D. Xygalatas, R. McKay, et al. 2017. Global evidence of extreme intuitive moral prejudice against atheists. *Nature Human Behaviour* 1: 0151. https://doi.org/10.1038/s41562-017-0151.

Giberson, Karl, and Randall Stephens. 2011. The evangelical rejection of reason. *New York Times*, October 17. https://www.nytimes.com/2011/10/18/opinion/the-evangelical-rejection-of-reason.html

Goldhill, Oliva. 2017. Bill Nye, the science guy, says I convinced him that philosophy is not just a load of self-indulgent crap. *Quartz*, April 15. https://qz.com/960303/bill-nye-on-philosophy-the-science-guy-says-he-has-changed-his-mind/

Goodman, Lenn E. 1971. Ghazali's argument from creation. *International Journal of Middle East Studies* 2 (1): 67–85. https://www.jstor.org/stable/162272.

Gramlich, John. 2020. 5 Facts about Fox News. Pew Research Center, April 8. https://www.pewresearch.org/fact-tank/2020/04/08/five-facts-about-fox-news/

Grewal, Daisy. 2012. In atheists we distrust. *Scientific American*, January 17. https://www.scientificamerican.com/article/in-atheists-we-distrust/

Hawking, Stephen, and Leonard Mlodinow. 2012. *The grand design: New answers to the ultimate questions of life*. New York: Bantam Books.

Hepburn, Brian, and Hanne Anderson. 2021. Scientific method. *Stanford Encyclopedia of Philosophy*. https://plato.stanford.edu/entries/scientific-method
Hick, John. 1975. *Evil and the god of love*. Norfolk: Collins.
Hister. n.d. *Nostradamus Wiki*. https://nostradamus.fandom.com/wiki/Hister
Hoyle, Fred. 1948. A new model for the expanding universe. *MNRAS* 108 (5): 372–382.
Hubble, E. 1929. A relation between distance and radial velocity among extra-galactic nebulae. *The Proceedings of the National Academy of Sciences* 15: 168–173.
Humanist International. 2020. The humanists at risk: Action report *Humanist International*. https://humanists.international/wp-content/uploads/2020/06/3098_Humanists-International_Humanists-at-Risk-Action-Report_Amends-V2_LR.pdf
Hume, David. (1748). *Enquiry concerning human understanding. Section X: Of miracles*. Part I.
Interobang Staff. 2012. Penn Jillette rapes all the women he wants to. *The Interro Bang*, April 30. https://theinterrobang.com/penn-jillette-morality-without-religion/
James, Emily St. 2014. God's Not Dead is a mess even by Christian film standards. *AvClub.com*. https://www.avclub.com/god-s-not-dead-is-a-mess-even-by-christian-film-standar-1798179908?utm
Johnson, David Kyle. 2011. Natural evil and the simulation hypothesis. *Philosophy* 14 (2): 161–175. https://doi.org/10.5840/philo201114212.
———. 2013a. The failure of Plantinga's solution to the logical problem of natural evil. *Philosophy* 15 (2): 145–157. https://doi.org/10.5840/philo20121528.
———. 2013b. A refutation of skeptical theism. *Sophia* 52 (3): 425–445. https://doi.org/10.1007/s11841-012-0326-0.
———. 2015. *The myths that stole Christmas: Seven misconceptions that hijacked the holiday (and how we can take it back)*. Humanist Press.
———. 2016. A friendly open letter to Bill Nye (about philosophy). *Psychology Today*, February 27. https://www.psychologytoday.com/us/blog/logical-take/201602/friendly-open-letter-bill-nye-about-philosophy
———. 2017. Moral culpability and choosing to believe in god. In *Atheism and the Christian faith*, ed. Bill Anderson, 11–32. Vernon Press.
———. 2018. Mystery therefore magic. In *Bad arguments: 100 of the most important fallacies in western philosophy*, ed. Robert Arp, Bruce Robert, and Steve Barbone. Wiley-Blackwell.
———. 2021. Refuting skeptical theism. In *God and horrendous suffering*, ed. John Loftus. GCRR Publishing.
———. 2022. Free will, the holocaust, and the problem of evil. *SHERM* 4 (1): 81–96. https://doi.org/10.33929/sherm.2022.vol4.no1.06.
———. 2022a. God's prime directive: Non-interference and why there is no (viable) free will defense. *Religion* 13: 871.
———. 2022b. Does god exist? *Thinking* 21 (61): 5–22. https://doi.org/10.1017/S1477175621000415.
Kauffman, Frank. 2014. Point misses real point in lawsuit. *Springfield News-Leader*, May 9. https://www.news-leader.com/story/opinion/readers/2014/05/09/point-misses-real-point-lawsuit/8904345/
Kowalski, Dean. 2017. *Joss Whedon as philosopher*. Lexington Books.
Lemaître, Georges. 1927. Un Univers homogène de masse constante et de rayon croissant rendant compte de la vitesse radiale des nébuleuses extra-galactiques. *Annales de la Société Scientifique de Bruxelles* 47: 49. [(Translated in: A Homogeneous Universe of Constant Mass and Increasing Radius Accounting for the Radial Velocity of Extra-galactic Nebulae. *Monthly Notices of the Royal Astronomical Society* 91(5): 483–490. 1931.
———. 1931. Expansion of the universe, the expanding universe. *Monthly Notices of the Royal Astronomical Society* 91: 490–501. https://academic.oup.com/mnras/article/91/5/490/985169.
———. 1958. The primeval atom hypothesis and the problem of clusters of galaxies. In *La Structure et l'Evolution de l'Univers*, ed. R. Stoops, 1–32. As translated in Helge Kragh,

Cosmology and Controversy: The Historical Development of Two Theories of the Universe (1996): 39–60.

Lipka, Michael. 2014. Americans are somewhat more open to the idea of an atheist president. *Pew Research Center*, May 29. https://www.pewresearch.org/fact-tank/2014/05/29/americans-are-somewhat-more-open-to-the-idea-of-an-atheist-president/

Lisle, Jason. 2010. Does the Big Bang fit with the Bible? *AnswersInGensis.com.* https://answersingenesis.org/big-bang/does-the-big-bang-fit-with-the-bible/

Loftus, John. 2021. *God and horrendous suffering*. GCRR Press.

Mainland, G.B., and Bernard Mulligan. 2019. *Journal of Phychology: Conference Series* 1239. https://iopscience.iop.org/article/10.1088/1742-6596/1239/1/012016/pdf

Malhotra, Deepak. 2010. (When) are religious people nicer? Religious salience and the 'Sunday Effect' on pro-social behavior. *Judgment and Decision making* 5 (2): 138–143. https://journal.sjdm.org/10/10216/jdm10216.pdf.

Martin, Michael, and Ricki Monnier. 2003. *The impossibility of god*. Amherst/New York: Prometheus Books.

Metha, Hemant. 2016. Let's debunk the 'Christian persecution' court cases that inspired the 'God's Not Dead' films. *Patheos*, April 8. https://friendlyatheist.patheos.com/2016/04/08/lets-debunk-the-christian-persecution-court-cases-that-inspired-the-gods-not-dead-films/

Mortenson, Terry. 2011. Young-earth creationist view summarized and defended. AnswersInGensis.com https://answersingenesis.org/creationism/young-earth/young-earth-creationist-view-summarized-and-defended/

Moss, Candida. 2013. *The myth of persecution: How early Christians invented a story of martyrdom*. Harper Collins.

Norris, Christopher. 2011. Hawking contra Philosophy. *Philosophy Now.* https://philosophynow.org/issues/82/Hawking_contra_Philosophy

Penzias, A.A., and R.W. Wilson. 1965. A measurement of excess antenna temperature at 4080 Mc/s. *Astrophysical Journal Letters* 142: 419–421.

Pew Research Center. 2021. Measuring Religion in Pew Research Center's American Trends Panel. https://www.pewresearch.org/religion/2021/01/14/measuring-religion-in-pew-research-centers-american-trends-panel/

Pfaff, Steven, Charles Crabtree, Holger L. Kern, and John B. Holbein. 2020. Do street-level bureaucrats discriminate based on religion? A large-scale correspondence experiment among American public school principals. *Public Administration Review* 81 (2): 244–259. https://doi.org/10.1111/puar.13235.

Postdiction. n.d. Wikipedia. https://en.wikipedia.org/wiki/Postdiction

Rovelli, Carlo. 2018. Physics needs philosophy/philosophy needs physics. *Scientific American*, July 18. https://blogs.scientificamerican.com/observations/physics-needs-philosophy-philosophy-needs-physics/

Rowe, William L. 1979. The problem of evil and some varieties of atheism. *American Philosophical Quarterly* 16: 335–341.

Russell, Bertrand. 1952. Is there a god? In *The collected papers of Bertrand Russell Vol. 11: Last philosophical testament 1943–1968*, ed. John G. Slater, 542–548. London: Routledge. https://doi.org/10.1108/rr.1997.11.5.10.278.

Sandstorm, Aleksandra. 2021. Biden is only the second Catholic president, but nearly all have been Christians. *Pew Research Center*. https://www.pewresearch.org/fact-tank/2021/01/20/biden-only-second-catholic-president-but-nearly-all-have-been-christians-2/

Savage, David. 1994. School Prayer Just a Start for Some Christian Activists: Religion: Conservatives say they need a constitutional amendment protecting their right to expressions of faith. *LA Times*, December 25. https://www.latimes.com/archives/la-xpm-1994-12-25-mn-12943-story.html

Schick, Theodore. 2003. Can god explain anything? *Thinking* 2 (4): 55–63.

———. 2004. A humanist theory of ethics: Inference to the best action. In *Toward a new political humanism*, ed. B.F. Seidman and N.J. Murphy. Prometheus.

Schick, Theodore, and Lewis Vaugh. 2020. *How to think about weird things*. McGraw Hill.

Schopf, J. William. 2006. The first billion years: When did life emerge? *Elements* 2 (4): 229–233. https://doi.org/10.2113/gselements.2.4.229.

Scott, Callum D. 2012. The death of philosophy: A response to Stephen Hawking. *South African Journal of Philosophy* 31 (2): 384–404. https://doi.org/10.1080/02580136.2012.10751783.

Sloan, Philip. 2019. Evolutionary thought before Darwin. *Stanford Encyclopedia of Philosophy*. https://plato.stanford.edu/entries/evolution-before-darwin/

Sterba, James. 2019. *Is a good god logically possible?* London: Palgrave Macmillan. https://doi.org/10.1007/978-3-030-05469-4.

———. 2020. Is a good god logically possible? *International Journal for Philosophy of Religion* 87: 203–208. https://doi.org/10.1007/s11153-020-09755-x.

Thayer, H., ed. 2005. *Newton's philosophy of nature: Selections from his writings*. Mineola/New York: Dover. Originally published by New York: Hafner, 1953. See, in particular, *Section III: God and Natural Philosophy*.

Tryon, E.P. 1973. Is the universe a vacuum fluctuation? *Nature* 246: 396–397.

Underwood, Emily. 2014. Religious or not, we all misbehave. *Science*, September 11. https://www.science.org/content/article/religious-or-not-we-all-misbehave

Williams, Bernard. 1973. The Makropulos case: Reflections on the tedium of immortality. In *Problems of the self: Philosophical papers 1956–1972*, 82–100. Cambridge: Cambridge University Press.

Wing, Nick. 2017. There are still no open atheists in congress. *HuffPost.com*, January 4. https://www.huffpost.com/entry/no-atheists-in-congress_n_586c074ae4b0de3a08f9d487

Withrow, Brandon. 2017. Can you be good without god?. *The Daily Beast*, September 3. https://www.thedailybeast.com/can-you-be-good-without-god?source=twitter&via=desktop

Xygalatas, Dimitris. 2017. Are religious people more moral? *The Conversation*, October 23. https://theconversation.com/are-religious-people-more-moral-84560

Zabala, Santiago, and Creston Davis. 2013. Which philosophy is dead? *AlJazerra*, July 11. https://www.aljazeera.com/opinions/2013/6/11/which-philosophy-is-dead/